HANDBOOK OF INTERPERSONAL PSYCHOLOGY

HANDBOOK OF INTERPERSONAL PSYCHOLOGY

Theory, Research, Assessment, and Therapeutic Interventions

Edited by
Leonard M. Horowitz
and
Stephen Strack

WILEY

John Wiley & Sons, Inc.

Library of Congress Cataloging-in-Publication Data:

Handbook of interpersonal psychology : theory, research, assessment and therapeutic interventions / edited by Leonard M. Horowitz, Stephen Strack.
    p. cm.
  Includes index.
  ISBN 978-0-470-47160-9 (cloth); 978-0-470-88103-3 (ebk); 978-0-470-88106-4 (ebk); 978-0-470-88107-1 (ebk)
  1.   Interpersonal relations. 2.   Social psychology. 3.   Psychology, Applied. I.   Horowitz, Leonard M. II.   Strack, Stephen.
   HM1106.H363 2011
   302.01--dc22

                                                                                  2010010872

ISBN 978-0-470-47160-9

Printed in the United States of America
10 9 8 7 6 5 4 3 2 1

This book is dedicated to:

The Society for Interpersonal Theory and Research (SITAR) for nurturing the science and practice of interpersonal psychology in the 21st century

CONTENTS

FOREWORD

Leslie C. Morey

The disciplines of personality, social, and clinical psychology have long struggled to identify an emergent paradigm that can help consolidate the many and disparate contributions that scholars have made to these fields. Dating back to Sigmund Freud (e.g., 1895, 1916–1917), various expansive theories have been offered, but these theories have typically demonstrated profound limitations in their capacity to generate specific and testable hypotheses regarding human behavior. This volume represents compelling evidence that the interpersonal tradition in psychology has matured to a point that it represents a viable contender to serve as such a consolidating model.

One of the earliest challenges to Freud's overarching model of personality came from Alfred Adler (e.g., 1951, 2002). For Freud, most of the dynamic elements of personality were intrapsychic; interpersonal relations were conceived as following relatively fixed templates with a limited number of characteristic outcomes. Adler observed that the interpersonal milieu of the developing person reflected a powerful and ever-changing source of motivation through social comparison, and the adaptations to this milieu resulted in diverse yet consistent patterns of motivations and behaviors, patterns that continued to

be responsive to the social environment throughout life. These themes were refined and expanded by Harry Stack Sullivan (e.g., 1953a, 1953b), who provided keen insight into how interpersonal mechanisms could help provide meaning even to the most severe forms of psychopathology. Such seminal ideas were further developed by succeeding generations of interpersonal scholars, such as Timothy Leary (1957), who proposed a revolutionary *circumplex* model for mapping interpersonal characteristics as well as a means for representing these elements at various levels of awareness and automaticity; and Jerry Wiggins (e.g., 2003; Wiggins, Trapnell, & Phillips, 1988), who provided both a strategy for understanding the origins of the salient dimensions of the model as well as critical refinements in measuring these dimensions. Many other important figures, such as Robert Carson (e.g., 1969), Donald Kiesler (e.g., 1983), and Maurice Lorr (e.g., 1996), introduced and elaborated principles (such as the principle of complementarity) to understand components of these models as dynamic processes as well as personological styles. Such giants in the field provided a rich and comprehensive foundation from which the contemporary field of interpersonal science could flourish.

And flourish it has. The contributor list to this volume is a veritable "Who's Who" of the leading scholars of the current generation of interpersonal theorists and researchers, as well as of extensions of interpersonal theory into essential areas of personality and psychopathology. The chapters bear testimony to the enduring impact of the foundational work, and the remarkable development, that the field has witnessed in recent years. The chapters make clear that the interpersonal approach provides both a structure by which key individual differences can be described and understood, as well as a representation for mapping the dynamic, transactional aspects of human interaction. These contributions demonstrate how the approach serves to help understand aspects of human experience as fundamental as empathy, attachment, alliance, and adaptation, and its failures. Despite the far-reaching impact of these principles, each chapter also documents the extensive empirical base that helps elaborate and refine our understanding of the application of the interpersonal paradigm within these specific areas—research that is the result of developing and testing hypotheses directly derived from theory, a progression uncharacteristic of many other broad theories of human behavior.

One wonders what pioneers such as Adler and Sullivan might think if they were able to review this volume. Surely they would be impressed by the steady progression and refinement of ideas and methods in this area, a progression that characterizes any science as it matures. Perhaps they might be a bit mystified by methodological developments that include applications of Cartesian geometric models or structural equation modeling. Nonetheless, because both were practitioners attempting to apply interpersonal principles to help alleviate human suffering, I suspect both would be pleased about the direct translation of the theory into practice and intervention. As shown in a number of the chapters, the interpersonal approach not only provides an explanation for what is observed, but also suggests a course of action with explicit predictions about what might be needed to bring about desired change.

Doctors Horowitz and Strack are to be commended for assembling a remarkable group of scholars whose work represents the cutting edge of interpersonal theory, research, and practice. The broad span of ideas and findings integrated here succeeds in collating and organizing a field that is growing in exciting ways. This book should serve as both an inspiration and a challenge to the next generation of interpersonal scientists, professionals, and students as the field continues to evolve over the next decades.

References

Adler, A. (1951). *The practice and theory of individual psychology* (2nd ed., rev.). Oxford, UK: Humanities Press. (Original work published 1924)

Adler, A. (2002). *The neurotic character: Fundamentals of individual psychology and psychotherapy.* Bellingham, WA: The Classical Adlerian Translation Project. (Original work published 1926)

Carson, R. C. (1969). *Interaction concepts of personality.* Chicago, IL: Aldine.

Freud, S. (1916–1917). Introductory lectures on psycho-analysis. In J. Strachey (Ed. & Trans.), *The standard edition of the works of Sigmund Freud* (Vol. 15–16, pp. 9–496). London: Hogarth Press.

Freud, S. (1895). Project for a scientific psychology. In J. Strachey (Ed. & Trans.), *The standard edition of the works of Sigmund Freud* (Vol. 14, pp. 109–140). London: Hogarth Press.

Kiesler, D. J. (1983). The 1982 Interpersonal Circle: A taxonomy for complementarity in human transactions. *Psychological Review, 90,* 185–214.

Leary, T. (1957). *Interpersonal diagnosis of personality.* New York: Ronald Press.

Lorr, M. (1996). The interpersonal circle as a heuristic model for interpersonal research. *Journal of Personality Assessment, 66,* 234–239.

Sullivan, H. S. (1953a). *The interpersonal theory of psychiatry.* New York: W. W. Norton.

Sullivan, H. S. (1953b). *Conceptions of modern psychiatry.* New York: W. W. Norton.

Wiggins, J. S. (2003). *Paradigms of personality assessment.* New York: Guilford Press.

Wiggins, J. S., Trapnell, P., & Phillips, N. (1988). Psychometric and geometric characteristics of the Revised Interpersonal Adjectives Scale (IAS-R). *Multivariate Behavioral Research, 23,* 517–530.

CONTRIBUTORS

Lynn E. Alden, PhD
Department of Psychology
University of British Columbia
Vancouver, BC, Canada

Ananda B. Amstadter, PhD
National Crime Victims Research
and Treatment Center
Department of Psychiatry
and Behavioral Sciences
Medical University of South Carolina
Charleston, SC

Kim Bartholomew, PhD
Department of Psychology
Simon Fraser University
Burnaby, BC, Canada

Julia Bear, PhD
Tepper School of Business
Carnegie Mellon University
Pittsburgh, PA

Lorna Smith Benjamin, PhD
Department of Psychology
University of Utah
Salt Lake City, UT

Kristy E. Benoit, MS
Department of Psychology
Virginia Polytechnic Institute
and State University
Blacksburg, VA

Sidney J. Blatt, PhD
Departments of Psychiatry and Psychology
Yale University
New Haven, CT

Peter Borkenau, PhD
Department of Psychology
University of Halle-Wittenberg
Halle, Germany

James F. Boswell, MS
Department of Psychology
Pennsylvania State University
University Park, PA

Franz Caspar, PhD
Department of Psychology
University of Bern
Bern, Switzerland

Louis G. Castonguay, PhD
Department of Psychology
Pennsylvania State University
University Park, PA

John F. Clarkin, PhD
Weill Medical College of Cornell University
White Plains, NY

Rebecca J. Cobb, PhD
Department of Psychology
Simon Fraser University
Burnaby, BC, Canada

Nancy L. Collins, PhD
Department of Psychology
University of California
Santa Barbara, CA

Michael J. Constantino, PhD
Department of Psychology
University of Massachusetts
Amherst, MA

Natalie M. Costa, PhD
Child Study Center
Virginia Tech University
Blacksburg, VA

Paul T. Costa, Jr., PhD
Laboratory of Personality and Cognition
NIH Biomedical Research Center
Baltimore, MD

Jenny M. Cundiff, MA
Department of Psychology
University of Utah
Salt Lake City, UT

Ronen Cuperman, MS
Department of Psychology
University of Texas
Arlington, TX

William D. Ellison, MS
Department of Psychology
Pennsylvania State University
University Park, PA

Nicole Ethier, MA
Department of Psychology
University of Waterloo
Waterloo, ON, Canada

Catherine Eubanks-Carter, PhD
Department of Psychiatry
Beth Israel Medical Center
New York, NY

Brooke C. Feeney, PhD
Department of Psychology
Carnegie Mellon University
Pittsburgh, PA

Máire B. Ford, PhD
Department of Psychology
Loyola Marymount University
Los Angeles, CA

Marc A. Fournier, PhD
Department of Psychology
University of Toronto Scarborough
Toronto, ON, Canada

Robert Gifford, PhD
Department of Psychology and School of
Environmental Studies
University of Victoria
Victoria, BC, Canada

Tilman Grande, PhD
Clinic for Psychosomatics and General
Clinical Medicine
University of Heidelberg
Heidelberg, Germany

Vladas Griskevicius, PhD
Carlson School of Management
University of Minnesota
Minneapolis, MN

Meredith Gunlicks-Stoessel, PhD
Division of Child and
Adolescent Psychiatry
Columbia University College of
Physicians and Surgeons
New York State Psychiatric Institute
New York, NY

Michael B. Gurtman, PhD
Department of Psychology
University of Wisconsin-Parkside
Kenosha, WI

Jeffrey A. Hayes, PhD
Counseling Psychology
Pennsylvania State University
University Park, PA

Jonathan Hill, MRCP FRCPsych
University of Manchester
Manchester, England
and Tavistock Clinic
London, England

John G. Holmes, PhD
Psychology Department
University of Waterloo
Waterloo, ON, Canada

Martin Grosse Holtforth, PhD
Department of Psychology
University of Bern
Bern, Switzerland

Leonard M. Horowitz, PhD
Department of Psychology
Stanford University
Stanford, CA

William Ickes, PhD
Department of Psychology
University of Texas
Arlington, TX

Daniel N. Jones, PhD
Department of Psychology
University of British Columbia
Vancouver, BC, Canada

John S. Kim, BA
Department of Psychology
University of Minnesota
Minneapolis, MN

Karestan C. Koenen, PhD
Departments of Society, Human
Development, and Health
and Epidemiology
Harvard School of Public Health
Boston, MA

David R. Kraus, PhD
Behavioral Health Labs
Marlborough, MA

Daniel Leising, PhD
Department of Psychology
University of Halle-Wittenberg
Halle, Germany

Hanna Levenson, PhD
Wright Institute
Berkeley, CA

Kenneth N. Levy, PhD
Department of Psychology
Pennsylvania State University
University Park, PA

Kenneth D. Locke, PhD
Department of Psychology
University of Idaho
Moscow, ID

Patrick Luyten, PhD
Department of Psychology
University of Leuven
Leuven, Belgium

Robert R. McCrae, PhD
Laboratory of Personality and Cognition
NIH Biomedical Research Center
Baltimore, MD

Mario Mikulincer, PhD
The New School of Psychology
Interdisciplinary Center
Herliya, Israel

Leslie C. Morey, PhD
Department of Psychology
Texas A&M University
College Station, TX

D. S. Moskowitz, PhD
Department of Psychology
McGill University
Montreal, QC, Canada

J. Christopher Muran, PhD
Department of Psychiatry
Beth Israel Medical Center
New York, NY

Sandra L. Murray, PhD
Psychology Department
State University of New York
Buffalo, NY

Nicole R. Nugent, PhD
Brown Medical School
Bradley/Hasbro Children's Research
Center
Providence, RI

Brian P. O'Connor, PhD
Department of Psychology
Barber School of Arts and Sciences
University of British Columbia-
Okanagan
Kelowna, BC, Canada

John S. Ogrodniczuk, PhD
Department of Psychiatry
University of British Columbia
Vancouver, BC, Canada

Thomas H. Ollendick, PhD
Department of Psychology
Child Study Center
Virginia Tech University
Blacksburg, VA

Delroy L. Paulhus, PhD
Department of Psychology
University of British Columbia
Vancouver, BC, Canada

Paul A. Pilkonis, PhD
Western Psychiatric Institute
and Clinic
Pittsburgh, PA

Aaron L. Pincus, PhD
Department of Psychology
Pennsylvania State University
University Park, PA

William E. Piper, PhD
Department of Psychiatry
University of British Columbia
Vancouver, BC, Canada

Marci J. Regambal, MA
Department of Psychology
University of British Columbia
Vancouver, BC, Canada

Kathryn H. Rollings, MS
Department of Psychology
University of Texas
Arlington, TX

Pamela Sadler, PhD
Department of Psychology
Wilfrid Laurier University
Waterloo, ON, Canada

Jeremy D. Safran, PhD
Department of Psychology
New School University
New York, NY

Henning Schauenburg, MD
Clinic for Psychosomatics and General
Clinical Medicine
University of Heidelberg
Heidelberg, Germany

Chris G. Segrin, PhD
Department of Communication
University of Arizona
Tucson, AZ

Phillip R. Shaver, PhD
Department of Psychology
University of California
Davis, CA

Jeffry A. Simpson, PhD
Department of Psychology
University of Minnesota
Minneapolis, MN

Timothy W. Smith, PhD
Department of Psychology
University of Utah
Salt Lake City, UT

Stephen Strack, PhD
Psychology Service
U.S. Department of Veterans Affairs
Los Angeles, CA

Andrea Thomas, PhD
Friedrich-Schiller-University of
Jena Medical Center
Institute for Psychosocial Medicine
Jena, Germany

Myrna M. Weissman, PhD
Division of Epidemiology
Columbia University College of
Physicians and Surgeons
New York State Psychiatric Institute
New York, NY

Erik Woody, PhD
Department of Psychology
University of Waterloo
Waterloo, ON, Canada

Aiden G. C. Wright, MS
Department of Psychology
Pennsylvania State University
University Park, PA

David C. Zuroff, PhD
Department of Psychology
McGill University
Montreal, QC, Canada

HANDBOOK OF INTERPERSONAL PSYCHOLOGY

1 INTRODUCTION

Stephen Strack

Leonard M. Horowitz

Interpersonal psychology emerged as a significant academic discipline in the 1950s, when the field was dominated by behaviorism and psychoanalysis. Many researchers and practitioners at the time, dissatisfied with the extreme positions of those two schools of thought, sought an integrative alternative. In place of either doctrine, they looked for a more moderate position that was scientifically sound but also addressed internal states (e.g., interpersonal motives) as well as observable behavior. "Interpersonalists" distinguished themselves from their mainstream counterparts with their assumption that human behavior is best understood within the context of transactional causality and reciprocal influence: Persons A and B mutually and reciprocally influence each other, in that the behavior of each is both a response to and a stimulus for the other's behavior.

During the past 60 years thousands of research articles, chapters, and books have been published that address interpersonal processes in personality, social, and abnormal psychology, behavior in dyads and groups, relationship patterns, and psychotherapy. Old models of interpersonal behavior have been modified and new models have been developed. Especially important during the past decade has been the implementation of new research methods that capitalize on the latest developments in communication technology (e.g., low-cost video equipment, miniature cameras, hand-held computers, wireless networks, and the Internet), which has made it possible to study aspects of interpersonal behavior that were previously off limits. See Table 1.1 for a list of milestones in the evolution of the field.

Interpersonal psychology is clearly at a point where advances need to be brought together and organized so that researchers, practitioners, and students can develop a clearer perspective about the territory that has been covered and what is new, different, and state-of-the art. This handbook was designed to fill this need. Its main purpose is to inform readers about the central issues that are being addressed by researchers and clinicians in the realm of interpersonal psychology, with the aim of providing individuals new to the area some of the basic tools they need to become participants in this important area of scientific inquiry. We also believe that the book can help define and shape the field as it evolves during the first half of the 21st century.

TABLE 1.1   Some Milestones in the History of Interpersonal Psychology

Year(s)	Event(s)
1922–1930	Treating schizophrenics on a special ward at the Sheppard and Enoch Pratt Hospital in Maryland, Harry Stack Sullivan develops his interpersonal theory of psychiatry.
1934	George Herbert Meade explains how individual personality and self-concept arise as a function of social processes in his monograph, *Mind, Self, and Society.*
1936	In *Principles of Topological Psychology*, Kurt Lewin describes behavior as a function of the individual's perceptive capacities in interaction with the dynamic forces that exist within specific environments.
	Sullivan helps found the Washington School of Psychiatry. The school becomes a forum for his work and attracts scholars from anthropology, political science, psychology, and sociology, including Ruth Benedict, Erick Fromm, Frieda Fromm-Reichmann, Karen Horney, and David and Margaret Rioch. Many of Sullivan's students make their own contributions to the budding field of interpersonal psychology.
1938–1945	The rise of Nazi Germany and World War II galvanize the interests of researchers and practitioners to study social and interpersonal processes, and to develop group treatments for soldiers suffering from "combat fatigue."
1940	The first widely disseminated summary of Sullivan's interpersonal model is published as *Conceptions of Modern Psychiatry.*
1946	The *Tavistock Institute of Human Relations* is founded in Britain as a charity concerned with studying group and organizational behavior, and the treatment of war casualties. Several key figures at the institute make seminal contributions to interpersonal psychology, including Wilfrid Bion, John Bowlby, Melanie Klein, and Ronald Laing.
1951	Professor Hubert Coffey's students at the University of California at Berkeley begin to publish the results of their cooperative studies on personality processes in group psychotherapy (Freedman, Leary, Ossorio, & Coffey, 1951).
1953	The first volumes in a series of posthumous works are published on Sullivan's interpersonal theory of psychiatry.
1957	Timothy Leary's monograph, *Interpersonal Diagnosis of Personality*, is published, offering the first circular model of interpersonal behavior.
1958	Fritz Heider's book, *The Psychology of Interpersonal Relations*, is published, serving as the foundation for the study of social cognition.
1963	Maurice Lorr and Douglas McNair (1963, 1965) revitalize interest in Leary's work with their factor analytic research demonstrating the robustness of a two dimensional, circular representation of behavior.
1969	The first of John Bowlby's books on *Attachment and Loss* is published. Bowlby offers a developmental perspective on the processes of early attachment that lead to internalized expectations for future relationships.
	In *Interaction Concepts of Personality*, Robert Carson focuses attention on the interpersonal processes that "pull" for symmetrical or complementary responses from others.
	Walter Mischel publishes his initial account of a social-cognitive theory of personality.
1974	Lorna Smith Benjamin's dimensional model of interpersonal behavior, *Structural Analysis of Social Behavior* (SASB), is published, leading to numerous empirical investigations of social processes in psychotherapy, as well as two books on interpersonal treatment of psychiatric disorders: *Interpersonal Diagnosis and Treatment of Personality Disorders* (1993) and *Interpersonal Reconstructive Therapy* (2003).
	Gerald Klerman and colleagues (Klerman, DiMascio, Weissman, et al., 1974) present their initial research on *Interpersonal Therapy* (IPT) for the treatment of depression, which is now recognized as one of the most effective interventions ever developed for the treatment of this disorder.
1979	Leonard M. Horowitz publishes the first of many studies on interpersonal problems expressed in psychotherapy. Horowitz's influential work on interpersonal problems and motives is summarized in his 2004 monograph, *Interpersonal Foundations of Psychopathology.*

TABLE 1.1 *Continued*

Year(s)	Event(s)
	Jerry S. Wiggins begins publishing a series of studies designed to clarify the interpersonal taxonomy of personality via psychometrics and factor analysis. He makes numerous contributions to interpersonal psychology, many of which are highlighted in his last major work, *Paradigms of Personality Assessment* (2003).
1983	Donald Kiesler publishes his *1982 Interpersonal Circle*, an updated taxonomy of interpersonal behavior based on a new interpretation of complementarity. Kiesler's considerable body of work is summarized in the 1996 book, *Contemporary Interpersonal Theory and Research*.
1984	Hans Strupp and Jeffrey Binder develop *Time-Limited Dynamic Psychotherapy* (TLDP), which facilitates awareness in the client of relationship patterns that foster dysfunctional behavior, and teaches healthy alternatives. TLDP has since been found to be effective in treating a wide range of psychiatric disorders.
1986	Albert Bandura publishes *Social Foundations of Thought and Action: A Social Cognitive Theory*.
1991	Michael B. Gurtman publishes the first of several articles and chapters that help illuminate and make accessible the unique methodologies for analyzing and interpreting assessments from circumplex measures.
1994	Timothy Leary's impact on contemporary interpersonal psychology is highlighted in an American Psychological Association symposium, *Interpersonal Theory and the Interpersonal Circumplex: Timothy Leary's Legacy*, later published as a Special Series in the *Journal of Personality Assessment* (Strack, 1996).
1997	Robert Plutchick and Hope Conte survey the wide range of two dimensional psychological models developed since the 1950s in their edited book, *Circumplex Models of Personality and Emotions*.
1998	The *Society for Interpersonal Theory and Research* (SITAR) meets for the first time in Snowbird, UT. Conceived the year before during a luncheon hosted by Leonard M. Horowitz following an American Psychological Association symposium, SITAR is now an international, multidisciplinary, scientific association. Goals of the Society are to encourage the development of interpersonal research; foster communication, understanding, and application of research findings; and to enhance the scientific and social value of interpersonal psychology.
2003	Aaron L. Pincus (Pincus & Ansell, 2003) begins offering a series of articles and chapters that expand and reinterpret traditional interpersonal theory, helping to widen its influence in clinical and personality psychology.
	Using new technology and sophisticated statistical methods (i.e., structural equation modeling), Pamela Sadler and Erik Woody offer an integrative model of interpersonal complementarity that can predict outcomes in interactions using interpersonal traits and situational patterns that incorporate the effects partners have on each other.
2004	Sidney J. Blatt publishes the first of two volumes summarizing his clinical and research work over a 30-year span, *Experiences of Depression: Theoretical, Clinical and Research Perspectives*. His more recent book, *Polarities of Experience: Relatedness and Self-Definition in Personality Development, Psychopathology, and the Therapeutic Process* (2008), offers a complex model of normal and abnormal interpersonal behavior using the metaconcepts of agency and communion.
	Debbie S. Moskowitz and David C. Zuroff present a dynamic view of interpersonal behavior based on a new method of data collection: Intensive repeated measures in naturalistic settings. Their work shows that interpersonal behavior can exhibit considerable variability within situations, and is measurable in terms of *flux*, *pulse*, and *spin*.
2007	Mario Mikulincer and Philip R. Shaver publish *Attachment Patterns in Adulthood: Structure, Dynamics, and Change*, summarizing 25 years of research based on Bowlby's clinical and theoretical formulations.

To set the stage for readers, we first present a history of modern interpersonal psychology that focuses on the theoretical roots that commonly underlie its major lines of science and practice. We then describe how the handbook evolved into its current form and offer a summary of what can be found in each section and chapter.

HISTORY OF MODERN INTERPERSONAL PSYCHOLOGY

Interpersonal psychology can trace its roots to ancient philosophy (e.g., Plato, Hippocrates, Aristotle, Galen), evolutionary biology (e.g., Darwin, 1859), and the pioneers who spawned the subfields of abnormal, organizational, personality, and social psychology (e.g., F. H. Allport, 1924; G. Allport, 1937; Münsterberg, 1915; Murray, 1938; Prince, 1914). However, it was the events of World War II that galvanized the interests of scientists and clinicians in this area. Seeking explanations for the decline of German society into Nazism during the 1930s, and the atrocities of the war that followed, one group of scientists began studying the social processes that shape intolerance and destructive behavior (e.g., Lewin, Lippitt, & White, 1939), while another focused on dispositional individual differences variables associated with aggression and the formation of dysfunctional groups (e.g., Adorno, Frenkel-Brunswik, Levinson, & Sanford, 1950). Clinicians were called to action to provide effective treatments for thousands of "combat fatigue" casualties that had to be seen in groups because of their vast numbers (Coffey, 1954).

The field as we know it today was initially shaped by theoretical developments in American and British psychiatry during the 1930s and 1940s, and by academic social psychologists, primarily from Europe, who developed the first models to explain human behavior as a function of the reciprocal influence among individuals and the social environment. In America, the clinical roots of modern interpersonal psychology can be traced to the psychiatrist Harry Stack Sullivan (e.g., 1940, 1953a, 1953b, 1954, 1956), who was trained as a psychoanalyst but dissatisfied with the lack of attention paid by psychoanalytic theory to interpersonal processes in the development and treatment of psychopathology. Sullivan was originally hired in 1921 by the psychiatrist William Alanson White to work with patients at St. Elizabeth's Hospital in Washington, D.C. He later transferred to the Sheppard and Enoch Pratt Hospital in Maryland where, in his work primarily with schizophrenics, he began developing his interpersonal theory of psychiatry. The data for his theory came mostly from his psychotherapy patients and, in particular, his observations of patients on a ward that he created as a kind of interpersonal field laboratory (Evans, 1996; D. M. Rioch, 1985).

Sullivan radically transformed psychoanalysis and psychiatry from the study of things and events that occur within an individual (particularly the patient) to the study of interpersonal living (Evans, 1996). Whereas psychoanalysis emphasized intrapsychic processes in the development of personality and psychopathology, and viewed the psychiatrist as a physician ministering to a sick individual, Sullivan believed that the psychological contents of a person are inextricably derived from social processes, and that a psychiatrist could never be a neutral observer in the presence of the patient; instead, he or she was a participant-observer because the interpersonal field is always active and every participant shapes, and is shaped by, its ongoing dynamics (Sullivan, 1953a). For Sullivan, personality wasn't something that resides in the individual; instead, it is "the relatively enduring pattern of recurrent interpersonal situations which characterize a human life" (Sullivan, 1953b, p. 18). He viewed the structure of personality as a system of security mechanisms for managing interpersonal anxiety. He used his one-genus hypothesis (i.e., "everyone is much more simply human than otherwise," Sullivan, 1953a, p. 32) as a guide for developing treatments that put the therapist and patient on equal footing.

Sullivan's ideas were originally presented as lectures to small groups of psychiatrists and residents, but his fame grew with the establishment of the Washington School of Psychiatry in the 1930s, which he helped found, and which attracted an eclectic, multidisciplinary group of students from anthropology, political science, psychiatry, psychology, and sociology, including Ruth Benedict (1934), Erich Fromm (1941), Frieda Fromm-Reichmann (1960), Karen Horney (1937), and David and Margaret Rioch (D. M. Rioch, 1959, 1985; M. J. Rioch, 1970, 1986). Sullivan's theoretical approach was not widely appreciated until the appearance of *Conceptions of Modern Psychiatry* in 1940, and much of the body of his work was not published until after his death in 1949 (Evans, 1996; D. M. Rioch, 1985). By the time his ideas were adopted by psychologists in the 1950s, there were a number of others making independent contributions to interpersonal theory and treatment, including Wilfrid Bion (1961) and Melanie Klein (1962) from Britain, who worked at the Tavistock Institute of Human Relations, Erik Erickson (1950), Jurgen Ruesch and Gregory Bateson (Ruesch & Bateson, 1951), and the individuals mentioned above.

During the same time that Sullivan was developing his interpersonal theory of psychiatry, the American social psychologist George Herbert Meade (1934) presented his ideas on how the human mind and self-concept arise from, and are shaped by, social processes, especially by way of linguistic communication or *symbolic interactionism*. Instead of approaching human experience from the standpoint of individual psychology, in *Mind, Self, and Society* (1934) Meade described experience from the standpoint of communication that occurs within a context of sociocultural rules and norms. He asserted that humans develop and organize their thoughts and behavior through interpersonal relations, the effects of which can be both conscious and unconscious.

Meade contended that mental phenomena are substantive because they can be traced to and correlated with social behavior. He rejected the traditional view of the mind as separate from the body, as well as the behaviorist attempt to account for mind solely in terms of physiology or neurology.

Also during the 1930s, the German-born social psychologist Kurt Lewin (1936) offered his influential Field Theory, which provided a framework for examining the dynamic "forces" or conditions present in specific environments that influence behavior within them. Breaking from person-centered accounts of human behavior, Lewin argued that both nature and nurture interact to shape individual development, and that behavior is best understood as a function of the interplay between person and environment: B = f(P, E). Lewin (1947, 1948) was strongly influenced in his early career by the Gestalt school of psychology, which primarily studied perception, and was later affiliated with the Tavistock Institute.

Another important development for interpersonal psychology came from Lewin's colleague, the Austrian-born social psychologist Fritz Heider, whose book *The Psychology of Interpersonal Relations* (1958) essentially founded the modern field of social cognition (e.g., Bandura, 1986; Mischel, 1973; Mischel & Shoda, 1995), which has attracted the attention of interpersonal psychologists. Heider argued that social perceptions follow many of the same rules of physical object perception, including the way such perceptions are organized within the individual. Just as errors in sense perception can lead to problems in performance, errors in social perception can lead to all sorts of miscommunications and social misfires. Heider is also credited with developing the concept of social attribution, and providing a framework for understanding how individuals make causal attributions using a mix of person-centered dispositions and situational factors that may be stable or transient.

In America in the 1950s, a new generation of scientist-practitioners began to operationalize Sullivan's interpersonal theory of psychiatry. Seeking to understand social influences on personality and behavior, University of California at Berkeley social psychologist David Krech became interested in Sullivan's work and attended lectures at the Washington School of Psychiatry in the 1940s (D. M. Rioch, 1985). Krech stimulated the interest of a young psychology professor, Hubert Coffey, who was brought to Berkeley to help spearhead a new department of clinical psychology. Coffey enlisted a group of bright graduate students returning from the war to help test Sullivan's ideas, which to that point had never been empirically investigated (LaForge, 2004).

Coffey and his students—Mervin Freedman, Rolfe LaForge, Timothy Leary, and Abel Ossorio—used group psychotherapy sessions and psychological test data as the raw material for developing a comprehensive model of interpersonal behavior in the form of an Interpersonal Circle (Freedman, Leary, Ossorio, & Coffey, 1951). Their work culminated in the publication of Timothy Leary's 1957 book, *Interpersonal Diagnosis of Personality*, which provided a taxonomy of normal and abnormal personality styles, and demonstrated that personality and the behavior of individuals can be fully understood only within an interpersonal context. By engineering Sullivan's ideas into a framework that could be understood and tested by personality, social, and clinical psychologists, Coffey and his students provided a scientific foundation for the proliferation of interpersonal research both inside and outside the clinic (Strack, 1996).

Although post-Freudian ego psychology and object relations theory provided views of child development that focused on the interaction of the infant and caregivers (e.g., A. Freud, 1946; Klein, 1962), it was the work of British psychologist John Bowlby (e.g., 1973, 1980, 1982, 1988) on attachment that stimulated the interests of interpersonal psychologists seeking to understand the roots of relationship patterns in children and adults. In the 1940s and 1950s, at the Tavistock Institute and Child Guidance Clinic in England, Bowlby worked with young children displaced from their families during World War II. His clinical observations provided the data for his monumental trilogy: *Attachment*, *Separation*, and *Loss*. Breaking with existing psychoanalytic models of child development, Bowlby asserted that attachment in infants is primarily a process of proximity-seeking to an identified caregiver in situations of perceived distress, for the purpose of survival. Infants become attached to adults who are sensitive and responsive in interactions with the infant, and who remain as consistent caregivers during the critical period of 6 to 24 months. Parental responses lead to the development of patterns of attachment that, in turn, lead to internal working models that guide the individual's feelings, thoughts, and expectations in subsequent relationships.

In the 1960s theory and research on interpersonal behavior began to grow at a pace that has quickened during each successive decade. Through the circular framework provided by Leary (1957) and colleagues, Sullivan's insights have continued to inspire new ideas in personality theory and assessment (e.g., Benjamin, 1974; Carson, 1969; Lorr, 1991; Wiggins, 1979, 2003), the study of psychopathology (e.g., Horowitz, 2004; Kiesler 1996; Pincus & Ansell, 2003), treatments for psychiatric disorders (e.g., Klerman, DiMascio, Weissman et al., 1974; Klerman, Weissman, Rounsaville, & Chevron, 1984; Strupp & Binder, 1984), and hundreds of studies on interpersonal processes (e.g., Plutchik & Conte, 1997). The work of Meade, Lewin, and Heider spawned sophisticated models of social behavior focusing on the mental representation of interaction patterns based on the interplay of cognitive, affective, and dispositional traits (e.g., Bandura, 1986; Mischel, 1973; Mischel & Shoda, 1995). With the help of his associate Mary Ainsworth

(Ainsworth & Bowlby, 1965; Ainsworth, Blehar, Waters, & Wall, 1978), Bowlby's ideas found their way into empirical studies of attachment behavior in many areas of psychology (e.g., Cassidy & Shaver, 2008).

Also noteworthy in the evolution of the field, particularly during the 1960s and 1970s, are the contributions of communications and systems theorists, who elaborated on Meade's (1934) early work to show how human behavior can be radically shaped through a complex system of shared cultural norms codified and operationalized in language and nonverbal behavior (e.g., Watzlawick, Beavin, & Jackson, 1967; Watzlawick & Weakland, 1977). Their ideas were particularly influential in shedding light on the communication patterns of families that foster psychopathology (e.g., Bateson, Jackson, Haley, & Weakland, 1956; Coyne, 1976; Laing, 1960), and the development of therapeutic interventions for couples and families (Broderick & Schrader, 1991).

To a great extent interpersonal psychology in the 21st century is based on, and driven by, the results of empirical investigations that have been conducted to test hypotheses generated by the theorists presented earlier. As methods have become more sophisticated (e.g., Gurtman & Balakrishnan, 1998; Moskowitz & Zuroff, 2004) researchers have been able to examine more complex hypotheses (e.g., Sadler & Woody, 2003), and new theoretical lines have been offered that integrate concepts from social, personality, and clinical perspectives on interpersonal behavior (e.g., Horowitz, 2004; Mikulincer & Shaver, 2007; Pincus, 2005a, 2005b). Throughout the pages of this handbook, readers will note both the sustaining power of early interpersonal theorists as well as the creativity of current researchers and clinicians in using research findings and new methods to generate increasingly complex models of interpersonal behavior and effective treatment interventions.

PUTTING THE HANDBOOK TOGETHER

Developing the scope and content of this volume was a group effort that took place over 18 months. Recognizing that the territory of interpersonal science had never been fully mapped, we believed it was important to seek the advice of as many insiders as possible. We first discussed with our colleagues, including members of the Society for Interpersonal Theory and Research (SITAR), the perceived boundaries of the field and areas of research and practice that had evolved enough to have a sound empirical base. We asked what could be reasonably covered in a single book that would capture the range of topics being addressed today, and also be of greatest benefit to an audience of researchers and clinicians. Next, we asked people to nominate specific chapter topics as well as prospective authors who were "leaders in the area" and/or "the person you would most like to see write the chapter." Our survey yielded over 50 topics and many more potential authors. We divided the topics according to themes (e.g., theory, interpersonal processes) and then had our colleagues rank-order them according to what they thought was absolutely essential, important but not essential, good but not essential, and so forth.

Based on the ratings we selected 38 potential topics and authors that were grouped into several sections. We prepared a book proposal with the list and negotiated a publishing contract for 35 chapters. After this we began contacting prospective authors with an invitation that asked them to provide a comprehensive review of their topic from the standpoint of theory, research, and applications. We asked that they address the empirical validity of their approach, and to write for an audience that would include advanced undergraduates, graduate students, and professionals. They were encouraged to write in such a way that people new to the field—those who are not familiar with terms, ideas, and methods unique to interpersonal psychology—will understand the material. We did not provide an outline for authors to follow but asked everyone to provide a conclusion or summary section at the end that gave a synopsis of their contribution.

The job of preparing the handbook has been a labor of love. We were fortunate to have the support and guidance of SITAR, whose members are well represented in the list of contributors, understanding and accommodating wives (Suzanne Horowitz and Lèni Ferrero), and a charming executive editor at John Wiley & Sons, Patricia Rossi, who shared our vision but never lost track of deadlines and space limitations. We were blessed to have chapter authors who offered not only their time, expertise, and scholarship, but their enthusiasm, patience, and tact throughout the sometimes lengthy review process. Because of them, we feel confident that we can offer you, the reader, a comprehensive overview of the field of interpersonal psychology written by those most qualified to present it.

ORGANIZATION AND CONTENT

Divided into six parts, the handbook covers major theories, methods, measures, therapeutic interventions, and empirical research that take as their parentage the interpersonal concepts and models of the last half of the 20th century. The handbook summarizes data from the vast domain of interpersonal phenomena (both within and between persons), with the goal of elucidating the complex interplay of biopsychosocial variables that make up the interpersonal world of human beings across all cultures and ages.

Part I, Theoretical Perspectives, includes five chapters addressing traditional and new ways of organizing and understanding the entire spectrum of interpersonal behavior. In Chapter 2, Shaver and Mikulincer offer a complex, developmental model of interpersonal behavior based on a blend of Bowlby's (1973, 1980, 1982, 1988) attachment theory, traditional interpersonal theory, and social-cognitive theory. Much of what is new and different about the field

of interpersonal psychology can be gleaned from their work, as well as that of Blatt and Luyten in Chapter 3. In the evolution of interpersonal theory, the circumplex dimensions of dominance-submission and love-hate were linked by Wiggins (1991) to the metaconcepts of agency and communion (Bakan, 1966) which have their roots in human evolution. Blatt and Luyten offer an intriguing model of relatedness (communion) and self-definition (agency) that integrates circumplex models, attachment theory, and psychodynamic views of normal and maladaptive interpersonal functioning.

Those who have followed the advance of circular models of interpersonal behavior from the 1950s to now will find in Chapter 4 by Fournier, Moskowitz, and Zuroff an elegant historical summary of this tradition, as well as a call for future researchers to think "outside the circle." To make their point, they present recent research findings that at once add to our knowledge base about the dynamics of interpersonal processes and go beyond a two-dimensional circle.

Chapter 5 by Simpson, Griskevicius, and Kim provides a perspective on interpersonal behavior that will be novel to many readers. The authors trace the roots of interpersonal needs, motives, and behavior patterns in human evolution and genetics. This perspective is important because we know that the "unit of survival" for human beings is the group. No one can survive or grow into maturity without the help of many others, and so we need to understand how interpersonal elements of survival and adaptation have been encoded in our biological make-up.

Rounding out the section is a contribution by Costa and McCrae (Chapter 6). They examine traditional interpersonal models of personality from the lens of the five-factor model, which has become the most widely applied framework for understanding personality traits in both normal and abnormal persons.

Part II, Basic Interpersonal Processes and Mechanisms, consists of five chapters that address fundamental elements of interpersonal behavior. Holtforth, Thomas, and Caspar (Chapter 7) argue that essentially all interpersonal behavior is motivationally directed, and so it is vital for both researchers and therapists to understand the implicit and explicit goals of those who participate in any interpersonal encounter. Chapter 8 by Sadler, Ethier, and Woody provides an historical account of interpersonal complementarity, which posits that certain kinds of interpersonal behaviors cause or "pull" specific responses from others. They argue for, and demonstrate, new ways of looking at complementarity as forms of relational adaptation over time that involve a variety of cognitive and motivational mediating processes.

The ability to be empathically attuned to others is important for success in many kinds of relationships, and is especially important for psychotherapists. In Chapter 9, Rollings, Cuperman, and Ickes introduce the reader to a growing body of research on empathic accuracy and inaccuracy, and provide evidence for the sometimes unusual consequences of being emotionally attuned or not in a variety of relationship situations.

Social cognition is now recognized by many interpersonal psychologists as an essential ingredient in shaping interpersonal behavior. Leising and Borkenau (Chapter 10) highlight some of the important consequences of how we perceive others (e.g., as potential threats or objects of affection), make judgments about motives and behaviors, and form stereotypes.

Gifford (Chapter 11) highlights the important role of nonverbal behavior in shaping our thoughts about people and situations, and how we respond interpersonally. He also describes a number of methodological challenges to researchers in this area of scientific inquiry.

In Part III, Personality and Interpersonal Interactions, there are six chapters focusing on a variety of dispositional individual difference variables known to impact interpersonal behavior. The topics in this section range in scope from specific behavioral triggers (social allergens) to pervasive, maladaptive patterns of relating to others in a wide variety of contexts (personality disorders). Starting off in Chapter 12, Murray and Holmes offer a lucid account of how trust (and the lack of it) mediates and moderates the interpersonal "dance" of partners in romantic relationships. Collins, Ford, and Feeney (Chapter 13) follow with an attachment-theory perspective on two forms of social support and care-giving, and provide a review of empirical findings.

Recent studies in personality, social, and clinical psychology are shedding light on the situational and interpersonal factors that influence aggressive acts in people whose potential for antisocial behavior might not otherwise be recognized. In Chapter 14 Bartholomew and Cobb discuss this work, which shows that violence in close relationships can be predicted by specific patterns of individual dispositions and relationship behaviors. Jones and Paulhus follow in Chapter 15 with a report on how contemporary interpersonal theory may be used to elucidate differences in three semantically similar constructs: Machiavellianism, narcissism, and psychopathy. They argue that temporal orientation (whether behavior is focused on short-term or long-term goals) and identity strength (strong or diffuse focus on self) can differentiate these personality styles and predict their varying responses to similar circumstances.

We are all aware of the everyday annoyances of others that shape whether and how we interact with them in the future. In Chapter 16, O'Connor reports on a new field of study that addresses these behaviors, termed "social allergens." The final chapter in this section, by Hill, Pilkonis, and Bear (Chapter 17), presents the importance of the social context of behavior in determining people's reactions. A bid for intimacy from a romantic partner is judged very differently from a similar bid from a co-worker.

Part IV highlights important topics in the Assessment of Interpersonal Characteristics. Gurtman (Chapter 18) discusses the methodological properties of the circular measurement models that are a hallmark of interpersonal psychology. Locke (Chapter 19) summarizes the family of instruments developed over the past 50-plus years to assess interpersonal aspects of personality and related constructs such as interpersonal motives and values. Benjamin (Chapter 20) offers a fresh perspective on Structural Analysis of Social Behavior (SASB), a three-dimensional model of interpersonal behavior that she originally developed in the 1970s to elucidate maladaptive patterns in psychotherapy clients. Following this, Schauenberg and Grande (Chapter 21) review interview-based measures of interpersonal behaviors and object relations, which show promise in providing data to clinicians and researchers that is not biased by self-report impression management tendencies.

Psychopathology and Health is the theme of Part V, where readers will find six chapters that highlight the contributions of interpersonal theory to the understanding of psychiatric and medical disorders. Starting off, Pincus and Wright (Chapter 22) provide a historical review of efforts by interpersonal psychologists to create a nosology for psychopathological conditions that would also inform treatment, and then offer suggestions for the future from recent research on interpersonal pathoplasticity, intraindividual variability, and behavioral signatures. Next, Clarkin, Levy, and Ellison (Chapter 23) focus their attention on the interpersonal features of personality disorders, and discuss the strengths and weaknesses of existing personality models for understanding the interpersonal processes that lead to the pervasive, maladaptive functioning of individuals with these disorders. Nugent, Amstader, and Koenen (Chapter 24) assert the view that there is a robust and reciprocal relationship between interpersonal processes and trauma. They offer strong empirical

evidence for this and note that there are a growing number of comprehensive models of coping with traumatic stress that include interpersonal processes as a central feature. Segrin (Chapter 25) follows with a survey of recent research on social skills deficits, interpersonal responses to depression, and dysfunctional family interactions as causes, consequents, maintaining forces, and vulnerabilities to depression.

In Chapter 26, Alden and Regambal review the interpersonal factors associated with the development and treatment of social anxiety disorder, generalized anxiety disorder, panic disorder, obsessive-compulsive disorder, and post–traumatic stress disorder. In the final chapter of this section, Smith and Cundiff (Chapter 27) review evidence for the importance of interpersonal behavior in the development, management, and treatment of coronary heart disease.

Completing our survey of the field is Part VI, Interpersonal Therapeutic Interventions, which offers six contributions on recent developments in interpersonal approaches to treating a wide variety of psychiatric and behavior problems in children, adolescents, and adults. Costa, Benoit, and Ollendick (Chapter 28) review the link between a variety of dispositional, familial, and peer variables and interpersonal development, discuss the interpersonal processes that influence the development and expression of psychopathology in childhood and adolescence, and explore the implications of interpersonal processes in the treatment of these disorders.

The relationship between therapist and client has been a focus of attention for interpersonal psychologists since the 1930s. Castonguay, Constantino, Boswell, and Kraus (Chapter 29) review current theory and research on the relationship factors of greatest impact on therapeutic success. In a companion chapter (30), Eubanks-Carter, Muran, Safran, and Hayes address a new generation of research that seeks to clarify how the therapeutic alliance develops, why strains or ruptures occur, and how the alliance can be repaired.

Interpersonal therapy for depression, originally developed by Gerald Klerman and Myrna Weissman in the 1970s (Klerman et al., 1974; Klerman et al., 1984), has become a treatment of choice for psychologists all over the world. In Chapter 31, Gunlicks-Stoessel and Weissman provide a concise but thorough overview of this intervention technique and review a large body of empirical evidence demonstrating its efficacy. Levenson (Chapter 32) follows with a report on another well-validated interpersonal treatment, Time-Limited Dynamic Psychotherapy (TLDP), which was developed by Hans Strupp and Jeffrey Binder in the 1980s (Strupp & Binder, 1984). TLDP has been shown to be effective in treating a wide range of psychiatric disorders by using the therapist-client relationship as the main focus of treatment. Interpersonal processes in group psychotherapy are the focus of Chapter 33 by Piper and Ogrodniczuk. They review therapeutic factors that are unique to group treatment, describe different approaches to treatment, and provide evidence for the efficacy and efficiency of group therapy.

The final contribution to the book (34), written by the editors, offers a synthesis of salient themes presented by chapter authors. It also provides a perspective on the process of confluence and integration over the past 60-plus years of the ideas that now form the mainstream of interpersonal psychology.

References

Adorno, T. W., Frenkel-Brunswik, E., Levinson, D. J., & Sanford, D. N. (1950). *The authoritarian personality*. New York: Harper and Row.

Ainsworth, M., & Bowlby, J. (1965). *Child care and the growth of love*. London: Penguin.

Ainsworth, M., Blehar, M., Waters, E., & Wall, S. (1978). *Patterns of attachment*. Hillsdale, NJ: Erlbaum.

Allport, F. H. (1924). *Social psychology*. Boston: Houghton Mifflin.

Allport, G. (1937). *Personality: A psychological interpretation*. New York: Henry Holt.

Bakan, D. (1966). *The duality of human existence: An essay on psychology and religion*. Chicago: Rand McNally.

Bandura, A. (1986). *Social foundations of thought and action: A social cognitive theory*. Englewood Cliffs, NJ: Prentice-Hall.

Bateson, G., Jackson, D. D., Haley, J., & Weakland, J. (1956). Toward a theory of schizophrenia. *Behavioral Sciences, 1*, 251–264.

Benedict, R. (1934). *Patterns of culture*. New York: Houghton Mifflin.

Benjamin, L. S. (1974). Structural analysis of social behavior (SASB). *Psychological Review, 81*, 392–425.

Benjamin, L. S. (1993). *Interpersonal diagnosis and treatment of personality disorders*. New York: Guilford Press.

Benjamin, L. S. (2003). *Interpersonal Reconstructive Therapy: Promoting change in nonresponders*. New York: Guilford Press.

Bion, W. (1961). *Experiences in groups*. London: Tavistock.

Blatt, S. J. (2004). *Experiences of depression: Theoretical, clinical and research perspectives*. Washington, DC: American Psychological Association.

Blatt, S. J. (2008). *Polarities of experience: Relatedness and self-definition in personality development, psychopathology, and the therapeutic process*. Washington, DC: American Psychological Association Press.

Bowlby, J. (1973). *Attachment and loss: Vol. 2. Separation: Anxiety and anger*. New York: Basic Books.

Bowlby, J. (1980). *Attachment and loss: Vol. 3. Sadness and depression*. New York: Basic Books.

Bowlby, J. (1982). *Attachment and loss: Vol. 1. Attachment* (2nd ed.). New York: Basic Books. (Original edition published 1969).

Bowlby, J. (1988). *A secure base: Clinical applications of attachment theory*. London: Routledge.

Broderick, C. B., & Schrader, S. S. (1991). The history of professional marriage and family therapy. In A. S. Gurman & D. P. Kniskern (Eds.), *Handbook of Family Therapy* (Vol. 2, pp. 3–40). New York: Brunner/Mazel.

Carson, R. C. (1969). *Interaction concepts of personality*. Chicago: Aldine.

Cassidy, J., & Shaver, P. R. (Eds.) (2008), *Handbook of attachment: Theory, research, and clinical applications* (2nd ed.). New York: Guilford Press.

Coffey, H. S. (1954). Group psychotherapy. In L. A. Pennington & I. A. Berg (Eds.), *An introduction to clinical psychology* (2nd ed., pp. 586–606). New York: Ronald Press.

Coyne, J. C. (1976). Toward an interactional description of depression. *Psychiatry, 39,* 28–40.

Darwin, C. R. (1859). *On the origin of species by means of natural selection.* London: Murray.

Erickson, E. (1950). *Childhood and society.* New York: Norton.

Evans, F. B. (1996). *Harry Stack Sullivan: Interpersonal theory and psychotherapy.* New York: Routledge.

Freedman, M. B., Leary, T. F., Ossorio, A. G., & Coffey, H. S. (1951). The interpersonal dimension of personality. *Journal of Personality, 20,* 143–161.

Freud, A. (1946) *The psycho-analytic treatment of children.* Oxford, England: Imago.

Fromm, E. (1941). *Escape from freedom.* New York: Rinehart & Co.

Fromm-Reichmann, F. (1960). *Principles of intensive psychotherapy.* Chicago: University of Chicago Press.

Gurtman, M. B. (1991). Evaluating the interpersonalness of personality scales. *Personality and Social Psychology Bulletin, 17,* 670–677.

Gurtman, M. B., & Balakrishnan, J. D. (1998). Circular measurement redux: The analysis and interpretation of interpersonal circle profiles. *Clinical Psychology: Science and Practice, 5,* 344–360.

Heider, F. (1958). *The psychology of interpersonal relations.* New York: John Wiley & Sons.

Horney, K. (1937). *The neurotic personality of our time.* New York: Norton.

Horowitz, L. M. (1979). On the cognitive structure of interpersonal problems treated in psychotherapy. *Journal of Consulting and Clinical Psychology, 47,* 5–15.

Horowitz, L. M. (2004). *Interpersonal foundations of psychopathology.* Washington, DC: American Psychological Association.

Kiesler, D. J. (1983). The 1982 Interpersonal Circle: A taxonomy for complementarity in human transactions. *Psychological Review, 90,* 185–214.

Kiesler, D. J. (1996). *Contemporary interpersonal theory and research: Personality, psychopathology, and psychotherapy.* New York: John Wiley & Sons.

Klein, M. (1962). *The psychoanalysis of children.* Oxford, England: Grove.

Klerman, G. L., DiMascio, A., Weissman, M., Prusoff, B., & Paykel, E. S. (1974). Treatment of depression by drugs and psychotherapy. *American Journal of Psychiatry, 131,* 186–191.

Klerman, G. L., Weissman, M. M., Rounsaville, B. J., & Chevron, E. S. (1984). *Interpersonal psychotherapy of depression.* New York: Basic Books.

LaForge, R. (2004). The early development of the interpersonal system of personality (ISP). *Multivariate Behavioral Research, 39,* 359–378.

Laing, R. D. (1960). *The divided self.* New York: Penguin.

Leary, T. (1957). *Interpersonal diagnosis of personality.* New York: Ronald Press.

Lewin, K. (1936). *Principles of topological psychology.* New York: McGraw-Hill.

Lewin, K. (1947). Frontiers in group dynamics. *Human Relations, 1,* 5–41.

Lewin, K. (1948). *Resolving social conflicts: Selected papers on group dynamics.* New York: Harper & Row.

Lewin, K., Lippitt, R., & White, R. K. (1939). Patterns of aggressive behavior in experimentally created social climates. *Journal of Social Psychology, 10,* 271–301.

Lorr, M. (1991). A redefinition of dominance. *Personality and Individual Differences, 12,* 877–879.

Lorr, M., & McNair, D. M. (1963). An interpersonal behavior circle. *Journal of Abnormal and Social Psychology, 67,* 68–75.

Lorr, M., & McNair, D. M. (1965). Expansion of the interpersonal behavior circle. *Journal of Personality and Social Psychology, 2,* 823–830.

Meade, G. H. (1934). *Mind, self, and society.* Chicago: University of Chicago Press.

Mikulincer, M., & Shaver, P. R. (2007). *Attachment patterns in adulthood: Structure, dynamics, and change.* New York: Guilford Press.

Mischel, W. (1973). Toward a cognitive social learning reconceptualization of personality. *Psychological Review, 80,* 252–283.

Mischel, W., & Shoda, Y. (1995). A cognitive-affective system theory of personality: Reconceptualizing situations, dispositions, dynamics, and invariance in personality structure. *Psychological Review, 102,* 246–268.

Moskowitz, D. S., & Zuroff, D. C. (2004). Flux, pulse, and spin: Dynamic additions to the personality lexicon. *Journal of Personality and Social Psychology, 86,* 880–893.

Münsterberg, H. (1915). *Psychology: General and applied.* New York: D. Appleton & Company.

Murray, H. A. (1938). *Explorations in personality*. New York: Oxford University Press.

Pincus, A. L. (2005a). A contemporary integrative interpersonal theory of personality disorders. In J. Clarkin & M. Lenzenweger (Eds.), *Major theories of personality disorder* (2nd ed., pp. 282–331). New York: Guilford Press.

Pincus, A. L. (2005b). The interpersonal nexus of personality disorders. In S. Strack (Ed.), *Handbook of personology and psychopathology* (pp. 120–139). Hoboken, NJ: John Wiley & Sons.

Pincus, A. L., & Ansell, E. B. (2003). Interpersonal theory of personality. In T. Millon & M. Lerner (Eds.), *Comprehensive handbook of psychology: Vol. 5. Personality and social psychology* (pp. 209–229). Hoboken, NJ: John Wiley & Sons.

Plutchik, R., & Conte, H. R. (Eds.) (1997). *Circumplex models of personality and emotions*. Washington, DC: American Psychological Association.

Prince, M. (1914). *The unconscious: The fundamentals of human personality, normal and abnormal*. Oxford, England: Macmillan.

Ruesch, J., & Bateson, G. (1951). *Communication: The social matrix of psychiatry*. New York: Norton.

Rioch, D. M. (1959). Problems of "perception" and "communication" in mental illness. *Archives of General Psychiatry, 1*, 81–92.

Rioch, D. M. (1985). Recollections of Harry Stack Sullivan and of the development of his interpersonal psychiatry. *Psychiatry, 48*, 141–158.

Rioch, M. J. (1970). Group relations: Rationale and technique. *International Journal of Group Psychotherapy, 20*, 340–355.

Rioch, M. J. (1986). Fifty years at the Washington School of Psychiatry. *Psychiatry, 49*, 33–44.

Sadler, P., & Woody, E. (2003). Is who you are who you're talking to? Interpersonal style and complementarity in mixed-sex interactions. *Journal of Personality and Social Psychology, 84*, 80–96.

Strack, S. (Ed.) (1996). Special series: Interpersonal theory and the interpersonal circumplex: Timothy Leary's legacy. *Journal of Personality Assessment, 66*, 211–307.

Strupp, H. H., & Binder, J. L. (1984). *Psychotherapy in a new key*. New York: Basic Books.

Sullivan, H. S. (1940). Conceptions of modern psychiatry: The first William Alanson White Memorial Lectures. *Psychiatry, 3*, 1–117.

Sullivan, H. S. (1953a). *The interpersonal theory of psychiatry*. New York: Norton.

Sullivan, H. S. (1953b). *Conceptions of modern psychiatry*. New York: Norton.

Sullivan, H. S. (1954). *The psychiatric interview*. New York: Norton.

Sullivan, H. S. (1956). *Clinical studies in psychiatry*. New York: Norton.

Watzlawick, P., Beavin, J., & Jackson, D. (1967). *Pragmatics of human communication*. New York: Norton.

Watzlawick, P., & Weakland, J. H. (Eds.) (1977). *The interactional view*. New York: Norton.

Wiggins, J. S. (1979). A psychological taxonomy of trait-descriptive terms: The interpersonal domain. *Journal of Personality and Social Psychology, 37*, 395–412.

Wiggins, J. S. (1991). Agency and communion as conceptual coordinates for the understanding and measurement of interpersonal behavior. In W. W. Grove & D. Cicchetti (Eds.), *Thinking clearly about psychology: Vol. 2. Personality and psychotherapy* (pp. 89–113). Minneapolis, MN: University of Minnesota Press.

Wiggins, J. S. (2003). *Paradigms of personality assessment*. New York: Guilford Press.

I THEORETICAL PERSPECTIVES

2 AN ATTACHMENT-THEORY FRAMEWORK FOR CONCEPTUALIZING INTERPERSONAL BEHAVIOR

Phillip R. Shaver

Mario Mikulincer

Attachment theory, created by Bowlby (1973, 1980, 1982) and initially rendered testable by Ainsworth (e.g., Ainsworth, Blehar, Waters, & Wall, 1978), has become one of the leading approaches to conceptualizing and studying close interpersonal relationships. (See Cassidy & Shaver, 2008, and Mikulincer & Shaver, 2007a, for overviews of attachment research in general and attachment theory applied to the study of adult relationships in particular.) The theory postulates core motivational, or behavioral, "systems" such as attachment, exploration, caregiving, and sexuality, which humans share to some extent with nonhuman primates (Bowlby, 1982). It characterizes these systems as having experientially modifiable parameters, which (in addition to modest genetic influences), account for relatively stable individual differences in what has come to be called "attachment style" (see Mikulincer & Shaver, 2007a, for a history of this construct).

In this chapter, we explore the relevance of attachment theory for understanding individual differences in interpersonal behavior, and we propose a general attachment-oriented framework for conceptualizing such behavior. We begin with a brief summary of attachment theory and an account of the two major dimensions of attachment style in adulthood, attachment anxiety and avoidance. We then review evidence concerning the associations between these dimensions and interpersonal behavior, proposing that the associations are mediated by both attachment-related cognitive-motivational predispositions and patterns of social information processing. Next we review studies of the ways in which attachment style contributes to a person's goal structures, mental representations of self and others, and mental scripts concerning interpersonal transactions as well as information-processing biases during social interactions. Finally, we consider factors responsible for individual differences in attachment style, including genetic and environmental influences.

BASIC CONCEPTS IN ATTACHMENT THEORY AND RESEARCH

One of the core tenets of attachment theory (Bowlby, 1973, 1980, 1982) is that human beings are born with a psychobiological system (the *attachment behavioral system*) that motivates them to seek proximity to significant others (*attachment figures*) in times of need. According to Bowlby (1982), the goal of this system is to maintain adequate protection and support, which is accompanied by a subjective sense of safety and security. This goal is made salient when people encounter actual or symbolic threats and notice that an attachment figure is not sufficiently near, interested, or responsive (Bowlby, 1982). In such cases, a person's attachment system is up-regulated and the person is motivated to increase or reestablish proximity to an attachment figure so that "felt security" (Sroufe & Waters, 1977) is attained.

Bowlby (1988) assumed that although age and development increase a person's ability to gain comfort from internal, symbolic representations of attachment figures, no one at any age is completely free from reliance on actual others. The attachment system therefore remains active over the entire life span, as indicated by adults' tendency to seek proximity and support when threatened or distressed (Hazan & Zeifman, 1999; Mikulincer & Shaver, 2009). Moreover, people of all ages are capable of becoming emotionally attached to a variety of close relationship partners (e.g., siblings, friends, romantic partners, coaches, and leaders), using such people as "stronger and wiser" (Bowlby, 1982) attachment figures—that is, as safe havens in times of need and secure bases from which to explore and develop skills—and suffering distress upon prolonged or permanent separation from these people (Bowlby, 1980; Shaver & Fraley, 2008).

Bowlby (1973) devoted a great deal of attention to the individual differences in attachment-system functioning that arise as a result of the availability, responsiveness, and supportiveness of a person's key attachment figures, especially in times of need. Interactions with attachment figures who are available and responsive facilitate optimal functioning of the attachment system and promote a lasting, pervasive sense of *attachment security*—a sense that the world is interesting and safe, that attachment figures are helpful when called upon, and that it is possible to explore the environment curiously and engage effectively with other people. During these interactions, a person learns that acknowledgment and display of distress elicit supportive responses from others, and that turning to others when threatened is an effective means of coping with problems and threats. These experiences generate positive mental representations of self and others (*attachment working models*) that increase both self-confidence and confidence in attachment figures' willingness to provide support. Bowlby (1988) viewed the sense of attachment security as crucial for maintaining emotional stability, developing positive attitudes toward self and others, and forming mature, mutually satisfying close relationships.

When attachment figures are not reliably available and supportive, a sense of security is not attained, negative working models of self and others are formed, and secondary strategies of affect regulation come into play. These secondary strategies are of two kinds: *hyperactivation* and *deactivation* of the attachment system (Cassidy & Kobak, 1988; Mikulincer & Shaver, 2003.) Hyperactivation is characterized by energetic, insistent attempts to induce a relationship partner, viewed as insufficiently available or responsive, to pay more attention and provide better care and support. Hyperactivating strategies include clinging, controlling, and coercive responses, cognitive and behavioral efforts to establish proximity, and overdependence on relationship partners as a source of protection

(Shaver & Mikulincer, 2002). Deactivation refers to suppression or inhibition of proximity-seeking inclinations and actions, discounting of threats that might activate the attachment system, and determination to handle undeniable stresses alone. These strategies involve maintaining physical and emotional distance from others, being uncomfortable with intimacy and interdependence, downplaying threat- and attachment-related cues, and suppressing threat- and attachment-related thoughts (Shaver & Hazan, 1993).

In examining individual differences in attachment-system functioning in adolescence and adulthood, researchers have focused on a person's *attachment style*—the chronic pattern of relational expectations, emotions, and behaviors that results from a particular history of attachment experiences (Fraley & Shaver, 2000). Beginning with Ainsworth et al.'s (1978) studies of infant attachment, and continuing through Hazan and Shaver's (1987) conceptualization of romantic attachment, followed by many studies conducted by social and personality psychologists (reviewed by Mikulincer & Shaver, 2007a), researchers have found that individual differences in attachment style can be measured along two dimensions, attachment-related *avoidance* and *anxiety* (Brennan, Clark, & Shaver, 1998). A person's position on the avoidant attachment dimension indicates the extent to which he or she distrusts others' good will and relies on deactivating strategies for coping with attachment insecurities. A person's position on the anxiety dimension indicates the degree to which he or she worries that relationship partners will be unavailable or unhelpful in times of need and relies on hyperactivating strategies. People who score low on both dimensions have a chronic sense of security and are said to be secure or to have a secure attachment style.

The two dimensions can be measured with reliable and valid self-report scales (e.g., Brennan et al., 1998) and are associated in theoretically predictable ways with relationship quality, adjustment, and

mental health (see Mikulincer & Shaver, 2003, 2007a; Shaver & Hazan, 1993, for reviews). Throughout this chapter we refer to people with secure, anxious, and avoidant attachment styles, or people who are relatively anxious or avoidant. Although the convenient categorical shorthand (secure, anxious, and avoidant) can mistakenly foster typological thinking, we will always be referring to fuzzy regions in a two-dimensional space, a space in which research participants are continuously rather than categorically distributed.

ATTACHMENT-STYLE DIFFERENCES
IN INTERPERSONAL BEHAVIOR

Individual differences in attachment anxiety and avoidance are important for understanding characteristic differences in a wide variety of interpersonal reactions and behaviors. For example, attachment insecurities encourage negative, dysfunctional construals of social interactions. In studies assessing the quality of daily interactions over the course of one to two weeks, for example, more avoidant people reported lower levels of satisfaction, intimacy, self-disclosure, supportive behavior, and positive emotions than less avoidant (i.e., more secure) people as well as higher levels of negative emotions, such as boredom and tension (e.g., Kafetsios & Nezlek, 2002; Tidwell, Reis, & Shaver, 1996). These studies also revealed that, as compared to less anxious people, ones who scored higher on attachment anxiety reported more negative emotional experiences and more frequent feelings of rejection during daily interactions. There is also evidence that attachment insecurity (of both the anxious and avoidant varieties) is associated with less constructive, less sensitive patterns of dyadic communication (e.g., Guerrero, 1996) and less effective attempts to resolve relational conflicts (e.g., Scharfe & Bartholomew, 1995).

Attachment insecurities are also related to more negative reactions to interpersonal transgressions and offenses. Whereas relatively secure people tend to react with functional, constructive expressions of anger (nonhostile protests), insecure people (either anxious or avoidant) exhibit more destructive forms of anger, such as animosity, hostility, vengeful criticism, or vicious retaliation (e.g., Simpson, Rholes, & Phillips, 1996). In addition, more avoidant people tend to be less inclined to forgive a hurtful partner and more likely to withdraw or seek revenge (Mikulincer, Shaver, & Slav, 2006). Mikulincer et al. (2006) also found that more avoidant people felt less grateful than less avoidant people during interactions in which someone behaved positively toward them.

Attachment insecurities also interfere with prosocial attitudes and behavior during interactions with people who are distressed or in need. On the negative side, attachment anxiety and avoidance are associated with lower scores on self-report scales measuring sensitivity and responsiveness to a relationship partner's needs (e.g., Kunce & Shaver, 1994) and less supportive actual behaviors toward a distressed partner (e.g., Simpson, Rholes,

& Nelligan, 1992). On the positive side, both dispositional and experimentally augmented attachment security are associated with heightened empathy and compassion for a person who is suffering or struggling (e.g., Mikulincer, Shaver, Gillath, & Nitzberg, 2005).

In this chapter, we propose a general model of the ways in which individual differences in attachment-system functioning (operationalized in terms of attachment anxiety and avoidance) affect behavior in social interactions. Specifically, we propose a double-mediation model (see Figure 2.1) that involves (a) cognitive-motivational predispositions (interpersonal goals, beliefs about self and others, and mental scripts) that influence behavior during interpersonal encounters and (b) patterns of information processing during such encounters. According to this model, individual differences in attachment-system functioning shape cognitive-motivational predispositions (the first mediation path), which in turn bias the way people attend, interpret, and respond to information that arises during a social interaction (the second mediation path).

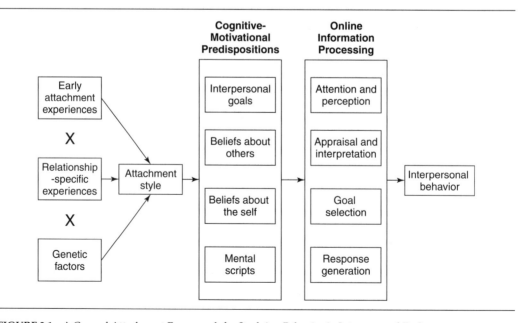

FIGURE 2.1   A General Attachment Framework for Studying Behavior in Interpersonal Exchanges

These attachment-related patterns of social information processing are the proximal antecedents of interpersonal behavior.

ATTACHMENT-RELATED COGNITIVE-MOTIVATIONAL PREDISPOSITIONS

People enter social interactions with knowledge and attitudes that they acquired during past interactions with the same relationship partner, or they transfer and apply knowledge and attitudes based on previous relationships (Brumbaugh & Fraley, 2006). These personal predispositions are manifested in a person's goal structure (the goals he or she frequently seeks during social interactions), in declarative knowledge about self and others (beliefs about one's worth, skills, and efficacy; beliefs about a partner's likely motives and actions), and procedural knowledge about interpersonal exchanges (mental scripts representing the ways in which interpersonal exchanges typically unfold). These predispositions can bias the acquisition and use of social information during an interaction via top-down, schematic processes that favor attention to and encoding of information that reinforces expectations and encourages the ignoring or dismissal of information that invalidates expectations. More important, as explained later, these predispositions are parts or implications of a person's attachment style, and they tend to be the main vehicles by which individual differences in attachment-system functioning are transferred to new social interactions and relationships.

Interpersonal Goals

According to attachment theory, each of the two main kinds of attachment insecurity (anxiety and avoidance) involves particular wishes and fears concerning security, closeness, dependency, and autonomy (e.g., Cassidy & Kobak, 1988; Mikulincer & Shaver, 2007a), which can influence the pursuit of particular goals during social interactions. Attachment-anxious people tend to select interpersonal goals compatible with their intense need for closeness and to strongly fear rejection and separation. In contrast, avoidant people tend to organize their interactions around desires for distance and self-reliance and to perceive interdependence and intimacy as threatening or aversive. For example, Collins, Guichard, Ford, and Feeney (2004) found that attachment anxiety was associated with overemphasizing the importance of a romantic partner's love and support, and avoidant attachment was associated with downplaying such closeness-related goals. Research has shown that avoidant attachment is associated with intimacy-aversion (e.g., Doi & Thelen, 1993), conceiving of relationship partners as more distant from one's "core self" (Rowe & Carnelley, 2005), and expressing discomfort when another person moves into one's personal space (e.g., Kaitz, Bar-Haim, Lehrer, & Grossman, 2004). In addition, attachment anxiety is associated with rejection sensitivity (e.g., Downey & Feldman, 1996) and quick recognition of rejection words in a lexical decision task (e.g., Baldwin & Kay, 2003).

Mental Representations of the Self

Bowlby (1973) argued that children construct mental representations of themselves while interacting with attachment figures in times of need. Whereas episodes of attachment-figure availability can promote perceptions of the self as valuable, lovable, and special, because one is actually valued, loved, and regarded as special by a caring attachment figure, frustrating interactions with unsupportive attachment figure can shatter these positive self-representations. Indeed, adult attachment research consistently shows that attachment insecurities are associated with negative self-representations (see Mikulincer & Shaver, 2007a, for a review). For example, more anxiously attached individuals tend to report lower self-esteem (e.g., Mickelson,

Kessler, & Shaver, 1997), to view themselves as less competent and efficacious (e.g., Cooper, Shaver, & Collins, 1998), and to possess less optimistic expectations about their ability to cope with stress (e.g., Berant, Mikulincer, & Florian, 2001). Moreover, both attachment anxiety and avoidance are associated with having a less-coherent model of self (Mikulincer, 1995).

In a series of laboratory experiments, Mikulincer (1998a) showed that both of the secondary attachment strategies (anxious hyperactivation and avoidant deactivation) distort self-representations, but in different ways. Whereas hyperactivation negatively biases anxious people's self-representations, deactivating strategies favor defensive processes of self-enhancement and self-inflation. On the one hand, anxious strategies cause attention to be directed to self-relevant sources of distress (e.g., expectations of interpersonal rejection) and exacerbate self-defeating self-presentational tendencies, which involve emphasizing helplessness and vulnerability as a way of eliciting other people's compassion and support. On the other hand, avoidant strategies divert attention away from self-relevant sources of distress and encourage the adoption of a self-reliant attitude, which requires exaggeration of strengths and competences.

Mental Representations of Others

According to attachment theory, people with different attachment styles also differ in their perceptions of other people (Bowlby, 1973). Whereas security-enhancing interactions with available and responsive attachment figures promote a positive view of others, emotionally painful, frustrating interactions with unavailable or rejecting attachment figures contribute to negative views of others (Shaver & Hazan, 1993). Indeed, avoidant attachment is correlated with negative views of human nature (e.g., Collins & Read, 1990), lack of esteem for others (e.g., Luke, Maio, & Carnelley, 2004),

doubts about other people's trustworthiness (e.g., Cozzarelli, Hoekstra, & Bylsma, 2000), and negative expectations about others' behavior (e.g., Baldwin, Fehr, Keedian, Seidel, & Thompson, 1993). For example, Baldwin et al. (1993) examined the cognitive accessibility of expectations regarding a partner's behavior, using a lexical-decision task, and found that avoidant people had readier mental access to representations of negative partner behaviors (e.g., the partner being hurtful) than secure people.

Mikulincer and Shaver (2007a) concluded that anxious attachment is associated with more ambivalent views of others. Although people scoring high on attachment anxiety have a history of frustrating interactions with attachment figures, they nevertheless tend to believe that if they intensify their proximity-seeking efforts, they may compel relationship partners to pay attention and provide adequate support (Cassidy & Berlin, 1994). As a result, they do not form a simple, strongly negative view of others, because such a view would imply that proximity seeking is hopeless. Rather, even if they are angry as well as frightened, they tend to take some of the blame for a partner's unreliable attention and care (Mikulincer & Shaver, 2003). These mental gyrations can lead to simultaneous appraisals of others' potential value and their likely unavailability or unsupportiveness.

Mental Scripts

Recent theoretical analyses propose that working models of self and others—the heart of attachment styles—also include procedural knowledge about how social interactions unfold and how one can best handle stress and distress (e.g., Mikulincer & Shaver, 2007b; Waters, Rodrigues, & Ridgeway, 1998; H. S. Waters & Waters, 2006). According to Mikulincer and Shaver (2007b), interactions with warm, loving, and supportive attachment figures are embodied in a relational if-then script, which Waters et al. (1998) called a *secure-base script*. This script is thought to include something like the following if-then propositions: "If I encounter an obstacle and/or become distressed, I can approach a significant other for help; he or she is likely to be available and supportive; I will experience relief and comfort as a result of proximity to this person; I can then return to other activities." Once activated, this script serves as a guide for interacting with others and can, by itself, mitigate distress, promote optimism and hope, and help secure individuals cope well with life problems.

There is already evidence for the psychological reality of the secure-base script. Mikulincer, Shaver, Sapir-Lavid, and Avihou-Kanza (2009) presented study participants with a picture of a needy person (an injured person in a hospital bed who had a sad facial expression) and asked them to write a story about what would happen next. More secure participants were more likely to write stories that included the key elements of the secure-base script (support seeking, support provision, and distress relief). Using a prompt-word outline method, H. S. Waters and Waters (2006) also showed that securely attached participants produced more stories organized around the secure-base script than insecurely attached participants. In addition, Mikulincer et al. (2008) found that relatively secure participants generated more inferences concerning the secure-base-script information they received and made faster and more confident judgments about it.

Following this line of research, Ein-Dor, Mikulincer, and Shaver (2009) argued that insecurely attached people also possess mental scripts of distress management. They claimed that anxiously attached individuals rely on a *sentinel script*—one that includes high sensitivity to clues of impending danger and a tendency to warn others about the danger while staying close to those others in the dangerous situation. Ein-Dor et al. (2009) also hypothesized that avoidant people's responses are organized around what they called *a rapid fight-flight script*—one that includes rapid self-protective responses to

danger without consulting other people or seeking to receive help from them. In a series of five studies, Ein-Dor et al. (2009) found that more anxiously attached participants had readier mental access to the core components of the sentinel script when writing a story about threatening events, and they processed sentinel-script information more quickly and more deeply. More avoidant participants had readier mental access to the core components of the rapid fight-flight script and better encoding and deeper processing of rapid-fight-flight-script information.

Summary

Evidence is growing that individual differences in attachment-system functioning are involved in shaping interpersonal goals, beliefs about self and others, and mental scripts representing interpersonal exchanges. However, more research is needed to determine how the cognitive-motivational predispositions a person brings to a given social interaction influence his or her behavior during the interaction, and to determine whether and how these predispositions mediate the connection between attachment insecurities and interpersonal behavior.

ATTACHMENT-RELATED DIFFERENCES IN THE PROCESSING OF SOCIAL INFORMATION

In this section we review evidence concerning the influence of attachment style on the processing of information about social interactions as they unfold in time. However, before reviewing the evidence, we explain how we understand the processing of information during interpersonal transactions, its proximal antecedents, and its immediate behavioral consequences.

Social Information Processing

In analyzing attachment-related biases in the processing of information during interpersonal exchanges, we consider the cognitive steps that lead to behavior according to sequential models of social information processing (e.g., Andersen & Glassman, 1996; Dodge, 2003, in press; Vogel, Wester, Larson, & Wade, 2006). In these models, the initial steps of processing involve attention, perception, and interpretation of information, and the later steps involve judgments and decisions about behavioral alternatives in a given situation (see Figure 2.1).

The first step is attention to and perception of informational cues. Because multiple cues appear simultaneously and the stimulus array is so large, selective attention to some cues over others is inevitable. When a dating partner smiles at an attractive opposite-sex person at a cocktail party, for example, one person might attend to the smile and the pain it causes oneself, another person might attend to the potential rival and his or her attractiveness, and a third person might attend to others' reactions to the event. Attention to certain cues can obviously influence subsequent information processing and behavior based on it, such as when attention to the dating partner's expression of apology or guilt tinged with embarrassment might mitigate one's chagrin and jealousy and encourage a forgiving or conciliatory response.

Closely following upon the perception of social cues is the assembly of a mental representation of the current situation, the other person's reactions, and the self in relation to this person. This more complex and reflective process often initiates a series of causal attributions regarding the other's behavior (e.g., Why is my dating partner smiling at this attractive opposite-sex person?), interpretations of the other's motives and intentions, expectations concerning what he or she will do next, appraisal of the situation as a threat, a loss, a challenge, or a benefit (which Lazarus & Folkman, 1984, called primary appraisal), and appraisal of one's coping capabilities and response alternatives (which Lazarus & Folkman, 1984, called secondary appraisal). Such

mental representations form online in microseconds and can be updated over the course of a social interaction. Forming such representations is not usually a conscious process, although it can become so if prompted (Dodge, 2003).

Of course, there are numerous variations on this process. For example, a romantic partner's complaint about one's behavior can be interpreted as reflecting a partner's hostility and intention to break off the relationship or as a constructive attempt to improve the quality and reliability of the relationship. Moreover, one can appraise a partner's response as a threat to oneself or to the relationship or as a challenging opportunity. Similarly, one can appraise oneself as able to change and become more considerate of a partner's needs or freedom, or as unable to make this change. In any case, the way a person appraises a situation, a partner's behavior, and one's own emotional reactions to that behavior is likely to influence the relationship—for example when one attributes hostile intent to a partner's comments, appraises the comments as a deliberate provocation, and appraises oneself as forceful in the situation and in the relationship, one might well act aggressively, perhaps even violently, toward the insulting partner (e.g., Dodge, 2003).

The third step in the process is goal selection. As with the formation of a mental representation, people are not usually aware of this step, but they may reflect afterward on the goals and impulses that became salient. In the example discussed above, the appraisal of the partner's insulting comment might lead to the selection of prorelationship or reparatory goals, approval or pacifying goals, withdrawal or defensive goals, or aggressive, retaliatory goals. Such goal selection is accompanied by discrete emotional reactions that are triggered by specific patterns of cognitive appraisals (e.g., Frijda, 1986; Lazarus, 1991). For example, whereas feelings of love or gratitude may predispose a person to behave in ways that promote the relationship, fear may predispose a person to withdraw, and anger may predispose the person to retaliate aggressively.

The subsequent decision phase of processing includes response generation, response evaluation, and enactment. Mental representations trigger one or more possible behavioral responses, such as prorelationship responses, withdrawal, or aggression. According to Dodge (2003), the linkages between certain mental representations and the responses that get generated are neural associations that may be either innate, and therefore "ready" at birth, or conditioned through observations of others and personal experience. However, generation of a response does not lead inevitably to its enactment. Fontaine and Dodge (2006) proposed a sequence of response evaluation and decision (RED), during which a person can quickly (and often unconsciously) decide either to enact the generated response without any consideration of the consequences or to consider and evaluate the consequences. The considerations include estimating how likely it is that one will be successful in carrying out the response, assigning personal value to the response, estimating the likelihood of various consequences of the behavior; and the assigning value to these consequences. Fontaine and Dodge (2006) hypothesized that different possible responses are compared (*response comparison*) before the most appropriate response is selected (*response selection*).

All of these steps can be influenced by contextual factors, including the interpersonal setting, the other person's verbal and nonverbal behavior, and his or her responses to one's own behavior. However, they can also be influenced by factors that people bring with them to the situation, such as the knowledge they have gathered about the other person's traits and motives during previous interactions as well as more general cognitive-motivational predispositions. We suppose that social information processing is shaped by complex person-by-situation interactions, in which contextual factors exacerbate or mitigate the influences

of cognitive-motivational predispositions through bottom-up processes while the predispositions fuel or reduce the effects of the contextual factors via top-down processes. We view individual differences in attachment-system functioning as important antecedents of top-down influences on social information processing, because, as mentioned earlier, they shape both partner-specific and more general cognitive-motivational predispositions.

Attachment Insecurities and Patterns of Social Information Processing

Early stages of information processing. There is considerable evidence linking attachment insecurities to biases in the perception of others' nonverbal messages. For example, Noller and Feeney (1994) asked one member of a newlywed couple to send a set of nonverbal messages expressing particular emotions (e.g., sadness, anger) to the other member of the couple and found that more anxious or avoidant spouses were less accurate in decoding their partner's nonverbal messages. Similarly, using Ekman and Friesen's (1975) facial action coding system, Magai, Distel, and Liker (1995) found that less-secure people were less accurate in decoding facial expressions of emotions.

In another study of facial affect decoding, Fraley, Niedenthal, Marks, Brumbaugh, and Vicary (2006) used a "morph" movie paradigm in which participants were shown computerized movies of faces in which a neutral facial expression gradually changed to an expression of a particular emotion. Participants were instructed to stop the display when they perceived that the emotional expression was coming into view, and to judge which emotion the face was expressing (anger, happiness, or sadness). More attachment-anxious individuals tended to perceive the onset of facial expressions of emotion earlier and made more errors in judging which emotion the face was expressing. These results suggest that anxious people's difficulties in decoding emotions might be a result of heightened vigilance to emotional cues and a tendency to make premature judgments.

Studies examining avoidant people's defensiveness also provide evidence concerning the early stages of social information processing. For example, Fraley, Garner, and Shaver (2000) examined the hypothesis that avoidant people would direct attention away from, or encode in a shallow way, distressing attachment-related information. Participants listened to an interview about the loss of a close relationship partner and were later asked to recall details of the interview, either soon after hearing it or at various delays ranging from half an hour to 21 days. An analysis of forgetting curves revealed that (a) avoidant people initially encoded less information from the interview, and (b) people with different attachment styles forgot encoded information at the same rate. Thus, avoidant defenses seem to block threatening interpersonal material from awareness before it is encoded.

Following up these findings, Maier et al. (2005) examined the hypothesis that avoidant people would be vigilant to attachment-related information in order to block it out and keep it from being processed further. Indeed, avoidant attachment was associated with lower identification thresholds (less exposure time needed to identify a picture) for pictures depicting affect-laden human faces and social interactions. This association was not significant for pictures of neutral faces, natural scenes, or inanimate objects. Thus, avoidant defenses seem to involve perceptual vigilance to emotional and social stimuli.

Appraisals of interpersonal events. Several studies have shown that attachment insecurities contribute to more pessimistic and catastrophic appraisals of threatening interpersonal events, such as divorce (e.g., Birnbaum, Orr, Mikulincer, & Florian, 1997), the birth of an ill child (e.g., Berant et al., 2001), and abortion (e.g., Cozzarelli, Sumer, & Major, 1998). In a study of hurt feelings in couple relationships, J. Feeney (2004) found that less secure people were more likely to appraise a hurtful event as having negative long-term effects on their self-esteem and relationship.

Appraisals of others. Studies have shown that people who differ in attachment style also differ in the way they interpret and explain others' aversive behaviors (e.g., Collins, Ford, Guichard, & Allard, 2006; Gallo & Smith, 2001). For example, Collins (1996) presented study participants with six hypothetical vignettes about a romantic partner's troubling behavior (e.g., "Your partner didn't comfort you when you were feeling down") and asked them to write an open-ended explanation of each event and to complete an attribution questionnaire assessing the extent to which the behavior was attributed to internal, stable, controllable, and intentional causes. Insecure individuals' explanations emphasized the partner's poor intentions and negative traits. Specifically, more insecure people were more likely to believe that their partner's negative behaviors were caused by the partner's lack of love, to attribute these behaviors to stable and global causes, and to view them as unkindly motivated. A similar attributional bias was noted by Mikulincer (1998b), who found that insecure people tended to attribute hostility to another person even when this person did not show signs of having hostile intentions.

Biases have also been recorded in insecure individuals' appraisal of other people's supportiveness or lack of supportiveness. For example, Collins and Feeney (2004, Study 1) experimentally manipulated a partner's supportiveness and assessed attachment-style differences in perceptions of this support. Dating couples were brought into the lab; one member of the couple was informed that he or she would perform a stressful task (deliver a speech while being videotaped); and the couple was then observed for five minutes. Next, couple members were separated, and support was manipulated by having the non-speech-making partner copy either two clearly supportive notes or two ambiguously supportive notes to send to the partner who would be giving a speech. The speech-giver then read the notes and rated both their supportiveness and the partner's behaviors during the prior interaction. Insecure participants rated the ambiguous notes as less supportive and more upsetting and inferred more negative intent than did secure participants. More important, after receiving the ambiguous notes, insecure participants rated their prior interaction as less supportive than would be expected on the basis of judges' ratings of the interactions. These findings were replicated in a second study (Collins & Feeney, 2004, Study 2) in which partners were allowed to write their own authentic notes.

Zhang and Hazan's (2002) study of person perception provides another example of how attachment insecurities can bias the interpretation of others' behavior. Participants received a list of positive and negative traits and were asked to estimate the number of behavioral instances they would need to confirm or disconfirm the possession of each trait by a hypothetical romantic partner. Anxious participants required less evidence to confirm the presence of both positive and negative traits and disconfirm the possession of negative traits. That is, anxious individuals tended to make positive and negative judgments about others relatively quickly and without much behavioral evidence. More avoidant participants requested more behavioral evidence before concluding that others possessed positive traits or that their possession of negative traits was disconfirmed. This finding suggests that avoidance fosters hard-to-refute, negative appraisals of others' traits. Moreover, it implies that avoidant people's negative views of others may be more stable and pervasive than those of anxiously attached people, who tend to be more receptive to others' positive behaviors.

Attachment style interacts with context to influence appraisals of others. Adult attachment studies have also turned up person × situation interactions, or attachment style × context interactions, that affect the appraisal of relationship partners. For example, Rholes, Simpson, Campbell, and Grich (2001) reported that both attachment-related cognitive biases and a partner's actual behavior influenced insecure women's perceptions of support during the transition to parenthood. More anxious wives perceived their spouses to be less supportive than their husbands claimed to be before and after the delivery. Moreover, men married to more anxiously attached women reported being less supportive than men married to less anxious women. Taken together, the findings suggest that, although anxious women may be biased in appraising their partner's supportiveness, there is also a degree of accuracy in their complaints about their husband's lack of support. Whether that lack of support was partly a reaction to early biased appraisals is still unknown. Interestingly, anxiously attached women were no more prone to postpartum depression than less anxious women when they perceived their husband to be supportive. This is an example of how important such perceptions can be for mental health and family functioning.

Attachment-oriented studies of marital relationships provide further information about the role of a partner's actual characteristics in influencing appraisals of his or her supportiveness (e.g., Gallo & Smith, 2001; Volling, Notaro, & Larsen, 1998). For example, secure couples (i.e., those in which both partners were securely attached) were more confident about their spouse's support than doubly insecure couples (those in which both spouses were insecurely attached). No difference was found between secure couples and mixed couples (those in which only one partner was secure), implying that the negative perceptions of the insecure partner can sometimes be mitigated by the other partner's attachment security. Moreover, since secure spouses tend actually to be more sensitive, responsive, and supportive than insecure spouses (see Mikulincer & Shaver, 2007a, for a review), this finding suggests that insecure people's perceived support from a spouse can be positively affected by the spouse's truly supportive behaviors.

Although insecure people tend to be predisposed to offer pessimistic explanations of other people's behavior, two studies show that this tendency can be moderated by contextual forces. Pereg and Mikulincer (2004) subjected study participants to a negative-mood or neutral-mood induction and found that anxious people's pessimistic attributions were strengthened by the negative-mood induction. Collins et al. (2006) found that anxious people's tendency to offer pessimistic attributions was attenuated for those who were involved in a satisfying relationship. In both studies, avoidant people's pessimistic explanations remained the same regardless of variations in mood or relationship satisfaction. That is, whereas anxious people's negative cognitive biases seemed to be responsive to fluctuations in mood and relationship-specific factors, avoidant people's biases were stable and likely to yield pessimistic inferences even when a satisfactory relationship encouraged more benign attributions.

Self-appraisals during social interactions. Attachment insecurities also bias people's self-appraisals during social interactions. For example, Pietromonaco and Barrett (1997) examined attachment-style differences in daily-diary self-evaluations over the course of a week. Anxiously attached students made more negative self-evaluations after everyday interactions, and avoidant students' ratings fell between those of anxious and secure students.

Attachment researchers have also found attachment anxiety to be associated with self-defeating, hopeless interpretations of negative experiences in relationships—an attribution pattern that includes taking responsibility for a disappointing interaction and attributing it to a temporally stable lack of ability, skill, or personal value (e.g., Gamble & Roberts, 2005; Sumer & Cozzarelli, 2004). Studies assessing beliefs about personal control have also shown that attachment-anxious individual often feel relatively hopeless about their relationship

prospects (e.g., Fass & Tubman, 2002; Mickelson, Kessler, & Shaver, 1997). They also tend to believe that powerful others have a great deal of control of their lives.

Several studies have found that less-secure individuals rely more on external sources of validation for their sense of worth, whereas relatively secure individuals rely on an internal, relatively stable sense of worth. For example, Srivastava and Beer (2005) asked people to take part in four weekly small-group discussions and, following each group session, to rate their own likeability and the extent to which they liked each other person in the group. Participants who were more liked by others following a group session had more positive self-evaluations at a later session. However, a dependence on others' liking was mainly found among participants scoring high on attachment anxiety. For more securely attached group members, self-evaluations were relatively high regardless of what other group members thought.

In a laboratory setting, Carvallo and Gabriel (2006) found that avoidant individuals' self-appraisals also relied on external sources of validation. Specifically, they reported more positive self-appraisals after receiving information that they were accepted by others or that their prospects of future success in interpersonal domains was good than after receiving no information. But again, the self-appraisals of less avoidant participants were not significantly affected by the experimental feedback. Maier, Bernier, Pekrun, Zimmermann, and Grossmann (2004) obtained a similar pattern of findings while assessing implicit responses to subliminal priming with a rejection statement. Study participants were subliminally primed with either "My mother rejects me" or a neutral message, and their reaction times for endorsing positive statements about their self-worth or self-efficacy were assessed. Avoidant and anxious individuals had longer reaction times after being primed with the rejection message, implying that rejection-related primes interfered with retrieving positive self-representations.

Response generation. Adult attachment researchers have begun to study insecure people's difficulties in evaluating possible responses and deciding among them. For example, Tangney, Baumeister, and Boone (2004) reported that more anxious and more avoidant people scored lower on a measure of self-control, and Learner and Kruger (1997) found that adolescents who scored lower on a measure of secure attachment to parents reported less planning and poorer organization of their daily activities. Mikulincer and Shaver (2007a) reported correlational findings showing that more anxious and avoidant undergraduates scored lower on problem analysis, plan rehearsal, task concentration, task persistence, and behavioral reorganization, and scored higher on procrastination. Moreover, attachment anxiety was associated with relatively fruitless deliberation and difficulties in concentrating, prioritizing goals, and making decisions, perhaps reflecting a tendency to ruminate on negative possibilities.

Findings from our laboratories also showed that insecurely attached people have interpersonal coordination problems when they attempt to increase closeness and cooperation (Mikulincer & Shaver, 2007a). In one study, participants were invited to engage in a problem-solving interaction (a "desert survival" task) with another participant whom they had not previously met. Participants were explicitly instructed to encourage closeness and cooperation during the interaction, but their partners were unaware of this instruction. The interaction was videotaped, and five independent judges later rated participants' and partners' behaviors. Attachment-anxious and avoidant participants were rated by judges as displaying less effective goal-oriented behavior, seeming to feel less relaxed and calm during the interaction, reacting in less appropriate ways to their partner's responses, and being less able to promote closeness and cooperation. Furthermore, partners of more attachment-anxious or avoidant participants were rated by judges as seeming less calm and relaxed during the interaction.

ANTECEDENTS OF INDIVIDUAL DIFFERENCES IN ATTACHMENT STYLE

Given the pervasive problems associated with insecure attachment styles, it is important to learn more about the determinants of these styles. According to Bowlby (1973) and Ainsworth et al. (1978), attachment orientations are shaped by interactions with one's attachment figures across the lifespan, beginning very early in childhood. In their view, parental caregiving is the most important antecedent of an infant's attachment pattern, with more sensitive and responsive parents encouraging a more secure pattern of infant attachment. In the earliest studies of infant attachment, Ainsworth et al. (1978) conducted home observations of mother-child interactions and found identified predictors of infants' subsequent emotional reactions and behaviors in a laboratory Strange Situation. The relevant maternal behaviors included, for example, being responsive to the infant's crying, sensitive to the infant's signals and needs, and being psychologically accessible when the infant was distressed, cooperating with the infant's efforts, and accepting the infant's needs and behavior. Together, these behaviors have come to be called "sensitive and responsive" parenting (e.g., De Wolff & van IJzendoorn, 1997).

Since the pioneering studies reported by Ainsworth et al. (1978), dozens of other studies have been conducted on the link between maternal sensitivity and infant attachment security, and their findings have been summarized in three meta-analytic studies that have found clearly significant but only moderately sized mean correlations (Atkinson et al., 2000; De Wolff & van IJzendoorn, 1997; Goldsmith & Alansky, 1987). Experimental intervention studies aimed at improving parental sensitivity during infancy have provided further evidence for a link between parenting and infant attachment. For example, in a meta-analytic review of 23 experimental intervention studies (including 1,255 mother-child dyads), Bakermans-Kranenburg, van IJzendoorn, and Juffer (2003) reported a moderate, but statistically significant, mean effect size (.20) linking interventions aimed at improving maternal sensitivity (as compared to control groups) with a higher probability of secure infant attachment. Recently, H. Steele and Steele (2008) compiled examples of numerous intervention studies that have shown good results with low SES and otherwise at-risk mother child and foster-mother/foster-child dyads.

Longitudinal studies examining the association between parental care during childhood and an offspring's attachment patterns during adolescence or adulthood are scarce, but the findings obtained so far provide evidence for the formative influence of early experiences on later adult attachment. For example, Beckwith, Cohen, and Hamilton (1999) found that maternal sensitivity during mother-child interactions when the children were 1, 8, and 24 months old was associated with more secure attachment to mother when they were 18 years old. Relying on data from the Bielefeld Project in Germany, Grossmann et al. (2005) found that secure attachment at age 22 was positively associated with (a) father's sensitivity during the participants' first 3 years of life and (b) supportive experiences with either mother or father during later childhood.

Parents' own attachment patterns can also affect infant attachment. High rates of concordance (between 60% and 85%) have been found between mother's attachment security and her child's degree of security or insecurity in her presence (e.g., Benoit & Parker, 1994; Fonagy, H. Steele, & Steele, 1991). According to Main, Kaplan, and Cassidy (1985), the quality of parent-children interactions mediates this intergenerational transmission of attachment. However,

van IJzendoorn's (1995) meta-analysis of 10 studies revealed what he called a "transmission gap." Although there was a sizeable mean effect size linking mother's secure attachment and sensitive responsiveness to children's needs, much of the association between parent's and child's attachment status seemed to occur through processes other than the quality of parental-child interactions, at least as this quality had been measured so far.

The "transmission gap" opened the door to possible genetic explanations of inter-generational transmission of attachment patterns, which challenged Bowlby's (1982) almost exclusive emphasis on the importance of early social experiences. Behavioral genetic studies that have assessed concordance of attachment patterns in monozygotic and dizygotic twins have indicated that genetic factors may explain between 14% and 40% of the variance in attachment patterns at various phases of the lifespan (e.g., Brussoni, Jang, Livesley, & Macbeth, 2000; Crawford et al., 2007; O'Connor & Croft, 2001). Studies exploring possible molecular genetic markers associated with adult attachment patterns have produced preliminary evidence for such associations (e.g., Donnellan, Burt, Levendosky, & Klump, 2008; Gillath, Shaver, Baek, & Chun, 2008). However, studies involving children have so far failed to find a strong, direct genetic contribution to attachment patterns, although they have found evidence for interactions between genetic and parenting influences (e.g., Bakermans-Kranenburg & van IJzendoorn, 2004). Recently, Belsky and Pluess (2009) reported another kind of gene-parenting interaction, in which children with difficult temperaments as infants were more susceptible to the detrimental effects of poor maternal care (i.e., exhibited more behavior problems in kindergarten) than children with easy temperaments.

In sum, a comprehensive model of the development of attachment style must take into account environmental main effects, gene main effects, and gene-by-environment interaction effects. Moreover, when considering environmental effects, one should distinguish between early experiential factors (e.g., parenting) that are likely to influence attachment styles across many relationships and under many relationship conditions, on one hand, and more local environmental factors such as a relationship partner's characteristics, on the other, which are likely to influence attachment behaviors within a particular relationship. These days, in addition, it is becoming important to consider how environmental influences have their effects through regulating gene expression (Meaney & Szyf, 2005).

CONCLUDING REMARKS

The model proposed here builds on models published previously by Fraley and Shaver (2000) and Mikulincer and Shaver (2003, 2007a), but it is unique in positing that both attachment-related cognitive-motivational predispositions and within-situation patterns of interpersonal information processing mediate the effects of genes, history of attachment interactions, and the combination of these factors on interpersonal behavior. The model (Figure 2.1) posits that specific (albeit mostly unidentified, as of yet) genes and early experiences with insensitive, unsupportive, unreliable, rejecting, or abusive attachment figures pose risks for the long-term development of insecure attachment styles and maladaptive patterns of cognitive-motivational predispositions that people bring with them into new social interactions and close relationships. These distal factors operate as main effects and in interaction with each other. Throughout development, experiences in particular kinds of relationships also lead to the development of relationship-specific attachment styles that influence specifiable patterns of cognitive-motivational predispositions within those relationships. In particular, in interpersonal exchanges, these cognitive-motivational predispositions shape the way people process information and generate and choose among possible behaviors. All stages of this process have begun to receive researchers' attention, but the complete story is still a work in progress.

References

Ainsworth, M. D. S., Blehar, M. C., Waters, E., & Wall, S. (1978). *Patterns of attachment: Assessed in the Strange Situation and at home.* Hillsdale, NJ: Erlbaum.

Andersen, S. M., & Glassman, N. S. (1996). Responding to significant others when they are not there: Effects on interpersonal inference, motivation, and affect. In R. M. Sorrentino & E. T. Higgins (Eds.), *Handbook of motivation and cognition* (Vol. 3, pp. 262–321). New York: Guilford Press.

Atkinson, L., Niccols, A., Paglia, A., Coolbear, J., Parker, K. C. H., Poulton, L., Guger, S., & Sitarenios, G. (2000). A meta-analysis of time between maternal sensitivity and attachment assessments: Implications for internal working models in infancy/toddlerhood. *Journal of Social and Personal Relationships, 17,* 791–810.

Bakermans-Kranenburg, M. J., & van IJzendoorn, M. H. (2004). No association of the dopamine D4 receptor (DRD4) and -521 C/T promoter polymorphisms with infant attachment disorganization. *Attachment and Human Development, 6,* 211–218.

Bakermans-Kranenburg, M. J., van IJzendoorn, M. H., & Juffer, F. (2003). Less is more: Meta-analyses of sensitivity and attachment interventions in early childhood. *Psychological Bulletin, 129,* 195–215.

Baldwin, M. W., Fehr, B., Keedian, E., Seidel, M., & Thompson, D. W. (1993). An exploration of the relational schemata underlying attachment styles: Self-report and lexical decision approaches. *Personality and Social Psychology Bulletin, 19,* 746–754.

Baldwin, M. W., & Kay, A. C. (2003). Adult attachment and the inhibition of rejection. *Journal of Social and Clinical Psychology, 22,* 275–293.

Beckwith, L., Cohen, S. E., & Hamilton, C. E. (1999). Maternal sensitivity during infancy and subsequent life events relate to attachment representation at early adulthood. *Developmental Psychology, 35,* 693–700.

Belsky, J., & Pluess, M. (2009). Differential susceptibility to rearing experience: The case of childcare. *Journal of Child Psychology and Psychiatry, 50*, 396–404.

Benoit, D., & Parker, K. C. H. (1994). Stability and transmission of attachment across three generations. *Child Development, 65*, 1444–1456.

Berant, E., Mikulincer, M., & Florian, V. (2001). The association of mothers' attachment style and their psychological reactions to the diagnosis of infant's congenital heart disease. *Journal of Social and Clinical Psychology, 20*, 208–232.

Birnbaum, G. E., Orr, I., Mikulincer, M., & Florian, V. (1997). When marriage breaks up: Does attachment style contribute to coping and mental health? *Journal of Social and Personal Relationships, 14*, 643–654.

Bowlby, J. (1973). *Attachment and loss: Vol. 2. Separation: Anxiety and anger.* New York: Basic Books.

Bowlby, J. (1980). *Attachment and loss: Vol. 3. Sadness and depression.* New York: Basic Books.

Bowlby, J. (1982). *Attachment and loss: Vol. 1. Attachment* (2nd ed.). New York: Basic Books. (Original edition published 1969)

Bowlby, J. (1988). *A secure base: Clinical applications of attachment theory.* London: Routledge.

Brennan, K. A., Clark, C. L., & Shaver, P. R. (1998). Self-report measurement of adult romantic attachment: An integrative overview. In J. A. Simpson & W. S. Rholes (Eds.), *Attachment theory and close relationships* (pp. 46–76). New York: Guilford Press.

Brumbaugh, C. C., & Fraley, R. C. (2006). Transference and attachment: How do attachment patterns get carried forward from one relationship to the next? *Personality and Social Psychology Bulletin, 32*, 552–560.

Brussoni, M. J., Jang, K. L., Livesley, W., & MacBeth, T. M. (2000). Genetic and environmental influences on adult attachment styles. *Personal Relationships, 7*, 283–289.

Carvallo, M., & Gabriel, S. (2006). No man is an island: The need to belong and dismissing avoidant attachment style. *Personality and Social Psychology Bulletin, 32*, 697–709.

Cassidy, J., & Berlin, L. J. (1994). The insecure/ambivalent pattern of attachment: Theory and research. *Child Development, 65*, 971–981.

Cassidy, J., & Kobak, R. R. (1988). Avoidance and its relationship with other defensive processes. In J. Belsky & T. Nezworski (Eds.), *Clinical implications of attachment* (pp. 300–323). Hillsdale, NJ: Erlbaum.

Cassidy, J., & Shaver, P. R. (Eds.) (2008). *Handbook of attachment: Theory, research, and clinical applications* (2nd ed.). New York: Guilford Press.

Collins, N. L. (1996). Working models of attachment: Implications for explanation, emotion, and behavior. *Journal of Personality and Social Psychology, 71*, 810–832.

Collins, N. L., & Feeney, B. C. (2004). Working models of attachment shape perceptions of social support: Evidence from experimental and observational studies. *Journal of Personality and Social Psychology, 87*, 363–383.

Collins, N. L., Ford, M. B., Guichard, A. C., & Allard, L. M. (2006). Working models of attachment and attribution processes in intimate relationships. *Personality and Social Psychology Bulletin, 32*, 201–219.

Collins, N. L., Guichard, A. C., Ford, M. B., & Feeney, B. C. (2004). Working models of attachment: New developments and emerging themes. In W. S. Rholes & J. A. Simpson (Eds.), *Adult attachment: Theory, research, and clinical implications* (pp. 196–239). New York: Guilford Press.

Collins, N. L., & Read, S. J. (1990). Adult attachment, working models, and relationship quality in dating couples. *Journal of Personality and Social Psychology, 58*, 644–663.

Cooper, M. L., Shaver, P. R., & Collins, N. L. (1998). Attachment styles, emotion regulation, and adjustment in adolescence. *Journal of Personality and Social Psychology, 74*, 1380–1397.

Cozzarelli, C., Hoekstra, S. J., & Bylsma, W. H. (2000). General versus specific mental models of attachment: Are they associated with different outcomes? *Personality and Social Psychology Bulletin, 26*, 605–618.

Cozzarelli, C., Sumer, N., & Major, B. (1998). Mental models of attachment and coping with abortion. *Journal of Personality and Social Psychology, 74*, 453–467.

Crawford, T. N., Livesley, W. J., Jang, K. L., Shaver, P. R., Cohen, P., & Ganiban, J. (2007). Insecure attachment and personality disorder: A twin study of adults. *European Journal of Personality, 21*, 191–208.

De Wolff, M., & van IJzendoorn, M. H. (1997). Sensitivity and attachment: A meta-analysis on parental antecedents of infant attachment. *Child Development, 68*, 571–591.

Dodge, K. A. (2003). Do social information process-ing patterns mediate aggressive behavior? In B. Lahey, T. Moffitt, & A. Caspi (Eds.), *Causes of conduct disorder and juvenile delinquency* (pp. 254–274). New York: Guilford Press.

Dodge, K. A. (in press). Social information process-ing patterns as mediators of the interaction between genetic factors and life experiences in the development of aggressive behavior. In M. Mikulincer & P. R. Shaver (Eds.), *Under-standing and reducing aggression, violence, and their consequences*. Washington, DC: American Psychological Association.

Doi, S. C., & Thelen, M. H. (1993). The Fear-of-Intimacy Scale: Replication and extension. *Psychological Assessment, 5,* 377–383.

Donnellan, M. B., Burt, S. A., Levendosky, A. A., & Klump, K. L. (2008). Genes, personality, and attachment in adults: A multivariate behav-ioral genetic analysis. *Personality and Social Psychology Bulletin, 34,* 3–16.

Downey, G., & Feldman, S. I. (1996). Implications of rejection sensitivity for intimate relationships. *Journal of Personality and Social Psychology, 70,* 1327–1343.

Ein-Dor, T., Mikulincer, M., & Shaver, P. R. (2009). *Attachment insecurities and the processing of threat-related information: Studying the scripts involved in insecure people's coping strategies.* Manuscript submitted for publication.

Ekman, P., & Friesen, W. Y. (1975). *Unmasking the face: A guide to recognizing emotions from facial clues.* Oxford, UK: Prentice-Hall.

Fass, M. E., & Tubman, J. G. (2002). The influence of parental and peer attachment on college students' academic achievement. *Psychology in the Schools, 39,* 561–574.

Feeney, J. A. (2004). Hurt feelings in couple rela-tionships: Towards integrative models of the negative effects of hurtful events. *Journal of Social and Personal Relationships, 21,* 487–508.

Fonagy, P., Steele, H., & Steele, M. (1991). Maternal representations of attachment during pregnancy predict the organization of infant-mother attachment at one year of age. *Child Development, 62,* 891–905.

Fontaine, R. G., & Dodge, K. A. (2006). Real-time decision making and aggressive behavior in youth: A heuristic model of response evalua-tion and decision (RED). *Aggressive Behavior, 32,* 604–624.

Fraley, R. C., Garner, J. P., & Shaver, P. R. (2000). Adult attachment and the defensive regula-tion of attention and memory: Examining the role of preemptive and postemptive defensive processes. *Journal of Personality and Social Psy-chology, 79,* 816–826.

Fraley, R. C., Niedenthal, P. M., Marks, M., Brum-baugh, C., & Vicary, A. (2006). Adult attach-ment and the perception of emotional expres-sions: Probing the hyperactivating strategies underlying anxious attachment. *Journal of Per-sonality, 74,* 1163–1190.

Fraley, R. C., & Shaver, P. R. (2000). Adult romantic attachment: Theoretical developments, emerg-ing controversies, and unanswered questions. *Review of General Psychology, 4,* 132–154.

Frijda, N. H. (1986). *The emotions.* New York: Cam-bridge University Press.

Gallo, L. C., & Smith, T. W. (2001). Attachment style in marriage: Adjustment and responses to interaction. *Journal of Social and Personal Rela-tionships, 18,* 263–289.

Gamble, S. A., & Roberts, J. E. (2005). Adolescents' perceptions of primary caregivers and cog-nitive style: The roles of attachment security and gender. *Cognitive Therapy and Research, 29,* 123–141.

Gillath, O., Shaver, P. R., Baek, J-M., & Chun, D. S. (2008). Genetic correlates of adult attachment style. *Personality and Social Psychology Bulletin, 34,* 1396–1405.

Goldsmith, H. H., & Alansky, J. A. (1987). Mater-nal and infant temperamental predictors of attachment: A meta-analytic review. *Journal of Consulting and Clinical Psychology, 55,* 805–816.

Grossmann, K., Grossmann, K. E., & Kindler, H. (2005). Early care and the roots of attachment and partnership representations: The Bielefeld and Regensburg longitudinal studies. In K. E. Grossmann, K. Grossmann, & E. Waters (Eds.), *Attachment from infancy to adulthood: The major longitudinal studies* (pp. 98–136). New York: Guilford Press.

Guerrero, L. K. (1996). Attachment-style differences in intimacy and involvement: A test of the four-category model. *Communication Monographs, 63,* 269–292.

Hazan, C., & Shaver, P. R. (1987). Romantic love conceptualized as an attachment process. *Journal of Personality and Social Psychology, 52,* 511–524.

Hazan, C., & Zeifman, D. (1999). Pair-bonds as attachments: Evaluating the evidence. In

J. Cassidy & P. R. Shaver (Eds.), *Handbook of attachment: Theory, research, and clinical applications* (pp. 336–354). New York: Guilford Press.

Kafetsios, K., & Nezlek, J. B. (2002). Attachment styles in everyday social interaction. *European Journal of Social Psychology, 32*, 719–735.

Kaitz, M., Bar-Haim, Y., Lehrer, M., & Grossman, E. (2004). Adult attachment style and interpersonal distance. *Attachment and Human Development, 6*, 285–304.

Kunce, L. J., & Shaver, P. R. (1994). An attachment-theoretical approach to caregiving in romantic relationships. In K. Bartholomew & D. Perlman (Eds.), *Advances in personal relationships: Attachment processes in adulthood* (Vol. 5, pp. 205–237). London: Jessica Kingsley.

Lazarus, R. S. (1991). *Emotion and adaptation.* New York: Oxford University Press.

Lazarus, R. S., & Folkman, S. (1984). *Stress, appraisal, and coping.* New York: Springer.

Learner, D. G., & Kruger, L. J. (1997). Attachment, self-concept, and academic motivation in high-school students. *American Journal of Orthopsychiatry, 67*, 485–492.

Luke, M. A., Maio, G. R., & Carnelley, K. B. (2004). Attachment models of the self and others: Relations with self-esteem, humanity-esteem, and parental treatment. *Personal Relationships, 11*, 281–303.

Magai, C., Distel, N., & Liker, R. (1995). Emotion socialization, attachment, and patterns of adult emotional traits. *Cognition and Emotion, 9*, 461–481.

Maier, M. A., Bernier, A., Pekrun, R., Zimmermann, P., Strasser, K., & Grossmann, K. E. (2005). Attachment state of mind and perceptual processing of emotional stimuli. *Attachment and Human Development, 7*, 67–81.

Maier, M. A., Bernier, A., Pekrun, R., Zimmermann, P., & Grossmann, K. E. (2004). Attachment working models as unconscious structures: An experimental test. *International Journal of Behavioral Development, 28*, 180–189.

Main, M., Kaplan, N., & Cassidy, J. (1985). Security in infancy, childhood, and adulthood: A move to the level of representation. *Monographs of the Society for Research in Child Development, 50*, 66–104.

Meaney, M. J., & Szyf, M. (2005). Maternal care as a model for experience-dependent chromatin plasticity? *Trends in Neurosciences, 28*, 456–463.

Mickelson, K. D., Kessler, R. C., & Shaver, P. R. (1997). Adult attachment in a nationally representative sample. *Journal of Personality and Social Psychology, 73*, 1092–1106.

Mikulincer, M. (1995). Attachment style and the mental representation of the self. *Journal of Personality and Social Psychology, 69*, 1203–1215.

Mikulincer, M. (1998a). Adult attachment style and affect regulation: Strategic variations in self-appraisals. *Journal of Personality and Social Psychology, 75*, 420–435.

Mikulincer, M. (1998b). Adult attachment style and individual differences in functional versus dysfunctional experiences of anger. *Journal of Personality and Social Psychology, 74*, 513–524.

Mikulincer, M., & Shaver, P. R. (2003). The attachment behavioral system in adulthood: Activation, psychodynamics, and interpersonal processes. In M. P. Zanna (Ed.), *Advances in experimental social psychology* (Vol. 35, pp. 53–152). New York: Academic Press.

Mikulincer, M., & Shaver, P. R. (2007a). *Attachment patterns in adulthood: Structure, dynamics, and change.* New York: Guilford Press.

Mikulincer, M., & Shaver, P. R. (2007b). Boosting attachment security to promote mental health, prosocial values, and inter-group tolerance. *Psychological Inquiry, 18*, 139–156.

Mikulincer, M., & Shaver, P. R. (2009). An attachment and behavioral systems perspective on social support. (Special Issue: Social Support.) *Journal of Social and Personal Relationships, 26*, 7–19.

Mikulincer, M., Shaver, P. R., Gillath, O., & Nitzberg, R. A. (2005). Attachment, caregiving, and altruism: Boosting attachment security increases compassion and helping. *Journal of Personality and Social Psychology, 89*, 817–839.

Mikulincer, M., Shaver, P. R., Sapir-Lavid, Y., & Avihou-Kanza, N. (in press). What's inside the minds of securely and insecurely attached people? The secure-base script and its associations with attachment-style dimensions *Journal of Personality and Social Psychology.*

Mikulincer, M., Shaver, P. R., & Slav, K. (2006). Attachment, mental representations of others, and gratitude and forgiveness in romantic relationships. In M. Mikulincer & G. S. Goodman (Eds.), *Dynamics of romantic love: Attachment, caregiving, and sex* (pp. 190–215). New York: Guilford Press.

Noller, P., & Feeney, J. A. (1994). Relationship satisfaction, attachment, and nonverbal accuracy in early marriage. *Journal of Nonverbal Behavior, 18,* 199–221.

O'Connor, T. G., & Croft, C. M. (2001). A twin study of attachment in preschool children. *Child Development, 72,* 1501–1511.

Pereg, D., & Mikulincer, M. (2004). Attachment style and the regulation of negative affect: Exploring individual differences in mood congruency effects on memory and judgment. *Personality and Social Psychology Bulletin, 30,* 67–80.

Pietromonaco, P. R., & Barrett, L. F. (1997). Working models of attachment and daily social interactions. *Journal of Personality and Social Psychology, 73,* 1409–1423.

Rholes, W. S., Simpson, J. A., Campbell, L., & Grich, J. (2001). Adult attachment and the transition to parenthood. *Journal of Personality and Social Psychology, 81,* 421–435.

Rowe, A. C., & Carnelley, K. B. (2005). Preliminary support for the use of a hierarchical mapping technique to examine attachment networks. *Personal Relationships, 12,* 499–519.

Scharfe, E., & Bartholomew, K. (1995). Accommodation and attachment representations in young couples. *Journal of Social and Personal Relationships, 12,* 389–401.

Shaver, P. R., & Fraley, R. C. (2008). Attachment, loss, and grief: Bowlby's views and current controversies. In J. Cassidy & P. R. Shaver (Eds.), *Handbook of attachment: Theory, research, and clinical applications* (2nd ed., pp. 48–77). New York: Guilford Press.

Shaver, P. R., & Hazan, C. (1993). Adult romantic attachment: Theory and evidence. In D. Perlman & W. Jones (Eds.), *Advances in personal relationships* (Vol. 4, pp. 29–70). London, UK: Kingsley.

Shaver, P. R., & Mikulincer, M. (2002). Attachment-related psychodynamics. *Attachment and Human Development, 4,* 133–161.

Simpson, J. A., Rholes, W. S., & Nelligan, J. S. (1992). Support seeking and support giving within couples in an anxiety-provoking situation: The role of attachment styles. *Journal of Personality and Social Psychology, 62,* 434–446.

Simpson, J. A., Rholes, W. S., & Phillips, D. (1996). Conflict in close relationships: An attachment perspective. *Journal of Personality and Social Psychology, 71,* 899–914.

Srivastava, S., & Beer, J. S. (2005). How self-evaluations relate to being liked by others: Integrating sociometer and attachment perspectives. *Journal of Personality and Social Psychology, 89,* 966–977.

Sroufe, L. A., & Waters, E. (1977b). Attachment as an organizational construct. *Child Development, 48,* 1184–1199.

Steele, H, & Steele, M. (Eds.) (2008). *Clinical applications of the Adult Attachment Interview.* New York: Guilford Press.

Sumer, N., & Cozzarelli, C. (2004). The impact of adult attachment on partner and self-attributions and relationship quality. *Personal Relationships, 11,* 355–371.

Tangney, J. P., Baumeister, R. F., Boone, A. L. (2004). High self-control predicts good adjustment, less pathology, better grades, and interpersonal success. *Journal of Personality, 72,* 271–322.

Tidwell, M. C. O., Reis, H. T., & Shaver, P. R. (1996). Attachment, attractiveness, and social interaction: A diary study. *Journal of Personality and Social Psychology, 71,* 729–745.

van IJzendoorn, M. (1995). Adult attachment representations, parental responsiveness, and infant attachment: A meta-analysis on the predictive validity of the Adult Attachment Interview. *Psychological Bulletin, 117,* 387–403.

Vogel, D. L., Wester, S. R., Larson, L. M., & Wade, N. G. (2006). An information-processing model of the decision to seek professional help. *Professional Psychology: Research and Practice, 37,* 398–406.

Volling, B. L., Notaro, P. C., & Larsen, J. J. (1998). Adult attachment styles: Relations with emotional well-being, marriage, and parenting. *Family Relations, 47,* 355–367.

Waters, H. S., Rodrigues, L. M., & Ridgeway, D. (1998). Cognitive underpinnings of narrative attachment assessment. *Journal of Experimental Child Psychology, 71,* 211–234.

Waters, H. S., & Waters, E. (2006). The attachment working models concept: Among other things, we build scriptlike representations of secure base experiences. *Attachment and Human Development, 8,* 185–198.

Zhang, F., & Hazan, C. (2002). Working models of attachment and person perception processes. *Personal Relationships, 9,* 225–235.

3 RELATEDNESS AND SELF-DEFINITION IN NORMAL AND DISRUPTED PERSONALITY DEVELOPMENT

Sidney J. Blatt

Patrick Luyten

A remarkable recent convergence, across a number of theoretical models, emphasizes the developmental psychological dimensions of interpersonal relatedness and self-definition as a basic conceptual structure in both normal and disrupted personality development (Blatt, 2008; Luyten & Blatt, 2009). In particular, both contemporary interpersonal (e.g., Benjamin; 2003; Pincus, 2005; Ravitz, Maunder, and McBride, 2008; Wiggins, 2003) and attachment theory and research (e.g., Mikulincer & Shaver, 2007) emphasize the centrality of interpersonal relatedness and self-definition in personality organization. In this chapter, we review this theoretical and empirical convergence between contemporary interpersonal and attachment theories, and then demonstrate how the two-configurations model of personality development and psychopathology developed by Sidney Blatt and colleagues is consistent with and substantially extends this theoretical convergence. More specifically, Blatt

and colleagues demonstrate how the developmental dimensions of interpersonal relatedness and self-definition provide the basis for understanding normal personality development throughout the life cycle, and how disruptions, at different developmental levels, of this normal developmental process can lead to various forms of psychopathology, thereby avoiding many of the conceptual pitfalls of the DSM model, such as unacceptably high levels of comorbidity and the arbitrary differentiation between normality and pathology and between Axis I and Axis II disorders. The two-configurations model not only maintains conceptual continuity between normal and disrupted personality development, but is also applicable to the reparative developmental processes that can occur in psychotherapy. In sum, the two-configurations model, based on the fundamental developmental dimensions of interpersonal relatedness and self-definition, establishes conceptual continuity between personality development, variations in normal personality organization, various forms of psychopathology, and the processes of therapeutic change—a continuity consistent with the emphasis in contemporary interpersonal and attachment theory and research on interpersonal relatedness and self-definition as the primary dimensions of a fundamental conceptual system.

RELATEDNESS AND SELF-DEFINITION IN CONTEMPORARY INTERPERSONAL AND ATTACHMENT THEORIES

Interpersonal relatedness (the development of the capacity to establish and maintain reciprocal relationships) and self-definition (the development of the capacity to establish and maintain a differentiated, integrated, realistic, essentially positive identity) are fundamental dimensions in both contemporary interpersonal (Pincus, 2005; Ravitz et al., 2008; Wiggins, 2003) and attachment theory (Mikulincer & Shaver, 2007) approaches to personality development and personality organization (Luyten & Blatt, 2009). Contemporary interpersonal theory is organized around two orthogonal dimensions—agency (or social dominance) and communion (or nurturance and affiliation) that underlie interpersonal traits, attitudes, and behavior that define both normal and disrupted psychological development (Benjamin, 2003; Pincus, 2005; Wiggins, 1991). These two dimensions are also central to contemporary attachment theory and research. Using a variety of assessment procedures (e.g., interviews and questionnaires), with both clinical and nonclinical samples, studies indicate that the two fundamental dimensions of interpersonal relatedness and self-definition underlie different attachment styles (Meyer & Pilkonis, 2005; Mikulincer & Shaver, 2007 and this volume; Roisman, Holland, Fortuna, Fraley, Clauser, & Clarke, 2007). Attachment anxiety—"fear of rejection and abandonment" (Mikulincer & Shaver, 2007; Sibley, 2007)—is clearly

linked to the relatedness dimension, while attachment avoidance—"discomfort with closeness and discomfort depending on others"—is conceptually linked to the self-definitional dimension. Attachment anxiety and avoidance are not only related to the dimensions of interpersonal relatedness and self-definition, they also reflect important aspects of the representation of self and of others that underlie these dimensions (Bartholomew & Horowitz, 1991; Horowitz, 2004). In brief, all three theoretical systems converge in exposing a similiar pair of dimensions: X = interpersonal relatedness, Y = self-definition; X = communion, Y = agency; X = preferred avoidance (vs. closeness), Y = attachment anxiety (vs. self-confidence). Furthermore, when the attachment dimensions are represented graphically, the four quadrants correspond to the four organized attachment styles (secure, preoccupied, fearful-avoidant, and dismissive).

Both interpersonal theory and attachment approaches also converge to suggest that normal or adaptive personality development involves a balance between agency and communion or comfort with both attachment and separation. Maladaptive personality organization, in contrast, is hypothesized to result from an overemphasis on relatedness as expressed in an excessive emphasis on communion or attachment anxiety, or in a defensive preservation of self-definition expressed in high levels of dominance or attachment avoidance. As noted by Mikuliciner and Shaver (2007, p. 254), "Attachment-anxious people overemphasize the need for protection and intimacy, and avoidant people overemphasize the need for autonomy and interpersonal distance." In contrast, "secure people do not view closeness and autonomy as antagonistic goals.... Secure individuals can flexibly move along the closeness-distance dimension of the circumplex without being afraid of losing autonomy or a partner's love. In contrast, insecurely attached people are less able to balance or coordinate closeness and autonomy" (Mikulincer & Shaver, 2007, p. 255). Anxiously attached individuals fear rejection and abandonment while avoidantly attached individuals fear closeness and a loss of autonomy and independence. Moreover, studies suggest that maladaptive levels of relatedness and self-definition are expressed in different combinations of attachment anxiety and avoidance in preoccupied, fearful-avoidant, or dismissive attachment styles (e.g., Levy & Blatt, 1999).

Furthermore, the distinction between anxiously seeking or avoiding interpersonal contact also provides the basis for distinctions within disorganized attachment. Main and colleagues (Main et al., 1985) distinguished two types of controlling behavior patterns in disorganized insecurely attached children at age six, which involve issues with self-definition and relatedness respectively: Controlling-punitive children tended to harshly order the parent around or even try to humiliate the parent, while controlling-caregiving children, in contrast, tended to be excessively solicitous. Likewise, Lyons-Ruth and colleagues (e.g., Lyons-Ruth, 2001; Lyons-Ruth & Block, 1996; Lyons-Ruth, Zeanah, & Beloit, 2003) distinguished two types of parental caregiving styles within disorganized attachment. One is a hostile-avoidant style in which the mother identifies with her own malevolent punitive caregiver and interacts with her infant in a hostile distant way, attempting to avoid experiencing her vulnerability by suppressing emotions and constantly controlling others. These mothers discipline their children by coercion, suppression of the child's anger, and prematurely encouraging the child's autonomy. The second is a helpless/fearful style in which the mother adopts a lifelong caregiving style of attending to the needs of others, often at the expense of her own needs, resulting in a repression of her own affect. These mothers tend to be fearful and easily overwhelmed by the demands of others. They feel powerless to control their children, especially when the child's emotions are aroused.

Hence, issues of self-definition predominate in controlling-punitive children and in mothers with hostile-avoidant disorganized attachment; issues of relatedness predominate in controlling- caregiving children and in mothers with helpless/fearful disorganized attachment.

THE TWO-CONFIGURATIONS MODEL OF PERSONALITY DEVELOPMENT AND PSYCHOPATHOLOGY

Over the past several decades, Blatt and colleagues have developed a developmentally based two-configurations model in which the two fundamental psychological dimensions, that is, *interpersonal relatedness* and *self-definition,* provide a coordinated theoretical matrix for understanding personality development, variations in normal personality organization, and concepts of psychopathology, as well as mechanisms of therapeutic change (Blatt, 2006, 2008). These formulations are consistent with contemporary interpersonal and attachment theory and research as well as with a wide range of personality theories, from psychoanalytic to empirically derived formulations. Throughout psychoanalytic thought, a number of theorists in addition to Freud (e.g., Abraham, Jung, Adler, Rank, Horney, Tausk, Bowlby, Balint, Shor and Sanville, Sullivan, Kohut, M. Slavin, and Kriegman), as well as many nonpsychoanalytic personality theorists (e.g., Angyal, Bakan, Carson, Deci and Ryan, U. Foa, Gilligan, Hogan, Leary, McClelland, McAdams, Winter, Hegelson, Markus and colleagues, Maddi, Spiegel and Spiegel, White) made the dimensions of interpersonal relatedness and self-definition central to their theoretical formulations (see Blatt, 2008, for a detailed discussion).

Relatedness and Self-Definition in Personality Development

Blatt and colleagues (e.g., Blatt 1974, 1995, 2006, 2008; Blatt & Blass, 1990, 1996; Blatt

& Luyten, 2009; Blatt and Shichman, 1983) propose that personality development evolves, from infancy to senescence, through a *complex dialectic transaction* between the two fundamental psychological dimensions—between the development of increasingly mature (e.g., intimate, mutually satisfying, reciprocal) interpersonal relationships and the development of an increasingly differentiated, integrated, realistic, essentially positive sense of self or identity. These two fundamental developmental processes evolve through a life-long, *complex, synergistic, hierarchical, dialectic transaction* such that progress in one developmental line facilitates progress in the other. An increasingly differentiated, integrated and mature sense of self emerges out of constructive interpersonal relationships and, conversely, the continued development of increasingly mature interpersonal relationships is contingent on the development of a more differentiated and integrated self-definition and identity. Meaningful and satisfying relationships contribute to the evolving concept of self; and a revised sense of self leads, in turn, to a capacity for more mature levels of interpersonal relatedness.

Based on an extension of Erikson's (e.g., 1950) epigenetic psychosocial developmental model, Blatt and colleagues (e.g., Blatt & Blass, 1990, 1996; Blatt & Shichman, 1983) illustrate how the two fundamental dimensions of interpersonal relatedness and self-definition evolve developmentally and are eventually integrated in a mature self-identity—a self-in-relation with others. Expanding Erikson's developmental model by including an additional psychosocial stage, cooperation versus alienation, around the age of 4 to 6 years with the emergent awareness of the triadic structure of the family (the Oedipal phase), the development of operational thinking (e.g., Piaget, 1954) and the emergence of cooperative peer play (e.g., Whiteside, Busch, & Horner, 1976), Blatt and Shichman (1983) placed this stage at the appropriate point in Erikson's developmental sequence, between the stage of "initiative versus guilt" and "industry versus inferiority." Figure 3.1 illustrates this dialectic synergistic developmental sequence in an expanded version of Erikson's epigenetic psychosocial model.

Progress in one developmental line, in the development of the self or in the

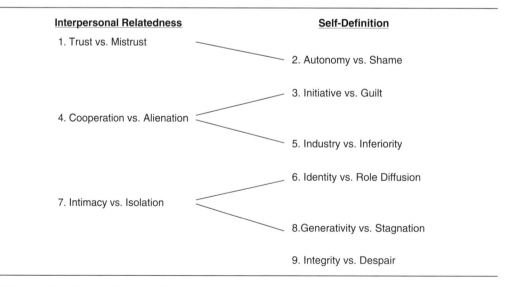

Interpersonal Relatedness	Self-Definition
1. Trust vs. Mistrust	
	2. Autonomy vs. Shame
	3. Initiative vs. Guilt
4. Cooperation vs. Alienation	
	5. Industry vs. Inferiority
	6. Identity vs. Role Diffusion
7. Intimacy vs. Isolation	
	8.Generativity vs. Stagnation
	9. Integrity vs. Despair

FIGURE 3.1 The Dialectic Iteration of Interpersonal Relatedness and Self-Definition Implicit in E. Erikson's Psychosocial Model

development of a capacity for interpersonal relatedness, facilitates development in the other. Throughout life, meaningful interpersonal experiences contribute to a fuller articulation, differentiation and integration of the sense of self that, in turn, facilitates the establishment of more mature forms of interpersonal relatedness. Though the relative balance between these two developmental dimensions and the specific life experiences that contribute to the development of a sense of self and the capacity for interpersonal relatedness varies across individuals and across cultures, these two fundamental developmental dimensions evolve through a basic synergistic process throughout life in a wide range of cultures (e.g., Triandis, 1995).

This dialectical rendering of Erikson's formulations defines one developmental dimension (*self-definition or individuality*) as evolving from (a) early experiences of separation and autonomy from the primary caregiver, to (b) a capacity to initiate activity first in opposition to the other and later more proactively, to (c) industry with sustained goal-directed activity that has direction and purpose, to (d) the emergence of a "self-identity." And the addition of an intermediate stage of cooperation to the Erikson theoretical model defines phases in the development of *interpersonal relatedness* that evolves from (a) the sharing of affective experiences between mother and infant (e.g., Stern, 1985) with a concomitant sense of basic trust (e.g., Erikson, 1950), to (b) a capacity for cooperation and collaboration with peers, to (c) the evolution of a close friendship with a same-sex chum, to (d) the development of a capacity for mutual, reciprocal, enduring intimacy.

The evolving capacities for autonomy, initiative, and industry in the self-definitional developmental dimension progress in an alternating sequence with the growth of relational capacities. For example, one needs a sense of basic trust to venture in opposition to the need-gratifying other in asserting one's autonomy and independence, and later one needs a sense of autonomy and initiative to establish cooperative and collaborative relationships with peers. Development begins with a focus on interpersonal relatedness—specifically with the stage of trust versus mistrust—before proceeding to two early self-definitional stages: autonomy versus shame and initiative versus guilt. These early expressions of self-definition are then followed by the newly identified stage of interpersonal relatedness, cooperation versus alienation, and then by two later stages of self-definition: industry versus inferiority and identity versus role diffusion. These more mature expressions of self-definition are followed by the more advanced stage of interpersonal relatedness, intimacy versus isolation, before development proceeds to two mature stages of self-definition, generativity versus stagnation and integrity versus despair.

This broadened Erikson model articulates the reciprocal development of these two dimensions throughout life, from infancy through the early developmental years until adolescence, at which time the developmental task is to integrate the two developmental dimensions of relatedness and self-definition into the comprehensive structure Erikson called "self-identity" (Blatt & Blass, 1990, 1996) or a self-in-relation (Blatt, 2006, 2008). Thus, according to this view, adolescence is a crucial time for a synthesis in the formation of a consolidated identity or the emergence of many forms of psychopathology, particularly personality disorders that are characterized by failures to integrate various aspects of the two fundamental developmental processes of interpersonal relatedness and self-definition (Blatt & Luyten, 2009).

Relatedness and Self-Definition in Personality Organization

Based on these formulations, well-functioning personality organization involves an integration (or balance) in the development of interpersonal relatedness and of self-definition. Each individual, however, even within the normal range, tends to place a somewhat greater emphasis on one or the other of these dimensions. This relative emphasis delineates two basic personality or character styles, each with a particular experiential mode; preferred forms of cognition, defense, and adaptation; unique aspects of interpersonal relatedness; and specific forms of object and self-representation (Blatt, 2006, 2008; Blatt & Zuroff, 1992; Luyten, Blatt, & Corveleyn, 2005b, 2005c).

Some individuals, more often women, tend to place somewhat greater emphasis on relatedness (an anaclitic or relational personality organization), while other individuals, more often men, place somewhat greater emphasis on self-definition (an introjective or self-definitional personality organization). Blatt (1974) and Blatt and Shichman (1983) used the term *anaclitic* for the personality organization that focuses predominantly on interpersonal relatedness—a term taken by Freud (1905, 1915) from the Greek *anklitas*, to rest or lean on, to characterize all interpersonal relationships that derive from dependency experienced in the satisfying mother-child relationship. Blatt (1974) and Blatt and Shichman (1983) used the term *introjective* for the personality organization primarily focused on self-definition—a term used by Freud (1917) to describe processes whereby values, patterns of culture, motives, and restraints are assimilated into the self (e.g., made subjective), consciously or unconsciously, as guiding personal principles through learning and socialization.

Though much more research is needed, emerging findings indicate that thought processes in the *anaclitic personality style* are more figurative and focused primarily on affects and visual images, characterized by simultaneous rather than sequential processing and an emphasis on the reconciliation and synthesis of elements into an integrated cohesion rather than a critical analysis of separate elements and details (Szumotalska, 1992). The predominant tendency in the anaclitic personality style is to seek fusion, harmony, integration, and synthesis. The focus is upon personal experiences—on meanings, feelings, affects, and emotional reactions. These individuals are primarily field dependent (Witkin, 1965), aware of and influenced by environmental factors. Thought processes in the *introjective personality style*, in contrast, are much more literal, sequential, linguistic, and critical. Concerns are focused on action, overt behavior, manifest form, logic, consistency, and causality. These individuals tend to place emphasis on analysis rather than on synthesis, on the critical dissection of details and part properties rather than on achieving a total integration and an overall gestalt (Szumotalska, 1992). These individuals are predominantly field independent (Witkin, 1965), their experiences and judgments are primarily influenced by internal rather than environmental factors.

Extensive research demonstrates the validity of the distinction of anaclitic (relatedness) and introjective (self-definitional) personality styles in nonclinical samples (see summaries in Blatt, 2004, 2008; Blatt & Zuroff, 1992; Luyten, Blatt, & Corveleyn, 2005a; Zuroff, Mongrain, & Santor, 2004) and demonstrates that these two types of individuals engage and experience life differently. Findings (Smith, O'Keefe, & Jenkins, 1988) also indicate a vulnerability to stress of gender-incongruent individuals (i.e., anaclitic males and introjective females, especially anaclitic males).

Relatedness and Self-Definition in Psychopathology

The specification of the normal synergistic development of relatedness and self-definition also provides a basis for identifying maladaptive variations of the fundamental developmental process. In particular, research has demonstrated that biological predispositions and severely disruptive environmental events interact in complex ways to distort the integrated synergistic developmental process of relatedness and self-definition and lead to defensive, markedly exaggerated emphasis on one developmental dimension at the expense of the other (Blatt & Luyten, 2009). These deviations can be relatively mild in normal personality or character variations, as discussed above, but these deviations can also be quite extreme. The more extensive the deviation, that is, the greater the exaggerated emphasis on one developmental line at the expense of the other, the greater the possibility of psychopathology. Severe disruptions of the synergistic dialectic developmental process at different points in development can lead to the various forms of psychopathology described in Axis I and Axis II of the DSM, from schizophrenia and depression to personality disorders (Blatt & Luyten, in press; Luyten & Blatt, 2009).

Individuals tend to deal with severe disruptions of the normal dialectic developmental process by attempting to achieve some degree of equilibrium by placing exaggerated emphasis on one of these dimensions to the neglect of the other. This distorted, one-sided emphasis thus identifies two primary configurations of psychopathology. *Anaclitic forms of psychopathology*, including undifferentiated schizophrenia, abandonment depression, and the borderline, dependent and histrionic personality disorders, all involve, at different developmental levels, a distorted one-sided preoccupation with issues of interpersonal relatedness. *Introjective forms of psychopathology*, such as paranoid schizophrenia and the paranoid, obsessive-compulsive, self-critical depressive, and narcissistic personality disorders, in contrast, are characterized, at different developmental levels, by a distorted and one-sided preoccupation with issues of self-definition (Blatt, 2006, 2008; Blatt & Shichman, 1983).

Again, considerable research evidence (e.g., Blatt, 2004, 2006, 2008; Blatt & Zuroff, 1992) supports the validity of this distinction of two primary configurations of psychopathology. Anaclitic patients who have a distorted one-sided preoccupation with issues of interpersonal relatedness and introjective patients who have a distorted one-sided preoccupation with issues of self-definition have very different early and later life experiences and different concerns and preoccupations (e.g., Blatt & Homann, 1992; Blatt & Zuroff, 1992) and respond differentially to different types of therapeutic interventions (e.g., for reviews, see Blatt, 2008; Blatt, Zuroff, Hawley, & Auerbach, 2010).

IMPLICATIONS FOR THE CONCEPTUALIZATION AND CLASSIFICATION OF PSYCHOPATHOLOGY

The two-configurations model is a dynamic structural developmental approach to personality development and psychopathology—as Fonagy (2008, p. xi) notes, the "first genuinely psychodynamic developmental psychopathology"—a model of personality and psychopathology supported by extensive research in which personality dimensions provide the basis for understanding the motivational organization and dynamic factors that contribute to a wide range of symptomatic expressions of fundamental psychological disturbance. In particular, this model suggests a hierarchical organization of psychopathology in which many different symptomatic expressions of psychological disturbances derive from more basic dimensions of personality development and organization, avoiding the complex and vexing problem of comorbidity that plagues more conventional, symptom-based approaches to the diagnosis and classification of psychopathology (Blatt & Luyten, 2009, in press).

A central assumption of the two-configurations model is that *exaggerated distortions of one developmental line to the neglect of the other reflects compensatory or defensive maneuvers in response to developmental disruptions.* Hence, different forms of psychopathology are not static developmental deficits, but *dynamic, conflict-defense constellations that reflect struggles to deal with disruptions of the normal synergistic developmental interaction between relatedness and self-definition* (Luyten & Blatt, 2009). Thus, psychopathological disorders in both Axis I and II of the DSM involve exaggerated and distorted preoccupations, at different developmental levels, with either of the two fundamental personality dimensions of interpersonal relatedness and self- definition.

The Anaclitic Configuration of Psychopathology

Anaclitic psychopathology involves exaggerated preoccupations with establishing and maintaining satisfying intimate relationships—with feeling loved and being able to love. Anaclitic patients are desperately concerned about trust, closeness, and the dependability of others, as well as with their capacity to receive and give love and affection. The development of the self is disrupted by these intense conflicts about feeling deprived of care, affection, and love. This excessive preoccupation with establishing and maintaining satisfying interpersonal relatedness can occur at several developmental levels—in a lack of differentiation and a sense of merger between self and other as in some forms of schizophrenia (e.g., Blatt & Wild, 1976), in severe conflicts between dependency and the need for separateness as in hysteroid borderline personality disorder, in intense dependent attachment as in dependent or infantile personality disorder, to difficulties in more mature, reciprocal types of relationships as in hysterical personality organization. Patients with these anaclitic disorders use primarily avoidant defenses (e.g., withdrawal, denial, repression) to cope with psychological conflict and stress and to avoid intense erotic longings and competitive strivings, because these intense feelings potentially threaten their tenuous interpersonal relations.

The Introjective Configuration of Psychopathology

Introjective psychopathology involves an excessive preoccupation with issues of self at varying developmental levels that range from a basic sense of separation and differentiation from others, through concerns about autonomy and control of one's mind and body, to more internalized issues of self-worth, identity, and integrity. The development of interpersonal relations is interfered with by exaggerated struggles to establish and maintain a viable sense of self. Introjective patients are more ideational and issues of anger and aggression, directed toward the self or others, are usually central to their difficulties. Introjective disorders, ranging developmentally from more to less severely disturbed, include paranoid schizophrenia, the over-ideational or schizoid borderline, and the paranoid, obsessive–compulsive, introjective (guilt-ridden) depressive, and narcissistic personality disorders. Patients with introjective disorders use primarily counteractive defenses (e.g., projection, rationalization, negativism, isolation, intellectualization, doing and undoing, reaction formation, and overcompensation) such that the underlying impulse and conflict are partially expressed, but in disguised form. The basic issue for introjective patients is to achieve separation, control, independence, and self-definition, and to be acknowledged, respected, and admired. Conflicts within the introjective configuration usually involve profound feelings of inadequacy, inferiority, worthlessness, guilt, and difficulty managing affect, especially anger and aggression, toward others and the self (Blatt, 1974; Blatt and Shichman, 1983).

An Alternative to the Symptom-Based DSM Classification Schema

These views of psychopathology as disruptions of normal psychological development differ markedly from the symptom-based formulations of the *Diagnostic and Statistical Manual (DSM) of Mental Disorders* (APA, 1994) of the American Psychiatric Association. The identification of commonalities across normal and disrupted psychological development suggests that various forms of psychopathology are not separate independent diseases that derive from presumed, but often as yet undocumented, specific biological and genetic disturbances, as implied in most psychiatrically informed diagnostic manuals. Rather, research deriving from this unifying theoretical model indicates that most forms of psychopathology are the consequence of severe disruptions of basic developmental psychological processes. The differentiation between anaclitic and introjective configurations of psychopathology is, as noted, based on dynamic considerations, including differences in primary motivational focus (libidinal versus aggressive), types of defensive organization (avoidant versus counteractive), and predominant character style (emphasis on an interpersonal versus self-orientation, on affects versus cognition), and developmental factors.

The anaclitic and introjective configurations of personality development and psychopathology thus provide a comprehensive theoretical structure for identifying fundamental similarities among many forms of psychopathology and for maintaining conceptual continuity across processes of psychological development, normal variations in character or personality organization, and different forms of psychological disturbance. Even further, this view facilitates fuller understanding of potential pathways of regression and progression, as well as the nature of therapeutic change (see clinical examples in Blatt, Auerbach, & Behrends, 2008; Blatt, Besser, & Ford, 2007; Blatt & Ford, 1994; Blatt & Shahar, 2005; Blatt et al., 2010).

These formulations also facilitate understanding the relationships among different disorders as various levels of psychopathology within the anaclitic or the introjective configurations, *defining different points*

of organization in the two developmental dimensions along which patients can progress or regress. Thus, an individual's difficulties can usually be identified as predominantly in one or the other configuration, at a particular developmental level, with a differential potential to regress or progress to other developmental levels within that configuration. Various forms of psychopathology are no longer seen as isolated, independent diseases. But, congruent with the developmental principles of equifinality and multifinality, different types of psychopathology can now be considered as *interrelated modes of adaptation to difficult early and later life experiences in interaction with biological endowment—modes of adaptation organized at different developmental levels within two basic configurations.*

Congruent with these assumptions, findings of a number of studies suggest that the differentiation between Axis I and Axis II of the DSM is arbitrary and unproductive (e.g., Blatt et al., 2007; Blatt & Ford, 1994; Blatt & Levy, 1998; Krueger et al., 2005; Kupfer, First, & Reiger, 2002; Westen, Novotny, & Thompson-Brenner, 2004). Personality factors are inherent in Axis I disorders such as in unipolar (Blatt, 2004; Blatt et al., 1976, 1982; Beck, 1983; Luyten & Blatt, 2007) and bipolar (Lam, Wright, & Smith, 2004) depression, but also in eating disorders (Thompson-Brenner & Westen, 2005), anxiety disorders, and even in severe psychopathology, such as psychotic disorders (Shahar, Trower, Iqbal, Birchwood, Davidson, & Chadwick, 2004; Tsuang, Stoen, Tarbox, & Faraone, 2003) as well as in the clinical course of neoplastic immunological and cardiovascular disease (e.g., Blatt, Cornell, & Eshkol, 1993; Helgeson, 1994). Additionally, evidence increasingly suggests that categorical symptom-based diagnostic distinctions of the DSM limit clinical practice and research (Luyten & Blatt, 2007).

The formulations of two primary configurations of psychopathology not only provides a theoretical model for establishing continuities between normality, subclinical disturbances, and manifest clinical disorders (Blatt, 1974, 2004; Blatt & Shichman, 1983; Luyten & Blatt, 2007; Tsuang et al., 2003), but they may also provide the basis for integrating clinical disorders in Axis I with the personality disorders of Axis II of the DSM. These formulations also suggest the possibility of identifying a hierarchical organization in which many symptom-based disorders can be subsumed within one of several major clinical disorders (Blatt, 2004; Krueger et al., 2005; Luyten & Blatt, 2009; Watson, 2005). One of the primary advantages of these formulations is that they are based on the identification of continuities among processes in personality development, normal variations in personality organization, and various forms of psychopathology—formulations that avoid many of the pitfalls that have been discussed in frequent contemporary criticisms of the DSM approach to the diagnosis of psychopathology, including the problematic issue of extensive comorbidity (e.g., Blatt & Levy, 1998; Luyten, 2006; Luyten & Blatt, 2007; Luyten, Blatt, Van Houdenhove, & Corveleyn, 2006; Widiger & Trull, 2007). Thus, it is now possible to begin to develop a classification system of disorders based on systematic empirical research on both the etiologic development and treatment response—a classification system that has important implications for clinical practice as well as for clinical research (Luyten & Blatt, 2009).

The differentiation of relatedness and of self-definition as two fundamental psychological dimensions has, for example, enabled investigators from different theoretical orientations (e.g., Arieti & Bemporad, 1978; 1980; Beck, 1983; Blatt, 1974, 1998, 2004; Bowlby, 1988) to identify two fundamental independent dimensions in depression (Blatt & Maroudas, 1992)—an anaclitic dimension centered on feelings of loneliness, abandonment, and neglect and an introjective dimension focused on issues of self-worth and feelings of failure and guilt (e.g., Blatt, 1974, 1998, 2004; Luyten et al., 2005; Zuroff et al., 2004).

Extensive empirical and clinical investigations (e.g., Besser, Vliegen, Luyten, & Blatt, 2008; Blatt, 1998, 2004; Blatt & Zuroff, 1992; Luyten et al., 2005) indicate consistent differences in the current and early life experiences of these two types of depressed individuals (Blatt and Homann, 1992) as well as major differences in their basic character style, their relational and attachment style (Luyten, Blatt, & Corveleyn, 2005a, 2005c), their clinical expression of depression (Blatt, 2004; Blatt & Zuroff, 2005), and in their therapeutic response (Blatt, 2008; Blatt & Zuroff, 2005). Increasing evidence indicates that these differences can also be found in postpartum depression, and that these differences have important implications for intervention (Besser, Luyten, Vliegen, & Blatt, 2008). These findings indicate that it is more productive to focus on underlying personality dynamics as the basis for the classification of depression than on manifest symptoms.

The differentiation between individuals preoccupied with issues of relatedness and with issues of self-definition has also enabled several independent investigators to identify an empirically derived taxonomy for the diverse personality disorders described in Axis II of the DSM. Systematic empirical investigation of both inpatients and outpatients (Clark et al., 1997; Cogswell & Alloy, 2006; Goldberg et al., 1989; Levy et al., 1995; Morse, Robins, and Gittes-Fox, 2002; Nordahl & Stiles, 2000; Overholser & Freiheit, 1994; Ouimette & Klein, 1993; Ouimette, Klein, Anderson, Riso, and Lizardi, 1994; Pilkonis, 1988; Ryder, McBride, & Bagby, 2008) found that various Axis II personality disorders are organized, in meaningfully and theoretically consistent ways, into two primary configurations—one around issues of relatedness and the other around issues of self-definition. Congruent with theoretical assumptions, these studies have generally found that individuals with a dependent, histrionic, or borderline personality disorder have significantly greater concern with issues of interpersonal relatedness than with issues of self-definition, while individuals with a paranoid, schizoid, schizotypic, antisocial, narcissistic, avoidant, obsessive-compulsive, or self-defeating personality disorder usually have significantly greater preoccupation with issues of self-definition than with issues of interpersonal relatedness. These findings are further supported by attachment research demonstrating that personality disorders can be similarly organized in a two-dimensional space defined by attachment anxiety, reflecting anaclitic concerns, and by attachment avoidance, reflecting introjective issues (Meyer & Pilkonis, 2005), and in the two-dimensional space defined by communion and agency based on interpersonal theory (see Horowitz et al., 2006, for a detailed review). In addition, several studies have provided evidence for a distinction between a more anaclitic hysteroid versus a more introjective type of borderline personality disorder (Blatt & Auerbach, 1988; Levy, Edell, & McGlashan, 2007; Ryder et al., 2008; Westen et al., 1992; Wixom, Ludolph, & Westen, 1993; see also Southwick, Yehuda, & Giller, 1995).

Thus, systematic empirical investigations indicate that the personality disorders in Axis II of the DSM can be integrated parsimoniously into two configurations of anaclitic and introjective personality disorders. At the same time, these studies also show that there is no one-to-one relationship between the two configurations of psychopathology and symptoms and other characteristics that define various disorders in the current DSM Axis II classification. Ouimette & Klein (1993), for example, studying both students and depressed outpatients, using five different measures of anaclitic and introjective features, found that not all of their predicted convergent and discriminant relationships between anaclitic and introjective features and the DSM personality disorder criteria were significant. While a number of reasons may account for this, including the limitations of Axis II and the two-configurations model, as well as methodological limitations

of the measurement instruments, the findings suggest that similar symptoms and characteristics can be expressed in different disorders (multifinality) or the same disorder may be expressed by different symptoms (equifinality). As Levy et al. (2006) argue, current DSM criteria are unable to identify different underlying dynamics of patients who have similar characteristics (see also Westen et al., 2006). For example, patients who received a DSM-IV diagnosis of borderline personality disorder show considerable heterogeneity as indicated by marked differences in interpersonal distress, self-destructive behavior, and impulsivity. These differences, however, can be accounted for in theoretically predicted ways by the two-configurations model that differentiates between a more anaclitic or hysteroid and a more introjective or paranoid type of borderline personality disorder (Blatt & Auerbach, 1988). Fundamental differences in personality organization appear to provide a more coherent way of differentiating among various disorders than a focus on manifest symptoms and characteristics.

The anaclitic and introjective differentiation in personality organization and psychopathology based on personality dimensions establishes a coherent diagnostic classificatory system in which psychopathological disorders are viewed on a continuum from normal personality organization, to subclinical pathology, to manifest clinical disorders, congruent with other recent dimensional models (Haslam, 2003; Luyten & Blatt, 2007; J. Ruscio & Ruscio, 2000; Tsuang et al., 2003; Widiger & Clark, 2000). Moreover, this model also suggests the possibility of identifying a hierarchical organization in which many *symptom-based disorders* (e.g., eating disorders and conduct disorders) can be subsumed within one of several major clinical disorders (Blatt, 2004; Blatt & Shichman, 1981; Clark, 2005; Krueger, Markon, Patrick, & Iacono, 2005; Watson, 2005). This hierarchical view of clinical disorders provides a parsimonious way of dealing with the problematic and vexing issue of comorbidity (Shafran & Mansell, 2001). Symptom-based diagnoses, such as conduct and antisocial disorders (e.g., Blatt, 2004; Blatt & Shichman, 1981), substance abuse (e.g., Blatt, Rounsaville, Eyre, & Wilbur, 1984; T. Lidz, Lidz, & Rubenstein, 1976), eating disorders (e.g., Bers, Blatt, & Dolinsky, 2004; Claes, Vandereycken, Luyten, Soenens, Pieters, & Vertommen, 2006; Thompson-Brenner & Westen, 2005), sleep disturbance (Norlander et al., 2005), posttraumatic stress disorder (PTSD; Gargurevich, 2006; Southwick et al., 1995) and chronic fatigue syndrome (e.g., Luyten, Van Houdenhove, Cosyns, & Van den Broeck, 2006), for example, are often *behavioral expressions of difficulties with interpersonal relatedness or self-definition and therefore are symptomatic expressions of more primary disorders in either the anaclitic or introjective configuration.*

These formulations have important implications for intervention because they indicate, for instance, that disruptive behavior in many symptom-based disorders, including conduct and antisocial disorders, are frequently defensive and distorted attempts to establish some form of interpersonal relatedness or some sense of self-worth (Blatt & Shichman, 1981)—issues that should be a central focus of treatment in addition to the more manifest symptomatic expressions of the disorder (Blatt & Shichman, 1981; First et al., 2004; Kupfer et al., 2002).

RELATEDNESS AND SELF-DEFINITION AND PROCESSES OF THERAPEUTIC CHANGE

The mechanisms of therapeutic change are elusive. Yet there is growing consensus that therapeutic change results from an interaction between patient, therapist and therapeutic alliance factors, as well as the specific techniques, creating a very complex interpersonal matrix, the investigation of which could be facilitated by

a comprehensive theoretical model of personality development (Blatt et al., 2010). The two-configurations model provides such a theoretical structure: a paradigm for psychotherapy research across theoretical orientations.

Recent research (e.g., Blatt & Shahar, 2004; Fertuck, et al, 2004; Vermote et al., 2009) indicates that interpersonally oriented anaclitic patients are responsive primarily to the supportive aspects of treatment, whereas self-oriented introjective patients are responsive primarily to the exploratory, interpretive aspects of the psychotherapeutic process. Other research (Blatt, Besser, & Ford, 2007; Blatt & Ford, 1994) indicates that therapeutic change in anaclitic patients occurs primarily initially in interpersonal dimensions whereas therapeutic change in introjective patients occurs primarily initially in aspects of self-presentation (i.e., clinical symptoms) and in cognitive efficacy (e.g., IQ). Beyond these initial changes in the treatment process that are congruent with the patient's personality organization, the two-configurations model is based on the assumption of a parallel between normal psychological development and the processes of therapeutic change. Consolidated therapeutic change in psychotherapy, as in normal development, occurs as a synergistic developmental interaction of experiences of interpersonal relatedness and self-definition—the consequence of the reactivation of the normal synergistic developmental process. Moreover, if various forms of psychopathology are the consequence of disruptions of the normal synergistic developmental process as a result of disrupted interpersonal experiences, then interpersonal experiences in the therapeutic relationship should contribute to constructive development in the sense of self, leading to more mature expressions of interpersonal relatedness that in turn contribute to further refinements in the sense of self (Blatt, 2002). Alternating experiences of gratifying involvement (e.g., attachment) and experienced incompatibility (e.g., separation) in the treatment process (Blatt & Behrends, 1987) reactivates a normal synergistic developmental process in which more mature expressions of interpersonal relatedness and of self-definition develop in reciprocal interaction.

Recent findings by Safran and Muran (2000; see also Chapter 30 in this volume) provide some empirical support for this view of the reactivation of the normal synergistic developmental process in the later phases of the treatment process. Safran and Muran, studying disruptions in the treatment process, distinguish between withdrawal ruptures more typical for interpersonally oriented anaclitic patients, and confrontation ruptures more characteristic of self-oriented introjective patients. They note differences in the process leading to the resolution of these two types of therapeutic ruptures. In withdrawal ruptures, empathic statements by the therapist evoke experiences of disavowed unmet needs for nurturance that underlay the extensive demands of the patient. They (2000, p. 154) view the direct expression of these intense needs for nurturance late in treatment as "an important act of self-assertion" because it enables the patient "to begin to take responsibility for . . . (these) demands, rather than expressing them indirectly." Thus, the resolution of withdrawal ruptures, more typical of interpersonally oriented anaclitic patients, involves direct expression of disavowed needs for nurturance in assertive, agentic self-expression. In contrast, for the resolution of confrontational ruptures, more typical of self-oriented introjective patients, Safran and Muran (2000, p. 174) note the importance of exploring the "construal of the futility of the situation . . . and the underlying feelings of desperation," and how these explorations lead to the emergence of underlying "fears of abandonment . . . and access to feelings of vulnerability and the need for nurturance." Thus, the resolution of confrontational ruptures of self-oriented introjective patients leads to the emergence of underlying anaclitic

qualities and an interest in interpersonal relatedness (anaclitic issues). In contrast, the resolution of withdrawal ruptures in interpersonally-oriented anaclitic patients, lead to the emergence of self-assertive (introjective) activity. These findings and formulations by Safran and Muran suggest that successful treatment involves the emergence of the other voice—of self-assertion in interpersonally oriented anaclitic patients and of interpersonal concerns and interests in self-oriented introjective patients. Thus, a successful therapeutic process appears to involve the resumption of the normal dialectic process in which the synergistic developmental interaction between anaclitic interpersonal and introjective self-definitional processes is reactivated in the resolutions of ruptures in the treatment process. As anaclitic patients feel more secure in the treatment relationship they can, for example, venture to disagree with the therapist; and when introjective patients feel more secure in their autonomy and independence, they can allow themselves to experience and express feelings of gratitude and affection for the therapist. Therapists should intervene in a timely fashion to facilitate the emergence of this "other voice," and the generalization of these experiences in the therapeutic relationship to interpersonal relationships external to the treatment process. As suggested by Safran and Muran, ruptures in the therapeutic alliance as expressions of experienced incompatibilities appear to play a key role in the treatment process. Thus, the findings of Safran & Muran about the importance of ruptures and repairs in the therapeutic process are consistent with the formulations of Blatt & Behrends (1987) that alternating experiences of gratifying involvement (e.g., attachment) and experienced incompatibility are central in the treatment process, especially in reactivating a normal developmental process in which more mature expressions of interpersonal relatedness and of self-definition develop in reciprocal interaction.

CONCLUSIONS

Extensive empirical research demonstrates that the two fundamental developmental dimensions of interpersonal relatedness and self-definition provide a basis for a coherent model of personality development and of personality organization, and a diagnostic schema of psychopathology. Thus, the two fundamental dimensions of interpersonal relatedness and self-definition facilitate the identification of continuities among dimensions in personality development, personality organization, and various psychopathological disorders in both Axis I and Axis II of the current DSM. These conceptualizations not only avoid the complex and vexing problems of comorbidity associated with DSM-IV, but they provide the conceptual structure for integrating research on psychopathology and the therapeutic process with investigations of personality development and organization based on attachment theory and research as well as on contemporary approaches to the study of interpersonal processes with the circumplex model.

Future research should further explore the role these two fundamental personality dimensions play in the emergence of psychopathology across the life span, and explore the similarities and differences with other two-polarities models. More specifically, there is an urgent need to address the genetic, neurobiological, and neural underpinnings of these two polarities. Rather than post-hoc searches for specific genetic, neurobiological, and neural markers of particular psychiatric disorders, an approach troubled by complex issues of the equifinality and multifinality of symptoms and of etiological pathways, the two-configurations approach provides a comprehensive theoretical approach to more theory-driven studies of the interaction between psychosocial and biological factors. Gunnar and Quevedo (2007), for instance, argued that individual differences in the regulation of stress in mother-infant interactions can provide a lens for examining the impact and management of stress throughout development. In this context, a study by Beebe and colleagues (2007) illustrates how mother's personality organization around issues of interpersonal relatedness and self-definition influence the infant's development of self- and interactive regulation as early as four months of age. Together with growing evidence for a close link between such (early) attachment experiences and the development of stress and affect regulation, of mental representations, and of metareflective capacities (Lupien et al., 2009; Luyten, Mayes, Fonagy, & Van Houdenhove, 2009), this focus also provides powerful links to neuroscience research that is increasingly studying the neural circuits involved in our understanding of oneself and others and the "processes that occur at the interface of self and others" (Lieberman, 2007, p. 259). Hence, insights into the neural circuits involved in issues of relatedness and self-definition could greatly increase our understanding of both normal and pathological personality development.

Concerning possible intervention strategies, research based on the two-configuration model suggests that the development, implementation, and training in different treatments for different disorders may be in part misguided. In contrast, it may be more fruitful to identify spectra of disorders that involve different disruptions in the capacity for relatedness (attachment) and self-definition (autonomy), and develop age-sensitive treatment principles, strategies and techniques for these spectra, rather than for specific disorders. Moreover, from this perspective, the aim of treatment is not simply to reduce symptoms or improve interpersonal functioning, but to enable individuals to resume normal development. This also implies that outcome studies should routinely include age-sensitive measures of specific developmental tasks and capacities that assess the extent to which treatment has brought individuals closer to normative developmental trajectories (Luyten et al., 2008).

References

American Psychiatric Association (1994). *Diagnostic and statistical manual of mental disorders* (4th ed.). Washington, DC: American Psychiatric Association.

Arieti, S., & Bemporad, J. R. (1978). *Severe and mild depression: The therapeutic approach*. New York: Basic Books.

Arieti, S., & Bemporad, J. R. (1980). The psychological organization of depression. *American Journal of Psychiatry, 137*, 1360–1365.

Bartholomew, K., & Horowitz, L. (1991). A four category model of attachment. *Journal of Personality and Social Psychology, 61*, 226–241.

Beck, A. T. (1983). Cognitive therapy of depression: New perspectives. In P. J. Clayton & J. E. Barrett (Eds.), *Treatment of depression: Old controversies and new approaches* (pp. 265–290). New York: Raven.

Beebe, B., Jaffe, J., Buck, K., Chen, H., Cohen, P., Blatt, S. J., ... Andrews, H. (2007). Six-week postpartum maternal self-criticism and dependency predict 4-month mother-infant self- and interactive regulation. *Developmental Psychology, 43*, 1360–1376.

Benjamin, L. S. (2003). *Interpersonal reconstructive therapy: Promoting change in nonresponders*. New York: Guilford Press.

Bers, S. A., Blatt, S. J., & Dolinksy, A. (2004). The sense of self in Anorexia-Nervosa patients: A psychoanalytically informed method for studying self-representation. *Psychoanalytic Study of the Child, 59*, 294–315.

Besser, A., Vliegen, N., Luyten, P., & Blatt, S. J. (2008). Systematic empirical investigation of vulnerability to postpartum depression from a psychodynamic perspective: Commentary on issues raised by Blum (2007). *Psychoanalytic Psychology, 25*, 392–410.

Besser, A., Luyten, P. Vliegen, N., & Blatt, S. J. (2008). Women and depression: Contemporary psychodynamic perspectives. In W. Hansson & E. Olsson (Eds.), *New Perspectives on Women and Depression*. Hauppauge, NY: Nova Publishers.

Blatt, S. J. (1974). Levels of object representation in anaclitic and introjective depression. *Psychoanalytic Study of the Child, 29*, 107–157.

Blatt, S. J. (1995). Representational structures in psychopathology. In D. Cicchetti & S. Toth (Eds.), *Rochester Symposium on Developmental Psychopathology: Vol. 6. Emotion, Cognition, and Representation* (pp. 1–33). Rochester, NY: University of Rochester Press.

Blatt, S. J. (1995b). The destructiveness of perfectionism: Implications for the treatment of depression. *American Psychologist, 50*, 1003–1020.

Blatt, S. J. (1998). Contributions of psychoanalysis to the understanding and treatment of depression. *Journal of the American Psychoanalytic Association, 46*, 723–752.

Blatt, S. J. (2002). Patient variables: Anaclitic and introjective dimensions. In W. Sledge & M. Hershen (Eds.), *Encyclopedia of Psychotherapy* (pp. 349–357). New York: Academic Press.

Blatt, S. J. (2004). *Experiences of depression: Theoretical, clinical and research perspectives*. Washington, DC: American Psychological Association.

Blatt, S. J. (2006). A fundamental polarity in psychoanalysis: Implications for personality development, psychopathology, and the therapeutic process. *Psychoanalytic Inquiry, 26*, 492–518.

Blatt, S. J. (2008). *Polarities of experience: Relatedness and self-definition in personality development, psychopathology, and the therapeutic process*. Washington, DC: American Psychological Association Press.

Blatt, S. J., & Auerbach, J. S. (1988). Differential cognitive disturbances in three types of "borderline" patients. *Journal of Personality Disorders, 2*, 198–211.

Blatt, S. J., Auerbach, J. S., & Behrends, R. S. (2008). Changes in representation of self and significant others in the therapeutic process: Links among representation, internalization, and mentalization. In A. Slade, E. Jurist, & S. Bergner (Eds.), *Mind to Mind: Infant research, neuroscience and psychoanalysis* (pp. 225–253). New York: Other Press.

Blatt, S. J., & Behrends, R. S. (1987). Internalization, separation-individuation, and the nature of therapeutic action. *International Journal of Psychoanalysis, 68*, 279–297.

Blatt, S. J., Besser, A., & Ford, R. Q. (2007). Two primary configurations of psychopathology and change in thought disorder in long-term, intensive, inpatient treatment of seriously disturbed young adults. *American Journal of Psychiatry, 164*, 1561–1567.

Blatt, S. J., & Blass, R. B. (1990). Attachment and separateness: A dialectic model of the products and processes of psychological development. *Psychoanalytic Study of the Child, 45*, 107–127.

Blatt, S. J., & Blass, R. (1996). Relatedness and self-definition: A dialectic model of personality development. In G. G. Noam & K. W. Fischer (Eds.), *Development and vulnerabilities in close relationships* (pp. 309–338). Hillsdale, NJ: Erlbaum.

Blatt, S. J., Cornell, C. E., & Eshkol, E. (1993). Personality style, differential vulnerability and clinical course in immunological and cardiovascular disease. *Clinical Psychology Review, 13,* 421–450.

Blatt, S. J., D'Afflitti, J. P., & Quinlan, D. M. (1976). Experiences of depression in normal young adults. *Journal of Abnormal Psychology, 85,* 383–389.

Blatt, S. J., & Ford, R. (1994). *Therapeutic change: An object relations perspective.* New York: Plenum.

Blatt, S. J., & Homann, E. (1992). Parent-child interaction in the etiology of dependent and self-critical depression. *Clinical Psychology Review, 12,* 47–91.

Blatt, S. J., & Levy, K. N. (1998). A psychodynamic approach to the diagnosis of psychopathology. In J. W. Barron (Ed.), *Making diagnosis meaningful* (pp. 73–109). Washington, DC: American Psychological Association Press.

Blatt, S. J., & Luyten, P. (2009). A structural developmental psychodynamic approach to psychopathology: Two polarities of experience across the life span. *Development and Psychopathology, 21,* 793–814.

Blatt, S. J., & Luyten, P. (2010). Reactivating the psychodynamic approach to classify psychopathology. In T. Millon, R. Krueger, & E. Simonsen (Eds.), *Contemporary directions in psychopathology: Toward the DSM-V, ICD-11, and beyond* (pp. 483–514). New York: Guilford Press.

Blatt, S. J., & Maroudas, C. (1992). Convergence of psychoanalytic and cognitive behavioral theories of depression. *Psychoanalytic Psychology, 9,* 157–190.

Blatt, S. J., Quinlan, D. M., Chevron, E. S., McDonald, C., & Zuroff, D. (1982). Dependency and self-criticism: Psychological dimensions of depression. *Journal of Consulting and Clinical Psychology, 50,* 113–124.

Blatt, S. J., Rounsaville, B. J., Eyre, S., & Wilber, C. (1984). The psycho-dynamics ofopiate addiction. *Journal of Nervous and Mental Disease, 172,* 342–352.

Blatt, S. J., & Shahar, G. (2004). Psychoanalysis: For what, with whom, and how: A comparison with psychotherapy. *Journal of the American Psychoanalytic Association, 52,* 393–447.

Blatt, S. J., & Shahar, G. (2005). A dialectic model of personality development and psychopathology: Recent contributions to understanding and treating depression. In Corveleyn, J., Luyten, P., & Blatt, S. J. (Eds.), *The theory and treatment of depression: Towards a dynamic interactionism model* (pp. 137–162). Leuven: University of Leuven Press.

Blatt, S. J., & Shichman, S. (1981). Antisocial behavior and personality organization. In S. Tuttman, C. Kaye, & M. Zimmerman (Eds.), *Object and self: A developmental approach: Essays in honor of Edith Jacobson* (pp. 325–367). Madison: International Universities Press.

Blatt, S. J., & Shichman, S. (1983). Two primary configurations of psychopathology. *Psychoanalysis and Contemporary Thought, 6,* 187–254.

Blatt, S. J., & Wild, C. M. (1976). *Schizophrenia: A developmental analysis.* New York: Academic Press.

Blatt, S. J., & Zuroff, D. C. (1992). Interpersonal relatedness and self-definition: Two prototypes for depression. *Clinical Psychology Review, 12,* 527–562.

Blatt, S. J., & Zuroff, D. C. (2005). Empirical evaluation of the assumptions in identifying evidence based treatments in mental health. *Clinical Psychology Review, 25,* 459–486.

Blatt, S. J., Zuroff, D. C., Hawley, L. L., & Auerbach, J. S. (2010). An attempt to identify processes that contribute to sustained therapeutic change. *Psychotherapy Research, 20,* 37–54.

Bowlby, J. (1988). *A secure base: Clinical applications of attachment theory.* London: Routledge & Kegan Paul.

Claes, L., Vandereycken, W., Luyten, P., Soenes, B., Pieters, G., & Vertommen, H. (2006). Personality prototypes in eating disorders based on the big five model. *Journal of Personality Disorders, 20,* 401–416.

Clark, D. A., Steer, R. A., Haslam, N., Beck, A. T., & Brown, G. K. (1997). Personality vulnerability, psychiatric diagnoses, and symptoms: Cluster analyses of the Sociotropy and Autonomy subscales. *Cognitive Therapy and Research, 21,* 267–283.

Clark, L. A. (2005). Temperament as a unifying base for personality and psychopathology. *Journal of Abnormal Psychology, 114,* 505–521.

Cogswell, A., & Alloy, L. B. (2006). The relation of neediness and Axis II pathology. *Journal of Personality Disorders, 20,* 16–21.

Erikson, E. H. (1950). *Childhood and society* (2nd ed.). New York: Norton.

Fertuck, E., Bucci, W., Blatt, S. J., & Ford, R. Q. (2004). Verbal representation and therapeutic change in anaclitic and introjective patients. *Psychotherapy: Theory, Research, Practice, Training, 41,* 13–25.

First, M. B., Pincus, H. A., Levine, J. B., Williams, J. B., Ustun, B., & Peele, R. (2004). Clinical utility as a criterion for revision psychiatric diagnoses. *American Journal of Psychiatry, 161,* 946–954.

Fonagy, P. (2008). Foreword in S. J. Blatt, *Polarities of Experience: Relatedness and self-definition in personality development, psychopathology and the therapeutic process* (pp. ix–xiii). Washington, DC: American Psychological Association.

Freud, S. (1905/1963). Three essays on sexuality. In J. Strachey (Ed. & Trans.), *The standard edition of the complete psychological works of Sigmund Freud* (Vol. 7, 135–243. London: Hogarth Press.

Freud, S. (1957). Instincts and their vicissitudes. In J. Strachey (Ed. & Trans.), *The standard edition of the complete psychological works of Sigmund Freud* (Vol. 23, 144–207. London: Hogarth Press. (Original work published 1915)

Freud, S. (1957). Mourning and melancholia. In J. Strachey (Ed. and Trans.), *The standard edition of the complete psychological works of Sigmund Freud* (Vol. 14, pp. 243–258). London: Hogarth Press. (Original work published 1917)

Gargurevich, R. (2006). *Post-traumatic stress disorder and disasters in Peru.* Unpublished doctoral dissertation. Leuven, Belgium: University of Leuven.

Goldberg, J. O., Segal, Z. V., Vella, D. D., & Shaw, B. (1989). Depressive personality: Millon Clinical Multiaxial Inventory profiles of sociotropic and autonomous subtypes. *Journal of Personality Disorders, 3,* 193–198.

Gunnar, M., & Quevedo, K. (2007). The neurobiology of stress and development. *Annual Review of Psychology, 58,* 145–173.

Haslam, N. (2003). Categorical versus dimensional models of mental disorders: The taxonometric evidence. *Australian and New Zealand Journal of Psychiatry, 37,* 696–704.

Helgeson, V. S. (1994). Relation of agency and communion to well-being: Evidence and potential exploration. *Psychological Bulletin, 116,* 412–428.

Horowitz, L. M. (2004). *Interpersonal foundations of psychopathology.* Washington, DC: American Psychological Association.

Horowitz, L. M., Wilson, K. R., Turan, B., Zolotsev, P., Constantino, M. J., & Henderson, L. (2006). How interpersonal motives clarify the meaning of interpersonal behavior: A revised circumplex model. *Personality and Social Psychology Review, 10,* 67–86.

Krueger, R. F., Markon, K. E., Patrick, C. J. & Iacono, W. G. (2005). Externalizing psychopathology in adulthood: A dimensional-spectrum conceptualization and its implications for DSM-V. *Journal of Abnormal Psychology, 114,* 537–550.

Kupfer, D. J., First, M. B. & Reiger, D. A. (2002). Introduction. In D. J. Kupfer, M. B. First, & D. E. Reiger (Eds.), *A research agenda for DSM-V* (pp. xv–xxiii). Washington, DC: American Psychiatric Association.

Lam, D. H., Wright, K., & Smith, N. (2004). Dysfunctional assumptions in bipolar disorder. *Journal of Affective Disorders, 79,* 193–199.

Levy, K. N., & Blatt, S. J. (1999). Attachment theory and psychoanalysis: Further differentiation within insecure attachment patterns. *Psychoanalytic Inquiry, 19,* 541–575.

Levy, K. N., Edell, W. S., Blatt, S. J., Becker, D. F., Quinlan, D. M., Kolligan, J., & McGlashan, T. H. (1995). *Two configurations of psychopathology: The relationship of dependency, anaclitic neediness, and self-criticism to personality pathology.* Unpublished manuscript.

Levy, K. N., Edell, W. S., & McGlashan, T. H. (2007). Depressive experiences in inpatients with borderline personality disorder. *Psychiatric Quarterly, 78,* 129–143.

Levy, K. N., Meehan, K. B., Nelly, K. M., Reynoso, J. S., Weber, M., Clarkin, J. F., & Kernberg, O. F. (2006). Change in attachment paterns and reflective function in a randomized control trial of transference-focused psychothearpy for borderline personality disorder. *Journal of Consulting and Clinical Psychology, 74,* 1027–1040.

Lidz, T., Lidz, R. W., & Rubenstein, R. (1976). An anaclitic syndrome in adolescent amphetamine addicts. *The Psychoanalytic Study of the Child, 31,* 317–348.

Lieberman, M. D. (2007). Social cognitive neuroscience: A review of core processes. *Annual Review of Psychology, 58*, 259–289.

Lupien, S. J., McEwen, B. S., Gunnar, M. R., & Heim, C. (2009). Effects of stress throughout the lifespan of the brain, behaviour and cognition. *Nature Reviews Neuroscience, 10*, 434–445.

Luyten, P. (2006). Psychopathology: A simple twist of fate or a meaningful distortion of normal development? Toward an etiologically based alternative for the DSM approach. *Psychoanalytic Inquiry, 26*, 521–535.

Luyten, P., & Blatt, S. J. (2007). Looking back towards the future: Is it time to change the DSM approach to psychiatric disorders? The case of depression. *Psychiatry: Interpersonal and Biological Processes, 70*, 85–99.

Luyten, P., & Blatt, S. J. (2009). Reconciling theory-driven and empirically-derived models of psychopathology: Relatedness and self-definition as central coordinates in personality development, psychopathology, and the therapeutic process. (In review).

Luyten, P., Blatt, S. J., & Corveleyn, J. (2005a). The convergence among psychodynamic and cognitive-behavioral theories of depression: Theoretical overview. In J. Corveleyn, P. Luyten, & S. J. Blatt (Eds.), *The theory and treatment of depression: Towards a dynamic interactionism model* (pp. 67–94). Leuven: University of Leuven Press.

Luyten, P., Blatt, S. J., & Corveleyn, J. (2005b). Introduction. In J. Corveleyn, P. Luyten, & S. J. Blatt (Eds.), *The theory and treatment of depression: Towards a dynamic interactionism model* (pp. 5–15). Leuven: University of Leuven Press.

Luyten, P., Blatt, S. J., & Corveleyn, J. (2005c). Towards integration in the theory and treatment of depression. In J. Corveleyn, P. Luyten, & S. J. Blatt (Eds.), *The theory and treatment of depression: Towards a dynamic interactionism model* (pp. 253–284). Leuven, Belgium: Leuven University Press.

Luyten, P., Blatt, S. J., van Houdenhove, B., & Corveleyn, J. (2006). Depression research and treatment: Are we skating to where the puck is going to be? *Clinical Psychology Review, 26*, 985–999.

Luyten, P., Mayes, L., Fonagy, P., & Van Houdenhove, B. (2009). *The interpersonal regulation of stress*. Manuscript submitted for publication.

Luyten, P., Vliegen, N., Van Houdenhove, B., & Blatt, S. J. (2008). Equifinality, multifinality, and the rediscovery of the importance of early experiences: Pathways from early adversity to psychiatric and (functional) somatic disorders. *The Psychoanalytic Study of the Child, 63*, 27–60.

Luyten, P., Van Houdenhove, B., Cosyns, N., & Van den Broeck, A. (2006). Are patients with Chronic Fatigue Syndrome perfectionistic—or were they? A case-control study. *Personality and Individual Differences, 40*, 1473–1483.

Lyons-Ruth, K. (2001). The two-person construction of defenses: Disorganized attachment strategies, unintegrated mental states and hostile/helpless relational processes. *Psychologist-Psychoanalyst, 21*, 40–45.

Lyons-Ruth, K., & Block, D. (1996). The disturbed caregiving system: Relations among childhood trauma, maternal caregiving, and infant affect and attachment. *Infant Mental Health Journal, 17*, 257–275.

Lyons-Ruth, K., Zeanah, C. H., & Benoit, D. (2003). Disorder and risk for disorder during infancy and toddlerhood. In E. J. Mash & R. A. Barkley (Eds.), *Child psychopathology* (2nd ed., pp. 589–631). New York: Guilford Press.

Main, M., Kaplan, L., & Cassidy, J. (1985). Security in infancy, childhood and adulthood: A move to the level of representation. In I. Bretherton & E. Waters (Eds.), Growing Points in Attachment Theory and Research, *Monographs of the Society for Research in Child Development 50* (1–2, Serial No. 209), 66–104.

Meyer, B., & Pilkonis, P. A. (2005). An attachment model of personality disorders. In. M. F. Lenzenweger & J. F. Clarkin (Eds.), *Major theories of personality disorder* (2nd ed., pp. 231–281). New York: Guilford Press.

Mikulincer, M., & Shaver, P. (2007). *Attachment in adulthood: Structure, dynamics, and change.* New York: Guilford Press.

Morse, J. Q., Robins, C. J., & Gittes-Fox, M. (2002). Sociotropy, autonomy, and personality disorder criteria in psychiatric patients. *Journal of Personality Disorders, 16*, 549–560.

Nordahl, H., & Stiles, T. C. (2000). The specificity of cognitive personality dimensions in Cluster C personality disorder. *Behavioural and Cognitive Psychotherapy, 28*, 235–246.

Norlander, T., Johansson, A., & Bood, S. A. (2005). The affective personality: Its relation to quality of sleep, well-being, and stress. *Social Behavior and Personality, 33,* 709–722.

Ouimette, P. C., & Klein, D. N. (1993). Convergence of psychoanalytic and cognitive-behavioral theories of depression: A review of the empirical literature and new data on Blatt's and Beck's models. In J. Masling & R. Bornstein (Eds.), *Empirical studies of psychoanalytic theories: Vol. 4. Psychoanalytic perspectives on psychopathology* (pp. 191–223). Washington, DC: American Psychological Association.

Ouimette, P. C., Klein, D. N., Anderson, R., Riso, L. P., & Lizardi, H. (1994). Relationship of sociotropy/autonomy and dependency/self-criticism to DSM–III-R personality disorders. *Journal of Abnormal Psychology, 103,* 743–749.

Overholser, J. C., & Freiheit, S. R. (1994). Assessment of interpersonal dependency using the Millon Clinical Multiaxial Inventory-II (MCMI-II) and the Depressive Experiences Questionnaire. *Personality and Individual Differences, 17,* 71–78.

Piaget, J. (1954). *The construction of reality in the child* (M. Cook, Trans.). New York: Basic Books. (Original work published 1937)

Pilkonis, P. A. (1988). Personality prototypes among depressives: Themes of dependency and autonomy. *Journal of Personality Disorders, 2,* 144–152.

Pincus, A. L. (2005). The interpersonal nexus of personality disorders. In S. Strack (Ed). *Handbook of personology and psychopathology* (pp. 120–139). Hoboken, NJ: John Wiley & Sons.

Ravitz, P., Maunder, R., & McBride, C. (2008). Attachment, contemporary interpersonal theory and IPT: An integration of theoretical, clinical, and empirical perspectives. *Journal of Contemporary Psychotherapy, 38,* 11–21.

Roisman, G. I., Holland, A., Fortuna, K., Fraley, R. C., Clausell, E., & Clarke, A. (2007). The Adult Attachment Interview and self-reports of attachment style: An empirical rapprochement. *Journal of Personality and Social Psychology, 92,* 678–697).

Ruscio, J., & Ruscio, A. M. (2000). Informing the continuity controversy: A taxometric analysis of depression. *Journal of Abnormal Psychology, 109,* 473–487.

Ryder, A. G., McBride, C., & Bagby, R. M. (2008). The association of affiliative and achievement personality styles with DSM-IV personality disorders. *Journal of Personality Disorders, 22,* 208–216.

Safran, J. D., & Muran, J. C. (2000). *Negotiating the therapeutic alliance: A relational treatment guide.* New York: Guilford Press.

Shafran, R., & Mansell, W. (2001). Perfectionism and psychopathology: A review of research and treatment. *Clinical Psychology Review, 21,* 879–906.

Shahar, G., Blatt, S. J., & Ford, R. Q. (2003). The identification of mixed anaclitic-introjective psychopathology in young adult inpatients. *Psychoanalytic Psychology, 20,* 84–102.

Shahar, G., Trower, P., Iqbal, Z., Birchwood, M., Davidson, L., & Chadwick, P. (2004). The person in recovery from acute and severe psychosis: The role of dependency, self-criticism, and efficacy. *American Journal of Orthopsychiatry, 74,* 480–488.

Sibley, C. G. (2007). The association between working models of attachment and personality: Toward an integrative framework operationalizing global relational models. *Journal of Research in Personality, 41,* 90–109.

Southwick, S. M., Yehuda, R., & Giller, E. L. (1995). Psychological dimensions of depression in borderline personality disorder. *American Journal of Psychiatry, 152,* 789–791.

Stern, D. N. (1985). *The interpersonal world of the infant: A view from psychoanalysis and developmental psychology.* New York: Basic.

Szumotalska, E. (1992). *Severity and type of depressive affect as related to perceptual styles: Relationship of anaclitic versus introjective depressive configuration to holistic versus analytic similarity judgment.* Unpublished doctoral dissertation, New School for Social Research, New York, N.Y.

Thompson-Brenner, H., & Westen, D. (2005). Personality subtypes in eating disorders: Validation of a classification in a naturalistic sample. *British Journal of Psychiatry, 186,* 516–524.

Triandis, H. C. (1995). *Individualism and collectivism.* Boulder, CO: Westview Press.

Tsuang, M. T., Stone, W. S., Tarbox, S. I., & Faraone, S. V. (2003). Implications of schizotaxia for the prevention of schizophrenia. In A. Grispini (Ed.), *Preventive strategies for schizophrenic disorders: Basic principles, opportunities and limits* (pp. 225–243). Rome, Italy: Giovanni Fioriti Editore.

Vermote, R., Fonagy, P., Vertommen, H., Verhaest, Y., Stroobants, R., Vandeneede, B. Corveleyn, J., Lowyck, B., Luyten, P., & Peuskens, J.

(2009). Outcome and outcome trajectories of personality disorder patients during and after a psychoanalytic hospitalization-based treatment. *Journal of Personality Disorders, 23,* 294–307.

Watson, D. (2005). Rethinking the mood and anxiety disorders: A quantitative hierarchical model for DSM-V. *Journal of Abnormal Psychology, 114,* 522–532.

Westen, D. Moses, M. J., Silk, K. R., Lohr, N. E., Cohen, R., & Segal, H. (1992). Quality of depressive experience in borderline personality disorder and major depression: When depression is not just depression. *Journal of Personality Disorders, 6,* 382–393.

Westen, D., Novotny, C. M. & Thompson-Brenner, H. (2004). The empirical status of empirically supported psychotherapies: Assumptions, findings, and reporting in controlled clinical trials. *Psychological Bulletin, 130,* 631–663.

Westen, D., Shedler, J., & Bradley, R. (2006). A prototype approach to personality disorder diagnosis. *American Journal of Psychiatry, 163,* 846–856.

Whiteside, M. F., Busch, F. & Horner, T. (1976). From egocentric to cooperative play in young children: A normative job study. *Journal of the American Academy of Child Psychiatry, 15,* 294–313.

Widiger, T. A., & Clark, A. (2000). Toward DSM-V and the classification of psychopathology. *Psychological Bulletin, 126,* 946–963.

Widiger, T. A., & Trull, T. J. (2007). Plate tectonics in the classification of personality disorder: Shifting to a dimensional model. *American Psychologist, 62,* 71–83.

Wiggins, J. S. (1991). Agency and communion as conceptual coordinates for the understanding and measurement of interpersonal behavior. In W. W. Grove & D. Cicchetti (Eds.), *Thinking clearly about psychology, Vol. 2: Personality and psychotherapy* (pp. 89–113). Minneapolis: University of Minnesota Press.

Wiggins, J. S. (Ed.). (2003). *Paradigms of personality assessment.* New York: Guilford Press.

Witkin, H. A. (1965). Psychological differentiation and forms of pathology. *Journal of Abnormal Psychology, 70,* 317–336.

Wixom, J., Ludolph, P., & Westen, D. (1993). The quality of depression in adolescents with borderline personality disorder. *Journal of the American Academy of Child & Adolescent Psychiatry, 32,* 1172–1177.

Zuroff, D. C., Mongrain, M., & Santor, D. A. (2004). Conceptualizing and measuring personality vulnerability to depression: Commentary on Coyne and Whiffen (1995). *Psychological Bulletin, 130,* 489–511.

4 ORIGINS AND APPLICATIONS OF THE INTERPERSONAL CIRCUMPLEX

Marc A. Fournier

D. S. Moskowitz

David C. Zuroff

In the 60 years since Timothy Leary and colleagues first introduced the interpersonal circumplex, the interpersonal tradition has matured into a methodologically sophisticated, theoretically rich approach to the study of personality processes and individual differences. In this chapter, we review the history of the interpersonal tradition, from Sullivan's (1953) definition of personality in terms of the recurrent patterns in our interpersonal relationships to the introduction of the Leary (1957) Circle and its subsequent variations. We then describe how contextually sensitive approaches to interpersonal assessment have contributed to resolving longstanding controversies concerning the consistency, variability, and patterning of interpersonal behavior, and discuss how such approaches now raise new challenges for contemporary interpersonalists.

Tracing the Origins of the Interpersonal Circumplex

The origins of contemporary interpersonal theory and research can be found in the writings of Harry Stack Sullivan (1940, 1953), who emphasized the importance of interpersonal relationships to healthy personality development and adaptive personality functioning. Sullivan contended that the psychological contents of the individual are intrinsically interpersonal, and went so far as to define personality as *"the relatively enduring pattern of recurrent interpersonal situations which characterize a human life"* (Sullivan, 1953, pp. 110–111).

According to Sullivan, individuals express *integrating tendencies* that bring them together in the mutual pursuit of both the satisfaction of their biologically based needs and the feeling of security (anxiety-free functioning). The resulting interpersonal experience can range on a gradient from rewarding to anxiety-inducing to terrifying, at which point states of dissociation and disintegration are likely to occur. The patterning and repatterning of interpersonal experience across recurrent interpersonal situations subsequently give rise to latent conceptions or cognitive templates of self and other that Sullivan called *personifications*. Personifications are elaborated organizations of past interpersonal experiences, and as such are intrinsically subjective. Sullivan firmly believed that we react not to how things really are, but rather to our subjective experience of them and the meaning they have for us: "I would like to make it forever clear that the relation of personifications to that which is personified is always complex and sometimes multiple; and that personifications are not adequate descriptions of that which is personified" (Sullivan, 1953, p. 167). The importance of the *psychological situation* is a point to which we return later in this chapter.

The earliest attempts to formalize Sullivan's concepts were documented in a series of publications by Hubert Coffey and his students at the University of California, Berkeley, and the Kaiser Foundation Research Hospital (Freedman, Leary, Ossorio, & Coffey, 1951; LaForge, Leary, Naboisek, Coffey, & Freedman, 1954; LaForge & Suczek, 1955), and subsequently in Timothy Leary's (1957) seminal work, *Interpersonal Diagnosis of Personality*. The clinical goal of this research was to understand the relations between personality and group interaction by observing patients' behavior in session. The Kaiser Group's research culminated in a circular framework of interpersonal variables with which they could characterize both everyday and extreme aspects of interpersonal behavior. The Kaiser Group selected verbs for describing the *actions* of individuals (e.g., dominate) and adjectives for describing their *traits* (e.g., dominating). Segments of action verbs and trait adjectives were selected to encompass both everyday (i.e., statistically frequent) and extreme (i.e., statistically infrequent) categories of behavior. Sixteen categorical segments in all were selected, lettered A through P, and then ordered in a circular arrangement around the orthogonal axes of dominance–submission and love–hate.

The model itself came to be known as the interpersonal circle (IPC) or circumplex,

an early representation of which can be seen in Figure 4.1. Although interpersonal researchers still debate critical features of the model (e.g., Horowitz, Wilson, Turan, Zolotsev, Constantino, & Henderson, 2006; Moskowitz, 2005), virtually all contemporary interpersonal researchers see the interpersonal domain as having a two-dimensional structure. The vertical (or *agentic*) dimension concerns autonomy and control and ranges from submissiveness to dominance. The horizontal (or *communal*) dimension concerns affiliation and connection and ranges from quarrelsomeness to agreeableness. All forms of social behavior can in turn be viewed as combinations of the four poles. For instance, *being critical* represents a combination of dominance and quarrelsomeness. In contrast, *being deferential* represents a combination of submissiveness and agreeableness.

It is worth noting that the Kaiser Group researchers did not set out in search of a circle, even though one was found: "A close fought battle with empirical fact, not lofty considerations of logical symmetry, produced the sixteen categories. In the final stages, the circle emerged" (LaForge, 1977, p. 8). In fact, the original IPC framework appeared some time before Guttman (1954) introduced the circumplex. However, knowing that a set of interpersonal variables conforms to a circumplex, the following three inferences can then be made: first, that variables close together on the circumference of the circle are conceptually and statistically similar (e.g., dominance and extraversion); second, that variables separated by ninety degrees on the circumference of the circle are conceptually and statistically unrelated (e.g., dominance and affiliation); and third, that variables on opposing sides of the circle are conceptual and statistical opposites (e.g., dominance and submission).

The IPC constitutes a formal geometric model in a two-dimensional space (Wiggins, 1982), in which distance from the origin serves to indicate the extremity or

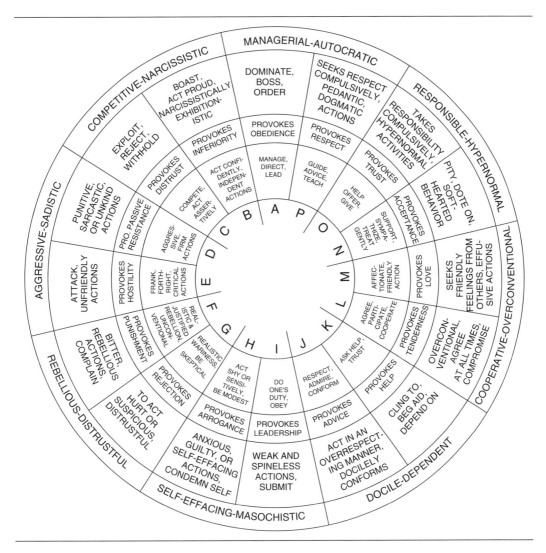

FIGURE 4.1 An Early Representation of the Interpersonal Circle (IPC)
Source: From *Interpersonal Diagnosis of Personality* (p. 65), by T. Leary, 1957, New York: Ronald Press.

intensity of the interpersonal characteristic in question. The dimensions of dominance and affiliation can be seen as latent variables that give rise to a circular continuum (Guttman, 1954) in which every interpersonal characteristic can be understood as a specific blend of the two basic dimensions. However, it should be noted that although two dimensions are necessary, they are not in and of themselves sufficient to infer circumplexity. In order to conclude that a circumplex exists, evidence of interstitiality, equal spacing, and constant radius must also be found. In other words, variables must be distributed around the circle, variables must be spaced equally around the circle, and variables must have a constant radius from the center of the circle, such that all variables have equal communality on the two circumplex dimensions. Numerous psychometric criteria have been proposed to assess for circumplex structure, which Acton and Revelle (2004) have evaluated.

Although a range of terms has been used to refer to the axes of the IPC, Wiggins (1991) advocated that the dimensions be interpreted in reference to the metaconcepts of *agency* and *communion* (Bakan, 1966). The metaconcept of agency refers to the condition of being a differentiated individual, which manifests in strivings for expansion and elevation that serve to protect that differentiation. The metaconcept of communion refers to the condition of being part of a larger social or spiritual entity, which manifests in strivings for contact and congregation within that larger entity. Wiggins (2003) commented on how themes of agency and communion could be seen throughout the social sciences, from the evolutionary literature on *status hierarchy negotiation* versus *reciprocal alliance formation* (Buss, 1991) to the cross-cultural literature on *individualism* versus *collectivism* (Triandis, 1990) to the clinical literature on *control* versus *affiliation* (Kiesler, 1996). Themes of agency and communion were clearly evident to Wiggins (1991, 2003) in Sullivan's ideas of self-esteem and security, respectively.

Measures soon followed the model. Maurice Lorr (Lorr & McNair, 1963, 1965) was among the first to systematically validate and extend Leary's conceptions, and pioneered the application of multivariate statistics to interpersonal measurement. Although the Interpersonal Check List (ICL; LaForge and Suczek, 1955) had already been developed to assess the 16 segments of the IPC, the authors of the ICL had relied on their intuition to determine the circular ordering of its segments (Lorr, 1996). It remained to be seen whether multivariate statistical procedures would confirm their intuitions. Lorr and McNair thus developed the Interpersonal Behavior Inventory (IBI) and found, from factor-analyzing ratings of psychiatric patients and normal participants, that the IBI's scales adhered to the expected circular order. Lorr and colleagues then showed that the IPC could be used to identify distinct interpersonal types among samples of psychiatric patients

(Lorr, Bishop, & McNair, 1965), a practice that later became endemic to the field of interpersonal research.

Interpersonal trait measurement continued to develop over the following decades. Building on the work of Allport, Norman, and Goldberg, Jerry Wiggins sought to develop a taxonomy with which to classify trait-descriptive adjectives from the interpersonal domain (Wiggins, 1979). The Interpersonal Adjective Scales (IAS; Wiggins, 1995) eventually emerged from these research efforts. Operating with a working definition of the interpersonal domain as involving *"dyadic interactions that have relatively clear-cut social (status) and emotional (love) consequences for both participants (self and other)"* (Wiggins, 1979, p. 398), Wiggins identified approximately 800 adjectives as having interpersonal content. Factor-analytic procedures were then used to reduce the original pool of 800 terms first to 128 terms (Wiggins, 1979) and then to 64 terms (Wiggins, Trapnell, & Phillips, 1988). The final version of the IAS (Wiggins, 1995) consisted of eight scales, each consisting of eight adjectives, reflecting the octants of the IPC.

Clinically informed measurement instruments were developed over this same period. Recognizing that interpersonal problems are among the most common complaints that patients report during clinical interviews, Leonard Horowitz and colleagues (Horowitz, 1979; Horowitz, Rosenberg, Baer, Ureño, & Villaseñor, 1988) sought to develop the Inventory of Interpersonal Problems (IIP) to systematically organize patients' interpersonal complaints. The IIP item set was originally developed by transcribing and cataloguing the complaints voiced by prospective psychotherapy patients during their intake interviews. Complaints judged by a panel of experts to be interpersonal were then reduced and rewritten to have a common, standardized format, from which a 127-item version of the IIP was developed (Horowitz et al., 1988). Items took the form of self-statements capturing the level of distress associated with a variety of interpersonal deficits ("things you find hard to do") and forms of interpersonal excess ("things you do too much"). To strengthen the instrument's circumplex properties, Alden, Wiggins, and Pincus (1990) subsequently proposed a 64-item subset of the IIP (IIP-C). The IIP-C was later reintroduced as the IIP, with slight modifications to the labeling of the scales and with new normative data (Horowitz, Alden, Wiggins, & Pincus, 2000).

The development of the IAS and the IIP introduced an era of paradigm refinement during which interpersonal researchers sought to clarify the content and meaning of the many existing personality scales by correlating them with interpersonal scales (i.e., by projecting them onto the surface of the IPC). To the extent that a personality scale correlated with the IAS or IIP, the scale in question could be said to be interpersonal (or to have interpersonal content). The goal of such research was two-fold (Wiggins & Broughton, 1985). First, the researchers intended to clarify the content and meaning of existing personality scales by establishing their locations in interpersonal space. Second, the researchers intended to enrich the nomological network in which the IAS and IIP are embedded by establishing their external correlates. Such work led to the conceptual refinement and clarification of several personality characteristics of longstanding interest to researchers and clinicians alike, including attachment (Bartholomew & Horowitz, 1991), dependency (Pincus & Gurtman, 1995), narcissism (Dickinson & Pincus, 2003), and social anxiety (Alden & Taylor, 2004).

Sullivan was acutely sensitive not only to the importance of the interpersonal situation, but to the dynamic transactional processes that continuously emerge between interaction partners in the interpersonal situation, as each individual attempts to negotiate with and exert influence upon the social environment. Sullivan's *theorem*

of reciprocal emotion spoke of the integration of the interpersonal situation as *"a reciprocal process in which (1) complementary needs are resolved, or aggravated; (2) reciprocal patterns of activity are developed, or disintegrated; and (3) foresight of satisfaction, or rebuff, of similar needs is facilitated"* (Sullivan, 1953, p. 198). In other words, Sullivan argued that interpersonal integration occurs when the behavior of individuals falls into a complementary pattern of mutually satisfying, need-gratifying activity. Although a provocative theoretical claim, Sullivan's theorem lacked specificity (Kiesler, 1983), and ultimately only conveyed the notion that the behavior of interaction partners are, in Kiesler's words, "redundantly interrelated . . . over the sequence of transactions" (p. 198).

Leary's (1957) *principle of reciprocal interpersonal relations* provided a more systematic accounting of the patterned regularities that tend to occur in the behavior of interaction partners. Leary (1957) proposed that "interpersonal reflexes tend (with a probability significantly greater than chance) to initiate or invite reciprocal interpersonal responses from the 'other' person in the interaction that lead to a repetition of the original reflex" (p. 123). Central to Leary's system was the idea that the behavior of each individual performs, in Sullivan's terms, a kind of *security operation* that staves off anxiety and maintains the individual's sense of security and self-esteem. For example, a narcissist's hostile-competitive behavior can prompt feelings of inferiority and fearful submission from others, thereby preserving the narcissist's fragile sense of security. Human behavior thus serves a basic security-maintenance function for each individual.

Surprisingly, Leary (1957) did not explicitly relate his principle of reciprocity to the IPC. It fell to Robert Carson (1969) to show how the patterned regularity of interpersonal transactions, which he called *interpersonal complementarity*, could be explicitly framed in terms of the IPC. "Generally speaking," Carson (1969) wrote, "complementarity occurs on the basis of reciprocity in respect to the dominance–submission axis (dominance tends to induce submission, and vice versa), and on the basis of correspondence in respect to the hate–love axis (hate induces hate, love induces love)" (p. 112). Carson (1969) suggested that complementary interactions are those in which the interpersonal needs of both partners are met. He assumed that such interactions would be mutually rewarding, and so likely to enhance the felt security of both interactants.

Donald Kiesler (1983) elaborated upon and extended Carson's (1969) reasoning by adapting interpersonal complementarity to the geometry of the IPC model. Given that the IPC constitutes a circular continuum, the principles of reciprocity and correspondence can be used to specify points of complementarity around the entire circumference of the circle. Kiesler (1983) thus asserted that complementary interactions occur when one individual reacts to another with interpersonal acts that are both reciprocal in terms of dominance–submission and corresponding in terms of love–hate. As such, not only should dominance pull for submission, but friendly-dominance should pull for friendly-submission and hostile-dominance should pull for hostile-submission. Furthermore, Kiesler (1983) asserted that complementary interactions occur only between acts at the same level of behavioral intensity, such that interpersonal acts at a particular level of intensity tend (with a probability significantly greater than chance) to initiate, invite, or evoke from interactants complementary responses at an equivalent level of intensity. As such, a mild-to-moderate act should elicit a mild-to-moderate complementary response, whereas a more extreme act should elicit a more extreme complementary response.

Lorna Smith Benjamin (1974) has offered a compelling and clinically informed alternative to the traditional Leary-Carson-Kiesler approach to interpersonal complementarity. In an attempt to reconcile historical differences in the interpretation of the agentic dimension either as dominance–submission (Leary, 1957) or as control–autonomy (Schaefer, 1965), Benjamin put forward a three-tiered circumplex (called the Structural Analysis of Social Behavior, or SASB) comprising: (1) a *transitive* plane for active (or parentlike) behavior, (2) an *intransitive* plane for reactive (or childlike) behavior, and (3) an *introjective* plane for intrapsychic behavior. The vertical axis of the transitive plane ranges from *control* to *emancipate*. The vertical axis of the intransitive plane ranges from *submit* to *separate*. Partitioning the transitive and intransitive planes has enabled Benjamin to distinguish *opposites* (antithetical terms on the same plane) from *complements* (parallel terms on different planes). Therefore, the opposite of "to control" is "to emancipate," whereas the complement of "to control" is "to submit." Benjamin's SASB has also enabled her to document the *copy processes* through which individuals internalize their interaction patterns with significant others: *identification*, the process through which individuals treat others as they themselves were once treated by their significant others; *recapitulation*, the process through which individuals react to others as they once reacted to their significant others; and *introjection*, the process through which individuals treat themselves as they themselves were once treated by their significant others. Hailed early on as "the most detailed, clinically rich, ambitious, and conceptually demanding of all contemporary models" (Wiggins, 1982, p. 193), Benjamin has offered a complex alternative to the prevailing single-plane circumplex representation of interpersonal behavior.

In summary, the legacy of Harry Stack Sullivan and his focus on interpersonal functioning can be seen in the efforts of interpersonal researchers over the last 60 years to develop models with which to characterize the lawful organization of interpersonal behavior (i.e., the structural framework that later came to be known as the *interpersonal circumplex*) and a delimited set of transactional constructs with which to characterize the field-regulatory aspects of interpersonal behavior (i.e., postulates concerning dynamic transactional processes that later came to be known as *interpersonal complementarity*). Circular representations of interpersonal behavior proliferated in the years following the publication of the Kaiser Group's papers and Leary's (1957) seminal work. Wiggins (1980) identified 20 circular models of interpersonal characteristics that had been independently constructed over the preceding 30-year period, all with the same two principal axes. Although subsequent categorical systems have differed in how they partition the circle, occasionally collapsing adjacent segments into octants or quadrants, a common paradigm for the investigation of interpersonal behavior has clearly emerged across different populations, instruments, and theoretical perspectives. The interpersonal tradition has shown the potential to become an integrative framework for personality and psychopathology (e.g., Horowitz, 2004; Pincus & Gurtman, 2006) and continues to become increasingly methodologically sophisticated (e.g., Sadler, Ethier, Gunn, Duong, & Woody, 2009).

Applying the Interpersonal Circumplex to the Study of Persons-in-Context

The interpersonal tradition has long been aligned with the multivariate approach to personality assessment, in which the behavior of individuals is explained through reference to their essential qualities (i.e., personality traits). The essentialist view assumes substantial consistency in the behavior of individuals, and argues that the most meaningful behavioral variation is to be found in the pervasive and enduring differences between individuals. The essential qualities of individuals are evident in their general tendencies (i.e., behavioral mean levels). If individuals are able and willing to report on their essential qualities, then such qualities can be reliably assessed through one-occasion self-report questionnaires.

These assumptions were put on trial during what has become known as the person-situation debate, when Mischel (1968) reported that cross-situational consistency coefficients between single behavioral indices rarely surpass a ceiling of .30. Mischel concluded that there was little evidence for the cross-situational consistency of behavior, and that behavior seemed to be far more situation-specific than the trait theorists would like to believe. In reply to Mischel, researchers argued that single indices of behavior invariably contain a sizable component of error variance. If error is randomly distributed across occasions, situations, or behavioral referents, then the process of aggregating or smoothing across repeated assessments should provide a closer approximation of each individual's true score, which in turn should reveal greater consistency in the behavior of individuals (Epstein, 1979, 1980; Moskowitz, 1982).

Such a strategy, however, requires researchers to repeatedly assess behavior across occasions and/or across situations. In a collaborative program of research that has spanned the last two decades, Moskowitz and colleagues have developed a contextually sensitive approach to the assessment of interpersonal behavior using intensive repeated measurements in naturalistic settings (IRM-NS; Moskowitz, Russell, Sadikaj, & Sutton, 2009). IRM-NS procedures require participants to repeatedly report on their cognitions, affects, and/or behaviors soon after their occurrence over extended periods of time, thereby focusing the participant's attention on specific experiences and limiting the delay between an event's occurrence and the participant's report. Consequently, IRM-NS procedures are less vulnerable to the reconstructive processes that potentially threaten the validity of global and retrospective one-occasion assessment procedures.

IRM-NS procedures are consistent with a social-cognitive approach to personality assessment (Bandura, 1986; Mischel, 1973; Rotter, 1954). In contrast to the multivariate approach, social-cognitive approaches to personality assessment seek to explain the behavior of an individual through reference to the system of interacting forces occurring between that individual and the environment in which he or she is embedded. These reciprocal person-environment interactions are presumed to account for both the typical behavior of the individual and his or her idiosyncratic behavior patterns. The social-cognitive approach emphasizes the importance of assessing *persons-in-context*. Contextualized assessments are important because some personality processes are inherently domain-specific and are only activated contextually. Situational variation in observable behavior can thus serve to reveal the underlying personality characteristics of the individual (Cervone, Shadel, & Jencius, 2001). IRM-NS procedures represent one way of assessing persons-in-context.

We use a form of IRM-NS known as *event-contingent recording*, in which we ask participants to report on their social behavior immediately following each significant social interaction that lasts at least five minutes over the course of a 20-day period. Participants are typically recruited from the working community, demonstrating that the event-contingent recording method is suitable for individuals of varying ages, education levels, and occupations. Participants report on their behavior and affective experience, as well as their role relationship to, and situational appraisals of, their primary interaction partner. Participants typically complete an average of 6 to 7 forms per day, or 120 to 140 forms over the 20-day period.

Behavioral scales were developed to assess the four poles of the IPC (Moskowitz, 1994). Items were worded to be independent of context. Dominance was sampled through such items as "I expressed an opinion" and "I made a suggestion." Submissiveness was sampled through such items as "I did not state my own views" and "I gave in." Agreeableness was sampled through such items as "I expressed affection with words or gestures" and "I

expressed reassurance." Quarrelsomeness was sampled through such items as "I confronted the other about something I did not like" and "I made a sarcastic comment." A complete listing of the social behavior items used in event-contingent recording studies can be found in the appendix to this chapter.

IRM-NS procedures reveal how behavior fluctuates across occasions and situations. To characterize the ongoing stream of behavior, we have found it helpful to depict the behavior of individuals using two types of profiles: *occasion-behavior profiles* (in which behavior is plotted across a set of occasions) and *situation-behavior profiles* (in which behavior is plotted across a set of situations). Doing so has allowed us to examine the extent of consistency in behavior, both across time and across contexts.

Moskowitz (1994) examined the extent of consistency in the behavior of individuals across sets of situations defined as agentic (i.e., occupational situations involving supervisors, coworkers, and supervisees) or as communal (i.e., personal situations involving acquaintances, friends, and romantic partners). The extent of cross-situational generality was assessed by calculating Cronbach's coefficient alpha for each of the behavioral characteristics across each prespecified set of interpersonal situations. Relatively high levels of cross-situational generality were observed, although higher levels of cross-situational generality were observed across communal situations than across agentic situations.

Brown and Moskowitz (1998) examined the extent of consistency in the behavior of individuals across time by calculating Cronbach's coefficient alpha across days for each of the four behavioral dimensions. Findings revealed levels of stability in behavior comparable to those typically found for personality traits. Separate alphas were also calculated on smaller samples of days. Mean levels of stability in behavior rose steadily as a function of the time frame over which aggregation occurred, presumably because aggregating helped to separate the true variance from the error variance.

Although the stability of behavior is low when scores are disaggregated, the behavioral dimensions become increasingly stable when scores are aggregated over increasingly long time intervals. Whether a behavioral dimension seems more like a trait or more like a state thus depends on the time frame over which the characteristic is observed.

However, it may not always be appropriate to aggregate scores to a single point. To the extent that an individual's behavior varies *systematically* and *meaningfully* across situations, the process of aggregation throws away true variance with error variance. Fortunately, IRM-NS procedures are highly sensitive to situational variation. Several features of the situation, such as social roles and situated appraisals of the other person, are systematically associated with fluctuations in behavior (Moskowitz, Ho, & Turcotte-Tremblay, 2007; Moskowitz, Suh, & Desaulniers, 1994). For example, levels of agentic behavior fluctuate predictably as a function of variation in one's social status. Individuals demonstrate higher levels of dominant behavior when in a high-status role and higher levels of submissive behavior when in a low-status role. Consistencies in the behavior of individuals thus do not rule out meaningful within-person variability.

Mischel and Shoda (1995, 1998, 1999) proposed a metatheoretical framework—the cognitive-affective processing system, or CAPS—in which to conceptualize such within-person variability. According to the CAPS framework, individuals encode the psychological features of the situation through a complex configuration of within-person cognitive-affective units (CAUs), including competencies ("I feel capable of performing behavior X"), expectancies ("If I perform behavior X, then outcome Y will follow"), values ("Outcome Y is important to me"), and goals. Individuals differ with respect to the accessibility or availability of CAUs and with respect to the organization of relations between CAUs. This complex and dynamic behavioral system gives rise to stable but conditional *if . . . then . . .* dispositions (Wright & Mischel, 1987), such that each individual demonstrates stable levels of behavior within situations and stable patterns of behavior, called *signatures*, across situations.

An emerging body of evidence suggests that, consistent with Mischel & Shoda's theorizing, there is stability in the organization and patterning of within-person behavioral variability. In their classic demonstration, Shoda, Mischel, and Wright (1994) examined the stability of situation-behavior profiles through a large-scale field research program conducted at a residential summer camp for children characterized by significant adjustment problems. Hourly observations of the children were collected over a six-week period by the camp counselors, who recorded the class of situation that each child encountered (e.g., peer approach, peer tease) and whether or not the child responded with any of the behavioral categories of interest (e.g., compliance, prosocial talk). To test the stability of the children's situation-behavior profiles, the data for each child from each situation were randomly divided in half, thereby yielding two situation-behavior profiles for each child from nonoverlapping samples of occasions. Stability of the situation-behavior profiles was indexed by the within-subject correlation coefficient, which estimated the degree of resemblance between the two profiles for each child. Moderate but significant levels of profile stability were obtained, leading Shoda, Mischel, and Wright to conclude that the behavior of a substantial number of the children from the summer camp could be characterized by idiographic signatures, stable and unique patterns of within-person variability across salient psychological situations.

We believe that the interpersonal model can serve to clarify key aspects of the CAPS framework and address critical limitations to the empirical research that has been published to date in support of it. CAPS leaves several theoretical questions unanswered, including how to conceptualize the domains of situations and behavior that constitute the "inputs" and "outputs" of the cognitive-affective processing system. In their camp data, Shoda and colleagues (1994) relied on ad hoc categories of situations and behavior that had been developed for pragmatic rather than theoretical purposes. Furthermore, Shoda and colleagues (1994) relied on objective (i.e., observer-rated) descriptions of each situation, which may not have mapped directly onto the psychological situation as the child experienced it. From an interpersonal perspective, it is critical that the individual's subjective experience of the situation is obtained.

In our recent work, we have focused our efforts on integrating CAPS with the IPC (Fournier, Moskowitz, & Zuroff, 2008). CAPS can benefit from the dual utility of the IPC, which can serve as a framework for conceptualizing both the domain of interpersonal behavior and the domain of interpersonal situations. From the vantage point of the interpersonal theorist, the most salient psychological features of the situation are found in the behavior of the individual with whom one is interacting. Consequently, we can rely on the structure of the IPC both to conceptualize the behavior that individuals exhibit with their interaction partners and to conceptualize the perceived behavior of the interaction partner, which defines the immediate psychological situation for the individual.

To assess the psychological situation, we have used the interpersonal grid (Moskowitz & Zuroff, 2005; see Figure 4.2), a single-item instrument developed to assess perceptions of others' interpersonal behavior. The grid consists of an 11 by 11 arrangement of squares depicting the agentic and communal dimensions of interpersonal behavior. The vertical (or agentic) axis of the grid is anchored by "assured-dominant" on the top and by "unassured-submissive" on the bottom. The horizontal (or communal) axis of the

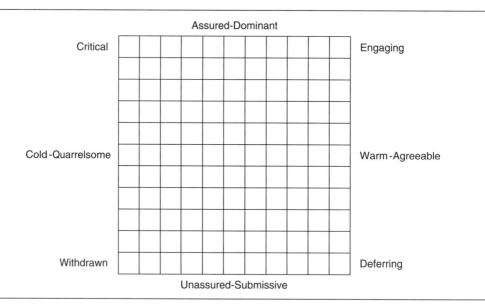

FIGURE 4.2   The Interpersonal Grid
Participants are asked to place a mark on the grid to indicate how they perceived the other person behaving toward them during a particular social interaction. The vertical and horizontal axes of the grid respectively correspond to the agentic and communal dimensions of interpersonal behavior.
Source: From "Assessing Interpersonal Perceptions with the Interpersonal Grid," by D. S. Moskowitz and D. C. Zuroff, 2005, *Psychological Assessment, 17.*

grid is anchored by "cold-quarrelsome" on the left and by "warm-agreeable" on the right. The corners are anchored by "engaging" (top-right), "deferring" (bottom-right), "withdrawn" (bottom-left), and "critical" (top-left). Participants rate their perceptions of their primary interaction partners by placing a single "X" in any square on the grid, thereby indicating the extent to which they perceived the other person as dominant (vs. submissive) and as agreeable (vs. quarrelsome). The psychological situation is then classified in terms of whether the primary interaction partner was perceived as having been agreeable-dominant, agreeable-submissive, quarrelsome-submissive, or quarrelsome-dominant.

In one study (Fournier et al., 2008), participants provided event-contingent records of their own social behavior and that of their interaction partners over a 20-day period. Situation-behavior profiles were constructed for each individual by averaging behavioral scores in each of the four situations. Normative situational influences were observed in the situation-behavior profiles of individuals. Along the agentic dimension of behavior, individuals reported that they displayed higher levels of submissive behavior when they perceived the other as dominant and higher levels of dominant behavior when they perceived the other as submissive (i.e., reciprocity). Along the communal dimension of behavior, individuals reported that they displayed higher levels of quarrelsome behavior when they perceived the other as quarrelsome and higher levels of agreeable behavior when they perceived the other as agreeable (i.e., correspondence). These normative situational influences reflect the principles of complementarity discussed previously, and speak directly to how the interpersonal situation can influence the behavior of the individual.

However, participants also showed idiosyncratic patterns of variability around these normative influences. Participants' distinct behavioral patterns become evident

when we rescale participants' profiles within situations as z-scores. Standardizing scores within situations removes systematic differences in behavior across situations, thereby allowing each profile to reflect the participant's own unique pattern of situation-behavior contingencies. Figure 4.3 displays one such idiographic pattern or signature. Compared to other participants, this participant reported unexpectedly high levels of quarrelsome behavior in all four situations and unexpectedly low levels of submissive behavior in situations where others were seen as having behaved dominantly (i.e., in either an agreeable-dominant or a quarrelsome-dominant manner).

We wanted to know whether the idiographic signatures of individuals constitute a stable organizing feature of their behavior. The following steps were taken. First, we randomly divided the situation-behavior data for each participant in half. Second, we aggregated the scores from each half within situations to produce

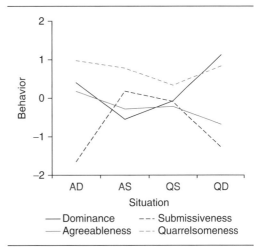

FIGURE 4.3   The Four Situation-Behavior Profiles of a Sample Participant
In comparison to others, this participant reported high levels of quarrelsome behavior in all four situations and low levels of submissive behavior in situations where others were seen as having behaved dominantly. AD = agreeable-dominant. AS = agreeable-submissive. QS = quarrelsome-submissive. DQ = quarrelsome-dominant.

two situation-behavior profiles for each participant. Third, we rescaled the profiles within situations as z-scores to identify each participant's distinct profile of behavioral variability across the four interpersonal situations. Fourth, we indexed the stability of the situation-behavior profiles by the within-subject correlation coefficient, which indicated the degree of similarity between the shapes of the two profile halves. Finally, as each stability estimate was to some extent dependent on how the data had been randomized, we repeated this process 1,000 times for each participant and then aggregated the stability estimates together. As Mischel and Shoda (1995, 1998, 1999) would have predicted, we found the interpersonal signature to be a stable facet of behavioral organization.

We also wanted to know whether the idiographic signatures of individuals would covary intraindividually in a manner consistent with the IPC. In other words, could we look inside the behavior of a single individual and find the structure of the IPC in his or her behavior? To obtain within-person evidence of the IPC, we required individuals to show that in those situations in which they behaved more dominantly, they were also less submissive, and in those situations in which they behaved more agreeably, they were also less quarrelsome. We thus calculated within-subject correlation coefficients for all pairs of behavioral scales. These *linkage estimates* (i.e., within-subject correlation coefficients) indexed the extent to which the cross-situational patterning of an individual's behavior along one dimension (e.g., dominance) correlated with the cross-situational patterning of that same individual's behavior along another dimension (e.g., submissiveness). As expected, we found that behavioral scales on opposing sides of the circle were significantly and inversely correlated. We also found that the correlations between behavioral scales at right angles on the circle were about half the size of the correlations obtained between opposing behavioral scales and generally not significantly different from zero. The

normative organization of behavior within the individual was thus observed to adhere to the two-dimensional structure of the IPC.

However, the within-subject correlations for many individuals departed from this normative arrangement. Some individuals blended dominance with agreeableness, some individuals blended dominance with quarrelsomeness, and some even blended dominance with submissiveness. It became evident that the behavior of some individuals did not adhere to the IPC. We therefore conducted additional analyses in which we factor-analyzed the linkage estimates in order to extract nomothetic dimensions of individual differences from the idiographic signatures of individuals (Fournier, Moskowitz, & Zuroff, 2009). These analyses revealed two new forms of meaningful individual differences: *polarity*, which captures the extent to which the behaviors anchoring the agentic dimension (dominance and submissiveness) and the behaviors anchoring the communal dimension (agreeableness and quarrelsomeness) are inversely correlated within the individual; and *orthogonality*, which captures the extent to which the underlying agentic and communal dimensions are uncorrelated within the individual. Taken together, polarity and orthogonality describe how individuals systematically adhere to or depart from the normative two-dimensional structure of the IPC. Polarity speaks to the degree to which the four behavioral dimensions produce two clear bipolar axes (agency and communion) in the behavior of a single individual. Orthogonality speaks to the degree to which the agentic and communal dimensions are independent or correlated in the behavior of a single individual.

Polarity and orthogonality raise important questions for interpersonalists. Given the common departures from the shape of the IPC that we have observed at the level of the individual, is it possible that the IPC is simply a statistical artifact that arises from the aggregation of many individuals' data? Although the IPC is clearly capable of depicting the between-person organization of interpersonal behavior, the data described here demonstrate marked variation across individuals in the within-person organization of interpersonal behavior. Given that departures from the IPC observed at the level of the individual seem to be systematic and meaningful, additional psychological constructs—e.g., interpersonal competencies, expectancies, values, and goals—will be needed to account for the structural variation observed across individuals. A proper accounting of the departures that individuals show from the structure of the IPC is likely to present a considerable challenge for the interpersonal researchers of tomorrow.

Future Directions

We suggest that interpersonal theory and research in the 21st century will be driven by the integration of multilevel thinking about persons and situations, with the consequent clear delineation of person-level (or dispositional) and situation-level (or contextual) structures and processes, as well as cross-level interactions (i.e., person-level differences in situation-level influences). Regarding cross-level interactions, our findings demand attention to person-level moderators of circumplexity and complementarity. For instance, we have found that neuroticism and self-esteem both moderate circumplexity (Fournier et al., 2009) and that levels of depression moderate complementarity (Zuroff, Fournier, & Moskowitz, 2007). A multilevel framework further invites us to consider moderators of circumplexity and complementarity beyond the level of the individual, such as social-organizational variables (hierarchical vs. egalitarian environments) and cultural variables (individualism vs. collectivism).

We see several directions for the use of the IPC and the intensive repeated measurement of interpersonal behavior. One promising direction involves using behavioral data to characterize the interpersonal dynamics of individuals sharing a common personality configuration and/or psychodiagnostic classification (e.g., dependency, narcissism). As described previously, there has been a longstanding practice in the interpersonal tradition to characterize the generalized interpersonal dispositions of individuals with common personality traits and psychopathological disorders. Can we now go beyond the dispositional to describe the more dynamic interpersonal qualities of these individuals? For instance, can we determine whether individuals who share a common personality configuration or psychodiagnostic classification also leave a common signature across the range of their social interactions? Such an interactionist approach has the potential to offer a richer clinical description of the interpersonal functioning of individuals.

Another promising direction involves using event-contingent recording procedures in combination with neuroimaging, neurochemical/electrophysiological methods, and/or proteomic mapping to determine the biological bases of these interpersonal processes and dynamics. We have already taken some preliminary steps in this direction. In one variation on our standard research design, participants received 12 days of tryptophan (a precursor of the neurotransmitter serotonin) and 12 days of placebo as part of a double-blind, crossover study. Tryptophan was found to enhance the adaptive behavior of individuals, raising their levels of dominance and lowering the levels of quarrelsomeness (Moskowitz, Pinard, Zuroff, Annable, & Young, 2001). Tryptophan was also found to reduce the extent of individuals' interpersonal spin (Moskowitz, Zuroff, aan het Rot, Pinard, & Young, 2005). Similar effects have been observed in response to naturalistic environmental events that are believed to increase serotonin, such as exposure to bright light (aan het Rot, Moskowitz, & Young, 2008). We imagine that the search for the biological bases of interpersonal behavior will hold promise for years to come.

CONCLUSION

Harry Stack Sullivan first introduced the interpersonal conceptualization of personality, a view that Timothy Leary and others then helped to codify into the interpersonal circumplex. The interpersonal tradition has since become a vibrant intellectual community, with its foundations in the structural framework of the IPC and the dynamic transactional processes of complementary interaction. We can now characterize not only the cross-situational consistencies in the behavior of individuals, but also how variability in behavior is patterned across situations with what we call the interpersonal signature. The development of these constructs has been intertwined with methodological advances, such as the refinement of event-contingent recording procedures, permitting the intensive repeated assessment of individuals in their naturalistic settings. However, IRM-NS technologies will no doubt continue to evolve (e.g., Mehl, Pennebaker, Crow, Dabbs, & Price, 2001), which in turn should permit new insights into the dispositional, contextual, and interactive factors that give rise to the observed consistency, variability, and patterning of interpersonal behavior.

References

aan het Rot, M., Moskowitz, D. S., & Young, S. N. (2008). Exposure to bright light is associated with positive social interaction and good mood over short time periods: A naturalistic study in mildly seasonal people. *Journal of Psychiatric Research, 42,* 311–319.

Acton, G. S., & Revelle, W. (2004). Evaluation of ten psychometric criteria for circumplex structure. *Methods of Psychological Research, 9,* 1–27.

Alden, L. E., & Taylor, C. T. (2004). Interpersonal perspectives on social phobia. Special Issue. *Clinical Psychology Review, 24,* 857–882.

Alden, L. E., Wiggins, J. S., & Pincus, A. L. (1990). Construction of circumplex scales for the Inventory of Interpersonal Problems. *Journal of Personality Assessment, 55,* 521–36.

Bakan, D. (1966). *The duality of human existence.* Chicago: Rand McNally.

Bandura, A. (1986). *Social foundations of thought and action: A social cognitive theory.* Englewood Cliffs, NJ: Prentice-Hall.

Bartholomew, K., & Horowitz, L. M. (1991). Attachment styles among young adults: A test of a four-category model. *Journal of Personality and Social Psychology, 61,* 226–244.

Benjamin, L. S. (1974). Structural analysis of social behavior (SASB). *Psychological Review, 81,* 392–425.

Brown, K. W., & Moskowitz, D. S. (1998). Dynamic stability of behavior: The rhythms of our interpersonal lives. *Journal of Personality, 66,* 105–134.

Buss, D. M. (1991). Evolutionary personality psychology. *Annual Review of Psychology, 42,* 459–491.

Carson, R. C. (1969). *Interaction concepts of personality.* Chicago, IL: Aldine.

Cervone, D., Shadel, W. G., & Jencius, S. (2001). Social-cognitive theory of personality assessment. *Personality and Social Psychology Review, 5,* 33–51.

Dickinson, K. A., & Pincus, A. L. (2003). Interpersonal analysis of grandiose and vulnerable narcissism. *Journal of Personality Disorders, 17,* 188–207.

Epstein, S. (1979). The stability of behavior: I. On predicting most of the people much of the time. *Journal of Personality and Social Psychology, 37,* 1097–1126.

Epstein, S. (1980). The stability of behavior: II. Implications for psychological research. *American Psychologist, 35,* 790–806.

Fournier, M. A., Moskowitz, D. S., & Zuroff, D. C. (2008). Integrating dispositions, signatures, and the interpersonal domain. *Journal of Personality and Social Psychology, 94,* 531–545.

Fournier, M. A., Moskowitz, D. S., & Zuroff, D. C. (2009). The interpersonal signature. *Journal of Research in Personality, 43,* 155–162.

Freedman, M. B., Leary, T. F., Ossario, A. G., & Coffey, H. S. (1951). The interpersonal dimension of personality. *Journal of Personality, 20,* 143–161.

Guttman, L. (1954). A new approach to factor analysis: The Radex. In P. F. Lazarsfeld (Ed.), Mathematical thinking in the social sciences (pp. 258–348). New York: Free Press.

Horowitz, L. M. (1979). On the cognitive structure of interpersonal problems treated in psychotherapy. *Journal of Consulting and Clinical Psychology, 47*, 5–15.

Horowitz, L. M. (2004). *Interpersonal foundations of psychopathology.* Washington, DC: APA.

Horowitz, L. M., Alden, L. E., Wiggins, J. S., & Pincus, A. L. (2000). *IIP-64/IIP-32 professional manual.* San Antonio, TX: The Psychological Corporation.

Horowitz, L. M., Rosenberg, S. E., Baer, B. A., Ureño, G., & Villaseñor, V. S. (1988). Inventory of Interpersonal Problems: Psychometric properties and clinical applications. *Journal of Consulting and Clinical Psychology, 56*, 885–892.

Horowitz, L. M., Wilson, K. R., Turan, B., Zolotsev, P., Constantino, M. J., & Henderson, L. (2006). How interpersonal motives clarify the meaning of interpersonal behavior: A revised circumplex model. *Personality and Social Psychology Review, 10*, 67–86.

Kiesler, D. J. (1983). The 1982 Interpersonal Circle: A taxonomy for complementarity in human transactions. *Psychological Review, 90*, 185–214.

Kiesler, D. J. (1996). *Contemporary interpersonal theory and research: Personality, psychopathology, and psychotherapy.* New York: John Wiley & Sons.

LaForge, R. (1977). *Using the IPC: 1976.* Mill Valley, CA: Author.

LaForge, R., Leary, T. F., Naboisek, H., Coffey, H. S., & Freedman, M. B. (1954). The interpersonal dimension of personality: II. An objective study of repression. *Journal of Personality, 23*, 129–153.

LaForge, R., & Suczek, R. F. (1955). The interpersonal dimension of personality: III. An interpersonal check list. *Journal of Personality, 24*, 94–112.

Leary, T. (1957). *Interpersonal diagnosis of personality.* New York: Ronald Press.

Lorr, M. (1996). The interpersonal circle as a heuristic model for interpersonal research. *Journal of Personality Assessment, 66*, 234–239.

Lorr, M., Bishop, P. F., & McNair, D. M. (1965). Interpersonal types among psychiatric patients. *Journal of Abnormal Psychology, 70*, 468–472.

Lorr, M., & McNair, D. M. (1963). An interpersonal behavior circle. *Journal of Abnormal and Social Psychology, 67*, 68–75.

Lorr, M., & McNair, D. M. (1965). Expansion of the interpersonal behavior circle. *Journal of Personality and Social Psychology, 2*, 823–830.

Mehl, M. R., Pennebaker, J. W., Crow, D. M., Dabbs, J., & Price, J. H. (2001). The electronically activated recorder (EAR): A device for sampling naturalistic daily activities and conversations. *Behavior Research Methods, Instruments & Computers, 33*, 517–523.

Mischel, W. (1968). *Personality and assessment.* New York: John Wiley & Sons.

Mischel, W. (1973). Toward a cognitive social learning reconceptualization of personality. *Psychological Review, 80*, 252–283.

Mischel, W., & Shoda, Y. (1995). A cognitive-affective system theory of personality: Reconceptualizing situations, dispositions, dynamics, and invariance in personality structure. *Psychological Review, 102*, 246–268.

Mischel, W., & Shoda, Y. (1998). Reconciling processing dynamics and personality dispositions. *Annual Review of Psychology, 49*, 229–258.

Mischel, W., & Shoda, Y. (1999). Integrating dispositions and processing dynamics within a unified theory of personality: The cognitive-affective personality system. In L. A. Pervin & O. P. John (Eds.), *Handbook of personality: Theory and research* (2nd ed.) (pp. 197–218). New York: Guilford Press.

Moskowitz, D. S. (1982). Coherence and cross-situational generality in personality: A new analysis of old problems. *Journal of Personality and Social Psychology, 43*, 754–768.

Moskowitz, D. S. (1994). Cross-situational generality and the interpersonal circumplex. *Journal of Personality and Social Psychology, 66*, 921–933.

Moskowitz, D. S. (2005). Unfolding interpersonal behavior. *Journal of Personality, 73*, 1607–1632.

Moskowitz, D. S., Ho, M.-H. R, & Turcotte-Tremblay, A.-M. (2007). Contextual influences on interpersonal complementarity. *Personality and Social Psychology Bulletin, 33*, 1051–1063.

Moskowitz, D. S., Pinard, G., Zuroff, D. C., Annable, L., & Young, S. N. (2001). The effect of tryptophan on social interaction in every day life: A placebo-controlled study. *Neuropsychopharmacology, 25*, 277–289.

Moskowitz, D. S., Russell, J. J., Sadikaj, S., & Sutton, R. (2009). Measuring people intensively. *Canadian Psychology, 50*, 131–140.

Moskowitz, D. S., Suh, E. J., & Desaulniers, J. (1994). Situational influences on gender differences in agency and communion. *Journal of Personality and Social Psychology, 66*, 753–761.

Moskowitz, D. S., & Zuroff, D. C. (2005). Assessing interpersonal perceptions with the interpersonal grid. *Psychological Assessment, 17*, 218–230.

Moskowitz, D. S., Zuroff, D. C., aan het Rot, M., Pinard, G., & Young, S. N. (January, 2005). Serotonin inhibits and facilitates interpersonal behavior. Presentation at the annual meeting of the Association for Research in Personality, New Orleans.

Pincus, A. L., & Gurtman, M. B. (1995). The three faces of interpersonal dependency: Structural analyses of self-report dependency measures. *Journal of Personality and Social Psychology, 69*, 744–758.

Pincus, A. L., & Gurtman, M. B. (2006). Interpersonal theory and the interpersonal circumplex: Evolving perspectives on normal and abnormal personality. In S. Strack (Ed.), *Differentiating normal and abnormal personality* (2nd ed., pp. 83–111). New York: Springer.

Rotter, J. B. (1954). *Social learning and clinical psychology*. New York: Prentice-Hall.

Sadler, P., Ethier, N., Gunn, G. R., Duong, D., & Woody, E. (2009). Are we on the same wavelength? Interpersonal complementarity as shared cyclical patterns during interactions. *Journal of Personality and Social Psychology, 97*, 1005–1020.

Schaefer, E. S. (1965). A configurational analysis of children's reports of parent behavior. *Journal of Consulting Psychology, 29*, 552–557.

Shoda, Y., Mischel, W., & Wright, J. C. (1994). Intraindividual stability in the organization and patterning of behavior: Incorporating psychological situations into the idiographic analysis of personality. *Journal of Personality and Social Psychology, 67*, 674–687.

Sullivan, H. S. (1940). Conceptions of modern psychiatry: The first William Alanson White Memorial Lectures. *Psychiatry, 3*, 1–117.

Sullivan, H. S. (1953). *The interpersonal theory of psychiatry*. New York: Norton.

Triandis, H. C. (1990). Cross-cultural studies of individualism and collectivism. In J. J. Berman (Ed.), *Nebraska Symposium on Motivation: Vol.*

37. Cross-cultural perspectives (pp. 41–133). Lincoln: University of Nebraska Press.

Wiggins, J. S. (1979). A psychological taxonomy of trait-descriptive terms: The interpersonal domain. *Journal of Personality and Social Psychology, 37*, 395–412.

Wiggins, J. S. (1980). Circumplex models of interpersonal behavior. In L. Wheeler (Ed.), *Review of personality and social psychology* (Vol. 1, pp. 265–294). Beverly Hills, CA: Sage.

Wiggins, J. S. (1982). Circumplex models of interpersonal behavior in clinical psychology. In P.C. Kendall & J. N. Butcher (Eds.), *Handbook of research methods in clinical psychology* (pp. 183–221). New York: John Wiley & Sons.

Wiggins, J. S. (1991). Agency and communion as conceptual coordinates for the understanding and measurement of interpersonal behavior. In W. Grove & D. Cicchetti (Eds.), *Thinking clearly about psychology: Essays in honor of Paul E. Meehl* (Vol. 2, pp. 89–113). Minneapolis, MN: University of Minnesota Press.

Wiggins, J. S. (1995). *Interpersonal Adjective Scales: Professional manual*. Odessa, FL: Psychological Assessment Resources, Inc.

Wiggins, J. S. (2003). *Paradigms of personality assessment*. New York: Guilford Press.

Wiggins, J. S., & Broughton, R. (1985). The interpersonal circle: A structural model for the integration of personality research. In R. Hogan & W. H. Jones (Eds.), *Perspectives in personality* (Vol. 1, pp. 1–47). Greenwich, CT: JAI Press.

Wiggins, J. S., Trapnell, P., & Phillips, N. (1988). Psychometric and geometric characteristics of the Revised Interpersonal Adjective Scales (IAS-R). *Multivariate Behavioral Research, 23*, 517–530.

Wright, J. C., & Mischel, W. (1987). A conditional approach to dispositional constructs: The local predictability of social behavior. *Journal of Personality and Social Psychology, 53*, 1159–1177.

Zuroff, D. C., Fournier, M. A., & Moskowitz, D. S. (2007). Depression, perceived inferiority, and interpersonal behavior: Evidence for the involuntary defeat strategy. *Journal of Social and Clinical Psychology, 26*, 751–778.

APPENDIX

Social behavior items used in event-contingent recording studies (Moskowitz, 1994).

Dominance

I set goal(s) for the other(s) or for us.
I gave information.
I expressed an opinion.
I criticized the other(s).
I took the lead in planning/organizing a project or activity.
I asked for a volunteer.
I spoke in a clear firm voice.
I asked the other(s) to do something.
I got immediately to the point.
I tried to get the other(s) to do something else.
I made a suggestion.
I assigned someone to a task.

Submissiveness

I waited for the other person to act or talk first.
I went along with the other(s).
I did not express disagreement when I thought it.
I spoke softly.
I let other(s) make plans or decisions.
I gave in.
I spoke only when I was spoken to.
I did not say what I wanted directly.
I did not state my own views.
I did not say how I felt.
I avoided taking the lead or being responsible.
I did not say what was on my mind.

Agreeableness

I listened attentively to the other.
I went along with the other(s).
I spoke favorably of someone who was not present.
I compromised about a decision.
I complimented or praised the other person.
I smiled and laughed with the other(s).
I showed sympathy.
I exchanged pleasantries.
I pointed out to the others where there was agreement.
I expressed affection with words or gestures.
I made a concession to avoid unpleasantness.
I expressed reassurance.

Quarrelsomeness

I did not respond to the other(s)' questions or comments.
I criticized the other(s).
I raised my voice.
I made a sarcastic comment.
I demanded that the other(s) do what I wanted.
I discredited what someone said.
I confronted the other(s) about something I did not like.
I gave incorrect information.
I stated strongly that I did not like or that I would not do something.
I ignored the other(s)' comments.
I withheld useful information.
I showed impatience.

5 EVOLUTION, LIFE HISTORY THEORY, AND PERSONALITY

Jeffry A. Simpson

Vladas Griskevicius

John S. Kim

EVOLUTION, LIFE HISTORY THEORY, AND PERSONALITY

The study of personality is central not only to psychology, but also to the social and life sciences. The way individuals perceive, process, interpret, and remember daily events is filtered through the lens of who they are. In the past two decades, evolutionary scientists have turned their attention toward understanding personality. Many of the important ideas and findings from this body of work, however, have not yet crossed over into mainstream theorizing and research in personality psychology. As a consequence, the field of personality has not taken full advantage of one of the most powerful sets of ideas in the social and life sciences—the modern evolutionary perspective.

One can begin studying personality from an evolutionary perspective by asking a *specific* type of "why" question. Consider Joe, a male in his early twenties. Joe is highly extraverted, open to new experiences, uninhibited, and sexually promiscuous. To understand Joe's personality, a psychologist would generally ask: Why does Joe have this specific profile of traits? One answer might be that these traits are simply a genetic product of Joe's mother and father. From an evolutionary perspective, however, this answer is unsatisfactory. For example, it does not address why Joe's parents—as well as his grandparents—possess the specific personality profiles they do. Instead, the key to understanding personality from an evolutionary perspective is to recognize that individual differences in personality traits are not randomly determined. Personality trait scores, in other words, are not dictated by whimsical genetic reshuffling in each generation. Instead, they are likely to be *adaptive*, meaning that specific clusters of traits may have had historical evolutionary benefits.

The realization that certain personality profiles may be adaptive, however, is only the beginning to the study of personality. After all, if it was evolutionarily advantageous to have Joe's traits, why doesn't everyone have them? The reason is that high and low scores on a given trait typically entail potential benefits *and* potential costs. For example, Joe's trait profile of being highly extraverted, open to novel experiences, uninhibited, and sexually active is likely to have certain adaptive benefits. This cluster of traits, for instance, may enable Joe to make friends, gain status, and attract romantic partners quickly. But these traits may also carry debilitating costs and liabilities. For example, they might lead Joe to take more physical and social risks, which could result in premature death, social exploitation, or sexually transmitted diseases. The main point is that all trait clusters involve *trade-offs*, and evolutionary approaches seek to explain why and how these trade-offs occur.

Central to an examination of trade-offs is the premise that, although all major personality traits are partly heritable (Bouchard, 2004), a person's standing on a given trait (i.e., high, moderate, or low) is not "pre-programmed" from birth. Rather, a person's standing on a trait emerges partly in response to environmental events. When Joe was born, for instance, he was not "prewired" to be highly extraverted, open to new experiences, uninhibited, and sexually promiscuous. Rather, he was "pre-pared" to assess and then respond to specific features of his childhood and current environment. Depending on what those features were, Joe eventually came to have a trait profile that was generally well adapted to his local environment, with his genetics being influential but not deterministic. This of course does not imply that Joe consciously chose to adopt a specific personality profile. Rather, adaptive psychological mechanisms led him to eventually adopt a specific profile in response to particular features of his upbringing and current environment.

The primary goal of this chapter is to show how the infusion of evolutionary principles into the field of personality might yield novel and important insights into how and why certain personality traits, and variability on these traits, came to exist. This chapter is divided into four sections. In the first section, we describe hallmark features of an evolutionary approach and outline some of the unique ways in which it can contribute to our understanding of

personality. In section 2, we briefly discuss how circumplex models of personality, which are relevant to an evolutionary perspective, have been applied to explain important facets of social behavior. We then review major evolutionary theories that explain why certain personality traits (e.g., the Big Five) are prevalent across cultures. In section 3, we review evolutionary theories and models that elucidate why variation exists within nearly all major traits and individual differences. In the final section, we combine various models to explain why, from an evolutionary perspective, someone such as Joe possesses the specific trait profile he does. We then propose directions in which future theory and research on evolutionary personality psychology might head.

SECTION 1: KEY FEATURES OF AN EVOLUTIONARY APPROACH

Evolutionary approaches to understanding social behavior are rooted in the seminal work of Charles Darwin (1859, 1871). Darwin proposed that, just as natural selection shapes morphological features such as the design of a bat's wing or a monkey's hand, it also shapes psychological and behavioral tendencies. Bats, for example, have specialized brain mechanisms that analyze the sonarlike echoes of the unique sounds emitted by their prey in order to locate moving prey in the dark. Monkeys, in comparison, have brain mechanisms that are specially designed to analyze binocular color vision, which enables them to gauge distances more accurately while leaping between branches to determine the ripeness of fruit. These examples illustrate how different mental mechanisms have evolved to meet different evolutionary needs.

According to an evolutionary approach, all animals have inherited brains and bodies that are equipped to respond in ways that tend to be *adaptive*—that typically match the unique demands of the environments in which our ancestors evolved, resulting in greater reproductive fitness. Some adaptations are shared by common descent, some are shared by virtue of similar ecological demands, and some are uniquely designed to solve the particular problems routinely encountered by a species during its evolutionary history (Tooby & Cosmides, 1992).

This same evolutionary logic applies to *Homo sapiens* in that natural selection also designed complex human traits such as those involved in the generation and expression of language, emotion, and mating behavior. Just as human morphological features—opposable thumbs, larynxes, noses, and upright postures—have been shaped by evolutionary pressures, humans have also inherited brain mechanisms that are specially designed to solve recurrent problems associated with survival and reproduction. Along with the larynx, for example, humans have also inherited brain mechanisms for learning to communicate and use language. All languages share the same basic universal structure that reflects evolved human mechanisms for language, even if the specific words and sounds of a language differ across cultures (Pinker, 1994).

From an evolutionary perspective, the key question one asks about a physical or behavioral feature is: What might its ultimate adaptive function be? In other words, how might a given trait or behavior have helped our ancestors survive, reproduce, and parent? Consider two types of answers to the same "why" question that a psychologist might ask: When asking why children prefer products containing corn syrup to spinach, one type of answer is that sweet foods taste better and produce more pleasure than spinach. An evolutionary approach, however, would take this a step further and also ask why highly sweetened foods taste good and produce more pleasure than spinach in the first place. In this case, the reason is because humans have inherited a preference for fatty and sweet foods. These kinds of foods, such as meat and ripe fruit, provided our ancestors with much-needed calories in a food-scarce environment, and did so more

effectively than foods lower in fat or sugar (e.g., roots, leaves, or unripe fruit). Thus, the more specific "why" question posed from an evolutionary perspective asks if—and how—a given behavior or trait might be adaptive.

Note that the kind of "why" question asked by an evolutionary approach is not the only type of "why" question that could be asked. For this reason, it is important to distinguish between four distinct yet compatible levels of analysis—evolutionary history, adaptive function, ontogenetic development, and proximate determinants (see Kenrick, Griskevicius, Neuberg, & Schaller, in press; Simpson & Gangestad, 2001; Tinbergen, 1963). Consider the following question: "Why are dominance displays more likely to be witnessed in male than female chimpanzees?" This "why" question can be addressed at four levels of analysis, with explanations at one level usually complementing those at other levels. Although evolutionary scientists are primarily interested in adaptive function, all four levels of analysis inform the evolutionary approach.

1. *Historical* (phylogenetic) explanations consider the ancestral roots of a given trait or behavior in relation to other species. Researchers adopting this approach, for example, might view sex differences in chimpanzee dominance in relation to other primate species or other social mammals (increasingly more distant relatives), noting that males are larger and more competitive in most mammalian species (see Eastwick, in press).

2. *Functional* (ultimate) explanations are concerned with the *ultimate adaptive* purposes of a given trait or behavior. A functional explanation, for instance, might focus on associations between dominance and reproductive success in males and females, noting that dominance is more germane to reproductive success in males than females.

3. *Developmental* (ontogenetic) explanations are concerned with lifespan-specific inputs that sensitize an organism to particular cues. A developmental explanation, for

example, might suggest that maturing male chimpanzees experience hormonal changes during this period in their life, making them more likely to engage in dominance-related behaviors than females.

4. *Proximate* explanations focus on the immediate triggers of a given trait or behavior. A proximate explanation, for example, might note that displays of male dominance are usually triggered by threats from other males, and that such responses to other males' displays are facilitated by higher levels of circulating testosterone.

Sometimes there is a straightforward connection between the different levels of analysis. For instance, the four types of answers to the question "Why do mothers nurse their young?" have clear connections: a *historical* explanation—all mammalian females nurse their young, given the way in which mammals reproduce; a *functional* explanation—infants who are nursed and given nourishment are more likely to survive; a *developmental* explanation—pregnancy produces hormonal and other bodily changes that enable lactation; and a *proximate* explanation— suckling the nipple produces the immediate release of milk in the mother. In other cases, however, clear connections between the different levels of analysis are less obvious. Consider the question "Why do birds migrate each year?" The *proximate* explanation is that birds migrate because days are getting shorter, and the amount of daylight is a cue that triggers migration. The *functional* explanation, however, is that migration increases birds' chances of survival, given that the distribution of desirable food varies seasonally. Individual birds, however, neither observe nor understand the connection between day length and survival. Similarly, with respect to human traits and behavior, evolutionary theorists do not assume that the links between proximate, developmental, functional, and historical levels of analysis will always be direct or obvious (Alcock & Crawford, 2008).

As previously noted, an evolutionary approach begins by asking the "why" question at the second level of analysis—the functional level concerned with the ultimate adaptive purposes of a given trait or behavior. Evolutionary researchers, however, are not limited to focusing on only one level of analysis. Indeed, much of the power of an evolutionary approach comes from *integrating* research questions and answers along the four levels of analysis, which leads to a more complete understanding of a given psychological phenomenon. Consider once again the case of Joe, who is extraverted, open to new experiences, uninhibited, and sexually promiscuous. To fully understand why and how Joe has this particular combination of traits, we need to consider all four levels of analysis: (1) *Historical*: Do other mammalian species exhibit this type of personality trait profile and, if so, which ones?; (2) *Functional*: What are the adaptive benefits of having these specific traits?; (3) *Developmental*: Are there sensitive periods in childhood that partially determine whether Joe develops these trait patterns in adulthood?; and (4) *Proximate*: What are the environmental triggers—both in childhood and in adulthood—that lead Joe to manifest this constellation of traits? By asking "why" questions at all four levels of analysis, we gain a richer and more nuanced understanding of how and why Joe developed to become the person he is.

SECTION 2: INTERPERSONAL MODELS AND EXPLANATIONS OF WHY PERSONALITY EXISTS

Historically, many facets of interpersonal behavior have been explained by interpersonal circumplex models of personality (e.g., Horowitz, Wilson, Turan, Zolotsev, Constantino, & Henderson, 2006; Leary, 1957). All of these models assume that two broad motivational dimensions have contributed to human survival and reproduction throughout evolutionary history. The first dimension, labeled *communion*, reflects motives associated with developing and maintaining connections, closeness, or affiliation with other people; the second dimension, labeled *agency*, refers to motives related to one's own influence, dominance, or control over others. Interpersonal theorists have used the core motives that anchor each dimension to interpret an assortment of interpersonal phenomena, ranging from attachment behavior in children and adults, to the establishment of dominance hierarchies, and to courtship behaviors. Interestingly, the more "interpersonal" factors of the Big Five (e.g., extraversion) fit very nicely within the two-dimensional space defined by communion and agency, which are orthogonal dimensions (see Costa & McCrae, Chapter 6). People who score higher on the trait of extraversion, for example, possess motives that are positive with respect to both communion and agency (dominance). Returning to our earlier example, one can conceptualize Joe as someone who is strongly motivated to achieve both contact/connection with other people as well as exert influence/control over them. The more "intrapersonal" dimensions of the Big Five (e.g., conscientiousness, openness to experience) may lead Joe to find other novel ways to act on these two core motives, which define Joe's interpersonal orientation to the social world.

Circumplex models have played important and generative roles in helping personality psychologists predict and understand links between personality traits, motives, and social behavior (see Horowitz et al., 2006). These models, however, were not intended to address other important issues. For example, they do not tackle the deeper "why" questions to which evolutionary approaches seek answers (see above), and they do not fully explain why so much variability exists on so many different personality traits. Several evolutionary theories, however, have been advanced to explain the existence of different personality traits (see Buss, 2009; Nettle, 2006, for reviews). Although these theories vary somewhat in their specific features, all of them share a common assumption: Personality is *adaptive* in the sense that certain traits should have helped our ancestors survive and/or reproduce

more successfully in the social and physical environments in which they lived.

Buss (1991), for example, proposes that the Big Five traits—Agreeableness, Conscientiousness, Extraversion, Neuroticism, and Openness to Experience—were a critical part of the "adaptive landscape" of our ancestors. According to this view, other humans were probably the most important and salient feature of ancestral environments. Our ancestors, therefore, had to find ways to successfully interact with, respond to, and infer the intentions of other people in order to survive, reproduce, and raise offspring. Consistent with this model, most of the items used to measure the Big Five traits are evaluative adjectives that describe how other people typically think, feel, and behave, especially as potential contributors to or exploiters of group resources (Buss, 1991). This may explain why the Big Five are found in some form in all known cultures: these traits represent five of the most evolutionarily relevant dimensions on which other people had to be assessed in order for individuals to achieve sufficient reproductive fitness in early human groups (Brewer & Caporael, 1990, 2006).

Given this evolutionary perspective on the Big Five, the salience of extraversion may reflect the fact that early human groups were organized hierarchically. To the extent that more extraverted individuals were at or near the top of group leadership hierarchies, it would have been important to identify such people; helping them or working with them might have garnered more resources that could then be shared with friends and coalition partners. The salience of agreeableness could reflect the importance of establishing and maintaining harmonious, reciprocal relationships with other members of early human groups. To the extent that more agreeable people tended to be more trustworthy and better reciprocators, it would have been important to discern who these good potential cooperators were. The salience of neuroticism, by comparison, may have resulted from the chronic costs associated with becoming involved with emotionally unstable and perhaps less productive individuals.

Extending the "adaptive landscape" notion, MacDonald (1998) hypothesizes that midlevel theories from evolutionary biology may also explain individual differences in certain personality traits. Parental investment theory (Trivers, 1972), for instance, predicts that the sex within a species that initially invests more in offspring (typically females) should be more cautious and discriminating when selecting mates, whereas the sex that invests less in offspring (typically males) should be more risky and competitive. Although human males invest more in their offspring than do males of other mammalian species, human females still have significantly higher obligatory parental investment (Trivers, 1985). Consistent with predictions from parental investment theory, men across cultures tend to score higher than women on traits that are good markers of the behavioral approach system (e.g., extraversion, sensation-seeking, dominance, and risk-taking). Women, by comparison, tend to score higher on measures assessing nurturance and communal orientation. MacDonald argues that these small yet reliable sex differences evolved to facilitate the different reproductive strategies that many women and men enacted during evolutionary history (see also Figueredo et al., 2005).

In summary, an evolutionary approach posits that personality traits are evolutionarily adaptive. This realization, however, sets up a more intriguing question to which we turn next: If certain traits are more adaptive than others, why do personality traits vary from person to person?

SECTION 3: WHY IS THERE VARIABILITY IN PERSONALITY?

If personality is an adaptive feature, one might expect that there would be little if any variation in personality traits (Tooby & Cosmides, 1990). For example, because having two eyes is so highly adaptive for humans and other mammals, there is no variability in the number of eyes that individuals possess—everyone has two. Individual differences in personality traits, however, show substantial variation, suggesting that we must ask a different evolutionary question: How and why was it adaptive for there to be *variability* in certain personality traits?

Some trait variation is attributable to heritable differences between people. Twin and adoption studies have found that 40 to 55% of the variance underlying major personality traits is heritable, with the remaining variance being due to nonshared environmental effects or measurement error (Bouchard, 2004). Though considerable room remains for environmental influences on personality, the genes-personality link is more complicated—and much more interesting—than previously thought. Specifically, even if a significant portion of a given personality trait is heritable, this does not suggest that the trait is biologically predetermined at birth. As discussed earlier, it is more accurate to think of individuals at birth being "genetically prepared" to take on any of several different personality profiles later in life. Adopting a particular profile does not imply that a person is consciously choosing one personality type over another. Instead, it suggests that a person's adaptive psychological mechanisms are nonconsciously responding to certain features of his or her past and/or present environment. Evolutionary researchers are now trying to identify the factors that lead people to adopt different personality profiles, especially in response to early environmental experiences.

To understand how childhood environments might influence personality, we turn to Life History Theory (LHT). As explained in greater detail below, LHT proposes that an individual ought to adopt a specific personality profile depending on three early environmental factors: (1) Parental Investment (e.g., Is the father present or absent?); (2) Mortality Level (e.g., Is the environment dangerous or safe?); and

(3) Frequency of other personality types in the local environment (e.g., Are my traits similar to or different from other people?).

Life History Theory

Life History Theory (Charnov, 1993; Kaplan & Gangestad, 2005; Stearns, 1992) focuses on how traits arise from specific life experiences encountered at different points of social development. According to LHT, because time and resources are inherently limited, all organisms must make important *trade-offs* in how they divide up and use their resources at any given phase of life. Due to structural and resource constraints, organisms cannot simultaneously maximize each major component of fitness (i.e., survival, reproduction, caring for offspring and kin). As a result, LHT suggests that all organisms have been selected to prioritize the specific life-domain(s) on which current resources are spent. Most relevant for personality, LHT focuses on the specific selection pressures in our ancestral past that should have determined when, and the conditions under which, individuals allocated time, energy, and resources to physical development, growth, reproduction, and parenting.

According to LHT, individuals must make three basic types of trade-offs when "deciding" (nonconsciously) how to best allocate their energy at different stages of their lives: (1) whether to invest effort in current (immediate) reproduction *or* future (delayed) reproduction; (2) whether to invest effort in higher quantity *or* higher quality of offspring; and (3) whether to invest effort in mating *or* parenting. An individual cannot concurrently invest energy into both sides of any trade-off. Consider the trade-off involving investment in current (immediate) reproduction or future (delayed) reproduction. Investing in current reproduction means that an individual does *not* invest in future reproduction. In modern Western societies, for example, people who have children as teenagers often do not have sufficient resources (e.g., time, money,

energy) to acquire higher education and job experiences, which they might have had if they delayed reproduction.

It is important to emphasize that organisms (including people) are not necessarily consciously aware of these trade-offs. In other words, individuals do not consciously and carefully deliberate about when and how to make certain trade-offs. Instead, LHT suggests that an organism's motivational systems are calibrated to respond to specific environmental cues. Accordingly, some environments nonconsciously motivate individuals to favor one trade-off decision, whereas others nonconsciously motivate individuals to favor a different decision. In what follows, we review three types of environmental factors that should contribute to the development of specific personality traits or trait profiles.

Personality as a Function of Parental Investment

Inspired by LHT and research on father-absence during childhood (Draper & Harpending, 1982), Belsky, Steinberg, and Draper (1991) developed the first major evolution-based lifespan theory of human social and personality development. This theory focuses on the trade-off between offspring quantity and quality. According to the model, the main evolutionary function of early social experience is to "prepare" individuals for the environments they are likely to inhabit during their lifetime. Certain information gleaned from the early environment should help individuals adopt an appropriate reproductive strategy—one that, on average, increases fitness the best—in their future environments.

Belsky et al. (1991) hypothesize that two developmental trajectories culminate in two distinct reproductive strategies (i.e., personality profiles) in adulthood. One strategy entails a short-term, opportunistic orientation toward relationships, especially to mating and parenting, in which sexual intercourse happens earlier in life, romantic pair bonds are shorter and less stable, and parental investment is lower. This orientation is geared toward increasing the *quantity* of offspring. The second strategy is characterized by a long-term, investing orientation toward relationships in which sexual intercourse occurs later in life, romantic pair bonds are more enduring, and parental investment is greater. This orientation focuses on maximizing offspring *quality*. A critical prediction of this model, one that distinguishes it from nonevolutionary theories of psychological and behavioral development, is that early rearing experiences should affect when puberty occurs. Specifically, puberty should take place earlier in individuals who develop along the "quantity trajectory" than in those who develop along the "quality trajectory." A growing body of evidence supports the Belsky et al. (1991) model, particularly the early predictors of pubertal timing in girls (see Ellis, 2004; Simpson & Belsky, 2008, for reviews).

Blending ideas from Belsky et al. (1991), Draper and Harpending (1982), and parental investment theory (Trivers, 1972), Ellis and colleagues (1999) hypothesize that fathers assume a special role in the development of girls' reproductive strategies. Whereas Belsky et al. (1991) viewed early father absence as a marker of stress in the family of origin and focused on the quality of mothering and fathering, Ellis (2004) suggests that father absence or stepfather presence may be an important cue of paternal investment, signaling low, unpredictable, or changing levels of paternal investment within families. Recent research has confirmed that there are good empirical and theoretical reasons for *not* treating mothers and fathers as interchangeable agents of influence in understanding how childhood experiences shape reproductive strategies. Greater attention must be paid to the presence of biologically unrelated male figures in the home during development and to the differential influence of maternal and paternal investment (i.e., the quality of parenting by mothers and fathers). Emerging evidence supports the basic tenets of

Ellis' model (see Ellis, 2004; Simpson & Belsky, 2008, for reviews).

More recently, Ellis, Figueredo, Brumbach, and Scholmer (2009) have differentiated two types of difficult early environments: those that are consistently *difficult* or *harsh*, and those that are *unpredictable* (shifting between harsh and benign). According to this model, exposure to consistently difficult/harsh environments leads to receiving more rejecting, punitive, or neglectful care from parents. This, in turn, produces more avoidant attachment styles and unrestricted mating strategies in adulthood, whereby romantic ties are more emotionally distant and impersonal. Exposure to unpredictable (variable) environments, on the other hand, should result in receiving sporadic and unpredictable care from parents. This should culminate in more anxious attachment styles and unrestricted mating strategies in adulthood in which romantic ties are emotionally tempestuous and enmeshed.

In summary, the type of parental investment that children receive ought to shunt them down different developmental and reproductive pathways. Beginning early in life, children should use the type and amount of parental investment they receive to gauge the demands, challenges, and opportunities that may be posed by their later social environments. This, in turn, should shape the specific personality traits and associated reproductive strategies they eventually adopt in adulthood.

Personality as a Function of Mortality Levels

Drawing on LHT, Chisholm (1993, 1996, 1999) claims that the nature of life-history trade-offs should also depend on the environmental factor of local mortality rates. According to Chisholm (1993), local mortality rates should be the pivotal environmental cue that directs people down different developmental and reproductive pathways. When mortality rates are high in a local area, the optimal reproductive strategy is to mate early so that current fertility is maximized (Horn & Rubenstein, 1984; Promislow & Harvey, 1990). When mortality rates are low, the best strategy is deferred, long-term reproduction in which fewer children are given better and longer care. Thus, in abundant and safe environments that signal longer life-expectancies, a delayed/high-investment reproductive strategy should increase the total number of descendants across several generations by minimizing the *variance* of surviving offspring within each generation. This, in turn, should decrease the likelihood that an entire generation fails to reproduce.

High mortality rates, which should have been an excellent barometer of the difficulty of local environments during evolutionary history (Chisholm, 1999), should also have resulted in poorer caregiving. Chisholm (1993, 1996) suggests that parental indifference or insensitivity might have been a valid cue of local mortality rates, motivating children to develop appropriate traits and behaviors (e.g., more aggression, less cooperative orientations) that were better suited to increasing fitness in such arduous environments. Low mortality rates, which probably signaled more hospitable environments, should have been associated with better and more attentive caregiving. Sensitive parenting, in other words, may have conveyed to children that premature death was less likely, resulting in different traits and behaviors (e.g., less aggression, more cooperative orientations) that enhanced fitness in more benign environments.

Chisholm (1999) also proposes another personality mediator that might link early childhood experience and adult reproductive strategies—time preference. Time preference, which is related to delay-of-gratification tendencies, reflects the degree to which individuals prefer—or believe they will achieve—their desires either now (immediately) or later (sometime in the future). Individuals who are raised in dangerous or uncertain environments in which waiting for rewards could result in leaving no descendants should prefer immediate payoffs, even if delayed ones might be superior (Wilson & Daly, 2005). Mounting evidence also supports components of Chisholm's model (see Ellis, 2004; Simpson & Belsky, 2008, for reviews).

In sum, mortality levels in early environments should shunt individuals down different developmental and reproductive pathways. Cues indicative of local death rates may "signal" the need to reproduce earlier versus later in life. These specific cues, gleaned from early social environments, ought to shape the personality traits and associated reproductive strategies that individuals eventually adopt in adulthood.

Personality as a Function of the Frequency of Other Personalities

Another environmental feature that should shape the development of personality traits is the traits of other people, especially potential competitors. When one considers an individual's traits in social isolation (i.e., one person living on an island), possessing a certain set of traits is not necessarily "good" or "bad" in an evolutionary sense. However, when one views those same traits *in relation to* the distribution of traits possessed by other people within the local population, certain traits can increase or decrease in adaptive value. For example, it might be more adaptive for an individual to be highly open to new experiences when 70% of the local population is highly risk-averse. Greater openness may allow an individual to find or create new solutions to problems that impair survival, mating, and/or parenting, which could give such individuals a fitness advantage over their risk-averse counterparts. Greater openness may, however, lose its fitness value if 80% of the local population is risk-takers. Thus, according to frequency-dependency models (see Gangestad & Simpson, 1990), the adaptive value of a trait score depends on its value and base-rate within a population.

One critical insight from evolutionary models of trait variability is that there are inherent trade-offs in being high or low on certain traits. For example, being high (or low) on any Big Five trait affords both benefits *and* costs (MacDonald, 1995; Nettle, 2006). Greater agreeableness, for example, probably conferred myriad benefits in evolutionary history. It most likely enabled individuals to be more attuned to what others were thinking and feeling, to forge more enduring relationships, and to form stronger ties with coalition partners. However, high agreeableness should also have had some costs, such as the greater likelihood of being cheated by others and not acting on one's self-interest when it was opportune to do so. Less agreeable people would be less likely to reap these benefits, but they also would be less vulnerable to these potential costs. Highly conscientious people might have benefited from paying closer attention to long-term fitness benefits and living longer, but they may have engaged in obsessive thinking, rigid ways of doing tasks, and might have been less inclined to pursue short-term fitness gains. More "open" people may have been more creative and better at attracting mates, but they may also have been prone to psychoses or delusional thoughts. Highly neurotic individuals may have been more vigilant to possible danger and more willing to compete with others for valuable resources, but they also should have been more vulnerable to depression, more stress-reactive, and less likely to have stable relationships. Finally, highly extraverted people might have had more mates, more social allies, and should have been more willing to explore new environments, but they also should have been more prone to physical injuries and tenuous or unstable relationships (see Nettle, 2006, for relevant citations for these claims).

Although natural selection typically removes heritability on traits that are essential to reproductive fitness (Fisher, 1930; Tooby & Cosmides, 1990), there are circumstances in which interindividual variation can be maintained in heritable traits. Nettle (2006) argues that personality traits can have high heritability and substantial interindividual variability. Especially if a trait is influenced by several genes, it can retain genetic variation even when directional selection forces are powerful (Houle, 1998). For example, if frequency-dependent selection has occurred, traits can have both high heritability (i.e., they have a strong genetic basis) and considerable interindividual variation (i.e., some people are low on the trait, whereas others are moderate or high).

Clear examples of this process are found in the animal literature, where different mating strategies and tactics are enacted by members of the same species (see Nettle, 2006). For example, there is a species of guppy in Trinidad that has heritable variation in behavioral traits linked to their survival in particular local habitats. The most reproductively successful guppies that live in high mountain streams where fewer predators exist are bolder and more aggressive. The most successful guppies that live downstream—where predators flourish—tend to be timid and cautious. When predators are introduced to upstream environments or are moved from downstream ones, these modal behavioral strategies (aggressive vs. cautious) change, with upstream guppies becoming more timid within a few generations and with downstream guppies becoming more aggressive. Nettle (2006) proposes that the same general processes could also be true of people who score high and low on certain personality traits, which may have evolved to facilitate the enactment of different survival and mating strategies in humans.

In sum, the development of personality traits is also likely to be influenced by the frequency of other personality traits within the local environment. More specifically, a person may nonconsciously develop different adult personality traits, depending on the traits of the people with whom she or he interacts across the lifespan.

SECTION 4: SOCIOSEXUALITY
AS AN EXAMPLE OF AN ADAPTIVE
CLUSTER OF TRAITS

In this chapter, we have discussed two fundamental points with regard to how personality traits can be viewed from an evolutionary perspective. First, when viewed from an evolutionary lens, certain personality traits may be adaptive in specific environments. Being highly extraverted, for instance, can be advantageous in terms of making friends, gaining status, and attracting romantic partners. The ability to accomplish these goals would have helped our ancestors survive and reproduce. However, despite the adaptive benefits of being high (or low) on a given trait, individuals do not have the same personality profiles. This highlights the second major point of the chapter: An evolutionary perspective also considers *variability* in personality traits as reflecting adaptive trade-offs. Being high or low on extraversion (or other traits), for example, has benefits *and* costs, and there are several different processes by which adaptive variability in personality can be sustained across time (e.g., frequency-dependency processes, life-history processes).

To this point, we have focused on the purported functions of individual personality traits such as the Big Five. However, the evolutionary literature suggests that certain traits may cluster, together in the service of enacting reproductive strategies leading people to adopt unique personality profiles. Because all organisms have evolved to enhance their reproductive fitness, an evolutionary perspective predicts that personality traits should *cluster* around different types of mating strategies. Humans do, in fact, engage in different types of mating strategies (see Buss & Schmitt, 1993; Gangestad & Simpson, 2000). Given that different mating strategies are differentially successful in certain environments, individuals should adopt the mating strategy that, on average, tends to be most successful for their specific environment.

Reproduction, of course, involves much more than merely copulation; it also involves sexual competition to attract mates, courtship rituals, and parenting in the aftermath of mating. Consequently, mating strategies should entail clusters of different personality characteristics that are "applied" to different aspects of reproduction (e.g., attracting a mate, competing with same-sex competitors, parenting children). Recall the case of Joe, a man in his early twenties who is highly extraverted, open to new and exciting experiences, uninhibited, and sexually promiscuous. It is conceivable that these traits "cohere" because they constitute a specific mating strategy, namely a short-term, opportunistic one in which emotional ties with partners are weaker and more fleeting (termed an *unrestricted* strategy; Simpson & Gangestad, 1991a). This mating strategy is related to specific life-history trade-offs discussed earlier, especially those that favor earlier reproduction (rather than delayed reproduction) and offspring quantity (rather than offspring quality). To successfully enact an unrestricted mating strategy, an individual must be motivated to enter new situations and novel environments in order to meet new mates and then captivate and retain their interest. Individuals who adopt an unrestricted mating strategy, therefore, must continually approach the potential rewards offered by novel and changing opportunities, including new mating opportunities. They cannot be inhibited, afraid, or constrained because such tendencies could negate, hinder, or derail interactions with new potential partners. Unrestricted individuals, in other words, cannot be risk-averse or overly concerned about making mistakes that could, on occasion, result in bad outcomes. During evolutionary history, these personality trait clusters should have facilitated the successful enactment of unrestricted mating strategies, given the demands and pressures of the environment in which individuals lived.

A very different personality profile is required to enact a restricted mating strategy successfully. A restricted strategy is a long-term, committed one in which emotional ties with partners are stronger and more enduring (Simpson & Gangestad, 1991a). This strategy is tied to life-history trade-offs that favor delayed (rather than earlier) reproduction and offspring quality (rather than offspring quantity). Individuals who pursue a restricted mating strategy cannot be easily drawn away from current partners and relationships by the lure of attractive but temporary alternative partners. They need to focus on and remain committed to the partners and relationships they have already invested in, assuming that their current partners are satisfactory. Thus, the combination of lower extraversion and higher constraint ought to facilitate the enactment of restricted mating strategies.

These trait clusters have been examined empirically. Gangestad and Simpson (1990; Simpson & Gangestad, 1991b) investigated how scores on the Sociosexual Orientation Inventory (SOI; Simpson & Gangestad, 1991a) correlate with trait scales from Tellegen's (1982) Multidimensional Personality Questionnaire (MPQ) in young, single adults. The MPQ contains several scales that tap different personality traits, including the Big Five. As shown in Figure 5.1, higher scores on the SOI (i.e., having a more short-term, unrestricted mating orientation) load on two higher-order factors: *extraversion* (SOI factor loading = .39) and *lack of constraint* (SOI loading = .47). In other words, people who have a more unrestricted mating strategy tend to be both more extraverted/socially potent and less constrained/inhibited, less harm-avoidant, and poorer at self-regulation. Those who have a more restricted mating strategy, in contrast, are more introverted and more constrained. These results are consistent with previous research by Eysenck (1976), who found similar connections between sexual attitudes/behaviors and personality traits.

This leads us back to the case of Joe. Why, from an evolutionary perspective, does Joe have the specific profile of traits he does? The answer may be that this cluster of traits is the set that is "best suited" for Joe in order to compete for and attract mates, to successfully interact with others, and to parent, given his developmental history along with his current life circumstances. According to the Belsky et al. (1991) model, for example, Joe is likely to have been raised in a conflict-ridden home by parents who had an unstable relationship and did not invest considerable time or effort into parenting him. He may have learned from an early age that he had to be self-sufficient, he had to compete with others and take risks in order to gain attention and "get ahead" in life, and he could not get too close to others without becoming vulnerable or being taken advantage of. Joe's early experiences, in other words, shunted him down an unrestricted pathway. And the specific profile of personality traits that he developed should facilitate the successful enactment of his unrestricted mating strategy.

Interestingly, the two higher-order factors shown in Figure 5.1 roughly map onto two biologically based systems that underlie personality. Greater extraversion, which entails a mixture of communal and agentic motives, is believed to facilitate action and produce positive affect (emotion), reflecting the *approach* motivational system. Greater constraint is believed to inhibit action and produce negative affect, reflecting the *avoidance* motivational system (Cacioppo & Berntson, 1994; Lang, 1995; Panksepp, 1998). Gray (1990) has demonstrated that individual differences exist on both of these dimensions—one that promotes behavior and positive affect (the Behavior Activation System), and one that inhibits behavior and is associated with negative affect (the Behavioral Inhibition System).

According to frequency-dependency models (e.g., Gangestad & Simpson, 1990), selection can produce alternate genotypes—genetically-based traits or sets of traits—that result in different mating

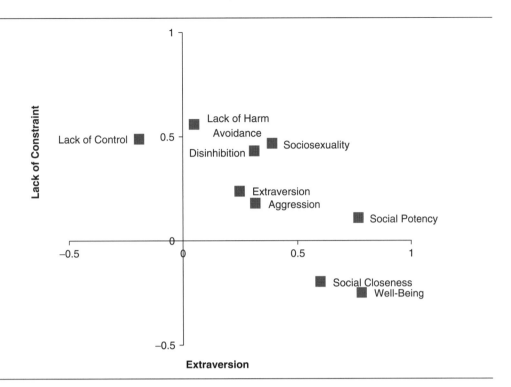

FIGURE 5.1   The Horizontal Axis Reflects Extraversion, and the Vertical Axis Reflects Lack of Constraint
The trait scales are from the Multidimensional Personality Questionnaire (Tellegen, 1982). A more unrestricted sociosexual orientation is associated with motives characteristic of high extraversion and low constraint, whereas a more restricted orientation is associated with motives characteristic of low extraversion (introversion) and high constraint.
Source: This figure is based on one originally published in "Toward an Evolutionary History of Female Sociosexual Variation," by S. Gangestad and J. A. Simpson, 1990, *Journal of Personality, 58.* Reprinted with permission.

strategies. Each genotype can have good reproductive fitness outcomes across time as long as individuals adopt a reproductive strategy that is suited to their personal motivations, talents, skills, and assets. As we have seen, specific clusters of traits ought to promote the enactment of different reproductive strategies, including restricted and unrestricted forms of sociosexuality. Indeed, Gangestad and Simpson (1990) have provided evidence that both restricted and unrestricted mating strategies could have enhanced reproductive fitness especially in women during evolutionary history, depending on whether a woman needed greater paternal investment or better genes from male partners, given the specific demands of her environment. The specific cluster of traits that would

have facilitated an unrestricted mating strategy should have been those that led ancestral women to meet and draw the attention of highly desirable mates (e.g., greater extraversion) while not being overly restrained or excessively regulated (e.g., greater disinhibition). The opposite cluster of traits should have promoted a restricted mating strategy.

In conclusion, evolutionary theories and principles have a great deal to offer personality psychology. One of the primary objectives of this chapter was to highlight how certain evolutionary theories—especially those related to Life History Theory—can generate novel and important insights into not only why certain personality traits such as the Big Five exist, but how and why people have different scores on traits and why certain traits may "cluster" more than others. One reason why evolutionary theories provide unique insights is that they address deeper "why" questions that focus on the ultimate origins, purposes, and functions of a given trait or behavior. The field of personality is well-positioned to take full advantage of one of the most powerful sets of ideas in the social and life sciences—the modern evolutionary perspective. It is time to do so.

References

Alcock, J., & Crawford, C. (2008). Evolutionary questions for evolutionary psychologists. In C. Crawford & D. Krebs (Eds.), *Foundations of evolutionary psychology* (pp. 25–46). New York: Taylor & Francis.

Belsky, J., Steinberg, L., & Draper, P. (1991). Childhood experience, interpersonal development, and reproductive strategy: An evolutionary theory of socialization. *Child Development, 62,* 647–670.

Bouchard, T. J., Jr. (2004). Genetic influence of human psychological traits. *Current Directions in Psychological Science, 13,* 148–151.

Brewer, M. B., & Caporael, L. R. (1990). Selfish genes versus selfish people: Sociobiology as origin myth. *Motivation and Emotion, 14,* 237–243.

Brewer, M. B., & Caporael, L. R. (2006). An evolutionary perspective of social identity: Revisiting Groups. In M. Schaller, J. A. Simpson, & D. T. Kenrick (Eds.), *Evolution and social psychology* (pp. 143–161). New York: Psychology Press.

Buss, D. M. (1991). Evolutionary personality psychology. *Annual Review of Psychology, 42,* 459–491.

Buss, D. M. (2009). How can evolutionary psychology successfully explain personality and individual differences? *Perspectives on Psychological Science, 4,* 359–366.

Buss, D. M., & Schmitt, D. P. (1993). Sexual Strategies Theory: A contextual evolutionary analysis of human mating. *Psychological Review, 100,* 204–232.

Cacioppo, J. T., & Berntson, G. G. (1994). Relationship between attitudes and evaluative space: A critical review, with emphasis on the separability of positive and negative substrates. *Psychological Bulletin, 115,* 401–423.

Charnov, E. L. (1993). *Life history invariants.* Oxford, UK: Oxford University Press.

Chisholm, J. S. (1993). Death, hope, and sex: Life-history theory and the development of reproductive strategies. *Current Anthropology, 34,* 1–24.

Chisholm, J. S. (1996). The evolutionary ecology of attachment organization. *Human Nature, 7,* 1–38.

Chisholm, J. S. (1999). *Death, hope, and sex.* New York: Cambridge University Press.

Darwin, C. (1859). *On the origins of species.* London: John Murray.

Darwin, C. (1871). *The descent of man, and selection in relation to sex.* Princeton, NJ: Princeton University Press, 1981.

Draper, P., & Harpending, H. (1982). Father absence and reproductive strategy: An evolutionary perspective. *Journal of Anthropological Research, 38,* 255–273.

Eastwick, P. W. (in press). Beyond the Pleistocene: Using phylogeny and constraint to inform the evolutionary psychology of human mating. *Psychological Bulletin.*

Ellis, B. J. (2004). Timing of pubertal maturation in girls. *Psychological Bulletin, 130,* 920–958.

Ellis, B. J., Figueredo, A. J., Brumbach, B. H., & Schlomer, G. L. (2009). Fundamental dimensions of environmental risk: The impact of harsh versus unpredictable environments on the evolution and development of life history strategies. *Human Nature, 20,* 204–268

Ellis, B. J., McFadyen-Ketchum, S., Dodge, K. A., Pettit, G. S., & Bates, J. E. (1999). Quality of early family relationships and individual differences in the timing of pubertal maturation in girls. *Journal of Personality and Social Psychology, 77,* 387–401.

Eysenck, H. J. (1976). *Sex and personality.* London: Open Books.

Figueredo, A. J., Sefcek, J. A., Vasquez, G., Brumbach, B. H., King, J. E., & Jacobs, W. J. (2005). Evolutionary personality psychology. In D. M. Buss (Ed.), *The handbook of evolutionary psychology* (pp. 851–877). Hoboken, NJ: John Wiley & Sons.

Fisher, R. A. (1930). *The genetical theory of natural selection.* Oxford, UK: Clarendon Press.

Gangestad, S., & Simpson, J. A. (1990). Toward an evolutionary history of female sociosexual variation. *Journal of Personality, 58,* 69–96.

Gangestad, S. W., & Simpson, J. A. (2000). The evolution of human mating: Trade-offs and strategic pluralism. *Behavioral and Brain Sciences, 23*, 573–587.

Gray, J. A. (1990). Brain systems that mediate both emotion and cognition. *Cognition and Emotion, 4*, 269–288.

Horn, H., & Rubenstein, D. (1984). Behavioral adaptations and life history. In J. Krebs & N. Davies (Eds.), *Behavioral ecology: An evolutionary approach* (2nd ed.). Oxford, UK: Blackwell.

Horowitz, L. M., Wilson, K. R., Turan, B., Zolotsev, P., Constantino, M. J., & Henderson, L. (2006). How interpersonal motives clarify the meaning of interpersonal behavior: A revised circumplex model. *Personality and Social Psychology Review, 10*, 67–86.

Houle, D. (1998). How should we explain variation in the genetic variance of traits? *Genetica, 102/103*, 241–253.

Kaplan, H. S., & Gangestad, S. W. (2005). Life history theory and evolutionary psychology. In D. M. Buss (Ed.), *The handbook of evolutionary psychology* (pp. 68–95). Hoboken, NJ: John Wiley & Sons.

Kenrick, D. T., Griskevicius, V., Neuberg, S. L. & Schaller, M. (in press). Renovating the pyramid of needs: Contemporary extensions built upon ancient foundations. *Perspectives in Psychological Science.*

Lang, P. J. (1995). The emotion probe: Studies of motivation and attention. *American Psychologist, 50*, 372–385.

Leary, T. F. (1957). *Interpersonal diagnosis of personality.* New York: Ronald Press.

MacDonald, K. B. (1995). Evolution, the five-factor model, and levels of personality. *Journal of Personality, 63*, 525–567.

MacDonald, K. B. (1998). Evolution, culture, and the five–factor model. *Journal of Cross Cultural Psychology, 29*, 119–149.

Nettle, D. (2006). The evolution of personality variation in humans and other animals. *American Psychologist, 61*, 622–631.

Panksepp, J. (1998). *Affective neuroscience: The foundations of human and animal emotions.* New York: Oxford University Press.

Pinker, S. (1994). *The language instinct.* New York: William Morrow.

Promislow, D., & Harvey, P. (1990). Living fast and dying young: A comparative analysis of life-history variation among mammals. *Journal of the Zoological Society of London, 220*, 417–437.

Simpson, J. A., & Belsky, J. (2008). Attachment theory within a modern evolutionary framework. In J. Cassidy & P. R. Shaver (Eds.), *Handbook of attachment: Theory, research, and clinical applications* (2nd ed.) (pp. 131–157). New York: Guilford Press.

Simpson, J. A., & Gangestad, S. (1991a). Individual differences in sociosexuality: Evidence for convergent and discriminant validity. *Journal of Personality and Social Psychology, 60*, 870–883.

Simpson, J. A., & Gangestad, S. W. (1991b). Personality and sexuality: Empirical relations and an integrative theoretical model. In K. McKinney & S. Sprecher (Eds.), *Sexuality in close relationships* (pp. 71–92). Hillsdale, NJ: Erlbaum.

Simpson, J. A., & Gangestad, S. W. (2001). Evolution and relationships: A call for integration. *Personal Relationships, 8*, 341–355.

Stearns, S. (1992). *The evolution of life histories.* New York: Oxford University Press.

Tellegen, A. (1982). *Brief manual for the Multidimensional Personality Questionnaire.* Unpublished manuscript, University of Minnesota, Minneapolis, MN.

Tinbergen, N. (1963). On the aims and methods of ethology. *Z. Tierpsychol., 20*, 410–433.

Tooby, J., & Cosmides, L. (1990). The past explains the present: Emotional adaptations and the structure of ancestral environments. *Ethology and Sociobiology, 11*, 375–424.

Tooby, J., & Cosmides, L. (1992). Psychological foundations of culture. In J. Barkow, L. Cosmides, & J. Tooby (Eds.), *The adapted mind* (pp. 19–136). New York: Oxford University Press.

Trivers, R. L. (1972). Parental investment and sexual selection. In B. Campbell (Ed.), *Sexual selection and the descent of man, 1871–1971* (pp. 136–179). Chicago: Aldine-Atherton.

Trivers, R. L. (1985). *Social evolution.* Menlo Park, CA: Benjamin/Cummings.

Wilson, M., & Daly, M. (2005). Carpe diem: Adaptation and devaluing the future. *Quarterly Review of Biology, 80*, 55–60.

6 THE FIVE-FACTOR MODEL, FIVE-FACTOR THEORY, AND INTERPERSONAL PSYCHOLOGY

Paul T. Costa, Jr.

Robert R. McCrae

The Five-Factor Model (FFM; Digman, 1990; McCrae & John, 1992) is an account of the structure of individual differences in personality; it is an empirical taxonomy of traits open to many different theoretical interpretations (Wiggins, 1996). Five-Factor Theory (FFT; McCrae & Costa, 2008b) is our account of the development and functioning of the individual; it is a theory of personality. We called it "Five-Factor Theory" because it was formulated to account for a host of findings from research conducted using measures of the FFM. By contrast, interpersonal psychology is not, in the usual sense, a theory of personality; it has its focus outside the individual, in interactions among people, especially dyads. One might imagine that there is a relatively limited intersection of FFT's intrapersonal perspective with the approach of interpersonal psychology that could be exhaustively covered in the space of this small chapter, but in fact the two

perspectives are so deeply intertwined that they are better seen as two different views of the same topic. Human personality is invariably expressed in cultural, social, and interpersonal forms; interpersonal and social behaviors always emanate from individual human beings with their own personalities. Our goal here is to sketch the more important ways in which the two views converge or complement each other. We begin with empirical correspondences at the level of FFM traits, then present a theoretical framework—FFT—that can be applied to interpersonal psychology, and finally discuss attachment as an illustration of how FFT might be used to reinterpret topics of central importance to interpersonal theory.

TRAITS

Perhaps the clearest and best-established link between these two research traditions comes from the study of individual differences. Half a century ago, Leary (1957) and others noted that people differ in their characteristic interpersonal behaviors, and that the behaviors, and corresponding

AUTHOR NOTE: This research was supported entirely by the Intramural Research Program of the National Institute on Aging, NIH. Paul T. Costa, Jr., and Robert R. McCrae receive royalties from the NEO-PI-R.

traits, showed a circular order, the interpersonal circumplex (Kiesler, 1983; Wiggins & Broughton, 1985). Behaviors, and people, were contrasted in terms of two dimensions, typically called Love or Affiliation and Dominance or Status. In contrast to the simple structures generally sought by factor analysts, interpersonal theorists were equally concerned with the intermediate positions between these two dimensions. Thus, a person high in both Love and Dominance might be considered sociable; one high in Love but low in Dominance might be cooperative.

Trait researchers spent many decades enumerating important individual differences in enduring dispositions; eventually it became clear that most traits are related to one or more of just five basic factors. These are now commonly called Neuroticism versus Emotional Stability, Extraversion, Openness to Experience, Agreeableness versus Antagonism, and Conscientiousness. A good deal is now known about these factors (McCrae & Costa, 2008a): They recur across cultures, are strongly heritable, can be assessed by self-reports or the ratings of knowledgeable informants, and characterize individuals for long periods during adulthood.

Wiggins (1979) extracted interpersonal trait adjectives from the dictionary and created a measure called the Interpersonal Adjective Scales (IAS), later revised as the IAS-R (Wiggins, Trapnell, & Phillips, 1988). In 1989, we showed that the interpersonal plane defined by IAS-R scales coincided with a plane defined by measures of the FFM trait factors Extraversion and Agreeableness (McCrae & Costa, 1989), as measured by the NEO Personality Inventory. That instrument included six facet scales each for Neuroticism, Extraversion, and Openness factors, but only global scales for Agreeableness and Conscientiousness. A subsequent revision (Costa & McCrae, 1992) included facet scales for all five factors.

Figure 6.1 shows the results of a joint factor analysis of self-reports on the IAS-R and spouse ratings on the Revised NEO Personality Inventory (NEO-PI-R). Because the data are from an ongoing longitudinal study, they were collected at different times: The IAS-R was administered in 1985, spouse ratings on the original NEO-PI were obtained in 1986, and spouse ratings on the new Agreeableness and Conscientiousness items were gathered in 1991. However, because personality traits are quite stable in adulthood, these different times of administration probably had little effect on the structure (Costa & McCrae, 1985). Figure 6.1 replicates earlier findings with regard to Extraversion facets, which occupy the upper right quadrant. It shows further that facets of Agreeableness are arrayed in the lower right quadrant, moving clockwise from Altruism to Modesty. These new data on facets of Agreeableness make perfect sense: IAS-R Warm-Agreeable (LM) is closest to the Altruism and Tender-Mindedness facets of Agreeableness; IAS-R Unassuming-Ingenuous (NO) is closest to Modesty and Straightforwardness.

The orientation of the Love and Dominance axes in Figure 6.1 is based on Wiggins's model—Procrustes rotation was used so that PA best approximates 90 degrees, NO 45 degrees, and so on. Other orientations for Dominance and Love are sometimes advocated, and Tracey, Ryan, and Jaschik-Herman (2001) reported evidence that a clockwise rotation of 22.5 degrees from the Wiggins orientation yields a position in which the principle of complementarity seems to work best. Note that such an orientation would make the axes of Dominance and Love pass near the centroids of the Extraversion and Agreeableness facets, respectively. One might then conclude that interpersonal behaviors tend to elicit complementary behaviors that are similar with regard to Agreeableness and opposite with regard to Extraversion.

Several conclusions can be drawn from Figure 6.1. Because IAS-R and NEO-PI-R scales define the same factors, the figure shows that interpersonal characteristics are largely isomorphic with some facets of general personality traits. In fact,

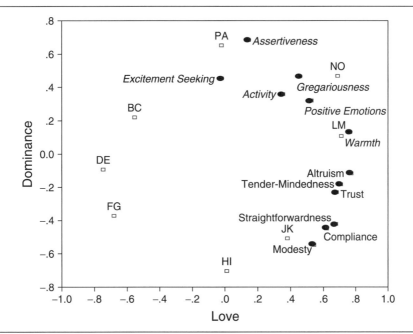

FIGURE 6.1 Joint Factor Analysis of Self-Reported IAS-R Scales (Open Squares) with Spouse-Rated NEO-PI-R Extraversion and Agreeableness Facets (Ovals), N = 71

Factors have been rotated toward Wiggins et al.'s (1988) circumplex orientation. Extraversion facets are in italics. PA = Dominant-Assured. BC = Arrogant-Calculating. DE = Cold-hearted. FG = Aloof-Introverted. HI = Unassured-Submissive. JK = Unassuming-Ingenuous. LM = Warm-Agreeable. NO = Gregarious-Extraverted.

Traupman and colleagues (2009) have created a measure of the full Interpersonal Circumplex using items from the NEO-PI-R. Because there is a six-year interval between the IAS-R and NEO-PI-R data, the figure testifies to the enduring nature of interpersonal traits. Because this is a joint analysis of self-reports and spouse ratings, it demonstrates that interpersonal traits are consensually valid. That is, at least among married couples, interpersonal person perception is generally accurate.

Careful consideration of Figure 6.1, however, points to another conclusion as well. Although this might easily be deemed a diagram of the interpersonal plane (defined by the two dimensions of Love and Dominance), it clearly contains traits that are not intrinsically interpersonal. Three of the Extraversion facets—Excitement Seeking, Activity, and Positive Emotions—are sometimes considered temperamental rather than interpersonal, because they need not

involve other people at all. The Agreeableness facet of Tender-Mindedness is only indirectly interpersonal; it is fundamentally a dimension of personality-relevant attitudes. Human nature, it seems, does not necessarily respect the neat conceptual categories we invent: Not all traits in the interpersonal plane are interpersonal.

The converse is also true: Traits outside the interpersonal plane may also be interpersonal, in the sense that they powerfully influence social interactions. Wiggins and Trapnell (1996; see also Ansell & Pincus, 2004) attempted to link all five factors to the interpersonal dimensions by broadening Dominance and Love to the more abstract metaconcepts of Agency and Communion. Thus, for example, they considered the Vulnerability facet of Neuroticism an example of (low) Agency, whereas the Angry Hostility facet was seen as representing (low) Communion.

There are more direct ways to link the remaining FFM factors to interpersonal concerns. Consider Openness to Experience. This is fundamentally an intrapsychic experiential dimension, concerned with how individuals filter and process cognitive, emotional, and perceptual information (McCrae & Costa, 1997). Open individuals value novelty and variety, generate remote associates to ideas, become intensely absorbed in their activities, and tolerate—even cultivate—ambiguity; whereas closed people are traditional, down-to-earth, and compartmentalized in their thinking. These distinctive forms of handling experiential input have pervasive influences on social interactions at almost all levels: People seek friends and spouses (McCrae et al., 2008) who resemble them in their level of Openness and tend to work most effectively in like-minded groups. Open people have more egalitarian family structures. Closed people provide more practical social support and show greater in-group loyalty. Openness is an important determinant of social attitudes, including prejudice and political affiliation. Open leaders facilitate organizational change, and cultures whose members (on average) score higher on measures of Openness are more progressive and innovative in social policies (McCrae, 1996; McCrae & Sutin, 2009).

Conscientiousness—or its lack—also has major repercussions in the interpersonal sphere. Imagine a roommate who borrows your belongings without asking, leaves clothes and trash on the floor, makes but rarely keeps promises, and forgets to pay the rent. Such behaviors, though not directed at you personally, are likely to affect your well-being and may well sour your relationship with your roommate. It is hardly surprising that people uniformly prefer mates high in Conscientiousness (Botwin, Buss, & Shackelford, 1997), or that low Conscientiousness in men is a predictor of subsequent divorce (Kelly & Conley, 1987). It is curious that *trust* is traditionally considered an interpersonal trait, but that *trustworthiness* is not.

Individuals high in Neuroticism are prone to experience a variety of distressing emotions, including fear, anger, dejection, and shame; these affective responses often disturb interpersonal functioning. This is seen most clearly in extreme cases, such as individuals diagnosed with Borderline Personality Disorder, who typically score high on all facets (Morey et al., 2002). *DSM-IV* (American Psychiatric Association, 1994) notes that patients with this disorder have intense but unstable relationships, in which their perceptions of others are unrealistic and can shift dramatically. They are helplessly dependent on others, but can resort to outbursts of temper if they feel slighted; in consequence, "broken marriages are common" (p. 652).

More generally, there are entire categories of problems in living that are classified as *interpersonal*. Analyses of instruments that assess these problems (Horowitz, Alden, Wiggins, & Pincus, 2000; Horowitz, Rosenberg, Baer, Ureño, & Villaseñor, 1988) typically show a general factor that is associated with negative affectivity (Tracey, Rounds, & Gurtman, 1996) or Neuroticism (Becker & Mohr, 2005); after controlling for this general factor, the familiar circular arrangement of interpersonal traits is found. From the perspective of the FFM, we might say that people high in Neuroticism are prone to interpersonal problems; the nature of the predominant problems is a function of levels of Extraversion and Agreeableness. Thus, dependency might be associated with high Agreeableness and high Neuroticism; jealousy with low Agreeableness and high Neuroticism.

Some researchers have been so fascinated by the circular arrangement of traits in the interpersonal circumplex and by the intriguing but sometimes elusive (Oxford, 1986) notion of complementary behaviors it affords that they have neglected other traits that are also essential to a complete understanding of interpersonal behaviors and relationships. The FFM offers a broader perspective that should be helpful here. That fact was acknowledged by Wiggins, who supplemented his Interpersonal Circumplex measure with scales for Neuroticism, Openness, and Conscientiousness (Trapnell & Wiggins, 1990).

THE PERSONALITY SYSTEM

Interpersonal psychology is as much about process as it is about traits, whereas the FFM is, in itself, only a structural model of traits. In his 1996 volume, Wiggins asked FFM researchers to make explicit the theoretical basis of their understanding of traits, and we did so by spelling out the metatheoretical assumptions behind trait psychology (including variability, proactivity, rationality, and scientific knowability) and by outlining a theory of personality, complete with definitions and postulates (McCrae & Costa, 1996). The metatheoretical assumptions assert that human nature is variable (surely an axiom of differential psychology!); that behavior is not merely reactive, but also expresses the inner nature of the individual; that lay persons have some insight into their own motives and behaviors (and those of others); and that human personality is a proper object of scientific inquiry. No one imagines that human beings are perfectly rational, or absolute masters of their own actions, or infallibly correct in how they see themselves. But as general principles, these metatheoretical premises have proven to be useful, and they set trait psychology apart from radical behaviorism, which sees humans as uniformly reactive to a history of reinforcements; from psychoanalysis, which regards motives as hidden and behavior as fundamentally irrational; and from some forms of existential psychology, which grant human beings a freedom that defies scientific understanding. It is noteworthy that interpersonal psychologists by-and-large adopt the same metatheoretical premises (variability, proactivity, rationality, knowability) as trait psychologists, although they might prefer to describe personality as *interactive* rather than *proactive*.

In fact, most modern forms of personality psychology share these basic tenets of trait psychology. What sets FFT apart from other contemporary theories of personality is the particular set of postulates it proposes. These in turn are not based primarily on the nature of the five factors, but rather on findings that have emerged from research on the FFM. For example, the existence of five factors says nothing about where these factors come from, but a large body of research shows that they are substantially heritable (Bouchard & Loehlin, 2001). We have known for some time that traits (like Extraversion) that were traditionally considered temperamental have a genetic basis (Eaves & Eysenck, 1975), but it was not until all five major trait dimensions were systematically studied (e.g., Riemann, Angleitner, & Strelau, 1997) that psychologists learned that essentially all personality traits are heritable. We now know that the FFM structure itself is genetically based (Yamagata et al., 2006). Such findings inspired FFT's postulate 1b. *Origin*, which asserts that personality traits are endogenous basic tendencies (McCrae & Costa, 2008b). Note that this postulate applies to the interpersonal NEO-PI-R facets in Figure 6.1, which showed additive genetic influences in German and Canadian samples (Jang, McCrae, Angleitner, Riemann, & Livesley, 1998).

FFT is an attempt to synthesize many such lines of research, and it is summarized in Figure 6.2 (a more elaborate version of this figure is presented in McCrae & Costa, 2008b). Personality is here viewed as a system whose central components are basic tendencies (specifically personality traits) and characteristic adaptations, with inputs from biology and the environment, and with the stream of experience and behavior as its output. The arrows in the figure indicate the causal pathways that are postulated by the theory.

FFT draws a crucial distinction between *basic tendencies* (including personality traits) and acquired *characteristic adaptations* (including skills, habits, attitudes, roles, relationships, and so on). Basic tendencies

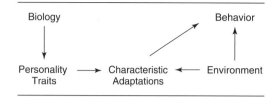

FIGURE 6.2 A Simplified Representation of the Personality System
Arrows indicate the direction of postulated causal influences.
Source: Adapted from "Human Nature and Culture," by R. R. McCrae, 2004, *Journal of Research in Personality, 38.*

are abstract potentials that give rise to specific patterns of thought and behavior that are learned in particular social environments. The clearest analogy is with language: Every healthy infant has a capacity for human language, but the particular language acquired—Norwegian, Japanese, or Hindi—is purely a function of the environment. FFT claims that traits like Openness to Experience and Conscientiousness—indeed, all personality traits—are also abstract capacities that come to be expressed in culturally conditioned patterns of behavior (this is why traits appear only on the left side of the figure). The patterns of behavior are not the trait, but the trait can usually be inferred from the behaviors. Indeed, traits *must* be inferred from behaviors, wishes, attitudes, and other characteristic adaptations: They are no more directly observable than the abstract capacity for language. Such a view has important consequences for trait assessment. Personality inventories can only ask questions about habits, beliefs, goals, and other characteristic adaptations, but they are intended to allow inferences about underlying traits.

The arrow from biology to traits in Figure 6.2 reflects the known heritability of personality traits, and many theories of personality would acknowledge some constitutional basis for personality. What is most distinctive, and controversial, about FFT is its postulated independence of traits from the environment—indicated in

Figure 6.2 by the lack of an arrow from the environment to traits. This radical position is surely an oversimplification, but it is arguably a heuristically valuable one, and it is consistent with a surprising array of well-documented findings: The essential absence of any effect of the environment shared by children in the same family (Plomin & Daniels, 1987), the limited influence of child-rearing variables on adult traits (McCrae & Costa, 1988), the presence of the same five factors in widely different cultures (McCrae, Terracciano, & 78 Members of the Personality Profiles of Cultures Project, 2005), the stability of traits in adults despite intervening life experiences (Costa, Metter, & McCrae, 1994), and the weakness of historical cohort effects in studies of adult age differences (McCrae et al., 2000). All of these findings are understandable if one assumes that personality traits are insulated from the environment in their origin and development.

In FFT, saying that traits are *endogenous* does not necessarily mean that they are early-appearing. Infants do have temperaments that correspond to personality traits, but early temperament tends to be weakly related to adult personality (e.g., Caspi & Silva, 1995). This might reflect modifying influences of the environment on early temperamental traits during development, but FFT offers a different interpretation: Postulate 1c. *Development* states that traits change over time as a result of intrinsic maturation, in large part because of the unfolding over time of genetic influences. Hair color, too, is genetically determined, but a blond infant may become a brunette in adolescence and gray-haired in middle-age.

Although genetics are important in FFT, the theory has a broader conception of biological bases. Antidepressant medications, for example, affect personality trait levels (Costa, Bagby, Herbst, & McCrae, 2005) in ways that are consistent with FFT. Conditions such as Alzheimer's disease also alter personality (Strauss, Pasupathi, & Chatterjee, 1993).

The postulated independence of FFM traits from the environment most certainly does not mean that the environment does not matter; it is crucial for the development of characteristic adaptations. A person may be born with the disposition to be talkative, but the language he or she speaks is determined solely by the environment. Indeed, culture and the social environment are central in the formation of a whole host of phenomena of great importance to psychologists, including knowledge, skills, beliefs, tastes, values, prejudices, habits, routines, roles, relationships, and the self-concept. All of these are also shaped by personality traits, which is why these adaptations are characteristic of the person.

The personality system in Figure 6.2 can be interpreted as operating on two time scales. In the moment, specific behaviors and experiences arise as a joint function of characteristic adaptations and the immediate environmental situation: One's choice of dinner at a restaurant reflects both one's food preferences (and one's habits of thrift) and the offerings on the menu. Over a lifetime, accumulated behaviors and experiences constitute the *objective biography*, "every significant thing that a man [or woman] felt and thought and said and did from the start to the finish of his [or her] life" (Murray & Kluckhohn, 1953, p. 30). On this broader time scale, characteristic adaptations themselves are a joint function of personality traits and the social environment. Becoming a physician (a role that is likely central to one's self-concept), for example, may result from intellectual interests, altruistic motives, and a degree of self-discipline and achievement striving that all reflect personality traits such as Openness, Agreeableness, and Conscientiousness; but it also depends on one's educational opportunities, financial resources, and the support of one's family and spouse.

FFT AT THE INTERPERSONAL LEVEL

From the perspective of interpersonal psychology, the major shortcoming of Figure 6.2 is that it says very little about interactions between people. From Sullivan (1953) to Wiggins (2003), interpersonal theorists have focused their attention outside the person and onto relationships between people. Carson (1969) went so far as to define personality as "nothing more (or less) than the patterned regularities that may be observed in an individual's relations with other persons" (p. 26; cited in Wiggins, 2003). Clearly, FFT takes a broader view of personality, but it is one that can accommodate interpersonal concerns.

Consider the diagram in Figure 6.3, which expands FFT to represent interpersonal interactions. Here the personality systems of two people (P_1 and P_2) are shown together; for P_2 the usual arrangement from Figure 6.2 has been inverted to bring it face-to-face with P_1. These two systems mesh though the identification of P_1's output (Behavior$_1$) with P_2's input (Environment$_2$), and vice-versa. These two people can be seen as conducting a conversation, in which each makes a statement in turn in response to the other's communication. It is in such a model that the principle of complementarity is supposed to operate: An assertive behavior on the part of P_1 should be answered by a submissive behavior from P_2, which in turn should stimulate further assertive behaviors from P_1.

Sadler and Woody (2003) provided clear support for this model in a study of mixed-sex couples who interacted over a 20-minute period. Using self-, partner-, and observer ratings of interpersonal behavior, they showed that dominant behaviors in one partner elicited submissive behaviors in the other, and that affiliative behaviors were reciprocated. However, other studies of complementarity show that this simple and elegant pattern is often violated, especially at the level of individual behaviors. Strong and colleagues (1988) used a confederate in a dyad to initiate behaviors and coded the response of the subject. They found many significant effects, often in the overall direction of complementarity, but noted

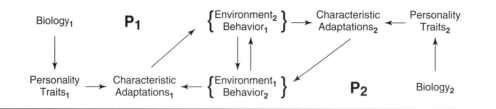

FIGURE 6.3   A Simplified Representation of Interacting Personality Systems for Person 1 (P_1) and Person 2 (P_2)

that "a specific interpersonal behavior does not impel a specific response from the other."

FFT offers one explanation for that finding: Behavior is not simply a function of the environment (that is, the behavior of the other); it is also shaped by preexisting characteristic adaptations that reflect enduring personality traits. Individuals high in Assertiveness and low in Compliance are not likely to adopt the role of submissive followers simply because they are paired with an assertive partner. Some interpretations of the complementarity principle recognize the role of interpersonal traits, and Sadler and Woody (2003) also showed that enduring traits (as rated by self and friends) were independent predictors of situational dominance and affiliation. Trait and interpersonal psychologists should be able to agree that human behavior is both interactive and proactive.

However, from the perspective of the FFM, it seems clear that traits outside the interpersonal circumplex can also affect the interpretation and evaluation of others' behaviors in complex ways. For example, Bollmer, Harris, Milich, and Georgesen (2003) examined responses of experimental subjects to teasing by a confederate. Participants who were closed to experience were put off by this behavior, apparently because it violated their norm expectations for proper behavior from experimental subjects; open participants took it in stride (McCrae & Sutin, 2009).

Some researchers have been concerned with complementarity in terms of the reciprocal roles that individuals develop (Tracey,

Ryan, & Jaschik-Herman, 2001). Because roles and relationships are characteristic adaptations, such a view is consistent with FFT. Surely complementary role theory does explain much human behavior. Army privates learn to take orders from sergeants; coworkers may become fast friends or bitter enemies; spouses may negotiate an enduring division of household labor. Behavioral responses are then more predictable.

But even that model fails to take into account the fact that characteristic adaptations are shaped in part by personality traits, which are themselves largely immune to influence from the environment. Some privates receive dishonorable discharges because they can never adjust to taking orders. Some workers avoid emotional involvement with their fellow employees. Some household chores never get done, despite repeated negotiations. Traits, like truth, will out.

THE ORIGINS OF INTERPERSONAL ORIENTATIONS AND ATTACHMENTS

If interpersonal relationships do not exhaust the personality sphere, they clearly occupy a very important place in it. We may be devoted to completing tasks, or to discovering truths, or to avoiding dangers, but for most people the significance of the task lies in its importance to others; the thrill of discovery is tied to its public announcement; the dangers we shun and the protection we seek are usually social in nature. Our lives are continually grounded in social interaction and evaluation—even if only in the imagination, as when Maslow addressed his thoughts "to people I love and respect. To Socrates and Aristotle and Spinoza and Thomas Jefferson" (Maddi & Costa, 1972, p. 147). People whose lives are not essentially social are considered pathological; they may suffer a form of autism.

Clinicians have always had a particular interest in patterns of interpersonal relationships, because disturbances in relationships are among the chief features of mental disorders, and among the major reasons individuals consult therapists. Psychodynamic theorists have frequently noted that patients repeat the same dysfunctional interpersonal patterns across a succession of relationships, never seeming to learn from past experience. The psychoanalytic notion of transference is based on the idea that significant interpersonal patterns are unconsciously transferred to the therapist. Attachment theory (Bowlby, 1969) assumes that basic patterns of relating to others are established early in life and played out again (often inappropriately) in adult relationships.

Voluminous research on adult attachment styles shows that people can be meaningfully characterized by the ways in which they relate to significant others (Shaver & Mikulincer, 2005), and this might seem to pose a challenge to FFT. At least in its simplest form, attachment theory suggests that early environmental influences, rather than biologically based traits, ultimately shape adults' social, especially intimate, interactions.

Is this true, and is it inconsistent with FFT? If there were strong evidence for enduring influences of infant or child attachment experiences on adult behavior, FFT might accommodate it by classifying attachment style as an early-formed characteristic adaptation. After all, at an early age most children acquire a regional speech accent that they usually retain throughout their life. This is clearly a characteristic adaptation, and the same might be true of attachment styles: Analogously, they might function like interpersonal accents that are early acquired and long retained.

A strong case for this interpretation might be made if adult attachment were relatively isolated from other aspects of personality. Suppose we found an individual who was generally well-adjusted, optimistic, and well able to handle stress at work, but who was chronically insecure in intimate relationships. We might diagnose this as a case of anxious attachment style, perhaps attributable to early life experience, in an individual temperamentally low in Neuroticism. More generally, if attachment style were a purely environmentally determined characteristic adaptation—as regional accent presumably is—FFT would predict that it would be uncorrelated with personality traits. The literature, however, is clear on this point: Adult attachment is rather strongly related to (though not entirely explained by) general personality traits (Shaver & Brennan, 1992). In particular, anxious attachment is consistently related to trait measures of Neuroticism (Noftle & Shaver, 2006).

The classic psychodynamic interpretation of this correlation would be that early life experience affects general personality traits—a view explicitly disputed by FFT, which allows no arrow of influence from experience to traits. Experimental studies manipulating attachment experiences in infants and children would be most revealing, but surely unethical. Longitudinal studies linking experiences assessed in childhood with adult personality would be the best feasible design, but (considering the importance of childhood experience as an explanatory variable in the history of personality theory) there are astoundingly few such studies (e.g., Kagan & Moss, 1962; see McCrae & Costa, 1994). Results from these few studies are meager and mixed. For example, Harrington (1993) examined associations of observed and self-reported *poisonous pedagogy* (PP; Miller, 1983) in mothers and fathers of four- to five-year-olds and related it to rated personality when the children were 18 and 23. He found predicted associations of poorer adult adjustment with observed maternal

PP, but not with observed paternal PP or self-reported PP from either parent. Harris (1998) later argued that any associations between parenting styles and adult personality may be due to shared genes: Neurotic parents may have maladjusted children not because they are poor at child-rearing, but because they pass along the genes for Neuroticism. That interpretation is bolstered by evidence from adoption studies that parental personality is essentially unrelated to adopted children's adult personality: Bouchard and Loehlin (2001) summarized the correlations as ranging from $-.03$ to $.08$.

If parenting does not causally influence personality traits, why are personality and attachment style linked in adults? FFT would suggest two possibilities. First, the child's (P_1) personality might influence the parent's (P_2) behavior, and thereby the child's own learned attachment style (via the path in Figure 6.3: Personality Traits$_1$ → Characteristic Adaptations$_1$ → Behavior$_1$/Environment$_2$ → Behavior$_2$/Environment$_1$ → Characteristic Adaptations$_1$). In this scenario, a child with a difficult temperament might elicit punitive parenting that would teach the child that intimate relationships are dangerous. Second, FFT might suggest that adult personality traits are an independent contributor to adult attachment style. Both innate dispositions and early learning might be reflected in the way adults react in intimate relationships.

The first of these explanations may well describe what happens in childhood, but as an account of adult associations, it depends on the further assumption that both personality traits and attachment styles are very stable from childhood to adulthood. Those assumptions are questionable. Although traits in children as young as three years old show some associations with adult personality, the correlations are very small (Caspi & Silva, 1995), consistent with a large literature showing that personality stability increases with age (Roberts & DelVecchio, 2000). Despite the importance of early experience in attachment theory,

meta-analytic data show only modest associations of attachment between age one and age 19, weighted $r = .27$, total $N = 218$ (Fraley, 2002). The modest magnitude of this correlation may reflect the modifying influence of other environmental inputs during childhood and adolescence, but the bottom line is that early attachment in itself has limited influence on attachment styles in young adults. By contrast, adult attachment styles are rather strongly predicted by adult personality traits (e.g., Noftle & Shaver, 2006), and because traits endure for decades, these associations are likely to remain strong for many years (Costa & McCrae, 1985).

Both trait and developmental (e.g., Blatt & Luyten, in press) approaches have long influenced interpersonal psychology, and both are well-represented in contemporary research. Conceptually, attachment theory has captured the imagination of a generation of personality researchers (Shaver & Mikulincer, 2005), and empirically, measures of adult attachment have been shown to predict relationship quality above and beyond the contribution of general personality traits (Noftle & Shaver, 2006). Our intention in discussing the theory was not to minimize its importance. Instead, we hoped to show that FFT provides a fresh perspective on the concepts of attachment in intimate relationships.

SUMMARY AND CONCLUSIONS

The Five-Factor Model is a taxonomy of traits; two of its factors (Extraversion and Agreeableness) define the plane of the interpersonal circumplex. However, the three other factors (Neuroticism, Openness, and Conscientiousness) are also relevant to interpersonal behavior. Five-Factor Theory is an attempt to make sense of a body of findings from research on the FFM; its most distinctive claim is that personality traits (including interpersonal traits) are endogenous tendencies, essentially independent of environmental influences. At the interpersonal level, FFT provides a model that can accommodate social influences on behavior but also explains some of the limits of social influence. Interpersonal psychologists may find other ways to extend the scope of FFT.

We used FFT in an attempt to shed new light on attachment theory. Other topics in interpersonal psychology, such as person perception, personality disorders (McCrae, Löckenhoff, & Costa, 2005), and psychotherapy (Harkness & McNulty, 2002) may also benefit from the FFT perspective. There is no doubt that the Five-Factor Model has proven useful in integrating empirical trait research (John, Naumann, & Soto, 2008); it remains to be seen whether Five-Factor Theory will be equally useful in integrating the theoretical concepts of personality and interpersonal theory.

References

American Psychiatric Association. (1994). *Diagnostic and statistical manual of mental disorders* (4th ed.). Washington, DC: Author.

Ansell, E. B., & Pincus, A. L. (2004). Interpersonal perceptions of the Five-Factor Model of personality: An examination using the structural summary method for circumplex data. *Multivariate Behavioral Research, 39*, 167–201.

Becker, P., & Mohr, A. (2005). Psychometric arguments for the use of non-ipsatized scores in the Inventory of Interpersonal Problems (IIP-D) [in German]. *Zeitschrift für Klinische Psychologie und Psychotherapie: Forschung und Praxis,, 34*, 205–214.

Blatt, S. J., & Luyten, P. (in press). Relatedness and self-definition: Basic dimensions in personality development. In S. Strack & L. M. Horowitz (Eds.), *Handbook of interpersonal psychology*. New York: Guilford Press.

Bollmer, J. M., Harris, M. J., Milich, R., & Georgesen, J. C. (2003). Taking offense: Effects of personality and teasing history on behavioral and emotional reactions to teasing. *Journal of Personality, 71*, 557–603.

Botwin, M. D., Buss, D. M., & Shackelford, T. K. (1997). Personality and mate preferences: Five factors in mate selection and marital satisfaction. *Journal of Personality, 65*, 107–136.

Bouchard, T. J., & Loehlin, J. C. (2001). Genes, evolution, and personality. *Behavior Genetics, 31*, 243–273.

Bowlby, J. (1969). *Attachment and loss: Vol. 1. Attachment*. New York: Basic Books.

Carson, R. C. (1969). *Interaction concepts of personality*. Chicago: Aldine.

Caspi, A., & Silva, P. A. (1995). Temperamental qualities at age 3 predict personality traits in young adulthood: Longitudinal evidence from a birth cohort. *Child Development, 66*, 486–498.

Costa, P. T., Jr., Bagby, R. M., Herbst, J. H., & McCrae, R. R. (2005). Personality self-reports are concurrently reliable and valid during acute depressive episodes. *Journal of Affective Disorders, 89*, 45–55.

Costa, P. T., Jr., & McCrae, R. R. (1985). Concurrent validation after 20 years: Implications of personality stability for its assessment. In J. N. Butcher & C. D. Spielberger (Eds.), *Advances in personality assessment* (Vol. 4, pp. 31–54). Hillsdale, NJ: Erlbaum.

Costa, P. T., Jr., & McCrae, R. R. (1992). *Revised NEO Personality Inventory (NEO-PI-R) and NEO Five-Factor Inventory (NEO-FFI) professional manual*. Odessa, FL: Psychological Assessment Resources.

Costa, P. T., Jr., Metter, E. J., & McCrae, R. R. (1994). Personality stability and its contribution to successful aging. *Journal of Geriatric Psychiatry, 27*, 41–59.

Digman, J. M. (1990). Personality structure: Emergence of the Five-Factor Model. *Annual Review of Psychology, 41*, 417–440.

Eaves, L. J., & Eysenck, H. J. (1975). The nature of extraversion: A genetical analysis. *Journal of Personality and Social Psychology, 32*, 102–112.

Fraley, R. C. (2002). Attachment stability from infancy to adulthood: Meta-analysis and dynamic modeling of developmental mechanisms. *Personality and Social Psychology Review, 6*, 123–151.

Harkness, A. R., & McNulty, J. L. (2002). Implications of personality individual differences science for clinical work on personality disorders. In P. T. Costa, Jr., & T. A. Widiger (Eds.), *Personality disorders and the Five-Factor Model of personality* (2nd ed., pp. 391–403). Washington, DC: American Psychological Association.

Harrington, D. M. (1993). Child-rearing antecedents of suboptimal personality: Exploring aspects of Alice Miller's concept of poisonous pedagogy.

In D. C. Funder, R. D. Parke, C. Tomlinson-Keasey, & K. Widaman (Eds.), *Studying lives through time: Personality and development* (pp. 289–313). Washington, DC: American Psychological Association.

Harris, J. R. (1998). *The nurture assumption: Why children turn out the way they do*. New York: The Free Press.

Horowitz, L. M., Alden, L. E., Wiggins, J. S., & Pincus, A. L. (2000). *Inventory of Interpersonal Problems manual*. San Antonio, TX: Psychological Corporation.

Horowitz, L. M., Rosenberg, S. E., Baer, B. A., Ureño, G., & Villaseñor, V. S. (1988). Inventory of Interpersonal Problems: Psychometric properties and clinical applications. *Journal of Consulting and Clinical Psychology, 56*, 885–892.

Jang, K. L., McCrae, R. R., Angleitner, A., Riemann, R., & Livesley, W. J. (1998). Heritability of facet-level traits in a cross-cultural twin sample: Support for a hierarchical model of personality. *Journal of Personality and Social Psychology, 74*, 1556–1565.

John, O. P., Naumann, L., & Soto, C. J. (2008). Paradigm shift to the integrative Big Five taxonomy: Discovery, measurement, and conceptual issues. In O. P. John, R. W. Robins, & L. A. Pervin (Eds.), *Handbook of personality: Theory and research* (3rd ed., pp. 114–158). New York: Guilford Press.

Kagan, J., & Moss, H. A. (1962). *From birth to maturity*. New York: John Wiley & Sons.

Kelly, E. L., & Conley, J. J. (1987). Personality and compatibility: A prospective analysis of marital stability and marital satisfaction. *Journal of Personality and Social Psychology, 52*, 27–40.

Kiesler, D. J. (1983). The 1982 interpersonal circle: A taxonomy for complementarity in human transactions. *Psychological Review, 90*, 185–214.

Leary, T. (1957). *Interpersonal diagnosis of personality*. New York: Ronald Press.

Maddi, S. R., & Costa, P. T., Jr. (1972). *Humanism in personology: Allport, Maslow and Murray*. Chicago: Aldine.

McCrae, R. R. (1996). Social consequences of experiential openness. *Psychological Bulletin, 120*, 323–337.

McCrae, R. R. (2004). Human nature and culture: A trait perspective. *Journal of Research in Personality, 38*, 3–14.

McCrae, R. R., & Costa, P. T., Jr. (1988). Recalled parent-child relations and adult personality. *Journal of Personality, 56*, 417–434.

McCrae, R. R., & Costa, P. T., Jr. (1989). The structure of interpersonal traits: Wiggins's circumplex and the Five-Factor Model. *Journal of Personality and Social Psychology, 56*, 586–595.

McCrae, R. R., & Costa, P. T., Jr. (1994). The paradox of parental influence: Understanding retrospective studies of parent-child relations and adult personality. In C. Perris, W. A. Arrindell, & M. Eisemann (Eds.), *Parenting and psychopathology* (pp. 107–125). New York: John Wiley & Sons.

McCrae, R. R., & Costa, P. T., Jr. (1996). Toward a new generation of personality theories: Theoretical contexts for the Five-Factor Model. In J. S. Wiggins (Ed.), *The Five-Factor Model of personality: Theoretical perspectives* (pp. 51–87). New York: Guilford Press.

McCrae, R. R., & Costa, P. T., Jr. (1997). Conceptions and correlates of Openness to Experience. In R. Hogan, J. A. Johnson, & S. R. Briggs (Eds.), *Handbook of personality psychology* (pp. 825–847). Orlando, FL: Academic Press.

McCrae, R. R., & Costa, P. T., Jr. (2008a). Empirical and theoretical status of the Five-Factor Model of personality traits. In G. Boyle, G. Matthews, & D. Saklofske (Eds.), *Sage Handbook of personality theory and assessment* (Vol. 1, pp. 273–294). Los Angeles: Sage.

McCrae, R. R., & Costa, P. T., Jr. (2008b). The Five-Factor Theory of personality. In O. P. John, R. W. Robins, & L. A. Pervin (Eds.), *Handbook of personality: Theory and research* (3rd ed., pp. 159–181). New York: Guilford Press.

McCrae, R. R., Costa, P. T., Jr., Ostendorf, F., Angleitner, A., Hřebíčková, M., Avia, M. D., et al. (2000). Nature over nurture: Temperament, personality, and lifespan development. *Journal of Personality and Social Psychology, 78*, 173–186.

McCrae, R. R., & John, O. P. (1992). An introduction to the Five-Factor Model and its applications. *Journal of Personality, 60*, 175–215.

McCrae, R. R., Löckenhoff, C. E., & Costa, P. T., Jr. (2005). A step towards *DSM-V*: Cataloging personality-related problems in living. *European Journal of Personality, 19*, 269–270.

McCrae, R. R., Martin, T. A., Hřebíčková, M., Urbánek, T., Boomsmaa, D. I., Willemsen, G., & Costa, P. T. (2008). Personality trait similarity between spouses in four cultures. *Journal of Personality, 76,* 1137–1163.

McCrae, R. R., & Sutin, A. R. (2009). Openness to Experience. In M. R. Leary & R. H. Hoyle (Eds.), *Handbook of individual differences in social behavior* (pp. 257–273). New York: Guilford Press.

McCrae, R. R., Terracciano, A., & 78 Members of the Personality Profiles of Cultures Project. (2005). Universal features of personality traits from the observer's perspective: Data from 50 cultures. *Journal of Personality and Social Psychology, 88,* 547–561.

Miller, A. (1983). *For your own good: Hidden cruelty in child-rearing and the roots of violence.* New York: Farrar, Straus & Giroux.

Morey, L. C., Gunderson, J., Quigley, B. D., Shea, M. T., Skodol, A. E., McGlashan, T. H., … Zanarini, M. C. (2002). The representation of Borderline, Avoidant, Obsessive-Compulsive, and Schizotypal personality disorders by the Five-Factor Model of personality. *Journal of Personality Disorders, 16,* 215–234.

Murray, H. A., & Kluckhohn, C. (1953). Outline of a conception of personality. In C. Kluckhohn & H. A. Murray (Eds.), *Personality in nature, society, and culture* (2nd ed., pp. 3–52). New York: Knopf.

Noftle, E. E., & Shaver, P. R. (2006). Attachment dimensions and the Big Five personality traits: Associations and comparative ability to predict relationship quality. *Journal of Research in Personality, 40,* 179–208.

Oxford, J. (1986). The rules of interpersonal complementarity: Does hostility beget hostility and dominance, submission? *Psychological Review, 93,* 365–377.

Plomin, R., & Daniels, D. (1987). Why are children in the same family so different from one another? *Behavioral and Brain Sciences, 10,* 1–16.

Riemann, R., Angleitner, A., & Strelau, J. (1997). Genetic and environmental influences on personality: A study of twins reared together using the self- and peer report NEO-FFI scales. *Journal of Personality, 65,* 449–475.

Roberts, B. W., & DelVecchio, W. F. (2000). The rank-order consistency of personality traits from childhood to old age: A quantitative review of longitudinal studies. *Psychological Bulletin, 126,* 3–25.

Sadler, P., & Woody, E. (2003). Is who you are who you're talking to? Interpersonal style and complementarity in mixed-sex interactions. *Journal of Personality and Social Psychology, 84,* 80–96.

Shaver, P. R., & Brennan, K. A. (1992). Attachment styles and the "Big Five" personality traits: Their connection with each other and with romantic relationship outcomes. *Personality and Social Psychology Bulletin, 18,* 536–545.

Shaver, P. R., & Mikulincer, M. (2005). Attachment theory and research: Resurrection of the psychodynamic approach to personality. *Journal of Research in Personality, 39,* 22–45.

Strauss, M. E., Pasupathi, M., & Chatterjee, A. (1993). Concordance between observers in descriptions of personality change in Alzheimer's disease. *Psychology and Aging, 8,* 475–480.

Strong, S. R., Hills, H. I., Kilmartin, C. T., DeVries, H., Lanier, K., Nelson, B. N., … Meyer, C. W. (1988). The dynamic relations among interpersonal behaviors: A test of complementarity and anticomplementarity. *Journal of Personality and Social Psychology, 54,* 798–810.

Sullivan, H. S. (1953). *The interpersonal theory of psychiatry.* New York: Norton.

Tracey, T. J. G., Rounds, J., & Gurtman, M. (1996). Examination of the general factor with the interpersonal circumplex structure: Application to the Inventory of Interpersonal Problems. *Multivariate Behavioral Research, 31,* 441–466.

Tracey, T. J. G., Ryan, J. M., & Jaschik-Herman, B. (2001). Complementarity of interpersonal circumplex traits. *Personality and Social Psychology Bulletin, 27,* 786–797.

Trapnell, P. D., & Wiggins, J. S. (1990). Extension of the Interpersonal Adjective Scales to include the Big Five dimensions of personality. *Journal of Personality and Social Psychology, 59,* 781–790.

Traupman, E., Smith, T. W., Uchino, B. N., Berg, C. A., Trobst, K., & Costa P. T., J. (2009). Interpersonal Circumplex octant, dominance, and affiliation scales for the NEO-PI-R. *Personality and Individual Differences, 47,* 457–463.

Wiggins, J. S. (1979). A psychological taxonomy of trait-descriptive terms: The interpersonal domain. *Journal of Personality and Social Psychology, 37,* 395–412.

Wiggins, J. S. (2003). *Paradigms of personality assessment*. New York: Guilford Press.

Wiggins, J. S. (Ed.). (1996). *The Five-Factor Model of personality: Theoretical perspectives*. New York: Guilford Press.

Wiggins, J. S., & Broughton, R. (1985). The interpersonal circle: A structural model for the integration of personality research. In R. Hogan & W. H. Jones (Eds.), *Perspectives in personality* (Vol. 1, pp. 1–47). Greenwich, CT: JAI Press.

Wiggins, J. S., & Trapnell, P. D. (1996). A dyadic-interactional perspective on the Five-Factor Model. In J. S. Wiggins (Ed.), *The Five-Factor Model of personality: Theoretical perspectives* (pp. 88–162). New York: Guilford Press.

Wiggins, J. S., Trapnell, P., & Phillips, N. (1988). Psychometric and geometric characteristics of the Revised Interpersonal Adjective Scales (IAS-R). *Multivariate Behavioral Research, 23,* 119–134.

Yamagata, S., Suzuki, A., Ando, J., Ono, Y., Kijima, N., Yoshimura, K., . . . Jang, K. L. (2006). Is the genetic structure of human personality universal? A cross-cultural twin study from North America, Europe, and Asia. *Journal of Personality and Social Psychology, 90,* 987–998.

II BASIC INTERPERSONAL PROCESSES AND MECHANISMS

7 INTERPERSONAL MOTIVATION

Martin Grosse Holtforth

Andrea Thomas

Franz Caspar

INTERPERSONAL MOTIVATION

Why does my colleague always put me down in front of others? Why does my tennis partner never complain, even after I have cancelled our matches three times in a row? Psychological answers to these questions might relate to interpersonal motivation; for example, the colleague needs to feel superior, or the tennis partner strongly fears retaliation. Such explanations refer to motivation that is directed toward other people, that is, interpersonal motivation. In this chapter, we will approach the construct of interpersonal motivation from theoretical, diagnostic, empirical, and clinical angles. We will first explicate interpersonal motivation in terms of a more general concept of human goals. Within human goals, we will distinguish between two types of goals (i.e., approach and avoidance goals) and two descriptive dimensions of goals (i.e., goal intensity and goal satisfaction). As interpersonal goals can be involved in the development of psychological problems, we will describe a goal-related conception

of the development of psychological problems and disorders. We will first present heterogeneous methods of goal assessment that include interpersonal goals. To demonstrate research applications of these measures, we will present results of studies that explore the relationships between interpersonal goals and interpersonal problems. Finally, we will demonstrate the application of interpersonal goal theory and goal assessment in clinical practice.

Goals and Interpersonal Goals

Motivation is generally concerned with the directing and activating processes that determine the selection and the intensity of behavioral tendencies. An increasing body of research supports the view that human behavior is driven by two separate motivational systems: (1) an emotion-driven implicit system and (2) a cognition-based explicit system (McClelland, Koestner, & Weinberger, 1989; Schmalt & Sokolowski, 2000). *Motives* are often assumed to be unconscious and associated with the implicit motivational system. Therefore, motives can only be measured indirectly, for example, by projective techniques such as Murray's Thematic Apperception Test (TAT; Smith, 1992). In contrast, *goals* are stored in the explicit system, are consciously accessible in a way that can be verbalized, and consequently can be assessed directly via self-report. Goals can generally be defined as "states that people seek to obtain, maintain or avoid" (Emmons, 1996, p. 314; see also Austin & Vancouver, 1996, for a review of goal concepts in psychology). Thus, according to this definition, approach goals (e.g., wishes) as well as avoidance goals (e.g., fears) can be considered goals. Goals may concern varying "objects" (purposes), for example, individual achievements, personal growth, or interactions with other people. *Interpersonal goals* are a specific subset of all possible human goals and subsume strivings that can be satisfied or frustrated, respectively, only in interpersonal situations. It is generally assumed that goals are functionally related to superordinate motivational constructs such as motives or needs, as well as to subordinate strategies and behaviors (Austin & Vancouver, 1996; Michalak & Grosse Holtforth, 2006). In other words, the same goal may serve as the master for subordinate behaviors, but at the same time as the servant for superordinate needs.

The concept of a *Plan*[1] (Miller, Galanter, & Pribram, 1960) links goal concepts at several levels in the goal hierarchy. The criterion for the position in the hierarchy is the instrumental relation between elements: Means are positioned below the purposes to which they serve, and vice versa. The same element, which is a purpose when viewed from below, serves as a means when viewed from above. In Figure 7.1, "reduce tensions" is the purpose of binge eating, and so on (viewed from below); concurrently, it is the means for protecting oneself from injuries (viewed from above). A Plan includes the motivational component (a goal or purpose) and at least some minimal behavioral means of satisfying that goal. Furthermore, low-level Plans (e.g., interrupt the therapist in order to exert control in the therapy situation) have a motivational component by definition. A *Plan structure* is the entire set of instrumental strategies that an individual has acquired throughout life to realize his or her most important needs.

When speaking of *motives*, one usually refers to motivational constructs at a higher level in the goal hierarchy. Convention dictates at which level high-level goals are called *motives*. To be consistent with research on goal constructs, we will continue to speak of *goals*, even when we refer to goal constructs at a higher level of abstraction. Needs are assumed to be at the top of the goal hierarchy, i.e., they do not *serve* any other motivational construct. The related concept of *values* also describes motivational constructs at a higher level of abstraction. By definition, values are consciously accessible. Thus when it comes to assessment by self-report (see the next paragraph), goals resemble values in that they have to be consciously accessible to be reported.

Interpersonal motives are central concepts in human development. According to attachment theory (Bowlby, 1977), two fundamental motives, *agency* and *communion*, emerge as consequences of a child's specific experiences made when trying to satisfy his or her needs in interpersonal interactions during the course of individual development. An innate human attachment system is assumed to regulate the building and maintaining of an inner emotional bond to others. A child's secure attachment toward primary caregivers is seen as the prerequisite for autonomously taking charge of the self and exploring the environment. Early interpersonal experiences are internalized in an attachment system, the so-called "inner working model" that is assumed to structure interpersonal perception as well as behavior. In later development, the communion motive may differentiate into interactional goals of intimacy, sociality, or community, whereas agentic

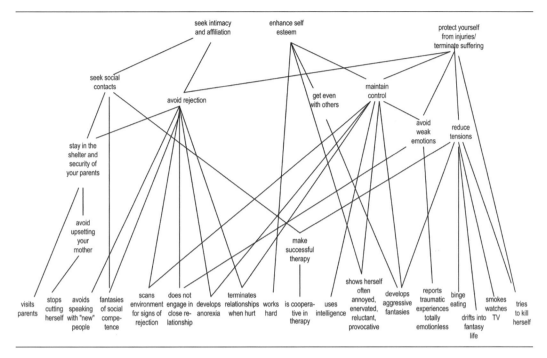

FIGURE 7.1 A Sample Plan

goals may differentiate into goals of autonomy, achievement, or control.

Consequently in adults, agency and communion represent the top of a person's hierarchy of interpersonal goals. Agency (also called *efficacy* or *control*) refers to the pursuit of independence and autonomy of the individual and aims at control, assertiveness, and self-enhancement. Communion (also called *community* or *love*) refers to the self as a part of a community and is geared toward closeness, affection, and cooperation. From an evolutionary perspective (e.g., Hogan & Roberts, 2000), the motives of agency and communion reflect two fundamental life tasks, that is, "getting along" (communion) and "getting ahead" (agency; Bakan, 1966). The concepts of agency and communion also correspond well with two of the four basic psychological needs as proposed by Grawe (2004, 2007), i.e., attachment and control. In interpersonal theory, agency and communion define the two dimensions of the interpersonal circle (Kiesler, 1983; Leary,

1957) that systematically captures various kinds of interpersonal phenomena. The interpersonal circle is described in more detail in chapters 4 and 19 of this volume.

Types and Dimensions of Goals

Two distinctions are important in the analysis of goals: (1) Approach versus avoidance goals, as well as (2) goal intensity versus goal satisfaction. Elliot and Covington (2001) explained that

> Approach and avoidance motivation differ as a function of valence: In approach motivation, behavior is instigated or directed by a positive/desirable event or possibility; in avoidance motivation, behavior is instigated or directed by a negative/undesirable event or possibility. (p. 73f)

Similarly, approach and avoidance goals can be distinguished. Whereas approach goals are thought to satisfy psychological needs, avoidance goals serve to prevent need frustration (Grawe, 2004). On closer inspection, however, taking the person's whole Plan structure into account, an apparently approach-oriented goal (e.g., to be an excellent worker or to be a caring husband) might turn out to serve predominantly avoidance purposes (to avoid criticism by overcritical parents or to avoid losing one's spouse) at a higher level of the goal hierarchy. Similarly, predominantly approach-oriented goals might involve lower-level avoidance strategies and behaviors. For example, trying to please one's spouse might also involve not smoking in his or her presence to avoid upsetting him or her. Thus, the question of whether a person's behavior is dominated by his or her approach or avoidance system (Gray, 1987) turns out to be a complex question of *more or less* rather than of *either-or*.

As illustrated by the popular wisdom in the song "You Can't Always Get What You Want" (Jagger & Richards, 1969), intense wishes are by no means always satisfied. Luckily, intense fears do not always come true either. In fact, this adage suggests that two different dimensions need to be distinguished for the description of goals: (a) the intensity and (b) the satisfaction of goals (Little, 1989). Insufficient satisfaction of needs is regarded as a necessary condition for the development of psychological disorders, whereas overly intense goals may contribute to the development of disorders via goal frustration (Grawe, 2004).

Goals and Psychological Problems

Goal satisfaction determines a person's affective reaction to an interpersonal encounter. If a person can satisfy an important goal, then he or she is likely to experience positive feelings. In contrast, if a goal is frustrated, then negative feelings like anger or sadness result (Shechtman & Horowitz, 2006). Consistency theory (Grawe, 2004) assumes that a person can achieve happiness by finding suitable ways to satisfy all of the four psychological needs postulated to exist in a person's life, i.e., the need for attachment, control, self-worth, and pleasure (see also Epstein, 1990). This

includes developing higher-level goals that have the potential to satisfy the person's psychological needs, finding strategies and behaviors that adequately serve to reach the goals, as well as preventing the goals, strategies, and behaviors from inhibiting each other, i.e., from being in conflict with each other. In other ways, happiness requires developing a need-fulfilling Plan structure. In consistency theory, the failure to sufficiently satisfy one's psychological needs (incongruence) chiefly contributes to the development and maintenance of deficient well-being, psychological problems, and psychological disorders.

If goals are repeatedly frustrated, a person might conceptualize the failure to satisfy important wishes or the failure to prevent important fears from coming true together with the associated negative feelings as a psychological *problem*. Correspondingly, interpersonal problems can be viewed as chronic frustrations of important interpersonal goals (Grosse Holtforth, Pincus, Grawe, & Mauler, 2007). For example, people who perceive themselves as constantly being misunderstood by significant others may experience aversive feelings such as anxiety, anger, sadness, or worthlessness. Applying the assumptions of Grawe's (2004) consistency theory to the interpersonal domain, the insufficient satisfaction of important interpersonal goals (*interpersonal incongruence*) may be one of the most important factors contributing to the development and maintenance of psychological problems, psychological disorders, and reduced well-being.

Insufficient need satisfaction may have various sources, a part of which is related to goals. For example, goals may be too strong or too weak, or parts of the Plan structure might conflict with each other. With regard to overly strong goals, Reiss and Havercamp (1996) pointed out:

> People who crave too much love, too much attention, too much acceptance, too much companionship, or too much of some other fundamental reinforcer are at risk for aberrant behavior because normative behavior

does not produce the desired amounts of reinforcement. (p. 621)

Thus, an overemphasis on particular interpersonal goals might prevent a person from cultivating behaviors that are necessary to satisfy other needs. However, problems may arise in other ways as well. In the extreme, a person may completely sacrifice one goal in order to satisfy another overly strong goal. For example, if an individual has been told from childhood onward that success is the most important thing in life, he or she might neglect friendship or altruism in favor of trying to excel. Along these lines, Helgeson and Fritz (1999) distinguished between agency and unmitigated agency as well as between communion and unmitigated communion. In unmitigated agency, the individual focuses exceedingly on the self to the total neglect of other people's interests; and, in unmitigated communion, the individual excessively highlights the needs of others to the neglect of his or her own self-interests. In mitigated agency or mitigated communion, the individual balances his or her agentic goals with communal goals. Empirically, unmitigated agency and communion seem to be associated with interpersonal and health problems (Helgeson & Fritz, 1999).

Unmitigated agency and unmitigated communion are instances of the more general concept of motivational conflicts. If conflicting responses (e.g., approach and avoidance responses) are activated simultaneously in the same social situation, the conflict may leave both goals insufficiently satisfied. Thus, goal conflicts (e.g., Emmons, King, & Sheldon, 1993; Lauterbach, 1996) are assumed to be powerful sources of interpersonal incongruence (Grawe, 2004). In the interpersonal realm, such inner conflicts may arise between agency- and communion-oriented interpersonal goals (Exline & Lobel, 1999; Santor & Zuroff, 1997). For example, in a close relationship, an agentic goal such as to assert oneself regarding the next vacation destination might be at odds with the communion-oriented goal of being close to one's spouse.

Depending on the strength of each goal, one or the other goal might be frustrated (e.g., touring a bustling city contrary to the wishes of one's spouse for a quiet holiday versus spending two weeks in a reclusive mountain cottage to please the spouse).

Under the wider perspective of Plans, motivational conflicts usually originate as a negative effect of one Plan upon another. Means that are used as a part of one Plan can have negative side effects for another Plan. For example, an employee's assertive request for a promotion, serving the Plans of earning more money, and/or achieving a more powerful position in a company, may create tension with his/her superior, and thus have a real or imagined negative side effect upon the Plan of avoiding tension, which serves the Plan of maintaining a good relationship with the superior. As a result of such conflicts, the employee may abolish ideas that she or he might ask for a promotion altogether, or utter the wish for a promotion in such a nonassertive way (e.g., taking back nonverbally what he or she states verbally, as a compromise between demanding promotion and avoiding tension), that the behavior is overall ineffective. As the examples demonstrate, the Plan perspective helps to analyze and pinpoint such conflicts in terms of concrete side effects. A special case is so-called "conflict schemata": Grawe (2004) has used this term for schemata, the activation of which automatically triggers negative emotions and avoidance tendencies as soon as the approach component of the schema is activated. For example, an attachment schema may include strategies to satisfy attachment needs, but might also include biographically engraved links to fears of vulnerability and of being abandoned as soon as one lets oneself into relationships, and therefore lead to tendencies to run away and terminate relationships when they become significant.

Motivational conflicts may result in ambiguous behaviors or behavioral inhibition. Like Buridan's donkey who starves to death while being unable to choose from which heap of hay to eat, an attempt to satisfy too many goals at the same time may lead to behavioral paralysis so that none are sufficiently satisfied. Ambiguous behaviors that result from inner conflicts might also create problems in relationships (Horowitz, 2004). For example, a woman might want to become close with a man and go on a date with him. At the same time, she may behave in a distant manner during a supposedly romantic dinner because she fears humiliation arising from her own self-disclosures due to negative experiences in previous close relationships. As a result, the man may doubt her interest in him and distance himself from her.

To empirically study the relationships among interpersonal goals, interpersonal behaviors, and interpersonal problems, as well as the relationships of these constructs with well-being and psychopathology, adequate measures of these constructs are needed, which will be described in the following section.

INTERPERSONAL GOALS

Benjamin's well-known Structural Analysis of Social Behavior (SASB; Benjamin, Rothweiler, & Critchfield, 2006; see Chapter 20) has been successfully used for the observer-coding of human interactions. There is also The Inventory of Interpersonal Problems (IIP-C; Alden, Wiggins, & Pincus, 1990; Horowitz, Rosenberg, Baer, Ureno, & Villasenor, 1988) which is also widely used as the gold standard for the assessment of interpersonal problems via self-report. Still, the development of measures of motivational constructs in the interpersonal realm is rather new (e.g., Elliot, Gable, & Mapes, 2006; Gable, 2006; Grosse Holtforth et al., 2007). We will first describe motivational measures that have originated directly from clinical applications. These measures assess interpersonal as well as noninterpersonal constructs. Second, we will describe a measure that has been constructed specifically

to assess interpersonal motivation, i.e., interpersonal values.

To assess clinically relevant goals, either idiographic or standardized methods can be used. *Plan analysis* (Caspar, 2007; Caspar, Grossmann, Unmussig, & Schramm, 2005; Grawe & Dziewas, 1978) is an idiographic method for deriving individual Plan structures "A person's Plan structure is the total of conscious and unconscious strategies this person has developed to satisfy his or her needs" (Caspar et al., 2005, p. 92). The client's Plan structure is derived from various sources of information (e.g., biographical information, behavioral observations, and the client's impact on others). The main question guiding the assessment process is: What is the explicit or implicit purpose of this client's behavior? The structure is primarily inferred by and for the therapist. Mostly a patient is not able to confirm the therapist's inferences at the beginning of treatment. However, inferences may be of pivotal clinical importance, so that therapists do not limit themselves to conclusions validated by the patient. Yet, in a simplified form (normally without jargon, and focusing on a part of the patient's functioning), Plan Analysis can be done and used in collaboration with the patient to enhance his or her understanding of certain parts of his or her functioning (Caspar, 2007). The result of a Plan analysis is a graphic display of the structure of the client's most important approach and avoidance goals as well as his or her individual means (Plans and behaviors) toward pursuing these goals. Figure 7.1 shows a simplified Plan structure.

The Inventory of Approach and Avoidance Motivation (IAAM [German: FAMOS]; Grosse Holtforth & Grawe, 2000) is a standardized measure of clinically relevant goals. On the basis of case formulations constructed by therapists using the Plan analysis method, the authors identified approach and avoidance goals that are particularly relevant for psychotherapy.

Through a stepwise test-construction process, the IAAM was developed and psychometrically evaluated. Whereas the IAAM assesses the intensity dimension of goals, the Incongruence Questionnaire (INC, German: INK, Grosse Holtforth & Grawe, 2003) was constructed to assess the satisfaction of those goals, using the same items and scale structure as the IAAM, but a different response format. Table 7.1 presents an overview of the IAAM and INC scales along with the corresponding response formats. Seven of 14 approach goals and six of nine avoidance goals can be considered as predominantly interpersonal (indicated by an asterisk in Table 7.1).

The Circumplex Scales of Interpersonal Values (CSIV; Locke, 2000) is a measure of interpersonal motivation that was developed to conform to circumplex structure.

TABLE 7.1 Goals Assessed by the Inventory of Approach and Avoidance Motivation (IAAM) and the Incongruence Questionnaire (INC), Sample Items, and Response Formats

	IAAM	INC
	Approach goals	
Intimacy[a]	Being in an intimate relationship	I've been in an intimate relationship
Affiliation[a]	Having contact with many people	I've had contact with many people
Altruism[a]	Sticking up for the weak or needy	I've stuck up for the weak or needy
Help[a]	Being taken care of by someone	I've been taken care of by someone
Recognition[a]	Being respected by others	I've been respected by others
Status[a]	Impressing others	I've impressed others
Autonomy[a]	Being independent	I've been independent
Performance	Being productive	I've been productive
Control	Being in control of myself	I've been in control of myself
Education	Pursuing broad interests	I've pursued broad interests
Spirituality	Finding meaning in life	I've found meaning in life
Variety	Living a life full of variety	I've lived a life full of variety
Self-confidence	Having faith in myself	I've had faith in myself
Self-reward	Treating myself to something	I've treated myself to something
	For me, what the item says is: 1 (*not at all*) to 5 (*extremely important*)	How satisfied have you recently been with regard to the following experiences? 1 (*not at all*) to 5 (*a lot*)
	Avoidance goals	
Separation[a]	Being left by a spouse, partner, or significant other (e.g., boyfriend, girlfriend)	I've been left by a spouse, partner, or significant other (e.g., husband, girlfriend)
Deprecation[a]	Not receiving recognition	I've not received recognition
Humiliation[a]	Humiliating myself	I've humiliated myself
Accusations[a]	Being criticized	I've been criticized
Dependency[a]	Not being able to make my own decisions	I've not been able to make my own decisions
Being hostile[a]	Treating others aggressively	I've treated others aggressively
Vulnerability	Showing my weaknesses to others	I've had to show my weaknesses to others
Helplessness	Being powerless	I've been powerless
Failure	Being inadequate	I've been inadequate
	For me, what the item says is: 1 (*not at all*) to 5 (*extremely terrible*)	Recently, I've experienced what the item says: 1 (*hardly ever*) to 5 (*very often*)

[a]Predominantly interpersonal goals.

The principle of a circumplex structure implies that variables that measure interpersonal relations are arranged around a circle in a two-dimensional space (Leary, 1957; see Chapter 19). The CSIV consists of 64 items (behavioral interpersonal goals). Eight items from each octant are used to measure the interpersonal value described by that octant. These are summed to form scales representing particular octants of interpersonal values (see Figure 7.2). Scales for the higher ranking motive dimensions of agency and communion can be computed by summarizing the single scales via specific weighted scale combinations (see Chapter 19).

As the development of tools to assess interpersonal motivation is still in its infancy, the future holds promise for the optimization of assessment in this domain.

INTERPERSONAL GOALS/VALUES AND INTERPERSONAL PROBLEMS

Given the rather recent development of measures to assess interpersonal motivation, empirical research that links interpersonal problems, goals, values, and motives is still scant. In this section, we report the results of first studies of the relationships of interpersonal goals and values to interpersonal problems.

A large part of the problems that psychotherapy patients experience are interpersonal in nature (Grosse Holtforth & Grawe, 2002; Horowitz, 1979; Uebelacker et al., 2008). In addition, the reduction of interpersonal problems is a significant part of psychotherapeutic effects (e.g., Grosse Holtforth, Lutz, & Grawe, 2006; Vittengl, Clark, & Jarrett, 2003). Correspondingly, interpersonal problems play a major role in the conceptualization, measurement, and therapy of psychological disorders. As noted above, interpersonal problems can be understood as the result of repeated frustrations of important interpersonal goals (Grosse Holtforth et al., 2007). Therefore, gaining more information about

the associations between interpersonal problems and their potential motivational sources promises to be theoretically informative as well as clinically helpful.

In a survey with clinical and nonclinical samples, Grosse Holtforth et al. (2007) analyzed the associations of various goals with diverse interpersonal problems as assessed by the German circumplex version of the IIP-64 (Horowitz, Strauss, & Kordy, 2000). Two goal types (approach and avoidance goals) and two goal dimensions (goal intensity and goal satisfaction) were analyzed. Association with interpersonal problems was specified by locating the goals in the interpersonal space via their correlations with the Dominance and Love dimensions of the interpersonal circle. As hypothesized, the results indicated that the intensity and satisfaction of approach and avoidance goal scales could be reliably localized in the interpersonal space across samples. Problems at the positive poles of the interpersonal circumplex (e.g., being too domineering or being overly nurturing) were consistently associated with strong approach goals (e.g., striving for status or intimacy). Problems at the negative poles were consistently associated with strong avoidance goals (e.g., avoiding feelings of vulnerability or humiliation). People who described themselves as too cold towards other people (an interpersonal problem) also reported insufficient intimacy in their lives (incongruence).

The observed correlations were significant but not striking. Therefore, it is important to note that one should not overgeneralize. For example, it may very well be that some people who are too submissive might actually have strong approach goals (to be advised, directed, or led). The observed locations of interpersonal goals in the interpersonal problem space yield testable hypotheses for future research regarding potential causal links between goals and behavior. For example, interpersonal problems (e.g., being too submissive) could also be explained by the suppression of dominant interpersonal behaviors

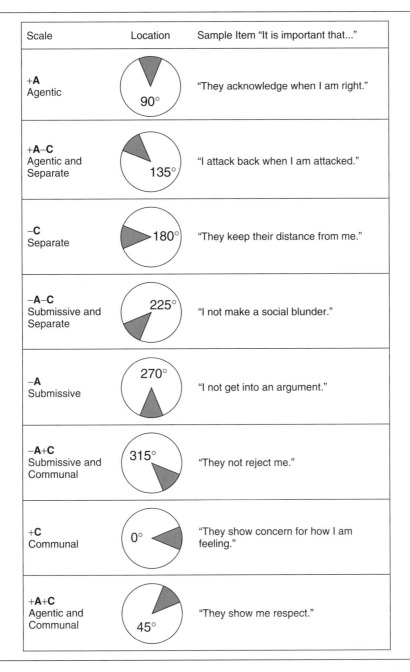

Scale	Location	Sample Item "It is important that..."
+A Agentic	90°	"They acknowledge when I am right."
+A–C Agentic and Separate	135°	"I attack back when I am attacked."
–C Separate	180°	"They keep their distance from me."
–A–C Submissive and Separate	225°	"I not make a social blunder."
–A Submissive	270°	"I not get into an argument."
–A+C Submissive and Communal	315°	"They not reject me."
+C Communal	0°	"They show concern for how I am feeling."
+A+C Agentic and Communal	45°	"They show me respect."

FIGURE 7.2   Localization and Sample Items of the Circumplex Scales of Interpersonal Values (CSIV) within the Interpersonal Space

Note: The orthogonal dimensions are defined as A = agency and C = communion.

owing to avoidance goals, thereby resulting in a submissive self-perception (Grosse Holtforth, Bents, Mauler, & Grawe, 2006).

In another study using the CSIV as a measure of interpersonal values, Bräutigam, Thomas, Suess, and Strauss (2008) observed the change of interpersonal motivation over time. The authors investigated the extent to which changes in the subjective importance of interpersonal values over psychotherapy go along with symptom reduction. The authors hypothesized that a reduction in the subjective importance of interpersonal values in the lower quadrants of the circumplex (low agentic/low communal values) would be related to therapeutic success. In their survey of 245 psychotherapy inpatients, results generally confirmed this hypothesis. Among others, changes in the subjective importance of the interpersonal goal *avoiding ridicule and rejection* (low agency and low communion), and also *avoiding arguments and anger* (low agency), were associated with larger reductions in symptom distress and interpersonal problems. Apparently, pronounced interpersonal goals that are low in agency or in both agency and communion may endanger need satisfaction and, hence, are promising targets for therapeutic interventions.

INTERPERSONAL MOTIVATION IN CLINICAL PRACTICE

For the practicing psychotherapist, interpersonal goals can be of interest in at least three ways. First, the therapist may try to foster a maximally beneficial therapeutic relationship by attuning his or her behavior to the patient's goals. Second, the therapist may try to change problematic interpersonal behavior by helping the patient modify interpersonal goals. Third and correspondingly, the therapist who understands the problem from a motivational perspective can then encourage behavior that helps the patient satisfy important goals that previously have been frustrated.

Motivational Attunement

Interpersonal behavior may or may not be well-received by another person. From a motivational perspective, how well a behavior is received by the other person depends on how effectively a behavior helps to satisfy that person's goals (i.e., satisfies a wish or disconfirms a feared expectation, or both). Interpersonal behavior is motivationally attuned if the perceived behavior of the *sender* corresponds to the goals of the *receiver* (Grosse Holtforth & Castonguay, 2005). Thus, the overarching goal of motivational attunement in psychotherapy is for the therapist to foster the therapeutic alliance (see also Chapter 30). The therapist facilitates this by providing the patient with need-satisfying experiences by means of attuning his or her interventions to the patient's most important goals. In this way, the therapist attempts to satisfy approach goals while activating avoidance goals no more than necessary. To optimally prepare motivational attunement, the therapist may assess the patient's motivation and integrate these findings into an individualized case formulation. Once the therapist has identified the patient's most salient Plans and goals, motivational attunement can be used to foster each of the essential parts of the therapeutic alliance: therapeutic bond, therapeutic tasks, and therapeutic goals (Bordin, 1979).

For example, in order to foster the therapeutic bond, the therapist may express empathy by integrating the patient's idiosyncratic goals into his or her verbal statements. The therapist could say, "It must have been very difficult for you to take care of your father after his accident, given your strong urge for personal freedom." The therapist may also try to foster the therapeutic bond by adapting the nonverbal and paraverbal behavior to the patient's goals. For example, if the patient values close relationships, he or she probably will prefer the therapist to display a warm and caring nonverbal behavior. In contrast, if the patient has a strong need for autonomy, the therapist may leave as many decisions as possible in the therapeutic process to the patient. To foster goal agreement, the therapist may help the patient to formulate explicit treatment goals that closely match his or her important approach goals. For instance, a motivationally attuned treatment goal for a patient with agoraphobia who strongly values altruistic behavior could be: "I want to be able again to take the subway to my old grandmother and help her with the groceries." Finally, the therapist may foster task agreement by selecting techniques that are motivationally appealing to the patient. For example, patients with a strong need for control might particularly benefit from a detailed explanation of the treatment rationale, from agenda setting, from continuously explicating each step in the therapy process, and so forth. In this strategy, the therapist continuously tries to find a middle way between supporting the "healthy" part of a motive that is usually at a higher level of abstraction and being specific enough to target the patient's individual concerns.

The therapist may also use motivational attunement to prevent alliance ruptures (see Chapter 31). Based on empirical studies, Ackerman and Hilsenroth (2001) categorized potential precipitants of alliance ruptures either in terms of the "therapist does something that the patient does not want or need" or "the therapist fails to do something that the patient wants or needs" (p. 183). In motivational terms, failing to do something that the patient wants or needs can be translated as "failing to satisfy the patient's approach goals," and doing something that the patient does not want as "activating the patient's avoidance goals" (Grosse Holtforth & Castonguay, 2005, p. 450). By preparing a motivation-based case formulation, the therapist will be better prepared to avoid alliance ruptures by specifically attending to the patient's wishes and fears. Consider, for example, a patient who strongly values

personal status and respect. If the therapist assumes a very directive role in therapy, the patient may perceive it as an expression of disrespect because the control of the therapeutic process is not in his or her hands. Consequently, the patient may react with withdrawal or engage in power struggles with the therapist. Therefore, the therapist must be careful when giving directions to the patient.

Changing Problematic Interpersonal Behavior by Changing Underlying Goals

If goals are hypothesized to be the potential reasons behind interpersonal problems, a therapist may try to approach the change of interpersonal problems by helping to change the supposedly underlying goals and Plans. This should lead to more adaptive interpersonal strategies and behaviors that, in turn, should lead to a better satisfaction of the full range of the person's goals. Early in the therapeutic process, the therapist might provide the patient with powerful corrective interpersonal experiences by disconfirming negative expectations or fears (Alexander & French, 1946). In addition, the therapist may develop idiographic hypotheses about what motivates a patient's problematic interpersonal behaviors. The hypotheses will guide the therapist in planning specific interventions to change the patient's interpersonal behavior by attempting to modify the patient's motivation (approach and avoidance goals).

The results of the aforementioned studies that link interpersonal motivation to interpersonal problems promise to be helpful for this purpose (Bräutigam et al., 2008; Grosse Holtforth et al., 2006; Grosse Holtforth et al., 2007). For example, the finding that submissive interpersonal problems (e.g., being too exploitable) were consistently associated with strong avoidance goals (e.g., avoiding feelings of vulnerability or humiliation) suggests that directly addressing and disconfirming such fears will be fruitful targets in therapy with overly submissive people. In addition, the finding that changes in the fears of ridicule and rejection were associated with larger reductions in symptom distress and interpersonal problems further support this notion.

The treatment of personality disorders, in particular, might profit from a motivation-focused approach. This assertion is based on the assumption that interpersonal problems as key features of personality disorders may be explained by salient frustrated motives (Horowitz, 2004). Consequently, the goal of motivation-focused interventions for personality disorders is to change problematic interpersonal behavior by changing the assumed underlying motivation. We will present two motivation-focused approaches to the conceptualization and treatment of personality disorders. Whereas the first approach was developed within the interpersonal tradition (Horowitz, 2004), the second approach emerged from clinical practice in humanistic and process-experiential psychotherapy (Sachse, 2004). Another well-established, yet not explicitly motivation-focused, interpersonal approach to the understanding and treatment of "difficult to treat patients" is that of Benjamin (1996, 2004), which is discussed in Chapter 20 of this volume.

According to their classification in the *Diagnostic and Statistical Manual of Mental Disorders* (*DSM-IV-TR*; American Psychiatric Association, 2000), personality disorders are defined as fuzzy sets. In order to diagnose a given personality disorder, a certain number of heterogeneous criteria have to be fulfilled. If a certain number of these criteria are fulfilled in a patient, he or she will be diagnosed with a specific personality disorder regardless of the specific criteria being fulfilled. For example, a person diagnosed with a narcissistic personality disorder displays a pervasive pattern of grandiosity, appears arrogant, seeks admiration, lacks empathy and/or exploits other people, whereas persons diagnosed with a dependent personality disorder display an excessive need to be taken care of, show submissive and clinging behavior, and/or experience strong fears of separation. The

DSM classification of personality disorders has been repeatedly criticized (e.g., Livesley, 2001; Westen & Shedler, 2000). Major criticisms of the *DSM-IV-TR* classification are that it does not offer a coherent conceptualization of personality disorders, that it does not provide a convincing justification for the use of fuzzy definitions, that it does not explain the co-occurrence of several personality disorders, and that it does not allow for deriving concrete interventions for the treatment of personality disorders.

In contrast, Horowitz's (2004) model of interpersonal motives (Horowitz et al., 2006) offers a comprehensive conception of personality disorders. To avoid conceptual confusion, it is important to note that Horowitz's use of the term *motives* is largely equivalent with our use of the term *higher-level goals*. In Horowitz's model, a person with a certain personality disorder is assumed to feel frustrated with respect to some salient motive. The person fails to satisfy that motive in interaction with the environment due to too rigid or too intense behaviors. As a result, the person reports characteristic recurring cognitions, fears, and interpersonal problems, which are described as the diagnostic criteria in the *DSM-IV-TR*. According to Horowitz et al. (2006), the defining criteria of most of the personality disorders can be characterized using the following four dimensions: (1) the predominant interpersonal motive, (2) the strategies employed to satisfy the motive, (3) negative emotions resulting from the frustration of the predominant motive, and (4) specific strategies to regulate these negative emotions. For example, whereas the organizing motive of a narcissistic personality disorder is the unrestricted admiration by other people, the organizing motive of a dependent personality disorder is the avoidance of helplessness. People who behave narcissistically may brag about their exceptional achievements, whereas dependent people may cling to others and be overly compliant with whatever another person says or wants. As a consequence, people with a narcissistic personality disorder often appear rather arrogant and repel other people. Conversely, interacting with a person who has a dependent personality disorder might leave another person frustrated—for example, feeling used or excessively burdened. In response to failures to satisfy the predominant interpersonal motive, a person with a personality disorder may experience negative emotions, show maladaptive behavioral strategies (e.g., oversensitive counterattacks), or retreat to maladaptive coping strategies (e.g., abusing drugs or alcohol). In the treatment of personality disorders according to Horowitz's model, a therapist will try to clarify and modify the various sources of the patient's motive frustrations on all four descriptive dimensions (motives, strategies, emotions, and emotion regulation).

Departing from clinical practice in process-experiential therapy ("clarification-oriented therapy"), Sachse (2004) proposed a similar conceptualization and treatment of personality disorders. Sachse's model of dual action regulation assumes that over their lives, people with personality disorders have developed a preponderance of certain motives as well as dysfunctional interactional goals, strategies, behaviors, and cognitions for the satisfaction of these motives. These *game structures* constitute the characteristics of people with personality disorders and, in turn, make up the diagnostic criteria of a personality disorder. Thus, the actions of a patient with a personality disorder are dually governed by predominant motives and developed game structures. For example, people with a narcissistic personality disorder are assumed to strongly value personal importance and autonomy as well as recognition by others. In contrast, people with a dependent personality disorder exceedingly dread isolation and seek out solidarity and reliability by other people. Therefore, at a strategic level, people with a narcissistic personality disorder may present as being achievement oriented, prone to set the rules, and sensitive to critique, whereas people with a dependent personality disorder may be submissive, dependent, and unable to make decisions.

Based on these assumptions, Sachse (2004) formulated the Clarification-Oriented Psychotherapy for Personality Disorders (COP-PD), which is part of a more general psychotherapy approach that is based on process-experiential and cognitive therapies (Sachse, 2003). After building an effective therapeutic relationship via motivational attunement, the general approach in COP-PD is to help the patient explicate his or her interpersonal motives, change the associated dysfunctional interpersonal schemas (goals, strategies, and behaviors), and establish new need-satisfying motivational-behavioral patterns in real-life interactions. For example, with patients who have a narcissistic personality disorder, therapists attune their behavior to the assumed narcissistic motives by normalizing the patient's problems, maximally validating the patient's resources (but not the dysfunctional strategies), and cautiously directing attention to the discrepancy between the patient's self-doubts and his or her resources. This discrepancy in conjunction with awareness of the costs of the maladaptive behavior is assumed to fuel the patient's motivation for change. In contrast, in the treatment of patients with a dependent personality disorder, the therapist strongly conveys reliability and solidarity while, at the same time, refraining from accepting responsibility for the patient's life. In a nonblaming manner, the therapist cautiously raises the patient's awareness about his or her motivation to defer responsibility and readiness to adapt to other people's needs, both of which are motivated by a strong urge to avoid being alone. Subsequently, the therapist slowly moves to reconstructing the schemas and to practicing new, more adaptive strategies and behaviors for motive satisfaction in real-life interactions. A case formulation based on the Plan analysis can help to identify maladaptive strategies and to find more adaptive alternatives with less adverse side effects.

Need Satisfaction as the Primary Therapy Goal

Viewed from a motivational perspective, the overarching treatment goal of psychotherapeutic interventions is to help the person better satisfy his or her psychological needs (Grawe, 2007). This can be achieved via developing clear and unambivalent goals, and by finding appropriate strategies to reach these goals. If the person has developed goals and strategies in the service of his or her needs, but they do not lead to need satisfaction (as in personality disorders), psychotherapy will help the person gain awareness of this mismatch and find more effective ways to attain need satisfaction. A case formulation that (a) integrates interpersonal behaviors and problems with interpersonal Plans and goals, (b) embeds these within the whole of the person's Plan structure, and (c) relates Plans and goals to general psychological needs—attachment, control, self-enhancement, pleasure—prepares a therapist to foster sustainable well-being in patients.

CONCLUSION

Interpersonal motivation, as well as the related constructs of interpersonal motives, goals, plans, and values, can be used to explain observable interpersonal behavior and interpersonal problems. Conceptually, it has proved useful to distinguish two types of goals (i.e., approach and avoidance goals) and two evaluative dimensions of goals (i.e., goal intensity and satisfaction). Interpersonal motive constructs can be measured idiographically or by various standardized measures. Empirically studying the associations between interpersonal motivation and problematic interpersonal behaviors may both advance interpersonal theory and optimize clinical interventions. Future diagnostic research may develop measures that assess all four dimensions of interpersonal goals (approach/avoidance × intensity/satisfaction), while at the same time taking the circumplex structure of

the measures into account. Using such instruments, further studies are needed to test hypotheses about the causal links between interpersonal motivation, interpersonal problems, and psychopathology. Psychotherapy research may examine the effects of motivation-based intervention strategies, particularly for personality disorders, and test hypotheses about modifying interpersonal motivation in these therapies. In conclusion, the concept of interpersonal motivation holds great potential toward enhancing the understanding of and the change in interpersonal behavior.

References

Ackerman, S. J., & Hilsenroth, M. J. (2001). A review of therapist characteristics and techniques negatively impacting the therapeutic alliance. *Psychotherapy, 38*(2), 171–185.

Alden, L. E., Wiggins, J. S., & Pincus, A. L. (1990). Construction of circumplex scales for the Inventory of Interpersonal Problems. *Journal of Personality Assessment, 55*, 521–536.

Alexander, F., & French, T. M. (1946). *Psychoanalytic therapy: Principles and applications.* New York: Ronald Press.

American Psychiatric Association (2000). *Diagnostic and statistical manual of mental disorders* (4th ed., text revision). Washington, DC: Author.

Austin, J. T., & Vancouver, J. B. (1996). Goal constructs in psychology: Structure, process, and content. *Psychological Bulletin, 120*(3), 338–375.

Bakan, D. (1966). *The duality of human existence. An essay on psychology and religion.* Chicago: Rand McNally.

Benjamin, L. S. (1996). *Interpersonal diagnosis and treatment of personality disorders.* New York: Guilford Press.

Benjamin, L. S. (2004). Interpersonal reconstructive therapy for individuals with personality disorder. In J. J. Magnavita (Ed.), *Handbook of personality disorders* (pp. 151–168). Hoboken, NJ: John Wiley & Sons.

Benjamin, L. S., Rothweiler, J. C., & Critchfield, K. L. (2006). The use of structural analysis of social behavior (SASB) as an assessment tool. *Annual Review of Clinical Psychology, 2*(12), 1–27.

Bordin, E. (1979). The generalizability of the psychoanalytic concept of the working alliance.

Psychotherapy: Theory, Research and Practice, 16, 252–260.

Bowlby, J. (1977). The making and the breaking of affectional bonds. *Psychiatry* (130), 201–210.

Bräutigam, S., Thomas, A., Suess, H., & Strauss, B. (June, 2008). *Interpersonal motives and their relevance for symptom distress and symptom reduction.* Paper presented at the 39th annual meeting of the Society for Psychotherapy Research, Barcelona, Spain.

Caspar, F. (2007). Plan analysis. In T. Eells (Ed.), *Handbook of psychotherapeutic case formulations* (2nd ed., pp. 251–289). New York: Guilford Press.

Caspar, F., Grossmann, C., Unmussig, C., & Schramm, E. (2005). Complementary therapeutic relationship: Therapist behavior, interpersonal patterns, and therapeutic effects. *Psychotherapy Research, 15*(1–2), 91–102.

Elliot, A. J., & Covington, M. V. (2001). Approach and avoidance motivation. *Educational Psychology Review, 13*(2), 73–92.

Elliot, A. J., Gable, S. L., & Mapes, R. R. (2006). Approach and avoidance motivation in the social domain. *Personality and Social Psychology Bulletin, 32*(3), 378–391.

Emmons, R. A. (1996). Striving and feeling: Personal goals and subjective well-being. In P. M. Gollwitzer & J. A. Bargh (Eds.), *The psychology of action* (pp. 313–337). New York: Guilford Press.

Emmons, R. A., King, L. A., & Sheldon, K. (1993). Goal conflict and the self-regulation of action. In D. M. Wegner & J. M. Pennebaker (Eds.), *Handbook of mental control* (pp. 528–550). Englewood Cliffs, NJ: Prentice-Hall.

Epstein, S. (1990). Cognitive-experiental self-theory. In L. A. Pervin (Ed.), *Handbook of personality: Theory and research* (pp. 165–192). New York: Guilford Press.

Exline, J. J., & Lobel, M. (1999). The perils of outperformance: Sensitivity about being the target of a threatening upward comparison. *Psychological Bulletin, 125*(3), 307–337.

Gable, S. L. (2006). Approach and avoidance social motives and goals. *Journal of Personality, 74*(1), 175–222.

Grawe, K. (2004). *Psychological therapy.* Ashland, OH: Hogrefe & Huber.

Grawe, K. (2007). *Neuropsychotherapy: How the neurosciences inform effective psychotherapy.* Mahwah, NJ: Erlbaum.

Grawe, K., & Dziewas, H. (1978). Interaktionelle Verhaltenstherapie. *Mitteilungen der DGVT. Sonderheft 1,* 27–49.

Gray, J. A. (1987). *The psychology of fear and stress.* New York: Cambridge University Press.

Grosse Holtforth, M., Bents, H., Mauler, B., & Grawe, K. (2006). Interpersonal distress as a mediator between avoidance goals and goal satisfaction in psychotherapy inpatients. *Clinical Psychology and Psychotherapy, 13,* 172–182.

Grosse Holtforth, M., & Castonguay, L. G. (2005). Relationship and techniques in CBT—A motivational approach. *Psychotherapy: Theory, Research, Practice, Training, 42*(4), 443–455.

Grosse Holtforth, M., & Grawe, K. (2000). Fragebogen zur Analyse Motivationaler Schemata (FAMOS) [Inventory of Approach and Avoidance Motivation (IAAM)]. *Zeitschrift für Klinische Psychologie, 29*(3), 170–179.

Grosse Holtforth, M., & Grawe, K. (2002). Bern Inventory of Treatment Goals (BIT), Part 1: Development and First Application of a Taxonomy of Treatment Goal Themes (BIT-T). *Psychotherapy Research, 12*(1), 79–99.

Grosse Holtforth, M., & Grawe, K. (2003). Der Inkongruenzfragebogen (INK)—Ein Messinstrument zur Analyse motivationaler Inkongruenz. *Zeitschrift für Klinische Psychologie und Psychotherapie, 32}* (4), 315–323.

Grosse Holtforth, M., Lutz, W., & Grawe, K. (2006). The structural stability of the IIP-C pre- and post treatment: A replication using a Swiss clinical sample. *European Journal of Psychological Assessment, 22*(2), 98–103.

Grosse Holtforth, M., Pincus, A., Grawe, K., & Mauler, B. (2007). What you want is not what you get: Goal importance, goal satisfaction, and interpersonal problems. *Journal of Social and Clinical Psychology, 26*(10), 1095–1119.

Helgeson, V. S., & Fritz, H. L. (1999). Unmitigated agency and unmitigated communion: Distinctions from agency and communion. *Journal of Research in Personality, 33*(2), 131–158.

Hogan, R., & Roberts, B. W. (2000). A socioanalytic perspective on person-environment interaction. In K. H. C. W. B. Walsh, & R. H. Price (Eds.), *New directions in person-environment psychology* (pp. 1–24). Hillsdale, NJ: Erlbaum.

Horowitz, L. M. (1979). On the cognitive structure of interpersonal problems treated in psychotherapy. *Journal of Consulting and Clinical Psychology, 47*(1), 5–15.

Horowitz, L. M. (2004). *Interpersonal foundations of psychopathology*. Washington, DC: American Psychological Association.

Horowitz, L. M., Rosenberg, S. E., Baer, B. A., Ureno, G., & Villasenor, V. S. (1988). Inventory of interpersonal problems: Psychometric properties and clinical applications. *Journal of Consulting and Clinical Psychology, 56*, 885–892.

Horowitz, L. M., Strauss, B., & Kordy, H. (2000). *Inventar zur Erfassung Interpersonaler Probleme (IIP-D)—Deutsche Version* (2nd ed.). Göttingen, Germany: Beltz.

Horowitz, L. M., Wilson, K. R., Turan, B., Zolotsev, P., Constantino, M. J., & Henderson, L. (2006). How interpersonal motives clarify the meaning of interpersonal behavior: A revised circumplex model. *Personality and Social Psychology Review, 10*(1), 67–86.

Jagger, M., & Richards, K. (1969). You can't always get what you want. On *Let it bleed* [LP]. London: Decca Records.

Kiesler, D. J. (1983). The 1982 Interpersonal Circle: A taxonomy for complementarity in human transactions. *Psychological Review, 90*(3), 185–214.

Lauterbach, W. (1996). The measurement of personal conflict. *Psychotherapy Research, 6*(3), 213–225.

Leary, T. F. (1957). *Interpersonal diagnosis of personality: A functional theory and methodology for personality evaluation*. New York: Ronald Press.

Little, B. R. (1989). Personal project analysis: Trivial pursuits, magnificient obsessions, and the search for coherence. In A. R. Buss & N. Cantor (Eds.), *Personality Psychology: Recent trends and emerging directions* (pp. 15–31). New York: Springer.

Livesley, W. J. (2001). Conceptual and taxonomic issues. In J. Livesley (Ed.), *Handbook of personality disorders*. New York: Guilford Press.

Locke, K. D. (2000). Circumplex scales of interpersonal values: Reliability, validity, and applicability to interpersonal problems and personality disorders. *Journal of Personality Assessment, 75*(2), 249–267.

McClelland, D. C., Koestner, R., & Weinberger, J. (1989). How do self-attributed and implicit motives differ? *Psychological Review, 96*, 690–702.

Michalak, J., & Grosse Holtforth, M. (2006). Where do we go from here?—The goal perspective in psychotherapy. *Clinical Psychology: Science and Practice, 13*, 346–365.

Miller, G. A., Galanter, E., & Pribram, K. H. (1960). *Plans and the structure of behavior*. New York: Holt.

Reiss, S., & Havercamp, S. (1996). The sensitivity theory of motivation: Implications for psychopathology. *Behavioural Research and Therapy, 34*(8), 632–632.

Sachse, R. (2003). *Klärungsorientierte Psychotherapie*. Göttingen: Hogrefe.

Sachse, R. (2004). *Persönlichkeitsstörungen*. Göttingen: Hogrefe.

Santor, D. A., & Zuroff, D. C. (1997). Interpersonal responses to threats to status and interpersonal relatedness: Effects of dependency and self-criticism. *British Journal of Clinical Psychology, 36*, 521–541.

Schmalt, H. D., & Sokolowski, K. (2000). The current status of motive measurement. *Diagnostica, 46*(3), 115–123.

Shechtman, N., & Horowitz, L. M. (2006). Interpersonal and noninterpersonal interactions, interpersonal motives, and the effect of frustrated motives. *Personality and Social Psychology Bulletin, 32*(8), 1126–1139.

Smith, C. (1992). *Motivation and personality: Handbook of thematic content analysis*. New York: Cambridge University Press.

Uebelacker, L. A., Battle, C. L., Friedman, M. A., Cardemil, E. V., Beevers, C. G., & Miller, I. W. (2008). The importance of interpersonal treatment goals for depressed inpatients. *Journal of Nervous and Mental Disease, 196*(3), 217–222.

Vittengl, J. R., Clark, L. A., & Jarrett, R. B. (2003). Interpersonal problems, personality pathology, and social adjustment after cognitive therapy for depression. *Psychological Assessment, 15*(1), 29–40.

Westen, D., & Shedler, J. (2000). A prototype matching approach to diagnosing personality disorders: Toward DSM-V. *Journal of Personality Disorders, 14*(2), 109–126.

NOTES

1. *Plan* is capitalized following a suggestion by Miller, Galanter, and Pribram (1960) to distinguish the meaning from the common language definition of a plan as being rational/conscious.

8 INTERPERSONAL COMPLEMENTARITY

Pamela Sadler

Nicole Ethier

Erik Woody

The word *complementarity* is unusual and relatively unfamiliar. So to begin, let's consider some examples of the type of phenomena that this chapter addresses. Jill has a warm and friendly interpersonal style. Linda, who has a similarly warm style, finds that she interacts easily and enjoyably with Jill. However, Susan, who has a colder, more distant style, finds that interaction with Jill is somewhat awkward and unsatisfying. For example, she wishes that Jill would be less smarmy and more task-focused.

Dick tends to have a strongly dominant interpersonal style. Bill, who has a similarly dominant style, finds that he tends to clash with Dick and cannot work with him effectively. He wishes that Dick would "get off his high horse." However, Stuart, who has a more submissive style, enjoys Dick's sense of direction and self-confidence, and finds that they work together very well.

As these examples illustrate, any two people bring to an interaction their own consistent traits, called interpersonal styles. In addition, particular combinations of interpersonal styles may fit together in distinctive ways and yield different emotional and objective outcomes.

Now consider another type of example. Judy is a manager who is concerned about the work of her employee, David. She finds herself becoming increasingly blunt and directive toward him, but instead of improving, David seems only to become more sullen and lacking in initiative. Although she realizes the interaction patterns between them may be spiraling unproductively, she finds it difficult to interact with him in other ways, because he seems to "pull for" certain behaviors from her. For his part, David is bewildered that Judy, who once seemed like a reasonable person, has become so overbearing toward him.

As this example illustrates, when two people interact, they tend to modify their interactional behaviors in response to each other. These shifts can occur over a wide range of time scales—from a few minutes to several months or more. Although such shifts may make people happier with each other, this is not always the case, as the example also indicates.

Interpersonal complementarity is a general term referring to the ways in which the interactional behavior of pairs of people may fit together and influence each other. It

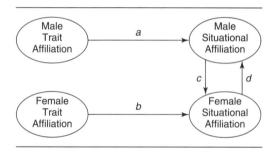

FIGURE 8.1   Integrative Model of Complementarity
Source: Adapted with permission from Sadler and Woody, 2003.

consists of two related, but separable phenomena: the initial match versus mismatch of people's interaction styles, as in the first two examples, and the tendency of people to change their behavior in reaction to each other, as in the third example.

There is an important sense in which interpersonal styles and shifts in interpersonal behavior as a result of interaction are interlocking issues. Figure 8.1 shows an integrative model of complementarity (Sadler & Woody, 2003). In the ovals to the left are the interactants' interpersonal styles—in this case, their levels of trait affiliation. In the ovals to the right are the interactants' situational patterns of behavior—in this case, their levels of expressed affiliation during an interaction. The paths labeled *a* and *b* represent the consistent impact of the relevant underlying traits on situational behavior, whereas the paths labeled *c* and *d* represent the impact of each person's expressed behavior on the partner's situational behavior. The trait-to-situational-behavior relations (paths *a* and *b*) serve as the levers, so to speak, by which each person exerts an effect on the behavior of the other (paths *c* and *d*).

It is possible to predict outcomes of interactions either by using the pairing of interpersonal styles (that is, the underlying traits, at the left) or by using the pairing of behavior patterns evident during the interaction (the situational patterns, at the right, which incorporate the effects of the partners on each other). These two types of predictors are not the same—for example, although partners may be able to shift during an interaction toward behavior patterns that fit together better than their respective interpersonal styles, these shifts could be stressful or attention-demanding. Finally, patterns of mutual influence sustained over substantial periods of time may, in turn, eventually lead to changes in general interpersonal style as an outcome. To illustrate, interpersonal therapists attempt to promote lasting changes in the client's interpersonal style by altering situational patterns of behavior—for example, in interactions during therapy sessions.

Fitting Interpersonal Complementarity Into a Broader Scientific Context

The predominant framework for studying complementarity has been the interpersonal circle or circumplex (Leary, 1957), defined by the orthogonal dimensions of affiliation and dominance, portrayed, respectively, as horizontal and vertical axes of a Cartesian plane (Kiesler, 1996). Using this framework, Carson (1969) posited that complementary behaviors are defined by sameness on the affiliation dimension (referred to as *correspondence*) and oppositeness on the dominance dimension (referred to as *reciprocity*). For example, friendly dominant behavior by one person invites friendly submissive behavior from an interaction partner. Kiesler (1983) elaborated on these dimensional principles by applying them to 16 stylistic prototypes around the interpersonal circle and specifying all hypothesized complementary pairings of interpersonal behavior. However, this finely grained conception is based on exactly the same two underlying, dimensional principles: greater affiliation pulls for greater affiliation, and greater dominance pulls for greater submissiveness (and vice versa). (For alternative, less widely adopted conceptions of interpersonal complementarity, see Wiggins, 1982, and Benjamin, 1974.)

Although the concept of complementarity arose within interpersonal theory, it has much wider implications across the broad landscape of ideas in social, personality, and clinical psychology. For instance, complementarity is a paradigmatic case of dyadic interdependence, a major emerging theme in current psychological theory and research (e.g., Kenny, Kashy, & Cook, 2006). In addition, complementarity is highly consistent with the recent upsurge of interest in the role of synchronization and coregulation in social cognition and behavior (e.g., Semin, 2007; Semin & Cacioppo, 2008). Further, there is great potential for cross-fertilization of research in interpersonal complementarity with research in communication (e.g., Burgoon, Stern, & Dillman, 1995; Cappella, 1996) and systems theory (e.g., Boker & Wenger, 2007).

In view of all this potential, it is unfortunate that, by tradition, interpersonal theorists use key terms—*complementarity, reciprocity*, and *correspondence*—in ways that are surprisingly inconsistent with what most other researchers, outside the tradition of interpersonal theory, mean by the same words. In interpersonal theory, *complementarity* is a blanket term covering both similarity of behavior across partners (e.g., friendliness pulls for friendliness) and dissimilarity (e.g., dominance pulls for submissiveness). In contrast, in the communications literature (Burgoon et al., 1995) and in the romantic relationships literature (e.g., Beach, Whitaker, Jones, & Tesser, 2001; Pilkington, Tesser, & Stephens, 1991), the term *complementarity* refers only to instances of dissimilarity. In interpersonal theory, *reciprocity* refers to oppositeness on the dominance dimension and *correspondence* refers to sameness on the affiliation dimension. In contrast, in the communications literature and in social psychology more generally, the term *reciprocity* refers to sameness and the term *compensation* refers to oppositeness (Burgoon et al., 1995). Thus, what interpersonal researchers call *correspondence* (on the affiliation axis) would be called *reciprocity* by researchers outside of this tradition, and what interpersonal researchers call

reciprocity (on the dominance axis) would be called *compensation* by most other researchers.

This situation brings to mind Humpty Dumpty's famous quip from Lewis Carroll's *Through the Looking Glass*: "When *I* use a word, it means just what I choose it to mean—neither more nor less." Our experience is that, at a social psychology convention, even the statement, "I do research on complementarity" will be misunderstood by most listeners. It is not only social psychologists who may be confused by this term. For example, Tracey (2007) described how an attendee of his poster presentation on complementarity in psychotherapy misunderstood this key term, and consequently engaged him in a long conversation about the importance of saying nice things to others (i.e., *complimenting* them). Clearly, researchers working within the tradition of interpersonal theory, with its rather parochial use of key terms, need to be careful to communicate effectively with other social scientists.

EMPIRICAL EVIDENCE FOR COMPLEMENTARITY

Having discussed key concepts and terminology, we now turn to a brief review of the empirical evidence regarding complementarity. There are three broad types of relevant research, which we consider in the following order:

1. Studies comparing different combinations of partners' interpersonal styles: What pairings of interpersonal traits have what effects? Under what circumstances do these effects occur?
2. Studies addressing mutual influence and adaptation: What interpersonal characteristics pull for each other? Over what time frame do these effects occur, and under what circumstances? In addition, what outcomes do patterns of mutual adjustment have?
3. Studies addressing processes underlying complementarity: *Why* might

interactions and relationships tend to be complementary?

Studies of Complementarity in Interpersonal Styles

A range of studies has evaluated how the complementarity of interaction partners' trait interpersonal style predicts various outcomes. Generally speaking, these studies tend to show that greater complementarity (i.e., sameness on the affiliation dimension and oppositeness on the dominance dimension) in trait interpersonal style tends to bring about positive outcomes, whereas anticomplementarity (i.e., oppositeness on the affiliation dimension and sameness on the dominance dimension) tends to yield detrimental outcomes. It is worthwhile to distinguish between two types of outcomes: *subjective* perceptions of how the partners feel about each other and their interaction, such as feelings of satisfaction; and *objective* measures of dyadic outcomes, such as quality of performance on a joint task.

Concerning subjective perceptions, one important outcome studied has been partners' satisfaction with a particular interaction, or more broadly, with their relationship. Indeed, one of the core tenets of interpersonal theory is that more complementary interpersonal styles should produce more satisfying, harmonious relationships (Kiesler, 1996). Several empirical studies support this principle. For example, Dryer and Horowitz (1997) showed that participants were more satisfied with their interaction when their interpersonal styles were opposite on dominance to an experimental confederate's scripted behavior. Participants were also more satisfied when their own dominance goals were opposite to the other person's dominance-related behavior. Likewise, Shechtman and Horowitz (2006) showed that when dominant participants perceived an interaction partner to be expressing similarly high levels of dominance, they were less satisfied (i.e., more angry toward the interaction partner) than when the interaction partner

was not dominating. In a similar vein, Locke and Sadler (2007) studied how satisfaction is related to complementarity on trait interpersonal efficacy. In previously unacquainted, same-sex interactions, satisfaction with the interaction was positively associated with similarity in partners' levels of affiliative interpersonal efficacy. Thus, in these lab-based studies we see evidence that complementary matching of trait interpersonal styles tends to produce increased satisfaction in a dyadic interaction and noncomplementary matching results in decreased satisfaction.

Closely akin to the construct of satisfaction, liking and comfort between interaction partners are also higher when interaction partners have more complementary traits. Subjective perceptions of this nature have been studied with different types of relationships, such as interactions between strangers, friends, and colleagues. Two studies that looked at interactions between strangers both showed that increased complementarity led to increases in how much the interaction partners liked and were comfortable with each other. For instance, Tiedens and Fragale (2003; Study 2) had same-sex strangers (one being a confederate) interact in the lab, and the researchers manipulated the posture of each individual to be either expansive or constrictive. Their findings suggested that when individuals were matched such that one partner had expansive posture and the other partner had a more constricted posture (indicative of dominance reciprocity in nonverbal behavior), participants tended to experience more liking toward and comfort with the confederate, in comparison to when both had the same postures. Likewise, Nowicki and Manheim (1991) matched same-sex, female dyads based on trait interpersonal style and showed that complementary dyads (who were reciprocal on dominance and correspondent on friendliness) tended to show signs of greater liking and comfort, such as engaging in more conversation and sitting closer to each other, in comparison to anticomplementary dyads.

Several studies have also examined the impact of complementary interpersonal styles on perceptions of closeness in contexts outside the lab. In a study on relationships between friends, Yaughn and Nowicki (1999) collected information about the interpersonal styles of friends who varied in the closeness of the friendship. They found that in women, interpersonal complementarity was related to perceived relationship closeness. Likewise, both college roommates tend to feel more cohesive when there is a high degree of complementarity (Ansell, Kurtz, & Markey, 2008), and members of musical "bar bands" who show increased levels of complementarity perceive greater positive regard and group cohesion (Dyce & O'Connor, 1992; O'Connor & Dyce, 1997). Married couples also report greater relationship quality, characterized by greater love and harmony, when the trait interpersonal styles of each person complement each other (Markey & Markey, 2007). Thus, there is fairly broad support for the idea that higher levels of complementarity between interaction partners leads to more positive perceptions of each other and the relationship.

Although less research has focused on objective outcomes that may be related to complementary interpersonal styles, there is some support for these relations, too. Estroff and Nowicki (1992) found that complementarity is related to dyadic productivity. Specifically, when dyads were matched so that their interpersonal styles complemented each other, they were significantly more productive at putting together a jigsaw puzzle than partners who were anticomplementary. Smith and Ruiz (2007) examined objective indices of interpersonal distress in partners who were matched to be either correspondent or opposite on trait friendliness. They showed that when dyads were mismatched on trait friendliness, the participants tended to display increased blood pressure and heart rate.

Overall, this group of studies suggests that complementarity in trait interpersonal style plays a potentially important role in a variety of subjective and objective outcomes, both in controlled lab settings involving strangers and in real-life interactions between people in established relationships. Furthermore, these results generalize across same-sex and mixed-sex dyads. However, the number of studies that show evidence for these outcomes is relatively modest, suggesting that more research is needed. This is particularly the case for objective outcomes, for which there is limited, but promising, evidence. For instance, the few studies looking at more objective outcomes, such as task performance or distress level, have been conducted in the lab between two strangers. More research is needed to evaluate whether these findings generalize to other circumstances outside the lab, between individuals who are previously acquainted.

Studies of Mutual Influence and Adaptation

As mentioned earlier, a second major area of complementarity research concerns how partners influence each other's interpersonal behavior, either within a single interaction or over many interactions. In 1983, Kiesler reviewed the available evidence and concluded there was convincing evidence that responses to interpersonal behaviors tend to be complementary: Hostile dominant behavior tends to evoke hostile submissive behavior (and vice versa), whereas friendly dominant behavior tends to evoke friendly submissive behavior (and vice versa). However, in response, Orford (1986) argued that the evidence was actually more mixed. He agreed that there is fairly strong evidence for complementarity on the right side of the circumplex (i.e., friendly dominant behavior pulls for friendly submissive behavior and vice versa). However, his review of studies indicated that the evidence on the left side of the circumplex is less straightforward. In particular, some research suggested that hostile dominant behavior elicits similar levels of hostile dominance, rather than the expected complementary behavior of hostile submissiveness. Furthermore, hostile submissive behavior may often be met with friendly dominant behavior, rather than the expected complementary behavior of hostile dominance.

Subsequently, further studies and review (e.g., see Kiesler, 1996) have shed more light on the question of whether mutual influence follows the principles of complementarity. There are three main types of studies, representing various time scales as follows:

1. Act-by-act behavioral complementarity. At the most micro level of assessment, some work has evaluated complementarity in specific moment-to-moment behavioral acts. What is the probability that a particular type of interpersonal behavior will be followed immediately by a complementary behavioral response from an interaction partner?
2. Aggregated situational mutual influence. Taking a more molar approach to studying single interactions, other work has aggregated the behavior of each partner across the interaction into overall indices. Over the course of an interaction, do partners adjust their interpersonal behavior so that they become more complementary?
3. Mutual influence over multiple interactions. At the most macro level, some work has evaluated complementarity over multiple interactions. Are different types of interactions characterized by different degrees or types of complementarity?

Act-by-act behavioral complementarity. Strong, Hills, Kilmartin et al. (1988) studied interactions between same-sex, previously unacquainted individuals, where one of these individuals was a confederate who was enacting one of the eight octants of the interpersonal circle. Based on written transcripts, each speaking turn was categorized as falling into one of the eight octants of the interpersonal circle. This study showed evidence for complementarity on an act-by-act basis, such that the behavior of one individual (the confederate) increased

the probability of a subsequent complementary act from the interaction partner. For instance, a dominant (i.e., leading) act produced an increased probability for a subsequent submissive (i.e., docile) act.

Tracey (1994, 2004) also investigated complementarity at the level of specific behavioral acts. He demonstrated that, controlling for base rates of the interpersonal behaviors corresponding with each octant, there is clear evidence for complementarity on both the left and right side of the circumplex. Similarly, Gurtman (2001) reanalyzed Strong, Hill, and Kilmartin's (1988) data controlling for base rates in a different way, and again found general support for act-by-act complementarity.

It is noteworthy that all but one study (Tracey, 2004; Study 1) of this type involved lab paradigms in which one of the interaction partners was a confederate; also, both partners were always female. These limitations suggest that more research is needed to evaluate whether act-by-act complementarity generalizes to more naturalistic, unscripted social interactions.

Aggregated situational mutual-influence. Of the studies that examine the process of mutual influence in aggregated situational behavior, the majority are between unacquainted pairs of people who are interacting in a lab setting. Overall, there tends to be very good support for interpersonal complementarity within this type of setting. Several studies have shown that during the course of an interaction, previously unacquainted dyads tend to exhibit both correspondence on affiliation and reciprocity on dominance (Locke & Sadler, 2007; Markey, Funder, & Ozer, 2003; Sadler & Woody, 2003). Furthermore, the results for such studies generalize across mixed-sex and same-sex dyads, across interactions that range in duration from five minutes to twenty minutes, and across a variety of joint activities, including relatively unstructured, cooperative, and competitive tasks.

To illustrate this type of finding, Panel A of Figure 8.2 shows a structural equation

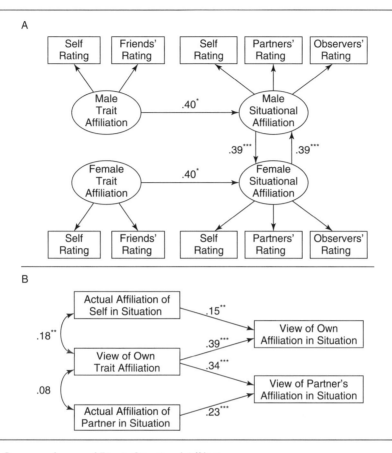

FIGURE 8.2 Correspondence and Bias in Situational Affiliation
Panel A: Mutual-influence model of correspondence in affiliation. Panel B: Bias in perceptions of situational affiliation.
Notes: * p < .05. ** p < .01. *** p < .001. All coefficients are standardized; error variables have been omitted from the diagrams.
Source: Adapted with permission from Sadler and Woody, 2003.

model from Sadler and Woody (2003), who studied unacquainted dyads engaged in a cooperative task. The ovals denote latent or conceptual variables, and the rectangles denote measured variables. As the diagram indicates, the interactants' underlying levels of trait affiliation (to the left) were measured both by self-report and the report of friends. The interactants' situational patterns of behavior (to the right)—namely, their levels of expressed affiliation during the interaction—were also measured in a variety of ways: by self-report observations, partner-report observations, and the ratings of independent observers. The obtained

coefficients for the paths among the latent variables, shown on the diagram, reveal that the impact of partners on each other's level of expressed affiliation is positive and just as strong as the contribution of their respective trait interpersonal styles. Using a similar model, Sadler and Woody also found that partners had a substantial negative effect on each other's levels of expressed dominance.

In a lab study involving female dyads (one member of each dyad was a confederate), Bluhm, Widiger, & Meile (1990) found support for correspondence on affiliation: Participants showed friendly behavior in response to a friendly confederate and hostile behavior in response to a hostile confederate. Although no such mutual adjustment seemed to be occurring on dominance, it is likely that the scripted nature of interactions with a confederate interferes with the natural give and take that occurs in social interaction.

To date, these findings supporting complementarity in overall situational behavior mainly involve previously unacquainted pairs of individuals interacting in a lab setting. Thus, future research should address the phenomenon in contexts outside the lab.

Mutual influence over multiple interactions. In addition to studies of mutual influence processes within a single interaction, there is a growing body of literature that examines mutual influence over longer periods of time. Studies of this nature typically involve real-life circumstances such as interactions at home and in the workplace, between individuals who are well acquainted, such as friends, coworkers, and romantic partners.

One major type of investigation examines the extent to which individuals adopt complementary stances across multiple situations and interaction partners. An advantage of this approach is that it allows for the study of the ways in which context may influence expression of complementarity. For example, Moskowitz, Ho, and Turcotte-Tremblay (2007) collected information about people's interpersonal behavior over multiple interactions with a variety of individuals. Specifically, these authors had people complete self-report measures of their own interpersonal behavior and the behavior of their interaction partners for each social interaction that occurred in their everyday life over a 20-day period. The authors were interested in examining how the process of complementarity might differ depending on whether people were interacting in work versus nonwork settings, or in higher status versus lower status roles. They found that individuals tend to exhibit greater reciprocity on dominance in work than in nonwork settings, and less reciprocity when in a lower status role, compared to those in a higher status role.

On the friendliness dimension, those in higher-status roles tend to show greater correspondence than those in lower-status roles. In a similar study, rather than examining type of setting and role, Fournier, Moskowitz, and Zuroff (2008) defined four interpersonal situations based on the partners' behavior: friendly-dominant, friendly-submissive, hostile-dominant, and hostile-submissive. Using these situational categories, they found strong evidence of complementarity.

A major second type of study investigates how mutual influence evolves over time *within the same dyad.* For instance, Markey and Kurtz (2006) studied the process of complementarity between female college roommates who had just moved in with each other. The authors collected information about the interpersonal behavior of each roommate at two time points: at the beginning of their time living together and then 13 weeks later. Within this period of time, the roommates' behavioral styles moved from being unrelated to each other to being highly reciprocal on dominance and highly correspondent on friendliness. In a similar vein, Tracey, Ryan, and Jaschik-Herman (2001) found that long-standing romantic partnerships and close friendships tend to be characterized by a high degree of complementarity: Those with trait styles that are friendly dominant tend to have relationship partners who are friendly submissive (and vice versa), whereas those with trait styles that are hostile dominant tend to have relationship partners who are hostile submissive (and vice versa). However, because the styles were measured at only one time point, a possible confound is that partners, at least to some extent, may have selected into complementary relationships rather than developing them through a mutual influence process over time.

Another important circumstance involving the same dyad over multiple interactions is the therapeutic relationship. Tracey, Sherry, and Albright (1999) collected information about complementarity between therapists and clients over the course of six cognitive-behavioral therapy sessions and showed that therapists and clients tend to display a U-shaped function of complementarity over the course of treatment. Complementarity tends to be greatest at the beginning of therapy, followed by a decline during the middle sessions, and then a subsequent rise toward the termination phase.

One study investigated complementarity processes in larger groups. Wright and Ingraham (1986) had classes of eight students complete retrospective measures of interpersonal style for each of their classmates based on the students' interactions over the course of a school term. Using a social relations model to test actor, partner, and relationship effects, the authors showed that a large proportion of the dyads within the group exhibited correspondence on the affiliation dimension, and there were trends toward reciprocity on the dominance dimension.

Mutual Influence Processes and the Prediction of Outcome Variables

The foregoing body of research makes a strong case for the hypothesis that as people interact, they reshape each other's interactional behaviors; in addition, this mutual-influence process occurs on a range of time scales. But what are the effects of such mutual adjustments?

A few studies have investigated how mutual-influence processes may predict subjective and objective outcomes. In both therapist/client dyads and university undergraduate dyads, Tracey (2004) demonstrated that base-rate-corrected act-by-act complementarity was a strong predictor of perceptions of satisfaction and positivity. Similarly, Tiedens and Fragale (2003) found that individuals who adopt a complementary postural stance in relation to their interaction partner have more positive feelings about them.

There is also some evidence that objective outcomes are affected by this mutual influence process. For example, Tracey et al. (1999) showed that when therapist/client

dyads have a more U-shaped pattern of complementarity over the course of therapy, clients tend to experience better treatment outcomes, such as reduction in the number and severity of symptoms. Thus, complementarity appears to contribute to the efficacy of interaction partners who are working together toward a common goal. Some work has also examined how low complementarity may produce detrimental outcomes. In particular, Tracey (2005) showed that dyads with decreased levels of act-by-act complementarity tend to experience greater levels of interpersonal distress in their lives. In summary, these studies, although few in number, suggest that further work on the effects of the mutual-influence process might be quite promising.

Studies of Processes Underlying Complementarity

It has often been assumed that adjustments toward greater complementarity are reinforced and maintained by their consequences for the partners (e.g., Kiesler, 1983; Tracey, 1994). In particular, as shown by some of the research reviewed earlier, complementary interactions may be more pleasant and satisfying for both partners. Thus, at least to some extent, adjustments that increase complementarity probably occur because of their reward value.

Although such reward value applies readily to the range of behaviors on the right side of the circumplex, involving some degree of friendliness (i.e., positive complementarity), it is not as clear how it would apply to the range of behaviors on the left side of the circumplex, involving various degrees of unfriendliness (i.e., negative complementarity) (e.g., Friedlander, 1993; Tracey, 1993). It is counterintuitive that negative complementarity, in which both partners are acting in an unfriendly fashion toward each another, would bring about feelings of satisfaction and harmony. Likewise, many people seeking psychotherapy for interpersonal difficulties have interaction styles that consistently evoke complementary, but deeply unsatisfying responses from others, yet these patterns of behavior may be highly stable and resistant to change (Carson, 1969, 1982).

Proposed resolutions to this apparent paradox invoke the theme of self-validation, whereby people may unwittingly create a social environment that confirms their own preconceptions about themselves and others (Bowers, 1973; Carson, 1969; Wachtel, 1973). Specifically, people's preconceptions color their perceptions of an interaction, and these biased perceptions affect their actions toward other people. These actions, in turn, may evoke responses from others that confirm the preconceptions, in a circle of self-fulfilling prophecy. The apparent confirmation of expectancies (i.e., a sense of prediction and control) may reinforce behavior patterns even when these patterns lead to unsatisfying or self-defeating outcomes. For example, a person's hostile dominant style may be maintained by observations that most other people are feckless toadies (i.e., hostile submissive), awaiting direction. Such a person may not realize that it is actually his or her own behavior that is evoking this behavioral consistency in others. Kiesler (1996) called this important phenomenon the *interpersonal transaction cycle*.

In support of this idea, it is crucial to show that interpersonal styles are associated with biases in social perception that would tend to confirm or foster those styles. Panel B of Figure 8.2 shows a representative example of such a finding, again drawn from Sadler and Woody (2003).

The results for this regression model show that, controlling for the actual levels of affiliation shown by participants and their partners during an interaction, participants' self-perceived interpersonal style (View of Own Trait Affiliation) is an important predictor of their perceptions of both their own and their partner's levels of expressed affiliation. In short, people are biased to view both their own behavior and the responses of others in ways that are consistent with their own self-conception.

Similarly, Dodge and Somberg (1987) demonstrated that when presented with an ambiguous situation, aggressive children tend to perceive others as being more aggressive than do nonaggressive children. These findings, pertaining to the left side of the circumplex, suggest that those who are hostile tend to see their interaction partners as being more hostile than they actually are. This perceived hostility in others, in turn, would lend apparent confirmation to the person's hostile style, in the sense that it is better to "beat others to the punch." Some other research also demonstrates that people have cognitive expectancies for others to behave in ways that are complementary to their own style. Tiedens, Unzueta, and Young (2007) showed that people tend to expect others to behave in ways that are reciprocal to their own trait dominance, even when the participants have not met the other person.

It is worth mentioning that cognitive and related social factors may also inhibit complementarity. To illustrate, consider some factors that could interfere with Henry responding in a complementary fashion to Tom. First, if Tom sends mixed messages— for example, conveying a friendly message with a hostile tone of voice (Patterson, 1995)—or is otherwise inept about signaling his wishes, Henry may not be able to tell what kind of response Tom is inviting. Second, even if Tom's messages are reasonably clear to others, Henry may lack the required social-perception skill to decode Tom's behavior correctly. Third, even if Henry decodes Tom's overtures correctly, he may lack some of the social skills necessary to enact the complementary behavior in a clear or consistent way. Work by Duke and Nowicki (1992, 2005; Nowicki & Duke, 1994) on deficits in receptive and expressive nonverbal skills is consistent with the two foregoing scenarios, respectively (see also Lieberman & Rosenthal, 2001). Finally, even if all three of the preceding factors are favorable, Henry may have a motivational agenda that conflicts with behaving in a complementary fashion (see Dryer & Horowitz, 1997; Horowitz et al., 2006).

Much research remains to be done to shed further light on the circle of linkages implied by the interpersonal transaction cycle. However, the central idea—that people unwittingly shape their social world, whether it is one they find satisfying or not—is intuitively appealing, as suggested by the following anecdote:

> A man was moving to a new town and stopped at a gas station there. While filling up, he asked the attendant, "Are people friendly here?" The attendant paused, looked him over, and replied, "It all depends; what were people like where you came from?"

COMPLEMENTARITY AS INTERDEPENDENT SHIFTS, BURSTS, AND OSCILLATIONS

Having discussed previous research on complementarity, we now turn to advancing some new ideas about its component phenomena, ideas that we believe hold much promise. Although some of these ideas could conceivably be applied over larger time frames, here we will focus on understanding the phenomena that transpire over the course of a single interaction.

There are three fundamentally different ways in which two partners may adapt to each other's style. Figure 8.3 uses reciprocity

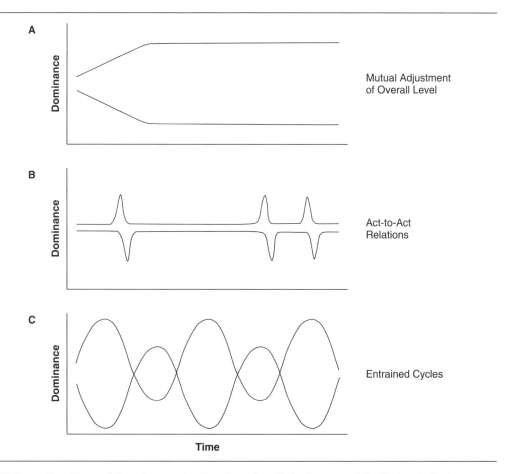

FIGURE 8.3 Pure Types of Complementarity. Interdependent Shifts, Bursts, and Oscillations in Reciprocity on Dominance

on dominance to depict each of these possibilities as pure types.

First, partners may demonstrate mutual adjustment of overall level, as shown in Panel A. The left side of the plot at the top depicts an early phase of the interaction in which partners show opposite slopes as they make overall adjustments toward more reciprocal stances to each other. Eventually, these adjustments of overall level would typically stabilize, yielding the steady overall levels depicted across the rest of the plot. Thus, one major component of complementarity is *interdependent shifts*.

Second, partners may demonstrate interdependence in act-to-act relations, as depicted in Panel B. At irregular intervals, one person acts more dominant than his or her baseline, and the partner immediately responds by being more submissive than his or her respective baseline. The notion of irregularity—that is, more or less random occurrence across time—is important to distinguish this type of adjustment from the next one. Thus, a second major component of complementarity is *interdependent bursts*.

Third, partners may demonstrate entrained cycles, as depicted in Panel C. The partners show coordinated rhythms, occurring more or less regularly across time, in which as one partner becomes more dominant, the other becomes more submissive, and vice versa. These coordinated rhythms represent a form of dynamic equilibrium in which each partner's behavior varies over time but stays within desired limits, a process of attunement (Field, 1985). Thus, a third major component of complementarity is *interdependent oscillations*.

These three types of complementarity can coexist in various combinations. For example, one can imagine sine-wave oscillations superimposed on the shifts in overall levels depicted in Panel A. If the oscillations for one partner were 180 degrees out of phase with the oscillations for the other partner (that is, the peaks in one person coincided with the valleys in the other person, and vice versa), then the pattern would represent the expected reciprocity in entrained cycles. In contrast, if the oscillations for one partner were in phase with the oscillations for the other partner (with coinciding peaks and coinciding valleys), then the pattern would represent theoretically surprising anticomplementarity of dominance in the entrained cycles. It is important to note, as this example illustrates, that the issue of complementarity at the level of entrained cycles is completely distinguishable from the issue of complementarity at the level of overall adjustment of means—a dyad could be complementary at one level and not at the other level.

It is useful to briefly relate this threefold breakdown, which we adopted from the work of Warner (1998), to the insights and terminology of some other researchers. Cappella (1996) argued that it is essential to draw a clear distinction between correlated adjustments of overall level, which he termed *mutual influence*, and correlated patterns of change within an interaction (controlling for adjustments of overall level), which he termed *mutual adaptation*. Interdependent bursts and interdependent oscillations are two forms of mutual adaptation, whereas interdependent shifts are the same phenomenon as mutual influence. The possibility of interdependent oscillations in social interaction has attracted the attention of several researchers (e.g., Bernieri & Rosenthal, 1991; Burgoon, Buller, & Woodall, 1989; Condon & Ogston, 1971; Chapple, 1970, 1982; Davis, 1982; Hatfield, Cacioppo, & Rapson, 1994; Warner, 1988). Burgoon and colleagues (1995) proposed that such enmeshing of recurrent cycles be termed *interactional synchrony*.

Are We on the Same Wavelength?

In the study by Sadler and Woody (2003) that we have used as an example (Figure 8.2), all the behavior ratings—whether by self, partner, or independent observers—reflected an overall judgment over the entire interaction. For example, observers watched the video of the interaction separately for each partner. As they watched the target person, they mentally tallied behaviors across time, and then at the end of the video they filled out a Social Behavior Inventory (SBI; Moskowitz, 1994). These SBIs provide overall levels of dominance and affiliation for each partner aggregated over the entire period of observation.

Thus, this study was purely an investigation of interdependent shifts; without time-dependent observations, it is not possible to capture interdependent bursts or oscillations. Kenny (1996) used the term *mutual influence model* to describe the type of structural equation model that Sadler and Woody (2003) applied to analyze these data, and this term is entirely consistent with the meaning reserved for *mutual influence* by Cappella (1996)—that is, *mutual influence* refers to the same phenomenon as *interdependent shifts*.

Sadler, Ethier, Gunn, Duong, and Woody (2009) used the same cooperative dyadic task as Sadler and Woody (2003), but added a new measurement technology to accommodate investigation of interdependent bursts and oscillations. In particular, as the observer watched the target person during an interaction, he or she made moment-to-moment, continuous ratings of behavioral dominance and affiliation using a computer joystick device. The observer could see on a display where his or her current rating was lying in the plane of the interpersonal circle, and the computer recorded the joystick position every half-second. To improve the reliability of the ratings, we had four observers independently watch the videos and use the joystick to record their moment-to-moment impressions, and then for each target person we averaged the four observers' ratings at each time point.

During the first few minutes of the 20-minute interaction period, dyads are often getting used to the task and settling into a stable pattern of interaction. Thus, we had observers make the continuous joystick ratings for the last 10 minutes of the interaction. This 10-minute observational period

generates more than a thousand successive observations for each partner.

The top panels in Figure 8.4 show the resulting data for one dyad. The plot to the left provides the bivariate time series for affiliation (*bivariate* simply means that we include both partners), with the solid trajectory representing the female and the dashed trajectory the male. The plot to the right provides the corresponding bivariate time series for dominance.

Note that the plot for affiliation shows a clear difference in overall levels—namely that the female is always more affiliative than the male. In addition, both trajectories show a negative linear slope. However, our main interest is in the similarity of moment-to-moment variation between the two partners. There appears to be a somewhat modest tendency for the partners to share peaks in affiliation. In the plot for dominance, the overall levels are more similar and linear slopes are less evident. However, the strong inverse relation in the moment-to-moment variation between partners is quite striking.

How can we quantify the degree of coordination in moment-to-moment variation between the partners? One relatively obvious approach is simply to calculate the correlation between partners' scores over time. This is called a *cross-correlation*. In this dyad, the cross-correlation for affiliation is .45, and the cross-correlation for dominance is −.50. The signs of these correlations are consistent with the hypotheses of complementarity—that is, a tendency toward sameness on affiliation versus a tendency toward oppositeness on dominance.

Unfortunately, the cross-correlation is susceptible to a number of potential confounds. For example, one contributor to the cross-correlation is similarity of linear slopes, which is usually regarded as distinct from similarity of patterning over time. To correct for this problem, we can remove the linear trend from each time series and recompute the correlations. They turn out to be .31 for affiliation and −.57 for dominance. These detrended cross-correlations capture

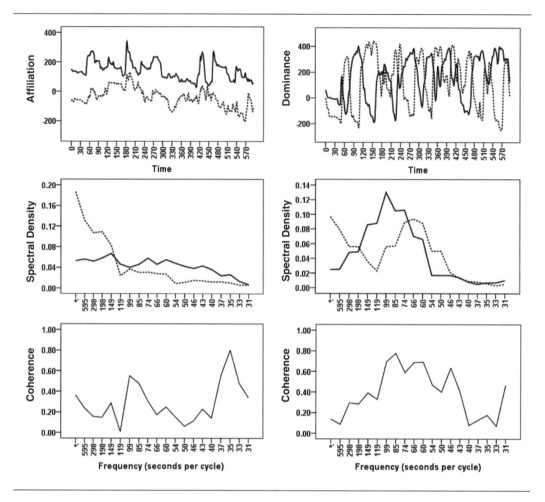

FIGURE 8.4   Plots of Times Series, Spectral Density, and Coherence for Affiliation (left column) and Dominance (right column): Data from One Dyad

Note: The solid trajectory represents the female's data and the dashed trajectory represents the male's data. The spectral analysis extrapolates back to a cycle of unlimited length, denoted here with an asterisk.

better what is evident visually—that the coordination of patterning is stronger for dominance than for affiliation. Other ways to attempt to overcome potential confounds in cross-correlations are covered in some detail in Sadler et al. (2009).

For present purposes, the main short-coming of the cross-correlation is that it does not distinguish among interdependent shifts, bursts, and oscillations; all three con-tribute to it. Distinguishing among these different types of effects requires a variance-decomposition strategy and the use of spec-tral analysis (Warner, 1998).

The first step is to model and remove overall trends. A regression analysis for each partner's time series provides the intercept at the beginning of the observation period, which indexes the average level at the beginning, and the linear slope, which indexes overall change over time. As detailed in Sadler et al. (2009), analysis of these intercepts and slopes over the entire sample of dyads yielded very strong evidence for interdependent shifts (that is, mutual adjustment of overall levels), in directions consistent with the hypotheses of complementarity.

Next, we can submit the detrended data to a procedure called *cross-spectral analysis*, which allows us to quantify the extent and nature of interdependent oscillations. The details of this procedure are somewhat technical and covered in Sadler et al. (2009); here we simply convey the gist. The lower panels of Figure 8.4 show some results of cross-spectral analyses of the bivariate time series at the top. Let's walk through these results for dominance (the right column):

In the middle is a plot of *spectral density profiles* for each partner. These tell us what proportion of the variance, along the Y-axis, is occurring at each component frequency, along the X-axis. The frequencies are the duration in seconds of a full sine wave. Here the female has a predominant tendency to show cycles with a duration of about a minute and a half (highest density at 99 s), whereas the male tends to show slightly shorter cycles (highest density at 66 s). However, the partners share substantial variance in cycles of around one to one-and-a-half minutes duration.

At the bottom is a plot showing the profile of the *coherence* across this spectrum of frequencies. The coherence indexes how closely related the partners' variations in amplitude are at each frequency. Akin to a squared correlation, it tells us how attuned the partners are at that frequency. Here the coherence values in the shared range of frequencies (one to one-and-a-half minutes duration) are quite high, above .60.

These rather detailed results need to be integrated into a simpler index. As our overall index of entrainment between partners, we computed the *average weighted coherence*. In computing this average, we weighted the coherence at each frequency by the proportions of variance for each partner at this frequency. The resulting value, which varies from 0 to 1, indexes how strongly entrained the partners are. Here, for dominance the average weighted coherence was .55.

Finally, a cross-spectral analysis provides us with information about the *phase relation* between the partners—that is, who is leading or lagging whom. A phase of 0 degrees would mean that the partners tend to be perfectly in synch, with peaks coinciding and troughs coinciding. In contrast, according to the hypothesis of reciprocity on dominance, we would expect this value to be near 180 degrees, because 180 degrees means that one partner's peaks occur at the same time as the other partner's troughs, and vice versa. Here the average phase was 174 degrees, which is very close to 180.

The corresponding results for the cross-spectral analysis of affiliation appear in the lower panels to the left in Figure 8.4. Compared to the results for dominance, on affiliation the partners show much less tendency to cycle at comparable frequencies, and the coherence values are generally lower. Accordingly, the resulting value for the average weighted coherence was a more modest .26. The average phase was –2 degrees, which is very close to zero and hence strongly consistent with moment-to-moment correspondence.

Such an analysis may be performed on the data from each dyad. Figure 8.5 shows the distribution of such results across a sample of 50 dyads. The results for coherence of affiliation (upper left) show values ranging from near zero, indicating no entrainment, to almost one, indicating near-perfect entrainment. The mean is about .5, indicating that the norm is moderate entrainment. For dominance (lower left), the range is just as striking, and the mean is about .4. (Coherence is like a squared correlation, so we do not expect it to have a negative value even for dominance.)

The results for average phase (shown on the right) require a scale that wraps around in a circle. The main thing to note here is that for affiliation and dominance there is no overlap at all in the distributions of phase. On the basis of phase alone, one could tell with perfect accuracy whether any bivariate time series is for affiliation or for dominance.

Moving beyond the cross-spectral analyses, the remaining issue is how to quantify interdependent bursts. For this purpose, trends and cycles are removed from the data and an entity called the cross-correlation

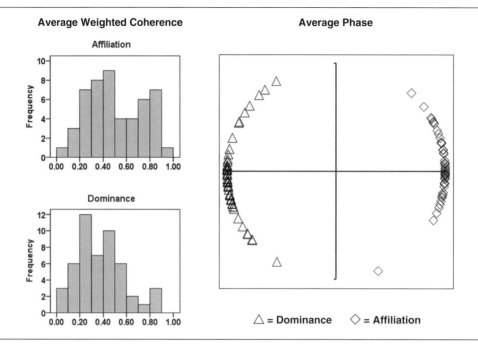

FIGURE 8.5   Distributions of Average Weighted Coherence and Average Phase for Affiliation and Dominance across 50 Dyads
Source: Based on data from Sadler et al., 2009.

function is examined. Sadler et al. (2009) provide the details of this procedure. The results indicated a statistically significant tendency toward interdependent bursts in almost all the dyads, in the theoretically expected directions (i.e., positive correlations for affiliation and negative correlations for dominance). However, these phenomena accounted for far less variance than the interdependent oscillations.

In summary, the results of this study verified that interdependent shifts are a very important component of interpersonal complementarity, but added to this picture as a second important, reasonably independent component the phenomenon of interdependent oscillations. In future research, the very large entrainment differences between dyads may be used to predict interesting subjective and objective outcomes. Along these lines, Markey, Lowmaster, and Eichler (2010) used the joystick method and showed that positive cross-correlations on affiliation predict

faster completion time and higher quality of collaborative tasks. Finally, although interdependent bursts occur in most dyads, they seem to be a more minor phenomenon.

SUMMARY AND CONCLUSIONS

In this chapter, we characterized interpersonal complementarity as the diverse ways in which the interpersonal behaviors of people may fit together and influence each other. As we pointed out, it is unfortunate that the terminology classically adopted by interpersonal theorists (e.g., Kiesler, 1996) to describe such phenomena clashes with how the same terms are used by other psychologists (including the term *complementarity* itself). Nonetheless, the resulting literature, which we reviewed in some detail, is definitely of considerable interest to personality, social, clinical, and I/O psychologists. In particular, this literature shows that there are important subjective and objective effects of different pairings of interpersonal styles, that people modify each other's interpersonal behaviors during interaction in lawful and important ways, and that a variety of mediating processes, involving cognitive and motivational factors, are involved in these effects.

A theme we would like to emphasize in closing is the key importance of variability in interpersonal behavior (Moskowitz & Zuroff, 2004). In previous accounts of the interpersonal circle, there has usually been much emphasis on relatively invariant behavior, which becomes more dramatic as one moves away from the center. For example, in Kiesler's (1983) depiction of the circle, as we move out from the origin in the direction of 10 o'clock, we pass from "suspicious/resentful" to "paranoid/vindictive" and the rigid interpersonal pathologies such as paranoia which, according to the model, lie on the periphery of the circumplex (Wiggins, 1982).

In contrast, the center area, near the origin, can seem comparatively dull and even ill-defined. For instance, consider the midpoint on the affiliation dimension. A person whose interpersonal behavior is so unvarying and nondescript that he or she shows neither distinctly friendly nor distinctly unfriendly acts would fall here. However, so would a person who varies a great deal and shows very friendly and very unfriendly behaviors with about equal frequency. Surely these patterns need to be distinguished.

Furthermore, other distinctions involving variability may be essential as well—namely, those having to do with entrainment. For example, consider a person whose level of friendliness varies widely, but who fails to entrain these variations to those of partners. This person, characterized by unpredictable or expectancy-violating fluctuations, may be just as problematic to others as a person who, say, is consistently very unfriendly.

In conclusion, there may be many interesting phenomena, vibrating and more or less entrained, that are hiding around the origin of the interpersonal circle. To study them we need to use, in effect, a temporal microscope that brings these patterns into focus.

References

Ansell, E. B., Kurtz, J. E., & Markey, P. M. (2008). Gender differences in interpersonal complementarity within roommate dyads. *Personality and Social Psychology Bulletin, 34,* 502–512.

Beach, S. R. H., Whitaker, D. J., Jones, D. J., & Tesser, A. (2001). When does performance feedback prompt *complementarity* in romantic relationships? *Personal Relationships, 8,* 231–248.

Benjamin, L. S. (1974). Structural analysis of social behavior. *Psychological Review, 81,* 392–425.

Bernieri, F. J., & Rosenthal, R. (1991). Interpersonal coordination: Behavioral matching and interactional synchrony. In R. S. Feldman & B. Rimé (Eds.), *Fundamentals of nonverbal behavior* (pp. 401–432). Cambridge, UK: Cambridge University Press.

Bluhm, C., Widiger, T. A., & Miele, G. M. (1990). Interpersonal complementarity and individual differences. *Journal of Personality and Social Psychology, 58,* 464–471.

Boker, S. M., & Wenger, M. J. (2007). *Data analytic techniques for dynamical systems.* Mahwah, NJ: Erlbaum.

Bowers, K. S. (1973). Situationism in psychology: An analysis and a critique. *Psychological Review, 80,* 307–336.

Burgoon, J. K., Buller, D. B., & Woodall, W. G. (1989). *Nonverbal communication: The unspoken dialogue.* New York: HarperCollins.

Burgoon, J. K., Stern, L. A., & Dillman, L. (1995). *Interpersonal adaptation: Dyadic interaction patterns.* New York: Cambridge University Press.

Cappella, J. N. (1996). Dynamic coordination of vocal and kinesic behavior in dyadic interaction: Methods, problems, and interpersonal outcomes. In J. H. Watt & C. A. Van Lear (Eds.), *Dynamic patterns in communication processes.* Thousand Oaks, CA: Sage.

Carson, R. C. (1969). *Interaction concepts of personality.* Chicago: Aldine.

Carson, R. C. (1982). Self-fulfilling prophesy, maladaptive behavior, and psychotherapy. In J. C. Anchin & D. J. Kiesler (Eds.), *Handbook of Interpersonal Therapy* (pp. 64–77). Elmsford, NY: Pergamon.

Chapple, E. D. (1970). *Culture and biological man: Explorations in behavioral anthropology.* New York: Holt, Rinehart & Winston.

Chapple, E. D. (1982). Movement and sound: The musical language of body rhythms in interaction. In M. Davis (Ed.), *Interaction rhythms: Periodicity in communicative behavior* (pp. 31–52). New York: Human Sciences.

Condon, W. S., & Ogston, W. D. (1971). Speech and body motion synchrony of the speaker-hearer. In D. L. Horton & J. J. Jenkins (Eds.), *Perception of language* (pp. 150–173). Columbus, OH: Charles E. Merrill.

Davis, D. (1982). Determinants of responsiveness in dyadic interaction. In W. I. Ickes & E. S. Knowles (Eds.), *Personality, roles, and social behaviors* (pp. 85–139). New York: Springer-Verlag.

Dodge, K. A., & Somberg, D. R. (1987). Hostile attributional biases among aggressive boys are exacerbated under conditions of threats to the self. *Child Development, 58,* 213–224.

Dryer, D. C., & Horowitz, L. M. (1997). When do opposites attract? Interpersonal complementarity versus similarity. *Journal of Personality and Social Psychology, 72,* 592–603.

Duke, M., & Nowicki, S. Jr. (1992). *Helping the child who doesn't fit in.* Atlanta: Peachtree.

Duke, M., & Nowicki, S. Jr. (2005). The Emory Dyssemia Index. In V. Manusov (Ed.), *The sourcebook of nonverbal measures: Going beyond words* (pp. 35–46). Mahwah, NJ: Erlbaum.

Dyce, J., & O'Connor, B. P. (1992). Personality complementarity as a determinant of group cohesion in bar bands. *Small Group Research, 23,* 185–198.

Estroff, S., & Nowicki, S. Jr. (1992). Interpersonal complementarity, gender of interactants, and performance on puzzle and word tasks. *Personality and Social Psychology Bulletin, 18,* 351–356.

Field, T. (1985). Attachment as psychobiological attunement: Being on the same wavelength. In M. Reite & T. Field (Eds.), *Psychobiology of attachment.* New York: Academic Press.

Fournier, M. A., Moskowitz, D. S., & Zuroff, D. C. (2008). Integrating dispositions, signatures, and the interpersonal domain. *Journal of Personality and Social Psychology, 94,* 531–545.

Friedlander, M. L. (1993). When complementarity is uncomplimentary and other reactions to Tracey (1993). *Journal of Counseling Psychology, 40,* 410–412.

Gurtman, M. B. (2001). Interpersonal complementarity: Integrating interpersonal measurement with interpersonal models. *Journal of Counseling Psychology, 48,* 97–110.

Hatfield, E., Cacioppo, J. T., & Rapson, R. (1994). *Emotional contagion.* Cambridge: Cambridge University Press.

Horowitz, L. M., Wilson, K. R., Turan, B., Zolotsev, P., Constantino, M. J., & Henderson, L. (2006). How interpersonal motives clarify the meaning of interpersonal behavior: A revised circumplex model. *Personality and Social Psychology Review, 10,* 67–86.

Kenny, D. A. (1996). Models of nonindependence in dyadic research. *Journal of Social and Personal Relationships, 13,* 279–294.

Kenny, D. A., Kashy, D. A., & Cook, W. L. (2006). *Dyadic data analysis.* New York: Guilford Press.

Kiesler, D. J. (1983). The 1982 Interpersonal Circle: A taxonomy for complementarity in human transactions. *Psychological Review, 90,* 185–214.

Kiesler, D. J. (1996). *Contemporary interpersonal theory and research: Personality, psychopathology, and psychotherapy.* New York: John Wiley & Sons.

Leary, T. (1957). *Interpersonal diagnosis of personality.* New York: Ronald Press.

Liebermann, M. D., & Rosenthal, R. (2001). Why introverts can't always tell who likes them: Multitasking and nonverbal decoding. *Journal of Personality and Social Psychology, 80,* 294–310.

Locke, K. D., & Sadler, P. (2007). Self-efficacy, values, and complementarity in dyadic interactions: Integrating interpersonal and social-cognitive theory. *Personality and Social Psychology Bulletin, 33,* 94–109.

Markey, P. M., Funder, D. C., & Ozer, D. J. (2003). Complementarity of interpersonal behaviors in dyadic interactions. *Personality and Social Psychology Bulletin, 29,* 1082–1090.

Markey, P. M., & Kurtz, J. E. (2006). Increasing acquaintanceship and complementarity of behavioral styles and personality traits among college roommates. *Personality and Social Psychology Bulletin, 32,* 907–916.

Markey, P. M., Lowmaster, S. E., & Eichler, W. C. (2010). A real-time assessment of interpersonal complementarity. *Personal Relationships, 17,* 13–25.

Markey, P. M., & Markey, C. N. (2007). Romantic ideals, romantic obtainment, and relationship experiences: The complementarity of interpersonal traits among romantic partners. *Journal of Social and Personal Relationships, 24,* 517–533.

Moskowitz, D. S., Ho, M.-H. R., & Turcotte-Tremblay, A.-M. (2007). Contextual influences on interpersonal complementarity. *Personality and Social Psychology Bulletin, 33,* 1051–1063.

Moskowitz, D. S., & Zuroff, D. C. (2004). Flux, pulse, and spin: Dynamic additions to the personality lexicon. *Journal of Personality and Social Psychology, 86,* 880–893.

Nowicki, S. Jr., & Duke, M. (1994). Individual differences in the nonverbal communication of affect: The diagnostic analysis of the nonverbal accuracy scale. *Journal of Nonverbal Behavior, 18,* 9–34.

Nowicki, S. Jr., & Manheim, S. (1991). Interpersonal complementarity and time of interaction in female relationships. *Journal of Research in Personality, 25,* 322–333.

O'Connor, B. P., & Dyce, J. (1997). Interpersonal rigidity, hostility, and complementarity in musical bands. *Journal of Personality and Social Psychology, 72,* 362–372.

Orford, J. (1986). The rules of interpersonal complementarity: Does hostility beget hostility and dominance, submission? *Psychological Review, 93,* 365–377.

Patterson, M. L. (1995). A parallel process model of nonverbal communication. *Journal of Nonverbal Behavior, 19,* 3–29.

Pilkington, C. J., Tesser, A., & Stephens, D. (1991). Complementarity in romantic relationships: A self-evaluation maintenance perspective. *Journal of Social and Personal Relationships, 8,* 481–504.

Sadler, P., & Woody, E. (2003). Is who you are who you're talking to? Interpersonal style and complementarity in mixed-sex interactions. *Journal of Personality and Social Psychology, 84,* 80–96.

Sadler, P., Ethier, N., Gunn, G. R., Duong, D., & Woody, E. (2009). Are we on the same wavelength? Interpersonal complementarity as shared cyclical patterns during interactions. *Journal of Personality and Social Psychology, 97,* 1005–1020.

Shechtman, N., & Horowitz, L. M. (2006). Interpersonal and noninterpersonal interactions, interpersonal motive, and the effect of frustrated motives. *Personality and Social Psychology Bulletin, 32,* 1126–1139.

Semin, G. R. (2007). Grounding communication: Synchrony. In A. W. Kruglanski & W. T. Higgins (Eds.), *Social psychology: Handbook of basic principles* (2nd ed., pp. 630–649). New York: Guilford Press.

Semin, G. R., & Cacioppo, J. T. (2008). Grounding social cognition: Synchronization, coordination, and coregulation. In G. R. Semin & E. R. Smith (Eds.), *Embodied grounding: Social, cognitive, affective, and neuroscientific approaches* (pp. 119–147). New York: Cambridge University Press.

Smith, J. L., & Ruiz, J. M. (2007). Interpersonal orientation in context: Correlates and effects of interpersonal complementarity on subjective and cardiovascular experiences. *Journal of Personality, 75,* 679–708.

Strong, S. R., Hills, H. I., Kilmartin, C. T., DeVries, H., Lanier, K., Nelson, B. N., ... Meyer III, C. W. (1988). The dynamic relations among interpersonal behaviors: A test of complementarity and anticomplementarity. *Journal of Personality and Social Psychology, 54,* 798–810.

Tiedens, L. Z., & Fragale, A. R. (2003). Power moves: Complementarity in dominant and submissive nonverbal behavior. *Journal of Personality and Social Psychology, 84,* 558–568.

Tiedens, L. Z., Unzueta, M. M., & Young, M. J. (2007). An unconscious desire for hierarchy? The motivated perception of dominance complementarity in task partners. *Journal of Personality and Social Psychology, 93,* 402–414.

Tracey, T. J. (1993). An interpersonal stage model of the therapeutic process. *Journal of Counseling Psychology, 40,* 396–409.

Tracey, T. J. (1994). An examination of the complementarity of interpersonal behavior. *Journal of Personality and Social Psychology, 67,* 864–878.

Tracey, T. J. G. (2004). Levels of interpersonal complementarity: A simplex representation. *Personality and Social Psychology Bulletin, 30,* 1211–1225.

Tracey, T. J. G. (2005). Interpersonal rigidity and complementarity. *Journal of Research in Personality, 39,* 592–614.

Tracey, T. (2007, June). The construct of complementarity: *I* is not equal to *E. Society for Interpersonal Theory and Research Newsletter, 7*(3), 1,6.

Tracey, T. J., Ryan, J., & Jaschik-Herman, B. (2001). Complementarity of interpersonal circumplex traits. *Personality and Social Psychology Bulletin, 27*, 786–797.

Tracey, T. J. G., Sherry, P., & Albright, J. (1999). The interpersonal process of cognitive-behavioral therapy: An examination of complementarity over the course of treatment. *Journal of Counseling Psychology, 46*, 80–91.

Wachtel, P. (1973). Psychodynamics, behavior therapy, and the implacable experimenter: An inquiry into the consistency of personality. *Journal of Abnormal Psychology, 82*, 324–334.

Warner, R. M. (1988). Rhythm in social interaction. In J. E. McGrath (Ed.), *The social psychology of time: New perspectives*. Beverly Hills, CA: Sage.

Warner, R. M. (1998). *Spectral analysis of time-series data*. New York: Guilford Press.

Wiggins, J. S. (1982). Circumplex models of interpersonal behavior in clinical psychology. In P. C. Kendall & J. N. Butcher (Eds.), *Handbook of research methods in clinical psychology* (pp. 183–221). New York: John Wiley & Sons.

Wright, T. L., & Ingraham, L. J. (1986). A social relations model test of the interpersonal circle. *Journal of Personality and Social Psychology, 50*, 1285–1290.

Yaughn, E., & Nowicki, S. Jr. (1999). Close relationships and complementary interpersonal styles among men and women. *Journal of Social Psychology, 139*, 473–478.

9

EMPATHIC ACCURACY AND INACCURACY

Kathryn H. Rollings

Ronen Cuperman

William Ickes

A college freshman is walking into his first class of the semester when he notices a beautiful girl sitting in the front row of the lecture hall. He walks over and sits down next to her, striking up a conversation about school and the class. Later, he meets his friends in the dining hall and tells them about the encounter.

"She was totally into me," he brags. "She even gave me her phone number."

He looks up and sees her walking across the dining hall, and waves at her. She waves back nervously, and hurries to sit with her friends.

"See?" the boy says to his jealous friends. "She wants me."

"Who was that?" The girl's friends ask her as she sits down at the table with them.

"Some guy in my English class," she replies. "He hit on me first thing this morning. He's so not my type. I gave him a fake phone number."

As this example illustrates, people don't always understand the thoughts and feelings of the people they meet. Although misunderstandings are common in interactions with strangers (Colvin, Vogt, & Ickes, 1997), they also occur with the people we

know well (Sillars, 1998; Sillars, Koerner, & Fitzpatrick, 2005).

The male character in our scenario made an empathic inference when he decided that the attractive woman was interested in him; the term *empathic inference* refers to the guesses we make about the contents of others' thoughts and feelings. However, based on the woman's comment to her friends ("*He's so not my type*"), we might conclude that the young man does not have much *empathic accuracy*, a term that refers to how accurately a person can infer the content of another person's thoughts and feelings. Empathic inferences are made by virtually everyone on a regular basis (Goleman, 2006), but the extent to which such inferences are accurate is a topic worthy of study in its own right (Ickes, 1997, 2003).

In this chapter, we explore the topic of empathic accuracy and its logical complement, empathic *in*accuracy. We begin with a discussion of the measurement of empathic accuracy, reviewing the three research paradigms that have been developed to study this phenomenon. We next consider whether empathic accuracy is greater for women than for men, and for friends than for strangers. We then discuss the relevance of empathic accuracy to clinical settings, suggesting how to improve the empathic accuracy of psychotherapists and how to apply the findings of empathic accuracy research to the study of autism, borderline personality disorder, and couples therapy. In this clinically relevant section of the chapter, the work on motivated accuracy and motivated *in*accuracy will be featured.

MEASURING EMPATHIC ACCURACY:
THREE PARADIGMS

In the various studies of empathic accuracy that have been conducted during the past two decades, the concept has been studied in three ways: with the *unstructured dyadic interaction paradigm*, the *standard stimulus paradigm*, and the *standard interview paradigm*. Below, we describe each of these methods, explore their respective advantages and disadvantages, and note the kind of research problem that each method is best suited to address.

The Unstructured Dyadic Interaction Paradigm

The original procedure for collecting empathic accuracy data involves an "unstructured dyadic interaction paradigm," in which two individuals who may or may not already be acquainted are escorted to a laboratory "waiting room" by an experimenter. The experimenter asks the two participants to sit on a couch, but then has to leave them alone under the pretext of having to retrieve something that is needed for the experiment. At this point, the unstructured dyadic interaction occurs. During the next six minutes, the two participants are unobtrusively video and audio recorded. At the end of this time, the experimenter returns to the room and reveals to the participants that they have been taped. At this point, both participants must give their written consent to have the video and

audio recordings used as data sources; if this occurs, they continue to the next part of the study, which proceeds as follows.

The participants are seated in separate cubicles, where each watches playback of the tape that was made while they were interacting. While they are watching the tape, the participants are asked to stop the tape whenever they remember having had a thought or a feeling at a particular point during the interaction. Using a supply of thought/feeling recording forms, they are asked to note the specific time when their thought or feeling occurred, whether they are reporting a thought or a feeling, and the content of that thought or feeling. They continue with this procedure until they have made a complete list of all of the thoughts and feelings they experienced.

When both participants have completed this task, the thought/feeling inference phase of the procedure begins. This phase of the procedure has been modified over the years, and a few variations exist (Ickes, 2003). In one variation, the participants are asked to infer the content of their partner's thoughts and feelings and to rate the overall valence of each thought or feeling as positive, neutral, or negative. In a second variation, the participants infer each of their partner's thoughts and feelings and go on to rate how accurate they thought they were after making each inference. In a third variation, more recent studies of empathic accuracy have not asked participants to evaluate their inferences at all.

In all three variations, the tape is paused for each "perceiver" at each of the times when his or her partner reported having a specific thought or feeling. The perceiver begins by deciding whether the partner had a thought or a feeling, and after noting this decision, writes the inferred content of the thought or feeling (as a phrase or a sentence) in one of the spaces provided on the thought/feeling inference form.

Empathic accuracy is judged by a group of five to eight raters. The raters are asked to review all of the thoughts and feelings that have been reported by each participant and inferred by his or her interaction partner. Raters then assign a rating to each inference according to how similar it is in content to the thought or feeling that was reported by the interaction partner. For instance, a reported thought of "This guy is nice" and an inferred thought of "This guy is a jerk" would be rated with a 0, as they have essentially different content. In contrast, ratings of 1 or 2 denote "similar, but not the same, content" and "essentially the same content," respectively. By aggregating and transforming these ratings, an overall empathic accuracy score can then be calculated for each participant. Higher scores indicate higher levels of empathic accuracy on a scale that has a potential range of 0 (zero accuracy) to 100 (perfect accuracy).

The unstructured dyadic interaction paradigm has been used to study interactions between strangers (e.g., Garcia, Stinson, Ickes, Bissonnette, & Briggs, 1986; Ickes, Stinson, Bissonnette, & Garcia, 1990) and between individuals who know each other well (e.g., friends, dating partners, and marriage partners). This paradigm can be used to study asymmetries in empathic accuracy within relationships (Clements, Holtzworth-Munroe, Schweinle, & Ickes, 2007) and differences in empathic accuracy across relationships that vary in their degree of intimacy/acquaintanceship (Stinson & Ickes, 1992; Thomas, Fletcher, & Lange, 1997). Another important advantage of this paradigm is that it provides a very rich data source. In addition to the empathic accuracy data, the videotaped interaction can be coded to measure interpersonal (physical) distance, body language, eye contact, and a variety of conversational and linguistic elements (see Garcia et al., 1991; Ickes, 2003).

The major disadvantage of the unstructured dyadic interaction paradigm is that each perceiver infers a unique interaction partner's thoughts and feelings, making the inference task different for each perceiver, and confounding the perceiver's empathic ability with the partner's "readability." For a statistical solution to these problems, see Simpson, Oriña, and Ickes (2003) and Flury, Ickes, and Schweinle (2008).

The Standard Stimulus Paradigm

The standard stimulus paradigm was originally developed to assess empathic accuracy in a clinically relevant research setting (Marangoni, Garcia, Ickes, & Teng, 1995). This paradigm employs a standard stimulus video, usually composed of excerpts from a set of previously videotaped interactions. This videotape is used as a standard stimulus tape in subsequent studies, in which participants are asked to make thought and feeling inferences at those points on the tape where the target person(s) reported having had a thought or feeling. The inferred thoughts and feelings are compared to the actual reported thoughts and feelings (as described in the previous section), and participants are assigned an overall empathic accuracy score.

The major advantage of the standard stimulus paradigm is the fact that the task is the same for all perceivers. This feature allows empathic accuracy scores to be compared across perceivers and correlated with relevant perceiver characteristics. Researchers can therefore assess individual differences in empathic ability and then use these data to explore issues such as cross-target consistency (Marangoni et al., 1995) and the correlates of empathic ability (Gleason, Jensen-Campbell, & Ickes, 2009).

The standard stimulus paradigm is particularly well-suited to studies of individual differences in therapists' empathic ability (studies relevant to this topic are discussed below in the section titled "Empathic Accuracy of Clinical Psychologists"). On the other hand, the standard stimulus paradigm is not well-suited to the study of interpersonal behavior (for this purpose, researchers should use the unstructured dyadic interaction paradigm instead).

The Standard Interview Paradigm

The standard interview paradigm (Dugosh, 1998, as described in Ickes, 2009) takes participants in a slightly different direction than either the unstructured dyadic interaction paradigm or the standard stimulus paradigm. In the standard interview paradigm, participants are asked to view a videotaped interview of a person or person(s) that they may or may not know well. The target person(s) in the videotape are asked a standard set of interview questions by an interviewer. The perceiver watches the videotape, which is stopped immediately after each question has been posed, and is asked to write down the content of the predicted answer that the target person will give. In this case, empathic accuracy is determined by the degree to which the perceiver's predicted answers are similar to the actual answers given by the target (once again, predicted answer/actual answer similarity is judged by a group of trained raters).

The standard interview paradigm is useful in studying acquaintanceship, making it possible to compare the predicted answers of those who know an individual well with those who don't. A potential problem with this paradigm occurs, however, if the perceivers watch unedited recordings, since they receive immediate feedback after each inference when the recording proceeds and the target partner's answer is revealed. As discussed later in this chapter, Marangoni et al. (1995) found that receiving feedback during the course of performing the empathic accuracy task can significantly improve a perceiver's empathic accuracy. It is therefore possible that effects found in studies using the standard interview paradigm may be inflated due to the effect of feedback. To avoid this problem, researchers should delete the target person's actual answers to the interviewer's questions from the videotaped interview before it is shown to the perceiver.

EXPLORATIONS OF GENDER DIFFERENCES AND ACQUAINTANCESHIP EFFECTS

Early in the history of empathic accuracy research, William Ickes and his colleagues explored two factors that were widely believed to play a role in empathic accuracy: the gender of the perceiver and the degree of acquaintanceship between the perceiver and the target person. As the reader will see, the research on gender differences produced unexpected findings, whereas the research on acquaintanceship did not.

Gender Differences in Empathic Accuracy

The social stereotype of "women's intuition" suggests that the average woman should have greater empathic ability than the average man. Surprisingly, however, there was no evidence to support this stereotype in the results of the first seven studies in which the empathic accuracy of male and female perceivers could be compared (Graham & Ickes, 1997). Following these seven studies of empathic accuracy, the empathic accuracy data collection procedure was changed so that perceivers rated the accuracy of their empathic inferences immediately after making each of them. Interestingly, after this procedural change, evidence for the expected gender difference emerged in the form of greater empathic accuracy scores for women than for men.

Subsequent research has clarified these findings. First, it revealed that gender differences favoring female perceivers tend to be the exception rather than the rule. Second, it revealed that when such differences do occur, they reflect gender-based differences in empathic *motivation* rather than empathic *ability* (i.e., when women are "reminded" that they are supposed to excel on empathy-relevant tasks, it motivates them to outperform men). For overviews of the evidence that supports this motivational interpretation, see Graham and Ickes (1997), Ickes, Gesn, and Graham (2000), Klein and Hodges (2001), and Thomas and Maio (2008).

Acquaintanceship Effects in Empathic Accuracy

One would expect that individuals who are familiar with one another would have better empathic accuracy than would complete strangers. Friends often have intimate knowledge of each others' backgrounds. They also have shared experiences and inside jokes that can be referenced with a few words or a facial expression (Graham, 1994; Colvin et al., 1997).

In a study of male dyads, some composed of friends and some composed of strangers, Stinson and Ickes (1992) found that the average empathic accuracy score of the friends (about 30 on the 0 to 100 scale) was 50% greater than that of the strangers (about 20 on the same scale). Graham (1994) replicated and extended this finding in a study that also included female friends and strangers. Not surprisingly, Graham found that friends tended to rely on "shared information" about events that had taken place in the past, such as shared experiences or shared knowledge. Strangers did not have this "shared information" on which to rely, but when they were able to find "common ground" regarding subjects and events about which they both had similar information, their empathic accuracy performance was improved. Strangers who found such common ground were able to perform the empathic accuracy task better than those who did not; however, friends still performed the empathic accuracy task better than strangers, in general.

We should note that although friends demonstrate an enhanced ability to infer each other's thoughts and feelings, they still perform this task well below the theoretically possible limit of 100 on the 0-to-100 empathic accuracy scale. Although increasing acquaintance does lead to better empathic accuracy, friends do not possess the ability to literally "read each others' minds." For additional evidence of the role of acquaintanceship in empathic accuracy, see the subsequent studies reported by Gesn (1995) and Thomas, Fletcher, and Lange (1997).

EMPATHIC ACCURACY AND PSYCHOTHERAPY

Empathy is important to the development of rapport between a therapist and a patient, and has been identified as an essential element of the client-therapist relationship (Ickes, Marangoni, & Garcia, 1997; Kagan, 1977; Rogers, 1957, 1975). Not surprisingly, therefore, there have been some attempts to study empathic accuracy in clinically relevant contexts.

The Empathic Accuracy of "Amateur Psychotherapists"

Marangoni et al. (1995) recognized the benefit of studying empathic accuracy in a clinically relevant setting. Using the standard stimulus paradigm, they asked college student participants to act as amateur psychotherapists. Specifically, these participants viewed videotapes of the client-centered therapy sessions of three women who had not been diagnosed with a psychological disorder, but who had personal relationship problems in their lives. Each video was edited so that participants made 30 thought/feeling inferences for each of the three targets.

All participants established a baseline level of their empathic accuracy during the first eight thought/feeling inferences, and then an experimental group was given feedback on each of their subsequent 16 inferences (the control group also made inferences about these 16 thoughts and feelings, but was not given any feedback). In the final test phase, all participants made inferences without feedback for the last set of eight thoughts and feelings.

Overall, the researchers observed strong evidence for a short-term "acquaintanceship effect." Regardless of the feedback/no feedback manipulation, the empathic accuracy of perceivers was greater during the final test phase than it was during the baseline phase. In other words, as the therapy session proceeded from beginning to end, the perceivers became more accurate at judging what the target person was thinking or feeling.

But was the feedback successful in improving the perceivers' empathic accuracy? It was: the participants who received feedback during the middle portion of the videos had significantly higher levels of empathic accuracy during the test phase than those who did not (Marangoni, et al., 1995). There was even some evidence to suggest that the feedback given to the participants during the first of the three videotapes may have helped to improve their empathic accuracy during the other two videos they viewed. The results of this study suggest that empathic accuracy is a skill that can be improved when feedback is provided. People who desire to improve their empathic accuracy might therefore attempt to solicit such feedback by means of feedback-seeking statements such as "Do I understand you correctly? Are you saying that . . . ?"

In addition to these effects, Marangoni et al. (1995) reported significant target-based differences in the perceivers' empathic accuracy, such that accuracy was relatively high for two of the targets but low for the third target, who was clearly more "difficult to read." There was evidence that this target was quite ambivalent in her underlying feelings, making it difficult for the perceivers to accurately infer how she felt from one minute to the next. Interestingly, substantial differences in "target readability" appear to be the rule, rather than the exception. In fact, the results of a small-scale meta-analysis by Ickes, Buysse, et al. (2000) revealed that there is much more variance in the readability of targets than in the empathic ability of perceivers.

The Empathic Accuracy of Psychotherapists-in-Training

Using the Marangoni et al. (1995) study as their precedent, Barone et al. (2005) sought to examine the effect of feedback training on perceivers who were studying to become clinical psychologists. All of these student therapists completed interview training sessions. However, the students in the experimental group inferred the thoughts and feelings of "clients" in a role-play and were given feedback regarding their accuracy, whereas the students in the control group

did not practice inferring the thoughts and feelings of any "clients." Barone and his colleagues found that the students who had practiced the thought/feeling inference task were more accurate in inferring the feelings of an actual client at a posttest than were the students who had not practiced the thought/feeling inference task. Interestingly, they did not find a difference in participants' abilities to infer the client's thoughts.

Taken together, these studies highlight the usefulness of studying empathic accuracy in a clinically relevant context. Although the empathic accuracy of therapists will tend to improve with increasing exposure to their clients, therapists can accelerate this improvement by obtaining feedback regarding the accuracy of their empathic inferences. They can also benefit from knowing that there are substantial differences in client "readability," and that some clients will inevitably be more difficult to read than others.

Autism

Baron-Cohen and his colleagues have characterized autistic individuals as "mind-blind," acting as if they are unaware that other people have thoughts and feelings, and failing to accurately infer them (Baron-Cohen, 1995, 2003; Baron-Cohen et al., 2001). Such individuals fall within an "autism spectrum" that ranges from severely autistic to normally functioning. Baron-Cohen (2003) has argued that males are less empathically accurate than females because there are more males who are closer to the autistic pole of the continuum.

Remember, however, that in the empathic accuracy research with college student samples, a gender difference was found in regard to empathic motivation, but not in regard to empathic ability (Ickes, Gesn, & Graham, 2000; Schmid Mast & Ickes, 2007). These results suggest that although a gender difference in empathic ability might indeed exist at the autistic end of the autism spectrum (males are four to five times more likely than females to be diagnosed with autism), there is no gender difference in empathic ability at the normal end of the spectrum.

In fact, in a study of young adolescents, Gleason, Johnson, et al. (2004) found that empathic accuracy and an autistic-like behavior pattern had additive and *independent* effects on the children's personal and social adjustment. These findings suggest that odd, autistic-like behaviors (e.g., remembering license plate numbers, persisting in repetitive acts) can co-occur with high as well as with low empathic accuracy, and that there is a danger in conflating these two predictors. Perhaps, as Goleman (2006, p. 92) has suggested, only a minority of children with odd social behaviors are indeed autistic, whereas the majority have simply failed to acquire the kinds of social experiences that are needed to learn to relate to others in a normatively appropriate way.

Borderline Personality Disorder

When examining the relationship between empathic accuracy and borderline personality disorder (BPD), Flury, Ickes, and Schweinle (2008) initially found support for an assumption made by several clinicians over the years: that people with the symptoms of BPD are better at inferring the thoughts and feelings of others than is the average individual. In their study, same-sex strangers who fell on opposite poles of a measure of borderline symptomology were paired together in a waiting-room scenario. Although the results initially revealed that high-BPD members were more empathically accurate than their low-BPD counterparts, this difference was no longer significant after controlling for the inferential difficulty of the dyad members' reported thoughts and feelings. In other words, because the high-BPD individuals reported thoughts and feelings that were more difficult to infer than those of their low-BPD partners, the high-BPD individuals achieved better

empathic accuracy because they had more "readable" partners, and *not* because they had greater empathic ability.

When applying these findings to a clinical setting, therapists should remember that the thoughts and feelings of their BPD patients may be more difficult to infer than they realize. Due to the non-normative content of these thoughts and feelings, therapists should continually seek to reconsider and reinterpret them, a process that may provide new and unexpected insights. Perhaps future versions of the *Diagnostic and Statistical Manual of Mental Disorders* should include difficult-to-infer thoughts and feelings as one of the defining characteristics of BPD.

Couples Therapy

A common assumption is that as couples become more accurate in inferring each other's thoughts and feelings, they feel closer to each other and more satisfied with their relationship. This assumption is plausible because a mutual understanding of one another's thoughts and feelings should enable relationship partners to satisfy and respond to each other's needs more effectively (Kilpatrick, Rusbult, & Bissonnette, 2002). It is now apparent, however, that in certain cases involving relationship-threatening information, the link between empathic accuracy and relationship satisfaction is not as simple as it first appeared.

These special cases are a central focus of the empathic accuracy model developed by Ickes and Simpson (1997, 2001). According to this model, in situations where a partner's thoughts or feelings are not threatening to the relationship, greater empathic accuracy can help the relationship and allow the partners to grow closer and communicate better. For example, if a wife can accurately infer that her husband is in need of having his spirits boosted, she can offer him some encouraging words that might end in a long mutual embrace. However, in cases where the partner's thoughts and feelings have the potential to threaten and destabilize the relationship, displaying a *low* level of empathic accuracy can actually help maintain the stability of the relationship. "Not going there" is often a wise strategy from an inferential standpoint, and partners display discretion when they seem to intuitively understand both when *and when not* to accurately infer their spouse's current thoughts and feelings (Ickes, 2003).

In a test of Ickes and Simpson's empathic accuracy model that examined the relationship between empathic accuracy and relationship satisfaction in married couples, Simpson, Oriña, and Ickes (2003) found that when the spouses were accurate about their partner's nonthreatening thoughts and feelings, they felt closer to each other. On the other hand, when the spouses accurately inferred each other's relationship-threatening thoughts and feelings, their reported feelings of closeness to each other decreased.

Motivated inaccuracy. Because a low level of empathic accuracy can help to preserve a relationship in situations in which partners are confronted with potentially damaging thoughts and feelings, people who find themselves in such situations may be intentionally *in*accurate in their empathic inferences. Depending on the threat potential and ambiguity of the partner's thoughts and feelings, relationship partners may be motivated *not* to confront each other's thoughts and feelings in order to keep things as pleasant as possible, particularly when the partner's thoughts and feelings are believed to present short-term (i.e., transient) threats.

If the content of the partner's thoughts or feelings is sufficiently ambiguous, motivated inaccuracy can be achieved by ignoring or "tuning out" revealing aspects of the partner's behavior, or by using certain defense mechanisms such as denial, repression, or rationalization. By intentionally tuning out evidence that the partner harbors relationship-threatening thoughts and feelings, perceivers can save themselves from having to deal with potentially distressing insights that could damage their relationship. On the other hand, if the threatening

content of the partner's thoughts and feelings is perceived to be unambiguous, the sheer clarity of the resulting insights may make it impossible for individuals to engage in motivated inaccuracy. They may instead have no choice but to confront the distressing information they just received and deal with the consequences.

It is important to note, however, that although motivated inaccuracy may provide temporary relief from relationship threats, continuing to ignore recurring threats may be quite harmful in the long run. Refusing to address relationship-threatening issues that continue to resurface may cause them to build to a point where they can no longer be ignored, resulting in a future confrontation that is even more unpleasant than the present one would be.

The phenomenon of motivated *in*accuracy was first documented by Simpson, Ickes, and Blackstone (1995), who asked heterosexual dating partners to rate pictures of people of the opposite sex for their physical attractiveness and sexual appeal (and to do this task together, with the dating partners sitting next to each other). Each couple was randomly assigned to view pictures that were pre-rated as being attractive (i.e., high-threat condition) or unattractive (i.e., low-threat condition). Every session was videotaped, and the partners were asked to review the tape individually and report their thoughts and feelings at the points where they occurred. The participants then reviewed the videotapes and attempted to infer their partner's thoughts and feelings at each of the designated "stop points."

As predicted, the partners in the high-threat condition were less accurate in inferring each other's thoughts and feelings than were those in the low-threat condition. Interestingly, when these couples were contacted four months after completion of the study, those who had been motivated to be inaccurate in their inferences (i.e., high-threat condition) were all still dating, whereas 30% of the couples in the low-threat condition were no longer together. It seems that being "strategically inaccurate" during a period of transient but high-level threat enabled the dating partners to avoid confronting thoughts and feelings that could have harmed their relationship, and thereby enabled them to preserve the stability of the relationship in the face of this short-term threat.

Motivated accuracy. Although there are circumstances in which most people actively avoid confronting their relationship partner's threatening thoughts and feelings, there are some people who counter this trend. For example, women with an anxious-ambivalent attachment style have been found to display greater empathic accuracy in relationship-threatening situations (Simpson, Ickes, & Grich, 1999). Instead of wanting to keep things pleasant and avoid any short-term confrontations, these women act as if they *have* to know about their partners' threatening thoughts and feelings, despite the negative consequences that such knowledge might bring. Simpson, Ickes, and Grich (1999) not only documented the motivated accuracy of anxiously attached women, but also found that such women reported feeling more jealous and less close to their romantic partners at the end of the experimental session.

Further evidence of motivated accuracy comes from the use of a self-report measure of the motivation to acquire relationship-threatening information (MARTI questionnaire; Ickes, Dugosh, et al., 2003). As the name of the scale suggests, its purpose is to identify individuals who are motivated to acquire even the most relationship-threatening information about their current dating partners. In a series of studies conducted by Ickes et al. (2003), participants completed the MARTI questionnaire . They then completed a relational trust scale that specifically focused on their current relationships, and an 11-item checklist that measured the extent to which they engaged in various "suspicion behaviors" in order to test their partner's loyalty (e.g., eavesdropping on the partner's phone conversations, spying on the partner). The results of

these studies revealed that the individuals who scored higher on the MARTI questionnaire also scored lower on the relational trust scale. Moreover, these same individuals were more likely to express their distrust by engaging in a variety of "suspicion behaviors."

Implications of Motivated Accuracy and Inaccuracy for Relationship Therapy

According to Ickes (2003), in order to properly treat a couple seeking therapy, a therapist must first appreciate the fact that focusing on what their clients are saying is, in general, likely to be more useful than interpreting the nonverbal behaviors they may display. Support for this idea comes from a study conducted by Gesn and Ickes (1999) that examined differences in empathic accuracy after manipulating the kinds of "information channels" that were available. Specifically, the participants were instructed to infer the thoughts or feelings of a client in a previously recorded therapy session from a videotape that had been edited to include only sound, only video, or both.

The results of this study showed that participants who had only the audio component of the therapy session were almost as accurate in their empathic inferences as those who had both the auditory and visual components. In other words, removing the visual component made little to no difference in their empathic accuracy. On the other hand, participants who only had the visual information were significantly less accurate than those in the other two conditions, a finding that emphasizes the importance of the words client use—and how they use them. Similar results were later reported by Hall and Schmid Mast (2007) and by Zaki, Bolger, and Ochsner (in press).

Ickes (2003) also recommends that therapists who perform couples' therapy should try to recognize when their clients might be engaging in either motivated accuracy or motivated inaccuracy when confronted with their partner's relationship-threatening thoughts or feelings. Because spouses who engage in *motivated inaccuracy* typically do so to "keep things calm" by avoiding the danger-zone issues in their relationship, a therapist who pushes these individuals to confront such issues before they are ready may be doing more harm than good. Therefore, in order to prepare married or cohabiting partners to confront information that may seriously threaten their relationships, therapists should begin by addressing issues that are less threatening, and then gradually build up to more difficult ones.

Being able to recognize when a spouse is displaying *motivated accuracy* in relationship-threatening situations is crucial for successful therapy as well. Therapists should understand that although people who engage in motivated accuracy (i.e., females with an anxious-ambivalent attachment style, and those with an overly suspicious nature) seem prepared to address relationship-threatening issues, this readiness to constantly "look for trouble" may do more harm than good. Labeling clients who habitually rely on motivated accuracy as overly suspicious and intrusive may be justified, but it may also harm the effectiveness of the treatment that is being provided. Such individuals are particularly in need of support and reassurance. Knowing how to identify these individuals should therefore increase a therapist's ability to help them—and their partners—more effectively.

The Empathic Accuracy and Inaccuracy of Maritally Aggressive Men

Maritally aggressive men also engage in motivated inaccuracy, but not with the motive of trying to "keep things calm." On the contrary, abusive men avoid inferring their female partner's thoughts and feelings as a way of both maintaining control within the relationship and justifying their abuse of the partner. The research on this topic shows that maritally aggressive men are predisposed to believe that their female partners harbor inappropriately critical and rejecting thoughts and feelings towards them (Schweinle, Ickes, & Bernstein, 2002; Schmid Mast & Ickes, 2007).[1] Given this bias, it is not surprising that Clements, Holtzworth-Munroe, Schweinle, and Ickes (2007) found that violent husbands were less accurate in inferring their wives' thoughts and feelings when compared to nonviolent husbands and objective observers. Interestingly, however, the violent husbands in this study were no less accurate than the other two groups when they inferred the thoughts and feelings of women who were *not* their wives.

Overall, the pattern of data suggests that abusive men are motivated to inaccurately "read" their wives in order to exert control over them. If these men can maintain a biased perception that their wives are chronically harboring critical and rejecting thoughts and feelings about them, they can ignore what their wives are actually thinking and feeling and feel justified in abusing them. In order to maintain this biased perception, abusive husbands appear to use either or both of two strategies: (1) disattending a female partner's complaints and (2) expressing contempt, rather than sympathy, in response to them (Schweinle and Ickes, 2007).

In a clinical setting, therapists should begin by helping abusive husbands become aware of the biased attributions they are inclined to make about their wives' thoughts and feelings. Because these biased attributions eventually harden into automatic schemas that are activated on a regular basis, abusive men may not even realize that they are present. Therapists must therefore encourage abusive husbands to recognize and challenge these biased attributions, so that they can begin to accurately infer their wives' thoughts and feelings and treat them with attention and sympathy, instead of with disattention and contempt.

Empathic Accuracy and Inaccuracy in Couples Over Time

Although one would expect couples to become more empathically accurate as they spend more time together, this predicted linear increase in accuracy has not been supported by the relevant research. In a study focusing on the empathic accuracy of couples that had been married for at least 15 years, Thomas, Fletcher, and Lange (1997) found an inverse relationship between empathic accuracy and length of marriage, such that couples who had been married for several years had lower empathic accuracy than couples who were more recently married. This finding might be surprising to some, because it is easy to assume that when couples have been married for a long period of time, they will have closer relationships and the opportunity to learn to understand each other better.

Thomas and colleagues explained this surprising finding by comparing the content of the spouses' thoughts and feelings at the same points in an interaction episode. They found that, in couples who had been married for a long period of time, the content of the spouses' thoughts and feelings was more discrepant than that of couples who had been married for a much shorter period. This finding suggests that longer-married couples tend to pursue more individual and idiosyncratic "lines of thought," whereas shorter-married couples tend to maintain a common cognitive focus during their discussions.

To better understand the changes in empathic accuracy that occur over time, Kilpatrick, Rusbult, and Bissonnette (2002) examined a group of married couples during their first three years of marriage. The partners' ability to infer each other's thoughts and feelings was measured after six months of marriage, and then again after a period of 18 to 24 months. The results of this study revealed that the degree to which partners could accurately infer each other's thoughts and feelings showed evidence of a decline from the first testing to the second. In other words, the couples were more empathically accurate after being married for six months than they were after being married for 18 to 24 months. Although this decline was not statistically significant, it was enough to suggest that with sufficient time, the reduced accuracy of these couples would eventually match that of the longer-married couples in Thomas, Fletcher, and Lange's (1997) study.

Other results from this study revealed that the couples who were better at inferring each other's thoughts and feelings during the first six months of marriage also felt more committed to their relationship, tended to accommodate each other more often, and generally felt more satisfied with their marriage. At the end of their second year of marriage, however, being empathically accurate was no longer necessary for them to accommodate each other or to feel committed to their marriage.

In other words, the data suggest that couples seem to benefit the most from being empathically accurate during their first two years of marriage when things are still new and unpredictable. It is at this early stage when newlyweds are more concerned with "staying on the same page" and trying to keep each other happy. As time progresses, however, empathic accuracy declines as a husband and wife begin to acquire their own individual roles that demand their attention, making it harder for them to maintain the cognitive synchrony that was a common occurrence at the beginning of their marriage. At this later point in the marriage, couples may overestimate the degree to which they know and understand each other. A compensatory factor, however, is that the ways they have learned to accommodate each other have already turned into habits that no longer require them to be as empathically accurate. Thus, empathic accuracy can decline without seriously compromising commitment and accommodation within the marriage.

SUMMARY AND IMPLICATIONS

As illustrated in the prelude to this chapter, failing to accurately infer the thoughts or feelings of others can have serious interpersonal consequences. However, as described in the section on romantic partners, there are times when failing to accurately infer a partner's thoughts and feelings can help to preserve one's relationship in the face of a strong situational threat. Although greater empathic accuracy usually benefits relationships, greater accuracy about a partner's relationship-threatening thoughts and feeling can have the opposite effect.

Individual differences are also important. Anxious-ambivalent women are motivated to be highly accurate when inferring their partner's relationship-threatening thoughts and feelings, even though they may be devastated by the consequences. In contrast, maritally abusive men seem motivated to inaccurately infer their wives' thoughts and feelings, both to maintain control within the relationship and to justify their abuse. And despite the stereotype of "women's intuition," which suggests that the average woman has greater empathic ability than the average man, the data suggest that there is no gender difference in empathic ability in normal persons, although there is a difference in empathic motivation (one that favors female perceivers).

Many topics related to empathic accuracy remain to be explored. For example, although several studies have addressed the empathic accuracy of maritally aggressive men, there is a need for comparable research on maritally aggressive women (Clements et al., 2007). Similarly, although researchers have examined the empathic accuracy of individuals with the symptomology of BPD, other personality disorders with similar characteristics, such as Antisocial Personality Disorder and Narcissistic Personality Disorder, also deserve to be the focus of empathic accuracy research. Another new direction for the study of empathic accuracy lies in the realm of computer-mediated communication. Empathic accuracy research has been conducted with individuals interacting in real life; however, in an age when more and more of our interactions occur online, understanding how empathic accuracy and other interpersonal processes are affected by this mode of communication will become increasingly important.

Empathic accuracy is a fascinating and complex construct. More than two decades after the first dyad sat in Ickes's "waiting room," interest in the topic has not waned. Although empathic inference is a daily preoccupation of most individuals, their levels of empathic accuracy can vary widely. As we have seen, when one delves deeply into the topics of *who* is empathically accurate, *when* they are empathically accurate, and *why* they are empathically accurate, some very interesting patterns of effects are revealed.

References

Baron-Cohen, S. (1995). *Mindblindness: An essay on autism and theory of mind*. Cambridge: MIT Press.

Baron-Cohen, S. (2003). *The essential difference: The truth about the male and female brain*. New York: Basic Books.

Baron-Cohen, S., Wheelwright, S., Skinner, R., Martin, J., & Clubley, E. (2001). The Autism-Spectrum Quotient (AQ): Evidence from Asperger Syndrome/high-functioning autism, males and females, scientists and mathematicians. *Journal of Autism and Communication Disorders, 31,* 5–17.

Barone, D. F., Hutchings, P. S., Kimmel, H. J., Traub, H. L., Cooper, J. T., & Marshall, C. M. (2005). Increasing empathic accuracy through practice and feedback in a clinical interviewing course. *Journal of Social and Clinical Psychology, 24*(2), 156–171.

Clements, K., Holzworth-Munroe, A., Schweinle, W., & Ickes, W. (2007). Empathic accuracy of intimate partners in violent versus nonviolent relationships. *Personal Relationships, 14*(3), 369–388.

Colvin, C. R., Vogt, D., & Ickes, W. (1997). Why do friends understand each other better than strangers do? In W. Ickes (Ed.), *Empathic accuracy* (pp. 169–193). New York: Guilford Press.

Dugosh, J. W. (1998). *Adult attachment style influences on the empathic accuracy of female dating partners.* Unpublished master's thesis, The University of Texas at Arlington.

Flury, J. M., Ickes, W., & Schweinle, W. (2008). The borderline empathy effect: Do high BPD individuals have greater empathic ability? Or are they just more difficult to "read"? *Journal of Research in Personality, 42,* 312–332.

Garcia, S., Stinson, L. L., Ickes, W., Bissonnette, V., & Briggs, S. R. (1991). Shyness and physical attractiveness in mixed-sex dyads. *Journal of Personality and Social Psychology, 61,* 35–49.

Gesn, P. R. (1995). *Shared knowledge between same-sex friends: Measurement and validation.* Unpublished master's thesis, The University of Texas at Arlington.

Gesn, P. R., & Ickes, W. (1999). The development of meaning contexts for empathic accuracy: Channel and sequence effects. *Journal of Personality and Social Psychology, 77,* 746–761.

Gleason, K. A., Jensen-Campbell, L. A., & Ickes, W. (2009). The role of empathic accuracy in adolescents' peer relations and adjustment. *Personality and Social Psychology Bulletin.*

Gleason, K. A., Johnson, B., Ickes, W., & Jensen-Campbell, L. (2004). *Autistic characteristics, empathic accuracy, and prosocial skills in adolescents.* Poster presentation given at the Annual Conference of the Society for Personality and Social Psychology, Austin, Texas, 20 January, 2004.

Goleman, D. (2006). *Emotional intelligence: 10th anniversary edition: Why it can matter more than IQ.* New York: Bantam Books.

Graham, T. (1994). *Gender, relationship, and target differences in empathic accuracy.* Unpublished master's thesis, The University of Texas at Arlington.

Graham, T., & Ickes, W. (1997). When women's intuition isn't greater than men's. In W. Ickes (Ed.), *Empathic accuracy* (pp. 117–143). New York: Guilford Press.

Hall, J. A., & Schmid Mast, M. (2007). Sources of accuracy in the empathic accuracy paradigm. *Emotion, 7,* 438–446.

Ickes, W. (1997). *Empathic accuracy.* New York: Guilford Press

Ickes, W. (2003). *Everyday mind reading: Understanding what other people think and feel.* Amherst: Prometheus Books.

Ickes, W. (2009). Empathic accuracy: Its links to clinical, cognitive, developmental, social, and physiological psychology. In J. Decety and W. Ickes (Eds.), *The social neuroscience of empathy* (pp. 57–70). Cambridge: MIT Press

Ickes, W., Buysse, A., Pham, H., Rivers, K., Erickson, J. R., Hancock, M., . . . Gesn, P. J. (2000). On the difficulty of distinguishing "good" and "poor" perceivers: A social relations analysis of empathic accuracy data. *Personal Relationships, 7,* 219–234.

Ickes, W., Dugosh, J. W., Simpson, J. A., & Wilson, C. L. (2003). Suspicious minds: The motive to acquire relationship-threatening information. *Personal Relationships, 10,* 131–148.

Ickes, W., Gesn, P. R., & Graham, T. (2000). Gender differences in empathic accuracy: Differential ability or differential motivation? *Personal Relationships, 7*(1), 95–109.

Ickes, W., Marangoni, C., & Garcia, S. (1997). Studying empathic accuracy in a clinically relevant context. In W. J. Ickes (Ed.), *Empathic accuracy* (pp. 282–310). New York: Guilford Press.

Ickes, W., & Simpson, J. A. (1997). Managing empathic accuracy in close relationships. In W. J. Ickes (Ed.), *Empathic accuracy* (pp. 218–250). New York: Guilford Press.

Ickes, W., & Simpson, J. A. (2001). Motivational aspects of empathic accuracy. In G. J. O. Fletcher & M. Clark (Eds.), *The Blackwell handbook in social psychology: Interpersonal processes* (pp. 229–249). Oxford, England: Blackwell.

Ickes, W., Stinson, L., Bissonnette, V., & Garcia, S. (1990). Naturalistic social cognition: Empathic accuracy in mixed-sex dyads. *Journal of Personality and Social Psychology, 59*(4), 730–742.

Kagan, N. (1977). *Interpersonal process recall.* East Lansing: Michigan State University Press.

Kilpatrick, S. D., Rusbult, C. E., & Bissonnette, V. (2002). Empathic accuracy and accommodative behavior among newly married couples. *Personal Relationships, 9,* 369–393.

Klein, K. J. K., & Hodges, S. D. (2001). Gender differences, motivation, and empathic accuracy: When it pays to understand. *Personality and Social Psychology Bulletin, 27,* 720–730.

Kwong, M. J., Bartholomew, K., & Dutton, D. G. (1999). Gender differences in patterns of relationship violence in Alberta. *Canadian Journal of Behavioural Science, 31,* 150–160.

Marangoni, C., Garcia, S., Ickes, W., & Teng, G. (1995). Empathic accuracy in a clinically relevant setting. *Journal of Personality and Social Psychology, 68*(5), 854–869.

Rogers, C. R. (1957). The necessary and sufficient conditions of therapeutic personality change. *Journal of Consulting Psychology, 21,* 95–103.

Rogers, C. R. (1975). Empathic: An unappreciated way of being. *Counseling Psychologist, 5,* 2–10.

Schmid Mast, M. S., & Ickes, W. (2007). Empathic accuracy: Measurement and potential clinical applications. In T. F. D. Farrow and P. W. R. Woodruff (Eds.), *Empathy and mental illness and health* (pp. 408–427). Cambridge, UK: Cambridge University Press.

Schweinle, W. E., & Ickes, W. (2007). The role of men's critical/rejecting overattribution bias, affect, and attentional disengagement in marital aggression. *Journal of Social and Clinical Psychology, 26*(2), 173–198.

Schweinle, W., Ickes, W., & Bernstein, I. (2002). Empathic inaccuracy in husband to wife aggression: The overattribution bias. *Personal Relationships, 9,* 141–158.

Sillars, A. L. (1998). (Mis)understanding. In B. H. Spitzberg & W. R. Cupach (Eds.), *The dark side of close relationships* (pp. 73–102). Mahwah, NJ: Erlbaum.

Sillars, A. L., Koerner, A., & Fitzpatrick, M. A. (2005). Communication and understanding in parent-adolescent relationships. *Human Communication Research, 31*(1), 102–128.

Simpson, J. A., Ickes, W., & Blackstone, T. (1995). When the head protects the heart: Empathic accuracy in dating relationships. *Journal of Personality and Social Psychology, 69,* 629–641.

Simpson, J. A., Ickes, W., & Grich, J. (1999). When accuracy hurts: Reactions of anxious-ambivalent dating partners to a relationship-threatening situation. *Journal of Personality and Social Psychology, 76,* 754–769.

Simpson, J. A., Oriña, M. M., & Ickes, W. (2003). When accuracy hurts, and when it helps: A test of the empathic accuracy model in marital interactions. *Journal of Personality and Social Psychology, 85,* 881–893.

Stinson, L., & Ickes, W. (1992). Empathic accuracy in the interactions of male friends versus male strangers. *Journal of Personality and Social Psychology, 62*(5), 787–797.

Thomas, G., Fletcher, G. J. O., & Lange, C. (1997). Online empathic accuracy in marital interaction. *Journal of Personality and Social Psychology, 72*(4), 839–850.

Thomas, G., & Maio, G. R. (2008). Man, I feel like a woman: When and how gender-role motivation helps mind-reading. *Journal of Personality and Social Psychology, 95*(5), 1165–1179.

Zaki, J., Bolger, N., & Ochsner, K. (in press). Unpacking the informational bases of empathic accuracy. *Emotion.*

NOTES

1. Although the current line of research focuses on marital violence initiated by men, it is clear that a great deal of marital violence is also initiated by women (e.g. Kwong, Bartholomew, & Dutton, 1999). Perhaps future research will reveal that the results discussed in this section may not be limited to aggressive men, but may apply to aggressive women as well.

10 PERSON PERCEPTION, DISPOSITIONAL INFERENCES, AND SOCIAL JUDGMENT

Daniel Leising

Peter Borkenau

PERSON PERCEPTION, DISPOSITIONAL INFERENCES, AND SOCIAL JUDGMENT

Paula and Percy are managers at an international company. Now an influential business partner from Japan is about to pay them a visit, to negotiate some very important new contract with them. Paula and Percy would like to make their guest feel as comfortable as possible during his stay, but unfortunately both of them do not have much time. So they wonder which of their employees they should ask to take care of him (take him to dinner, show him around, etc.). "It should be someone who is *really* polite", says Percy. "The Japanese value politeness a lot, you know. So whom should we pick? There's Tracy, Terry, Tim, Todd, Tina. . . ."

Judgments like these constitute the focus of interest of a research field that is commonly referred to as "interpersonal perception" (Kenny, 1994). Researchers in this field study how people judge each others' personality traits. Therein, the people who do the judgments (e.g., Paula and Percy) are often called "perceivers," whereas the people who are being judged (e.g., Tracy, Terry, Tim, Todd, and Tina) are

called "targets." Research in interpersonal perception addresses questions like "Under what conditions will perceivers *agree* in judging the personality traits of targets?" or "Under what conditions will a perceiver's judgments of targets' personality traits be *correct*?" The first of these questions refers to what is commonly called "consensus," whereas the second question refers to what is called "accuracy" (cf. Funder & West, 1993). In this chapter, we will give an overview of the factors that may affect consensus and accuracy in personality judgments. A third question ("Under what conditions will a perceiver's judgments of targets' personality traits agree with the targets' *own* views of their personalities?") refers to what is called "self-other agreement." We will only occasionally touch on this issue, because it is more difficult to account for with the models that are used in the study of *inter*personal perception (i.e., judgments that take place *between* people).

Personality judgments are highly relevant in everyday life. It seems that people do not judge each others' personalities just for fun, but for a good reason. But what may that reason be? What is the *advantage* of judging another person's personality? Many scholars agree that this advantage may be seen in the greater *predictability* of other people's future behavior. More specifically, by judging someone's personality, a judge makes a prediction as to whether the person's future behavior is likely to satisfy, or interfere with, his or her own personal needs (cf. Horowitz et al., 2006). For example, if Paula infers that Todd is the most polite of their employees, she makes a prediction about Todd's future behavior (e.g., "He will know how to behave in the presence of our business partner and make a good impression"). Such a prediction may then directly influence the judge's own behavior. For example, Paula may try to convince Percy of choosing Todd, because she thinks this choice would increase, or at least not impair, their chances of having successful negotiations with the Japanese guest. Generally speaking, it can be very useful to make accurate inferences about the behavioral inclinations of other people. The more accurate these inferences are, the better for our own welfare.

In this chapter, we will address the issue of personality judgment broadly, by presenting some of the most influential theoretical approaches and empirical findings in this field. We will begin by describing two widely known models that have proven to be useful in studying interpersonal perception. These models will then help us organize the next section, which focuses on various important factors that may affect consensus and accuracy. Two things should be noted: First, when speaking of consensus we will only refer to the case in which the *same* raters judge all of the targets. Second, in talking about consensus and accuracy we will always refer to *Pearson* correlations, that is, we will employ a "consistency definition" of agreement (e.g., perceivers agree to the extent that they assign the same *differences* in trait levels to targets). Several alternatives are conceivable (e.g., a different perceiver for each target, an "absolute agreement" definition of consensus), and they would lead

to slightly different conclusions regarding some of the issues that are discussed below (cf. Shrout & Fleiss, 1979). However, for illustration purposes we think it will be most useful to stick with this very simple case, which is also representative of much of interpersonal perception research so far.

TWO USEFUL MODELS OF PERSON PERCEPTION

The Social Relations Model

In his Social Relations Model (SRM), Kenny (1991, 1994) addresses interpersonal perception in terms of Analysis of Variance (ANOVA): If a group of perceivers makes dispositional inferences about a group of targets, a matrix like the one displayed in Table 10.1 will result. Let us assume that these data reflect judgments that three hypothetical perceivers (Allan, Barry, and Carl) have provided about the *friendliness* of three hypothetical targets (David, Ernie, and Frank). Apart from the individual judgments, the table also displays the average judgments of each target by all (bottom row), and the average judgments of all targets by each perceiver (right column). Finally, the bottom right corner of the table displays the average of all judgments, that is, the "grand mean" of all numbers in the table.

Let us first have a look at the targets. Obviously, the average ratings that the three targets received differ from each other. In Kenny's terminology, the difference between the average rating of a given target (see bottom row of Table 10.1) and the grand

TABLE 10.1   Judgments of Three Targets by Three Perceivers

Perceivers	Targets			Mean
	David	Ernie	Frank	
Allan	0	2	4	2
Barry	2	4	6	4
Carl	4	6	8	6
Mean	2	4	6	4

mean is called the "target effect" of that person. In our example, David has a target effect of −2 (i.e., he is judged as being less friendly than the average target), Ernie has a target effect of 0 (i.e., his friendliness is judged as being just average), and Frank has a target effect of +2 (i.e., he is judged as being more friendly than the average target).

Likewise, we may have a look at the perceivers. The difference between the average rating by a given perceiver (see right column) and the grand mean is called the "perceiver effect" of that person. In our example, Allan has a perceiver effect of −2 (i.e., he perceives the targets as being less friendly than the average perceiver does), Barry has a perceiver effect of 0 (i.e., his perception of the targets' friendliness is just average), and Carl has a perceiver effect of +2 (i.e., he perceives the targets as being more friendly than the average perceiver does).

Perceiver and target effects in interpersonal perception may have direct consequences for people's interpersonal behavior. For example, people who enjoy friendly interactions would probably approach a person like Frank, who is generally perceived as being a nice guy, but rather avoid a person like David. And someone like Carl (who perceives others as being quite friendly) would probably approach other people more easily than would someone like Allan. However, people like Carl may tend to *overestimate* how friendly others are, and thus experience some unexpected rejections.

Speaking in terms of ANOVA, the values in Table 10.1 only reflect the *main effects* of targets and perceivers, as each cell value is completely predictable from the marginal means. In reality, however, one will never encounter such a situation. Therefore, let us consider Table 10.2.

Although the marginal means (and thus, the perceiver and target effects) of the two tables are identical, the individual cell values differ. For example, in Table 10.1 Allan had assigned David a friendliness score of zero, which is exactly what would be expected from Allan's perceiver effect (−2) and David's target effect (−2). In

TABLE 10.2   Judgments of Three Targets by Three Perceivers

Perceivers	Targets			Mean
	David	Ernie	Frank	
Allan	1	2	3	2
Barry	2	4	6	4
Carl	3	6	9	6
Mean	2	4	6	4

contrast, Allan assigns David a friendliness score of 1 in Table 10.2. Such differences may reflect two influences: First, a specific perceiver may judge a specific target in a particular way. This is what Kenny (1994) calls a "relationship effect." For example, David may be a good friend of Allan's; thus Allan judges David more favorably. Second, however, the difference may be due to measurement error. In order to separate relationship effects from measurement error, each perceiver would have to assess each target at least twice. With two observations for each cell, we could determine to which extent the differences between Table 10.1 and Table 10.2 are stable (indicating relationship effects) or unstable over time (indicating measurement error). Note that this approach presupposes that relationship effects do not change over time (e.g., Allan becoming more critical of David).

The SRM emphasizes that not only the targets, but also the perceivers, as well as the unique relationships between targets and perceivers, contribute to interpersonal perception in systematic ways. It is interesting to note that a given perceiver's tendency to make dispositional inferences of a particular kind is *itself* a disposition. Some of the DSM-IV (APA, 2000) personality disorder criteria even *define* personality pathology in terms of characteristic ways of perceiving other people. Paranoid persons, for example, generally perceive others as being malicious, deceptive, and manipulative. This represents a perceiver effect (although the term is not used in DSM-IV). What's more important, such a perceiver effect is likely to have direct consequences for the perceiver's own interpersonal behavior. For example, a paranoid person may find it very difficult to open up to other people and thus be unable to obtain emotional support in times of need.

The problem of accuracy. Given that different people may have different views on a target's personality, and given that it is common to speak of "biased" interpersonal perception, we have to deal with the question of "What is the truth?" in interpersonal perception. This question is one of the most difficult issues in the field. It necessarily involves conceptual, theoretical and philosophical considerations. For example, if we are to assess how accurately perceivers estimate the intelligence of targets, we need a measure of the targets' "actual" intelligence levels with which the perceivers' estimates may be compared. Such a measure is called an "accuracy criterion." It is important to note that the choice of an accuracy criterion needs to be justified in terms of theoretical, conceptual, and philosophical deliberations. We can not "compute" what the truth is. Rather, we have to rationally decide which measure, or whose perspective, is most acceptable as an accuracy criterion, and why. Only then may we compute how accurately people, or tests, capture that criterion.

In some cases, the choice of an accuracy criterion may be relatively straightforward. For example, a good measure of people's general intelligence may be the average of several well-established intelligence tests. This choice of an accuracy criterion would essentially be justified by assuming (or demonstrating) that most intelligence researchers would probably agree with it. However, the choice of appropriate tests may not be completely unanimous, because there is some controversy as to which abilities constitute the intelligence domain (Sternberg, 1987).

In other domains, such as judgments of interpersonal behavior or traits, the choice of an accuracy criterion is even more disputable (cf. Funder, 1995; Horowitz et al.,

2006; Horowitz & Turan, 2008). We argue that the best possible approximation of a person's "true" standing on an interpersonal trait like friendliness or dominance would be the person's *target effect*, provided that (a) the sample of perceivers is large, (b) the perceivers have no particular loyalties or dislikes toward the target, and (c) the perceivers have observed the target in various circumstances. This is for several reasons: First, by aggregating across perceivers, systematic and unsystematic judgment errors are likely to cancel each other out, leading to a more reliable composite score (cf. Hofstee, 1994). Second, the judgments should reflect characteristics of the target, rather than the personal preferences of the perceivers. Third, the judgments should be representative of the target's behavior across situations. Finally, what *other* people think about a target's interpersonal behavior is often what matters the most, because the *consequences* of the behavior will largely depend on how other people perceive it. For example, if the average other person thinks that Jason is "sleazy," he will experience a lot of social rejection, regardless of how sociable, friendly, and outgoing he may consider himself to be.

In reality, it is very difficult and effortful to use such an accuracy criterion. Thus, most empirical studies have to employ some simplified version of it. There are exceptions, however: Oltmanns and Turkheimer (2006), for example, assessed self- and other-ratings of personality in army recruits who had been assigned to training groups of about 40 people and then lived and worked together for several weeks. The composite other-ratings in that study come as close as we think is possible to an "optimal" accuracy criterion regarding interpersonal behavior. Note, however, that in other domains of psychological functioning the targets themselves have "privileged access" by definition (cf. Vazire & Mehl, 2008). For example, the best accuracy criterion regarding a target's subjective feelings is probably the target's *self-report*, as long as it can be assumed that the target reports them honestly.

The Lens Model

Whereas Kenny's SRM deals with how much of the variance in a set of personality judgments is accounted for by targets and perceivers, Egon Brunswik's (1956) lens model addresses the *process* that enables perceivers to make more or less accurate inferences about the dispositions of targets. In fact, the model is applicable to all sorts of judgments (e.g., judgments of emotional states, biological sex, or profession), but we will concentrate on judgments of personality traits here. The term "lens model" refers to the shape of the model when it is depicted graphically as in Figure 10.1.

Here, the targets' trait levels are depicted on the left-hand side, whereas the impressions that a perceiver (or a group of perceivers, on average) has of the targets' trait levels are depicted on the right-hand side. Note that both of the larger circles represent *vectors* of numbers, that is, a

vector containing the actual trait levels of the targets and a vector containing the impressions that the perceiver has of each target. For example, George may be asked to estimate the intelligence levels of a group of targets. Which processes would be involved in these judgments?

Brunswik's answer would be that the targets emit so-called "cues" which the perceiver may use in estimating the targets' intelligence. The cues are depicted in the middle of Figure 10.1. Note that each of these smaller circles represents a *vector* of numbers as well. For example, the targets may differ from each other in how much they use foreign words (Cue_1), wear glasses (Cue_2), read fluently (Cue_3), and wear a tie (Cue_4). In theory, the number of cues that the targets may emit is unlimited, but let us stick with these four for now.

The most important parts of the model are the associations of the cues with the

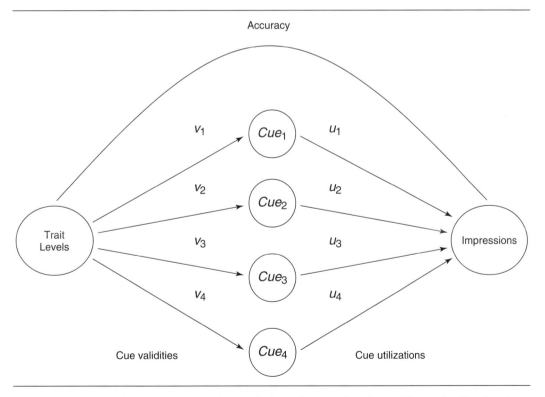

FIGURE 10.1   Brunswik's (1956) Lens Model as Applied to Inferences about Targets' Personality Trait Levels
Key: u_1–u_4 = cue utilization correlations, v_1–v_4 = cue validity correlations.

targets' actual trait levels (v_1 to v_4), and with the perceiver's impressions of the targets' trait levels (u_1 to u_4). The correlations of the cues with the targets' actual trait levels reflect the "validities" (v) of the cues. They indicate how much each cue is *actually* informative about the targets' trait levels. For example, the correlation between the targets' using many foreign words (Cue_1) and the targets' actual intelligence levels may be $r = .25$. In Figure 10.1, this correlation would be denoted as v_1.

The correlations between the cues and the perceiver's impressions reflect the "utilizations" (u) of the cues. They indicate how much the perceiver makes use of each cue in inferring the trait levels of the targets. For example, the correlation between the targets' using many foreign words (Cue_1) and the perceiver's estimates of the targets' intelligence levels may be $r = .35$. In Figure 10.1, this correlation would be denoted as u_1.

Accuracy also has its place in the model. It is represented by the arch that connects the targets' actual trait levels with the perceiver's impressions. Like cue validities and cue utilizations, accuracy is expressed in terms of a correlation coefficient.

Brunswik's lens model has been the theoretical framework for hundreds of empirical studies. Among them are so-called "thin slice studies," in which raters are exposed to highly controlled information about target persons whom they have never met before. For example, Borkenau and Liebler (1992, 1993) videotaped targets who were reading a weather forecast. They also collected self-ratings and partner ratings of the targets' personalities, administered intelligence tests, and collected measures of observable attributes (cues) of the targets. The video footage was then presented to unacquainted judges who were asked to rate each target's personality and intelligence.

The judges assigned high levels of intelligence to targets who read the weather forecast fluently. In terms of the lens model, reading fluently was a cue that the perceivers *utilized* in estimating the targets' intelligence. Moreover, targets who read fluently had higher intelligence test scores. In terms of the lens model, reading fluently was a *valid* cue to the targets' intelligence (Borkenau & Liebler, 1995; Borkenau, Mauer, Riemann, Spinath, & Angleitner, 2004). The perceivers' *accuracy* in estimating the targets' intelligence was better than would be expected by chance, and the lens model offers an explanation of how such accuracy may emerge: The targets emitted valid cues, which the perceivers utilized in making their judgments.

However, cue validity and cue utilization do not always have to be such a good match: For example, in Borkenau and Liebler's study some valid cues that the targets emitted were overlooked by the perceivers, such as the use of standard language versus dialect. Use of standard language was a valid cue to intelligence, but it was not utilized as a cue by the perceivers. Also, the perceivers utilized some cues that were not valid. For example, they attributed higher levels of intelligence to targets who were physically attractive, although in reality there was no such association. Finally, there was a great number of cues that were neither valid nor utilized.

Brunswik's model not only clarifies how people can make accurate inferences about others' dispositions, but also offers an explanation why accuracy is usually far from perfect: Cue validity and cue utilization are connected in a multiplicative fashion. Thus if *either* the validity *or* the utilization of a cue is zero, the cue may not contribute to accuracy. Accuracy is only fostered by cues that are *both* valid and utilized. Perceivers may fail in judging the personalities of targets for various reasons: Valid cues may not be available, or valid cues may be available but not utilized, or perceivers may utilize cues that are not valid, or they may utilize valid cues in inappropriate ways (e.g., if the perceivers in Borkenau and Liebler's study had attributed *higher* levels of intelligence to targets who spoke with a dialect). Given all these pitfalls, it may be surprising that people can make accurate inferences about other people's personalities at all

(Funder, 1989, 1995). Brunswik's model is widely used, because it is broadly applicable. For example, recent studies have investigated offices and bedrooms (Gosling, Ko, Mannarelli, & Morris, 2002), music preferences (Rentfrow & Gosling, 2003), and personal websites (Vazire & Gosling, 2004) as sources of cues to personality.

FACTORS THAT INFLUENCE DISPOSITIONAL INFERENCES

A large variety of factors that may affect personality judgments have been identified over the last few decades. Several, but not all, of these are represented in David Kenny's *Weighted Average Model* (Kenny, 1994) and his *PERSON* model (Kenny, 2004), both of which we will not address in detail here. Rather, we will introduce what we think are the most important factors, in an order that roughly follows the structure of Brunswik's lens model. Where possible, we will discuss how each factor may influence consensus and accuracy.

Characteristics of the Trait

A factor that is directly associated with the respective trait is *trait evaluativeness*. It refers to how much some levels of the trait are seen as being "better" or "worse" than other levels. Peabody (1967) had emphasized that all personality-descriptive terms contain both a substantive component (reflecting actual differences between targets' behavioral dispositions), and an evaluative component (reflecting how "good" or "bad" it is to have those dispositions). For example, the Affiliation dimension of the Interpersonal Circumplex model (Kiesler, 1983; Leary, 1957; Wiggins, 1979) is strongly evaluative, as being "friendly" is much more socially desirable than being "hostile." For other traits, however, high levels, low levels, and intermediate levels are quite similar with regard to social desirability. For example, the Dominance axis of the Interpersonal Circumplex model is less evaluative,

because being "assertive" is not much more desirable than being "obedient" (Anderson, 1968; Saucier, Ostendorf, & Peabody, 2001). Note, however, that for most traits the relationship between trait level and social desirability is not perfectly linear, but has a curvilinear component as well: Extreme trait levels hardly ever represent the "optimal" level, except for attributes that are almost exclusively evaluative like "lovely" (cf. Borkenau, Zaltauskas, & Leising, 2009).

Studies (e.g., Funder & Colvin, 1988; Funder & Dobroth, 1987; John & Robins, 1993) suggest that consensus and self-other agreement are lower for more evaluative traits, implying that perceivers agree more on the substantive component than on the evaluative component of personality judgments (Saucier, Ostendorf, & Peabody, 2001). However, the issue is more complex than that. For example, trait evaluativeness may function as a moderator variable that determines to which extent the targets' impression management motivation or the perceivers' leniency may affect the perceivers' judgments of the targets (see the following).

Factors Associated With Cue Availability and Cue Validity

A large number of factors that influence dispositional inferences are associated with the availability and validity of cues. We address them jointly here, because discussing cue validities without considering the cues themselves makes no sense.

The first important factor operating at this stage is the *amount of information* that is available to the perceivers. Targets differ in how active they are. Within a given time interval, active targets (i.e., targets that do a lot) emit more cues than do inactive targets. If two targets with equal activity levels are observed, the target that is observed for a longer time will emit more cues. We may conceptualize the overall amount of information as the aggregate of all cues that a target emits (taking into account the possibility that the information that is carried by individual cues may be partly redundant with each other). To the extent that the perceivers utilize the cues *in similar ways* (see below), more information about the targets will contribute to better consensus (as long as the information that the perceivers receive is not perfectly identical; cf. Kenny, 2004). And to the extent that the perceivers utilize those cues that are valid indicators of the targets' actual trait levels, more information will contribute to better accuracy.

The amount of valid information that the perceivers receive also depends on how observable the valid cues of the trait are from outside. For example, whether a person is extraverted can be inferred from the person's overt interpersonal behavior (e.g., laughing, talking in a loud voice, approaching people) with relative ease. In contrast, the indicators of a trait like neuroticism (e.g., ruminating about one's past mistakes) are more internal, and thus more difficult to access. In theory, the fact that the valid cues of a trait are observable from the outside does not guarantee that perceivers will utilize them in making their judgments, but empirical research has shown they do: Traits with more observable cues like extraversion are usually judged with better consensus and accuracy (Funder & Colvin, 1988; Funder & Dobroth, 1987; Kenrick & Stringfield, 1980; Paunonen, 1989).

Studies have demonstrated that targets may convey a lot of relevant information about themselves within very brief amounts of time. Observing "thin slices" (i.e., small segments) of the behavior stream may already result in considerable consensus and accuracy (Borkenau et al., 2004; Leising, Sporberg, & Rehbein, 2006). Even still images of targets' faces may be judged with some consensus and accuracy regarding the targets' personalities (Borkenau & Liebler, 1992), even if these images are displayed for 50 milliseconds only (Borkenau, Brecke, Möttig, & Paelecke, 2009).

When raters who were formerly unacquainted with targets receive the first bits of information about the targets, consensus and accuracy increase very quickly. This implies that at least some of the cues that targets emit must be valid *and* utilized. At later stages, when the raters already have received considerable information about the targets, adding more information results in smaller increases in consensus and accuracy (Borkenau et al., 2004; Kenny, 2004). Generally speaking, consensus and accuracy are asymptotic functions of the amount of information.

A second and related factor is *information overlap*. It describes the extent to which the information that different raters receive about the targets is the same. Let us imagine a study in which two raters (Tom and Nick) judge the personalities of targets they have never met before. For each target, four videos of equal length are available, showing how the target behaves in different situations (e.g., classroom, date, party, and gym). Now each rater is randomly assigned to two of these situations, watches the respective videos, and rates the targets on, say, extraversion. All other things being equal, consensus among the raters will be highest if they both rate the targets in the same two situations (e.g., classroom and date). In this case, information overlap is 100%. If Tom judges the targets in the classroom and on a date, but Nick judges them in the classroom and at a party, information overlap is only 50%, and consensus is likely be lower. If Tom judges the targets in the classroom and on a date, but Nick judges them at a party and in the gym, information overlap is 0%, and consensus is likely to be lower still. Even in this latter situation, however, consensus will probably be above chance level, because the targets' actual extraversion levels will influence their behavior in all four situations (Kenny, 1994; 2004).

A third factor is the targets' willingness and ability to present themselves strategically, in an attempt to evoke specific impressions in the perceivers. We will call this factor *impression management* (cf. Goffman, 1959; Paulhus, 1984). For example, if Andy has a crush on Cathy, and wants to make her believe he is "boyfriend material," he may decide to get a neat haircut and dress up in a tuxedo before he goes on his first date with her. Impression management implies that a target voluntarily emits cues (e.g., neat haircut, tuxedo) that he or she thinks will be utilized by the perceiver in ways that evoke the desired impression.

The motivation to engage in impression management clearly depends on the situation. For example, when Andy and Cathy go on their first date together, both of them may be highly motivated to make good impressions on each other, but after 20 years of being married, that motivation may decrease. Moreover, the specific impression that a target wishes to evoke in the perceiver (e.g., intimidating, pitiful, likeable, or competent) may also vary with the circumstances (Jones & Pittman, 1982; Leary, 1995; Paulhus & John, 1998). To the extent that targets *differ* in how successfully they engage in impression management, cue validities, and, as a consequence, accuracy will be reduced.

The impression management factor is closely related to what has traditionally been called "socially desirable responding." Socially desirable responding implies that people attempt to present themselves in overly positive ways. In fact, there is more than one way of doing that (Paulhus & John, 1998), but for the sake of simplicity we will stick with a simple positive-negative continuum here. The bulk of research on socially desirable responding has dealt with targets' responses to personality questionnaires, and specifically with how the "substance" component of these responses (= how the targets actually are) may be disentangled from the "style" component (= how the targets would like to be seen). In terms of the lens model, questionnaire responses may be interpreted as cues. The problem is to determine the extent to which these cues are valid indicators of the targets' personalities, or rather indicators of their motivation and ability to present themselves in a positive fashion.

Some of the first attempts at solving this problem used scales (so-called "lie scales" or "social desirability scales") in which the targets were asked to report how often they engage in behaviors that are (a) desirable but rare, or (b) undesirable but common (e.g., Crowne & Marlowe, 1960). Targets endorsing the first and denying the second kind of behaviors were classified as presenting themselves in overly positive ways, based on the reasoning that such a response pattern is just "too good to be true."

If social desirability scales actually captured people's tendencies to present themselves in overly positive ways, then using these scales as covariates should improve self-other agreement in personality ratings (Wiggins, 1973). However, numerous studies (e.g., Borkenau & Ostendorf, 1992; McCrae & Costa, 1983; Piedmont, McCrae, Riemann, & Angleitner, 2000) failed to confirm this prediction. Rather, self-other agreement often *decreased*. This finding may be explained by the fact that most social desirability scales correlate not only with the targets' own reports of their personalities (as one would expect), but also with descriptions of the targets by knowledgeable informants (Borkenau & Ostendorf, 1992; McCrae & Costa, 1983; Ones, Viswesvaran, & Reiss, 1996; Piedmont, McCrae, Riemann, & Angleitner, 2000), indicating that the scales at least partly assess actual personality differences (= "substance"). In fact, people *do* vary in how much their everyday behavior is socially desirable (Hofstee & Hendriks, 1998). Accordingly, Crowne and Marlowe (1964) concluded that their lie scale measured a trait, rather than a response style. As Paulhus (2002) has pointed out, a proper measure of socially desirable responding should be independent of actual personality differences. To date, we know of no social desirability scale that meets this requirement.

A fourth factor associated with the availability and validity of cues is *situation strength*. A "strong" situation exerts pressure on individuals to behave in certain ways, and thus reduces interindividual variance in behavior (cf. Leising & Müller-Plath, 2009; Mischel, 1977; Murray, 1938). As a consequence, the cues emitted by the targets become more similar to each other, and also less valid as indicators of the targets' personalities. For example, as the range of acceptable behaviors at a funeral is rather limited, one should probably not draw dispositional inferences from people's behaviors in just this situation.

A "weak situation," in contrast, imposes little constraints on people's behavior. Being alone in one's room after school, for example, is a relatively weak situation. Here, people have a large range of behavioral alternatives to choose from (e.g., calling a friend, watching TV, reading, exercising, eating, doing homework). Weak situations are usually informative about personality differences. In order to get accurate impressions of targets' personalities, it is advisable to assess the targets across several weak situations.

Factors Associated With Cue Utilization and Impression Formation

A factor that is associated with cue utilization is *shared vs. non-shared meaning systems* (Kenny, 1994). It refers to the extent that perceivers assign similar trait levels to targets, based on the same information. For example, if targets do not talk much, this may be seen as an indicator of extreme shyness by one rater, but as an indicator of only moderate shyness by another rater. The other rater may even interpret the very same behavior (not talking much) as indicating high levels of a different trait (e.g., thoughtfulness) (Bem & Allen, 1974; Chaplin & Panter, 1993; Horowitz & Turan, 2008). Such discrepancies in subjective behavior-to-trait relations may account for a considerable proportion of the misunderstandings and communication problems that people encounter when they are interpreting each others' interpersonal behaviors (Horowitz et al., 2006; Horowitz & Turan, 2008).

In terms of Brunswik's lens model, shared meaning refers to how much the cue utilizations by different perceivers resemble each other. This resemblance can be estimated by providing perceivers with exactly the same information about a sample of formerly unknown target persons, and then letting them judge the targets' personalities. Any disagreement among the perceivers would reflect nonshared meaning systems plus measurement error, the two of which could be disentangled by letting the perceivers repeat their judgments after a while.

Several studies have investigated the contribution of shared meaning to interrater agreement. McCrae, Stone, Fagan, and Costa (1998), for example, let married couples discuss the reasons why they disagreed in judging each other's personalities. Nonshared meaning was among the most influential factors. Chaplin and Panter (1993) directly assessed which behaviors perceivers associated with certain trait terms (so called "meaning profiles"). Perceivers with similar meaning profiles agreed better with each other in judging target persons (cf. Horowitz & Turan, 2008). Note that these studies only addressed the explicit, conscious components of people's meaning systems. It is highly likely, however, that a considerable proportion of how people infer traits from behaviors is not reportable by those very people.

An issue that is related to shared meaning involves what Kenny (2004) calls "categorical" information: Perceivers may partly base their judgments on nonbehavioral information like the targets' ethnicity or sex. To the extent that perceivers hold *shared* stereotypes about associations between category membership and personality, their judgments will agree better with each other. For example, if Joss and Kevin share the belief that women are less intelligent than men, their agreement in judging the intelligence of male and female targets will be better than if they did not share this belief. Despite their agreeing with each other, however, their judgments may still be wrong. Only to the extent that the perceivers' stereotypes reflect actual associations between category membership and personality (a so-called "kernel-of-truth"), will use of the categorical information enhance accuracy. For example, if Alma is convinced that men perform better at mental rotation tasks than do women, then her estimates of targets' mental rotation capacity are likely to be somewhat accurate, as long as (and even if only) she knows the sex of the targets. That is because her stereotype reflects a reality (Voyer, Voyer, & Bryden, 1995).

A second factor, which we will call *perceiver leniency*, has to do with social desirability again. Perceivers differ in how lenient or critical they are regarding targets. As long as a perceiver's positive or negative attitude applies to all targets equally (i.e., a perceiver effect for leniency), consensus and accuracy would remain unaffected. But if—which is often the case—a perceiver prefers some targets over other targets (i.e., a relationship effect for leniency), accuracy will be reduced to the extent that the respective trait is evaluative. For example, if Paula has a secret crush on Todd, her accuracy in picking the most polite of her employees would probably be impaired. With regard to consensus, the pattern is even more complex: To the extent that different perceivers prefer the *same* targets over other targets, consensus among them will be *higher* than if they did not have any shared preferences (note that higher trait evaluativeness would *amplify* this effect of shared preferences on consensus). To the extent that the perceivers *differ* in which targets they prefer, consensus will be *lower*.

Finally, judgments of personality may also be affected by *communication among perceivers*. This factor refers to how much the perceivers talk about their impressions of the targets. Communication among perceivers is likely to make their ratings more similar to each other (Chaplin & Panter, 1993), because extreme judgments by one perceiver will probably be challenged by the other perceiver(s). The effect that communication among perceivers has on accuracy is not exactly clear, because there is only little empirical evidence regarding this issue. On the one hand, it is well established that communication increases accuracy in solving so-called "Eureka problems," that

is, problems for which a solution is difficult to find but highly convincing once it is suggested (e.g., a mathematical problem). On the other hand, communication may *reduce* accuracy in situations where the correct solution is less clearly identifiable, such as judgments of personality and interpersonal behavior. Specifically, group-dynamic processes (e.g., one dominant rater talking the others into adopting his or her incorrect view of the target) may have a negative impact under such circumstances (cf. Borkenau & Liebler, 1994).

CONCLUSION

Let us return once again to our example from the introductory section: Paula and Percy judging the politeness of their employees. What Kenny's (1994) SRM teaches is that judgments like these are influenced by (a) how polite each of the employees is judged to be by others in general (target-effects), (b) how polite Paula and Percy generally find other persons to be (perceiver-effects), (c) the *specific* views that Paula and Percy have of each of the targets (relationship-effects), and (d) measurement error. Brunswik's lens model explicates the intermediary steps of the perceptual process that takes place, and that may enable Paula and Percy to agree with each other (*consensus*) and/or to be correct (*accuracy*) in judging the politeness of their employees.

The consensus between Paula and Percy will be higher (a) the more information about the targets each of them has received in the past (as long as information overlap is not perfect), (b) the more the situations in which they have observed the targets overlap, (c) the more they communicate with each other about their impressions, (d) the more they are similarly lenient or critical towards individual targets, and (e) the more their individual conceptions of which cues indicate which levels of politeness (= cue utilization) resemble each other.

Importantly, even if Paula and Percy agree perfectly in judging the politeness of their employees, they may still be totally wrong. Their judgments will only be accurate to the extent that they (a) have received *valid* information about the targets in the past, and (b) utilize that information appropriately (Brunswik, 1956; Funder, 1995). The amount of valid information that they received will be higher (b1) the greater the number of valid cues of politeness that are observable from the outside; (b2) the greater the amount of time or the number of occasions they have had to observe the targets; (b3) the weaker the situations were in which they have observed the targets; and (b4) the less the targets differ in how successfully they have engaged in impression management in the past. Appropriate use of the valid information would imply that Paula and Percy give more weight to more valid cues, and less weight to less valid cues. It would also imply that they should not have any particular preferences or dislikes towards certain targets.

The more accurate Paula's and Percy's assessments of their employees' politeness, the better they will be able to make an informed decision as to whom they should let take care of their guest. By basing their decision on a most accurate assessment, they would maximize their gains and minimize their losses. Generally speaking, accuracy in judging other people's personalities often "pays off," whereas for inaccuracy we sometimes have to "pay a price."

References

American Psychiatric Association (2000). *Diagnostic and statistical manual of mental disorders* (4th ed., text rev.). Washington: American Psychiatric Association.

Anderson, N. H. (1968). Likeableness ratings of 555 personality trait words. *Journal of Personality and Social Psychology, 3*, 272–279.

Bem, D., & Allen, A. (1974). On predicting some of the people some of the time. *Psychological Review, 81*, 506–520.

Borkenau, P., Brecke, S., Möttig, C., & Paelecke, M. (in press). Extraversion is accurately perceived after a 50-ms exposure to a face. *Journal of Research in Personality, 43*, 702–705.

Borkenau, P., & Liebler, A. (1992). Trait inferences: Sources of validity at zero acquaintance. *Journal of Personality and Social Psychology, 62*, 645–657.

Borkenau, P., & Liebler, A. (1993). Convergence of stranger ratings of personality and intelligence with self-ratings, partner ratings, and measured intelligence. *Journal of Personality and Social Psychology, 65*, 546–553.

Borkenau, P., & Liebler, A. (1994). Effects of communication among judges on the validity of their judgments. *European Journal of Psychological Assessment, 10*, 10–14.

Borkenau P., & Liebler, A. (1995). Observable attributes as cues and manifestations of personality and intelligence. *Journal of Personality, 63*, 1–25.

Borkenau, P., Mauer, N., Riemann, R., Spinath, F. M., & Angleitner, A. (2004). Thin Slices of behavior as cues of personality and intelligence. *Journal of Personality and Social Psychology, 86*, 599–614.

Borkenau, P., & Ostendorf, F. (1992). Social desirability scales as moderator and suppressor variables. *European Journal of Personality, 6*, 199–214.

Borkenau, P., Zaltauskas, K., & Leising, D. (2009). More may be better but there may be too much: Optimal trait level and self-enhancement bias. *Journal of Personality, 77*, 825–858.

Brunswik, E. (1956). *Perception and the representative design of psychological experiments.* Berkeley, CA: University of California Press.

Chaplin, W. F., & Panter, A. T. (1993). Shared meaning and the convergence among observers' personality descriptions. *Journal of Personality, 61*, 553–585.

Crowne, D. P., & Marlowe, D. (1960). A new scale of social desirability independent of psychopathology. *Journal of Consulting Psychology, 24*, 349–354.

Crowne, D. P., & Marlowe, D. (1964). *The approval motive.* New York: John Wiley & Sons.

Funder, D. (1989). Accuracy in personality judgment and the dancing bear. In D. M. Buss & N. Cantor (Eds.), *Personality psychology: Recent trends and emerging directions* (pp. 210–223). New York: Springer.

Funder, D. (1995). On the accuracy of personality judgment: A realistic approach. *Psychological Review, 102*, 652–670.

Funder, D., & Colvin, C. (1988). Friends and strangers: Acquaintanceship, agreement, and the accuracy of personality judgement. *Journal of Personality and Social Psychology, 55*, 149–158.

Funder, D. C., & Dobroth, K. (1987). Differences between traits: Properties associated with interjudge agreement. *Journal of Personality and Social Psychology, 52*, 409–418.

Funder, D. C., & West, S. G. (1993). Consensus, self-other agreement, and accuracy in personality judgment: An introduction. *Journal of Personality, 61*, 457–476.

Goffman, E. (1959). *The presentation of self in everyday life*. New York: Doubleday / Anchor Books.

Gosling, S. D., Ko, S. J., Mannarelli, T., & Morris, M. E. (2002). A room with a cue: Personality judgments based on offices and bedrooms. *Journal of Personality and Social Psychology, 82*, 379–398.

Hofstee, W. K. B. (1994). Who should own the definition of personality? *European Journal of Personality, 8*, 149–162.

Hofstee, W. K. B., & Hendriks, A. A. J. (1998). The use of scores anchored at the scale midpoint in reporting individuals' traits. *European Journal of Personality, 12*, 219–228.

Horowitz, L. M., & Turan, B. (2008). Prototypes and personal templates: Collective wisdom and individual differences. *Psychological Review, 115*, 1054–1068.

Horowitz, L. M., Wilson, K. R., Turan, B., Zolotsev, P., Constantino, M. J., & Henderson, L. (2006). How interpersonal motives clarify the meaning of interpersonal behavior: A revised circumplex model. *Personality and Social Psychology Review, 10*, 67–86.

John, O. P., & Robins, R. W. (1993). Determinants of interjudge agreement on personality traits: The Big Five domains, observability, evaluativeness, and the unique perspective of the self. *Journal of Personality, 61*, 521–551.

Jones, E. E., & Pittman, T. S. (1982). Towards a general theory of strategic self-presentation. In J. Suls (Ed.), *Psychological perspectives on the self* (Vol. 1, pp. 231–262). Hillsdale, NJ: Erlbaum.

Kenny, D. A. (1991). A general model of consensus and accuracy in interpersonal perception. *Psychological Review, 98*, 155–163.

Kenny, D. A. (1994). *Interpersonal perception: A social relations analysis*. New York: Guilford Press.

Kenny, D. A. (2004). PERSON: A general model of interpersonal perception. *Personality and Social Psychology Review, 8*, 265–280.

Kenrick, D. T., & Stringfield, D. O. (1980). Personality traits and the eye of the beholder: Crossing some traditional philosophical boundaries in the search for consistency in all of the people. *Psychological Review, 87*, 88–104.

Kiesler, D. J. (1983). The 1982 interpersonal circle: A taxonomy for complementarity in human transactions. *Psychological Review, 90*, 185–214.

Leary, T. (1957). *Interpersonal diagnosis of personality*. New York: Ronald Press.

Leary, M. R. (1995). *Self-presentation: Impression management and interpersonal behavior*. Madison, WI: Brown & Benchmark.

Leising, D., & Müller-Plath, G. (2009). Person-situation integration in research on problematic personality characteristics. *Journal of Research in Personality, 43*, 218–227.

Leising, D., Sporberg, D., & Rehbein, D. (2006). Characteristic interpersonal behavior in dependent and avoidant personality disorder can be observed within very short interaction sequences. *Journal of Personality Disorders, 20*, 319–330.

McCrae, R. R., & Costa, P. T. (1983). Social desirability scales: More substance than style. *Journal of Consulting and Clinical Psychology, 51*, 882–888.

McCrae, R. R., Stone, V., Fagan, P. J, & Costa, P. T. (1998). Identifying causes of disagreement between self-reports and spouse ratings of personality. *Journal of Personality, 66*, 285–313.

Mischel, W. (1977). The interaction of person and situation. In D. Magnusson & N. S. Endler (Eds.), *Personality at the crossroads: Current issues in interactional psychology* (pp. 333–352). Hillsdale, NJ: Erlbaum.

Murray, H. A. (1938). *Explorations in Personality*. New York: Oxford University Press.

Oltmanns, T. F., & Turkheimer, E. (2006). Perceptions of self and others regarding pathological personality traits. In R. F. Krueger & J. L. Tackett (Eds.), *Personality and psychopathology* (pp. 71–111). New York: Guilford Press.

Ones, D. S., Viswesvaran, C., & Reiss, A. D. (1996). Role of social desirability in personality testing for personnel selection: The red herring. *Journal of Applied Psychology, 81*, 660–679.

Paulhus, D. L. (1984). Two-component models of socially desirable responding. *Journal of Personality and Social Psychology, 46*, 598–609.

Paulhus, D. L., & John, O. P. (1998). Egoistic and moralistic biases in self-perception: The interplay of self-deceptive styles with basic traits and motives. *Journal of Personality, 66,* 1025–1060.

Paulhus, D. L. (2002). Socially desirable responding: The evolution of a construct. In H. I. Braun, D. N. Jackson, & D. E. Wiley (Eds.), *The role of constructs in psychological and educational measurement* (pp. 49–69). Mahwah NJ: Erlbaum.

Paunonen, S. V. (1989). Consensus in personality judgments: Moderating effects of target-rater acquaintanceship and behavior observability. *Journal of Personality and Social Psychology, 56,* 823–833.

Peabody, D. (1967). Trait inferences: Evaluative and descriptive aspects. *Journal of Personality and Social Psychology Monographs, 7* (4, Whole No. 644).

Piedmont, R. L., McCrae, R. R., Riemann, R., & Angleitner, A. (2000). On the invalidity of validity scales: Evidence from self-reports and observers ratings in volunteer samples. *Journal of Personality and Social Psychology, 78,* 582–593.

Rentfrow, P. J., & Gosling, S. D. (2003). The do re mi's of everyday life: The structure and personality correlates of music preferences. *Journal of Personality and Social Psychology, 84,* 1236–1256.

Saucier, G., Ostendorf, F., & Peabody, D. (2001). The nonevaluative circumplex of personality adjectives. *Journal of Personality, 69,* 537–582.

Shrout, P. E. & Fleiss, J. L. (1979). Intraclass correlations: Uses in assessing rater-reliability. *Psychological Bulletin, 2,* 420–428.

Sternberg, R. J. (1987). *Beyond IQ: A triarchic theory of human intelligence.* Cambridge, MA: Cambridge University Press.

Vazire, S., & Gosling, S. D. (2004). E-perceptions: personality impressions based on personal websites. *Journal of Personality and Social Psychology, 87,* 123–132.

Vazire, S., & Mehl, M. R. (2008). Knowing me, knowing you: The accuracy and unique predictive validity of self-ratings and other-ratings of daily behavior. *Journal of Personality and Social Psychology, 95,* 1202–1216.

Voyer, D., Voyer, S., & Bryden, M. P. (1995). Magnitude of sex differences in spatial abilities: A meta-analysis and consideration of critical variables. *Psychological Bulletin, 117,* 250–270.

Wiggins, J. S. (1973). *Personality and prediction: Principles of personality assessment.* Reading, Mass: Addison-Wesley.

Wiggins, J. S., (1979). A psychological taxonomy of trait-descriptive terms: The interpersonal domain. *Journal of Personality and Social Psychology, 37,* 395–412.

11 THE ROLE OF NONVERBAL COMMUNICATION IN INTERPERSONAL RELATIONS

Robert Gifford

Imagine, for a moment, interpersonal relations *without* nonverbal behavior. A first scenario might feature two immobile people who are conversing: no expressive movements. However, their frozen postures, clothing, and interpersonal distance would, nevertheless, be nonverbally communicative. To remove those cues, they could be placed in separate rooms, so that they communicate by phone only. However, their paraverbal behavior (style of speaking, such as vocal intensity, tone, rhythm, and pitch; Trager, 1958) would still convey messages beyond the content of the words they use. To expunge these paraverbal cues, the two people would have to be restricted to typing out messages.[1] Although this sort of interpersonal interaction exists, and in fact is increasingly frequent with the advent of computer-mediated communication (e.g., e-mail, texting, and social networking), all our other interpersonal interactions are informationally rich from a myriad of gesture, posture, glance, gaze, expression, distance, tone, clothing, and grooming cues. Face-to-face nonverbal communication consists of complex sequences in which a huge number of events are constantly occurring and recurring (Agliati, Vescovo, & Anolli, 2006), and therefore poses an enormous challenge for behavioral scientists.

Nonverbal communication is an essential part of interpersonal psychology, perhaps more essential than is generally recognized. Although the following estimates apply only to the expression of emotion or liking rather than all interpersonal communication, researchers have reported that nonverbal and paraverbal messages are about four times more influential than verbal messages (Argyle et al., 1970; Hsee, Hatfield, & Carlson, & Chemtob, 1992), or that they account for 93% of inferred meaning (e.g., Mehrabian & Weiner, 1967). Even if these estimates are too high, nonverbal aspects of interpersonal communication clearly are crucial for understanding interpersonal relations.

Nonverbal behavior communicates messages between persons. This communication includes dynamic movements, static appearance-related choices of clothing and grooming, and paraverbal acts by senders and impressions of those actions and choices formed by receivers. The sender's messages may be intended or not, received or not, and interpreted as having been intended or not. They are sent via numerous channels, forcefully or subtly. Some nonverbal messages are universal, or nearly so, and others are specific to particular cultures, subcultures, or intimates. Nonverbal communication is a very complex, essential part of interpersonal relations, and it serves a number of important psychological functions. However, a simple initial framework for thinking about it is depicted in the following diagram, which presents nonverbal communication as a special case of a classic communication model (Hovland & Janis, 1959), in which one person sends a message (intended or not) to another person via one medium or another (e.g., face-to-face or video), stimulating a response from the receiver that reaches the sender, and the process continues.

This chapter will begin with a brief history of research in the area, followed by a brief discussion of the original influence of evolution on nonverbal communication. Next, I describe modern social psychological theories and research methods, with a special emphasis on current adaptations of Brunswik's (1956) lens model, a very useful framework for understanding the process. The complexity of nonverbal communication means that studying it has many pitfalls, and a section is devoted to cautionary notes for researchers and readers. We communicate nonverbally in a variety of contexts, including everyday interpersonal relations, but also where power and deception are involved and, increasingly, we must consider computer-mediated nonverbal communication. Finally, I present a brief review of nonverbal communication as a way to predict the eventual outcomes of relationships.

A BRIEF HISTORY

Although a number of fairly simple studies were conducted in the early part of the 20th century (e.g., Pintner, 1918), the first important scientific study that is pertinent here was that of Allport and Vernon (1933), who sought to find unity (or something close to it) *among* the expressive movements of their subjects. Their hypothesis appears to have been rooted in the Aristotelian proposition that one's whole body and personality are a kind of unity, in which every aspect is mirrored in every other aspect. This view was championed by German psychologists such as William Stern (1935), who profoundly influenced Allport. Their results showed promise, in that two clusters of expressive movements, one "general" and one "specific," were found, albeit with lower-than-desirable reliability.

Allport and Vernon's book did not stimulate much new published research over the next three decades; only a few scattered studies may be found from the 1930s until the early 1960s. Perhaps the first modern study of interest was Exline's (1963) investigation of visual interaction in groups of men and groups of women who had been categorized in terms of their need for affiliation. He found that need for affiliation was related to mutual glances, but differently for men and women. Exline's study had the further distinction of recognizing that nonverbal behavior should be examined *within interacting groups*, rather than implicitly assuming that people express themselves nonverbally without reference to others, that is, always in the same way.

EVOLUTIONARY BASES OF NONVERBAL COMMUNICATION

Darwin (1872/1998) proposed in *Expression of the Emotions in Man and Animals* that nonverbal expressive displays evolved to signal the sender's motivations and emotions to others. Although this idea is very plausible, particularly for other animals' displays, it has been challenged in the case of humans by Hauser (1996), who countered that senders who communicate their true state are at an evolutionary *dis*advantage; Hauser suggested that true displays leave the sender vulnerable to exploitation by the receiver. This view, consistent with Dawkins' (1989) *selfish gene theory*, asserts that displays are designed to deceive and manipulate the receiver. In turn, the receiver, it is said, attempts to decode the sender's true motivational state, and thus social interaction proceeds as a kind of war of interpretation and impression management. Others have offered a more complex compromise: dishonest displays are more likely when the sender does not trust the receiver, and honest displays are more likely when the sender trusts the receiver (e.g., Boone & Buck, 2003).

SOCIAL PSYCHOLOGICAL THEORIES OF NONVERBAL COMMUNICATION

Theoretical approaches from social psychologists began with simple *one-channel studies*. Fifty years ago, Robert Sommer (1959) investigated interpersonal distance as a form of nonverbal communication, one that presumably balanced too-close with too-far, an idea also discussed by Hall (1959). A few years later, the very influential *equilibrium theory* expressed by Argyle and Dean (1965) proposed that people seek such a balance across several "channels" (physical distance, gaze, smiling, as well as a verbal dimension, topic intimacy), rather than any single channel. Their theory suggested, for example, that if two people were forced closer together than they would prefer (for example, in an elevator), that they would compensate by increasing interpersonal "distance" in another channel, such as by gazing less at one another.

Theory next developed, in the 1970s, to explain the bases for these equilibratory adjustments. Several of these formulations focused on *arousal* as the psychological basis for the adjustments (Andersen, 1985;

Burgoon, 1978; Cappella & Greene, 1982). In Patterson's (1976) original version of this approach, *arousal-labeling theory*, a move "closer" to the other person (receiver) in any of the channels causes that person to label the arousal, for example, as positive if the receiver is attracted to the sender (which tends to lead to a reciprocation of the adjustment toward closer) or negative (which tends to lead to the receiver resetting the distance to the equilibrium, or even increasing the distance). In a similar vein, Mehrabian and Diamond (1971) viewed these nonverbal adjustments as ways to vary interpersonal *immediacy*.

In the next theoretical development, Patterson (1982) proposed his *functional perspective*. The essence of the functional approach is that nonverbal behavior serves a variety of social purposes. Nonverbal behavior was now seen as not merely reactive (to the sender's moves), but could also involve the initiation of movement or expression on the part of the sender to serve a social goal. Sometimes these actions do not reflect the sender's emotions and attitudes, but reflect a goal that is inconsistent with them, such as obtaining the compliance of a receiver, or deceiving them, or creating a desired impression (Patterson, 1991). Nonverbal behavior can and often does serve to communicate one's social role in a social interaction, to manage one's presentation of self to others, to signal rapport or the lack of it, to express emotion, to reveal one's personality, and to indicate whether or not one is telling the truth. Some of these functions are more, and some less, under the sender's control (e.g., Choi et al., 2005).

As theory in the area matured further, these ideas were expanded into *interaction adaptation theory* (Burgoon et al., 1998). Functionality is seen in this approach as consisting of three sorts: required, expected, and desired. Required functionality refers to biological drives and imperatives that may operate outside of consciousness. Expected functionality reflects norms and typical behavior for the context and culture.

Desired functionality reflects such idiosyncratic influences as personality, attitudes, and moods. Together, these are said to comprise the person's interaction position— the averaged or main thrust of the sender's nonverbal predisposition in a given situation and with a specific receiver. The dynamics of the interpersonal exchange are posited to be the result of the sender's interaction position and the receiver's behavioral response to it. Like each succeeding approach, interaction adaptation theory presumably was intended to incorporate and supersede the previous equilibrium, arousal, and functional approaches.

The other contemporary development is *parallel processing theory* (Patterson, 1995), which proposes that nonverbal interaction is not merely about behavior, but requires understanding the social cognitive judgment processes involved. The latter are often automatic or overlearned, but sometimes under control and in the service of a particular goal. Interactants not only send (encode); they also receive (decode), and Patterson believes that decoding has been underemphasized in earlier theories. Plausible and seemingly complete as parallel processing theory is, it is complex (as is interaction adaptation theory) and both theories have become difficult to properly test. As theory in the area struggles to capture the multidimensional nature of nonverbal interaction in context, it tends to become more descriptive than testable.

RESEARCH METHODS

Nonverbal researchers may focus on (a) the interpersonal, organizational, or cultural context of the interaction; (b) the personal qualities, strategies, or background of the sender, the receiver, or both; (c) the dynamic or static nonverbal cues displayed by the sender; (d) the receiver's interpretations of those cues; and (e) the receiver's dynamic or static responses. Of course, receivers become senders, and the process is a dynamic interaction that unfolds over time. Most studies focus on one slice or aspect of the full process, usually the receiver's impressions of the sender, who is presented in different *channels* (e.g., silent video versus video with sound; e.g., Hall & Schmid Mast, 2007), or with different alleged qualities (e.g., in a relationship or not; e.g., Parker & Burkley, 2009).

Studies of nonverbal communication in the interpersonal context typically have focused on liking or attraction, usually between strangers, to control for the influence of preexisting interactions (e.g., Mehrabian & Weiner, 1971). Organizational contexts have often included job interviews (e.g., Gifford, Ng, & Wilkinson, 1985). Cultural studies have often investigated presumed similarities or universalities in the meaning of cues such as facial expressions (e.g., Ekman & Friesen, 1971) or the lack thereof. The qualities of the sender and receiver typically include attractiveness, intelligence, personality, culture, race, formal status, relationship status, social class, and stigma.

Presenting the sender. The typical ways that senders have been presented to receivers include photographs, video clips, vocal clips, and *in vivo*, with or without role-playing. This choice must be made carefully, because no presentation technique is universally appropriate or infallible (Gray & Ambady, 2006). The sender has been presented in very brief "slices" of time (e.g., Ambady & Rosenthal, 1993) and at length.

Measuring the sender's cues. Much effort has been expended creating scoring systems for nonverbal behavior. Ekman and Friesen's (1978) Facial Action Coding System (FACS) is the best-known of these, although others exist—for example, the Maximally Descriptive Facial Movement Coding System (Izard, 1979) and the Pride Coding System (Tracy & Robins, 2007). Others have created systems that assess the whole body's dynamic movements and static cues (e.g., Birdwhistell, 1952) and the Seated Kinesic Activity Notation System (SKANS 5.2), in which 38 kinesic and facial behaviors are measured in one of three ways: frequency, duration, or time-sampling (Gifford, 1994b), and numerous other systems exist (see Riggio, 2006).

A framework for understanding the process. For experimental-theoretical and efficiency reasons, researchers usually focus on slices of the many possibilities. No study can include all the potential influences, but perhaps the best framework for including at least selected elements of the full process is that envisioned by Brunswik as early as the mid-1940s, but best described in the posthumous book assembled by his colleagues (Brunswik, 1956, pp. 26–29). His *lens model* is a seemingly simple overview of the whole nonverbal communication process but, once delved into, emerges as one rich with possibility and complexity (e.g., Hammond, 1955; Hoffman, 1960; Wiggins, 1973; also see Leising & Borkenau, this volume). Those who have attempted to further develop and use the full lens model, that is, by measuring the sender's background and qualities, the sender's cues, the receiver's background and qualities, and the accuracy or lack of it on the receiver's part, find it rewarding (e.g., Bernieri & Gillis, 2001; Borkenau & Liebler,

1992; Gifford, 1994a; Gifford, Ng, & Wilkinson, 1985; Scherer, 1978). Because it may be the best (if labor-intensive) overall framework for investigating nonverbal communication, the lens model, its advantages and its challenges, will be described in more detail, beginning with its main elements.

The paradigm's structure is an adaptation of Brunswik's (1956) lens model (Figure 11.1). Encoding (or what Brunswik called *ecological validity*) is represented by the lines connecting sender qualities to nonverbal behavior. Encoding occurs when reliable sender assessments significantly correlate with the sender's reliably scored nonverbal behaviors. Decoding (or what Brunswik called *cue utilization*) is represented by the lines connecting nonverbal behavior and impression formation on the part of the observers; it occurs when reliable receiver assessments are correlated with reliably scored sender nonverbal behaviors. The curved line linking the ratings of the actors' dispositions with the observers' ratings of those dispositions represents what Brunswik (1956) called *achievement*, or what is sometimes called agreement or accuracy. The large oval signifies the social

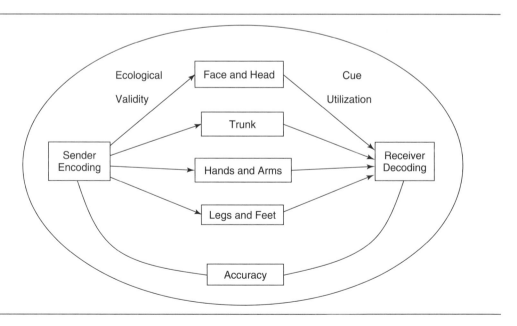

FIGURE 11.1   Social and Cultural Context

and cultural context in which the interaction process unfolds. Encoding and decoding are influenced by the context in which they occur. What transpires in a hallway conversation probably does not flow the same way as during a romantic evening, a business discussion, a criminal interrogation, or in interactions in different cultures.

A primary principle is that the personal qualities of senders should be investigated in contexts in which they may reasonably be expected to manifest themselves or to be salient. Sociability should be investigated in a context that permits or encourages it. Dominance should be investigated in a setting that permits or encourages it (but does not force it) because then nonverbal behaviors associated with it might involve self-conscious acting on the part of the sender, perhaps borrowed from some film or television show, that does not reflect the palette of natural dominance behavior.

The goal on the left half of the lens is to determine which nonverbal behaviors *actually* encode the sender's interpersonal-related quality of interest, and the goal on the right side of the lens is to determine which nonverbal behaviors are *believed* by receivers to be cues that reveal the quality. This distinction follows from Brunswik's original labels for the two sides of the lens model: ecological *validity* (left half) and cue *utilization* (right half). Thus, e*ncoding* is the outward, objective, visible manifestation of a sender's personal quality that is presumed to be, or to relate to, some aspect or quality of interpersonal relations. The fundamental hypothesis of lens model researchers is that valid encoding does occur or, alternatively, that *predictable* failures of encoding occur (e.g., in studies of bias or stereotyping).

Decoding is the use by receivers of nonverbal behavior to infer these aspects of interpersonal relations in the sender. It certainly occurs; the two interesting questions concern (1) its accuracy, by different kinds of receivers for different aspects of interpersonal relations in different conditions, and (2) the nature of systematic errors in decoding, which may signal bias or stereotyping.

Achievement is the degree of connection between encoding and decoding. How, and equally or even more importantly, *why* is the receiver correct or incorrect about the sender's true interpersonal feelings, intentions, or motivations?

The study of achievement is challenged in two important and related ways: (1) the validity of the measures of the sender's qualities themselves (e.g., emotion, motivation, attraction, intention, personality); and (2) the accuracy of receivers as they employ nonverbal cues to decode these qualities in others. These measures usually are self-reported by the sender or rated by others who know the sender well. However, important problems with both sorts of measures have been identified (cf. Funder, 2003; Kenny, 1994). Nevertheless, many researchers seem to assume that sender measures are valid. Sometimes this presumption is defensible (e.g., that the sender is lying or not, because this is an experimental manipulation), and sometimes it is worthy of question (e.g., the sender's motivation or attractiveness). Because they can be multiple, and thus have a natural psychometric edge, ratings of the sender's qualities by several significant others may be the "least-worst" approach to the validity problem when the criterion does not have an objective or experimental-manipulation basis. The second main problem with achievement is, as its definition implies, that receivers may or may not accurately decode the (true) level of the sender's interpersonal qualities from the sender's nonverbal behavior.

However, even if accuracy is low for these reasons, or not examined at all, decoding can be important, depending on the study's purpose. Receivers' assessments have inherent value as their view of senders' qualities, whether correct or not, as explanations of receivers' subsequent actions or attitudes toward the sender (e.g., Carney, Hall, & LeBeau, 2005).

Achievement can be enhanced or compromised depending on the mode in which the sender is presented. For example, decoders in an interview study saw either a silent videotape of an interview with a manager (that is, only the nonverbal behavior), or read a transcript of the same interview (thus, no nonverbal behavior) (Motowidlo, Burnett, Maczynski, & Witkowski, 1996). Decoders agreed well among themselves in their assessments of two encoder dispositions within each mode of presentation, but the correlations between the assessments of the two dispositions across the two conditions were $r = .27$ and $r = .30$; that is, they shared about nine percent of their variance. Given this low level of agreement between the assessments made in the two conditions, the decodings cannot both have been accurate.

HOW ENCODING AND DECODING ARE RELATED

In a full lens model, the relations between encoding and decoding fall into two categories, each with two forms. First, *matched links* may be identified. One form of matched link occurs when a nonverbal behavior significantly encodes self-assessments and is also used to a significant degree by receivers to decode or infer that self-assessment. Another form of matched link occurs when a link is significant on *neither* side of the lens: Receivers are saying that a given behavior does not encode a given sender quality and, based on the self-assessments, it does not.

Second, *mismatched links* may be identified. One form of mismatched link occurs when a nonverbal behavior does encode a self-assessed sender quality, but receivers do not utilize that cue. The other form of mismatched link occurs when receivers utilize a particular nonverbal cue to form their impression, but that cue does *not* encode that sender quality.

Achievement is greater, in general, when there are more matched links. The existence of matched links, with their lines going from the sender quality to a behavior and from the behavior to the receiver's assessment, clearly suggests that agreement

increases when information "flows" via such matched links. Conversely, agreement is lower when many mismatched links occur. When information does *not* flow, either encoding has not occurred (no behaviors measured encode the sender quality) or the receiver has used cues other than those that the encoding analysis suggests are valid indicators of the sender's quality.

Depending on the magnitudes of these links, which are discussed below, the findings in lens model studies show exactly *how* information appears to flow from the sender to the receiver. Its beauty and utility are that it shows precisely how a quality of the sender is reflected (or not) in nonverbal behavior and how receivers infer (and misinfer) that quality. Receivers may utilize "power codes" (Carney, Hall, & LeBeau, 2005; Schwartz, Tesser, & Powell, 1982), and postures may have shared meaning for receivers (Kudoh & Matsumoto, 1985). However, this does not necessarily mean that the sender's dominance is encoded by this same set of acts; it merely means that receivers believe that it is. In an early study, personnel managers were quite confident that job application photographs revealed the applicants' character (Viteles & Smith, 1932). Receivers' inferences may be reliable, which *suggests* accuracy, but they often correlate sporadically or not at all with senders' cues (e.g., Cleeton & Knight, 1924). Decoding studies report that "high-persuasive" nonverbal behavior patterns in senders (direct gaze, more gestures, fewer self-touches) are decoded as more assertive, forceful, powerful, and intelligent (Hart & Morry, 1997).

However, are these accurate assessments of sender qualities or mere "decoding errors" (Bull, 1983)? Observers appear to decode *confidently* and with greater consensus (Gifford, 1994a; Lippa & Dietz, 2000), but the evidence that they do so *accurately* is mixed or even discouraging, as shown for example by Cleeton and Knight's study. On the positive side, some research shows that, *if* one is willing to define accuracy as agreement between receiver assessments with sender self-assessments, then removing nonverbal behavior from a job interview (by conducting it by telephone, as opposed to in person) reduces accuracy (Blackman, 2002). Thus, nonverbal behavior certainly *can* contribute to accurate judgments. Again, lens model studies would enhance understanding of the full nonverbal communication process, including claims about accuracy or achievement.

Let us consider a concrete example. Gifford (1994a) used the lens model to identify nonverbal behaviors that (a) were valid indicators of particular interpersonal dispositions and (b) were correctly utilized by receivers, thereby forming matched links. In his study, unacquainted students conversed with each other in groups of three. Often, however, encoding and decoding do not result in optimal communication. The encoding and decoding of ambitiousness-dominance, for example, seems to involve largely different nonverbal acts (Gifford, 1994a). In the sample of behaviors examined, it was encoded by four acts, but receivers appear to have believed in a "power code" that included 10 acts. Only two acts were used in both encoding and decoding. Achievement depends on the receivers' appropriate use of ecologically valid cues. For example, the receivers believed that 14 nonverbal cues were good indicators of sender cold-quarrelsomeness, but not one of the 14 cues encoded self-rated cold-quarrelsomeness (Gifford, 1994a). Thus, achievement depends heavily on the receiver's use of appropriate nonverbal cues (i.e., those that actually encode the sender's qualities). "Dis-agreement" occurs when observers use inappropriate cues.

The strength of encoding and decoding. The magnitude of encoding and decoding is computed as the multiple correlation and percent of variance in each quality accounted for by the nonverbal behaviors. One general tendency is that decoding is stronger than encoding. Many more significant decoding links than encoding links typically are found (e.g., Borkenau and Liebler, 1992; Hall, Coats, & LeBeau,

2005). Despite this, decoding by individuals actually may not be much stronger than encoding. Decoding is usually based on ratings by multiple raters because multiple ratings almost necessarily increase the reliability of ratings. When ratings are more reliable, correlations involving them are stronger because less error is involved. Stronger correlations are more likely to be statistically significant. Analyses in one study that corrected for attenuation and estimated the reliability of single judges (Gifford, 1994a), showed that one typical decoding link shrank from $r = -.58$ to $-.35$. The matched encoding link for this decoding link was $r = -.29$, not much less than $r = -.35$. Thus, observers as a *group* decode strongly, but researchers who wish to generalize to typical *individual* observers, would conclude that decoding is not particularly reliable, and this would attenuate the seemingly large magnitude of decoding.

Whether researchers examine population or individual group decoding depends on the study's purpose. If it is to understand how observers (in general, nomothetically) decode, one would use the full observer sample; if it is to estimate the decoding skill of a single "typical" observer, the attenuation approach should be used, and if the goal is to understand how one particular observer decodes (for example, a clinician in training), one could study decoding with an n of 1. The question for the researcher is, do I wish to learn how and how well observers in general decode, how and how well a typical single observer (e.g., a typical human resource officer in a large organization) decodes, or how and how well *this* observer (for example, a person applying for a job as a human resource officer) decodes?

Potential outcomes of lens model studies. What are the generic potential outcomes of studies that use this paradigm? The first assumption is that all the judgments (e.g., self- and significant-other ratings, behavior scoring by independent raters, and receiver ratings) are reliable; any that are not cannot be used with any pretence of validity. In general, encoding, decoding, and achievement may be weak or strong for any sender quality, and the pattern of results probably will be different for each sender quality.

The first type of potential outcome occurs when, for a given quality, encoding, decoding, and achievement are all weak. In this case, (a) the sender's quality is not consistently reflected in his or her nonverbal behavior (at least not in the behaviors studied), (b) receivers do not use this set of behavior cues to arrive at their inferences, and (c) receiver inferences do not agree with the self- or significant-other assessments of the sender.

Second, if decoding is strong but encoding is weak, receivers apparently are employing invalid stereotypes. Achievement should be weak in such a case, because there are no true relations between the sender's quality and nonverbal behavior for receivers to validly decode.

Third, if strong encoding but weak decoding is found, receivers are unable to deduce correctly which nonverbal cues reflect the sender's quality. The potential for strong agreement is present but unrealized.

Fourth, if achievement is strong but both encoding and decoding are weak, receivers must be using nonverbal behaviors for decoding that the researcher has not measured. Some nonverbal cue or other must have been providing valid information about the sender's quality, or strong achievement would not be possible. The researcher must explore the receiver's impression formation process, perhaps through interviews with them, to learn which unstudied nonverbal cues they might have been using to succeed in matching the assessments of the senders.

Fifth, if weak encoding and high agreement are found, receivers again must be using valid but unmeasured nonverbal cues, unless the receivers are clairvoyant (Reichenbach, 1938). As Wiggins (1973, p. 159) wryly noted, "(s)uch a possibility is assigned rather low priority as a contemporary scientific explanation." This is a case in which researchers must rethink their choice of cues, seeking other ones that *do* encode the sender's quality. Again, this might be accomplished by asking receivers to reflect on their inferences: What was it about the senders' actions that caused you to assess them as you did?

Finally, if strong encoding, strong decoding, *and* strong agreement are found, one may conclude that the whole process is working as researchers in this area dream, and they may be able to supply a satisfying account of the nonverbal inference process. A sober second thought, however, is that senders (or their intimates) and receivers *might* be agreeing on an inaccurate view of the sender's quality, something akin to a *folie à deux*. A more likely interpretation is that the strong mediation of objective nonverbal behaviors, reliably assessed by independent raters, would be substantial evidence that the receivers' decoding is valid, given that they have been demonstrated to rely on the same objective (visible) aspects of reality as encoding.

TEN TROUBLESOME COMPLEXITIES

Many studies have not adequately dealt with all the difficulties inherent in this area of research; to learn how nonverbal behavior truly illuminates the nature of interpersonal interaction, researchers must grapple with at least ten design and analysis complexities (Gifford, 2006). By "complexity" is meant a Type I or Type II error in interpreting the relations between nonverbal behavior and the target aspect of interpersonal interaction that may occur if the study fails to take into account one or more of the accuracy or agreement issues.

Some of these complexities are familiar and some less so; some are easier to manage than others. They are that (1) true encoding can be obscured through the use of unreliable measures, (2) encoding should be studied in a context in which the dimension of interpersonal interaction of interest is salient, (3) others involved in the interaction might influence an individual's encoding,

(4) encoding might occur differently when a person is engaged in different activities or purposes, (5) encoding may depend on who (e.g., self or significant others) assesses the dimension of interpersonal interaction of interest, (6) nonverbal behavior may encode combinations of these dimensions without encoding that combination's constituent dimensions, (7) combinations of nonverbal behaviors may encode a dimension of interpersonal interaction of interest without the individual behaviors doing so, (8) encoding may depend on the gender composition of the group, (9) encoding sometimes differs for male and female individuals, and (10) cultural groups vary in their encoding patterns.

The lens model to the rescue. The lens model paradigm deals with the crucial accuracy problems in the most useful way. Its essential feature is that encoding and decoding both are included in the same study. Most studies examine either encoding or decoding, which disallows the possibility of understanding the relations between the two processes, or compare sender and receiver ratings without investigating the intervening nonverbal behavior. For example, one study showed that self and acquainted observer ratings were more highly correlated than self and unacquainted observer ratings, but the behavioral cues on which the ratings were based were not measured (Funder & Colvin, 1988). Watson (1989) noticed this gap and called for studies of judgments that also include behavioral cues. Nevertheless, "cueless" studies are still reported. For example, "sociable" actors were found to be more legible (that is, easier to "read" or accurately decode) than less sociable actors, based on actor-observer agreement, but the pathways or mediating behaviors underlying this phenomenon were not examined (e.g., Ambady, Hallahan, & Rosenthal, 1995). A few years later, these results were replicated, and many potential mediating cues were investigated. Extraverts used more energetic gestures, kept their hands farther from their bodies, and changed their facial expression more than introverts (Lippa, 1998).

The full lens model paradigm includes the following elements: reliably measured sender qualities that are investigated within the context to which they apply, and three independent groups of raters are used: (1) senders' self-rated qualities or raters who know the sender well, (2) raters trained in a carefully developed nonverbal behavior scoring system, and (3) observer-raters, who are unacquainted typically with the actors, so that their ratings are not influenced by previous personal experience with the actor. A full lens study investigates all three processes, and the relative strengths of encoding, decoding, and agreement—and it takes the context into account in order to provide some understanding of *how* nonverbal behavior communicates (and miscommunicates). Some notable exceptions include those by Borkenau and Liebler (1992) and Lippa (1998).

Which receivers? The paradigm can be employed to understand the cue-utilization policies of either an individual receiver or an aggregate of receivers. Some early studies focused on individual abilities, such as those of clinicians (e.g., Hoffman, 1960) and found that their judgments, as revealed through their use of cues, did not match well with their own impressions of how they use those cues. Later, the individual-level focused on the differential sensitivity of individual receivers (e.g., Rosenthal, 1979). When the researcher has "aggregate" (nomothetic) goals, the ratings of a sample of receivers are used on the decoding side—if those ratings show adequate interrater reliability. If interrater agreement is low, it will be inappropriate to correlate their ratings with the nonverbal behavior scores (decoding correlations) or with the targets' own self-ratings (achievement correlations). Thus, studies with any sort of nomothetic goals depend on, and therefore must hypothesize, that a group of observers will reliably agree on actors' dispositions. If a specified group of observers do not agree, then conclusions about their cue-utilization policies cannot be stated, probably because members of that group do not use the same cues.

In one study that fulfilled most of the goals of the proposed paradigm, behavioral cues were examined as mediators of the encoding-decoding process (Borkenau & Liebler, 1992). The same judges served as raters of the physical cues and as decoders, however, which compromised the independence of the behavior scores and trait ratings. Gifford, Ng, and Wilkinson (1985) examined nonverbal behavioral mediators and used behavior scorers who were independent of both targets and observers. The study identified nonverbal cues exhibited by job applicants that mediated (and failed to mediate) agreement between job applicant and personnel officer assessments of the applicant's social skill and motivation to work.

INFLUENCES ON NONVERBAL COMMUNICATION

The relations between nonverbal communication and interpersonal relations are complex, and a complete description of them is not possible here; the interested reader is referred to Manusov and Patterson (2006). This section offers sample findings for the influences of personality, gender, culture, decoding skill, and decodability.

Personality. An example of relatively straightforward encoding results comes from a study of interacting female dyads (Berry & Hansen, 2000). More agreeable women gestured more, used more open body postures, visually attended to their interaction partner more, used fewer visual dominance behaviors, and displayed fewer negative facial expressions than did less-agreeable women. Women who were more open to experience visually attended to their interaction partners more than those who were less open to experience.

More extraverted persons seem to use more animated, expressive, and animated gestures, that is, faster and more energetic gestures using the hands farther from the body (Lippa, 1998) than more introverted persons. Children with more internal, rather than external, locus of control tendencies smile more and engage in fewer off-task activities (Carton & Carton, 1998). Individuals with avoidant attachment styles tend to choose larger interpersonal distance (Kaitz, Bar-Haim, Lehrer, & Grossman, 2004), as do those with greater trait anxiety (e.g., Patterson, 1973) and weaker affiliative tendencies (e.g., Mehrabian & Diamond, 1971). Senders who speak in a tight-lipped manner or who turn their heads while speaking may be judged as "uptight," those who speak with a hand over their mouths or smile with a closed mouth as shy, and those who smile less as too serious (Ferrari & Swinkels, 1996). The encoded nonverbal behaviors of conversing senders as a function of eight interpersonal circle dispositions (Wiggins, 1979) was reported by Gifford (1994a), and nonverbal behaviors clearly map onto the interpersonal circle (Gifford, 1991; Gifford & O'Connor, 1987). Personality and gender, the next topic, often interact. For example, using most of one's body when gesturing validly signals extraversion for women, but not for men (Lippa, 1998).

Gender. Differences in nonverbal behavior for males and females are relatively small in magnitude, but they do exist and can have important consequences (Hall, 2006). On average, males generally choose larger interpersonal distances and females tend to orient themselves more directly to their interaction partner. Women usually are nonverbally more animated and warm, that is, they smile and laugh more, stand closer, look at and touch others more. These tendencies vary or even reverse under different circumstances (Gifford, 2007). As one example, girls with depressive symptoms look less at their peers than boys with depressive symptoms (van Beek, van Dolderen, & Dubas, 2006). Women decode more accurately and are more decodable (legible) to others of both genders, on average. Men are likely to misinterpret women's nonverbal encoding of friendliness as sexual interest; and new work suggests that men also misinterpret women's encoded sexual interest as friendliness (Farris, Treat, Viken, & McFall, 2008).

Culture. A primary goal and issue in the study of nonverbal behavior across cultures has been universality versus specificity. One general conclusion is that facial expressions for the main emotions are universal, but the rules for how and when to use them, as well as how to decode them in others, vary across cultures. For example, Americans and Russians express anger and contempt more than do Japanese (Matsumoto, Yoo, Hirayama, & Petrova, 2005), and Asians decode emotions as having lower intensity than do Americans (Ekman et al., 1987).

The expression of other nonverbal actions varies considerably across cultures; perhaps the primary example is preferred interpersonal distance, which roughly increases with latitude in Western societies (apart from Australia and New Zealand), but is more finely tuned than such a generalization implies. For example, Colombians choose smaller distances than Costa Ricans (Shuter, 1976). Among many possible examples, Arabs tend to gaze longer and more directly at their partners than do Americans (Hall, 1966). Newly immigrated Jews and Italians in New York City had traditional gesturing patterns, but assimilation attenuated them (Efron, 1941).

Decoding ability. A variant on the study of decoding is the study of decoding *ability*, sometimes called nonverbal sensitivity (e.g., Riggio, 2006; Rosenthal, 1979). Decoding as a skill related to the receiver's own experience and background has often been applied to decoding the sender's emotions (e.g., Mullins & Duke, 2004). Apparently, more intelligent judges are more accurate (Lippa & Dietz, 2000), at least for some qualities: more intelligent university-student receivers assessed dispositional extraversion and an omnibus (across-dispositions) measure more accurately than less-intelligent university-student receivers.

Decodability. On the other side of the lens, which qualities are easiest to decode from nonverbal behavior? Several studies

(e.g., Ambady, Hallahan, & Rosenthal, 1995; Borkenau & Liebler, 1992; Gifford, 1994a; Lippa & Dietz, 2000) report that sociability or extraversion is the most legible or accurately discernable disposition. However, this may be a function of context: Most studies use conversations as the activity, and extraversion is particularly salient in conversations. As noted earlier, women are, on average, more legible than men.

CONTEXTS OF NONVERBAL COMMUNICATION

Nonverbal communication is part of every face-to-face interaction, and even many electronically mediated interactions. Some interaction contexts are more common or more important, and this section focuses on close relationships, power relationships, deception, and computer-mediated interactions, although many more could be included, as in the following sections.

Close Relationships

Positively valenced nonverbal behavior is essential to the development and maintenance of close relationships, or what has been called, in reference to the interpersonal circle (Leary, 1957; Wiggins, 1979), the horizontal dimension of social interaction. Among these are touch, smiling, mutual gaze, forward lean, and interpersonal distance, which together have been called *immediacy* (Mehrabian, 1967) or *positive involvement behavior* (Prager, 2000). Each of these behavioral elements helps to distinguish an intimate relationship from a casual one (Andersen, Guerrero, & Jones, 2006).

Involvement is said to be encoded in terms of five dimensions (Burgoon & Newton, 1991): immediacy in terms of touch, expressiveness of the face, attention paid to the other, smooth and coordinated conversational turn-taking, and few vocal pauses. Perhaps less obviously, because it is not a nonverbal behavior in the sense of what occurs *during* an interaction, is simply the amount of time spent together, a nonverbal behavior of another sort. In fact, in one study this was the most powerful of 20 nonverbal behaviors in predicting relational satisfaction (Egland, Stelzner, Andersen, & Spitzberg, 1997).

Decoding is also important in close relationships: The accurate decoding of the other's emotions is important for relationship satisfaction (Gottman & Porterfield, 1981). People in satisfying relationships generally decode one another more accurately, an outcome in which the causal arrows probably run in both directions. However, this is not always easy: nonverbal behavior can be ambiguous, both in terms of encoding and decoding. Ambiguity leads to misinterpretation which, particularly in developing and in close relationships, can have serious consequences. For example, faces can convey different dispositional impressions to receivers depending on the sender's emotional state (Montepare & Dobish, 2003). Intimate partners are more likely to notice negative nonverbal cues than positive ones (Manusov, Floyd, & Kerssen-Griep, 1997). Other studies suggest that the accuracy of emotional decoding in couples is almost impossibly complex: it depends on the positive or negative valence of the emotion, whether the emotion is related to the relationship itself or not, and on the sender's and receiver's degree of relationship satisfaction (Koerner & Fitzpatrick, 2002).

Apart from encoding and decoding, a number of nonverbal trends in relationships have been found. For example, unhappy couples display more negative nonverbal behavior (Burgoon, Buller, & Woodall, 1996), and men tend to nonverbally withdraw (less gaze, turning their head down and away) (Noller, Feeney, Roberts, & Christensen, 2005).

Power and dominance. An important aspect of interpersonal interaction is dominance or power, sometimes called the vertical dimension of social relations. If one focuses on beliefs about cues that define sender power ("power codes"), without considering sender encoding, receivers apparently believe that as many as 35 cues reveal sender power (Carney, Hall, & LeBeau, 2005). Among the strongest of these are manifesting a self-assured expression, successfully interrupting others, and initiating hand-shaking. As for most qualities, however, decoding is much stronger than encoding (Hall, Coats, & LeBeau, 2005). When beliefs are stronger than reality, the potential for misunderstanding is great.

Decoding depends to some extent on power relations. Subordinates in one study were more accurate at decoding superiors than superiors were at decoding subordinates, probably because subordinates send less clear messages to superiors than superiors sent to subordinates (Hall et al., 2006).

Deception. Unfortunately (in most cases), people lie to one another (DePaulo et al., 1996). A long tradition in nonverbal communication research investigates this phenomenon, usually with the goal of distinguishing between instances of lying and truth-telling. In an illustration of usually faulty decoding, most police and parents think that they can distinguish the difference, but most people are poor at detecting lies (e.g., Bond & DePaulo, 2005). Part of the problem for decoders is that liars do not always use different nonverbal behavior from when they are telling the truth (Strömwall, Hartwig, & Granhag, 2006; Vrig, 2006).

When people do lie, one perspective asserts that it often is reflected in nonverbal behaviors associated with (a) fear, guilt, or delight emotions; (b) the complexity of the content, that is, having to think hard to create a story; and (c) attempts at behavior control, that is, controlling actions that liars believe might reveal that they are indeed lying (Zuckerman, DePaulo, & Rosenthal, 1981). Others have suggested that truth-tellers sometimes are subject to these same influences (DePaulo et al., 2003), for example, when convincing others that something is very important. Thus, distinguishing between lying and truth-telling can be difficult, but the distinction may be apparent if the liar presents the story unconvincingly or too deliberately.

Another perspective recognizes that liars are senders, but someone else is receiving the message, and that person influences the sender with his or her own actions (Buller & Burgoon, 1996) or knowledge. For example, knowing or thinking that a sender is lying influences what receivers perceive in the sender's behavior (Levine, Asada, & Park, 2006). As in any nonverbal interaction, one person's gazing, smiling, nodding, and posture may influence the other's. Obviously, then, particularly if receivers do not take this into account, they may influence the actions of the sender, and then begin to interpret the sender's lying or truth-telling in terms of some nonverbal pattern that they themselves influenced.

No single cue is an extremely valid cue to lying, but some are more reliable than others. In a comprehensive meta-analysis, De Paulo et al. (2003) found the largest effect sizes for a lack of vocal and verbal immediacy and certainty, less time spent talking, discrepant or ambivalent actions, and nervousness. Even larger effect sizes were found for number of foot movements, changes in pupil size, false smiles, and an indifferent or unconcerned appearance, but these effect sizes are based on a smaller number of studies and thus are less well established. Obviously they deserve more research attention. Other studies report that fewer movements, for example of the hands, signals deception, at least among senders with higher levels of public self-consciousness (Vrij, Akehurst, & Morris, 1997).

Can receivers be trained to detect deception? The evidence is mixed, but leans toward slight or moderate improvement in detection rates, depending on the type of message. Interestingly, even bogus training can improve detection rates, because "trained" receivers increase their attention to nonverbal cues as they process cues more critically (Levine, Feeley, McCornack, Hughes, & Harms, 2005).

Computer-Mediated Communication

The past several decades have seen an enormous increase in communication via computers. One might think this is outside the realm of nonverbal communication because for the most part, sender and receiver simply type messages. However, senders seem to want to embellish their words with more-than-verbal meaning, and so emoticons and avatars were invented.

Emoticons (combinations of punctuation marks or small graphic depictions of emotion-indicating faces) have been used since the early 1980s, and come in many type-symbolic forms, such as :) or ☺. Despite, or perhaps because of, their simplicity, emoticons are actually more reliably recognized than human facial expressions (Walther, 2006). Females use them more often than males, and the frown emoticon ☹ seems to be the only one that can actually change the meaning of a verbal statement, as opposed to reinforcing a statement (Walther, 2006).

Avatars, cartoon-like full-body graphic images, up the nonverbal ante, because senders choose a virtual body to represent themselves, one that is not stuck in a sentence and restricted to keyboard symbols, but can move around in a virtual world. Thus, avatars open up the possibility of studying senders' chosen "interpersonal" distances (Krikorian, Lee, & Chock, 2000) and appearance (Nowak & Biocca, 2003) as they interact with (virtual) others.

Chronemics refers to the temporal aspect of computer-mediated communication, that is, the study of the time it takes for a recipient to reply to a sender. Is it important that someone replies to your e-mail in five minutes versus five days? Apparently it is (Hesse, Werner, & Altman, 1988; Rice, 1990). When responses are slower, receivers tend toward making personal rather than situational attributions about senders (Cramton, 2001). Waiting longer than expected for a reply in instant-message conversations understandably leads to frustration or even hostility (Rintel & Pittam, 1997). Task-oriented messages sent late in the evening (as opposed to those sent in the morning) lead to attributions of dominance on the part of the sender by the receiver (Walther & Tidwell, 1995). Expectations of a fast e-mail reply appear to be relaxed when the sender and receiver are in an established social relationship (Walther, 2006).

USING NONVERBAL BEHAVIOR TO PREDICT INTERPERSONAL OUTCOMES

Whether through very brief presentations of a sender or longer and involved inter-actions such as marriage (e.g., Gottman & Porterfield, 1981), nonverbal communica-tion researchers concerned with the future impact of current interactions have tried to predict the future from the present. The classic example is a study that demon-strated that evaluations of 30-second silent clips of instructors by college students were strongly predictive of those instructors' end-of-term ratings by students in their classes (Ambady & Rosenthal, 1993). Many other studies have supported the idea that fairly accurate evaluations occur with quite brief exposures to senders (e.g., Curhan & Pentland, 2007).

IMPLICATIONS FOR EVERYDAY INTERPERSONAL INTERACTIONS

One important implication of the findings is that when sender and receiver believe that different behaviors signify a given sender quality (or that a given behavior signifies different sender qualities), misinterpreta-tion and conflict can result. For example, if a receiver believes that a sender is open to the development of a deeper relationship—or not—he or she may well behave toward the sender in accordance with this percep-tion. The sender consequently may then be pleasantly *or* unpleasantly moved by these actions and may then respond accord-ingly (or not). The receiver may then react to the sender's reaction negatively if the inference was incorrect, and so on. In this

way, the innocent use of, and consequent misinference from, certain nonverbal behav-iors can seriously damage the development of social relations. A very general problem is the overly strong and often incorrect infer-ence of sender qualities by receivers. This can be, and probably is, the root of many interpersonal problems.

CONCLUSION

Nonverbal communication clearly is a very important part of interpersonal interaction, yet pinning down the specific ways in which its behavioral dimensions are encoded and decoded, and how social judgment pro-cesses influence and are influenced by it, remain as challenges.

The possibilities, however, when con-trasted with the challenges, help to account for the variations in researchers' optimism and enthusiasm from the 1930s until now. Researchers have been both aided and daunted by advances in theory and technol-ogy, and they face important methodolog-ical complexities. However, if researchers are, at minimum, careful to describe how their studies deal with the complexities, understanding will grow. This will be a step toward a fuller understanding of both social judgment and the delicate behavioral dance involved in nonverbal communication.

References

Agliati, A., Vescovo, A., & Anolli, L. (2006). A new methodological approach to nonverbal behav-ior analysis in cultural perspective. *Behavior Research Methods, 38*, 364–371.

Ambady, N., Hallahan, M., & Rosenthal, R. (1995). On judging and being judged accurately in zero-acquaintance situations. *Journal of Person-ality and Social Psychology, 69*, 518–529.

Ambady, N., & Rosenthal, R. (1993). Half a minute: Predicting teacher evaluations from thin slices of nonverbal behavior and physical attractive-ness. *Journal of Personality and Social Psychology, 64*, 431–441.

Allport, G., & Vernon, P. (1933). *Studies in expressive movement*. New York: MacMillan.

Andersen, P. A. (1985). Nonverbal immediacy in interpersonal communication. In A. W. Siegman & S. Feldstein (Eds.). *Multichannel integrations of nonverbal behavior* (pp. 1–36). Hillsdale, NJ: Erlbaum.

Andersen, P. A., Guerrero, L. K., & Jones, S. M. (2006). Nonverbal behavior in intimate interactions and intimate relationships. In V. Manusov & M. L. Patterson (Eds.), *The Sage handbook of nonverbal communication* (pp. 259–278). Thousand Oaks, CA: Sage.

Argyle, M., Salter, V., Nicholson, H., Williams, M., & Burgess, P. (1970). The communication of inferior and superior attitudes by verbal and non-verbal signals. *British Journal of Social and Clinical Psychology, 9*, 222–231.

Argyle, M., & Dean, J. (1965). Eye contact, distance, and affiliation. *Sociometry, 28*, 289–304.

Bernieri, F. J., & Gillis, J. S. (2001). Judging rapport: Employing Brunswik's lens model to study interpersonal sensitivity. In J. A. Hall & F. J. Bernieri (Eds.), *Interpersonal sensitivity: Theory and measurement* (pp. 3–20). Mahwah, NJ: Erlbaum.

Berry, D. S., & Hansen, J. S. (2000). Personality, nonverbal behavior, and interaction quality in female dyads. *Personality and Social Psychology Bulletin, 26*, 278–292.

Birdwhistell, R. L. (1952). *An introduction to kinesics: An annotation system for analysis of body motion and gesture.* Washington, DC: U.S. Department of State Foreign Service Institute.

Blackman, M. C. (2002). The employment interview via the telephone: Are we sacrificing accurate personality judgments for cost efficiency? *Journal of Research in Personality, 36*, 208–233.

Boone, R. T., & Buck, R. (2003). Emotional expressivity and trustworthiness: The role of nonverbal behavior in the evolution of cooperation. *Journal of Nonverbal Behavior, 27*, 163–182.

Bond, C. F., & De Paulo, B. M. (2005). *Accuracy of deception judgments.* Unpublished manuscript.

Borkenau, P., & Liebler, A. (1992). Trait inferences: Sources of validity at zero acquaintance. *Journal of Personality and Social Psychology, 62*, 645–657.

Brunswik, E. (1956). *Perception and the representative design of psychological experiments.* Berkeley, CA: University of California Press.

Bull, P. (1983). *Body movement and interpersonal communication.* New York: John Wiley & Sons.

Buller, D. B., & Burgoon, J. K. (1996). Interpersonal deception theory. *Communication Theory, 6*, 203–242.

Burgoon, J. K. (1978). A communication model of personal space violations: Explication and an initial test. *Human Communication Research, 4*, 129–142.

Burgoon, J. K., Buller, D. B., & Woodall, W. G. (1996). *Nonverbal communication: The unspoken dialogue* (2nd ed.). New York: McGraw-Hill.

Burgoon, J. K., & Newton, D. A. (1991). Applying social meaning model to relational message interpretations of conversational involvement: Comparing observer and participant perspectives. *Southern Communication Journal, 56*, 96–113.

Burgoon, J. K., Ebesu, A. H., White, C. H., Koch, P., Alvaro, E. M., & Kikuchi, T. (1998). The many faces of interaction adaptation. In M. T. Palmer & G. A. Barnett (Eds.), *Progress in communication sciences* (Vol. 14, pp. 191–220). Stamford, CT: Ablex.

Cappella, J. N., & Greene, J. O. (1982). A discrepancy-arousal explanation of mutual influence on expressive behavior for adult and infant-adult interaction. *Communication Monographs, 49*, 89–114.

Carney, D. R., Hall, J. A., & LeBeau, L. S. (2005). Beliefs about the nonverbal expression of power. *Journal of Nonverbal Behavior, 29*, 105–123.

Carton, J. S., & Carton, E. E. R. (1998). Nonverbal maternal warmth and children's locus of control of reinforcement. *Journal of Nonverbal Behavior, 22*, 77–86.

Choi, V. S., Gray, H. M., & Ambady, N. (2005). The glimpsed world: Unintended communication and unintended perception. In R. R. Hassin, J. S. Uleman, & J. A. Bargh (Eds.), *The new unconscious* (pp. 309–333). New York: Oxford University Press.

Cleeton, G. U., & Knight, F. B. (1924). Validity of character judgments based on external criteria. *Journal of Applied Psychology, 8*, 215–231.

Cramton, C. D. (2001). The mutual knowledge problem and its consequences for dispersed collaboration. *Organization Science, 12*, 346–371.

Curhan, J. R., & Pentland, A. (2007). Thin slices of negotiation: Predicting outcomes from conversational dynamics within the first 5 minutes. *Journal of Applied Psychology, 92*, 802–811.

Darwin, C. (1872/1998). *The expression of the emotions in man and animals.* New York: Oxford University Press.

Dawkins, R. (1989). *The selfish gene* (2nd ed.). New York: Oxford University Press.

DePaulo, B. M., Kashy, D. A., Kirkendol, S. E., Wyer, M. M., Epstein, J. A. (1996). Lying in everyday life. *Journal of Personality and Social Psychology, 70,* 979–995.

DePaulo, B. M., Lindsay, J. L., Malone, B. E., Muhlenbruck, L., Charlton, K., & Cooper, H. (2003). Cues to deception. *Psychological Bulletin, 129,* 74–118.

Efron, D. (1941). *Gesture and environment.* Oxford, UK: King's Crown Press.

Egland, K. I., Stelzner, M. A., Andersen, P. A., & Spitzberg, B. S. (1997). Perceived understanding, nonverbal communication, and relational satisfaction. In J. E. Aitken & L. J. Shedletsky (Eds.), *Intrapersonal communication processes* (pp. 386–396). Annandale, VA: Speech Communication Association.

Ekman, P., & Friesen, W. V. (1971). Constants across culture in the face and emotion. *Journal of Personality and Social Psychology, 17,* 124–129.

Ekman, P., & Friesen, W. V. (1978). *Facial Action Coding System: A technique for the measurement of facial movement.* Palo Alto, CA: Consulting Psychologists Press.

Ekman, P., Friesen, W. V., O'Sullivan, M., Chan, A., Diacpoyanni-Tarlatzis, I., & Heider, K. (1987). Universals and cultural differences in the judgments of facial expressions of emotion. *Journal of Personality and Social Psychology, 53,* 712–717.

Exline, R. V. (1963). Explorations in the process of person perception: Visual interaction in relation to competition, sex, and need for affiliation. *Journal of Personality, 31,* 1–20.

Farris, C., Treat, T. A., Viken, R. J., & McFall, R. M. (2008). Perceptual mechanisms that characterize gender differences in decoding women's sexual intent. *Psychological Science, 19,* 348–354.

Ferrari, J. R., & Swinkels, A. (1996). Classic coverups and misguided messages: Examining facetrait associations in stereotyped perceptions of nonverbal behavior. *Journal of Social Behavior and Personality, 11,* 27–42.

Funder, D. C. (2003). Toward a social psychology of person judgments: Implications for person perception accuracy and self-knowledge. In Forgas, J. P., & Williams, K. D. (Eds.) Social judgments: Implicit and explicit processes (pp. 115–133). New York: Cambridge University Press.

Funder, D. C., & Colvin, C. R. (1988). Friends and strangers: Acquaintanceship, agreement, and the accuracy of personality judgment. *Journal of Personality and Social Psychology, 55,* 149–158.

Gifford, R. (1991). Mapping nonverbal behavior on the interpersonal circle. *Journal of Personality and Social Psychology, 61,* 279–288.

Gifford, R. (1994a). A lens-mapping framework for understanding the encoding and decoding of interpersonal dispositions in nonverbal behavior. *Journal of Personality and Social Psychology, 66,* 398–412.

Gifford, R. (1994b). *SKANS 5.2: The seated kinesic activity notation system.* Technical report. Victoria, BC: University of Victoria. (Available from the author.)

Gifford, R. (2006). Personality and nonverbal behavior. In V. Manusov & M. L. Patterson (Eds.), *The Sage handbook of nonverbal communication* (pp. 201–218). Thousand Oaks, CA: Sage.

Gifford, R. (2007). *Environmental psychology: Principles and practice.* Colville, WA: Optimal Books.

Gifford, R., Ng, C. F., & Wilkinson, M. (1985). Nonverbal cues in the employment interview: Links between applicant qualities and interviewer judgments. *Journal of Applied Psychology, 70,* 729–736.

Gifford, R., & O'Connor, B. (1987). The interpersonal circumplex as a behavior map. *Journal of Personality and Social Psychology, 52,* 1019–1026.

Gottman, J. M., & Porterfield, A. L. (1981). Communicative competence in the nonverbal behavior of married couples. *Journal of Marriage and the Family, 43,* 817–824.

Gray, H. M., & Ambady, N. (2006). Methods for the study of nonverbal communication. In V. Manusov & M. L. Patterson (Eds.), *The Sage handbook of nonverbal communication* (pp. 41–58). Thousand Oaks, CA: Sage.

Hall, E. T. (1959). *The silent language.* Garden City, NY: Doubleday.

Hall, E. T. (1966). *The hidden dimension.* Garden City, NY: Doubleday.

Hall, J. A. (2006). Women's and men's nonverbal communication: Similarities, differences, stereotypes, and origins. In V. Manusov & M. L. Patterson (Eds.), *The Sage handbook of nonverbal communication* (pp. 201–218). Thousand Oaks, CA: Sage.

Hall, J. A., Coats, E. J., & LeBeau, L. S. (2005). Nonverbal behavior and the vertical dimension of social relations: A meta-analysis. (Full text available.) *Psychological Bulletin, 131*(6), 898–924.

Hall, J. A., Rosip, J. C., Smith LeBeau, L., Horgan, T. G., & Carter, J. D. (2006). Attributing the sources of accuracy in unequal-power dyadic communication: Who is better and why? *Journal of Experimental Social Psychology, 42*, 18–27.

Hall, J. A., & Schmid Mast, M. (2007). Sources of accuracy in the empathic accuracy paradigm. *Emotion, 7*, 438–446.

Hammond, K. R. (1955). Probabalistic functioning and the clinical method. *Psychological Review, 62*, 255–262.

Hauser, M. D. (1996). *The evolution of communication.* Cambridge, MA: MIT Press.

Hesse, B. W., Werner, C. M., & Altman, I. (1988). Temporal aspects of computer-mediated communication. *Computers in Human Behavior, 4*, 147–165.

Hoffman, P. J. (1960). The paramorphic representation of clinical judgment. *Psychological Bulletin, 57*, 116–131.

Horgan, T. G., & Smith, J. L. (2006). Interpersonal reasons for interpersonal perceptions: Gender-incongruent purpose goals and nonverbal judgment accuracy. *Journal of Nonverbal Behavior, 30*, 127–140.

Hovland, C. I., & Janis, I. L. (1959). *Personality and persuasibility.* New Haven, CT: Yale University Press.

Hsee, C. K., Hatfield, E., Carlson, J. G., & Chemtob, C. (1992). Assessments of the emotional state of others—conscious judgments versus emotional contagion. *Journal of Social and Clinical Psychology, 11*, 119–128.

Izard, C. E. (1979). *The maximally discriminative facial movement coding system (MAX).* Newark, NJ: The University of Delaware Information Technologies and University Media Services.

Kaitz, M., Bar-Haim, Y., Lehrer, M., & Grossman, E. (2004). Adult attachment style and interpersonal distance. *Attachment and Human Development, 6*, 285–304.

Kenny, D. A. (1994). *Interpersonal perception: A social relations analysis.* New York: Guilford Press.

Koerner, A. F., & Fitzpatrick, M. A. (2002). Nonverbal communication and marital adjustment and satisfaction: The role of decoding of relationship relevant and relationship irrelevant affect. *Communication Monographs, 69*, 33–51.

Krikorian, D. H., Lee, J., & Chock, T. M. (2000). Isn't that spatial? Distance and communication in a 2D virtual environment. *Journal of Computer-Mediated Communication, 5*. Retrieved August 25, 2009, from http://jcmc.indiana.edu/vol5/issue4/krikorian.html

Kudoh, T., & Matsumoto, D. (1985). Cross-cultural examination of the semantic dimensions of body postures. *Journal of Personality and Social Psychology, 48*, 1440–1446.

Leary, T. (1957). *Interpersonal diagnosis of personality.* New York: Ronald Press.

Levine, T. R., Asada, K. J. K., & Park, H. S. (2006). The lying chicken and the gaze-avoidant egg: Eye contact, deception, and causal order. *Southern Communication Journal, 71*, 401–411.

Levine, T. R., Feeley, T. H., McCornack, S. A., Hughes, M., & Harms, C. M. (2005). Testing the effects of nonverbal behavior training on accuracy in deception detection with the inclusion of a bogus training control group. *Western Journal of Communication, 69*, 203–217.

Lippa, R. (1998). The nonverbal display and judgment of extraversion, masculinity, femininity, and gender diagnosticity: A lens model analysis. *Journal of Research in Personality, 32*, 80–107.

Lippa, R., & Dietz, J. K. (2000). The relation of gender, personality, and intelligence to judges' accuracy in judging strangers' personality from brief video segments. *Journal of Nonverbal Behavior, 24*, 25–43.

Manusov, V., Floyd, K., & Kerssen-Griep, J. 1997. Yours, mine, and ours: Mutual attributions for nonverbal behaviors in couples' interactions. *Communication Research, 24*, 234–260.

Manusov, V., & Patterson, M. L. (Eds.) (2006). *The Sage handbook of nonverbal communication.* Thousand Oaks, CA: Sage.

Matsumoto, D., Yoo, S. H., Hirayama, S., & Petrova, G. (2005). Validation of an individual-level measure of display rules: The display rule assessment inventory (DRAI). *Emotion, 5*, 23–40.

Mehrabian, A. (1967). Orientation behaviors and nonverbal attitude in communicators. *Journal of Communication, 17*, 324–332.

Mehrabian, A., & Diamond, S. G. (1971). Seating arrangement and conversation. *Sociometry, 34*, 281–289.

Mehrabian, A., & Weiner, M. (1967). Decoding of inconsistent communications. *Journal of Personality and Social Psychology, 6*, 108–114.

Montepare, J. M., & Dobish, H. (2003). The contribution of emotion perceptions and their overgeneralizations to trait impressions. *Journal of Nonverbal Behavior, 27,* 237–254.

Motowidlo, S. J., Burnett, J. R., Maczynski, J., & Witkowski, S. (1996). Predicting managerial job performance from personality ratings based on a structured interview: An international replication. *Polish Psychological Bulletin, 27,* 139–151.

Mullins, D. T., & Duke, M. P. (2004). Effects of social anxiety on nonverbal accuracy and response time I: Facial expressions. *Journal of Nonverbal Behavior, 28,* 3–33.

Noller, P., Feeney, J. A., Roberts, N., & Christensen, A. (2005). Withdrawal in couple interactions: Exploring the causes and consequences. In R. E. Riggio & R. S. Feldman (Eds.), *Applications of nonverbal communication* (pp. 195–213). Mahwah, NJ: Erlbaum.

Nowak, K. L., & Biocca, F. (2003). The effect of the agency and anthropomorphism on users' sense of telepresence, co-presence, social presence in virtual environments. *Presence, 12,* 481–494.

Parker, J., & Burkley, M. (2009). Who's chasing whom? The impact of gender and relationship status on mate poaching. *Journal of Experimental Social Psychology, 45,* 1016–1019.

Patterson, M. L. (1973). Stability of nonverbal immediacy behaviors. *Journal of Experimental Social Psychology, 9,* 97–109.

Patterson, M. L. (1976). An arousal model of interpersonal intimacy. *Psychological Review, 83,* 235–245.

Patterson, M. L. (1982). A sequential functional model of nonverbal exchange. *Psychological Review, 89,* 231–249.

Patterson, M. L. (1991). A functional approach to nonverbal exchange. In R. S. Feldman, & B. Rime (Eds.), *Fundamentals of nonverbal behavior* (pp. 458–495). Cambridge, UK: Cambridge University Press.

Patterson, M. L. (1995). A parallel process model of nonverbal communication. *Journal of Nonverbal Behavior, 19,* 3–29.

Pintner, R. (1918). Intelligence estimated from photographs. *Psychological Review, 25,* 286–296.

Prager, K. J. (2000). Intimacy in personal relationships. In C. Hendrick & S. S. Hendrick (Eds.), *Close relationships: A sourcebook* (pp. 229–242). Thousand Oaks, CA: Sage.

Reichenbach, H. (1938). *Experience and prediction.* Chicago: University of Chicago Press.

Rice, R. E. (1990). Computer-mediated communication system network data: Theoretical concerns and empirical examples. *International Journal of Man-Machine Studies, 32,* 627–647.

Riggio, R. E. (2006). Nonverbal skills and abilities. In V. Manusov & M. L. Patterson (Eds.), *The Sage handbook of nonverbal communication* (pp. 79–95). Thousand Oaks, CA: Sage.

Rintel, E. S., & Pittam, J. (1997). Strangers in a strange land: Interaction management on Internet Relay Chat. *Human Communication Research, 23,* 507–534.

Rosenthal, R. (Ed.) (1979). *Skill in nonverbal communication: Individual differences.* Cambridge, MA: Oelgeschlager, Gunn & Hain.

Scherer, K. R. (1978). Personality inference from voice quality: The loud voice of extroversion. *European Journal of Social Psychology, 8,* 467–487.

Schwartz, B., Tesser, A., & Powell, E. (1982). Dominance cues in nonverbal behavior. *Social Psychology Quarterly, 45,* 114–120.

Shuter, R. (1976). Proxemics and tactility in Latin America. *Journal of Communication, 26,* 46–52.

Sommer, R. (1959). Studies in personal space. *Sociometry, 22,* 247–260.

Stern, W. (1935). *Allgemeine psychologie auf personalistischer grundlage.* The Hague: Nijhoff.

Strömwall, L. A., Hartwig, M., & Granhag, P. A. (2006). To act truthfully: Nonverbal behavior and strategies during a police interrogation. *Psychology, Crime, and Law, 12,* 207–219.

Tracy, J. L., & Robins, R. W. (2007). The prototypical pride expression: Development of a nonverbal behavior coding system. *Emotion, 7,* 789–801.

Trager, G. L. (1958). Paralanguage: A first approximation. *Studies in Linguistics, 13,* 1–12.

van Beek, Y., van Dolderen, M. S. M., & Dubas, J. J. S. D. (2006). Gender-specific development of nonverbal behaviors and mild depression in adolescence. *Journal of Child Psychology and Psychiatry, 47,* 1272–1283.

van Beek, Y., & Dubas, J. S. (2008). Age and gender differences in decoding basic and non-basic facial expressions in late childhood and early adolescence. *Journal of Nonverbal Behavior, 31,* 32–52.

Viteles, M. S., & Smith, K. R. (1932). The prediction of vocational aptitude and success from photographs. *Journal of Experimental Psychology, 15,* 615–629.

Vrij, A. (2006). Nonverbal communication and deception. In V. Manusov & M. L. Patterson (Eds.), *The Sage handbook of nonverbal communication* (pp. 341–359). Thousand Oaks, CA: Sage.

Vrij, A., Akehurst, L., & Morris, P. (1997). Individual differences in hand movements during deception. *Journal of Nonverbal Behavior, 21,* 87–102.

Walther, J. B. (2006). Nonverbal dynamics in computer-mediated communication. In V. Manusov & M. L. Patterson (Eds.), *The Sage handbook of nonverbal communication* (pp. 461–479). Thousand Oaks, CA: Sage.

Walther, J. B., & Tidwell, L. C. (1995). Nonverbal cues in computer-mediated communication, and the effect of chronemics on relational communication. *Journal of Organizational Computing, 5,* 355–378.

Watson, D. (1989). Strangers' ratings of the five robust personality factors: Evidence of a surprising convergence with self-report. *Journal of Personality and Social Psychology, 57,* 120–128.

Wiggins, J. S. (1973). *Personality and prediction: Principles of personality assessment.* Reading, MA: Addison-Wesley.

Wiggins, J. S. (1979). A psychological taxonomy of trait-descriptive terms: The interpersonal domain. *Journal of Personality and Social Psychology, 37,* 395–412.

Zuckerman, M., DePaulo, B. M., & Rosenthal, R. (1981). Verbal and nonverbal communication of deception. In L. Berkowitz (Ed.), *Advances in experimental social psychology* (Vol. 14, pp. 1–57). New York: Academic Press.

NOTES

1. In fact, even in these typing-only circumstances, senders often use emoticons (symbolic smiles, frowns, winks, etc.) to increase the odds that receivers correctly understand their meaning.

III PERSONALITY AND INTERPERSONAL INTERACTIONS

12 TRUST AS MOTIVATIONAL GATEKEEPER IN ADULT ROMANTIC RELATIONSHIPS

Sandra L. Murray

John G. Holmes

I know a maiden fair to see,

Take care!

She can both false and friendly be,

Beware! Beware!

Trust her not,

She is fooling thee.

—Henry Wadsworth Longfellow, "In Hyperion"

Better trust all, and be deceived,

And weep that trust and that deceiving,

Than doubt one heart, that if believed

Had blessed one's life with true believing.

—Frances Anne Kemble, "Faith"

The contradictory advice each of these sentiments offers captures the paradoxical nature of trust in romantic relationships. Trust is both cautious and audacious (Murray & Holmes, in press). To safeguard against

Acknowledgments: The preparation of this chapter was supported by a grant awarded to the first author from the National Institute of Mental Health (MH 060105).

the pain of rejection, trust in the partner's responsiveness needs to be extended with some trepidation. To experience the benefits of connection, trust also needs to be extended with great faith.

This chapter examines the duality inherent to the expression of trust in adult romantic relationships. We use two terms, "interpersonal vigilance" and "interpersonal abandon" to describe this duality. Interpersonal vigilance reflects a cautious reluctance to connect with a partner (i.e., an avoidance tendency), whereas interpersonal abandon reflects an unrestrained readiness to do so (i.e., an approach tendency). In the model we propose, trust regulates both interpersonal vigilance and abandon. Trust functions as this motivational gatekeeper by summarizing the status of five cues that signal one's special value to the partner (Murray & Holmes, 2009). When the status of these cues warrants being less trusting, it motivates interpersonal vigilance—a suspicious mind-set that imbues ambiguous partner behavior with negative intent and directs behavioral avoidance (e.g., reacting in anger, withholding emotional support). When the status of these cues warrants being more trusting, it motivates interpersonal abandon—a hopeful mind-set that imbues ambiguous partner behavior with positive intent and directs behavioral approach (e.g., soliciting support, acceding decision-making power).

We describe the role trust plays as motivational gatekeeper by describing how trust controls the specific interpersonal goals people pursue in conflict-of-interest situations (Murray & Holmes, 2009). Imagine that Gayle and Ron both want to work, but their house needs cleaning (customarily torpedoed by a toddler's antics). Gayle can reap gains through trade if she volunteers to sacrifice some work time to do the laundry, a chore Ron loathes, in exchange for Ron taking the time to clean the hardwood, a chore she loathes. In extending herself, Gayle stands to gain work time and a clean house, but she also exposes herself to risk at Ron's hands. Her outcomes suffer most if she launders and Ron succumbs to his temptation to skip the hardwood. Mixed-motive situations such as these put the state goal to connect in conflict with the state goal to self-protect against rejection (Murray, Holmes, & Collins, 2006). Trust functions to resolve the approach-avoidance goal conflict in these types of situations.

Our chapter contains three parts. In the first part, we describe the nature of trust. Trust is paradoxical. To some extent, trust is grounded in cues that provide evidence of one's value to the partner. But, to some extent, trust is also independent of such cues, requiring a leap of faith that goes beyond the evidence at hand. In the second part of the chapter, we build on this grounded-faith conceptualization of trust to describe how trust regulates behavior in conflict-of-interest situations. In the third part, we characterize the behavioral dynamics likely in relationships where being more trusting often motivates connectedness-seeking (i.e., interpersonal abandon) in mixed-motive situations and being less

trusting often motivates self-protection-seeking (i.e., interpersonal vigilance). We accomplish these objectives by drawing on a theoretical model of the social-cognitive structure of the interdependent mind (Murray & Holmes, 2009). The mind we posit motivates responsive behavior in conflict-of-interest situations through a system of interconnected procedural or "if-then" rules that regulate when trust primarily motivates vigilance (i.e., self-protection and avoidance) and when trust primarily motives abandon (i.e., connection and approach).

GROUNDED FAITH: THE NATURE OF TRUST

Trust is an interpersonal expectation. It captures the anticipated strength of the partner's willingness to meet one's needs (Holmes, 2002; Holmes & Rempel, 1989). Because people cannot have direct access to the contents of another person's motives or consciousness, trust is a supposition. Based on the available evidence, Ron assumes that Gayle is more (or less) motivated to meet his needs. He grounds this inference in five evidential cues that signal how readily he could be replaced (Murray & Holmes, 2008; Murray & Holmes, 2009; Murray, Leder, et al., 2009).

Being hard to replace grounds trust because having special or unique value to one's partner helps solve the adaptive problem that being in an objective state of need creates. When something is wrong—when people are sick, or distressed, or fearful—they need the aid afforded by close interpersonal ties. However, when something is wrong, people are least able to reciprocate any help they receive. Tooby and Cosmides (1996) describe this adaptive problem as a "bankers' paradox." People most need loans of interpersonal sacrifice and good will when they are bad credit risks. This paradox led Tooby and Cosmides (1996) to a specific insight. For people to survive long enough to reproduce, there needs to be a mechanism in place for discriminating good and sacrificing friends from fair-weather ones. These theorists contend that specific cognitive mechanisms evolved to track which specific others perceive one's qualities as special because they could not imagine finding those qualities in others. Securing a niche among friends—possessing some quality that makes one special, and thus, valuable to one's social ties—ensures the responsiveness of these friends when it is costly. Why? Because filling a niche guarantees that others have some *reason* to be loyal. Being special to at least one person provides liability insurance that someone will meet one's needs in times of crisis. Such loyalty minimizes the chance of rejections that could threaten the transmission of one's genes (Bowlby, 1969; Gilbert, 2005; Reis, Clark, & Holmes, 2004; Tooby & Cosmides, 1996).

Grounding Trust: Five Evidential Cues

The evidential cues that ground trust correspond to five "if-then" inference rules. These rules link specific "if" inputs to the contingent "then" response to trust or distrust. We describe each of these five rules in turn. Each rule links the perceiver's assessment of a specific piece of evidence (i.e., "if") to the tendency to trust the partner more or less. (In the specification of each rule, "I" refers to the perceiver and "P" refers to the partner.)

If P sacrifices for me, then I trust P. In assessing how readily they could be replaced, people can look to their partner's behavior. Directly observing the partner's willingness to forgo personal interests on one's own behalf signals one's special value to the partner and heightens trust (Holmes, 1981; Kelley, 1979; Simpson, 2007; Turan & Horowitz, 2007). People in both dating and marital relationships report greater trust in their partner's caring when they witness signs of their partner's commitment, such as self-sacrificing responsiveness to their needs or willingness to excuse their

transgressions (Wieselquist, Rusbult, Foster, & Agnew, 1999).

If P values my traits, then I trust P. Trust is a prediction about the future as much as it is a commentary on past behavior (Holmes & Rempel, 1989). Because the future may not mirror the past, people also rely on indirect cues to gauge the likelihood of their continued value to their partner. The qualities Gayle believes Ron perceives in her provide one such barometer (Leary & Baumeister, 2000). In gauging their partner's regard for their traits, people behave like naïve realists and assume that their partner sees the same qualities in them that they see in themselves (Kenny, 1994; Murray, Holmes, & Griffin, 2000; Murray, Holmes, Griffin, Bellavia, & Rose, 2001). When such self-assessments are positive, as they typically are for people high in self-esteem or secure in attachment style, they strengthen confidence in one's value as special and heighten trust (Murray, et al., 2000; Murray et al., 2001). When self-assessments are relatively negative, they undermine trust.

If I am equal in worth to P, then I trust P. People also compare their own worth to their partner's perceived worth to judge their special value to the partner. Such comparisons cue valuing because fair-trade principles constrain one's own romantic options (Berscheid & Walster, 1969; Feingold, 1988; Rubin, 1973; E. Walster, Walster, & Berscheid, 1978). Social exchange theorists argue that people implicitly understand fair-trade principles and limit romantic aspirations to those who have an equivalent "social net worth" (Berscheid, Dion, E. Walster, & Walster, 1971; Montoya, 2008; Murstein, 1970). For instance, people who perceive themselves less positively on interpersonal traits, such as warm, intelligent, and attractive, expect less from their ideal partner (Campbell, Simpson, Kashy, & Fletcher, 2001; Murray, Holmes, & Griffin, 1996a; Murray, Holmes, & Griffin, 1996b). On dating Web sites, people also maximize the odds of success by pursuing equal matches (Lee, Loewenstein,

Ariely, Hong, & Young, 2008). Such pragmatism is prudent. The real world pressure toward matching is so powerful that dating partners who are unfairly matched on physical attractiveness are more likely to break up (White, 1980). Because fairness norms constrain one's options, believing one's own worth falls short of the partner's worth threatens one's value as special and undermines trust (Derrick & Murray 2007; Murray et al., 2005).

If I am better than P's alternatives, then I trust. People also compare their own desirability to the desirability of the potential suitors whom *their partner* might reasonably hope to attract (Murray, Leder, et al., 2009). Such comparisons further cue valuing because fair trade norms also constrain the partner's romantic options (Thibaut & Kelley, 1959). Partners' commitments are constrained by their alternatives to the current relationship (Thibaut & Kelley, 1959; Rusbult & Van Lange, 2003). Their affections can waiver when the life that might be had with a possible alternative partner looks better than the life with the current partner (Rusbult, 1983). Because one's partner can be tempted by the interest of available and attractive alternatives (Rusbult, Martz, & Agnew, 1998; White, 1980), gauging the partner's responsiveness also involves tracking how one stacks up against the partner's best options. With this cue, believing that one's own worth or contribution exceeds the partner's most viable alternatives signals trust because one's superiority to the partner's alternatives makes one harder to replace (Murray, Leder, et al., 2009).

If P faces barriers, then I trust P. People can also look to the barriers constraining their partner's commitment to gauge their partner's trustworthiness (Frey, McNulty, & Karney, 2008; Levinger, 1976; Rusbult & Van Lange, 2003). The salience of such barriers, such as familial or religious prohibitions (Levinger, 1976) make Gayle feel harder to replace and, therefore, heighten her trust in Ron.

GOING BEYOND THE EVIDENCE: THE ESSENCE OF FAITH

The cues that signal one's special value to the partner are grounded in the present. In assessing how he measures up, Ron might compare his muscular physique to Gayle's shapely figure. He might also note how favorably he compares to the single men she encounters at the grocery store or church. Although the evidential cues ground trust, they are not sufficient for its experience. Trust is a prediction about a future state of affairs that cannot be fully justified by current circumstances, because the future will never be a mirror of the past (Holmes & Rempel, 1989). Even if a 30-year-old Ron measures up to Gayle's value, he has no guarantee that his 40-year-old self will stack up nearly as well. The intervening decade invites uncertainty. His six-pack abs might slip into a middle-aged paunch while Gayle steps up her outings to the gym. He might lose his job, while she advances her education. Gayle might start to resent the sacrifices she once made happily on Ron's behalf. Because Ron cannot know what the future holds, trusting in Gayle requires going beyond the available evidence. It requires a leap of faith.

To trust in Gayle, Ron must set aside his uncertainties and conclude that his relationship future will be a mirror of its past (Rempel, Holmes, & Zanna, 1985). Making such a leap of faith involves suspending the "if-then" evidence rules at least on occasion. Even in the best of relationships, reasons to doubt one's value to the partner are abundant because partner interests can diverge at multiple levels of interdependence (Kelley, 1979). No matter how much Gayle values Ron, there will be times when she behaves selfishly, there will be times when she outperforms him, and there will be times when her eyes seem to linger on an attractive alternative. In adding an element of faith to his trust in Gayle, Ron essentially ignores such perturbations. In fact, people who are more trusting even perceive greater reason to trust their partner in evidence that points to the opposite conclusion (Holmes & Rempel, 1989; Murray, Holmes, MacDonald, & Ellsworth, 1998; Murray, Bellavia, Rose, & Griffin, 2003; Simpson, Rholes, & Phillips, 1996). A daily diary study involving married couples provides an apt example of this dynamic (Murray, Bellavia, Rose, & Griffin, 2003). In this study, both partners completed measures of the partner's rejecting behaviors and perceptions of the partner's acceptance each day for three weeks. For people who trusted in their partner's responsiveness, perceiving more partner transgressions on a given day actually increased their daily confidence in their partner's acceptance the next day. Cross-lagged analyses revealed that people who generally trusted in their partner's responsiveness actually felt more loved and accepted by their partner on days after they thought their partner had behaved particularly badly. People who generally questioned their partner's responsiveness evidenced no such compensatory effect.

In this sense, solidifying trust is akin to suspending disbelief (Brickman, 1987). The imperative to suspend the "if-then" rules and sometimes discount the evidence means that extending trust requires the dispositional capacity for faith in others. Attachment theorists argue that people develop the basic capacity for faith in the most basic of relationships, that between a parent and a child (Mikulincer & Shaver, 2003). Experiences with a consistently available and responsive caregiver in infancy provide a basic sense of felt security—optimism about the nature of one's relationship to others. This state communicates that one is worthy of the love that others are willing to provide. However, experiences with inconsistently available or nonresponsive caregivers make this state of felt security elusive. Such experiences leave people doubtful of their own value and hesitant to trust in the responsiveness of others. The capacity for faith that felt security provides then shapes subsequent experiences with new relationship partners (Collins & Read, 1994). For instance, people who are higher in global self-esteem

and more secure in attachment style report greater trust in their partner's love and commitment in both dating and marital relationships. In contrast, people troubled by self-doubt have difficulty trusting even loving and committed partners (Collins & Read, 1994; Murray et al., 2001).

MOTIVATIONAL GATEKEEPING: HOW TRUST REGULATES RESPONSIVENESS IN SPECIFIC SITUATIONS

A grounded faith conceptualization of trust offers unique insights for understanding how responsive (and nonresponsive) behavior results in specific conflict-of-interest situations. Figure 12.1 presents a simplified version of our model of how the "if-then" structure of the mind motivates partner responsiveness in specific situations (Murray & Holmes, 2009).[1]

The dynamics begin with the social coordination dilemmas that diagnose and test trust. Partners are interdependent in multiple ways (Kelley, 1979). Ron and Gayle not only negotiate responsibilities for laundry versus hardwood (i.e., life task dilemmas), but they must also blend Ron's extraversion with Gayle's introversion (i.e., personality dilemmas), and reconcile Gayle's desire to spend their free time together with Ron's desire for greater autonomy (i.e., relationship goal dilemmas). For interaction in such a marriage to be smooth and rewarding, each partner needs to accommodate his or her own goals in order to be responsive to the needs of the other partner (Reis et al., 2004).

In a utopian relationship in which Ron and Gayle shared entirely convergent interests, responsiveness would be easy to enact, requiring only that each partner behave in his or her own self-interest. In the imperfect reality of most relationships, partner interests inevitably conflict (Holmes, 2002; Kelley, 1979). The capacity to perspective-take also allows people to anticipate how divergent personal interests can tempt the partner *not* to be responsive (Enfield & Levinson,

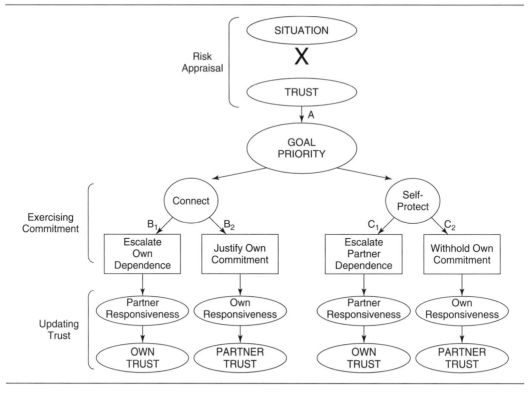

FIGURE 12.1   The Social Cognitive Structure of Interdependent Minds
Source: From "The Architecture of Interdependent Minds: A Motivation-Management Theory of Mutual Responsiveness," by S. L. Murray and J. G. Holmes, 2009, *Psychological Review, 116,* 908–928. Adapted by permission.

2006; Thibaut & Kelley, 1959). The resulting perception of risk creates a major structural barrier to responsiveness (Murray, Holmes, and Collins, 2006). Gayle's selfish temptation to pursue her own goals makes it prudent for Ron to self-protect against her possible exploitation by limiting his willingness to put his outcomes in her hands in conflict-of-interest situations. To transcend such self-interested concerns and promote rewarding interactions, the interdependent mind needs to motivate Ron's commitment to being responsive when Gayle relies on him to meet her needs.

Coordinating the particular behavioral goals each partner adopts in *specific* conflict-of-interest situations within the relationship begins and ends with trust. Chronic trust in the partner's responsiveness occupies a directive role because trust is the psychological precondition for how people express

commitment in specific situations (Murray et al., 2006; Wieselquist et al., 1999). Why would this be the case? Relationships are unstable, and inherently less safe, when one partner is more committed than the other partner (Waller, 1938; Sprecher, Schmeeckle, & Felmless, 2006). People minimize the potential for such disruptive power imbalances to develop by making their own commitment very much contingent on trust in the partner's reciprocated commitment (Murray et al., 2000; Murray et al., 2006). By regulating vigilance and avoidance, the evidential grounding of trust ensures that people risk being dependent on their partner only when it seems sufficiently safe to do so.

The Situational Dynamics

Conflict-of-interest situations offer both the potential for gain *and* the potential for loss in putting one's outcomes in the partner's hands. Consequently, such situations pose an acute approach-avoidance goal conflict. Imagine that Gayle has had a taxing day at work and she wants to ask Ron to take her turn preparing dinner. In such a situation, Gayle stands to benefit from Ron's sacrifice by getting needed time to relax. She also stands to gain the benefits that come from feeling loved. Those benefits motivate her to connect, put her outcomes in Ron's hands, and ask for help. But Gayle also stands to lose both relaxation and confidence in Ron's caring if he refuses to take her turn. The costs that might be incurred motivate her to self-protect, keep her outcomes in her own hands, and cook dinner herself. Indecision is no recipe for action (Cacioppo, Gardner, & Berntson, 1999). Gayle's trust and Ron's commitment step in to resolve this situational goal conflict.

Risk appraisal. Trust arbitrates interpersonal goal pursuit in conflict-of-interest situations by controlling the subjective perception of risk. Namely, trust interacts with objective features of the situation to reveal the partner's likely motivation to be responsive (Holmes & Rempel, 1989; Murray et al., 2006). The subjective appraisal of risk that results captures the likelihood of the partner being accepting or rejecting of one's needs in that particular situation. The person by situation analysis assumes that chronic trust in a partner's responsiveness plays a larger role in shaping the risks perceived in ambiguous than clear-cut situations (Mischel & Shoda, 1995). How does trust have such an effect?

In most situations, trust in a partner's responsiveness renders the prospect of a specific rejection by the partner less hurtful and less likely to foretell future costs (Murray, Griffin, Rose, & Bellavia, 2003). For these reasons, people who are more chronically trusting of their partner can afford to see more opportunity for gain than loss in conflict-of-interest situations. By contrast, people who are less trusting are likely to see more opportunity for loss than gain (Murray et al., 2006). Considerable research

(utilizing convergent conceptualizations of trust) supports the assumption that trust and situation features interact to signal risk in conflict-of-interest situations.

Trust generally only signals risk given the trigger of a mixed motive situation where such gains and losses are relatively ambiguous. For instance, in a daily diary study, married intimates who felt less positively regarded by their partner felt all the more rejected on days after their partner criticized or disappointed them (Murray, Bellavia, et al., 2003). Less trusting intimates also interpret their spouse's behavior more negatively during a conflict discussion than more trusting intimates (Rempel, Ross, & Holmes, 2001). Less trusting intimates also react to reminders of a past misdeed by interpreting their spouse's current behavior more negatively (Holmes & Rempel, 1989). However, married intimates who are more trusting reaffirm their partner's general acceptance in the face of limited criticisms (Murray, Bellavia, et al., 2003) and potentially contentious comments (Holmes & Rempel, 1989; Rempel et al., 2001).

People who are more or less trusting of their partner by virtue of being more or less dispositionally trusting exhibit similarly discrepant appraisals of the risks inherent in specific conflicts-of-interest. People who chronically anticipate interpersonal rejection are so sensitive to violations of trust that they attribute negative intent to a new partner's hypothetical behaviors (Downey & Feldman, 1996). People high in attachment-related anxiety similarly perceive their partner as more rejecting when discussing a more important conflict than a less important conflict (Simpson, Rholes, & Phillips, 1996). People who are high on attachment-related anxiety about acceptance also interpret a partner's hypothetical misdeeds (Collins, 1996), actual misdeeds (Mikulincer, 1998), and daily conflicts as a sign of their waning commitment (Campbell, Simpson, Boldry, & Kashy, 2005).

State behavioral goals: To connect or self-protect? As these examples illustrate, trust controls the level of risk people perceive in specific conflict-of-interest situations. By controlling situational appraisals, trust then regulates whether the state goal to connect or the state goal to self-protect takes behavioral priority in given situations (Path A in Figure 12.1). In particular, anticipating the partner's acceptance strengthens the goal to connect in that situation. Anticipating rejection instead strengthens the goal to self-protect against exploitation in that situation. The goal to connect or self-protect that results from risk appraisal then elicits specific behavioral strategies in memory for fulfilling each of these goals. The "if-then" *implementation* rules central to Figure 12.1 satisfy connectedness (Paths B_1 and B_2) and self-protection goals (Paths C_1 and C_2), respectively. These rules extract as much responsiveness as situations allow by regulating each partner's expression of commitment. The implementation rules regulate both dependence on the partner for need fulfillment and the value people attach to the relationship itself—the psychological substrates of commitment (Drigotas & Rusbult, 1992; Rusbult et al., 1998). Table 12.1 lists the implementation rules. We discuss each rule in turn.

The "if-then" rules for implementing the goal to connect express trust with reasonable abandon. First, the "escalate own dependence" rule links Gayle's anticipation of Ron's acceptance to her propensity to behave in ways that increase Ron's opportunity to be responsive to her request. Anticipating gains motivates Gayle to increase her commitment to Ron by putting her personal outcomes more squarely in his hands (Murray, Bellavia, et al., 2003). Such expectations might motivate her to disclose something embarrassing, seek Ron's

support in coping with a personal crisis, solicit an onerous favor, reciprocate Ron's disclosure, or let Ron make financial decisions for her. In escalating her dependence, Gayle provides Ron with more behavioral opportunities to prove his responsiveness. Nonetheless, heightened dependence can have unfortunate and unintended costs. In drawing closer to Ron, Gayle exposes herself to more situations where Ron can interfere with her goals. The frustrations that result could undermine Gayle's motivation to be responsive to Ron (Grote & Clark, 2001). The "justify commitment" rule keeps Gayle's commitment to being responsive from being sidetracked. This rule motivates Gayle to justify costs incurred by actually valuing Ron more when his plans for the evening interfere with her hopes for a night out with friends (Murray, Holmes, Aloni, Pinkus, Derrick, & Leder, 2009).

The "if-then" rules for implementing the goal to self-protect express trust with vigilance. The "escalate partner dependence" implementation rule links Gayle's anticipation of Ron's rejection to behavioral propensities that increase Ron's motivation to be responsive to her. Anticipating nonresponsiveness motivates Gayle to escalate the instrumental benefits Ron gains from the relationship and limits his freedom to find such benefits elsewhere. Such expectations might motivate her to make his appointments, cook his favorite meal, or limit his time with friends. In escalating Ron's dependence, Gayle limits his incentive to be selfish because he cannot afford to lose her (Murray, Aloni, Holmes, Derrick, Stinson, & Leder, 2009). Such a response serves self-protection goals. Gayle brings Ron closer, and protects against his rejection, without taking the risk of making herself more vulnerable to him. Nevertheless, dependent partners can sometimes still behave negatively. The "withhold own dependence" implementation rule further minimizes the potential for rejection. It links Gayle's anticipation of Ron's rejection to the propensity to behave in ways that minimize Ron's opportunity to

TABLE 12.1   The If-Then Implementation Rules

Rule
If connect goal, then escalate own dependence
If connect goal, then justify own commitment
If self-protect goal, then escalate partner dependence
If self-protect goal, then withhold own dependence

be hurtful and nonresponsive. Anticipating rejection motivates Gayle to withdraw her commitment by lessening her practical and psychological dependence on Ron (Murray, Bellavia, et al., 2003). Such expectations might motivate her to divulge only superficial details of her day or spend more time with her family. In so doing, she makes it more difficult for Ron to be nonresponsive because she asks little of him.

The "if-then" implementation rules govern what Gayle is willing to do for Ron, what Gayle needs Ron to do for her, what Ron is willing to do for Gayle, and what Ron needs Gayle to do for him. The implementation rules thus govern behavioral expressions of mutual responsiveness. For instance, in mixed-motive situations that offer reasonable potential for gain, the "escalate own dependence" rule might motivate Ron to disclose a personal worry to Gayle—a behavior that gives her the opportunity to be responsive. In turn, the "justify commitment rule" motivates Gayle to listen to Ron's disclosure even though she would rather work. In conflict-of-interest situations that offer reasonable potential for loss, the "withhold own dependence" rule might motivate Gayle to keep her own feelings to herself in the face of Ron's impatience. The "promote partner dependence" rule might in turn motivate Ron to fix Gayle's computer in the hope of eliciting her forgiveness. Such behavioral expressions of (non)responsiveness then inform and update feelings of trust.

Efficiency and Flexibility

The "if-then" rules govern the interpersonal mind in a way that is both *efficient* and *flexible*. Ongoing and complex problems have automatic and effortless solutions (Bargh, 2007; Dijksterhuis, Chartrand, & Aarts, 2007; Dijksterhuis & Nordgren, 2006). The "efficiency" criterion stipulates that the "if-then" rules are *implicit* procedural features of relationship representations (Baldwin, 1992; Holmes & Murray, 2007). By implicit, we mean that these rules

can operate without conscious mediation (Bargh, 2007: Dijksterhuis et al., 2007). Situations that prime the "if" automatically elicit the propensity to engage in the "then" without any conscious intent on Ron's part (Murray, Derrick, Leder, & Holmes, 2008; Murray, Aloni, et al., 2009; Murray, Holmes, et al., 2009).

By *flexible*, we mean that the power of these rules to compel overt behavior shifts with motivation and opportunity to correct or override the rules (Olson & Fazio, 2008). Flexibility implies that an automatic urge to think, feel, or behave in a particular way is less likely to translate into correspondent action if people are motivated *and* able to correct it (Murray, Aloni, et al., 2009; Murray, Derrick, et al., 2008; Murray, Holmes, et al., 2009). Consistent with this logic, models of attitudes, impression formation, and stereotyping assume that such automatic propensities control behavior unless people have the motivation, opportunity, and capacity to override them (Fazio & Towles-Schwen, 1999; Fiske & Neuberg, 1990; Gilbert & Malone, 1995; Kunda & Spencer, 2003; Olson & Fazio, 2008; Wilson, Lindsey, & Schooler, 2000). Indeed, the behavioral effects of automatically activated goals can be overridden by situational cues that suggest goal pursuit might be hazardous or costly (Aarts, Custers, & Holland, 2007; Macrae & Johnston, 1998; Kunda & Spencer, 2003; Macrae & Johnston, 1998).

CAUTIOUS OR AUDACIOUS? TRUST CAPTURES VARIABILITY IN AFFECT, COGNITION, AND BEHAVIOR

Because trust is the precondition for commitment (Murray et al., 2006), being unable to set aside issues of trust sets the stage for a qualitatively different experience of commitment (Murray & Holmes, 2009). Trust has its behavioral effects through the social cognitive structure of the mind. First, trust controls the subjective appraisal of risk and, thus, the interpersonal goals and "if-then" behavioral strategies for goal implementation most likely to be activated automatically in specific mixed-motive situations in the relationship. Second, trust controls which of the specific implementation rules are likely to be enacted in overt behavior.

An influential model of the attitude-behavior relation suggests that such automatically activated propensities control behavior unless people have the motivation *and* opportunity to override them (Olsen & Fazio, 2008). Applied to our analysis, this logic suggests that trust determines how often the automatic propensity to think or behave in a particular way translates into *correspondent* action in specific situations. It does so because trust provides the motivation to correct impulses compelled by "if-then" implementation rules that run counter to a person's more chronic goal orientation toward the relationship (Murray, Aloni, et al., 2009; Murray, Holmes, et al., 2009). Sufficient executive or conscious control over behavior supplies the opportunity to correct (Gilbert & Malone, 1995; Muraven & Baumeister, 2000).

High levels of trust in the partner's responsiveness foster the *chronic* pursuit of connection in relationships (Mikulincer & Shaver, 2003; Murray et al., 2006). People who are more trusting can more readily afford to set aside self-protection goals in mixed-motive situations because the partner's nonresponsiveness is not that likely or that hurtful (Murray, Griffin, et al., 2003). Low levels of trust in the partner's responsiveness instead foster the *chronic* pursuit of self-protection in relationships. People who are less trusting can less readily afford to pursue connectedness goals in mixed-motive situations because the partner's nonresponsiveness is more likely and more hurtful (Holmes & Rempel, 1989; Murray et al., 2006). Because trust shapes chronic goal pursuit, it provides the motivation to correct the behavioral impulse to pursue contradictory state *goals*. For instance, being less trusting might motivate Ron to curb his automatic impulse to value Gayle more when she interferes

with his capacity to watch his favorite television show in peace and quiet. We detail such dynamics next.

Cautious Trust

Being less trusting has three systematic effects on relationships. First, being vigilant for evidential cues to trust increases the tendency to perceive rejection in ongoing events (Downey & Feldman, 1996; Gable, 2005; Holmes & Rempel, 1989; Murray, Bellavia, et al., 2003). Imagine that Gayle thinks the gains that Ron would get from taking her turn cooking dinner are pretty much equal to the gains he would get from *not* helping. Being less trusting gives Gayle reason to expect Ron to be rejecting (i.e., not cooking) and reason to fear being hurt (Murray, Griffin, et al., 2003). Being less trusting, Gayle might notice incidental cues, such as Ron's bad mood, that forecast rejection and ignore those cues, such as Ron's affectionate glance, that forecast acceptance (Murray, Bellavia, et al., 2003). Consistent with this logic, Downey and Feldman (1996) argue that chronic differences in the tendency to expect and perceive rejection reflect the operation of the defensive motivational system. This system serves the goal of avoiding threatening situations by decreasing the threshold for identifying threats (Lang, Bradley, & Cuthbert, 1990; MacLeod, Mathews, & Tata, 1986; Mineka, & Sutton, 1992).

Second, quicker to perceive rejection, Gayle is then better equipped to avoid it. For people who are less trusting, the goal to self-protect is activated more often in mixed-motive situations because the partner is more likely to be perceived as rejecting. Models of attitudes, habit, and stereotyping assume that frequent associations between signals and responses compel stronger behavioral leanings (Fazio, 1986; Wood & Neal, 2007). More often anticipating Ron's rejection strengthens the accessibility of the "escalate partner dependence" and the "withhold dependence" rules for implementing self-protection goals in Gayle's memory. As a result, she frequently does things to escalate Ron's dependence on her (e.g., shop for his clothes) and limit her dependence on him (e.g., going to her friends for support; Murray, Aloni, et al., 2009).

Third, being less trusting provides the motivation to override the automatic impulse to escalate dependence and value the partner on the (relatively rarer) occasion when the state goal to connect is activated. Imagine Gayle comes home to find Ron in a good mood and already happily ensconced in the kitchen. Such a scenario might automatically elicit her desire to ask him to cook. Asking Ron to take her turn cooking dinner (i.e., escalating dependence) might solicit his help, but it might also solicit his rejection. Acting on the impulse to escalate dependence has compromised utility if Gayle is less trusting because chronic self-protection goals compete with the situated impulse to connect (Murray, Griffin, et al., 2003). Therefore, being less trusting motivates people to overturn the impulse to escalate dependence and closeness when they have the opportunity to do so. When the goal to connect is activated automatically, people who are less trusting (i.e., low in self-esteem) actually report feeling less close to their partner on self-report measures that provide the opportunity to correct (Murray, Derrick et al., 2008). Similarly, valuing a costly partner more (i.e., justify commitment) has the potential cost of making rejection more painful (because losing a valued partner hurts more). A less trusting Gayle is motivated to correct this impulse when she can. For instance, people primed with the ways in which their romantic partner thwarts their goals are actually quicker to associate their partner with positive traits. But low self-esteem people correct this automated impulse and evaluate their partner more negatively on self-report measures that provide the opportunity to correct (Murray, Holmes, et al., 2009). In sum, for people who are less trusting, the easy activation of the self-protect-goal rules and the curbing of the connect-goal

rules elicit a *cautious* interaction pattern. Namely, it elicits responsiveness that puts firm boundaries on the amount of risk encountered, such as the tit-for-tat exchange of practical benefits or rigid roles, such as caretaker/provider (Murray & Holmes, in press).

Audacious Trust

Being more trusting has three parallel, but opposite, effects on relationships. First, faith in the partner's responsiveness increases the tendency to perceive signs of the partner's acceptance in ongoing events. In fact, people who are more trusting actually interpret their partner's negative behaviors as signs of caring (Holmes & Rempel, 1989; Murray, Bellavia, et al., 2003). Second, the goal to connect is activated more frequently in mixed-motive situations because the partner is more likely to be perceived as accepting. More often anticipating Gayle's acceptance then strengthens the accessibility of the "escalate dependence" and "justify commitment" rules for implementing the goal to connect in Ron's memory. As a result, Ron frequently does things to escalate his own dependence on Gayle (e.g., asking for her support) and justify any costs he incurs as a result of this stronger connection (e.g., deciding Gayle's need for his attention is endearing, Murray, Holmes, et al., 2009).

Third, being more trusting provides the motivation to override the automatic impulse to promote the partner's dependence and limit one's own dependence on the (relatively rarer) occasion when the state goal to self-protect is activated. Actual rejections, such as a partner breaking a major promise, automatically elicit suspicion and anger and provoke retaliation goals (i.e., "withhold dependence"; Murray, Bellavia, et al., 2003). Such an automatic response has compromised utility for a more trusting Ron because restricting dependence forfeits gains of connection he desires and has every reason to anticipate (Murray, Bellavia, et al., 2003). Being more trusting results in people curbing the automatic impulse to retaliate or withhold one's dependence when they have the opportunity to do so (Cavallo, Fitzsimons, & Holmes, 2009; Murray, Derrick, et al., 2008). Warning signs of a partner's rejection, such as feeling inferior to the partner, automatically elicit behavioral efforts to increase the partner's dependence (Murray, Aloni et al., 2009). Such automatic efforts have compromised utility for people who are more trusting because seeing one's partner as trapped or dependent threatens faith (Seligman, Fazio, & Zanna, 1980). Therefore, being more trusting results in people curbing the automated will to curry the partner's dependence when they have the opportunity to do so. In sum, for people who are more trusting, the repeated activation of the connect-goal rules and the frequent curbing of the self-protect goal rules elicit an *audacious* interaction pattern. Namely, it elicits responsiveness that does not restrict opportunities for closeness on the basis of risk, such as the communal giving of benefits, the provision of major sacrifices, and the solicitation and provision of identity support.

SUMMARY AND CONCLUSIONS

Trust is necessarily cautious and audacious. To protect against rejection, people attend to the "if-then" evidential cues that signal their value to the partner (see Table 12.1). To connect to the partner, people also need to go beyond these cues and make a leap of faith. Because trust is a precondition for commitment (Murray et al., 2006), being vigilant to rejection and preoccupied with self-protection creates a qualitatively different experience of the relationship. This vulnerability is most evident in the conflict-of-interest situations that are the proving ground for trust. When trust is relatively low, and tethered to the evidential cues, people are quick to perceive signs of the partner's impending rejection. Being sensitized to rejection then results in people more often pursuing the state goal to self-protect in mixed-motive situations. They

focus on promoting their partner's dependence and limiting their own dependence. When trust is relatively high, and reasonably divorced from the evidential cues, people are quick to perceive signs of their partner's acceptance. Being desensitized to rejection then results in people more often pursuing the state goal to connect in mixed-motive situations. They focus instead on escalating their own dependence and justifying the costs incurred through greater closeness. A grounded-faith conceptualization of trust thus offers unique insights for understanding why dispositional factors (e.g., self-esteem, attachment style) matter in relationships and how behavioral differences emerge between relationships.

References

Aarts, H., Custers, R., & Holland, R. W. (2007). The nonconscious cessation of goal pursuit: When goals and negative affect are coactivated. *Journal of Personality and Social Psychology, 92*, 165–178.

Baldwin, M. W. (1992). Relational schemas and the processing of social information. *Psychological Bulletin, 112*, 461–484.

Bargh, J. A. (2007). *Social psychology and the unconscious: The automaticity of higher mental processes*. New York: Psychology Press.

Berscheid, E., Dion, K., Walster, E., & Walster, G. W. (1971). Physical attractiveness and dating choice: A test of the matching hypothesis. *Journal of Experimental Social Psychology, 7*, 173–189.

Berscheid, E., & Walster, E. H. (1969). *Interpersonal attraction*. Reading, MA: Addison-Wesley.

Bowlby, J. (1969). *Attachment and loss: Vol. 1. Attachment*. London: Hogarth Press.

Brickman, P. (1987). *Commitment, conflict, and caring*. Englewood Cliffs, NJ: Prentice-Hall.

Cacioppo, J. T., Gardner, W. L., & Berntson, G. G. (1999). The affect system has parallel and integrative processing components: Form follows function. *Journal of Personality and Social Psychology, 76*, 839–855.

Campbell, L., Simpson, J. A., Boldry, J., & Kashy, D. A. (2005). Perceptions of conflict and support in romantic relationships: The role of attachment anxiety. *Journal of Personality and Social Psychology, 88*, 510–531.

Campbell, L., Simpson, J. A., Kashy, D. A., & Fletcher, G. J. O. (2001). Ideal standards, the self, and flexibility of ideals in close relationships. *Personality and Social Psychology Bulletin*, 27, 447–462.

Cavallo, J., Fitzsimons, G. M., & Holmes, J. G. (in press). When self-protection overreaches: Relationship-specific threat activates domain-general avoidance motivation. *Journal of Experimental Social Psychology*.

Collins, N. L. (1996). Working models of attachment: Implications for explanation, emotion and behavior. *Journal of Personality and Social Psychology*, 71, 810–832.

Collins, N. L., & Read, S. J. (1994). Cognitive representations of attachment: The structure and function of working models. In K. Bartholomew & D. Perlman (Eds.), *Attachment processes in adulthood: Vol. 5. Advances in personal relationships* (pp. 53–90). Philadelphia: Jessica Kingsley.

Derrick, J. L., & Murray, S. L. (2007). Enhancing relationship perceptions by reducing felt inferiority: The role of attachment style. *Personal Relationships*, 14, 531–549.

Dijksterhuis, A., Chartrand, T. L., & Aarts, H. (2007). Effects of priming and perception on social behavior and goal pursuit. In J. A. Bargh (Ed.), *Social psychology and the unconscious: The automaticity of higher mental processes* (pp. 51–132). New York: Psychology Press.

Dijksterhuis, A., & Nordgren, L. F. (2006). A theory of unconscious thought. *Perspectives on Psychological Science*, 1, 95–109.

Downey, G., & Feldman, S. I. (1996). Implications of rejection sensitivity for intimate relationships. *Journal of Personality and Social Psychology*, 70, 1327–1343.

Drigotas, S. M., & Rusbult, C. E. (1992). Should I stay or should I go? A dependence model of breakups. *Journal of Personality and Social Psychology*, 62, 62–87.

Enfield, N. J., & Levinson, S. C. (2006). *Roots of human sociality: Culture, cognition, and interaction.* New York: Berg.

Fazio, R. H. (1986). How do attitudes guide behavior? In R. M. Sorrentino & E. T. Higgins (Eds.), *The handbook of motivation and cognition: Foundations of social behavior* (pp. 204–243). New York: Guilford Press.

Fazio, R. H., & Towles-Schwen, T. (1999). The MODE model of attitude-behavior processes.

In S. Chaiken & Y. Trope (Eds.), *Dual process models in social psychology* (pp. 97–116). New York: Guilford Press.

Feingold, A. (1988). Matching for attractiveness in romantic partners and same-sex friends: A meta-analysis and theoretical critique. *Psychological Bulletin*, 104, 226–235.

Fiske, S. T., & Neuberg, S. L. (1990). A continuum of impression formation, from category-based to individuating processes: Influences of information and motivation on attention and interpretation. In M. P. Zanna (Ed.), *Advances in experimental social psychology* (Vol. 23, pp. 1–74). New York: Academic Press.

Frey, N. E., McNulty, J. K., & Karney, B. R. (2008). How do constraints on leaving a marriage affect behavior within the marriage? *Journal of Family Psychology*, 22, 153–161.

Gable, S. L. (2005). Approach and avoidance social motives and goals. *Journal of Personality*, 74, 175–222.

Gilbert, P. (2005). Social mentalities: A biopsychosocial and evolutionary approach to social relationships. In M. Baldwin (Ed.), *Interpersonal cognition* (pp. 299–333). New York: Guilford Press.

Gilbert, D. T., & Malone, P. S. (1995). The correspondence bias. *Psychological Bulletin*, 117, 21–38.

Grote, N. K., & Clark, M. S. (2001). Perceiving unfairness in the family: Cause or consequence of marital distress. *Journal of Personality and Social Psychology*, 80, 281–293.

Holmes, J. G. (1981). The exchange process in close relationships: Microbehavior and macromotives. In M. L. Lerner & S. Lerner (Eds.), *The justice motive in social behavior* (pp. 261–284). New York: Plenum.

Holmes, J. G. (2002). Interpersonal expectations as the building blocks of social cognition: An interdependence theory perspective. *Personal Relationship*, 9, 1–26.

Holmes, J. G., & Murray, S. L. (2007). Felt security as a normative resource: Evidence for an elemental risk regulation system? *Psychological Inquiry*, 18, 163–167.

Holmes, J. G., & Rempel, J. K. (1989). Trust in close relationships. In C. Hendrick (Ed.), *Review of personality and social psychology: Close relationships* (Vol. 10, pp. 187–219). Newbury Park, CA: Sage.

Kelley, H. H. (1979). *Personal relationships: Their structures and processes.* Hillsdale, NJ: Erlbaum.

Kenny, D. A. (1994). *Interpersonal perception: A social relations analysis*. New York: Guilford Press.

Kunda, Z., & Spencer, S. J. (2003). When do stereotypes come to mind and when do they color judgment? A goal-based theoretical framework for stereotype activation and application. *Psychological Bulletin, 129*, 522–544.

Lang, P. J., Bradley, M. M., & Cuthbert, B. N. (1990). Emotion, attention, and startle reflex. *Psychological Review, 97*, 377–395.

Leary, M. R., & Baumeister, R. F. (2000). The nature and function of self-esteem: Sociometer theory. In M. P. Zanna (Ed.), *Advances in experimental social psychology* (Vol. 32, pp. 2–51). San Diego, CA: Academic Press.

Lee, L., Loewenstein, G., Ariely, D., Hong, J., & Young, J. (2008). If I'm not hot, are you hot or not? Physical attractiveness evaluations and dating preferences. *Psychological Science, 19*, 669–677.

Levinger, G. (1976). A social psychological perspective on marital dissolution. *Journal of Social Issues, 32*, 21–49.

MacLeod, C., Mathews, A., & Tata, P. (1986). Attentional bias in emotional disorders. *Journal of Abnormal Psychology, 95*, 15–20.

Macrae, C. N., & Johnston, L. (1998). Help, I need somebody: Automatic action and inaction. *Social Cognition, 16*, 400–417.

Mikulincer, M. (1998). Attachment working models and the sense of trust: An exploration of interaction goals and affect regulation. *Journal of Personality and Social Psychology, 74*, 1209–1224.

Mikulincer, M., & Shaver, P. R. (2003). The attachment behavioral system in adulthood: Activation, psychodynamics, and interpersonal processes. In M. Zanna (Ed.), *Advances in experimental social psychology* (Vol. 35, pp. 52–153). New York: Academic Press.

Mineka, S., & Sutton, S. K. (1992). Cognitive biases and the emotional disorders. *Psychological Science, 3*, 65–69.

Mischel, W., & Shoda, Y. (1995). A cognitive-affective system theory of personality: Reconceptualizing situations, dispositions, dynamics, and invariance in personality structure. *Psychological Review, 102*, 246–268.

Murray, S. L., & Holmes, J. G. (2009). The architecture of interdependent minds: A motivation-management theory of mutual responsiveness. *Psychological Review, 116*, 908–928.

Muraven, M., & Baumeister, R. F. (2000). Self-regulation and depletion of limited resources:

Does self-control resemble a muscle? *Psychological Bulletin, 126*, 247–259.

Murray, S. L., Aloni, M., Holmes, J. G., Derrick, J. L., Stinson, D. A., & Leder, S. (2009). Fostering partner dependence as trust-insurance: The implicit contingencies of the exchange script in close relationships. *Journal of Personality and Social Psychology, 96*, 324–348.

Murray, S. L., Bellavia, G., Rose, P., & Griffin, D. (2003). Once hurt, twice hurtful: How perceived regard regulates daily marital interaction. *Journal of Personality and Social Psychology, 84*, 126–147.

Murray, S. L., Derrick, J., Leder, S., & Holmes, J. G. (2008). Balancing connectedness and self-protection goals in close relationships: A levels of processing perspective on risk regulation. *Journal of Personality and Social Psychology, 94*, 429–459.

Murray, S. L., Griffin, D. W., Rose, P., & Bellavia, G. (2003). Calibrating the sociometer: The relational contingencies of self-esteem. *Journal of Personality and Social Psychology, 85*, 63–84.

Murray, S. L., & Holmes, J. G. (2008). The commitment-insurance system: Self-esteem and the regulation of connection in close relationships. In M. P. Zanna (Ed.), *Advances in experimental social psychology* (Vol. 40, pp. 1–60). Amsterdam: Elsevier Press.

Murray, S. L., Holmes, J. G., Aloni, M., Pinkus, R. T., Derrick, J. L., & Leder, S. (2009). Commitment insurance: Compensating for the autonomy costs of interdependence in close relationships. *Journal of Personality and Social Psychology, 97*, 256–278.

Murray, S. L., Holmes, J. G., & Collins, N. L. (2006). Optimizing assurance: The risk regulation system in relationships. *Psychological Bulletin, 132*, 641–666.

Murray, S. L., Holmes, J. G., & Griffin, D. (1996a). The benefits of positive illusions: Idealization and the construction of satisfaction in close relationships. *Journal of Personality and Social Psychology, 70*, 79–98.

Murray, S. L., Holmes, J. G., & Griffin, D. W. (1996b). The self-fulfilling nature of positive illusions in romantic relationship: Love is not blind, but prescient. *Journal of Personality and Social Psychology, 71*, 1155–1180.

Murray, S. L., Holmes, J. G., & Griffin, D. W. (2000). Self-esteem and the quest for felt security: How perceived regard regulates attachment processes. *Journal of Personality and Social Psychology, 78,* 478–498.

Murray, S. L., Holmes, J. G., Griffin, D. W., Bellavia, G., & Rose, P. (2001). The mismeasure of love: How self-doubt contaminates relationship beliefs. *Personality and Social Psychology Bulletin, 27,* 423–436.

Murray, S. L., Holmes, J. G., MacDonald, G., & Ellsworth, P. (1998). Through the looking glass darkly? When self-doubts turn into relationship insecurities. *Journal of Personality and Social Psychology, 75,* 1459–1480.

Murray, S. L., Leder, S., McGregor, J. C. D., Holmes, J. G., Pinkus, R. T., & Harris, B. (2009). Becoming irreplaceable: How comparisons to a partner's alternatives differentially affect low and high self-esteem people. *Journal of Experimental Social Psychology, 45,* 1180–1191.

Murstein, B. I. (1970). Stimulus-value-role: A theory of marital choice. *Journal of Marriage and the Family, 32,* 465–481.

Olson, M. A., & Fazio, R. H. (2008). Implicit and explicit measures of attitudes: The perspective of the MODE model. In R. E. Petty, R. H. Fazio, & P. Brinol (Eds.), *Attitudes: Insights from the new implicit measures* (pp. 19–63). Mahwah, NJ: Erlbaum.

Reis, H. T., Clark, M. S., & Holmes, J. G. (2004). Perceived partner responsiveness as an organizing construct in the study of intimacy and closeness. In D. Mashek & A. P. Aron (Eds.), *Handbook of closeness and intimacy* (pp. 201–225). Mahwah, NJ: Erlbaum.

Rempel, J. K., Holmes, J. G., & Zanna, M. P. (1985). Trust in close relationships. *Journal of Personality and Social Psychology, 49,* 95–112.

Rempel, J. K., Ross, M., & Holmes, J. G. (2001). Trust and communicated attributions in close relationships. *Journal of Personality and Social Psychology, 81,* 57–64.

Rubin, Z. (1973). Liking and loving: An invitation to social psychology. New York: Holt, Rinehart & Winston.

Rusbult, C. (1983). A longitudinal test of the investment model: The development (and deterioration) of satisfaction and commitment in heterosexual involvements. *Journal of Personality and Social Psychology, 45,* 172–186.

Rusbult, C. E., Martz, J. M., & Agnew, C. R. (1998). The investment model scale: Measuring commitment level, satisfaction level, quality of alternatives, and investment size. *Personal Relationships, 5,* 357–391.

Rusbult, C. E., & Van Lange, P. A. M. (2003). Interdependence, interaction, and relationships. *Annual Review of Psychology, 54,* 351–375.

Seligman, C., Fazio, R. H., & Zanna, M. P. (1980). Effects of salience of extrinsic rewards on liking and loving. *Journal of Personality and Social Psychology, 38,* 453–460.

Simpson, J. A. (2007). Psychological foundations of trust. *Current Directions in Psychological Science, 16,* 264–268.

Simpson, J. A., Rholes, W. S., & Phillips, D. (1996). Conflict in close relationships: An attachment perspective. *Journal of Personality and Social Psychology, 71,* 899–914.

Sprecher, S., Schmeeckle, M., & Felmless, D. (2006). The principle of least interest: Inequality in emotional involvement in romantic relationships. *Journal of Family Issues, 27,* 1–26.

Thibaut, J. W., & Kelley, H. H. (1959). *The social psychology of groups.* New York: John Wiley & Sons.

Tooby, J., & Cosmides, L. (1996). Friendship and the banker's paradox: Other pathways to the evolution of adaptations for altruism. *Proceedings of the British Academy, 88,* 119–143.

Turan, B., & Horowitz, L. M. (2007). Can I count on you to be there for me? Individual differences in knowledge structure. *Journal of Personality and Social Psychology, 93,* 447–465.

Waller, W. (1938). *The family: A dynamic interpretation.* Austin: Holt, Rinehart and Winston.

Walster, E., Walster, G. W., & Berscheid, E. (1978). *Equity: Theory and research.* Boston: Allyn and Bacon.

White, G. L. (1980). Physical attractiveness and courtship progress. *Journal of Personality and Social Psychology, 39,* 660–668.

Wieselquist, J., Rusbult, C. E., Foster, C. A., & Agnew, C. R. (1999). Commitment, prorelationship behavior, and trust in close relationships. *Journal of Personality and Social Psychology, 77,* 942–966.

Wilson, T. D., Lindsey, S., & Schooler, T. Y. (2000). A dual model of attitudes. *Psychological Review, 107,* 101–126.

Wood, W., & Neal, D. T. (2007). A new look at habits and the habit-goal interface. *Psychological Review, 14,* 843–863.

NOTES

1. Murray and Holmes (2009) present an extended treatment of this model.

13

AN ATTACHMENT-THEORY PERSPECTIVE ON SOCIAL SUPPORT IN CLOSE RELATIONSHIPS

Nancy L. Collins

Máire B. Ford

Brooke C. Feeney

Individuals of all ages are most likely to thrive when they have significant people in their lives who care deeply about their welfare and are willing and able to come to their aid should difficulties arise (Bowlby, 1973). Just as children look to parents for protection and nurturance when coping with stress or uncertainty, adults look to their spouses, family, and friends for support and care during times of adversity and personal challenge. A large body of research shows that social support plays a vital role in fostering health and emotional well-being at all stages in the lifespan (e.g., Cohen, 2005; Reblin & Uchino, 2008; Sarason, Sarason, & Gurung, 1997); and there is growing evidence that it also plays a central role in the development and maintenance of secure and satisfying intimate relationships (e.g., Collins & Feeney, 2000; Gleason, Iida, Shrout, & Bolger, 2008; Julien & Markman, 1991; Pasch, Bradbury, & Sullivan, 1997).

Nevertheless, adults differ greatly in their desire to seek care from others and in their willingness and ability to provide responsive care to others in need. As a result, many people find it difficult to navigate social support interactions and to develop the type of mutually caring and supportive relationships that are necessary for optimal functioning. How can we explain these individual differences? What personality, relationship, and contextual factors facilitate or impede effective social support dynamics in close relationships? And how do these dynamics affect individual well-being and relationship functioning?

Until recently, researchers knew surprisingly little about the interpersonal processes that take place during support interactions, or about the factors that facilitate or impede effective social support dynamics in close relationships. One reason for this gap is that most prior research on social support has taken an intrapersonal perspective, one that focuses on the link between a support-recipient's health outcomes and his or her general perceptions of available support (i.e., the belief that close others will be available if needed). Relatively few studies have examined the role of the support-provider, or the interpersonal dynamics that unfold between providers and recipients during actual support interactions. Fortunately, researchers have begun to examine social support as an interpersonal process within the context of close relationships (e.g., Barbee & Cunningham, 1995; Collins & Feeney, 2000; Cutrona & Suhr, 1994; Feeney & Collins, 2001; Gleason et al., 2008; Pasch et al., 1997; Simpson, Rholes, & Nelligan, 1992). Much of this new research has emerged within the adult attachment literature. Adult attachment researchers have been especially interested in social support dynamics because seeking and giving care are viewed as core elements of attachment bonds at all stages in the lifespan. Attachment theory provides a valuable framework for understanding both the normative patterns of support-seeking and caregiving that occur in close relationships, and the ways in which these patterns are shaped by individual differences in adult attachment style. Most of the empirical work in this area has focused on support processes in romantic couples, which will be the focus of this chapter; however, we believe that the basic processes discussed in this work apply to other adult relationships of emotional significance (e.g., close friendships, sibling relationships, and adult parent-child relationships).

Our goal in this chapter is to provide an overview of research on social support from an attachment theoretical perspective. We begin by describing three major behavioral systems—attachment, exploration, and caregiving—that are relevant to understanding social support processes in close relationships. Next, we provide an attachment theoretical framework for understanding social support dynamics in couples. Finally, we summarize empirical work in this area and discuss implications of these findings for individual and relationship well-being.

SEEKING AND GIVING SUPPORT: THE INTERFACE OF THREE BEHAVIORAL SYSTEMS

Attachment theory provides an ideal framework for studying social support because it considers the interplay of three important aspects of human nature that are relevant to support-seeking and support-provision in close relationships: *attachment, exploration,* and *caregiving.*

The Attachment Behavioral System

Attachment theory regards the propensity to form strong emotional bonds with particular individuals as a basic component of human behavior (Bowlby, 1973, 1982; Bretherton, 1985). According to the theory, infants enter the world equipped with an innate *attachment behavioral system* that functions to promote safety and survival through contact with nurturing caregivers. The attachment system becomes activated most strongly in adversity so that when a child is frightened, anxious, tired, or ill, he or she will tend to seek protection and care from a primary attachment figure, typically a parent (Bowlby, 1973, 1982). Furthermore, the quality of the relationship that develops between a parent and child is expected to be largely determined by the parent's emotional availability and responsiveness to the child's needs. A child's ability to rely trustingly on a parent as a *safe haven* of comfort when distressed, and a *secure base* for exploration when not distressed, is a key component of well-functioning attachment bonds and a key predictor of healthy emotional development (Ainsworth, Blehar, Waters, & Wall, 1978; Bowlby, 1973).

Although attachment theory was originally developed to explain the nature of the relationship that develops between a child and a parent, Bowlby (1982) emphasized that the basic functions of the attachment system continue to operate across the lifespan, and that attachment behavior is not limited to children. Although it is less readily activated in adults than in children, attachment behavior can be seen whenever adults are faced with events that they perceive as stressful or threatening. For example, adults often seek proximity to the significant people in their lives (often romantic partners) in response to illness, physical pain, fear of new situations, feelings of attack or rejection by others, achievement problems or failures, and threats of loss. Attachment behavior, and an associated increase in desire for care, is considered to be the norm in these situations. Moreover, attachment theory emphasizes that the desire for comfort and support during times of adversity is neither childish nor immature (Feeney, 2007). Indeed, Bowlby (1982) argued that healthy self-reliance involves the "capacity to rely trustingly on others when occasion demands and to know on whom it is appropriate to rely" (p. 359). Accordingly, adult attachment researchers view support-seeking behavior as a manifestation of the attachment behavioral system in intimate relationships (Collins & Feeney, 2000; Shaver, Mikulincer, & Shemesh-Iron, 2009).

Although the need for security is believed to be universal, adults as well as children will develop characteristic strategies for coping with distress and regulating feelings of security; and these strategies are thought to be contingent on an individual's history of regulating distress with attachment figures (Bartholomew, Cobb, & Poole, 1997; Kobak & Sceery, 1988; Mikulincer & Shaver, 2003). This has led researchers to identify systematic individual differences in *attachment style* in infants and adults (Ainsworth et al., 1978; Bartholomew & Horowitz, 1991; Hazan & Shaver, 1987). Bowlby (1973) postulated that these individual differences are rooted in *internal working models* of the self (as worthy or unworthy of love and care)

and others (as responsive or unresponsive in times of need), which develop in the context of transactions with caregivers and other important attachment figures. Working models of attachment are thought to be cognitive-affective-motivational schemas that regulate the attachment system by directing not only feelings and behavior, but also attention, memory, and cognition in attachment-relevant contexts (for a review, see Collins, Guichard, Ford, & Feeney, 2004).

For adults, individual differences in attachment styles are typically assessed in terms of two underlying dimensions: anxiety and avoidance (Bartholomew & Horowitz, 1991; Brennan, Clark, & Shaver, 1998; Fraley & Waller, 1998). Attachment *anxiety* reflects the degree to which individuals worry about being rejected, abandoned, or unloved by significant others. Attachment *avoidance* reflects the degree to which individuals limit intimacy and interdependence with others. Additional information regarding individual differences can be obtained by considering interactions between these two dimensions (Bartholomew & Horowitz, 1991). *Secure* individuals are low in both anxiety and avoidance. They feel valued by others and worthy of affection, and they perceive attachment figures as generally responsive, caring, and reliable. They are comfortable developing close relationships and depending on others when needed. Various forms of *insecure* attachment are defined by high levels of anxiety and/or avoidance. *Preoccupied* individuals (high anxiety, low avoidance) have an exaggerated desire for closeness but lack confidence in others' availability and responsiveness in times of need. They depend on the approval of others for a sense of personal well-being but have heightened concerns about being rejected or abandoned. *Fearful-avoidant* individuals (high anxiety, high avoidance) experience a strong sense of distrust in others coupled with heightened expectations of rejection, which result in discomfort with intimacy and avoidance of close relationships.

Finally, *dismissing-avoidant* individuals (low anxiety, high avoidance) value independence and self-reliance and view close relationships as relatively unimportant. They perceive attachment figures as generally unreliable and unresponsive. They attempt to maintain a positive self-image in the face of potential rejection by minimizing attachment needs, distancing from others, and restricting expressions of emotionality.

These individual differences in attachment style are thought to be rooted in underlying differences in working models of self and others, and can be understood in terms of rules that regulate the attachment system and guide responses to emotionally distressing situations (Fraley & Shaver, 2000; Kobak & Sceery, 1988; Shaver & Mikulincer, 2007). For example, secure attachment is organized by rules that allow acknowledgment of distress and turning to others for comfort and support when needed. In contrast, avoidant attachment is organized by rules that restrict acknowledgment of distress and inhibit dependence on others (a deactivating strategy), whereas anxious attachment is organized by rules that direct attention toward distress and attachment figures in a hypervigilant manner that inhibits autonomy and self-reliance (a hyperactivating strategy). These different strategies of emotion regulation should have important implications for understanding how relationship partners cope with their own distress as well as how they respond to the emotional distress of others. Thus, attachment styles should play a key role in shaping support-seeking and support-provision dynamics in adult close relationships.

The Exploration System

According to attachment theory, the urge to explore the environment—to work, play, discover, create, and take part in activities with peers—is another basic component of human nature (Ainsworth et al., 1978; Bowlby, 1988). For adults, these exploratory activities may take many forms, including

pursuing a career, traveling, developing hobbies, and working toward important personal goals (Brunstein, Dangelmayer, & Schultheiss, 1996; Carnelley & Ruscher, 2000; Feeney, 2004; Hazan & Shaver, 1990). The ability to pursue personal goals and to confidently explore the environment is assumed to be critical to learning and personal adaptation (Bowlby, 1988). However, the attachment and exploratory systems are thought to be antithetic to each other, such that focused and productive exploration is likely to occur only when attachment needs have been satisfied and the attachment system is deactivated (Bowlby, 1982, 1988). That is, when an individual of any age is feeling secure, he or she is likely to explore away from attachment figures; but when alarmed or distressed, the attachment system will take priority and he or she will tend to desire proximity to attachment figures.

Whereas children use their parents as a secure base for exploration by keeping note of a parent's whereabouts, exchanging glances, and from time to time returning to the parent to share in enjoyable mutual contact, adults are likely to engage in similar forms of behavior. For example, an adult is likely to keep track of a spouse's whereabouts, maintain phone contact when exploring away for an extended period of time, or share details of his or her explorations with the spouse (Feeney, 2004; Feeney & Collins, 2004). Adults may also look to their partner for encouragement, advice, or instrumental aid in achieving their exploratory goals.

Because a sense of felt security is necessary for productive exploration, people of all ages will be more likely to explore the environment and take on challenges when they are confident that an attachment figure will be available, accessible, and responsive should the need arise. Thus, according to attachment theory, the ability to confidently explore the environment stems in part from having an attachment figure who can serve as a secure base—one who both encourages and supports such exploration and in the past has proven himself or herself to be readily available and responsive when comfort, assistance, or protection has been sought (Bowlby, 1982, 1988). Because a sense of security is necessary for productive exploration, it is not surprising that individual differences in attachment style have been linked to differences in exploratory behavior in both children (Ainsworth et al., 1978) and adults (Carnelley & Ruscher, 2000; Elliot & Reis, 2003; Hazan & Shaver, 1990). As would be expected, secure individuals show more adaptive patterns of exploration and have a healthier balance between attachment behavior and exploratory behavior, compared to their insecure counterparts.

The Caregiving Behavioral System

In order for attachment bonds to function effectively, the attachment and exploratory behavior of one partner must be coordinated with the caregiving behavior of his or her attachment figure. Thus, the propensity to care for the needs of others is regarded by attachment theory as another major component of human nature. Whereas the attachment system is a normative safety-regulating system that reduces the risk of the *self* coming to harm, the caregiving system is a safety regulating system that reduces the risk of a *close other* coming to harm (Bowlby, 1982; George & Solomon, 1999; Kunce & Shaver, 1994). From a normative perspective, the caregiving system alerts individuals to the needs of others and motivates them to provide protection, comfort, and assistance to those who are either generally dependent upon them or temporarily in need (Collins & Feeney, 2000; Feeney & Collins, 2001). Although the caregiving behavioral system is most often discussed in the context of parent-child relationships, Bowlby (1982, 1988) recognized the profound importance of caregiving in adult intimate relationships, and he suggested that secure and well-functioning relationships are possible only when intimate partners are aware of their vital role as caregivers to one another

(see also Bretherton, 1987). Accordingly, adult attachment researchers view the provision of social support to an intimate partner as a manifestation of the caregiving behavioral system (Collins, Ford, Guichard, Kane, & Feeney, 2009; Shaver et al., 2009).

In its optimal form, caregiving should include a broad array of behaviors that complement a partner's attachment and exploratory behavior (George & Solomon, 1999; Kunce & Shaver, 1994; Reis & Patrick, 1996). Thus, according to attachment theory, caregiving serves two major functions: (1) to meet the dependent partner's need for security by responding to signals of distress or potential threat (providing a safe haven), and (2) to support the attached person's autonomy and exploration when not distressed (providing a secure base). Regardless of the specific form of care being offered, optimal caregiving should be characterized by two key features: (1) sensitivity to the partner's signals, and (2) interpersonal responsiveness (Collins, Ford, Guichard, Kane, & Feeney, 2009; Collins, Ford, Guichard, & Feeney, 2006). *Sensitivity* reflects the degree to which the caregiver's behavior is in synchrony with, and appropriately contingent upon, the partner's needs (Ainsworth et al., 1978; Bowlby, 1982; George & Solomon, 1999). A sensitive caregiver is attuned to the care-seeker's signals, interprets them correctly, and responds promptly and appropriately (providing the type and amount of support that is wanted and needed). In contrast, insensitive caregivers may be neglectful, overinvolved, intrusive, or otherwise out of synch with their partner's needs. The second key feature of effective caregiving is *interpersonal responsiveness*, which reflects not the type or amount of support that is provided but the *manner* in which it is provided. Specifically, responsive care is provided in a way that leads the recipient to feel understood, validated, and cared for (Reis & Shaver, 1988). To accomplish this, caregivers must offer support in a way that expresses generous intentions, protects their partner's esteem, validates their partner's feelings and needs, respects their partner's point of view, and conveys love, acceptance, and understanding.

Of course, providing responsive care is not always easy, and even well-intended support efforts can have unintended negative consequences (Dunkel-Schetter, Blasband, Feinstein, & Herbert, 1992; Rini et al., 2006). For example, when offering support in response to a partner's distress (providing a safe haven), caregivers may provide support in a way that makes their partner feel weak, helpless, needy, or inadequate, that induces guilt or indebtedness, or that makes their partner feel like a burden. Caregivers may also minimize or discount their partner's problem, or may blame or criticize their partner for his or her own misfortune. When offering support in response to a partner's challenging or growth-related opportunities (providing a secure base), caregivers may provide support in a way that undermines their partner's confidence, belittles their partner's goals and personal strivings, or fails to respect their partner's desire for autonomy by (explicitly or implicitly) discouraging or impeding the pursuit of explorations outside of the relationship. Such interference may be especially likely for support-providers whose own insecurities lead them to be threatened by their partner's desire for autonomous exploration and personal growth.

According to attachment theory, one important factor determining whether caregivers have the capacity for providing optimal care is the caregiver's own degree of attachment security. Bowlby suggested that the caregiving and attachment behavioral systems will be antithetic to each other, such that effective support-provision is likely to occur only when the caregiver's own attachment needs have been satisfied and the attachment system is deactivated (Bowlby, 1982, 1988). That is, when a caregiver is feeling secure, he or she will be able to devote attention and resources to the needs of others; but when the caregiver's *own security* is threatened (either chronically or temporarily), caregiving behavior is likely

to be impaired to some degree (Collins et al., 2009). This suggests that individuals with an insecure attachment style—who are either preoccupied with their own attachment needs or defensively distancing from such needs—may be less willing or able to be sensitive and responsive to the needs of others. Consistent with this assumption, a number of studies (reviewed below) show that insecure adults are less effective support-providers than their secure counterparts.

AN ATTACHMENT THEORY PERSPECTIVE ON SOCIAL SUPPORT

Attachment theory has clear relevance to understanding social support in intimate relationships, and offers important insights and research ideas that may not be considered in other theoretical approaches. Based on attachment theory, Collins and Feeney (2010; Feeney, 2004; Feeney & Collins, 2004) developed an integrative framework for studying the interpersonal processes involved in support-seeking (attachment), support-giving (caregiving), and exploration in close relationships. In doing so, they conceptualize social support as an interpersonal process that involves one partner's support-seeking efforts and the other partner's caregiving responses. Their model identifies two general forms of social support—*secure base* and *safe haven*—and examines normative processes and individual differences. Below, we provide a brief overview of this framework as a backdrop for the empirical review that follows. We begin with a description of the two forms of support identified by the model. Next we discuss the interpersonal dynamics involved in social support transactions. Finally, we consider how these dynamics are shaped by individual differences in attachment styles.

Two Forms of Social Support: Safe Haven and Secure Base Support

Drawing from attachment theory, Feeney and Collins (2004; Collins & Feeney, 2010) differentiate between two distinct forms of social support. First, *safe-haven support* occurs when relationship partners seek or provide support in response to stress or adversity. This conceptualization is based on attachment theory's notion of a safe haven (Bowlby, 1988), which functions to support behaviors that involve "coming in" to the relationship for comfort, reassurance, and assistance in times of stress. Although the term *safe haven* has not generally been used in the social support literature, this is the type of support (support during stress or adversity) that is most often studied in prior work. Adults provide a safe haven for their relationship partners when they respond sensitively and appropriately to their partners' distress. Safe-haven support behaviors may include (a) encouraging communication of thoughts and feelings; (b) showing interest in the partner's problems, and validating his or her concerns, worries, and fears; (c) conveying a sense of confidence in a partner's ability to handle the stressful situation; (d) affirming the partner's worth and reassuring the partner that he or she is loved and valued; (e) providing physical closeness, affection, and comfort; (f) providing instrumental assistance as needed (e.g., information, advice, problem-solving, task assistance, provision of material resources); and (g) conveying continued availability if needed.

The second form of support is called *secure base support*, which occurs when relationship partners seek or provide support for exploration behavior (e.g., the desire to learn, grow, discover, and accomplish goals). This term is based on attachment theory's notion of a secure base, which functions to support behaviors that involve "going out" from the relationship for autonomous exploration in the environment (Bowlby, 1988; Feeney, 2004, 2007; Waters & Cummings, 2000). Bowlby (1988) describes the concept of a secure base as one in which support-providers act as a base from which an attached person can engage in autonomous exploration, knowing that he or she can return for comfort, reassurance, or assistance should he or she encounter difficulties along the way. Adults provide a secure base for their relationship partners when they respond sensitively and appropriately to their partners' exploratory behavior and to their need for encouragement in their exploratory activity (Feeney, 2004). Secure base support may include (a) encouraging the partner to accept challenges and try new things; (b) showing interest in, and validation of, the partner's personal goals and plans; (c) conveying a sense of confidence in a partner's ability to handle challenges and to succeed; (d) providing instrumental assistance as needed (information, advice, assistance in removing obstacles); (e) avoiding behaviors that interfere with the partner's explorations; (f) celebrating the partner's successes and responding sensitively to his or her failures; and (g) balancing an acceptance of the partner's need for self-growth with the conveyance of continued availability, if needed.

In summary, Feeney and Collins suggest that in well-functioning close relationships, partners provide one another with a safe haven to which they can retreat when distressed and a secure base from which they can explore when not distressed. Thus, they view social support as an ongoing process that occurs even when a partner's security is not being immediately threatened. This view of social support is different from the broader support literature, which has defined support almost exclusively in terms of the provision of emotional or instrumental aid in response to stress or adversity (i.e., *safe haven* support). Attachment theory suggests that secure base support will play a vital role in personal adaptation and optimal relationship functioning (Feeney, 2004, 2007), and yet this form of support has been largely overlooked in the social support literature. By differentiating between these two forms of support, the framework advanced here provides a basis for exploring the unique functions and benefits of each form of support, and the unique negative consequences that may ensue when individuals fail to satisfy one or both of these distinct support needs.

Social Support as an Interpersonal Process

In addition to identifying two forms of social support, attachment theory also draws our attention to the importance of studying social support as an interpersonal process. Accordingly, Collins and Feeney conceptualize social support as a transactional process that involves one partner's support-seeking efforts and the other partner's caregiving responses (see Collins & Feeney, 2000; Collins & Feeney, 2010; Feeney, 2004). A simplified version of this model is shown in Figure 13.1, which depicts a prototypical support interaction involving safe-haven and/or secure-base dynamics. We begin by discussing normative safe-haven and secure-base processes; then we consider how these processes are shaped by individual differences in adult attachment styles. For ease of presentation, we refer to the person who could potentially benefit from support as the *support-recipient* (or *support-seeker*) and the close other who is expected to provide support as the *support-provider* (or *caregiver*). However, it is important to keep in mind that in adult relationships, the support-seeking and caregiving roles are not exclusively assigned to one member of the dyad

(as they are in parent-child relationships). Indeed, Bowlby (1979) suggested that healthy attachment bonds in adulthood require that individuals have the ability to comfortably adopt either role—to rely trustingly on others for care when occasion demands, and to provide others with the same responsive care and support in return.

Normative safe haven dynamics. The *safe haven* function of support is set into motion when an individual's *attachment* system is activated in response to a life stressor, which should lead an individual to desire proximity to and support from a close relationship partner (path *a*). This attachment behavior should, in turn, motivate the partner to provide safe-haven support (path *b*). Next, the support-recipient's subjective perception of support should be grounded, at least to some degree, in actual features of the support-provider's behavior (path *c*). Support behaviors that are sensitive to the support recipient's needs and interpersonally responsive should be perceived as supportive, whereas insensitive (e.g., neglectful, over-involved) and unresponsive (e.g., critical, controlling, undermining) behaviors should be viewed as unsupportive (Collins et al., 2006, 2009). Finally, perceptions of effective safe-haven support should result in both short-term and long-term benefits for support-recipients (path *d*). Collins and Feeney assume that effective

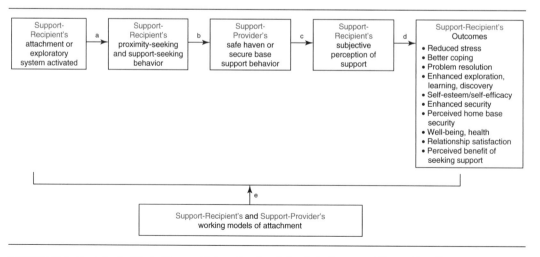

FIGURE 13.1   Prototypical Social Support Interaction Involving Safe Haven and Secure Base Processes

support of either form (safe haven or secure base) will result in some important common benefits including (a) healthy relationship functioning, (b) psychological well-being, (c) better health/physical well-being, and (d) general views that it is worthwhile to seek support from others. However, because safe-haven and secure-base support serve different functions, each form of support will have some unique benefits (Feeney, 2004; Feeney & Collins, 2004). Some unique benefits of safe-haven support include (a) reduced stress (both psychological and physiological), (b) improved coping capacity, (c) perceived (and actual) safety, and (d) problem resolution. In sum, immediate (and long-term) improvements in emotional well-being are likely to be an important benefit of safe haven support.

Normative secure base dynamics. The *secure base* function of support is set into motion when an individual's *exploratory* system is activated. The experience of an exploratory opportunity should increase exploratory behavior and a willingness to seek goal-relevant support (path *a*). Goals that are perceived to be more daunting should lead individuals to solicit more active forms of support (e.g., assistance, encouragement). In other cases, simply the perception that one's home base is secure and available if needed should suffice. Next, the support-recipient's behavior should motivate his or her partner to provide secure base support (path *b*), and the support-recipient's subjective perception of support should depend on the degree to which this support is sensitive and responsive (path *c*). Support behaviors that encourage exploratory behavior and validate the pursuit of personally rewarding challenges, as well as behaviors that convey availability if needed, should be perceived as supportive. In contrast, intrusive, interfering, or discouraging behaviors should be viewed as unsupportive. Finally, perceptions of effective secure base support should result in both short-term and long-term benefits for support-recipients (path *d*). In addition to the shared benefits noted above, secure base support should

have some important benefits that are distinct from those afforded by safe-haven support. These include (a) positive self-construals (self-esteem, self-efficacy, self-confidence), (b) greater willingness/efforts to pursue goals, accept challenges, and take risks, and (c) increased personal growth and successful goal strivings. In sum, immediate (and long-term) improvements in the self (personal growth, successful goal strivings, positive self-construals) are likely to be important benefits of secure base support.

Individual Differences

The interpersonal processes discussed thus far reflect normative or prototypical social support processes. However, individual difference factors are expected to influence these processes in numerous ways—facilitating or interfering with all of the pathways shown in Figure 13.1. For example, people differ in their willingness to express distress, engage in exploratory behavior, and seek support when needed. They also differ in their willingness and ability to provide sensitive and responsive care to others in need. In addition, preexisting beliefs and expectations may act as interpretative filters, shaping the way that partners perceive one another's behavior. One theoretically important individual difference factor is the role of adult attachment styles in shaping support dynamics (Figure 13.1, path *e*). Working models of attachment have obvious relevance to social support because they are assumed to guide cognitive, affective, and behavioral responses in attachment-relevant situations. Moreover, individual differences in adult attachment styles are presumed to emerge (at least in part) from care-seeking and caregiving dynamics that occur during childhood and adolescence. Thus, attachment styles should play a key role in shaping the interpersonal dynamics surrounding safe-haven and secure-base support processes. Overall, secure individuals should be more willing and better able to engage in effective support-seeking behavior and to provide sensitive and responsive care to others in need. In contrast, insecure adults are likely to have deficits in their willingness and ability to seek and provide effective support; although (as discussed below) the specific type of deficit should depend on the specific form of insecurity.

Summary

The theoretical perspective advanced here provides an integrative framework for considering the unique functions of safe-haven and secure-base support in close relationships. It also emphasizes the importance of viewing social support as an interpersonal process that involves the thoughts, feelings, and behaviors of *two* individuals. Finally, this framework integrates behavior, emotion, motivation, and perception; and identifies normative processes as well as individual differences in these processes. In the sections that follow, we provide a review of empirical research on safe haven and secure base processes in couples. We organize our review around the conceptual framework shown in Figure 13.1.

RESEARCH ON SAFE HAVEN PROCESSES: SUPPORT IN TIMES OF STRESS

In one line of work, attachment researchers have investigated the normative ways in which relationship partners seek and provide support during times of stress or adversity—as well as the ways in which individual differences in attachment style shape these dynamics. Below we review the key research questions and findings addressed in this work and their implications for understanding how partners help one another cope with stress.

Normative Safe Haven Processes

Mobilization of attachment and caregiving behavior in response to stress. An assumption of attachment theory—and the theoretical

framework presented here—is that when individuals are distressed (attachment system activation) they will desire proximity to close others, and that attachment behavior will be activated with greater intensity as the degree of threat increases (Figure 13.1, path *a*). The support-seeker's attachment behavior should, in turn, mobilize the support-provider's behavior (caregiving system activation) such that greater support-seeking efforts (or expressions of distress) should be associated with increased support-provision (path *b*). Observational studies of couples reveal strong evidence for these normative dynamics. In one study, couples were videotaped while discussing stressful life events (Collins & Feeney, 2000). Support-seekers who evaluated their problems as more distressing exhibited more support-seeking behavior during their discussion (path *a*); this increased support-seeking effort was then associated with increased caregiving behavior from their partner (path *b*). Similar effects were obtained in a study in which couples were unobtrusively videotaped after one member of the couple was asked to perform a stressful public speaking task (Collins, Kane, Guichard, & Ford, 2009). In this study, participants who felt more nervous and anxious about the speech task sought more emotional support from their spouses (path *a*); and spouses responded with greater emotional and instrumental support efforts (path *b*). Diary studies provide additional support for these normative dynamics. For example, in a 21-day diary study of romantic couples, Collins and Feeney (2005) found that people sought more support from their partners on days when they experienced more stressful life events (path *a*), and partners responded to these needs by providing more support on these high stress days (path *b*). Along similar lines, when couples were followed over time as one member of the couple prepared to take the bar exam, partners increased their emotional support efforts as the bar exam approached and their partner's degree of anxiety increased (Iida,

Seidman, Shrout, Fujita, & Bolger, 2008; Gleason et al., 2008).

Experimental studies provide further evidence for the normative activation of the attachment and caregiving systems. In a series of studies, Mikulincer and colleagues showed that attachment concepts (Mikulincer, Birnbaum, Woddis, & Nachmias, 2000) and attachment figures (Mikulincer, Gillath, & Shaver, 2002) are automatically activated in memory in response to threat (path *a*). For example, after being subliminally primed with threat related words (e.g., death, separation, failure), participants showed increased cognitive accessibility to the names of people they had previously identified as serving attachment functions (i.e., serving as a safe haven or secure base; Mikulincer et al., 2002). In other work, Feeney and Collins (2001; Ford, Guichard, & Collins, 2009) examined the normative activation of the caregiving system (path *b*) by experimentally manipulating the caregiver's perception of the support-seeker's need for support (by providing caregivers with false information about their partner's degree of emotional distress about an upcoming speech task). In these studies, caregivers experienced greater sympathy and empathic concern for their partner, were more mentally focused on their partner, and increased their support efforts when they believed that their partner was highly distressed and in greater need of support. These results suggest that support-providers modulate their support efforts in line with their partner's needs by deploying greater cognitive, emotional, and behavioral resources when their partners most need them.

Taken together, these studies provide clear evidence for a normative increase in attachment behavior (desire for proximity/support) in response to life stressors, and a normative increase in caregiving behavior in response to these needs. These studies also reveal that support-seeking and caregiving behaviors are highly interdependent and that *both* members of a dyad play important roles in determining the nature and quality of their support interactions.

Subjective perceptions of support received. The theoretical framework presented here assumes that a support-recipient's subjective perceptions of a support interaction— the degree to which a support effort is judged to be caring, helpful, and well-intended—will depend heavily on objective features of the caregiver's behavior (Figure 13.1, path *c*). Consistent with this assumption, studies indicate that subjective perceptions of support are grounded, at least to some extent, in the quality of the support provided by caregivers. For example, when discussing personal worries, support-recipients perceived their interaction to be more supportive when their partner provided more emotional and instrumental support and less negative support (e.g., dismissing the importance of the problem or blaming the support-receiver), and when their partner behaved in ways that were judged (by independent raters) to be more responsive (Collins & Feeney, 2000). Likewise, in an experimental study in which support quality was experimentally *manipulated* (by asking partners to copy prewritten messages), support-recipients rated their partners' messages as more supportive when they were indeed more thoughtful and less ambiguous (Collins & Feeney, 2004b). Another experimental study revealed that support-seekers are highly attuned to their partner's degree of responsiveness and emotional availability during stressful situations (Kane, McCall, Collins, & Blascovich, 2009). In this study, virtual reality technology was used to experimentally manipulate the caregiver's presence and nonverbal attentiveness (attentive versus inattentive/neglectful) while the support-recipient crossed a dangerous cliff in a virtual world; support-recipients perceived the attentive (vs. inattentive) partner as more caring and responsive to their needs, and they reported feeling more comforted in the presence of the attentive partner.

As these results suggest, just as a child's sense of emotional security is rooted in the parent's emotional availability and responsiveness to the child's needs, adults are similarly attuned to their partner's responsiveness; support recipients are most likely to feel supported and comforted when social support is offered in a generous manner that is appropriately contingent on their needs.

Outcomes associated with safe haven support. Attachment theory highlights the benefits of safe-haven support not only for individual health and well-being, but also for the development and maintenance of happy and secure relationships. When relationship partners provide caring support to one another in times of adversity, they not only foster an environment of kindness and goodwill in their relationship, they also provide one another with diagnostic evidence of their deep engagement in one another's welfare (Collins & Feeney, 2004a). Thus, attachment researchers have been interested in understanding the role of effective safe-haven support in promoting a variety of positive outcomes for support-recipients and their relationships (Figure 13.1, path *d*). Laboratory studies show that small acts of caring (or neglect) can have immediate effects on well-being and relationship functioning. For example, in Collins and Feeney's (2000) observational study of couples in which one partner disclosed a personal worry to the other, support-recipients experienced immediate improvements in emotional well-being (increases in positive mood) when their partner provided more responsive support. Likewise, in their daily diary study, Collins and Feeney (2005) found that couple members felt happier and more secure in their relationship (more loved and valued) on days when their partner provided more caring support, and these positive effects lingered during the following day. In addition, self-report studies show that people are happier and more satisfied in their relationships when they view their partners as good caregivers and support providers (Carnelley, Pietromonaco, & Jaffe, 1996; Cutrona, 1996; Feeney, 1996; Kane et al., 2007).

In addition to these correlational studies, experimental studies show that caring support can have immediate (causal) effects on physical and emotional well-being, as well as on relationship functioning. For example, in their virtual reality study—in which they manipulated caregiver presence and attentiveness while participants engaged in a frightening cliff-walking task—Kane et al. (2009) found that participants who crossed the cliff in the presence of an attentive partner reported lower anxiety during the task (compared to those who crossed the cliff alone); they also reported feeling safer during their task (compared to those who crossed the cliff in the presence of an inattentive partner). Furthermore, participants who had an inattentive/neglectful partner kept greater *physical* distance between themselves and their partner during a subsequent, unrelated task in the virtual world. A recent brain-imaging study provides further evidence that caring support can reduce the appraisal of threat (Coan, Schaefer, & Davidson, 2006). In this study, when women were holding (vs. not holding) their spouses hand while anticipating mild shocks in an fMRI scanner, they showed less neural activation in brain regions associated with threat. Along similar lines, Collins, Jaremka, & Kane (2009) showed that caring support can reduce stress hormones in response to a social evaluative stressor. In this study, they manipulated social support in the context of a stressful speech task by asking caregivers to copy pre-prepared notes that were designed to be highly supportive. Participants who received supportive messages (vs. those who did not receive messages) had lower levels of stress hormones (salivary cortisol) during their speech task and more rapid emotional recovery. Caring support also had immediate relationship benefits; those who received support felt emotionally closer to their partner, desired more proximity, and rated their partner as more responsive to their needs. Taken together, these findings indicate that small acts of kindness can attenuate stress (both psychologically and physiologically), promote health, and enhance relationship closeness and intimacy.

Individual Differences in Safe Haven Processes

Individual differences in support seeking. An attachment framework assumes that stressful events will motivate people to seek support from (and proximity to) close others; but it also acknowledges that people differ in their willingness and ability to effectively mobilize support. Asking for help can be risky, and individuals may only be willing to reach out to others if they have confidence that their efforts will be met with kindness and understanding. Thus, people with different attachment styles—who differ in their comfort with intimacy and their expectations of responsiveness from others—should differ in their support seeking behavior (moderating path *a* in Figure 13.1). Consistent with this assumption, self-report (Ognibene & Collins, 1998; Florian, Mikulincer, & Bucholtz, 1995; Mikulincer & Florian, 1995) and observational (Collins & Feeney, 2000; Fraley & Shaver, 1998; Rholes, Simpson, & Orina, 1999; Simpson et al., 1992) studies find consistent evidence that attachment avoidance is associated with less—and less effective—support-seeking behavior. For example, in an observational study of couples discussing personal stressors (Collins & Feeney, 2000), avoidant individuals sought relatively low levels of support regardless of how stressful their problem was; and when they did seek support, they tended to use indirect support-seeking strategies that were less effective at eliciting support. These findings, as well as findings from other studies, suggest that avoidant individuals behave in ways that make it difficult for others to provide support—they tend to withdraw from their partners when feeling distressed and are less direct in expressing their needs.

In general, studies have failed to find systematic links between attachment anxiety and support-seeking behavior. In self-report studies, anxious adults report greater use of social support as a coping strategy (Ognibene & Collins, 1998; Mikulincer & Florian, 1995), but laboratory studies find no association between anxiety and increased support-seeking behavior (e.g., Collins & Feeney, 2000; Simpson et al., 1992). However, a few studies suggest that anxious individuals may seek support in less effective ways (Feeney, Cassidy, & Ramos-Marcuse, 2008; Rholes, Simpson, & Orina, 1999). For example, in an observational study of adolescents interacting with new acquaintances, Feeney et al. (2008) found that anxious individuals mixed support-seeking behavior with expressions of negativity toward their interaction partner, perhaps because they wanted support but did not expect it to be forthcoming or because they perceived the support they did receive as less helpful and well-intended.

Individual differences in subjective perceptions of support received. Although support-perceptions are grounded in reality (as discussed above), subjective perceptions of support should also be shaped by characteristics of the support-recipient. Thus, attachment researchers have examined the extent to which secure and insecure support-recipients differ in their construal of the *same objective* support messages (moderating path *c* in Figure 13.1). In one study, support messages were experimentally manipulated by asking partners to copy preprepared notes that were either highly supportive or ambiguously supportive (Collins & Feeney, 2004b, Study 1). These notes were then delivered to support-recipients (before and after a stressful speech task), who later rated their subjective perceptions of the notes. Although secure and insecure recipients did not differ in their appraisals of highly supportive notes, they did differ in their appraisals of ambiguous notes. Secure adults made benign attributions for the ambiguous notes, whereas insecure individuals (those high in anxiety and/or avoidance) made more negative attributions. Furthermore, after receiving ambiguous support messages, insecure individuals misremembered an earlier support interaction as having been negative when, in reality (as indicated by observer ratings), it had not been. Similar findings were obtained in a conceptual replication in which partners were allowed to write genuine notes (Collins & Feeney, 2004b, Study 2). In this study, insecure support-recipients rated their partner's note as less supportive, but only when the notes were judged (by independent raters) to be less supportive. Taken together, these studies suggest that insecure individuals are predisposed to perceive their partner's behavior as less supportive, but primarily when the support effort is ambiguous and therefore open to greater subjective construal.

Individual differences in support-provision/ caregiving. The studies reviewed above show that caregiving behavior is normatively activated when a romantic partner is facing adversity. However, this normative pattern is often moderated by individual differences in attachment style (moderating path *b* in Figure 13.1). Overall, the theoretical framework presented here assumes that secure individuals will find it easier than insecure individuals to respond to their partner's attachment needs. One reason for this prediction is that sensitive and compassionate reactions to the needs of others are products of a well-functioning caregiving behavioral system, which cannot function effectively when one's own needs for security have not been met (Collins et al., 2009; Mikulincer & Shaver, 2005). Support-providers who are preoccupied with their own attachment needs (those high in anxiety) or wish to distance themselves from attachment needs (those high in avoidance) should be less capable of giving spontaneously to others.

Consistent with these ideas, questionnaire studies provide strong evidence that secure caregivers are more effective at providing support to close others (Carnelley et al., 1996, Feeney & Collins, 2001; Feeney, 1996; Kane et al., 2007; Kunce & Shaver, 1994). For example, Feeney and

Collins (2001) found that secure adults are sensitive to their partner's cues and willing to provide physical comfort when needed; they are more cooperative than controlling, and are less likely to be overinvolved in their caregiving efforts. In contrast, avoidant individuals are relatively neglectful and controlling, whereas anxious individuals are relatively intrusive, overinvolved, and controlling.

Observational studies provide further evidence of individual differences in support provision. For example, in the study by Collins and Feeney (2000)—in which couples were observed discussing personal stressors—anxious caregivers provided less instrumental support to their partners, were less responsive during their conversations, and exhibited more negative caregiving behavior, especially when their partner's needs were less clear. Other observational studies of couples provide evidence that attachment avoidance, but not anxiety, is associated with less effective support-provision in dyadic interaction (Rholes, Simpson, & Orina, 1999; Simpson et al., 1992).

To examine individual differences in greater depth, Feeney and Collins (2001; Ford et al., 2009) created a laboratory paradigm for studying responsiveness by manipulating the caregiver's belief that his or her partner was either extremely distressed about an upcoming speech task (high need for support) or not at all distressed (low need for support). As discussed previously, caregivers in these studies showed a normative increase in their support effort in response to greater need. However, this increase was much more characteristic of secure than insecure caregivers. For example, in one study (Ford et al., 2009, Study 1), anxious caregivers showed clear evidence of being out of synch with their partner's needs. They failed to increase their support behavior in response to their partner's need, and showed high levels of empathy, mental distraction, and partner focus regardless of their partner's level of distress (a pattern of overinvolvement). Avoidant caregivers showed a clear pattern of relative neglect. Regardless of partner need, they felt less empathy and compassion for their partner, reported less partner focus during their own task, and wrote less supportive messages to their partner. This basic pattern of findings was replicated using a slightly modified procedure in which the speech-giver's level of distress (speech-anxiety) was measured rather than manipulated (Ford et al., 2009, Study 2). Once again, secure spouses displayed a pattern of responsiveness, whereas insecure spouses showed various patterns of unresponsiveness and negative emotional reactions to their partner's distress. For example, insecure-anxious support-providers became more self-focused and reported feeling more angry and frustrated as their partner's level of distress increased; perhaps because they depend heavily on their partners as a source of their own care, and therefore felt threatened when their partner was emotionally needy. Insecure-avoidant support-providers were more tense and angry when their partners were more distressed about the speech (see also Rholes, Simpson, & Orina, 1999).

Taken together, laboratory work provides clear evidence that secure individuals are more sensitive to the needs of their partner and better able to modulate their cognitive, emotional, and behavioral resources in ways that are contingent on their partner's needs (for additional evidence with new acquaintances, see Feeney et al., 2008). In contrast, avoidant individuals are relatively neglectful and unmotivated to provide support, whereas anxious individual are motivated to care for their partners, but have difficulty modulating their responses in accordance with their partner's needs. (See also Mikulincer et al., (2001) and Mikulincer, Shaver, Gillath, & Nitzberg (2005) for causal evidence that the temporary activation of attachment security increases empathy and prosocial responses to nonclose others.)

What mechanisms explain individual differences in support provision? It is important not only to document attachment differences in support behaviors, but also to identify the mechanisms that explain these differences. Collins and colleagues (Collins et al., 2006, 2009; Feeney & Collins, 2001) have suggested that effective support provision requires a constellation of (a) skills and abilities (including support knowledge and adaptive attitudes about support); (b) cognitive, emotional, and tangible resources; and (c) adaptive motives (e.g., felt responsibility for the needs of others, altruistic vs. egoistic motives) that individuals possess to varying degrees. Thus, attachment differences in support provision may be mediated by differences in these factors. Consistent with this idea, Feeney and Collins (2001) found that avoidant adults were unresponsive because they lacked knowledge about how to support others, lacked prosocial orientation, and failed to develop the deep sense of relationship closeness, commitment, and trust that is critical for motivating effective support behavior. The results also revealed that anxious adults tended to be over-involved as support providers because, although they felt close and committed to their partners, they simultaneously distrusted their partners and their support was motivated by self-serving purposes.

In another study, Feeney and Collins (2003) examined in greater depth the degree to which specific motives underlie the provision of responsive or unresponsive support in couples. Because support-provision involves a good deal of responsibility—as well as cognitive, emotional, and sometimes tangible resources—support-providers must be motivated to accept that responsibility and to use their resources in the service of others. Using a self-report measure of support motives that they developed, Feeney and Collins found that avoidant individuals helped their partners for relatively egoistic or selfish reasons (e.g., because they felt obligated to help and wanted to avoid sanctions for not helping, or because they expected to get something in return), whereas anxious individuals helped for both egoistic and altruistic reasons (e.g., because they felt concern for their partner's welfare, but also because they wanted to gain their partner's love or make their partner dependent upon them). These motives, in turn, predicted the quality of support that was provided in the relationship. For example, people who endorsed altruistic motives were more likely to have a high-quality, responsive caregiving style, whereas those who endorsed egoistic motives were more likely to have either a neglectful style or an overinvolved caregiving style. These findings suggest that the underlying motives that people have for helping play a vital role in determining the quality of care that is provided.

More recently, Monin, Feeney, and Schultz (2009) explored emotional mechanisms that might underlie differences in support provision. In two studies, they examined support-providers' emotional reactions to their partners' expressions of anxiety. They predicted that witnessing a partner experience or express anxiety would have negative emotional consequences for insecure support providers (who are unable to regulate their own emotions or who are uncomfortable with emotion expression and with being in a caregiving role). The first study was an observational study in which one member of a couple was exposed to a stressor (a public speech task) and was unobtrusively observed; the second study was an experimental study in which participants watched standardized videos of clear versus ambiguous expressions of emotion (anxiety) in a stressful situation. Consistent with predictions, insecure-avoidant individuals felt angry (as reported by couple members and coded by independent observers) in response to their partners' expression of anxiety, whereas insecure-anxious individuals felt anxious. These negative emotional reactions to others' distress are likely to impede effective support-provision.

Research on Secure-Base Support Processes: Support of Exploration

People routinely assign credit for their accomplishments to the support of significant people in their lives who have helped them achieve their goals and reach their potential. However, with few exceptions (e.g., Brunstein et al., 1996; Ruehlman & Wolchik, 1988) there has been virtually no empirical work on how support from others may contribute to an individual's goal seeking and exploratory behavior. In response to this gap, Feeney and colleagues (Feeney, 2004; 2007; Feeney & Thrush, 2010) have launched a program of research to explore normative secure base processes (and individual differences) using the attachment theoretical framework described above.

Normative Secure Base Processes

In an initial exploration of some of the basic interpersonal processes involved in the provision of secure base support, Feeney (2004) investigated the paths described in Figure 13.1 (paths a–d), in order to determine whether this model accurately captured secure base processes. To test this model, couples were given an opportunity to discuss personal goals in the laboratory. Couple members then reported on a variety of cognitive and emotional responses, and the videotapes were coded by independent raters. Findings supported the basic processes outlined in Figure 13.1. Specifically, support-recipients sought more support from their partner when they viewed their goals as more daunting (i.e., when they were lower in self-efficacy and felt that their goals were less achievable; path a). In addition, support-provider and recipient behaviors were also meshed in complementary ways (path b). For example, when support-providers were more sensitive and responsive to their partner (as coded by observers), support-recipients discussed their goals in a more confident manner and showed warmth and positivity during the discussion. Findings also showed that specific support-provision behaviors exhibited during the discussion predicted the recipients' perceptions of having been supported (path c). For example, when support providers were more sensitive and responsive during the discussion (as coded by observers), support-recipients rated their partner as having been more encouraging and supportive, and less disappointing or critical. In contrast, when support-providers minimized the importance of their partner's goals or maximized the negative features of these goals, then support-recipients rated their partner as having been rude and critical. Lastly, perceptions of secure base support predicted immediate changes in support recipients' well-being and goal strivings (path *d*). Specifically, when participants perceived their partner as supportive of their goals during the discussion, they experienced significant increases in state self-esteem and positive mood, and increased likelihood of achieving their goals.

In another phase of this study, Feeney (2004) investigated paths *c* and *d* of the model by experimentally manipulating an important aspect of secure base support (via an instant messaging system) to examine immediate consequences for support-recipients. Specifically, an important function of a secure base is to be ready to respond when called upon, but to intervene actively in a partner's explorations only when necessary. Support that is excessive and not in synch with a partner's needs may be ineffective, as it may actually undermine the partner's striving. Thus, according to the theoretical model outlined earlier, intrusive secure base support should be perceived by recipients as unresponsive (path *c*) and should therefore lead to poor outcomes (path *d*). To test this assumption, Feeney manipulated support-provider intrusiveness as one member of each couple (the support-recipient) worked on a laboratory exploration activity (a computer puzzle). There were two intrusive conditions and two nonintrusive conditions. In the *intrusive* conditions, the support-recipient was interrupted frequently with supportive messages that were either controlling (providing answers or telling the partner what to do—an *intrusive-controlling* condition) or emotionally supportive (providing positive feedback

or encouragement—an *intrusive-supportive* condition). In the *nonintrusive* conditions, the support-recipient received either two encouraging messages (*nonintrusive-supportive* condition) or no messages at all (*control* condition). First, as predicted, the intrusive conditions were rated as less supportive than the nonintrusive conditions (path *c*). Specifically, support-recipients in the two intrusive conditions (especially the intrusive-controlling condition) perceived their partners' *messages* as being more frustrating and insensitive than the nonintrusive supportive condition; they also rated their *partner* as being more intrusive and interfering than the nonintrusive supportive or the control conditions. Second, as predicted, these perceptions of unresponsive support had some immediate negative consequences for the support recipient's well-being (path *d*). Specifically, support-recipients who rated their partner as less supportive overall (i.e., unhelpful, insensitive, intrusive) experienced declines in state self-esteem and positive mood from before to after the puzzle activity.

Feeney and Collins (2004; Feeney, 2004) view the relationship dynamics depicted in Figure 13.1 as processes in which individuals are able to *move in* toward a relationship partner to derive comfort and security when feeling threatened (safe haven) and to *move out* from a relationship partner to learn, explore, and discover when feeling secure and content (secure base). Although it is generally believed that yielding to expressions of dependence creates *less* self-sufficiency, their work presents an alternative view. According to this view (referred to as the "dependency paradox"), independence and self-reliance emerge *because* of an individual's ability to depend on relationship partners in times of need (Bowlby, 1979, 1988).

To test this hypothesis, Feeney (2007) measured the acceptance of dependency needs and independent functioning in four ways—through self-reports, observations of each couple's laboratory interactions, the participant's responses to experimentally manipulated assistance from the partner during a laboratory task, and their subsequent goal strivings over time as a function of the degree to which they had accepted dependency. Results provided converging evidence that when one relationship partner accepts the other's dependence, the other partner engages in *more* (not less) autonomous functioning, greater self-sufficiency, greater goal-striving, and greater goal accomplishment.

What Are the Characteristics and Function of a Secure Base?

Another step in this program of research has been to advance theory and research identifying the important characteristics of a secure base, and then examining the influence of the presence/absence of these characteristics on exploration behavior in adulthood. To accomplish this goal, Feeney and Thrush (2010) studied married couples who, in two laboratory sessions, provided reports of relationship dynamics involving exploration and then participated in an exploration activity that was videotaped and coded by independent observers. First, Feeney and Thrush identified three important characteristics of a secure base: A secure base supports exploration in several ways, if they are needed—(1) *being available* (e.g., to assist in removing obstacles, to respond to distress cues, to accept dependence); (2) *not interfering with exploration*; and (3) *encouraging and accepting exploration*. Second, they showed that these secure base support features predicted the support-recipient's performance-related outcomes. For example, when support-providers expressed more encouragement, their partners showed greater enthusiasm in exploration; when support-providers displayed more interference, their partners were less likely to persist at their exploratory task. Finally, the three secure base qualities also predicted changes in the recipients' self-esteem and mood. For example, spouse encouragement predicted positive changes in mood, whereas interference predicted decreases in state self-esteem.

Individual Differences in Secure Base Processes

Do individual differences in attachment style predict the provision and receipt of secure base support? In an initial investigation of this question, Feeney and Thrush (2010) examined attachment style differences in self-report, partner-report, and observational assessments of three components of secure base support in couples. Results indicated that insecure-avoidant spouses were less available to their partners during exploration, whereas insecure-anxious spouses were available but less likely to encourage exploration and more likely to interfere with it. With regard to who is more or less likely to receive secure base support from their partners, results indicated that the spouses of insecure individuals (avoidant and anxious) were less available to them during exploration, and insecure-avoidant individuals were less likely to receive encouragement to explore. Although more work needs to be done in this area, these results demonstrate that the characteristics of *both* interaction partners matter in predicting secure base support, consistent with the view that social support is an *interpersonal* process that is shaped by the needs, skills, motives, and resources of both members of a dyad.

Finally, Feeney and Collins (2009) have shown that secure and insecure individuals also differ in their motives for providing, or failing to provide, secure base support. Using a new measure that parallels the measure they designed for safe-haven support, this study indicates that insecure caregivers (high anxiety and/or avoidance) support their spouse's exploratory efforts for relatively egoistic reasons—to avoid pursuing their own goals, to avoid negative partner responses, and to get something in return. Anxious providers also reported supporting their spouse as a way of staying connected and keeping their partner committed. With regard to motives for *not* helping, anxious and avoidant caregivers reported that they sometimes fail to support their spouse's exploration because they feel jealous of their spouse's activities, lack skills, lack a sense of responsibility, perceive their partner's goals as unimportant, and desire to punish their partner. In addition, anxious caregivers reported that they sometimes fail to support their spouse's exploration because they worry that their partner's goal pursuits will harm or threaten their relationship. These findings help explain *why* insecure individuals may be less willing and able to serve as a secure base for their romantic partners; and, more broadly, they provide important insights into the many different factors that may enhance or inhibit effective secure base support in couples.

CONCLUDING STATEMENT

. . . human beings of all ages are happiest and able to deploy their talents to best advantage when they are confident that, standing behind them, there are one or more trusted persons who will come to their aid should difficulties arise. (Bowlby, 1979, p. 103)

Our goal in this chapter was to explore some of the intra- and interpersonal mechanisms that shape social support dynamics in close relationships, and to consider the importance of social support for healthy personality and relationship functioning. Consistent with attachment theory, the findings reviewed in this chapter suggest that adults—like children—are most likely to thrive when they have close relationship partners who provide a safe haven of comfort when needed and a secure base from which to explore. The findings also make it clear that individual differences in attachment style play an important role in determining whether people develop the type of mutually supportive relationships that are necessary for optimal functioning.

The systematic study of social support as an interpersonal process is still in its early stages and much more work is needed to examine specific components of safe-haven and secure-base support processes, and the

ways in which these processes are facilitated or impeded by attachment styles and other important individual differences variables (e.g., personality factors, gender roles, cultural norms). We look forward to future work on these topics. In addition, although most of the empirical work has focused on romantic couples, we believe that the basic processes discussed in this chapter apply to other relationships of emotional significance in adulthood; but these applications await further investigation. We hope that this chapter inspires additional empirical work in this area, and moves the field toward more refined and integrative theoretical models.

References

Ainsworth, M. D. S., Blehar, M. C., Waters, E., & Wall, S. (1978). *Patterns of attachment: psychological study of the strange situation*. Hillsdale, NJ: Erlbaum.

Barbee, A. P., & Cunningham, M. R. (1995). An experimental approach to social support communications: Interactive coping in close relationships. *Communication Yearbook, 18,* 381–413.

Bartholomew, K., Cobb, R. J., & Poole, J. (1997). Adult attachment patterns and social support processes. In G. R. Pierce, B. Lakey, I. G. Sarason, & B. R. Sarason (Eds.), *Sourcebook of social support and personality*. New York: Plenum Press.

Bartholomew, K., & Horowitz, L. M. (1991). Attachment styles among young adults: A test of a four-category model. *Journal of Personality and Social Psychology, 61,* 226–244.

Bowlby, J. (1973). *Attachment and loss: Vol. 2. Separation*. New York: Basic Books.

Bowlby, J. (1979). *The making and breaking of affectional bonds*. London: Tavistock.

Bowlby, J. (1982). *Attachment and loss: Vol. 1. Attachment* (2nd ed.). New York: Basic Books.

Bowlby, J. (1988). *A secure base*. New York: Basic Books.

Brennan, K. A., Clark, C. L., & Shaver, P. R. (1998). Self-report measurement of adult attachment: An integrative overview. In J. A. Simpson & W. S. Rholes (Eds.), *Attachment theory and close relationships* (pp. 46–76). New York: Guilford Press.

Bretherton, I. (1985). Attachment theory: Retrospect and prospect. *Monographs of the Society for Research in Child Development*, 50, 3–35.

Bretherton, I. (1987). New perspectives on attachment relations: Security, communication, and internal working models. In J. D. Osofsky (Ed.), *Handbook of infant development* (2nd ed., pp. 1061–1100). New York: John Wiley & Sons.

Brunstein, J. C., Dangelmayer, G., & Schultheiss, O. C. (1996). Personal goals and social support in close relationships: Effects on relationship mood and marital satisfaction. *Journal of Personality and Social Psychology*, 71, 1006–1019.

Carnelley, K. B., Pietromonaco, P. R., & Jaffe, K. (1996). Attachment, caregiving, and relationship functioning in couples: Effects of self and partner. *Personal Relationships*, 3, 257–278.

Carnelley, K., & Ruscher, J. (2000). Adult attachment and exploratory behavior in leisure. *Journal of Social Behavior and Personality*, 15, 153–165.

Coan, J., Schaefer, H. S., & Davidson, R. J. (2006). Lending a hand: Social regulation of the neural response to threat. *Psychological Science*, 17, 1032–1039.

Cohen, S. (2005). The Pittsburgh common cold studies: Psychosocial predictors of susceptibility to respiratory infectious illness. *International Journal of Behavioral Medicine*, 12, 123–131.

Collins, N. L., & Feeney, B. C. (2000). A safe haven: An attachment theory perspective on support-seeking and caregiving in adult romantic relationships. *Journal of Personality and Social Psychology*, 78, 1053–1073.

Collins, N. L., & Feeney, B. C. (2004a). An attachment theory perspective on closeness and intimacy. In D. Mashek, & A. Aron (Eds.), *Handbook of Closeness and Intimacy*. Mahwah, NJ: Erlbaum.

Collins, N. L., & Feeney, B. C. (2004b). Working models of attachment shape perceptions of social support: Evidence from experimental and observational studies. *Journal of Personality and Social Psychology*, 87, 363–383.

Collins, N. L., & Feeney, B. C. (2005, May). *Attachment processes in intimate relationships: Support-seeking and caregiving behavior in daily interaction*. Paper presented at the meeting of the American Psychological Society, Los Angeles, CA.

Collins, N. L., & Feeney, B. C. (2010). An attachment theoretical perspective on social support dynamics in couples: Normative processes and individual difference. In K. Sullivan & J. Davila (Eds.), *Support processes in intimate relationships* (pp. 89–120). New York: Oxford University Press.

Collins, N. L., Ford, M. B., Guichard, A. C., & Feeney, B. C. (2006). Responding to need in intimate relationships: Normative processes and individual differences. In M. Mikulincer & G. Goodman (Eds.), *The dynamics of love: Attachment, caregiving, and sex*. New York: Guilford Press.

Collins, N. L., Ford, M. B., Guichard, A. C., Kane, H. S., & Feeney, B. C. (2009). Responding to need in intimate relationships: Social support and caregiving processes in couples. In M. Mikulincer & P. R. Shaver (Eds.), *Prosocial motives, emotions, and behavior* (pp. 367–389). Washington DC: American Psychological Association.

Collins, N. L., Guichard, A. C., Ford, M. B., & Feeney, B. C. (2004). Working models of attachment: New developments and emerging themes. In W. S. Rholes & J. A. Simpson (Eds.), *Adult attachment: Theory, research, and clinical implications* (pp. 196–239). New York: Guilford Press.

Collins, N. L., Jaremka, L., & Kane, H. S. (2009). *Social support during a stressful task attenuates cortisol reactivity and promotes relationship closeness and security: An experimental study*. Unpublished manuscript, University of California, Santa Barbara.

Collins, N, L., Kane, H. S., Guichard, A. C., & Ford, M. B. (2009). *Will you be there when I need you? Perceived partner responsiveness shapes support-seeking behavior and motivations*. Unpublished manuscript, University of California, Santa Barbara.

Cutrona, C. E. (1996). Social support as a determinant of marital quality: The interplay of negative and supportive behaviors. In G. R. Pierce, B. R. Sarason, & I. G. Sarason (Eds.), *Handbook of social support and the family* (pp. 173–194). New York: Plenum Press.

Cutrona, C. E., & Suhr, J. A. (1994). Social support communication in the context of marriage: An analysis of couples' supportive interactions. In B. R. Burleson, T. L. Albrecht, & I. G. Sarason (Eds.), *Communication of social support: Messages, interactions, relationships, and community*. Thousand Oaks, CA: Sage.

Dunkel-Schetter, C., Blasband, D. E., Feinstein, L. G., & Herbert, T. B. (1992). Elements of supportive interactions: When are attempts to help effective? In S. Spacapan & S. Oskamp (Eds.), *Helping and being helped: Naturalistic studies. The Claremont Symposium on Applied Psychology* (pp. 83–114). Newbury Park, CA: Sage.

Elliot, A. J., & Reis, H. T. (2003). Attachment and exploration in adulthood. *Journal of Personality and Social Psychology, 85*, 317–331.

Feeney, B. C. (2004). A secure base: Responsive support of goal strivings and exploration in adult intimate relationships. *Journal of Personality and Social Psychology, 87*, 631–648.

Feeney, B. C. (2007). The dependency paradox in close relationships: Accepting dependence promotes independence. *Journal of Personality and Social Psychology, 92*, 268–285.

Feeney, B. C., Cassidy, J., & Ramos-Marcuse, F. (2008). The generalization of attachment representations to new social situations: Predicting behavior during initial interactions with strangers. *Journal of Personality and Social Psychology, 95*, 1481–1498.

Feeney, B. C., & Collins, N. L. (2001). Predictors of caregiving in adult intimate relationships: An attachment theoretical perspective. *Journal of Personality and Social Psychology, 80*, 972–994.

Feeney, B. C., & Collins, N. L. (2003). Motivations for caregiving in adult intimate relationships: Influences on caregiving behavior and relationship functioning. *Personality and Social Psychology Bulletin, 29*, 950–968.

Feeney, B. C., & Collins, N. L. (2004). Interpersonal safe haven and secure base caregiving processes in adulthood. In J. Simpson & S. Rholes (Eds.), *Adult attachment: New directions and emerging issues.* New York: Guilford Press.

Feeney, B. C., & Collins, N. L. (2009). *Motivations for providing secure base support in couples: Influences on support behavior and relationship functioning.* Unpublished raw data, Carnegie Mellon University.

Feeney, B. C., & Thrush, R. L. (2010). Relationship influences on exploration in adulthood: The characteristics and function of a secure base. *Journal of Personality and Social Psychology, 98*, 57–76.

Feeney, J. A. (1996). Attachment, caregiving, and marital satisfaction. *Personal Relationships, 3*, 401–416.

Ford, M. B., Guichard, A. C., & Collins, N. L. (2009). *Responding to need in intimate relationships: Cognitive, emotional, and behavioral responses to partner distress.* Unpublished manuscript, University of California Santa Barbara.

Florian, V., Mikulincer, M., & Bucholtz, I. (1995). Effects of adult attachment style on the perception and search for social support. *The Journal of Psychology, 129*, 665–676.

Fraley, R. C., & Shaver, P. R. (1998). Airport separations: A naturalistic study of adult attachment dynamics in separating couples. *Journal of Personality and Social Psychology, 75*, 1198–1212.

Fraley, R. C., & Shaver, P. R. (2000). Adult romantic attachment: Theoretical developments, emerging controversies, and unanswered questions. *Review of General Psychology, 4*, 132–154.

Fraley, R. C., & Waller, N. G. (1998). Adult attachment patterns: A test of the typological model. In J. A. Simpson & W. S. Rholes (Eds.), *Attachment theory and close relationships* (pp. 77–114). New York: Guilford Press.

George, C., & Solomon, J. (1999). Attachment and caregiving: The caregiving behavioral system. In J. Cassidy & P. P. Shaver (Eds.), *Handbook of attachment: Theory, research, and clinical applications* (pp. 649–670). New York: Guilford Press.

Gleason, M. E. J., Iida, M., Shrout, P. E., & Bolger, N. (2008). Receiving support as a mixed blessing: Evidence for dual effects of support on psychological outcomes. *Journal of Personality and Social Psychology, 94*, 824–838.

Hazan, C., & Shaver, P. R. (1987). Romantic love conceptualized as an attachment process. *Journal of Personality and Social Psychology, 52*, 511–524.

Hazan, C., & Shaver, P. R. (1990). Love and work: An attachment-theoretical perspective. *Journal of Personality and Social Psychology, 59*, 270–280.

Ida, M., Seidman, G., Shrout, P. E., Fujita, K., & Bolger, N. (2008). Modeling support provision in intimate relationships. *Journal of Personality and Social Psychology, 94*, 460–478.

Julien, D., & Markman, H. J. (1991). Social support and social networks as determinants of individual and marital outcomes. *Journal of Social and Personal Relationships, 8*, 549–568.

Kane, H. S., Jaremka, L. M., Guichard, A. C., Ford, M. B., Collins, N. L., & Feeney, B. C. (2007). Feeling supported and feeling satisfied: How one partner's attachment style predicts the other partner's relationship experiences. *Journal of Social and Personal Relationships, 24*, 535–555.

Kane, H. S, McCall, C., Collins, N. L., & Blascovich, J. A. (2009). Mere presence is not enough: the effects of partner responsiveness on coping with stress in an immersive virtual environment. Manuscript under review, *Psychological Science*.

Kobak, R. R., & Sceery, A. (1988). Attachment in late adolescence: Working models, affect regulation, and representations of self and others. *Child Development, 59*, 135–146.

Kunce, L. J., & Shaver, P. R. (1994). An attachment-theoretical approach to caregiving in romantic relationships. In K. Bartholomew & D. Perlman (Eds.), *Advances in personal relationships* (Vol. 5, pp. 205–237). London: Jessica Kingsley.

Mikulincer, M., & Florian, V. (1995). Appraisal of and coping with a real-life stressful situation: The contribution of attachment styles. *Personality and Social Psychology Bulletin, 21*, 406–414.

Mikulincer, M., Birnbaum, G., Woddis, D., & Nachmias, O. (2000). Stress and accessibility of proximity-related thoughts: Exploring the normative and intraindivdiual components of attachment theory. *Journal of Personality and Social Psychology, 78*, 509–523.

Mikulincer, M., Gillath, O., & Shaver, P. R. (2002). Activation of the attachment system in adulthood: Threat-related primes increase the accessibility of mental representations of attachment figures. *Journal of Personality and Social Psychology, 83*, 881–895.

Mikulincer, M., Gillath, O., Halevy, V., Avihou, N., Avidan, S., & Eshkoli, N. (2001). Attachment theory and reactions to others' needs: Evidence that activation of the sense of attachment security promotes empathic responses. *Journal of Personality and Social Psychology, 81*, 1205–1224.

Mikulincer, M., & Shaver, P. R. (2003). The attachment behavioral system in adulthood: Activation, psychodynamics, and interpersonal processes. In M. P. Zanna (Ed.), *Advances in experimental social psychology* (Vol. 35, pp. 53–152). New York: Academic Press.

Mikulincer, M., & Shaver, P. R., (2005). Attachment security, compassion, and altruism. *Current Directions in Psychological Science, 14*, 34–38.

Mikulincer, M., Shaver, P. R., Gillath, O., & Nitzberg, R. A. (2005). Attachment, caregiving, and altruim: Boosting attachment security increases compassion and helping. *Journal of Personality and Social Psychology, 89*, 817–839.

Monin, J. K., Feeney, B. C., & Schultz, R. (2009). *Individual differences in emotional reactions to partners' anxiety expression.* Unpublished manuscript, Carnegie Mellon University.

Ognibene, T. C., & Collins, N. L. (1998). Adult attachment styles, perceived social support, and coping strategies. *Journal of Social and Personal Relationships, 15*, 323–345.

Pasch, L. A., Bradbury, T. N., & Sullivan, K. T. (1997). Social support in marriage: An analysis of intraindividual and interpersonal components. In G. R. Pierce, B. Lakey, I. G. Sarason, & B. R. Sarason (Eds.), *Sourcebook of social support and personality* (pp. 229–256). New York: Plenum Press.

Reblin, M., & Uchino, B. N. (2008). Social and emotional support and its implications for health. *Current Opinions in Psychiatry, 21*, 201–205.

Reis, H. T., & Patrick, B. C. (1996). Attachment and intimacy: Component processes. In E. T. Higgins, & A. W. Kruglanski (Eds.), *Social psychology: Handbook of basic principles* (pp. 523–563). New York: Guilford Press.

Reis, H. T., & Shaver, P. (1988). Intimacy as an interpersonal process. In S. Duck & D. F. Hay (Eds.), *Handbook of personal relationships: Theory, research, and interventions* (pp. 367–389). Chichester, UK: John Wiley & Sons.

Rholes, W. S., Simpson, J. A., & Orina, M. M. (1999). Attachment and anger in an anxiety-provoking situation. *Journal of Personality and Social Psychology, 76*, 940–957.

Rini, C., Dunkel-Schetter, C., Hobel, C. J., Glynn, L. M., & Sandman, C. A. (2006). Effective social support: Antecedents and consequences of partner support during pregnancy. *Personal Relationships, 13*, 207–229.

Ruehlman, L. S., & Wolchik, S. A. (1988). Personal goals and interpersonal support and hindrance as factors in psychological distress and well-being. *Journal of Personality and Social Psychology, 55*, 293–301.

Sarason, B. R., Sarason, I. G., & Gurung, R. A. R. (1997). Close personal relationships in health outcomes: A key to the role of social support. In S. Duck (Ed.), *Handbook of personal relationships: Theory, research, and interventions* (2nd ed., pp. 547–573). Chichester, UK: John Wiley & Sons.

Shaver, P. R., & Mikulincer, M. (2007). Adult attachment strategies and the regulation of emotions.

In J. J. Gross (Ed.), *Handbook of emotion regulation* (pp. 446–465). New York: Guilford Press.

Shaver, P. R., Mikulincer, M., & Shemesh-Iron, M. (2009). A behavioral systems perspective on prosocial behavior. In M. Mikulincer & P. R. Shaver (Eds.), *Prosocial motives, emotions, and behavior* (pp. 73–92). Washington, DC: American Psychological Association.

Simpson, J. A., Rholes, W. S., & Nelligan, J. S. (1992). Support seeking and support giving within couples in an anxiety-provoking situation: The role of attachment styles. *Journal of Personality and Social Psychology, 62*, 434–446.

Waters, E., & Cummings, E. (2000). A secure base from which to explore close relationships. *Child Development, 71*, 164–172.

14 CONCEPTUALIZING RELATIONSHIP VIOLENCE AS A DYADIC PROCESS

Kim Bartholomew

Rebecca J. Cobb

All couples face situations in which partners have conflicting personal or relational goals. The strong interdependence between intimate partners creates ample opportunities for such conflict, conflict that sometimes results in violence. Intimate partner violence (IPV) is disturbingly common in marital relationships (e.g., 16% prevalence in the past year; Straus & Gelles, 1986) and even more common in dating and same-sex relationships (e.g., Straus, 2004; Statistics Canada, 2005). Contrary to the stereotype that IPV consists of men aggressing against female partners, men and women report similar rates of IPV (Archer, 2000). We present a framework for organizing the IPV research literature based on the premise that relationships are inherently interactional. Relationships reside in the interplay of both partners' dispositions and how this interplay unfolds over time in a range of contexts. Therefore, any relationship behavior, including IPV, can only be fully understood in the context of the couple system (cf. Reiss, Capobianco, & Tsai, 2002).

Feminist perspectives on IPV have traditionally asked "Why do men beat their wives?" (Bograd, 1988), and answered that men control their wives through violence as part of a patriarchal system of male privilege and female subordination. Thus, IPV is defined as primarily a sociological problem, rather than a psychological or relationship problem. Feminist perspectives have been instrumental in galvanizing societal attention and action on violence against women. However, there are major problems with the patriarchal perspective on IPV: some of its core tenets are contradicted by empirical research, it fails to address the full range of partner abuse (including IPV by women and same-sex partners), and interventions based on this perspective are generally ineffective (Babcock, Canady, Graham, & Schart, 2007; Dutton & Corvo, 2006; Dutton & Nicholls, 2005). As well, work from this perspective has been conducted with little reference to literature on intimate relationships or to the broader literatures on aggression and interpersonal processes.

Although feminist perspectives continue to guide public policy and popular discourse on IPV, the research and clinical communities are moving toward more complex, empirically based understandings of

Acknowledgments: We thank Don Dutton, Erika Lawrence, and the editors for their helpful comments on earlier drafts of this chapter.

IPV (Hamel & Nicholls, 2007). Psychological perspectives on IPV ask "Why do some individuals abuse their intimate partners?" (e.g., Dutton, 2007; Ehrensaft, 2008). These perspectives have been fruitful in explaining the developmental trajectories and psychological makeup of perpetrators of IPV, but are limited by a failure to consider the dyadic context of IPV (cf. Bartholomew & Allison, 2006). Interactional perspectives—a more recent development—ask "What are the relational and situational contexts in which IPV occurs?" (e.g., Winstok, 2007). These approaches have greatly expanded our understanding of IPV, but they have not generally incorporated personality and background factors of relationship partners.

In Figure 14.1, we present a model for organizing the IPV literature. The model addresses individual background and dispositional characteristics of partners (P1 and P2), how partners' predispositions interact to establish their relationship context, and the situational contexts in which relational

patterns give rise to violent interactions (cf. Capaldi & Kim, 2007). At each stage of the model, partners may reciprocally influence one another, and (though not depicted in Figure 14.1) later stages may feedback to earlier stages. Generally, we expect factors earlier in the model to impact IPV to the extent that they are mediated by subsequent steps. Thus, regardless of individual dispositions toward violence, partners in mutually satisfying relationships characterized by trust, benevolent partner attributions, and constructive communication would not be at risk for IPV. (Unfortunately, vulnerable individuals may find it challenging to establish and maintain such a positive relationship!) Moreover, even in distressed relationships with entrenched patterns of hostility, IPV does not occur randomly. It occurs when the situational and interactional context triggers and sustains violent impulses by one or both partners.

We selectively review research relevant to each step of the model, with particular focus on the situational context because

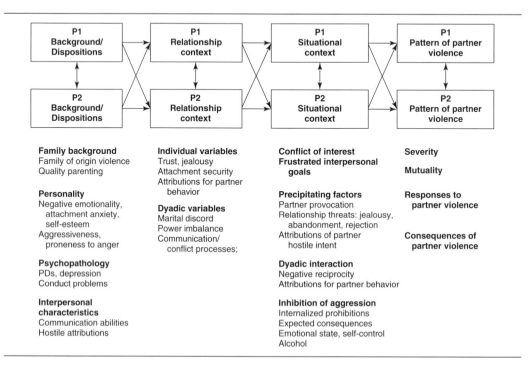

FIGURE 14.1   A Dyadic Model of Partner Violence

it has received the least attention. There are some limitations to the framework in Figure 14.1. First, the model does not explicitly incorporate the broader social and cultural systems in which individual, relational, and situational contexts are embedded. Second, reflecting the empirical literature, we focus on the perpetration of IPV. However, given the high level of reciprocal abuse in intimate relationships, predictors of IPV receipt are generally similar (e.g., Magdol et al., 1997). Also reflecting the empirical literature, we focus on physical rather than psychological abuse. However, psychological abuse (including verbal aggression and controlling behavior) predicts the onset of IPV, coexists with IPV, and can have just as deleterious effects as IPV on individuals and relationships (O'Leary, 1999). We expect the proposed model to apply to psychological abuse, with one caveat: for women, IPV appears to exist on a continuum with psychological abuse, but for men IPV may represent a qualitative increase in abusiveness, given the strong normative prohibitions against men assaulting women (cf. Stets, 1990). Finally, although research has focused on risk factors for male-to-female IPV, similar patterns of findings generally hold across gender and across relationship type (gay, heterosexual; dating, marital, and cohabiting) (e.g., Medeiros & Straus, 2006, 2007; Bartholomew, Regan, Oram, & Landolt, 2008). Therefore, we address gender only when there are theoretical or empirical reasons to expect that gender moderates associations with IPV.

BACKGROUND AND DISPOSITIONAL FACTORS

A large body of psychological research addresses the question of why some people in a given culture perpetrate violence against intimate partners and others do not (the link between Background/Dispositions and IPV in Figure 14.1). The rationale guiding much of this work is that childhood experiences in the family impact emotional and social functioning, putting individuals at greater or lesser risk for future IPV. For example, social learning perspectives suggest that exposure to family violence teaches children that aggression is a viable means of dealing with interpersonal conflict, which increases the likelihood of future IPV in conflict situations (Dutton, 2006). Alternatively, attachment perspectives suggest that inadequate parenting leads to anxious attachment orientations in children, leading to hypersensitivity to abandonment in intimate relationships, and to a risk of aggressing against partners as a form of protest behavior to maintain contact with an intimate partner (Bartholomew & Allison, 2006).

Consistent with developmental models of IPV, retrospective reports of adverse experiences in the family of origin (including witnessing interparental violence, maltreatment, parental rejection, and negative family environment) predict IPV in adult relationships (Dutton, 2006). IPV is also concurrently associated with a host of personal and interpersonal qualities: personal vulnerability (notably attachment insecurity, dependency, and low self-esteem); aggressive, angry, and antisocial tendencies (including childhood conduct problems); psychopathology (notably borderline personality, depression, and trauma symptoms); dysfunctional interpersonal patterns (e.g., hostile/dominance, poor social skills, hostile attribution bias); and attitudes toward the acceptability of IPV (Dutton, 2006).

Most research linking individual factors with IPV is cross-sectional, raising the possibility that experiences of IPV influence retrospective childhood reports and even enduring dispositions. For example, the link between anxious attachment and IPV could indicate that abusive relationships undermine attachment security. Similarly, the link between attitudes toward IPV and perpetration of IPV (found consistently only for men) could indicate a post hoc justification for IPV. In the last decade, prospective studies have examined how childhood family and personal factors relate to subsequent IPV. Across studies, the strongest and most consistent predictors of IPV are child and adolescent conduct problems (e.g., Ehrensaft, Moffit, & Caspi, 2004; Woodward, Fergusson, & Horwood, 2002), negative emotionality (indicating vulnerability, reactivity, and proneness to anger) (e.g., Moffitt, Krueger, Caspi, & Fagan, 2000), and adolescent depression (e.g., Ehrensaft, Moffit, & Caspi, 2006). These studies confirm cross-sectional associations between adverse childhood experiences and adult IPV (e.g., Ehrensaft et al., 2003) and confirm that this link is mediated, at least in part, by adolescent behavioral and emotional problems (Ehrensaft, 2008). Though not consistent across studies, there is some indication of more severe pathology and deviance in adolescent boys who go on to perpetrate IPV than in girls who go on to perpetrate IPV (e.g., Ehrensaft et al., 2004; Magdol et al., 1997).

Because individual risk factors are assessed before entry into romantic relationships, prospective studies provide an opportunity to consider *both* partners' contributions to the development of IPV. In a New Zealand birth cohort, negative emotionality (assessed at 18 years of age) predicted abuse perpetration by both partners in established heterosexual relationships three years later (Moffitt, Robins, & Caspi, 2001). Moreover, each partner's negative emotionality was as strong a predictor of their partner's abuse as of their own abuse (cross-partner effects). Another analysis from the same cohort indicated that the most severely violent relationships at ages 24 to 26 were comprised of *two* partners characterized by adolescent risk factors (Ehrensaft et al., 2004). Similarly, in a longitudinal study of at-risk youth, women's antisocial behavior and depression predicted their male partners' later aggression (Kim & Capaldi, 2004).

Longitudinal studies also indicate a moderate degree of assortative mating on antisocial behavior (Kim & Capaldi, 2004; Krueger, Moffitt, Caspi, Bleske, & Silva,

1998). Thus, young people tend to select mates who share risk factors for future IPV, and then they mutually influence each other's tendencies to engage in partner abuse. These effects are consistent with conceptualizing IPV as arising in a relational context and highlight the inadequacy of focusing on only one member of the dyad to understand a dyadic phenomenon.

RELATIONSHIP CONTEXT

Dyadic relationships emerge from the interaction of the enduring characteristics of two partners in specific contexts. There is considerable indirect evidence that IPV is a dyadic phenomenon. For instance, both partners' background characteristics predict IPV perpetration and victimization, and there is strong mutuality of abuse in intimate relationships (Bartholomew & Allison, 2006). Individuals' IPV is more stable within relationships than across relationships in young adulthood, indicating that dyadic factors impact IPV (Capaldi, Shortt, & Crosby, 2003; Robins, Caspi, & Moffitt, 2002). However, studies linking both partners' characteristics to IPV do not directly address the relationship context in which IPV arises.

Violence by one or both partners is robustly associated with relationship dissatisfaction (e.g., Williams & Frieze, 2005). Thus, it is not surprising that the relational predictors of IPV parallel the predictors of global relationship dissatisfaction. Various individual-level variables indicative of insecurity and distrust in a relationship are associated with IPV. Notably, individuals who aggress against partners tend to make negative attributions for their partners' behavior, and tend to view their partners as critical, rejecting, intentionally hurtful, and malicious (e.g., Scott & Straus, 2007). Other established correlates of IPV include marital discord (Coleman & Straus, 1990), skills deficits in dealing with marital problems (e.g., Anglin & Holtzworth-Munroe, 1997), and a lack of egalitarian decision making (in favor of either spouse), which likely contributes to marital conflict (e.g., Coleman & Straus, 1990).

Not only are various relational variables predictive of IPV, but the relationship context moderates the impact of individual risk factors for perpetrating IPV. For example, husband hostility and alcohol abuse predict partner abuse only among men who are maritally distressed (Leonard & Senchak, 1993). Moreover, partners' personal qualities likely predict IPV to the extent that they impact experiences in their relationships. In the few studies that include background/dispositional and relational predictors of IPV, relational variables, such as marital satisfaction and attributions for partner behavior, are stronger correlates of partner aggression than background predictors and largely mediate associations between background factors and aggression (e.g., O'Leary, Smith Slep, & O'Leary, 2007).

Predispositions of both partners likely interact in predicting IPV. For example, Roberts and Noller (1998) found that couples comprised of one partner high in attachment anxiety and one partner high in avoidance of intimacy had elevated risk for IPV. They speculate that incompatibilities in desired levels of closeness lead the more anxious partners to use violence in an attempt to gain their partners' attention. Such aggressive demands lead avoidant partners to withdraw further, exacerbating anxious partners' fear of abandonment. Thus, both partners play a role in establishing relational patterns, and partners mutually impact one another over time.

The most direct approach to assessing the relational context of partner abuse may be to examine conflict behavior of couples with IPV. With few exceptions, behavioral studies have focused on male violence in marital and cohabiting relationships. Virtually no work considers IPV in same-sex relationships, in dating relationships, or in relationships characterized by women's abuse of men (for a notable exception, see Capaldi & Crosby, 1997). However, in couples selected for husband violence, wives also report perpetrating high levels of IPV (e.g., Cordova, Jacobson, Gottman, Rushe, & Cox, 1993).

Thus, this literature also sheds light on the context in which mutual violence arises.

In observational studies, both partners in couples with a violent husband show high levels of aversive behavior and affect, and high reciprocity of negativity in problem-solving discussions (Holtzworth-Munroe, Smutzler, & Bates, 1997). Partners tend to respond to each other's negativity (e.g., hostile anger and expressions of criticism, contempt, and belligerence) with negativity, resulting in escalation. In contrast, satisfied couples do not tend to reciprocate aversive partner behavior with further negativity, thereby containing the conflict and avoiding escalation (e.g., Cordova et al., 1993). The importance of negative reciprocity in setting the context for IPV is also indicated by cross-dyad influences on partner aggression in short-term longitudinal studies of couples; over time, aggression by one partner tends to elicit aggression by the other (e.g., O'Leary & Smith Slep, 2003; Schumacher & Leonard, 2005).

Of interest, there is some evidence that in dissatisfied but nonviolent couples, wives tend to show higher negativity and verbal aggressiveness than husbands, while husbands tend to show higher withdrawal and defensiveness (e.g., Jacobson et al., 1994; Babcock, Waltz, Jacobson, & Gottman, 1993). This pattern suggests that as long as only one person acts overtly aggressive (most often the wife), and the partner does not reciprocate, the conflict is unlikely to escalate to severe violence (at least by the husband) (cf. Leonard & Senchak, 1996). Consistent with this interpretation, young heterosexual couples with low, nonclinical levels of partner abuse were characterized by higher IPV by female partners, whereas severely abusive relationships were characterized by high IPV by both partners (Ehrensaft et al., 2004).

SITUATIONAL CONTEXT

Given partners' personal risk factors for IPV and their mutually constructed relationship, what are the situational factors that affect the occurrence of IPV? This question has received little systematic attention (for exceptions, see Wilkinson & Hamerschlag, 2005; Winstok, 2007). We do know that arguments typically precede IPV (Cascardi & Vivian, 1995; R. E. Dobash & Dobash, 1984), suggesting that IPV occurs during attempts to resolve conflicts of interest. Anger, and potentially IPV, arise when one or both partners are frustrated in meeting their goals, whether the goal is to gain a partner's attention, to have time alone to pursue personal interests, or to have the partner fulfill a household duty. Situational perspectives on IPV examine the interpersonal contexts in which IPV is likely, and the interactional processes leading to IPV. We expect relationship factors to affect the occurrence and nature of conflict situations. For instance, distressed, insecure partners are more likely to experience situations in which they perceive relationship threat. Further, couples with established patterns of negative communication will find it especially difficult to deal constructively with conflicts that arise.

Interpersonal situations may interact with dispositions toward aggression in predicting aggressive outcomes. In a meta-analysis of personality and aggressive behavior, traits indicating vulnerability to provocation (e.g., emotional sensitivity and impulsivity) were only related to aggression under provoking conditions (Bettencourt, Talley, Benjamin, & Valentine, 2006). In a review of the literature linking interpersonal rejection with aggression, Leary, Twenge, and Quinlivan (2006) suggested that individuals who are sensitive to rejection (such as those high in attachment anxiety) are most prone to aggression when faced with rejection. Dutton and Browning (1988) found that violent husbands responded with greater anger and anxiety to videotaped couple arguments related to wife abandonment than did control husbands. Specifically, violent husbands reported more anger in response to a conflict about a wife's demands for independence (such as wanting to spend more time with friends), but did not react more negatively than other husbands to a conflict about a

wife's demands for intimacy (a desire for her husband to open up more) or to a neutral conflict (a disagreement over vacation plans). Person-situation interaction is also evident in the finding that violent husbands can be distinguished from nonviolent husbands by their inability to provide competent responses to scenarios involving wife rejection (Holtzworth-Munroe & Anglin, 1991).

The importance of attachment-related threats (such as abandonment and rejection) in setting the stage for IPV is also evident in qualitative studies of participants' descriptions of IPV. In a study of heterosexual couples identified for male IPV, Allison, Bartholomew, Mayseless, and Dutton (2008) found that male and female violence could often be understood as part of a coherent strategy to regulate closeness and distance. When other strategies failed, individuals sometimes resorted to violence to pursue or to hold on to a partner they perceived to be withdrawing or, conversely, to force distance from a partner making excessive demands for closeness (cf. Roberts & Noller, 1998). Although these strategies were related to dispositional attachment insecurities, the dynamics of these relationships could only be understood by examining the interplay of both partners' attachment orientations and current attachment-related goals. Similarly, in a study of gay men describing violent incidents in same-sex relationships, Stanley, Bartholomew, Taylor, Oram, and Landolt (2006) observed that most violent conflicts involved attachment-relevant threats (such as partner rejection or infidelity) or incompatible needs for closeness versus autonomy. Also, jealousy is one of the most commonly reported precipitants of male IPV against women (for a review, see Wilkinson & Hamerschlag, 2005).

Though the motivational context for IPV can be inferred from conflict descriptions, it may not be feasible to identify motives for specific acts of IPV. Self-reported motives for IPV are subject to reconstruction and may be more accurately thought of as attributions or post hoc justifications for IPV. It is also problematic to assess motives for IPV as though they reside in individuals and are independent of the shifting relational and situational context. Moreover, as conflict escalates, the conflict process can become a source of anxiety and threat, and couples often shift their attention from the original source of conflict to the course of the conflict itself (Winstok & Eisikovits, 2008). Partners may then strike out violently to retaliate against partner abuse (e.g., "He insulted me, so I slapped him"), to escape conflict when faced with a partner who physically blocks exit, or to force engagement with a fleeing partner (Allison et al., 2008). There may also be multiple motives at play in a given situation. For example, an attempt to control a partner's Internet use may also reflect a desire to spend more time with a partner seen as lacking in interest. There is even evidence that motivational conflict—when partners differ in their perceptions of each other's motives in a conflict situation—is associated with elevated verbal aggression (Winstok, 2006b). Hostile attributions for partner behavior likely contribute to misunderstandings of each other's interpersonal goals, further fuelling frustration and anger.

Given the complexities of identifying motives for IPV, it may not be worthwhile to assess specific motives. Rather, aggressive conflict tactics can be seen as attempts to influence or control the partner when more conventional means of influence (e.g., requests, discussion, and compromise) have failed (Archer & Coyne, 2005). More generally, anger and aggression stem from frustration in meeting interpersonal goals (Berkowitz, 1993), and goals related to acceptance, closeness, and autonomy tend to be especially salient in intimate relationships.

The few studies to examine individuals' accounts of the interaction processes leading to IPV suggest that violence typically follows an escalating pattern of negativity by both partners. Consistent with the couple interaction research previously reviewed, Burman, Margolin, and John (1993) found, based on home reenactment of conflicts, that aggressive couples displayed high levels of hostile affect and engaged in reciprocal patterns of hostility. Perpetrators overwhelmingly self-report that their aggressive acts are precipitated by their partners' verbal or physical abuse or by some other negative partner behavior (O'Leary & Smith Slep, 2006). Even in couples selected for severe male violence against female partners, violence is preceded by mutual escalation and each partner views their actions as reactions to their partners' actions (Winstok & Eisikovits, 2008). A priority for future research is to employ daily-diary methods to test whether patterns in retrospective reports of violent episodes are replicated when partners report closer in time to their conflicts. Another priority is to explore the role of hostile attributions for partner behavior in escalating conflict leading to violence (Eckhardt & Dye, 2000).

During couple conflict, individuals experience violent impulses toward intimate partners much more frequently than they act upon them (Finkel, DeWall, Slotter, Oaten, & Foshee, 2009). Finkel (2007) argues that theory and research on factors that impel individuals to perpetrate IPV need to be complemented with attention to factors that *inhibit* aggressive impulses. Notably, internalized norms about the unacceptability of IPV and related expectations about the negative consequences of IPV for the self, the partner, and the relationship may serve to inhibit IPV in conflict situations. We are not aware of research examining the direct role of IPV norms and outcome expectancies in inhibiting impulses toward IPV. However, the literature on IPV norms indicates that men have much stronger attitudes prohibiting male IPV and much more negative outcome expectations for IPV (especially social sanctions) than women have about female IPV (e.g., Miller & Simpson, 1991; Sorenson & Taylor, 2005). In contrast, women might be more likely than men to inhibit IPV out of fear of retaliatory violence by a stronger partner. We speculate that whereas the factors predictive of IPV are generally similar across gender, the inhibiting factors in conflict situations may be more strongly gendered.

Finkel and colleagues (2009) demonstrate that self-regulatory failure may undermine the capacity of individuals to control violent impulses toward intimate partners. Self-regulation is affected by various dispositional, relational, and situational factors. Of note, the strong negative emotions elicited in couple conflict can undermine self-control (Winstok & Eisikovits, 2008). Alcohol consumption may also compromise the capacity of individuals to control violent impulses. In a diary study of men in IPV treatment, drinking was strongly associated with the likelihood of IPV on a given day (Fals-Stewart, 2003). In a laboratory study of marital conflict, both partners in couples in which men received alcohol (relative to a placebo) showed increased verbal negativity (Leonard & Roberts, 1998). This finding demonstrates the power of the dyadic system; a change in one partner (the husband's level of intoxication) was immediately reflected in increased negativity by the other partner. Other laboratory research suggests that alcohol may exacerbate conflict by increasing relational insecurity and hostile partner attributions in men with low-esteem (MacDonald, Zanna, & Holmes, 2000). Thus, disinhibiting situational factors interact with individual and relational factors to affect the likelihood of IPV.

PATTERNS OF INTIMATE
PARTNER VIOLENCE

Partner violence varies dramatically in form and severity from occasional pushing to serious acts of violence such as beating up a partner. Although there are extensive data on rates and severity of IPV in various populations, little information is available on the topography of IPV in specific incidents. We briefly review the literature on reciprocity of IPV, initiation of IPV, responses to IPV, and consequences of IPV. Unfortunately, current research does not provide a basis for linking dispositional, relational, and situational factors with specific patterns of IPV.

At least half of violent relationships are characterized by bidirectional or mutual violence (e.g., Anderson, 2002; Whitaker, Haileyesus, Swahn, & Saltzman, 2007). IPV severity is strongly positively associated across partners in heterosexual and same-sex relationships (e.g., Bartholomew, Regan, Landolt, & Oram, 2008; Fergusson, Horwood, & Ridder, 2005), and IPV is more severe and harmful when both partners are violent than when one partner is violent (e.g., Anderson, 2002; Whitaker et al., 2007). From summary IPV measures, we cannot conclude that partners are mutually violent in the same incidents. Even if partners report comparable IPV levels, it could be that only one partner is violent or one partner is more severely violent than the other in a given incident. However, mutuality is suggested by some qualitative data and by the interactional context of reciprocal hostility in violent incidents. Contrary to traditional views that violent relationships consist of a violent (often male) abuser and a helpless (often female) victim, IPV arises in the context of reciprocal interaction and often involves mutual abuse.

Women are more likely than men: (a) to initiate IPV in heterosexual relationships (e.g., Archer, 2000; Fergusson et al., 2005), (b) to report that they would be violent in response to unacceptable partner behavior (e.g., Winstok, 2006a), and (c) to perpetrate IPV when only one partner is violent (e.g., Whitaker et al., 2007). However, we cannot conclude from such findings that women are more likely to be aggressors and men to be victims in one-sided patterns of abuse. Further, the concept of initiation makes little sense from an interactional perspective. Each partner responds to the behavior of the other, and even if one partner is first to bring up an issue or to act out physically during a heated conflict, both partners' reciprocal interaction sets the stage for IPV by either partner. We expect that women are less inhibited in escalating conflict with violence because of weaker norms against female relative to male IPV.

The scanty research on individuals' responses to IPV focuses on accounts of women identified as victims of severe male violence. Contrary to the stereotype that battered women passively comply with violent partners, female partners of men in batterer programs reported that they complied with their partner's wishes in less than 5% of violent episodes (Gondolf & Beeman, 2003). In another sample of women selected for high levels of victimization, 86% reported that they refused to do what their partner asked of them and 82% reported fighting back physically (Goodman, Dutton, Weinfurt & Cook, 2003). These findings are consistent with what is known about the situational context of IPV; IPV arises in a context of mutual conflict, with both partners struggling to fulfill interpersonal goals. The few larger studies comparing women's and men's responses to IPV indicate that women are much more likely to seek formal and informal help and to end relationships (e.g., Povey, Coleman, Kaisa, Hoare, & Jansson, 2008). This gender difference could stem from any number of sources, such as greater shame associated with male victimization, the lack of services available to aid male victims, or men finding their victimization less distressing than women.

IPV is associated with a range of adverse health outcomes for both genders. However, the majority of studies indicate that female recipients of male IPV are more likely than male recipients of female IPV to sustain severe injury (at a rate of about 2:1; Archer, 2000), to fear physical harm (e.g., Tjaden & Thoennes, 2000), and to report mental health symptoms (e.g., Anderson, 2002). These outcomes could reflect men's greater intent to harm, women's greater vulnerability to harm, and/or men's greater strength and competence with physical aggression. Unfortunately, no research of which we are aware systematically examines reasons for gender differences in IPV outcomes. Based on the dispositional predictors of IPV for both genders, and the relational and situational contexts of IPV, we suspect that the greater harm to women from IPV stems primarily from the greater capacity of men to physically harm their female partners.

PROCESS AND CONTEXTUAL ISSUES

The processes leading to IPV are dynamic—they shift over time in individuals, in relationships, and in situations—and later stages in the process leading to IPV can feed back to earlier stages. In particular, the experience of IPV may undermine partners' relational trust and security, contributing to marital discord and dissatisfaction (e.g., Lawrence & Bradbury, 2007). Relational experiences can also affect personal dispositions, exacerbating or moderating individual risk factors for IPV, such as impulsivity and negative emotionality (Robins et al., 2002).

Some risk factors for IPV cannot readily be categorized as dispositional, relational, or situational. For example, attitudes about the acceptability of IPV operate on a number of levels. IPV attitudes may derive from cultural norms, individual experiences in childhood and prior intimate relationships (background factors), and from experiences in current relationships. Given that no populations studied ascribe to norms promoting IPV, we hypothesize that attitudes affect IPV primarily through inhibiting IPV in violence-conducive situations (cf. Finkel, 2007). Thus, IPV attitudes may affect responses in violence-eliciting situations without being mediated by the relational context. Similarly, outcome expectancies for violence likely derive from cultural, background, and relational contexts, but they operate on the likelihood of violence in specific conflict situations. Expectancies may shift in a given situation; for instance, if a stronger partner threatens to retaliate physically or if a partner threatens to call the police if assaulted, then IPV expectancies will become more negative.

Cultural and Social Contexts

Although we expect the proposed model to apply cross-culturally, the social and cultural communities in which relationships are embedded provide an overarching context for all steps in the process leading to IPV. To date, few studies have examined the background, relational, or situational contexts of IPV cross-culturally, making it difficult to interpret cultural differences in IPV rates. For instance, national rates of corporal punishment of children are strongly associated with national IPV attitudes and rates of dating IPV (Douglas & Straus, 2006). These national differences in IPV could be mediated through personality dispositions and/or the quality of intimate relationships. Alternatively, cross-cultural norms for interpersonal violence may directly affect the degree to which individuals inhibit their IPV.

Cultural differences in gender roles and marital processes (how partners are selected, expectations about marriage, availability of divorce, etc.) also likely impact the relational context in which IPV develops. For instance, there may be less evidence of assortative mating on dispositions conducive to violence when marriages are arranged. We would expect conflicts of interest and frustration of interpersonal goals to set the context for IPV cross-culturally (e.g., Kim & Emery, 2003; Winstok & Eisikovits, 2008), though the particular content of conflicts and goals and the form of abuse may be moderated by culture. Whereas patterns of IPV in dating relationships appear to be similar cross-culturally (e.g., comparable rates of male and female IPV; Straus, 2004), patterns of marital IPV differ, with higher rates of male to female IPV in countries with greater gender inequality (Archer, 2006). It is therefore important to examine how culture provides a broader context for the development of IPV.

What About Power and Control?

Feminist perspectives view men's IPV as part of a general strategy to maintain men's control over women, and IPV is associated with acting in a controlling way toward a partner (Graham-Kevan, 2007b). However, there is little evidence that even severe IPV typically reflects a general pattern of one partner controlling the other across relational domains (cf. Felson & Outlaw, 2007). Rather, IPV perpetration may be associated with having *less* power across domains than one's partner (at least for men) (e.g., Babcock et al., 1993), as might be expected if IPV stems from a failure to meet interpersonal goals. Moreover, there is a strong *positive* association between the degree to which partners attempt to control one another (O'Leary & Smith Slep, 2003; Winstok, 2006b), suggesting a dyadic struggle for influence rather than the unilateral control of one partner by the other.

Escalating hostility and IPV are most likely when both partners actively seek to fulfill conflicting goals and resort to coercion when other means have failed. In relationships where a general pattern of dominance does exist, where one partner consistently accedes to the preferences and demands of the other, the conditions for escalating conflict and IPV as a coercive tactic are absent. Presumably, dominant partners are able to meet their goals, and dominated partners, though likely dissatisfied, are putting their desire for relational harmony (or avoidance of conflict) above other personal goals. This analysis is consistent with various findings we have reviewed, notably, that severe IPV is most likely when IPV is mutual, that both partners' negative reciprocity predicts IPV, and that victims of severe IPV rarely accede to their partners' demands.

What About Typologies of Partner Violence?

Researchers have proposed various typologies to describe the heterogeneity in violent individuals and violent relationships (Graham-Kevan, 2007a). For example, Holtzworth-Munroe and Stuart (1994) identified Borderline and Antisocial subtypes of severely violent men. In our proposed model, borderline/emotionally reactive and antisocial/aggressive features may predict somewhat different relational and situational contexts for IPV and different IPV patterns. We might, for instance, expect perceptions of situational threats to the relationship to be especially provocative for persons with borderline features. Moreover, dispositional factors may interact in predicting IPV outcomes, with individuals high in borderline and antisocial features being at elevated risk for severe IPV across a range of contexts. Thus, dimensional models are well suited for capturing variability in IPV predictors. They allow for the possibility of various paths to varying patterns of IPV, and interactions between IPV risk factors (dispositional, relational, and situational) (cf. Capaldi & Kim, 2007; Holtzworth-Munroe & Meehan, 2004).

Recently, some researchers have made a categorical distinction between *situational* and *characterological* IPV (e.g., Babcock et al., 2007). Situational IPV is described as less severe, likely to be reciprocal, and determined by relational and situational factors. Characterological IPV is severe, asymmetrical (with clear perpetrator and victim roles), and "internally generated" or primarily due to stable dispositional features of the perpetrator. This distinction serves a political purpose of affirming that victims of severe IPV do not bear responsibility for their victimization, but it is inconsistent with evidence of negative reciprocity and mutual IPV in the relationships of highly violent men. Further, severity and mutuality of IPV lie on continuums (Hamel, 2005) that tend to be positively associated (i.e., severe IPV is most common in relationships with mutual IPV); they are not mutually exclusive as proposed subtypes would suggest. More fundamentally, characterological notions of IPV fail to recognize that IPV is inherently interpersonal and situational. Individuals with strong vulnerabilities toward violence may have a stronger impact on the quality of their intimate relationships than do their partners; they may be hypersensitive to indications of their partner's rejection or hostility; and they may have weaker inhibitions against the use of violence in conflict situations. However,

violence-prone individuals are not consistently violent across relationships or across situations. IPV is perpetrated in a dyadic context in specific situations in response to perceived partner behaviors.[1]

Future Directions

In the past couple of decades, models of the etiology of IPV have shifted from single-variable models (such as a focus on societal norms or individual pathology) to multifactor models that incorporate cultural, social, and individual predictors of IPV. More recently, researchers have begun to move beyond individually focused perspectives to incorporate the dyadic context in which IPV takes place. However, the majority of IPV research still examines either perpetrators or victims of IPV in isolation. Just as marital researchers routinely study both partners in a marriage to understand marital processes and outcomes, violence researchers need to routinely include both partners to understand IPV. A dyadic approach will require researchers to consider interactions between predispositions of both partners in a violent relationship in the development of abusive dynamics, and to acknowledge the possibility of mutual abuse. We especially encourage study of the situational context in which episodes of IPV take place, including a focus on factors that inhibit and disinhibit aggression toward an intimate partner. Across domains of inquiry, we encourage a move beyond a focus on married couples and samples chosen for male-to-female IPV, to include the study of IPV in dating couples, in same-sex couples, and in couples distinguished by female-to-male violence.

A range of methods are available to tackle the difficult task of understanding the situational context of IPV, including lab-based studies of couple interactions, and qualitative and daily-diary studies of couples' descriptions of their abuse-related experiences. The study of IPV has greatly benefited by the perspectives and methods brought to bear by other fields of study, notably developmental psychopathology (e.g., Ehrensaft et al., 2003), couple and family research (e.g., Jacobson et al., 1994), and adult attachment (e.g., Dutton, Saunders, Starzomki, & Bartholomew, 1994). More progress could be made by incorporating insights from the broader literatures on interpersonal aggression and on interpersonal processes. For instance, greater understanding of the process whereby couples' conflicts escalate to the point of violence may be gained from examining the interpersonal motives of each partner and how each partner's failure to respond with a complementary response to a partner's expressed desire for a particular outcome can lead to mutual frustration and anger (Horowitz et al., 2006).

Clinical Implications

Psychoeducational interventions for violent men, the dominant treatment approach, have limited effectiveness (e.g., Babcock, Green, & Robie, 2004). This is not surprising given that they are based on outdated models of IPV that do not address the relational or situational contexts of IPV. In recent years, researchers and clinicians have advocated for a broader range of treatments informed by current IPV research (Hamel & Nicholls, 2007). In particular, couples treatments may be appropriate when the risk of injury from IPV is low. It also may be fruitful to focus treatment on proximal predictors of IPV, such as situational triggers and self-regulatory capacity to control violence, rather than targeting dispositional variables (e.g., Finkel, 2007).

Domestic violence advocates have expressed concern that dyadic models shift attention from the perpetrator as an independent agent to the dyadic context and thereby raise the possibility that identified victims may be partially responsible for their own victimization (e.g., Yllo & Bograd, 1988). We do not suggest that perpetrators are not responsible for their abusive behavior. To the contrary, all perpetrators of

IPV should be held personally responsible, regardless of gender. Developing a deeper and more accurate understanding of developmental, relational, and situation contexts of IPV can only further the goal of helping couples to establish satisfying, nonabusive relationships.

SUMMARY

Partners in close relationships inevitably encounter situations in which they perceive their interpersonal goals and aspirations to be incompatible, and a disturbing number of partners resort to violence when confronted by these challenges. We have presented a dyadic framework integrating theory and research on IPV. We have considered the enduring characteristics of both partners (background/dispositional factors), how partners come together and interact to create an intimate relationship (the relationship context), and how IPV can arise when partners respond to and interact in particular situations (the situational context). Difficult childhood experiences are associated with dispositions conducive to violence, especially emotional reactivity and aggressive interpersonal tendencies. These vulnerabilities put people at risk for future intimate relationships characterized by mutual distrust in which partners become locked in patterns of reciprocal hostility when dealing with conflicts of interest. However, partners in such relationships only become violent in specific situations. IPV typically arises during conflicts characterized by escalating hostility, with each partner reacting to perceived provocation from their partner. IPV may be especially likely in situations involving attachment threats if vulnerable individuals respond with extreme anger to perceived abandonment or rejection by their partner. We also considered factors that may inhibit and disinhibit the expression of IPV in provoking situations. We hope that a more inclusive dyadic framework for understanding IPV will help in the development of more effective approaches to prevention and treatment.

References

Allison, C. J., Bartholomew, K., Mayseless, O., & Dutton, D. G. (2008). The relationship dynamics of couples identified for male partner violence: An attachment perspective. *Journal of Family Issues, 29*, 125–150.

Anderson, K. L. (2002). Perpetrator or victim? Relationships between intimate partner violence and well-being. *Journal of Marriage and Family, 64*, 851–863.

Anglin, K., & Holtzworth-Munroe, A. (1997). Comparing the responses of maritally violent and nonviolent spouses to problematic marital and nonmarital situations: Are the skill deficits of physically aggressive husbands and wives global? *Journal of Family Psychology, 11*, 301–313.

Archer, J. (2000). Sex differences in aggression between heterosexual partners: A meta-analytic review. *Psychological Bulletin, 126*, 651–680.

Archer, J., & Coyne, S. (2005). An integrated review of indirect, relational, and social aggression. *Personality and Social Psychology Review, 9*, 212–230.

Archer, J. (2006). Cross-cultural differences in physical aggression between partners: A social-role analysis. *Personality and Social Psychology Review, 10*, 133–153.

Babcock, J. C., Canady, B. E., Graham, K., & Schart, L. (2007). The evolution of battering interventions: From the dark ages into the scientific age. In J. Hamel & T. L. Nicholls (Eds.), *Family interventions in domestic violence* (pp. 215–244). New York: Springer.

Babcock, J. C., Green, C. E., & Robie, C. (2004). Does batterers' treatment work? A meta-analytic review of domestic violence treatment. *Clinical Psychology Review, 23*, 1023–1053.

Babcock, J. C., Waltz, J., Jacobson, N. S., & Gottman, J. M. (1993). Power and violence: The relation between communication patterns, power discrepancies, and domestic violence. *Journal of Consulting and Clinical Psychology, 61*, 40–50.

Bartholomew, K., & Allison, C. J. (2006). An attachment perspective on abusive dynamics in intimate relationships. In M. Mikulincer & G. S. Goodman (Eds.). *Romantic love: Attachment, caregiving, and sex* (pp. 102–127). New York: Guilford Press.

Bartholomew, K., Regan, K. V., Landolt, M. A., & Oram, D. (2008). Patterns of abuse in male same-sex relationship. *Violence and Victims, 23*, 617–636.

Bartholomew, K., Regan, K. V., Oram, D., & Landolt, M. A. (2008). Correlates of partner abuse in male same-sex relationships. *Violence and Victims, 23*, 348–364.

Berkowitz, L. (1993). *Aggression: Its causes, consequences, and control.* New York: Mcgraw-Hill.

Bettencourt, B. A., Talley, A., Benjamin, A. J., & Valentine, J. (2006). Personality and aggressive behavior under provoking and neutral conditions: A meta-analytic review. *Psychological Bulletin, 132*, 751–777.

Bograd, M. (1988). Feminist perspectives on wife abuse: An introduction. In M. Bograd & K. Yllo (Eds.), *Feminist perspectives on wife abuse* (pp. 11–26). Beverly Hills, CA: Sage.

Burman, B., Margolin, G., & John, R. S. (1993). America's angriest home videos: Behavioral contingencies observed in home reenactments of marital conflict. *Journal of Consulting and Clinical Psychology, 6*, 28–39.

Capaldi, D. M., & Crosby, L. (1997). Observed and reported psychological and physical aggression in young, at-risk couples. *Social Development, 6*, 184–206.

Capaldi, D. M., & Kim. H. K. (2007). Typological approaches to violence in couples: A critique and alternative conceptual approach. *Clinical Psychology Review, 27*, 253–265.

Capaldi, D. M., Shortt, J. W., & Crosby, L. (2003). Physical and psychological aggression in at-risk young couples: Stability and change in young adulthood. *Merrill-Palmer Quarterly, 49*, 1–27.

Cascardi, M., & Vivian, D. (1995). Context for specific episodes of marital violence: Gender and severity of violence differences. *Journal of Family Violence, 10*, 265–293.

Coleman, D. H., & Straus, M. A. (1990). Marital power, conflict, and violence in a nationally representative sample of American couples. In M. A. Straus & R. J. Gelles (Eds.), *Physical violence in American families: Risk factors and adaptations to violence in 8,145 families* (pp. 287–304). New Brunswick, NJ: Transaction.

Cordova, J. V., Jacobson, N. S., Gottman, J. M., Rushe, R., & Cox, G. (1993). Negative reciprocity and communication in couples with a violent husband. *Journal of Abnormal Psychology, 102*, 559–564.

Dobash, R. E., & Dobash, R. P. (1984). The nature and antecedents of violent events. *British Journal of Criminology, 24*, 269–288.

Douglas, E. M., & Straus, M. A. (2006). Assault and injury of dating partners by university students in 19 countries and its relation to corporal punishment experienced as a child. *European Journal of Criminology, 3*, 293–318.

Dutton, D. G. (2006). *Rethinking domestic violence.* Vancouver, BC: UBC Press.

Dutton, D. G. (2007). *The abusive personality* (2nd Ed.). New York: Guilford Press.

Dutton, D., & Browning, J. (1988). Power struggles and intimacy anxieties as causative factors of wife assault. In G. W. Russell (Ed.), *Violence in intimate relationships* (pp. 163–175). Costa Mesa, CA: PMA Publishing Corp.

Dutton, D. G., & Corvo, K. (2006). Transforming a flawed policy: A call to revive psychology and science in domestic violence research and practice. *Aggression and Violent Behavior, 11*, 457–483.

Dutton, D. G., & Nicholls, T. L. (2005). The gender paradigm in domestic violence research and theory: The conflict of theory and data. *Aggression and Violent Behavior, 10*, 680–714.

Dutton, D. G., Saunders, K., Starzomski, A. J., & Bartholomew, K. (1994). Intimacy-anger and insecure attachment as precursors of abuse in intimate relationships. *Journal of Applied Social Psychology, 24*, 1367–1386.

Eckhardt, C. I., & Dye, M. L. (2000). The cognitive characteristics of maritally violent men: Theory and evidence. *Cognitive Therapy and Research, 24*, 139–158.

Ehrensaft, M. K. (2008). Intimate partner violence: Persistence of myths and implications for intervention. *Children and Youth Services Review, 30*, 276–286.

Ehrensaft, M. K., Cohen, P., Brown, J., Smailes, E., Chen, H., & Johnson, J. G. (2003). Intergenerational transmission of partner violence: A 20-year prospective study. *Journal of Consulting and Clinical Psychology, 71*, 741–753.

Ehrensaft, M. K., Moffitt, T. E., & Caspi, A. (2004). Clinically abusive relationships in an unselected birth cohort: Men's and women's participation and developmental antecedents. *Journal of Abnormal Psychology, 113*, 258–271.

Ehrensaft, M., Moffitt, T., & Caspi, A. (2006). Is domestic violence followed by an increased risk of psychiatric disorders among women but not among men? A longitudinal cohort study. *American Journal of Psychiatry, 163*, 885–892.

Fals-Stewart, W. (2003). The occurrence of partner physical aggression on days of alcohol consumption: A longitudinal diary study. *Journal of Consulting and Clinical Psychology, 71*, 41–52.

Felson, R., & Outlaw, M. (2007). The control motive and marital violence. *Violence and Victims, 22*, 387–407.

Fergusson, D. M., Horwood, L. J., & Ridder, E. M. (2005). Partner violence and mental health outcomes in a New Zealand birth cohort. *Journal of Marriage and the Family, 67*, 1103–1119.

Finkel, E. J. (2007). Impelling and inhibiting forces in the perpetration of intimate partner violence. *Review of General Psychology, 11*, 193–207.

Finkel, E. J., DeWall, C. N., Slotter, E. B., Oaten, M., & Foshee, V. A. (2009). Self-regulatory failure and intimate partner violence perpetration. *Journal of Personality and Social Psychology, 97*, 483–499.

Gondolf, E. W., & Beeman, A. K. (2003). Women's accounts of domestic violence versus tactics-based outcome categories. *Violence against Women, 9*, 278–301.

Goodman, L., Dutton, M. A., Weinfurt, K., & Cook, S. (2003). The Intimate Partner Violence Strategies Index: Development and application. *Violence Against Women, 9*, 163–186.

Graham-Kevan, N. (2007a). Partner violence typologies. In J. Hamel & T. L. Nicholls (Eds.), *Family interventions in domestic violence* (pp. 145–163). New York: Springer.

Graham-Kevan, N. (2007b). Power and control in relationship aggression. In J. Hamel & T. L. Nicholls (Eds.), *Family interventions in domestic violence* (pp. 87–108). New York: Springer.

Hamel, J. (2005). *Gender inclusive treatment of intimate partner abuse: A comprehensive approach.* New York: Springer.

Hamel, J., & Nicholls, T. L. (Eds.). (2007). *Family interventions in domestic violence.* New York: Springer.

Holtzworth-Munroe, A., & Anglin, K. (1991). The competency of responses given by maritally violent versus nonviolent men to problematic marital situations. *Violence and Victims, 6*, 257–269.

Holtzworth-Munroe, A., & Meehan, J. C. (2004). Typologies of men who are maritally violent. *Journal of Interpersonal Violence, 19*, 1369–1389.

Holtzworth-Munroe, A., Smutzler, N., & Bates, L. (1997). A brief review of the research on husband violence: Part III. Sociodemographic factors, relationship factors, and differing consequences of husband and wife violence. *Aggression and Violent Behavior, 2*, 285–307.

Holtzworth-Munroe, A., & Stuart, G. (1994). Typologies of male batterers: Three subtypes and the differences among them. *Psychological Bulletin, 116,* 476–497.

Horowitz, L. M., Wilson, K. R., Turan, B., Zolotsev, P., Constantino, M. J., & Henderson, L. (2006). How interpersonal motives clarify the meaning of interpersonal behavior: A revised circumplex model. *Personality and Social Psychology Review, 10,* 67–86.

Jacobson, N. S., Gottman, J. M., Waltz, J., Rushe, R., Babcock, J., & Holtzworth-Munroe, A. (1994). Affect, verbal content, and psychophysiology in the arguments of couples with a violent husband. *Journal of Consulting and Clinical Psychology, 62,* 982–988.

Johnson, M. P. (1995). Patriarchal terrorism and common couple violence: Two forms of violence against women. *Journal of Marriage and the Family, 57,* 283–294.

Kim, H. K., & Capaldi, D. M. (2004). The association of antisocial behavior and depressive symptoms between partners and risk for aggression in romantic relationships. *Journal of Family Psychology, 18,* 82–96.

Kim, J., & Emery, C. (2003). Marital power, conflict, and marital violence in a nationally representative sample of Korean couples. *Journal of Interpersonal Violence, 18,* 197–219.

Krueger, R. F., Moffitt, T. E., Caspi, A., Bleske, A, & Silva, P. A. (1998). Assortative mating for antisocial behavior: Developmental and methodological implications. *Behavior Genetics, 28,* 173–185.

Lawrence, E., & Bradbury, T. N. (2007). Trajectories of change in physical aggression and marital satisfaction. *Journal of Family Psychology, 21,* 236–247.

Leary, M. R., Twenge, J. M., & Quinlivan, E. (2006). Interpersonal rejection as a determinant of anger and aggression. *Personality and Social Psychology Review, 10,* 111–132.

Leonard, K. E., & Roberts, L. J. (1998). The effects of alcohol on the marital interactions of aggressive and nonaggressive husbands and their wives. *Journal of Abnormal Psychology, 107,* 602–615.

Leonard, K. E., & Senchak, M. (1993). Alcohol and premarital aggression among newlywed couples. *Journal of Studies on Alcohol, 11,* 96–108.

Leonard, K. E., & Senchak, M. (1996). Prospective prediction of husband marital aggression within newlywed couples. *Journal of Abnormal Psychology, 105,* 369–380.

Magdol, L., Moffitt, T. E., Caspi, A., Newman, D. L., Fagan, J., & Silva, P. A. (1997). Gender differences in partner violence in a birth cohort of 21-year-olds: Bridging the gap between clinical and epidemiological approaches. *Journal of Consulting and Clinical Psychology, 65,* 68–78.

MacDonald, G., Zanna, M. P., & Holmes, J. G. (2000). An experimental test of the role of alcohol in relationship conflict. *Journal of Experimental Social Psychology, 36,* 182–193.

Medeiros, R. A., & Straus, M. A. (2006). *A review of research on gender differences in risk factors for physical violence between partners in marital and dating relationships.* Family Research Laboratory, University of New Hampshire. Durham, NH.

Medeiros, R. A., & Straus, M. A. (2007). Risk factors for physical violence between dating partners: Implications for gender-inclusive prevention and treatment of family violence. In J. Hamel & T. L. Nicholls (Eds.), *Family interventions in domestic violence* (pp. 59–86). New York: Springer.

Miller, S. L., & Simpson, S. S. (1991). Courtship violence and social control: Does gender matter? *Law & Society Review, 25,* 335–365.

Moffitt, T. E., Krueger, R. F., Caspi, A., & Fagan, J. (2000). Partner abuse and general crime: How are they the same? *Criminology, 38,* 199–232.

Moffitt, T. E., Robins, R. W., & Caspi, A. (2001). A couples analysis of partner abuse with implications for abuse-prevention policy. *Criminology and Public Policy, 1,* 5–36.

O'Leary, K. D. (1999). Psychological abuse: A variable deserving critical attention in domestic violence. *Violence and Victims, 14,* 3–23.

O'Leary, K. D., & Smith Slep, A. M. (2003). A dyadic longitudinal model of adolescent dating aggression. *Journal of Clinical Child and Adolescent Psychology, 32,* 314–327.

O'Leary, S. G., & Smith Slep, A. M. (2006). Precipitants of partner aggression. *Journal of Family Psychology, 20,* 344–347.

O'Leary, K. D., Smith Slep, A. M., & O'Leary, S. G. (2007). Multivariate models of men's and women's partner aggression. *Journal of Consulting and Clinical Psychology, 75,* 752–764.

Povey, D. Coleman, K., Kaisa, P., Hoare, J., & Jansson, K. (2008). Homicides, firearm offences and intimate violence 2006/07. Home Office Statistical Bulletin 03/08. London: Home Office.

Reis, H., Capobianco, A., & Tsai, F. (2002). Finding the person in personal relationships. *Journal of Personality, 70,* 813–850.

Roberts, N., & Noller, P. (1998). The associations between adult attachment and couple violence: The role of communication patterns and relationship satisfaction. In J. A. Simpson & W. S. Rholes (Eds.), *Attachment theory and close relationships* (pp. 317–350). New York: Guilford Press.

Robins, R. W., Caspi, A., & Moffitt, T. E. (2002). It's not just who you're with, it's who you are: Personality and relationship experiences across multiple relationships. *Journal of Personality, 70,* 925–964.

Schumacher, J. A., & Leonard, K. E. (2005). Husbands' and wives' marital adjustment, verbal aggression, and physical aggression as longitudinal predictors of physical aggression in early marriage. *Journal of Consulting and Clinical Psychology, 73,* 28–37.

Scott, K., & Straus, M. (2007). Denial, minimization, partner blaming, and intimate aggression in dating partners. *Journal of Interpersonal Violence, 22,* 851–871.

Sorenson, S. B., & Taylor, C. A. (2005). Female aggression towards male intimate partners: An examination of social norms in a community-based sample. *Psychology of Women Quarterly, 29,* 78–96.

Stanley, J. L, Bartholomew, K., Taylor, T., Landolt, M., & Oram, D. (2006). An exploration of partner violence in male same-sex relationships. *Journal of Family Violence, 21,* 31–41.

Statistics Canada (2005). *Family violence in Canada: A statistical profile, 2005.* Ottawa, ON: Canadian Centre for Justice Statistics.

Stets, J. E. (1990). Verbal and physical aggression in marriage. *Journal of Marriage and the Family, 52,* 501–514.

Straus, M. (2004). Prevalence of violence against dating partners by male and female university students worldwide. *Violence Against Women, 10,* 790–811.

Straus, M. A., & Gelles, R. J. (1986). Societal change and change in family violence from 1975 to 1985 as revealed by two national surveys. *Journal of Marriage and the Family, 48,* 465–479.

Tjaden, P., & Thoennes, N. (2000). Prevalence and consequences of male-to-female and female-to-male intimate partner violence as measured by the national violence against women survey. *Violence against Women, 6,* 142–161.

Whitaker, D. J., Haileyesus, T., Swahn, M., & Saltzman, L. (2007). Differences in frequency of violence and reported injury between relationships with reciprocal and nonreciprocal intimate partner violence. *American Journal of Public Health, 97,* 941–947.

Wilkinson, D. L., & Hamerschlag, S. J. (2005). Situational determinants in intimate partner violence. *Aggression and Violent Behavior, 10,* 333–361.

Williams, S. L., & Frieze, I. H. (2005). Patterns of violent relationships, psychological distress, and marital satisfaction in a national sample of men and women. *Sex Roles, 52,* 771–784.

Winstok, Z. (2006a). Gender differences in the intention to react to aggressive action at home and in the workplace. *Aggressive Behavior, 32,* 433–441.

Winstok, Z. (2006b). The why and what of intimate conflict: Effect of the partners' divergent perceptions on verbal aggression. *Journal of Family Violence, 21,* 461–468.

Winstok, Z. (2007). Toward an interactional perspective on intimate partner violence. *Aggression and Violent Behavior, 12,* 348–363.

Winstok, Z., Eisikovits, Z. (2008). Motives and control in escalatory conflicts in intimate Relationships. *Children and Youth Services Review, 30,* 287–296.

Woodward, L. J., Fergusson, D. M., & Horwood, L. J. (2002). Romantic relationships of young people with childhood and adolescent onset antisocial behavior problems. *Journal of Abnormal Child Psychology, 30,* 231–243.

Yllo, K., & Bogard, M. (1988). *Feminist perspectives on wife abuse.* Beverly Hills: Sage.

NOTES

1. Johnson's (1995) influential distinction between IPV as part of a general pattern of domination stemming from stable intrapersonal characteristics of the perpetrator (referred to as *patriarchal* or *intimate terrorism*) and mutual lower-level IPV stemming from dyadic and situational factors (referred to as *common couple violence*) suffers from the same limitations.

15 DIFFERENTIATING THE DARK TRIAD WITHIN THE INTERPERSONAL CIRCUMPLEX

Daniel N. Jones

Delroy L. Paulhus

INTRODUCTION

The Dark Triad of personality consists of three conceptually distinct, but empirically overlapping constructs: Machiavellianism, narcissism, and psychopathy (Paulhus & Williams, 2002). Psychopathy is a personality trait characterized by callousness, impulsive thrill-seeking, and criminal behavior. Narcissism, on the other hand, is associated with grandiosity, egocentrism, and a sense of personal entitlement. Machiavellianism is marked by strategic manipulation. Although conceptually distinct, all three project onto Quadrant 2 of the interpersonal circumplex. In this chapter, we investigate which aspects of the dark personalities can be captured within interpersonal space and which cannot. We conclude that additional moderating variables are necessary to elucidate the distinctive behavioral style of the Dark Triad members.

To begin, we examine and then refute the notion that these three personalities are the same construct. Our refutation draws on a review of recent empirical evidence showing key differences. To determine the fundamental roots of these differences, we return to the seminal theorists of each construct and uncover two systematic moderators: temporal orientation and identity need. We go on to discuss in detail several new studies supporting the efficacy of these two moderators for differentiating the Dark Triad. We conclude with an attempt to integrate the two moderators within interpersonal theory.

If successful, this approach will permit us to predict the distinct behavioral patterns of the Dark Triad without losing sight of their overlapping nature. At a broader level, we seek to articulate what it may mean for personality variables to share similar interpersonal space while displaying different behavioral manifestations.

UNIFICATIONIST THEORIES

Not all researchers agree that it is worthwhile to discriminate the Dark Triad. Evidence for that unificationist position can be organized into three sources: circumplex research, trait research, and evolutionary arguments. In each of the three subsections below, we provide the strongest case for the unificationist position.

Evidence From Circumplex Research

In terms popularized by Bakan (1966), two basic themes underlie social interactions: agency (getting ahead) and communion (getting along). When positioned as the axes of a two-dimensional space, agency and communion provide a powerful framework for representing individual differences in both normal and abnormal behavior (Leary, 1957). A plot of all possible blends of the two tendencies maps out a circular pattern now known as the interpersonal circumplex (e.g., Wiggins, 1979). The same circular pattern emerges whether the plotted variables are trait adjectives (Gurtman, & Pincus, 2000; Wiggins & Broughton, 1985), trait statements (P. M. Markey & Markey, 2009), motives (Locke, 2000), values (Trapnell & Paulhus, in press), or interpersonal problems (Horowitz, Alden, Wiggins, & Pincus, 2000). The blends are held to capture more than the weighted sum of the two motives: Each quadrant represents a unique interpersonal perspective (for a recent review, see Horowitz, 2004a).

For example, Quadrant 2 of the interpersonal circumplex (i.e., high-agency low-communion) is inhabited by individuals variously characterized as arrogant, calculating, callous, and manipulative. Another label, unmitigated agency, highlights the emphasis on personal achievement to the neglect of interpersonal connectedness. As indicated in Figure 15.1, circumplex projections invariably land the Dark Triad of personalities in Quadrant 2.

To date, only a handful of studies have simultaneously projected all three of the Dark Triad onto the circumplex (Paulhus, 2001, August). Those studies confirmed the location of the Dark Triad as depicted in Figure 15.1. Many other studies have included one or two of the Dark Triad in the context of the circumplex. We discuss the evidence for each triad member one at a time.

Psychopathy. As a rule, personality disorders with antisocial implications tend to fall in Quadrant 2 of the circumplex (e.g.,

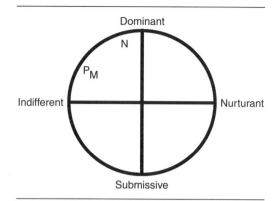

FIGURE 15.1   Typical Location of the Dark Triad on the Interpersonal Circumplex N = narcissism; P = psychopathy; M = Machiavellianism.

Pincus, 2006; Ruiz, Dickinson, & Pincus, 2002; Strack & Lorr, 1994). This pattern holds for self-report measures of psychopathy collected on normal samples, that is, subclinical psychopathy (Blackburn & Maybury, 1985; Hicklin & Widiger, 2005; Salekin, Trobst, & Krioukova, 2001). The same pattern holds whether the circumplex is represented in terms of traits, values, or motives. This same circumplex location has even been found in adolescent psychopaths (Salekin, Leistico, Trobst, Schrum, & Lochman, 2005) suggesting a developmental continuity of psychopathic traits.

Machiavellianism. The same circumplex pattern has been found for Machiavellianism (see Jones & Paulhus, 2009). Measures of the construct are invariably positively correlated with agency and negatively correlated with communion, thus locating them in Quadrant 2 of the interpersonal circumplex of traits (Gurtman, 1992; Wiggins & Broughton, 1985) or values (Trapnell & Paulhus, in press).

Narcissism. Finally, narcissism (as measured with the Narcissistic Personality Inventory) shows the same pattern of associations with agency and communion (Bradlee & Emmons, 1992; Emmons, 1987; Ruiz, Smith, & Rhodewalt, 2001). The overall pattern was partially corroborated by Rhodewalt and Morf (1995), who found that total NPI scores were uncorrelated with communion, but positively associated with agency.[1] Summarizing across all the relevant research, we conclude that narcissism is associated negatively (albeit weakly) with communion and positively with agency. Again, it lands in Quadrant 2 of the interpersonal circumplex.

Summary. It is evident from Figure 15.1 that the circumplex projections of Machiavellianism and psychopathy are virtually identical. Narcissism is nearby, although it loads more positively on both agency and communion. Nonetheless, the overall message is that the Dark Triad members all fall in Quadrant 2 of the interpersonal circumplex. This location applies whether the circumplex is measured in terms of traits, goals, values, or psychological problems.

Evolutionary Psychology

Several evolutionary theorists have implied that the Dark Triad personalities are adaptive for the same reason and, therefore, can be subsumed within a single concept. Mealey (1995), for example, detailed how exploitative tendencies can flourish up to a point. A given population can sustain only a limited number of such chronic "cheaters" because the advantage conferred on each of them decreases as their frequency increases. In making these arguments, Mealey uses the term *psychopathy* interchangeably with *Machiavellianism.*

Another evolutionary group, Wilson, Near, and Miller (1996), further reinforced the notion that Machiavellians are but one of a variety of societal cheaters. Wilson and colleagues argued that those who cheat in a society of noncheaters would best restrict themselves to short-term social interaction, after which they move on. Otherwise, they will be detected and reported, and repercussions will ensue as a consequence of their actions (Wilson et. al., 1996, p. 4).

A third group, Book and Quinsey (2004) articulated how individuals who pursue exploitative strategies have benefited from both impulsive aggression and a lack of empathy: the adaptiveness of this style has created and sustained psychopathy. The authors draw the distinction between the exploitative "cheater" and the impulsive "aggressor" (i.e., warrior-hawk). But they conclude that the two would naturally have coevolved to create a deceptive, aggressive, and impulsive character.

Other researchers have drawn on evolutionary theories to explain similar correlates obtained with measures of the Dark Triad. Jonason, Li, Webster, and Schmitt (2009), for example, reported that all three of the Dark Triad members were high in short-term mating. This finding is consistent with a previous report of similar (positive) correlations between Dark Triad members and rates of sexual activity (Harms, Williams, and Paulhus, 2001; Reise & Wright, 1996). The latter writers, however, argued that these similar associations ensued from different strategies and motivations.

Jonason and colleagues also reported no correlation between each member of the Dark Triad and long-term mating. More recent research has not supported these findings, suggesting instead that the Dark Triad members actually have very different long-term mating strategies as well as other sexual behaviors (Jones & Paulhus, 2010c).

The Jonason data found modest correlations among the Dark Triad (.28, .39, .20)—values that are similar to those from other studies. Surprisingly, Jonason and colleagues concluded that these modest associations provided evidence that the Dark Triad are interchangeable.

Evidence From Trait Approaches

Other researchers have been led by trait research to conclude that members of the Dark Triad are simply three labels for previously established personality constructs.

For example, in a series of studies, McHoskey, Worzel, and Szyarto (1998) compared various members of the Dark Triad to a variety of personality correlates. Dark Triad measures overlapped substantially and shared similar relationships to variables such as disinhibition, forcefulness, self-reported antisocial behavior, prosocial behavior, and cooperativeness. All three were negatively related to impression management. McHoskey and colleagues concluded that Machiavellianism is nothing more than a mild form of psychopathy.

Evidence for unifying the Dark Triad can also be found in Big Five research. The most common finding is that all three members score low on agreeableness (Egan, 2009; Jakobwitz & Egan, 2006; Paulhus, 2001; Paulhus & Williams, 2002; Vernon, Villani, Vickers, & Harris, 2008; Widiger & Lynam, 1998). Although other personality correlates have been found, the correlation between the Dark Triad and disagreeableness is robust and consistent.

Interestingly, the relation of the Dark Triad to fundamental personality traits appears to shift under the six-factor model (Ashton et al., 2004). Subsequent factor analytic work by these researchers showed that measures of the Dark Triad can jointly be defined by a sixth personality factor called honesty-humility (Lee & Ashton, 2005). The convergence of the Dark Triad could not be explained with the Big Five alone. Thus the convergence of the Dark Triad members on their sixth factor helped advance the authors' "Big Six" model of personality (Lee & Ashton, 2005). Incidentally, their findings also support the unificationist view of the Dark Triad.

Summary

Research based on the interpersonal circumplex appears to support the unificationist position. All three members of the Dark Triad locate in Quadrant 2: In other words, they score high on agency and low on communion. In Big Five trait terms, they share a common element of disagreeableness. Finally, research within an evolutionary framework supports the unificationist claim in that all three of the Dark Triad have a sexually promiscuous mating style. In sum, the unificationist arguments outlined in this section appear to justify the allegation: Personality psychologists have unwittingly been referring to the same (dark) wine in three different bottles.[2]

CONTRADICTORY EVIDENCE: YES, THEY DO DIFFER!

We will dispute the unificationist claim by pointing to several key studies. Because of their overlap, The Dark Triad members should often show the same correlates. If, however, they show some distinctive correlates, that evidence should suffice to indicate that the Dark Triad constructs require separate measurement.[3]

Even in the original paper, Paulhus and Williams (2002) provided evidence that the Dark Triad members have distinctive correlates. For example, narcissism was associated with openness and extraversion, whereas the other two were not. Machiavellianism and psychopathy were negatively correlated with conscientiousness whereas narcissism was not. Jakobowitz and Egan (2006) also showed differential correlates among the Dark Triad, although they were not entirely consistent with those found by Paulhus and Williams (2002).

Differences in associations with self-enhancement were also evident in the original Paulhus and Williams data. Narcissism was associated with higher scores on two objective measures of self-enhancement. A small association was observed with psychopathy but no association emerged for Machiavellianism. Interestingly, there were differences in cognitive functioning as well: Those high in Machiavellianism and psychopathy had higher than average verbal-nonverbal discrepancy scores, and those high in narcissism scored the highest on global IQ (Paulhus & Williams, 2002).

Dark Triad differences have also emerged with respect to antisocial behavior. Whereas psychopathy is a robust predictor of delinquency, Machiavellianism and narcissism are not (Williams & Paulhus, 2004). Psychopathy also is uniquely associated with violent and antisocial entertainment (Williams, McAndrew, Learn, Harms & Paulhus, 2001) and with sporting piercings and tattoos (Nathanson, Paulhus, & Williams, 2006a).

In relation to aggression, psychopathy has been established as a consistent predictor across a range of conditions (Blackburn & Maybury, 1985; Patrick & Zempolich, 1998; Reidy, Zeichner, & Martinez, 2008). This indiscriminant aggression contrasts with research on Machiavellianism, which shows no overall association with aggression, revenge, or violence (Williams & & Paulhus, 2004). Narcissists do aggress, but only after provocation (Bettencourt, Talley, Benjamin, & Valentine, 2006).[4]

Differences among the Dark Triad have also emerged in work on behavior genetics. Machiavellianism has a substantial shared-environment component whereas narcissism and psychopathy were accounted for almost entirely by genetic and nonshared environmental factors (Vernon, Villani, Vickers, & Harris, 2008). The shared-environment component suggests that individuals acquire Machiavellian traits over time, and possess enough phenotypic plasticity to adjust to their environment. In contrast, results with the other members of the Dark Triad suggest a genetic etiology.

The same research team extended this line of research in an even more recent study addressing the origins of moral reason (Campbell, Shermer, Villani, Vickers, & Vernon, 2009). Machiavellianism and psychopathy share a positive phenotypic and genetic correlation with the lowest level of moral development—that based on a "personal interest schema" (e.g., it is right to do what benefits the self). By contrast, psychopathy was the only member of the Dark Triad correlated (negatively) with higher stages of abstract moral reasoning. This finding suggests that those high on Machiavellianism, unlike those high in psychopathy, are not impaired in their ability to reason through moral dilemmas; they can see others' perspectives, but act selfishly nonetheless.

Taken together, the studies in this section indicate that—contrary to the unificationist claim—the Dark Triad members differ in important ways. While helpful, those studies do not specify the precise nature of those differences.

Note that we are not arguing the Dark Triad members are entirely different—some overlap does exist. Indeed, the range of data cited under the unificationist section above points to substantial overlap. But what characteristics overlap? And what characteristics are distinct? To tease apart the array of similarities and differences, we must return to the conceptual roots of each Dark Triad member.

A CONCEPTUAL REVIEW: GUIDED BY THE MASTERS

Our original rationale for studying narcissism, psychopathy, and Machiavellianism as a triad was their conceptual similarity (Paulhus & Williams, 2002). All three show an indifference to the harm they cause to others in the course of achieving their goals. We will summarize this common behavioral style under the label "exploitative," that is, agentic striving at the expense of communal welfare.

This shared exploitativeness is consistent with the notion of convergent evolution: It is the process whereby selective pressures culminate in similar behaviors in different organisms, despite unique evolutionary roots (e.g., Buss, 1994). The concept has recently been addressed with respect to individual differences in humans (Fraley, Brumbaugh, & Marks, 2005). Applying the notion to the Dark Triad, we note the possibility that some behavioral similarities have emerged despite different evolutionary adaptations. That is, the exploitativeness common to the Dark Triad members may originate in three different personality dynamics.

Our review of the empirical literature above, however, leaves us with the task of tracking down the systematic differences among the Dark Triad members. To clarify the nature of these differences, it is necessary to delve into the seminal works on each of the triad. Ideally we will be able to pinpoint cardinal features that distinguish the three.

Machiavellianism (According to Machiavelli and Sun Tzu)

Machiavellianism, as expounded and measured by Christie and Geis (1970), was based almost entirely on the 16th-century writings of Niccolo Machiavelli. The most recent review (Jones & Paulhus, 2009), however, reaches further back in intellectual history to include the writings of the Chinese philosopher Sun Tzu.

Originally written in 500 B.C., Sun Tzu's *Art of War* predates Machiavelli's (1513) advice to use duplicitous tactics. Sun Tzu placed special importance on strategic planning. Below we detail a number of strategies subsumed by this broad theme: long-term goals, planning and preparation, impulse control, situational adaptation, alliance building, and reputation maintenance. Because Machiavelli and Sun Tzu offered similar profiles for success, we will allude to their ideal characters more-or-less interchangeably and refer to them as Machiavellians.

Long-term goals. Possibly of greatest importance in characterizing Machiavellianism is his emphasis on long-term achievement through any means necessary (e.g., " . . . a prince who wishes to remain in power is often forced to be other than good"; Machiavelli, p. 75). Both Machiavelli and Sun Tzu consistently emphasized the avoidance of any behavior that might impair the realization of the long-term goal. Sun Tzu specified five such pitfalls: Recklessness, cowardice, a hot temper, pride, overconcern for his soldiers (i.e., empathy). To win in the long-term, one must be pragmatic, cautious, slow to anger, self-aware, and callous.

Planning and preparation. The advantage of preparatory work is also discussed by both master writers (e.g., " . . . never submit to idleness in time of peace, but rather endeavor to turn such time to advantages

so as to profit from it in adversity. Thus when fortune turns against him, he will be prepared to resist it" (Machiavelli, p. 61). In short, Machiavellians employ long-term preparations and planning in order to accomplish their goals. By contrast, Cleckley (1976) characterizes the psychopathic character by a dearth of preparation, planning, and strategy. These writers do not address the degree of planning by narcissists.

Impulse control. Both masters emphasized impulse control as key to victory. A commander should keep outright warfare to a minimum because of the toll it can take on morale (e.g., "No nation has ever benefited from protracted war"; Sun Tzu, p. 10). Tempting the enemy to make that mistake is ideal (e.g., "He causes the enemy to make a move and awaits him with full force"; Sun Tzu, p. 29).

A cautious style helps facilitate a rational cost-benefit analysis: "The wise leader in his deliberations always blends consideration of gain and harm" (Sun Tzu, p. 48). Similarly, Machiavelli recommended that a leader should take risks only when well-calculated. For example, one should cheat or aggress only when there is little cost or risk involved or the payoffs are sufficient (e.g., "Prudence lies in knowing how to distinguish between degrees of danger and in choosing the least danger as the best"; Machiavelli, p. 86).

Situational adaptation. Unlike the psychopathic individual who is rigidly locked into short-term orientation, Machiavelli and Sun Tzu (similar to Machiavelli) suggested that leaders should be able to adapt to the situation and be flexible in applying tactics both in the short-term and long-term. Long-term strategies need to be executed skillfully and include honesty as well as outright deception. Accordingly, Machiavellian tactics can take the form of alternating ruthlessness and benevolence (e.g., Machiavelli: " . . . he must stick to the good so long as he can, but, being compelled by necessity, he must be ready to take the way of evil"; Machiavelli, p. 69; Sun Tzu: "victory belongs to the man who can master the stratagem of the crooked and the straight"; p. 43).

Alliance building. Accumulating supporters can be especially challenging for the callous individual bent on selfishness. But one can exploit the fact that others are selfish. Hence, both masters argued that one should divide the spoils judiciously to build alliances: "Plunder the countryside and divide the spoil; extend territory and distribute the profits" (Sun Tzu, p. 42).

Reputation. Both Machiavelli and Sun Tzu elucidated the complexities of creating optimal reputations. Inspirational and persuasive messages can be effective in garnering support or raising fear. But Machiavellian theory discourages the use of excessive force because it creates distrust, ill-will, and poor morale among those who may help you later (" . . . in seizing a state, one ought to consider all the injuries he will be obligated to inflict and then proceed to inflict them all at once so as to avoid a frequent repetition of such acts" (Machiavelli, p. 42) and "The skillful strategist defeats the enemy without ever doing battle" (Sun Tzu, p. 16). Such advice would be lost on a psychopath who has no ability to put the brakes on temptation and seeks immediate gratification (Cleckley, 1976).

Summary. Based on insights gleaned from the masters—Sun Tzu and Machiavelli—a key theme has emerged: The successful Machiavellian must exploit long-term strategies that incorporate careful planning and flexible execution. Cold instrumentality is a great asset because it facilitates the application of deceptive and manipulative tactics, useful in the service of greater goals. However, criminal activity or coercion is appropriate only when the payoffs are sufficient; maladaptive responses such as revenge are to be eschewed. As a result, we would expect only select kinds of antisocial behavior (financial fraud, white-collar crime) to be exhibited by Machiavellians: Such crimes should be typified by high gain and low probability of detection.

Of course, the fact that these two historical figures offered such recommendations does not guarantee their existence in contemporary societies. Nonetheless, they are abundant and they can be diagnosed via standard measures such as the Mach IV (Jones & Paulhus, 2009).

Psychopathy (According to Cleckley)

Cleckley's seminal work continues to influence how psychopathy is defined. Along with the exploitativeness common to the Dark Triad, Cleckley pointed to a unique feature of psychopaths, namely, their impulsive and inconsistent behavior (Cleckley, 1976). This maladaptive behavior is so pervasive that it seems to imply a self-sabotage dynamic. Although they practice lying, psychopaths fail to coordinate their duplicitous behaviors in such a way that would allow them to reap the benefits. Lacking impulse control, they appear to show no concern for reputation.

The result is a wide variety of maladaptive behaviors ranging from violence to casual irresponsibility and erratic inconsistency. A hair-trigger aggression is part of a reckless and hot-tempered profile. In seeking to obtain a goal through coercion, those high in psychopathy often strike for little benefit at high-risk times (e.g., "He will commit theft, forgery, adultery, fraud, and other deeds for astonishingly small stakes and under much greater risks of being discovered than will the ordinary scoundrel. He will, in fact, commit such deeds in the absence of any apparent goal at all"; Cleckley, p. 390).

Psychopaths are also theorized to be rigid in their tactics, seemingly unable to learn from mistakes (Cleckley, 1976). This rigidity makes sense insofar as the psychopath never feels regret, and does not engage in long-term planning. There exists little to no impulse control in the psychopath: Rather than the right time, they strike at any time. Unable to adjust, psychopaths are seemingly locked into a short-term frame of mind.

In sum, Cleckley argued that psychopaths are driven by impulsive gratification: that is, getting what they want and getting it now. Interestingly psychopaths seem to break several basic rules of the Machiavellian philosophy: they are reckless, impulsive, and hot-tempered. Of key importance to this chapter is the fact that a similar profile is evident in subclinical psychopaths (Lilienfeld & Andrews, 1996; Williams, Paulhus, & Hare, 2007).

Narcissism (According to Kernberg and Kohut)

The two writers most associated with theoretical conceptions of narcissism are Otto Kernberg and Heinz Kohut. Although there are subtle differences in their approaches, their contributions are typically cited together and interchangeably (e.g., Mollon, 1986; Morf & Rhodewalt, 2001). We will follow suit.

The masters concur that narcissism is characterized primarily by the presence of grandiosity in self-perception. As articulated by Kernberg (1975), "The main characteristics of these narcissistic personalities are grandiosity, extreme self-centeredness, and remarkable absence of interest in and empathy for others in spite of the fact that they are so very eager to obtain admiration and approval from other people" (p. 228). Grandiosity is driven ultimately by fragility of self (Kohut, 1951, p. 28).

According to both writers, there are strong identity elements to narcissism. In traditional psychoanalytic language, the narcissistic identity involves object relations (Kernberg, 1975, p. 29). The vulnerability of the grandiose self requires symbolic objects for confirmation (p. 43). Because the ego is insatiable in its need for continual reinforcement, the behavioral manifestations are chronic. One reason offered by Kohut and Kernberg is that narcissists remain psychologically tethered to long-past parental conflicts.

Consider how concern with one's identity might relate to exploitativeness of those in Quadrant 2. The subset high on identity need must come up with a satisfying interpretation of their exploitativeness. A grandiose self-image would provide the identity that they seek. After all, if one is truly superior to others, it is quite appropriate to exploit them and ignore their feelings. Narcissists feel entitled to take what they want, and can rationalize it; the ensuing grandiosity then feeds back into their sense of entitlement (Kernberg, 1975, p. 17).

Narcissists will also praise those who provide them with narcissistic reinforcement, but shun, avoid, or openly derogate those who cease (or refuse) to do so (e.g., "... They envy others, tend to idealize some people from whom they expect narcissistic supplies and to depreciate and treat with contempt those from whom they do not expect anything (often their former idols)" (1975, p. 17). This rigid strategy involving a lofty elusive goal runs in stark contrast to the Machiavellian strategy. It even contrasts with that of the psychopath, who is motivated by more pedestrian, short-term goals.

Summary. For reasons offered above, the grandiose identity of narcissists provides a symbolic satisfaction of their motives. They seize any opportunity that would reinforce (and strike out at any threat to) their identity. Narcissists rarely engage in criminality per se, perhaps because such behavior brings about only practical or instrumental goals; it rarely helps to reinforce the ego.

Although they share exploitativeness with the other members of the Dark Triad, the etiology is different: Narcissists are callous and manipulative because their grandiosity and sense of entitlement lead to a disregard for others. The grandiose identity ensues from their attempt to extract meaning from knowledge of their exploitative interpersonal style: The only sensible interpretation is that they are indeed superior individuals and entitled to such interpersonal liberties.

Summary and Moderator Extraction

We have gleaned two major themes from our review of the seminal writers.[5] The first theme concerns a set of behavioral tendencies that distinguish Machiavellianism from the other two members of the Dark Triad: They are planning, preparation, flexibility, impulse control, long-term goals, and reputation. Together they suggest a long-term strategist. When combined with exploitativeness, they yield a malevolent but cautious character.

It is this long-term and flexible orientation that distinguishes Machiavellians. It stands in sharp contrast with the short-term tactics associated with psychopathy and narcissism. This individual difference variable moderates the link between circumplex location and behavior and will henceforth be referred to as temporal orientation.

A second theme that emerges from the masters has to do with the tangibility of the goals pursued by the members of the Dark Triad. Those high in psychopathy and Machiavellianism focus on concrete goals such as sex and money. Narcissism, however, involves the pursuit of goals at an abstract level. The reinforcement of a grandiose identity is the consuming motive of these individuals. In sum, we argue for the necessity of a second overarching moderator that distinguishes narcissism: We will refer to this moderator as identity need.

EXPLICATING THE MODERATORS

Moderator 1: Temporal Orientation

The first moderator is captured in Aesop's fable contrasting the ant with the grasshopper. Some people more closely resemble the grasshopper (short-term focused) than the ant (long-term focused). Some individuals may sacrifice the long-term for short-term gain and some will not. We refer to this distinction as temporal orientation. Note that the long-term strategy subsumes well-known constructs such as impulse control and delay of gratification, but goes well beyond them. It also includes planning, flexibility, and reputation-building.

In evolutionary terms, short-term orientation (STO) may be adaptive in situations where cues to appropriate behavior are not reliable or where life expectancy is short. Otherwise, in social species like humans, a long-term orientation (LTO) tends to be more adaptive (Figueredo et al., 2009).

Let's apply this notion to the interpersonal circumplex. The behavioral display of agency and communion should vary with the temporal orientation of the individual. Differences on this moderator should predict the different tactics to achieve their ends.

Key to our argument is that Quadrant 2 inhabitants differ along this dimension. Machiavellian individuals, in particular, are distinctive. Their exploitativeness is played out over time and in the service of long-term, higher order goals. By contrast, psychopathic and narcissistic individuals exhibit their exploitativeness with little regard for the future consequences.

To incorporate this moderator geometrically, a third dimension needs to be appended to the circumplex. Geometrically, this new dimension is represented by the vertical axis in Figure 15.2. Therefore, the similar locations of the Dark Triad in the interpersonal circumplex mask their distinct locations in three-dimensional space.

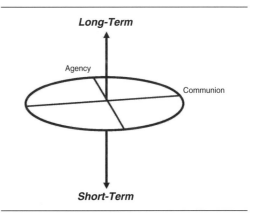

FIGURE 15.2 Interpersonal Circumplex Plus Moderator 1

Recent Research

Recently, we have conducted several studies expressly designed to evaluate the moderating power of temporal orientation. The first example applied the distinction to academic dishonesty (Nathanson, Paulhus, & Williams, 2006b; Williams, Nathanson, & Paulhus, in press). Although both Machiavellianism and psychopathy were linked with academic dishonesty, they differed with respect to the preferred behavioral strategies. Impulsively driven "opportunistic" cheating (e.g., copying someone's multiple choice answers), was predicted by psychopathy scores (Williams et al., in press). Machiavellianism did not predict this risky and impulsive cheating strategy. By contrast, planned dishonesty (e.g., plagiarism on term papers) was predicted by Machiavellianism (Nathanson et al., 2006b).

A second study showed how temporal orientation influences behavioral tactics in the domain of sexual and romantic relationships. Jones and Paulhus (2010c) used a new and improved measure of sociosexuality that assesses both long-term as well as short-term mating orientation (Jackson & Kirkpatrick, 2007). Results showed that psychopathy was the only one of the Dark Triad associated with an exclusively short-term profile: They are sexually promiscuous, short-term focused, and strongly averse to any long-term romantic commitment. Psychopaths also have an abundance of casual sex, lifetime partners, and act unfaithfully.

A third study showed that Machiavellians adjust their mate retention tactics according to the type of relationship they are pursuing (long-term vs. short-term), whereas the other two personality types do not. For example, mate retention tactics, which are often coercive and ultimately destructive to a relationship, may serve the short-term benefit of keeping a partner from straying, even if it leads to the dissolution of the relationship in the future. Jones and Paulhus (2010c) showed that all three members of the Dark Triad engage in similar mate retention tactics for short-term relationships, but only Machiavellianism was associated with a mitigation of those tactics when a long-term relationship was the goal.

A fourth study by Jones and Paulhus (2010b) directly contrasted the Dark Triad with respect to measures of impulsivity. Overall, psychopathy showed the strongest association. The correlation with narcissism was in the same direction, but weaker. Machiavellianism was either neutral or negatively associated with all forms of impulsivity. Interestingly, narcissism was exclusively associated with "functional" impulsivity or confidence, whereas psychopathy was exclusively associated with "dysfunctional" impulsivity (Dickman, 1990).

Summary

We have detailed the need for a moderator variable to differentiate Machiavellians from the other two Dark Triad members. There is sufficient evidence to suggest that Machiavellians are long-term oriented whereas the other two members are short-term in orientation. Although exploitative like other members of the Dark Triad, Machiavellians have long-term relationships, are behaviorally flexible, are less impulsive, and cheat in a calculated fashion.

Moderator 2: Identity Need

We now turn to a second moderator variable—identity need—which helps distinguish narcissism from the other two Dark Triad members. This construct captures the distinction between (a) goals of a concrete, instrumental nature, and (b) goals of an abstract, symbolic nature.[6] The latter goals involve making subjective meaning out of (often chaotic) objective life events (Frankl, 1968; May, 1953).

This distinction was anticipated in the social exchange theory of U. G. Foa and Foa (1974). They laid out an exchange dimension ranging from concrete to abstract.

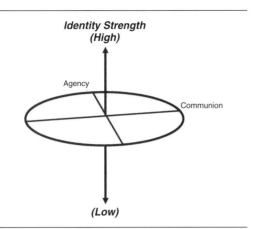

**Identity Strength
(High)**

Agency

Communion

(Low)

FIGURE 15.3   Interpersonal Circumplex Plus Moderator 2

Abstract goals included status, esteem, and identity, whereas concrete goals included the attainment of goods or services. Another example may be found in the literature on communication theorists: Clark and Delia (1979) included a higher order dimension labeled "identity making," along with two others labeled "instrumental" and "relational" (e.g., Clark & Delia, 1979). Needless to say, instrumental and relational dimensions map onto the agentic and communal motives of the interpersonal circumplex, respectively. The identity dimension corresponds to our identity need moderator.

Experimental work from contemporary social psychology corroborates the motivational power of meaning-making: Temporarily undermining meaning creates anxiety, which then motivates the extraction of new meaning from the situation (Heine, Proulx, & Vohs, 2006). For example, individuals who encounter an inexplicable event are motivated to find meaning in their situation. Consistent with existential psychologists such as Frankl and May, meaning-making quells the inevitable anxiety of everyday life.

Application to personality. Personality researchers deal with meaning-making at the level of identity (see special issue edited by Singer, 2004). Indeed, personality can be defined as the creation and maintenance of an abstract integration of a broad range of information about the self (Baumeister,

1986; McAdams, 1985). Included in one's identity are historical narratives as well as static traits (Singer, 2004). To Hogan and Smither (2001), identity-seeking represents a third motive on equal footing with the circumplex axes of "getting ahead" (agency) and "getting along" (communion). Figure 15.3 shows a third dimension along with communion and agency; this dimension concerns the strength of a motive to affirm one's identity.

Only recently have social scientists called for empirical attention to individual differences in identity need. Ryff (1989), for example, showed that concepts such as purpose in life and personal growth are missing from common conceptions of health, and are a dimension that must be explored when considering human goals (Ryff & Singer, 1998). Horowitz (2004b) described how strength of self-image has repercussions for psychopathology.

The proposition that the identity process has an interpersonal basis is not a new one. As the symbolic interactionists argued many years ago, identity emerges primarily from information inferred from others' reactions to the self (Cooley, 1956). Feedback from interactions is continually integrated into the self-concept and, if consistent, creates a strong identity (Singer, 2004).

In sum, identity need is a second individual difference variable that moderates the relation between circumplex location and observable behavior. We have argued that the concept is especially apt for articulating the process of turning meaning-making inward, that is, interpreting ongoing behavior and events in relation to the self. As such, it provides the moderator necessary for distinguishing narcissism from the other two members of the Dark Triad.

Narcissism: A strong and positive identity. This moderator of identity need explains where narcissists part company from subclinical psychopaths and Machiavellians. Whereas the latter two pursue functional goals such as sex, money, or status, narcissistic goals are abstract in nature. For the narcissist, the desired identity is clear: "I am a superior and entitled individual."

Attaining this identity requires status, admiration, and respect rather than tangible resources or outcomes (Kernberg, 1975).

In searching for an identity that justifies their dispositions, narcissistic individuals face the difficult task of incorporating low communion into a positive identity. A strong sense of superiority and entitlement is necessary to justify their indifferent dominance of others. Moreover, the narcissistic need for maintaining this positive identity is a never-ending pursuit (Brown & Bosson, 2001).

By contrast, neither Machiavellians nor psychopaths appear to have the continual self-enhancement needs of the narcissistic individual. Without a strong identity need, these personalities remain unconcerned about their self-concept and focus on the instrumental benefits of their behavior.

Our aggression study. Recently, we designed an experiment that directly addresses the role that identity need plays in triggering aggression (Jones & Paulhus, 2010a). We drew on previous research indicating that narcissists aggress when their egos are threatened (e.g., Bushman & Baumeister, 1998; Twenge & Campbell, 2003). Our rationale was that interference with the identity need process (via ego threat) should upset narcissistic individuals but not Machiavellians or psychopathic individuals.

Two forms of provocation were manipulated: Participants were randomly assigned to be threatened with an abstract ego threat (an insult or no insult to an essay they wrote). Their aggression was also measured before and after a physical threat (a blast of white noise). Results indicated that only the narcissists responded to the symbolic threat whereas only psychopaths responded to the physical threat. Machiavellians responded to neither threat.

Narcissists' identity as superior was threatened by the insult: At an abstract level it represented an identity threat (Vohs & Heatherton, 2001). Psychopaths did not respond to the insult; however, they did respond to a direct physical threat.

Although not on a par with other forms of physical threat (i.e., a punch in the face), a blast of white noise fits the definition of physical aggression because it is an act intended to do physical harm to another.

Also as predicted, Machiavellianism did not predict aggression under either provocation. Under the proper conditions, we suspect, Machiavellianism could be related to aggression: But such aggression would only occur for those high in Machiavellianism when the context was one of high profit and low risk (see Jones & Paulhus, 2009).

Summary

We have called for a second moderator variable to differentiate narcissists from the other two Dark Triad members. Exploitative individuals (those in Quadrant 2), trying to interpret their own behavior and traits, find identity in a narcissistic self. For them, the question is: "Why am I indifferent to other people's feelings and want to manipulate them?" ... and the answer is: "I am a superior person who is entitled to do so."[7]

INTEGRATION

Our challenge was to reconcile the distinctiveness of the Dark Triad within a common framework of the interpersonal circumplex. Although the three exploitative personalities project into the same quadrant in interpersonal space, their overt behavior often differs.

Our solution was to undo the knot with two twists—that is, two conceptual moderators. The first moderator is temporal orientation. An individual's interpersonal predispositions can be played out strategically in the long-term or impulsively in the short-term. Compared to the other two inhabitants of Quadrant 2, Machiavellians are more long-term in the pursuit of their goals.

A second conceptual moderator honors individual differences in identity need. Self-construals may or may not be transformed into a meaningful identity. In Quadrant 2, individuals high in identity need develop the grandiose self-image characteristic of narcissists. That choice of identities is necessary to explain a combination of interpersonal motives that appears exploitative. By contrast, Machiavellians and psychopaths may be aware of their traits and behaviors but have no need to formulate them as an identity.

In sum, we combined two moderator variables with the two-dimensional IPC plane to form a four-dimensional system. We believe that it has applications beyond our goal of reconciling the Dark Triad variables.

Beyond Quadrant 2

Our two-moderator model may help explain the behavioral tactics of individuals in any quadrant of the IPC. Consider the first moderator: temporal orientation. Behaviors typically associated with Quadrant 1 can be short-term or long-term. For example, one could express these (agentically communal) values through activities such as street protests for the homeless, a short-term tactic. Alternatively, one could manifest these values by fashioning a political movement, a long-term tactic.

Similar to temporal orientation, the identity need distinction is not limited to Quadrant 2 of the circumplex. In Quadrant 3 (indifferent and submissive), identity need might differentiate two other characters. Those high in identity need might invoke an identity of "alienated victim" whereas those low on the moderator might simply acknowledge their negative traits. Quadrant 4 (submissive and communal) could also be differentiated by the identity need moderator. Those high on the moderator might create an identity out of their connections with others, whereas others might not (e.g., Aron, Paris, & Aron, 1995).

We do not argue that every finding in circumplex research needs to be reevaluated with respect to these two moderators. For one thing, much interpersonal research is concerned with self-perceptions: The structure of self-reported traits or values

can usefully be analyzed independently of observed behavior. Even behavioral analyses are likely to show that similar locations in the circumplex are matched by similar behavioral tactics. In some cases, there are no striking phenotypic differences to be explained. In the case of Quadrant 2, it seems impossible to understand our three exploitative personalities without the two moderators.

Nor should the addition of moderators be limited to our two offerings. Other moderators are likely to be necessary to deal with other sets of variables that project adjacently on the IPC. Tracey and colleagues, for example, have demonstrated the conceptual richness of adding moderators such as anxiety and self-esteem (Tracey, Rounds, & Gurtman, 1996). They went further to evaluate the shape of the IPC at different levels of the moderators.

Our two moderators were derived from seminal writers with the explicit purpose of clarifying three distinct personalities that are all associated with high agency and low communion. Although the circumplex is powerful on its own, moderators may help to disentangle apparently overlapping constructs that are actually distinct in other important ways. Left on the agenda is the examination of the shape of the IPC within various levels of the IPC (Tracey, Rounds, & Gurtman, 1996).

Underlying Personality Processes

From a process point of view, the IPC confluence of the Dark Triad members in Quadrant 2 may seem misleading. It is likely that their common tendency to be exploitative juxtaposes them in Quadrant 2. However, the underlying psychological mechanisms that led Machiavellians, psychopaths, and narcissists to exhibit these predispositions may differ substantially. Without clarifying the underlying motivations, it is difficult to fully understand personality constructs (Horowitz et al., 2006).

In fact, the IPC location of the Dark Triad may not jibe with the necessity to use interpersonal theory for distinguishing them. A fully noninterpersonal interpretation is worth considering (cf. Shechtman & Horowitz, 2006). First is the case of narcissism.[8] That personality can be manifested without the involvement of other people (e.g., gazing into the mirror). The exploitation of others may simply be a side effect of self-centeredness. Other narcissistic behaviors, such as self-enhancement, derogation, and self-handicapping, are also consistent with this overriding egocentrism.

For psychopaths, exploitation of others may simply be a side effect of poor impulse-control. Assuming that their temptations are similar to nonpsychopaths, psychopathic individuals will cause more harm to more people. As their inadvertent harm to others accumulates, their callousness hardens much as a physical callus forms from consistent use (Blair, 2005).

Similarly, Machiavellian individuals may be motivated by goals similar to non-Machiavellians. If other people interfere with their goals, their indifference (lack of empathy) will play a role. Others are no different from inanimate pawns to be maneuvered. But Machiavellians often manifest their exploitativeness in noninterpersonal domains: For example, on tax returns they attempt to cheat businesses or society as a whole. In none of these cases is it necessary to engage directly with another person. In sum, the strong IPC projection of the Dark Triad may be misleading in implying that the Dark Triad behaviors are intrinsically interpersonal.

Two Interpersonal Views?

Finally, we reflect on the Dark Triad in terms of interpersonal theory in the Sullivanian sense (e.g., Carson, 1969; Sullivan, 1953). All three of the variables can be construed as fundamentally interpersonal. Consider narcissism: It can be construed as an interpersonal trait to the extent that narcissists require others' praise to counter their underlying insecurity. According to Morf and Rhodewalt (2001), narcissists report that others' praise is more important than personal accomplishments. One can also argue that Machiavellians require others to manipulate: Without others, they cannot satisfy their motivation for duping delight (Ekman, 1980). Finally, psychopathy may be interpersonal to the degree that psychopaths need someone to hurt. Their exploitation of others may reflect an intrinsic motivation to see others suffer.

Interestingly, these conjectures appear to undermine the claim that the low end of communion is indifference. Instead, low communion scores may entail an intrinsic motivation to exploit others. For example, some degree of interpersonal connection is required to explain such behaviors as aggression, hostility, mate-poaching, mating interference, cruelty, and torture. They go well beyond detachment; they are consistent with studies locating aggression as the polar opposite of communion (Hopwood, Koonce, & Morey, in press).

Yet we hesitate to dismiss the indifference interpretation because it has a solid theoretical and empirical basis (Horowitz, Wilson, Turan, Zolotsev, Constantino, & Henderson, 2006). Instead, a reconciliation of the interpersonal circumplex and interpersonal theory may require yet another moderator variable—one that distinguishes hot versus cold versions of low communion. Such an orthogonal moderator would help explain why many studies of the circumplex have landed variables such as hostile and cold adjacent to each other on the circumplex (e.g., Horowitz et al., 2006; Wiggins & Pincus, 1992).

Resolving these issues is well beyond the scope of the current chapter. A great deal of further empirical and theoretical work is required. One possible approach to determining the interpersonal saturation of the Dark Triad is to apply techniques developed by Shechtman and Horowitz (2006).

CONCLUSION

The interpersonal circumplex harbors a wealth of information about interpersonal values, goals, motives, and traits. For the most part, evaluation of these attributes does not require the moderators proposed here; the attributes are fully characterized by the circumplex alone. Specifically with respect to the Dark Triad, the circumplex captures perfectly their overlap: they are all high agency and low communion because of their common exploitative tendencies.

An accurate evaluation of the behavioral tactics of the Dark Triad, however, requires both the circumplex location and a specification of one or both of the moderators—temporal orientation and identity need. If the moderators prove equally useful in the other quadrants, a more wholesale integration with the circumplex might be in order.

References

Aron, A., Paris, M., & Aron, E. N. (1995). Falling in love: Prospective studies of self-concept change. *Journal of Personality and Social Psychology, 69*, 1102–1112.

Ashton, M .C., Lee, K., Perugini, M., Szarota, P., de Vries, R. E., & Di Blas, L., ... De Raad, B. (2004). A six-factor structure of personality-descriptive adjectives: Solutions from psycholexical studies in seven languages. *Journal of Personality and Social Psychology, 86*, 356–366.

Bakan, D. (1966). *The duality of human existence: Isolation and communion in Western man*. Boston: Beacon Press.

Baumeister, R. F. (1986). *Identity: Cultural change and the struggle for self*. New York: Oxford Books.

Bettencourt, B. A., Talley, A., Benjamin, A. J., & Valentine, J. (2006). Personality and aggressive behavior under provoking and neutral conditions: A meta-analytic review. *Psychological Bulletin, 132*, 751–777.

Blackburn, R., & Maybury, C. (1985). Identifying the psychopath: The relation of Cleckley's criteria to the interpersonal domain. *Personality and Individual Differences, 6*, 375–386.

Blair, R. J. R. (2005). Responding to the emotions of others: Dissociating forms of empathy through the study of typical and psychiatric populations. *Consciousness and Cognition, 14*, 698–718.

Book, A. S., & Quinsey, V. L. (2004). Psychopaths: cheaters or warrior-hawks? *Personality and Individual Differences, 36*, 33–45.

Bradlee, P. M., & Emmons, R. A. (1992). Locating narcissism within the interpersonal circumplex and the five-factor model. *Personality and Individual Differences, 13*, 821–830.

Brown, R. P., & Bosson, J. K. (2001). Narcissus meets Sisyphus: Self-love, self-loathing, and the never-ending pursuit of self-worth. *Psychological Inquiry, 12*, 210–213.

Bushman, B. J., & Baumeister, R. F. (1998). Threatened egotism, narcissism, self esteem, and direct and displaced aggression: Does self-love or self-hate lead to violence? *Journal of Personality and Social Psychology, 75*, 219–229.

Campbell, J., Schermer, J. A., Villani, V. C., Nguyen, B., Vickers, L., & Vernon, P. A. (2009). A behavioral genetic study of the Dark Triad of personality and moral development. *Twin Research and Human Genetics, 12*, 132–136.

Carson, R. (1969). *Interaction concepts of personality*. Chicago: Aldine Press.

Christie, R., & Geis, F. (1970). *Studies in Machiavellianism*. New York: Academic Press.

Clark, R. A., & Delia, J. G. (1979). Topoi and rhetorical competence. *The Quarterly Journal of Speech, 65*, 187–206.

Cleckley, H. (1976). *The mask of sanity* (5th ed.). St. Louis, MO: Mosby.

Cooley, C. H. (1956). *Human nature and the social order*. New York: Free Press.

Dickinson, K. A., & Pincus, A. L. (2003). Interpersonal analysis of grandiose and vulnerable narcissism . *Journal of Personality Disorders, 17*, 188–203.

Dickman, S. J. (1990). Functional and dysfunctional impulsivity: Personality and cognitive correlates. *Journal of Personality and Social Psychology, 58*, 95–102.

Egan, V. (2009, July). *The main predictors of aggression: Low A, low A, and low A?* Paper presented at meeting of the International Society for the Study of Individual Differences, Evanston, Illinois.

Emmons, R. A. (1987). Narcissism: Theory and measurement. *Journal of Personality and Social Psychology, 52*, 11–17.

Figueredo, A. J., Wolf, P. S. A. Gladden, P. R., Olderbak, S. G., Andrzejczak, D. J., & Jacobs, W. J. (2009). Ecological approaches to personality. In Buss, D. M., & Hawley, P. H., (Eds.), *The evolution of personality and individual differences*. New York: Oxford University Press.

Foa, U. G., & Foa, E. B. (1974). *Societal structures of the mind*. Springfield, IL: Charles C. Thomas.

Fraley, C. R., Brumbaugh, C. C., & Marks, M. J. (2005). The evolution and function of adult attachment: A comparative and phylogenetic analysis. *Journal of Personality and Social Psychology, 89,* 731–746.

Frankl, V. (1968). *Man's search for meaning.* New York: Washington Square Press.

Gurtman, M. B. (1992). Trust, distrust, and interpersonal problems: A circumplex analysis. *Journal of Personality and Social Psychology, 62,* 989–1002.

Gurtman, M. B., & Pincus, A. (2000). Interpersonal adjective scales: Confirmation of circumplex structure from multiple perspectives. *Journal of Personality and Social Psychology, 26,* 374–384.

Harms, P. D., Williams, K. M., & Paulhus, D. L. (2001). *Predictors of love-proneness vs. lust-proneness.* Poster presented at the 109th annual convention of the American Psychological Association, San Francisco.

Heine, S. J., Proulx, T., & Vohs, K. D. (2006). The Meaning Maintenance Model: On the coherence of social motivations. *Personality and Social Psychology Review, 10,* 88–110.

Hicklin, J., & Widiger, T. A. (2005). Similarities and differences among antisocial and psychopathic self-report inventories from the perspective of general personality functioning. *European Journal of Personality, 19,* 325–342.

Hogan, R., & Smither, R. (2001). *Personality: Theories and applications.* Boulder, CO: Westview Press.

Hopwood, C. J., Koonce, E. A., & Morey, L. C. (in press). An exploratory study of integrative personality pathology systems and the interpersonal circumplex. *Journal of Psychopathology and Behavioral Assessment.*

Horowitz, L. M. (2004a). *Interpersonal foundations of psychopathology.* Washington, DC: American Psychological Association.

Horowitz, L. M., (2004b). The self-image and interpersonal processes. In L. M. Horowitz, *Interpersonal foundations of psychopathology* (pp. 81–100). Washington, DC: American Psychological Association.

Horowitz, L. M., Alden, L. E., Wiggins, J. S., & Pincus, A. L. (2000). *Inventory of interpersonal problems.* San Antonio, TX: Psychological Corporation.

Horowitz, L. M., Wilson, Kelly, R., Turan, B., Zolotsev, P., Constantino, M. J., & Henderson, L. (2006). How interpersonal motives clarify the meaning of interpersonal behavior: A revised circumplex model. *Personality and Social Psychology Review, 10,* 67–86.

Jackson, J. J., & Kirkpatrick, L. (2007). The structure and measurement of human mating strategies: Toward a multidimensional model of sociosexuality. *Evolution and Human Behavior, 28,* 382–391.

Jakobwitz, S., & Egan, V. (2006). The dark triad and normal personality traits. *Personality and Individual Differences, 40,* 331–339.

Jonason, P. K., Li, N. P., Webster, G. D., & Schmitt, D. P. (2009). The Dark Triad: Facilitating a short-term mating strategy in men. *European Journal of Personality, 23,* 5–18.

Jones, D. N., & Paulhus, D. L. (2009). Machiavellianism. In M. R. Leary & R. H. Hoyle (Eds.), *Handbook of individual differences in social behavior* (pp. 102–120). New York: Guilford Press.

Jones, D. N., & Paulhus, D. L. (2010a). Differential provocations trigger aggression in psychopaths and narcissists. *Social Psychological and Personality Science, 1,* 33–45.

Jones, D. N., & Paulhus, D. L. (2010b). How impulsivity differentiates the Dark Triad. Manuscript submitted for publication.

Jones, D. N., & Paulhus, D. L. (2010c). Mating Strategies among the Dark Triad: Retention, infidelity, and short- vs. long-term relationship focus. Manuscript submitted for publication.

Kernberg, O. (1975). *Borderline conditions and pathological narcissism.* New York: Jason Aronson.

Kohut, H. (1951). "The function of the analyst in the therapeutic process" by Samuel D. Lipton. In P. H. Ornstein (Ed.) (1978), *The search for the self: Selected writings of Heinz Kohut: 1950–1978* (pp. I: 159–166). New York: International Universities Press.

Leary, T. F. (1957). *Interpersonal diagnosis of personality.* New York: Ronald Press.

Lee, K., & Ashton, M. C. (2005). Psychopathy, Machiavellianism, and narcissism in the Five-Factor Model and the HEXACO model of personality structure. *Personality and Individual Differences, 38,* 1571–1582.

Lilienfeld, S. O., & Andrews, B. P. (1996). Development and preliminary validation of a self-report measure of psychopathic personality traits in non-criminal populations. *Journal of Personality Assessment, 66,* 488–524.

Locke, K. D. (2000). Circumplex scales of interpersonal values: Reliability, validity, and applicability to interpersonal problems and personality disorders. *Journal of Personality Assessment, 75,* 249–267.

Machiavelli, N. (1513/1981). *The prince*. New York: Bantam Classics.

Markey, P. M., & Markey, C. N. (2009). A brief assessment of the interpersonal circumplex. *Assessment, 16*, 352–361.

May, R. (1953). *Man's search for himself*. New York: Norton.

McAdams, D. P. (1985). *Power, intimacy, and the life story: Personological inquiries into identity*. New York: Guilford.

McHoskey, J. W., Worzel, W., & Szyarto, C. (1998). Machiavellianism and psychopathy. *Journal of Personality and Social Psychology, 74*, 192–210.

Mealey, L. (1995). The sociobiology of sociopathy: An integrated evolutionary model. *Behavioral and Brain Sciences, 18*, 523–599.

Mollon, P. (1986). An appraisal of Kohut's contribution to the understanding of narcissism. *British Journal of Psychotherapy, 3*, 151–161.

Morf, C. C., & Rhodewalt, F. (2001). Unraveling the paradoxes of narcissism: A dynamic self-regulatory processing model. *Psychological Inquiry, 12*, 177–196.

Nathanson, C., Paulhus, D. L. & Williams, K. M. (2006a). Personality and misconduct correlates of body modification and other cultural deviance markers. *Journal of Research in Personality, 40*, 779–802.

Nathanson, C., Paulhus, D. L., & Williams, K. M. (2006b). Predictors of a behavioral measure of scholastic cheating: Personality and competence but not demographics. *Contemporary Educational Psychology, 31*, 97–122.

Patrick, C. J., & Zempolich, K. A. (1998). Emotion and aggression in the psychopathic personality. *Aggression and Violent Behavior, 3*, 303–338.

Paulhus, D. L. (2001). Normal narcissism: Two minimalist accounts. *Psychological Inquiry, 8*, 228–230.

Paulhus, D. L. (August, 2001). *Shedding conceptual light on the Dark Triad of personality*. Presented at the meeting of the American Psychological Association convention, San Francisco.

Paulhus, D. L., & Williams, K. M. (2002). The dark triad of personality: Narcissism, Machiavellianism, and psychopathy. *Journal of Research in Personality, 36*, 556–563.

Pincus, A. (2006). A contemporary integrative interpersonal theory of personality disorders. In M. F. Lensenweger & J. F. Clarkin (Eds.), *Major theories of personality disorder* (2nd ed.). New York: Guilford Press.

Reidy, D. E., Zeichner, A., & Martinez, M. A. (2008). Effects of psychopathy traits on unprovoked aggression. *Aggressive Behavior, 34*, 319–328.

Reise, S. P., & Wright, T. M. (1996). Personality traits, cluster B personality disorders, and sociosexuality. *Journal of Research in Personality, 30*, 128–136.

Rhodewalt, F., & Morf, C.C. (1995). Self and interpersonal correlates of the narcissistic personality inventory: A review and new findings. *Journal of Research in Personality, 29*, 1–23.

Ruiz, M. A., Dickinson, K. A., & Pincus, A. L. (2002). Concurrent validity of the Personality Assessment Inventory Alcohol Problems (ALC) Scale in a college student sample. *Assessment, 9*, 261–270.

Ruiz, J. M., Smith, T. W., & Rhodewalt, F. (2001). Distinguishing narcissism and hostility: Similarities and differences in interpersonal circumplex and five-factor correlates. *Journal of Personality Assessment, 76*, 537–555.

Ryff, C. D. (1989). Happiness is everything, or is it? Explorations on the meaning of psychological well-being. *Journal of Personality and Social Psychology, 57*, 1069–1081.

Ryff, C. D., & Singer, B. (1998). The contours of positive human health. *Psychological Inquiry, 9*, 1–28.

Salekin, R. T., Leistico, A. M. R., Trobst, K. K., Schrum, C. L., & Lochman, J. E. (2005). Adolescent psychopathy and personality theory: The interpersonal circumplex: Expanding evidence of a nomological net. *Journal of Abnormal Child Psychology, 33*, 445–460.

Salekin, R. T., Trobst, K. K., Krioukova, M. (2001). Construct validity of psychopathy in a community sample: A nomological net approach. *Journal of Personality Disorders, 15*, 425–441.

Shechtman, N., & Horowitz, L. M. (2006). Interpersonal and noninterpersonal interactions, interpersonal motives, and the effect of frustrated motives. *Personality and Social Psychology Bulletin, 32*, pp. 1126–1139.

Singer, J. A. (Ed.) (2004). Special Issue: Narrative identity and meaning-making across the adult lifespan. *Journal of Personality, 72*, 437–658.

Strack, S., & Lorr, M. (Eds.) (1994). *Differentiating normal and abnormal personality*. New York: Springer.

Sullivan, H. S. (1953). The interpersonal theory of psychiatry. New York: Norton.

Sun Tzu (1998). *The art of war* (Y. Shibing & J. J. L. Duyvendak, Trans.). New York: Wordsworth.

Tracey, T. J. G., Rounds, J., & Gurtman, M. (1996). Examination of the general factor with the interpersonal circumplex structure: Application to the Inventory of Interpersonal Problems. *Multivariate Behavioral Research, 31,* 36–44.

Trapnell, P. D., & Paulhus, D. L. (in press). Agentic and communal values. *Journal of Research in Personality.*

Twenge, J. M., & Campbell, W. K. (2003). "Isn't it fun to get the respect that we are going to deserve?" Narcissism, social rejection, and aggression. *Personality and Social Psychology Bulletin, 29,* 261–272.

Vernon, P. A., Villani, V. C., Vickers, L. C., & Harris, J. A. (2008). A behavioral genetic investigation of the Dark Triad and the Big 5. *Personality and Individual Differences, 44,* 445–452.

Vohs, K. D., & Heatherton, T. F. (2001). Self-esteem and threats to self: Implications for self-construals and interpersonal perceptions. *Journal of Personality and Social Psychology, 81,* 1103–1118.

Widiger, T. A., & Lynam, D. R. (1998). Psychopathy as a variant of common personality traits: Implications for diagnosis, etiology, and pathology. In T. Millon (Ed.), *Psychopathy: Antisocial, criminal, and violent behavior* (pp. 171–187). New York: Guilford Press.

Williams, K. M., McAndrew, A., Learn, T., Harms, P. D., & Paulhus, D. L. (2001). *The Dark Triad returns: Antisocial behavior and entertainment preferences among narcissists, Machiavellians, and psychopaths.* Poster presented at the meeting of the American Psychological Association, San Francisco

Williams, K. M., & Paulhus, D. L. (2004). Factor structure of the Self-Report Psychopathy scale (SRP II) in nonforensic samples. *Personality and Individual Differences, 37,* 765–778.

Williams, K. M., Nathanson, C., & Paulhus, D. L. (in press). Identifying and profiling scholastic cheaters: Their personality, cognitive ability, and motivation. *Journal of Experimental Psychology: Applied.*

Williams, K. M., Paulhus, D. L., & Hare, R. D. (2007). The four facet structure of psychopathy in non-forensic samples. *Journal of Personality Assessment, 88,* 118–129.

Wilson, D. S., Near, D. C., & Miller, R. R. (1996). Machiavellianism: A synthesis of the evolutionary and psychological literatures. *Psychological Bulletin, 119,* 285–299.

Wiggins, J. S. (1979). A psychological taxonomy of trait-descriptive terms: The interpersonal domain. *Journal of Personality and Social Psychology, 37,* 395–412.

Wiggins, J. S., & Broughton, R. (1985). The interpersonal circle: A structural model for the integration of personality research. In R. Hogan, & W. H. Jones (Eds.), *Perspectives in personality* (Vol. 1, pp. 1–47). Greenwich, CT: JAI Press.

Wiggins, J. S., & Pincus, A. (1992). Agency and communion as conceptual coordinates for understanding and measurement of interpersonal behavior. In P. T. Costa & T. A Widiger (Eds.), *Personality disorders and the five-factor model of personality* (pp. 73–93). Washington, DC: American Psychological Association.

NOTES

1. Most similar in location to the other Dark Triad members is the NPI facet labeled "exploitative-entitled."

2. Convinced by the unificationist arguments, Lilienfeld has concretized the unificationist position in his influential measure of antisocial behavior. The Psychopathic Personality Inventory (PPI) subsumes all three Dark Triad members under one label, "psychopathy" (Lilienfeld & Andrews, 1996).

3. Later in this chapter, we detail several other studies designed specifically to explain this distinctiveness within a moderated circumplex.

4. Our most recent research on this issue is detailed in the moderator section later in this chapter.

5. We acknowledge that other important writers on these topics take rather different theoretical positions.

6. The notion of meaning-making has strong philosophical roots. In the existential literature, the creation of symbolic representations out of mundane human events was central to the writings of

philosophers such as Kierkegaard and Nietzsche, and psychologists such as Frankl and May. Frankl (1968), for example, argued that meaning-making was a motive that transcended biological systems and concrete goals. May (1953) argued that extracting meaning from the chaos of life is necessary to overcome the inevitable anxieties of life.

7. We must acknowledge alternatives to grandiosity as the key element of this moderator dimension. Fundamental insecurity, for example, may be the psychological mechanism that distinguishes narcissists from the other Dark Triad members. May (1953), for example, argued that anxiety drives a fundamental search for meaning, which at the personality level creates an identity need.

8. A less explored variant, *vulnerable narcissism*, entails an even more complex process model (Dickinson & Pincus, 2003). It also falls in Quadrant 2, but may require another moderator—neuroticism, perhaps.

16   SOCIAL ALLERGENS

Brian P. O'Connor

SOCIAL ALLERGENS

Jack and I were friends in graduate school. We had a lot of interests in common and often enjoyed having lunch together. But after a while I noticed that, whenever I expressed an opinion, Jack would interrupt me and begin his reply with "Yes, but..." and then proceed to criticize my opinion. After a while, I was counting the number of "Yes, but" interruption-criticisms whenever we had lunch together. I became increasingly annoyed, and in time, I let our friendship cool. Eventually I lost contact with Jack.

Perhaps all human beings have had the experience of being annoyed or repulsed by another person at some time in their lives. "Social allergens" are behaviors or characteristics of others that generate negative experiences in us. While some behaviors, such as outright physical assaults, likely generate negative reactions in just about everyone, social allergens are often

objectively minor from the perspectives of outside observers. Conversational interruptions, unwanted suggestions, possessive jealousy, inattentiveness, insensitivity, and monologues may bother some people very much and others not at all. Emotionally major aversive personal experiences can nevertheless develop once a particular social behavior begins to grate on our nerves.

Cunningham, Barbee, and Druen (1997) were the first researchers to use the term "social allergens" in this context. In their words, a social allergen is "a behavior or situation created by another person that may be seen as unpleasant, but not as strongly aversive, to objective observers." According to these authors, a social allergy is a "reaction of hypersensitive disgust or annoyance to a social allergen" (p. 191). Cunningham et al. claimed that there are close parallels between psychological reactions to social allergens and the reactions that some persons have to physical allergens, such as pollen or poison ivy. Initial exposures prompt mild and slow-developing aversive reactions, whereas repeated exposures can elicit immediate and intensely uncomfortable emotions. Although social allergies may sometimes seem trivial and petty, they are presumably very common, and

Acknowledgments: This work was supported by a grant from the Social Sciences and Humanities Research Council of Canada. Address correspondence to Brian P. O'Connor, Department of Psychology,, University of British Columbia–Okanagan, 3333 University Way, Kelowna, British Columbia, Canada, V1V 1V7; e-mail: brian.oconnor@ubc.ca; phone: 250-807-9636; fax: 250-807-8439.

relationships may deteriorate because sensitive individuals often say nothing about their discomfort and because individuals sometimes explode with hostile expressions of irritation and annoyance.

Although the concept of social allergens has strong intuitive appeal to many people, there have been surprisingly few empirical studies of the phenomenon reported in the literature. This chapter provides a review of the available evidence and relevant theoretical issues. The first section of the chapter describes empirical findings concerning the features of social allergens and social allergies, and outlines definitional and conceptual issues that have emerged from the research. Subsequent sections focus on social allergens in relation to interpersonal theory, the five-factor model of personality, and close relationships. Theoretical reasons why some interpersonal behaviors become aversive to some people are then discussed. The closing section focuses on directions for further research.

FEATURES OF SOCIAL ALLERGENS
AND SOCIAL ALLERGIES

Research Findings

Cunningham et al. (1997) asked 150 respondents to describe cases in which someone had exhibited a behavior that produced such strong feelings in them that "it takes very little for the person to irritate, offend you, or cause physical symptoms" (p. 193). Every respondent was able to nominate at least one such person. The most commonly nominated persons were friends (30%), romantic partners (18%), coworkers (18%), bosses and teachers (17%), and relatives (14%). Cunningham et al. classified every social allergen to show (a) whether it seemed to be intentional and (b) whether it seemed to be directed personally at the person reporting it. The resulting four categories produced the following results: (1) Of all the allergens, 34% were classified as intentional and personal; they were called "intrusions and dominance"—for example, *gives commands without having*

legitimate authority. (2) Thirty percent were unintentional but personal; they were called "insensitivity and nonreciprocity"—for example, *is inattentive in conversations.* (3) Twenty-three percent were intentional but impersonal: They were called "annoying habits and personal qualities"—for example, *norm violations and discrepant behaviors*— for example, *cheats or tells lies to other people.* (4) Fourteen percent were unintentional and impersonal; they were called "annoying habits and personal qualities"— for example, *frequently expresses negative emotions.* Further research is needed to determine whether and how these categories differ in aversiveness.

The respondents in this study reported that they interacted with the offending persons in their lives five times per week on average, with a median exposure time of 4 to 5 hours. They said that they were able to spend about 1 hour with such persons before experiencing negative emotions. According to their reports, the negative emotions typically took nearly three hours to subside once activated. In addition, the respondents said they had known the offending persons approximately one year before the negative feelings began to develop, and the strongest negative feelings occurred after 18 months. Their reports also suggested that the longer it took for an allergic reaction to develop, the longer the negative emotion lasted.

O'Connor and Nadin (2009) surveyed 545 female and 167 male undergraduates (total $N = 712$; mean age $= 21$ years) using essentially the same nomination instructions (quoted above) that were used by Cunningham et al. (1997). Every respondent reported at least one social allergy. The offending persons were typically friends or acquaintances (67%), family members (15%), or coworkers (9%). Most respondents had known the offending persons a long time (mean $= 5.8$ years), and 19% of respondents lived with the person. Most respondents said they saw the offending person rather frequently, and they typically spent an average of 2.2 hours a week with the individuals. There was great variation among the respondents in how long they reported having known the offending person before the negative emotions became strong, but once the allergy had developed, the negative emotions were typically experienced within minutes of being in the presence of the offending persons. Only 43% of respondents said that they had ever talked about the problem with the offending persons. They reported much less positive regard for the offending persons than they did for people in their lives toward whom they had no allergic reactions. The respondents believed that the offending persons had more positive regard for them than they themselves had for the offending persons. Participants also reported that their relationships with the offending persons were much less positive, stable, and strong, compared to their relationships with persons who did not generate such reactions in them.

Definitional and Conceptual Issues

Further research on social allergens and social allergies may benefit from refinements to our definitions. The original definition of a social allergy, a "reaction of hypersensitive disgust or annoyance to a social allergen" (Cunningham et al., 1997, p. 191), may be unnecessarily specific and restrictive. Assuming that displeasure of any form may help identify a social allergy, we may redefine a social allergy as a "hypersensitivity involving negative affect to another person's social behavior." There is a separate, growing literature on disgust per se (Oaten, Stevenson, Case, 2009; Olatunji & Sawchuck, 2005), for which many of the stimuli are not social or interpersonal. Therefore, there seems to be no advantage to incorporating such specific kinds of negative affect (such as disgust) into the definition of social allergies.

The original definition of a social allergen may be overly restrictive and problematic in another way as well: It describes an allergen as "a behavior or situation created by another person that may be seen as unpleasant (to the allergic person), but not as strongly aversive to objective observers" (Cunningham et al., 1997, p. 191). This definition would be difficult to operationalize for research purposes: First, researchers would have to get participants to name such social behaviors. Then objective observers would have to evaluate the aversiveness of each described social behavior; and criteria for aversiveness would have to be established and assessed. Instead of refining the definition at this time, however, it seems prudent to rely on the experiences that people recognize in themselves that meet such criteria as producing aversive reactions (e.g., "I just can't stand it when you do that.") For this reason, I will not belabor the definition issue, but instead sample people's reports of experiences that they recognize from prior definitions and then determine how the reported experiences relate to well-established theoretical constructs.

SOCIAL ALLERGENS AND INTERPERSONAL THEORY

Theoretical Relevance

Interpersonal theory provides an established theoretical context for the common, important, but rarely studied phenomenon of social allergens. Social allergens, in turn, provide a practical, intense, and real-life grounding for comparatively abstract features of interpersonal theory. The seemingly mundane behaviors that get some people "really ticked off" can serve as a challenging and immediate testing ground for interpersonal theorizing.

As described in earlier chapters of this volume, the two orthogonal dimensions of dominance-submissiveness and friendliness-hostility theoretically underlie the universe of terms that describe interpersonal behavior. These two dimensions together provide a map or circle upon which interpersonal traits, behaviors, and individuals can be positioned or located (Andrews, 1991; Carson, 1991; Kiesler, 1983, 1996; Leary, 1957; Wiggins, Phillips,

& Trapnell, 1989). If the interpersonal circle is truly comprehensive, then we should be able to locate every *social* allergen within the circle. But where on the interpersonal circle do they fall? Interpersonal theory suggests two characteristics that locate each behavior in the interpersonal space: (1) angular location and (2) distance from the origin (the zero-point intersection of the axes). Angular location refers to the region of the circle, as in north-south-east-west, in which a behavior, person, or trait is located. It is the angle, with respect to the horizontal axis, from 0- to 360-degrees, made by a line (vector) from the origin to that point. The angular location defines the quality or kind of interpersonal behavior. Distance from the origin—that is, the vector length—is thought of as an index of extremity. Angular location and distance from the origin are independent. Both features can be assessed using familiar measures of interpersonal traits (e.g., Wiggins, Trapnell, & Phillips, 1988), and both features are relevant to social allergens (see Gurtman, Chapter 18).

Interpersonal behaviors that are the most strongly or intensely expressed are located on the outer perimeter of the circle. They are much farther from the origin than are typical, less extreme behaviors. According to a number of interpersonal theorists, extreme behaviors are annoying and aversive to other people (Andrews, 1991; Carson, 1991; Kiesler, 1983, 1996; Leary, 1957; Wiggins et al., 1989). For example, extreme-dominance-and-minimal-submissiveness would lead to a great vector length along the dominance axis and should, theoretically, reflect rigidity and possibly pathology. This proposition therefore suggests a hypothesis: Because extreme behaviors are thought to be annoying and aversive, we would expect social allergens to be located farther from the origin of the circle than less offensive behaviors. In addition, I hypothesized that (a) social allergens reported by different people would be found in all regions of the circle, including regions on the "friendly" side of the graph,

but (b) they would more often appear in the negative regions of the graph.

Research Findings

O'Connor and Nadin (2009) reported two studies on the interpersonal angular locations and vector lengths of social allergens. In both studies individuals were asked to describe behaviors from others that they had experienced as aversive (following the instructions of Cunningham et al., 1997). The participants then used the Interpersonal Adjective Scales (IAS) to rate, on eight-point Likert scales, each behavior as well as each person who had displayed the corresponding behavior. The procedures described by Wiggins et al. (1989) and LaForge (1977) were then applied to the IAS octant scores to determine the regional location and vector length for each allergen and for each person. Regional location and vector length scores were also obtained for IAS self-ratings and for IAS ratings that participants had provided for another person in their lives who did not produce an allergic reaction in the participant. Details about computing these values are provided in Chapter 18 (Gurtman).

In Study 1 (N = 712), the vector lengths for the allergens and for the persons who displayed them were significantly greater than those for baseline self-ratings and for the ratings of other persons who did not generate allergic reactions in the participants. The effect sizes were large, with Cohen *d* values well over 2.0. Social allergens were thus perceived as extreme behavioral manifestations that were situated near the outer edges of the interpersonal circle, at least in the perceptions of the affected individuals.

The vector lengths for the allergens were strongly correlated with the vector lengths for the personality trait ratings of the persons who displayed them, *r* = .70. However, the vector lengths obtained from ratings of the self and from ratings of the nonoffensive person were not significantly associated with those of (a) the allergens or (b) the offending persons. In other words, an allergic reaction to one aspect of another person's behavior was associated with more extreme descriptions of the individual's general personality. The aversive reactions apparently colored the general impressions of the individuals who displayed the offending behaviors. Thus, people who display behaviors that are aversive to others would seem to be at risk for broader negative evaluations: Their personalities in general seem to be perceived as extreme. Apparently, strong trait attributions are inferred from narrower annoying behavior patterns.

There were also meaningful correlations between the allergen vector lengths and ratings of other features of the allergens and persons who displayed them. Higher vector lengths were associated with more perceived intentionality behind the offending behavior; participants apparently believed that the behavior was directed at them personally. They judged the offensive behavior to be more controllable than the offending person was willing to exercise. They also reported that (a) negative emotions were aroused sooner and lasted longer, (b) they had less mutual positive regard in the relationship, and (c) the relationship was less stable. Vector lengths thus summarized a variety of important and harmful correlates of social allergens.

The results concerning angular locations of the allergens, however, were unexpected. Ninety-seven percent of the nominated behaviors fell on the hostile side of the circle, and fewer than 1% of the allergens were on the friendly side of the circle. Yet one would think that excessive neediness (for example) would not be judged to be hostile, so some explanation is needed for this finding. Similar results also occurred for IAS ratings of the offending persons: Ninety-one percent of these placements were on the unfriendly side of the circle and only 3.2% were on the friendly side. In contrast, self-ratings and ratings of the nonoffensive persons were evenly distributed across angular locations of the circle.

Is it possible that participants would describe allergens from a variety of regions if the interpersonal circle and its regions were more carefully described to them? In Study 2 (N = 151) we asked participants to name possible allergic reactions to behaviors from different regions of the interpersonal circle. A description of each octant of the circle was provided to participants, who then described "annoying behaviors from as many regions of the circle as you can." With these instructions, behaviors were nominated from all regions of the space. An example of a nominated behavior for each octant of the interpersonal space is shown in Table 16.1.

Participants also completed IAS ratings of the allergens, of the offending persons, and of themselves. The ratings of allergens from octants that reflect hostile or dominant behavior (or both) all fell on the hostile side of the circle (dominating behavior was perceived as hostile). But there was much greater variability in the ratings of allergens from octants that reflect friendly or submissive behavior (or both). About 50% of the ratings of nominated behaviors were located on the friendly side of the circle. The remaining nominated behaviors (from nonhostile octants) were subsequently rated as being hostile. Thus, participants were able to generate allergenic behaviors from (for example) the friendly-yielding octant (e.g., too needy), but in many cases they later rated that allergen as hostile. In addition, discrepancies may have occurred between *private* evaluations of allergens (as hostile) and the *overt* ("objective") description of the offensive behaviors (e.g., as friendly-submissive). The following is a prototypical description of an allergen from the friendly-controlling octant:

> [The person] makes me feel slightly annoyed and agitated as I don't like being the recipient of an overbearing, perky someone who thinks they are in charge of me.

The discrepancy between a participant's private evaluation of the allergen-bearing

TABLE 16.1   Selected Allergens Nominated by Participants for Octants of the Interpersonal Circle

Octant of the Interpersonal Circle	Nominated Allergen
Submissive	When people won't speak up and share their opinion on a certain subject. Even if it is as simple as trying to figure out what to do for the evening, and their only response is, "I don't care." Because it is obvious that they do care. They do have some sort of a preference; they just for some reason won't say what it is.
Friendly-Submissive	They want to help, but don't know what to do, so end up getting in the way, messing stuff up, or feeling unconfident so continually ask if they're doing it right
Friendly	People can act friendly...but there's a fine line between BEING friendly, and ACTING friendly...—what's REALLY annoying is when someone is friendly with you and yet they're really just being FAKE...you can see right through them—they're either mad at you or holding something back and just ACTING friendly to avoid conflict—PHONY FRIENDLINESS is ANNOYING
Friendly-Dominance	when you walk into a store and there is an overly friendly salesperson who follows you all over and tries to talk to you about selling and all you want to do is browse
Dominance	I find it very annoying when someone loudly begins speaking before I am finished and always contradicts everything that I say
Hostile-Dominance	People who are very confident with themselves and their work and are very rude about it because you don't do yours the EXACT same way
Hostile	People who yell at referees or other officials and do not show respect for authority
Hostile-Submissive	I think it's really annoying when someone is mad at you and you ask them what is wrong and they just say nothing and continue to be angry. They just remain mad at you without telling you what you did

person (hostile, negative) and the way the behavior is overtly described (perky, overbearing) is reminiscent of a phenomenon described by interpersonal theorists: In Coyne's (1976) interactional model, depressed people are said to exert strong pulls on others for support and reassurance. Other people then often reply with support for the depressed person. But frequently they also eventually report (or "leak") expressions of annoyance, as though the support they provided, to some extent, has been "insincere." Discrepancies between overt behaviors and covert impacts are also prominent features of Kiesler's (1996) model of maladaptive interpersonal transactions and psychopathology. The same kinds of public-private discrepancies are apparently involved in many "friendly-behavior" social allergens, so (in private) they are mainly perceived to be negative.

Thus, in Study 2, O'Connor and Nadin (2009) demonstrated that social allergens, when described "objectively," can be found at all angular locations of the interpersonal circle. This result exposes the ambiguity in behavior per se: The method used to ask participants to describe a social allergen influences the results obtained. When people are asked to nominate a behavior from a friendly region of the graph, they can do so. But when they are then asked to (privately) rate that behavior, their responses generally fall into a smaller number of hostile regions of the interpersonal space. When the instructions are more explicit, however, and participants are asked to describe the behavior objectively, they can locate allergenic behaviors for each region (octant) of the interpersonal circle.

In Study 2, the vector lengths of the described allergens were again higher than the vector lengths of the baseline self-ratings on the IAS. This was true for allergens from all eight octants of the IPC. However, there was variation in the vector lengths of allergens from different octants. Those from the dominant, hostile-dominant, hostile, and hostile-submissive octants had the greatest vector lengths—significantly greater than the mean vector lengths for allergens from the submissive, friendly-submissive, friendly, and friendly-dominant octants. In brief, extremity is a feature of most allergens—particularly those in the hostile and dominant octants. Future research is needed to determine whether these allergens are also more irritating.

Although pathology is often thought to involve extreme behaviors in interpersonal theory, it is interesting to note that extreme behaviors are not necessarily signs of pathology. Nonetheless, in some personality disorders the extreme behavior may be maladaptive, partly because of the allergenic effect that it produces on other individuals. As one example, a person with a dependent personality disorder may be judged to be "clingy," producing one kind of allergenic effect in some people. Similarly, a person with a histrionic personality disorder may be judged to be "manipulative," producing a different kind of allergenic effect. A person with a narcissistic personality may be judged to be "a know-it-all," producing yet another kind of allergenic effect, and so on. Such effects of different personality disorders need to be examined in future research.

To summarize, the findings from both studies provide empirical support for the claim that extremity, as operationalized by vector lengths, does characterize aversive behaviors.

THE LOCATION OF SOCIAL ALLERGENS IN FIVE-FACTOR MODEL SPACE

Features of social allergens may extend beyond the two dimensions of the interpersonal circle. The five-factor model (FFM; see Costa & McCrae, Chapter 6 in this volume) consists of five basic dimensions (neuroticism, extraversion, openness to experience, agreeableness, and conscientiousness, or N, E, O, A, and C) that have repeatedly emerged in lexical research and in research on popular personality inventories (Digman, 1990; McCrae & John, 1992; Wiggins, 1996). The first two dimensions of the FFM correspond to the two dimensions of the IPC, and O'Connor and Dyce (2001) demonstrated how the two-dimensional conceptualization of extremity described in interpersonal theory can be extended to the more comprehensive FFM.

Therefore, in previous research we also examined the location of allergenic behaviors on all five dimensions as well as the five-dimensional vector lengths (O'Connor & Nadin, 2009). In this study, 712 participants rated social allergens using the IASR-B5 (Trapnell & Wiggins, 1990). This measure assesses the two primary dimensions of the interpersonal circumplex—dominance-submissiveness and friendliness-hostility—as well as the remaining dimensions of the FFM: neuroticism (N), conscientiousness (C), and openness to experience (O). The mean vector lengths for all five dimensions showed the same pattern as the one described above for two dimensions: The FFM vector lengths were highest for the allergen, second highest for the offending persons, and considerably lower for self-ratings and for ratings of nonoffending persons. Furthermore, the mean FFM vector length was somewhat higher than the mean of the two-dimensional vector lengths: $d = 2.16$ for the allergens, and $d = 2.17$ for offending persons. These large effect sizes for the differences between the interpersonal circle and FFM vector lengths (2.2 vs. 2.0) indicate that the three noninterpersonal dimensions of the FFM (i.e., N, O, and C) are also highly relevant to social allergens: the behavior is judged to be more neurotic, less conscientious, and less open. Allergenic vector lengths in the FFM space were significantly greater than the vector lengths in the two-dimensional interpersonal space because of these added effects. The broader FFM is thus more comprehensive and potentially important in elucidating the nature of social allergens.

We also found that social allergens did not fall into all regions of the FFM. That is, we used each participant's ratings to sort every allergen into a region of the FFM using a simple categorization procedure. For each dimension, allergens with standardized scores above zero were assigned a "+," and allergens with standardized scores below zero were assigned a "–." These above-or-below values for each of five orthogonal dimensions together result in ($2^5 =$) 32 possible FFM regions. The results showed that 56% of the allergens fell within two of the regions defined by low A, high N, low O, and low C (and either high or low E).

SOCIAL ALLERGENS AND CLOSE RELATIONSHIPS

Cunningham, Shamblen, Barbee, and Ault (2005) reported findings from two studies on social allergens in close relationships that built upon "fatal attraction" research by Felmlee (2001). That term refers to a phenomenon in which the very characteristics in others that are the initial basis of attraction later get despised and are experienced as aversive. According to these authors, initial passion leads individuals to overlook particular behaviors; therefore, over time, as passion declines, social allergens become more evident, causing individuals in close relationships to experience negative emotions towards the partner (called a "deromantization").

The authors therefore examined beliefs about changes in the likelihood of unpleasant behaviors in close relationships. Respondents (161 undergraduates) indicated the frequency with which they believed typical males and females performed specific behaviors, either in the first two months of a dating relationship or after one year. It was found that uncouth habits were believed to increase over time. Men and

women both believed that men engage in more uncouth habits than women. Women perceived the grooming and manners of men as boorish after two months, and as barely tolerable after one year. (Men may be unaware that their own individual behavior is uncouth and offensive.) On the other hand, men perceived women to be more intrusive. Both men and women believed that women engaged in more inconsiderate acts than men (i.e., that women are more self-absorbed) and that men engaged more often in norm violations than women.

The authors also examined the impact of allergenic behaviors on emotions, dissatisfaction, and relationship dissolution in dating couples. Both members of 137 dating couples (one member of the couple was an introductory psychology student) reported on the frequency of both their partner's and their own allergenic behaviors. They also rated the valence and intensity of the emotions that they had experienced when the partner performed each behavior, as well as their satisfaction with the relationship. The researchers also determined whether the couples were still together or had separated one year later.

The results showed that uncouth habits (e.g., flatulating) were the most frequent allergens, followed by inconsiderate acts (e.g., selfishness), intrusive behaviors (e.g., rudeness), and norm violations (e.g., avoiding work). In line with the stereotype, men seemed to display more uncouth habits than women, and women seemed to engage in more inconsiderate acts than men. Men reported (about themselves) higher frequencies of uncouth habits than women, and women admitted higher frequencies of inconsiderate acts than men. On the other hand, women did not perceive men to perform more norm violations, but men acknowledged more norm violations than women did. Men judged their female partners to engage more frequently in intrusive behaviors, but women did not endorse this description. Men, however, seemed to be particularly sensitive to intrusive behaviors from women.

Relationship dissatisfaction was associated with frequent offensive behaviors. This was true for both self-reports of allergens and for partner perceptions of allergens. However, judgments of the frequency of the partner's offensive behavior was the best predictor of the individual's relationship satisfaction. The partner's *self-reports* of performing allergenic behaviors did seem to match the participants' *perceptions* in that actual behaviors (i.e., both self-reported and partner-perceived) seemed to predict the partner's distress.

Emotional impact scores for social allergens were obtained by computing the product of the frequency of the allergen and the strength of the reported emotion. Couples with higher scores reported lower relationship satisfaction. This effect persisted even when the frequency of contact and relationship length were statistically controlled. Intrusive behaviors had the greatest emotional impact, followed by norm violations. Women reported higher emotional impact from uncouth habits than did men, probably because men displayed such behaviors more frequently than women. Furthermore, relationship dissolutions after one year were associated with intrusive behaviors and, marginally, with norm violations.

THEORETICAL REASONS WHY SOCIAL BEHAVIORS CAN BECOME ALLERGENIC

There has been very little speculation in the literature as to why a social behavior becomes aversive to one person but not to another. Three related explanations will be described in this section of the chapter. The focus will be on prototypical *social* allergens.

One explanation for social allergies follows directly from traditional interpersonal theory. Intense (extreme) displays by other persons exert a strong pull for overt complementary responses that the affected partner is reluctant to provide (Kiesler, 1983, 1996; Leary, 1957). That is, we *expect* certain types of dyadic interactions, and become annoyed when behaviors of other people exert strong pulls (e.g., for supportive, encouraging reactions) that are different from our expectations (based on the way we normally behave). Although we may overtly tolerate extreme behaviors from others (and provide the complementary reaction), the *covert* emotional impact may be unpleasant (Kiesler, 1983, 1996). To some extent, expectations are consistent with our self-concept, and an unpleasant experience may arise when a dyadic interaction requires us to behave in a way that differs from our own self-concept and self-relevant expectations (Andrews, 1989). That is, we devote some of our psychological resources to serving another person's purposes and expect to receive in return complementary behaviors from the other person that confirm our own self-concept (Andrews, 1989; Kiesler, 1983, 1996). For example, a narcissist's consistent unidirectional pulls for admiring reactions from others become annoying to us when they violate our expectation that this "service" will be reciprocated.

A recent revision of interpersonal theory has been proposed by Horowitz, Wilson, Turan, Zolotsev, Constantino, and Henderson (2006) that expresses this hypothesis in motivational terms. According to their view, every interpersonal behavior is driven by one or more interpersonal motives, which may be communal or agentic (or a blend of both). Furthermore, an interpersonal behavior "invites" a complementary reaction from the partner, that is, it invites a reaction that would satisfy the motive that drives the behavior. The "invited" reaction, like any complementary reaction, is similar with respect to communion and reciprocal with respect to agency. If the desired class of reactions does not occur, the person's motive is frustrated, resulting in negative affect (e.g., irritation).

This theory has been extended to social allergens by Henderson and Horowitz (2006). In their view, a social allergy implies that the offending person is expressing a motivated behavior ("admire me," "take care of me," "do as I tell you to do," "be intimate with me"). Thus, the offending person is inviting a particular class of reactions that would satisfy that person's own "wants." But a partner (the offended person), for his or her own reasons, may not wish to satisfy the offending person's wants: After all, a partner has interpersonal motives, too, and may not wish to admire (or take care of, or obey, or be intimate with) the offending person. The partner's own motives are therefore frustrated by the "invitation," producing negative affect (irritation, anger). In brief, then, the offended partner may or may not provide the "invited" behavioral reaction, but either way, the person is displeased. Then the displeased partner may reveal the negative affect or keep it private.

If these two theoretical interpretations are correct, the most aversive behaviors to a person should be ones that conflict with our usual *interpersonal expectations* (Andrews, 1991; Kiesler, 1996) or *interpersonal motives* (Horowitz & Henderson, 2006). Thus, interpersonal theory can potentially account for the large individual differences among partners in developing an allergenic reaction to a person's behavior.

A third explanation for the development of social allergies is simultaneously cognitive, motivational, and interpersonal: People develop beliefs about themselves and others—beliefs about the meaning of a particular behavior, beliefs about proper ways of behaving and treating others, and so on. These various beliefs are integrated into our own unique worldviews, which we believe to be real and correct—and which we want to confirm and maintain (O'Connor & Gabora, in press). Our self-worth and sense of psychological stability stem largely from our maintaining the validity and standards in our worldviews and from securing positions of value for ourselves within these systems (Solomon, Greenberg, & Pyszczynski, 1991). An allergenic behavior may be a behavior that challenges this concept: A social allergy may develop when another person's appearance or behavior repeatedly and strongly is

at odds with the "truths" of our belief system—"truths" that we want to confirm. Another person's behavior becomes offensive, for example, because it threatens cultural standards that our belief system values, or because it directly or indirectly threatens cherished beliefs about ourselves.

This perspective can account for the wide variation across persons in the behaviors from others that trigger allergic reactions. Our preferred beliefs about ourselves and about other people are idiosyncratic (unique). Therefore, it is possible for a social allergen to affect a single person idiosyncratically (or just a few people). The perspective can also explain why social allergies may be slow to erupt, and why allergic reactions may rapidly ignite once they have developed. Interpersonal behaviors are often ambiguous. When we are first exposed to a behavior pattern from another person, our attention may first be drawn to content: "That is a peculiar T-shirt, hairstyle, manner of speaking . . . " However, over time, we may become more focused on the interpersonal implications of the behavior in question (Watzlawick, Beavin, & Jackson, 1967): "The fact that you dress yourself in that particular way, or that you behave in that particular way, implies that you perceive yourself and other people in a particular way, and that you have particular values that really contradict what I like to believe and uphold." Once we connect the inferred message to our relationship with the allergenic partner and fix on a particular interpretation of the allergenic behavior, we may become more quickly annoyed the next time we are exposed to the behavior: "There you go again! I now know what you are probably thinking (about me, yourself, or others) or wanting from me when you do that, and I don't like it."

This perspective can also explain why allergic persons rarely discuss the offensive behaviors with the persons who display them. The reasons go beyond the obvious difficulties that are involved in confronting other people. It is much easier for people to discuss neutral issues with a partner than it is for us to discuss issues about "our relationship" (Teyber, 2005; Watzlawick et al., 1967).

SUMMARY AND DIRECTIONS FOR FURTHER RESEARCH

Social allergies are pervasive. Every participant in every study of social allergens so far has been able to describe at least one behavior from others that they find annoying or disgusting. Social allergens, by definition, are aversive personal experiences. But they are also clearly harmful to relationships. Persons who display offensive behaviors are less liked; relationships with such persons are experienced as less positive and stable, and the intensity of social allergens is associated with relationship dissolutions. Social allergens can be found in all regions of the interpersonal circle, although hostile behaviors more readily come to mind and explicit prompts are required to obtain nominations of behaviors that explicitly involve friendly behavior. Social allergens are strongly associated with greater vector lengths on the interpersonal circle and in the five-factor model space. They are experienced as extreme behaviors by recipients. Thus, research on social allergens has also provided empirical support for a postulate of interpersonal theory concerning "extreme" behaviors.

Research on this phenomenon has only just begun, and there are many important questions for further investigations. The existing studies have all focused on the more general category of annoying and/or disgusting behaviors. We need a set of norms that systematically classify the type of social allergens that exist, including ones that would seem entirely harmless. We also need to better understand the theoretical reasons that allergens come to offend some people but not others. Further research might also examine social allergens in samples other than undergraduate students. People may differ in their susceptibility to social allergens, and an easily irritated person may suffer specific consequences. The pervasiveness and effects of social allergens on long-term relationships have not been studied adequately. We also need to learn more about adaptive and maladaptive methods that people use to cope with social allergens and effective ways of reducing a social allergen once it begins to develop or has already become acute. Finally, more research is required on the kinds of interpersonal behaviors that are most apt to become offensive to others, on the reasons that some people readily exhibit offensive behaviors whereas others do not, and on the reasons that some behaviors readily become strongly allergenic whereas others do not.

References

Andrews, J. D. (1989). Psychotherapy of depression: A self-confirmation model. *Psychological Review, 96*, 576–607.

Andrews, J. (1991). *The active self in psychotherapy.* Boston: Allyn & Bacon.

Carson, R. C. (1991). The social-interactional viewpoint. In M. Hersen, A. Kazdin, & A. Bellack (Eds.), *The clinical psychology handbook* (pp. 185–199). New York: Pergamon.

Coyne, J. C. (1976). Toward an interactional description of depression. *Psychiatry, 39*, 28–40.

Cunningham, M. R., Barbee, A. P., & Druen, P. B. (1997). Social allergens and the reactions that they produce: Escalation of annoyance and disgust in love and work. In R. M. Kowalski (Ed.), *Aversive interpersonal behaviors* (pp. 190–215). New York: Plenum.

Cunningham, M. R., Shamblen, S. R., Barbee, A. P., & Ault, L. K. (2005). Social allergies in romantic relationships: Behavioral repetition, emotional sensitization, and dissatisfaction in dating couples. *Personal Relationships, 12*, 273–295.

Digman, J. M. (1990). Personality structure: Emergence of the five-factor model. *Annual Review of Psychology, 41*, 417–440.

Felmlee, D. H. (2001). From appealing to appalling: Disenchantment with a romantic partner. *Sociological Perspectives, 44*, 263–280.

Henderson, L., & Horowitz, L. M. (2006). Social allergens and frustrated interpersonal motives.

Programs and Abstracts of the Seventh Annual Meeting of the Society for Interpersonal Theory and Research, Philadelphia, PA.

Horowitz, L. M., Wilson, K. R., Turan, B., Zolotsev, P., Constantino, M. J., & Henderson, L. (2006). How interpersonal motives clarify the meaning of interpersonal behavior: The revised circumplex model. *Personality and Social Psychology Review, 10*, 67–86.

Kiesler, D. J. (1983). The 1982 Interpersonal Circle: A taxonomy for complementarity in human transaction. *Psychological Review, 90*, 185–214.

Kiesler, D. J. (1996). *Contemporary interpersonal theory and research: Personality, psychopathology, and psychotherapy*. New York: John Wiley & Sons.

LaForge, R. (1977). *Using the ICL: 1976*. Unpublished manuscript, Mill Valley, Ca.

Leary, T. (1957). *Interpersonal diagnosis of personality*. New York: Ronald Press.

McCrae, R. R., & John, O. P. (1992). An introduction to the five-factor model and its applications. *Journal of Personality, 60*, 175–215.

Oaten, M. J., Stevenson, R. J., & Case, T. I. (2009). Disgust as a disease-avoidance mechanism. *Psychological Bulletin, 135*, 303–321.

O'Connor, B., & Gabora, L. (in press). A general dynamical process model of the development of pathological belief systems. In F. Orsucci (Ed.), *Mind force*. Nova Science.

O'Connor, B. P., & Dyce, J. A. (2001). Rigid and extreme: A geometric representation of personality disorders in five-factor model space. *Journal of Personality and Social Psychology, 81*, 1119–1130.

O'Connor, B. P., & Nadin, S. (2009). "I can't stand it when you do that!": The location of social allergens in interpersonal and five-factor model space. Manuscript submitted for publication.

Olatunji, B. O., & Sawchuck, C. N. (2005). Disgust: Characteristics features, social manifestations, and clinical implications. *Journal of Social and Clinical Psychology, 24*(7), 932–962.

Solomon, S., Greenberg, J., & Pyszczynski, T. (1991). A terror management theory of social behavior: The psychological functions of self-esteem and cultural worldviews. In M. P. Zanna (Ed.), *Advances in experimental social psychology* (Vol. 24, pp. 93–159). New York: Academic Press.

Teyber, E. (2005). *Interpersonal process in psychotherapy: An integrative model*. New York: Brooks/Cole.

Trapnell, P. D., & Wiggins, J. S. (1990). Extension of the Interpersonal Adjective Scales to include the Big Five dimensions of personality. *Journal of Personality and Social Psychology, 59*, 781–790.

Watzlawick, P., Beavin, J., & Jackson, D. (1967). Pragmatics of human communication: A study of interactional patterns, pathologies and paradoxes. New York: W. W. Norton.

Wiggins, J. S. (Ed.) (1996). *The five–factor model of personality*. New York: Guilford Press.

Wiggins, J. S., Phillips, N., & Trapnell, P. (1989). Circular reasoning about interpersonal behavior: Evidence concerning some untested assumptions underlying diagnostic classification. *Journal of Personality and Social Psychology, 56*, 296–305.

Wiggins, J. S., Trapnell, P., & Phillips, N. (1988). Psychometric and geometric characteristics of the Revised Interpersonal Adjective Scales (IAS-R). *Multivariate Behavioral Research, 23*, 517–530.

17 SOCIAL DOMAINS, PERSONALITY, AND INTERPERSONAL FUNCTIONING

Jonathan Hill

Paul A. Pilkonis

Julia Bear

A woman in treatment described her bitterness at the behavior of her friend at work.

Acknowledgments: We are pleased to acknowledge the contributions of Helen Stein, PhD, to the development of the Revised Adult Personality Functioning Assessment during her tenure at the Child and Family Center, Menninger Clinic.

We thank Helen Taylor and Holly Hope at the University of Liverpool for their contributions to the ideas in this chapter while working on the project "The Relationship between the Caretaking Environment of Young Children and Personality Functioning in Mothers," funded by the Health Foundation, grant 1823/1442.

We thank the members of the Personality Studies research group at the University of Pittsburgh School of Medicine for their observations and discussion of the relevance and limitations of a domain-based approach to personality disorders throughout the implementation of NIMH grant R01 MH56888, "Interpersonal Functioning in Borderline Personality" (PI: P. A. Pilkonis, PhD).

This friend was another woman, about 10 years older and also her boss, whom she had gotten to know well because each had confided about their histories of childhood abuse. They often spent lunch breaks together but did not meet outside of work. Recently this friend had been upset because her ex-partner had run up debts, and she did not know how she would cope financially. The patient had lent her friend $1,000, which she now needed back to help pay for medical treatment. The patient described how her friend had responded to her requests for repayment by reminding her of her subordinate position in the company and reducing the time they spent together. The patient felt badly treated, and she commented that this kind of disappointment had happened throughout her life.

The framework described in this chapter will make plain how the interpersonal context in which these events occurred failed to provide an adequate platform for solving the problems that emerged. The patient's interactions with her boss had elements of work relationships, friendship, and negotiated financial transactions, three social domains with distinctive procedural rules governing behavior, problem-solving, and emotional expression. In this case, elements of all three domains were present simultaneously, creating confusion and depriving the patient of an easily identified means for dealing with the specific problem of repayment. This chapter describes the domain organization of social relationships, how it emerges over development, and the implications of disorganization of domain structure for personality disorders.

Limitations in the current conceptualization of personality disorder are widely acknowledged, and several valuable approaches to reconceptualization have been proposed (Livesley, Jang, & Vernon, 1998; Parker et al., 2002). Rather contrasting requirements are apparent. On the one hand, the personality disorders are so heterogeneous that a single model is unlikely to fit the range of phenomena. Therefore, some disorders may need to be partitioned off for separate study (Hill, 2008). For example, schizotypal personality disorder may be best understood in the context of the schizophrenia spectrum rather than the personality disorders. On the other hand, the distinctiveness of many of the disorders in the DSM and International Classifications of Diseases (ICD; World Health Organization, 1992) classifications is not proven, and a more general conceptualization may help move the field forward. The aim of this chapter is to contribute to the generation of a coherent conceptualization that leads to empirically testable predictions and has therapeutic potential.

The organizing principle in our view of personality disorders is the observation that the "characteristic that seems to define them all is a pervasive persistent abnormality in maintaining social relationships" (Rutter, 1987; see also Henry, 1996). Chronic difficulties in interpersonal relationships do not exhaust, of course, the descriptive features associated with personality disorders: early onset, subjective distress, dysfunction in role performance, and the rigid behavioral styles defined in the DSM and ICD. They do, however, include aspects of chronicity, style, and role dysfunction that are apparent to both patients and others, and this transparency provides valuable leverage—both scientific and clinical—for understanding and treating personality disorders.

The key specific concept considered in this chapter is the "social domain." This is defined as an area of mutual social understanding in which participants share a set of rules regarding the interpretation of each others' motives, behaviors, and emotions, and about appropriate ways of responding. This characterization leads to the idea that the conceptualization must be interpersonal and social, and also intrapersonal and psychological. Understanding the social organization of cognitions and emotions, and hence of behaviors, then becomes central to the study of normal personality development and adult personality functioning. Socially competent individuals are able to monitor and manage movement within and across several domains—in some instances with the same person and, in others, from one person to another. In this domain-based analysis, we (a) explicate the functions of domain organization, (b) identify relevant areas of normal functioning, (c) show how variations in these areas may contribute to dysfunction, (d) indicate ways in which such dysfunction is associated with personality disorder, (e) outline the implications for empirical studies, and (f) indicate the therapeutic potential of the approach. Although there is a substantial body of developmental findings consistent with this domain-based analysis, few address the topic directly. The framework outlined here implies a program of research into the normal functioning of domain processes from social, psychological, biological, and developmental perspectives, the identification of abnormalities in these processes, and their contributions to personality disorder.

DOMAIN-BASED FUNCTIONING

Domain Organization

The analysis of the organization of social cognitions and behaviors into domains has its origins in biological and evolutionary considerations considered in detail elsewhere (Bugental, 2000, Bolton & Hill, 2004; Simpson et al., Chapter 5 in this volume). In brief, all living organisms must be able to represent aspects of the environment in order to respond appropriately to them. Representations must reference the kind of event, circumstance, or object in the environment as well as its specific features. Communication in social systems requires that aspects of the environment relevant to effective behaviors are presented in social interactions, and that there are shared rules for passing on the information. For example, bees communicate the direction and distance of nectar from the hive in the length and angle of the central run of a figure-of-eight dance. The utility of this communication for nectar gathering behaviors depends on a shared convention that what is referenced are "nectar," "direction," and "distance," including the specifics of location and distance of nectar. These features are hard-wired and not open to creation or revision.

By contrast, in systems of human communication and social interaction, information is transmitted in numerous ways, in different languages, and in varying contexts. Establishing the ability to navigate through complex social interactions appears to be a developmental priority, given that the newborn infant attends selectively to social stimuli and is able to participate skillfully in social interactions with caregivers within a few weeks (Stern, 2001). Events that differ in subtle ways are capable of being interpreted differently and of being reviewed even in early childhood. The capacity to interpret events in the environment in multiple ways, and to elaborate novel actions, is a central aspect of the creative intelligence of humans, but it has also introduced major demands on social understanding and participation. If social organizations are comprised of individuals, each capable of interpreting events in the environment in multiple ways, then achieving shared frameworks for the interpretations of behaviors, emotions, and motives is a major challenge. It is essential, however, for effective social interactions. Furthermore it must be efficient. If each social encounter were to entail consideration of multiple possibilities regarding the interpretation of another person's behavior, the result would be information overload and painstakingly slow social interactions.

We suggest that the key function served by the organization of social life into domains is the creation of flexibility, together with a limit on the number of interpersonal possibilities that must be considered in any particular sequence of social interactions. Provided that participants can rely on the identity of the domain, they can focus on a restricted range of potential topics, based on shared assumptions about the motives, emotions, behaviors, and responses that are appropriate in that domain.

Principal Features of Domain Functioning in Adults

A domain is a family of interpersonal interactions between individuals that share a specifiable set of procedural rules for each partner that are defined and reviewed both in moment-to-moment interactions and over longer periods. When individuals are relating in the same domain, behaviors are assumed to be occurring according to the shared rules unless they fall close to the limits of (or outside) what is expected, in which case the identity of the domain is reviewed. Behaviors here include what is said and emotions that are expressed. Their range and appropriateness to the domain are monitored moment to moment by the participants.

Domains differ in the ways their long-term identity is established. In work, for example, it is usually defined explicitly at the outset by contractual arrangements, hierarchical positions, and prescribed responsibilities. More subtly, there may also be implicit "psychological contracts" (Rousseau, 1996) between employer and employee concerning their mutual expectations, which are not necessarily explicated in a formal contract, but which are present early on. In romantic relationships, by contrast, there are stages in the establishment and development of the shared space. Much of this is made explicit in talk about feelings and the progress of the relationship, and stages are marked both by publicly sanctioned commitments (engagement and marriage) and by taking personal steps with important consequences such as establishing a joint household and having children. In friendships, however, long-term development and maintenance of the relationship is generally accompanied neither by talk about the relationship nor by explicit or implicit markers of the evolution of the relationship. Wider social interactions with people brought together solely by circumstance (living in the same neighborhood, routine encounters of daily life) involve only moment-to-moment monitoring and responding without the guidelines provided by a contract or long-term relationship.

Most people have social encounters in several domains on a regular basis—for example, with romantic partners, colleagues at work, friends, and acquaintances of daily life. Thus, not only does an individual have to participate accurately and efficiently in different domains, but also to manage the transition from one to another domain as contexts change. Interactions with any particular person occur commonly in only one domain, such as work or education, friendships, or routine social interactions, but a relationship in one domain may be moved into another. Indeed, some domains, notably school or work, often act as gateways to friendships or romantic relationships. This movement is not achieved, however, without considerable restructuring of the relationship, and a failure to accomplish this can lead to "boundary violations" and a disorganization of domain structure. In contrast to the example at the beginning of the chapter, a friendship becomes established with a work colleague only when the participants make arrangements that are independent of their roles in the work place, and they develop pleasurable shared activities that are not task-oriented. The development of a romantic relationship requires even greater consciousness of the steps necessary to establish the relationship on a new footing and, therefore, not to confuse the content of different domains.

Domains have structure in cross-section and over time. In each domain, there is a set of practices that are found together and generally developed to a similar degree. For example, friendships commonly include confiding, but they also entail a range of activities that are less intense, such as conversations about recent work and leisure, and shared interests and activities. These different activities may be undertaken more or less equally with the same friend, or there may be friends within a circle in which there are variations in the predominant activities. The development of interactions across separate domains varies in time course. For example, in work, the onset and termination of relationships is defined by a contract, and their intensity and scope may not change much between those two points. By contrast, in romantic relationships, there are incremental changes over time, and steps are taken within the relationship (e.g., bids for greater intimacy and attachment) that have implications for its subsequent intensity and scope.

The domain also provides pointers to the range of resources that are likely to be available. In work, colleagues may devote considerable time to helping each other complete a task but less time to resolving a personal issue. In romantic relationships, the expectations regarding resources change as the level of commitment increases, but in established relationships, help in resolving personal issues and provision of physical comfort are expected. The resources of friendship are different again because they consist primarily of opportunities to discuss events and problems, and to offer new perspectives, without highly intense emotional expression and comfort.

When the domains of work, romance, and friendship involve continuity with the same people, they also include concepts of responsibility to the job or relationship, with the nature of the responsibility differing across domains. Thus, in work, the responsibilities focus on productivity and fair behavior with colleagues in relation to the outputs demanded. If people behave in a way that violates these responsibilities, they expect such behavior to elicit a response. This generally happens in work, unless arrangements are very informal or special allowances are made. However, in romantic relationships and friendships, there may be more variability in the acknowledgment and negotiation of disappointments and conflict.

Thus, the smooth operation of domain functioning entails five functions:

1. Interpreting others' behaviors accurately, regulating affect, and responding appropriately in order to maintain coherence within the boundaries of the domain.
2. Managing the movement from one domain to another.
3. Maintaining domain structure in cross-section and over time.
4. Recognizing appropriately the resources available in the domain.
5. Negotiating mutual responsibilities to others in the domain.

THEORIES OF NORMAL PERSONALITY FUNCTIONING

Substantial work has established systematic links between individual differences in normal personality features, such as temperamental variations in childhood, and personality disorder. For example, in a study of adolescents, the combination of high novelty seeking (high need for stimulation), low harm avoidance (low anxiety), and low reward dependence (unresponsiveness to social rewards) was associated with the emergence of antisocial problems that are precursors of antisocial personality disorder (Kerr, Tremblay, Pagini, & Vitaro, 1997). Trait-based theories of personality, however, have to contend with the evidence for situational variability in the behavior of most individuals (Mischel & Shoda, 1995). Interestingly, as far as we know, no studies have tested the simple prediction that people with personality disorder show more cross-situational consistency than others because of the predominance of inflexible, maladaptive traits. In the absence of such evidence, it is important to draw on work that examines the interface between the individual and the social context. In doing this, it is essential to consider not only behaviors emitted in contrasting social contexts, but also the cognitive and affective processes that mediate between the environment and the individual's behaviors (Mischel, 2004). In this approach, personality is construed as a system of mediating units (e.g., encodings, expectancies, goals) and psychological processes, conscious and unconscious, that interact with situations. Different cognitive-affective, and possibly also neuroanatomical, units are thought to map onto contrasting social contexts. Therefore, stable individual differences are sought at the level of the organization of these units rather than in undifferentiated tendencies to behave in certain ways.

Studies informed by this perspective have yielded findings compatible with a domain-based approach. For example, Shoda, Mischel, and Wright (1994) showed that there were groups of children in a summer camp that displayed distinctive profiles of behaviors that were context specific. The authors refer to individuals having "behavioral signatures" reflecting a tendency to respond similarly in situations that have the same "if . . . then" characteristics. They define "if . . . then" in terms such as "if punished by an adult" contrasted with "if threatened by a peer." Many of the contextual differences they describe map on to domain differences. The similarity between their and our concepts lies in the proposal that individual differences in personality can be understood in terms of profiles of context-specific behaviors.

The aim of the framework described in this chapter is to provide a descriptive, yet dynamic, account of the way relationships are structured. We anticipate that domain organization requires a range of skills, and that difficulties may arise in many ways. Thus exploring the causes of domain-based problems is a further clinical and empirical task. Note, however, that work on interpersonal motivation has many points of contact with the domain framework, which places considerable emphasis on social cognition. Horowitz et al. (2006) proposed that interpersonal misunderstandings may arise when participants have conflicting motives. They gave the example of a woman who competes with a good friend for an elective office and wins: "In the process of satisfying her own agentic motive, she may have disappointed and alienated her friend, thereby jeopardizing the friendship." From a domain perspective, competing for election generally takes place within a work or social setting where consideration of others' feelings and concern for personal implications of winning or losing are not prominent. Thus, the election, in a similar way to the loan of money in our opening example, took place under rules for more than one domain, giving rise not only to distress, but also to questions about how a solution might be found. An understanding of these kinds of interpersonal difficulties is likely to benefit from an analysis in terms of both motives and domains.

Developmental Considerations

The developmental evidence suggests that even young children are adept at judging social context. Initially, interactions are confined to caregivers, but in the second year, the interpersonal world begins to encompass other children and a widening number and variety of adults. However, the developing child does not interact in the same way with these different groups. This is seen strikingly with the emergence of stranger anxiety and selective attachments between six and nine months. In the presence of a stranger, most children become wary or even fearful and seek comfort or protection from a familiar caregiver (Sroufe, Cooper, & DeHart, 1996). Later, as sibling and peer interactions develop, further differences are apparent. Children engage in playful and aggressive exchanges with other children but rarely turn to them for comfort in contrast to familiar adults. Thus, individual development entails an increasingly sophisticated organization in the child's mind of different kinds of social interaction.

Sroufe and Waters (1976) provided an excellent example of such organization in the first year of life. They asked mothers to put masks over their faces in the presence of their 9-month-old infants under a range of conditions. The typical responses of the infants included an initial cessation of activity and a period during which the infants looked closely at their mothers, often with an expression of puzzlement. This was followed either by crying and other manifestations of distress or by laughter. The type of reaction was influenced significantly by factors such as the familiarity of the infants' surroundings. Thus, the central question that the experiment seemed to present to the child was, "Has my mother gone and am I under threat, or is she still here and am I okay?" In either case, the interpretation of the circumstance as playful or threatening was key to the subsequent interactions with the parent.

Children's capacities to differentiate the rules of behavior and emotion regulation in different kinds of relationships appear to be undermined by early privation. Studies of children in the United Kingdom who were adopted after spending their early years in institutions with multiple caretakers (Hodges & Tizard, 1989) and studies of children adopted from Romanian orphanages

(O'Connor, Marvin, Rutter, Olrick, & Britner, 2003) indicate that they commonly display poorly demarcated organization of social interactions, e.g., indiscriminate friendliness and difficulties in forming close relationships. These children appear to lack an understanding of the boundary between interactions where friendliness and self-disclosure contribute to enduring relationships and where they are inappropriate. Studies are needed of the ways in which less extreme child-rearing circumstances foster or undermine a child's capacity to manage the domain organization of social life.

A DEVELOPMENTAL MODEL OF SOCIAL DOMAIN ORGANIZATION: FROM EARLY FAMILY EXPERIENCES TO ADULT PERSONALITY FUNCTIONING

The general proposition is that the organization of social interactions entails differentiating expectations regarding the roles of the participants, the range of emotions that may be expressed, and the nature of the actions that may be anticipated. Even in the young child, this process appears to be sophisticated, turning, for example, on whether the surroundings are familiar or not. Rather than being prepared to engage in identical responses across contexts, the young child may be seen as acquiring conditional responses of an "if-then" nature (Mischel & Shoda, 1995).

Considerable attention has been paid to behaviors in particular domains in development, particularly attachment between parents and children and play between peers. However, few comprehensive attempts have been made to outline the range of domains. Bugental (2000) argued for the domains of attachment, hierarchical power, coalitional group processes, reciprocity, and mating. Hill, Fonagy, Safier, and Sargent (2003) suggested that, within families, attachment, discipline, and safety are three domains with different demands and expectations, each characterized by a need to forestall or cope with negative

emotions. In addition, there are other exploratory domains characterized by neutral or pleasurable emotions that include companionable conversation, play, and learning. Hill et al. (2003) argued that key processes in the organization of domains in families, and therefore also in development, are the management of (a) the boundaries between domains and (b) the cues for movement from one to another. In this formulation, the supportive family provides a setting for the child to practice the skills of domain organization and management, optimally with the same people over time.

In applying this domain-based analysis to the development of individual personality functioning during childhood, we argue that the skills that the child is able to practice with the same people within the family are then deployed in interactions outside the family with different people, who are not long-term attachment or authority figures. Social interactions outside of the family do not cover the range of domains that are experienced with parents. For example, most children will have experienced joint exploration, perhaps with some teaching, with a parent who reads to them, and at other times, they will have been cared for physically and emotionally by the same parent. When they start school, they participate in similar exploratory and instructional activities, but not intimate caring interactions, with other adults—their teachers. However, the increasing complexity does not stop there. The child at school moves constantly between the rules of interaction with teachers and peers and, within interactions with peers, between those with friends and those among the wider circle. Strikingly, children know the difference between the demands and expectations of interactions in these domains (Hay, Payne, & Chadwick, 2004). We assume that adaptive personality development entails the continued safe practice of the skills of domain organization in the family, supporting the even more demanding tasks of domain organization across different relationships, and settings outside the family. Bowlby (1988) characterized the good parent, when serving as an attachment figure, as a "secure base." By extension, the good family provides a "secure and mapped terrain" in which a broader repertoire of role definition, problem-solving, teamwork, exploration, and learning can be developed in addition to attachment.

APPLICATION OF A DOMAIN-BASED APPROACH TO PERSONALITY DISORDERS

Personality disorders are associated with social dysfunction in cross-section (Skodol et al., 2002) and over time for as much as a decade or more (Seivewright, Tyrer, & Johnson, 2004). Within DSM-IV, the assumption is made that social dysfunction arises from the disorder: "The enduring pattern [of inner experience and behavior, i.e., personality] leads to clinically significant distress or impairment in social, occupational, or other important areas of functioning" (American Psychiatric Association, 1994, p. 633). This view is consistent with personality theories that emphasize the role of abnormal traits influencing behavior across a wide range of social contexts, but less so with theories, such as the one outlined in this chapter, that emphasize person-context interactions. In this case social dysfunction is not a consequence of trait abnormalities, but instead reflects personality processes that are inherently social.

In this section, we make the case that the domain-based conception of social processes provides us with a model of personality that can lead to an understanding of some features of personality disorders. In each subsection, we describe the organization of domain-based processes and the likely consequences that arise from their disorganization. Our aim here is to show how the domain analysis of effective personality functioning can be used to understand interpersonal and affective dysfunction commonly seen in the personality disorders. In the next section, we turn to recent empirical findings on domain disorganization in personality disorder.

The maintenance of responding within domains involves a complex set of processes and skills. For example, interactions between peers in education or work, who are not friends outside of that setting, generally entail low to moderate levels of affective expression and a focus on work outcomes. Higher levels of affective expression, whether positive or negative, or conversation that is not clearly in the service of the educational or work tasks, are likely to alert others that a bid is being made for interactions in another domain. This may occur, for example, when a work colleague talks about a personal problem and becomes distressed about it. A sympathetic response will generally be accompanied by attempts to restore the work context, for example, by asking whether the person is getting support from family or friends, or has seen a doctor. The effectiveness of social maneuvers such as these is judged by their success in returning the intensity and direction of interactions to the anticipated range within work. They may also fail in ways that have serious consequences. For example, the bid to restore the work context may be experienced by distressed persons as failing to understand their predicament and to provide adequate help, leading them either to escalate the intensity of affect or to withdraw. Such a course implies that they are looking for attachment needs to be addressed within a setting not defined primarily by affection and the provision of comfort. Such domain confusion may lead to continued subjective distress, difficult work relationships, and poor role performance.

In a related vein, the management of one's public display of emotions in the workplace, a process that is also referred to as "emotional labor," is an important precursor to success at work (Hochschild, 1983). For example, the skillful implementation of display rules that are specific to different jobs, for example, displays of upbeat happiness by salespeople (Pugh, 2001), has been shown to be linked with effective performance. Such emotional labor, however, may be especially difficult for individuals who fail to discern norms concerning emotional expression across different contexts, leading to inappropriate displays of emotions. In this case, individuals with impaired domain organization may fail to grasp the nature of normative affective expression at work, as well as being unable to enact strategic displays of emotion necessary for successful performance in certain jobs.

Interpersonal interactions can be moved from one domain to another. It is common for close relationships, whether romantic or friendships, to start in the less intimate settings of work or wider social interactions. However, this evolution requires a further set of skills. Resuming the example above, a colleague may respond by suggesting a meeting outside of work to provide more time to talk, implying a willingness to relate under a different set of rules, such as those of friendship. The effective ''translation'' from work to friendship requires more, however, because the starting point is an asymmetrical interaction in which one person is needy and the other a potential caregiver. Friendship entails the development of activities independent of the work setting in which the participants contribute to a similar degree. A further possibility is that one or more of the work colleagues respond with the intensity and concern that the person is seeking, and also share their own personal preoccupations, while remaining in the work setting. Then relationships may develop that have some features of friendships or romance but that remain constrained by the terms and conditions of work. This progression is likely to leave the participants vulnerable to confusion and the possibility that expectations generated in one domain are frustrated by responses from another. This was seen in the example that opened the chapter.

Deficits in the cross-sectional structure of domains occur where some elements are present but others are absent or rudimentary. This may be evident, for example, in friendships when considerable time is spent with friends in interactions that focus exclusively on a narrow topic, such as a sport, antisocial behaviors, or illness. Alternatively, the focus may not be narrow but rather unbalanced. This is seen in friendships conducted at a high level of intensity, and confiding by phone or e-mail, but in which the participants rarely meet for other activities. Difficulties in generating structure over time are seen particularly clearly in romantic relationships, which involve the different but related neurobiological systems regulating lust, attraction, and attachment (Fisher, Aron, Mashek, Li, & Brown, 2002). These systems operate over different time courses in that lust and attraction may be instantaneous but the development of attachment implies trust and commitment over longer periods. Furthermore, the cues that lead a person to respond with lust or attraction may be quite different from those relevant to attachment. The structure of the developing relationship may be undermined when individuals entrust other persons with confidential information or make commitments to them prior to establishing their capacity to provide genuine intimacy. On the other hand, the structuring of a romantic relationship may fail because, although initial steps are taken, the participants reach a plateau, with progress neither to greater intimacy and commitment nor to separation in order to provide opportunities for an alternative relationship.

Inaccurate location of interpersonal resources is a common consequence of confusions and deficits in domain structure. Confiding intimacies at work, seeking intimacy in friendships that lack other structural features, or rapidly deepening a romantic relationship without an adequate assessment of the qualities of the prospective partner are all processes in which mistakes are made regarding where to locate sources of intimacy and emotional support. Conversely, it is likely that when people make this kind of mistake, they also fail to locate accurately the resources that are available in less intense interactions. For example, interactions with work colleagues can validate a person's sense of competence and self-efficacy. Interactions with friends can widen horizons, improve problem-solving, and create a sense of solidarity that is as important as closeness based on emotional intensity and self-disclosure. Therefore, we suggest that processes relevant to the personality disorders involve both the mistaken location of intense closeness in domains where it is not available (frustrated bids for attachment), and a failure to locate other less intense but important resources in those domains.

Participants also have different responsibilities in each domain. These are substantial and enduring in work and established romantic relationships and friendships, but generally slight and brief in broader social interactions and day-to-day negotiations. Failure to meet responsibilities is often met with a structured response in work, but the response in more personal relationships depends on the engagement of the participants. For example, in romantic relationships, infidelity, violence, or attempts by one partner to control another, violate the responsibilities of the domain and call for a response—which may or may not be forthcoming, depending on the personalities of the participants and the history and context of the relationship. Tension, discord, and expression of distress reflect problems in a relationship, but the absence of "corrective" reactions suggests a more fundamental difficulty in the management of the domain.

In this section, we have described difficulties that reflect problems in domain management. It is important to emphasize that this is not intended to be an exhaustive account of dysfunction that may be found in the personality disorders. Many quite severe difficulties occur in the context of clear domain organization. Poor work performance, marital discord, and lack of friendships are all examples of such problems. It remains a question for further investigation whether there are some forms of personality disorder that arise predominantly from domain disorganization, that is,

difficulties in organizing domains properly, both within and across domains.

The Measurement of Domain Functioning

Measures reflecting a domain-based approach are needed if this framework is to be examined empirically. The Adult Personality Functioning Assessment (APFA; Hill, Harrington, Fudge, Rutter, & Pickles, 1989; Hill, Fudge, Harrington, Pickles, & Rutter, 2000) was designed to assess social role performance in the six domains of work, romantic relationships, friendships, nonspecific social interactions, negotiations, and day-to-day coping. A key discriminator of the domains is the social role of the participants. Thus, negotiations in work are conducted in the role assigned by the job and are not included in the negotiations domain. By contrast, in negotiations with shopkeepers, plumbers, or doctors, the role has to be established in the interaction, and performance in this role is assessed in the negotiations domain. Ratings are made of the subject's contribution to functioning over substantial periods, generally five years. The aim is to assess stable functioning reflecting competencies in each domain without prejudging issues of change in the even longer term. Ratings are made for each domain independently so that contextual differences as well as consistencies can be detected.

The APFA is an investigator-based measure, in which the interviewer uses flexible questioning to obtain adequate information, and makes ratings on the basis of detailed rules, a dictionary of examples, and training. The interviews are recorded, and detailed reports are prepared from the recordings. More recently, the Revised Adult Personality Functioning Assessment (RAPFA) has been developed to assess specific aspects of domain dysfunction in the personality disorders (Hill & Stein, 2002). Ratings are made in each domain on a scale from 1 to 9 where "1" reflects a high level of adaptation and "9" very poor functioning over the rating period. Ratings are also made of the predominant type of dysfunction: discordant, avoidant, or other (unstable). The RAPFA also includes "dysfunction scales" that assess more specific interpersonal processes, such as whether the respondent repeatedly intensifies romantic relationships where problems are already evident. The dysfunction scales identify processes that are taken into account when rating domain disorganization (DD). Domain organization refers to the accurate identification of the demands of the domain and the expectations that each participant in the domain can have of one another, the appropriate level of emotional expression and its intentionality, and the extent of intimacy and emotional resources to be found in the domain. DD is identified (a) where the balance of the components in one or more domains is markedly disrupted (domain incoherence), (b) where processes that are appropriate in one domain appear in another (domain boundary violation), and (c) where the balance of intensity or intimacy across the domains is skewed. DD is rated on a 0 to 6 scale. Zero is rated where there are no markers for DD, "1 to 2" where there are some markers but no convincing examples, "3 to 4" where there are definitely some relevant features but there are also aspects of functioning in which domain clarity is preserved, and "5 to 6" where most or all functioning lacks domain clarity.

We used the RAPFA in a study in Pittsburgh of patients with borderline personality disorder (BPD), contrasting them with two groups—patients with avoidant personality disorder (APD) and patients suffering from an Axis I disorder but no personality disorder. Both BPD and APD patients had substantially higher levels of dysfunction within each domain than non-PD psychiatric patients, but BPD patients differed from APD patients in having higher levels of romantic dysfunction (consistent with a role for attachment processes) and of DD (Hill et al., 2008). Thus, APD appears to be characterized by limitations in the performance of tasks within domains, without difficulties in domain organization of the kind outlined

earlier, whereas DD is a core feature of the social dysfunction of BPD.

We extended these analyses by incorporating measures of temperament (anxiety and anger) and of attachment into a joint examination of the effects of temperament, preoccupied attachment, and DD on BPD traits and diagnosis (Morse et al, 2009). The results suggest that these factors contribute to BPD both independently and in interaction, even when controlling for other personality disorder traits and Axis I symptoms. In regression analyses, the interaction between anger (but not anxiety) and DD predicted BPD traits. In recursive partitioning analyses, two possible paths to BPD were identified: high anger combined with high domain DD and low anger combined with preoccupied attachment (with examples of the first pathway considerably more prevalent). These results suggest possible subtypes of BPD and possible mechanisms by which BPD traits are established and maintained. More generally, they illustrate the value of a domain-based approach for generating assessment tools and hypotheses that are theoretically meaningful for research on personality disorders.

Illustrative Examples of Difficulties in Domain Organization

We provide here some descriptions of interpersonal functioning obtained using the RAPFA from ongoing studies of personality disorders being conducted in Pittsburgh. A woman in her early 30s had an unstable work history resulting both from being fired and leaving jobs. Within weeks of starting one of the jobs, she was crying at work every day and complaining that people did not know how to respond to her or what to do because of the frequency and intensity of the episodes. She was fired after two months "because the supervisors didn't have empathy for or know how to deal with a person who had been diagnosed with a mental illness." In this example, the participant presented her work colleagues with emotional upset that posed a demand to respond empathetically with an intensity of emotion associated with intimate relationships. A second kind of domain mismanagement was evident in her next job where she became sexually involved with a work colleague and began to argue with him at work. In this example, intense emotions were located appropriately in a romantic relationship, but the participants failed to maintain the boundary between that relationship and functioning at work.

Another problematic pattern was illustrated in an account of a romantic relationship from a woman in her mid 30s who worked as a prostitute. She fell in love with a client, and the feelings were said to be mutual. However, the relationship was conducted entirely within the confines of the hotel where she saw her clients. This meant that it had the intensity and sexual passion of a romantic relationship but none of the other features, such as a range of shared activities, mutual support, or links with wider social interactions. It was also unclear what were the underlying rules of the relationship, summed up in the report of the interviewer that, "She would be angry if he didn't leave her money and would also be sad and disappointed if he did pay her."

Consider another class of examples in which there is confusion between romance and friendship. A woman in her mid 20s had a discordant and violent relationship with her partner, and an intense friendship with a woman three years younger, with daily confiding and considerable mutual reliance. This relationship was not perceived as a romantic relationship by either of the participants, it was not sexual, and it did not have the dynamic of romantic relationships moving either towards commitment or an ending. Thus, this was a friendship; however, it was conducted at a level of emotional intimacy found usually in romantic relationships, but without the underpinning of a shared view of it as a romantic relationship. This left one or both participants vulnerable to misidentifying the resources available, as if they were similar to those found in a romantic relationship. Furthermore, this person did not have any other friends, suggesting difficulties in practicing the skills of less intense relationships, as well as lacking the resources available from a wider circle.

The vulnerability associated with misidentifying resources available in friendships was also illustrated in the friendship of a woman in her late 30s who moved to a new city to stay close to a male friend. After moving, they lived together on the basis that she supported him in various difficult decisions regarding his sexuality, and he paid the rent. However, their relationship was not sexual, and they did not establish a joint household. After some time, he decided to move again, leaving the subject behind. In this example, not only was there an intensity more characteristic of romantic relationships, but also the subject, in moving with the friend, behaved like a romantic partner without the underpinning of the expectations and responsibilities of a romantic relationship. This person's vulnerability was also underlined by her lack of other friendships conducted over a range of intensities.

DEVELOPING EMPIRICAL AND CLINICAL AGENDAS

Our aim has been to contribute to the generation of a coherent conceptualization for the personality disorders that leads to empirically testable predictions and has therapeutic potential. We have argued that, once the processes that under normal personality functioning have been identified, predictions can be made regarding the ways in which these may be undermined in disordered functioning. We have also suggested that an examination of the organization of personality functioning through childhood and adolescence will provide indications of the ways in which personality disorders develop over time. The central concept is social domain organization, which is evident over development from infancy. Clarifying the interpersonal competencies required to manage domain functioning provides indicators of the ways in which domain management may fail in the personality disorders.

This point can be illustrated, for example, by the processes associated with the initiation of romantic relationships. These include the interpretation of social signals prior to the initiation of the relationship, which is followed by a phase of intensification involving powerful emotions and their regulation, monitoring of the qualities of the potential partner and the emerging relationship, and the exploration of areas of common interest and enjoyment. Different methodologies are required to explore different elements and how they may vary in individuals with personality disorders. Experimental methods could be employed to explore how normal individuals interpret the domains to which social cues belong, and how they react to cues that appear to be at odds with the prevailing domain, either to restore interactions to that domain or to explore alternative domains. For example, social cues at work suggesting intimacy are likely to be met with responses that restore interactions to the work domain, or ones that explore more intimate possibilities. Individuals with personality disorders may interpret everyday cues as bids for attachment and, therefore, make inappropriate domain interpretations in work or school; in a related vein, they may have difficulties in responding to bids for attachment in ways that restore the usual interactions of work or school.

Such processes could be examined using a range of techniques, such as measures of attributions about the behaviors of others and assessment of responses to imagined scenarios. Further studies could explore the cognitive boundaries of domains. These would test how reliably individuals identify the domains of social interactions portrayed in pictures, audiotaped or videotaped conversations, and written text. Once unambiguous cues for domains have been identified, cues signaling domain confusions or violations could be investigated. A related set of studies could examine the psychophysiology of domains. The prediction would be that cues that do not meet the prevailing assumptions regarding

domain identity lead to autonomic arousal reflecting an alerting response and affects of anxiety or excitement. In all such studies, it would be essential to attend to possible variations by age, gender, social class, and culture, as well as the kind of personality disorder. Further aspects of the normal and dysfunctional development of romantic relationships in personality disorders can be evaluated using interviews such as the RAPFA that ask about the details of the initiation, intensification, maintenance, and ending of such relationships.

It is important to emphasize that, although this analysis makes a number of specific predictions, it is intended to encourage the assessment of competing possibilities regarding causal mechanisms. For example, it is a common clinical observation that borderline adolescents and young adults have difficulty maintaining a level of emotional expression and intensity of relationships appropriate to different domains. This problem may arise from processes as diverse as misinterpretations of social cues, a generalized failure of affect regulation, a more specific difficulty in maintaining the distinction between attachment contexts and task-oriented contexts, or problems in managing the demands of task-based social interactions. This range of possibilities has implications for empirical studies, clinical formulations, and interventions. As we have outlined, such phenomena first need to be identified at a behavioral level using a measure such as the RAPFA. Then, observational and experimental studies are needed to differentiate the competing explanations. These, in turn, will inform treatment.

There are implications for treatment, however, prior to evidence from such studies being available. We illustrate this using the example that opened the chapter. Responding to the patient's distress regarding her friend's failure to repay the loan, there are themes that a therapist may identify without reference to social domains— for example, the patient's expectations in a relationship with someone older and more senior, and her motives in lending the money. Using the domain framework, the therapist might discuss the general concept of a friend, exploring issues such as equality and choice in friendship, participants' motives in friendships, and how problems are solved. The characteristics of friendship could be contrasted with those for work relationships, and relationships in which money may be lent, and then the "identity" of this relationship could be examined.

Other relationships in the patient's life might be reviewed with a focus on emotional expression and regulation. Using the domain framework, patient and therapist might conclude that a tendency to react to social situations with high emotional intensity where it is not readily accommodated has created a pattern of difficulties in emotion regulation. Provided it is consistent with the overall approach, treatment might include an element of psychoeducation in which the therapist explains features of social domains and their demarcating characteristics. In this vein, Stein, Allen, and Hill (2003) have described group work developed from the APFA definitions of social domain organization. The aim is for psychoeducation not only to enhance a specific understanding of social domains and their management, but also to promote increased reflection about the general ways in which one creates one's own social environment.

Second, the pervasiveness of social dysfunction in personality disorder implies that treatment approaches need to address processes across multiple domains. This assertion is consistent with the comprehensive approaches of dialectical behavior therapy (DBT; Linehan, 1993), mentalization-based partial hospitalization (Bateman & Fonagy, 2004), multisystemic therapy (MST; Henggeler, Clingempeel, Brondino, & Pickrel, 2002), and treatment foster care (Chamberlain & Reid, 1998) for juvenile delinquency.

Third, some perspectives that are viewed as competing can be adapted and integrated within the domain-based framework. For example, working with difficulties in affect regulation is central to DBT. Affect regulation is a key concept in a domain-based approach, together with the idea that affect is regulated at different levels of intensity, and in different ways across domains. Therefore, solutions to problems in affect regulation need to address the different requirements and resources of the domains. In turn, this encourages competing alternatives to be considered for diagnosing problems—a generalized problem in affect regulation is then only one of a number of possibilities.

Fourth, for work with patients with severe personality disorders, the use of a treatment team is indicated (Pilkonis, 2001). The emotional burden of treating patients with severe personality disorders is often too great for the individual therapist to bear comfortably. A team helps to "metabolize" affect, and to provide organization and support in the face of discouragement, slow progress, and incentives to give up the work. The use of a treatment team can also foster attachments to members of a larger group and a sense of social integration that many patients find sustaining. The domain-based approach implies that there needs to be a differentiation of roles in therapeutic teams reflecting the demarcation of the domains. This will enhance the potential for clarity of communication and in appropriately identifying the available interpersonal resources in different domains. Crucially, this differentiation reflects not only roles but also skills. For example, one member of a team may focus on social interactions outside of intimate relationships using expertise in social skills training, whereas another trained in relationship-oriented psychotherapy may work on issues in more intimate relationships. The aim is integration across domains, so clinicians with demarcated roles need to exchange information freely, and to review constantly, the domain appropriateness of patients' behaviors. Finally, the demarcation in a domain-based approach between (a) processes that involve emotion regulation and mood-dependent action, and (b) processes that entail reconsideration and reflection, suggests a combination of interventions that are active and behavioral, on the one hand, and reflective and meta-cognitive, on the other.

SUMMARY

Social dysfunction in the personality disorders has generally been assumed to be a consequence of individual trait abnormalities. However, from a developmental perspective, personality and social functioning are inseparable. In this chapter, we have outlined the case that the capacity for accurate and efficient partitioning of interpersonal functioning into social domains is central to personality development, and that deficits in domain organization underlie many of the phenomena seen in the personality disorders. Social domains, such as work and romantic relationships, involve a shared understanding among the participants as to the focus and purpose of their interactions. They provide rules for the prediction and interpretation of each others' behaviors and emotions, and a common expectation regarding responsibilities and the likely interpersonal resources that are available. Adaptive functioning involves effective performance within each domain, and movement from one domain to another, making demands on social information processing, regulation of emotions and behaviors, and modulation of expressions of need. Disorganization of these processes is seen in the personality disorders. Studies of the social, psychological, and biological underpinning of domain organization over normal development have the potential to inform mechanisms in domain disorganization, and hence in the etiology and maintenance of personality disorders.

References

American Psychiatric Association. (1994). *Diagnostic and statistical manual of mental disorders* (4th ed.). Washington, DC: Author.

Bateman, A., & Fonagy, P. (2004). *Psychotherapy for borderline personality disorder: Mentalization-based treatment*. New York: Oxford University Press.

Bolton, D., & Hill, J. (2004). *Mind, meaning and mental disorder: The nature of causal explanation in psychology and psychiatry* (2nd ed.). New York: Oxford University Press.

Bowlby, J. (1988). *A secure base*. New York: Basic Books.

Bugental, D. B. (2000). Acquisition of the algorithms of social life: A domain-based approach. *Psychological Bulletin, 126*, 187–219.

Chamberlain, P., & Reid, J. B. (1998). Comparison of two community alternatives to incarceration for chronic juvenile offenders. *Journal of Consulting and Clinical Psychology, 66*, 624–633.

Cloninger, C. R. (2005). Antisocial personality disorder: A review. In M. Maj, H. S. Akiskal, J. E. Mezzich, & A. Okasha (Eds.), *WPA series: Evidence and experience in psychiatry: Vol. 8. Personality disorders*. (pp. 125–200). Chichester, UK: John Wiley & Sons.

Fisher, H. E., Aron, A., Mashek, D., Li, A., & Brown, L. L. (2002). Defining the brain systems of lust, romantic attraction, and attachment. *Archives of Sexual Behavior, 31*, 413–419.

Hay, D. F., Payne, A., & Chadwick, A. (2004). Peer relations in childhood. *Journal of Child Psychology and Psychiatry, 45*, 84–108.

Henggeler, S. W., Clingempeel, W. G., Brondino, M. J., & Pickrel, S. G. (2002). Four-year follow-up of multisystemic therapy with substance-abusing and substance-dependent juvenile offenders. *Journal of the American Academy of Child and Adolescent Psychiatry, 41*, 868–874.

Henry, W. P. (1996). Structural Analysis of Social Behavior as a common metric for programmatic psychopathology and psychotherapy research. *Journal of Consulting and Clinical Psychology, 64*, 1263–1275.

Hill, J. (2008). Disorders of personality. In M. Rutter, D. Bishop, D. Pine, S. Scott, J. Stevenson, E. Taylor, & Thapar, A. (Eds.), *Rutter's Child and adolescent psychiatry* (5th ed.). Hoboken, NJ: John Wiley & Sons.

Hill, J., Fonagy, P., Safier, E., & Sargent, J. (2003). The ecology of attachment in the family. *Family Process, 42*, 205–221.

Hill, J., Fudge, H., Harrington, R., Pickles, A., & Rutter, M. (2000). Complementary approaches to the assessment of personality disorder: The Personality Assessment Schedule and Adult Personality Functioning Assessment compared. *British Journal of Psychiatry, 176*, 434–439.

Hill, J., Harrington, R., Fudge, H., Rutter, M., & Pickles, A. (1989). Adult Personality Functioning Assessment (APFA): An investigator-based standardised interview. *British Journal of Psychiatry, 155*, 24–35.

Hill, J., Pickles, A., Rollinson, L., Davies, R., & Byatt, M. (2004). Juvenile versus adult onset depression: Multiple differences imply different pathways. *Psychological Medicine, 34,* 1483–1493.

Hill, J., Pilkonis, P. A., Morse, J. Q., Feske, U., Reynolds, S. K., Hope, H., ... Broyden, N. (2008). Social domain dysfunction and disorganization in borderline personality disorder. *Psychological Medicine, 38,* 135–146.

Hill, J., & Stein, H. (2002). Revised Adult Personality Functioning Assessment (RAPFA). Technical Report No. 02-0052. Topeka, KS: Menninger Clinic.

Hochschild, A. (1983). *The managed heart: Commercialization of human feeling.* Berkeley: University of California Press.

Hodges, J., & Tizard, B. (1989). Social and family relationships of ex-institutional adolescents. *Journal of Child Psychology and Psychiatry, 30,* 77–97.

Horowitz, L., Wilson, K., Turan, B., Zolotsev, P., Constantino, M. & Henderson, L. (2006). How interpersonal motives clarify the meaning of interpersonal behavior: A revised circumplex model. *Personality and Social Psychology Review, 10,* 67–86.

Kerr, M., Tremblay, R. E., Pagini, L., & Vitaro, F. (1997). Boys' behavioral inhibition and the risk of later delinquency. *Archives of General Psychiatry, 54,* 809–816.

Linehan, M. (1993). *Cognitive-behavioral treatment of borderline personality disorder.* New York: Guilford Press.

Livesley, W. J., Jang, K. L., & Vernon P. A. (1998). Phenotypic and genetic structure of traits delineating personality disorder. *Archives of General Psychiatry, 55,* 941–948.

Mischel W. (2004). Toward an integrative science of the person. *Annual Review of Psychology, 55,* 1–22.

Mischel, W., & Shoda, Y. (1995). A cognitive-affective system theory of personality: Reconceptualizing situations, dispositions, dynamics and invariance in personality structure. *Psychological Review, 102,* 246–268.

Morse, J. Q., Hill, J., Pilkonis, P. A., Yaggi, K., Broyden, N., Stepp, S., Reed, L. I., & Feske, U. (2009). Anger, preoccupied attachment, and domain disorganization in borderline personality disorder. *Journal of Personality Disorders, 23,* 240–257.

O'Connor, T. G., Marvin, R. S., Rutter, M., Olrick, J. T., & Britner, P. A. (2003). Child-parent attachment following early institutional deprivation. *Development and Psychopathology, 15,* 19–38.

Parker, G., Both, L., Olley, A., Hadzi-Pavlovic, D., Irvine, P., & Jacobs, G. (2002). Defining disordered personality functioning. *Journal of Personality Disorders, 16,* 503–522.

Pilkonis, P. A. (2001). Treatment of personality disorders in the context of symptom disorders. In W. J. Livesley (Ed.), *Handbook of personality disorders* (pp. 541–554). New York: Guilford Press.

Pugh, S. D. (2001). Service with a smile: Emotional contagion in the service encounter. *Academy of Management Journal, 44,* 1018–1027.

Rousseau, D. M. (1996). *Psychological contracts in organizations: Understanding written and unwritten agreements.* Newbury Park, CA: Sage.

Rutter, M. (1987). Temperament, personality and personality disorder. *British Journal of Psychiatry, 150,* 443–458.

Seivewright, H., Tyrer, P., & Johnson, T. (2004). Persistent social dysfunction in anxious and depressed patients with personality disorder. *Acta Psychiatrica Scandinavica, 109,* 104–109.

Shoda, Y., Mischel, W., & Wright, J. C. (1994). Intraindividual stability in the organization and patterning of behavior: Incorporating psychological situations into the idiographic analysis of personality. *Journal of Personality and Social Psychology, 67,* 674–687.

Skodol, A. E., Gunderson, J. G., McGlashan, T. H., Dyck, I. R., Stout, R. L., Bender, D. S., ... Oldham, J. M. (2002). Functional impairment in patients with schizotypal, borderline, avoidant, or obsessive-compulsive personality disorder. *American Journal of Psychiatry, 159,* 276–283.

Sroufe, A., Cooper, R., & DeHart, G. (1996). *Child development: Its nature and course* (3rd ed.). New York: McGraw Hill.

Sroufe, A., & Waters, E. (1976). The ontogenesis of smiling and laughter: A perspective on the organization of development in infancy. *Psychological Review, 83,* 173–189.

Stein, H., Allen, J. G., & Hill, J. (2003). Roles and relationships: A psychoeducational approach to reviewing strengths and difficulties in adulthood functioning. *Bulletin of the Menninger Clinic, 67,* 281–313.

Stern, D. N. (2001). Face-to-face play: Its temporal structure as a predictor of socio-affective development. *Monographs of the Society for Research in Child Development, 66,* 144–149.

World Health Organization. (1992). The ICD-10 classification of mental and behavioural disorders: Clinical descriptions and diagnostic guidelines. Geneva, Switzerland: Author.

IV ASSESSMENT OF INTERPERSONAL CHARACTERISTICS

18 CIRCULAR REASONING ABOUT CIRCULAR ASSESSMENT

Michael B. Gurtman

There are a number of strong geometric and substantive assumptions involved when assessment instruments are used to classify persons into typological categories defined by the coordinates of the Interpersonal Circle ([IPC]; Wiggins, Phillips, & Trapnell, 1989, p. 296). In an article likely familiar to many readers (and nearly all contributors to this volume), Jerry Wiggins and his coauthors set forth some of the basic assumptions—or as they described it, the "circular reasoning"—behind the "diagnostic use" of the IPC for personality assessment. These assumptions were largely in the form of predictions about the diagnostic implications of certain structural and substantive products of IPC-based assessments. At the same time, the article provided a set of principles and demonstrations for how such products could be incorporated into personality assessment.

The purpose of this chapter is to provide what is best described as an amplification and extension of some of the circular reasoning—the principles and themes of circular assessment—that are presented in this essential work. Several newer ideas and developments will be introduced, but, at the same time, I will try to stay grounded in the approach that Wiggins and his colleagues so effectively and persuasively advocated in this article and in related works. I will begin by describing the features of the *circular model*, its relation to the *interpersonal circumplex* (Wiggins, 1979), and then present the derivations and implications of the model for the assessment of individual differences, including circular profiles, vector scoring, and circular distributions. Both the statistics and the graphics of circular assessment will be illustrated. As I have noted in previous places (e.g., Gurtman, 2009, Gurtman & Balakrishnan, 1998; Gurtman & Pincus, 2003), circular-based assessments offer new ways—and opportunities—for analyzing, representing, and construing interpersonal data. These methods, as Wiggins et al. (1989) noted, offer "exciting possibilities" that help further the potential and creativity of our interpersonal assessments and research activities.

WHAT IS THE CIRCULAR MODEL?

In a history well-covered elsewhere (e.g., Freedman, 1985; Kiesler, 1996; LaForge, 2004; Wiggins, 1996), the circular model of interpersonal behavior can be traced to the pioneering work of the Kaiser

Foundation Research Group of the 1950s (e.g., Freedman, Ossorio, & Coffey, 1951; Leary, 1957), who developed the IPC as a way of "systematizing" the array of interpersonal traits and behaviors at different levels of personality. A 1955 version of that model appears as Figure 18.1, and shows a 16-segment circle that served to operationalize the basic organization and contents of that system.

The spark of genius or insight that ultimately led the Kaiser Group to adopt a circular model to represent the interpersonal domain remains somewhat uncertain (see, in particular, Freedman, 1985). Nevertheless, the implications of a circle, once adopted, can be easily deduced.

As has been noted elsewhere (e.g., Gurtman, 2009; Gurtman & Balakrishnan, 1998), circular models of personality are implicitly defined by three features: *two-dimensionality*, *constant radius*, and *continuous distribution of variables*. In the order given, these are increasingly particularistic

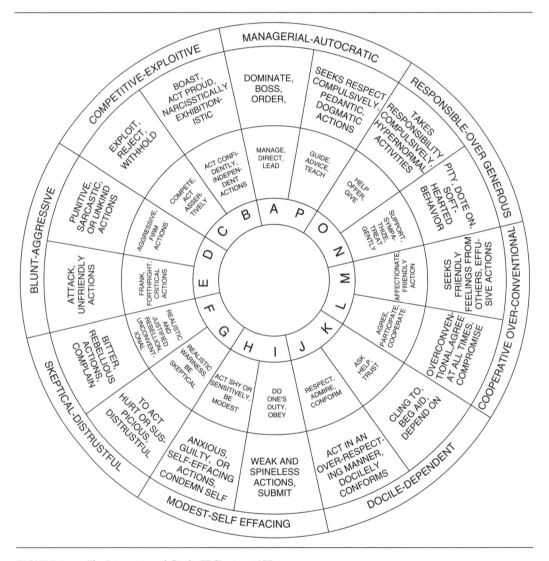

FIGURE 18.1   The Interpersonal Circle (IPC), circa 1955
Source: "Interpersonal Diagnosis: Some Problems of Methodology and Validation," by T. Leary and H. Coffey, 1955, *The Journal of Abnormal and Social Psychology*, 50(1), 110–124.

to circular models (i.e., in comparison to other structural models of personality).

Two-dimensionality (see also Fournier, Moskowitz, & Zuroff, Chapter 4, this volume) implies that the differences between the variables comprising that domain are reducible to differences along two dimensions; hence the relationships can be represented in a two-dimensional plane. Wiggins and Trapnell (1996) argued that, for the interpersonal domain of personality, "conceptual priority" (pp. 89–90) should be given to the factors of *Dominance* and *Nurturance* as the dimensions (or axes) that define the space; hence, they serve to provide a coordinate system for locating interpersonal variables and tendencies. In part, this priority is due to their relation to the broader meta-concepts of *Agency* and *Communion*, respectively (Bakan, 1966; Wiggins, 1991). The *constant radius property* is best understood (as the Kaiser Group did) by thinking of each variable as a vector emanating from the origin and having constant or unit length. (Figure 18.2). This implies that each variable has equal "communality" (in the factor-analytic sense) in that space; at the same time, each variable represents a particular "blend" of the two dimensions that define that space (e.g., Dominance and Nurturance). Lastly, the feature of a continuous distribution suggests that, theoretically, variables are arrayed along a circular continuum, with no major gaps in coverage around the circumference of the circle (Gurtman, 1997). In an *interpersonal taxonomy* (Wiggins, 1979), this would imply that, at any given point on the circular continuum, it should be possible to specify a meaningful interpersonal variation (and thus presumably a word to express that variation, e.g., De Raad, 1995). For measurement purposes, however, the circular continuum is typically sampled at equal intervals, and hence the circle is segmented into equally spaced *octants* (8ths) or *sectors* (16ths); see, for example, Kiesler (1983). Each octant or sector essentially cumulates content over a particular span of the circle.

Finally, Figure 18.2 reveals another distinctive feature of the circular model—the polar coordinate system that is used to locate variables, and ultimately people, along the circumference of the circle. As can be seen, in a polar coordinate system (versus a rectangular system), locations are specified by angular displacement (in degrees)

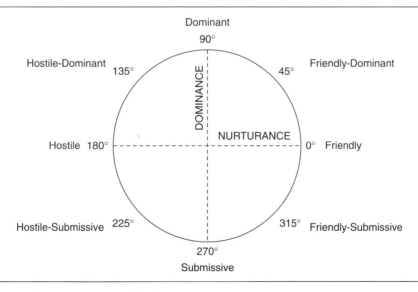

FIGURE 18.2 A Generic Interpersonal Circle

from a fixed position. Traditionally, in interpersonal models, the fixed point is at the "three o'clock" position (pure Nurturance, corresponding to Friendly in the figure), and displacement is measured in degrees, in a counterclockwise direction.

THE INTERPERSONAL CIRCUMPLEX

Although the IPC (e.g., Kiesler, 1983) and *the interpersonal circumplex* (Wiggins, 1979) are terms often employed interchangeably, it may be useful to consider some distinctions. In their article on "circular reasoning," Wiggins et al. (1989) described both a weak form and a strong form of the circular model, relevant to this distinction. In its weak form, the circle is simply "a convenient pictorial representation of concepts associated with an interpersonal theory of personality" (p. 296). Although the circle does suggest certain testable hypotheses about the properties of a particular domain (as presented previously), an IPC may simply be regarded as an interpersonal circle—with little surplus meaning intended.

Wiggins et al. (1989) also identified a clearly preferred, strong form of the model—the circle as a "formal geometric model of the interrelations among indicants of constructs derived from an interpersonal theory of personality" (p. 296). Psychometrically, this meaning is clearly attached to that of the *circumplex*, or *circulant correlation matrix*, as originally proposed by Guttman (1954). Like the circle itself, the circumplex matrix, as depicted in Table 18.1, has an order with "no beginning or end." Its main feature is a repeating pattern in which values fall and then rise again based on the proximity to the main diagonal. As many have noted (e.g., Browne, 1992; Tracey, 2000), the ideal of the circulant offers a formal model of how variables within a circular system are expected to relate. Specifically, two variables' correlation should be a direct function of their (angular) proximity on the circle (e.g., Browne, 1992; Gurtman &

TABLE 18.1   The Circumplex or Circulant Correlation Matrix

Defining Correlational Pattern							
Angle	0°	45°	90°	135°	180°	225°	270°	315°
0°	1							
45°	ρ_1	1						
90°	ρ_2	ρ_1	1					
135°	ρ_3	ρ_2	ρ_1	1				
180°	ρ_4	ρ_3	ρ_2	ρ_1	1			
225°	ρ_3	ρ_4	ρ_3	ρ_2	ρ_1	1		
270°	ρ_2	ρ_3	ρ_4	ρ_3	ρ_2	ρ_1	1	
315°	ρ_1	ρ_2	ρ_3	ρ_4	ρ_3	ρ_2	ρ_1	1

where $\rho_1 > \rho_2 > \rho_3 > \rho_4$

An Example of a Perfect Circumplex

Angle	0°	45°	90°	135°	180°	225°	270°	315°
0°	1.00							
45°	.50	1.00						
90°	.00	.50	1.00					
135°	−.50	.00	.50	1.00				
180°	−1.00	−.50	.00	.50	1.00			
225°	−.50	−1.00	−.50	.00	.50	1.00		
270°	.00	−.50	−1.00	−.50	.00	.50	1.00	
315°	.50	.00	−.50	−1.00	−.50	.00	.50	1.00

Note: Values in the example assume the facet composition of interpersonal variables proposed by Wiggins, 1979.

Pincus, 2003), and variables at the same distance should have equal correlations. The extent to which this is true for a given system can be evaluated using confirmatory methods designed to fit an obtained correlation matrix to the hypothesized covariance model (e.g., Fabrigar, Visser, & Browne, 1997; Tracey, 2000; Wiggins, Steiger, & Gaelick, 1981). At the same time, maximum-likelihood estimates of the correlation parameters comprising the circumplex can be computed, as shown, for example, in Gurtman and Pincus (2000).

WHAT IS AN INTERPERSONAL CIRCUMPLEX?

Although, arguably, the interpersonal circumplex is the most prominent of the various circular models in the personality field, circular models have also been proposed for other domains of interest (Plutchik & Conte, 1997). Among these are well-established models for the domains of affect (e.g., Russell, 1980; Yik, Russell, & Barrett, 1999), emotion (e.g., Plutchik, 1980), universal human values (e.g., Schwartz, 1992), and vocational interests (e.g., Tracey & Rounds, 1993, 1997). Circumplex models have also been created by pairing together various Big Five personality factors, thus extending the model beyond the traditional interpersonal factors of the Big Five (i.e., Extraversion/Surgency and Agreeableness; McCrae & Costa, 1989) to the other *non-interpersonal* factor combinations (see Hofstee, De Raad, & Goldberg, 1992, and the AB5C model). Finally, besides the Wiggins circumplex, alternative circumplex (or circumplexlike) models for the interpersonal domain have been proposed (e.g., Benjamin, 1996; Kiesler, 1983; Lorr & McNair, 1963), including some variants intended to be specific to constructs such as interpersonal problems (e.g., Horowitz, 2004), values (Locke, 2000), supports (Trobst, 1999), and impacts (Kiesler, Schmidt, & Wagner, 1997).

Given the number and variety of circular models, the question of what kind of content makes a circumplex "interpersonal" is especially relevant. Wiggins and Trobst (1997) addressed this question by noting that an interpersonal interpretation requires a "plausible substantive rationale" (p. 58): "A circumplex is an *interpersonal* circumplex when there are good reasons to interpret it as such" (p. 58) (emphasis in original). An interpersonal circumplex can be constructed either top-down or bottom-up. An example of bottom-up process is De Raad's (1995) *psycholexical* interpersonal circumplex. Starting with a pool of 1,203 personality adjectives, experts culled words that fit a definition of interpersonal ("the behavior assumes one or two other people," p. 92). Factor analysis of self-ratings based on the selected subset of 454 adjectives led to a two-dimensional solution with a circular distribution similar to that of the Wiggins (1979) circumplex.

The top-down approach, typified at least in part by Wiggins's (1979) interpersonal taxonomy, begins with an overarching theory about the nature of the interpersonal world. Perhaps the most relevant example is Wiggins's adaptation of Foa and Foa's (1974) facet theory of social exchange to define an "interpersonal event" as an exchange between two people (self and other) involving the "resource classes" of love and status (Wiggins & Trapnell, 1996, p. 106). A facet analysis would therefore define a certain behavior or trait as interpersonal on a deductive basis. Additionally, the facet compositions of particular interpersonal events or variables—the resource classes involved and the implications for self and other—would necessarily suggest a certain circumplex ordering (see Wiggins & Trapnell, 1996, pp. 120–124). In an elegant analysis, Wiggins (1979) showed how the variables comprising his interpersonal circumplex would meet these criteria.

FROM MODEL TO MEASUREMENT

Beginning with the pioneering work of the Kaiser Foundation Research Group, circular models and systems have given rise to various measures designed to operationalize the assessment of interpersonal characteristics. Still today, perhaps the most ambitious project was the IPC, which was intended to capture 16 interpersonal variables arranged on a circular continuum, at different intensities (moderate and severe), and across three different levels of personality data (public, conscious, symbolic). (See Figure 18.1 and articles by Freedman, Ossorio, & Coffey, 1951; Laforge, Leary, Naboisek, Coffey, & Freedman, 1954; and LaForge & Suczek, 1955.) To assess interpersonal traits in relation to that system, the group developed the Interpersonal Checklist (ICL; LaForge & Suczek, 1955). At the same time, the group also pioneered some of the statistical methods and graphical devices for representing interpersonal tendencies within a circular system, like that afforded by the ICL. Two of these contributions are the *circular profile* and the *vector method*; both figure prominently in Wiggins et al.'s (1989) article on "circular reasoning." They will be discussed, in turn.

The Circular Profile

As I have indicated in a number of places (e.g., Gurtman, 2009; Gurtman & Balakrishnan, 1998), circular assessments call for new and distinctly different ways of analyzing and presenting summary personality data. A basic presentation device is the circular profile. Its features and particular advantages can best be appreciated by contrasting it with the traditional approach for summarizing personality data, which I call the *linear profile* (Gurtman, 2009).

Figure 18.3 conveys a generic example of the traditional linear profile—the kind of personality profile commonly associated with popular, omnibus tests of personality and psychopathology, such as the NEO-PI-R (Costa & McCrae, 1992), MMPI-2 (Butcher, Graham, Ben-Porath, Tellegen, Dahlstrom, & Kaemmer, 2001), and CPI (Gough & Bradley, 1996). Typically, the pattern of each individual's standard scores is displayed along a linear continuum,

progressing from the test's first scale to its last. Although reasonably informative, two features of the linear profile make it less than optimal as a "picture" of an individual's personality tendencies. First, as noted in Gurtman and Balakrishnan (1998), the order of the scales comprising the test is usually arbitrary, sometimes simply a function of the order in which the scales were developed or published. Thus, there is no substantively meaningful "law of neighboring" that applies. Second, although such tests may broadly cover a particular domain (e.g., for the MMPI-2, personality psychopathology), they may also have gaps, redundancies, and imbalances in coverage. (Arguably, this is one reason for the recent "restructuring" of the MMPI-2 as the new MMPI-2 RC scales; Tellegen, Ben-Porath, McNulty, Arbisi, Graham, & Kaemmer, 2003).

In contrast, Figure 18.4 shows an example of a circular profile, as would typically be available from a circumplex measure such as Wiggins's Interpersonal Adjective Scales (IAS; Wiggins, 1995), the Inventory of Interpersonal Problems-Circumplex (IIP-C; Alden, Wiggins, & Pincus, 1990; Horowitz, Alden, Wiggins, & Pincus, 2000),

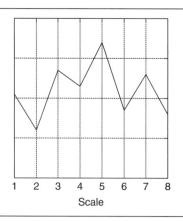

FIGURE 18.3   A Generic Example of a Traditional Linear Profile
The *y*-axis presents the scores and the *x*-axis lists the scales

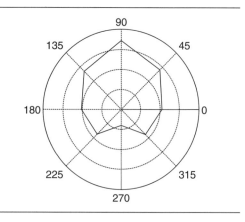

FIGURE 18.4   An Example of a Circular Profile
Source: Scores are based on Table 1 of "Circular Reasoning about Interpersonal Behavior: Evidence Concerning Some Untested Assumptions Underlying Diagnostic Classification," by J. Wiggins, N. Phillips, and P. Trapnell, 1989, *Journal of Personality and Social Psychology, 56*(2), p. 298.

or the Circumplex Scales of Interpersonal Values (CSIV; Locke, 2000). (For a more comprehensive list and discussion, see Locke, 2006, and Chapter 19 in this volume.) In this case, the standard scores of the eight octants of the circumplex are arranged in a radial fashion, conforming to the circular configuration of the particular measure. Each score can be thought of as a vector, with a certain direction and length. The result is, in effect, a polar coordinate graph of the individual's tendencies. As noted in Gurtman and Balakrishnan (1998), psychometrically, circular profiles developed from valid measures have two particular advantages: (1) they sample uniformly and systematically from a particular theoretically-defined domain (e.g., the domain of interpersonal traits, defined by the circumplex), and (2) the order of the scales follows the "law of neighboring" that is inherent to circumplex models—closer scales are more similar, theoretically and empirically, than are scales further apart.

Given these qualities, circular profiles are often structured—not surprisingly—in the general sinusoidal pattern that is the circle. This pattern is especially obvious for prototypic profiles (e.g., Wright, Pincus, Conroy, & Hilsenroth, 2009) and those that are group composites. Wiggins et al. (1989, p. 300) refered to this pattern as the "interpersonal spaceship" and note that: "the highest elevation occurs on the defining octant . . . followed by adjacent octants . . . and diminishing to the highly truncated opposite octant" (p. 300). This structuring, and the natural ordering of the circular measure, greatly facilitate interpretation. As illustrated in Figure 18.4, the profile is literally "shifted" in the direction of the profile's central tendency, thus conveying the predominant theme in the personality data (Gurtman, 2009).

Many examples of circular profiles are available in the interpersonal literature, including in Wiggins et al.'s (1989) circular reasoning article. From an historical perspective, perhaps the most interesting examples are the hand-drawn (and apparently hand-shaded) profiles appearing in the original series of articles by the Kaiser Foundation Research Group (see, in particular, LaForge et al., 1954, pp. 137, 139; LaForge & Suczek, 1955, pp. 103, 109; and Leary & Coffey, 1955, pp. 113, 118, 122, 123).

The Vector Method

As was apparent to the Kaiser Group (e.g., LaForge et al., 1954), circular profiles offer an opportunity for basic structural analyses that can reduce the profile to its essential features. Given that scores on a circular measure are vectors with both a magnitude and direction (see Figure 18.4), it would therefore make sense to summarize a profile by calculating a resultant vector—which would, in effect, indicate the overall trend in the profile, and reduce it to a single, summary point in the two-dimensional, interpersonal space. Wiggins et al. (1989) described this as "one of the exciting possibilities of the Interpersonal Circle" (p. 297), and linked it to the important task of "diagnostic classification" (see also Leary & Coffey, 1955).

Wiggins et al. (1989) provided a computational example (p. 298, Table 1); their formulas were adapted from those originally developed and presented by LaForge et al. (1954). The method by which the eight vectors (of the profile) were reduced to a single resultant is straightforward, and indeed involves simple vector arithmetic. As a first step, each (standardized) score in the profile is weighted (multiplied) by the sine (to obtain the y-component) or cosine (to obtain the x-component) of that vector's angular direction (θ) in the circle. These components are summed to yield the x, y coordinates of the resultant, usually referred to as *Lov* and *Dom*, respectively. Hence:

$$Lov = .25 * \Sigma z_i * \cos(\theta_i) \qquad (1)$$

$$Dom = .25 * \Sigma z_i * \sin(\theta_i) \qquad (2)$$

where .25 is a scaling factor for an eight-octant circle,[1] z_i is the person's standard score on octant or scale$_i$, and θ_i is the angular location of the scale (0°, 45°, 90°, etc., as per Figure 18.1).

As a final step, these rectangular coordinates are converted to polar coordinates, which thus yields the resultant vector's angular displacement (or *angle*) and its length (or *vector length*). Angle is derived using the arctangent formula (modified for a result in degrees), and vector length is obtained using the Pythagorean theorem:

$$\text{Angle} = \tan^{-1}(Dom/Lov) * 180/\pi \quad (3)$$

$$\text{Vector length} = \text{sqrt}(Dom^2 + Lov^2) \quad (4)$$

Table 18.2 provides a worked-out example, using the same sample data used previously to produce Figure 18.4.

The vector method, of course, produces a simplification of the profile (LaForge et al., 1954), obscuring its internal variations (or "fluctuations," LaForge et al., 1954), but at the same time highlighting its important features. These are given by the vector's direction (angle) and extremity (vector length) in interpersonal space. Of the two,

angle is especially important. Mathematically, angle indicates the "center of gravity" or "mean direction" of the profile vectors (e.g., Upton & Fingleton, 1989), and, as such, suggests the predominant interpersonal *theme* of the person's profile of scores (Gurtman, 1994; Gurtman & Pincus, 2003). For example, an angle of 45 degrees suggests a friendly form of dominance (equal parts of +*Dom* and +*Lov*); in comparison, an angle of 60 degrees would indicate relatively more dominance, and an angle of 30 degrees would suggest more friendliness in that mixture. Beyond this, different angles would suggest different interpersonal styles or typologies, which could be embellished either conceptually or empirically to yield general descriptions (not unlike MMPI-2 "code types"). As an example, Wiggins (1995) provided prototypic descriptions of individuals who fall at different segments of the IAS circle. Ultimately, angle may serve the broad purpose of diagnostic classification (Wiggins et al., 1989).

The proper interpretation of vector length is a bit more complex. Wiggins et al.

TABLE 18.2 Solving for Angle and Vector Length

Interpersonal Category	Angle (θ)	Z-score	cos(θ)	sin(θ)	Z*cos(θ)	Z*sin(θ)
Friendly	0	.10	1.00	.00	.10	.00
Friendly-Dominant	45	.82	.71	.71	.58	.58
Dominant	90	1.45	.00	1.00	.00	1.45
Hostile-Dominant	135	.70	−.71	.71	−.49	.49
Hostile	180	.05	−1.00	.00	−.05	.00
Hostile-Submissive	225	−.25	−.71	−.71	.18	.18
Submissive	270	−1.20	.00	−1.00	.00	1.20
Friendly-Submissive	315	−.23	.71	−.71	−.16	.16
				.25* Σ =	.04	1.02
					Lov	Dom
Angle = tan⁻¹ (Dom/Lov)*180/π	87.90					
Vector Length = sqrt (Dom² + Lov²)	1.02					

Notes:
Standard Scores (Z) are from Table 1, Wiggins et al. (1989), p. 298.
Calculations are precise beyond the (2-digit) intermediate values displayed in the table.
A live (Excel) version of this worksheet can be obtained from the author.

Adapted from "Circular Reasoning about Interpersonal Behavior: Evidence Concerning Some Untested Assumptions Underlying Diagnostic Classification," by J. Wiggins, N. Phillips, and P. Trapnell, February 1989, *Journal of Personality and Social Psychology*, 56(2), 296–305. Table 1, p. 298. Published by the American Psychological Association. Adapted with permission.

(1989) demonstrated that vector length is highly correlated with profile variability. Beyond that, some have also conceived of vector length as a measure of interpersonal deviance or maladjustment, suggesting that high vector length may be associated, clinically, with interpersonal behaviors that are rigid, intense, or extreme (see, e.g., Leary, 1957). Gurtman and Balakrishnan (1998) argued for a distinction between the *descriptive* and *clinical significance* of profile statistics like vector length. In a descriptive sense, vector length is indeed related to the variability among the profile scores—but it is also a function of the fit of the profile to the prototypic pattern of the circle (a sinusoidal curve) (see Gurtman & Balakrishnan, 1998, p. 351). Hence, I regard vector length as more a measure of the profile's *structured* variability or patterning, and consequently an indication of the distinctiveness of the profile. Clinically, evidence that vector length is associated with, or is an index for psychopathology, is limited, and perhaps difficult to interpret (e.g., McCarthy, Gibbons, & Barber, 2008; O'Connor & Dyce, 1997, 2001). Wiggins et al. (1989) found that vector length was associated with psychological distress, but only when the distress measures themselves shared the same variance as the IAS scale in which subjects were classified. Vector length, by itself, was uncorrelated with distress (see also O'Connor & Dyce, 2001, for a similar pattern). Thus, although the question remains open, the clinical significance of vector length—and perhaps more importantly its direct relation to the main concepts of interpersonal adjustment (Kiesler, 1996)—seems tenuous.

FROM INDIVIDUAL TO GROUP

The circular reasoning that applies to the individual case can easily and meaningfully be extended to situations where groups of individuals are the focus of study. Many examples of this are available in the interpersonal literature, and the key methodologies have recently been presented by Wright et al. (2009). (See also Gurtman and Pincus, 2003.)

Profile Averaging

An easy and intuitive method of combining individual data is simply to average the circular profiles of group members. Referred to by Gurtman and Pincus (2003) as *profile averaging* (p. 419), this produces a composite or mean profile that shows the general pattern for the group while "smoothing over" the individual differences. As illustrated in Wiggins et al. (1989, p. 300), mean profiles often conform closely to the ideal for a circle (i.e., a cosine curve; Gurtman & Pincus, 2003). Thus, they can be meaningfully reduced to their main structural features, including angle and vector length. Recently, Pincus and colleagues (e.g., Ansell, & Pincus, 2004) showed how my *structural summary method* (e.g., Gurtman, 1994) could be meaningfully applied to the analysis of group profiles.

Although profile averaging is a suitable technique in many research situations, its main disadvantage is that it obscures individual differences (Gurtman & Pincus, 2003). Hence, it is uncertain how individual profiles contribute to, and relate to, the group average.

The Circular Distribution

As indicated earlier, the vector method allows an individual's interpersonal tendencies to be represented as a single point in the two-dimensional space. When many individuals are studied and their test results plotted in that common space, their point locations show how group members are concentrated in different areas of the circle. Early examples of this approach appear in LaForge et al. (1954, pp. 141, 142, 143).

Although such scatterplots are useful, a simpler and perhaps more effective method of communicating group trends is the *circular distribution* or *circular plot* (Gurtman & Pincus, 2003). In this case, individual points are projected onto the circumference of the circle (that is, to unit length). Information on each person's angular position is thus retained, while vector length is disregarded.

Circular distributions are particularly useful for showing where individuals are centered and how they are dispersed on the circular continuum. Circular distributions are also amenable to both descriptive and inferential analyses through the methods of circular statistics (e.g., Upton & Singleton, 1989; Wright et al., 2009).

As an example, consider a hypothetical group of 100 individuals who report experiencing problems of being overcontrolling and domineering (e.g., Horowitz et al., 2000). Figure 18.5 shows the circular distribution of their projections on an interpersonal problems circle. Clearly, these individuals are concentrated near the Dominance octant of the circle. Using circular statistics (see, e.g., Gurtman & Pincus, 2003; Upton & Fingelton, 1989), it is possible to augment this visual impression by calculating the group's circular mean and variability. The circular mean is the center point of the distribution, determined by solving for the angle, θ_M, that minimizes the angular deviations, and hence maximizes the quantity:

$$\Sigma \cos(\theta_M - \theta_i) \qquad (5)$$

where θ_M is the circular mean and θ_i is angular projection of individual$_i$ on the

circle. The circular variance, as described in Gurtman and Pincus (2003), is the average of this sum (Equation 5), converted to degrees through the inverse cosine formula (see Wright et al., 2009). Of course, the higher this value, the more dispersed are groups members around the center point of the distribution. For the data presented in Figure 18.5, the circular mean is 111 degrees, and the circular variance is 21 degrees.

Obviously, it is also possible to extend this approach to include plots of multiple groups (distributions) on the circle. In this case, group comparisons are possible, as well as inferential statistics calculated on the basis of (circular) confidence intervals. The interested reader is directed to Wright et al. (2009) for relevant examples based on published research.

CONCLUSIONS

Now 20 years later, Wiggins et al's (1989) article on circular reasoning continues to guide and inspire the work of the current generation of interpersonal researchers and theoreticians. Jerry's vision of an interpersonal personality psychology—informed by history, directed by theory, and empirically and methodologically rigorous—is clearly evident in that key article. While, by design, this chapter gave particular focus to the circular reasoning article, his many books, articles, and chapters provide numerous examples of the depth and consistency of that vision. And they also hint at his ever-present wit and whimsy—the pun of "circular reasoning," although prominently placed in the title, is never once repeated in the article!

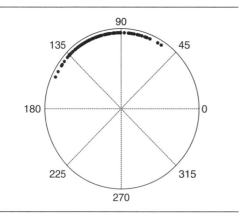

FIGURE 18.5 A Circular Distribution of 100 Cases Each projection represents an individual case.

References

Alden, L. E., Wiggins, J. S., & Pincus, A. L. (1990). Construction of circumplex scales for the Inventory of Interpersonal Problems. *Journal of Personality Assessment, 55,* 521–536.

Ansell, E., & Pincus, A. (2004). Interpersonal perceptions of the Five-Factor Model of personality: An examination using the structural summary method for circumplex data. *Multivariate Behavioral Research*, *39*(2), 167–201.

Bakan, D. (1966). *The duality of human existence: Isolation and communication in Western man.* Boston: Beacon Press.

Benjamin, L. (1996). A clinician-friendly version of the Interpersonal Circumplex: Structural Analysis of Social Behavior (SASB). *Journal of Personality Assessment*, *66*(2), 248–266.

Browne, M. W. (1992). Circumplex models for correlation matrices. *Psychometrika*, *57*, 469–497.

Butcher, J. N., Graham, J. R., Ben-Porath, Y. S., Tellegen, A., Dahlstrom, W. G., & Kaemmer, B. (2001). *MMPI–2 (Minnesota Multiphasic Personality Inventory—2): Manual for the administration, scoring, and interpretation* (Rev. ed.). Minneapolis: University of Minnesota Press.

Costa, P. T., Jr., & McCrae, R. R. (1992). *NEO PI-R professional manual: Revised NEO Personality Inventory (NEO PI-R) and NEO Five-Factor Inventory (NEO-FFI).* Odessa, FL: Psychological Assessment Resources.

De Raad, B. (1995). The psycholexical approach to the structure of interpersonal traits. *European Journal of Personality*, *9*(2), 89–102.

Fabrigar, L. R., Visser, P. S., & Browne, M. W. (1997). Conceptual and methodological issues in testing the circumplex structure of data in personality and social psychology. *Personality and Social Psychology Review*, *1*, 184–203.

Foa, U. G., & Foa, E. B. (1974). *Societal structures of the mind.* Springfield, IL: Charles C. Thomas.

Freedman, M., Ossorio, A., & Coffey, H. (1951). The interpersonal dimension of personality. *Journal of Personality*, *20*, 143–161.

Freedman, Mervin B. (1985). Interpersonal circumplex models (1948–1983). *Journal of Personality Assessment*, *49*(6), 622–625.

Gough, H. G., & Bradley, P. (1996). *California Psychological Inventory manual* (3rd ed.). Palo Alto, CA: Consulting Psychologists Press.

Gurtman, M. B. (1994). The circumplex as a tool for studying normal and abnormal personality: A methodological primer. In S. Strack & M. Lorr (Eds.), *Differentiating normal and abnormal personality* (pp. 243–263). New York: Springer.

Gurtman, M. B. (1997). Studying personality traits: The circular way. In R. Plutchik & H. R. Conte (Eds.), *Circumplex models of personality and emotions* (pp. 81–102). Washington, DC: American Psychological Association.

Gurtman, M. B. (2009). Exploring personality with the interpersonal circumplex. *Social and Personality Psychology Compass*, *3/4*, 601–619.

Gurtman, M. B., & Balakrishnan, J. D. (1998). Circular measurement redux: The analysis and interpretation of interpersonal circle profiles. *Clinical Psychology: Science and Practice*, *5*, 344–360.

Gurtman, M. B., & Pincus, A. L. (2000). Interpersonal Adjective Scales: Confirmation of circumplex structure from multiple perspectives. *Personality and Social Psychology Bulletin*, *26*, 374–384.

Gurtman, M. B., & Pincus, A. L. (2003). The circumplex model: Methods and research applications. In J. Schinka & W. Velicer (Eds.), *Handbook of psychology: Research methods in psychology* (Vol. 2, pp. 407–428). Hoboken, NJ: John Wiley & Sons.

Guttman, L. (1954). A new approach to factor analysis: The radex. In P. F. Lazarsfeld (Ed.), *Mathematical thinking in the social sciences* (pp. 258–348). Glencoe, IL: Free Press.

Hofstee, W., de Raad, B., & Goldberg, L. (1992, July). Integration of the Big Five and circumplex approaches to trait structure. *Journal of Personality and Social Psychology*, *63*(1), 146–163.

Horowitz, L. M. (2004). *Interpersonal foundations of psychopathology.* Washington, DC: American Psychological Association.

Horowitz, L. M., Alden, L. E., Wiggins, J. S., & Pincus, A. L. (2000). *Inventory of Interpersonal Problems: Manual.* San Antonio, TX: Psychological Corporation.

Kiesler, D. (1983, July). The 1982 Interpersonal Circle: A taxonomy for complementarity in human transactions. *Psychological Review*, *90*(3), 185–214.

Kiesler, D. J. (1996). *Contemporary interpersonal theory and research.* New York: John Wiley & Sons.

Kiesler, D., Schmidt, J., & Wagner, C. (1997). A circumplex inventory of impact messages: An operational bridge between emotion and interpersonal behavior. *Circumplex models of personality and emotions* (pp. 221–244). Washington, DC: American Psychological Association.

LaForge, R. (2004). The early development of the Interpersonal System of Personality (ISP). *Multivariate Behavioral Research*, *39*(2), 359–378.

LaForge, R., & Suczek, R. F. (1955). The interpersonal dimensions of personality: III. An interpersonal check list. *Journal of Personality*, *24*, 94–112.

Laforge, R., Leary, T., Naboisek, H., Coffey, H., & Freedman, M. (1954). The interpersonal dimension of personality: II. An objective study of repression. *Journal of Personality, 23,* 129–153.

Leary, T. (1957). *Interpersonal diagnosis of personality.* New York: Ronald Press.

Leary, T., & Coffey, H. (1955). Interpersonal diagnosis: Some problems of methodology and validation. *The Journal of Abnormal and Social Psychology, 50*(1), 110–124.

Locke, K. (2000, October). Circumplex scales of interpersonal values: Reliability, validity, and applicability to interpersonal problems and personality disorders. *Journal of Personality Assessment, 75*(2), 249–267.

Locke, K. D. (2006). Interpersonal Circumplex Measures. In S. Strack (Ed.), *Differentiating normal and abnormal personality* (2nd ed., pp. 383–400). New York: Springer.

Lorr, M., & McNair, D. (1963, July). An interpersonal behavior circle. *The Journal of Abnormal and Social Psychology, 67*(1), 68–75.

McCarthy, K., Gibbons, M., & Barber, J. (2008). The relation of rigidity across relationships with symptoms and functioning: An investigation with the revised Central Relationship Questionnaire. *Journal of Counseling Psychology, 55*(3), 346–358.

McCrae, R., & Costa, P. (1989, April). The structure of interpersonal traits: Wiggins's circumplex and the five-factor model. *Journal of Personality and Social Psychology, 56*(4), 586–595.

O'Connor, B., & Dyce, J. (1997, February). Interpersonal rigidity, hostility, and complementarity in musical bands. *Journal of Personality and Social Psychology, 72*(2), 362–372.

O'Connor, B., & Dyce, J. (2001, December). Rigid and extreme: A geometric representation of personality disorders in five-factor model space. *Journal of Personality and Social Psychology, 81*(6), 1119–1130.

Plutchik, R. (1980). A general psychoevolutionary theory of emotion. In R. Plutchik & H. Kellerman (Eds.), *Emotion: Theory, research, and experience: Vol. 1. Theories of emotion* (pp. 3–33). New York: Academic Press.

Plutchik, R., & Conte, H. (1997). *Circumplex models of personality and emotions.* Washington, DC: American Psychological Association.

Russell, J. A. (1980). A circumplex model of affect. *Journal of Personality and Social Psychology, 39,* 1161–1178.

Schwartz, S. H. (1992). Universals in the content and structure of values: Theoretical advances and empirical tests in 20 countries. In M. P. Zanna (Ed.), *Advances in experimental social psychology* (Vol. 25, pp. 1–65). San Diego, CA, and London: Academic Press.

Tellegen, A., Ben-Porath, Y. S., McNulty, J. L., Arbisi, P. A., Graham, J. R., & Kaemmer, B. (2003). *The MMPI–2 restructured clinical (RC) scales: Development, validation, and interpretation.* Minneapolis: University of Minnesota Press.

Tracey, T. J. G. (2000). Analysis of circumplex models. In H. E. A. Tinsley & S. D. Brown (Eds.), *Handbook of applied multivariate statistics and mathematical modeling* (pp. 641–664). San Diego: Academic Press.

Tracey, T., & Rounds, J. (1993, March). Evaluating Holland's and Gati's vocational-interest models: A structural meta-analysis. *Psychological Bulletin, 113*(2), 229–246.

Tracey, T., & Rounds, J. (1997). Circular structure of vocational interests. In R. Plutchik & H. R. Conte (Eds.), *Circumplex models of personality and emotions* (pp. 183–201). Washington, DC: American Psychological Association.

Trobst, K. (1999). Social support as an interpersonal construct. *European Journal of Psychological Assessment, 15*(3), 246–255.

Upton, G. J. G., & Fingleton, B. (1989). *Spatial data analysis by example: Vol. 2. Categorical and directional data.* New York: John Wiley & Sons.

Wiggins, J. (1979). A psychological taxonomy of trait-descriptive terms: The interpersonal domain. *Journal of Personality and Social Psychology, 37*(3), 395–412.

Wiggins, J. (1991). Agency and communion as conceptual coordinates for the understanding and measurement of interpersonal behavior. In W. M. Grove & D. Cicchetti (Eds.), *Thinking clearly about psychology: Vol. 2. Personality and psychopathology* (pp. 89–113). Minneapolis, MN: University of Minnesota Press.

Wiggins, J. (1995). *Interpersonal adjective scales professional manual.* Odessa, FL: Psychological Assessment Resources.

Wiggins, J. (1996). An informal history of the interpersonal circumplex tradition. *Journal of Personality Assessment, 66*(2), 217–233.

Wiggins, J., & Trapnell, P. (1996). A dyadic-interactional perspective on the five-factor model. In J. S. Wiggins (Ed.), *The five-factor model of personality: Theoretical perspectives* (pp. 88–162). New York: Guilford Press.

Wiggins, J., & Trobst, K. (1997). When is a circumplex an "interpersonal circumplex"? The case of supportive actions. In R. Plutchik & H. R. Conte (Eds.), *Circumplex models of personality and emotions* (pp. 57–80). Washington, DC: American Psychological Association.

Wiggins, J., Phillips, N., & Trapnell, P. (1989). Circular reasoning about interpersonal behavior: Evidence concerning some untested assumptions underlying diagnostic classification. *Journal of Personality and Social Psychology, 56*(2), 296–305.

Wiggins, J., Steiger, J., & Gaelick, L. (1981, July). Evaluating circumplexity in personality data. *Multivariate Behavioral Research, 16*(3), 263–289.

Wright, A. G. C., Pincus, A. L., Conroy, D. E. & Hilsenroth, M. J. (2009). Integrating methods to optimize circumplex description and comparison of groups. *Journal of Personality Assessment, 91*(4), 311–322

Yik, M., Russell, J., & Barrett, L. (1999, September). Structure of self-reported current affect: Integration and beyond. *Journal of Personality and Social Psychology, 77*(3), 600–619.

NOTES

1. When calculating *Dom* and *Lov*, multiplying by .25 returns each sum to the original scale of the octant scores.

19 CIRCUMPLEX MEASURES OF INTERPERSONAL CONSTRUCTS

Kenneth D. Locke

The interpersonal circle or interpersonal circumplex (IPC) has in recent decades become the most popular model for conceptualizing, organizing, and assessing interpersonal dispositions (Wiggins, 2003). The IPC is defined graphically by two orthogonal axes: a vertical axis (of status, dominance, power, control, or, most broadly, *agency*) and a horizontal axis (of solidarity, friendliness, warmth, love, or, most broadly, *communion*). Thus, each point within the IPC can be specified as a weighted mixture of agency and communion. Simple interpersonal characteristics (such as "introverted" or "forceful") may be located graphically as a distinct combination of the two broad underlying factors; in other words, there is a particular location within the IPC space for each interpersonal disposition.

IPC inventories are designed to measure interpersonal dispositions from every segment of the IPC. IPC inventories comprise a family of related instruments: All members of the family are based on the same theoretical model, but each member focuses on a different type of construct (e.g., traits, motives, problems). In this chapter, I first summarize the IPC model that unites the diverse IPC inventories. Second, I describe the IPC inventories that are currently in use and provide examples of how each one is being used to advance contemporary interpersonal research. Third, I describe some simple methods for scoring, graphing, and interpreting IPC inventories, and for using IPC inventories to identify maladaptive interpersonal patterns.

THE INTERPERSONAL CIRCUMPLEX MODEL

Multiple literatures support the centrality of agency and communion in human behavior. Evolutionary psychology highlights how, throughout our evolutionary history, natural selection has favored those who could master the challenges of negotiating and coordinating both communion (e.g., attachments and coalitions) and agency (e.g., hierarchical power) (Bugental, 2000). Evidence that different hormones and neurotransmitters are associated with regulating communion (e.g., oxytocin; Bartz & Hollander, 2006) and agency (e.g., testosterone; Archer, 2006) supports the view that they are both essential yet distinct tasks. From a psychometric perspective, factor analyses show that the dimensions of agency and communion account for a large proportion of the variance in ratings of interpersonal behaviors and traits (Foa, 1961; Wiggins, 1979). Additional psychometric support comes from studies showing that extraversion and agreeableness (the interpersonal factors of the solidly supported five-factor model of personality) are rotational variants of agency and communion (McCrae & Costa, 1989).

The IPC can be divided into broad segments (such as fourths) or narrow segments (such as sixteenths), but most IPC inventories partition the circle into eight octants as shown in Figure 19.1. As one moves around the circle, each octant reflects a different blend of the two axial dimensions. By convention, each octant has a generic two-letter code (shown in parentheses in Figure 19.1).

To be considered an IPC measure, an inventory's octant scales should have the following properties: (a) scales that are closer to one another on the circle should have higher correlations than scales that are farther apart; (b) the scales' communalities on the two underlying dimensions of agency and communion should all be high

and approximately equal; and (c) plotting the octant scales on the two underlying axes should show them to be distributed at approximately equal 45-degree intervals. Unless otherwise noted, all of the inventories reviewed in this chapter meet these criteria (as well as the usual psychometric criteria for scale reliability and convergent validity with related measures).

For the sake of simplicity, some researchers (e.g., Moskowitz, 2009) assess only the dimensions of agency and communion rather than the 8 or 16 segments assessed by the IPC inventories reviewed below. Indeed, theoretically the IPC can be defined by any two orthogonal bipolar axes that align largely within the IPC plane. Thus, to the extent that measures of the extraversion and agreeableness dimensions of the five-factor model can be mapped onto the IPC (McCrae & Costa, 1989), such measures also can be used to locate interpersonal dispositions within the IPC space.

As described in the following section, there now exist IPC measures for many different constructs, such as traits, problems,

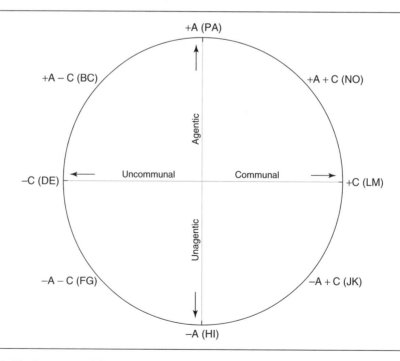

FIGURE 19.1   The Interpersonal Circumplex (IPC)

and self-efficacy. For each inventory reviewed below, I will first provide a brief description of the inventory (e.g., purpose, length, items) and then summarize at least one example of recent research which successfully employed that inventory.

CIRCUMPLEX MEASURES OF INTERPERSONAL CONSTRUCTS

Although the IPC inventories reviewed below typically are used as self-report measures of global dispositions, they can be—and most have been—used in other ways. For example, many of the self-report measures have (with minor changes to the instructions or items) been used to obtain ratings by peers or observers. Likewise, many of the inventories have been used to assess not only general dispositions, but also dispositions in specific situations (e.g., at work), in specific relationships (e.g., with your therapist), or under specific conditions (e.g., when under stress). Finally, short-forms are available for most of the inventories.

The first IPC measure was the Interpersonal Check List (ICL; LaForge & Suczek, 1955). The 128-item ICL assesses 16 segments of the IPC; eight adjectives or verb-phrases assess each segment. Each item is weighted according to one of four levels of extremity. Although the ICL has been used in numerous studies (Clark & Taulbee, 1981), its scales provide uneven coverage of the IPC space. Since the introduction of the ICL, interpersonal scales have been constructed for a variety of domains, as described below.

Assessing Interpersonal Traits

The psychometric and circumplex properties of the Interpersonal Adjective Scales (IAS; Wiggins, 1995; Wiggins, Trapnell, & Phillips, 1988) are superior to that of the ICL, and so it is now the preferred measure of interpersonal traits. IAS respondents rate each of 64 interpersonal adjectives with respect to how accurately it describes the target (usually the self) on a scale from 1 (very inaccurate) to 8 (very accurate). The adjectives are combined into eight 8-item octant scales. Table 19.1 shows an illustrative adjective from each octant. Some respondents may be unfamiliar with certain adjectives (e.g., "uncrafty"), so a glossary can be provided (Adams & Tracey, 2004).

IPC measures have often been used to study "interpersonal complementarity" (Sadler, Ethier, & Woody, Chapter 8 in this volume). A complementary response to another's behavior is a response that is similar in communion but differs in agency. Some people are less likely than others to make complementary responses, perhaps because they rigidly rely on a narrow range of interpersonal behaviors. One potential indicator of rigidity is the distance the vector sum of an individual's eight octant scores extends from the origin of the IPC. Vector length indexes trait strength, or rigidity, in that scores are especially high in one segment of the IPC and especially low in the opposite segment. Thus, the longer the vector, the more that individual expresses behaviors exclusively and intensively from that particular segment of the IPC. To test this hypothesis, Tracey (2005, Study 2) had observers watch two participants working together (to concoct a story about an ambiguous picture) and locate the interpersonal meaning of each partner's behavior on the IPC. The results confirmed that participants with longer IAS vectors were less likely to behave in ways that were complementary to their partner's behavior.

The IAS also can help clarify the interpersonal meaning of behaviors or dispositions whose meaning may not be obvious. For example, in order to explore the interpersonal meaning of sexual promiscuity, Markey and Markey (2007) had young men and women complete the IAS and also indicate how many people they had engaged with in various sexual activities. Warm, cold, and dominant individuals reported having more partners for each type of sexual activity than did submissive individuals. Cold and warm individuals reported similar numbers of partners, but presumably cold individuals were driven more by self-focused motives (such as pleasure or narcissistic self-enhancement) and warm individuals were driven more by other-focused motives (such as closeness and intimacy).

Assessing Interpersonal Problems

The eight 8-item scales of the Inventory of Interpersonal Problems (IIP; Horowitz, Alden, Wiggins, & Pincus, 2000) assess problematic dispositions associated with each octant of the IPC. Table 19.1 shows illustrative items. Respondents indicate how distressed they have been by each problem on 0 (not at all) to 4 (extremely) scales. The items are divided into two sections: "things you find hard to do with

other people" and "things that you do too much."

A number of studies of psychotherapy process and outcome have employed the IIP (Ruiz et al., 2004). Another common use of the IIP has been to identity the interpersonal problems associated with various forms of psychopathology. Whereas some disorders (including most Axis II personality disorders) show distinct and consistent IIP profiles, others (including most Axis I disorders) do not. For example, Salzer et al. (2008) conducted a cluster analysis on the IIP scores of individuals with generalized anxiety disorder (i.e., chronic, excessive, subjectively uncontrollable worrying about multiple everyday concerns). Four clusters—cold, submissive, intrusive, and exploitable—were identified, suggesting that generalized anxiety may be associated with multiple distinct patterns of interpersonal problems.

TABLE 19.1   Examples of Items from Each Octant of the IAS, IIP, CSIV, and CSIE

Octant Scale	Example IAS Items (Rate how accurately each describes you)	Example IIP Items (Rate how distressing each problem has been)	Example CSIV Items "When I am with him/her/them, it is important that…"	Example CSIE Items "Rate how confident you are that you can…"
LM (communal)	Sympathetic	I try to please other people too much	…I feel connected to them	…be helpful
NO (agentic and communal)	Perky	I tell personal things to other people too much	…they respect what I have to say	…express myself openly
PA (agentic)	Forceful	I try to control other people too much	…they acknowledge when I am right	…be assertive
BC (agentic and uncommunal)	Boastful	I fight with other people too much	…I keep the upper hand	…be aggressive if I need to
DE (uncommunal)	Ruthless	It is hard for me to show affection to people	…they keep their distance from me	…get them to leave me alone
FG (unagentic and uncommunal)	Unsociable	I am too afraid of other people	…I not say something stupid	…hide my thoughts and feelings
HI (unagentic)	Timid	It is hard for me to be assertive with another person	…I not make them angry	…be a follower
JK (unagentic and uncommunal)	Unargumentative	I am too gullible	…they like me	…get along with them

The IIP can help guide therapeutic interventions for interpersonal problems. For example, I demonstrated that the interpersonal problems assessed by the IIP are linked to the types of beliefs or interpersonal expectations that are readily targeted by therapeutic interventions (Locke, 2005). To assess everyday interpersonal expectations over a one-week period, every time participants imagined how another person might react to them, they wrote down how they expected the other person to react and how that reaction would make them feel. I found clear associations between these interpersonal expectations and the interpersonal problems assessed by the IIP. For example, expecting others to be uninviting or unsupportive predicted problems with being too uncommunal; expecting others to be critical (and expecting oneself in response to feel angry) predicted problems with being too agentic; and expecting others to be dismissive (and expecting oneself in response to feel ashamed) predicted problems with being too communal. Reducing the frequency or intensity of these negative interpersonal expectations may help people overcome their chronic interpersonal problems.

Assessing Interpersonal Values and Motives

Interpersonal values or motives also shape individuals' reactions to interpersonal experiences. For example, being told what to do may be a relief to someone who values submission, but a humiliation to someone who values dominance. Consequently, many psychotherapies try to change feelings and behavior by changing values; for example, cognitive and rational-emotive therapists may help clients question the extreme value they place on certain interpersonal experiences, such as *needing* approval. The eight 8-item scales of the Circumplex Scales of Interpersonal Values (CSIV; Locke, 2000) assess the worth individuals place on interpersonal experiences associated with each octant of the IPC. For each item, respondents indicate how important that type of

interpersonal experience is for them on 0 (not important) to 4 (extremely important) scales. Table 19.1 shows illustrative items.

Interpersonal values can magnify or dampen emotional reactions to interpersonal events. One common interpersonal event is comparing the self with another person (i.e., *social comparison*). I tested if interpersonal values moderate reactions to social comparisons (Locke, 2003). To assess social comparisons, participants kept a diary of evaluations they made during their everyday lives. For each comparison, they noted (a) whether the other person was better-off, worse-off, similar, or different; and (b) how the comparison made them feel. People with stronger communal values (as assessed by the CSIV) reported stronger positive reactions to noticing that someone was similar, but they did not report stronger—and on some measures reported weaker—reactions to noticing that someone was better-off or worse-off. Thus, interpersonal values moderated the emotional impact of social comparisons.

Locke and Christensen (2007) found that stronger communal values (as assessed by the CSIV) also predict describing oneself and others in similar terms. (I have since replicated this finding both in the United States and in Korea [Locke, 2009].) Self-other similarity also correlated negatively with the Machiavellianism scale (MACH; Christie & Geis, 1970), which measures a detached and manipulative attitude towards others, and positively with the Relational-Interdependent Self-Construal scale (RISC; Cross, Bacon, & Morris, 2000), which measures tendencies to define oneself in terms of one's close relationships. Because MACH correlates negatively and RISC correlates positively with communal traits and values, inventing separate explanations for the effects of each specific measure was unnecessary; instead, the dimension of communion could explain all three effects. This singular explanation is (a) more parsimonious than having different models for different measures and (b) more generative because it suggests that *any* interpersonal quality associated with communal motives should predict describing the self and others in similar terms. The broader message is that many measures exist—such as MACH and RISC—that are designed to assess specific interpersonal dispositions that may not be fully captured by the two-dimensional IPC. Yet, these measures typically correlate with IPC dimensions (Wiggins & Broughton, 1991), and locating these measures within the IPC may help us interpret them more effectively. In this way, by using the IPC as an integrative model, we can avoid repeatedly "reinventing the [interpersonal] wheel."

Assessing Interpersonal Self-Efficacy

Self-efficacy is a person's confidence that he or she can successfully perform a specific type of action (Bandura, 1997). The eight 4-item scales of the Circumplex Scales of Interpersonal Efficacy (CSIE; Locke & Sadler, 2007) assess a person's confidence that he or she can successfully perform behaviors associated with each octant of the IPC. For each item, respondents indicate on a 0 (not at all confident) to 10 (absolutely confident) scale how sure they are that they could act that way with other people. Table 19.1 lists illustrative items.

Locke and Sadler (2007) had pairs of strangers complete the CSIE and 30 minutes later work together to solve a murder mystery. Greater self-efficacy for enacting dominant than yielding behavior predicted the expression of more dominant behavior during the interaction (as indicated by amount of time spent talking and observers' ratings of dominance). Moreover, pairs who were more similar in self-efficacy for communal actions were more satisfied with their interaction, suggesting that people who are more confident they can be tough than nice, and people who are more confident they can be nice than tough, may be unlikely to negotiate satisfying working relationships. Collectively, studies using the CSIE and CSIV (plus the study linking the IIP to interpersonal expectations) show

the utility of joining the person variables of social-cognitive theory (such as subjective values and self-efficacy) with the IPC model of interpersonal behavior.

Observer Ratings of Interpersonal Behavior

The Chart of Interpersonal Reactions in Closed Living Environments (CIRCLE; Blackburn & Renwick, 1996) is a 49-item observer rating scale designed to assess the interpersonal behavior of psychiatric inpatients. Examples of items are "dominates conversations" (PA) and "sits alone or keeps to himself" (FG). The frequency of each behavior is rated on a 4-point scale. The CIRCLE may be particularly useful for inpatient and forensic populations, and when self-reports are likely to be invalid. One area of application has been to predict future aggressive behavior in high-risk populations. For example, Doyle and Dolan (2006) had nurses complete the CIRCLE on forensic inpatients. Staff (who had not completed the CIRCLE) then monitored patients' aggressive behavior during the next 12 weeks. Higher ratings on the dominant, coercive, and hostile (PA, BC, DE) scales, and lower ratings on the compliant (JK) scale, predicted future aggression.

The Check List of Interpersonal Transactions (CLOIT; Kiesler, Goldston, & Schmidt, 1991) is a 96-item rating measure of interpersonal behaviors from each of 16 segments of the IPC. Examples of items are "act in a relaxed, informal, warm, or nonjudgmental manner" (LM) and "act in a stiff, formal, unfeeling, or evaluative manner" (DE). For each item the rater indicates whether or not the target enacted that behavior. The Check List of Psychotherapy Transactions (CLOPT) is a version specifically made for ratings of clients or counselors. The CLOIT and CLOPT are not measures of enduring dispositions, and so are most appropriate for identifying patterns of behavior within particular situations or interactions, such as within a therapy session. In recent years researchers have rarely used the entire

CLOIT or CLOPT, and instead have been selecting and modifying items from these scales to create their own observational measures. For example, Schmid Mast and Hall (2004) had coders use an aggregate of the CLOIT's dominant and submissive items to rate the dominance of members of male or female dyads engaged in brief interactions. Different coders counted how many times each participant smiled. Perceived dominance was negatively related to smiling among female participants, but positively related to smiling among male participants, suggesting that perceivers may be biased to interpret a woman's smile as deference and a man's smile as confidence.

Assessing Interpersonal Impacts

The eight 7-item octant scales of the Impact Message Inventory-Circumplex (IMI; Kiesler & Schmidt, 2006; Kiesler, Schmidt, & Wagner, 1997) assess the interpersonal dispositions of a target person, not by asking the target person directly, but by assessing the "impact messages" (feelings, thoughts, and action tendencies) that the target typically evokes in the respondent. Thus, dominant (PA) scale items assess the reactions a dominant target is likely to evoke such as "[makes me feel] bossed around," whereas submissive (HI) scale items assess the reactions a submissive target is likely to evoke such as "[makes me feel] in charge." Respondents indicate how well each item describes their reaction to the target on *not at all* (1) to *very much so* (4) scales. Although the octant scales show a circular ordering around the interpersonal axes, they also show unequal spacing and inconsistent vector lengths, and so do not meet circumplex criteria as well as the other measures reviewed here (Hafkenscheid & Rouckhout, 2009; Schmidt, Wagner, & Kiesler, 1999).

The IMI is generally used to assess the impacts of a specific individual, but it can also be used to assess the impacts of an entire social environment. Gallo, Smith, and Cox (2006) asked participants from community settings to describe their typical social experiences at home, with work supervisors, with coworkers, and with people in their neighborhood on a brief version of the IMI. Having less educational attainment predicted experiencing these social environments as more agentic and uncommunal (i.e., more hostile and controlling). The perception of the social context, particularly the perception of communion, partially mediated the negative association between educational attainment and various self-reported health outcomes. In sum, having less socioeconomic status may result in experiencing less supportive social environments, which, in turn, may negatively impact health.

Assessing Social Support Behaviors

The eight 8-item octant scales of the Support Actions Scale-Circumplex (SAS-C; Trobst, 2000) measure dispositions to provide agentic or communal support to those in need of assistance. Examples of items are "give advice" (PA) and "give them a hug" (LM). The SAS-C might be particularly useful for describing the actions of people who are members of support groups, or who are providing support to individuals with illnesses or disabilities. Hamann et al. (2008) asked adult siblings to use the SAS-C to describe their supportive behaviors when their brother or sister had a health problem. Specifically, they compared pairs of siblings in which (a) both tested positive for a mutation in the BRCA1/2 gene (which increases cancer risk), (b) both tested negative, or (c) one tested positive and the other tested negative. Siblings with the same test results reported more friendly support behaviors than siblings with different test results, suggesting that having different test results may cause siblings to experience more tension and distance. Also, members of "both positive" dyads reported more dominant support behaviors than did members of "both negative" dyads, suggesting that positive dyads may get more actively involved in each other's health needs.

Circles for Children

Although most research with the IPC has involved measures developed on and for adults, recently there have been efforts to create IPC inventories specifically for children and adolescents. For example, Sodano and Tracey (2006) created the Child and Adolescent Interpersonal Survey (CAIS), which consists of interpersonal trait descriptions accessible to children such as "I am fun to be around" (NO) and "I call people names" (BC). As another example, Ojanen, Gronroos, and Salmivalli (2005) modified the CSIV to create an "Interpersonal Goals Inventory for Children;" they tried to make the inventory more accessible to children by removing some items and altering others (e.g., changing "not make a social blunder" to "not do anything ridiculous").

SCORING AND INTERPRETING
IPC INVENTORIES

Having chosen and administered an IPC inventory, the next step is to score and interpret the responses. The following section describes simple analytic procedures that can be done without a computer. (For more sophisticated procedures that more fully exploit the inventories' circumplex properties, see Gurtman, Chapter 18 in this volume.) I will illustrate the procedures using CSIE data, but these same procedures can be used on data from *any* IPC inventory.

First, compute the raw scale score for each octant. On most IPC inventories, the raw scale scores are positively correlated with each other; this is referred to as the *general factor*. The general factor may have a substantive meaning or may reflect response tendencies unrelated to item content; for example, both general interpersonal confidence and an acquiescent response style may contribute to the CSIE's general factor. Regardless, for *any* IPC inventory, the general factor and the individual octant scores have different meanings, and so must be examined separately. To accomplish this, for each individual separately, (1) compute the general factor score by averaging the individual's eight octant scores, and then (2) ipsatize the octant scores by subtracting that individual's general factor score from each raw octant score.

To illustrate, I will analyze the CSIE responses from two participants from Locke and Sadler's (2007) study in which pairs of strangers completed the CSIE before working together to solve a murder mystery. Specifically, I will examine an extremely dissatisfied pair (whose satisfaction with their interaction was 2.4 standard deviations below average). First I computed the raw scale scores and overall mean (or general factor score) for each partner. (Recall that the scores could range from 0 to 10). The overall mean was 7.0 for Partner A and 8.2 for Partner B. I then ipsatized the scores by subtracting the overall mean from each scale score. Figure 19.2 plots the ipsatized octant scores for each partner (on scales ranging from a low value of −2.5 at the center of the circle to a high value of 1.5 at the edge of the circle). The figure shows that the two partners were similar in efficacy for being agentic/unagentic, but differed greatly in efficacy for being communal/uncommunal: Partner A was more confident that he could be communal than uncommunal, whereas Partner B was more confident that he could be uncommunal than communal.

The next step is to summarize the individual's overall agentic, unagentic, communal, and uncommunal dispositions by combining the ipsatized octant scores as follows:

Agentic Vector = (0.414)(PA + (0.707)(BC + NO))

Unagentic Vector = (0.414)(HI + (0.707)(FG + JK))

Communal Vector = (0.414)(LM + (0.707) (JK + NO))

Uncommunal Vector = (0.414)(DE + (0.707) (BC + FG))

The agentic vector minus the unagentic vector yields the individual's overall

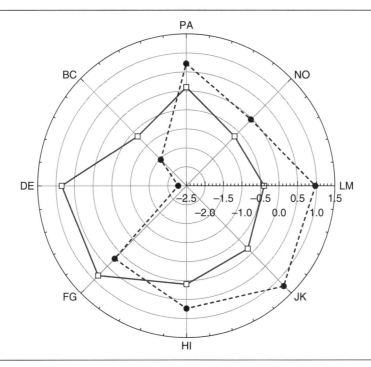

FIGURE 19.2   CSIE Octant Scores of a Pair of Dissatisfied Partners
Partner A's scores are connected by a dashed line; Partner B's scores are connected by a solid line.
Source: "Self-Efficacy, Values, and Complementarity in Dyadic Interactions: Integrating Interpersonal and Social-Cognitive Theory," by K. D. Locke and P. Sadler, 2007, *Personality and Social Psychology Bulletin, 33,* Study 2.

tendency to be agentic versus unagentic (the vertical or "*y*" coordinate). The communal vector minus the uncommunal vector yields the individual's overall tendency to be communal versus uncommunal (the horizontal or "*x*" coordinate). These *x* and *y* coordinates define a vector sum in the IPC space. The angle of this vector shows the individual's predominant interpersonal tendency. The vector length shows how intensely and consistently the target manifests this interpersonal disposition; the longer the vector, the more the scores define a clear interpersonal pattern with a peak in one region and a clear trough in the opposite region. For example, returning to our dissatisfied dyad, Partner B's vector angle was 216 degrees (in the FG octant), whereas Partner A's vector angle was 337 degrees (in the JK octant), which is several times greater than B's (indicating a more pronounced interpersonal pattern). This mismatch in communal

self-efficacy—which may have contributed to a corresponding mismatch in communal behaviors—may be partly to blame for their dissatisfaction.

Because all IPC inventories share the same structure, the same procedures just used to analyze data from the CSIE can be used to analyze data from any IPC inventory. Note also that the procedures just used to analyze an individual's scores also can be used to analyze the scores of a group of individuals—for example, the typical interpersonal style of depressed patients.

USING IPC MEASURES TO ASSESS
MALADAPTIVE INTERPERSONAL STYLES

The IPC model does not define any particular segment of the interpersonal space as necessarily adaptive or maladaptive (Leary, 1957). Indeed, the wide variations in agency and communion across persons, and within persons across situations, may exist precisely because different levels of agency and communion have both costs and benefits. For example, communion creates opportunities not only for beneficial resource exchange and social support, but also for acquiring costly social obligations and diseases. Likewise, agency can increase not only access to valued resources, but also the likelihood of costly rivalries.

Nonetheless, although only the IIP assesses interpersonal problems directly, all IPC measures can help identify maladaptive interpersonal styles. The interpersonal tradition assumes that an adaptive interpersonal style is flexible—that is, able (if necessary) to embody interpersonal behaviors and experiences from any IPC region (Kiesler, 1996; Leary, 1957). In contrast, a maladaptive style is too narrow or extreme to be appropriate in many situations. As discussed earlier, one indicator of overly narrow and extreme interpersonal traits is the length of the vector sum of an individual's octant scores (Tracey, 2005).

In addition, conflicted interpersonal profiles (high scores on opposing vectors) may indicate internal ambivalence and a tendency to convey unclear or inconsistent messages (Kiesler, 1996). For example, a person who strongly values both closeness and distance (i.e., who wishes to be loved and embraced but fears being exploited or constrained) may experience distressing internal conflicts and send shifting and confusing messages to others regarding what they want from their relationships.

Finally, particular patterns of scores may be associated with specific psychological disorders, especially personality disorders (PDs) (Horowitz, 2004; Locke, 2006). For example, antisocial and paranoid PDs are associated with interpersonal dispositions that are "high agency, low communion;" avoidant and schizoid PDs are associated with "low agency, low communion" interpersonal dispositions; dependent PD is associated with "low agency, high communion" interpersonal dispositions; histrionic PD is associated with "high agency, high communion" interpersonal dispositions; and narcissistic PD is associated with high agency interpersonal dispositions.

CONCLUSIONS

IPC inventories offer a balance of comprehensiveness and simplicity: They fully and evenly sample the domain of interpersonal dispositions defined by agency and communion, but enable that information to be distilled into just a few numbers or graphed as a single point on the IPC. In this chapter, I showed how the various IPC inventories are being successfully used to investigate a wide range of topics, including interpersonal complementarity, maladaptive expectations, psychopathology, social comparisons, sexuality, relationship satisfaction, and even how socioeconomic factors influence health outcomes. IPC inventories are also being employed in a variety of clinical and therapeutic settings.

The successful use of IPC inventories in diverse settings show how the IPC provides a solid two-dimensional foundation—grounded in both theory and research—on which to build a multidimensional understanding of the interpersonal world. Cumulative scientific progress depends on using a consistent set of constructs and locating specific constructs within a more encompassing conceptual framework. By providing a simple yet powerful framework for organizing interpersonal constructs and measures, the IPC is expediting this type of cumulative progress and broad understanding.

If a healthy family is characterized by both differentiation and integration, then the family of IPC inventories I have reviewed in this chapter—while imperfect and open for improvement—does appear healthy. The sundry inventories are differentiated by their focus on distinct constructs, such as traits, problems, values, self-efficacy, supportive actions, and impacts on others. At the same time, the inventories are anchored in, and integrated by, the IPC which remains the most popular and robust model of the cardinal vectors upon which people map and navigate their interpersonal lives.

References

Adams, R. S., & Tracey, T. J. G. (2004). Three versions of the Interpersonal Adjective Scales and their fit to the circumplex model. *Assessment, 11,* 263–270.

Archer, J. (2006). Testosterone and human aggression: An evaluation of the challenge hypothesis, *Neuroscience and Biobehavioral Reviews, 30,* 319–345.

Bandura, A. (1997). *Self-efficacy: The exercise of control.* New York: Freeman.

Bartz, J. A., & Hollander, E. (2006). The neuroscience of affiliation: Forging links between basic and clinical research on neuropeptides and social behavior. *Hormones and Behavior, 50,* 518–528.

Blackburn, R., & Renwick, S. J. (1996). Rating scales for measuring the interpersonal circle in forensic psychiatric patients. *Psychological Assessment, 8,* 76–84.

Bugental, D. B. (2000). Acquisition of the algorithms of social life: A domain-based approach. *Psychological Bulletin, 26,* 187–209.

Christie, R., & Geis, F. (1970). *Studies in Machiavellianism.* San Diego, CA: Academic Press.

Clark, T. L., & Taulbee, E. S. (1981). A comprehensive and indexed bibliography of the Interpersonal Check List. *Journal of Personality Assessment, 45,* 505–525.

Cross, S. E., Bacon, P. L., & Morris, M. L. (2000). The relational-interdependent self-construal and relationships. *Journal of Personality and Social Psychology, 78,* 791–808.

Doyle, M., & Dolan, M. (2006). Evaluating the validity of anger regulation problems, interpersonal style, and disturbed mental state for predicting inpatient violence. *Behavioral Sciences and the Law, 24,* 783–798.

Foa, U. G. (1961). Convergences in the analysis of the structure of interpersonal behavior. *Psychological Review, 68,* 341–353.

Gallo, L. C., Smith, T. W., & Cox, C. (2006). Socioeconomic status, psychosocial processes, and perceived health: An interpersonal perspective. *Annals of Behavioral Medicine, 31,* 109–119.

Hafkenscheid, A., & Rouckhout, D. (2009). Circumplex structure of the Impact Message Inventory (IMI-C): An empirical test with the dutch version. *Journal of Personality Assessment, 91,* 187–94.

Hamann, H., Smith, T. W., Smith, K. R., Ruiz, J. M., Kircher, J. C., & Botkin, J. R. (2008). Interpersonal responses among sibling dyads tested for BRCA1/2 gene mutations. *Health Psychology, 27,* 100–109.

Horowitz, L. M. (2004). *Interpersonal foundations of psychopathology.* Washington, DC: American Psychological Association.

Horowitz, L. M., Alden, L. E., Wiggins, J. S., & Pincus, A. L. (2000). *Inventory of Interpersonal Problems manual.* Odessa, FL: The Psychological Corporation.

Kiesler, D. J. (1996). *Contemporary interpersonal theory and research: Personality, psychopathology, and psychotherapy.* New York: John Wiley & Sons.

Kiesler, D. J., Goldston, C. S., & Schmidt, J. A. (1991). *Manual for the Check List of Interpersonal Transactions-Revised (CLOIT-R) and the Check List of Psychotherapy Transactions-Revised (CLOPT-R).* Richmond: Virginia Commonwealth University.

Kiesler, D. J., & Schmidt, J. A. (2006). *Manual for the Impact Message Inventory-Circumplex (IMI-C).* Menlo Park, CA: Mind Garden.

Kiesler, D. J., Schmidt, J. A., & Wagner, C. C. (1997). A circumplex inventory of impact messages: An operational bridge between emotional and interpersonal behavior. In R. Plutchik, & H. R. Conte (Eds.), *Circumplex models of personality and emotions* (pp. 221–244). Washington, DC: American Psychological Association.

LaForge, R., & Suczek, R. F. (1955). The interpersonal dimension of personality: An interpersonal check list. *Journal of Personality, 24,* 94–112.

Leary, T. (1957). *Interpersonal diagnosis of personality.* New York: Ronald Press.

Locke, K. D. (2000). Circumplex Scales of Interpersonal Values: Reliability, validity, and applicability to interpersonal problems and personality disorders. *Journal of Personality Assessment, 75,* 249–267.

Locke, K. D. (2003). Status and solidarity in social comparison: Agentic and communal values and vertical and horizontal directions. *Journal of Personality and Social Psychology, 84,* 619–631.

Locke, K. D. (2005). Interpersonal problems and interpersonal expectations in everyday life. *Journal of Social and Clinical Psychology, 24*, 915–931.

Locke, K. D. (2006). Interpersonal circumplex measures. In S. Strack (Ed.), *Differentiating normal and abnormal personality* (2nd ed., pp. 383–400). New York: Springer.

Locke, K. D., & Christensen, L. (2007). Re-construing the relational self-construal and its relationship with self-consistency. *Journal of Research in Personality, 41*, 389–402.

Locke, K. D. (2009). *Communal values and perceived self-other similarity.* Poster session presented at the annual meeting of the Society for Interpersonal Theory and Research, Toronto, Canada.

Locke, K. D., & Sadler, P. (2007). Self-efficacy, values, and complementarity in dyadic interactions: Integrating interpersonal and social-cognitive theory. *Personality and Social Psychology Bulletin, 33*, 94–109.

Markey, P. M., & Markey, C. N. (2007). The interpersonal meaning of sexual promiscuity. *Journal of Research in Personality, 41*, 1199–1212.

Moskowitz, D. S. (2009). Coming full circle: Conceptualizing the study of interpersonal behaviour. *Canadian Psychology, 50*, 33–41.

McCrae, R. R., & Costa, P. T., Jr. (1989). The structure of interpersonal traits: Wiggins' circumplex and the five-factor model. *Journal of Personality and Social Psychology, 56*, 586–595.

Ojanen, T., Gronroos, M., & Salmivalli, C. (2005) Applying the interpersonal circumplex model to children's social goals: Connections with peer reported behavior and sociometric status. *Developmental Psychology, 41*, 699–710.

Ruiz, M., Pincus, A., Borkovec, T., Echemendia, R., Castonguay, L., & Raguesa, S. (2004). Validity of the Inventory of Interpersonal Problems for predicting treatment outcome: An investigation with the Pennsylvania Practice Research Network. *Journal of Personality Assessment, 83*, 213–222.

Salzer, S., Pincus, A. L., Hoyer, J., Kreische, R., Leichsenring, F., & Leibing, E. (2008). Interpersonal subtypes within generalized anxiety disorder. *Journal of Personality Assessment, 90*, 292–299.

Schmid Mast, M., & Hall, J. A. (2004). When is dominance related to smiling? Assigned dominance, dominance preference, trait dominance, and gender as moderators. *Sex Roles, 50*, 387–399.

Schmidt, J. A., Wagner, C. C., & Kiesler, D. J. (1999). Psychometric and circumplex properties of the octant scale impact message inventory (IMI-C): A structural evaluation. *Journal of Counseling Psychology, 46*, 325–334.

Sodano, S. M., & Tracey, T. J. G. (2006). Interpersonal traits in childhood and adolescence: Development of the Child and Adolescent Interpersonal Survey. *Journal of Personality Assessment, 87*, 317–329.

Tracey, T. J. G. (2005). Interpersonal rigidity and complementarity. *Journal of Research in Personality, 39*, 592–614.

Trobst, K. K. (2000). An interpersonal conceptualization and quantification of social support transactions. *Personality and Social Psychology Bulletin, 26*, 971–986.

Wiggins, J. S. (1979). A psychological taxonomy of trait-descriptive terms: The interpersonal domain. *Journal of Personality and Social Psychology, 33*, 409–420.

Wiggins, J. S. (1995). *Interpersonal Adjective Scales: Professional manual.* Odessa, FL: Psychological Assessment Resources.

Wiggins, J. S. (2003). *Paradigms of personality assessment.* New York: Guilford Press.

Wiggins, J. S., & Broughton, R. (1991). A geometric taxonomy of personality scales. *European Journal of Personality, 5*, 343–365.

Wiggins, J. S., Trapnell, P., & Phillips, N. (1988). Psychometric and geometric characteristics of the Revised Interpersonal Adjective Scales (IAS-R). *Multivariate Behavioral Research, 23*, 517–530.

20 STRUCTURAL ANALYSIS OF SOCIAL BEHAVIOR (SASB)

Studying the Nature of Nature

Lorna Smith Benjamin

SASB (Benjamin, 1979, 1987, 1996) is a model that describes interpersonal and intrapsychic interactions in terms of three underlying dimensions, shown in Figure 20.1. The first dimension is discontinuous and is shown as three planes (surfaces) representing interpersonal focus on other (transitive action), interpersonal focus on self (intransitive state), and intrapsychic focus on other turned inward (introjection). The first plane describes behavior that is prototypically parentlike; the second describes behavior that is prototypically childlike; and the third describes what happens when parentlike behavior is turned inward. Each plane is defined by two continuous axes placed at right angles: love and hate appear on the horizontal axis, while enmeshment (Control/Submit) and differentiation (Emancipate/Separate) define the vertical axis. Highlights of the intellectual history of SASB and studies of its validity appear below.

The full SASB model shown in Figure 20.1 has the highest degree of resolution (36 points per plane) of all versions. Two simpler versions have eight points or clusters per plane (the two-word cluster model appeared in Benjamin, 1987; the one word simplified cluster model appeared in 1996).

An even simpler version has four quadrants per plane (Benjamin, 1979). The SASB model is build upon "primitive basics," as can be seen by the names on the poles of the axes of each plane of Figure 20.1. These relate directly to sexuality, power, murder, and separate territory. Construct, concurrent, content, and predictive validity of the SASB model have been discussed elsewhere (e.g., Benjamin, 1974, 2000; Benjamin, Rothweiler, & Critchfield, 2007). In this chapter, I touch on highlights of theory, research, and applications of SASB in assessment and treatment of psychopathology. The emphasis is on important methodological points that have been underdeveloped elsewhere. The main topical area is SASB theory and related methodological issues in research and practice.

THE SASB MODEL

The theory reflected by the SASB model developed from rational analysis of extant models and data prior to 1968, when the first draft of SASB was prepared. The first peer-reviewed publication was in Benjamin, 1974. Subsequently, the model was refined using a dimensional ratings method that

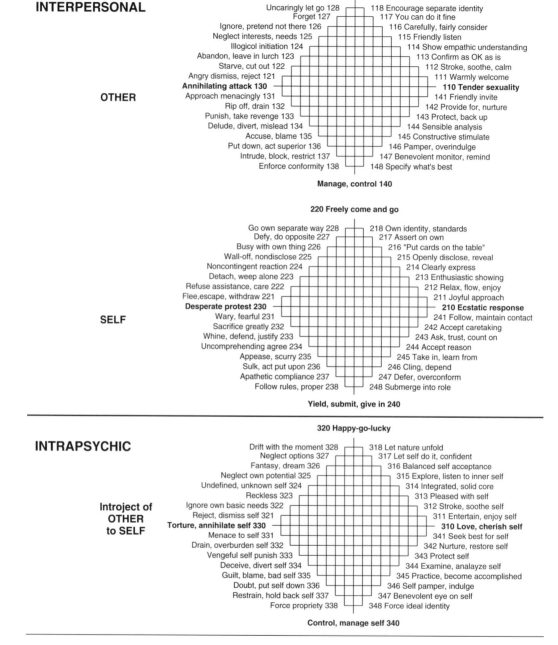

FIGURE 20.1 SASB Model

Source: From "Structural Analysis of Differentiation Failure," by L. S. Benjamin, 1979, *Psychiatry: Journal for the Study of Interpersonal Processes, 42,* p. 6.

directly assesses content validity of the items describing each of the model points. The most important prior model was Schaefer's (1965) circumplex model of parenting behavior. His circumplex, a single plane, placed love versus hate on one axis and control versus emancipate on the other. It described the natural opposites of control (emancipate) as well as for love (hate). Leary's circumplex predated Schaefer's. It also placed love and hate as opposites on the horizontal axis. However, the Leary circumplex placed control and submit as "opposites" on the vertical. The dimension of focus included in the SASB model resolves the disagreement about the opposite of Control (Dominate). According to SASB, Emancipate is the opposite of Control, while Submit is the *complement* of Control. This view of the vertical axis was affirmed by Lorr (1991). Logical and geometric definitions of the terms "opposite" and "complement" appear in the next section.

Geometry and Predictive Principles in the SASB Model

Code numbers identify location. Names for each point on Figure 20.1 have code numbers that describe its location. The hundreds digits describe the plane (1, 2, or 3); the tens digits describe the Cartesian quadrant (1, 2, 3, 4); the ones digits describe the subdivision of the quadrant (0 to 8). For example, 143, "Protect, back up" is on the first surface (or 1), the fourth quadrant (or 4), and the third subdivision (or 3). The geometric coordinates of 143 are (+6, −3). In other words, 143, "Protect, back up" is made up of about two-thirds love and one-third control.

Predictive principles. Each point has a *complement*, an *opposite*, and an *antithesis*. Complements are represented by pairs of points at the same geometric location (e.g., 4:30 o'clock for point 143) on the top and middle planes of Figure 20.1. They have the same theoretical values for affiliation (horizontal axis) and interdependence (vertical axis). They differ only in interpersonal focus. For

example, 143, "Protect, back up," and its complement, 243, "Ask, trust, count on," have coordinates (+6, −3), while one is on the parentlike plane and the other is on the childlike plane. Opposites have the same coordinates, except signs are reversed. For example, the psychological opposite of 143 is 123, "Abandon, leave in lurch," with the coordinates (−6, +3). The complement of 123 is 223, "Detach, weep alone" (−6, +3), which is the logical and psychological opposite of 243, "Ask, trust, count upon." Point 223, "Detach, weep alone" (coordinates −6, +3) also is the antithesis of 143, "Protect, back up" (coordinates +6, −3). Antitheses, which are complements of opposites, reverse signs and also shift focus. For example, if a caregiver shows behaviors classified as focus on other that is friendly and mildly influential (+6, −3), that is, 143, "Protect, back up," the baby is likely to complement that with 243, "Ask, trust, count on." However, if a baby does not respond to warm influence, and instead shows 223, "Detach, weep alone," the antithesis to try to improve its attachment would be to provide more behaviors that amount to 143, "Protect, back up."[1] 143 would provide antithetical corrective intervention that might maximize the chances of pulling a child out of its depressive withdrawal (e.g., after separation from its caregiver) into appropriate trust, which is required to develop a secure base (described later). Antithesis can work in a destructive direction, too. If a trusting baby (243) is abandoned (123) for too long, it will withdraw and become lethargic (223).

Assessment With the SASB Model

Data are generated either by questionnaire or by objective observer ratings, and processed by SASB software.[2] Raters of the questionnaires endorse SASB items for aptness and frequency jointly on a scale from 0 to 100, with 50 being a marker between True and False. There are different sets of items that correspond either to the full model (36 items per plane = the SASB Intrex Long

Form) or the octant models (eight items per plane = the SASB Intrex Short Form, version 1 or version 2; SASB Intrex Medium Form uses both versions combined). The Medium form is recommended as the most useful because it is considerably shorter than the Long Form, yet provides better sampling than the Short form because it has two rather than one item per octant. Objective observer ratings are based on videotapes of selected samples of interactions. Scores are in terms of the percentage of occurrence of a given model point in each given relationship.

Output is mostly the same, whether data were gathered by questionnaire or objective observer coding. It is based on octants (clusters), which have shorter names than the names on the full model in Figure 20.1. Octant names in the software and user's manual are from the two-word cluster model (Benjamin, 1987), but the simplest version is the one-word cluster model (Benjamin, 1996/2003). For convenience, the one-word names are cited in the rest of this chapter. In clockwise order, starting at 12 o'clock, they are: **Emancipate**, **Affirm**, **Active Love**, **Protect**, **Control**, **Blame, Attack**, **Ignore** (focus on other is indicated by boldface); Separate, Disclose, Reactive Love, Trust, Submit, Sulk, Wall off (focus on self is indicated by underlining); *Self-Emancipate*, *Self-Affirm*, *Self-Love*, *Self-Protect*, *Self-Control*, *Self-Blame*, *Self-Attack*, *Self-Ignore* (introjected focus is indicated by italics). The main parameters from the output are cluster scores that provide profiles in terms of octants; weighted affiliation (AF) and autonomy scores (AU) that show a vector (AF, AU) describing position on each plane of the model; pattern coefficients that assess affiliation, interdependence, and conflict (endorsement of opposites) in terms of patterns rather than, as is the case for (AF, AU), position in terms of absolute levels of endorsement. For data based on questionnaires, assessments of internal consistency are available. For data based on objective observer coding, information about sequences is available.

SASB is unusual among assessments of personality in its focus on specific interpersonal contexts. The standard set of questionnaires includes: rater in relation to self (introject) in the best and worst states; a significant other (marital) person in the best and worst states; parents as remembered from childhood; parental modeling observed in childhood. Clinically relevant variations unique to each rater also are encouraged (e.g., incestually abusing big brother; father when drunk). Data from many contexts have shown that ratings can be markedly different for different situations and states. Those differences have, among other things, provided important clinical information about relationships between recalled interactions with loved ones and current interactional patterns in different states. The observer system is contextualized by rating each individual within specific interpersonal contexts (e.g., person X in relation to Y and to Z). Comparisons of self-ratings with objective observer ratings of the same relationships can be highly informative. For example, Humes and Humphrey (1994) showed that objective observer coding of family interactions was in closer agreement to the questionnaire ratings provided by adolescent bulimic patients than to questionnaire ratings by their parents. General surveys of publications using either system appear in Benjamin (1995) and Benjamin, Rothweiler, and Critchfield (2006).

Utility of Factor Analysis in Testing the Validity of Models of Personality

The validity of most measures of personality in academic psychology is based on factor analysis. Typically, principal components that factor analysis identifies are orthogonal axes (i.e., axes at right angles) that define the underlying space in which every subject can be located by his or her factor scores. A given factor score is generated by summing the product of each individual's score on every item in the instrument times the given factor loadings for each item. Theoretically, there are as many factors as there are dimensions in the underlying space. A two-dimensional reconstruction of a circumplex is based on two factors. In reconstruction of a model, each variable, rather than each individual,[3] is plotted according to its factor loading. The convention in circumplex model testing is to perform a varimax rotation before plotting factor loadings for the respective model points.

Validity of the IAS-R Circumplex According to Factor Analysis

The most widely published contemporary version of the eight-octant single-circle circumplex model (generally called the IPC, or Interpersonal Circle) is the IAS-R (Interpersonal Adjective Scale–Revised; Wiggins, 1982; Wiggins, Trapnell, & Phillips, 1988). The structure of the IAS-R is very similar to the IPC, first published by Freedman, Leary, Ossorio, and Coffey (1951) and fully developed by Leary (1957). Data for the IAS-R come from a checklist of eight words per model point (64 in all). Reconstructions of the IAS-R model consistently deliver a virtually perfectly circle via principal components analysis and varimax rotation. Opposites are located precisely at 180 degrees, and all points are exactly 45 degrees apart. IAS-R scores make interesting predictions in relation to other variables. For example, they can plot the DSM Axis II personality categories in a two-dimensional space defined by love versus hate and dominate versus submit. Results make clinical sense (Gurtman, 1994). Within the academic field of personality, the IAS-R has substantial concurrent validity in that it behaves reasonably in relation to other measures, such as measures of personality disorder, health, marital interactions, interpersonal difficulties, the NEO-5 (Costa & McCrae, 1992) universal description of personality, and more.

Validity of SASB According to Tests by Factor Analysis

Tests of SASB are performed by principal components only,[4] and have never delivered a perfect circle (even with varimax rotation). Reconstructions of SASB intransitive surface (middle of Figure 20.1) almost always approximate a circle.[5] The axes are distinctive enough to yield the predicted circular order, but they are not at right angles and the points are not dispersed at equal intervals. Reconstructions of the SASB transitive surface, and the introject (transitive action turned inward) surfaces, are in an "oval shape" for many, but not all, states and situations.[6] The oval always tilts from the lower left-hand corner (hostile enmeshment) to the upper right-hand corner (friendly differentiation). Sometimes the vertical axis is not well articulated in reconstructions based on factor analysis. These problems have been noted, and questions have been raised about the validity of the SASB items and/or model (Lorr & Strack, 1999; Monson et al. 2007; Pincus et al., 1998). The emphasis on a perfect circle, and the requirement that structure be confirmed without regard to context, raises the question: What should be the purpose of theory in personality and clinical psychology? To answer that question, it is important briefly to review the history of theory in modern science.

A Gold Standard for Theory in Modern Science: Understanding "The Nature of Nature"

Modern scientific method evolved during the Renaissance and was distinguished from what came before by its "radical objectivity." Scientific theories must be tested by objective evidence in pursuit of the goal of understanding the nature of nature. Modern scientists presume the universe is real, otherwise, how can there be "objective evidence" about it? In the quest to understand Nature, a modern scientist makes careful observations, interprets them with a theory that is specific enough to be proven wrong, uses the theory to make predictions about the nature of nature, and tests the predictions via using new data that support or refute the theory. If data do not support the theory, the theory must be modified, and new data must be gathered to check the modified theory. If there is too little empirical support for the theory, or if another theory provides and accounts for more predictions, the less supported theory is abandoned. Scientific theory is at its best when its predictions provide surprises[7] that are confirmed by data. It is important to note that the predictions are about the nature of nature, and not merely about what statistical result is expected.[8] Hume summarized the vital role of theory in science: "Data without theory are as a heap of stones is to a house" (Hume, 1748/1947).

To set such goals in clinical psychology is reasonable. Theorists in the hard sciences have shown the way. For example, Darwin's (1952; reprint of original 1859 paper[9]) theory of evolution interpreted data that he gathered during a five-year voyage around the world. He catalogued multitudes of plants and animals in widely diverging environments. After returning to England, Darwin worked for over a decade to construct the theory that would explain his data. Without his *theory* about why animals and plants varied in relation to their environments, Darwin's reams of notebooks full of observations would have been uninterpretable. Many years later, others discovered mechanisms that explained the speciation[10] that Darwin had described so accurately and interpreted in terms of the principle of natural selection. Highlights of the sequence of solving the mystery of the varieties of life forms began with Mendel's theory of inheritance, which was based on the study of successive generations of plants. Mendel could not actually see chromosomes (or the genes on chromosomes), but after microscopes were developed to higher degrees of resolution, the entities (chromosomes) predicted by his theory were seen. Almost a century later (1953), Watson and Crick's model of DNA "broke the code" for genes and explained the mechanisms for how information is transmitted during meiosis, as well as during mitosis. Presently, studies in epigenetics (e.g.,

Higgs et al., 2007) enhance understanding about how adaptation to the environment affects the developing organism as it provides detail about the mechanisms for the expression and suppression of genes. This entire sequence within biology, the study of life, is directed by the goal of palpating the nature of nature. The theory of evolution, and the gene theory of inheritance, provide a gold standard for testing the validity of a theory.

Note to Clinical Psychology on the Consequences of Forgetting About the Study of Nature

Why review all this, the reader might ask. We learn about it as undergraduates and know it all very well. The answer is that, in its enthusiasm for objectivity, clinical psychology seems to have stripped the meaning of theory down to levels that barely go beyond the data themselves. By avoiding the development of rich theories to interpret data and guide the collection of new data, clinical psychology has lost sight of the goal of discovering the nature of nature. Instead, there is a highly codified, narrowly defined set of rules that seek usually to determine whether a narrowly defined hypothesis is "right" or "wrong." Typical questions are: does treatment A have a better outcome than treatment B? Is Trait X correlated significantly with symptom Y? Does group X score higher than group Y on instrument Z? Does instrument X account for more of the variance than does instrument Y? Although any of these methods could in fact inform us about the nature of nature if framed within testable and generative theory, that step is usually missing. Two examples follow to illustrate unrecognized problems in failing to provide theory that seeks to understand the nature of nature by posing internal logic that generates an unlimited number of specific generalizations that can be empirically tested. There is: (1) an analysis of the method of constructing and validating IAS-R theory; and (2) consideration of theoretical implications for two different rotations of factor analysis of DSM-IV items describing personality disorder.

The IAS-R perfect circle and the nature of nature. SASB's validity has been challenged because its oval shape falls short of the perfection in the IAS-R circle. It is worthwhile to compare the Platonic standard of a perfect circle to the standard of studying the nature of nature. Moving in a clockwise direction, the IAS-R circle is defined by **Assured/Dominant** at the top, followed by Gregarious/Extraverted, *Warm/Agreeable*, Unassuming/Ingenuous, **Unassured/Submissive**, Aloof/Introverted, *Cold-Hearted*, Arrogant/Calculating. The horizontal poles are shown here in italics and the vertical poles in boldface type. Opposition is bolstered by grammar, in that the prefix "un-" and the suffix "-less" occur frequently in the IAS-R. Consider this set of opposite octants: Gregarious/Extroverted is defined by these words: cheerful, neighborly, extraverted, enthusiastic, outgoing, perky, and jovial. Its opposite, Aloof/Introverted, is defined by uncheery, unneighborly, distant, dissocial, unsociable, antisocial, unsparkling, and introverted. The method for assuring 45-degree spacing between IAS-R model points is not discussed in the literature. The frequency of strange words in the checklists suggests items may have been selected on the basis of their contribution to the location of their octant on the model during factor analytic reconstructions. This idea is supported by Rothweiler's (2004) dimensional ratings of the content of the IAS-R items (described later), which showed substantial variability in angular placement of individual items that make up a given IAS octant score. For example, within the octant Aloof/Introverted, the item "unsociable" has an angular placement exactly where it was predicted to be. But other items within that octant were rated by Rothweiler's 135 subjects at substantial angular distances away from prediction. "Unneighborly" was off target by 41 degrees in the counterclockwise direction, while "Introverted" was off target by 30 degrees in the clockwise

direction. This range of 70 degrees is considerably more than the 45 degrees represented by an octant.

The net geometry of the IAS-R is perfect, but the use of grammar to define opposites, and the use of very unusual words within groups of eight items that average to locate the model point, introduce uncertainty if the instrument measures interactional social "reality." That concern is heightened by the fact that the method of constructing the instrument (factor analysis) is the same as the method of testing the validity of the theory (factor analysis). Suppose that, in nature, underlying interpersonal space has three dimensions that compare to length, width, and height in physical space. If true, the procedure just described for IAS-R could be used to define a two-dimensional figure of any arbitrary shape within that three-dimensional space. Although a perfect circle[11] can be identified within the three-dimensional space, it would not describe the general nature of nature if there are really three dimensions (of any sort). The possibility that the IAS-R circle does not include all relevant dimensionality is raised by noting that the IAS-R covers the bottom two parts of the SASB model in Figure 20.1 (the enmeshment half), but does not address the many varieties of ways of being differentiated (separate) marked by the upper half of Figure 20.1.

Factor analytic descriptions of personality and the nature of nature. Not all models of personality based on factor analysis seek to take a particular geometric form. Well-known examples of personality theory based on factor profiles are offered by Barrett and Eysenck, 1984; Cloninger, 1987; Costa and McCrae, 1992. Like the IAS, each has demonstrated useful concurrent validity. However, relating one empirically derived measure to another (i.e., concurrent validity) does not necessarily establish construct validity that directly contributes to the effort to understand the nature of nature. The need for independent theory to guide interpretation of data is heightened when the method of analysis involves, as is the case with factor analysis, many arbitrary procedural decisions that can affect interpretation of results. Examples of decisions that need guidance from theory are: deciding how many factors to extract (note: eigenvalue of 1 has only a statistical rationale); whether to rotate; and, if rotating, when to stop. Although performing factor analysis is well operationalized, *naming the factors* (e.g., neurosis) is quite subjective and not operationalized at all. This is manifest by the fact that there are many theories of personality with no standard for choosing which, if any, comes close to palpating nature in relation to the principle of natural selection—the defining feature of biological science.

In sum, descriptions of personality based on questionnaires interpreted by factor analysis generate data in a highly reliable fashion (e.g., pass out questionnaires; score them according to statistical algorithms based on factor analysis; refer profiles to norms or other data-based criteria). However, interpretation is vulnerable to some important arbitrary decisions and is expressed in terms of names that are of indeterminate meaning and quite subjective. For example, there is no potential for the word *neurotic* (as used in the NEO-5) to be used in the same infinitely generative and testable way that the word *gene* can be used.

The Challenge of Moving From Raw Empiricism Toward Theory-Based Science

Staying very close to data processed by a few favored statistical algorithms has become the accepted methodology in clinical psychology. There are many reasons why there is little effort to engage in the difficult process of developing and testing theory about the nature of nature. For one thing, the politics of contemporary university (or corporate) life would never support the research time that Darwin required as he spent five years gathering his data and more than 10 years developing and preparing a book describing a viable theory to account for the data. Another problem for contemporary clinical psychology is attitudinal. The word *theory* has

come to mean little more than "unverifiable fantasy of the investigator."[12] This likely derives from the fate of psychoanalytic theory, which was criticized as untestable, unverifiable, and lacking generality by Mischel (1973), and (more indirectly) by the creators of the DSM-III (APA, 1980). Psychoanalytic theory may be untestable as claimed, but it is a mistake to ignore the possibility of more testable versions of psychoanalytic or other theories of psychopathology, personality, and psychotherapy. In failing to use integrative, data-based theory, we cannot provide a naturalistic definition of what is normal. The operating definition of "normal" is in terms of absence of symptoms and/or being within one standard deviation of the mean provided by normal subjects on a given measure. This says nothing at all about how things work in nature. A scientific theory of personality that seeks to understand the nature of nature might instead consider the possibility that normal personality can be defined in relation to what our anatomy and physiology prepare us to do under various conditions relevant to the biological principle of natural selection. In other words, it might attend to the ways that evolution is directly relevant to the study of psychology, including the study of personality.

SASB AND THE NATURE OF NATURE

The SASB model and its associated theory of psychopathology and treatment, Interpersonal Reconstructive Therapy (IRT, Benjamin, 2003/2006) aspire to the status of a modern scientific (i.e., testable) theory that has the goal of enhancing our understanding (ability to better predict and control) of the nature of nature. Some, but not all, relevant scientific features are discussed below.

SASB Theory Has Internal Logic Consistent With the Evolutionary Principle of Natural Selection

The SASB model is based on the hypothesis that all social interactions are made up of underlying simpler fundamental components (1 = focus; 2 = attachment; 3 = interdependence). These components[13] derive from the idea that the human is a herd animal, and they are consistent with the evolutionary principle of natural selection. Social interactions must define and protect the herd, and allocate supplies so that chances for survival of this generation and creation of the next are maximized. Components of the model are expressed in terms that are consistent with observations of interactions among domestic animals, monkeys, and humans of all ages. Here is a brief review of three components and their evolutionary functions:

1. "Attentional focus" is an important component of any social interaction. When meeting another member of the troop, it is adaptive to be able to discern whether the other is taking action toward oneself (focusing on other). It is also adaptive to consider what to do or not do in relation to that other member (focusing on self). The two orientations have very different messages and effects. For example, a paranoid personality has a different attentional baseline ("he may hurt me"/focus on other) than does a narcissistic personality ("I am here, let the celebration begin"/focus on self). Responses to these personalities differ predictably (Benjamin, 1996/2003, Chapters 13 and 6).

2. The component "affiliation" (love to hate axis) reflects attachment, and functions to keep members of the herd together. The bonding pole (**Active Love**/Reactive Love) assures the herd will stick together. Its opposite, the Fight-or-flight pole (**Attack**/Recoil), describes forces that have the function of mediating control of, or distance from, members, supplies, or the territory itself.

3. The component "interdependence" details where and how available resources are allocated. The territorial poles (**Emancipate**/Separate) provide a mechanism to preserve and protect available resources from appropriation by others within and between herds. Its opposite (**Control**/Submit), the enmeshment pole, determines the use of resources within a territory by allocating them first to dominant members.

The primitive basics of survival are necessarily extreme, and so the items representing them in the questionnaire that assess positions on the poles of the SASB full model likewise are extreme.[14] In the octant versions of SASB, the intensity of the polar points diminishes as the primitive basics are averaged conceptually with adjacent points. The moderation is reflected by softer names and items for the poles in the octant version of the SASB model: **Emancipate**/Separate; **Active Love**/Reactive Love; **Control**/Submit; **Attack**/Recoil.

SASB ITEMS WERE WRITTEN TO REFLECT THEORY DIRECTLY

SASB items were not selected on an empirical basis from a pool of words that seem relevant to personality. Instead, the items describing the SASB model were *constructed* to represent theoretically assigned amounts of the underlying primitive basics for each point. That is, a given point represented by a vector (X,Y) should have a location defined by X units of Affiliation and Y units of Interdependence. The rules for constructing opposites were that the opposition has to be inherent in the language and could not be achieved by the use of negation. An opposite point is defined by inverse signs in its (X, Y) vector, and the language for an opposing item must inherently reflect that opposition. For example, a short form item for Trust is: "X trustingly depends on, willingly takes in what Y offers." Its theoretical opposite is Wall off: "X is closed off from Y and mostly stays alone in his or her own world."

Successive samples of naïve subjects assessed the content validity of proposed items using rating scales that reflected their theoretical dimensionality. As is the case for the SASB questionnaires themselves, the dimensional ratings questionnaires present items in a randomly determined order. Each item was rated by a scale that ranged from −100 to +100 with 0 at the neutral point. Affiliation extremes for the parentlike domain were anchored at "Attacking destructive, extremely hostile" and "Actively loving, extremely friendly." Anchors for the affiliation extremes for the childlike domain were: "Full of hateful protest, extremely hostile" and "Actively loving, extremely friendly." Interdependence extremes for the parentlike domain were: "Leaving others to be free, separate, different" and "Extremely influencing or controlling; telling others what to do, be, think." Interdependence items for the childlike domain had these anchors: "Extremely independent; separated, differentiated," "Free to be one's own person" on one end, and "Extremely submissive, yielding, very influenced, affected by others" on the other. Affiliation anchors for the introject were: "Attacking self, destructive, extremely hostile" and "Actively loving self, extremely friendly." Interdependence items for the introject were: "Leaving self as is," and "Extremely influencing and controlling of self." All items also were rated for interpersonal focus. Raters assigned all items 1, 2 or 3, corresponding to the definitions of the three planes in Figure 20.1. Focus was represented by stick figures, accompanied by the words. A rating of "1" means that X directs a transitive action toward Y. The emphasis is on what is happening to Y. A rating of "2" means that X is in an intransitive state in reaction to Y. The emphasis is on what is happening to X. A rating of "3" means that X directs a transitive action inward upon himself.

Reconstruction of the SASB model was based on average dimensional ratings for the items. Items that were far from where they were supposed to be were rewritten to add whatever dimension was over- or underemphasized. However, the words and grammar needed to be ordinary and simple. The items in the short and medium form were written at the sixth-grade level. The long is at about the ninth-grade level.[15] The goal was to create circumplex order

for the content of every item, to have the poles of axes opposite each other, and to have model points be dispersed as evenly as possible. Logically this should result in the two axes (affiliation, interdependence) located at right angles. Every single item was held to these standards. This means that items could not be added to, or deleted from, a group only on the basis of their impact on the average. Instead, the ideal was to write each item so accurately that plots of single items on the model would be as good as plots of averages of items. The results of dimensional-ratings assessments were quite successful but not perfect. Figure 20.2 shows a reconstruction of the interpersonal surfaces of the model based on items from the Short Form, versions 1 and 2 (Benjamin, 2000), while Figure 20.3 presents dimensional ratings for the introject surface. Inspection of these figures reveals that there is circumplex order for all surfaces of both versions. Dispersion of points is adequate but not perfect.

There is a discernable oval shape for transitive action (parentlike in Figure 20.2; introject in Figure 20.3). The axes (3 versus 7; 1 versus 5) are opposed but not orthogonal, and points are not evenly dispersed. The reconstruction of the introject in Figure 20.3 rather directly parallels the distortions shown by the transitive action group in Figure 20.2. Results for intransitive action shown in the lower half of Figure 20.2 (childlike) are much closer to theory. Axes are opposite and orthogonal, and the points are more or less evenly dispersed. The difference between ovallike reconstructions of parentlike (Figure 20.2, upper half) and parentlike turned inward (Figure 20.3), compared to circlelike reconstructions of childlike items reconstructions (Figure 20.2, lower half) is interesting. The distortions in the domain representing transitive action may mean those items need rewriting; it may mean the model should be different for transitive actions, whether focused on other or inward; or it may mean there is rater (cultural/gender/developmental) bias that is marked when

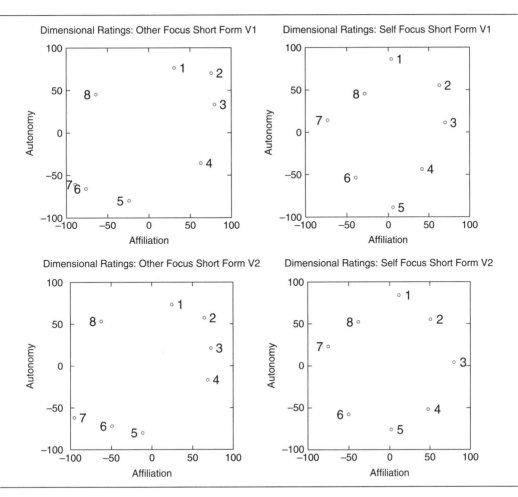

FIGURE 20.2   Dimensional Ratings of Short Form Single Items, Versions 1 and 2
Key (top/bottom): 1 = Emancipate/Separate; 2 = Affirm/Disclose; 3 = Active/Reactive Love; 4 = Protect/Trust; 5 = Control/Submit; 6 = Blame/Sulk; 7 = Attack/Recoil; 8 = Ignore/Wall off. There is a discernible tendency for an oval shape in the transitive set (focus on other), and for the oval to tilt, reflecting a correlation of hostility and control, and of emancipation and love.

there is transitive action. At this point, it is impossible to choose among these alternatives or perhaps others. I am unable to imagine writing the items differently without violating the theory regarding the polar points, the rules prohibiting "un, not, less," and without selecting words simply on the basis of their contribution to the desired average for a given point.

To illustrate what would happen if the shape of the model was the goal rather than attempting to palpate the configuration of the nature of nature, consider that the oval would disappear if the language describing the poles were damped down. More

neutral descriptions of **Attack** and **Love** would shrink the horizontal scale (which is longer than the vertical) and create a "better" circle. But the resulting approximation of the platonic perfect circle would violate the hypothesis that primitive basics of the SASB model describe primitive basics, presumably given in nature.

On the other hand, consider for a moment the possibility that the oval shape reflects interpersonal reality. The oval shape itself would suggest that the affiliation axis carries more variance than the interdependence axis when there is transitive action because an oval is defined when one axis

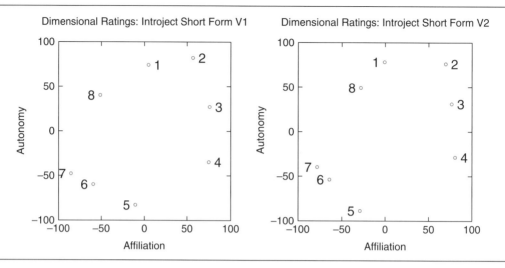

FIGURE 20.3   Dimensional Ratings of the Short Form Single Items Describing the Introject
The tilted oval seen for transitive items in Figure 20.2 can also be seen here.

is longer than the other. The tilt of the oval is a separate issue. It suggests that hostility is linked to (not independent of) control; emancipation and separation are linked to attachment. However, before concluding that one or both of these attributes reflect the nature of nature, it is important to note that the raters were mostly college students. Their linking of hostility with control and emancipation/separation with love might reflect their developmental concern with differentiation of self and the high value that is placed on independence in Western culture. Having dimensional ratings from mature adults, and raters of all ages in other cultures,[16] is needed to better inform these questions about ovals.

Another feature of SASB that centers on evolution is the fact that assessments are, as mentioned above, always interactional and contextualized by state and situation. According to SASB, behavior is supported by affect and cognition, and the triumvirate is adaptive when the behaving organism interacts with the environment. There are affective and cognitive models that parallel the SASB model (Benjamin, 2003/2006, chapter 4), but these are not yet well validated. Additional features of the SASB

model that are consistent with the theory of evolution are mentioned in the last section on Interpersonal Reconstructive Therapy (IRT), a clinical application of SASB principles and data.

IAS, FACTOR ANALYSIS, AND THE NATURE OF PERSONALITY

Dimensional ratings of IAS. Rothweiler (2004) asked a sample of 135 volunteers from college and adult education populations to make dimensional ratings of each word in the IAS (eight each for eight clusters).[17] He used scales that ranged from −9 to +9 rather than the −100 to +100 scales I have used (Figures 20.2 and 20.3). In Rothweiler's study, anchor points for the horizontal IAS axis were *Coldhearted* on one extreme and *Warm/Agreeable* on the other. Anchor points on the vertical axis were *Assured/Dominant* on one end, and *Unassured/Submissive* on the other.[18] Results are presented in Figure 20.4. The points are in circumplex order and the poles are opposite (1 versus 5; 3 versus 7). The axes are not orthogonal and the points between the axes are not evenly distributed. Figure 20.4 is a facsimile to the IAS model but is not a perfect circle. It compares unfavorably to the reconstructions of the SASB model based on dimensional ratings of the single items (Figures 20.2 and 20.3) for the Short and Medium Forms. The difference most likely can be attributed to the fact the SASB items were written to succeed at dimensional reconstruction for every item, while the IAS was not. Figures 20.2 to 20.4 show that, when directly assessed for content according to the theory about underlying dimensionality, SASB items are truer to its stated theory than IAS-R items.

Revisiting Factor Analytic Tests of SASB Structure

Factor analysis of data gathered when subjects use SASB items to rate themselves in social context yield different results for different contexts. Reconstructions of the SASB model based on factor analysis tend to be more orderly in normative situations, like "my introject at best," "my

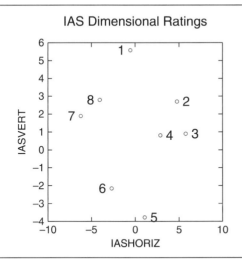

FIGURE 20.4 Rothweiler's (2004) Dimensional Ratings of IAS-R Clusters
The points are ordered in a circumplex, the axes are opposite (1 vs. 5; 3 vs. 7), but they are not orthogonal. The other points are not placed at 45 degree angles. 1 = Assured/Dominant, 2 = Gregarious/Extroverted, 3= Warm/Agreeable, 4 = Unassuming/Ingenuous, 5 = Unassured/Submissive, 6 = Aloof/Introverted, 7 = Coldhearted, 8 = Arrogant/Calculating.

mother/father focused on me" (parentlike domain), "I reacted to mother/father" (childlike domain).[19] By contrast, reconstructions of the model based on factor analyses of role reversals, as in "I focused on my mother/father," tend to collapse on the vertical axis because normative subjects do not rate themselves highly on items saturated with control.

Testing the SASB Predictive Principle of Complementarity

If appropriate independent information can be developed to explain why the variations are seen in the structure of models reconstructed from different contexts, such deviations actually validate rather than challenge the usefulness of the model. They simply mean that greater precision is needed to describe the conditions under which different predictive principles operate. This is normal in science. One does not predict, for example, that a given chemical reaction will always occur. There are contingent circumstances involving context: temperature, concentration, purity, ambient pressure, and so on. Despite the challenge posed by possible deviations in the model's structure and/or in the predictive principles, data testing complementarity in contextually appropriate samples are strong. Table 20.1 illustrates this for the role-appropriate complementary match: "mother focused on me" (parentlike); "I reacted to mother" (childlike). The table contains correlations for 187 psychiatric inpatients rating their mother's parentlike transitive focus on them (top of Figure 20.1), and their childlike intransitive reactions to her (middle of Figure 20.1), as remembered from ages 5 to 10. Data were gathered by SASB Intrex Long form items, which, as usual for SASB, appear in a randomly determined order.[20] The eight rows and eight columns of Table 20.1 are named for clusters (octants) that represent average scores for 4 or 5 adjacent full-model items. For example, the row labeled **Control** is defined by correlations involving the average of scores for

TABLE 20.1 Psychiatric Inpatients (N = 187) Rating the SASB Intrex Long-Form Items Describing "Mother Focused on Me" and "I Reacted to mother," both of which Occurred "When I Was Aged 5 to 10"

Mother	RATER							
	Separate	Disclose	Reactive Love	Trust	Submit	Sulk	Recoil	Wall Off
Emancipate	.668	.378	.337	.277	.035	.036	.229	.251
Affirm	.270	.712	.750	.626	−.012	−.374	−.350	−.336
Active Love	.209	.663	.788	.669	.113	−.194	−.314	−.250
Protect	.128	.567	.704	.671	.155	−.237	.331	−.274
Control	−.045	−.048	.008	.230	.621	.522	.330	.302
Blame	.142	−.315	−.405	−.310	.269	.663	.688	.631
Attack	.165	−.303	−.370	−.361	.178	.581	.682	.605
Ignore	.199	−.355	−.419	−.348	.236	.616	.672	.646
Rho theory And data	.869**	.807*	.932**	.711*	.769*	.832*	.874**	.676*

The diagonal, which has the darkest shading, shows pairings expected to have maximal correlations according to complementarity theory, with the lightest shading marking antithetical parings between "opposites of complements." If complementarity holds, antithesis should not. To assess the degree of complementary ordering of parentlike: childlike pairings, the numbers at the bottom of each column present nonparametric correlations between the theoretical rank order of entries in a column and the observed order. For 8 data points, rho of .643 marks the .05 level, and .833 marks the .01 level.

the five items from Figure 20.1 that are clustered around the power pole: 137, 138, 140, 148, 147.

Table 20.1 is shaded according to predictions based on circumplex theory if it is operative in any 8 x 8 table (Guttman, 1966). Because of the choice of variables on rows and columns, this table represents a harsh test of complementarity. Circumplex order will be confirmed only if it exists within each domain (parentlike/childlike) *and also* if complementarity is operating. Shading represents the predicted magnitudes of correlations. The diagonal, which has the darkest shading, should have maximal correlations because it shows exact complementary matches: **Emancipate** with Separate, **Affirm** with Disclose, and so on, stepwise around the octant model. The lightest shading marks pairings expected to have minimal correlations (and representing antitheses when comparing complementary sets). The numbers in the extra row (9th) at the bottom of each column in Table 20.1 present rho, a distribution free correlation between theoretical and observed orders of the cells in the columns. The theoretical values for column 1 are 0, 1, 2, 3, 4, 3, 2, 1; they represent the

stepwise distances that each successive cell should have from the maximum r for the column. The values for column 2 are: 1, 0, 1, 2, 3, 4, 3, 2. And so on to column 8, which has the values of 1, 2, 3, 4, 3, 2, 1, 0. The bottom row of Table 20.1 shows that correspondence between predicted and observed values is significant for every pairing. The two best-ordered columns are labeled Reactive Love and Recoil. These are the theoretical opposites for the extremes of attachment in the childlike domain. The columns with the weakest, but still significant, associations are Trust and Wall off. These are opposites that relate most directly to the development of a secure base, which is central to healthy attachment.[21]

INTERPERSONAL RECONSTRUCTIVE
THERAPY (IRT)

IRT (Benjamin, 2003/2006) offers a developmental theory of psychopathology, and an associated theory of treatment, that evolved from decades of using SASB theory to guide clinical practice and research. Brief reviews of it, with emphasis on relevance to personality theory, are available in Benjamin 2008, and Benjamin, in press.

Stated most simply, IRT theory proposes that personality is based on social learning that is particularly powerful if it happens in relation to loved ones (especially early caregivers, and long-term sexual partners). The mechanisms are simple: as in DNA, copying is central to the transmission of information regarding survival from one generation to the next. There are three basic copy processes: Be like him or her (identification); continue to act as you always did with him or her (recapitulation); treat yourself as he or she treated you (introjection). These can be tracked by SASB predictive principles and a number of them have been confirmed statistically in different samples, correcting for their base rates (Critchfield and Benjamin, 2008).

Copy process is recorded as a "family in the head," whose perceived rules and values sustain the copied patterns even when they are maladaptive. In psychiatric patients, the loyalty to the family in the head is so powerful that it can lead to devastating self-sabotage. A common and tragic version is the introjection of harsh messages: "You hated me and told me I am horrible and worthless. I agree with you and I know you will be happy when I am no longer around."

Engaging the will to change is a complex and very difficult, sometimes dangerous procedure. An entire book (Benjamin, in progress) is devoted to the problem of understanding and helping patients let go of their loyalties to self-sabotaging rules and values. The procedure invokes affective exploration of the fact that an individual's "safety system" (secure base) is defined primarily by proximity, and that when the caregiver is abusive, the safety system is fused with the "threat system," and self-sabotage is the result. Differentiation from the problem aspects of the "family in the head" is required before one can learn to practice friendly differentiation and enmeshment, behaviors that are defined as the therapy goal by SASB theory and data. Normal social interactions are basically friendly, with moderate degrees of enmeshment (**Control**/Submit)

and differentiation (**Emancipate**/Separate). A baseline of friendliness, and only moderate separation or enmeshment and reciprocity of focus, is totally unfamiliar to many patients. According to SASB theory and IRT practice, these behaviors are optimal for herd animals and are accompanied by pleasant affects and effective cognition. When they are firmly in place, symptoms of mental disorder are no longer present, and personality is reconstructed in a normative way. Preliminary pre-/posttests, and correlations between adherence to the IRT model and treatment outcome, are very promising in a highly comorbid, often rehospitalized, dysfunctional, and suicidal population.

SUMMARY AND CONCLUSIONS

The SASB model describes relationships with self and others in terms of underlying "primitive basics." Its structure is founded on a rational theory about the "nature of nature." Items describing the model points were written to conform to theoretical underlying dimensionality. Content validity is assessed by raters' dimensional ratings of the items themselves. The applicability of the items is tested by factor analyses of self-descriptions of normative and psychiatric raters. Interactional context is considered as separate assessments are made for others as well as for self in different states and situations. Predictive principles can be tested by assessing circumplex order in eight-by-eight matrixes, placing correlations between octant scores for one member of a dyad on rows and octant scores for the other member in columns.

Factor analytic and other correlational results confirm structure and predictions in some contexts, but not others. Deviations make sense and can be seen as informing us about the nature of nature, if not as problems with the theory or the items. SASB-based descriptions and predictions have led to Interpersonal Reconstructive Therapy (IRT), which offers a testable view of connections between early patterns in attachment and specific forms of subsequent psychopathology. IRT has been successful with "treatment resistant" patients, and illustrates the practical importance of going beyond raw empiricism via a testable theory about the nature of nature.

References

American Psychiatric Association. (1980). *Diagnostic and statistical manual of mental disorders* (3rd ed.). Washington, DC: Author.

Barrett, P., & Eysenck, S. (1984). The assessment of personality factors across 25 countries. *Personality and Individual Differences, 5,* 615–632

Benjamin, L. S. (1974). Structural analysis of social behavior (SASB). *Psychological Review 81,* 392–425.

Benjamin, L. S. (1979). Structural analysis of differentiation failure. *Psychiatry: Journal for the Study of Interpersonal Processes, 42,* 1–23.

Benjamin, L. S. (1987). *Use of the SASB dimensional model to develop treatment plans for personality disorders: Vol. I. Narcissism. Journal of Personality Disorders, 1,* 43–70.

Benjamin, L. S. (1996). *Interpersonal diagnosis and treatment of personality disorders* (2nd ed.). New York: Guilford Press. (Paperback ed., 2003)

Benjamin, L. S. (1996). Introduction to the special section on Structural Analysis of Social Behavior (SASB). *Journal of Consulting and Clinical Psychology, 64,* 1203–1212.

Benjamin, L. S. (2000). *SASB user's manual.* Salt Lake City: University of Utah Press.

Benjamin, L. S. (2003). *Interpersonal reconstructive therapy: Promoting change in nonresponders.* New York: Guilford Press. (Paperback edition 2006, with subtitle: *An integrative personality based treatment for complex cases*)

Benjamin, L. S. (2008). What is functional about functional autonomy? *Psychological Assessment, 90,* 412–420.

Benjamin, L. S. (in press). Interpersonal assessment and treatment of personality disorders. In J. Maddux & J. Tanguey (Eds.), *Social foundations of clinical psychology.* New York: Guilford Press.

Benjamin, L. S., & Friedrich, F. (1991). Contributions of Structural Analysis of Social Behavior (SASB) to the bridge between cognitive science and object relations psychotherapy. In M. J. Horowitz (Ed.), *Person schemas and maladaptive interpersonal patterns.* Chicago: University of Chicago Press, 379–412.

Benjamin, L. S., Rothweiler, J. C., & Critchfield, K. L. (2006). Use of Structural Analysis of Social Behavior as an assessment tool. *Annual Review of Clinical Psychology, 2.*

Cloninger, C. R. (1987). A systematic method for clinical description and classification of personality variants. A proposal. *Archives of General Psychiatry, 44,* 573–588.

Costa, P. T., & McCrae, R. R. (1992). Normal personality assessment in clinical practice: The NEO Personality Inventory. *Psychological Assessment, 4,* 5–13.

Critchfield, K. L., & Benjamin, L. S. (2008). Internalized representations of early interpersonal experience and adult relationships: A test of copy process theory in clinical and nonclinical populations. *Psychiatry: Interpersonal and Biological Processes, 71,* 71–92.

Darwin, C. (1952). *The origin of species.* In R. M. Hutchins (Ed.), *Great books of the Western world.* Chicago: Encyclopedia Britannica. (Original work published 1859)

Freedman, M. B., Leary, T. F., Ossorio, A. G., & Coffey, H. S. (1951). The interpersonal dimensions of personality. *Journal of Personality, 20,* 143–161.

Goldman, S. L. (2007). *Great scientific ideas that changed the world.* Chantilly, VA: The Teaching Company, 155 pp.

Gurtman, M. B. (1994). In S. Strack and M. Lorr (Eds.), *Differentiating normal and abnormal personality* (pp. 243–263). New York: Springer.

Guttman, L. (1966). Order analysis of correlation matrixes. In R. B. Cattell (Ed.), *Handbook of multivariate experimental psychology.* Chicago: Rand McNally.

Higgs, D. R., Vernimmen, D., Hughes, J., & Gibbons, R. (2007). Using genomics to study how chromatin influences gene expression, *Annual Review Genomics Human Genetics, 8,* 299–325.

Hume, D. (1748/1947). An enquiry concerning human understanding (Section IV). Reprinted in D. J. Bronstein, Y. H. Krikorian, & P. P. Wiener (Eds.), *Basic Problems of Philosophy.* New York: Prentice-Hall

Humes, D. L., & Humphrey, L. L. (1994). A multimethod analysis of families with a polydrug-dependent or normal adolescent daughter. *Journal of Abnormal Psychology, 103,* 676–685.

Leary, T. (1957). *Interpersonal diagnosis of personality: A functional theory and methodology for personality evaluation.* New York: Ronald Press.

Lorr, M. (1991). A redefinition of dominance. *Personality and Individual Differences, 12,* 877–979.

Lorr, M., & Strack, S. (1999). A study of Benjamin's eight-facet Structural Analysis of Social Behavior (SASB) Model. *Journal of Clinical Psychology, 55,* 207–215

Mischel, W. (1973). On the empirical dilemmas of psychodynamic approaches: Issues and alternatives. *Journal of Abnormal Psychology, 82,* 335–344.

Monson, J. T., van der Lippe, A., Havik, O. E., Halvorsen, M. S., & Eilertsen, D. E. (2007). Validation of the SASB Introject surface in a Clinical and Nonclinical Sample. *Journal of Personality Assessment, 88,* 235–245.

Pincus, A. L., Newes, S. L., Dickinson, K. A., & Ruiz, M. A. (1998). A comparison of three indexes to assess the dimensions of Structural Analysis of Social Behavior. *Journal of Personality Assessment, 70,* 145–170.

Rothweiler, J. C. (2004) An evaluation of the internal and external validity of Intrex and the Interpersonal Adjective Scale. *Dissertation Abstracts International: Section B.*

Schaefer, E. S. (1965). Configurational analysis of children's reports of parent behavior. *Journal of Consulting Psychology, 29,* 552–557.

Watson, J. D., & Crick, F. H. C. (1953). Molecular structure of nucleic acids. *Nature, 171,* 137–138.

Wiggins, J. S. (1982). Circumplex models of interpersonal behavior in clinical psychology. In P. C. Kendall and J. N. Butcher (Eds.), *Handbook of research methods in clinical psychology.* New York: John Wiley & Sons.

Wiggins, J. S., Trapnell, P., & Phillips, N. (1988). Psychometric and geometric characteristics of the Revised Interpersonal Adjective Scales (IAS-R), *Multivariate Behavioral Research, 23,* 517–530.

NOTES

1. Such a situation would also require behaviors shown adjacent to 143 on Figure 20.1 (142, nurturance; 144, consistent structuring of the environment; 145, constructive stimulation)

2. Available from the University of Utah by writing Intrex@psych.utah.edu.

3. This means that the plots of the factor loadings are not necessarily orthogonal, as is often assumed when using principal components factor analysis to argue that factor loadings per se represent underlying dimensions of personality.

4. Varimax rotation maximizes the variance associated with a given factor by assigning it to as few variables as possible. That standard is not logically consistent with circumplex theory, which hypothesizes continuous change in location on the underlying dimensions when moving around the circle. It happens to make little difference in practice, probably because stepwise changes that define progression around the circumplex are in fact the most efficient way of representing the variance.

5. Obviously, Figure 20.1 is not a circle. That is important because the poles of the axes in SASB are qualitatively distinct (primitive basics) from the other points. The uniqueness of the primitive poles is preserved by plotting points in terms of (X, Y) vectors, rather than locating points via the equation for a circle, $x^2 + y^2 = r^2$. Still, factor analysis is the most convenient method for reconstructing the SASB model based on self-ratings, because standard statistical software packages do not work with absolute values, which are required to test the diamond shape exactly.

6. Reasons for this are discussed in a later section headed: SASB items were written to reflect theory directly.

7. An example is Einstein's prediction that light rays are bent by gravity. It was first proved when Eddington and others gathered during an eclipse of the sun to see the apparent "shift" in a distant stars' positions as their light rays bent as they passed through the sun's gravitational field.

8. For example, the NEO-5 theory of personality is said to be "confirmed" by the fact that the same factors emerge in different cultures. The nature of reality

is not involved. When replication is said to confirm a "theory," the confirmation has no reference to an external reality.

9. Darwin was a graduate of a theological school, and an advocate of "natural theology," which holds that science enhances understanding and appreciation of God's work (Goldman, 2007).

10. Varieties of life forms.

11. In fact, any number of perfect circles. Since the only rule is that the $x^2 + y^2 = r$, the radius about any arbitrary origin, circles can vary in size and accompany any origin.

12. Postmodernism holds that there are many ways of "knowing," and there is not necessarily a "reality" to palpate. Postmodernists argue that accepted theories (and we might add in a postmodern environment, methods of knowing) are dominant primarily because they are sponsored by the most charismatic leaders.

13. The components likely have direct neurobiological correlates (Benjamin & Friedrich, 1991).

14. The items describing murder and sexuality are asked of every relationship, including when rating family members, or other "inappropriate" contexts. Despite the clear instruction to score an item "zero" if it does not apply, or to simply skip the item it if offends, responses to the very presence of these primitive realities by reviewers as well as raters have sometimes been quite passionate. A scientist nonetheless needs to explore all possibilities. An experienced clinician knows this is important as the amount of murderousness and sexuality that goes on within families needs discussion.

15. The reading levels of the IAS-R cannot be established because so many of its words do not exist in normal discourse.

For example, for the octant *Aloof, introverted* discussed earlier, half the items are not found in a search of an illustrative dictionary, *Encarta*. These invented words were *uncheery, unneighborly, dissocial, unsparkling*.

16. I have requested all translators to use the dimensional ratings method within the new language to test their items. Translations that are validated instead on "reverse translation" of my English versions do not necessarily adhere to SASB theory.

17. They were paid $20.

18. IAS-R words that describe the polar octants, and are assessed by the dimensional ratings task, appear here in parentheses. Horizontal: "Coldhearted" (uncharitable, ironhearted, unsympathetic, ruthless, coldhearted, cruel, hardhearted, warmthless) and **Warm-Agreeable** (Kind, sympathetic, tender, charitable, tenderhearted, gentlehearted, accommodating, softhearted). Vertical: **Assured-Dominant** (domineering, forceful, dominant, firm, persistent, assertive, self-confident, self-assured) and **Unassured-Submissive** (unaggressive, unbold, unauthoritative, forceless, meek, shy, bashful, timid).

19. Parentlike and childlike items are mixed by the randomly determined order used for all SASB questionnaires.

20. Questionnaires for the IAS-R, a widely used version of the interpersonal circle, present items according to the theoretical structure of the model. Opposites appear on opposite positions on the page; adjacent items follow in successive rows.

21. The full model has many features that evolved from the inherent logic used to write the items. For example, one rarely discussed but clinically powerful feature is the concept of (developmental) "tracks" (Benjamin, 1979).

21

INTERVIEW MEASURES OF INTERPERSONAL FUNCTIONING AND QUALITY OF OBJECT RELATIONS

Henning Schauenburg

Tilman Grande[1]

INTRODUCTION

Firmly established maladaptive interpersonal relationship patterns constitute a central cause of mental illness; those relationship patterns may also sustain mental illness (Strupp & Binder, 1984). Over the course of life, "automatic" relationship patterns (which take on a life of their own) develop from the "deposits" of earlier relationship experiences. Such inner-psychic affective-cognitive schemas are continually confirmed and modified in the process of transacting with other people. These schemas are, to a certain extent, observable and measurable (Anchin & Kiesler, 1982).

The assessment of such object-relation patterns using clinical interviews has a long tradition. A review of the literature reveals two types of instruments. The *first* of these aims to assess dysfunctional relationship patterns based on repetitive figures in interactions between the patient and his or her objects. This involves, for example, evaluating the desires and expectations of the patient, his or her manifest behavior towards others, the response of the object, and the patient's reaction to this response.

This way of "diagnosing a relationship" is generally strongly individualized: The elements can be very specifically determined in each individual case, leading to a wide range of different configurations when the elements are combined. Well-established examples of such approaches include the method of the Core Conflictual Relationship Theme (CCRT) developed by Luborsky and colleagues (Luborsky, 1990a), the Cyclic Maladaptive Pattern (CMP) developed by Strupp & Binder (1991), the Role-Relationship Model Configurations proposed by Horowitz (RRMC; Horowitz, 1991), and the Structural Analysis of Social Behavior (SASB) developed by Benjamin (1974, 1979, 1993; see Chapter 20 in this volume).

Among other benefits, the advantage of such approaches lies in the specificity of the resulting relationship formulations, which often provide a convincing clinical picture and can be used to focus on interpersonal processes in the therapeutic work with the patient. There are additional efforts to identify disorder-specific or group-specific relationship patterns based on empirical findings (e.g., Chance, Bakeman, Kaslow,

Farber, & Burg-Callaway, 2000; Staats, May, Herrmann, Kersting, & König, 1998) or clinical conceptualizations (Benjamin, 1993). The results are again relational forms with varying degrees of complexity that characterize recurrent relationship patterns within a certain patient or diagnosis group. Examples of such group-specific patterns may include, for example, aggressive and manipulative behavior (in the case of borderline patients) to avoid being left alone and sacrificial submission (in the case of some depressive patients) in order to ensure friendly and conflict-free relationships.

The *second* type of instrument for the assessment of object relations is based on dimensional models and evaluates relationships with respect to their functional level. Features that are assessed include, for example, the complexity of object representations, the quality of affect regulation, the regulation of self-esteem, self-cohesion, and relational involvement. The corresponding scales assess the degree of impairment or health. Developmental models of psychological maturity and integration generally form the basis of these instruments. Examples of such instruments include the Social Cognition and Object Relations Scale (SCORS) developed by Westen (1991) and the Quality of Object Relations Scale (QORS) developed by Azim, Duncan, Piper, and colleagues (Azim, Piper, Segal, Nixon, & Duncan, 1991; Piper & Duncan, 1999). A comprehensive summary is provided by Huprich and Greenberg (2003). A dimensional assessment of the quality of object relations is also possible via direct evaluations of countertransference reactions on the part of the clinician; Westen and his associates have also developed a questionnaire for this purpose (Betan, Heim, Cinklin, & Westen, 2005).

In capturing the quality of psychic functioning and the degree of pathology, this latter group of instruments is particularly useful clinically because therapeutic interventions and prognosis greatly depend on the functional and pathological level of the patient's relationships. Designed

as rating scales, these instruments can be economically applied to clinical interviews by trained raters. Compared to this procedure, the individualized assessment of repetitive interaction patterns described above is rather laborious. Furthermore, because they are based on a dimensional model, the second group of instruments offers a comparably wider range of possibilities for statistical analyses.

The two approaches complement one another in a useful way; the assessment of dysfunctional, repetitive patterns allows an evaluation of problematic internal working models of interpersonal relationships that the patient recurrently activates in his or her encounters with other people (Binder, 2004; Horowitz, 1994; Weiss, Sampson, & Mount Zion Group, 1986), while evaluating the quality of object relations draws attention to the psychological resources and skills that (a) can be used by the patient for relational regulation and (b) determine his or her interpersonal mode of functioning (Rudolf 2002; Westen 1991). In our view, gaining a comprehensive all-around picture of a relational disorder necessitates a consideration of both of these perspectives.

The Operationalized Psychodynamic Diagnostics (OPD) system systematically pursues such a twofold representation of relationships (OPD Task Force, 2001, 2007). The OPD Task Force was founded by a group of psychoanalysts, specialists in psychosomatic medicine, and psychiatrists with a background in psychotherapy research in Germany in 1992. The goal of the group was to broaden the descriptive and symptom-oriented ICD-10 classification system to include fundamental psychodynamic dimensions. This working group developed a diagnostic inventory and a handbook designed for training and clinical purposes for experienced therapists. Since then, the manual has been translated into many languages and is widely used in China, Italy, Spain, Chile, and Hungary. Further translations are in preparation.

The OPD system is based on four psychodynamically relevant diagnostic axes. These axes complement ICD classification, which is included as a fifth axis:

Axis I: Experience of illness and prerequisites for treatment
Axis II: Interpersonal relations
Axis III: Conflicts
Axis IV: Structure
Axis V: Mental and psychosomatic disorder (according to Chapter V [F] of the ICD-10)

With the help of a 1- to 2-hour patient examination, the clinician (or external observer) evaluates the patient's psychodynamics according to the requirements of the OPD. Interview guidelines ensure that relevant information is obtained in a standardized way. As will be shown below, Axes II and IV are suitable for a clinical evaluation of relationships in terms of the twofold perspective presented above.

THE OPD AXIS "INTERPERSONAL RELATIONS"

The diagnosis of relationships using the OPD is based on the patient's description of his or her relationships during the OPD interview, as well as on the observable, direct, interpersonal behavior manifested during the interview. Interview guidelines prompt exploration of the patient's accounts of encounters with other people in such a way that differentiated and reasonably complete relationship episodes emerge in line with Luborsky (1990b). For example, patients may be asked to elaborate on what the relationship to a significant other is like, what the important fears in this relationship are, or how they feel in typical interactions with important persons. Moreover, the interviewer must also observe the patient-interviewer patterns of interaction. Diagnostic judgments are made by extracting typical (i.e., repetitive) dysfunctional patterns from both of these information sources. Guidance in describing these patterns can be found in the OPD manual.

Two central aspects must be considered when diagnostically assessing relationship *patterns*: (1) The method must provide a matrix depicting the "circular" or "transactional" nature of human interaction. That is, it must describe the interplay between (a) subjective behavior and experience and (b) responses from the environment. And (2) there must be enough relationship dimensions described to cover the diversity of human behavior at a reasonably representative level.

Schacht and Henry's (1994) version of the Cyclic Maladaptive Patterns (CMP) is one example of a circular matrix. The maladaptive patterns describe a self-reinforcing figure of interpersonal pathological beliefs, behaviors resulting from these beliefs, and object reactions that in turn confirm the original beliefs. Benjamin's (1974) Structural Analysis of Social Behavior (SASB) is used for the standardized representation of interactional activity. Another well-established method is that of the Central Conflictual Relationship Pattern (CCRT) developed by Luborsky (1990a). This method describes problematic interpersonal transactions as sequences comprising wishes directed towards the object, the reactions of the object, and the ensuing reactions of the subject. Category systems and rating instruments have also been developed for the standardized assessment of these components (Albani, Kächele, Pokorny, & Blaser, 2008; Crits-Christoph, Demorest, & Connolly, 1990).

This approach is adopted by the OPD Task Force, but the method also includes an additional distinction: The patient's relational behavior is evaluated from two perspectives (see Figure 21.1). The first level involves an examination of the way in which patients experience themselves and other people within relationships: What is their experience of what other people do to them within interpersonal encounters, and how do they describe their own behavior towards others? The second level allows a representation from the perspective of another person interacting with the patient.

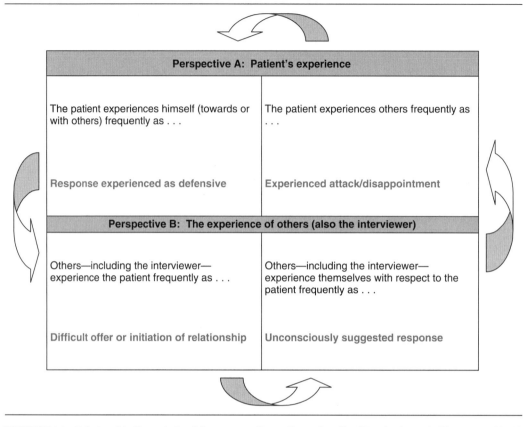

FIGURE 21.1   Relationship Formulation Schema according to Operationalized Psychodynamic Diagnostics (OPD)

Assessment at this level is based on the interviewer's experiences: What is the interviewer's experience of the patient (a clue to what the patient's significant others experience), and what impulses get generated (also a clue to the reactions of significant others)?

The authors consider the representation of transference, from the interviewer's perspective, to be of particular clinical importance. In evaluating this transference, the interviewer must be careful, however, to consider not only his or her own impulses and affective responses to the patient but also the reactions of other persons interacting with the patient as far as these can be gleaned from the patient's accounts (cf. OPD Task Force, 2007, pp. 144–145).

Integrating both of these perspectives enables the clinician or researcher to construct a transactional maladaptive pattern

(see Figure 21.1). The figure depicts cyclic links between the four fields representing the perspectives mentioned above. From the perspective of the patient's experience (top row), the sequence of events typically unfolds from right to left: The patient describes the recurrent relational acts of others that he or she experiences as disappointing or hostile and to which he or she must *respond*. From the perspective of others and the interviewer, events occur the other way around: That which the patient portrays as his or her *reaction* to the object instead appears to represent a problematic *offer* or initiation of a relationship that challenges and entangles the interaction partner. The third link connects the bottom two fields from left to right. The patient's way of relating tends to induce certain reactions that are experienced as feelings, fantasies, and impulses. The interviewer can subsequently consider the following question: *How would the patient experience my giving in to those impulses that he or she induces when beginning a relationship?* Would the patient perceive my behavior in exactly the same way that he or she recurrently experiences the behavior of others? These questions pertain to the fourth link that connects the bottom and top right-hand fields. If this connection can be coherently made, then reconstruction of the dynamics of the patient's relational interactions is complete. This reconstruction describes a self-reinforcing circle and reveals how the patient's ways of relating provoke the very reactions that the patient fears and tries to avoid.

As is also the case for other methods (e.g., Schacht & Henry, 1994), the OPD describes interactional behavior dimensionally by drawing upon the tradition of interpersonal circular models. These models represent human behavior using the dimensions *affection/communion* and *control/agency* (Benjamin, 1974, see also Chapter 20 in this volume; Kiesler, 1983). The OPD axis "interpersonal relations" is based on a list of items with 32 circularly arranged behaviors generated from the circumplex model. These are used to describe the two above-mentioned perspectives (OPD Task Force, 2008, Section 4.2.3). Based on the cyclic model depicted in Figure 21.1, these two perspectives are then combined to produce an integrative formulation comprising the reported behaviors of the patient and his or her significant others, the patient's relational "invitations," and the potential reactions of interaction partners. This formulation is more than a mere description of that which occurs within the patient's relationships; it deepens and expands the observed into a dynamic understanding (cf. Grande, Rudolf, & Jakobsen, 2004).

In summary, the procedure adopted by the OPD distinguishes itself from that employed by other instruments such as the CCRT with respect to its incorporation of the interviewer's experience and the empirical use of this experience in reconstructing a transactional pattern. It enables clinicians to reflect further upon their own experience and countertransference impulses, and to describe these reactions systematically in a structured manner that is based upon clinical evidence. Users of the instrument have found the procedure to be important and extremely helpful.

PSYCHOMETRIC PROPERTIES OF THE INTERPERSONAL RELATIONS AXIS

Reliability

Due to the complexity of diagnosing relationships using the OPD, an evaluation of its psychometric properties poses some difficulties. For the interpersonal relations axis, a weighted kappa approach is appropriate. In examining the reliability of the OPD, a procedure corresponding to that described by Grawe-Gerber and Benjamin (1989) for the SASB method has been employed. One study revealed moderate item-level kappa coefficients ranging from 0.56 to 0.62 (Stasch et al., 2002).

Validity

The diagnostic window of the interpersonal relations axis of the OPD, in particular, pertains to dysfunctions in interpersonal behavior. Cierpka et al. (1998) using Luborsky's CCRT demonstrated a positive association between rigidity of interpersonal wishes and degree of psychopathology. In an OPD-based study, 100 psychotherapy inpatients were examined regarding change in interpersonal flexibility based on the "behavior cluster" contained in the OPD circumplex model (Stasch & Cierpka, 2000). Diagnostic subgroups were individually compared before and after therapy, and correlations with the outcome of interpersonal distancing problems were calculated. For patients with affective disorders and those with adjustment disorders, an increase in interpersonal flexibility was found to be positively associated with symptomatic improvement. For patients with anxiety disorders, symptomatic improvement correlated negatively with flexibility. This can be interpreted as an increase in self-awareness and personal independence. Successful patients with anxiety disorders seem to have learned to become less dependent on the reactions and bids of others and are more able to follow their individual goals. These results show that certain relational-diagnostic facets of the OPD are able to discriminate between different diagnostic groups with respect to symptomatic outcomes.

The diagnosis of "interpersonal relations" on the OPD is based on the circumplex model of interpersonal behavior. This model represents a nomological network that can be used for construct validation. As methods that have been demonstrated to be valid for this criterion area, the Inventory of Interpersonal Problems (Horowitz, Rosenberg, Baer, Ureno, & Villasenor, 1988; German version, Horowitz, Straus, & Kordy, 2000) has been used to test concurrent validity of the OPD (in the sense of internal, criterion-related validity). The resulting validity coefficients have proven acceptable for a comparison of a self- versus observer-rated method (Stasch et al., 2004). This study also showed that the majority of the OPD relationship axis clusters are construct-conforming; that is, they possess specific interpersonal content, and they form a circular pattern when they are plotted on a two-dimensional graph (Stasch et al., 2004). A further study addressed the question concerning the degree to which the OPD relationship diagnosis and the independent results of the SASB correspond with the relationship episodes represented in the OPD interviews. Agreement between the OPD relationship diagnosis and the SASB ratings of the individual episodes were found to be greater than expected by chance (Leising, Stadler, Grande & Rudolf, 2000).

An elaborate test of the validity of the "interpersonal relations" axis of the OPD is currently being developed (Zimmermann et al., 2009). The authors constructed a Q-sort instrument based on the items of the OPD axis for patients and clinicians to assess typical versus non-typical patterns of interpersonal behavior. This is a feasible way to cope with the statistical and methodological problems when using circumplex item lists. In a first study Zimmermann et al. showed good interrater reliability of the measure, adequate variance of the individual profiles in the Q-sort, and good concurrent validity with the IIP (19 to 57% of IIP subscale variance explained by the OPD-Q-sort).

THE OPD AXIS "STRUCTURE"

Successful relationships require certain sociocommunicative skills and self-regulating capacities. The OPD structure axis provides an instrument to assess the availability of these skills and capacities with the help of a clinical interview. The concept of "structure" in the OPD is rooted in a developmental psychological model that is based on the work of Emde (1981), Fonagy (Fonagy et al., 2002; Fonagy & Target, 1997), Gergely (2002), Grossmann (Grossmann et al., 1989), Lichtenberg (1983), Papousek (1989), and Stern (1985, 1995). The structure of the self and that of the object relations develop in a closely intertwined manner. Over the course of development, the self progressively gains in coherence, differentiation, and the ability to self-organize. Attachment to others is concomitantly strengthened. Secure attachment to others favorably influences the development of self-autonomy, which in turn leads to the strengthened self beginning to detach itself from the objects and learning to deal with stressful situations by internalized self-regulating abilities This development results in a self that has formed a sense of identity, is capable of regulating its self-image and self-worth, and is able to regulate interpersonal behaviour in ever new ways.

According to the OPD, structural functions can thus not only be linked to the inner world of the psyche, but also to the external world of social relationships, that is, to both self and objects. Structure is therefore described along four dimensions, each of which distinguishes between the relationship to the self and the relationship to others.

1. Perception of self and objects

   Ability at self-perception
   Ability at object perception

2. Self-regulation and regulation of relationships

   Ability to regulate own impulses, affects, and self-worth
   Ability to regulate relations to others

3. Emotional internal communication and communication with the external world

   Ability to communicate internally via affects and fantasies
   Ability to communicate with others

4. Attachment capacity: Internal and external objects

   Ability to employ good internal objects for self-regulation
   Ability to attach and detach

Each of these eight primary scales contains three subscales, which form the basis to assess concrete and clinically relevant traits. For example, "Perception of self" consists of subscales that describe the ability to reflect upon oneself, to differentiate one's own affects, and to develop and maintain a sense of identity, "Ability to regulate relations to others" consists of scales for the abilities to protect relationships from one's own disturbing impulse, to maintain one's own interest and take account of those of others, and to develop a realistic picture of others. The Scale "Ability to communicate with others" comprises the competency to make emotional contact, express one's affects, let one be reached by the affects of others, and the capability for empathy. The description of the other subscales can be found in the OPD manual. Four levels of structural integration are distinguished for all these aspects. These are designated

as "high, moderate, low, and disintegrated integration" and also are described and graded in the OPD manual. Intermediate levels are also possible so that the eight aspects are rated on a seven-point Likert scale. A ninth scale is used to rate overall structural integration. A general description of the integration levels (which does not specifically refer to the individual dimensions) is provided in Table 21.1.

Assessment is based on the OPD interview described above. The interview examines patient-reported interactions and life experiences. Assessment also draws on the abilities the patient shows in interacting with the interviewer, the countertransference experienced by the interviewer, and the patient's introspective assessment of himself and his or her behavior revealed via enquiry or spontaneous utterances.

PSYCHOMETRIC PROPERTIES
OF THE "STRUCTURE" AXIS

Reliability

Reliability of the OPD Axis IV was investigated in a study with 269 patients from six psychosomatic clinics (Cierpka et al., 2001). Due to variation in rater conditions across clinics, this study was also able to examine which conditions led to improved reliability. Weighted kappas (Cohen, 1968) were used as a measure of reliability, and weights were determined based on the assumption of equal distance between each of the four levels of the rating scales. Obtained kappa values could thus be interpreted in a similar manner to Pearson correlation coefficients (Fleiss & Cohen, 1973).

Video-recorded interviews conducted for diagnostic purposes were independently rated and showed good reliability: In two of six clinics video-recorded interviews conducted for diagnostic purposes were independently rated and showed good reliability, with mean reliability values for all structural dimensions of 0.70 or 0.71.[2] These values approximately correspond to the results of an earlier OPD practicability

TABLE 21.1   Description of Levels of Structural Integration

1	High	Relatively autonomous self; well-structured internal psychic space in which intrapsychic conflicts may arise; capacity for self-reflection and reality-based perception of others; capacity for self-regulation; capacity for empathy; sufficiently good internal objects.
		Central fear: fear of losing care and attention of the object
1.5	High to moderate	
2	Moderate	Intrapsychic conflicts are more destructive; self-devaluing and auto-destructive tendencies; difficulty gaining self-image and identity; overregulation and reduced self-worth regulation; object images are limited to a few patterns; reduced ability to empathize; dyadic relationships predominate.
		Central fear: fear of losing the important object
2.5	Moderate to low	
3	Low	Little developed internal space and very limited differentiation of mental substructures; conflicts are interpersonal rather than intrapsychic; absence of self-reflection; identity diffusion; intolerance of negative affects; impulsive outbreaks and high sensitivity to being emotionally hurt or injured; defense; splitting, idealization, devaluation; lack of empathy and limited capacity for communication; internal objects are predominantly persecutory and punishing.
		Central fear: annihilation of the self through loss of the good object or through the bad object
3.5	Low to disintegrated	
4	Disintegrated	Lack of coherence of the self and floods of emotions are covered up by defensive patterns in the sense of postpsychotic, posttraumatic, or perverse forms of organization; self and object images appear confounded; empathic perception of the object is almost impossible; responsibility for own impulsive actions is not experienced (things just happen). Central fear: symbiotic merging of self- and object-representations leading to loss of self.

study conducted by Michels and colleagues (Michels, Siebel, Freyberger, Schönell, & Dilling, 2001), which was also conducted under routine clinical conditions. In another clinic, ratings were also made on the basis of videotaped interviews; however, the raters were clinically inexperienced students. Here, mean reliability for the structure axis was 0.55. Since these students had participated in systematic, standardized training, clinical inexperience can be assumed to be disadvantageous with respect to the reliability of OPD ratings. However, the results were still better than when the research interviews were squeezed into the clinical routine.

In a more recent study (Benecke et al., 2009), 139 individuals (comprising a diagnostically heterogeneous group of 120 patients and 19 healthy controls) were rated by three raters under research conditions.

Across all structure dimensions, a mean weighted kappa of 0.68 (ranging from 0.50 to 0.83) was obtained and a value of 0.72 for total structure ratings.

According to Fleiss (1981) and Cicchetti (1994), kappa values between 0.60 and 0.74 can be considered good. Therefore, in summary, the reliability of Axis IV is good when ratings are based on interviews conducted under research conditions.

Validity

An extensive review of the validity of the OPD structure axis can be found in Cierpka, Grande, Rudolf, von der Tann, and Stasch (2007). The studies reported below specifically refer to investigations that relate the structure axis to measures of disorder severity.

Schauenburg (2000) investigated the correlation between attachment security and structural integration in 49 consecutively admitted psychotherapy inpatients. Two measures were associated with a better structural level—secure attachment and excessive striving for rationality and independence. And three measures were associated with a poorer structural level—borderline traits, excessive dismissive and autonomous tendencies, and antisocial traits. In the same sample, Grütering and Schauenburg (2000) compared the Karolinska Psychodynamic Profile scales (Weinryb & Rössel, 1991) with the dimensions of the structure axis of the OPD rated by independent judges; they found the expected content-related correlations.

Grande, Schauenburg, and Rudolf (2002) compared the Scales of Psychological Capacities (SPC) developed by Wallerstein (1988) with structural characteristics measured using the OPD. Numerous associations were observed, as expected due to conceptual similarities of both instruments: for example, a significant correlation between the SPC scale "persistence" and the OPD dimension "self-control." Furthermore, low structure level measured using the OPD was significantly related to the SPC scales "emotional blunting" and "rarely able to rely on others." These two items relate to the interpersonal capacity of a person more than other items of the SPC, and are therefore especially associated with the theoretical concept of the OPD structure axis (which places the capabilities and vulnerabilities of the self in relation to others at the center of the structural analysis).

Based on a sample of 135 individuals (120 patients with varying diagnoses and 15 without mental disorders), Benecke et al. (2009) investigated the relationship between the OPD structure axis and the Inventory of Personality Organization (IPO; Clarkin, Foelsch, & Kernberg, 2000). Those investigators found consistently significant correlations between the individual scales of the structure axis and the total structure scale of the IPO, ranging from .40 to .51, and a correlation of .54 between the total scale of the OPD structure axis and that of the IPO. Both

the individual scales and the total scale of the OPD structure axis correlated even more highly with the number of diagnosed personality disorders (Axis II of DSM-IV). The correlation between total OPD structure and the number of diagnoses was $r = .64$.

In an investigation conducted by Müller, Kaufhold, Overbeck, and Grabhorn (2006), associations were found between the OPD structure axis and the Reflective Functioning Scale (RF Scale) developed by Fonagy and coworkers (Fonagy, Target, H. Steele, & Steele, 1998) in a sample of 24 (female) patients. The significant correlation between the measure of OPD total structure and the RF Scale was $r = .51$; as expected, high correlations were also found between the RF Scale and the individual scales of self-perception ($r = .54$) and communication (.52).

Diagnostic evaluation using the structure axis at the beginning of inpatient treatment was shown to be a significant predictor of treatment success, as judged by both the patient ($r = 0.30$) and the therapist ($r = 0.40$, Rudolf, Grande, Oberbracht, and Jakobsen, 1996). The study indicated that bonding capacity is especially relevant for predicting treatment outcome: For patient-ratings, $r = 0.42$; for therapist-ratings, $r = 0.46$. The capacity to imbue others with positive affect is often a good predictor of therapeutic success.

Finally, we mention a study conducted by Grande, Rudolf, and Oberbracht (1998) in which associations between the OPD Axis II "Interpersonal relations" and Axis IV "Structure" were examined in a sample of 81 patients. Two extreme groups with high and low structural level were formed, and comparisons were made with respect to the frequency with which the various circumplex octants were chosen in the course of the item selection (for details, see the earlier section on the OPD interpersonal relations axis). Relational acts of devaluation and withdrawal co-occurred more often in the group with low structural integration, whereas modes of protection and clinging co-occurred more often in the group with high structural integration.

DISCUSSION

In this overview, we have distinguished between instruments that are available for assessing (a) interpersonal functioning and (b) the quality of object relations. The difference between them depends on whether they evaluate transactional patterns between the patient and others or levels of interpersonal functioning. The Operationalized Psychodynamic Diagnostics (OPD) system combines both types of measures. From a clinical perspective, these aspects complement one another: Understanding a patient's relationship patterns lays the foundation for therapeutic work with an interpersonal focus (Luborsky, 1988; Strupp & Binder, 1984), while insight into the degree of a relational disorder provides important information regarding the general prognosis and therapeutic modifications that might be necessary as compared to standard psychodynamic treatment (Kernberg, 1989; Rudolf, 2006). These two levels of relationship-disorder assessment are only moderately correlated (Grande, Rudolf, & Oberbracht, 1998), since the focus is placed in one case on the relational *form* and in the other on the *intensity* of functional impairment: If, for example, a patient recurrently has the feeling that he or she is "ignored" by others, then the focus points to a problematic pattern without providing more precise information as to whether "being ignored" is simply "disappointing" (against the backdrop of a desire for closeness), or whether it possesses a "destructive" quality (accompanied by a paranoid perception of the object). The latter case would clearly be representative of a low level of interpersonal functioning.

Another unique aspect is the explicit use of countertransference in the construction of an individualized cyclic-maladaptive relationship pattern on Axis II of the OPD. As described previously, the question to be addressed concerns the way in which the patient would experience the interviewer's yielding to those impulses that arise in connection with the patient's specific way of initiating a relationship. Would he or she perceive the interviewer's response in the very same way that he or she recurrently experiences the behavior of others? If the association between perceptions of the interviewer's response and experiences with respect to the behavior of others is coherent, then the interviewer/therapist has gained direct insight into the self-fulfilling nature of the patient's interpersonal fears and at the same time begun to understand the damaging role that he or she is intended to play within this cyclic pattern.

Such insights can be used in a variety of ways in the therapeutic work with the patient. For instance, "traps" or tests, as described by Weiss et al. (1986), can be discovered and anticipated within the transference relationship. On the one hand, from a psychodynamic perspective, the desires and fears that lie beneath the patient's invitations to form a relationship motivate his or her dysfunctional behavior. On the other hand, from a structural viewpoint, the patient's deficits and vulnerabilities hinder his or her ability to regulate relationships (e.g., handicaps in self- and object- perception; impulsivity; vulnerability of self-esteem and self-coherence; perception, differentiation and regulation of one's own affect; and much more). The OPD Task Force (2007) provides guidelines regarding how these diagnostic findings can be used for the planning of therapy and the selection of therapeutic foci.

The clinical assessment of interpersonal patterns is thus, in our eyes, a central component of diagnostic indicators that provide guidance to therapists in treating patients. A certain degree of vagueness is associated with the fact that the diagnostic findings may potentially depend on the respective interviewer, especially when countertransference is systematically drawn upon for assessment purposes (Hamilton & Kivlighan, 2009). Also, while the interpersonal relations axis of the OPD assumes the presence of one central dysfunctional pattern, a single patient may have different patterns that are activated by specific situation or person characteristics. The obtrusiveness of a particular pattern—or conversely, the flexibility of interpersonal behavior—may in turn depend on the degree of the patient's functional impairment in terms of the OPD structure axis. It is precisely with respect to such associations that we consider the OPD particularly promising—with the simultaneous diagnosis of relational pattern and the degree of structural impairment.

In appraising the strengths of the OPD, it is necessary to mention its limitations. In the balancing act between validity and reliability, the interpersonal relations axis, in particular, is weighted to the detriment of reliability. Irrespective of its heuristic use in clinical applications, this limitation also limits the validity of the OPD in the context of research projects. Recent progress in the development of a Q-sort based version of the axis, however, is promising for future studies.

A further problem is that the OPD—and the assessment of interpersonal patterns of interaction in particular—are often too time-consuming. Efforts are necessary to develop short-form instruments and to compile frequent and typical global patterns; these aspects are currently being examined by the OPD group.

To sum up our overview, we think that there are important research perspectives in the field of interview-based interpersonal assessment. Researchers should continue developing empirically based prototype patterns for clinical use and in defining core features of structural (in)abilities, which will be clinically essential for the diagnosis of personality (disorders). Clinical interviews in psychiatry in general should be trying to capture basic interpersonal features, and the methods mentioned in this chapter can be helpful in this endeavor.

References

Albani, C., Kächele, H., Pokorny, D., & Blaser, G. (2008). *Beziehungsmuster und Beziehungskonflikte—Theorie, Klinik und* *Forschung* (eBook). Göttingen: Vandenhoeck & Ruprecht.

Anchin, J. C. & Kiesler, D. J. (1982). *Handbook of interpersonal psychotherapy.* New York: Pergamon.

Azim, H. F., Piper, W. E., Segal, P. M., Nixon, G. W. H., & Duncan, S. (1991). The Quality of Object Relations Scale. *Bulletin of the Menninger Clinic, 55,* 323–343.

Benecke, C., Koschier, A., Peham, D., Bock, A., Dahlbender, R. W., Biebl, W., & Doering, S. (2009). Erste Ergebnisse zu Reliabilität und Validität der OPD-2 Strukturachse. *Zeitischrift für Psychosomatik, Medizinische Psychologie und Psychotherapie, 55,* 84–96.

Benjamin, L. S. (1974). A structural analysis of social behavior (SASB). *Psychological Review, 81,* 392–425.

Benjamin, L. S. (1979). Use of structural analysis of social behavior (SASB) and Markov chains to study dyadic interactions. *Journal of Abnormal Psychology, 88,* 303–319.

Benjamin, L. S. (1993). *Interpersonal diagnosis and treatment of personality disorders.* New York/ London: Guilford Press.

Betan, E., Heim, A. K., Conklin, C. Z., & Westen, D. (2005). Countertransference phenomena and personality pathology in clinical practice: An empirical investigation. *American Journal of Psychiatry, 162,* 890–898.

Binder, J. L. (2004). *Key competencies in brief dynamic psychotherapy.* New York:, Guilford Press.

Chance, S., Bakeman, R., Kaslow, N., Farber, E., & Burg-Callaway, K. (2000). Core conflictual relationship themes in patients diagnosed with borderline personality disorder who attempted or who did not attempt suicide. *Psychotherapy Research, 10,* 337–350.

Cicchetti, D. V. (1994). Guidelines, criteria, and rules of thumb for evaluating normed and standardized assessment instruments in psychology. *Psychological Assessment, 6,* 284–290.

Cierpka, M., Grande, T., Stasch, M., Oberbracht, C., Schneider, W., Schüssler, G., & Heuft, G. (2001). Zur Validität der Operationalisierten Psychodynamischen Diagnostik (OPD). *Psychotherapeut, 46,* 122–133.

Cierpka, M., Strack, M., Benninghoven, D., Staats, H., Dahlbender, R., Pokorny, D., & Frevert, G. (1998). Stereotypical relationship patterns and psychopathology. *Psychotherapy and Psychosomatics, 67,* 241–248.

Cierpka, M., Grande, T., Rudolf, G., von der Tann, M., & Stasch, M. (2007). The Operationalized

Psychodynamic Diagnostics System: Clinical relevance, reliability and validity. *Psychopathology, 40*, 209–220.

Clarkin, J. F., Foelsch, P. A., & Kernberg, O. F. (2000). *Inventory of Personality Organization*. New York: Weill Medical College of Cornell University.

Cohen, J. (1968). Weighted kappa: Nominal scale agreement with provision for scaled disagreement or partial credit. *Psychological Bulletin, 70*, 213–220.

Crits-Christoph, P., Demorest, A., & Connolly, M. B. (1990). Quantitative assessment of interpersonal themes over the course of psychotherapy. *Psychotherapy, 27*, 513–522.

Cierpka, M., Grande, T., Rudolf, G., von der Tann, M., & Stasch, M. (2007). The Operationalized Psychodynamic Diagnostics System: Clinical relevance, reliability and validity. *Psychopathology. 40*, 209–220.

Emde, R. M. (1981). Changing models of infancy and the nature of early development: Remodelling the foundations. *Journal of the American Psychoanalytic Association, 29*, 179–219.

Fleiss, J. L., & Cohen, J. (1973). The equivalence of weighted kappa and the intraclass correlation coefficient as measures of reliability. *Educational and Psychological Measurement, 33*, 613–619.

Fleiss, J. L. (1981). *Statistical methods for rates and proportions* (2nd ed.). New York: John Wiley & Sons.

Fonagy, P., Gergely, G., Jurist, E. L., & Target, M. (2002). *Affect regulation, mentalization, and the development of the self*. New York: Other Press.

Fonagy, P., &, Target, M. (1997). Attachment and reflective function: The role in self-organization. *Development and Psychopathology, 9*, 679–700.

Fonagy, P., Target, M., Steele, H., & Steele, M. (1998). *Reflective Functioning manual. Version 5: for application to Adult Attachment Interviews*. Unpublished manual, University College, London.

Gergely, G. (2002). Ein neuer Zugang zu Margaret Mahler: Normaler Autismus, Symbiose, Spaltung, libidinöse Objektkonstanz aus der Perspektive der kognitiven Entwicklungspsychologie. *Psyche, 56*, 8009–8038.

Grande, T., Rudolf, G., & Oberbracht, C. (1998). Die Strukturachse der Operationalisierten Psychodynamischen Diagnostik (OPD)— Forschungsergebnisse zum Konzept und zur klinischen Anwendung. *Persönlichkeitsstörungen: Theorie und Therapie, 2*, 173–182.

Grande, T., Schauenburg, H., & Rudolf, G. (2002). Zum Begriff der "Struktur" in verschiedenen Operationalisierungen. In G. Rudolf, T. Grande, & P. Henningsen (Eds), *Die Struktur der Persönlichkeit. Vom theoretischen Verständnis zur therapeutischen Anwendung des psychodynamischen Strukturkonzepts* (pp. 177–196). Stuttgart: Schattauer.

Grande, T., Rudolf, G., & Jakobsen, T. (2004). Beziehungsdynamische Fallformulierung, Fokusbildung und Interventionsplanung auf der Grundlage der OPD-Beziehungsdiagnostik. In R.W. Dahlbender, P. Buchheim, & G. Schüssler (Eds.), *Lernen an der Praxis. OPD und Qualitätssicherung in der Psychodynamischen Psychotherapie* (pp. 95–109). Bern: Huber.

Grawe-Gerber, M., & Benjamin, L. S. (1989). *Structural Analysis of Social Behavior: Coding manual for psychotherapy research*. Forschungsberichte aus dem Psychologischen Institut der Universität Bern.

Grossmann, K. E., Becker-Stoll, F., Grossmann, K., Kindler, H., Schiechem, M., Spengler, G., ... Zimmermann, P. (1989). Die Bindungstheorie. Modell und entwicklungspsychologische Forschung. In H. Keller (Ed.), *Handbuch der Kleinkindforschung* (pp. 51–95). Heidelberg: Springer.

Grütering, T., &, Schauenburg, H. (2000). Die Erfassung psychodynamisch relevanter Persönlichkeitsmerkmale Vergleich zweier klinischer Instrumente: Karolinska Psychodynamic Profile (KAPP) und OPD–Strukturachse. In M. Bassler (Ed.), *Leitlinien in der stationären Psychotherapie: Pro und Kontra* (pp. 115–137). Giessen: Psychosozial Verlag.

Hamilton, J., & Kivlighan, D. (2009). Therapists' projection: The effects of therapists' relationship themes on their formulation of clients' relationship episodes. *Psychotherapy Research, 19* (3), 312–322.

Horowitz, M. (1989). Relationship schema formulation: Role-relationship models and intrapsychic conflict. *Psychiatry, 52*, 260–274.

Horowitz, M. J. (1991). Person schemas. In M. J. Horowitz (Ed.), *Person schemas and maladaptive interpersonal patterns* (pp. 13–31). Chicago/ London: University of Chicago Press.

Horowitz, L. M. (1994). Personenschemata, Psychopathologie und Psychotherapieforschung. *Psychotherapeut*, *39*, 61–72.

Horowitz, L. M., Rosenberg, S. E., Baer, B. A., Ureno, G., & Villasenor, V. S. (1988). Inventory of Interpersonal Problems: Psychometric properties and clinical applications. *Journal of Consulting and Clinical Psychology*, *56*, 885–892.

Horowitz, L. M., Strauss, B., & Kordy, H. (2000). *Inventar zu Erfassung interpersonaler Probleme* (2. Aufl.) (*Inventory of Interpersonal Problems*, 2nd ed.). Göttingen, Germany: Beltz.

Huprich, S. K., & Greenberg, R. P. (2003). Advances in the assessment of object relations in the 1990s. *Clinical Psychology Review*, *23*, 665–698.

Kernberg, O. F. (1989). *Psychodynamic psychotherapy of borderline patients*. New York: Basic Books.

Kiesler, D. J. (1983). The 1982 Interpersonal Circle: A taxonomy for complementarity in human transactions. *Psychological Review*, *90*, 185–214.

Leising, D., Stadler, K., Grande, T., & Rudolf G. (2000). *Lassen sich intrapsychische Konflikte anhand unterschiedlicher "Leitaffekte" unterscheiden? Eine Validierungsstudie zur OPD-Achse III*. Poster präsentiert auf der Tagung OPD in research and practice, Ulm, September 28–30, 2000.

Lichtenberg, J. D. (1983). *Psychoanalysis and infant research*. Hillsdale/London: Analytic Press.

Luborsky, L. (1988). *Einführung in die analytische Psychotherapie. Ein Lehrbuch*. Berlin: Springer.

Luborsky, L. (1990a). A guide to the CCRT method. In L. Luborsky & P. Crits-Christoph (Eds.), *Understanding transference* (pp. 15–36). New York: Basic Books.

Luborsky, L. (1990b). The Relationship Anecdote Paradigm (RAP) Interview as a versatile source of narratives. In L. Luborsky & P. Crits-Christoph (Eds.), *Understanding transference* (pp. 102–113). New York: Basic Books.

Michels, R., Siebel, U., Freyberger, H. J., Schönell, H., & Dilling, H. (2001). Evaluation of the multiaxial system of ICD-10 (preliminary draft): Correlations between multiaxial assessment and clinical judgements of aetiology, treatment indication and prognosis. *Psychopathology*, *34*, 69–74.

Müller, C., Kaufhold, J., Overbeck, G., & Grabhorn, R. (2006). The importance of reflective functioning to the diagnosis of psychic structure. *Psychology and Psychotherapy: Theory, Research, and Practice*, *79*, 485–494.

OPD Task Force (Eds.) (2001). *Operationalized Psychodynamic Diagnosis (OPD): Foundations and manual*. Kirkland: Hogrefe & Huber.

OPD Task Force (Eds.) (2007). *Operationalized Psychodynamic Diagnosis (OPD-2): Manual of diagnosis and treatment planning*. Göttingen: Hogrefe & Huber.

Papousek, M. (1989). Frühe Phase der Eltern-Kind-Beziehung. *Praxis der Psychotherapie und Psychosomatik*, *34*, 109–122.

Piper, W. E., & Duncan, S. C. (1999). Object relations theory and short-term dynamic psychotherapy: Findings from the Quality of Object Relations Scale. *Clinical Psychology Review*, *19*, 669–685.

Rudolf, G. (2002). Struktur als psychodynamisches Konzept der Persönlichkeit. Vom theoretischen Verständnis zur therapeutischen Anwendung des psychodynamischen Strukturkonzepts. In G. Rudolf, T. Grande, & P. Henningsen (Eds.), *Die Struktur der Persönlichkeit* (pp. 2–48). Stuttgart: Schattauer.

Rudolf, G. (2006). *Strukturbezogene Psychotherapie. Leitfaden zur psychodynamischen Therapie struktureller Störungen*. Stuttgart/New York: Schattauer.

Rudolf, G., Grande, T., Oberbracht, C., & Jakobsen, T. (1996). Erste empirische Untersuchungen zu einem neuen diagnostischen System: Die Operationalisierte Psychodynamische Diagnostik (OPD). *Zeitschrift für Psychosomatische Medizin und Psychoanalyse*, *42*, 343–357.

Schacht, T. E., & Henry, W.P. (1994). Modeling recurrent patterns of interpersonal relationship with Structural Analysis of Social Behavior: The SASB-CMP. *Psychotherapy Research*, *4*, 208–221.

Schauenburg, H. (2000). Zum Verhältnis zwischen Bindungsdiagnostik und psychodynamischer Diagnostik. In W. Schneider & H. W. Freyberger (Eds.), *Was leistet die OPD? Empirische Befunde und klinische Erfahrungen mit der Operationalisierten Psychodynamischen Diagnostik* (pp. 196–217). Bern: Huber.

Staats, H., May, M., Herrmann, C. H., Kersting, A., & König, K. (1998). Different patterns of change in narratives of men and women during analytical group psychotherapy. *International Journal of Group Psychotherapy*, *48*, 363–380.

Stasch, M., & Cierpka, M. (2000). Changes in patients' perceptions of their interpersonal behavior during inpatient psychotherapy.

31st Annual Meeting of Society of Psychotherapy Research, Chicago, June 2000.

Stasch, M., Cierpka, M., Dahlbender, R. W., Grande, T., Hillenbrand, E., Kraul, A., & Schauenburg, H. (2004). OPD und Repräsentation interpersonellen Beziehungsverhaltens: Ein Ansatz zur Konstruktvalidierung. In R. W. Dahlbender, P. Buchheim, & G. Schüssler (Eds.), Lernen an der Praxis. OPD und die Qualitätssicherung in der psychodynamischen Psychotherapie (pp. 85–94). Bern: Huber.

Stasch, M., Cierpka, M., Hillenbrand, E., & Schmal, H. (2002). Assessing reenactment in inpatient psychodynamic therapy. Psychotherapy Research, 12 (3), 355–368.

Stern, D. N. (1985). The interpersonal world of the infant. A view from psychoanalytic and development psychology. New York: Basic Books.

Stern, D. N. (1995). The motherhood constellation. New York: Basic Books.

Strupp, H. H., & Binder, J. L. (1984). Psychotherapy in a new key: A guide to time-limited dynamic psychotherapy. New York: Basic Books.

Wallerstein, R. S. (1988). Assessment of structural change in psychoanalytical therapy and research. Journal of the American Psychoanalytic Association 1988, 36, 241–261.

Weinryb, R. M., & Rössel, R. J. (1991). Karolinska Psychodynamic Profile KAPP. Acta Psychiatrica Scandinavia, 83, 1–23.

Weiss, J., Sampson, H., & Mount Zion Psychotherapy Research Group (1986). The psychoanalytic process: Theory, clinical observation and empirical research. New York: Guilford Press.

Westen, D. (1991). Social cognition and object relations. Psychological Bulletin, 109, 429–455.

Zimmermann, J., Stasch, M., Rost, R., Hunger, C., Schauenburg, H., Grande, T., & Cierpka, M. (2009). Can you see what I see? Tapping into the discrepancy between patients' and observers' interpersonal problem description using a Q-sort approach. Paper presented at the annual meeting of the Society for Psychotherapy Research, Santiago de Chile.

NOTES

1. Important contributions to the development of the OPD axes that are described in this chapter were also made by Manfred Cierpka, Reiner Dahlbender, Gerd Rudolf, and Michael Stasch.

2. In two other clinics, the interviews were performed under clinically routine conditions and were thus conducted under substantial time pressure. Ratings were performed by the interviewer and a second rater who was present during the interview. For these two clinics, reliability values ranged from 0.30 to 0.50.

V PSYCHOPATHOLOGY AND HEALTH

22 INTERPERSONAL DIAGNOSIS OF PSYCHOPATHOLOGY

Aaron L. Pincus

Aidan G. C. Wright

The symptomatic acts which are expressions of the mentally disordered are therefore most meaningful for psychiatry when their interpersonal contexts are known.

—H. S. Sullivan (1962, p. 303)

The earliest formal appearance of the term "interpersonal diagnosis" may be found in Leary and Coffey's (1955) predecessor to the publication of *Interpersonal Diagnosis of Personality: A Functional Theory and Methodology for Personality Evaluation* (Leary, 1957). Since then, many new developments have occurred in interpersonal psychology that rest firmly upon and usefully extend the fundamental scaffold developed by Leary and his colleagues. Thus today, interpersonal diagnosis is neither a unitary clinical assessment procedure nor a singular approach to the study of personality and psychopathology. Interpersonal diagnosis is a theoretically integrative paradigmatic approach to personality assessment (Wiggins, 2003), psychotherapeutic practice (Anchin & Pincus, 2010; Pincus & Cain, 2008), and the study of psychopathology (Horowitz, 2004). The term has been used to describe procedures that range dramatically in complexity, from basic typological assignment of interpersonal style (Wiggins,

Phillips, & Trapnell, 1989) to longitudinal examinations of interpersonal behavior over time and relationships (Moskowitz, 2005, 2009) to a comprehensive and developmentally informed clinical case conceptualization approach (Benjamin, 2003; Critchfield & Benjamin, 2008). Thus, a very molar definition of interpersonal diagnosis would be: *The use of those central and pluralistic practices employed by researchers and practitioners working within the interpersonal nexus of personality and psychopathology* (Pincus, 2005b; Pincus, Lukowitsky, & Wright, 2010; Pincus, Lukowitsky, Wright, & Eichler, 2009; see Figure 22.1).

The center of Figure 22.1 identifies four basic elements of interpersonal diagnosis that tie together its pluralistic procedures and applications. First, interpersonal diagnosis is anchored to the nomological net of interpersonal constructs contained in the interpersonal paradigm in personality and clinical psychology. In one way or another, this includes the application of the Agency and Communion metaframework (Wiggins, 1991) and its derivations of the Interpersonal Circle (IPC; Gurtman, Chapter 18 in this volume; Fournier, Moskowitz, & Zuroff, Chapter 4 in this volume; Locke, Chapter 19 in this volume;

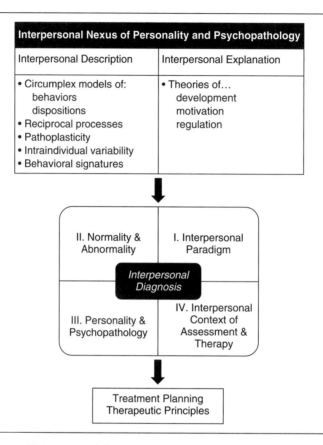

FIGURE 22.1   Interpersonal Diagnosis and the Interpersonal Nexus of Personality and Psychopathology

Wiggins, 1996) as a "key conceptual map" (Kiesler, 1996, p. 172) for an interpersonal *description* of psychopathology, in combination with the contemporary developmental, motivational, and regulatory assumptions of interpersonal theory (Benjamin, 2003, 2005b; Horowitz, 2004; Pincus, 2005a) for an interpersonal *explanation* of psychopathology. Second, interpersonal diagnosis assumes that normality and abnormality can be conceptualized with the same dimensions and are not wholly unique functional domains (O'Connor, 2002; Pincus & Gurtman, 2006). The implications of this assumption are that (a) interpersonal descriptions of normality and abnormality should be based on the same interpersonal models, constructs, and processes; and (b) abnormality is considered to be, in some way, a distortion

or disturbance of normal interpersonal functioning (Benjamin, 1993; Henry, 1994). Third, interpersonal diagnosis assumes that psychopathology and personality are inextricably linked. Although this is most notable in the conceptualization of personality disorders (e.g., Benjamin, 1996; Horowitz & Wilson, 2005; Pincus, 2005a), interpersonal diagnosis also views most psychiatric symptoms as embedded within the context of personality and interpersonal functioning (e.g., Horowitz & Vitkus, 1986; Kiesler, 1996; Millon, 2005; Pincus et al., 2010). Fourth, interpersonal diagnosis recognizes that diagnostic assessment and psychotherapy most commonly take place within an interpersonal context—the relationship between patient and clinician (e.g., Adams, 1964; Anchin & Kiesler, 1982; Andrews, 1989;

McLemore & Benjamin, 1979). This highlights the need to help clinicians identify and organize the salient interpersonal data involved in the verbal reports, nonverbal behaviors, affective shifts, and symptomatic expressions of those they assess and treat.

Over its 50-year history, the methods and theory underlying interpersonal diagnosis have continued to evolve. Since its nascent development in Sullivan's (1953a, 1953b, 1954, 1956, 1962, 1964) highly generative interpersonal theory of psychiatry, interpersonal diagnosis has consistently been employed in research on, and treatment of, the categories of psychopathology found within the existing nosologies of the day, ranging from pre-DSM (Sullivan, 1953a) to DSM-V (Pincus et al., 2010). Occasionally, calls to develop an altogether alternative nosology of psychopathology based in the interpersonal paradigm have arisen (e.g., Carson, 1996; McLemore & Benjamin, 1979; Pincus & Ansell, 2003). However, this goal remains more potentiality than reality.[1] Therefore, this chapter will emphasize the utility of interpersonal diagnosis by reviewing the interpersonal constructs and concepts that are typically employed to describe abnormality and psychopathology (see Figure 22.1). We begin with a brief review of the historical origins of interpersonal diagnosis found in the works of Sullivan and Leary. This is followed by a review of the evolving interpersonal constructs and methods that can be used to describe psychopathology. We will discuss a few specific disorders as exemplars, but in-depth coverage of specific classes of psychopathology can be found in the chapters that follow in this section.

ORIGINS OF INTERPERSONAL DIAGNOSIS

Sullivan's Views on Diagnosis of Psychopathology

Sullivan's formal discussions of diagnosis are quite sparse; even his well-known treatise on interviewing (Sullivan, 1954) does not contain a significant discussion on diagnosis per se. However, all four basic elements of interpersonal diagnosis reviewed above have their origins in Sullivanian thought and theory. Sullivan viewed diagnosis as serving both nomothetic and specific clinical aims. Regarding the former, he noted that, "The term *diagnosis*—literally a discrimination, and medically, a deciding as to the character of the situation before one—is, in the study of personality inextricably linked with prognosis—literally a foreknowing—the formulation of the probable outcome" (Sullivan, 1953b, p. 74). One goal of diagnosis is to discriminate and identify the class of psychopathology encountered. However, he goes on to assert that this is not enough, noting that, "Diagnosis and prognosis cannot be dissociated from therapeutic considerations" (p. 180), and to remind us that diagnosis must not only describe but also explain psychopathology in order that something can be done for the patient so that she or he might cease to be a patient (Sullivan, 1953a).

Perhaps the aspect of Sullivanian theory that most impacted interpersonal diagnosis was his view on the data used for diagnosis. This data is inherently interpersonal and what is diagnosed is the interpersonal *pattern* of psychopathology (*elements I & IV* of Figure 22.1). Sullivan considered mental disorders to be "patterns of inadequate or inappropriate interpersonal relations" (1953a, p. 313) and such disordered relational functioning was "characterized by the misuse of human dynamisms" (1954, p. 102).[2] Therefore, mental health is most meaningful as it pertains to interpersonal adjustment (Sullivan, 1964) and "One achieves mental health to the extent that one becomes aware of one's interpersonal relations" (Sullivan, 1953b, p. 207). *The goal of interpersonal diagnosis of psychopathology is to identify the pattern(s) of behavior that lead to disturbed interpersonal relations.* Sullivan saw the therapeutic relationship as an interpersonal situation, and thus, the therapist was considered a participant observer engaged in a real relationship with the patient. From this perspective, an interpersonal diagnosis is derived from the therapeutic relationship itself. Because the therapist is an active participant in an ongoing relationship, reactions to the patient reflect the prominent interpersonal impacts of the patient's behavior on others and are viewed as fundamental interpersonal communications that inform clinical understanding and intervention decisions.

But the therapist is more than a participant; he or she is also an observer. Sullivan was clear that a particular stance be taken when observing the therapeutic relationship. Specifically, therapists should be acutely attuned to (a) the interpersonal communication occurring via behavior, voice tone, gesture, and symptoms, and (b) indications of interpersonal anxiety or anxiety avoidance via the interpersonal communications of the patient's presentation. Such observation allows the therapist to identify those interpersonal behaviors and patterns that are associated with security and self-esteem, and those that are associated with anxiety and its avoidance. For example, some patients are secure when taking a passive, cooperative relational stance, but can be quite anxious with self-assertion or disagreement. For others, the opposite is true. Depressive symptoms may convey the submissive interpersonal message "Help me; I can't do it by myself." Suicidality may convey the hostile interpersonal message "You're to blame for my misery" in one context, and the affiliative interpersonal message "I desperately need someone to take care of me" in another context. While waiting for a consultation on an inpatient unit, a schizophrenic patient haltingly approached the first author and said glumly, "I'm being punished for breathing fire." One common reaction to such a statement in an inpatient context is to see it as a psychotic symptom and disregard it since human beings do not breathe fire. However, when the interpersonal communication was considered, the patient appeared to be relaying a sense of frustration and hurt. When I replied, "That must feel unfair," the patient relaxed and was able to explain that he was reprimanded

for smoking in his room rather than in a designated area.

According to Sullivan, the interpersonal communications of the patient's presentation will also demonstrate security operations, which serve to minimize anxiety via activation or inhibition of certain behaviors, and may operate outside the patient's awareness. Concretely, when, without awareness, a patient changes the subject abruptly, fails to comprehend the therapist, refuses to respond, exhibits nonverbal and affective shifts, or reports new symptoms, the therapist should consider "What is the interpersonal meaning of such phenomena?" Sullivan suggested that when such behaviors interfere with the integration of the therapeutic relationship, the patient is employing learned interpersonal strategies that minimize anxiety and increase security. Thus participant observation allows the therapist to conceptualize the patient's problems directly via relational experience. Since the same learned relational patterns are assumed to be common across the interpersonal situations that characterize the patient's life, this data can then be used to plan treatment that encourages new interpersonal learning within the therapeutic relationship.

Importantly, such patterns are neither random nor infinite. Sullivan (1964) noted that "While minor differences in personality are as numerous as are the cultural patterns of the homes from which people have come, the structure of society and the character of human potentialities combine to limit the conspicuous manifestations of mental disorder to a reasonably small number of patterns which can be discriminated" (p. 169). Such patterns are always defined by reference to an explicit or implicit formulation of personality (*element III* of Figure 22.1), which sets limits on the manifestations of human individuality and provides norms from which significant deviations can be regarded as disordered (Sullivan, 1962). Finally, description of normal and abnormal interpersonal patterns can be derived from a common interpersonal framework (*element II* of Figure 22.1). Sullivan repeatedly emphasized that disordered interpersonal patterns are deviations and distortions of normal interpersonal functioning, noting that "We all show everything that any mental patient shows, except for the pattern, the accents, and so on" (1954, p. 183), and "The course of life gives everyone some experience with everything that I know to be dynamisms of mental disorder" (1956, p. 358). It was Leary and colleagues who extended Sullivan's thinking and formalized the approach by developing operationalizations of Sullivan's concepts, leading to the initial derivation and empirical validation of the IPC, and the first formal interpersonal diagnostic system (LaForge, 2004; Pincus, 1994; Wiggins, 1996).

Leary's Contributions
to Interpersonal Diagnosis

Timothy Leary and the Kaiser Foundation research group (Freedman, Leary, Ossorio, & Coffey, 1951; LaForge, Leary, Naboisek, Coffey, & Freedman, 1954; Leary, 1957; Leary & Coffey, 1955) can be credited with providing the organizing framework and empirically validated structure for interpersonal diagnosis. Incorporating Sullivan's thinking and foreshadowing attachment theory, Leary (1957) argued for the primacy of the interpersonal domain in personality functioning by noting the biological reality of a child's frail nature and the necessity of social interaction for survival and achievement of maturity. Humans have biologically evolved to be social creatures and, via social learning principles, personality develops through the influence of others in interpersonal transactions across the lifespan.

Leary and his associates observed interactions among group psychotherapy patients and asked, "What is the subject of the activity, e.g., the individual whose behavior is being rated, doing to the object or objects of the activity?" (Freedman et al., 1951, p. 149). In this regard, topical

content was not of specific interest. Instead, observations reflected the interpersonal communications between group members, consistent with Sullivan's diagnostic data. This context-free cataloguing of patients' interpersonal behavior eventually led to an empirically derived IPC structure based on the two underlying dimensions of dominance-submission (Agency) on the vertical axis and nurturance-coldness (Communion) on the horizontal axis. While the IPC model has been empirically refined and extended over the years, its fundamental characteristics have been repeatedly validated (e.g., Gurtman & Pincus, 2000; Pincus, Gurtman, & Ruiz, 1998). Figure 22.2 presents a contemporary version of the IPC. Leary conceptualized this as the ordered classification of interpersonal mechanisms, reflexes, and behaviors around the two primary dimensions, and this circular space serves to organize the relationships between different types of interpersonal functioning at any given level of analysis (e.g., behaviors, traits, motives, etc). Importantly, in its original and subsequent incarnations, the IPC describes not only the static relations among the interpersonal variables (i.e., the ordering around the circle), but also the dynamic relations of human transaction based on the interpersonal bids and pulls of one behavior for another, i.e., complementarity (e.g., Carson, 1969; Kiesler, 1983; Sadler, Ethier, & Woody, Chapter 8 in this volume).

At the time of his book's publication, Leary was reacting strongly to the zeitgeist of symptom-focused psychiatry. In fact, the work appeared just five years after the publication of the DSM-I (American Psychiatric Association, 1952). He voiced his frustration with the common practice of the time of focusing on symptoms for diagnosis by pointing out that this limited the diagnostic nosology to those disorders that were prone to seeking out help, and further, that theories of personality were lopsidedly attendant to maladaptive rather than adaptive functioning. Among the other advances offered by Leary's volume,

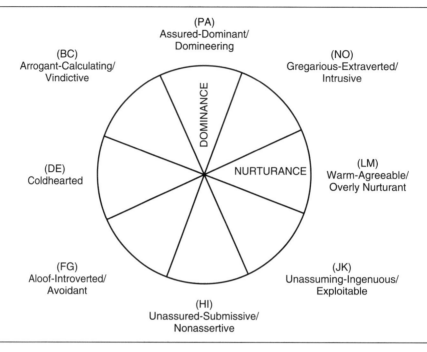

FIGURE 22.2   The Interpersonal Circle (Traits / Problems)

he argued that any system of personality needed to accommodate the full spectrum of normality and abnormality in functioning, which he considered dimensional in nature. To discriminate maladaptive from adaptive interpersonal functioning, Leary distinguished four ways to quantify patterns of interpersonal behavior: moderation versus *intensity*, flexibility versus *rigidity*, stability versus *oscillation*, and accuracy versus *inaccuracy* (i.e., the fit or match of behavior within a specific interpersonal context).[3] Importantly, these four patterns of interpersonal adjustment and maladjustment can be operationalized and quantified with specific reference to the IPC structure and they remain among the major constructs used to describe psychopathology in contemporary interpersonal diagnosis (see also Erickson, Newman, & Pincus, 2009; Pincus & Gurtman, 2006). At the time, Leary argued that the interpersonal system could serve as the foundation for an alternative taxonomy of personality styles, and that even the symptom

disorders could be diagnosed through the measurement of interpersonal patterns. The remainder of this chapter discusses these types of interpersonal patterns, as well as new developments in contemporary approaches to interpersonal diagnosis of psychopathology.

CONTEMPORARY INTERPERSONAL DIAGNOSIS

To identify interpersonal patterns of psychopathology, contemporary interpersonal diagnosis employs multiple constructs, methods, and levels of analysis in describing personality and behavior. Figure 22.3 lists three major classes of interpersonal variables associated with psychopathology. *Static individual differences* are traditional behavioral and dispositional characteristics that can be derived from established psychological assessment procedures (self-reports, other-ratings, interviews). These concepts served interpersonal diagnosis

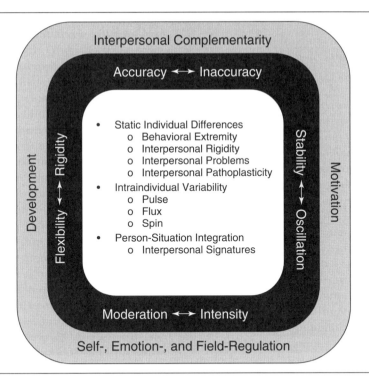

FIGURE 22.3 Variables of Interpersonal Diagnosis (white), Interpersonal Patterns of Psychopathology (black), and Assumptions of Interpersonal Theory (gray)

well, from Leary's initial formulations through the mid-1990s. In his encyclopedic review of that era, Kiesler (1996) recognized the limitations of the approach, noting, "If interpersonal diagnosis is to contribute to a full understanding of mental disorders, its assessment must systematically incorporate the important situational and temporal factors relevant to expression of each disorder's maladaptive interpersonal pattern" (p. 202). The very advances Kiesler called for nearly 15 years ago are now being realized. The last decade has witnessed a dramatic evolution in the conceptualization and measurement of personality (Fleeson & Noftle, 2008), leading to *intraindividual variability* approaches to the study of personality consistency (e.g., Fleeson, 2004), as well as new models of *person-situation integration* (e.g., Funder, 2009).

Figure 22.3 is organized to remind the reader that the variables of interpersonal diagnosis (white center), interpersonal patterns of psychopathology (black ring), and assumptions of interpersonal theory (gray ring) are interpenetrating rather than mutually exclusive. Each concentric ring holds a set of increasingly broader theoretical and empirical constructs associated with interpersonal diagnosis. As one moves from the white center to the black ring to the gray ring, the context and scope of interpersonal diagnosis expands substantially. The location of a given construct within a ring (i.e., top, bottom, left, right) is wholly arbitrary and does not imply a specific link to similarly located constructs at different levels—all constructs are interpenetrating. There are few one-to-one correspondences between interpersonal variables (white center) and interpersonal patterns (black ring). Rigidity and accuracy have been studied from both dispositional and variability approaches. Interpersonal problems may have implications for all interpersonal patterns. Rigidity as a trait has implications for aspects of variability, which in turn has implications for accuracy. Finally, as represented by the gray ring, interpersonal diagnosis is fundamentally embedded within interpersonal theory's conceptions of reciprocal transaction, development, motivation, and regulation.

Interpersonal Description of Psychopathology: Individual Differences

Static individual differences are, as typically defined, enduring, dispositional attributes of the individual expressed in distinctive patterns of thought, perception, feeling, and behavior. As McAdams (1995) points out, dispositions typically describe individual differences at a fairly broad or general level and are inherently "decontextualized" and relatively "nonconditional" (p. 365). Hence, the variables of interest here are assumed to reflect a general feature of the person's tendencies (e.g., "I am shy") that are presumed to be relatively stable over time and found in an aggregate of interpersonal situations. Importantly, however, there are not one-to-one relationships between traits and behaviors, leaving the interpersonal meaning of a given behavior ambiguous without consideration of the person's motive or goal in that interpersonal situation (Horowitz et al., 2006). Thus, a certain trait or behavior (whether adaptive or maladaptive) may not necessarily be expressed in a particular interpersonal situation, relationship, or episode; or dictate a particular emergent process. For this level of specificity, contemporary interpersonal diagnosis relies on additional theoretical constructs.

Behavioral extremity and interpersonal rigidity. When referenced to the IPC, extremity (i.e., enacting behaviors in intense forms) and rigidity (i.e., displaying a limited repertoire of interpersonal behaviors) are critical variables for conceptualizing patterns of psychopathology within the interpersonal tradition. Although the two are assumed to co-occur, they are conceptually distinct

(O'Connor & Dyce, 2001). In the context of IPC models, extremity reflects a specific behavior's intensity on a particular dimension, and is represented linearly, by the behavior's distance from the origin of the circle. Behaviors can vary from relatively mild expressions of a trait dimension close to the origin (e.g., expresses one's preferences) to extreme versions at the periphery of the circle (e.g., insists/demands others do his/her bidding). This intensity dimension is an inherent feature of the circle originally conceived by Leary and, more recently, by Kiesler's (1983, 1996) refined articulation of the IPC. Extreme behaviors that populate the circle's periphery are likely to be undesirable for both self and others. Their lack of moderation would rarely make them situationally appropriate or successful (for theoretical elaborations, consult Carson, 1969; Horowitz, 2004; or Kiesler, 1996).

As Pincus (1994) pointed out, whereas extremity (or intensity) is a property of an individual's single *behavior*, rigidity is a characteristic of a whole *person*, or more specifically, a summary of his or her limited number of different behaviors across various interpersonal situations. From Leary (1957) on, interpersonalists have argued that disordered individuals tend to enact or rely on a limited or restricted range of behaviors, failing to adapt their behaviors to the particular demands of a given situation. From a circumplex perspective, they tend to draw from a small segment of the IPC, rather than draw broadly as the situation requires. In contrast, interpersonally flexible individuals are capable of adjusting their behaviors appropriately to the cues of others in order to act effectively (see, e.g., Carson, 1991; Paulhus & Martin 1987, 1988). Hence, they are more likely to engage in and sustain behavior patterns that are mutually satisfying to their relational partners (e.g., Kiesler, 1996).

From the static dispositional perspective, rigidity has been assessed using methods for scoring a person's circular profile that derive originally from LaForge et al. (1954; see also Gurtman, 1994, Chapter 18 in this volume). Specifically, the profile's *vector length*, or VL, has been used as an index of rigidity (e.g., Leary, 1957; Tracey, 2005; Wiggins et al., 1989). Like behavioral intensity, VL is also a quantification of distance from the IPC origin. However, it is a geometric summary of an individual's ratings on dispositions around the entire IPC rather than the linear level of the relative intensity of a specific behavior or a direct measure of restricted behavioral range. A high VL profile tends to have greater differentiation across octant scale scores, which is commonly caused by a pronounced elevation in a single region of the circumplex. Gurtman and Balakrishnan (1998) have extensively discussed and critiqued the presumed link between VL and rigidity, drawing the distinction between VL as statistical index (known properties) and as potential clinical indicator (hypothesis). As a statistic, VL is technically a measure of a circular profile's differentiation moderated by the profile's "fit" to a circular model (Gurtman, 1994).

Whether VL is a valid indicator of rigidity, however, is an ongoing empirical matter. Research has demonstrated that in heterogeneous samples, VL is not highly correlated with general maladjustment (e.g., Paulhus & Martin, 1988; Gurtman, 1996; Gurtman & Balakrishnan, 1998; Ruiz et al., 2004; Wiggins et al., 1989; cf. O'Connor & Dyce, 2001), although when limited to a specific angular location (i.e., in samples selected as homogeneous in interpersonal style), VL is correlated with conceptually consistent forms of maladjustment (Wiggins et al., 1989). Further evidence suggests that the relationship between VL and maladjustment is complex and may be mediated "upstream" by accuracy, i.e., complementarity (Tracey, 2005), and moderated by cognitive adherence to IPC structure (Tracey & Rohlfing, 2010).

VL does not, in its calculation, include naturally occurring interpersonal behaviors sampled across time or situations (seemingly central to the full meaning of rigidity). The only study to investigate the association between IPC VL and variability in behavior sampled over time did not find evidence of a link (Erickson et al., 2009). We believe it is best to conceptualize VL calculated from self- or other-reports as IPC "profile differentiation," representing the degree to which a respondent discriminates between aspects of interpersonal functioning that are very much like the self or target, in contrast to those qualities that are not characteristic of the self or target (Gurtman & Balakrishnan, 1998; Wright, Pincus, Conroy, & Hilsenroth, 2009). It may be useful to add the interpretation of VL as "differentiation," and its social-cognitive implications, to the dispositional variables used in interpersonal diagnosis.

Interpersonal problems. Measures assessing maladaptive interpersonal characteristics and processes provide a proximal approach to describing patterns of psychopathology. In this respect, the development of the Inventory of Interpersonal Problems (IIP; Horowitz, Rosenberg, Baer, Ureño, & Villaseñor, 1988), along with explication of the interpersonal problems construct have been critical events in the recent history of interpersonal diagnosis (Gurtman, 1996; Horowitz et al., 2006). The evolution of the IIP has been described in detail by Horowitz and his colleagues in a number of sources (e.g., Horowitz, 1979, 1996; Horowitz & Vitkus, 1986). The IIP's item set was developed from the complaints voiced by prospective psychotherapy patients during intake interviews. This test construction method gives the IIP two appealing features. First, the items possess good ecological validity (Gurtman, 1996) that may be lacking in other instruments, and second, the item pool offers a fairly broad and comprehensive "universe of content" for delineating specific interpersonal difficulties. Interpersonal problems take two forms, interpersonal deficits or "things you find hard to do" (e.g., "It's hard for me to join in on groups"), and interpersonal excesses or "things you do too much" (e.g., "I argue with people too much"). On this basis, Horowitz et al. (1988)

published a 127-item version of the IIP. This version presents a superset of the current 64-item IIP-Circumplex Scales (IIP-C; Alden, Wiggins, & Pincus, 1990; Horowitz, Alden, Wiggins, & Pincus, 2000), which in turn was reduced to a 32-item short form (IIP-SC; Hopwood, Pincus, DeMoor, & Koonce, 2008; Soldz, Budman, Demby, & Merry, 1995). In its circumplex forms, the IIP captures the maladaptive variants of the basic IPC content domains (see Figure 22.2). IIP instruments exhibit sensitivity to change across psychodynamic, cognitive, and pharmacological treatments (Horowitz et al., 1988; Markowitz et al., 1996; Vittengl, Clark, & Jarrett, 2003), and are widely used in contemporary psychotherapy and psychopathology research (e.g., Borkovec, Newman, Pincus, & Lytle, 2002; Hopwood, Clarke, & Perez, 2007; Huber, Henrich, & Klug, 2007; Ruiz et al., 2004).

Limitations of static individual differences. Studies empirically linking psychopathology and static individual differences in interpersonal dispositions are numerous and, for some forms of psychopathology, such mapping is relatively successful in describing core maladaptive interpersonal patterns. For example, rigidity is most central to the concept of personality disorder. Research linking interpersonal dispositions to particular DSM personality disorder diagnoses (e.g., Pincus & Wiggins, 1990; Soldz, Budman, Demby, & Merry, 1993; Wiggins & Pincus, 1989) confirmed that personality disorder, consistent with the DSM definition, was reflected in overly extreme and rigid agentic and/or communal behavior that caused impairment and/or subjective distress. For example, histrionic personality disorder is consistently associated with IPC octant NO, implying extreme extraversion that, when rigidly enacted, leads to intrusive interpersonal problems (e.g., "I want to be noticed too much"). In contrast, avoidant personality disorder is consistently associated with IPC octants FG and HI, implying extreme introversion and submissiveness that, when rigidly enacted, leads to avoidant and nonassertive

interpersonal problems (e.g., "I find it hard to socialize with other people," "I find it hard to be self-confident when I am with other people"). However, static mapping research has only succeeded in capturing a subset of personality disorders. Specifically, the paranoid (BC—vindictive), schizoid (DE/FG—cold, avoidant), avoidant (FG/HI—avoidant, nonassertive), dependent (JK—exploitable), histrionic (NO—intrusive), and narcissistic (PA/BC—domineering, vindictive) personality disorders are associated with specific IPC locations. Beyond these results, the other personality disorders (e.g., borderline—Leihener et al., 2003; Ryan & Shean, 2007) and most symptom syndromes (e.g., anxiety disorders—Kachin, Newman, & Pincus, 2001; Salzer et al., 2008) do not appear to consistently present with a single, prototypic interpersonal phenomenology. Thus, to fully apply interpersonal diagnosis, we must move beyond basic descriptions of psychopathology founded on the covariation of symptoms/disorders with interpersonal characteristics assessed as static individual differences and investigate both pathoplastic and dynamic associations. We turn to these elements of interpersonal diagnosis next.

Advances in Interpersonal Diagnosis

Interpersonal Pathoplasticity

Whereas some forms of psychopathology can be summarized by relatively uniform interpersonal features across similarly diagnosed patients, others seem to have a kaleidoscopic relationship to the interpersonal system, wherein personality and psychopathology intertwine to produce variability in expression of the disorder. Interpersonal pathoplasticity can be said to occur when there exists a significant quantitative relationship between psychopathology and interpersonal behavior, but there is not a singular qualitative interpersonal signature associated with the form of psychopathology (Pincus et al., 2010; see also Klein, Wonderlich, & Shea, 1993; Widiger & Smith, 2008). Interpersonal pathoplasticity accounts for the lack of one-to-one coherence between some forms of psychopathology and interpersonal styles, in contrast to a purely etiological relationship that presumes that the same underlying process gives rise to the psychopathology and the interpersonal style. Pathoplasticity is part of the inextricable link between personality and psychopathology, in that the latter is always expressed within the larger context of the former (Millon, 2005), and it would be unreasonable to assume that the expression of pathology would not be influenced by one's characteristic manner of relating to others, and vice versa. Not only can interpersonal pathoplasticity describe the observed heterogeneity in expression of psychopathology (e.g., Cain, Pincus, & Grosse-Holtforth, in press; Kachin et al., 2001; Salzer et al., 2008), it can also predict variability in response to psychotherapy within a disorder (e.g., Alden & Capreol, 1993; Borkovec et al., 2002; Cain et al., in press; Salzer, Pincus, Winkelbach, Lechsenring, & Leibing, in press) and account for a lack of uniformity in regulatory strategies displayed by those who otherwise are struggling with similar symptoms (e.g., Slaney, Pincus, Wang, & Uliaszek, 2006; Wright, Pincus, Conroy, & Elliot, 2009). Differences in patients' interpersonal diagnoses will affect the manner in which they express their distress and make bids for the type of interpersonal situation they feel is needed to regulate their self, affect, and relationships.

Evidence is accruing that a number of symptom syndromes do not have a characteristic interpersonal profile, instead being associated with a broad range of interpersonal problems, and sometimes specific subtypes of problems (Wright et al., 2009). For example, a series of studies examining generalized anxiety disorder (GAD) have consistently found a relationship between this disorder and interpersonal problems generally—but failed to find a unitary interpersonal style, instead repeatedly identifying four distinct and prototypical interpersonal clusters within DSM-IV diagnosed GAD patients (Kasoff, 2002; Pincus et al., 2005; Salzer et al., 2008). Labeled Nonassertive, Cold, Exploitable, and Intrusive, these clusters, or subtypes, of patients reported distinct patterns of interpersonal problems but exhibited no significant differences in symptom severity or psychiatric co-occurrence. However, subtypes did vary in domains of worry content and controllability (Sibrava et al., 2007). Thus, GAD patients have increased interpersonal problems, but the types of problems an individual patient has varies as a function of their interpersonal diagnosis. These subtypes likely adopt different interpersonal regulatory strategies as they attempt to navigate the swells of their worry. For example, the interpersonally cold subtype may respond to increased worry by withdrawing from others in the hopes of avoiding the worries about outcomes. In contrast, the intrusive subtype may insert themselves into the interpersonal situations of others in the hopes that they will provide the needed assurance and social resources to manage their uncontrollable worry. In a similar fashion to GAD, two distinct groups of social phobics (one warmer and one colder) have been identified based on unique sets of interpersonal problems in both anxious student and patient samples (Cain et al., in press; Kachin et al., 2001), and these groupings were not better accounted for by symptom severity or co-occurring diagnoses. The relationship of eating disorders with interpersonal style also appears to be pathoplastic (Ambwani & Hopwood, 2009; Hopwood et al., 2007). Finally, theorists from multiple theoretical perspectives have suggested a pathoplastic model of depression vulnerability: Communal (dependent/sociotropic/anaclitic) versus Agentic (self-critical/automous/introjective) (Blatt, 2004; Beck, 1983), and evidence exists for pathoplasticity in perceived causal pathways (Keller, Neale, & Kendler, 2007), but it is not yet clear that there is a true interpersonal pathoplasticity in depressive phenomenology (see Barrett & Barber, 2007). More research is needed to elucidate the relationship between interpersonal problems and depression.

A number of studies have investigated the effect of interpersonal problem type on treatment outcome. Examination of treatment response of GAD patients to cognitive-behavioral therapy found that end-state functioning immediately after treatment was greater for the Nonassertive and Exploitable than the Cold and Intrusive GAD patients (Kasoff, 2002). At six-month follow-up, the functioning of Nonassertive and Exploitable GAD patients continued to improve, while the functioning of Cold and Intrusive GAD patients declined. Kasoff (2002) suggested that submissive GAD clusters had a better therapy outcome than more dominant GAD clusters due to their personality compatibility with the patient–therapist role relationships in cognitive-behavior therapy (Borkovec et al., 2002; Horowitz, Rosenberg & Bartholomew, 1993; for divergent results see also Puschner, Kraft, & Bauer, 2004). Cain et al. (in press) found that interpersonally warmer social phobics showed significantly greater symptomatic improvement and satisfaction following therapy than their colder counterparts. In a related study, Alden and Capreol (1993) found that the effective treatment components for social anxiety in patients with avoidant personality disorder also differed depending on their level of communion. While all patients exhibited significant nonassertive interpersonal problems, those whose nonassertiveness was colored by higher communion benefited best from intimacy-focused skills training, whereas those patients with lower communion benefited only from graduated exposure. Thus, interpersonal diagnosis informs treatment planning beyond symptom disorder diagnosis by identifying different maladaptive behavior patterns that cause relational disturbance and perpetuate negative outcomes (e.g., Benjamin, 2003, 2005a).

For many disorders, the lack of one-to-one correspondence with interpersonal functioning results in a rich and complex heterogeneity as the pathology is variously altered through an individual's characteristic interpersonal strengths, vulnerabilities, and self-, affect-, and field-regulation strategies (Pincus, 2005a; Wiggins & Trobst, 1999). Thus, interpersonal diagnosis contributes to the broader diagnostic enterprise by providing incrementally useful information about moderators that affect the description, explanation, and assessment of psychopathology, along with uniquely informed treatment planning and prognostic recommendations (Anchin & Kiesler, 1982; Anchin & Pincus, 2010; Pincus & Cain, 2008).

Intraindividual Variability

The addition of pathoplasticity greatly extends the empirical and practical utility of interpersonal diagnosis. However, describing psychopathology using dispositional personality concepts implying marked consistency of relational functioning is still insufficient, and does not exhaust contemporary interpersonal diagnostic approaches. Even patients described by a particular interpersonal style do not robotically emit the same behaviors without variation. Recent advances in the measurement and analysis of intraindividual variability (e.g., Baird, Le, & Lucas, 2006; Erickson et al., 2009; Heller, Watson, Komar, Min, & Perunovic, 2007; Shoda, Mischel, & Wright, 1994) converge to suggest that temporal intraindividual variability of behavior warrants assessment. This accumulating body of research indicates that individuals are characterized not only by their stable individual differences in trait levels of behavior, but also by stable differences in their variability in psychological states (Fleeson, 2001), behaviors (Moskowitz, 2010), and affect (Eid & Diener, 1999; Kuppens, Van Mechelen, Nezlak, Dossche, & Timmermans, 2007) across time and situations.

Interpersonal flux, pulse, and spin. Moskowitz and Zuroff (2004, 2005) introduced the terms *flux, pulse,* and *spin* to describe the stable levels of intraindividual variability in interpersonal behaviors sampled from the interpersonal circumplex. *Flux* refers to variability about an individual's mean behavioral score on agentic or communal dimensions (e.g., dominant flux, submissive flux, friendly flux, hostile flux). *Spin* refers to variability of the angular coordinate about the individual's mean interpersonal style. And *pulse* refers to variability of the overall extremity of the emitted behavior. Low spin would thus reflect a narrow repertoire of interpersonal behaviors enacted over time and is an alternative and more proximal measure of interpersonal rigidity than the computation of VL from self- or other-reports of interpersonal dispositions. Low pulse reflects little variability in behavioral intensity, and if it were associated with a high mean intensity generally, it would be consistent with the enactment of consistently extreme interpersonal behaviors. This dynamic lexicon has important implications for the assessment of normal and abnormal behavior. Theoretical analyses, as well as empirical results, suggest that the assessment of intraindividual variability offer unique and important new methods for the description of psychopathology.

For example, Russell, Moskowitz, Zuroff, Sookman, and Paris (2007) differentiated individuals with BPD from nonclinical control participants based on intraindividual variability of interpersonal behavior over a 20-day period. Specifically, individuals with BPD reported a similar mean level of agreeable (communal) behavior, as compared to their nonclinical counterparts, but BPD participants displayed greater flux in their agreeable behaviors, suggesting that control participants demonstrated consistent agreeable behavior across situations, while individuals with BPD varied greatly in their agreeable behaviors, vacillating between high and low levels. Results also suggested elevated mean levels of submissive behaviors in conjunction with low mean levels of dominant behavior coupled with greater flux in dominant behaviors for individuals with BPD relative to the control

participants. However, the groups did not differ in the variability of submissive behaviors. In other words, individuals with BPD were consistently submissive relative to normal controls, but also demonstrated acute elevations and declines in their relatively low level of dominant behavior. Finally, as predicted, individuals with BPD endorsed higher mean levels of quarrelsome behavior, and higher levels of flux in quarrelsome behavior, when compared to controls. Individuals with BPD also demonstrated greater spin than their nonclinical counterparts, suggesting greater behavioral lability. Future work on other personality disorders also appears promising. Although the DSM categories of dependent and narcissistic personality disorder (NPD) map onto consistent IPC locations cross-sectionally, recent theory and research characterizing broader conceptions of these disorders (e.g., Cain, Pincus, & Ansell, 2008; Bornstein, 2005) suggest they are actually characterized by variability in interpersonal behavior. Pincus (2005a) proposed using flux, pulse, and spin to differentiate the phenomenological expression of these broader conceptions of dependent and narcissistic personality disorders.

Describing psychopathology in terms of intraindividual variability in interpersonal behavior is not limited to personality disorders, although less theoretical rationale and research has been proposed for symptom syndromes. Consistent with the results suggesting greater spin in BPD patients than controls, Moskowitz and Zuroff (2005) found that trait neuroticism was positively correlated with interpersonal spin. Consider Mineka, Watson, and Clark's (1998) integrative hierarchical model of anxiety and depression. In this model, depression and anxiety share a common, higher-order factor of negative affectivity, and each disorder is differentiated by its own specific factor. This could suggest that high levels of negative affect, combined with individuals' agentic and communal motives and traits, could give rise to variable interpersonal behavior across interpersonal situations. Moskowitz and Zuroff

(2005) suggested that high levels of negative affectivity may lead individuals to experience interpersonal situations as threatening or dangerous and employ various interpersonal strategies to cope. For example, highly anxious individuals may try to cope with perceived interpersonal threats by arguing with the others, by smiling and laughing in order to build closer connections to others, or by passively giving in to others. They concluded that, "trying a variety of behaviors to cope with frequent perceptions of interpersonal danger would contribute to spin, frequent switching among the interpersonal circumplex behaviors" (p. 143). One can also imagine that individuals with dysthymia may exhibit chronic passivity (i.e., low spin around intense submissiveness), leading to a failure to engage in agentic actions to change the circumstances and promote self-esteem (e.g., Horowitz & Vitkus, 1986). In contrast, individuals with bipolar disorder or impulse control disorders may exhibit a high amount of flux, pulse, and spin contingent upon their mood states.

Person-Situation Integration

Advances in the study of intraindividual variability have stimulated a major reconceptualization of personality consistency (Fleeson & Noftle, 2008; Funder, 2006). Moving beyond traditional conceptions of cross-situational consistency, personality is considered to reflect stability of behavior within situations and variability of behavior across situations. This increases the salience of contextual factors without losing the essence of personality itself. Assessing personality consistency via the identification of stable *if-then* behavioral signatures (Shoda, Mischel, & Wright, 1993, 1994) has thus become an important arena of personality research (Mischel & Shoda, 1998; Mischel, Shoda, & Mendoza-Denton, 2002). In this approach, the stability of personality and core patterns of psychopathology are anchored to consistent contingent *if-then* structures of behavioral and emotional responses (*thens*) in situations the individual experiences as functionally equivalent (*ifs*).

Conceptualizing and measuring patterns of variability and stability of interpersonal behavior over time and across situations is an important development for interpersonal diagnosis that has the potential to enhance the sophistication of our current diagnostic systems (Pincus, 2005a, Pincus et al., 2009; Pincus et al., 2010). Some diagnoses, such as trichotillomania, imply rather classic conceptions of cross-situational consistency—chronic hair pulling without significant situational contingencies. The prominent features of others, such as bipolar disorder, are best characterized by variability in mood and behavior over time. Finally, many diagnostic features are actually based on implicit or explicit *if-then* behavioral signatures (see, e.g., Eaton, South, & Krueger, 2009; Leising & Müller-Plath, 2009). For example, a cardinal symptom of borderline personality disorder (BPD) could be phrased as, "*if* the person perceives abandonment, *then* frantic efforts to avoid it are enacted." Defining symptoms of social anxiety disorder could be phrased as, "*if* the person perceives scrutiny, dislike, or disapproval from others, *then* anxiety is experienced and avoidance behaviors are enacted."

A key implication of situation–behavior contingencies is the need to identify the psychologically salient features of situations, and this requires an organizing psychological theory. Consistent with our analysis of many *if-then* diagnostic features of psychopathology, recent work in personality, social, and clinical psychology converges in emphasizing the salience of interpersonal features of situations (e.g., Pincus et al., 2009; Reis, 2008). Importantly, this is directly incorporated into interpersonal diagnosis by the assessment of interpersonal behavior contextualized within interpersonal situations both assessed on the common metric of agentic and communal dimensions, i.e., *interpersonal signatures* (Fournier, Moskowitz, & Zuroff, 2008, 2009; Moskowitz, 2009). That is, the patterns of disturbed interpersonal functioning interpersonal diagnosis strives to identify can be contextualized by linking the perceived agentic and communal characteristics of the other person(s) in an interpersonal situation (*ifs*) with the symptomatic or maladaptive behavioral and emotional responses (*thens*) of the patient. Our view is that pathological interpersonal signatures often reflect coping behaviors (*thens*) activated by distorted perceptions of interpersonal situations (*ifs*). Consistent with the fundamental elements of interpersonal diagnosis, these contextualized patterns can be organized through the lens of Agency and Communion, and applied at a variety of descriptive levels, ranging from molar dispositional profiles (e.g., Pincus & Wiggins, 1990; Wiggins & Pincus, 1989) to highly articulated behavioral patterns (e.g., Benjamin, 1996) to the structure of social-cognitive schemas (e.g., Horowitz & Wilson, 2005) and articulations of internal object-relations (Pincus, 2005a).

At a descriptive level similar to DSM criteria, some of the cardinal symptoms of pathological narcissism or NPD could be phrased as interpersonal signatures: "*if* the person meets new peers, *then* self-promoting, attention-seeking, or competitive behaviors are enacted;" "*if* the person perceives lack of admiration, *then* he or she angrily devalues the other(s);" "*if* the person assumes authority over others, *then* self-serving and exploitative behavior is enacted;" or "*if* idealized expectations for self or others are disappointed, *then* he or she responds with shameful withdrawal and social avoidance." Problems arise because intense needs for self-esteem support, admiration, and superiority likely give rise to the characteristic schemas of the pathologically narcissistic individual, who consistently misinterprets a broad array of situations as opportunities for self-enhancement or threats to their ideal self-image (*ifs*), responding with characteristically narcissistic disaffiliative self-protective behaviors and agentic self-enhancement strategies (*thens*). In new

situations, these trump and violate normative behavioral patterns, and ultimately lead to vicious circles, self-fulfilling prophecies, disturbed interpersonal relations, and functional impairment (Pincus & Lukowitsky, 2010; Pincus & Roche, in press).[4]

Person-situation integration is a promising advance for contemporary interpersonal diagnosis for a number of reasons. First, it is possible to parsimoniously describe interpersonal behaviors and interpersonal situations using a common metric—the Agency and Communion metaframework. Second, empirical research confirms the normative behavioral contingencies of interpersonal situations described by the principles of interpersonal complementarity (Sadler et al., Chapter 8 in this volume), supporting the proposition that chronic deviations from complementarity may indicate the presence of psychopathology. Interpersonal signatures provide precise descriptions of contextualized behavioral patterns and strong tests of accuracy-inaccuracy (i.e., complementarity). Third, we propose that a focal question for the study of psychopathology is "Why do individuals deviate from their sociocultural conventions of dyadic interaction?" The framework points to multiple possible sources of disturbed interpersonal functioning (e.g., distortions in interpersonal perception and meaning-making processes; maladaptive, underdeveloped, or overvalued interpersonal goals, motives, expectancies, beliefs, and competencies).

CONCLUSIONS AND FUTURE DIRECTIONS

Although we have emphasized the interpersonal paradigm, and the agency and communion metaframework, it is important to note that one need not work exclusively from within the paradigm to focus on salient interpersonal factors in personality and psychopathology. More broadly, we see interpersonal diagnosis as reviewed here as having intersections with many emerging trends in psychological science. Advances in intraindividual variability and person-situation integration promote greater synthesis of social, personality, and clinical psychology (Lukowitsky, Pincus, Hill, & Loos, 2008; Swann & Seyle, 2005).[5] In addition, interpersonal diagnosis also intersects with advances in social neuroscience (Harmon-Jones & Winkielman, 2007), as contemporary theoretical (e.g., Depue, 2006) and empirical (e.g., aan het Rot et al., 2006) efforts are forging clear links between neural pathways and interpersonal behavior. The ease with which these advances, and others, can be operationalized within the interpersonal paradigm demonstrate that the approach is not only theoretically integrative (Horowitz et al., 2006; Pincus & Ansell, 2003), but highly interdisciplinary as well.

Given emerging advances in interpersonal diagnosis, the future appears vital and exciting. While we certainly hold no special prescience on the matter, we can offer some conclusions and suggested directions for the approach. First, although there have been occasional calls for developing an interpersonal diagnostic system that is an alternative to the DSM system (or other established systems), we believe there is substantial wisdom in psychology's and psychiatry's cumulative observations of psychopathology, such that the major classes of dysfunction (e.g., mood, anxiety, eating, psychosis, etc.) do seem reasonably identified, and we do not foresee development of a unique diagnostic nosology based solely on an agency and communion metaframework. Given that interpersonal functioning is an integrative pantheoretical nexus for the description and explanation of personality and psychopathology (Pincus, 2005b; Pincus et al., 2010), we feel interpersonal diagnosis can usefully augment existing and future psychiatric diagnoses in multiple ways.

First, we would advocate for interpersonal diagnosis of individual patients using agentic and communal interpersonal constructs (e.g., behaviors, traits, motives, problems, strengths) to provide a context for understanding presenting symptoms

and for treatment planning. Second, based on the contemporary scope of interpersonal diagnosis, augmentation of the DSM could include subclassification of disorders as characterized by (a) prototypical interpersonal characteristics (e.g., chronic submissiveness in dysthymia; chronic distrust in paranoia), (b) pathoplastic interpersonal subtypes (e.g., generalized anxiety disorder, social phobia), and (c) interpersonal variability (e.g., BPD; dissociative identity disorder). This descriptive augmentation is consistent with evolving models of personality disorder classification that integrate dimensional and categorical approaches (e.g., Krueger, Skodal, Livesley, Shrout, & Huang, 2008), and we see no reason such efforts cannot be extended to symptom syndromes.

The interpersonal nexus of psychopathology includes description and explanation of disorder. Explanation requires integration of the developmental, motivational, and regulatory concepts of interpersonal theory to generate testable hypotheses for future research. In this regard, the identification of pathological interpersonal signatures can point to potential underlying psychosocial mechanisms of disorder. Identifying stable *if-then* interpersonal signatures associated with the exacerbation or diminution of specific symptoms or symptom profiles allows for functional, etiological, and maintenance hypotheses integrating behavioral, social-cognitive, dispositional, and emotional constructs within the agency and communion metaframework.

Interpersonal aspects of description and explanation provide valuable information for the clinician above and beyond psychiatric diagnosis. Knowing a new patient's psychiatric diagnosis does not convey much about who this person is, how their symptoms manifest, and why they persist. If the patient's interpersonal problems are added to the diagnostic picture, the clinician may immediately have some initial ideas about what the patient experiences as significant interpersonal stressors, what social maintenance factors may be involved in the disorder, and what possibilities are indicated for tailoring treatment approaches effectively to the patient's personality. Initial sessions may further diagnosis by identifying pathological interpersonal signatures associated with symptom amplification (e.g., Sadikaj, Russell, Moskowitz, & Paris, in press), leading to targets for behavioral change. Although empirical investigations of interpersonal dispositions associated with psychopathology are abundant, research on interpersonal pathoplasticity, variability, and behavioral signatures has only emerged in the last decade, taking advantage of new developments in psychological science. While it is too early to provide definitive, empirically validated interpersonal augmentation of most disorders, we conclude by highlighting three fruitful interrelated areas for future research. First, psychopathology research should continue efforts to establish and clarify the nature of pathological interpersonal patterns (prototypic, pathoplastic, situationally-contingent) associated with different disorders. Second, psychotherapy research should aim to demonstrate the incremental utility of interpersonal diagnostic information for treatment planning, treatment effectiveness, and treatment efficacy. And third, empirical tests of the dynamics of behavior, emotion, and symptom change using multilevel modeling and latent growth curve frameworks can examine whether changes in interpersonal behavior predict changes in symptoms, further supporting the pantheoretical focus on interpersonal functioning in the conceptualization and treatment of psychopathology.

References

aan het Rot, M., Moskowitz, D., Pinard, G., & Young, S. (2006). Social behaviour and mood in everyday life: The effects of tryptophan in quarrelsome individuals. *Journal of Psychiatry and Neuroscience, 31,* 253–262.

Adams, H. B. (1964). "Mental illness" or interpersonal behavior? *American Psychologist, 19,* 191–197.

Alden, L. E., & Capreol, M. J. (1993). Avoidant personality disorder: Interpersonal problems as predictors of treatment response. *Behavior Therapy, 24,* 357–376.

Alden, L. E., Wiggins, J. S., & Pincus, A. L. (1990). Construction of circumplex scales for the inventory of interpersonal problems. *Journal of Personality Assessment, 55,* 521–536.

Ambwani, S., & Hopwood, C. J. (2009). The utility of considering interpersonal problems in the assessment of bulimic features. *Eating Behaviors, 10,* 247–253.

American Psychiatric Association (1952). *Diagnostic and statistical manual of mental disorders.* Washington, DC: Author.

Anchin, J. C., & Kiesler, D. J. (1982). *Handbook of interpersonal psychotherapy.* New York: Pergamon Press.

Anchin J. C., & Pincus, A. L. (2010). Evidence-based interpersonal psychotherapy with personality disorders: Theory, components, and strategies. In J. J. Magnavita (Ed.), *Evidence-based treatment of personality dysfunction: Principles, methods, and processes* (pp. 113–166). Washington, DC: American Psychological Association.

Andrews, J. D. W. (1989). Integrating visions of reality: Interpersonal diagnosis and the existential vision. *American Psychologist, 44,* 803–817.

Baird, B. M., Le, K., & Lucas, R. E. (2006). On the nature of intraindividual personality variability: Reliability, validity, and associations with well-being. *Journal of Personality and Social Psychology, 90*(3), 512–527.

Barrett, M. S., & Barber, J. P. (2007). Interpersonal profiles in major depressive disorder. *Journal of Clinical Psychology, 63,* 247–266.

Beck, A. T. (1983). Cognitive therapy of depression: New perspectives. In P. J. Clayton & J. E. Barrett (Eds.), *Treatment of depression: Old controversies and new approaches* (pp. 265–290). New York: Raven.

Benjamin, L. S. (1993). Every psychopathology is a gift of love. *Psychotherapy Research, 3,* 1–24.

Benjamin, L. S. (1996). *Interpersonal diagnosis and treatment of personality disorders* (2nd ed.). New York: Guilford Press.

Benjamin, L. S. (2003). *Interpersonal reconstructive therapy: Promoting change in nonresponders.* New York: Guilford Press.

Benjamin, L. S. (2005a). Addressing interpersonal and intrapsychic components of personality during psychotherapy. In S. Strack (Ed.),

Handbook of personology and psychopathology (pp. 417–441). Hoboken, NJ: John Wiley & Sons.

Benjamin, L. S. (2005b). Interpersonal theory of personality disorders: The Structural Analysis of Social Behavior and interpersonal reconstructive therapy. In M. F. Lenzenweger & J. F. Clarkin (Eds.), *Major theories of personality disorder* (2nd ed., pp. 157–230). New York: Guilford Press.

Blatt, S. J. (2004). *Experiences of depression: Theoretical, clinical, and research perspectives.* Washington, DC: American Psychological Association.

Borkovec, T. D., Newman, M. G., Pincus, A. L., & Lytle, R. (2002). A component analysis of cognitive-behavioral therapy for generalized anxiety disorder and the role of interpersonal problems. *Journal of Consulting and Clinical Psychology, 70,* 288–298.

Bornstein, R. F. (2005). *The dependent patient: A practitioner's guide.* Washington, DC: American Psychological Association.

Cain, N. M., Pincus, A. L., & Ansell, E. B. (2008). Narcissism at the crossroads: Phenotypic description of pathological narcissism across clinical theory, social/personality psychology, and psychiatric diagnosis. *Clinical Psychology Review, 28,* 638–656.

Cain, N. M., Pincus, A. L., & Grosse-Holtforth, M. (in press). Interpersonal subtypes in social phobia: Diagnostic and treatment implications. *Journal of Personality Assessment.*

Carson, R. C. (1969). *Interaction concepts of personality.* Chicago: Aldine.

Carson, R. C. (1991). The social-interactional viewpoint. In M. Hersen, A. Kazdin, & A. Bellack (Eds.), *The clinical psychology handbook* (2nd ed., pp. 185–199). New York: Pergamon Press.

Carson, R. C. (1996). Seamlessness in personality and its derangements. *Journal of Personality Assessment, 66,* 240–247.

Critchfield, K. L., & Benjamin, L. S. (2008). Internalized representations of early interpersonal experience and adult relationships: A test of copy process theory in clinical and non–clinical settings. *Psychiatry, 71,* 71–92.

Depue, R. A. (2006). Interpersonal behavior and the structure of personality: Neurobehavioral foundation of agentic extraversion and affiliation. In T. Canli (Ed.), *Biology of personality and individual differences.* (pp. 60–92). New York: Guilford Press.

Eaton, N. R., South, S. C., & Krueger, R. F. (2009). The Cognitive-Affective Processing System (CAPS) approach to personality and the concept of personality disorder: Integrating clinical and social cognitive research. *Journal of Research in Personality, 43,* 208–217.

Eid, M., & Diener, E. (1999). Intraindividual variability in affect: Reliability, validity, and personality correlates. *Journal of Personality and Social Psychology, 76,* 662–676.

Erickson, T. M., Newman, M. G., & Pincus, A. L. (2009). Predicting unpredictability: Do measures of interpersonal rigidity/flexibility and distress predict intraindividual variability in social perceptions and behavior? *Journal of Personality and Social Psychology 97,* 893–912.

Fleeson, W. (2001). Toward a structure- and process-integrated view of personality: Traits as density distributions of states. *Journal of Personality and Social Psychology, 80* (6), 1011–1027.

Fleeson, W. (2004). Moving beyond the person-situation debate: The challenge and the opportunity of within-person variability. *Current Directions in Psychological Science, 13,* 83–87.

Fleeson, W., & Noftle, E. E. (2008). Where does personality have its influence? A supermatrix of consistency concepts. *Journal of Personality, 76,* 1355–1386.

Fournier, M. A., Moskowitz, D. S., & Zuroff, D. C. (2008). Integrating dispositions, signatures, and the interpersonal domain. *Journal of Personality and Social Psychology, 94,* 531–545.

Fournier, M., Moskowitz, D. S., & Zuroff, D. (2009). The interpersonal signature. *Journal of Research in Personality, 43,* 155–162.

Fournier, M., Moskowitz, D. S., & Zuroff, D. (in press). Two-dimensional model of interpersonal behavior. In L. M. Horowitz & S. Strack (Eds.), *Handbook of interpersonal psychology: Theory, research, and therapeutic interventions.* Hoboken, NJ: John Wiley & Sons.

Freedman, M. B., Leary, T. F., Ossorio, A. G., & Coffey, H. S. (1951). The interpersonal dimension of personality. *Journal of Personality, 20,* 143–161.

Funder, D. C. (2006). Towards a resolution of the personality triad: Persons, situations, and behaviors. *Journal of Research in Personality, 40,* 21–34.

Funder, D. C. (2009). Persons, behaviors, and situations: An agenda for personality psychology in the postwar era. *Journal of Research in Personality, 43,* 120–126.

Gurtman, M. B. (1994). The circumplex as a tool for studying normal and abnormal personality: A methodological primer. In S. Strack & M. Lorr (Eds.), *Differentiating normal and abnormal personality* (pp. 243–263). New York: Springer.

Gurtman, M. B. (1996). Interpersonal problems and the psychotherapy context: The construct validity of the Inventory of Interpersonal Problems. *Psychological Assessment, 8,* 241–255.

Gurtman, M. B. (In press). Circumplex measures and circular reasoning. In L. M. Horowitz & S. Strack (Eds.), *Handbook of interpersonal psychology: Theory, research, and therapeutic interventions.* Hoboken, NJ: John Wiley & Sons.

Gurtman, M. B., & Balakrishnan, J. D. (1998). Circular measurement redux: The analysis and interpretation of interpersonal circle profiles. *Clinical Psychology: Science and Practice, 5,* 344–360.

Gurtman, M. B., & Pincus, A. L. (2000). Interpersonal adjective scales: Confirmation of circumplex structure from multiple perspectives. *Personality and Social Psychology Bulletin, 26,* 374–384.

Harmon-Jones, E., & Winkielman, P. (Eds.). (2007). *Social neuroscience: Integrating biological and psychological explanations of social behavior.* New York: Guilford Press.

Heller, D., Watson, D., Komar, J., Min, J., & Perunovic, W. Q. E. (2007). Contextualized personality: Traditional and new assessment procedures. *Journal of Personality, 75,* 1229–1254.

Henry, W. P. (1994). Differentiating normal and abnormal personality: An interpersonal approach based on the Structural Analysis of Social Behavior. In S. Strack & M. Lorr (Eds.). *Differentiating normal and abnormal personality* (pp. 316–340). New York: Springer.

Hopwood, C. J., Clarke, A. N., & Perez, M. (2007). Pathoplasticity of bulimic features and interpersonal problems. *International Journal of Eating Disorders, 40,* 652–658.

Hopwood, C. J., Pincus, A. L., DeMoor, R. M., & Koonce, E. A. (2008). Psychometric characteristics of the Inventory of Interpersonal Problems: Short Circumplex (IIP–SC) with college students. *Journal of Personality Assessment, 90,* 615–618.

Horowitz, L. M. (1979). On the cognitive structure of interpersonal problems treated in psychotherapy. *Journal of Consulting and Clinical Psychology, 47,* 5–15.

Horowitz, L. M. (1996). The study of interpersonal problems: A Leary legacy. *Journal of Personality Assessment, 66,* 283–300.

Horowitz, L. M. (2004). *Interpersonal foundations of psychopathology.* Washington, DC: American Psychological Association.

Horowitz, L. M., Alden, L. E., Wiggins, J. S., & Pincus, A. L. (2000). *IIP–64/IIP–32 professional manual.* San Antonio, TX: The Psychological Corporation.

Horowitz, L. M., Rosenberg, S. E., Baer, B. A., Ureño, G., & Villaseñor, V. S. (1988). Inventory of Interpersonal Problems: Psychometric properties and clinical applications. *Journal of Consulting and Clinical Psychology, 56,* 885–892.

Horowitz, L. M., Rosenberg, S. E., & Bartholomew, K. (1993). Interpersonal problems, attachment styles, and outcome in brief dynamic psychotherapy. *Journal of Consulting and Clinical Psychology, 61,* 549–560.

Horowitz, L. M., & Vitkus, J. (1986). The interpersonal basis of psychiatric symptoms. *Clinical Psychology Review, 6,* 443–469.

Horowitz, L. M., & Wilson, K. R. (2005). Interpersonal motives and personality disorders. In S. Strack (Ed.), *Handbook of personology and psychopathology* (pp. 495–510). Hoboken, NJ: John Wiley & Sons.

Horowitz, L. M., Wilson, K. R., Turan, B., Zolotsev, P., Constantino, M. J., & Henderson, L. (2006). How interpersonal motives clarify the meaning of interpersonal behavior: A revised circumplex model. *Personality and Social Psychology Review, 10,* 67–86.

Huber, D., Henrich, G., & Klug, G. (2007). The Inventory of Interpersonal Problems (IIP): Sensitivity to change. *Psychotherapy Research, 17,* 474–481.

Kachin, K. E., Newman, M. G., & Pincus, A. L. (2001). An interpersonal problem approach to the division of social phobia subtypes. *Behavior Therapy, 32,* 479–501.

Kaslow, F. W. (1996). *Handbook of relational diagnosis and dysfunctional family patterns.* Oxford, UK: John Wiley & Sons.

Kaslow, F., & Patterson, T. (2006). Relational diagnosis: A brief historical overview: Comment on the special section. *Journal of Family Psychology, 20,* 428–431.

Kasoff, M. B. (2002). Interpersonal subtypes of generalized anxiety disorder: Derivation and differentiation in patterns of adult attachment and psychiatric comorbidity. *Dissertation Abstracts International: Section B: The Sciences and Engineering, 62* (12-B).

Keller, M. C., Neale, M. C., & Kendler, K. S. (2007). Association of different adverse life events with distinct patterns of depressive symptoms. *American Journal of Psychiatry, 164,* 1521–1529.

Kiesler, D. J. (1983). The 1982 interpersonal circle: A taxonomy for complementarity in human transactions. *Psychological Review, 90,* 185–214.

Kiesler, D. J. (1996). *Contemporary interpersonal theory and research: Personality, psychopathology, and psychotherapy.* New York: John Wiley & Sons.

Klein, M. H., Wonderlich, S., & Shea, M. T. (1993). Models of relationships between personality and depression: Toward a framework for theory and research. In M. Klein, D. Kupfer, & M. Tracie (Eds.), *Personality and depression: A current view* (pp. 1–54). New York: Guilford Press.

Krueger R. F., Skodol A. E., Livesley, W. J., Shrout P. E., & Huang Y. (2008). Synthesizing dimensional and categorical approaches to personality disorders: Refining the research agenda for DSM-V axis II. In J. E. Helzer, H. C. Kraemer, R. F. Krueger, H.-U. Wittchen, P. J. Sirovatka, & D. E. Regier (Eds.), *Dimensional approaches in diagnostic classification: A critical appraisal* (pp. 85–99). Washington, DC: American Psychiatric. Association.

Kuppens, P., Van Mechelen, I., Nezlek, J. B., Dossche, D., & Timmermans, T. (2007). Individual differences in core affect variability and their relationship to personality and psychological adjustment. *Emotion, 7,* 262–274.

LaForge, R. (2004). The early development of the Interpersonal System of Personality (ISP). *Multivariate Behavioral Research, 39,* 359–378.

Laforge, R., Leary, T. F., Naboisek, H., Coffey, H. S., & Freedman, M. B. (1954). The interpersonal dimension of personality: II. An objective study of repression. *Journal of Personality, 23,* 129–153.

Leary, T. (1957). *Interpersonal diagnosis of personality.* New York: Ronald Press.

Leary, T. F., & Coffey, H. S. (1955). Interpersonal diagnosis: Some problems of methodology and validation. *Journal of Abnormal and Social Psychology, 50,* 110–124.

Leichsenring, F., Kunst, H., & Hoyer, J. (2003). Borderline personality organization in violent offenders: Correlations of identity diffusion and primitive defense mechanisms with antisocial features, neuroticism, and interpersonal problems. *Bulletin of the Menninger Clinic, 67,* 314–327.

Leihener, F., Wagner, A., Haff, B., Schmidt, C., Lieb, K., Stieglitz, R., & Bohus, M. (2003). Subtype differentiation of patients with borderline personality disorder using a circumplex model of interpersonal behavior. *The Journal of Nervous and Mental Disease, 191,* 248–254.

Leising, D., & Müller-Plath, G. (2009). Person-situation integration in research on personality problems. *Journal of Research in Personality, 43,* 218–227.

Locke, K. D. (in press). Measures of interpersonal constructs. In L. M. Horowitz & S. Strack (Eds.), *Handbook of interpersonal psychology: Theory, research, and therapeutic interventions.* Hoboken, NJ: John Wiley & Sons.

Lukowitsky, M. R., Pincus, A. L., Hill, L. L., & Loos, D. K. (2008). Enduring dispositions as points of contact for the social-clinical interface: Publication trends from 1965 to 2004. *Journal of Social & Clinical Psychology, 27,* 389–403.

Markowitz, J. C., Friedman, R. A., Miller, N., Spielman, L. A., Moran, M. E., & Kocsis, J. H. (1996). Interpersonal improvement in chronically depressed patients treated with desipramine. *Journal of Affective Disorders, 41,* 59–62.

McAdams, D. P. (1995). What do we know when we know a person? *Journal of Personality, 63,* 365–396.

McLemore, C. W., & Benjamin, L. S. (1979). Whatever happened to interpersonal diagnosis? A psychosocial alternative to DSM-III. *American Psychologist, 34,* 17–34.

Millon, T. (2000). Reflections on the future of DSM axis II. *Journal of Personality Disorders, 14,* 30–41.

Millon, T. (2005). Reflections on the future of personology and psychopathology. In S. Strack (Ed.), *Handbook of personology and psychopathology* (pp. 527–546). Hoboken, NJ: John Wiley & Sons.

Mineka, S., Watson, D., & Clark, L. A. (1998). Comorbidity of anxiety and unipolar mood disorders. *Annual Review of Psychology, 49,* 377–412.

Mischel, W., Shoda, Y., & Mendoza-Denton, R. (2002). Situation-behavior profiles as a locus of consistency in personality. *Current Directions in Psychological Science, 11,* 50–54.

Mischel, W., & Shoda, Y. (1998). Reconciling processing dynamics and personality dispositions. *Annual Review of Psychology, 49,* 229–258.

Moskowitz, D. S. (2005). Unfolding interpersonal behavior. *Journal of Personality, 73,* 1607–1632.

Moskowitz, D. S. (2009). Coming full circle: Conceptualizing the study of interpersonal behaviour. *Canadian Psychology/Psychologie Canadienne, 50,* 33–41.

Moskowtiz, D. S. (2010). Quarrelsomeness in daily life. *Journal of Personality, 78,* 39–66.

Moskowitz, D. S., & Zuroff, D. C. (2004a). Flux, pulse, and spin: Dynamic additions to the personality lexicon. *Journal of Personality and Social Psychology, 86,* 880–893.

Moskowitz, D. S., & Zuroff, D. C. (2005). Robust predictors of flux, pulse, and spin. *Journal of Research in Personality, 39,* 130–147.

O'Connor, B. P. (2002). The search for dimensional structure difference between normality and abnormality: A statistical review of published data on personality and psychopathology. *Journal of Personality and Social Psychology, 83,* 962–982.

O'Connor, B. P., & Dyce, J. A. (2001). Rigid and extreme: A geometric representation of personality disorders in five-factor model space. *Journal of Personality and Social Psychology, 81,* 1119–1130.

Paulhus, D. L., & Martin, C. L. (1987). The structure of personality capabilities. *Journal of Personality and Social Psychology, 52,* 354–365.

Paulhus, D. L., & Martin, C. L. (1988). Functional flexibility: A new conception of interpersonal flexibility. *Journal of Personality and Social Psychology, 55,* 88–101.

Pincus, A. L. (1994). The interpersonal circumplex and the interpersonal theory: Perspectives on personality and its pathology. In S. Strack & M. Lorr (Eds.), *Differentiating normal and abnormal personality* (pp. 114–136). New York: Springer.

Pincus, A. L. (2005a). A contemporary integrative interpersonal theory of personality disorders. In J. Clarkin & M. Lenzenweger (Eds.), *Major theories of personality disorder* (2nd ed., pp. 282–331). New York: Guilford Press.

Pincus, A. L. (2005b). The interpersonal nexus of personality disorders. In S. Strack (Ed.),

Handbook of personology and psychopathology (pp. 120–139). New York: John Wiley & Sons.

Pincus, A. L., & Ansell, E. B. (2003). Interpersonal theory of personality. In T. Millon & M. Lerner (Eds.), *Handbook of psychology: Personality and social psychology* (Vol. 5, pp. 209–229). Hoboken, NJ: John Wiley & Sons.

Pincus, A. L., & Cain, N. M. (2008). Interpersonal psychotherapy. In D. C. S. Richard & S. K. Huprich (Eds.), *Clinical Psychology: Assessment, treatment, and research* (pp. 213–245). San Diego, CA: Academic Press.

Pincus, A. L., & Gurtman, M. B. (2006). Interpersonal theory and the interpersonal circumplex: Evolving perspectives on normal and abnormal personality. In S. Strack (Ed.), *Differentiating normal and abnormal personality* (2nd ed., pp, 83–111). New York: Springer.

Pincus, A. L., Gurtman, M. B., & Ruiz, M. A. (1998). Structural Analysis of Social Behavior (SASB): Circumplex analyses and structural relations with the interpersonal circle and personality. *Journal of Personality and Social Psychology, 74,* 1629–1645.

Pincus, A. L., & Lukowitsky, M. R. (2010). Pathological narcissism and Narcissistic Personality Disorder. *Annual Review of Clinical Psychology, 6,* 421–446.

Pincus, A. L., Lukowitsky, M. R., & Wright, A. G. C. (2010). The interpersonal nexus of personality and psychopathology. In T. Millon, R. F. Krueger, & E. Simonsen (Eds.), *Contemporary directions in psychopathology: Scientific foundations for the DSM-V and ICD-11* (pp. 523–552). New York: Guilford Press.

Pincus, A. L., Lukowitsky, M. R., Wright, A. G. C., & Eichler, W. C. (2009). The interpersonal nexus of persons, situations, and psychopathology. *Journal of Research in Personality, 43,* 264–265.

Pincus, A. L., Przeworski, A., Yamasaki, A., Kasoff, M. B., Newman, M. G., Castonguay, L. G. & Borkovec, T. D. (2005, June). *Interpersonal Pathoplasticity in Generalized Anxiety Disorder: A Cluster Analytic Replication.* Paper presented at the Society for Interpersonal Theory and Research, Montreal, Quebec, Canada.

Pincus, A. L., & Roche, M. J. (in press). Narcissistic grandiosity and narcissistic vulnerability. In W. K. Campbell & J. D. Miller (Eds.), *The Handbook of Narcissism and Narcissistic Personality*

Disorder: Theoretical Approaches, Empirical Findings, and Treatment. Hoboken, NJ: John Wiley & Sons.

Pincus, A. L., & Wiggins, J. S. (1990). Interpersonal problems and conceptions of personality disorders. *Journal of Personality Disorders, 4,* 342–352.

Puschner, B., Kraft, S., & Bauer, S. (2004). Interpersonal problems and outcome in outpatient psychotherapy: Findings from a long-term longitudinal study in Germany. *Journal of Personality Assessment, 83,* 223–234.

Reis, H. T. (2008). Reinvigorating the concept of situation in social psychology. *Personality and Social Psychology Review, 12,* 311–329.

Ruiz, M. A., Pincus, A. L., Borkovec, T. D., Echemendia, R. J., Castonguay, L. G., & Ragusea, S. A. (2004). Validity of the Inventory of Interpersonal Problems for predicting treatment outcome: An investigation with the Pennsylvania Practice Research Network. *Journal of Personality Assessment, 83,* 213–222.

Russell, J. J., Moskowitz, D. S., Zuroff, D. C., Sookman, D., & Paris, J. (2007). Stability and variability of affective experience and interpersonal behavior in borderline personality disorder. *Journal of Abnormal Psychology, 116,* 578–588.

Ryan, K., & Shean, G. (2007). Patterns of interpersonal behaviors and borderline personality characteristics. *Personality and Individual Differences, 42,* 193–200.

Sadikaj, G., Russell, J. J., Moskowitz, D. S., & Paris, J. (in press). Affect dysregulation in individuals with borderline personality disorder: Persistence and interpersonal triggers. *Journal of Personality Assessment.*

Sadler, P., Woody, E., & Ethier, N. (in press). Complementarity in interpersonal relationships. In L. M. Horowitz & S. Strack (Eds.), *Handbook of interpersonal psychology: Theory, research, and therapeutic interventions.* Hoboken, NJ: John Wiley & Sons.

Salzer, S., Pincus, A. L., Hoyer, J., Kreische, R., Leichsenring, F., & Leibling, E. (2008). Interpersonal subtypes within generalized anxiety disorder. *Journal of Personality Assessment, 90,* 292–299.

Salzer, S., Pincus, A. L., Winkelbach, C., Leichsenring, F., & Leibing, E. (in press). Interpersonal subtypes and change of interpersonal problems in the treatment of patients with generalized anxiety disorder: A pilot study.

Psychotherapy: Theory, Research, Practice, Training.

Shoda, Y., Mischel, W., & Wright, J. C. (1993). Links between personality judgments and contextualized behavior patterns: Situation-behavior profiles of personality prototypes. *Social Cognition, 11,* 399–429.

Shoda, Y., Mischel, W., & Wright, J. C. (1994). Intraindividual stability in the organization and patterning of behavior: Incorporating psychological situations into the idiographic analysis of personality. *Journal of Personality and Social Psychology, 67,* 674–687.

Sibrava, N. J., Pincus, A. L., Przeworski, A., Yamasaki, A. S., Newman, M. G., & Borkovec, T. D. (2007, November). *Heterogeneity in the presentation of GAD.* Paper presented at the Association for Behavioral and Cognitive Therapies annual meeting, Philadelphia, PA.

Slaney, R., Pincus, A. L., Uliaszek, A. A., & Wang, K. (2006). Conceptions of perfectionism and interpersonal problems: Evaluating groups using the structural summary method for circumplex data. *Assessment, 13,* 138–153.

Soldz, S., Budman, S., Demby, A., & Merry, J. (1993). Representation of personality disorders in circumplex and five-factor model space: Explorations with a clinical sample. *Psychological Assessment, 5,* 41–52.

Soldz, S., Budman, S., Demby, A., & Merry, J. (1995). A short form of the Inventory of Interpersonal Problems Circumplex scales. *Assessment, 2,* 53–63.

Sullivan, H. S. (1953a). *The interpersonal theory of psychiatry.* New York: W. W. Norton.

Sullivan, H. S. (1953b). *Conceptions of modern psychiatry.* New York: W. W. Norton.

Sullivan, H. S. (1954). *The psychiatric interview.* New York: W. W. Norton.

Sullivan, H. S. (1956). *Clinical studies in psychiatry.* New York: W. W. Norton.

Sullivan, H. S. (1962). *Schizophrenia as a human process.* New York: W. W. Norton.

Sullivan, H. S. (1964). *The fusion of psychiatry and social science.* New York: W. W. Norton.

Swann, W. B., Jr., & Seyle, C. (2005). Personality psychology's comeback and its emerging symbiosis with social psychology. *Personality and Social Psychology Bulletin, 31,* 155–165.

Tracey, T. J. G. (2005). Interpersonal rigidity and complementarity. *Journal of Research in Personality, 39,* 592–614.

Tracey, T. J. G., & Rohlfing, J. E. (2010). Variations in the understanding of interpersonal behavior: Adherence to the interpersonal circle as a moderator of the rigidity-psychological well-being relation. *Journal of Personality, 78,* 711–746.

Vittengl, J. R., Clark, L. A., & Jarrett, R. B. (2003). Interpersonal problems, personality pathology, and social adjustment after cognitive therapy for depression. *Psychological Assessment, 15,* 29–40.

Widiger, T. A., & Smith, G. T. (2008). Personality and psychopathology. In O. P. John, R. Robins, & L. A. Pervin (Eds.), *Handbook of personality: Theory and research* (3rd ed., pp, 743–769). New York: Guilford Press.

Wiggins, J. S. (1996). An informal history of the interpersonal circumplex tradition. *Journal of Personality Assessment, 66,* 217–233.

Wiggins, J. S. (2003). *Paradigms of personality assessment.* New York: Guilford Press.

Wiggins, J. S., Phillips, N., & Trapnell, P. (1989). Circular reasoning about interpersonal behavior: Evidence concerning some untested assumptions underlying diagnostic classification. *Journal of Personality and Social Psychology, 56,* 296–305.

Wiggins, J. S., & Pincus, A. L. (1989). Conceptions of personality disorders and dimensions of personality. *Psychological Assessment, 1,* 305–316.

Wiggins, J. S., & Trobst, K. K. (1999). The fields of interpersonal behavior. In L. Pervin and O. P. John (Eds.), *Handbook of personality: Theory and research* (2nd ed., pp. 653–670). New York: Guilford Press.

Wright, A. G. C., Pincus, A. L., Conroy, D. E., & Elliot, A. J. (2009). The pathoplastic relationship between interpersonal problems and fear of failure. *Journal of Personality, 77,* 997–1024.

Wright, A. G. C., Pincus, A. L., Conroy, D. E., & Hilsenroth, M. J. (2009). Integrating methods to optimize circumplex description and comparison of groups. *Journal of Personality Assessment, 91,* 311–322.

NOTES

1. An example of a related approach to generating an alternative interpersonal nosology can be found in the systems-based "relational diagnosis" movement (e.g., Kaslow, 1996; Kaslow & Patterson, 2006). However, this approach does not necessarily incorporate the four basic elements of interpersonal diagnosis described here.

2. Dynamisms are the Sullivanian term for individuals' slowly changeable but recognizably recurrent and typical patterns of interpersonal behavior and emotion (e.g., a chronically irritable and argumentative interpersonal presentation).

3. Like Sullivan, Leary contended that those behaviors that are adaptive are those that are culturally valued and commonly socialized. This formulation offers flexibility in conceptualization by allowing for cultural framing of what is considered "disordered."

4. Note the consistency with Sullivan's conception of disturbed interpersonal relations as the "misuse" of human dynamisms.

5. This conclusion is certainly not new. Such possibilities were even discussed at length in Sullivan's (1964) final book, *The Fusion of Psychiatry and Social Science.*

23 PERSONALITY DISORDERS

John F. Clarkin

Kenneth N. Levy

William D. Ellison

Many avenues of research are contributing to a growing consensus that an interpersonal view of the human being is essential to understanding personality and the personality disorders (Andersen & Chen, 2002; Clark, 2007). The infant comes into the world utterly helpless and depends on a nurturing, protective interpersonal context for survival. The caregiver-infant interaction becomes an early training ground for the development of survival functions such as attention, memory, nurturance, and harm avoidance, in addition to the growing conception of others and their attitude toward the self (Rothbart, Ellis, & Posner, 2004). The human brain seems constructed for the ability to understand other people and interact with them (Bretherton & Munholland, 2008). An understanding of the normal development of cooperative, rewarding interpersonal interaction is crucial for an appreciation of how deviations from this trajectory lead to the distortions in interpersonal behavior that are termed the personality disorders.

Personality disorders are described as a pattern of inner experience and behavior that deviates from cultural norms. These patterns of perceiving, relating to, and thinking about the environment and oneself are pervasive, inflexible, and stable over time, and result in distress or impairment in functioning (American Psychiatric Association, 2000). Epidemiological studies across cultures suggest that the prevalence of any personality disorder is around 10% (Lenzenweger, 2008). Those with personality disorder are often comorbid with a range of Axis I symptom disorders. The impairment of functioning involved in the personality disorder can be substantial, and those with personality disorder are frequent users of medical and mental health services (Bender et al., 2001), so that treatment is difficult and with variable outcomes.

In this chapter we review the current part-theories of personality and its disorders, with special attention to the personality functions that are undeveloped or distorted in those with personality disorders. We focus specifically on the here-and-now functions of the normal personality and the abnormal personality. Focus on the process of personality functioning and dysfunction leads naturally and directly to assessment and intervention with those suffering from personality dysfunction. We speculate that in the near future an integration of personality theory, psychopathology of personality, and social-cognitive neuroscience will advance our understanding of the functioning of the individual person in a way that will more directly relate to understanding the personality disorders.

CONCEPTUAL ISSUES

Personality Disorder From the Perspective of Normal Personality Functioning

A theoretically comprehensive, coherent, and empirically supported theory of personality is basic to an understanding of deviations from normal personality. Personality theory has grappled with issues such as the core definition of personality, the appropriate scientific methodology to study personality, idiographic-nomothetic emphases, internal-external influences on the personality, nature-nurture, persistence and change, and conscious-unconscious processes (Pervin, 1990; John, Robins & Pervin, 2008). It is not surprising that many of the same issues are now surfacing in the investigation of personality disorders.

Importantly, most current theories of personality disorders involve the interpersonal and social aspects of personality functioning. Moreover, it has long been recognized that individuals with personality disorders display particular behaviors in response to specific interpersonal situations. For example, DSM-IV-TR suggests that individuals with borderline personality disorder (BPD) often display "frantic efforts to avoid real or imagined abandonment" (American Psychiatric Association, 2000). Although trait-based theories of personality, such as the Five-Factor Model (McCrae & Costa, 2008), have deservedly achieved a prominent status among empirically derived personality systems, it is unclear how global trait terms would capture this tendency, or indeed other maladaptive styles of interpersonal functioning. One contemporary grand theory of normal personality that takes both enduring dispositions and particular psychological situations into account is the cognitive-affective processing system (CAPS) theory (Mischel & Shoda, 1995, 2008).

CAPS theory conceives of personality in terms of distinct cognitive-affective units (CAUs) that describe an individual's encoding and construal of situations, beliefs about the world, affective tendencies, goals and values, and self-regulatory competencies (Mischel & Shoda, 1995). These units are seen as distinct representations that exist in a structured network and mediate between the objective situation and the individual's behavioral response to it. Although the roots of this personality system are in the idiographic study of person-situation interactions (Mischel, 1973; Shoda, Mischel, & Wright, 1994), nomothetic research is also possible within CAPS, based on particular structures and combinations of CAUs. As others have noted (Eaton, South, & Krueger, 2009), CAPS is thus able to capture both intraindividual, interindividual, and group differences in personality, making it a compelling model for personality dysfunction.

The CAPS system has been used to describe several interpersonal styles that are relevant to an understanding of personality disorders. For example, Susan Andersen has conducted a series of investigations into transference, or how representations of significant others, stored in memory, are activated in response to new people and affect the individual's reactions to them (Andersen & Chen, 2002). For example, subjects were presented cues about a stranger subliminally while engaged in a task with the stranger. When the subliminal cues related to subjects' past significant relationships, the subjects made stronger significant-other derived inferences about the stranger following the task.

In other situations, when a representation of a positive significant other is activated in interaction with a stranger, subjects were motivated to emotionally approach and be more open toward the stranger (Andersen & Chen, 2002).

Other research within the CAPS model has focused on rejection sensitivity, or the tendency to expect, perceive, and react strongly to rejection cues (Downey & Feldman, 1996). This interpersonal style has immediate relevance to the particular "if, then" behavioral signature observed in individuals with personality dysfunction. Recent research confirms this expectation. Ayduk and colleagues (2008) measured rejection sensitivity in college and community samples and found an association between this tendency and features of BPD. In addition, another component of the CAPS model, namely executive control (Metcalfe & Mischel, 1999), acted to buffer the effects of rejection sensitivity, such that even highly rejection sensitive individuals did not show BPD features if they were able to regulate their emotions effectively.

THEORIES OF PERSONALITY DISORDERS

Historically, theories of personality tended to describe the development of both normal and abnormal functioning (e.g., Cattell, 1946; Eysenck, 1952; Freud, 1933/1965; Millon, 1969). However, beginning with Murray (1938) and Allport (1937), the study of normal personality began to diverge from this tradition and developed separately in academic departments of psychology, where it acquired a theoretically and empirically rich body of findings in its own right. Because of this separation, theories of personality disorder are not carefully coordinated with the current prominent theories of personality, even though many authors argue that the personality disorders are essentially continuous with normal personality and simply represent extreme variations of the same traits or behaviors.

The study of personality pathology is only recently beginning to be shaped by research based on theories of normal personality. In addition, as will become clear, research into the personality disorders has been uneven, with BPD and antisocial personality disorder most prominently represented, perhaps because of the severity of pathology involved in these two disorders.

Three phases in the history of the study of personality disorders have been described (Livesley, 2001). The early phase dates from the 19th century and includes the work of pioneers in clinical psychiatry and psychopathology to formulate conceptions of character and its pathology (see Stone, 1997). Empirical work on personality pathology began in the 1960s and 1970s, and with the introduction of the personality disorder axis in 1980, the DSM phase of investigation was initiated. This official recognition of the personality disorders, along with the research criteria for separate disorders fostered assessment and diagnosis via semi-structured interview, which then led to reliability and validity studies and treatment investigations. These studies confirmed the enhanced reliability of the criterion sets, despite criticisms that the new system failed to promote validity (e.g., Blatt & Levy, 1998; Carson, 1991). In the current third phase of study, which Livesley has called the post DSM III-V phase, the problems with the DSM classification are so obvious that other ways to guide research are being sought. We suggest that this current and developing phase will focus more on the mechanisms of disorder, both in terms of examining the pathology cross-sectionally and longitudinally and in the treatment research. This focus on mechanisms will be enriched by the realization that the pathology involves genetic elements and other biological variables such as neurotransmitters and neural functioning.

There is a growing consensus that the essence of the personality disorder involves difficulties with self or identity and chronic interpersonal dysfunction (Bender & Skodol, 2007; Gunderson & Lyons-Ruth, 2008; Horowitz, 2004; Livesley, 2001; Pincus, 2005;). Clinicians across diverse orientations such as the cognitive (Pretzer & Beck, 2004), interpersonal (Benjamin, 2005), attachment (Levy, 2005; Meyer & Pilkonis, 2005), and object relations perspectives (Clarkin, Yeomans, & Kernberg, 2006) emphasize these essential areas of dysfunction. These difficulties are interrelated as conception of self and others, attention, and memory lead to the final common pathway of interpersonal behavior. Most relevant to personality disorders, their assessment, and the particular dysfunctions in need of clinical intervention are those personality theories that delineate mechanisms that allow individuals to function adequately in their interpersonal social and work environments.

Major Theories of the Personality Disorders

Theories of the personality disorders are in their infancy, and the existing theories are best described as part-theories, as they each emphasize a few salient aspects of the disorders. Many emphasize interpersonal relations as the heart of the pathology, conceptualized in terms of disturbed interpersonal schemas and strategies (Pretzer & Beck, 2004), object relations (Kernberg, 1975), attachment (Meyer & Pilkonis, 2005), and patterns of interpersonal behavior based on interactions with significant others (Benjamin, 1996). A sign of progress is evident in efforts to integrate functional psychological aspects of personality pathology with genetic abnormalities, neurotransmitters, and neuroimaging studies.

Trait theories. Trait models of the personality disorders are prominent in the academic world and in the discussions about the structure and revision of the DSM diagnostic system. Most prominent is research on the so-called Five-Factor Model, according to which the five dimensions of neuroticism, extraversion, openness, agreeableness, and conscientiousness capture normal personality (McCrae & Costa, 2008). Extreme deviations on these dimensions (or on lower-order factors) are understood to constitute the personality disorders (Widiger & Costa, 1994).

Although the Five-Factor Model is an important and well-researched model for relating normal personality traits to personality disorders, the manner in which these traits are related to pathology is varied. In addition, other personality factors are considered to be important by other theorists. Thus, one important issue for trait theories of personality disorders is which key (essential) traits are most important for personality and personality dysfunction. Cloninger (2000) sees variations in self-directedness, cooperativeness, affective stability, and self-transcendence as encompassing personality dysfunction. Other conceptualizations exist. Although not a trait theorist, Kernberg (1975) emphasizes moral values and aggression as traitlike qualities in personality disorders. Using the Five-Factor Model, Trull (2005) indicates that the most central traits that capture personality pathology are neuroticism/negative affectivity/emotional dysregulation, extraversion/positive affectivity, dissociality/antagonism, and constraint/compulsivity/conscientiousness. He recommends that the four higher-order factors be related to problem areas in the patient's life in the service of clinical utility. This suggestion implicitly recognizes that clinicians do not treat traits, but rather examine the patients' troubled interactions with the environment, especially other people.

Focus on self and others. An interpersonal approach to personality and its pathologies is based on the centrality of human interaction—involving the self and dyadic relationships—to human survival, striving, and satisfaction and/or disappointment and distress (Benjamin, 2005; Horowitz, 2004; Pincus, 2005). A number of clinical researchers have discussed the relationship between the development of self-definition and relatedness and personality disorders (Blatt & Levy, 2003; Levy & Blatt, 1999; Wiggins & Pincus, 1989). These two developmental lines of self-definition and relatedness not only provide a basis for considering personality development, but they have particular relevance for the conceptualization of psychopathology. Distortions of either developmental line, or an exaggerated emphasis on one or the other, leads to particular configurations of psychopathology (Blatt & Levy, 2003; Levy & Blatt, 1999). Blatt and Shichman (1983) contend that self-definition and relatedness are related to several types of personality disorder behaviors and diagnoses. They posit that exaggerated emphasis on the relatedness developmental line is associated with histrionic, dependent, and borderline personalities. In contrast, the self-definitional developmental line is related to paranoid, schizoid, schizotypal, narcissistic, obsessive-compulsive, and borderline personalities.

A plethora of research evidence generally supports these hypotheses (Cogswell & Alloy, 2006; Goldberg, Segal, Vella, & Shaw, 1989; Levy et al., 1994; Morse, Robins, & Gittes-Fox, 2002; Ouimette & Klein, 1993; O'Leary et al., 1991; Ouimette, Klein, Anderson, Riso, & Lizardi, 1994; Wiggins & Pincus, 1989). For instance, Goldberg, Segal, Vella, and Shaw (1989) found that need for approval was significantly related to dependent personality disorder traits and that perfectionism was significantly related to negativistic (or passive-aggressive) personality traits. Ouimette and colleagues (Ouimette & Klein, 1993; Ouimette et al., 1994) found that borderline, obsessive-compulsive, paranoid, passive-aggressive, schizoid, and narcissistic personality disorders were significantly correlated with concerns about issues of self-definition (e.g., autonomy and self-criticism), while dependent and histrionic personality disorders were significantly correlated with concerns about issues of interpersonal relatedness (e.g.,

sociotropy and dependency) in both college students and in an outpatient clinical sample. Levy and colleagues (1994) found similar results with a sample of seriously disturbed inpatients.

In addition to interpersonal theory (Horowitz, 2004), two other traditions that emphasize the interaction of the individual with significant others are especially relevant to understanding the personality disorders, namely, object relations theory (Kernberg & Caligor, 2005) and attachment theory (Fonagy, Target, Gergely, Allen, & Bateman, 2003; Levy, 2005; Meyer & Pilkonis, 2005).

Kernberg and colleagues (Clarkin, Yeomans, & Kernberg, 2006; Kernberg & Caligor, 2005) present a current object relations model of personality pathology that combines a dimensional scheme of personality disorders, according to severity of pathology, with a categorical or prototypic classification based on descriptive traits (see Figure 23.1). This approach characterizes the severity of personality pathology by assessing the nature, organization, and degree of integration of psychological structures, and then characterizes descriptive features of personality pathology to make a prototypic or categorical diagnosis of personality "type" or "style." The model attends in particular to the extent to which pathology is dominated by aggression (e.g., in malignant narcissism and antisocial personality), the extent to which affective dispositions to depression or anxiety influence personality functioning (as in depressive-masochistic personality), the potential role of a stable but pathological sense of self in psychological functioning (as in narcissistic personality), and the potential influence of a temperamental disposition to introversion or extroversion. We believe that this two-axis approach reflects the clinical reality that similar personality styles or maladaptive traits may be seen across a broad spectrum of pathology, with markedly different prognostic implications. We contend that, from a clinical perspective, the degree of severity of personality

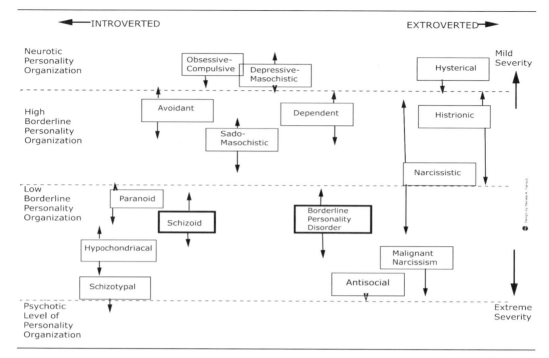

FIGURE 23.1   An Object Relations Model of Personality Pathology
Source: From "A Psychoanalytic Theory of Personality Disorders," by O. F. Kernberg and E. Caligor, 2005. In M. F. Lenzenweger and J. F. Clarkin (Eds.), *Major Theories of Personality Disorder* (2nd ed.), page 134. New York: Guilford Press. Reprinted with permission.

pathology is typically of greater importance with regard to prognosis and differential treatment planning than is personality "type." This view is consistent with a recent factor analytic study that has found that a severity dimension characterizes personality pathology (Verheul et al., 2008).

Another interpersonally focused theory of psychology that has great importance for personality disorder is attachment theory, which was initially formulated by Bowlby (1969, 1973, 1980), and has a large and growing body of empirical support. To date, attachment theory has provided a deeper understanding of the developmental aspects of the ability to form close relationships, and the link between disturbed interpersonal relationships and psychopathology, including the personality disorders (Levy, 2005). Attachment theory postulates that the emotional bond formed by the infant and its caretakers has important consequences

for the child's developing self-concept and representations of the social world. The behaviors used by the infant to maintain this bond correspond to discrete attachment "patterns" or "styles." Underlying these styles are "internal working models" of the interpersonal world, which are elaborated with further experience, and which the individual uses to anticipate interactions with significant others in the service of attachment.

Attachment can be used as a framework for understanding the maladaptive interpersonal styles of several of the personality disorders. For example, impoverished interpersonal relationships are a cardinal feature of both schizoid and avoidant personality disorders (American Psychiatric Association, 2000). The disturbance for both dependent and BPD centers around difficulties with aloneness and preoccupation with fears of abandonment and the dissolution of close relationships

(Adler & Buie, 1979; Livesley & Schroeder, 1991). Unstable, intense, and stormy relationships are a central feature of BPD (McGlashan, 1986; Modestin, 1987; Clarkin, Widiger, Frances, Hurt, & Gilmore, 1983).

Consistent with an attachment theoretical perspective, empirical findings point to the close overlap between personality pathology and attachment constructs. Brennan and Shaver (1998) found that most of the personality disorders could be found in a two-dimensional space composed of the attachment dimensions of insecurity and defensive emotional style. Attachment theory has been successful in differentiating between different personality disorders (West et al., 1994) as well as between those with personality disorders and those without (Sack, Sperling, Fagen, & Foelsch, 1996 Sheldon & West, 1990;). The link between insecure attachment and BPD is particularly well-researched and robust (Agrawal et al., 2004; Levy, 2005).

PERSONALITY DISORDERS: DEVELOPMENT AND LONGITUDINAL COURSE

There are a number of reasons why the developmental and longitudinal course of the personality disorders is important. Research into developmental factors involved in these disorders can provide an insight into some of their causes (Lenzenweger & Cicchetti, 2005). In looking at the longitudinal course, we can begin to differentiate between ephemeral aspects of the disorders, maintaining factors, and essential features. In all cases, developmental and longitudinal studies can inform what aspects of the disorders should be targeted for prevention and intervention. Empirical information on the course of personality disorder is crucial to our understanding of issues of consistency and inconsistency over time, and the mechanisms that relate to adjustment over time, including the relationship of personality disorders to the major symptom disorders such as substance

abuse, eating disorders, depression, and anxiety disorders.

Of special interest in the development and course of the personality disorders are the progression of social relations, their development, their deficiencies and failures across time, and the variables that relate to that trajectory. What contributes to the development of the individual's style and manner in relating to others? What factors lead to both consistency and change in the trajectory of social relations?

Longitudinal Course

It is assumed and has been built into the DSM definition of personality pathology that, in contrast to the clinical syndromes on Axis I, personality disorders are enduring aspects of the individual. Contrary to this assumption, a number of recent studies have revealed that personality disorder, as defined and detected by the Axis II criteria, tends to decline categorically and dimensionally over time. This has been found in community samples (Cohen, Crawford, Johnson, & Kasen, 2005; Lenzenweger, 1999;) and in clinical samples (Shea et al., 2002; Zanarini et al., 2003). For example, the Collaborative Longitudinal Personality Disorders Study (CLPS) found a significant decrease in personality disorder diagnoses over a two-year time period (Grilo et al., 2004; Shea et al., 2002) among patients with Axis II diagnoses in the community. A similar decline in personality pathology was found in a sample of university students followed for some 12 years (Lenzenweger, Johnson, & Willett, 2004).

Some important methodological issues must be mentioned in the face of these seemingly optimistic views that personality disorders decrease with time. A major confound in these studies is a reliance on Axis II criteria, which often do not reflect long-standing aspects of the person, but transient behavioral manifestations (e.g., suicidal acts). Longitudinal studies depend upon the Axis II criteria to identify the initial personality pathology, with arbitrary time frames for judging the stability of the criteria. The DSM criteria sets contain a mixture of feelings, symptomatic behaviors, more traitlike patterns of interacting with others, and internal constructs relating to social behavior such as identity diffusion. One would expect different degrees of stability and change among the individual criteria over time.

In addition, the Axis II diagnoses are polythetic, i.e., an arbitrary number of criteria among a larger set leads to the diagnosis. For example, the diagnosis of BPD requires the presence of any five from a set of nine criteria. The implication is that if an individual meets five criteria at the beginning of the longitudinal study, and meets only four criteria later, the individual is considered to be without personality disorder and the diagnosis is no longer present. Finally, it is important to note that in the CLPS study, although personality disorder as measured by the Axis II criteria declined, performance in social functioning remained consistently faulty (Skodol et al., 2005).

This general finding of decrease in Axis II criteria has led to important thinking about what is changing over time and what remains relatively stable. For example, Zanarini and colleagues (2005) make the distinction in reference to BPD between the remission of acute symptoms, such as suicidal behavior, and the more stable endurance of temperamental dimensions, such as chronic anger and stress reactivity. Clark (2005) has argued that basic temperamental dimensions are responsible for both the enduring aspects of the personality disorders and the comorbidities between symptom disorders and personality pathology.

Efforts to understand aspects of consistency and change in the personality disorders (crucial to assessment and treatment foci and goals) require clear theoretical conceptions carefully crafted into longitudinal designs. One recent and unique effort investigated change in personality disorder in a three-wave study over a 12-year duration (Lenzenweger & Willett, 2007). The authors hypothesized that change in personality disorder features would be related to changes in underlying neurobiological systems that relate to particular personality traits, such as sensitivity to rewards and incentives (which the authors called "agentic positive emotion"), affiliation, negative emotion, fear, and constraint. Latent growth modeling revealed: (a) lower levels of social closeness related to elevated Cluster A (odd, eccentric) personality disorder features; (b) elevated negative emotion, lower constraint, and elevated agentic positive emotion related to elevated Cluster B (dramatic, emotional) features; and (c) elevated negative emotion and decreased social closeness related to increased Cluster C (anxious, fearful) features. These initial levels of neurobehavioral systems generally related to personality disorder features as hypothesized. Lenzenweger and Willett also found that elevated initial levels of agentic positive emotion among those with Cluster B personality disorder features predicted accelerated declines in Cluster B features over time. The authors suggest that individuals with personality disorder features, who are nonetheless able to engage with the world and to use rewards and incentives for self-regulation, find themselves less susceptible to personality dysfunction over time. However, they did not detect statistically significant predictors of the rate of change for either the Cluster A or Cluster C personality disorder dimensions.

TAXONOMIES

Any adequate theory of the personality disorders would contain essential constructs that could be used to delineate or classify different manifestations of personality pathology. A number of clinical researchers contend that the prominent classification system of the American

Psychiatric Association, the DSM, has only limited empirical validity and clinical utility (Blatt & Levy, 1998; Carson, 1991; Westen & Shedler, 1999). The DSM system was designed to be atheoretical in order to be useful to clinicians and researchers of different backgrounds (Spitzer, 2001); however, because the diagnostic criteria were developed by committee, in many cases the criteria for a given disorder represent a hodgepodge of different theoretical perspectives instead of a single objective list.

The DSM system is, however, extremely influential as it dictates the method for diagnosing individuals in clinical delivery systems, and it has guided most research in the area. The personality disorders are described in terms of criteria, and the diagnosis is made if a sufficient number of criteria are met in the context of impaired functioning due to the presence of these criteria. Ten different personality disorders are described, grouped into three clusters of heuristic value but little empirical basis. This typology based on specific criteria has resulted in reliable diagnosis which fosters clinical communication and clinical research. However, the deficiencies of this diagnostic system and typology have become apparent, leading to many anticipated changes in the next iteration of the system. The major difficulties of the system are the lack of construct validity of most of the diagnoses and the extensive "comorbidity" among the disorders, suggesting that the disorders are neither mutually exclusive nor separable, and that a categorical system is less well-fitted to reality than a dimensional orientation (Krueger, 1999).

More interesting than the actual 10 disorders described in Axis II are the discernable dimensions embedded in the diagnostic system, as described by Clarkin, Lenzenweger, and colleagues (2007). First, the disorders vary in terms of extroversion and introversion. A second dimension of aggression extends across the disorders, including paranoid (in the expectation of aggression from the environment) and the narcissistic and antisocial personality disorders (both of which involve the instrumental utilization of aggression). A third discernable dimension is affect and its dysregulation. A final dimension is one concerning moral values, which vary from relatively absent in borderline, narcissistic, and antisocial personality disorders, to rigid and pervasive in obsessive-compulsive personality disorder.

A much discussed possible alternative to the current Axis II is the use of traits to differentiate the personality disorders, and a growing consensus that the "Big Five" factors capture the pathology of the personality disorders (Clark, 2007; Costa & Widiger, 2002; Miller, Lynam, Widiger, & Leukefeld, 2001; Trull, Widiger, Lynam, & Costa, 2003). In this conceptualization, personality pathology is understood as an extreme of normal traits, and the five factors of neuroticism, extraversion, openness, agreeableness, and conscientiousness capture the pathology. Thus, for example, borderline personality pathology is characterized by very high neuroticism and low agreeableness (Clarkin, Hull, Cantor, & Sanderson, 1993) (see Table 23.1).

One criterion for evaluating the taxonomies of personality and/or personality disorders is the clinical usefulness of the system. It has become clear that the DSM classification is of limited usefulness to clinicians. Westen's (Shedler & Westen, 2004a, 2004b) survey of clinicians indicates that they are attentive not to individual diagnostic criteria but to the narratives the patients weave in describing their relations with others including their relationship with the therapist. Clearly therapists of all persuasions are using interpersonal theory, implicitly or explicitly, to assess clients and plan treatment. In this regard, Shedler and Westen's (2004a) survey of clinician's descriptions of prototypic personality disorders, and patients with specific personality disorders, reveals difficulties with the Axis II descriptions (see Table 23.1). Most importantly, the clinicians' descriptions

TABLE 23.1   Borderline Personality Disorder (BPD): Three Descriptions

DSM Criteria (American Psychiatric Association, 2000)	NEO-PI Traits (Clarkin, Hull, Cantor, & Sanderson, 1993)	SWAP-200 Description (Shedler & Westen, 2004)
1. Frantic efforts to avoid real or imagined abandonment	1. Very high Neuroticism (subscales of Anxiety, Hostility, Depression, Self-Consciousness, Impulsiveness, Vulnerability)	1. Tends to become attached quickly or intensely
2. Pattern of unstable and intense interpersonal relationships	2. Low Agreeableness	2. Interpersonal relationships tend to be unstable, chaotic, rapidly changing
3. Identity disturbance: markedly and persistently unstable self-image or sense of self	3. Low Conscientiousness	3. Lacks a stable image of who she or he is or would like to become
4. Impulsivity in at least two areas that are potentially self-damaging		4. Emotions tend to spiral out of control
5. Recurrent suicidal behavior, gestures, or threats, or self-mutilating behavior		5. Tends to fear she or he will be rejected or abandoned by those who are emotionally significant
6. Affective instability due to a marked reactivity of mood		6. Tends to express intense and inappropriate anger
7. Chronic feelings of emptiness		7. Tends to make repeated suicidal threats or gestures
8. Inappropriate intense anger or difficulty controlling anger		8. Tends to see certain others as "all bad", and loses the capacity to perceive any positive qualities the person may have
9. Transient stress-related paranoid ideation or severe dissociative symptoms		9. Emotions tend to change rapidly and unpredictably
		10. Is unable to soothe or comfort self when distressed
		11. Tends to become irrational when strong emotions are stirred up
		12. Tends to idealize certain others in unrealistic ways
		13. Tends to engage in self-mutilating behavior
		14. Tends to be angry or hostile
		15. Tends to react to criticism with feelings of rage or humiliation
		16. Tends to act impulsively, without regard for consequences
		17. Tends to elicit extreme reactions or stir up strong feelings in others
		18. Tends to feel empty or bored
		19. Appears to fear being alone
		20. Tends to be overly needy or dependent

using the Shedler-Westen Assessment Procedure (SWAP-200; Westen & Shedler, 1999a; 1999b) are richer and more complex than the description arising from the few criteria in the Axis II sets. In addition, therapists of all treatment orientations are attentive to the inner experience of the patient and use the SWAP-200 items to describe this troubled experience of their patients. Finally, a comparison of the description of personality disordered patients with the SWAP-200 as compared to the Five-Factor Model suggests that the latter omits essential constructs used in clinical practice (Shedler & Westen, 2004b), and a recent study suggests that clinicians have difficulty using the Five-Factor Model to diagnose personality disorders (Rottman, Ahn, Sanislow, & Kim, 2009). It is not surprising that practicing clinicians prefer the clinical relevance and utility of the SWAP-200 over the Five-Factor Model (Spitzer, First, Shedler, Westen, & Skodol, 2008).

DISTURBED PROCESSES IN INDIVIDUALS WITH PERSONALITY DISORDERS

Disturbed and disturbing interpersonal behavior is the final common pathway of a number of dysfunctional processes in individuals with personality disorder. This pathway includes selective attention to incoming stimuli filtered through the lens of past experience, the nature and degree of affective stimulation, cognitive appraisal of the situation, and patterned responses to intrapsychic and external events. Livesley (2001) has argued that the central issue in the personality disorders is what functions of the human organism are essential to adaptation, and thus, what functions are disordered in those with personality disorders. Similarly, we take the view that a firm conceptualization of normal development and functioning is critical to an understanding of dysfunction. Two important domains in normal adaptive functioning appear to be disordered in several of the personality disorders: representations of self and others, and self-regulatory capacity.

Representations of Self and Others

A number of personality theorists and clinical researchers have discussed representations of self and others as central to their conception of personality development and personality pathology (Bowlby, 1988; Kernberg, 1975; Mischel, 2004; Pretzer & Beck, 2004). The concepts of cognitive-affective units as applied to representations of self and others (Mischel, 2004), object relations dyads (Kernberg, 1975), internal working models (Bowlby, 1988), and schemas (Pretzer & Beck, 2004) are similar in their focus on representations of the self in the context of interpersonal events and relationships. In the normal personality, these representations of self and other are relatively accurate, positive, and coherent. However, among those with personality disorders, these representations of self and others are impaired and distorted in various ways.

Research findings demonstrate that individuals with personality disorders show disturbed representations. This is perhaps especially true with BPD (Bender & Skodol, 2007; Horowitz, 2004). Barone (2003) found that individuals with BPD have a much higher likelihood than controls of insecure attachment as measured by the Adult Attachment Interview, which assesses the coherence of one's view of significant others. Nigg and colleagues (1991, 1992; Baker, Silk, Westen, Nigg, & Lohr, 1992) have found that borderline individuals show more "malevolent" representations of caregivers than those with major depressive disorder, and these malevolent representations were especially characteristic of those with BPD who had a history of sexual abuse. Research by Fonagy and colleagues (1996) provides some evidence that reflective function, or the capacity to reflect upon one's own representations of others' thoughts and intentions, provides a buffer between abuse experiences and a diagnosis of BPD. This finding suggests that, at least among individuals with a history of abuse, the formation of malevolent representations of others may be a risk factor for a BPD diagnosis. Evidence also shows that at least one successful treatment of BPD leads to both higher reflective function and more adaptive representations of others (Levy, Meehan, et al., 2006). Similar changes in representations have been observed after long-term treatment in a predominantly personality-disordered sample of adolescent inpatients (Blatt & Auerbach, 2001; Blatt, Stayner, Auerbach, & Behrends, 1996).

Researchers using the tools of neuroscience (e.g., neuroimaging) are beginning to elucidate the neural processes involved in manipulating representations of self and others, which has important theoretical implications for understanding interpersonal processes (Lieberman, 2007) and the personality disorders. For example, a growing body of neuroimaging research has implicated prefrontal areas, notably the medial prefrontal cortex (MPFC), in the retrieval of self-relevant knowledge from memory (D'Argembeau et al., 2005; Johnson et al., 2005; Kelley et al., 2002; Macrae, Moran, Heatherton, Banfield, & Kelley, 2004; Moran, Macrae, Heatherton, Wyland, & Kelley, 2006; Ochsner et al., 2005; Seger, Stone, & Keenan, 2004; Schmitz, Kawahara-Baccus, & Johnson, 2004). Interestingly, these studies typically show that the MPFC shows decreased activation during self-knowledge retrieval, perhaps suggesting that this type of processing is less effortful (or more similar to baseline) than many control tasks. Consistent with this idea, children display higher MPFC activity during self-knowledge retrieval than do adults (Pfeifer, Lieberman, & Dapretto, 2007). Thus, the capacity for smooth and efficient use of representations of self seems to correspond to a well-developed and efficient MPFC. Evidence is beginning to emerge that links borderline personality pathology with hyperactivity

in the MPFC during autobiographical memory retrieval (Schnell et al., 2007).

Another important aspect of normal personality functioning involves appropriate and realistic representations of significant others, which allow the individual to anticipate the actions of others and the likely consequences of his or her own behavior, leading to appropriate, adaptive interactions. Neuroimaging studies also shed light on particular deficits in this domain among individuals with personality disorders. For example, a recent study (King-Casas et al., 2008) examined the behavior of borderline patients when playing a multiround economic exchange game with healthy partners. The borderline patients were unable to maintain cooperation and were impaired in their ability to repair broken cooperation. The imaging results showed that the borderline patients were distinguished from normals in responsiveness of the anterior insula, a brain region involved in monitoring social norms. In particular, individuals with BPD showed much less activation of the anterior insula when they received an offer from a partner. The authors concluded from the neural and behavioral data that borderline patients may be less adept at cooperative social exchanges because they have difficulty interpreting the social gestures of others.

Self-Regulation

The infant is dominated by affective responses (Panksepp, 2003), and the caregiver and his or her relationship with the infant are essential in gradually enabling the growing child, through modeling and explicit teaching, to modulate and control affective responses in socially acceptable ways (Kochanska, Murray, & Harlan, 2000). Effortful control and the underlying attentional network in the child have a developmental course that begins to level off at age 7, after which it becomes a traitlike factor. An important point is that effortful control is related to other important interpersonal developmental factors, such as positive affect, compliance and the development of a conscience, prosocial behavior, empathy, social competence, and adjustment (Eisenberg, Smith, Sadovsky, & Spinrad, 2004; Eisenberg et al., 2007). The appropriate modulation of affective experience is receiving increasing empirical attention (Ochsner & Gross, 2005).

Emotion regulation is a broad concept, encompassing both deliberate and automatic efforts to modify diverse kinds of emotional experience. Difficulties in the complicated processes of emotional regulation may be central to the personality disorders. Several personality disorders involve difficulties with affective control, especially in response to interpersonal events. For example, Raine and colleagues (2000) have found that individuals with antisocial personality disorder (ASPD) show reduced autonomic arousal during a stressful social interaction compared to individuals without the disorder, including those with substance use disorders and psychiatric controls. Those with ASPD also had reduced prefrontal grey matter volume. The authors speculated that deficits in affective control (which requires activation of the autonomic nervous system and moderating activity by the prefrontal cortex) underlie the poor decision-making, lack of conscience, and decreased response to fear conditioning that characterize individuals with ASPD.

BPD is also associated with dysfunction in emotion regulation. In fact, some theorists (e.g., Linehan, 2003) consider emotional dysregulation to be the central aspect of BPD. A survey of practicing clinicians suggested that individuals with BPD show more difficulties in regulating their emotions than those with dysthymic disorder (Conklin, Bradley, & Westen, 2006), and further research demonstrates that the emotion dysregulation observed in BPD is not accounted for by co-morbid depression (Yen, Zlotnick, & Costello, 2002). As a whole, electrophysiological and neuroimaging studies suggest BPD is associated with deficits in several neural systems involved in emotion regulation (Johnson et al., 2003), although it remains to be seen whether dysfunction in any of these diverse systems is either necessary or sufficient to describe the disorder.

TREATMENT OF THE PERSONALITY DISORDERS

There are a growing number of treatments for the personality disorders, and these treatments are effective in changing symptoms. Taking BPD as an example, effective treatments include Dialectical Behavior Therapy (Linehan, Armstrong, Suarez, Allmon, & Heard, 1991), Mentalization-Based Therapy (Bateman & Fonagy, 1999), Transference-Focused Psychotherapy (Clarkin, Levy, Lenzenweger, & Kernberg, 2007), Schema-Focused Therapy (Giesen-Bloo et al., 2006), and Dynamic Deconstructive Therapy (Gregory et al., 2008). These treatments come from a variety of theoretical approaches, and yet each includes a substantial interpersonal component. Some focus on a reduction in interpersonal problems (Levy, Meehan, et al., 2006), while others posit interpersonal mechanisms, such as attachment or therapeutic alliance, as important elements of change (Bateman & Fonagy, 1999; Levy, Meehan, Weber, Reynoso, & Clarkin, 2005; Levy, Meehan, et al., 2006; Markowitz, Bleiberg, Christos, & Levitan, 2006).

The fact that different treatments from different theoretical orientations are effective in reducing symptoms suggests that common elements contained in the various treatment approaches might be at least partially responsible for change. Bateman and Fonagy (2000) point out that each successful treatment for personality disorder is "a carefully considered, well-structured and coherent interpersonal endeavour" (p. 142). This commonality may indicate that a key element in the treatment of personality disorders is the provision of a structured interpersonal situation within which to reform the distorted patterns of interpersonal relating that characterize these patients. In addition, another factor common to each of these successful treatments is the availability of intensive supervision for the therapist. Levy and Scott (2006) suggest that this component helps the therapist maintain an appropriate, therapeutic stance while engaging in the stressful interpersonal world of those with personality disorders. Nevertheless, research into the specific mechanisms of change in psychotherapy for personality disorders is scant. (Clarkin & Levy, 2006).

Despite the increasing prevalence of empirically supported treatments for personality disorders, several limitations to this body of research exist. First, with the exception of Mentalization-Based Therapy (Bateman & Fonagy, 2008), no long-term follow-up studies have been conducted. Outcomes are typically measured for a short period after cessation of treatment (if any posttreatment assessments are conducted at all), so we have little idea whether the gains attributed to these therapies persist over time. Given that personality disorders are conceptualized as persistent, nonepisodic problems, this inattention to long-term outcomes is especially problematic. Second, the existing treatments have shown much more evidence for the alleviation of symptomatic distress than for change in broader, arguably more important domains, such as interpersonal behavior, social and intimate relationships, and occupational functioning. This stems in part from the fact that symptomatic change is somewhat easier to document, but when change in functioning is assessed, the effects of therapy are typically small (Levy, 2008). Third, it is clear from the research that even the best treatments for personality disorders help only a subset of patients improve by any measure. For example, a substantial proportion of individuals were still engaging in parasuicidal behavior at the end of one year of Dialectical Behavior Therapy (Linehan et al., 1991) and

Mentalization-Based Therapy (Bateman & Fonagy, 1999). It is unknown whether other treatments would have been more beneficial to those patients who did not improve, or whether a variable exists that would allow clinicians to prescribe one form of therapy over another. Finally, although there is abundant evidence that several forms of psychotherapy effectively treat some symptoms for some patients, very little research has been geared toward the question of how these treatments work (Levy, Clarkin, et al., 2006). The developers of various treatments have proposed specific mechanisms of change, but very little evidence exists to support these ideas. Research into treatments for personality disorders is still rudimentary and focused on "validating" various manualized psychotherapies.

SUMMARY

Personality disorders are conceptualized as pervasive, inflexible patterns of dealing with the world that are stable in the individual and lead to distress or impairment. The study of personality disorders has been carried out by scholars and researchers in the psychiatric tradition and has historically been separate from inquiry into "normal" personality in academic psychology. Nevertheless, the two fields are becoming better integrated, and personality theory is increasingly being used to inform the study of personality disorders. Trait theories, such as the Five-Factor Model, and social-cognitive theories, such as CAPS, can be applied to a wide range of personality pathology (e.g., Costa & Widiger, 2002; Eaton et al., 2009). Paradigms that can be used to describe both adaptive and maladaptive interpersonal functioning, such as interpersonal theory, attachment theory, and object relations, are especially valuable.

A developmental and longitudinal perspective is essential for the personality disorders, given that they are conceptualized as beginning by adolescence and persisting well into adulthood. Despite this view, the evidence shows that certain aspects of personality pathology undergo substantial changes in adulthood, with many individuals no longer meeting criteria for a personality disorder (e.g., Zanarini et al., 2003). However, this remission is not total and tends to apply more to externalizing symptoms of the pathology (e.g., impulsivity and aggression) than to the inner experience of the individual (Skodol et al., 2005) or to overall functioning (Levy, 2008).

Current taxonomies of the personality disorders suffer from extensive comorbidity among theoretically distinct entities, both within the personality disorders and between these and other forms of psychopathology. Efforts are currently underway to reform the dominant diagnostic system, very likely by adding a dimensional component to the assessment of personality pathology. This approach takes into account the presence of a number of dimensional constructs (such as extraversion and aggression) that can be used to describe what are currently conceived of as categorical disorders. However, one important problem with a dimensional system is its apparent lack of clinical utility. Another approach that appears to have good clinical utility and deserves further study is the prototype-matching approach of Westen and Shedler (1999a, 1999b).

The personality disorders involve disturbed functioning in several domains, such as information processing related to the self-concept, representations of others, and emotion regulation (e.g., King-Casas et al., 2008). These factors are mutually influencing, and there are likely to be common (or interrelated) underlying neural pathways involved in each of these areas. Although most research to date has focused on BPD, it is probable that the other personality disorders involve distinct deficits in these important functions.

The psychotherapeutic treatment of personality disorders, until recently thought to be prohibitively difficult, has now been shown to be possible through a variety of approaches. These treatments, which are derived from several distinct theoretical traditions, share some common elements: a relatively long duration, a strong treatment frame, and intensive supervision for the therapist (Bateman & Fonagy, 2000; Levy & Scott, 2006). Nevertheless there are a number of important limitations that need to be addressed in future research.

References

Adler, G., & Buie, D. H., Jr. (1979). Aloneness and borderline psychopathology: The possible relevance of child development issues. *International Journal of Psycho-Analysis, 60*, 83–96.

Agrawal, H. R., Gunderson, J., Holmes, B. M., & Lyons-Ruth, K. (2004). Attachment studies with borderline patients: A review. *Harvard Review of Psychiatry, 12*, 94–104.

Allport, G. W. (1937). *Personality: A psychological interpretation*. Oxford, UK: Holt.

American Psychiatric Association (2000). *Diagnostic and statistical manual of mental disorders DSM-IV-TR* (4th ed.). Washington, DC: American Psychiatric Association.

Andersen, S. M., & Chen, S. (2002). The relational self: An interpersonal social-cognitive theory. *Psychological Review, 109*, 619–645.

Ayduk, Ö., Zayas, V., Downey, G., Cole, A. B., Shoda, Y., & Mischel, W. (2008). Rejection sensitivity and executive control: Joint predictors of borderline personality features. *Journal of Research in Personality, 42*, 151–168.

Baker, L., Silk, K. R., Westen, D., Nigg, J. T., & Lohr, N. E. (1992). Malevolence, splitting, and parental ratings by borderlines. *Journal of Nervous and Mental Disease, 180*, 258–264.

Barone, L. (2003). Developmental protective and risk factors in borderline personality disorder: A study using the Adult Attachment Interview. *Attachment & Human Development, 5*, 64–77.

Bateman, A., & Fonagy, P. (1999). Effectiveness of partial hospitalization in the treatment of borderline personality disorder: A randomized controlled trial. *American Journal of Psychiatry, 156*, 1563–1569.

Bateman, A., & Fonagy, P. (2000). Effectiveness of psychotherapeutic treatment of personality disorder. *British Journal of Psychiatry, 177*, 138–143.

Bateman, A., & Fonagy, P. (2008). 8-year follow-up of patients treated for borderline personality disorder: Mentalization-based treatment versus treatment as usual. *American Journal of Psychiatry, 165,* 631–638.

Bender, D. S., & Skodol, A. E. (2007). Borderline personality as self-other representational disturbance. *Journal of Personality Disorders, 21,* 500–517.

Bender, D. S., Dolan, R. T., Skodol, A. E., Sanislow, C. A., Dyck, I. R., McGlashan, T. H., . . . Gunderson, J. G., (2001). Treatment utilization by patients with personality disorder. *American Journal of Psychiatry, 158,* 295–302.

Benjamin, L. S. (1996). *Interpersonal diagnosis and treatment of personality disorders* (2nd ed.). New York: Guilford Press.

Benjamin, L. S. (2005). Interpersonal theory of personality disorders: The structural analysis of social behavior and interpersonal reconstructive therapy. In M. F. Lenzenweger, & J. F. Clarkin (Eds.), *Major theories of personality disorder* (2nd ed., pp. 157–230). New York: Guilford Press.

Blatt, S. J., & Auerbach, J. S. (2001). Mental representation, severe psychopathology, and the therapeutic process. *Journal of the American Psychoanalytic Association, 49,* 113–159.

Blatt, S. J., & Levy, K. N. (1998). A psychodynamic approach to the diagnosis of psychopathology. In J. W. Barron (Ed.), *Making diagnosis meaningful* (pp. 73–109). Washington, DC: American Psychological Association.

Blatt, S. J., & Levy, K. N., (2003). Attachment theory, psychoanalysis, personality development, and psychopathology. *Psychoanalytic Inquiry, 23,* 102–150.

Blatt, S. J., & Shichman, S. (1983). Two primary configurations of psychopathology. *Psychoanalysis and Contemporary Thought, 6,* 187–254.

Blatt, S. J., Stayner, D. A., Auerbach, J. S., & Behrends, R. S. (1996). Change in object and self-representations in long-term, intensive, inpatient treatment of seriously disturbed adolescents and young adults. *Psychiatry: Interpersonal and Biological Processes, 59,* 82–107.

Bowlby, J. (1969). *Attachment and loss: Vol. 1. Attachment.* New York: Basic Books.

Bowlby, J. (1973). *Attachment and loss: Vol. 2. Separation, anxiety, and anger.* New York: Basic Books.

Bowlby, J. (1980). *Attachment and loss: Vol. 3. Loss.* New York: Basic Books.

Bowlby, J. (1988). *A secure base.* New York: Basic Books.

Brennan, K. A., & Shaver, P. R. (1998). Attachment styles and personality disorders: Their connection to each other and parental divorce, parental death, and perception of parental caregiving. *Journal of Personality, 66,* 835–878.

Bretherton, I., & Munholland, K. A. (2008). Internal working models in attachment relationships: Elaborating a central construct in attachment theory. In J. Cassidy & P. R. Shaver (Eds.), *Handbook of attachment: Theory, research, and clinical applications* (2nd ed.). New York: Guilford Press.

Carson, R. C. (1991). Dilemmas in the pathway of the DSM-IV. *Journal of Abnormal Psychology, 100,* 302–307.

Cattell, R. B. (1946). *Description and measurement of personality.* Yonkers-on-Hudson, NY: World Book.

Cicchetti, D., Beeghly, M., Carlson, V., & Toth, S. (1990). The emergence of the self in atypical populations. In D. Cicchetti & M. Beeghly (Eds.), *The self in transition: Infancy to childhood* (pp. 309–344). Chicago: University of Chicago Press.

Clark, L. A. (2005). Temperament as a unifying basis for personality and psychopathology. *Journal of Abnormal Psychology, 114,* 505–521.

Clark, L. A. (2007). Assessment and diagnosis of personality disorder: Perennial issues and an emerging reconceptualization. *Annual Review of Psychology, 58,* 227–257.

Clarkin, J. F., Hull, J. W., Cantor, J., & Sanderson, C. (1993). Borderline personality disorder and personality traits: A comparison of SCID-II BPD and NEO-PI. *Psychological Assessment, 5,* 472–476.

Clarkin, J. F., Lenzenweger, M. F., Yeomans, F., Levy, K. N., & Kernberg, O. F. (2007). An object relations model of borderline pathology. *Journal of Personality Disorders, 21,* 474–499.

Clarkin, J. F., Levy, K. N., Lenzenweger, M. F., & Kernberg, O. F. (2007). Evaluating three treatments for borderline personality disorder: A multiwave study. *American Journal of Psychiatry, 164,* 922–928.

Clarkin, J. F., Widiger, T., Frances, A., Hurt, S. W., & Gilmore, M. (1983). Prototypic typology and the borderline personality disorder. *Journal of Abnormal Psychology, 92,* 263–275.

Clarkin, J. F., Yeomans, F., & Kernberg, O. F. (2006). *Psychotherapy of borderline personality: Focusing on object relations.* Washington, DC: American Psychiatric Publishing.

Clarkin, J. F., & Levy, K. N. (2006). Psychotherapy for patients with borderline personality disorder: Focusing on the mechanisms of change. *Journal of Clinical Psychology, 62,* 405–516.

Cloninger, C. R. (2000). A practical way to diagnosis personality disorder: A proposal. *Journal of Personality Disorders, 14,* 99–108.

Cogswell, A., & Alloy, L. B. (2006). The relation of neediness and Axis II pathology. *Journal of Personality Disorders, 20,* 16–21.

Cohen, P., Crawford, T. N., Johnson, J. G., & Kasen, S. (2005). The Children in the Community Study of developmental course of personality disorders. *Journal of Personality Disorders, 19,* 131–140.

Conklin, C. Z., Bradley, R., & Westen, D. (2006). Affect regulation in borderline personality disorder. *Journal of Nervous and Mental Disease, 194,* 69–77.

Costa, P. T. Jr., & Widiger, T. A. (Eds.) (2002). *Personality disorders and the five-factor model of personality* (2nd ed.). Washington, DC: American Psychological Association.

D'Argembeau, A., Collette, F., Van der Linden, M., Laureys, S., Del Fiore, G., Degueldre, C., ... Salmon, E., (2005). Self-referential reflective activity and its relationship with rest: A PET study. *Neuroimage, 25,* 616–624.

Downey, G., & Feldman, S. I. (1996). Implications of Rejection Sensitivity for intimate relationships. *Journal of Personality and Social Psychology, 70,* 1327–1343.

Eaton, N. R., South, S. C., & Krueger, R. F. (2009). The Cognitive-Affective Processing System (CAPS) approach to personality and the concept of personality disorder: Integrating clinical and social-cognitive research. *Journal of Research in Personality, 43,* 208–217.

Eisenberg, N., Guthrie, I. K., Fabes, R. A., Reiser, M., Murphy, B. C., Holmgren, R., ... Losoya, S., (1997). The relations of regulation and emotionality to resiliency and competent social functioning in elementary school children. *Child Development, 68,* 367–383.

Eisenberg, N., Smith, C. L., Sadovsky, A., Spinrad, T. L. (2004). Effortful control. In R. F. Baumeister & K. D. Vohs (Eds.), *Handbook of self-regulation: Research, theory and applications* (pp. 259–282). New York: Guilford Press.

Eysenck, H. J. (1952). *The scientific study of personality.* London: Routledge & Kegan Paul.

Fonagy, P., Leigh, T., Steele, M., Steele, H., Kennedy, R., Mattoon, G., ... Gerber, A., (1996). The relation of attachment status, psychiatric classification, and response to psychotherapy. *Journal of Consulting and Clinical Psychology, 64,* 22–31.

Fonagy, P., Target, M., Gergely, G., Allen, J. G., & Bateman, A. W. (2003). The developmental roots of borderline personality disorder in early attachment relationships: A theory and some evidence. *Psychoanalytic Inquiry, 23,* 412–459.

Freud, S. (1933/1965). *New introductory lectures on psychoanalysis* (J. Strachey, Trans.). New York: W. W. Norton.

Giesen-Bloo, J., van Dyck, R., Spinhoven, P., van Tilburg, W., Dirksen, C., van Asselt, T., ... Arntz, A., (2006). Outpatient psychotherapy for borderline personality disorder: A randomized clinical trial of schema-focused therapy versus transference-focused psychotherapy. *Archives of General Psychiatry, 63,* 649–658.

Goldberg, J. O., Segal, Z. V., Vella, D. D., & Shaw, B. F. (1989). Depressive personality: Millon Clinical Multiaxial Inventory profiles of sociotropic and autonomous subtypes. *Journal of Personality Disorders, 3,* 193–198.

Greenberg, M. T. (1999). Attachment and psychopathology in childhood. In J. Cassidy & P. R. Shaver (Eds.), *Handbook of attachment, theory, research, and clinical applications* (pp. 469–496). New York: Guilford Press.

Gregory, R. J., Chlebowski, S., Kang, D., Remen, A. L., Soderberg, M. G., Stepkovitch, J., & Virk, S. (2008). A controlled trial of psychodynamic psychotherapy for co-occurring borderline personality disorder and alcohol use disorder. *Psychotherapy: Theory, Research, Practice, Training, 45,* 28–41.

Grilo, C. M., Sanislow, C. A., Gunderson, J. G., Pagano, M. E., Yen, S., Zanarini, M. C., ... McGlashan, T. H., (2004). Two-year stability and change in schizotypal, borderline, avoidant, and obsessive-compulsive personality disorders. *Journal of Consulting and Clinical Psychology, 72,* 767–775.

Gunderson, J. G., & Lyons-Ruth, K. (2008). BPD's interpersonal hypersensitivity phenotype. *Journal of Personality Disorders, 22*, 22–41.

Harter, S. (1999). *The construction of the self: A developmental perspective.* New York: Guilford Press.

Horowitz, L. M. (2004). *Interpersonal foundations of psychopathology.* Washington, DC: American Psychological Association.

John, O. P., Robins, R. W., & Pervin, L. A. (Eds.) (2008). *Handbook of personality: Theory and research* (3rd ed.). New York: Guilford Press.

Johnson, M. K., Raye, C. L., Mitchell, K. J., Greene, E. J., Cunningham, W. A., & Sanislow, C. A. (2005). Using fMRI to investigate a component process of reflection: Prefrontal correlates of refreshing a just-activated representation, *Cognitive, Affective, and Behavioral Neuroscience, 5*, 339–361.

Johnson, P. A., Hurley, R. A., Benkelfat, C., Herpertz, S. C., & Taber, K. H. (2003). Understanding emotion regulation in borderline personality disorder: Contributions of neuroimaging. *Journal of Neuropsychiatry and Clinical Neurosciences, 15*, 397–402.

Kelley, W. M., Macrae, C. N., Wyland, C. L., Caglar, S., Inati, S., & Heatherton, T. F. (2002). Finding the self?: An event-related fMRI study. *Journal of Cognitive Neuroscience, 14*, 785–794.

Kernberg, O. F. (1975). *Borderline conditions and pathological narcissism.* New York: Jason Aronson.

Kernberg, O. F., & Caligor, E. (2005). A psychoanalytic theory of personality disorders. In M. F. Lenzenweger & J. F. Clarkin (Eds.), *Major theories of personality disorder* (2nd ed., pp. 114–156). New York: Guilford Press.

King-Casas, B., Sharp, C., Lomax-Bream, L, Lohrenz, T., Fonagy, P., & Montague, P. R. (2008). The rupture and repair of cooperation in borderline personality disorder. *Science, 321*, 806–810.

Kochanska, G., Murray, K. L., & Harlan, E. T. (2000). Effortful control in early childhood: Continuity and change, antecedents, and implications for social development. *Developmental Psychology, 36*, 220–232.

Krueger, R. F. (1999). The structure of common mental disorders. *Archives of General Psychiatry, 56*, 921–926.

Lenzenweger, M. F. (1999). Stability and change in personality disorder features: The longitudinal study of personality disorders. *Archives of General Psychiatry, 56*, 1009–1015.

Lenzenweger, M. F. (2008). Epidemiology of personality disorders. *Psychiatric Clinics of North America, 31*, 395–403.

Lenzenweger, M. F., & Cicchetti, D. (2005). Toward a developmental psychopathology approach to borderline personality disorder. *Development & Psychopathology, 17*, 893–898.

Lenzenweger, M. F., Johnson, M. D., & Willett, J. B. (2004). Individual growth-curve analysis illuminates stability and change in personality disorder features. *Archives of General Psychiatry, 61*, 1015–1024.

Lenzenweger, M. F., & Willett, J. B. (2007). Predicting individual change in personality disorder features by simultaneous individual change in personality dimensions linked to neurobehavioral systems: The longitudinal study of personality. *Journal of Abnormal Psychology, 116*, 684–700.

Levy, K. N. (2005). The implications of attachment theory and research for understanding borderline personality disorder. *Development and Psychopathology, 17*, 959–986.

Levy, K. N. (2008). Psychotherapies and lasting change. *American Journal of Psychiatry, 165*, 556–559.

Levy, K. N., & Blatt, S. J. (1999). Attachment theory and psychoanalysis: Further differentiation within insecure attachment patterns. *Psychoanalytic Inquiry, 19*, 541–575.

Levy, K. N., Clarkin, J. F., Yeomans, F. E., Scott, L., Wasserman, R., & Kernberg, O. F. (2006). The mechanisms of change in the treatment of borderline personality disorder with transference focused psychotherapy. *Journal of Clinical Psychology, 62*, 481–501.

Levy, K. N., Kolligan, J., Quinlan, D. M., Becker, D. F., Edell, W. S., & McGlashan, T. H. (1994, May). *Depressive experiences in borderline inpatients.* Paper presented at the annual meeting of the American Psychiatric Association, Philadelphia, PA.

Levy, K. N., Meehan, K. B., Kelly, K. M., Reynoso, J. S., Weber, M., Clarkin, J. F., & Kernberg, O. F. (2006). Change in attachment patterns and reflective functioning in a randomized control trial of transference focused psychotherapy for borderline personality disorder. *Journal of Consulting and Clinical Psychology, 74,* 1027–1040.

Levy, K. N., Meehan, K. B., Weber, M., Reynoso, J., & Clarkin, J. F. (2005). Attachment and borderline personality disorder: Implications for psychotherapy. *Psychopathology, 38,* 64–74.

Levy, K. N., & Scott, L. N. (2006). The "art" of interpreting the "science" and the "science" of interpreting the "art" of the treatment of borderline personality disorder. In S. G. Hofmann & J. Weinberger (Eds.), *The art and science of psychotherapy* (pp. 269–298). New York: Routledge.

Lieberman, M. D. (2007). Social cognitive neuroscience: A review of core processes. *Annual Review of Psychology, 58,* 259–289.

Linehan, M. M., Armstrong, H. E., Suarez, A., Allmon, D., & Heard, H. L. (1991). Cognitive-behavioral treatment of chronically parasuicidal borderline patients. *Archives of General Psychiatry, 48,* 1060–1064.

Linehan, M. M. (1993). *Cognitive-behavioral treatment of borderline personality disorder.* New York: Guilford Press.

Livesley, W. J. (2001). Conceptual and taxonomic issues. In W. J. Livesley (Ed.), *Handbook of personality disorders: Theory, research, and treatment* (pp. 3–38). New York: Guilford Press.

Livesley, W. J., & Schroeder, M. (1991). Dimensions of personality disorder: The DSM-III-R cluster B diagnosis. *Journal of Nervous and Mental Disease, 179,* 320–328.

Macrae, C. N., Moran, J. M., Heatherton, T. F., Banfield, J. F., & Kelley, W. M. (2004). Medial prefrontal activity predicts memory for self. *Cerebral Cortex, 14,* 647–654.

McCrae, R. R., & Costa, P. T. (2008). The five-factor theory of personality. In O. P. John, R. W. Robins, & L. A. Pervin (Eds.), *Handbook of personality: Theory and Research* (3rd ed., pp. 159–181). New York: Guilford Press.

Markowitz, J. C., Bleiberg, K. L., Christos, P., & Levitan, E. (2006). Solving interpersonal problems correlates with symptom improvement in interpersonal psychotherapy: Preliminary findings. *Journal of Nervous and Mental Disease, 194,* 15–20.

McGlashan, T. H. (1986). The Chestnut Lodge follow-up study: III. Long-term outcome of borderline personalities. *Archives of General Psychiatry, 43,* 20–30.

Metcalfe, J., & Mischel, W. (1999). A hot/cool system analysis of delay of gratification: Dynamics of willpower. *Psychological Review, 106,* 3–19.

Meyer, B., & Pilkonis, P. A. (2005). An attachment model of personality disorders. In M. F. Lenzenweger & J. F. Clarkin (Eds.), *Major theories of personality disorder* (2nd ed., pp. 231–281). New York: Guilford Press.

Miller, J. D., Lynam, D. R., Widiger, T. A., & Leukefeld, C. (2001). Personality disorders as extreme variants of common personality dimensions: Can the Five-Factor Model adequately represent psychopathy? *Journal of Personality, 69,* 253–276.

Millon, T. (1969). *Modern psychopathology.* Philadelphia: Saunders.

Mischel, W. (1973). Toward a cognitive social learning reconceptualization of personality. *Psychological Review, 80,* 252–283.

Mischel W. (2004). Toward an integrative science of the person. *Annual Review of Psychology, 55,* 1–22.

Mischel, W., & Shoda, Y. (1995). A cognitive-affective system theory of personality: Reconceptualizing situations, dispositions, dynamics, and invariance in personality structure. *Psychological Review, 102,* 246–268.

Mischel, W., & Shoda, Y. (2008). Toward a unified theory of personality: Integrating dispositions and processing dynamics within the cognitive-affective processing system. In O. P. John, R. W. Robins, & L. A. Pervin (Eds.), *Handbook of personality: Theory and Research* (3rd ed., pp. 208–241). New York: Guilford Press.

Modestin, J. (1987). Counter-transference reactions contributing to completed suicide. *British Journal of Medical Psychology, 60,* 379–385.

Moran, J. M., Macrae, C. N., Heatherton, T. F., Wyland, C. L., & Kelley, W. M. (2006). Neuroanatomical evidence for distinct cognitive and affective components of self. *Journal of Cognitive Neuroscience, 18,* 1586–1594.

Morse, J. Q., Robins, C. J., & Gittes-Fox, M. (2002). Sociotropy, autonomy, and personality disorder criteria in psychiatric patients. *Journal of Personality Disorders, 16,* 549–560.

Murray, G. (1938). *Explorations in personality.* Oxford, UK: Oxford University Press.

Nigg, J., Lohr, W., Westen, D., Gold, L., & Silk, K. (1992). Malevolent object representations in borderline personality disorder and major depression. *Journal of Abnormal Psychology*, *101*, 61–67.

Nigg, J. T., Silk, K. R., Westen, D., Lohr, W. E., Gold, L. J., Goodrich S., & Ogata, S. (1991). Object representations in the early memories of sexually abused borderline patients. *American Journal of Psychiatry*, *148*, 864–869.

Ochsner, K. N., & Gross, J. J. (2005). The cognitive control of emotion. *Trends in Cognitive Sciences*, *9*, 242–249.

Ochsner, K. N., Beer, J. S., Robertson, E. R., Cooper, J. C., Gabrieli, J. D. E., Kihsltrom, J. F., & D'Esposito, M. (2005). The neural correlates of direct and reflected self-knowledge. *Neuroimage*, *28*, 97–814.

O'Leary, K. M., Cowdry, R. W., Gardner, D. L., Leibenluft, E., Lucas, P., & deJong-Meyer, R. (1991). Dysfunctional attitudes in borderline personality disorder. *Journal of Personality Disorders*, *5*, 233–242.

Ouimette, P. C., & Klein, D. N. (1993). Convergence of psychoanalytic and cognitive-behavioral theories of depression: An empirical review and new data on Blatt's and Beck's models. In J. M. Masling & R. F. Bornstein (Eds.), *Psychoanalytic perspectives on psychopathology*. Washington, DC: American Psychological Association.

Ouimette, P., Klein, D. N., Anderson, R., Riso, L. P., & Lizardi, H. (1994). Relationship of sociotropy/autonomy and dependency/self-criticism to DSM-III-R personality disorders. *Journal of Abnormal Psychology*, *103*, 743–749.

Panksepp, J. (2003). At the interface of the affective, behavioral, and cognitive neurosciences: Decoding the emotional feelings of the brain. *Brain and cognition*, *52*, 4–14.

Pervin, L. A. (1990). A brief history of modern personality theory. In L. A. Pervin (Ed.), *Handbook of personality: Theory and research* (pp. 3–18). New York: Guilford Press.

Pfeifer, J. H., Lieberman, M. D., & Dapretto, M. (2007). "I know you are but what am I?!": Neural bases of self- and social knowledge retrieval in children and adults. *Journal of Cognitive Neuroscience*, *19*, 1323–1337.

Pincus, A. L. (2005). A contemporary interpersonal theory of personality disorders. In M. F. Lenzenweger & J. F. Clarkin (Eds.), *Major theories of personality disorder* (2nd ed., pp. 282–331). New York: Guilford Press.

Pretzer, J. L., & Beck, A. T. (2004). A cognitive theory of personality disorders. In M. F. Lenzenweger & J. F. Clarkin (Eds.), *Major theories of personality disorder* (2nd ed., pp. 36–105). New York: Guilford Press.

Raine, A., Lencz, T., Bihrle, S., Lacasse, L., & Colletti, P. (2000). Reduced prefrontal gray matter volume and reduced autonomic activity in antisocial personality disorder. *Archives of General Psychiatry*, *57*, 119–127.

Rothbart, M. K., Ellis, L. K., & Posner, M. I. (2004). Temperament and self-regulation. In R. F. Baumeister & K. D. Vohs (Eds.), *Handbook of self-regulation: Research, theory and applications* (pp. 357–370). New York: Guilford Press.

Rottman, B. M., Ahn, W., Sanislow, C. A., & Kim, N. S. (2009). Can clinicians recognize DSM-IV personality disorders from five-factor model descriptions of patient cases? *American Journal of Psychiatry*, *166*, 427–433.

Sack, A., Sperling, M. B., Fagen, G., & Foelsch, P. (1996). Attachment style, history and behavioral contrasts for a borderline and normal sample. *Journal of Personality Disorders*, *10*, 88–102.

Schmitz, T. W., Kawahara-Baccus, T. N., & Johnson, S. C. (2004). Metacognitive evaluation, self-relevance, and the right prefrontal cortex. *Neuroimage*, *22*, 941–947.

Schnell, K., Dietrich, T., Schnitker, R., Daumann, J., & Herpertz, S. C. (2007). Processing of autobiographical memory retrieval cues in borderline personality disorder. *Journal of Affective Disorders*, *97*, 253–259.

Seger, C. A., Stone, M., & Keenan, J. P. (2004). Cortical activations during judgments about the self and another person. *Neuropsychologia*, *42*, 1168–1177.

Shea, M. T., Stout, R., Gunderson, J., Morey, L. C., Grilo, C. M., McGlashan, T., ... Keller, M. B. (2002). Short-term diagnostic stability of schizotypal, borderline, avoidant, and obsessive-compulsive personality disorders. *American Journal of Psychiatry*, *159*, 2036–2041.

Shedler, J., & Westen, D. (2004a). Refining personality disorder diagnosis: Integrating science and practice. *American Journal of Psychiatry*, *161*, 1350–1365.

Shedler, J., & Westen, D. (2004b). Dimensions of personality pathology: An alternative to the five-factor model. *American Journal of Psychiatry*, *161*, 1743–1754.

Sheldon, A. E., & West, M. (1990). Attachment pathology and low social skills in avoidant personality disorder: An exploratory study. *Canadian Journal of Psychiatry, 35*, 596–599.

Shoda, Y., Mischel, W., & Wright, J. C. (1994). Intraindividual stability in the organization and patterning of behavior: Incorporating psychological situations into the idiographic analysis of personality. *Journal of Personality and Social Psychology, 67*, 674–687.

Skodol, A. E., Pagano, M. F., Bender, D. S., Shea, M. T., Gunderson, J. G., Yen, S., . . . McGlashan, T. H., (2005). Stability of functional impairment in patients with schizotypal, borderline, avoidant, or obsessive-compulsive personality disorder over two years. *Psychological Medicine, 35*, 443–451.

Spitzer, R. L. (2001). Values and assumptions in the development of DSM-III-R: An insider's perspective and a belated response to Sadler, Hulgus, and Agich's "On values in recent American psychiatric classification." *Journal of Nervous & Mental Disease, 189*, 351–359.

Spitzer, R. L., First, M. B., Shedler, J., Westen, D., & Skodol, A. E. (2008). Clinical utility of five dimensional systems for personality diagnosis: A consumer preference study. *Journal of Nervous and Mental Disease, 196*, 356–374.

Stone, M. H. (1997). *Healing the mind: A history of psychiatry from antiquity to the present*. New York: W. W. Norton.

Trull, T. J. (2005). Dimensional models of personality disorder: Coverage and cutoffs. *Journal of Personality Disorders, 19*, 262–282.

Verheul, R., Andrea, H., Berghout, C. C., Dolan, C., Busschbach, J. J. V., van der Kroft, P. J. A., & Fonagy, P. (2008). Severity Indices of Personality Problems (SIPP-118): Development, factor structure, reliability, and validity. *Psychological Assessment, 20*, 23–34.

West, M., Rose, S., & Sheldon-Keller, A. (1994). Assessment of patterns of insecure attachment in adults and application to dependent and schizoid personality disorders. *Journal of Personality Disorders, 8*, 249–256

Westen, D. (1993). The impact of sexual abuse on self-structure. *Rochester Symposium on Developmental Psychopathology: Disorders and Dysfunctions of the Self, 5*, 223–250.

Westen, D., & Shedler, J. (1999a). Revising and assessing Axis II, part I: Developing a clinically and empirically valid assessment method. *American Journal of Psychiatry, 156*, 258–272.

Westen, D., & Shedler, J. (1999b). Revising and assessing Axis II, part 2: Toward an empirically based and clinically useful classification of personality disorders. *American Journal of Psychiatry, 156*, 273–285.

Widiger, T. A., & Costa, P. T. (1994). Personality and personality disorders. *Journal of Abnormal Psychology, 103*, 78–91.

Wiggins, J. S. (1991). Agency and communion as conceptual coordinates for the understanding and measurement of interpersonal behavior. In W. W. Grove and D. Cicchetti (Eds.), *Thinking clearly about psychology: Vol. 2. Personality and psychotherapy* (pp. 89–113). Minneapolis: University of Minnesota Press.

Wiggins, J. S. (1997). Circumnavigating Dodge Morgan's interpersonal style. *Journal of Personality, 65*, 1069–1086.

Wiggins, J. S. (2003). *Paradigms of personality assessment*. New York: Guilford Press.

Wiggins, J. S., & Pincus, A. L. (1989). Conceptions of personality disorders and dimensions of personality. *Psychological Assessment, 1*, 305–316.

Yen, S., Zlotnick, C., & Costello, E. (2002). Affect regulation in women with borderline personality disorder traits. *Journal of Nervous and Mental Disease, 190*, 693–696.

Zanarini, M. C., Frankenburg, F. R., Hennen, J., Reich, D. B., & Silk, K. R. (2005). The McLean Study of Adult Development (MSAD): Overview and implications of the first six years of prospective follow-up. *Journal of Personality Disorders, 19*, 505–523.

Zanarini, M. C., Vujanovic, A. A., Parachini, E. A., Boulanger J. L., Frankenburg, F. R., & Hennen, J. (2003). Zanarini Rating Scale for Borderline Personality Disorder (ZAN-BPD): A continuous measure of DSM-IV borderline psychopathology. *Journal of Personality Disorders, 17*, 233–242.

24

INTERPERSONAL PROCESS AND TRAUMA: AN INTERACTIONAL MODEL

Nicole R. Nugent

Ananda B. Amstadter

Karestan C. Koenen

The Indian Ocean tsunami in December of 2004 resulted in more than 150,000 deaths as well as widespread destruction to eleven countries. Thousands were orphaned. In the sea of images documenting trauma and destruction, a picture of an orphaned baby hippopotamus (later called Owen)

Author Note: From the Departments of Society, Human Development, and Health and Epidemiology, Harvard School of Public Health (Dr. Koenen). From the Bradley/Hasbro Children's Research Center/Rhode Island Hospital and the Warren Alpert Medical School of Brown University (Dr. Nugent). From the Departments of Psychiatry and Behavioral Science, Medical University of South Carolina (Dr. Amstadter). Dr. Amstadter is supported by US-NIMH 083469 and US-NICHD HD055885. Dr. Nugent is supported by US-NIMH K01 MH087240. Dr. Koenen is supported by US-NIMH K08 MH070627 and MH078928.

seeking comfort from an unlikely adopted friend, a 130-year-old tortoise (called Mzee), inspired international news coverage and two books.

> At first, Owen wouldn't eat any of the leaves left out for him. Stephen and the other caretakers were worried.... Then they noticed Owen feeding right beside Mzee, as if Mzee were showing him how to eat. Or perhaps it was Mzee's protective presence that helped Owen feel calm enough to eat. No one will ever know. But it was clear that the bond between Owen and Mzee was helping the baby hippo to recover....
>
> —*From* Owen & Mzee: The True Story of a Remarkable Friendship, *by Isabella Hatkoff, Craig Hatkoff, and Paula Kahumbu*

The story of Owen and Mzee provides an illustration of the critical, and unique, role of social support in adjustment following trauma. In fact, a lack of social support has been found to be the strongest predictor of posttraumatic stress disorder (PTSD) in a meta-analysis (Brewin, Andrews, & Valentine, 2000). Social support may take the shape of (a) instrumental/informational support (e.g., showing an orphaned tsunami survivor how to eat) or emotional support (e.g., providing a calming or reassuring presence), as proposed in the Stress-Buffering Model; or of (b) active interactions between individual and support (e.g., an inherently social orphan seeks support), as proposed by an Interactional Model. Regardless of the precise model, interpersonal relationships are critical to individual traumatic response, with trauma also influencing the individual's relationships with others. Indeed, traumatic experiences often involve a fundamental shift in the individual's perceptions of themselves, the world, and others, and affect future interactions with the social world around them (e.g., Ehlers & Clark, 2000; Resick & Schnicke, 1992).

This chapter provides an overview of a trauma's influence on interpersonal processes, both the individual's approach to engaging in relationships with others and the way in which relationships can influence the individual's response to trauma, with a focus on interpersonal traumatic events. Models of coping with traumatic stress as related to interpersonal process are also reviewed. Our discussion first provides an overview of aspects of the trauma itself that are relevant to interpersonal processes. It then summarizes (a) the individual's ability to engage with others following trauma, (b) the impact of others on an individual following trauma, and (c) models in which interpersonal relationships are influenced by interactions between characteristics of the traumatized individual and characteristics of relevant others. Figure 24.1 illustrates the complicated contributions of the traumatic context, the affected individual,

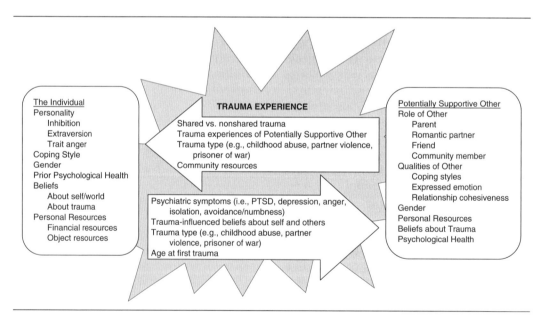

FIGURE 24.1   Interpersonal Process and Trauma: Interactions of Individual, Other, and the Trauma
Note: Figure 24.1 illustrates the impact of trauma on interpersonal interactions between the trauma-exposed Individual and a Potentially Supportive Other. As discussed throughout the chapter, distinct qualities of the Individual (indicated in the left box), the Trauma Experience (indicated by directional arrows), and the Potential Supportive Other (indicated by the right box) reciprocally influence posttrauma relationships.

and other people in interpersonal relationships following trauma.

THE TRAUMA: HOW THE TYPE OF TRAUMA AND ITS TIMING SHAPE THE POSTTRAUMATIC TRAJECTORY

Epidemiological studies estimate that between 50 to 70% of individuals in the United States have experienced at least one traumatic event during their lifetime (Kessler, Sonnega, Bromet, Hughes, & Nelson, 1995; Kilpatrick, Resnick, Ruggiero, Conoscenti, & McCauley, 2007; Kilpatrick et al., 2003). Traumatic stress can occur in many forms and can be intentionally inflicted (e.g., physical assault, robbery, unwanted sexual contact) or can be accidental/unintentional in nature (e.g., motor vehicle accident, natural disaster). Although any form of potentially traumatic event can affect the individual, there is evidence to suggest that some traumatic events may constitute more ''potent'' forms of stressors than others. As depicted by the arrows in Figure 24.1, aspects of the traumatic event may impact both the support provided by a potentially supportive other as well as the individual's ability to accept/recruit support from a potentially supportive other.

Type of Trauma

The first type of interpersonal trauma, *interpersonal victimization* (e.g., sexual assault, physical assault), tends to be associated with higher rates of PTSD than other forms of traumatic events, particularly relative to traumatic experiences that do not involve intentionality, such as natural disasters (Resnick, Kilpatrick, Dansky, Saunders, & Best, 1993). Interpersonal violence is prevalent, ranging from 10% to over 30% of adults, depending on the violence type and definition (Elliott, 1997; Finkelhor, 1990; Resnick et al., 1993). For example, the Adverse Childhood Experiences study (Felitti et al., 1998) reported that

approximately one in four adults disclosed childhood sexual abuse histories, and one in 10 reported childhood physical abuse histories. Domestic violence is also a prevalent problem in the United States, as approximately 20 to 30% of marriages and 33% of dating relationships are characterized by violence (National Women's Study, 1992), affecting two to four million women each year (National Women's Study, 1992). Estimates of lifetime histories of interpersonal victimization are also high. A recent epidemiologic study found that 20 million out of 112 million women (18.0%) in the United States have been raped during their lifetime (Kilpatrick, Resnick et al., 2007). In other words, approximately one in five women in our country will likely be raped in their lifetime, an increase since the 1990s.

There is no doubt that interpersonal victimization can have detrimental effects. A meta-analysis of 50 studies found a clinically significant increase in psychological distress associated with victimization (Weaver & Clum, 1995). Interestingly, this meta-analysis reported that subjective factors (e.g., self-blame, perceived life threat) were more predictive of distress than were objective factors (e.g., physical injury, weapon presence). Subjective appraisals of an experience may continue to evolve in the acute aftermath of trauma and for years to come, with social relationships serving as one critical influence on perceptions of the traumatic experience and their worldview. Exposure to interpersonal violence has been shown to alter people's views of themselves and their ability to cope (Janoff-Bulman, 1989; Owens & Chard, 2001). Strongly held assumptions (e.g., personal invulnerability, the world is meaningful and just, positive self-perceptions) may be challenged or even shattered following exposure to traumatic events, especially interpersonal victimization (Janoff-Bulman, 1989).

Notably, victims of interpersonal violence frequently experience chronic, repeated, and varied forms of trauma such as extended periods of emotional and physical abuse from parents. Such chronicity of exposure likely leads to greater severity of symptoms and a more complex clinical picture than single and nonintentional trauma (Amstadter, McCart, & Ruggiero, in press). Further, these features distinguish interpersonal violence victims from those exposed to other traumatic events where repeated exposure to the same stressor is less common (e.g., natural disaster). Although interpersonal victimization as a whole is generally associated with more detrimental effects than is nonintentional trauma, these effects may vary as a function of the specific nature of the interpersonal trauma. For example, intimate partner violence is often characterized not only by physical abuse but also by the sustained psychological trauma involving disempowerment, decreased autonomy, and social isolation and consequent feelings of terror and helplessness (Dutton & Painter, 1993a, 1993b). Sexual assault or rape has been associated with other outcomes, such as difficulties with intimacy and trust, and has also been associated with lower sexual satisfaction (Feldman-Summers, Gordon, & Meagher, 1979; Thelen, Sherman, & Borst, 1998).

A second type of interpersonal trauma is *war/combat exposure*. Since 2001, U.S. forces in Iraq and Afghanistan have engaged in a variety of major operations including ground combat, hazardous peacekeeping, security details, and humanitarian efforts (Hoge, Auchterlonie, & Milliken, 2006; Hoge et al., 2004; Seal, Bertenthal, Miner, Saunak, & Marmar, 2007). Whether in combatant or peacekeeping roles, missions are characterized by probable exposure to traumatic events, including life threatening patrols and direct fire, witnessing violence and human suffering, and receiving hostile responses from civilian populations (Wright, Huffman, Adler, & Castro, 2002). In addition to the mental health problems associated with traumatic event exposure, many veterans who do not meet full diagnostic criteria for a mental health

disorder nonetheless struggle to return to predeployment functioning (Hoge et al., 2006; Hoge et al., 2004; Kang, Natelson, Mahan, Lee, & Murphy, 2003). Psychosocial adjustment problems are also prevalent amongst returning veterans (Hankin & Abramson, 1999; Hoge et al., 2006; Hoge et al., 2004; Seal et al., 2007), including severe impairments in domestic functioning (Taft et al., 2005) as well as social and occupational functioning (Frueh, Turner, Beidel, & Cahill, 2001; Kang et al., 2003; Prigerson, Maciejewski, & Rosenheck, 2002).

A third relevant type of trauma consists of *disasters*. Although the focus of this chapter is on interpersonal trauma, traumatic event exposure that is not specifically interpersonal in nature (e.g., disasters, accidents) has also been shown to influence interpersonal relationships and therefore warrant brief mention. Disasters (i.e., natural disasters, technological disasters, terrorist attacks, or other large-scale incidents that affect one or more communities) represent a unique set of stressors that have received increased research attention in recent years. Disasters are a unique type of trauma in the discussion of interpersonal relationships, as many individuals are affected at the same time, which in turn directly impacts the availability of social support. In disaster-stricken settings, social ties are often disrupted and victims are unable to reach the social networks they may have formed prior to the disaster (Weems et al., 2007). In the postdisaster context, community and social resources may jointly influence an individual's functioning. Social support, in particular, has been identified as a protective factor for postdisaster mental health problems (Acierno, Ruggiero, Kilpatrick, Resnick, & Galea, 2006; Galea, Acierno, Ruggiero, Resnick, & Kilpatrick, 2006; Norris et al., 2002).

Timing of the Trauma

In addition to the distinct effects of the *type* of trauma, posttraumatic adjustment of the individual depends on temporal factors—the time of life in which the trauma occurs and the time when support becomes available. To some extent, the stage of development determines the key social relationships: whereas parents represent the most important social relationship for children, key social supports shift over the course of the lifespan to include peers, romantic others, and adult offspring. Studies of trauma-exposed children and adolescents (ranging in age from 5 to 18) consistently highlight the importance of parental posttrauma response to child posttraumatic adjustment (Daviss et al., 2000; Korol, Green, & Gleser, 1999; McFarlane, Policansky, & Irwin, 1987; Nugent, Ostrowski, Christopher, & Delahanty, 2007). However, developmental differences have been observed in the posttrauma effects of social support, even over the course of late childhood and adolescence. For example, a motor vehicle accident study of youth 7 to 16 years of age assessed perceived social support received from others (e.g., police, hospital staff, peers) shortly following the accident (Keppel-Benson, Ollendick, & Benson, 2002). Although the presence of social support seemed to be unrelated to child PTSD in zero-order correlations, when age and degree of physical injury were statistically held constant, social support significantly predicted PTSD. The authors attributed this finding to a suppressor effect, in which age appeared to have suppressed the relationship between social support and posttraumatic symptoms. Further research is needed to clarify how age-related differences may have masked these associations. For example, it is possible that perceived social support in the hours following an accident is differently influential over the course of development. Notably, findings also indicated that parental worry and increased vigilance posttrauma actually *increased* the likelihood that children would go on to develop PTSD.

Studies focusing on narrower developmental ranges provide further information about *who* provides key posttraumatic support. For example, an investigation of third- to fifth-graders found that symptoms of posttraumatic stress at 3, 7, and 10 months following a hurricane were inversely associated with levels of social support, including support provided by parents, friends, classmates, and teachers (La Greca, Silverman, Vernberg, & Prinstein, 1996). However, as the authors report elsewhere (Vernberg, La Greca, Silverman, & Prinstein, 1996), unique effects for PTSD symptoms at three months were found for social support provided by teachers and classmates. Although shared variance associated with support received from parents and close friends was also associated with subsequent PTSD symptoms, it appeared that supportive relationships within the classroom were uniquely important for children's adjustment after the disaster, suggesting that youth exposed to disaster may benefit from school-based interventions targeting socially supportive classroom environments.

Youth, especially young children, are highly dependent on adults in talking about and negotiating traumatic experiences (Fivush, 1998). When children discuss an experience with adults following trauma, the discussion may serve to: "(a) reinstate the experience in memory and prevent forgetting; (b) help the child to appraise and interpret the experience; (c) correct misconceptions; (d) help the child manage or regulate his or her emotions; and (e) provide information about coping strategies and facilitate their enactment" (Salmon & Bryant, 2002, p. 175). Young trauma survivors who reported that they were able to talk (with family, friends, or a professional) about their road traffic accident, and understood by those with whom they talked within six weeks following the trauma were less likely to present with PTSD at 30 weeks posttrauma (Stallard, Velleman, & Baldwin, 2001). The importance of talking about trauma persists through adolescence. Adolescents who disclosed to any other person having experienced a sexual assault within one month of the event showed reduced risk for a concurrent major depressive episode or delinquency (Broman-Fulks et al., 2007). Interestingly, in this case, disclosure to mothers did reduce the risk for concurrent PTSD and delinquency. The "active ingredient" to this is unclear, although some insight is provided by efficacy of an informational intervention that normalized responses to the accident and encouraged (a) parents to provide emotional support and (b) children to feel free to talk with their parent (Kenardy, Thompson, Le Brocque, and Olsson, 2008). It is possible that talking with parents, particularly when parents are prepared for the conversation, provides concrete opportunities for provision of explicit support and normalization of traumatic responses. Additionally, most contemporary empirically supported interventions for trauma-exposed children include the development of a trauma narrative as a critical component of treatment (Cohen, Mannarino, Murray, and Ingelman, 2006), suggesting that the development of a coherent narrative of the trauma is itself therapeutic.

Beyond the provision of a supportive environment that permits youth to discuss and contextualize their experiences, parents may transmit their own abilities to cope with traumatic stressors by modeling or helping the child learn useful cognitive styles, coping mechanisms, and reactions to stress (Schwartz, Dohrenwend, & Levav, 1994). Pediatric injury patients who initially exhibit early biological markers of posttraumatic *resilience* report increased symptoms of PTSD at six months if their parents show high levels of PTSD symptoms at six weeks—but not if their parents show low levels of PTSD symptoms at six weeks (Nugent et al., 2007). Other family factors that have been shown to promote child adjustment following trauma include increased family cohesion (Conte & Schuerman, 1987), low levels of maternal distress (Deblinger, McLeer, & Henry, 1990), maternal support, and family help-seeking behavior (Waterman, 1993).

The timing of trauma also has important implications for the effects of trauma on an individual's overall understanding of interpersonal relationships. Traumatic experiences disrupt normative development; that is, nascent frameworks for interpersonal relationships are altered by the roles that other individuals play, both in the trauma itself and in the process of posttraumatic coping/adjustment. Thus, childhood interpersonal traumas such as physical, sexual, and emotional abuse, are believed to exert perhaps the strongest and most pervasive influence on individuals and their interactions with the world around them. Schemas for intimacy and trust may incorporate early traumas as part of their organizing life or word-view. Childhood exposure to trauma and maltreatment (including sexual abuse, physical abuse, emotional abuse, neglect, and witnessed domestic violence) has consistently been associated with impairments in subsequent interpersonal relationships throughout the lifespan. More specifically, early childhood emotional abuse has been associated with dating violence in adolescence (Wekerle et al., 2009). Further, childhood sexual abuse has been associated with alterations in sexual aspects of subsequent interpersonal relationships. These effects include first consensual intercourse at a younger age (Miller, Monson, & Norton, 1995; Nagy & Adcock, 1994; Raj, Silverman, & Amaro, 2000; Senn, Carey, & Vanable, 2008; Upchurch & Kusunoki, 2004) and more sexual risk behaviors during adolescence than nonabused peers (Arata, Langhinrichsen-Rohling, Bowers, & O'Brien, 2007; Brown, Kessel, Lourie, Ford, & Lipsitt, 1997; Brown, Lourie, Zlotnick, & Cohn, 2000; Cinq-Mars, Wright, Cyr, & McDuff, 2003; Lodico & DiClemente, 1994; Nagy & Adcock, 1994; Raj et al., 2000; Upchurch & Kusunoki, 2004). In adulthood, a history of childhood sexual abuse has been associated with negative attitudes about sexuality, lower levels of interpersonal power in sexual relationships (Finkelhor & Browne, 1985), decreased stability of sexual relationships, and an increased number of sexual relationships in adulthood (Kirkham & Lobb, 1998; Timms & Connors, 1992).

Further, sexual abuse during childhood or adolescence has been associated with increased risk for sexual revictimization during adulthood (Fargo, 2008; Gidycz, Coble, Latham, & Layman, 1993; Gidycz, Hanson, & Layman, 1995; Humphrey & White, 2000; Koss & Dinero, 1989; Messman & Long, 1996; Roodman & Clum, 2001; Siegel & Williams, 2001). For example, in a national sample of women, 41% of women who were crime victims reported having been revictimized (Resnick et al., 1993). As many as 62 to 82% of child sexual abuse victims have been revictimized as adults (Sorenson, Siegel, Golding, & Stein, 1991). A number of factors have been posited to play a role in the occurrence of revictimization, including low self-esteem, learned helplessness, faulty causal attributions, and relationship choices (e.g., Cloitre, 1998; Messman & Long, 1996). Although evidence has been found for the influence of factors such as alcohol and drug use, dissociation/posttraumatic symptomology, poor risk recognition, and interpersonal expectations or difficulties, perhaps the strongest empirical support has been found for differences in sex behavior (i.e., coercive sexual behavior, younger age at first intercourse, greater number of sexual partners, permissive attitudes about sexual behavior; see Messman-Moore & Long, 2003 for a review).

In addition to increasing a person's vulnerability to further maladaptive patterns in relationships (e.g., partner violence), childhood maltreatment is also associated with global deficiencies in adult interpersonal relationships. Adults with childhood maltreatment have smaller social support networks, are less satisfied with their networks, and perceive their relationships to be less supportive (Gibson & Harthorne, 1996; Harmer, Sanderson, & Mertin, 1999; Stroud, 1999). Further, following adult traumatic experiences, adults with a history of early childhood victimization perceive themselves as receiving less social support than others (Clapp & Beck, in press; Vranceanu, Hobfoll, & Johnson, 2007).

Finally, later stages of life present new challenges to coping with trauma, as older adulthood is often characterized by increased dependency on instrumental support and decreased availability of peer social supports. For example, although nearly half (44%) of older adults (defined as 60-plus years of age) report "very low" levels of social support, research has shown that posttrauma social support continues to be important throughout older adulthood (Acierno, Hernandez, Amstadter, Resnick, Steve, Muzzy, & Kilpatrick, in press). Although direct comparisons of trauma-exposed older and younger adults have identified some differences in PTSD risk factors, low social support consistently predicts increased risk for PTSD across age groups (Acierno, Ruggiero, Kilpatrick, Resnick, & Galea, 2006). Further, trauma-related social losses sustained early in life may influence the person's ability to cope with subsequent traumatic events even decades later. For example, both recent (i.e., terrorism) and distal (i.e., Holocaust) interpersonal losses strongly predicted PTSD symptoms as well as overall psychological distress in older adult Israeli Holocaust survivors (Dekel & Hobfoll, 2007). Not only is low social support a correlate of PTSD, but the relationship may be reciprocal in that PTSD may also lead to disruptions in social support. For example, older myocardial infarction patients who meet criteria for PTSD report greater social dysfunction than non-PTSD comparison patients (Chung, Berger, Jones, & Rudd, 2008). It is possible that traumatic experiences and consequent posttraumatic symptoms may impact an individual's ability to recruit, or benefit from, social support mechanisms.

Effects of Trauma on the Individual's Engagement With Others

A thorough discussion of the psychological consequences of traumatic event exposure is beyond the scope of this chapter, and the interested reader is referred to books devoted to these issues (e.g., Cloitre, Cohen, & Koenen, 2006; Janoff-Bulman, 1992; van der Kolk, 1987). However, a brief overview of psychopathology related to exposure is presented, with a focus on how these symptoms may affect the individual's social relationships. Many individuals are resilient following trauma; that is, they maintain healthy and relatively stable levels of psychosocial functioning (Bonanno, 2004). A second trajectory involves threshold or subthreshold psychopathology that subsides within several weeks or months of the traumatic event; such rapid recovery is common and may occur when an individual's personal and social resources obviate the need for treatment. A third possible trajectory in the aftermath of criminal victimization is the development of chronic psychopathology, particularly PTSD (Kessler et al., 1995; D. G. Kilpatrick et al., 2003; Resnick et al., 1993).

Posttraumatic stress disorder (PTSD). The disorder most closely related to trauma exposure is PTSD. We therefore focus our discussion on this condition and provide only a cursory discussion of associated conditions. PTSD is unique among the mental disorders in that it requires exposure to a potentially traumatic life event (Criterion A; American Psychiatric Association, 1994). PTSD is further defined by the presence of three symptom clusters: (1) reexperiencing, (2) avoidance and numbing, and (3) arousal (American Psychiatric Association, 1994). As previously noted, interpersonal victimization is associated with a higher prevalence of PTSD, compared to other types of traumatic events. For example, the National Women's Study (Resnick et al., 1993) found the lifetime prevalence of PTSD resulting from rape and sexual assault to be 32.0% and 30.8%, respectively, compared to a prevalence of 9.4% resulting from a noncrime related traumatic event (e.g., motor vehicle accident). Although early trauma research focused on the ways that social support may serve to

facilitate positive posttraumatic adjustment and growth, research has increasingly characterized the manner whereby, over time, posttraumatic psychopathology such as PTSD and associated symptoms may progressively erode social support (King, Taft, King, Hammond, & Stone, 2006; Laffaye, Cavella, Drescher, & Rosen, 2008).

1. *Reexperiencing.* In addition to the overall distress associated with symptoms of reexperiencing, some symptoms, such as "physiologic reactivity upon exposure to internal or external cues that symbolize or resemble an aspect of the traumatic event" (Criterion B-5; American Psychiatric Association, 1994), may be particularly problematic following interpersonal traumas. When traumatic experiences are interpersonal in nature, such as rape or physical abuse, later interpersonal interactions such as sex or physical closeness may trigger reexperiencing symptoms. For example, rape has been shown to decrease sexual satisfaction years after the trauma (Kilpatrick, Best, Saunders, & Veronen, 1988; Norris & Feldman-Summers, 1981; van Berlo & Ensink, 2000). Further, rape survivors report that the majority of experienced flashbacks occur during sexual activities (Burgess & Holmstrom, 1979). Female rape survivors show less confidence in others' dependability, less comfort with closeness/intimacy, and increased fear of abandonment (McEwan, de Man, & Simpson-Housley, 2002; Thelen et al., 1998). Diagnoses of PTSD and depression have been shown to partly explain the association between rape and subsequent sexual difficulties (Letourneau, Resnick, Kilpatrick, Saunders, & Best, 1996; van Berlo & Ensink, 2000).

2. *Avoidance and emotional numbing.* Common to PTSD, avoidance symptoms have also been shown to induce significant strain on relationships (Kilpatrick, Veronen, & Resick, 1979; Carrion & Steiner, 2000), as research has found that emotional numbing (a subset of avoidance symptoms) and emotional detachment were

significantly associated with relationship difficulties in World War II ex-prisoners of war (Cook, Riggs, Thompson, Coyne, & Sheikh, 2004; Bernstein, 1998). Relative to symptoms of reexperiencing and hyperarousal, symptoms of avoidance/numbing are particularly harmful to marital quality (Riggs, Byrne, Weathers, & Litz, 1998). Numbing in motor vehicle accident survivors is consistently associated with impairment in psychosocial functioning with family and friends (Kuhn, Blanchard, & Hickling, 2003) and has been associated with decreases in perceived social support (Beck, Grant, Clapp, & Palyo, in press). Even after controlling for resource loss at baseline, emotional numbing symptoms in inner-city abused women were associated with the loss of future interpersonal resources including perceived losses of family (e.g., intimacy with partner, family stability) and general interpersonal resources (e.g., feeling valuable to others, affection from others; Johnson, Palmieri, Jackson, & Hobfoll, 2007).

Yet another symptom of avoidance is the "feeling of detachment or estrangement from others." PTSD and other trauma-related disorders have been associated with increases in loneliness (defined as distress secondary to perceive inadequacy of existing social relationships) and social isolation (withdrawal from, or failure to engage, existing social relationships) (Solomon & Dekel, 2008; Solomon, Mikulincer, & Waysman, 1991). A year posttrauma, more than half of rape victims report restricted social life (Nadelson, Notman, Zackson, & Gornick, 1982). Researchers postulate that posttraumatic guilt and shame may prevent trauma survivors from accepting social support, thereby increasing both loneliness and social isolation (Herman, 1992). Former prisoners of war have been characterized as preferring solitude (Bernstein, 1998) and experience higher divorce rates (Nice, McDonald, & McMillian, 1981). Further, PTSD in combat veterans and prisoners of war has been linked to lower marital satisfaction, intimacy, and constructive communication (Carroll, Roeger, Foy, & Donahue, 1985; Cook, Riggs, Thompson, & Coyne, 2004).

3. *Negative emotional arousal.* Symptoms of hyperarousal appear to exert complicated effects on relationships. Some research has shown that hyperarousal may be harmful for interpersonal functioning (Beck et al., in press) and is associated with lower perceptions of safety (Fullerton, Ursano, Reeves, Shigemura, & Grieger, 2006). However, some research suggests that symptoms of hyperarousal in rape victims may increase sensitivity to cues that predict a sexually coercive interaction, promoting risk recognition and possibly reduced likelihood of revictimization (Wilson, Calhoun, & Bernat, 1999). Rape victims with high levels of hyperarousal may have an attentional bias to any cues (such as partner behaviors or situational factors) reminiscent of prior trauma. Although this attentional bias may partly serve to prevent subsequent traumas, in individuals with PTSD, this bias may also overextend to include innocuous cues that serve as traumatic reminders.

Anger, which can harm a relationship, is a particularly robust predictor of the development and maintenance of PTSD. The DSM-IV arousal symptom of "irritability or outbursts of anger" is frequently endorsed by trauma-exposed individuals. Feelings of anger are commonly elevated following traumatic experiences (Andrews, Brewin, Rose, & Kirk, 2000; Brewin, Andrews, & Rose, 2000; Connor, Davidson, & Lee, 2003; Novaco & Chemtob, 2002) and have been associated with subsequent PTSD severity (Feeny, Zoellner, & Foa, 2000; Orth, Cahill, Foa, & Maercker, 2008; Orth & Wieland, 2006; Sijbrandij, Olff, Opmeer, Carlier, & Gersons, 2008). Relative to male veterans without PTSD, male veterans with PTSD evidence increased hostility and aggression toward intimate partners (Beckham, Moore, & Reynolds, 2000; Byrne & Riggs, 1996). Similarly, women with PTSD evidence elevations in both violence and hostility (Beckham, Calhoun, Glenn, & Barefoot, 2002; Najavits, Sonn, Walsh, & Weiss,

2004; Stuart, Moore, Gordon, Ramsey, & Kahler, 2006). Anger, and particularly fear of experiencing anger, has been shown to predict aggressive behavior (Tull, Jakupcak, Paulson, & Gratz, 2007) and to adversely impact PTSD treatment outcome (Forbes, Creamer, Hawthorne, Allen, & McHugh, 2003; Forbes et al., 2008). Researchers have suggested that anger may interfere with the development of a healthy therapeutic relationship and/or may interfere with the use of social support, including helpful support from therapeutic groups and personal networks (Forbes et al., 2003). Posttraumatic affect such as anger may partly drive coping responses, with anger promoting posttraumatic growth *in the short term* (Park, Aldwin, Fenster, & Snyder, 2008), but maintaining PTSD *in the long term* (Jayasinghe, Giosan, Evans, Spielman, & Difede, 2008).

Other disorders related to traumatic stress. In addition to PTSD, other common Axis I mental health consequences of trauma exposure include major depression and substance-use disorders (Kilpatrick, Acierno, Resnick, Saunders, & Best, 1997; Resnick et al., 1993). Trauma exposure, especially if it occurs in childhood, has also been associated with borderline personality disorder, a severe Axis II condition with behavioral manifestations that include emotion instability, suicidality, and parasuicidal acts (American Psychiatric Association, 1994). Similar to PTSD, these disorders are prevalent, and are associated with increased risk of morbidity and mortality and high rates of functional impairment (Murray & Lopez, 1996), underscoring the need for effective interventions.

Social Support and Resilience: Stress-Buffering Model

Aside from the effects of trauma on social relationships, a wealth of research supports the importance of social relationships on coping with trauma. Meta-analysis has identified loss of social resources to be one of the strongest risk factors for PTSD (Brewin et al., 2000). As framed within Cohen and Wills's (1984) stress-buffering model, supportive social relationships facilitate coping with stressful life events and buffer against deleterious outcomes, such as psychopathology. For example, in a study of World War II veterans who were exposed to secret military tests of mustard gas, increased likelihood of developing PTSD was associated with having been "sworn to secrecy and threatened with criminal prosecution" if they disclosed any details of the traumatic event (Schnurr et al., 2000).

Numerous investigations have highlighted the critical role of social support of family following trauma, with adequacy of social support consistently associated with lower PTSD symptoms (Brewin et al., 2000; Ozer, Best, Lipsey, & Weiss, 2003). Some evidence suggests that social support experienced even years after trauma may be important. For example, decreased social support in adulthood partially mediates the effects of childhood maltreatment on PTSD in adults (Vranceanu et al., 2007). Furthermore, the loss of interpersonal resources independently contributes to the effects of childhood abuse on later adult abuse or assault-related PTSD (Schumm, Hobfoll, & Keogh, 2004). Social support also attenuates the risk of sexual problems following rape (Dahl, 1993), with women who have a loving partner more likely to continue to engage in positive sexual contact with their partner (van Berlo & Ensink, 2000). Thus, supportive others may buffer the effects of trauma by providing a range of supports (i.e., emotional support, instrumental support). Supportive relationships may also provide a safe context for approaching activities or places that may also serve as trauma reminders (i.e., engaging in sex), thereby allowing conditioned fear to extinguish. Finally, a loving partner may help by decreasing feelings of social isolation.

Conversely, inadequate supports in the face of trauma can exacerbate feelings of social isolation and loneliness that sometimes develop following trauma. For example, victims of severe partner violence who seek support from friends frequently find that their friends avoid them (Weisz, Tolman, Callahan, Saunders, & Black, 2007). Similarly, nonsupportive family environments, particularly familial interactions with high levels of expressed emotion (e.g., criticism), have been shown to adversely impact treatment outcome (Barrowclough, Gregg, & Tarrier, 2008; Tarrier, 1996; Tarrier, Sommerfield, & Pilgrim, 1999). Traumatic events impacting entire communities, such as natural disaster, may also place victims at higher risk for adverse mental health outcomes if (1) relationships or resources are disrupted or (2) similarly traumatized relevant others respond with poor coping strategies. For example, research has shown an increase in domestic violence and child abuse in the aftermath of disaster (Laudisio, 1993). Following Hurricane Andrew, telephone calls to the community helpline reporting domestic violence increased by 50% (Laudisio, 1993) and more than one third of those surveyed reported that someone in their home had lost verbal or physical control in the two months since the hurricane (Control, 1992). In sum, exposure to traumatic events of all forms can have detrimental effects on a variety of levels of functioning.

Aspects of the social environment on a group level (e.g., community, neighborhood) also influence an individual. For example, group-level variables (e.g., high levels of community crime or neighborhood unemployment) influence both the risk of exposure to traumatic events and the risk of mental health problems (DuMond, Widom, & Czaja, 2007; Eibner & Sturm, 2006), even after accounting for individual-level variables (e.g., socioeconomic status, education, ethnicity/race). A recent review (Ellen, Mijanovich, & Dillman, 2001) suggests that features of the social environment may affect the individual in many relevant ways—e.g., making institutions and resources less available or causing stress in the physical environment through crowding and crime. When resources are adequate, socioenvironmental factors may be protective, as community members band together to provide both types of support, namely, instrumental (e.g., rescue and safety, rebuilding) and social/emotional (e.g., understanding, reassurance, care). However, when resources are limited, the same factors may increase stress. Clearly, social support, both in the form of individual relationships and community supports, is a key factor influencing posttrauma adjustment. However, consistent with the reciprocal nature of interpersonal relationships, the availability and utility of social support cannot be divorced from personal qualities of the individual.

An Interactional Model

The effects of trauma on interpersonal relationships probably interact in complex ways with details of the trauma experience, the availability of social support, and the person's own ability to make use of social support systems. Separate from the impact of trauma and posttraumatic symptoms on an individual's ability to relate to social others, individual-specific factors such as coping style or trait/personality influences likely impact the individual's ability to recruit and benefit from social support. The concept of *network orientation* refers to an individual's beliefs or attitudes about seeking and accepting help from a range of social relationships (Tolsdorf, 1976). Network orientation may be one important contributor to a trauma survivor's ability to make use of available social supports (Clapp & Beck, in press). Negative network orientation in women with a history of sexual abuse has been associated with lower levels of trust, increased suspicion of others, and avoidance of interpersonal intimacy (Kallstrom-Fuqua & Weston, 2004).

Foy and colleagues proposed a PTSD Etiological Hypothesis in which ''an immediate crisis physiological reaction'' interacts with subsequent biological, psychological, and *social* factors to promote (or prevent) the development of PTSD (Foy, Madvig, Pynoos, & Camulleri, 1996). Mechanisms of that type would contribute to statistical interactions between, for example, social/interpersonal processes and the development of PTSD. Interactions between an initial biological response and subsequent social supports are supported by an investigation of children with serious injuries: the presence of symptoms of PTSD in the parents at six weeks moderated the relationship between peritraumatic biological risk factors (i.e., cortisol, heart rate) and the PTSD symptoms in the child at six months (Nugent et al., 2007). Similarly, genetic examinations of posttraumatic adjustment have identified important interactions between social support and genetic variants (Amstadter, Koenen et al., in press; Kilpatrick, Koenen et al., 2007). Koenen, Amstadter, & Nugent (in press) provide a review of posttraumatic gene-environment interactions.

Summary and Conclusions

An individual's social environment and support network are among the most important factors in adjustment following traumatic experiences. As depicted in Figure 24.1, potentially supportive others range from family members to friends to members of one's community and their response to a victim's traumatic experience may serve to buffer or enhance the potentially harmful effects of trauma. Importantly, however, the effects of trauma on relationships are not unidirectional and an individual's ability to recruit/accept support is influenced by many qualities of the individual (e.g., personality and coping style, beliefs, and personal resources). Finally, social interactions following traumatic event exposure occur within the context of important aspects of the traumatic event itself. Interpersonal relationships following trauma are impacted by the type

of trauma experienced (e.g., sexual abuse, domestic violence, or natural disaster), the degree to which the traumatic event is shared, and the ecology of the victim's interpersonal relationships within the larger community. Although investigations of adjustment following traumatic event exposure have evidenced increasing focus on the complex interactions between adjustment following trauma and social relationships, continued research is warranted. In particular, although the effects of trauma on interpersonal relationships have been extensively documented, many of the underlying mechanisms of these effects, and thus potential avenues for secondary prevention and treatment, are unknown.

References

Acierno, R., Hernandez, M. A., Amstadter, A. B., Resnick, H. S., Steve, K., Muzzy, W., & Kilpatrick, D. G. (in press). Prevalence and correlates of emotional, physical, sexual, neglectful, and financial abuse in the United States: The National Elder Mistreatment Study. *American Journal of Public Health*.

Acierno, R., Ruggiero, K. J., Kilpatrick, D., Resnick, H., & Galea, S. (2006). Risk and protective factors for psychopathology among older versus younger adults after the 2004 Florida hurricanes. *American Journal of Geriatric Psychiatry*, 14, 1051–1059.

American Psychiatric Association. (1994). *Diagnostic and statistical manual of mental disorders* (4th ed.). Washington, DC: Author.

Amstadter, A. B., Koenen, K. C., Ruggiero, K. J., Acierno, R., Galea, S., Kilpatrick, D. G., & Gelernter, J. (2009). Variant in RGS2 moderates posttraumatic stress symptoms following potentially traumatic event exposure. *Journal of Anxiety Disorders*, 23(3), 369–373.

Amstadter, A. B., McCart, M., & Ruggiero, K. J. (in press). Psychosocial interventions for adults with crime-related PTSD. *Professional Psychology: Research and Practice*.

Andrews, B., Brewin, C. R., Rose, S., & Kirk, M. (2000). Predicting PTSD symptoms in victims of violent crime: The role of shame, anger, and childhood abuse. *Journal of Abnormal Psychology*, 109(1), 69–73.

Arata, C. M., Langhinrichsen-Rohling, J., Bowers, D., & O'Brien, N. (2007). Differential correlates of multi-type maltreatment among urban youth. *Child Abuse & Neglect, 31*(4), 393–415.

Barrowclough, C., Gregg, L., & Tarrier, N. (2008). Expressed emotion and causal attributions in relatives of post–traumatic stress disorder patients. *Behaviour Research and Therapy, 46*(2), 207–218.

Beck, J. G., Grant, D. M., Clapp, J. D., & Palyo, S. A. (in press). Understanding the interpersonal impact of trauma: Contributions of PTSD and depression. *Journal of Anxiety Disorders,* doi:10.1016/j.janxdis.2008.09.001.

Beckham, J. C., Calhoun, P. S., Glenn, D. M., & Barefoot, J. C. (2002). Posttraumatic stress disorder, hostility, and health in women: A review of current research. *Annals of Behavioral Medicine, 24*(3), 219–228.

Beckham, J. C., Moore, S. D., & Reynolds, V. (2000). Interpersonal hostility and violence in Vietnam combat veterans with chronic posttraumatic stress disorder: A review of theoretical models and empirical evidence. *Aggression and Violent Behavior, 5,* 451–466.

Bernstein, M. (1998). Conflicts in adjustment: WW2 prisoners of war and their families. In Y. Danieli (Ed.), *International handbook of multigenerational legacies of trauma* (pp. 119–124). New York: Plenum Press.

Bleiberg, K., & Markowitz, J. (2005). Interpersonal psychotherapy for posttraumatic stress disorder. *American Journal of Psychiatry, 162,* 181–183.

Bonanno, G. A. (2004). Loss, trauma, and human resilience. Have we underestimated the human capacity to thrive after extremely aversive events? *American Psychologist, 59,* 20–28.

Brewin, C. R., Andrews, B., & Rose, S. (2000). Fear, helplessness, and horror in posttraumatic stress disorder: Investigating DSM-IV criterion A2 in victims of violent crime. *Journal of Traumatic Stress, 13*(3), 499–509.

Brewin, C. R., Andrews, B., & Valentine, J. D. (2000). Meta-analysis of risk factors for post–traumatic stress disorder in trauma-exposed adults. *Journal of Consulting and Clinical Psychology, 68,* 317–336.

Broman-Fulks, J. J., Ruggiero, K. J., Hanson, R. F., Smith, D. W., Resnick, H. S., Kilpatrick, D. G.,

& Saunders, B. A. (2007). Sexual assault disclosure in relation to adolescent mental health: Results from the National Survey of Adolescents. *Journal of Clinical Child and Adolescent Psychology, 36*(2), 260–266.

Brown, L. K., Kessel, S. M., Lourie, K. J., Ford, H. H., & Lipsitt, L. P. (1997). Influence of sexual abuse on HIV-related attitudes and behaviors in adolescent psychiatric inpatients. *Journal of American Academy of Child & Adolescent Psychiatry, 36*(3), 316–322.

Brown, L. K., Lourie, K. J., Zlotnick, C., & Cohn, J. (2000). Impact of sexual abuse on the HIV-risk-related behavior of adolescents in intensive psychiatric treatment. *American Journal of Psychiatry, 157*(9), 1413–1415.

Burgess, A. W., & Holmstrom, L. L. (1979). Rape, sexual disruption, and recovery. *American Journal of Orthopsychiatry, 49,* 648–657.

Byrne, C. A., & Riggs, D. S. (1996). The cycle of trauma: Relationship aggression in male veterans with symptoms of post–traumatic stress disorder. *Violence and Victims, 11,* 213–225.

Carroll, E. M., Roeger, D. B., Foy, D. W., & Donahue, C. P. (1985). Vietnam combat veterans with post–traumatic stress disorder: Analysis of marital and cohabiting adjustment. *Journal of Abnormal Psychology, 94,* 329–337.

Chung, M. C., Berger, Z., Jones, R., & Rudd, H. (2008). Post–traumatic stress and comorbidity following myocardial infarction among older patients: The role of coping. *Aging & Mental Health, 12*(1), 124–133.

Cinq-Mars, C., Wright, J., Cyr, M., & McDuff, P. (2003). Sexual at-risk behaviors of sexually abused adolescent girls. *Journal of Child Sexual Abuse, 12*(2), 1–18.

Clapp, J. D., & Gayle Beck, J. (in press). Understanding the relationship between PTSD and social support: The role of negative network orientation. *Behaviour Research and Therapy.*

Cloitre, M. (1998). Sexual revictimization: Risk factors and prevention. In V. M. Follette, J. I. Ruzek & F. R. Abueg (Eds.), *Cognitive behavioral therapies for trauma* (pp. 278–304). New York: Guilford Press.

Cloitre, M., Cohen, L. R., & Koenen, K. C. (2006). *Treating the trauma of childhood abuse: Therapy for the interrupted life.* New York: Guilford Press.

Cloitre, M., Koenen, K. C., Cohen, L. R., & Han, H. (2002). Skills training in affective and interpersonal regulation followed by exposure: A phase-based treatment for PTSD related to childhood abuse. *Journal of Consulting and Clinical Psychology, 70*(5), 1067–1074.

Cohen, S., & McKay, G. (1984). Social support, stress and the buffering hypothesis: A theoretical analysis. In A. Baum, S. E. Taylor, & J. E. Singer (Eds.), *Handbook of psychology and health* (pp. 253–267). Hillsdale, NJ: Erlbaum.

Connor, K. M., Davidson, J. R. T., & Lee, L.-C. (2003). Spirituality, resilience, and anger in survivors of violent trauma: A community survey. *Journal of Traumatic Stress, 16*(5), 487–494.

Conte, J. R., & Schuerman, J. R. (1987). Factors associated with an increased impact of child sexual abuse. *Child Abuse and Neglect, 11,* 201–211.

Control, C. F. D. (1992). Post-Hurricane Andrew Assessment of Health Care Needs and Access to Health Care in Dade County, Florida. EPI-AID 93–09. Miami: Department of Health and Rehabilitative Services.

Cohen, J. A., Mannarino, A. P., Murray, L. K., & Ingelman, R. (2006). Psychosocial interventions for maltreated and violence-exposed children. *Journal of Social Issues, 62,* 737–766.

Cook, J. M., Riggs, D. S., Thompson, R., & Coyne, J. C. (2004). Posttraumatic stress disorder and current relationship functioning among World War II ex-prisoners of war. *Journal of Family Psychology, 18,* 36–45.

Dahl, S. (1993). *Rape—A hazard to health.* Oslo: Scandinavian University Press.

Daviss, W. B., Mooney, D., Racusin, R., Ford, J. D., Fleischer, A., & McHugo, G. J. (2000). Predicting posttraumatic stress after hospitalization for pediatric injury. *Journal of the American Academy of Child and Adolescent Psychiatry, 39,* 573–583.

Deblinger, E., McLeer, S. V., & Henry, D. (1990). Cognitive behavioral treatment for sexually abused children suffering posttraumatic stress: Preliminary findings. *Journal of the American Academy of Child and Adolescent Psychiatry, 29,* 747–752.

Dekel, R., & Hobfoll, S. E. (2007). The impact of resource loss on Holocaust survivors facing war and terrorism in Israel. *Aging & Mental Health, 11*(2), 159–167.

DuMond, K. A., Widom, C. S., & Czaja, S. J. (2007). Predictors of resilience in abused and neglected children grown-up: The role of individual and neighborhood characteristics. *Child Abuse & Neglect, 31*(3), 255–274.

Dutton, D. G., & Painter, S. (1993a). The battered woman syndrome: Effects of severity and intermittency of abuse. *American Orthopsychiatric Association, 63*(4), 614–622.

Dutton, D. G., & Painter, S. (1993b). Emotional attachments in abusive relationships: A test of traumatic bonding theory. *Violence and Victims, 8*(2), 105–120.

Ehlers, A., & Clark, D. M. (2000). A cognitive model of posttraumatic stress disorder. *Behaviour Research and Therapy, 38,* 319–345.

Eibner, C., & Sturm, R. (2006). U.S.-based indices of area-level deprivation: Results from HealthCare for Communities. *Social Science & Medicine, 62*(2), 348–359.

Ellen, I. G., Mijanovich, T., & Dillman, K. (2001). Neighborhood effects on health: Exploring the links and assessing the evidence. *Journal of Urban Affairs, 23*(3–4), 391–408.

Elliott, D. M. (1997). Traumatic events: Prevalence and delayed recall in the general population. *Journal of Consulting and Clinical Psychology, 65*(5), 811–820.

Fargo, J. D. (2008). Pathways to adult sexual revictimization: Direct and indirect behavioral risk factors across the lifespan. *Journal of Interpersonal Violence, 24*(11), 1771–1791.

Feeny, N. C., Zoellner, L. A., & Foa, E. B. (2000). Anger, dissociation, and post–traumatic stress disorder among female assault victims. *Journal of Traumatic Stress, 13*(1), 89–100.

Feldman-Summers, S., Gordon, P. E., & Meagher, J. R. (1979). The impact of rape on sexual satisfaction. *Journal of Abnormal Psychology, 88*(1), 101–105.

Felitti, V. J., Anda, R. F., Nordenberg, D., Williamson, D. F., Spitz, A. M., & Edwards, V. (1998). Relationship of childhood abuse and household dysfunction to many of the leading causes of death in adults. The Adverse Childhood Experiences (ACE) Study. *American Journal of Preventive Medicine, 14*(4), 245–258.

Finkelhor, D. (1990). Early and long-term effects of child sexual abuse: An update. *Professional Psychology: Research and Practice, 21*(5), 325–330.

Finkelhor, D., & Browne, A. (1985). The traumatic impact of child sexual abuse: A conceptualization. *American Journal of Orthopsychiatry, 55,* 530–541.

Fivush, R. (1998). Children's recollections of traumatic and nontraumatic events. *Development and Psychopathology, 10,* 699–726.

Forbes, D., Creamer, M., Hawthorne, G., Allen, N., & McHugh, T. (2003). Comorbidity as a predictor of symptom change after treatment in combat-related posttraumatic stress disorder. *Journal of Nervous and Mental Disease, 191*(2), 93–99.

Forbes, D., Parslow, R., Creamer, M., Allen, N., McHugh, T., & Hopwood, M. (2008). Mechanisms of anger and treatment outcome in combat veterans with posttraumatic stress disorder. *Journal of Traumatic Stress, 21*(2), 142–149.

Foy, D. W., Madvig, B. T., Pynoos, R. S., & Camilleri, A. J. (1996) Etiologic factors in the development of posttraumatic stress disorder in children and adolescents. *Journal of School Psychology, 34*, 133–145.

Frueh, B. C., Turner, S. M., Beidel, D. C., & Cahill, S. P. (2001). Assessment of social functioning in combat veterans with PTSD. *Aggression & Violent Behavior, 6*(1), 79–90.

Fullerton, C. S., Ursano, R. J., Reeves, J., Shigemura, J., & Grieger, T. (2006). Perceived safety in disaster workers following 9/11. *The Journal of Nervous and Mental Disease, 194*(1), 61–.

Galea, S., Acierno, R., Ruggiero, K. J., Resnick, H. S., & Kilpatrick, D. G. (2006). Social context and the psychobiology of trauma. *Annals of the New York Academy of Sciences, 1071*, 231–241.

Gibson, R., & Harthorne, T. (1996). Childhood sexual and adult loneliness and network orientation. *Child Abuse and Neglect, 20*, 1087–1093.

Gidycz, C. A., Coble, C. N., Latham, L., & Layman, M. J. (1993). Sexual assault experience in adulthood and prior victimization experiences. *Psychology of Women Quarterly, 17*, 151–168.

Gidycz, C. A., Hanson, K., & Layman, M. J. (1995). A prospective analysis of the relationships among sexual assault experiences. *Psychology of Women Quarterly, 19*, 5–29.

Hankin, B. L., & Abramson, L. Y. (1999). Development of gender differences in depression: Description and possible explanations. *Annals of Medicine, 31*, 372–379.

Harmer, A., Sanderson, J., & Mertin, P. (1999). Influence of negative childhood experiences on psychological functioning, social support, and parenting for mothers recovering from addiction. *Child Abuse & Neglect, 23*, 421–433.

Herman, J. L. (1992). *Trauma and recovery.* New York: Basic Books.

Hoge, C. W., Auchterlonie, J. L., & Milliken, C. S. (2006). Mental health problems, use of mental health services, and attrition from military service after returning from deployment to Iraq or Afghanistan. *Journal of the American Medical Association, 295*(9), 1023–1032.

Hoge, C. W., Castro, C. A., Messer, S. C., McGurk, D., Cotting, D. I., & Koffman, R. L. (2004). Combat duty in Iraq and Afghanistan, mental health problems, and barriers to care. *New England Journal of Medicine, 351*(1), 13–22.

Humphrey, J. A., & White, J. W. (2000). Women's vulnerability to sexual assault from adolescence to young adulthood. *Journal of Adolescent Health, 27*(6), 419–424.

Janoff-Bulman, R. (1989). Assumptive worlds and the stress of traumatic events: Applications of the schema construct. *Social Cognition, 7*(2), 113–136.

Janoff-Bulman, R. (1992). *Shattered assumptions: Towards a new psychology of trauma.* New York: The Free Press.

Jayasinghe, N., Giosan, C., Evans, S., Spielman, L., & Difede, J. (2008). Anger and posttraumatic stress disorder in disaster relief workers exposed to the September 11, 2001, World Trade Center disaster: One-year follow-up study. *Journal of Nervous & Mental Disease, 196*, 844–846.

Johnson, D. M., Palmieri, P. A., Jackson, A. P., & Hobfoll, S. E. (2007). Emotional numbing weakens abused inner-city women's resiliency resources. *Journal of Traumatic Stress, 20*(2), 197–206.

Kallstrom-Fuqua, A. C., Weston, R., & Marshall, L. L. (2004). Childhood and adolescent sexual abuse of community women: mediated effects of psychological distress and social relationships. *Journal of Consulting and Clinical Psychology, 72*, 980–992.

Kenardy, J., Thompson, K., Le Brocque, R., & Olsson, K. (2008). Information-provision intervention for children and their parents following pediatric accidental injury. *European Child and Adolescent Psychiatry, 17*, 316–325.

Kang, H. K., Natelson, B. H., Mahan, C. M., Lee, K. Y., & Murphy, F. M. (2003). Post-traumatic stress disorder and chronic fatigue syndrome-like illness among Gulf War veterans: A population-based survey of 30,000 veterans. *American Journal of Epidemiology, 157*, 141–148.

Keppel-Benson, J. M., Ollendick, T. H., & Benson, M. J. (2002). Posttraumatic stress in children following motor vehicle accidents. *Journal of Child Psychology and Psychiatry, 43,* 203–212.

Kessler, R. C., Sonnega, A., Bromet, E., Hughes, M., & Nelson, C. B. (1995). Posttraumatic stress disorder in the National Comorbidity Survey. *Archives of General Psychiatry, 52,* 1048–1060.

Kilpatrick, D., Best, C. L., Saunders, B. E., & Veronen, L. J. (1988). Rape in marriage and in dating relationships: How bad is it for mental health? In R. A. Prentky & V. L. Quinsey (Eds.), *Human sexual aggression: Current perspectives* (pp. 335–344). New York: New York Academy of Sciences.

Kilpatrick, D. G., Acierno, R., Resnick, H. S., Saunders, B. E., & Best, C. L. (1997). A 2-year longitudinal analysis of the relationship between violent assault and substance abuse in women. *Journal of Consulting and Clinical Psychology, 65,* 834–847.

Kilpatrick, D. G., Koenen, K. C., Ruggiero, K. J., Acierno, R., Galea, S., Resnick, H. S., & Gelernter, J. (2007). Serotonin transporter genotype and social support and moderation of posttraumatic stress disorder and depression in hurricane-exposed adults. *American Journal of Psychiatry, 164*(11), 1693–1699.

Kilpatrick, D. G., Resnick, H. S., Ruggiero, K. J., Conoscenti, L. M., & McCauley, J. (2007). Drug-facilitated, incapacitated, and forcible rape: A national study. Final report submitted to the National Institute of Justice.

Kilpatrick, D. G., Ruggiero, K. J., Acierno, R., Saunders, B. E., Resnick, H. S., & Best, C. L. (2003). Violence and risk of PTSD, major depression, substance abuse/dependence, and comorbidity: Results from the National Survey of Adolescents. *Journal of Consulting and Clinical Psychology, 71*(4), 692–700.

Kilpatrick, D. G., Veronen, L. J., & Resick, P. A. (1979). The aftermath of rape: Recent empirical findings. *American Journal of Orthopsychiatry, 49,* 658–669.

King, D. W., Taft, C., King, L. A., Hammond, C., & Stone, E. R. (2006). Directionality of the association between social support and posttraumatic stress disorder: a longitudinal investigation. *Journal of Applied Social Psychology, 36,* 2980–2992.

Kirkham, C. M., & Lobb, D. J. (1998). The British Columbia Positive Women's Survey: A detailed profile of 100 HIV-infected women. *Canadian Medical Association Journal, 158,* 317–323.

Koenen, K. C., Amstadter, A., & Nugent, N. R. (in press). Gene-environment interactions in PTSD: An update. *Journal of Traumatic Stress.*

Korol, M., Green, B. L., & Gleser, G. C. (1999). Children's responses to a nuclear waste disaster: PTSD symptoms and outcome prediction. *Journal of the American Academy of Child and Adolescent Psychiatry, 38,* 368–375.

Koss, M. P., & Dinero, T. E. (1989). Discriminant analysis of risk factors for sexual victimization among a national sample of college women. *Journal of Consulting and Clinical Psychology, 57,* 242–250.

Krupnick, J. L., Green, B. L., Stockton, P., Miranda, J., Krause, E., & Mete, M. (2008). Group interpersonal psychotherapy for low-income women with posttraumatic stress disorder. *Psychotherapy Research, 18*(5), 497–507.

Kuhn, E., Blanchard, E. B., & Hickling, E. J. (2003). Posttraumatic stress disorder and psychosocial functioning within two samples of MVA survivors. *Behaviour Research and Therapy, 41,* 1105–1112.

La Greca, A. M., Silverman, W. K., Vernberg, E. M., & Prinstein, M. J. (1996). Symptoms of posttraumatic stress in children after Hurricane Andrew: A prospective study. *Journal of Consulting and Clinical Psychology, 64,* 712–723.

Laffaye, C., Cavella, S., Drescher, K., & Rosen, C. (2008). Relationships among PTSD symptoms, social support, and support source in veterans with chronic PTSD. *Journal of Traumatic Stress, 21,* 394–401.

Laudisio, G. (1993). Disaster aftermath: Redefining response—Hurricane Andrew's Impact on I & R. *Alliance of Information and Referral Systems, 15,* 13–32.

Letourneau, E. J., Resnick, H. S., Kilpatrick, D. G., Saunders, B. E., & Best, C. L. (1996). Comorbidity of sexual problems and posttraumatic stress disorder in female crime victims. *Behavior Therapy, 27,* 321–336.

Lodico, M. A., & DiClemente, R. J. (1994). The association between childhood sexual abuse and prevalence of HIV-related risk behaviors. *Clinical Pediatrics, 33*(8), 498–502.

Markowitz, J., Milrod, B., Bleiberg, K., & Randall, M. (2009). Interpersonal factors in understanding and treating posttraumatic stress disorder. *Journal of Psychiatric Practice, 15*(2), 133–140.

McEwan, S. L., de Man, A. F., & Simpson-Housley, P. (2002). Ego-identity achievement and perception of risk in intimacy in survivors of stranger and acquaintance rape. *Sex Roles*, 47(5), 281–287.

McFarlane, A. C., Policansky, S. K., & Irwin, C. (1987). A longitudinal study of the psychological morbidity in children due to natural disaster. *Psychological Medicine.*, 17, 727–738.

Messman, T. L., & Long, P. J. (1996). Child sexual abuse and its relationship to revictimization in adult women: A review. *Clinical Psychology Review*, 16, 397–420.

Messman-Moore, T. L., & Long, P. J. (2003). The role of childhood sexual abuse sequelae in the sexual revictimization of women: An empirical review and theoretical reformulation. *Clinical Psychology Review*, 23, 537–571.

Miller, B. C., Monson, B. H., & Norton, M. C. (1995). The effects of forced sexual intercourse on white female adolescents. *Child Abuse & Neglect*, 19(10), 1289–1301.

Murray, C. J. L., & Lopez, A. D. (Eds.). (1996). *The global burden of disease*. Cambridge, MA: Harvard University Press.

Nadelson, C. C., Notman, M. T., Zackson, H., & Gornick, J. (1982). A follow-up study of rape victims. *American Journal of Psychiatry*, 139, 1266–1270.

Nagy, S., & Adcock, A. G. (1994). A comparison of risky health behaviors of sexually active, sexually abused, and abstaining. *Pediatrics*, 93(4), 570.

Najavits, L. M., Sonn, J., Walsh, M., & Weiss, R. D. (2004). Domestic violence in women with PTSD and substance abuse. *Addictive Behaviors*, 29, 707–715.

Nice, D. S., McDonald, B., & McMillian, T. (1981). The families of U.S. Navy prisoners of war from Vietnam five years after reunion. *Journal of Marriage and Family*, 43, 431–437.

Norris, F. H., Friedman, M. J., Watson, P. J., Byrne, C. M., Diaz, E., & Kaniasty, K. (2002). 60,000 disaster victims speak: Part 1. An empirical review of the empirical literature, 1981–2001. *Psychiatry*, 65(3), 207–239.

Norris, J., & Feldman-Summers, S. (1981). Factors related to the psychological impacts of rape on the victim. *Journal of Abnormal Psychology*, 90(6), 562–567.

Novaco, R. W., & Chemtob, C. M. (2002). Anger and Combat-Related Posttraumatic Stress Disorder. *Journal of Traumatic Stress*, 15(2), 123–132.

Nugent, N. R., Ostrowski, S., Christopher, N. C., & Delahanty, D. L. (2007). Parental symptoms of PTSD as a moderator of child's acute biological response and subsequent symptoms of PTSD in pediatric trauma patients. *Journal of Pediatric Psychology*, 32, 309–318.

Orth, U., Cahill, S. P., Foa, E. B., & Maercker, A. (2008). Anger and posttraumatic stress disorder symptoms in crime victims: A longitudinal analysis. *Journal of Consulting and Clinical Psychology*, 76(2), 208–218.

Orth, U., & Wieland, E. (2006). Anger, hostility, and posttraumatic stress disorder in trauma-exposed adults: A meta-analysis. *Journal of Consulting and Clinical Psychology*, 74, 698–706.

Owens, G. P., & Chard, K. M. (2001). Cognitive distortions among women reporting childhood sexual abuse. *Journal of Interpersonal Violence*, 16(2), 178–191.

Ozer, E. J., Best, S. R., Lipsey, T. L., & Weiss, D. S. (2003). Predictors of posttraumatic stress disorder and symptoms in adults: A meta-analysis. *Psychological Bulletin*, 129, 52–73.

Park, C. L., Aldwin, C. M., Fenster, J. R., & Snyder, L. B. (2008). Pathways to posttraumatic growth versus posttraumatic stress: Coping and emotional reactions following the September 11, 2001, terrorist attacks. *American Journal of Orthopsychiatry*, 78(3), 300–312.

Prigerson, H. G., Maciejewski, P. K., & Rosenheck, R. A. (2002). Population attributable fractions of psychiatric disorders and behavioral outcomes associated with combat exposure among U.S. men. *American Journal of Public Health*, 92(1), 59–63.

Raj, A., Silverman, J., & Amaro, H. (2000). The relationship between sexual abuse and sexual risk among high school students: Findings from the 1997 Massachusetts Youth Risk Behavior Survey. *Maternal and Child Health Journal*, 4, 125–134.

Resick, P. A., & Schnicke, M. K. (1992). Cognitive processing therapy for sexual assault victims. *Journal of Consulting and Clinical Psychology*, 60(5), 748–756.

Resnick, H. S., Kilpatrick, D. G., Dansky, B. S., Saunders, B. E., & Best, C. L. (1993). Prevalence of civilian trauma and posttraumatic stress disorder in a representative national sample of women. *Journal of Consulting and Clinical Psychology, 61,* 984–991.

Riggs, D., Byrne, C., Weathers, F., & Litz, B. (1998). The quality of the intimate relationships of male Vietnam veterans: Problems associated with posttraumatic stress disorder. *Journal of Traumatic Stress, 11,* 87–101.

Roodman, A. A., & Clum, G. A. (2001). Revictimization rates and method variance: A meta-analysis. *Clinical Psychology Review, 21,* 183–204.

Salmon, K., & Bryant, R. A. (2002). Posttraumatic stress disorder in children: The influence of developmental factors. *Clinical Psychology Review, 22,* 163–188.

Schnurr, P. P., Ford, J. D., Friedman, M. J., Green, B. L., Dain, B. J., & Sengupta, A. (2000). Predictors and outcomes of posttraumatic stress disorder in World War II veterans exposed to mustard gas. *Journal of Consulting and Clinical Psychology, 68,* 258–268.

Schumm, J. A., Hobfoll, S. E., & Keogh, N. J. (2004). Revictimization and interpersonal resource loss predicts PTSD among women in substance-use treatment. *Journal of Traumatic Stress, 17*(2), 173–181.

Schwartz, S., Dohrenwend, B. P., & Levav, I. (1994). Nongenetic familial transmission of psychiatric disorders? Evidence from children of Holocaust survivors. *Journal of Health and Social Behavior, 35,* 385–402.

Seal, K. H., Bertenthal, D., Miner, C. R., Saunak, S., & Marmar, C. I. (2007). Bringing the war back home: Mental health disorders among 103 788 U.S. veterans returning from Iraq and Afghanistan seen at Department of Veterans Affairs Facilities. *Archives of Internal Medicine, 167,* 476–482.

Senn, T. E., Carey, M. P., & Vanable, P. A. (2008). Childhood and adolescent sexual abuse and subsequent sexual risk behavior: Evidence from controlled studies, methodological critique, and suggestions for research. *Clinical Psychology Review, 28,* 711–735.

Siegel, J. A., & Williams, L. M. (2001). *Risk factors for sexual victimization of women: Results from a prospective study.* Unpublished manuscript.

Sijbrandij, M., Olff, M., Opmeer, B. C., Carlier, I. V. E., & Gersons, B. P. R. (2008). Early prognostic screening for posttraumatic stress disorder with the Davidson Trauma Scale and the SPAN. *Depression and Anxiety, 25*(12), 1038–1045.

Solomon, Z., & Dekel, R. (2008). The contribution of loneliness and posttraumatic stress disorder to marital adjustment following war captivity: A longitudinal study. *Family Process, 47*(2), 261–275.

Solomon, Z., Mikulincer, M., & Waysman, M. (1991). Delayed and immediate onset posttraumatic stress disorder: II. The role of live events and social resources. *Social Psychiatry and Psychiatric Epidemiology, 19,* 231–236.

Sorenson, S. B., Siegel, J. A., Golding, J. M., & Stein, J. A. (1991). Repeated sexual victimization. *Violence and Victims, 6,* 299–308.

Stroud, D. (1999). Familial support as perceived by adult victims of childhood sexual abuse. *Sexual Abuse: Journal of Research and Treatment, 11*(2), 159–175.

Stuart, G. L., Moore, T. M., Gordon, K. C., Ramsey, S. E., & Kahler, C. W. (2006). Psychopathology in women arrested for domestic violence. *Journal of Interpersonal Violence, 21,* 376–389.

Taft, C. T., Pless, A. P., Stalans, L. J., Koenen, K. C., King, L. A., & King, D. W. (2005). Risk factors for partner violence among a national sample of combat veterans. *Journal of Consulting and Clinical Psychology, 73*(1), 151–159.

Tarrier, N. (1996). An application of expressed emotion to the study of PTSD: Preliminary findings. *Clinical Psychology and Psychotherapy, 3,* 220–229.

Tarrier, N., Sommerfield, C., & Pilgrim, H. (1999). Relatives' expressed emotion (EE) and PTSD treatment outcome. *Psychological Medicine, 29,* 801–811.

Thelen, M. H., Sherman, M. D., & Borst, T. S. (1998). Fear of intimacy and attachment among rape survivors. *Behavior Modification, 22*(1), 108–116.

Timms, R. J., & Connors, P. (1992). Adult promiscuity following childhood sexual abuse: An introduction. *Psychotherapy Patient, 8,* 19–27.

Tolsdorf, C. C. (1976). Social networks, support, and coping: An exploratory study. *Family Process, 15*(4), 407–417.

Tull, M. T., Jakupcak, M., Paulson, A., & Gratz, K. L. (2007). The role of emotional inexpressivity and experiential avoidance in the relationship between posttraumatic stress disorder symptom severity and aggressive behavior among men exposed to interpersonal violence. *Anxiety, Stress & Coping: An International Journal, 20*(4), 337–351.

Upchurch, D. M., & Kusunoki, Y. (2004). Associations between forced sex, sexual and protective practices, and sexually transmitted diseases among a national sample of adolescent girls. *Women's Health Issues, 14*(3), 75–84.

van Berlo, W., & Ensink, B. (2000). Problems with sexuality after sexual assault. *Annual Review of Sex Research, 11,* 235.

van der Kolk, B. (1987). *Psychological trauma.* Washington, DC: American Psychiatric Press.

Vernberg, E. M., La Greca, A. M., Silverman, W. K., & Prinstein, M. J. (1996). Prediction of posttraumatic stress symptoms in children after Hurricane Andrew. *Journal of Abnormal Psychology, 105,* 237–248.

Vranceanu, A.-M., Hobfoll, S. E., & Johnson, R. J. (2007). Child multi-type maltreatment and associated depression and PTSD symptoms: The role of social support and stress. *Child Abuse & Neglect, 31*(1), 71–84.

Waterman, J. (1993). Mediators of effects on children: what enhances optimal functioning and promotes healing. In J. Waterman, R. J. Kelly, J. McCord & M. K. Oliveri (Eds.), *Behind the playground walls: Sexual abuse in preschools.* New York: Guilford Press.

Weaver, T. L., & Clum, G. A. (1995). Psychological distress associated with interpersonal violence: A meta-analysis. *Clinical Psychology Review, 15*(2), 115–140.

Weems, C. F., Pina, A. A., Costa, N. M., Watts, S. E., Taylor, L. K., & Cannon, M. F. (2007). Predisaster trait anxiety and negative affect predict posttraumatic stress in youths after Hurricane Katrina. *Journal of Consulting & Clinical Psychology, 75*(1), 154–159.

Weisz, A. N., Tolman, R. M., Callahan, M. R., Saunders, D. G., & Black, B. M. (2007). Informal helpers' responses when adolescents tell them about dating violence or romantic relationship problems. *Journal of Adolescence, 30*(5), 853–868.

Wekerle, C., Leung, E., Wall, A.-M., MacMillan, H., Boyle, M., Trocme, N., & Waechter, R. (2009). The contribution of childhood emotional abuse to teen dating violence among child protective services-involved youth. *Child Abuse & Neglect, 33*(1), 45–58.

Wilson, A. E., Calhoun, K. S., & Bernat, J. A. (1999). Risk recognition and trauma-related symptoms among sexually revictimized women. *Journal of Consulting and Clinical Psychology, 67*(5), 705–710.

Wright, K. M., Huffman, A. H., Adler, A. B., & Castro, C. A. (2002). Psychological screening program overview. *Military Medicine, 167*(10), 858–861.

25 DEPRESSIVE DISORDERS AND INTERPERSONAL PROCESSES

Chris Segrin

Depression is one of the most common psychological disorders, affecting 10 to 15% of the population at some point in their lives (Kessler et al., 1994). It consists of affective (e.g., feeling sad), behavioral (e.g., social withdrawal), cognitive (e.g., difficulty concentrating), and somatic (e.g., loss of appetite) symptoms. In the *DSM-IV-TR* (American Psychiatric Association, 2000) it is recognized that these symptoms produce distress and impairment in social, occupational, or other areas of functioning. It is that impairment in social or interpersonal functioning that is the focus of this chapter. Scientists, practitioners, and theorists have for a long time been aware of the powerful and deleterious effect of depression on interpersonal functioning. For example, Sullivan (1953) described depression as "a chiefly destructive process. It cuts off impulses to integrate constructive situations with others. Only destructive situations are maintained, and these are extremely stereotyped" (p. 102). Since that time, a number of theories and research paradigms have been developed to explain how depression can cause problems with interpersonal relationships as well as how problematic interpersonal relationships can cause depression.

This chapter will focus on three major interpersonal processes in depression: social skills deficits, interpersonal responses to depression, and dysfunctional family interactions. Although these processes do not represent a comprehensive appraisal of all things interpersonal that covary with depression, they constitute a compelling account of how social well-being and psychological well-being are inextricably connected. From the outset, it is important to understand that there is substantial heterogeneity within the depressive disorders (Carragher, Adamson, Bunting, & McCann, 2009) and that different people with depression might describe substantially different experiences (Horowitz & Turan, 2008). Therefore, the interpersonal processes described in this chapter, although common, would not be expected to be evident in all cases of depression.

SOCIAL SKILLS DEFICITS AND DEPRESSIONS

One of the dominant theoretical statements and empirical evaluations of interpersonal processes and depression came from Peter Lewinsohn and his colleagues at the

University of Oregon. Lewinsohn (1974, 1975) developed a behavioral theory of depression in which problems with social skills figured prominently. According to the behavioral theory, people with depression were hypothesized to exhibit deficiencies in social skills that impede the acquisition of positive reinforcement from the social environment. In fact, this research team defined social skill as "the complex ability both to emit behaviors which are positively reinforced or negatively reinforced and not to emit behaviors which are punished or extinguished by others" (Libet & Lewinsohn, 1973, p. 304). Accordingly, the attendant lack of reinforcement from the social environment for those with poor social skills is true by definition. There is an inherently interpersonal flavor to Lewinsohn's behavioral theory, as he explained that social skill "involves sequences of behavior consisting of actions emitted by an individual together with the reactions he/she elicits from the social environment" (Lewinsohn, 1975, p. 41). Although the theory assumes that social skills deficits are antecedents to low reinforcement and consequent depression, Lewinsohn consistently recognized that the experience of depression would feed back to social skills and further impede the emission of skilled social behaviors.

Efforts to test the behavioral theory, and to describe the social skills deficits of people with depression more generally, have largely focused on the interpersonal behavior of people with depression. However, Lewinsohn's theorizing explicitly recognized the importance of reactions from the social environment as having teleological significance in the course of events that lead up to depression. He argued that interpersonal reactions to depressive behaviors start out sympathetic but eventually become rejecting.

> The social environment provides contingencies in the form of sympathy, interest, and concern which strengthen and maintain depressive behaviors. These reinforcements are typically provided by a small segment of the depressed person's social environment (e.g., his immediate family). However, since most people in the depressed person's environment (and eventually even his family) find these behaviors aversive, they will avoid him/her as much as possible, thus decreasing his/her rate of receiving positive reinforcement and further accentuating his/her depression. (Lewinsohn, 1975, p. 30)

This statement clearly foreshadowed what was to become a major paradigm in the interpersonal study of depression that was advanced by Coyne (1976a) and acutely focused on the interpersonal responses to people with depression. Coyne's interactional theory is examined in detail later in this chapter.

The behavioral theory of depression underwent a major expansion in the 1980s to incorporate cognitive variables, more feedback loops, and a more explicit recognition of the fact that social skills deficits could be consequents as well as causes of depression (Lewinsohn, Hoberman, Teri, & Hautzinger, 1985). Lewinsohn et al. explained "many of the social skill deficits shown by depressed individuals are secondary to being depressed" (p. 348). Although the causal order of social skills deficits and depression is still being investigated to this day, and will be discussed in more detail shortly, since the appearance of the behavioral theory, an impressive and diverse body of data has accumulated that highlights many of the problems with interpersonal behavior that appear to go hand in hand with depression (see Segrin, 1990, 2000; Tse & Bond, 2004, for reviews). Social skills are not easily measured, much less defined, and for that reason it is instructive to examine the evidence for the behavioral theory by the method with which researchers measured social skills or their selected elements.

Self-Reports of Social Skills Deficits Associated With Depression

Because the observation of socially skilled or unskilled behavior can be challenging for a variety of reasons, many researchers have employed self-report instruments for assessing the social skills of people with depression. These instruments typically assess traits (e.g., friendly, outgoing), perceived abilities to engage in various social tasks (e.g., relationship initiation, conflict management), or tendencies to engage in various domains of interpersonal behavior (e.g., impression management, emotional expression). Such self-reports have reasonable associations with actual behaviors under naturalistic conditions (Segrin, 1998). In general, people with depression evaluate their own social skills more negatively than nondepressed people do (e.g., Huprich, Clancy, Bornstein, & Nelson-Gray, 2004; Lewinsohn, Mischel, Chaplin, & Barton, 1980; Segrin & Dillard, 1993; Youngren & Lewinsohn, 1980). This pattern appears when both state (e.g., Edison & Adams, 1992) and trait (e.g., Gotlib, 1982) operationalizations of social skills are employed, and is evident in both adults (Meyer & Hokanson, 1985) and children (Garland & Fitzgerald, 1998).

Early on in the research on social skills and depression, it was discovered that people with depression were more accurate in rating their social skills than nondepressed people were (Lewinsohn et al., 1980). Lewinsohn et al. noted that even though depressed participants were rated by their conversational partners as exhibiting lower social skills than nondepressed people were, the depressed participants were more realistic in ratings of their social skills. In contrast, nondepressed participants appeared to overestimate their social skills relative to the ratings of their conversational partners (see also Edison & Adams, 1992). This pattern of depressive accuracy and nondepressed exaggeration of self-rated social skills fit well with the depressive realism effect (Alloy & Abramson, 1979) that has been documented in the cognitive literature on depression. However, later evidence showed that depressed people underestimate their social skills, relative to ratings provided by their conversational partners (Chau & Milling, 2006; Whitton, Larson, & Hauser, 2008). This negative distortion of self-ratings is not entirely consistent with the depressive realism effect. Accordingly, there remain unresolved issues in the assessment of social skills deficits in people with depression via self-report. Some findings show that these agree with those of conversational partners, whereas others show a downward bias in these self-ratings. Nevertheless, in the vast majority of cases, depressed people rate their own social skills lower than nondepressed people do.

Peer Ratings of Depressed Persons' Social Skills

The preceding discussion highlighted a second major approach to assessment of depressed people's social skills, that is, through the evaluations of their conversational partners or third parties who observe the interactions of people with depression. Even though there is presently some controversy about the accuracy versus downward bias of depressed people's self-rated social skills, those same studies that contributed to this mix of findings were consistent in revealing that people with depression were rated as exhibiting a lower degree of social skill than nondepressed people exhibit in their social interactions (e.g., Chau & Milling, 2006; Lewinsohn et al., 1980; Whitton et al., 2008). In the larger literature on peer-ratings of depressed people's social skills, there is further evidence of deficits relative to nondepressed targets (Dalley, Bolocofsky, & Karlin, 1994; Edison & Adams, 1992; Segrin, 1992). At the same time, there have been some cases where observers' ratings of social skills did not discriminate between depressed and nondepressed research participants (e.g., Ducharme & Bachelor, 1993; Gotlib & Meltzer, 1987). A meta-analysis of the literature back in 1990 revealed an effect size of $r = .22$ for depressed-nondepressed differences in peer-rated social skills, in favor of lower ratings for the depressed group (Segrin, 1990). The research has not been entirely consistent, but the preponderance of evidence shows that there is something in the social behavior of people with depression that is detectable to peers and conversational partners, resulting in lower ratings of the social skills of people with depression.

Behavioral Analysis of Social Skills Deficits and Depression

There presently exists a large literature on communication behaviors of people with depression that lends considerable insight into the specifics of depressive social behavior as instantiations of social skills deficits. An in-depth analysis of the connection between these behaviors and the construct of social skill is beyond the scope of this chapter, but such analyses are available elsewhere (e.g., McFall, 1982; Perez & Riggio, 2003). Also, it is important to note that for the majority of investigations of specific social behaviors and depression, investigators were rarely studying them under the guise of social skills deficits. Nevertheless, analysis of depression and such behaviors as gaze, paralanguage, and facial expression provide substantial information about the specifics of social skills deficits that are associated with depression.

Eye contact. Human beings use gaze, consciously and unconsciously, to indicate interest, attention, attraction, and a positive attitude toward another person. Accordingly, it is a vital behavioral element of social skill. Numerous studies show that people with depression make less eye contact with their conversational partners than nondepressed people do (Segrin, 1992; Troisi & Moles, 1999; Youngren & Lewinsohn, 1980). Rutter and Stephenson (1972) discovered an interaction between depression and the presence or absence of speech, such that depressed subjects were less likely than controls to be looking while speaking. As looking while speaking is a behavior associated with confidence and status (Exline, Ellyson, & Long, 1975), it

is likely that depressed people's negative feelings about themselves precipitate this gaze avoidance. Related evidence indicating that depression is sometimes associated with less eye contact when in this listening role (van Beek, van Dolderen, & Dubas, 2006) also illustrates how the enactment of gaze by people with depression often has the appearance of unskilled social behavior.

Facial expression. The human facial expression is an extremely complex, and at times subtle, behavior that can convey a multitude of emotional states, liking, and displeasure to an observer. At a general level, the facial expressions of people with depression are less animated and spontaneous than those of nondepressed controls (Gaebel & Wolwer, 2004; Tremeau et al., 2005) or simply less happy and more sad in appearance (Renneberg, Heyn, Gebbhard, & Bachman, 2005). For example, Schwartz and his colleagues (Schwartz, Fair, Salt, Mandel, & Klerman, 1976a; 1976b) connected people to electromyographic (EMG) electrodes that measure subtle facial activity from electrical discharge produced by muscle movements. They found that depressed subjects evidenced an attenuated EMG response while trying to imagine happy situations and images, and an exaggerated reaction (relative to controls) while trying to imagine sad situations and feelings. When no instructions were offered, the controls spontaneously assumed a happy expression while the depressed subjects showed no evidence of a happy expression (cf. Oliveau & Willmuth, 1979; Schwartz et al., 1978). Other inquiries revealed depressed-nondepressed differences in facial expressions of pleasantness and arousal (Youngren & Lewinsohn, 1980), smiles (Ellgring, 1986), expressions of anger and contempt (Berenbaum, 1992), and facial expressions of happiness, sadness, fear, surprise, and interest (less in the depressed group; Fossi, Faravelli, & Paoli, 1984). Depressed people also tend to control felt smiles in response to a comedy clip with negative facial expressions such as a frown (Reed, Sayette, & Cohn, 2007). Controlling felt smiles is evident when a person initially shows a genuine smile (e.g., movement of the zygomatic major muscle) followed by a smile control movement (e.g., "lip corner depressors") in the face (Reed et al.). The tendency to exert more control over positive facial expressions is perhaps one reason why the facial expressions of people with depression are generally difficult for others to accurately decode (Prkachin, Craig, Papageorgis, & Reith, 1977).

Naturally, social skills do not only involve the ability to enact behaviors appropriately and effectively, but to effectively decode the behaviors of others as well. Some evidence indicates that depression is associated with insensitivity to seeing happiness in human facial expressions, and an elevated propensity to see anger or sadness in otherwise low-intensity facial expressions of emotion (Joormann & Gotlib, 2006; van Beek & Dubas, 2008). This negative bias in perceiving facial expressions of emotion has been linked to rumination among depressed patients (Raes, Hermans, & Williams, 2006). These and other errors in decoding the facial expressions of others are associated not only with higher depression, but also with lower levels of relationship well-being (Carton, Kessler, & Pape, 1999). Presently, there is reason to conclude that both the expression, and at least in some cases, the perception of facial expressions is negatively altered by depression.

Posture and gesture. During social interaction, posture and gesture can indicate interest, boredom, agreement, disagreement, attitudes, and emotional states (Bull, 1987). Depressed patients tend to engage in significantly less gesturing and head nodding than healthy controls (Fossi et al., 1984; Troisi & Moles, 1999). Similarly, depressed children appear to have a diminished tendency to use illustrators, which are gestures that accompany speech in an expressive fashion (Kazdin, Sherick, Esveldt-Dawson, & Rancurello, 1985). Ekman and Friesen (1972) found that the tendency to use illustrators increased dramatically in depressed individuals as symptoms lifted (see also Ekman & Friesen, 1974). People with depression also engage in more body contact (gestures called self-adaptors) than nondepressed subjects (Ranelli & Miller, 1981). People ordinarily exhibit self-adaptors when over- or underaroused. Depressed individuals are also more likely to hold their head in a downward position than nondepressed persons are (Waxer, 1974).

Paralanguage. How people say things often has more social consequence than exactly what they say. The effective use of speech rate, intonation, and loudness creates interest, liveliness, drama, and enthusiasm in human speech. Studies of the temporal aspects of paralanguage indicate that people who are depressed speak slower (Siegman, 1987; Youngren & Lewinsohn, 1980), speak less (Edison & Adams, 1992; Fossi et al., 1984; Hale, Jansen, Bouhuys, Jenner, & van der Hoofdakker, 1997), exhibit more pauses (Mundt, Snyder, Cannizzaro, Chappie, & Geralts, 2007), longer pauses (Ellgring & Scherer, 1996), and take longer to respond to the speech behaviors of others (Talavera, Saiz-Ruiz, & Garcia-Toro, 1994) than nondepressed people do. Investigations of speech production indicate that people with depression generally speak with less volume (Darby, Simmons, & Berger, 1984; Gotlib, 1982), and more silences (Vanger, Summerfield, Rosen, & Watson, 1992) and hesitancies than nondepressed persons. When prompted by a topic, people with depression have more difficulty producing speech than nondepressed controls (Calev, Nigal, & Chazan, 1989). Investigations of the tonal quality of speech show that people with depression tend to speak in a monotonous tone and with a lower pitch than nondepressed persons (Alpert, Pouget, & Silva, 2001; Talavera et al., 1994; see Scherer, 1987, for review). It is perhaps only sadness that people with depression convey paralinguistically with some degree of skill (Levin, Hall, Knight, & Alpert, 1985), although in a culture with display rules that often prescribe concealing sad affect in most cases, clear communication of sadness might not always be considered a skill.

Language and speech content. Depression is associated with a propensity for negatively toned discourse reflective of sadness, complaining, anger, and in some cases, aggression and inappropriateness. For example, conversations of married couples with a depressed member are marked by verbal expression of dysphoric feelings, negative well-being, greater talk about well-being, and in the case of the depressed partner, negative self-evaluation (Hautzinger, Linden, & Hoffman, 1982). Depressed spouses also report being more verbally aggressive and less constructive in problem-solving in their marital interactions (Kahn, Coyne, & Margolin, 1985, Segrin & Fitzpatrick, 1992). When interacting with their infants, mothers with depression exhibit a failure to adjust the emotional versus informational aspects of their speech content to the age-appropriate level of their child (Herrera, Reissland, & Shepherd, 2004). In "get acquainted" interactions, depressed students made fewer statements reflecting a positive appraisal of their partner, and made more directly negative statements than their nondepressed peers (Gotlib & Robinson, 1982). Further evidence of negative verbal content has been documented in studies of stranger interactions, telephone conversations with confidants, and psychotherapy sessions that include people with depression (Belsher & Costello, 1991; Coyne, 1976b). Negative verbal content is especially pronounced in interactions between depressed people and intimate others (Hautzinger et al., 1982; Ruscher & Gotlib, 1988). Segrin and Flora (1998) coded the linguistic behavior of depressed and nondepressed students discussing the "events of the day" with either a friend or a stranger. An interaction between depression and relationship with partner indicated that the depressed speakers withheld their negativity when talking with strangers, but were more inclined to introduce negative topics into the conversation (e.g., criticize, disagree, negative self-disclosure) when talking with a friend. A propensity toward negative self-disclosures more generally

is a problem associated with depression (Gurtman, 1987; Jacobson & Anderson, 1982). People with depression emit negative statements about the self at a higher rate than their nondepressed counterparts (Jacobson & Anderson, 1982). On a related point, people with depression have been shown to use more negatively valenced words and more first-person pronouns than nondepressed controls (Alison & Burgess, 2003; Rude, Gortner, & Pennebaker, 2004), suggestive of negative focus and self-preoccupation.

Associations Between Social Skills Deficits and Depression

In Lewinsohn's (1974, 1975) behavioral theory of depression, the social skills deficit hypothesis predicted that poor social skills are a causal antecedent to depression. In a series of three longitudinal studies, social skills at time 1 were found to predict changes in depression over one- to two-month intervals, such that lower social skills scores at time 1 predicted a worsening of depressive symptoms by time 2 (Wierzbicki, 1984, Wierzbicki & McCabe, 1988, study 1 and study 2). Although such findings are consistent with Lewinsohn's social skills deficit hypothesis, other longitudinal investigations using diagnostic interviews for the assessment of depression (Lewinsohn et al., 1994), multiple indicators of social skills (Segrin, 1996), longer inter-wave intervals of 4-12 months (Hokanson, Rupert, Welker, Hollander, & Hedeen, 1989; Lewinsohn et al., 1994; Segrin, 1993a, 1996), very large samples (Lewinsohn, Hoberman, & Rosenaum, 1988; Lewinsohn et al., 1994), and more than two waves of assessment (Segrin, 1999) have not been able to establish poor social skills as antecedent of increased depression. These findings present something of a challenge to the original form of the social skills deficit hypothesis and suggest that other causal trajectories might be responsible for the well-established covariation between poor social skills and depression.

One obvious alternative possibility is that poor social skills are a consequent of depression, a hypothesis once proposed by Lewinsohn et al. (1985). Many of the symptoms of depression such as low motivation, sad affect, and slowed motor behaviors have obvious implications for disrupted production of skilled social behavior. Studies guided by the scar hypothesis provide some insight into this possibility. The scar hypothesis uses the metaphor of a scar to postulate that people might acquire distinguishing characteristics as a result of an episode of depression, and that these characteristics represent a vulnerability to relapse (Lewinsohn, Steinmetz, Larson, & Franklin, 1981). Rohde, Lewinsohn, and Seeley (1990) demonstrated that self-rated social skills of once-depressed people remain lower than those of never-depressed controls, even one to two years after the depressive episode had lifted (but see Cole & Milstead, 1989). A later investigation by Petty, Sachs-Ericsson, and Joiner (2004) found some evidence that people recently remitted from depression had lower interpersonal functioning than those in a never-depression comparison group. Even though there are some mixed findings in the literature, enough evidence exists to suggest depression can lead to social skills deficits in at least some cases.

A third possible relationship linking poor social skills and depression is that poor social skills may be a distal contributory cause, or vulnerability factor, in the development of depression (Segrin, 1996; Segrin & Flora, 2000; Vanger, 1987). Such a relationship could account for some of the mixed findings from past research. In the tradition of diathesis-stress models of psychopathology, I proposed that poor social skills might be as a diathesis in the development of depression (Segrin, 1996; Segrin & Flora, 2000). By this logic, only those people who have poor social skills *and* experience stressful events are predicted to develop depressive symptoms. The reasoning behind this model is that people with good social skills can marshal the kind and quantity of social support that will be effective for coping with the stressful events. In contrast, people with poor social skills are expected to experience more stress (Segrin, Hanzal, Donnerstein, Taylor, & Domschke, 2007) and be less able to secure assistance and social support for dealing with those stressors when they do occur. A longitudinal test of this model revealed that the relationship between stressful life events and depression was strongest among those with the poorest social skills (Segrin & Flora, 2000). On the other hand, those with high social skills scores exhibited a relationship near $r = 0$ between stressful life events and depression. In other words, poor social skills made people vulnerable to the development of depression when faced with stressors, while good social skills produced a prophylactic effect in the face of stressors for some people. Similar results were obtained by Cummins (1990) using a measure of social insecurity that is similar to many commonly used measures of social skills. Collectively, these studies indicate that poor social skills make people vulnerable to the ill effects of stress and subsequent depression.

Summary

Consistent with the social skills deficit hypothesis, a broad range of research evidence shows that many people exhibit social skills deficits while in a state of depression. Evidence to this effect has accumulated from research that assessed social skills with self-reports, observer ratings, or various nonverbal or verbal behaviors that are microcomponents of social skills. People with depression often behave in a way that does not demonstrate effective social skill or interpersonal competence. Attempts to document causal associations between social skills deficits and depression have not been as frequent, but show that in at least some cases, poor social skills predate the development of depression; in others, depression appears to lead to lower social skills, and in still other cases, social skills deficits may function as a vulnerability factor in the development of depression. At the present time, there is no single causal association between depression and social skills deficits that has overwhelming or unequivocal support. Nevertheless, there can be little question about whether ineffective interpersonal behaviors are a common problem for people with depression.

INTERPERSONAL RESPONSES TO DEPRESSION

In contrast to the social skills approach that focuses on the behavior of depressed people, Coyne (1976a, 1976b) proposed an interpersonal model of depression that focused more on interpersonal responses to people with depression. Coyne theorized that depressive behavior engages other people and places a burden on them. Others are assumed to offer sympathy and support but eventually tire of depressive displays, becoming angry and unhappy and culminating in what is often referred to as nongenuine reassurance. The depressed person is aware of this lack of authenticity; as Coyne (1976a) noted, "he is aware by now that this response from others is not genuine and that they have become critical and rejecting" (p. 35). The rejection from the interpersonal environment is assumed to maintain a state of depression, and accordingly "the symptoms have a mutually maintaining relationship with the response of the social environment" (Coyne, 1976a, p. 39).

Coyne's interactional model of depression is a highly influential approach to researching and understanding interpersonal processes in depression (see Coyne, Burchill, & Stiles, 1990; Joiner, 2002; Segrin & Abramson, 1994; Segrin & Dillard, 1992, for reviews). The various propositions embedded in the model have each generated a substantial body of data, and these include the following three discussions on (1) depression and excessive reassurance seeking, (2) interpersonal induction of negative mood states in others (the emotional contagion effect), and (3) interpersonal rejection of people with

depression. Although interpersonal rejection of depressed people is truly the fundamental element of this perspective, the processes that lead up to it, reassurance seeking and emotional contagion, have major theoretical importance as well.

Excessive Reassurance Seeking

Coyne (1976a) observed that "Much of the depressive's communication is aimed at ascertaining the nature of the relationship or context in which this interaction is taking place" (p. 33). He further explained that "the depressive uses his symptoms to seek repeated feedback in his testing of the nature of his acceptance and the security of his relationship" (p. 34). These statements suggest that a major factor prompting negative mood induction in, and rejection from, others is this annoying interpersonal style of excessively seeking reassurance. A substantial body of data shows that reassurance seeking is common in depressed people and can have corrosive relational effects (e.g., Joiner, 1995; Joiner & Metalsky, 2001). The tendency for depressed people to seek reassurance from others may be driven by their increased experience of negative life events and low self-esteem (Joiner, Katz, & Lew, 1999). Reassurance seeking has been shown to interact with depressive symptoms to predict rejection from others (Joiner, 1999) and to be somewhat unique to depression (Burns, Brown, Plant, Sachs-Ericsson, & Joiner, 2006). Joiner and his associates argued that excessive reassurance seeking is the key interpersonal variable in depression that is responsible for both the contagion of depression and interpersonal rejection from others (Joiner, 2002; Joiner, Metalsky, Katz, & Beach, 1999). However, there has been some controversy about the reliability of the depression-excessive reassurance seeking association and its role in perpetrating interpersonal rejection (e.g., Benazon, 2000; Benazon & Coyne, 1999).

A newly revised version of the circumplex model of interpersonal behavior, based in interpersonal motives (Horowitz et al.,

2006), may help to explain how excessive reassurance seeking can prompt negative affect in partners of people with depression. According to the revised circumplex model, interpersonal behaviors invite a desired reaction from partners. Partners who do not respond accordingly frustrate the motivations of actors, thereby causing negative affect. So in the case of depression, the partner's offer of assistance and reassurance invites acceptance and signs of resolution from the depressed person. However, when the depressed person responds with continued reassurance seeking, according to Horowitz et al., the partner's motivation to help would be frustrated, and the partner would consequently experience negative affect.

A recent meta-analysis of 38 studies on depression and excessive reassurance seeking found a weighted mean effect size for the correlation between the two variables to be $r = .32$ (Starr & Davila, 2008). The weighted mean effect size for excessive reassurance seeking and rejection from others was $r = .14$; still statistically significant but rather weak in magnitude. Current conceptualizations of excessive reassurance seeking view it as a vulnerability factor in depression (Joiner & Metalsky, 2001) that can increase the risk of depression, especially when it results in lower perceived social support (Haeffel, Voelz, & Joiner, 2007).

Emotional Contagion

In his original statement, Coyne (1976a) suggested that members of the depressed person's social environment will find themselves "irritated, yet inhibited and increasingly guilt-ridden" (p. 34). It is this negative mood induction that is created through social interaction that fuels interpersonal rejection. After talking on the phone with depressed outpatients, subjects in Coyne's (1976b) investigation were significantly more depressed, anxious, and hostile than those who talked to nondepressed controls. Some further attempts to test this mood induction effect

experimentally (e.g., Gotlib & Robinson, 1982; McNiel, Arkowitz, & Pritchard, 1987) and in preexisting relationships (e.g., Segrin, 2004) have not always confirmed the effect, although it may become more evident over repeated interactions with the depressed target (Hokanson & Butler, 1992). Two meta-analyses of this literature documented modest to moderate effects for emotional contagion following interaction with depressed targets (Joiner & Katz, 1999; Segrin & Dillard, 1992). Although there has been some debate in the literature as to the conditions under which the effect should be expected and the research design requirements for testing it (e.g., Segrin, 2004, 2006; van Orden & Joiner, 2006), it is clear that in many cases, people with depression can prompt a negative affective state in their conversational partners. Perhaps the most compelling evidence for emotional contagion and depression comes from longitudinal studies showing that a target person's depression predicts the development or worsening of depressive symptoms or mood in his or her relational partner (Joiner, 1994; Segrin et al., 2005).

Interpersonal Rejection of People With Depression

In Coyne's (1976a) original investigation, university students talked on the phone with depressed outpatients or nondepressed controls. After the conversations, the students were significantly less willing to engage in future interaction with the depressed compared to nondepressed target individuals. This rejection effect has since been replicated with a variety of operationalizations and appears to be a very reliable feature of depressive interpersonal interactions (e.g., Elliott, MacNair, Herrick, Yoder, & Byrme, 1991; Gurtman, 1987; Segrin & Dillard, 1992), holding up across different cultures (Vanger, Summerfield, Rosen, & Watson, 1991) and age groups (Rudolph, Hammen, & Burge, 1994). The interpersonal rejection of people with depression is moderated by a host of factors. For instance, men appear to elicit more rejection than women (Hammen & Peters, 1977; Joiner, 1996), friends are less rejecting than strangers (Segrin, 1993b), people who rely on advice-giving, and joking are more rejecting (Notarius & Herrick, 1988), physically attractive people elicit less rejection (Amstutz & Kaplan, 1987), people with autonomous personalities receive greater rejection (Bieling & Alden, 2001), and those low in self-esteem who seek reassurance from their partners are especially prone to eliciting rejection (Joiner, Alfano, & Metalsky, 1992). The receipt of rejection from others has been demonstrated to predict subsequent worsening of depression (Nolan, Flynn, & Gaber, 2003). One apparent upshot of the rejection of people with depression is the tendency for them to be in dissatisfying and turbulent interpersonal relationships (Davila, 2001; Segrin, Powell, Givertz, & Brackin, 2003).

There is reason to believe that the interpersonal behavior of depressed people may elicit negative responses from others by design. According to self-verification theory, people are motivated to preserve self-views to enhance their sense of prediction and control (Swann, 1990). In the case of depression, this would be expressed as seeking negatively valenced feedback from other people in order to confirm what are otherwise negative views of the self. Indeed, this appears to be exactly the pattern of feedback seeking that is observed among people with depression (Giesler & Swann, 1999; Joiner, Katz, & Lew, 1997). In fact, in the presence of negative feedback, people with depression will actually increase their efforts at seeking negative feedback (Casbon, Burns, Bradbury, & Joiner, 2005). This negative feedback seeking is also related to rejection from partners (Weinstock & Whisman, 2004) and may be part of the constellation of depressogenic interpersonal behaviors that cause others to reject people with depression. Self-verification is one obvious means by which the symptoms of depression have a mutually maintaining relationship with the responses of others, as Coyne originally theorized.

Summary

Coyne's (1976a) interpersonal model of depression has generated an enormous body of research on other people's reactions to interaction with a depressed person. Most of the model's major assumptions have been empirically verified in a variety of different populations. Research showing that people with depression are especially likely to engage in excessive reassurance seeking fits well with the research on social skills deficits associated with depression. Excessive reassurance seeking may indeed be a manifestation or example of a particular social skills deficit associated with depression. Although the effects are not especially powerful, interaction with a depressed person generally appears to result in elevated negative affect in their partners. Perhaps as a result of this negative affect, conversational and relational partners are more inclined to reject people with depression. Despite the obviously negative consequences of receiving interpersonal rejection from other people, in some cases this appears to fulfill the depressed person's desire for self-verifying information. This interpersonal model of depression is really a theory of depression maintenance, for it does not specify causal antecedents to depression nor does it specify factors associated with improvement in depression. Because depression tends to be a recurrent and sometimes recalcitrant problem, theories of depression maintenance have considerable utility and value. The hallmark of Coyne's interpersonal model is recognition that regardless of the actual cause of a depressive episode, it is likely to be maintained or exacerbated by the contentious interpersonal interactions of the person with depression and those in his or her social network.

FAMILY RELATIONS AND DEPRESSION

Among the numerous relational contexts that are disrupted by depression, family relationships figure quite prominently.

Research on family relationships and depression can be usefully organized around interpersonal processes in the family of origin (i.e., the family in which one grew up) and the family of orientation (i.e., the family constructed by an adult through child rearing, a committed relationship with another adult, etc.).

Family of Origin Experiences and Risk for Depression

There is presently abundant evidence to implicate a number of depressogenic interpersonal experiences in the family of origin in child, adolescent, and adult depression. These processes could essentially be summarized as variations of child maltreatment. On the less "severe" but still highly corrosive end of the continuum, people who are depressed will describe their family of origin as rejecting (Lewinsohn & Rosenbaum, 1987; Stuewig & McCloskey, 2005) and uncaring (Gotlib, Mount, Cordy, & Whiffen, 1988; Rodriguez et al., 1996). A powerful family of origin risk factor for depression is exposure to low parental care coupled with overprotection (Alloy, Abramson, Smith, Gibb, & Neeren, 2006; Parker, 1983). Parker found depressed outpatients to be 3.4 times more likely than matched control subjects to have at least one parent who exhibited low care coupled with high protection, or "affectionless control." Children exposed to affectionless control from their nondepressed parents have as much as a six-fold increase in major depression (Nomura, Wickramaratine, Warner, Mufson, & Weissman, 2002). Lack of affection may impede a child's development of self-worth and overprotective and intrusive parenting behaviors may similarly interfere with the development of self-efficacy. Incidentally, the Nomura et al. study is remarkable for being one of the few prospective longitudinal studies conducted to test the association between parental warmth/affection and subsequent depression (see also Liu, 2003). Such investigations are of particular importance for ruling out the possibility that the association between

affectionless parenting and offspring depression is merely an artifact of a depressive memory bias—something that purely retrospective studies cannot control for.

Several other family processes appear to function as risk factors for concurrent or subsequent depression among offspring. Allen et al. (2006) found an association between depression in adolescents and an interaction pattern with mothers that was characterized by struggles for autonomy and relatedness. Feeling that one's role in the family is devalued has also been linked with subsequent depression (Reinherz, Giaconia, Hauf, Wasserman, & Silverman, 1999). Harsh and punitive parenting practices (e.g., yelling, insulting) elevate the risk for subsequent depression among offspring (Stuewig & McCloskey, 2005). Both negativity (e.g., criticism) and positivity (e.g., acceptance) in the family of origin are significant risk and protective factors, respectively, for the development of offspring depressive symptoms (Park, Garber, Ciesla, & Ellis, 2008).

The family of origin processes described thus far (i.e., affectionless control, harsh parenting, criticism, rejection) are all instantiations of emotional abuse. There has been a great deal of attention to the mediators of these abusive processes that link them with subsequent depression. For example, emotional abuse in the family of origin appears to create a fear of criticism and rejection that mediates and explains the connection between abuse and subsequent major depressive disorder (Maciejewski & Mazure, 2006). Harsh parenting practices can also create shame-proneness in children that in turn leads to depression (Stuewig & McClosky, 2005).

One of the most developed theoretical models of family of origin abuse and depression focuses on the learning of a negative inferential style (Alloy et al., 2006; Rose & Abramson, 1992). Rose and Abramson hypothesized that emotional abuse is particularly pernicious in that it often imparts to the child depressogenic attributions that through repeated exposure become traitlike, representing a cognitive vulnerability to depression. So for example, when a parent tells a child "You are worthless," "This is all your fault," or "You will never amount to anything," the child has a ready-made depressogenic attribution in which the self is blamed for failure in global, stable, and internal terms. In this model, it is assumed that such emotional abuse represents a greater risk for subsequent depression than physical or sexual abuse. This is because in the case of emotional abuse the parent directly supplies, through his or her communication with the child, a negative inference for the child to internalize and generalize. In the case of physical and sexual abuse, the child must generate the inference on his or her own, in which case the negative inferential style is less likely to develop. The polar opposite of emotional abuse, a type of social support known as "adaptive inferential feedback" (i.e., trying to help people feel better in the presence of negative events by stressing their specificity and irrelevance to self-worth) markedly decreases the risk for depression (Panzarella, Alloy, & Whitehouse, 2006). One key mechanism of repeated emotional abuse and the failure to provide adaptive inferential feedback to children is that it tends to create a cognitive vulnerability to later depression (Mezulis, Hyde, & Abramson, 2006).

Physical abuse of children is widely recognized as a significant risk factor for the development of depression (Al-Modallal, Peden, & Anderson, 2008; Wise, Zierier, Krieger, & Harlow, 2001). There is evidence to suggest that recall of specific physically abusive experiences is more strongly associated with depression than global beliefs that one was physically abused as a child (Gibb, Alloy, & Abramson, 2003). Springer, Sheridan, Kuo, and Carnes (2007) examined data from the Wisconsin Longitudinal Study (with an n in excess of 2000) in which participants were asked whether their mothers or fathers ever "slapped, shoved, or threw things" at them. Approximately 11% of the respondents were exposed to this form of abuse and it was associated with a 24% increase in depression as assessed by the CES-D. This investigation is particularly noteworthy in that the authors extensively controlled for sex, age, a variety of childhood adversities (e.g., parental problem drinking, parental marital problems), and family background (e.g., parents' education, parental income) variables, and still found that child physical abuse was significantly associated with depression (19% increase) nearly 40 years after the abuse occurred. One must interpret these as conservative estimates of the impact of child physical abuse on depression given the relatively mild nature of the abuse operationalization.

Child sexual abuse while living in the family of origin is a significant risk factor for subsequent depression (Alloy et al., 2006; Carey, Walker, Rossouw, Seedat, & Stein, 2008). It is estimated that sexually abused children have a 2.0 to 2.5 times greater risk of depression compared to children who were not abused (Andrews, 1995; Fergusson, Boden, & Horwood, 2008). In one large sample study of Hungarian women ages 15 to 24, sexual abuse had an odds ratio of 6.44 in predicting severe depressive symptoms (Csoboth, Birkas, & Purebi, 2005). Several meta-analyses of this literature indicate moderate- or medium-sized effects for exposure to this form of abuse and subsequent depression (Neumann, Houskamp, Pollock, & Briere, 1996; Paolucci, Genuis, & Violato, 2001; but see Rind, Tromovitch, & Bauserman, 1998). Naturally, child sexual abuse almost never occurs in a family context that is free from other dysfunctional interpersonal processes such as conflict, low cohesion, chaos, and physical abuse (Meyerson, Long, Miranda, & Marx, 2002). When such family factors are statistically controlled, the association between child physical abuse and depression becomes statistically nonsignificant, but the association between child sexual abuse and depression remains significant (Fergusson et al., 2008). There are numerous mechanisms by which child sexual abuse imparts an elevated risk for subsequent depression and these include, but are not limited to, anxiety and fear of future abuse from a family member, shame, self-blame, interpersonal difficulties, avoidant coping strategies, and dysregulation of the hypothalamic-pituitary-adrenal axis, altering responses to stress (Csoboth et al.; Weiss, Longhurst, & Mazure, 1999; Whiffen & MacIntosh, 2005). Finkelhor and Browne (1985) argued that child sexual abuse creates a stigma in survivors that engenders a view of the self as "damaged goods." This stigma, and associated shame, in turn, lead to a variety of negative outcomes, including depression.

Family of Orientation Experiences and Depression

People with depression often encounter interpersonal difficulties in their family of orientation. Two major relational dynamics that have been studied in this context are relational difficulties (a) with the depressed person's spouse and (b) with his or her child. These problems in the family of orientation are commonly understood as expressions of the negative interpersonal responses to depression by spouses and children, and are indeed quite consistent with the interactional model of depression (Coyne, 1976a).

There is a remarkably reliable association between depression and marital distress (see Beach, 2001; Beach, Sandeen, & O'Leary, 1990, for reviews). Repeatedly, this research has shown that depression and marital distress go hand in hand (Beach & O'Leary, 1993; Beach et al., 1990). A review of 26 studies with community-based samples revealed an average correlation between depression and marital quality of $r = -.37$ for men and $r = -.42$ for women (Whisman, 2001). Among 10 studies of patients with clinical depression, the depression-marital quality association was $r = -.66$ (Whisman, 2001). The marriages of people with depression are marked by destructive conflict management tactics, fewer expressions of affection more complaints about the marriage, and regrets about getting married (Coyne, Thompson, & Palmer, 2002). Spouses who live with

a depressed person experience significant burden, and often experience clinical levels of depression themselves (e.g., Benazon & Coyne, 2000; Coyne et al., 1987). Living with a depressed person leads to profound family transformations, as spouses and other family members attempt to cope with and understand the symptoms of the disorder (Badger, 1996a, 1996b).

The marital interactions of depressed people and their spouses are often negative in tone and tend to generate more negative affect in each spouse than those of nondepressed couples (Gotlib & Whiffen, 1989; Ruscher & Gotlib, 1988). This negative affect often takes the form of anger and hostility (Goldman & Haaga, 1995). McCabe and Gotlib (1993) showed that, over the course of a marital interaction, the verbal behavior of depressed wives becomes increasingly negative. For both husbands and wives, a history of depression is associated with less positive reciprocity in marital interaction (Johnson & Jacob, 2000), meaning that depressed spouses are less likely to follow their partner's positive communication with positive messages of their own. Johnson and Jacob further discovered that depressed husbands' positive contributions to conversations actually suppressed their wives' positivity, and increased their wives' negativity. This pattern illustrates how some members of an interpersonal system may contribute to and maintain another's depression.

In addition to negative and contentious interactions, another factor that may link depression with poor marital adjustment is the haste with which young depressed people marry (Gotlib, Lewinsohn, & Seeley, 1998). Gotlib et al. found that depression among adolescents predicts higher rates of marriage at a younger age, diminished marital satisfaction, and increased marital disagreements. It is possible that depression may motivate young people to seek out marriage, perhaps indiscriminately, as a solution to problems. Perhaps because of the obviously truncated mate selection, such marriages are often doomed to failure.

There is reason to suspect that depression and marital distress have a reciprocal relationship. One longitudinal study showed that wives' depression followed a decrease in their marital satisfaction, whereas men's initial levels of depression led to decreases in their marital satisfaction over time (Fincham, Beach, Harold, Osborne, 1997). This suggested that women are more vulnerable than men to symptoms of depression following declines in marital satisfaction. More recently however, dyadic analyses have shown that poor marital adjustment predicts a worsening of depressive symptoms for both men and women (Beach, Katz, Kim, & Brody, 2003; Kurdek, 1998) and that this relationship is indeed bidirectional (Davila, Karney, Hall, & Bradbury, 2003).

In addition to difficulty with marriage, people with depression seem to have problems in their role as parents. Depression has repeatedly been linked to disrupted and dysfunctional parenting behavior (e.g., Lovejoy, Graczyk, O'Hare, & Neuman, 2000). Chiariello and Orvaschel (1995) explained that depression interferes with parenting skills by corrupting parents' capacity to relate to their children. In general, the parenting behavior of people with depression is characterized by similar patterns of negativity, hostility, complaining, and poor interpersonal problem solving as is associated with their other relationships. Depression appears to impede effective parenting through such mechanisms as disengagement from the child and negative maternal behavior (Lovejoy et al., 2000), less effective emotional and motivational scaffolding (Hoffman, Crnic, & Baker, 2006), and rejection and difficulties relating to infant children (Loh & Vostanis, 2004).

In light of the aforementioned parenting difficulties that are concomitant to depression, it is perhaps understandable that the children of depressed parents are at risk for a variety of behavioral and emotional problems. Chief among the problems experienced by children of depressed mothers is depression itself (Warner, Weissman, Fendrich, Wickramaratne, & Moreau, 1992)

and related internalizing problems (Shelton & Harold, 2008). Children of depressed mothers also tend to exhibit problems with emotion regulation (Hoffman et al., 2006; Maughan, Cicchetti, Toth, & Rogosch, 2007) which, in turn, is positively associated with peer rejection (Maughan et al.), as well as increased antisocial behavior (Kim-Cohen, Moffitt, Taylor, Pawlby, & Caspi, 2005). Observational research shows that children of depressed mothers exhibit a behavioral pattern indicative of rejection. During interaction with their parents, children of depressed parents express negative affect, are generally tense and irritable, spend less time looking at their parent, and appear less content than children who interact with their nondepressed parents (e.g., Cohn, Campbell, Matias, & Hopkins, 1990; Field, 1984).

Summary

The family of orientation relationships of depressed people perhaps illustrates one important interpersonal context in which poor social skills and negative reactions from others are evident. Spouses with depression, and parents with depression, often behave in ways that that are suggestive of interpersonal skills deficits. Naturally, these family relationships are often strained. As predicted by Coyne's interpersonal model of depression, the spouses and children of depressed people often react to them with signs of irritation, conflict, sadness, and rejection. The family of origin relationships of people with depression provides tremendous insights into the developmental antecedents of depression. People with depression often have a history of emotional, physical, or sexual abuse while growing up in their family of origin. Although these types of abuse are diverse in their form (e.g., harsh criticism, affectionless control, physical violence), they all convey a message of devaluation. These destructive family processes appear to create a template of depressogenic cognitions (e.g., negative view of self,

self-blame), emotions (e.g., shame, poor emotion regulation), and social behaviors (e.g., difficulty relating to others, distrust of others) that impart a substantial risk for both concurrent and subsequent depression.

CONCLUSION

As inherently social animals, human beings have a powerful drive to seek out and relate to other human beings. These social relationships play an enormous role in regulating human emotions and people's sense of well-being. When something goes wrong with these relationships or the processes that initiate and maintain them, symptoms of depression often follow. It is also the case that when people become depressed, disruption of interpersonal processes and relationships soon become evident.

This analysis has highlighted two potential interpersonal processes that can increase the risk of depression. First, some people never develop adequate and effective social skills. This creates an extreme handicap when it comes to seeking, generating, and preserving a wide variety of interpersonal relationships. The sort of interpersonal trouble that follows people with poor social skills is stressful, upsetting, and unflattering. For at least some people in this situation, depression is a likely consequent. Second, dysfunctional and abusive experiences in the family of origin appear to create a negative social-cognitive template that perseveres well into adulthood. This template includes negative views of the self, distrust of others, self-blame, and feeling unworthy of positive regard from others. This too often culminates in concurrent and/or later experiences with depression.

This review also showed how interpersonal processes can maintain depression. Many people with depression behave in ways that other people find irritating, or quite frankly, depressing. Indeed, other people will sometimes "catch" the negative emotional state conveyed by the person with depression. Accordingly, they will subsequently reject and avoid the person with depression, only serving to maintain that depressive state.

Finally, it is apparent that regardless of its causal origins, depression is highly disruptive to interpersonal behavior and relationships. When in a state of depression, it is difficult to behave in ways that ordinarily garner the approval and support of other people. The withdrawn, pessimistic, and sometimes hostile behavior that often accompanies depression does not serve interpersonal relationships very well. This is one reason why many depressed people also experience trouble in their relationships with their spouses, children, romantic partners, and friends.

There have been significant advances in the understanding of interpersonal processes in the development, course, and treatment of depression. However, numerous questions remain unanswered and in need of further research. For example, social skills deficits are evident among at least some people with depression, but it is not always clear if these are deficits in ability or performance, or both. Low motivation can cause people who possess adequate abilities to turn in poor performances, and depression is notorious for its association with low motivation. Also, research on family of origin experiences and subsequent depression has relied heavily on retrospective self-reports. It would be useful to have more prospective studies that make assessments of family environments and experiences to more precisely evaluate their role in precipitating subsequent depressive episodes. On a related point, much of the research on interpersonal processes and depression has focused understandably on interpersonal factors that predispose people to develop or at least maintain an episode of depression. However, much less research attention has been focused on interpersonal resilience. Some people with poor social skills or dysfunctional family backgrounds never develop depression. There may be additional interpersonal processes such as social support and intimacy, for example, that could impart resilience to, or protection from, depression. Further research on these interpersonal phenomena could potentially explain why some people experience known risk factors for depression but never become depressed.

Both scientific discovery and intellectual fashion have contributed extensively to the advancement of theories and paradigms that have been cataloged in the service of understanding and treating depression. These forces have highlighted the important role played by biological, cognitive, and environmental (e.g., life events and stress) factors in depression, to name but a few. It is now obvious that interpersonal processes play a role in depression that is equally monumental to those other, sometimes better publicized, factors. Accordingly, a comprehensive understanding of depressive disorders requires careful attention to the myriad interpersonal processes that are virtually inseparable from this condition.

References

Al-Modallal, H., Peden, A., & Anderson, D. (2008). Impact of physical abuse on adulthood depressive symptoms among women. *Issues in Mental Health Nursing, 29*, 299–314.

Alison, J., & Burgess, C. (2003). Effects of chronic nonclinical depression on the use of positive and negative words in language contexts. *Brain and Cognition, 53*, 125–128.

Allen, J. P., Insabella, G., Porter, M. R., Smith, F. D., Land, D., & Phillips, N. (2006). A social-interactional model of the development of depressive symptoms in adolescence. *Journal of Consulting and Clinical Psychology, 74*, 55–65.

Alloy, L. B., & Abramson, L. Y. (1979). Judgments of contingency in depressed and nondepressed students: Sadder but wiser? *Journal of Experimental Psychology: General, 108*, 441–485.

Alloy, L. B., Abramson, L. Y., Smith, J. M., Gibb, B. E., & Neeren, A. M. (2006). Role of parenting and maltreatment histories in unipolar and bipolar mood disorders: Mediation by cognitive vulnerability to depression. *Clinical Child and Family Psychology Review, 9*, 23–64.

Alpert, M., Pouget, E. R., & Silva, R. R. (2001). Reflections of depression in acoustic measures of the patient's speech. *Journal of Affective Disorders, 66*, 59–69.

American Psychiatric Association. (1994). *Diagnostic and statistical manual of mental disorders: DSM-IV-TR*. Washington, DC: Author.

Amstutz, D. K., & Kaplan, M. F. (1987). Depression, physical attractiveness, and interpersonal acceptance. *Journal of Social and Clinical Psychology, 5*, 365–377.

Andrews, B. (1995). Bodily shame as a mediator between abusive experiences and depression. *Journal of Abnormal Psychology, 104*, 277–285.

Badger, T. A. (1996a). Family members' experiences living with members with depression. *Western Journal of Nursing Research, 18*, 149–171.

Badger, T. A. (1996b). Living with depression: Family members' experiences and treatment needs. *Journal of Psychosocial Nursing, 34*, 21–29.

Beach, S. R. H. (Ed.). (2001). *Marital and family processes in depression: A scientific foundation for clinical practice*. Washington, DC: American Psychological Association.

Beach, S. R. H., Katz, J., Kim, S., & Brody, G. H. (2003). Prospective effects of marital satisfaction on depressive symptoms in established marriages: A dyadic model. *Journal of Social and Personal Relationships, 20*, 355–371.

Beach, S. R. H., & O'Leary, K. D. (1993). Marital discord and dysphoria: For whom does the marital relationship predict depressive symptomatology? *Journal of Social and Personal Relationships, 10*, 405–420.

Beach, S. R. H., Sandeen, E. E., & O'Leary, K. D. (1990). *Depression and marriage*. New York: Guilford Press.

Belsher, G., & Costello, C. G. (1991). Do confidants of depressed women provide less social support than confidants of nondepressed women? *Journal of Abnormal Psychology, 100*, 516–525.

Benazon, N. R. (2000). Predicting negative spousal attitudes toward depressed persons: A test of Coyne's interpersonal model. *Journal of Abnormal Psychology, 109*, 550–554.

Benazon, N. R., & Coyne, J. C. (1999). The next step in developing an interactional description of depression? *Psychological Inquiry, 10*, 279–304.

Benazon, N. R., & Coyne, J. C. (2000). Living with a depressed spouse. *Journal of Family Psychology, 14*, 71–79.

Berenbaum, H. (1992). Posed facial expression of emotion in schizophrenia and depression. *Psychological Medicine, 22*, 929–937.

Bieling, P. J., & Alden, L. E. (2001). Sociotropy, autonomy, and the interpersonal model of depression: An integration. *Cognitive Therapy and Research, 25,* 167–184.

Bull, P. E. (1987). *Posture and gesture.* Oxford: Pergamon Press.

Burns, A. B., Brown, J. S., Plant, E. A., Sachs-Ericsson, N., & Joiner, T. E. (2006). On the specific depressotypic nature of excessive reassurance-seeking. *Personality and Individual Differences, 40,* 135–145.

Calev, A., Nigal, D., & Chazan, S. (1989). Retrieval from semantic memory using meaningful and meaningless constructs by depressed, stable bipolar and manic patients. *British Journal of Clinical Psychology, 28,* 67–73.

Carey, P. D., Walker, J. L., Rossouw, W., Seedat, S., & Stein, D. J. (2008). Risk indicators and psychopathology in traumatised children and adolescents with a history of sexual abuse. *European Child and Adolescent Psychiatry, 17,* 93–98.

Carragher, N., Adamson, G., Bunting, B., & McCann, S. (2009). Subtypes of depression in a nationally representative sample. *Journal of Affective Disorders, 113,* 88–99.

Carton, J. S., Kessler, E. A., & Pape, C. L. (1999). Nonverbal decoding skills and relationship well-being in adults. *Journal of Nonverbal Behavior, 23,* 91–100.

Casbon, T. S., Burns, A. B., Bradbury, T. N., & Joiner, T. E. (2005). Receipt of negative feedback is related to increased negative feedback seeking among individuals with depressive symptoms. *Behaviour Research and Therapy, 43,* 485–504.

Chau, P. M., & Milling, L. S. (2006). Impact of dysphoria and self-consciousness on perceptions of social competence: Test of the depressive realism hypothesis. *Clinical Psychologist, 10,* 99–108.

Chiariello, M. A., & Orvaschel, H. (1995). Patterns of parent-child communication: Relationship to depression. *Clinical Psychology Review, 15,* 395–407.

Cohn, J. F., Campbell, S. B., Matias, R., & Hopkins, J. (1990). Face-to-face interactions of postpartum depressed and nondepressed mother-infant pairs at 2 months. *Developmental Psychology, 26,* 15–23.

Cole, D. A., & Milstead, M. (1989). Behavioral correlates of depression: Antecedents or consequences? *Journal of Counseling Psychology, 36,* 408–416.

Coyne, J. C. (1976a). Toward an interactional description of depression. *Psychiatry, 39,* 28–40.

Coyne, J. C. (1976b). Depression and the response of others. *Journal of Abnormal Psychology, 85,* 186–193.

Coyne, J. C., Burchill, S. A. L., & Stiles, W. B. (1990). An interactional perspective on depression. In C. R. Snyder & D. R. Forsyth (Eds.), *Handbook of social and clinical psychology* (pp. 327–349). New York: Pergamon Press.

Coyne, J. C., Kessler, R. C., Tal, M., Turnbull, J., Wortman, C. B., & Greden, J. F. (1987). Living with a depressed person. *Journal of Consulting and Clinical Psychology, 55,* 347–352.

Coyne, J. C., Thompson, R., & Palmer, S. C. (2002). Marital quality, coping with conflict, marital complaints, and affection in couples with a depressed wife. *Journal of Family Psychology, 16,* 26–37.

Csoboth, C. T., Birkas, E., & Purebl, G. (2005). Living in fear of experiencing physical and sexual abuse is associated with severe depressive symptomatology among young women. *Journal of Women's Health, 14,* 441–448.

Cummins, R. (1990). Social insecurity, anxiety, and stressful events as antecedents of depressive symptoms. *Behavioral Medicine, 13,* 161–164.

Dalley, M. B., Bolocofsky, D. N., & Karlin, N. J. (1994). Teacher-ratings and self-ratings of social competency in adolescents with low- and high-depressive symptoms. *Journal of Abnormal Child Psychology, 22,* 477–485.

Darby, J. K., Simmons, N., & Berger, P. A. (1984). Speech and voice parameters of depression: A pilot study. *Journal of Communication Disorders, 17,* 75–85.

Davila, J. (2001). Paths to unhappiness: The overlapping courses of depression and romantic dysfunction. In S. R. H. Beach (Ed.), *Marital and family processes in depression: A scientific foundation for clinical practice* (pp. 71–87). Washington, DC: American Psychological Association.

Davila, J., Karney, B. R., Hall, T. W., & Bradbury, T. N. (2003). Depressive symptoms and marital satisfaction: Within-subject associations and the moderating effects of gender and neuroticism. *Journal of Family Psychology, 17,* 557–570.

Ducharme, J., & Bachelor, A. (1993). Perception of social functioning in dysphoria. *Cognitive Therapy and Research, 17,* 53–70.

Edison, J. D., & Adams, H. E. (1992). Depression, self-focus, and social interaction. *Journal of Psychopathology and Behavioral Assessment, 14,* 1–19.

Ekman, P., & Friesen, W. V. (1972). Hand movements. *Journal of Communication, 22,* 353–374.

Ekman, P., & Friesen, W. V. (1974). Nonverbal behavior and psychopathology. In R. J. Friedman & M. M. Mintz (Eds.), *The psychology of depression* (pp. 203–224). Washington, DC: V. H. Winston.

Ellgring, H. (1986). Nonverbal expression of psychological states in psychiatric patients. *European Archives of Psychiatric and Neurological Sciences, 236,* 31–34.

Ellgring, H., & Scherer, K. R. (1996). Vocal indicators of mood change in depression. *Journal of Nonverbal Behavior, 20,* 83–110.

Elliot, T. R., MacNair, R. R., Herrick, S. M., Yoder, B., & Byrne, C. A. (1991). Interpersonal reactions to depression and physical disability in dyadic interactions. *Journal of Applied Social Psychology, 21,* 1293–1302.

Exline, R. V., Ellyson, S. L., & Long, B. (1975). Visual behavior as an aspect of power role relationships. In P. Pliner, L. Krames, & T. Alloway (Eds.), *Nonverbal communication of aggression* (Vol. 2, pp. 21–52). New York: Plenum Press.

Fergusson, D. M., Boden, J. M., & Horwood, L. J. (2008). Exposure to childhood sexual and physical abuse and adjustment in early adulthood. *Child Abuse & Neglect, 32,* 607–619.

Field, T. (1984). Early interactions between infants and their post-partum depressed mothers. *Infant Behavior and Development, 7,* 517–522.

Fincham, F. D., Beach, S. R. H., Harold, G. T., & Osborne, L. N. (1997). Marital satisfaction and depression: Different causal relationships for men and women? *Psychological Science, 8,* 351–357.

Finkelhor, D., & Browne, A. (1985). The traumatic impact of child sexual abuse: A conceptualization. *American Journal of Orthopsychiatry, 55,* 530–541.

Fossi, L., Faravelli, C., & Paoli, M. (1984). The ethological approach to the assessment of depressive disorders. *Journal of Nervous and Mental Disease, 172,* 332–341.

Gaebel, W., & Wolwer, W. (2004). Facial expressivity in the course of schizophrenia and depression. *European Archives of Psychiatry and Clinical Neuroscience, 254,* 335–342.

Garland, M., & Fitzgerald, M. (1998). Social skills correlates of depressed mood in normal young adolescents. *Irish Journal of Psychological Medicine, 15,* 19–21.

Giesler, R. B., & Swann, W. B. (1999). Striving for confirmation: The role of self-verification in depression. In T. Joiner & J. C. Coyne (Eds.), *The interactional nature of depression* (pp. 189–217). Washington, DC: American Psychological Association.

Gibb, B. E., Ally, L. B., & Abramson, L. Y. (2003). Global reports of child maltreatment versus recall of specific maltreatment experiences: Relationship with dysfunctional attitudes and depressive symptoms. *Cognition and Emotion, 17,* 903–915.

Goldman, L., & Haaga, D. A. F. (1995). Depression and the experience and expression of anger in marital and other relationships. *Journal of Nervous and Mental Disease, 183,* 505–509.

Gotlib, I. H. (1982). Self-reinforcement and depression in interpersonal interaction: The role of performance level. *Journal of Abnormal Psychology, 91,* 3–13.

Gotlib, I. H., Lewinsohn, P. M., & Seeley, J. R. (1998). Consequences of depression during adolescence: Marital status and marital functioning in early adulthood. *Journal of Abnormal Psychology, 107,* 686–690.

Gotlib, I. H., & Meltzer, S. J. (1987). Depression and the perception of social skills in dyadic interaction. *Cognitive Therapy and Research, 11,* 41–54.

Gotlib, I. H., Mount, J. H., Cordy, N. I., & Whiffen, V. E. (1988). Depression and perceptions of early parenting: A longitudinal investigation. *British Journal of Psychiatry, 152,* 24–27.

Gotlib, I. H., & Robinson, L. A. (1982). Responses to depressed individuals: Discrepancies between self-report and observer-rated behavior. *Journal of Abnormal Psychology, 91,* 231–240.

Gotlib, I. H., & Whiffen, V. E. (1989). Depression and marital functioning: An examination of specificity and gender differences. *Journal of Abnormal Psychology, 98,* 23–30.

Gurtman, M. B. (1987). Depressive affect and disclosures as factors in interpersonal rejection. *Cognitive Therapy and Research, 11,* 87–100.

Haeffle, G. J., Voelz, Z. R., & Joiner, T. E. (2007). Vulnerability to depressive symptoms: Clarifying the role of excessive reassurance seeking and perceived social support in an interpersonal model of depression. *Cognition and Emotion, 21,* 681–688.

Hale, W. W., Jansen, J. H. C., Bouhuys, A. L., Jenner, J. A., & van den Hoofdakker, R. H. (1997). Nonverbal behavioral interactions of depressed patients with partners and strangers: The role of behavioral social support and involvement in depression persistence. *Journal of Affective Disorders, 44,* 111–122.

Hammen, C. L., & Peters, S. D. (1977). Differential responses to male and female depressive reactions. *Journal of Consulting and Clinical Psychology, 45,* 994–1001.

Hautzinger, M., Linden, M., & Hoffman, N. (1982). Distressed couples with and without a depressed partner: An analysis of their verbal interaction. *Journal of Behavior Therapy and Experimental Psychiatry, 13,* 307–314.

Herrera, E., Reissland, N., & Shepherd, J. (2004). Maternal touch and maternal child-directed speech: Effects of depressed mood in the postnatal period. *Journal of Affective Disorders, 81,* 29–39.

Hoffman, C., Crnic, K. A., & Baker, J. K. (2006). Maternal depression and parenting: Implications for children's emergent emotion regulation and behavioral functioning. *Parenting: Science and Practice, 6,* 271–295.

Hokanson, J. E., & Butler, A. C. (1992). Cluster analysis of depressed college students' social behaviors. *Journal of Personality and Social Psychology, 62,* 273–280.

Hokanson, J. E., Rubert, M. P., Welker, R. A., Hollander, G. R., & Hedeen, C. (1989). Interpersonal concomitants and antecedents of depression among college students. *Journal of Abnormal Psychology, 98,* 209–217.

Horowitz, L. M., & Turan, B. (2008). Prototypes and personal templates: Collective wisdom and individual differences. *Psychological Review, 115,* 1054–1068.

Horowitz, L. M., Wilson, K. R., Turan, B., Zolotsev, P., Constantino, M. J., & Henderson, L. (2006). How interpersonal motives clarify the meaning of interpersonal behavior: A revised circumplex model. *Personality and Social Psychology Review, 10,* 67–86.

Huprich, S. K., Clancy, C., Bornstein, R. F., & Nelson-Gray, R. O. (2004). Do dependency and social skills combine to predict depression? Linking two diatheses in mood disorders research. *Individual Differences Research, 2,* 2–16.

Jacobson, N. S., & Anderson, E. A. (1982). Interpersonal skill and depression in college students: An analysis of the timing of self-disclosures. *Behavior Therapy, 13,* 271–282.

Johnson, S. L., & Jacob, T. (2000). Sequential interactions in the marital communication of depressed men and women. *Journal of Consulting and Clinical Psychology, 68,* 4–12.

Joiner, T. E. (1994). Contagious depression: Existence, specificity to depressive symptoms, and the role of reassurance seeking. *Journal of Personality and Social Psychology, 67,* 287–296.

Joiner, T. E. (1995). The price of soliciting and receiving negative feedback: Self-verification theory as a vulnerability to depression theory. *Journal of Abnormal Psychology, 104,* 364–372.

Joiner, T. E. (1996). Depression and rejection: On strangers and friends, symptom specificity, length of relationship, and gender. *Communication Research, 23,* 451–471.

Joiner, T.E. (1999). A test of interpersonal theory of depression in youth psychiatric inpatients. *Journal of Abnormal Child Psychology, 27,* 77–85.

Joiner, T. E. (2002). Depression in its interpersonal context. In I. H. Gotlib & C. L. Hammen (Eds.), *Handbook of depression* (pp. 295–313). New York: Guilford Press.

Joiner, T. E., Alfano, M. S., & Metalsky, G. I. (1992). When depression breeds contempt: Reassurance-seeking, self-esteem, and rejection of depressed college students by their roommates. *Journal of Abnormal Psychology, 101,* 165–173.

Joiner, T. E., & Katz, J. (1999). Contagion of depressive symptoms and mood: Meta-analytic review and explanations from cognitive, behavioral, and interpersonal viewpoints. *Clinical Psychology: Science and Practice, 6,* 149–164.

Joiner, T. E., Katz, J., & Lew, A. S. (1997). Self-verification and depression among youth psychiatric inpatients. *Journal of Abnormal Psychology, 106,* 608–618.

Joiner, T.E., Katz, J., & Lew, A. (1999). Harbingers of depressotypic reassurance seeking: Negative life events, increased anxiety, and decreased self-esteem. *Personality and Social Psychology Bulletin, 25,* 630–637.

Joiner, T. E., & Metalsky, G. I. (2001). Excessive reassurance seeking: Delineating a risk factor involved in the development of depressive symptoms. *Psychological Science, 12,* 371–378.

Joiner, T. E., Metalsky, G. I., Katz, J., & Beach, S. R. H. (1999). Depression and excessive reassurance-seeking. *Psychological Inquiry, 10,* 269–278.

Joormann, J., & Gotlib, I. H. (2006). Is this happiness I see? Biases in the identification of emotional facial expressions in depression and social phobia. *Journal of Abnormal Psychology, 115,* 705–714.

Kahn, J., Coyne, J. C., & Margolin, G. (1985). Depression and marital disagreement: The social construction of despair. *Journal of Social and Personal Relationships, 2,* 447–461.

Kazdin, A. E., Sherick, R. B., Esveldt-Dawson, K., & Rancurello, M. D. (1985). Nonverbal behavior and childhood depression. *Journal of the American Academy of Child Psychiatry, 24,* 303–309.

Kessler, R. C., McGonagle, K. A., Shanyang, Z., Nelson, C., Hughes, M., Eshleman, S., & Kendler, K. S. (1994). Lifetime and 12-month prevalence of DSM-III-R psychiatric disorders in the United States. *Archives of General Psychiatry, 51,* 8–19.

Kim-Cohen, J., Moffitt, T. E., Taylor, A., Pawlby, S. J., & Caspi, A. (2005). Maternal depression and children's antisocial behavior: Nature and nurture effects. *Archives of General Psychiatry, 62,* 173–181.

Kurdek, L. A. (1998). The nature and predictors of the trajectory of change in marital quality over the first 4 years of marriage for first-married husbands and wives. *Journal of Family Psychology, 12,* 494–510.

Levin, S., Hall, J. A., Knight, R. A., & Alpert, M. (1985). Verbal and nonverbal expression of affect in speech of schizophrenic and depressed patients. *Journal of Abnormal Psychology, 94,* 487–497.

Lewinsohn, P. M. (1974). A behavioral approach to depression. In R. J. Friedman & M. M. Katz (Eds.), *The psychology of depression: Contemporary theory and research* (pp. 157–185). Washington, DC: Winston-Wiley.

Lewinsohn, P. M. (1975). The behavioral study and treatment of depression. In M. Hersen, R. M.

Eisler, & P. M. Miller (Eds.), *Progress in behavior modification* (Vol. 1, pp. 19–64). New York: Academic Press.

Lewinsohn, P. M., Hoberman, H., Teri, L., & Hautzinger, M. (1985). An integrative theory of depression. In S. Reiss & R. R. Bootzin (Eds.), *Theoretical issues in behavior therapy* (pp. 331–359). New York: Academic Press.

Lewinsohn, P. M., Hoberman, H. M., & Rosenbaum, M. (1988). A prospective study of risk factors for unipolar depression. *Journal of Abnormal Psychology, 97,* 251–264.

Lewinsohn, P. M., Mischel, W., Chaplin, W., & Barton, R. (1980). Social competence and depression: The role of illusory self-perceptions. *Journal of Abnormal Psychology, 89,* 203–212.

Lewinsohn, P. M., Roberts, R. E., Seeley, J. R., Rohde, P., Gotlib, I. H., & Hops, H. (1994). Adolescent psychopathology: II. Psychosocial risk factors for depression. *Journal of Abnormal Psychology, 103,* 302–315.

Lewinsohn, P. M., & Rosenbaum, M. (1987). Recall of parental behavior by acute depressives, remitted depressives, and nondepressives. *Journal of Personality and Social Psychology, 52,* 611–619.

Lewinsohn, P. M., Steinmetz, J. L., Larson, D. W., & Franklin, J. (1981). Depression-related cognitions: Antecedent or consequent? *Journal of Abnormal Psychology, 90,* 213–219.

Libet, J. M., & Lewinsohn, P. M. (1973). Concept of social skill with special reference to the behavior of depressed persons. *Journal of Consulting and Clinical Psychology, 40,* 304–312.

Liu, Y. (2003). The mediators between parenting and adolescent depressive symptoms: Dysfunctional attitudes and self-worth. *International Journal of Psychology, 38,* 91–100.

Loh, C. C., & Vostanis, P. (2004). Perceived mother-infant relationship difficulties in postnatal depression. *Infant and Child Development, 13,* 159–171.

Lovejoy, M. C., Graczyk, P. A., O'Hare, E., & Neuman, G. (2000). Maternal depression and parenting behavior: A meta-analytic review. *Clinical Psychology Review, 20,* 561–592.

Maciejewski, P. K., & Mazure, C. M. (2006). Fear of criticism and rejection mediates an association between childhood emotional abuse and adult onset of major depression. *Cognitive Therapy and Research, 30,* 105–122.

Maughan, A., Cicchetti, D., & Toth, S. L. (2007). Early-occurring maternal depression and maternal negativity in predicting young children's emotional regulation and socio-emotional difficulties. *Journal of Abnormal Child Psychology, 35*, 685–703.

McCabe, S. B., & Gotlib, I. H. (1993). Interactions of couples with and without a depressed spouse: Self-report and observations of problems-solving interactions. *Journal of Social and Personal Relationships, 10*, 589–599.

McFall, R. M. (1982). A review and reformulation of the concept of social skills. *Behavioral Assessment, 4*, 1–33.

McNiel, D. E., Arkowitz, H. S., & Pritchard, B. E. (1987). The response of others to face-to-face interaction with depressed patients. *Journal of Abnormal Psychology, 96*, 341–344.

Meyer, E. B., & Hokanson, J. E. (1985). Situational influences on social behaviors of depression-prone individuals. *Journal of Clinical Psychology, 41*, 29–35.

Meyerson, L. A.,. Long, P., Miranda, R., & Marx, B. P. (2002). The influence of childhood sexual abuse, physical abuse, family environment, and gender on the psychological adjustment of adolescents. *Child Abuse & Neglect, 26*, 387–405.

Mezulis, A. H., Hyde, J. S., & Abramson, L. Y. (2006). The developmental origins of cognitive vulnerability to depression: Temperament, parenting, and negative life events in childhood as contributors to negative cognitive style. *Developmental Psychology, 42*, 1012–1025.

Mundt, J. C., Snyder, P. J., Cannizzaro, M. S., Chappie, K., & Geralts, D. S. (2007). Voice acoustic measures of depression severity and treatment response collected via interactive voice response (IVR) technology. *Journal of Neurolinguistics, 20*, 50–64.

Neumann, D. A., Houskamp, B. M., Pollock, V. E., & Briere, J. (1996). The long-term sequelae of childhood sexual abuse in women: A meta-analytic review. *Child Maltreatment, 1*, 5–16.

Nolan, S. A., Flynn, C., & Garber, J. (2003). Prospective relations between rejection and depression in young adolescents. *Journal of Personality and Social Psychology, 85*, 745–755.

Nomura, Y., Wickramaratine, P. J., Warner, V. M., Mufson, L., & Weissman, M. M. (2002). Family discord, parental depression, and psychopathology in offspring: Ten-year follow-up. *Journal of the American Academy of Child and Adolescent Psychiatry, 41*, 402–409.

Notarius, C. I., & Herrick, L. R. (1988). Listener response strategies to a distressed other. *Journal of Social and Personal Relationships, 5*, 97–108.

Oliveau, D., & Willmuth, R. (1979). Facial muscle electromyography in depressed and non-depressed hospitalized subjects: A partial replication. *American Journal of Psychiatry, 136*, 548–550.

Panzarella, C., Alloy, L. B., & Whitehouse, W. G. (2006). Expanded hopelessness theory of depression: On the mechanism by which social support protects against depression. *Cognitive Therapy and Research, 30*, 307–333.

Paolucci, E. O., Genuis, M. L., & Violato, C. (2001). A meta-analysis of the published research on the effects of child sexual abuse. *The Journal of Psychology, 135*, 17–36.

Park, I. J. K., Garber, J., Ciesla, J. A., & Ellis, B. J. (2008). Convergence among multiple methods of measuring positivity and negativity in the family environment: Relation to depression in mothers and their children. *Journal of Family Psychology, 22*, 123–134.

Parker, G. (1983). Parental "affectionless control" as an antecedent to adult depression. *Archives of General Psychiatry, 40*, 956–960.

Perez, J. E., & Riggio, R. E. (2003). Nonverbal social skills and psychopathology. In P. Philippot, R. S. Feldman, & E. J. Coats (Eds.), *Nonverbal behavior in clinical settings* (pp. 17–44). New York: Oxford University Press.

Petty, S. C., Sachs-Ericson, N., & Joiner, T. E. (2004). Interpersonal functioning deficits: Temporary or stable characteristics of depressed individuals? *Journal of Affective Disorders, 81*, 115–122.

Prkachin, K. M., Craig, K. D., Papageorgis, D., & Reith, G. (1977). Nonverbal communication deficits and response to performance feedback in depression. *Journal of Abnormal Psychology, 86*, 224–234.

Raes, F., Hermans, D., & Williams, M. G. (2006). Negative bias in the perception of others' facial emotional expressions in major depression: The role of depressive rumination. *The Journal of Nervous and Mental Disease, 194*, 796–799.

Ranelli, C. J., & Miller, R. E. (1981). Behavioral predictors of amitriptyline response in depression. *American Journal of Psychiatry, 138*, 30–34.

Reed, L. I., Sayette, M. A., & Cohn, J. F. (2007). Impact of depression on response to comedy:

A dynamic facial coding analysis. *Journal of Abnormal Psychology, 116*, 804–809.

Reinherz, H. Z., Giaconia, R. M., Hauf, A. M. C., Wasserman, M. S., & Silverman, A. B. (1999). Major depression in the transition to adulthood: Risks and impairments. *Journal of Abnormal Psychology, 108*, 500–510.

Renneberg, B., Heyn, K., Gebhard, R., & Bachman, S. (2005). Facial expression of emotions in borderline personality disorder and depression. *Journal of Behavior Therapy, 36*, 183–196.

Rind, B., Tromovitch, P., & Bauserman, R. (1998). A meta-analytic examination of assumed properties of child sexual abuse using college students. *Psychological Bulletin, 124*, 22–53.

Rodriguez, V. B., Cafias, F., Bayon, C., Franco, B., Salvador, M., Graell, M., & Santo-Domingo, J. (1996). Interpersonal factors in female depression. *European Journal of Psychiatry, 10*, 16–24.

Rohde, P., Lewinsohn, P. M., & Seeley, J. R. (1990). Are people changed by the experience of having an episode of depression? A further test of the scar hypothesis. *Journal of Abnormal Psychology, 99*, 264–271.

Rose, D. T., & Abramson, L. Y. (1992). Developmental predictors of depressive cognitive styles: Research and theory. In D. Cicchetti & S. Toth (Eds.), *Rochester symposium on developmental psychopathology* (pp. 323–349). Hillsdale, NJ: Erlbaum.

Rude, S. S., Gortner, E. M., & Pennebaker, J. W. (2004). Language use of depressed and depression-vulnerable college students. *Cognition and Emotion, 18*, 1121–1133.

Rudolph, K. D., Hammen, C., & Burge, D. (1994). Interpersonal functioning and depressive symptoms in childhood: Addressing the issues of specificity and comorbidity. *Journal of Abnormal Child Psychology, 22*, 355–371.

Ruscher, S. M., & Gotlib, I. H. (1988). Marital interaction patterns of couples with and without a depressed partner. *Behavior Therapy, 19*, 455–470.

Rutter, D. R., & Stephenson, G. M. (1972). Visual interaction in a group of schizophrenic and depressive patients. *British Journal of Social and Clinical Psychology, 11*, 57–65.

Scherer, K. R. (1987). Vocal assessment of affective disorders. In J. D. Maser (Ed.), *Depression and expressive behavior* (pp. 57–82). Hillsdale, NJ: Erlbaum.

Schwartz, G. E., Fair, P. L., Mandel, M. R., Salt, P., Mieske, M., & Klerman, G. L. (1978). Facial electromyography in the assessment of improvement in depression. *Psychosomatic Medicine, 40*, 355–360.

Schwartz, G. E., Fair, P. L. Salt, P., Mandel, M. R., & Klerman, G. L. (1976a). Facial muscle patterning to affective imagery in depressed and nondepressed subjects. *Science, 192*, 489–491.

Schwartz, G. E., Fair, P. L., Salt, P., Mandel, M. R., & Klerman, G.L. (1976b). Facial expression and imagery in depression: An electromyographic study. *Psychosomatic Medicine, 38*, 337–347.

Segrin, C. (1990). A meta-analytic review of social skill deficits in depression. *Communication Monographs, 57*, 292–308.

Segrin, C. (1992). Specifying the nature of social skill deficits associated with depression. *Human Communication Research, 19*, 89–123.

Segrin, C. (1993a). Social skills deficits and psychosocial problems: Antecedent, concomitant, or consequent? *Journal of Social and Clinical Psychology, 12*, 336–353.

Segrin, C. (1993b). Interpersonal reactions to depression: The role of relationship with partner and perceptions of rejection. *Journal of Social and Personal Relationships, 10*, 83–97.

Segrin, C. (1996). The relationship between social skills deficits and psychosocial problems: A test of a vulnerability model. *Communication Research, 23*, 425–450.

Segrin, C. (1998). The impact of assessment procedures on the relationship between paper and pencil and behavioral indicators of social skill. *Journal of Nonverbal Behavior, 22*, 229–251.

Segrin, C. (1999). Social skills, stressful life events, and the development of psychosocial problems. *Journal of Social and Clinical Psychology, 18*, 14–34.

Segrin, C. (2000). Social skills deficits associated with depression. *Clinical Psychology Review, 20*, 379–403.

Segrin, C. (2004). Concordance on negative emotion in close relationships: Emotional contagion or assortative mating? *Journal of Social and Clinical Psychology, 23*, 815–835.

Segrin, C. (2006). Understanding scope conditions and evidence for emotional contagion in interpersonal interactions: A reply to Van Orden and Joiner (2005). *Journal of Social and Clinical Psychology, 25*, 833–839.

Segrin, C., & Abramson, L. Y. (1994). Negative reactions to depressive behaviors: A communication theories analysis. *Journal of Abnormal Psychology, 103,* 655–668.

Segrin, C., & Dillard, J. P. (1992). The interactional theory of depression: A meta-analysis of the research literature. *Journal of Social and Clinical Psychology, 11,* 43–70.

Segrin, C., Badger, T. A., Meek, P., Lopez, A. M., Bonham, E., & Sieger, A. (2005). Dyadic interdependence on affect and quality-of-life trajectories among women with breast cancer and their partners. *Journal of Social and Personal Relationships, 22,* 673–689.

Segrin, C., & Dillard, J. P. (1993). The complex link between social skill and dysphoria: Conceptualization, perspective, and outcome. *Communication Research, 20,* 76–104.

Segrin, C., & Fitzpatrick, M. A. (1992). Depression and verbal aggressiveness in different marital couple types. *Communication Studies, 43,* 79–91.

Segrin, C., & Flora, J. (1998). Depression and verbal behavior in conversations with friends and strangers. *Journal of Language and Social Psychology, 17,* 494–505.

Segrin, C., & Flora, J. (2000). Poor social skills are a vulnerability factor in the development of psychosocial problems. *Human Communication Research, 26,* 489–514.

Segrin, C., Hanzal, A., Donnerstein, C., Taylor, M., & Domschke, T. J. (2007). Social skills, psychological well-being, and the mediating role of perceived stress. *Anxiety, Stress, and Coping, 20,* 321–329.

Segrin, C., Powell, H. L., Givertz, M., & Brackin, A. (2003). Symptoms of depression, relational quality, and loneliness in dating relationships. *Personal Relationships, 10,* 25–36.

Shelton, K. H., & Harold, G. T. (2008). Interpersonal conflict, negative parenting, and children's adjustment: Bridging links between parents' depression and children's psychological distress. *Journal of Family Psychology, 22,* 712–724.

Siegman, A. W. (1987). The pacing of speech in depression. In J. D. Maser (Ed.), *Depression and expressive behavior* (pp. 83–102). Hillsdale, NJ: Lawrence Erlbaum Associates.

Springer, K. W., Sheridan, J., Kuo, D., & Carnes, M. (2007). Long-term physical and mental health consequences of childhood physical abuse: Results from a large population-based sample of men and women. *Child Abuse and Neglect, 31,* 517–530.

Starr, L. R., & Davila, J. (2008). Excessive reassurance seeking, depression, and interpersonal rejection: A meta-analytic review. *Journal of Abnormal Psychology, 117,* 762–775.

Stuewig, J., & McCloskey, L. A. (2005). The relation of child maltreatment to shame and guilt among adolescents: Psychological routes to depression and delinquency. *Child Maltreatment, 10,* 324–336.

Sullivan, H. S. (1953). *Conceptions of modern psychiatry.* New York: W. W. Norton.

Swann, W. B. (1990). To be adored or to be known: The interplay of self-enhancement and self-verification. In R. M. Sorrentino & E. T. Higgins (Eds.), *Handbook of motivation and cognition* (Vol. 2, pp. 408–480). New York: Guilford Press.

Talavera, J. A., Saiz-Ruiz, J., & Garcia-Toro, M. (1994). Quantitative measurement of depression through speech analysis. *European Psychiatry, 9,* 185–193.

Tremeau, F., Malaspina, D., Duval, F., Correa, H., Hagar-Budny, M., Coin-Bariou, L., ... Gorman, J. M. (2005). Facial expressiveness in patients with schizophrenia compared to depressed patients and nonpatient comparison subjects. *American Journal of Psychiatry, 162,* 92–101.

Troisi, A., & Moles, A. (1999). Gender differences in depression: An ethological study of nonverbal behavior during interviews. *Journal of Psychiatric Research, 33,* 243–250.

Tse, W. S., & Bond, A. J. (2004). The impact of depression on social skills: A review. *The Journal of Nervous and Mental Disease, 192,* 260–268.

van Beek, Y., & Dubas, J. S. (2008). Decoding basic and nonbasic facial expressions and depressive symptoms in late childhood. *Journal of Nonverbal Behavior, 32,* 53–64.

van Beek, Y., van Dolderen, M. S. M., & Dubas, J. S. D. (2006). Gender-specific development of nonverbal and mild depression in adolescence. *Journal of Child Psychology and Psychiatry, 47,* 1272–1283.

van Orden, K. A., & Joiner, T. E. (2006). A role for the contagion of emotion? A comment on Segrin (2004). *Journal of Social and Clinical Psychology, 25,* 825–832.

Vanger, P. (1987). An assessment of social skill deficiencies in depression. *Comprehensive Psychiatry, 28,* 508–512.

Vanger, P., Summerfield, A. B., Rosen, B. K., & Watson, J. P. (1991). Cultural differences in interpersonal responses to depressives' nonverbal behaviour. *The International Journal of Social Psychiatry, 37,* 151–158.

Vanger, P., Summerfield., A. B., Rosen, B. K., & Watson, J. P. (1992). Effects of communication content on speech behavior of depressives. *Comprehensive Psychiatry, 33,* 39–41.

Warner, V., Weissman, M. M., Fendrich, M., Wickramaratne, P., & Moreau, D. (1992). The course of major depression in the offspring of depressed parents: Incidence, recurrence, and recovery. *Archives of General Psychiatry, 49,* 795–801.

Waxer, P. (1974). Nonverbal cues for depression. *Journal of Abnormal Psychology, 83,* 319–322.

Weinstock, L. M., & Whisman, M. A. (2004). The self-verification model of depression and interpersonal rejection in heterosexual dating relationships. *Journal of Social and Clinical Psychology, 23,* 240–259.

Weiss, E. L., Longhurst, J. G., & Mazure, C. M. (1999). Childhood sexual abuse as a risk factor for depression in women: Psychosocial and neurobiological correlates. *American Journal of Psychiatry, 156,* 816–828.

Whiffen, V. E., & MacIntosh, H. B. (2005). Mediators of the link between childhood sexual abuse and emotional distress. *Trauma, Violence, & Abuse, 6,* 24–39.

Whisman, M. A. (2001). Depression and marital distress: Findings from clinical and community studies. In S. R. H. Beach (Ed.), *Marital and family processes in depression* (pp. 3–24). Washington, DC: American Psychological Association.

Whitton, S. W., Larson, J. J., & Hauser, S. T. (2008). Depressive symptoms and bias in perceived social competence among young adults. *Journal of Clinical Psychology, 64,* 791–805.

Wierzbicki, M. (1984). Social skills deficits and subsequent depressed mood in students. *Personality and Social Psychology Bulletin, 10,* 605–610.

Wierzbicki, M., & McCabe, M. (1988). Social skills and subsequent depressive symptomatology in children. *Journal of Clinical Child Psychology, 3,* 203–208.

Wise, L. A., Zierier, S., Krieger, N., & Harlow, B. L. (2001). Adult onset of major depressive disorder in relation to early life violent victimization: A case-control study. *Lancet, 358,* 881–887.

Youngren, M. A., & Lewinsohn, P. M. (1980). The functional relation between depression and problematic interpersonal behavior. *Journal of Abnormal Psychology, 89,* 333–341.

26 INTERPERSONAL PROCESSES IN THE ANXIETY DISORDERS

Lynn E. Alden

Marci J. Regambal

In this chapter we examine the role of interpersonal processes in the anxiety disorders, a group of clinical conditions marked by persistent and severe physiological arousal and worry. While anxiety is a ubiquitous human experience, in the anxiety *disorders* anxiousness exceeds any objective danger and results in debilitating distress and impairment. Our current classification system, the *Diagnostic and Statistical Manual of Mental Disorders* (DSM-IV-TR), distinguishes a number of anxiety syndromes, including social anxiety disorder, generalized anxiety disorder, panic disorder, obsessive-compulsive disorder, post-traumatic stress disorder, and specific phobia (American Psychiatric Association [APA], 2000).

Anxiety disorders have plagued mankind throughout history. In 400 B.C., Hippocrates described cases of "men who fear that which need not be feared," that match the clinical picture we see in anxious individuals today. One such case involved a man who never went to parties or the theatre for fear he would say something unacceptable and disgrace himself, an early depiction of social phobia. Another experienced terror in open spaces, a common fear in individuals suffering from agoraphobia (Saul, 2004). Indeed, the term *panic* was derived from *Pan,* the Greek man-goat god who inspired sudden, groundless terror in lonely places (Papakostas, Eftychiadis, Papakostas, & Christodoulou, 2003). *Phobia* derives from *Phobos,* the Greek god who embodied fear, particularly in battle, and whose likeness was painted on the shields of Greek warriors (Berrios, Link, & Clark, 1995). Descriptions of panic and anxiety weave through writings over the centuries, reflecting the zeitgeist of each era, to arrive at our psychological conceptualizations today.

Contemporary theories of anxiety disorders emphasize biological and cognitive processes. The biological literature clearly shows that genetic vulnerabilities and innate temperament, for example, behavioral inhibition and negative affectivity, increase the risk of developing an anxiety disorder (e.g., Brown, 2007; Fox, Henderson, Marshall, Nichols, & Ghera, 2005; Hettema, Prescott, Myers, Neale, & Kendler, 2005; Kagan, Reznick, Snidman, Gibbons, & Johnson, 1988). Cognitive theorists emphasize the way in which selective processing of threat information biases the individual's interpretation of events and maintains fear-provoking thoughts (e.g., Beck, Emery, & Greenberger, 1985). While biological and cognitive factors help to create and maintain anxiety, they do not provide the complete picture. The biological literature reveals that people inherit a predisposition toward anxiety disorders in general, as well as toward depression (e.g., Middeldorp, Cath, Van Dyck, & Boomsma, 2005). Whether individuals develop one anxiety disorder or another is generally attributed to differences in life experiences (e.g., Brown 2007; Hettema et al., 2005; South & Krueger, 2008). Cognitive writers agree that the negative cognitive processes that maintain fear have their roots in historical events that shape vulnerable individuals toward specific sensitivities and concerns, for example, with physical versus social catastrophe (e.g., Beck et al, 1985).

Here we suggest that another factor that shapes and maintains anxiety disorders may be the relationships the individual has with other people. In this chapter, we will review the empirical literature from the perspective of interpersonal theory. This conceptual framework underscores the importance of social relationships to the individual's emotional well-being, and conversely the role of social relationships in the onset and maintenance of psychopathology. Interpersonal writers propose that early social experiences shape innate dispositions and establish interpersonal patterns that tend to perpetuate themselves across the lifespan. It is possible that differences in these interpersonal experiences and *maladaptive* transactional patterns contribute to the development and maintenance of the various anxiety disorders. Finally, interpersonal writers underscore the role of interpersonal factors in the process and outcome of psychotherapy and other treatments for psychological problems.

We begin the chapter with a brief description of anxiety disorders. We then provide a thumbnail sketch of the empirical literature on interpersonal factors associated with each disorder. We end with a short comparison of similarities and differences in the interpersonal features of the disorders that point to directions for future research. Before we begin, a few caveats are necessary. There is a paucity of interpersonal research on some of these conditions. We do not discuss specific phobias, for example, due to the lack of interpersonal studies. In addition, research on different disorders often addresses similar interpersonal factors without taking coexisting disorders (*comorbidity*) into consideration. Given that the typical anxiety disordered individual will meet criteria for at least one other anxiety disorder (Sanderson, DiNardo, Rapee, & Barlow, 1990), failure to consider comorbidity makes it difficult to draw definitive conclusions about links between specific disorders and various life events. Moreover, interpersonal studies of anxiety often fail to consider the effects of depression, which commonly accompanies anxiety disorders and is known to involve significant interpersonal elements (see Segrin, Chapter 25 in this volume). Comparative studies are rare, and those that exist typically include only two disorders. Finally, the majority of studies rely on retrospective self-report measures, and observational studies of interpersonal processes are lacking. Readers should keep these caveats in mind as they consider this literature.

Anxiety Disorders

The anxiety disorders are quite prevalent. More than one-quarter of the population will suffer from one of these conditions at some point in their lifetime, making anxiety disorders as a group the most common psychiatric diagnosis (Kessler, Berglund, Demler, Jin, Merikangas, & Walters, 2005). Anxiety disorders often begin early and become chronic, and therefore can shape and distort the person's life. In addition to individual distress, these conditions have costs for society as a whole. In the

United States alone, the economic burden of the anxiety disorders exceeds $42 billion dollars annually in direct medical and occupational costs (Greenberg et al., 1999). Thus, understanding the factors that create these conditions, and developing effective treatment strategies for them, has considerable social importance.

The anxiety disorders are found in all cultures, although the content and attributions for symptoms can vary (World Mental Health Survey Consortium, 2004). Prevalence rates across cultures vary widely. Interestingly, anxiety disorders are more common in North America than in other cultures. There are also a number of *culture-bound* syndromes specific to various ethnic groups that combine features of anxiety disorders with somatoform, mood, and dissociative symptoms (APA, 2000). For example, Latino groups refer to *ataque de nervios*, which is marked by emotional symptoms and perceptions of being out of control that often follow a familial stressful event. *Taijin kyofusho* is a Japanese syndrome that in many ways resembles North American *social anxiety disorder*, albeit with greater emphasis on fear of giving offense to others. Despite cultural variation in form or how various symptoms are combined into distinctive syndromes, disorders marked by anxiety and worry span the globe. We turn now to a summary of the research literature for each anxiety disorder.

Social Anxiety Disorder

Social Anxiety Disorder (SOC, Social phobia) is characterized by a marked and persistent fear of social or performance situations in which the person might be observed or evaluated by others (APA, 2000). SOC has high 12-month (6.8%) and lifetime (12.1%) prevalence rates (Kessler et al., 2005), making it the fourth most common psychiatric condition. SOC typically has an early age of onset, surfacing in either childhood or adolescence, and often follows a chronic, unremitting course that causes

significant impairment and diminished quality of life (e.g., Eng, Coles, Heimberg, & Safren, 2005).

Interpersonal dysfunction is a core feature of this disorder, and hence, there are more studies on interpersonal features in SOC than other anxiety disorders. Individuals with SOC, particularly those with generalized social fears, are less likely to date or marry, have fewer friends, lower perceived social support, and experience greater social isolation than people with nongeneralized social anxiety or nonanxious controls (e.g., Hart, Turk, Heimberg, & Liebowitz, 1999; Mendlowicz & Stein, 2000). Although current clinical theories highlight the role of biased processing of social information in perpetuating social anxiety (e.g., Clark & Wells, 1995), there is growing interest in the role of interpersonal factors in the onset and maintenance of these cognitive processes and the disorder itself (see Alden & Taylor, 2004, for a review).

Etiology. Retrospective reports of adults point to three types of early family environments associated with SOC: (1) parental intrusiveness and control; (2) parental hostility, abuse, and neglect; and (3) limited family socializing (see Alden & Taylor, 2004; Bruch, Heimberg, Berger, & Collins, 1989; Rapee & Spence, 2004). Observational studies of parent-child interactions confirm these patient reports. Relative to mothers of other children, the mothers of anxious-withdrawn children were found to display more controlling or intrusive involvement, use nonresponsiveness or criticism, and encourage social avoidance (e.g., Dadds, Barrett, & Rapee, 1996; Dumas, LaFreniere, & Serketich, 1995). Consistent with interpersonal theories, longitudinal studies reveal a bidirectional relationship between the behavior of children and their parents. Child wariness and behavioral inhibition was found to elicit restrictive and controlling parental behavior (e.g., Rubin Nelson, Hastings, & Asendorpf, 1999), and in return, overprotection, intrusiveness, and derisive maternal behavior tended to maintain the child's innate social reticence (e.g., Rubin, Burgess, & Hastings, 2002).

Adverse peer behaviors also can create or help to maintain social anxiety. Socially anxious young people experience more bullying, harassment, and rejection, as well as more subtle forms of exclusion and neglect from their peers relative to nonsocially anxious youth (e.g., Inderbitzen, Walters, & Bukowski, 1997; La Greca & Lopez, 1998; Spence, Donovan, & Brechman-Toussaint, 1999). Even when socially withdrawn children make friends, both they and their friends report lower friendship *quality* than their nonanxious counterparts (Rubin, Wojslawowicz, Rose-Krasnor, & Booth-LaForce, 2006). As with parent interactions, the relationship between socially anxious children and their peers is bidirectional, with social withdrawal leading to negative peer perceptions and difficulties over time (e.g., Hymel, Rubin, Rowden, & LeMare, 1990). In return, social exclusion or rejection maintains or increases avoidance in anxious solitary children (e.g., Gazelle & Rudolph, 2004).

Social cognitions. Relational theorists propose that the developmental experiences described above lead to negative relational schemata. Indeed, different types of developmental experiences are linked to different interpretations of contemporary events (Taylor & Alden, 2005). These schemata, in which the self is viewed as inadequate and others are viewed as critical or ignoring (e.g., Baldwin & Ferguson, 2001; Leary, 2007), bias the way in which people with SOC process complex and often ambiguous social cues (e.g., Winton, Clark, & Edelmann, 1995). For example, patients with SOC more rapidly identified angry than happy faces immersed in pictures of neutral crowds (Joorman & Gotlib, 2006; Gilboa-Schectman, Foa, & Amir, 1999), assigned more negative evaluations to those crowds, and made those negative evaluations more rapidly than did people with depression or nonclinical controls (Gilboa-Schectman, Presburger, Marom, & Hermesh, 2005). When speaking

in public, they selectively attended to negative audience behaviors and ignored positive behaviors, even when both were present in equal numbers (e.g., Veljacca & Rapee, 1998). In dyadic interactions, they underestimated their partner's liking for them (Alden & Wallace, 1995).

Individuals with SOC overestimate the likelihood and cost of negative social outcomes relative to people with other anxiety disorders or no disorder (e.g., Gilboa-Schectman, Franklin, & Foa, 2000). In addition, they underestimate the likelihood but overestimate the cost of positive social outcomes (Gilboa-Schectman et al., 2000). Consistent with that finding, individuals with SOC believe that positive social events lead to more social demands and herald future disappointment (Alden, Taylor, Mellings, & Laposa, 2008).

Interpersonal patterns. The anxiety that arises from biased cognitions affects the social behavior of people with SOC. Objective observers rate these individuals as anxious and unskilled (e.g., Glass & Arnkoff, 1989). In turn, their behavior evokes negative responses from friends as well as strangers (e.g., Creed & Funder, 1998; Heery & Kring, 2007). For example, college friends viewed socially anxious students as overly-sensitive, moody, self-pitying, brittle, and defensive (Creed & Funder, 1998). Moreover, during interactions between unacquainted people, partners of socially anxious individuals attempted to dominate the interaction, talked *at* rather than *with* them, and expressed irritability. Thus, not only did socially anxious students evoke negative reactions in friends, they also irritated and alienated strangers very rapidly.

As we noted earlier, people with SOC lack friends and can be socially isolated. Relational theorists have underscored the role of mutual openness in the development of close relationships (e.g., Reis & Shaver, 1988). Laboratory studies indicate that the socially anxious person's attempts at self-concealment and self-protection short-circuit this process. In "getting acquainted"–type discussions, SOC individuals engage in less self-disclosure and are seen by their conversational partners as less warm and interested in them. As a result, their partners are less likely to desire future interaction, hence shutting off the potential friendship (e.g., Alden & Bieling, 1998; Alden & Wallace, 1995; Meleshko & Alden, 1993). Social rejection appears to be the direct effect of the negative emotional reactions and sense of dissimilarity that people with SOC evoke in others (Vöncken, Alden, Bögels, & Roelofs, 2008).

Close relationships. Surprisingly few studies have directly examined how social anxiety affects close relationships. The picture that emerges from these few studies is similar to that found with peers. Socially anxious people avoid emotional expression and are nonassertive with family and romantic partners (Davila & Beck, 2002, Grant, Beck, Farrow, & Davila, 2007). Patients with SOC report lower levels of emotional intimacy in their close relationships and are more likely to display fearful or preoccupied adult attachment styles (Wenzel, 2002). In interactions with romantic partners, socially anxious individuals displayed more extremely negative behaviors and engaged in fewer positive behaviors than controls (Wenzel, Graff-Dolezal, Macho, & Brendle, 2005). Thus, across all levels of relationships, strangers, friends, and spouses, social anxiety is associated with deficits in the interpersonal strategies needed to maintain and enhance close relationships.

Treatment. In light of the interpersonal difficulties described previously, it is surprising that only a handful of studies examined how interpersonal factors might affect treatment process and outcome. This work reveals that response to group cognitive-behavioral therapy was positively related to group cohesion (Taube-Schiff et al., 2007). Interpersonal differences among people with SOC also affected the individual's treatment response. Specifically, interpersonal behavior marked by anger (Erwin, Heimberg, Schneier, & Liebowitz,

2003) or emotional detachment (Alden & Capreol, 1993) boded poorly for the patient's treatment outcome. Eng and her colleagues found that although SOC patients' satisfaction with social functioning improved following cognitive-behavioral therapy, it remained significantly below that of nonanxious individuals (Eng et al., 2005). Clearly more work is needed to determine how dysfunctional interpersonal processes play out in treatment and to develop better strategies for directly targeting the interpersonal features of social anxiety.

Generalized Anxiety Disorder

Generalized Anxiety Disorder (GAD) is a condition marked by chronic, uncontrollable worry across multiple life domains (APA, 2000). GAD is a common disorder with high 12-month (3.1%) and lifetime (5.1%) prevalence rates (e.g., Kessler et al., 2005). For many years, GAD was used to describe anxiety symptoms that failed to meet diagnostic criteria for the other anxiety disorders. The pioneering work of Borkovec and his colleagues was instrumental in documenting its unique features, and GAD has now emerged from the scientific shadows to become the topic of a growing body of research. Contemporary theorists generally view worry as a form of experiential avoidance adopted in a maladaptive attempt to regulate emotions that are perceived as potentially overwhelming (e.g., Borkovec, Alcain, & Behar, 2004; Mennin, Heimberg, Turk, & Fresco, 2005). From a different perspective, Dugas proposed that worry, and hence GAD, is fueled by an intolerance of uncertainty that leads to ineffective attempts to increase certainty through such actions as reassurance-seeking and excessive preparation (Dugas & Robichaud, 2007).

There is growing recognition that interpersonal processes play a key role in GAD. GAD-related worry most frequently involves interpersonal matters, particularly concerns about significant relationships, social acceptance, embarrassment, conflict, and the like (e.g., Breitholtz, Johansson, &

Ost, 1999; Ladouceur, Freeston, Fournier, Dugas, & Doucet, 2002; Roemer, Molina, & Borkovec, 1997). Worriers report greater public self-consciousness and social anxiety than nonworriers (Pruzinski & Borkovec, 1990). Not surprisingly then, SOC is one of the most prevalent comorbid conditions in people with a principal diagnosis of GAD, with estimates of 33 to 59% overlap (e.g., Sanderson et al., 1990). Unfortunately, most research does not control for this overlap.

Interpersonal patterns. Individuals with GAD report significantly more interpersonal problems than non-GAD controls (Borkovec, Newman, Pincus, & Lytle, 2002). Specifically, they describe themselves as intrusive, overly accommodating, and nonassertive in relationships (e.g., Borkovec et al., 2002; Eng & Heimberg, 2006). They also report an absence of close friends (Whisman, Sheldon, & Goering, 2000). Interestingly, studies that examined peer reactions paint a somewhat different picture. Friends of GAD individuals did not view them as having more problems or rate their friendship quality lower than did controls (Eng & Heimberg, 2006). In a similar vein, students with GAD symptoms did not differ from controls on a self-disclosure task, and their conversational partners liked them as much as non-GAD students (Erickson & Newman, 2007). The GAD group was less accurate, however, in rating their interpersonal impact on their partners, either overestimating or underestimating their negative effect. People with GAD more readily perceive signs of social threat (Moog, Millar, & Bradley, 2000). It may be that this tendency leads them to perceive peer interactions and relationships as more negative than they actually are. On the other hand, it may be that their intrusiveness, chronic reassurance-seeking, and fretting emerge primarily in intimate relationships.

Close relationships. People with GAD are more likely to enter into marriagelike relationships than people with other disorders or no disorder (Yoon & Zinbarg, 2007); however, those relationships do not fare well. GAD is associated with marital difficulties, including separation and divorce, and in fact, is more strongly associated with marital dissatisfaction than are the other anxiety disorders (e.g., Kessler, Walters, & Forthofer, 1998; Whisman, 2007). The association between GAD and marital problems remains even when the quality of other social relationships is controlled, indicating that the link is not due to general social dissatisfaction or negative reporting bias. This association also remains when the effects of comorbid conditions are controlled (Whisman et al., 2000). These findings indicate that some feature specific to GAD is particularly pernicious to intimate relationships

Treatment. Interpersonal problems bode poorly for treatment outcome. More severe interpersonal problems predicted worse outcomes in both dynamic supportive-expressive (Crits-Christoph, Gibbons, Narducci, & Schamberg, 2007) and cognitive-behavioral therapy (e.g., Borkovec et al., 2002). The same is true of marital distress, which has been shown to predict relapse in individual therapy (Durham, Allan, & Hackett, 1997) and failure to respond to medication in GAD patients (e.g., Mancuso, Townsend, & Mercante, 1993).

Etiology. In looking for the social developmental roots of GAD, researchers found that adults with GAD did not differ from panic disordered adults in childhood abuse or parental divorce. They did, however, report more parental loss, lower family cohesiveness, greater family dysfunction, and perceived their parents as hostile and controlling (e.g., Silove, Parker, Hadzi, Pavlovic, Manicavasagar, & Blaszezynski, 1991; Stein & Heimberg, 2004). Adults with GAD reported more insecure attachment to parents, marked by perceived rejection, alienation, less trust, and role-reversal enmeshment relative to controls (e.g., Cassidy, Lichtenstein-Phelps, Sibrava, Thomas, & Borkovec, 2009; Eng & Heimberg, 2006). Cassidy proposed that the child's ability to regulate emotions emerges from secure attachment relationships and proposed that the insecure parental attachment that characterizes GAD results in failure to learn those skills (Cassidy et al., 2009). Hence, these individuals engage in ever-shifting cognitive worry to avoid being overwhelmed by the emotion that would result from directly confronting deeper issues.

Panic Disorder

The hallmark of panic disorder (PD) is recurrent, unexpected panic attacks, which are characterized by sudden physical symptoms, such as heart palpitations, sweating, chest pain, dizziness, and associated fears of dying or losing control/going crazy (APA, 2000). Cognitive behavioral theories are now the most widely accepted theories of PD (e.g., Barlow, 2007; Clark, 1986). Accordingly, PD develops when an individual interprets normal physical sensations in a catastrophic manner and then develops concerns about another panic attack or the implications of the attack (e.g., "I am having a heart attack"). The worries and fears associated with bodily symptoms can result in accompanying agoraphobia (PDA), which is marked by anxiety about places in which escape would be difficult or help would be unavailable. Panic disorder is one of the most commonly experienced anxiety disorders, with a lifetime prevalence rate of 3.7% for PD and 1.1% for PDA (Kessler et al., 2006).

Onset. Researchers have examined whether interpersonal events precede and perhaps trigger the onset of PD/PDA. When compared to healthy matched controls, individuals with PD/PDA typically do not differ in the number of negative interpersonal events experienced prior to the onset of their disorder. However, they find these events to be more distressing, uncontrollable, and more impactful (Roy-Byrne, Geraci, & Uhde, 1987; Rapee, Litwin, & Barlow, 1990), which suggests that they may simply be more emotionally reactive to such events. The types of events most commonly reported in the year preceding the development of PD or PDA are marital/familial conflicts, divorce or separation, social isolation, death of a loved one, and marriage or the beginning of a new relationship (Horesh, Amir, Kedem, Goldberger, & Kotler, 1997; Kleiner & Marshall, 1987), which notably involve close relationships. Finally, there may be gender differences, with women being more likely to report events concerning a significant other, and men reporting events concerning their boss or illness of a close family member (Barzega, Maina, Venturello, & Bogetto, 2001).

Close relationships. There is conflicting evidence whether individuals with PD are less satisfied or adjusted in their marriages than healthy controls (for a review, see Marcaurelle, Bélanger, & Marchand, 2003). Whether or not they differ, low marital adjustment in either partner is associated with a number of factors known to maintain PD/PDA including catastrophic thoughts, fear of anxiety sensations, and panic-related phobias (Marcaurelle, Bélanger, Marchand, Katerelos, & Mainguy, 2005). Treatment of PDA can improve marital satisfaction (Lange & van Dyck, 1992; Monteiro, Marks, & Ramm, 1985). Conversely, a good marital relationship prior to treatment can improve the efficacy of exposure-based therapy (e.g., Carter, Turovsky, & Barlow, 1994; Dewey & Hunsley, 1990; see, however, Jansson, Ost, & Jerremalm, 1987, and Steketee & Shapiro, 1995, for exceptions). Thus, while a poor marriage may not cause PD/PDA, poor marital quality is associated with symptom severity and impedes treatment.

Panic with and without agoraphobia. Despite the high comorbidity and similar interpersonal difficulties of PD and PDA, the two disorders can be distinguished by the prevalence of social concerns. Individuals with PDA endorse more social cognitions such as looking foolish, being negatively evaluated, and being neglected, compared to individuals with just PD (Fleming & Faulk, 1989; Hoffart, Hackmann, & Sexton, 2006). They also have more social concerns about the consequences of panic (de Jong & Bouman, 1995). Not unexpectedly, the odds of having a concurrent diagnosis of SOC are higher for individuals with PDA than those with PD (Grant et al., 2006). Notably, although some of the studies excluded individuals with a comorbid diagnosis of SOC, none of the studies reviewed controlled for subclinical social anxiety symptoms, which makes it difficult to determine if these social concerns are specific to agoraphobia, or a by-product of the accompanying social anxiety symptoms.

Treatment. A body of research supports the notion that relationships with significant others affect treatment outcomes. Family member hostility is associated with treatment dropout and poorer outcomes (Chambless & Steketee, 1999). How the PD/PDA individual perceives familial behavior is also important. Over the course of treatment, the degree to which patients became upset by their perceptions of their relatives' criticism, but not the degree of perceived criticism per se, contributed to anxiety during exposure sessions, beyond that of anxious and depressive mood (Steketee, Lam, Chambless, Rodebaugh, & McCollouch, 2006). Interestingly, although individuals with more severe symptoms perceived their relatives as more critical, symptom severity was not related to the relative's actual hostility (Chambless, Bryan, Aiken, Steketee, & Hooley, 2001), which suggests that PD/PDA can result in exaggerated perceptions of hostility. This hypothesis is consistent with the finding that outpatients with PD/PDA tend to interpret nonangry faces as angry, compared to outpatients without PD/PDA (Kessler, Roth, von Wietersheim, Deighton, & Traue, 2007).

Including significant others directly in treatment can have benefits. Partner-assisted exposure therapy was found to lead to improvement for 23 to 45% of individuals (Byrne, Carr, & Clark, 2004). In discerning what factors lead to such improvement, research points to effective communication, which is associated with greater treatment

completion (Craske, Burton, & Barlow, 1989). However, addressing communication and problem solving in treatment produced mixed results, with some studies showing greater improvement in PD/PDA symptoms, compared to treatment without these components (Kleiner, Marshall, & Spevack, 1987), while other studies failed to show any added benefit (Chambless, Foa, Grobes, & Goldstein, 1982).

Etiology. Researchers have also looked for the social-developmental roots of PD/PDA. Some work indicates that childhood separation anxiety disorder (SAD) occurs more frequently in individuals with PD/PDA compared to controls (e.g., Bandelow et al., 2001). Other studies, however, have refuted the specificity of this relationship, finding that a diagnosis of childhood SAD puts adults at greater risk for a variety of anxiety disorders (Aschenbrand, Kendall, Webb, Safford, & Flannery-Schroder, 2003; Biederman et al., 2007; Craske, Poulton, Tsao, & Plotkin, 2001). The transmission of PD/PDA specific cognitions may also have developmental routes through the modeling of panic behaviors. When primed, children of adults with PD demonstrated more anxious interpretation of ambiguous vignettes depicting physical sensations compared to children of animal phobics and healthy controls. This effect was not found in the absence of priming, strengthening the assumption that the results were due to panic schemas developed in response to parental behavior (Schneider, Unnewehr, Florin, & Margraf, 2002).

Obsessive-Compulsive Disorder

Obsessive compulsive disorder (OCD) is characterized by recurrent and distressing obsessions and/or compulsions (APA, 2000). Obsessions take the form of thoughts, images, or impulses that are experienced by the individual as inappropriate. Horowitz (2004) noted that some common obsessions can be grouped into three categories: (1) fear of being harmed (e.g., contamination concerns); (2) fear of accidentally harming others; and (3) unwanted urges to harm someone else. Indeed, the most commonly reported obsessions include themes regarding dirt and contamination, aggression, doubt, unacceptable sexual acts, religion, and orderliness. All in all, obsessions represent a wide range of psychopathology. Compulsions, on the other hand, are behaviors or mental acts that a person feels driven to perform to prevent or reduce distress or a feared outcome, although they will not realistically prevent the feared outcome. Common compulsions include washing, checking, repeating specific behaviors/phrases, and ordering. It is estimated that 1.6% of adults will be diagnosed with OCD in their lifetime (Kessler et al., 2005).

Interpersonal patterns. Individuals with OCD experience extensive interpersonal difficulties. When compared to healthy controls, they are more likely to be unemployed, have relationship disturbances (i.e., be divorced/separated), decreased social functioning, less social support, and decreased sexual activity (e.g., Koran, Thienemann, & Davenport, 1996; Stengler-Wenzke, Kroll, Matschinger, & Angermeyer, 2006). However, comorbid depression may account for many of these results. Individuals with comorbid depression report a lower quality of life than individuals with only OCD, and depression is one of the strongest predictors of overall quality of life (Huppert, Simpson, Nissenson, Liebowitz, & Foa, 2009; Masellis, Rector, & Richter, 2003).

Close relationships. A large proportion of individuals with OCD are single (Steketee & Pruyn, 1998). Although married patients typically report distressed marital relations, this does not appear to be greater than with average couples (see Steketee & van Noppen, 2003). However, the severity of OCD symptoms is associated with less intellectually and sexually intimate romantic relationships, even when controlling for the impact of depressive symptoms (Abbey, Clopton, & Humphreys, 2007). Although OCD severity is associated with

less self-disclosure, this link appears to be accounted for by depression (Abbey et al., 2007). Regardless of the source, reduced self-disclosure is thought to be particularly detrimental in OCD as it prevents individuals from gathering information to challenge their catastrophic interpretations (e.g., "people will reject me if they know") of their thoughts (Newth & Rachman, 2001). Overall, most of this research is correlational, so it is unclear whether the OCD symptoms stress the relationship, or if an already-stressed relationship exacerbates OCD symptoms; most likely, it is a bidirectional relationship.

Relatives and partners of individuals with OCD also experience interpersonal costs. Up to 75% of relatives report disruption in their lives because of OCD, including loss of personal relationships, loss of leisure time, and financial problems (Cooper, 1993). Relatives most frequently complain of not being able to stand the situation any longer, of being completely at the individual's disposal, and of being unable to rest (Magliano, Posini, Guarneri, Marasco, & Catapano, 1996). The perceived burden is associated with patient OCD severity, and with their relatives' depressive symptoms (de Abreu Ramos-Cerqueira, Torres, Torresan, Negreiros, & Vitorino, 2008; Magliano et al., 1996). Overall, the demands of having a relative with OCD are associated with reduced physical, social, and psychological well-being, compared to the general population (Stengler-Wenzke et al., 2006).

It is likely that much of the stress and interference for relatives is associated with accommodating the individual's OCD symptoms. Common forms of accommodation include providing reassurance, and waiting for the individual. Approximately 59% of relatives report accommodating the patient on a daily basis, and accommodation is associated with the degree of OCD severity (Stewart et al., 2008). Relatives appear to be caught in a vicious cycle. Providing accommodation results in distress, depression, anxiety, personal burden, perceived family disharmony, and limited family opportunities (Calvocoressi et al., 1995); however, not providing accommodation can result in the relative with OCD becoming upset, thereby creating relational stress (Amir, Freshman, & Foa, 2000).

Treatment. These interpersonal difficulties have a detrimental impact on the treatment of OCD. The research on hostility overlaps with that reviewed in the section on panic disorder. Briefly, family hostility and how upset patients become by their perception of family members' criticism is associated with greater treatment-related anxiety, treatment dropout, and less treatment change (Chambless & Steketee, 1999; Steketee et al., 2007). When specifically examining *marital* relationships, there was no clear connection between marital satisfaction and treatment outcome (e.g., Emmelkamp, de Haan, & Hoogduin, 1990; Riggs, Hiss, & Foa, 1992). These apparently contradictory findings may arise because marital satisfaction is a broader construct than hostility per se, and often measures assess many aspects of a marriage that may or may not be directly associated with treatment outcomes (e.g., sexual adjustment, agreement on recreational activities). It is not surprising that relatives' accommodation is associated with fewer treatment gains (Amir et al., 2000). When relatives are educated about reducing accommodation, individuals with OCD show more gains than individuals whose relatives are not included (e.g., Grunes, Neziroglu, & McKay, 2001; Mehta, 1990). Other uncontrolled studies demonstrate treatment gains when family members are involved in exposure and response prevention treatment (Thornicroft, Colson, & Marks, 1991; van Noppen, Steketee, McCorkle, & Pato, 1997).

*Etiology.*Developmental research points to early family relationships characterized by control and overprotection. Individuals with OCD report their parents as being more overprotective compared to depressive or healthy controls, but not compared to individuals with PDA (Merkel, Pollard, Wiener, & Staebler, 1993; Turgeon, O'Connor, Marchand, & Freeston, 2002; Yoshida, Taga, Matsumoto, & Fukui, 2005). Interestingly, Chambless, Gillis, Tran, and Steketee (1996) found that although anxious individuals recalled their parents as being controlling, parents reported using optimal parenting. The authors concluded that it was unclear whether clients inflated these parenting characteristics, or if parents responded to the questionnaires in a self-protective fashion. However, when observed during a problem-solving task, families of children with OCD were rated as demonstrating less confidence in their child's ability, and less rewarding of independence than families of children with other disorders and no clinical problems (Barrett, Shortt, & Healy, 2002).

Post-Traumatic Stress Disorder (PTSD)

The majority of people will experience a potentially traumatic event during their lifetime (Lee & Young, 2001); however, only approximately 7% of individuals will develop post-traumatic stress disorder (PTSD) (Kessler et al., 2005). PTSD is marked by three clusters of symptoms: (1) reexperiencing the traumatic event (e.g., nightmares or intrusive memories); (2) avoidance of trauma-related cues (e.g., situations, objects, and people) and emotional numbing; and (3) chronic physiological arousal such as an increased startle response or sleep difficulties (APA, 2000).

*Onset.*PTSD arises following exposure to an emotionally traumatic event that presents a threat to the life or physical well being of one's self or other people. Traumas of an interpersonal nature appear to be particularly deleterious (D. W. King, King, Gudanowski, & Vreven, 1995), with conditional prevalence rates (i.e., percentage of people exposed to a specific trauma who develop PTSD) suggesting that more people develop PTSD from interpersonal traumas (21 to 48%), such as combat exposure, childhood neglect/abuse, and sexual assault, than from accidents (8%; Kessler, Sonnega, Bromet, Hughes, & Nelson, 1995). The higher conditional prevalence rates may be a result of a tendency to appraise these traumas as being more life-threatening than accidents (Ozer, Best, Lipsey, & Weiss, 2003). Notably, there is a bidirectional relationship between PTSD symptoms and the experience of traumatic events; PTSD symptoms also put women at risk to experience subsequent traumatic events, particularly those with interpersonal violence perpetrated by a nonintimate partner (Cougle, Resnick, & Kilpatrick, 2009).

Interpersonal patterns. Regardless of the etiological event, PTSD is associated with poor interpersonal functioning. A recent meta-analysis found a much lower quality of life (e.g., social and home/family domains) in individuals with PTSD compared to healthy controls (Olatunji, Cisler, & Tolin, 2007). Research with war veterans suggests that PTSD in particular, and not merely trauma exposure, results in wide-arching family difficulties, including marital distress, difficulties with intimacy, divorce/separation, and behavioral difficulties for their children (Caselli & Motta, 1995; Jordan et al., 1992; Riggs, Byrne, Weathers, & Litz, 1998). It is not surprising that caregivers of veterans with PTSD also report high levels of distress, adjustment problems, and burden (Beckham, Lytel, & Feldman, 1996; Jordan et al., 1992), even when compared to partners of veterans without PTSD (Calhoun, Beckham, & Bosworth, 2002). When other traumas are considered, PTSD is associated with sexual problems across varied types of interpersonal victimization (Letourneau, Resnick, Kilpatrick, Saunders, & Best, 1996).

Anger bodes particularly poorly for both the development of PTSD and the quality of interpersonal relationships. Anger experienced after the trauma predicts later PTSD symptom severity across trauma types (e.g., Ehlers, Mayou, & Bryant, 1998; Feeny, Zoellner, & Foa, 2000). For war veterans, an association exists between PTSD and elevated hostility and violent behavior

for both men (Beckham, Feldman, Kirby, Hertzberg, & Moore, 1997; Beckham et al., 1996) and women (Butterfield, Forneris, Feldman, & Beckham, 2000).

Nugent and colleagues (see Chapter 24 in this volume) discuss the complex relationship between social support and PTSD; in particular, how the quality of support can exacerbate (Andrews, Brewin, & Rose, 2003; Zoellner, Foa, & Brigidi, 1999) or ameliorate PTSD symptoms (King, King, Fairbank, Keane, & Adams, 1998; Schumm, Briggs-Phillips, & Hobfoll, 2006). Here, we devote particular attention to self-disclosure, which is hypothesized to reduce PTSD symptoms by creating a congruent understanding and memory of the trauma. Indeed, self-disclosure is linked to reduced PTSD symptoms after a variety of traumatic events (Green, Grace, Lindy, Gleser, & Leonard, 1990; Joseph, Andrews, Williams, & Yule, 1992), whereas not disclosing can exacerbate symptoms (Davidson & Moss, 2008; Ruggiero et al., 2004). However, it appears that the reaction to the disclosure is also important, with supportive reactions associated with reduced PTSD symptoms (Bolton, Glenn, Orsillo, Roemer, & Litz, 2003), and negative reactions exacerbating symptoms (Ullman & Filipas, 2001). Self-disclosure also plays an important role in building intimacy, and it was found to mediate the relationship between PTSD severity and marital intimacy in a sample of war veterans (Solomon, Dekel, & Zerach, 2008).

Social cognitions. There is increased recognition regarding the role of social cognitions in maintaining PTSD. In trauma-exposed populations, individuals with PTSD consistently report higher levels of social anxiety and related fears compared to individuals without PTSD (e.g., Collimore, Asmundson, Taylor, & Jang, 2009; Kashdan, Julian, Merritt, & Uswatte, 2006). Surprisingly, assaultive groups do not differ in their social fears compared to nonassaultive groups, regardless of the interpersonal nature of the trauma (Collimore et al., 2009). Authors have speculated that guilt and shame may prevent the individual from talking about the trauma, and indeed higher levels of these emotions are associated with social anxiety in PTSD (Orsillo, Heimberg, Juster, & Garrett, 1996; Zayfert, DeViva, & Hofmann, 2005).

Treatment. Interpersonal processes are also implicated in the treatment of PTSD. Most notably, individuals displaying higher levels of anger make fewer gains in treatment (Forbes et al., 2008; Taylor et al., 2001; however, see van Minnen, Arntz, & Keijsers, 2002). Anger likely interferes with the therapeutic alliance, which has been shown to be a very strong predictor of CBT treatment outcome for PTSD (Cloitre, Scarvalone, & Difede, 1997). The therapeutic alliance likely helps engender a sense of trust and safety to engage in trauma exploration/exposure (Charuvastra & Cloitre, 2008). Moreover, relatives' hostility and criticism also affect treatment outcomes, with studies suggesting that 20% of variance in CBT outcome can be attributed to high levels of these emotions (Tarrier, Sommerfield, & Pilgrim, 1999). Overall, anger and hostility bode poorly for treatment gains, regardless of the source.

Comparative Summary

If we examine the literature presented earlier through the lens of interpersonal theory, it becomes clear that interpersonal factors are involved at various stages in all of the anxiety disorders. As we noted earlier, interpersonal theory draws attention to social developmental experiences. For SOC, GAD, and PTSD, extant findings suggest that interpersonal processes contribute to the onset of the disorder. For PDA and OCD, the evidence on etiology is inconsistent, perhaps because of the disparate types of psychopathology that are found within each of these disorders: for example, different categories of obsessions (cf. Horowitz, 2004), and the presence or absence of coexisting agoraphobic avoidance. Second, interpersonal theory highlights the importance of other peoples' responses to the anxiety

disordered individual, and also the potentially maladaptive transactional cycles that arise between these individuals and others. Empirical findings clearly indicate that all of the anxiety disorders impact other people, with particular effects on close relationships, either preventing the development of those relationships, in the case of SOC, or creating strain between the anxiety-disordered individual and others. In turn, others' responses to the anxious person help to maintain symptoms and influence treatment outcome.

We speculated at the beginning that differences in social developmental experiences, and the ongoing interpersonal cycles they establish, may explain how individuals come to develop different conditions and why those conditions persist. Consistent with those speculations, research points to potential differences in the interpersonal patterns associated with the various anxiety disorders. As noted earlier, our ability to draw definitive conclusions about interpersonal differences are limited by the absence of comparative studies, failure to consider comorbid conditions, and so on. Still, we offer a tentative comparative summary of existing findings in the hope that this will facilitate future research to either confirm or correct our current knowledge.

Social anxiety disorder has the strongest interpersonal profile. For these individuals, a combination of behavioral inhibition and developmental events result in ongoing tendencies to view themselves as socially inadequate, and others as rejecting. As a result, they avoid self-expression and emotional contact, which impedes the development of close relationships and reduces emotional intimacy in the relationships they have, thereby maintaining their social and emotional isolation.

For the GAD individual, biological vulnerabilities and negative parenting may result in insecure attachment to significant others and failure to develop the emotion regulation strategies needed to manage emotion-evoking events. Individuals with GAD seek out marriage (or marriagelike) relationships; however, they engage in ongoing worry about those relationships, which along with their self-described intrusiveness, attempts at control, and safety behaviors like continual reassurance-seeking, strain close relationships and increase the likelihood of those relationships ending, which might be expected to fuel future worry.

Based on existing evidence, panic disorder per se appears to be the least interpersonal of the anxiety disorders with inconsistent findings about the role of interpersonal factors in the onset and maintenance of pure PD. This is notable, given research suggesting that panic has different biological roots than anxiety (e.g., Barlow, 2007). Interpersonal concerns do play a greater role in agoraphobia, although this may be due to comorbid social anxiety. Nonetheless, PD and PDA are associated with negatively biased interpretations of family behavior and a tendency to overreact to negative social events, which may strain close relationships. In addition, criticism from partners exacerbates PD/PDA symptoms, and addressing marital communication in treatment can have beneficial effects.

OCD is marked by reduced rates of involvement in romantic relationships. When individuals with OCD are in such relationships, there is extraordinary burden on their partners, who are drawn into accommodating, and thus maintaining, the individual's OCD symptoms. Involving significant others in treatment can help to reverse this pattern. The literature clearly demonstrates that interpersonal trauma is an important contributor to the onset of PTSD. Once present, PTSD is uniquely associated with interpersonal anger/hostility and violent behavior, particularly directed towards intimate partners, at least in male and female veterans. Additionally, PTSD can lead to social anxiety and reluctance to self-disclose to others, hence maintaining symptoms. Finally, social support plays a key role in ameliorating or exacerbating PTSD symptoms.

Conclusions

Despite limitations in current research, the literature as a whole supports the notion that interpersonal processes contribute to the anxiety disorders. Moreover, interpersonal theories have the potential to expand existing treatments and research on these conditions. Incorporating an interpersonal perspective would allow clinicians to extend the therapeutic focus beyond the intraindividual biological and cognitive factors that are the center of attention in current treatments for these conditions. As for research, interpersonal theory points to important outcome measures (e.g., number or quality of friendships), and suggests that it may be valuable to examine interactional effects and mediating/moderating relationships between social functioning and other cognitive/developmental and biological factors. Major avenues for future research include: (a) developmental/prospective studies to determine which social experiences shape biological predispositions and contribute to the development of specific anxiety disorders, (b) comparative studies that examine interpersonal patterns in both analogue studies and daily life, and (c) treatment outcome studies that examine the effects of interventions focused on the maladaptive interpersonal patterns associated with these conditions. For most of us, social relationships are at the heart of our sense of emotional well-being. Accordingly, they deserve greater emphasis in theories and treatments for anxiety.

References

Abbey, R. D., Clopton, J. R., & Humphreys, J. D. (2007). Obsessive-compulsive disorder and romantic functioning. *Journal of Clinical Psychology, 63*, 1181–1192.

Alden, L. E., & Bieling, P. M. (1998). Interpersonal consequences of the pursuit of safety. *Behaviour Research and Therapy, 36*, 1–9.

Alden, L. E., & Capreol, M. J. (1993). Interpersonal problem patterns in avoidant personality disordered outpatients: Prediction of treatment response. *Behavior Therapy, 24*, 356–376.

Alden, L. E., & Taylor, C. T. (2004). Interpersonal perspectives on social phobia. *Clinical Psychology Review*, 24, 857–882.

Alden, L. E., Taylor, C. T., Laposa, J. M., & Mellings, T. M. B. (2006). Social developmental experiences and response to cognitive-behavioral therapy for Generalized Social Phobia. *Journal of Cognitive Psychotherapy*, 20, 407–416

Alden, L. E., & Wallace, S. T. (1995). Social phobia and social appraisal in successful and unsuccessful interactions. *Behaviour Research and Therapy*, 33, 497–506.

American Psychiatric Association (2000). *Diagnostic and statistical manual of mental disorders* (4th ed.; DSM-IV-TR). Washington, DC: Author.

Amir, N., Freshman, M., & Foa, E. B. (2000). Family distress and involvement in relatives of obsessive-compulsive disorder patients. *Journal of Anxiety Disorders*, 14, 209–217.

Andrews, B., Brewin, C. R., & Rose, S. (2003). Gender, social support, and PTSD in victims of violent crime. *Journal of Traumatic Stress*, 16, 421–427.

Aschenbrand, S. G., Kendall, P. C., Webb, A., Safford, S. M., & Flannery-Schroder, E. (2003). Is childhood separation anxiety disorder a predictor of adult panic disorder and agoraphobia? A seven-year longitudinal study. *Journal of the American Academy of Child and Adolescent Psychiatry*, 42, 1478–1485.

Baldwin, M. W., & Ferguson, P. (2001). Relational schemas: The activation of interpersonal knowledge structures in social anxiety. In R. Crozier & L. E. Alden (Eds.), *International handbook of social anxiety: Concepts, research and intervention relating to the self and shyness* (pp. 137–158). London: John Wiley & Sons.

Bandelow, B., Tichauer, G. A., Späth, C., Broocks, A., Hajak, G., Bleich, S., & Rüther, E. (2001). Separation anxiety and actual separation experiences in childhood in patients with panic disorder. *Canadian Journal of Psychiatry*, 46, 948–952.

Barlow, D. H. (2007). *Anxiety and its disorders: The nature and treatment of anxiety and panic.* New York: Guilford Press.

Barrett, P., Shortt, A., & Healy, L. (2002). Do parent and child behaviours differentiate families whose children have obsessive-compulsive disorder from other clinic and nonclinic families? *Journal of Child Psychology and Psychiatry*, 43, 597–607.

Barzega, G., Maina, G., Venturello, S., & Bogetto, F. (2001). Gender-related difference in the onset of panic disorder. *Acta Psychiatrica Scandinavica*, 103, 189–195.

Beck, A. T., Emery, G., & Greenberg, R. L. (1985). *Anxiety disorders and phobias: A cognitive perspective.* New York: Basic Books.

Beckham, J. C., Feldman, M. E., Kirby, A. C., Hertzberg, M. A., & Moore, S. D. (1997). Interpersonal violence and its correlates in Vietnam veterans with chronic posttraumatic stress disorder. *Journal of Clinical Psychology*, 53, 856–869.

Beckham, J. C., Lytel, B. L., & Feldman, M. E. (1996). Caregiver burden in partners of Vietnam veterans with posttraumatic stress disorder. *Journal of Consulting and Clinical Psychology*, 64, 1068–1071.

Berrios, G. E., Link, C. G., & Clark, M. J. (1995). Anxiety disorders. In G. E. Berrios & R. Porter (Ed). *A history of clinical psychiatry: The origin and history of psychiatric disorders.* (pp. 545–572). New York: New York University Press.

Biederman, J., Petty, C. R., Hirshfeld-Becker, D. R., Henin, A., Faraone, S. V., Fraire, M., . . . Rosenbaum, J. F. (2007). Developmental trajectories of anxiety disorders in offspring at high risk for panic disorder and major depression. *Psychiatry Research*, 153, 245–252.

Bolton, E. E., Glenn, D. M., Orsillo, S., Roemer, L., & Liz, B. T. (2003). The relationship between self-disclosure and symptoms of posttraumatic stress disorder in peacekeepers deployed to Somalia. *Journal of Traumatic Stress*, 16, 203–210.

Borkovec, T. D., Alcaine, O., & Behar, E. (2004). Avoidance theory of worry and generalized anxiety disorder. In R. G. Heimberg, C. L. Turk, & D. S. Mennin (Eds.), *Generalized anxiety disorder: Advances in research and practice* (pp. 77–108). New York: Guilford Press.

Borkovec, T. D., Newman, M. G., Pincus, A., & Lytle, R. (2002). A component analysis of cognitive-behavioral therapy for generalized anxiety disorder and the role of interpersonal problems. *Journal of Consulting and Clinical Psychology*, 70, 288–298.

Breitholtz, E., Johansson, B., & Öst, L.-G. (1999). Cognitions in generalized anxiety disorder and panic disorder patients. A prospective approach. *Behaviour Research and Therapy*, 37, 533–544.

Brown, T. A. (2007). Temporal course and structural relationships among dimensions of temperament and DSM-IV anxiety and mood disorder constructs. *Journal of Abnormal Psychology, 116,* 313–328.

Bruch, M. A., Heimberg, R. G., Berger, P., & Collins, T. M. (1989). Social phobia and perceptions of early parental and personal characteristics. *Anxiety Research, 2,* 57–63.

Butterfield, M. I., Forneris, C. A., Feldman, M. E., & Beckham, J. C. (2000). Hostility and functional health status in women veterans with and without posttraumatic stress disorder: A preliminary study. *Journal of Traumatic Stress, 13,* 735–741.

Byrne, M., Carr, A., & Clark, M. (2004). The efficacy of couples-based interventions for panic disorder with agoraphobia. *Journal of Family Therapy, 26,* 105–125.

Calhoun, P. S., Beckham, J. C., & Bosworth, H. B. (2002). Caregiver burden and psychological distress of veterans with chronic posttraumatic stress disorder. *Journal of Traumatic Stress, 15,* 205–212.

Calvocoressi, L., Lewis, B., Harris, M., Trufan, S. J., Goodman, W. K., McDougle, C. J., & Price, L. H. (1995). Family accommodation in obsessive-compulsive disorder. *American Journal of Psychiatry, 152,* 441–443.

Carter, M. M., Turovsky, J., & Barlow, D. H. (1994). Interpersonal relationships in panic disorder with agoraphobia: A review of empirical evidence. *Clinical Psychology—Science and Practice, 1,* 25–34.

Caselli, L. T., & Motta, R. W. (1995). The effect of PTSD and combat level on Vietnam veterans' perceptions of child behavior and marital adjustment. *Journal of Clinical Psychology, 51,* 4–12.

Cassidy, J., Lichtenstein-Phelps, J., Sibrava, N. J., Thomas, C. L., & Borkovec, T. D. (2009). Generalized Anxiety Disorder: Connection with self-reported attachment. *Behavior Therapy, 40,* 23–38.

Chambless, D. L., Bryan, A. D., Aiken, L. S., Steketee, G., & Hooley, J. M. (2001). Predicting expressed emotion: A study of families of obsessive-compulsive and agoraphobic outpatients. *Journal of Family Psychology, 15,* 225–240.

Chambless, D. L., Foa, E. B., Groves, G. A., & Goldstein, A. J. (1982). Exposure and communications training in the treatment of agoraphobia. *Behaviour Research and Therapy, 20,* 219–231.

Chambless, D. L., Gillis, M. M., Tran, G. Q., & Steketee, G. (1996). Parental bonding reports of clients with obsessive-compulsive disorder and agoraphobia. *Clinical Psychology and Psychotherapy, 3,* 77–85.

Chambless, D. L., & Steketee, G. (1999). Expressed emotion and behavior therapy outcome: A prospective study with obsessive-compulsive and agoraphobic outpatients. *Journal of Consulting and Clinical Psychology, 67,* 658–665.

Charuvastra, A., & Cloitre, M. (2008). Social bonds and posttraumatic stress disorder. *Annual Review of Psychology, 59,* 301–328.

Clark, D. M. (1986). A cognitive approach to panic. *Behaviour Research and Therapy, 24,* 461–470.

Clark, D. M., & Wells, A., (1995). A cognitive model of social phobia. In R. G. Heimberg, M. Liebowitz, D. Hope, & F. Schneier (Eds.), *Social phobia: Diagnosis, assessment, and treatment* (pp. 69–93). New York: Guilford Press.

Cloitre, M., Scarvalone, P., & Difede, J. (1997). Posttraumatic stress disorder, self- and interpersonal dysfunction among sexually retraumatized women. *Journal of Traumatic Stress, 10,* 437–452.

Collimore, K. C., Asmundson, J. G., Taylor, S. & Jang, K. L. (2009). Socially related fears following exposure to trauma: Environmental and genetic influences. *Journal of Anxiety Disorders, 23,* 240–246.

Cooper, M. (1993). A group for families of obsessive-compulsive persons. *Families in Society, 74,* 301–307.

Cougle, J. R., Resnick, H., & Kilpatrick, D. G. (2009). A prospective examination of PTSD symptoms as risk factors for subsequent exposure to potentially traumatic events among women. *Journal of Abnormal Psychology, 118,* 405–411.

Craske, M. G., Burton, T., & Barlow, D. H. (1989). Relationships among measures of communication, marital satisfaction and exposure during couple's treatment of agoraphobia. *Behaviour Research and Therapy, 27,* 131–140.

Craske, M. G., Poulton, R., Tsao, J. C. I., & Plotkin, D. (2001). Paths to panic disorder/agoraphobia: An exploratory analysis from age 3 to 21 in an unselected birth cohort. *Journal of the American Academy of Child and Adolescent Psychiatry, 40,* 556–563.

Creed, A. T., & Funder, D. C. (1998). Social anxiety: From the inside and outside. *Personality and Individual Differences, 25*, 19–33.

Crits-Christoph, P., Gibbons, M., Narducci, J. & Schamberg, M. (2005). Interpersonal problems and the outcome of interpersonally oriented psychodynamic treatment of GAD. *Psychotherapy: Theory, Research, Practice, Training, 4*, 211–224.

Dadds, M. R., Barrett, P. M., & Rapee, R. M. (1996). Family process and child anxiety and aggression: An observational analysis. *Journal of Abnormal Child Psychology, 24*, 715–734.

Darcy, K., Davila, J., & Beck, J. G. (2005). Is social anxiety associated with both interpersonal avoidance and interpersonal dependence? *Cognitive Therapy and Research, 29*, 171–186.

Davidson, A. C., & Moss, S. A. (2008). Examining the trauma disclosure of police officers to their partners and officers' subsequent adjustment. *Journal of Language and Social Psychology, 27*, 51–70.

Davila, J., & Beck, J. G. (2002). Is social anxiety associated with impairment in close relationships? A preliminary investigation. *Behavior Therapy, 33*, 427–444.

de Abreu Ramos-Cerqueira, A. T., Torres, A. R., Torresan, R. C., Negreiros, A. P. M., & Vitorino, C. N. (2008). Emotional burden in caregivers of patients with obsessive-compulsive disorder. *Depression and Anxiety, 25*, 1020–1027.

de Jong, G. M., & Bouman, T. K. (1995). Panic disorder: A baseline period. Predictability of agoraphobic avoidance behavior. *Journal of Anxiety Disorders, 9*, 185–199.

Dewey, D., & Hunsley, J. (1990). The effects of marital adjustment and spouse involvement on the behavioral treatment of agoraphobia: A meta-analytic review. *Anxiety Research, 2*, 69–93.

Dugas, M. J., & Robichaud, M. (2007). *Cognitive-behavioral treatment for Generalized Anxiety Disorder.* New York: Routledge.

Dumas, J. E., LaFreniere, P. J., & Serketich, W. J. (1995). "Balance of power": A transactional analysis of control in mother-child dyads involving socially competent, aggressive, and anxious children. *Journal of Abnormal Psychology, 104*, 104–113.

Durham, R. C., Allan, T., & Hackett, C. A. (1997). On predicting improvement and relapse in generalized anxiety disorder following

psychotherapy. *British Journal of Clinical Psychology, 36*, 101–119.

Ehlers, A., Mayou, R. A., & Bryant, B. (1998). Psychological predictors of chronic post–traumatic stress disorder after motor vehicle accidents. *Journal of Abnormal Psychology, 107*, 508–519.

Emmelkamp, P. M. G., de Haan, E., & Hoogduin, C. A. L. (1990). Marital adjustment and obsessive compulsive disorder. *British Journal of Psychiatry, 156*, 55–60.

Eng, W., Coles, M. E., Heimberg, R. G., & Safran, S. A. (2005). Domains of life satisfaction in social anxiety disorder: relation to symptoms and response to cognitive-behavioral therapy. *Journal of Anxiety Disorders, 19*, 143–156.

Eng. W., & Heimberg, R. G. (2006). Interpersonal correlates of generalized anxiety disorder: Self- versus other perception. *Journal of Anxiety Disorders, 20*, 380–387.

Erickson, T. M., & Newman, M. G. (2007). Interpersonal and emotional processes in generalized anxiety disorder analogues during social interaction tasks. *Behavior Therapy, 38*, 364–377.

Erwin, B. A., Heimberg, R. G., Schneier, F. R., & Liebowitz, M. R. (2003). Anger experience and expression in social anxiety disorder: Pretreatment profile and predictors of attrition and response to cognitive-behavioral treatment. *Behavior Therapy, 34*, 331–350

Feeny, N. C., Zoellner, L. A., & Foa, E. B. (2000). Anger, dissociation, and posttraumatic stress disorder among female assault victims. *Journal of Traumatic Stress, 13*, 89–100.

Fleming, B., & Faulk, A. (1989). Discriminating factors of panic disorder with and without agoraphobia. *Journal of Anxiety Disorders, 3*, 209–219.

Forbes, D., Parslow, R., Creamer, M., Allen, N., McHugh, T., & Hopwood, M. (2008). Mechanisms of anger and treatment outcome in combat veterans with posttraumatic stress disorder. *Journal of Traumatic Stress, 21*, 142–149.

Fox, N. A., Henderson, H. A., Marshall, P. J., Nichols, K. E., & Ghera, M. M. (2005). Behavioral inhibition: Linking biology and behavior within a developmental framework. *Annual Reviews of Psychology, 56*, 235–262.

Gazelle, H., & Rudolph, K. D. (2004). Moving toward and away from the world: Social approach and avoidance trajectories in anxious solitary youth. *Child Development, 75*, 829–849.

Gilboa-Schectman, E., Foa, E. B., & Amir, N. (1999). Attentional biases for facial expression in social phobia: The effects of target and distractor in the "face-in-the-crowd" task. *Cognition and Emotion, 13*, 305–318.

Gilboa-Schechtman, E., Franklin, M. E., & Foa, E. B. (2000). Anticipated reactions to social events: Differences among individual with generalized social phobia, obsessive-compulsive disorder, and nonanxious controls. *Cognitive Therapy and Research, 24*, 731–746.

Gilboa-Schechtman, E., Presburger, G., Marom, S., & Hermesh, H. (2005). The effects of social anxiety and depression on the evaluation of facial crowds. *Behaviour Research and Therapy, 43*, 467–474.

Glass, C. R., & Arnkoff, D. B. (1989). Behavioral assessment of social anxiety and social phobia. *Clinical Psychology Review, 9*, 75–90.

Grant, B. F., Hasin, D. S., Stinson, F. S., Dawson, D. A., Goldstein, R. B., Smith, S., . . . Saha, T. D. (2006). The epidemiology of DSM-IV panic disorder and agoraphobia in the United States: Results from the national epidemiologic survey on alcohol and related conditions. *Journal of Clinical Psychiatry, 67*, 363–374.

Grant, D. M., Beck, J. G., & Farrow, S. M. (2007). Do interpersonal features of social anxiety influence the development of depressive symptoms? *Cognition and Emotion, 21*, 646–663.

Green, B. L., Grace, M. C., Lindy, J. D., Gleser, G. C., & Leonard, A. (1990). Risk factors for PTSD and other diagnosis in a general sample of Vietnam veterans. *American Journal of Psychiatry, 147*, 729–733.

Greenberg, P. E., Sisitsky, T., Kessler, R. C., Finkelstein, S. N., Berndt, E. R., Davidson, J. R., . . . Fyer, A. J. (1999). The economic burden of anxiety disorders in the 1990s. *Journal of Clinical Psychiatry, 60*, 427–35.

Grunes, M. S., Neziroglu, F., & McKay, D. (2001). Family involvement in the behavioral treatment of obsessive-compulsive disorder: A preliminary investigation. *Behavior Therapy, 32*, 803–820.

Hart, T. A., Turk, C. L., Heimberg, R. G., & Liebowitz, M. R. (1999). Relation of marital status to social phobia severity. *Depression and Anxiety, 10*, 28–32

Heerey, E. A., & Kring, A. M. (2007). Interpersonal consequences of social anxiety. *Journal of Abnormal Psychology, 116*, 125–134.

Hettema, J. M., Neale, M. C., Myers, J. M., Prescott, C. A., & Kendler, K. S. (2006). A population-based twin study of the relationship between neuroticism and internalizing disorders. *American Journal of Psychiatry, 163*, 857–864.

Hettema, J. M., Prescott, C. A., Myers, J. M., Neale, M. C., & Kendler, K. S. (2005). The structure of genetic and environmental risk factors for anxiety disorders in men and women. *Archives of General Psychiatry, 62*, 182–189.

Hoffart, A., Hackmann, A., & Sexton, H. (2006). Interpersonal fears among patients with panic disorder with agoraphobia.` *Behavioural and Cognitive Psychotherapy, 34*, 359–363.

Horesh, N., Amir, M., Kedem, P., Goldberger, Y., & Kotler, M. (1997). Life events in childhood, adolescence, and adulthood, and the relationship to panic disorder. *Acta Psychiatrica Scandinavica, 96*, 373–378.

Horowitz, L. M. (2004). Difficulty regulating impulses, thoughts, and behavior: Obsessive-compulsive and eating disorders. In L. M. Horowitz, *Interpersonal foundations of psychopathology* (pp. 169–186). Washington, DC: American Psychological Association.

Huppert, J. D., Simpson, H. B., Nissenson, K. J., Liebowitz, M. R., & Foa, E. B. (2009). Quality of life and functional impairment in obsessive-compulsive disorder: A comparison of patients with and without comorbidity, patients in remission, and healthy controls. *Depression and Anxiety, 26*, 39–45.

Hymel, S., Rubin, K. H., Rowden, L., & LeMare, L. (1990). Children's peer relationships: Longitudinal prediction of internalizing and externalizing problems from middle to late childhood. *Child Development, 61*, 2004–2021.

Inderbitzen, H. M., Walters, K. S., & Bukowski, A. L. (1997). The role of social anxiety in adolescent peer relations: Differences among sociometric status groups and rejected subgroups. *Journal of Clinical Child Psychology, 26*, 338–348.

Jansson, L., Ost, L.-G., & Jerremalm, A. (1987). Prognostic factors in the behavioral treatment of agoraphobia. *Behavioural Psychotherapy, 15*, 31–44.

Joormann, J., & Gotlib, I. H. (2006). Is this happiness I see? Biases in the identification of emotional facial expressions in depression and social phobia. *Journal of Abnormal Psychology, 115*, 705–714.

Jordan, B. K., Marmar, C. R., Fairbank, J. A., Schlenger, W. E., Kulka, R. A., Hough, R. L., & Weiss, D. S. (1992). Problems in families of male Vietnam veterans with post–traumatic stress disorder. *Journal of Consulting and Clinical Psychology, 60,* 916–926.

Joseph, S., Andrews, B., Williams, R., & Yule, W. (1992). Crisis support and psychiatric symptomatology in adult survivors of the Jupiter cruise ship disaster. *British Journal of Clinical Psychology, 31,* 63–73.

Kagan, J., Reznick, J. S., Snidman, N., Gibbons, J., & Johnson, M. O. (1988). Childhood derivatives of inhibition and lack of inhibition to the unfamiliar. *Child Development, 59,* 1580–1589.

Kashdan, T. B., Julian, T., Merritt, K., & Uswatte, G. (2006). Social anxiety and posttraumatic stress in combat veterans: Relations to well-being and character strengths. *Behaviour Research and Therapy, 44,* 561–583.

Kessler, H., Roth, J., von Wietersheim, J., Deighton, R. M., & Traue, H. C. (2007). Emotion recognition patterns in patients with panic disorder. *Depression and Anxiety, 24,* 223–226.

Kessler, R. C., Berglund, P., Demler, O., Jin, R., Merikangas, K. R., & Walters, E. E. (2005). Lifetime prevalence and age-of-onset distributions of DSM-IV disorders in the national comorbidity survey replication. *Archives of General Psychiatry, 62,* 593–602.

Kessler, R. C., Chiu, W. T., Jin, R., Ruscio, A. M., Shear, K., & Walters, E. E. (2006). The epidemiology of panic attacks, panic disorder, and agoraphobia in the national comorbidity survey replication. *Archives of General Psychiatry, 63,* 415–424.

Kessler, R. C., Sonnega, A., Bromet, E., Hughes, M., & Nelson, C. B. (1995). Posttraumatic stress disorder in the National Comorbidity Survey. *Archives of General Psychiatry, 52,* 1048–1060.

Kessler, R. C., Walters, E. E., & Forthofer, M. S. (1998). The social consequences of psychiatric disorders: III. Probability of marital stability. *American Journal of Psychiatry, 155,* 1092–1096.

King, L. A., King, D. W., Fairbank, J. A., Keane, T. M., & Adams, G. A. (1998). Resilience-recovery factors in post–traumatic stress disorder among female and male Vietnam veterans: Hardiness, postwar social support, and additional stressful life events. *Journal of Personality and Social Psychology, 74,* 420–434

King, D. W., King, L. A., Gudanowski, D. M., & Vreven, D. L. (1995). Alternative representations of war zone stressors: Relationships to posttraumatic stress disorder in male and female Vietnam veterans. *Journal of Abnormal Psychology, 104,* 184–195.

Kleiner, L., & Marshall, W. L. (1987). The role of interpersonal problems in the development of agoraphobia with panic attacks. *Journal of Anxiety Disorders, 1,* 313–323.

Kleiner, L., Marshall, W. L., & Spevack, M. (1987). Training in problem-solving and exposure treatment for agoraphobics with panic attacks. *Journal of Anxiety Disorders, 1,* 219–238.

Koran, L. M., Thienemann, M. L., & Davenport, R. (1996). Quality of life for patients with obsessive-compulsive disorder. *American Journal of Psychiatry, 153,* 783–788.

Ladouceur, R., Freeston, J. H., Fournier, S., Dugas, M. J., & Doucet, C. (2002). The social basis of worry in three samples: high school students, university students, and older adults. *Behavioural and Cognitive Psychotherapy, 30,* 427–438.

La Greca, A. M., & Lopez, N. (1998). Social anxiety among adolescents: Linkages with peer relations and friendships. *Journal of Abnormal Child Psychology, 26,* 83–94.

Lange, A., & van Dyck, R. (1992). The function of agoraphobia in the marital relationship. *Acta Psychiatrica Scandinavia, 85,* 89–93.

Leary, M. R. (2007). Motivational and emotional aspects of the self. *Annual Review of Psychology, 58,* 317–344.

Lee, D., & Young, K. (2001). Post–traumatic stress disorder: Diagnostic issues and epidemiology in adult survivors of traumatic events. *International Review of Psychiatry, 13,* 150–158.

Letourneau, E. J., Resnick, H. S., Kilpatrick, D. G., Saunders, B. E., & Best, C. L. (1996). Comorbidity of sexual problems and posttraumatic stress disorder in female crime victims. *Behavior Therapy, 27,* 321–336.

Lundh, L. G., & Öst, L. G. (1996). Recognition bias for critical faces in social phobics. *Behavioural Research and Therapy, 34,* 787–794.

Magliano, L., Posini, P., Guarneri, M., Marasco, C., & Catapano, F. (1996). Burden on the families of patients with obsessive-compulsive disorder: A pilot study. *European Psychiatry, 11,* 192–197.

Mancuso, D. M., Townsend, M. H., & Mercante, D. E. (1993). Long-term follow-up of generalized anxiety disorder. *Comprehensive Psychiatry, 34,* 441–446.

Masellis, M., Rector, N. A., & Richter, M. A. (2003). Quality of life in OCD: Differential impact of obsessions, compulsions, and depression comorbidity. *Canadian Journal of Psychiatry, 48,* 72–77.

Marcaurelle, R., Bélanger, C., & Marchand, A. (2003). Marital relationships and the treatment of panic disorder with agoraphobia: A critical review. *Clinical Psychology Review, 23,* 247–276.

Marcaurelle, R., Bélanger, C., Marchand, A., Katerelos, T. E., & Mainguy, N. (2005). Marital predictors of symptom severity in panic disorder with agoraphobia. *Journal of Anxiety Disorders, 19,* 211–232.

Mehta, M. (1990). A comparative study of family-based and patient-based behavioural management in obsessive-compulsive disorder. *British Journal of Psychiatry, 157,* 133–135.

Meleshko, K. A., & Alden, L. E. (1993). Anxiety and self-disclosure: Toward a motivational model. *Journal of Personality and Social Psychology, 64,* 1000–1009

Mendlowicz, M. V., & Stein, M. B. (2000). Quality of life in individuals with anxiety disorders. *American Journal of Psychiatry, 157,* 669–682.

Mennin, D. A., Heimberg, R. G., Turk, C. L., & Fresco, D. M. (2005). Preliminary evidence for an emotion dysregulation model of generalized anxiety disorder. *Behaviour Research and Therapy, 43,* 1281–1310.

Merkel, W. T., Pollard, C. A., Wiener, R. L., & Staebler, C. R. (1993). Perceived parental characteristics of patients with obsessive compulsive disorder, depression, and panic disorder. *Child Psychiatry and Human Development, 24,* 49–57.

Middeldorp, C. M., Cath, D. C., Van Dyck, R., & Boomsma, D. I. (2005). The comorbidity of anxiety and depression in the perspective of genetic epidemiology: A review of twin and family studies. *Psychological Medicine, 35,* 611–624.

Mogg, K., Millar, N., & Bradley, B. P. (2000). Biases in eye movements to threatening facial expression in generalized anxiety disorder and depressive disorder. *Journal of Abnormal Psychology, 109,* 695–704.

Monteiro, W., Marks, I. M., & Ramm, E. (1985). Marital adjustment and treatment outcome in agoraphobia. *British Journal of Psychiatry, 146,* 383–390.

Newth, S., & Rachman, S. (2001). The concealment of obsessions. *Behaviour Research and Therapy, 39,* 457–464.

Olatunji, B. O., Cisler, J. M., & Tolin, D. F. (2007). Quality of life in the anxiety disorders: A meta-analytic review. *Clinical Psychology Review, 27,* 572–581.

Orsillo, S. M., Heimberg, R. G., Juster, H. R., & Garrett, J. (1996). Social phobia and PTSD in Vietnam veterans. *Journal of Traumatic Stress, 9,* 235–252.

Ozer, E. J., Best, S. R., Lipsey, T. L., & Weiss, D. S. (2003). Predictors of posttraumatic stress disorder and symptoms in adults: A meta-analysis. *Psychological Bulletin, 129,* 52–73.

Pruzinski, T., & Borkovec, T. D. (1990). Cognitive and personality characteristics of worriers. *Behaviour Research and Therapy, 28,* 507–512.

Rapee, R. M., & Heimberg, R. G. (1997). A cognitive-behavioral model of anxiety in social phobia. *Behaviour Research and Therapy, 35,* 741–756.

Rapee, R. M., Litwin, E. M., & Barlow, D. H. (1990). Impact of life events on subjects with panic disorder and on comparison subjects. *American Journal of Psychiatry, 147,* 640–644.

Rapee, R. M., & Spence, S. H. (2004). The etiology of social phobia: Empirical evidence and an initial model. *Clinical Psychology Review, 24,* 737–767.

Reis, H. T., & Shaver, P. (1988). Intimacy as an interpersonal process. In S. Duck, D. F. Hay, S. E. Hobfoll, W. Ickes, & B. M. Montgomery (Eds.), *Handbook of personal relationships: Theory, research, and interventions* (pp. 367–389). Oxford, UK: John Wiley & Sons.

Riggs, D. S., Byrne, C. A., Weathers, F. W., & Litz, B. T. (1998). The quality of the intimate relationships of male Vietnam veterans: Problems associated with posttraumatic stress disorder. *Journal of Traumatic Stress, 11,* 87–101.

Riggs, D. S., Hiss, H., & Foa, E. B. (1992). Marital distress and the treatment of obsessive compulsive disorder. *Behavior Therapy, 23,* 585–597.

Roemer, L., Molina, S., & Borkovec, T. D. (1997). An investigation of worry content among generally anxious individuals. *Journal of Nervous and Mental Disease, 185,* 314–319.

Roy-Byrne, P. P., Geraci, M., & Uhde, T. W. (1987). Life events and the onset of panic disorder. *American Journal of Psychiatry, 143,* 1424–1427.

Rubin, K. H., Burgess, K. B., & Hastings, P. D. (2002). Stability and social-behavioral consequences of toddlers' inhibited temperament and parenting behavior. *Child Development, 73,* 483–495.

Rubin, K. H., Nelson, L. J., Hastings, P., & Asendorpf, J. B. (1999). Transaction between parents' perceptions of their children's shyness and their parenting styles. *International Journal of Behavioral Development, 23,* 937–957.

Rubin, K. H., Wojslawowicz, J., Burgess, K., Rose-Krasnor, L., & Booth-LaForce, C. (2006). The friendships of socially withdrawn and competent young adolescents. *Journal of Abnormal Child Psychology, 34,* 139–153.

Ruggiero, K. J., Smith, D. W., Hanson, R. F., Resnick, H. S., Saunders, B. E., & Kilpatrick, D. G. (2004). Is disclosure of childhood rape associated with mental health outcome? Results from the national women's study. *Child Maltreatment, 9,* 62–77.

Sanderson, W. C., DiNardo, P. A., Rapee, R. M., & Barlow, D. H. (1990). Syndrome comorbidity in patients diagnosed with a DSM-III-R anxiety disorder. *Journal of Abnormal Psychology, 99,* 308–312.

Saul, H. (2004). *Phobias: Fighting the fear.* New York: Arcade.

Schneider, S., Unnewehr, S., Florin, I., & Margraf, J. (2002). Priming panic interpretations in children of patients with panic disorder. *Journal of Anxiety Disorders, 16,* 605–624.

Schumm, J. A., Briggs-Phillips, M., & Hobfoll, S. E. (2006). Cumulative interpersonal traumas and social support as risk and resiliency factors in predicting PTSD and depression among inner-city women. *Journal of Traumatic Stress, 19,* 825–836.

Silove, D., Parker, G., Hadzi Pavlovic, D., Manicavasagar, V., & Blaszcznski, A. (1991). Parental representations of patients with panic disorder and generalized anxiety disorder. *British Journal of Psychiatry, 159,* 835–841.

Solomon, Z., Dekel, R., & Zerach, G. (2008). The relationships between posttraumatic stress symptom clusters and marital intimacy among war veterans. *Journal of Family Psychology, 22,* 659–666.

South, S. C., & Krueger, R. F. (2008). Marital quality moderates genetic and environmental influences on the internalizing spectrum. *Journal of Abnormal Psychology, 117,* 826–837.

Spence, S. H., Donovan, C., & Brechman–Toussaint, M. (1999). Social skills, social outcomes, and cognitive features of childhood social phobia. *Journal of Abnormal Psychology, 108,* 211–221.

Stein, M. B., & Heimberg, R. G. (2004). Well-being and life satisfaction in generalized anxiety disorder: Comparison to major depressive disorder in a community sample. *Journal of Affective Disorders, 79,* 161–166.

Steketee, G., Lam, J. N., Chambless, D. L., Rodebaugh, T. L., & McCollouch, C. E. (2006). Effects of perceived criticism on anxiety and depression during behavioral treatment of anxiety disorders. *Behaviour Research and Therapy, 45,* 11–19.

Steketee, G., & Pruyn, N. (1998). Family functioning in OCD. In R. P. Swinson, M. M. Antony, S. Rachman, & M. A. Richter (Eds.), *Obsessive compulsive disorder: Theory, research and treatment.* New York: Guilford Press.

Steketee, G., & Shapiro, L. J. (1995). Predicting behavioral treatment outcome for agoraphobia and obsessive compulsive disorder. *Clinical Psychology Review, 15,* 317–346.

Steketee, G., & van Noppen, B. (2003). Family approaches to treatment for obsessive compulsive disorder. *Journal of Family Psychotherapy, 25,* 43–50.

Stengler-Wenzke, K., Kroll, M., Matschinger, H., & Angermeyer, M. C. (2006). Subjective quality of life of patients with obsessive-compulsive disorder. *Social Psychiatry and Psychiatric Epidemiology, 41,* 662–668.

Stewart, S. E., Beresin, C., Haddad, S., Stack, D. E., Fama, J., & Jenike, M. (2008). Predictors of family accommodation in obsessive-compulsive disorder. *Annals of Clinical Psychiatry, 20,* 65–70.

Tarrier, N., Sommerfield, C., & Pilgrim, H. (1999). Relatives' expressed emotion (EE) and PTSD treatment outcome. *Psychological Medicine, 29,* 801–811.

Taube-Schiff, M., Suvak, M. K., Antony, M. M., Bieling, P. J., & McCabe, R. E. (2007). Group cohesion in cognitive-behavioral group therapy for social phobia. *Behaviour Research and Therapy, 45,* 687–698.

Taylor, C. T., & Alden, L. E., (2005). Social developmental experiences and social interpretation in generalized social phobia. *Behaviour Research and Therapy, 43,* 6, 759–777.

Taylor, S., Fedoroff, I. C., Koch, W. J., Thordarson, D. S., Fecteau, G., & Nicki, R. M. (2001). Post-traumatic stress disorder arising after road traffic collisions: Patterns of response to cognitive-behavior therapy. *Journal of Consulting and Clinical Psychology, 69*, 541–551.

Thornicroft, G., Colson, L., & Marks, I. M. (1991). An inpatient behavioural psychotherapy unit description and audit. *British Journal of Psychiatry, 158*, 362–367.

Turgeon, L., O'Connor, K. P., Marchand, A., & Freeston, M. H. (2002). Recollections of parent-child relationships in patients with obsessive-compulsive disorder and panic disorder with agoraphobia. *Acta Psychiatrica Scandinavica, 105*, 310–316.

Ullman, S. E., & Filipas, H. H. (2001). Predictors of PTSD symptom severity and social reactions in sexual assault victims. *Journal of Traumatic Stress, 14*, 369–389.

van Minnen, A., Arntz, A., & Keijsers, G. P. J. (2002). Prolonged exposure in patients with chronic PTSD: Predictors of treatment outcome and dropout. *Behaviour Research and Therapy, 40*, 439–457.

van Noppen, B., Steketee, G., McCorkle, B. H., & Pato, M. (1997). Group and multifamily behavioral treatment for obsessive compulsive disorder: A pilot study. *Journal of Anxiety Disorders, 11*, 431–446.

Veljaca, K. A., & Rapee, R. M. (1998). Detection of negative and positive audience behaviours by socially anxious subjects. *Behaviour Research and Therapy, 36*, 311–321.

Vöncken, M., Alden, L. E., Bögels, S. M., & Röelefs, J. (2008). Social rejection in social anxiety disorder: The role of performance deficits. *British Journal of Clinical Psychology, 47*, 439–450.

Wallace, S. T., & Alden, L. E. (1997). Social phobia and positive social events: The price of success. *Journal of Abnormal Psychology, 106*, 1–10.

Wenzel, A. (2002). Characteristics of close relationships in individuals with social phobia; A preliminary comparison with nonanxious individuals. In J. H. Harvey & A. Wenzel (Eds.). *Maintaining and enhancing close relationships: A clinician's guide.* (pp. 199–213). Mahwah, NJ: Erlbaum.

Wenzel, A., Graff-Dolezal, J., Macho, M., & Brendle, J. R. (2005). Communication and social skills in socially anxious and nonanxious individuals in the context of romantic relationships. *Behaviour Research and Therapy, 43*, 505–519.

Whisman, M. A. (2007). Marital distress and DSM-IV psychiatric disorders in a population-based national survey. *Journal of Abnormal Psychology, 116*, 638–643.

Whisman, M. A., Sheldon, C. T., & Goering, P. (2000). Psychiatric disorder and dissatisfaction with social relationships: Does type of relationship matter? *Journal of Abnormal Psychology, 108*, 803–808.

Winton, E. C., Clark, D., & Edelmann, R. J. (1995). Social anxiety, fear of negative evaluation, and the detection of negative emotion in others. *Behaviour Research and Therapy, 33*, 193–196.

WHO World Mental Health Survey consortium (2004). Prevalence, severity, and unmet need for treatment of mental disorders in the World Health Organization World Mental Health Surveys. *Journal of the American Medical Association, 291*, 2581–2590.

Yoon, K. L., & Zinbarg, R. E. (2007). Generalized anxiety disorder and entry into marriage or a marriage-like relationship. *Journal of Anxiety Disorders, 21*, 955–965.

Yoshida, T., Taga, C., Matsumoto, Y., & Fukui, K. (2005). Parental overprotection in obsessive-compulsive disorder and depression with obsessive traits. *Psychiatry and Clinical Neurosciences, 59*, 533–538.

Zayfert, C., DeViva, J. C., & Hofmann, S. G. (2005). Comorbid PTSD and social phobia in a treatment seeking population: An exploratory study. *The Journal of Nervous and Mental Disease, 193*, 93–101.

Zoellner, L. A., Foa, E. B., & Brigidi, B. D. (1999). Interpersonal friction and PTSD in female victims of sexual and nonsexual assault. *Journal of Traumatic Stress, 12*, 689–700.

27 AN INTERPERSONAL PERSPECTIVE ON RISK FOR CORONARY HEART DISEASE

Timothy W. Smith

Jenny M. Cundiff

Negative emotions, interpersonal conflict, social isolation and other psychosocial influences on physical health and illness are increasingly well documented, especially in the case of coronary heart disease (CHD) (Everson-Rose & Lewis, 2005; Smith & Ruiz, 2002; Williams, 2008). The ultimate goal of such research is threefold: to assemble a comprehensive set of robust psychological and social risk factors for CHD, to explicate the mechanisms linking these risk factors to the development and course of CHD, and ultimately to translate those research findings into effective risk-reducing interventions.

Despite major advances, several challenges complicate further progress toward these goals. Most research has examined risk factors individually, leading to a lengthy but piecemeal list of psychosocial influences on CHD. Further, such lists typically separate risk factors presumed to reflect characteristics of individuals (i.e., personality traits, negative emotions) from those presumed to reflect the social environment (e.g., quality of personal relationships, job stress), again potentially obscuring a more integrated

view. Measures of these risk factors are often used with little attention to their construct validity, especially explorations of the similarities and differences among these scales, possibly masking general dimensions of risk. Finally, robust associations between risk factors and CHD helps identify individuals who might benefit from preventive interventions, but optimal design and implementation of those interventions require better understanding of the processes through which these risk factors influence disease.

Previously, we have discussed the ways in which the interpersonal perspective in personality and clinical psychology (e.g., Horowitz, 2004; Horowitz et al., 2006; Kiesler, 1996; Pincus & Ansell, 2003) can address these challenges (Gallo & Smith, 1999; Smith, Gallo, & Ruiz, 2003; Smith, Glazer, Ruiz, & Gallo, 2004; Smith, Traupman, Uchino, & Berg, in press). Concepts, methods, and research findings in this tradition can facilitate efforts to synthesize, extend, and apply the current understanding of these risk factors. In this chapter, we present an overview of an emerging *interpersonal psychosomatics* of CHD.

AN OVERVIEW OF CORONARY HEART DISEASE

Coronary heart disease (CHD) comprises three clinical endpoints: myocardial infarction (MI) or "heart attack;" angina pectoris (AP), or chest pain of cardiac origin; and sudden cardiac death (SCD). The cause of each condition is coronary atherosclerosis or coronary artery disease (CAD), the progressive build-up of lesions within the wall of arteries that carry blood to the heart muscle (i.e., myocardium). CAD is often accompanied by similar lesions elsewhere (e.g., major arteries in the neck and lower body), indicating a systemic disease process. It begins as microscopic injuries to the endothelium or inner lining of artery walls and the development of fatty streaks, which have been observed in late childhood and adolescence. In addition to cholesterol deposits, the lesions include inflammatory processes, contributing further to their size and instability. Later, lesions encroach on the interior opening of the artery, reducing blood flow and limiting the heart's available oxygen supply. CAD typically progresses silently until midlife or later, when clinical indications of CHD appear. These lesions can rupture, causing a thrombus (i.e., blood clot) to form and break loose under the force of blood flow, a common cause of MI. SCD results from a catastrophic disturbance in the rhythm of the heart (i.e., ventricular fibrillation), which is more easily evoked during episodes of myocardial ischemia that are common with more severe underlying CAD.

The pathophysiology and time-course of CHD are the source of key considerations for psychosocial research and related interventions (Smith & Ruiz, 2002). Associations between risk factors and CHD (e.g., MI, death from CHD) among previously healthy people could reflect effects at several phases in the decades-long development and course of the disease, including the initial development of CAD, the progression of this asymptomatic condition, and the later emergence of clinically apparent disease. Risk factors that predict the course of clinically apparent CHD are potentially important intervention targets in the management of these patients. Risk factors that predict the initial development of CHD may be targets for earlier prevention efforts.

PSYCHOSOCIAL RISK FACTORS

Many personality traits, negative affective characteristics, and aspects of the social environment have been linked to CHD. In what follows, we review those with the most substantial evidence of robust associations with objective indicators of CHD (i.e., MI, cardiac death), because chest pain resembling angina frequently is unrelated to CHD.

The Legacy of the Type A Behavior Pattern: Hostility and Dominance

In their seminal work, Friedman and Rosenman (1959) described the Type A Behavior Pattern (TABP) as comprising impatience, time urgency, easily evoked hostility, competitiveness, excessive job involvement and achievement striving, and a distinct vocal style involving loud, rapid, and emphatic speech, and the tendency to "talk over" others. Inconsistent results of epidemiologic studies prompted examinations of the components of the TABP, which identified hostility as the most "toxic" element (Hecker, Chesney, Black, & Frautchi, 1988; Matthews et al., 1977). A quantitative review of over 40 prospective studies indicates that hostility and related constructs (i.e., trait anger) have significant associations with both the initial development and course of CHD (Chida & Steptoe, 2009).

However, hostility is not the only toxic element of the TABP. Verbal competitiveness evident during interview assessments of the TABP (i.e., short response latencies, interrupting and "talking over" the interviewer) also predicts CHD (Houston, Chesney, Black, Cates, & Hecker, 1992) and all-cause mortality (Houston, Babyak, Chesney, Black, & Ragland, 1997). This vocal style reflects dominant or controlling social behavior. Other measures of trait dominance also predict CHD (Siegman et al., 2000; Whiteman, Deary, Lee, & Fowkes, 1997) and the severity of CAD (Smith et al., 2008). Interestingly, social dominance in male cynomolgus macaques predicts the development of CAD in response to chronic social challenge (Kaplan, Chen, & Manuck, 2009). Hence, both hostility and social dominance appear to be CHD risk factors.

Depression, Anxiety, Pessimism, and Hopelessness

Symptoms of depression and related mood disorders also are reliably related to CHD. A quantitative review of 54 studies found significant effects for both the initial development of CHD and prognosis (e.g., recurrent coronary events, survival) among patients with established CHD (Nicholson, Kuper, & Hemingway, 2006). A smaller literature suggests that symptoms of anxiety and anxiety disorders similarly predict the development and course of CAD (Roy-Byrne et al., 2008). Both anxiety and depression have been linked to the development of CAD in otherwise healthy persons, as well (e.g., Smith et al., 2008).

Suls and Bunde (2005) suggested that, when combined with the previously described effects of anger, associations of depressive symptoms and anxiety and CHD implicate the broader trait of negative affectivity (Watson & Clark, 1984) or neuroticism (Costa & McCrae, 1992). Related research suggests that associations of anxiety, depression, and anger with CAD and CHD may indeed be overlapping, and the broader trait of negative affectivity predicts these cardiovascular outcomes, as well (e.g., Boyle, Michalek, & Suarez, 2006; Kubzansky, Cole, Kawachi, Volonas, & Sparrow, 2006; Smith et al., 2008). Individual differences in negative cognitive characteristics such as pessimism (i.e., low optimism) and hopelessness also predict the development and course of CHD and atherosclerosis (Scheier et al., 1999;

Tindle et al., 2009; Whipple et al., 2009), independently of other negative affective traits.

Social Support, Isolation, and Interpersonal Conflict

Social isolation (i.e., reports of few relationships) and low levels of social support are associated with more severe CAD, the initial development of CHD, and adverse medical outcomes (e.g., death, recurrent coronary events) among patients with established CHD (Lett et al., 2005; Uchino, 2004). Experimentally manipulated social isolation in animal models also accelerates development of atherosclerosis (McCabe et al., 2002). Conflict and disruption in close relationships (e.g., marital strain, separation, divorce) are associated with atherosclerosis (Gallo, Smith, & Kircher, 2003), initial occurrence of CHD (De Vogli, Chandola, & Marmot, 2007; Matthews and Gump, 2002), and adverse course of established CHD (Orth-Gomer et al., 2000). Hence, low levels of positive aspects of personal relationships, and high levels of aversive aspects, are associated with increased CHD risk across the various phases of disease development.

Job Stress and Socioeconomic Status

A large body of research indicates that low socioeconomic status is associated with increased risk of atherosclerosis, initial development of CHD, and an adverse course of established CHD (Everson-Rose & Lewis, 2005; Williams, 2008). These effects remain when potential confounding factors such as access to health care are controlled, and are reduced but not eliminated when behavioral risk factors (e.g., smoking, diet, physical activity levels) are controlled, perhaps indicating that the psychosocial risk factors described above could be an additional mechanism linking low SES and CHD (Gallo & Matthews, 2003). Several conceptual models of job stress have been studied as CHD risk factors, although the strongest evidence implicates high levels of perceived job demands as a robust predictor (Eller et al., 2009).

Conclusions Regarding Risk Factors

There is substantial evidence that various aspects of personality and social circumstances are associated with increased risk for the initial development of CHD, and a poor prognosis for patients with established CHD. Negative aspects of emotion and personality (e.g., anger, hostility, dominance, anxiety, depression, hopelessness) increase risk, whereas positive aspects (e.g., optimism) reduce it. Similarly, negative aspects of social circumstances (e.g., isolation, conflict, relationship disruption, high job demands, low SES) increase risk, whereas positive social circumstances (e.g., high perceived social support) reduce it. The extent to which these various psychosocial risk factors describe a smaller number of more basic risk processes remains unclear.

MECHANISMS UNDERLYING PSYCHOSOCIAL RISK

Explication of mechanisms linking psychosocial risk factors and CHD not only addresses age-old questions regarding the influence of psychological processes on physical health, but also informs the design of risk reducing interventions. Several behavioral risk factors (e.g., smoking, physical inactivity, diet, etc.) are consistently associated with the psychosocial risk factors described above, making them plausible mechanisms. However, associations of the psychosocial risk factors and CHD development and course typically remain even when such health behaviors are controlled. Hence, at best these behavioral mechanisms provide only a partial explanation of the effects of psychosocial variables on CHD (Smith & Ruiz, 2002; Williams, 2008).

The psychophysiology of stress plays a central role in current theory and research on these mechanisms. Traditionally, these efforts have focused on the magnitude of physiological reactivity to stressors, predicting that psychosocial risk factors are associated with larger increases in heart rate and blood pressure (i.e., cardiovascular reactivity; CVR) and neuroendocrine responses (e.g., catecholamines, cortisol). These responses, in turn, are hypothesized to hasten the development of atherosclerosis, and to precipitate clinical manifestations of CHD among persons with advanced CAD (Schwartz et al., 2003). More recently, stress-related increases in inflammatory processes have been examined as an additional physiological link between psychosocial risk factors and CHD (Miller, Chen, & Cole, 2009). Importantly, the psychosocial risk factors described above are related to these cardiovascular, neuroendocrine, and inflammatory responses to stress (Miller et al., 2009; Segerstrom & Smith, 2006; Smith et al., 2009; Uchino, 2006).

Models in which psychophysiological responses to stress link psychosocial risk factors with health outcomes have been expanded beyond the focus on stress *reactivity* to include stress *exposure, recovery,* and *restoration* (Uchino, Smith, Holt-Lunstead, Campo, & Reblin, 2007; Williams et al., in press). Some psychosocial risk factors (e.g., hostility, depression) are associated with increased exposure to unhealthy life circumstances that are themselves well-established CHD risk factors, especially interpersonal conflict and reduced social support (Hammen, 2006; Smith et al., 2004). Psychosocial risk factors have also been linked to delayed physiological recovery or prolonged activation following stressful experiences (Brosschot, Gerin, & Thayer, 2006; Chida & Hamer, 2008). Finally, these risk factors can interfere with restorative processes following stressful episodes, primarily in the form of reductions in the quantity and quality of sleep, and less recovery of stress-related physiological processes during sleep (Williams et al., in press). Sleep duration and quality, in turn, are related to the risk of CHD (e.g., Shankar, Koh, Yuan, Lee, & Yu, 2009).

Overall, the magnitude, duration, and frequency of cardiovascular, neuroendocrine, and inflammatory components of the physiological stress response, as well as the level of restoration of these processes, are seen as aspects of a multi-faceted mechanism linking psychosocial risk factors to the development and course of CAD and CHD. There are few meditational studies establishing these links in a definitive manner (Segerstrom & Smith, 2006), but a variety of forms of converging evidence is available.

APPLICATIONS OF THE INTERPERSONAL PERSPECTIVE

Concepts and methods in the interpersonal tradition can facilitate progress in research on psychosocial risk factors for CHD, and facilitate its application in efforts to reduce that risk. In what follows here, we review some of these applications, but interested readers can consult other references for more detailed discussions (e.g., Smith et al., 2003; Smith et al., 2004; Smith, Traupman, Uchino, & Berg, 2010; Smith & Traupman, in press).

Conceptualization and Measurement of Psychosocial Risk Factors

As noted above, psychosocial risk factors are most commonly studied individually, and the measures used are often not examined in terms of their potential overlap. Further, personality risk factors (e.g., hostility) and social-environmental risk factors (e.g., social isolation) are implicitly seen as qualitatively distinct types of influences on CHD. This creates a largely unintegrated literature, and could obscure the effects of more general dimensions or patterns of risk. The interpersonal circumplex (IPC) (see Figure 18.2) provides an integrative framework or nomological net (Gurtman, 1992) in this regard, as the dimensions of affiliation (i.e., warm, friendly versus cold, quarrelsome) and control (i.e., dominant, directive versus submissive, passive)

can be used to describe individual differences (i.e., personality traits), social behavior, and stable dimensions of interpersonal circumstances (e.g., relationship quality). Hence, the IPC can be used to identify similarities and differences among individual risk factors within a traditional class or category (e.g., personality traits), but also between such typically distinct categories. Motivational equivalents of the IPC dimensions provide an integrative view of broad related social motives (Horowitz et al., 2006; Wiggins & Trapnell, 1996); *communion* concerns connections with others (i.e., getting along), whereas *agency* concerns autonomy, achievement, power, and status (i.e., getting ahead). Importantly, well-developed methods are available for locating measures of psychosocial risk factors in the IPC conceptual space, using well-validated measures (Gurtman & Pincus, 2003). This approach has been used to compare and contrast various measures of anger and hostility (Gallo & Smith, 1998; Ruiz, Smith, & Rhodewalt, 2001) and social support (Trobst, 2000).

We recently extended this approach to identify the IPC locations of individual differences in anxiety, depression, and anger as measured by these facets of neuroticism in the NEO-PI-R (see Costa & McCrae, 1992; also, this volume), as well as aspects of anger and hostility as measured by the Buss-Perry Aggression Questionnaire (Buss & Perry, 1992), in a sample of 300 middle-aged and older married couples (Smith et al., 2010). We utilized self-report and spouse rating IPC octant scales, and affiliation and control dimension scales, developed from the NEO-PI-R (cf. Traupman et al., 2009). As depicted in Figure 27.1, scales measuring each of these psychosocial risk factors were associated with an unfriendly interpersonal style, ranging from hostile-submissiveness in the case of anxiety and depression to hostile-dominance in the case of verbal aggression. The results were highly similar when interpersonal style was rated through self-reports and spouse ratings, and hence the associations do not simply reflect the effects of common method variance. Importantly,

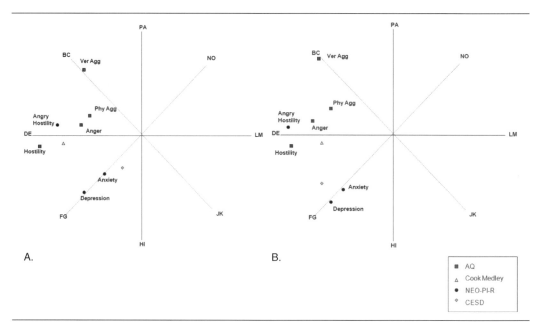

FIGURE 27.1   Plots of Associations of Personality Risk Factor Measures with Affiliation and Control in the IPC Panel A: Wives. Panel B: Husbands. (Radius of circumplex corresponds to multiple R = .5)
Source: From "Interpersonal Circumplex Descriptions of Psychosocial Risk Factors for Physical Illness: Application to Hostility, Neuroticism, and Marital Adjustment," by T. W. Smith, E. Traupman, B. N. Uchino, and C. A. Berg, 2010, *Journal of Personality*. Reprinted with permission.

even though in several cases (e.g., anxiety and depression scales) these measures included very little item content that was explicitly interpersonal in nature, the scales had at least moderately strong associations with the dimensions of the IPC, indicating that these affective traits were associated with a specific interpersonal style.

These couples also completed measures of self-reported marital satisfaction or adjustment, and the level of social support and conflict experienced with their spouse. We regressed these measures on ratings of the spouse's trait affiliation and control as measured by the NEO-PI-R IPC scales, as well as ratings of the spouse's affiliation and control evident in the specific context of marital interaction, using the Impact Message Inventory (IMI) (Schmidt, Wagner, & Kiesler, 1999). As depicted in Figure 27.2, participants who reported higher marital satisfaction and social support from their spouse rated their spouses as quite warm on the IPC measures. In contrast, participants

who reported high marital conflict rated the spouse as unfriendly and controlling. These measures of marital adjustment had similar associations with ratings *by* the spouse (Smith et al., 2010).

Taken together, these findings suggest that risk factors reflecting both personality and relationship quality are associated with a general pattern of interpersonal behavior; higher levels of risk are associated with a cold and unfriendly interpersonal style, when measured through both self-reports and ratings by significant others. Further, relationship qualities that are associated with greater CHD risk are associated with ratings of spouses as unfriendly and controlling, whereas relationship qualities that are associated with resilience are associated with ratings of spouses as warm. Most personality factors associated with higher risk are related to this cold and unfriendly interpersonal style, although they vary substantially along the control dimension from quite dominant to quite submissive. Hence,

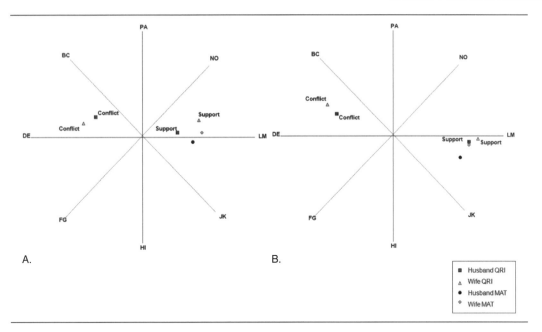

FIGURE 27.2   Plots of Associations of the Self-Report Marital Functioning Measures with Affiliation and Control in the IPC Ratings of Spouses
Panel A: NEO-IPC. Panel B: IMI–C. (Radius of circumplex corresponds to multiple R = 1.0)
Source: From "Interpersonal Circumplex Descriptions of Psychosocial Risk Factors for Physical Illness: Application to Hostility, Neuroticism, and Marital Adjustment," by T. W. Smith, E. Traupman, B. N. Uchino, and C. A. Berg, 2010, *Journal of Personality.* Reprinted with permission.

the IPC and related quantitative methods can identify common interpersonal patterns across a wide variety of risk factors.

The IPC has also been used directly in studies of CHD risk. For example, we utilized IPC-based measures of personality traits (i.e., interpersonal style) and marital interaction patterns as predictors of asymptomatic coronary atherosclerosis in 150 otherwise healthy older couples. Coronary atherosclerosis was assessed through CT scans of coronary artery calcification, a noninvasive assessment of the presence and extent of calcified "caps" in advanced coronary lesions. Spouse ratings of the participants' trait dominance and (low) trait affiliation were independent predictors of the extent of calcification (Smith et al., 2008). Interestingly, participants' self-reports of dominance and affiliation were much less closely related to the severity of coronary atherosclerosis.

These same couples participated in a video-taped discussion of an on-going marital interaction, later coded using the Structural Analysis of Social Behavior system (SASB) (Benjamin, Rothwieler, & Critchfield, 2006). We combined the SASB codes to form composite measures of each participant's affiliation and control during the six-minute interaction. For wives, low levels of affiliation during the disagreement discussion were significantly related to more severe atherosclerosis, such that women in couples where both they and their husbands displayed little warmth had particularly high levels of coronary calcification. The level of control couples displayed during the disagreement was unrelated to wives' coronary disease.

For husbands, a different pattern emerged. Couples' levels of affiliation during the interaction were unrelated to the severity of their calcification, but levels of control were significant predictors.

Specifically, dominant behavior displayed by the wives and the husbands themselves were associated with more severe atherosclerosis (Smith et al., under review). Hence, low levels of affiliative or communal behavior in the marital interaction was a risk factor for women, whereas high levels of controlling or agentic behavior was a risk factor for men. This pattern is consistent with a larger literature in which women are more concerned with communion in their social relations, whereas men are more concerned with agency (Helgeson, 2003). In general, our findings on personality traits and interactional behavior lend further support to the notion that the affiliation and control dimensions of the IPC are useful in describing psychosocial risk.

Understanding Correlated Risks

Although typically discussed separately, characteristics of personality and characteristics of the social environment studied as risk factors are typically correlated. For example, both hostility and depression are associated with increased levels of conflict and decreased levels of support in close relationships (Joiner & Coyne, 1999; Smith et al., 2004). Interpersonal theory provides a useful account of these aggregated risks. First, based on the principle of complementarity (Kiesler, 1983), the cold and unfriendly interpersonal style associated with most personality and emotional risk factors (e.g., anger, hostility, depression) would tend to, "pull, invite, or evoke restricted classes of responses from the other" (Pincus & Ansell, 2003, p.215) during social interactions. Specifically, this style would tend to invite or evoke similarly cold and unfriendly responses, likely promoting social isolation, higher conflict, and reduced social support. This suggests that a useful alternative to the usual single variable approach to studying psychosocial risk would entail the examination of co-occurring personality and social risks.

In a preliminary illustration of this approach (Gallo & Smith, 1999), two samples of undergraduates (total $n = 550$) completed multiple measures of hostility and social support, the Interpersonal Adjective Scales (IAS-R) as a measure of the IPC (Wiggins, Trapnell, & Phillips, 1988), and several other measures. Two independent cluster analyses of measures of hostility and social support identified three groups that were virtually identical across samples—an affiliative group reporting low hostility and high social support, a high hostility and high social support group, and a group reporting high hostility and low support. On the IPC measure, the affiliative group reported a warm and friendly interpersonal style, whereas the two hostile groups reported a considerably more cold and unfriendly style. The two hostile groups differed in that those who also reported low social support reported a more submissive style. Members of the latter group described their general social interactions as involving more negativity. They also described their interactions with parents during childhood as less warm, and they reported an anxious attachment style in their adult relationships, reflecting more insecurity. Hence, this third group represents a more severe and long-standing pattern of psychosocial risk.

An additional concept from the interpersonal perspective—the transactional cycle (Kiesler, 1996) depicted in Figure 27.3—provides a more detailed account of the processes underlying the aggregation of risk factors typically conceptualized as aspects of the person and those involving aspects of the social environment. Through recurring, reciprocally determined interactions between individuals and the social contexts they encounter, various patterns of low and high risk are maintained over time (Smith & Glazer, 2006). In this cycle, one person's *internal states* (e.g., goals, beliefs, expectations) lead the person to exhibit a particular style of *overt behavior* toward the interaction partner. The partner then *interprets* that initial actor's overt behavior (e.g., appraising the person's intentions and goals), but

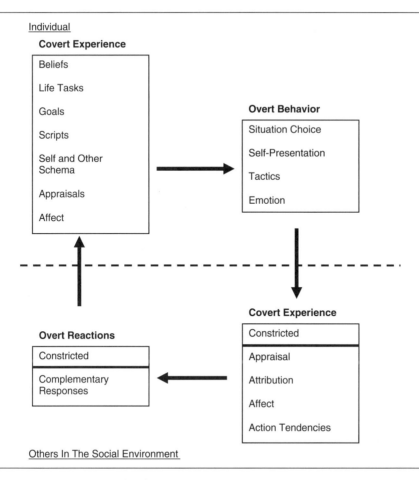

FIGURE 27.3   The Transactional Cycle (cf. Kiesler, 1996)

Individuals' covert experiences (e.g., goals, affect, beliefs) guide their overt behavior, in ways that tend to constrict the range of possible covert and overt reactions by their interaction partners.

Source: From "Patterns of Hostility and Social Support: Conceptualizing Psychosocial Risk Factors as Characteristics of the Person and the Environment," by L. C Gallo and T. W, Smith, 1999, *Journal of Research in Personality, 33,* 281–310. Reprinted with permission.

not all interpretations or appraisals are equally likely because the initial actor's overt behavior constricts or limits the range of the partner's plausible interpretations. For example, following a warm smile and friendly greeting by the initial actor, appraisals or attributions of hostile intent are much less likely.

The partner's interpretation then shapes the *partner's overt reactions* (behavior), and again not all overt reactions are equally likely, as the range has been constricted by the partner's prior (constricted) interpretations of the actor's initial behavior. That

overt reaction by the partner is then interpreted by the initial actor. Such cycles tend to promote behavior in the two participants that is similar along the affiliation axis of the IPC. That is, warmth invites and often evokes warmth in return, whereas hostility invites and often evokes hostility.

These dynamic and recurring interaction patterns may be a more accurate description of psychosocial risk than the conventional, largely static descriptions of personality and social environmental risk factors. These interpersonal processes are also relevant to other psychosocial risk factors. For example, low SES is associated with greater exposure to more hostility and less warmth during everyday social interactions, as well as to more dominance expressed by others (Gallo, Smith, & Cox, 2006). Low SES is also associated with greater risk of marital strain and disruption (Roberts, Kuncel, Shiner, Caspi, & Goldberg, 2007).

Explicating Mechanisms

The IPC and transactional cycle are also useful guides to research on the psychophysiological mechanisms believed to link psychosocial risk factors with CAD and CHD (Smith et al., 2003). The IPC can be used to describe the two central classes of stable influences on psychophysiological reactivity: individual differences in social behavior (i.e., personality traits) and aspects of the social environment (e.g., relationship quality, individual differences in perceived social support). It can also be used to describe momentary influences on reactivity in the form of the individual's own actions (e.g., expressing hostility, effortful attempts to exercise control over others) or the behavior of others (e.g., expressions of friendliness versus hostility). Variations in affiliation and control within these four classes of influences on physiological reactivity form the outlines of a comprehensive social psychophysiology of stress responses (Smith et al., 2003).

For example, trait hostility is generally associated with greater physiological responses to relevant social stressors (e.g., social conflict, harassment), whereas higher general levels of perceived social support are associated with less reactivity (Suls & Wan, 1993; Uchino, 2006). Experimentally manipulated efforts to exert influence over interaction partners (i.e., expressions of dominance) evoke heightened cardiovascular reactivity in the individual making such efforts, and sometimes in the interaction partner who is the target of such efforts, as well (Smith et al., 2003). In contrast, experimental manipulation of supportive behavior by interaction partners

generally attenuate such responses (Uchino, 2006).

Modeling the interpersonal processes that alter these psychophysiological processes entails complex laboratory manipulations of the social context (e.g., behavior of interaction partners). Here, too, the IPC can be quite useful, as the related well-validated measures (e.g., IMI, IAS-R) can be used to evaluate the psychological impact of these manipulations, and to evaluate the extent to which measured psychosocial risk factors are related to perceptions of, and behavioral responses to, those aspects of the social context (Gallo, Smith, & Kircher, 2000; Nealey-Moore, Smith, Uchino, Hawkins, & Olson-Cerny, 2007). For example, hostile persons sometimes appraise experimentally manipulated affiliative behavior of others as less warm and friendly than do more agreeable individuals (Smith et al., 2004), and they often respond to manipulations of conflict in close relationships with more hostile and controlling behavior (e.g., Smith & Gallo, 1999). These measured interpersonal processes can also be examined as mediators of the associations of manipulated aspects of the social context or measured psychosocial risk factors with physiological responses (Gallo et al., 2000). Hence, use of interpersonal measures in laboratory studies can help explicate associations between psychosocial risk factors and the psychophysiological mechanisms believed to link them with CHD.

The transactional cycle suggests an additional avenue for such research. From this perspective, associations of psychosocial risk factors with the *magnitude* of physiological reactivity provide an incomplete account of stress-related mechanisms, because the *frequency*, *duration*, and *severity* of episodes of reactivity will be influenced by transactional processes (cf., Smith, 1992; Smith et al., 2003). That is, personality risk factors such as hostility will be associated not only with heightened reactivity to social stressors such as interpersonal conflict, but also with increased exposure to such stressors. Through covert experiences (e.g., goals, appraisal, etc.) and overt behavior (e.g., situation choices, self-presentation, tactics) described in the transactional cycle (see Figure 27.4), hostile, chronically angry, or hostile-dominant persons are likely to evoke more frequent disagreeable behavior in interaction partners, thereby augmenting their heightened reactivity to such interaction with a greater frequency and severity of those stress exposures as additional determinants of an overall greater level of physiological activation. That is, hostile persons are at increased risk not only because they react to any given interpersonal stressor with larger physiological stress responses than those displayed by their more agreeable counterparts, but also because they create more frequent, severe, and prolonged social stressors in everyday life, through the transactional processes described previously. These combined effects of enhanced reactivity and exposure on overall physiological activation are depicted in Figure 27.4. For example, the hostile-dominant individual (top panel) displays greater reactivity than the friendly individual (bottom panel) when confronting the same laboratory stressor (e.g., a current events debate with an experimenter) and when confronting the same stressor in their everyday morning experience (e.g., heavy commuting traffic). Further, the hostile person displays overall greater blood pressure during a typical day because of a greater number, severity, and duration of stressors, due to the impact of their interpersonal behavior (e.g., pursuing versus ignoring differences of opinion with coworkers; choosing to argue with a spouse after work).

These transactional processes could also undermine the availability of stress-reducing socially supportive interactions, again raising overall activation levels. To evaluate combined effects of reactivity and exposure to beneficial and taxing social interactions on physiological activation, daily diary or experience sampling methods for assessing interpersonal events

(e.g., Moskowitz & Zuroff, 2005) can be combined with ambulatory physiological monitoring (e.g., blood pressure). Finally, these interpersonal processes can interfere with restorative mechanisms described above. For example, low marital quality and disruption of marriage (e.g., separation or divorce) are associated with poor sleep quality (Troxel, Buysse, Hall, Matthews, 2009; Troxel, Cyranowski, Hall, Frank, & Buysse, 2007).

Developmental Perspectives on Psychosocial Risk

The earliest signs of CAD have been observed in late childhood and adolescence, and individual differences in personality, emotional adjustment, and social relations that resemble psychosocial risk factors for CHD are apparent, as well. Further, childhood exposure to stressful social experiences is associated with increased risk of serious health difficulties during adulthood, including CHD (Miller et al., 2009). Thus, a developmental perspective on psychosocial risk could identify early intervention opportunities.

The concept of attachment is a cornerstone of the interpersonal perspective (Benjamin et al., 2006; Horowitz, 2004). Recurring patterns of early parent-child interactions (e.g., warm and responsive versus cold and neglectful parental behavior) contribute to the child's development of secure versus insecure attachment to parents. The quality of this attachment has far-reaching effects, as the internal representation of those early parent-child relationship patterns are an important determinant of emotional adjustment and the quality of future relationships (see Shaver & Mikulincer, Chapter 2 in this volume). From this perspective, individuals display continuities in the quality of important relationships across the lifespan, as early patterns shape later interpersonal experiences. These continuities can be conceptualized as adaptive or maladaptive interpersonal trajectories, comprising ongoing patterns of more or less adaptive

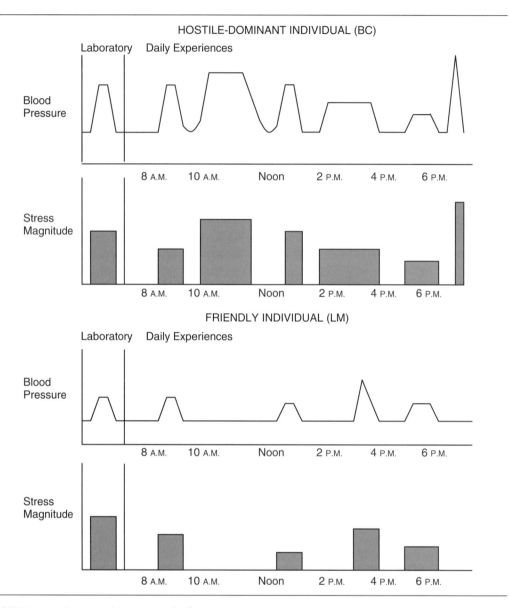

FIGURE 27.4   Conceptual Depiction of Effects of Individual Differences in Stress Reactivity and Exposure on Overall Levels of Blood Pressure

Observed during controlled laboratory conditions and during daily life for a hostile-dominant person (upper portion) and a friendly individual (lower portion). When experiencing the same stressor, the hostile dominant individual displays greater blood pressure increase than the friendly person. In everyday life, the hostile-dominant person also encounters more frequent, severe, and prolonged stressors as a result of the impact on others of their own interpersonal behavior.

transactional cycles recurring over time, as depicted in Figure 27.5.

In adaptive, health promoting trajectories, patterns of reciprocally determined transactions between the individual and important others (i.e., parents, siblings, peers) involve a preponderance of warmth. For example, positive internal representations of others promote warm and trusting overt behavior, which invites warmth from others in return. As these warm patterns develop early in life and continue over time, the individual's overall social context becomes progressively more favorable for health, as in the development of a robust network of supportive, low conflict relationships (upper portion of Figure 27.5). In contrast, in less adaptive or higher risk trajectories, transactional patterns involve greater levels of hostility and isolation and lower levels of warmth and support. In this latter pattern, negative internal representations of others, hostile expectations, and self-protective goals promote cold and antagonistic overt behavior, which invites hostility and isolation in return.

Beginning in childhood and continuing over time, these unhealthy trajectories (lower portion of Figure 27.5) lead to accumulating exposure to stress and reductions of stress-buffering psychosocial resources. These unhealthy transactional trajectories can also reflect hostile struggles involving contested dominance or recurring episodes of unwelcome or resentful submission to dominant others. Such patterns involve early exposure to stress, the development of increased psychosocial risk, and, as a result, likely increased levels of physiological activation. Thus, the social continuities at the heart of the interpersonal perspective may be a particularly informative way to conceptualize psychosocial risk factors over time and their cumulative effects on health.

Of course, recurring patterns of parent-child interaction could also reflect common genetic influences, as well as social learning. Further, early aversive experiences could alter the expression of genetic influences on emotions, self-regulation, social behavior, and physiological reactivity through epigenetic mechanisms (Miller et al., 2009).

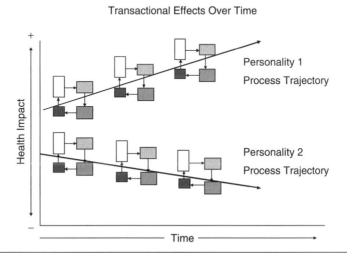

FIGURE 27.5 Conceptual Model of Developmental Trajectories Comprising Multiple, Ongoing Transactional Cycles

Individual transactional cycles depicted as four small linked boxes (see Figure 27.3), tend to maintain and magnify positive (i.e., high warmth) or negative (i.e., cold, quarrelsome, antagonistic) social interactions over time, creating low-risk, health enhancing trajectory in upper portion, or high-risk trajectory in lower portion, respectively.
Source: From Smith, Glazer, Ruiz, and Gallo, 2004. Reprinted with permission.

Even if genetic influences are important in these risk factors, an early social environment that includes low warmth, high hostility, and excessive or hostile control would likely maximize the emergence of a "high risk phenotype" which takes the form of an unhealthy transactional trajectory.

Interventions

A quantitative review of controlled intervention trials indicated that stress management and related psychosocial interventions can reduce recurrent coronary events (e.g., reinfarction, cardiac hospitalization, death) in patients with CHD (Linden, Phillips, & Leclerc, 2007). The interpersonal processes described here can guide such risk reduction efforts. IPC locations of coronary risk factors identify patterns of interpersonal behavior and experience that can be considered as general intervention targets, and the elements of the transactional cycle suggest more specific targets (e.g., covert experience, overt behavior, interactions with important others) and types of interventions (e.g., individual versus dyadic approaches). Many current interventions include such elements, but the IPC and transactional cycle can further inform their design and implementation.

The IPC analysis of psychosocial risk clearly identifies reduction of negative social interactions (e.g., hostility, conflict) and enhancement of positive interaction patterns (e.g., support) as important goals. These goals for the IPC affiliation axis are straightforward, but implications for the control axis are less clear, as both trait dominance and affective traits associated with submissive behavior (e.g., anxiety, depression) are associated with increased risk. Other interpersonal models may be useful in this regard. Specifically, in the SASB model (Benjamin et al., 2006; Chapter 20 in this volume), dominance and submissiveness are not opposite ends of a single continuum. Instead, the opposite of dominance is granting autonomy to

the interaction partner (i.e., *not* controlling them, but instead letting them go), and the opposite of submitting to an interaction partner is asserting one's own independence or autonomy. These behaviors and the related ones that include warmth (i.e., affirming an interaction partner; disclosing to an interaction partner) provide the outlines of interpersonal goals related to the control axis of the IPC for interpersonally-based interventions. That is, asserting one's own independence and granting it to others, with warmth when possible (i.e., warm autonomy), is an alternative to an otherwise unhelpful choice between exerting dominance or submitting to others (Smith & Traupman, in press).

CONCLUSIONS AND FUTURE DIRECTIONS

Whether studied as personality traits, emotional symptoms, or characteristics of the social environment, the best-established psychosocial risk factors involve a pattern of low levels of positive and supportive interactions with others, and high levels of antagonistic interactions. This seems to capture the major dimension of risk, perhaps because it impinges on the central human social motivation of belonging and attachment (Baumiester & Leary, 1995). A second dimension of risk involves efforts to exert social influence or control, and/or exposure to unwelcome dominance and control from others. Broader psychosocial risk factors such as low SES might be unhealthy in part because they promote both of these negative transactional patterns. These patterns are associated with the greater physiological activation believed to promote disease, through the specific mechanisms of stress exposure and reactivity, and impaired stress recovery and disrupted restorative processes. The IPC and transactional cycle help identify general and specific targets for risk-reducing interventions, which could prove useful in the prevention and management of CHD.

This interpersonal perspective is potentially applicable to other diseases. For example, a similar set of psychosocial risk factors predicts the course of cancer (Chida, Hamer, Wardle, & Steptoe, 2008), and physiological mechanisms involving stress have similarly been related to tumor growth and metastasis (Antoni et al., 2006). Although the topic is controversial (Coyne et al., 2007), in some cases psychosocial interventions have been found to improve prognosis among cancer patients (e.g., Andersen et al., 2008). Hence, the approach described here could prove useful in the development of a more generally applicable *interpersonal psychosomatics*. The model is also relevant beyond the general issue of stress and disease, as the interpersonal perspective has been fruitfully applied in research on coping with chronic disease (e.g., Lackner & Gurtman, 2005), patient-physician interactions (Kiesler & Auerbach, 2003), and the management of hypochondriasis or health anxiety (Williams, Smith, & Jordan, 2010).

Throughout the history of the species, humans have been highly social creatures, dependent on interpersonal processes for survival, as have our primate ancestors. Given this evolutionary context, we should not be surprised that the comforts and aggravations of social life play a central role in the effects of stress on CHD, and in physical health more generally. To a major extent, one's success in the general life task of *getting along* with others influences coronary risk, as does to a lesser extent one's approach to the goal of *getting ahead* (Hogan, 1983). The interpersonal tradition described in this volume has much to offer those seeking to understand such connections between mind and body, and ultimately to those who apply that knowledge in order to improve physical health.

References

Andersen, B. L., Yang, H., Farrar, W., Golden-Kreutz, D., Emery, C., Thornton, L., ... Carson, W. (2008). Psychologic intervention improves survival for breast cancer patients: A randomized clinical trial. *Cancer, 113,* 3450–3458.

Antoni, M. H., Lutgendorf, S., Cole, S., Dhabhar, F., Sephton, S., McDonald, P., ... Sood, A. (2006). The influence of biobehavioral factors on tumor biology: Pathways and mechanisms. *Nature Reviews Cancer, 6,* 240–248.

Baumeister, R. F., & Leary, M. (1995). The need to belong: Desire for human attachments as a fundamental human motivation. *Psychological Bulletin, 117,* 497–529.

Benjamin, L. S., Rothweiler, J. C., & Critchfield, K. L. (2006). The use of Structural Analysis of Social Behavior (SASB) as an assessment tool. *Annual Review of Clinical Psychology, 2,* 83–109.

Boyle, S. H., Michalek, J. E., & Suarez, E. C. (2006). Covariation of psychological attributes and incident coronary heart disease in U.S. Air Force veterans of the Vietnam War. *Psychosomatic Medicine, 68,* 844–850.

Brosschot, J. F., Gerin, W., & Thayer, J. F. (2006). The perserverative cognition hypothesis: A review of worry, prolonged stress-related physiological activation, and health. *Journal of Psychosomatic Research, 60,* 113–124.

Buss, A. H., & Perry, M. (1992). The aggression questionnaire. *Journal of Personality and Social Psychology, 63,* 452–459.

Chida, Y., & Hamer, M. (2008). Chronic psychosocial factors and acute physiological responses to laboratory-induced stress in health populations: A quantitative review of 30 years of investigations. *Psychological Bulletin, 134,* 829–885.

Chida, Y., Hamer, M., Wardle, J., & Steptoe, A. (2008). Do stress-related psychosocial factors contribute to cancer incidence and survival? *Nature Clinical Practice: Oncology, 5,* 466–475.

Chida, Y., & Steptoe, A. (2009). The association of anger and hostility with future coronary heart disease: A meta-analytic review of prospective evidence. *Journal of the American College of Cardiology, 53,* 774–778.

Costa, P. T., Jr., & McCrae, R. R. (1992). *Revised NEO Personality Inventory (NEO-PI-R) and NEO Five- Factor Inventory (NEO-FFI): Professional manual.* Odessa, FL: Psychological Assessment Resources.

Coyne, J. C., Stefanek, M., & Palmer, S. (2007). Psychotherapy and survival in cancer: The conflict between hope and evidence. *Psychological Bulletin, 133,* 367–394.

De Vogli, R., Chandola, T., & Marmot, M. G. (2007). Negative aspects of close relationships and heart disease. *Archives of Internal Medicine, 167,* 1951–1957.

Eller, N. H., Netterstrom, B., Gyntelberg, F., Kristensen, T., Nielsen, F., Steptoe, A., & Theorell, T. (2009). Work-related psychosocial factors and the development of ischemic heart disease: a systematic review. *Cardiology Reviews, 17,* 83–97.

Everson-Rose, S. A., & Lewis, T. T. (2005). Psychosocial factors and cardiovascular diseases. *Annual Review of Public Health, 26,* 469-500.

Friedman, M., & Rosenman, R. (1959). Association of a specific overt behavior pattern with increases in blood cholesterol, blood clotting time, incidence of arcus senilis, and clinical coronary artery disease. *JAMA, 169,* 1286–1296.

Gallo, L. C., & Matthews, K. A. (2003). Understanding the association between socioeconomic status and physical health: Do negative emotions play a role? *Psychological Bulletin, 129,* 10–51.

Gallo L. C., & Smith T. W. (1998). Construct validation of health-relevant personality traits: Interpersonal circumplex and five-factor model analyses of the aggression questionnaire. *International Journal of Behavioral Medicine, 5,* 129–147.

Gallo L. C., & Smith T. W. (1999). Patterns of hostility and social support: Conceptualizing psychosocial risk factors as characteristics of the person and the environment. *Journal of Research in Personality, 33,* 281–310.

Gallo, L. C., Smith, T. W., & Cox, C. (2006). Socioeconomic status, psychosocial processes, and perceived health: An interpersonal perspective. *Annals of Behavioral Medicine, 31,* 109–119.

Gallo, L. C., Smith, T. W., & Kircher, J. C. (2000). Cardiovascular and electrodermal responses to support and provocation: Interpersonal methods in the study of psychophysiological reactivity. *Psychophysiology, 37,* 289–301.

Gurtman, M. B. (1992). Construct validity of interpersonal personality measures: The interpersonal circumplex as a nomological net. *Journal of Personality and Social Psychology, 63,* 105–118.

Gurtman, M. B., & Pincus, A. L. (2003). The circumplex model: Methods and research applications. In J. A. Schinka & W. F. Velicer (Eds.), *Handbook of psychology: Vol. 2. Research methods in psychology* (pp. 407–428). Hoboken, NJ: John Wiley & Sons.

Hammen, C. (2006). Stress generation in depression: Reflections on origins, research, and future directions. *Journal of Clinical Psychology, 62,* 1065–1082.

Hecker, M., Chesney, M., Black, G., & Frautchi, N. (1988). Coronary-prone behaviors in the Western Collaborative Group Study. *Psychosomatic Medicine, 50,* 153–164.

Helgeson, V. S. (2003). Gender-related traits and health. In J. Suls & K. Wallston (Eds.), *Social psychological foundations of health and illness* (pp. 367–394). Oxford, UK: Blackwell.

Hogan, R. (1983). A socioanalytic theory of personality. In M. M. Page (Ed.), *Personality: Current theory and research* (pp. 55–89). Lincoln: University of Nebraska Press.

Horowitz, L. M. (2004). *Interpersonal foundations of psychopathology.* Washington, DC: American Psychological Association.

Horowitz, L. M., Wilson, K. R., Turan, B., Zolotsev, P., Constantino, M. J., & Henderson, L. (2006). How interpersonal motives clarify the meaning of interpersonal behavior: A revised circumplex model. *Personality and Social Psychology Review, 10,* 67–86.

Houston, B. K., Babyak, M. A., Chesney, M. A., Black, G., & Ragland, D. R. (1997). Social dominance and 22-year all-cause mortality in men. *Psychosomatic Medicine, 59,* 5–12.

Houston, B. K., Chesney, M., Black, G., Cates, D., & Hecker, M. (1992). Behavioral clusters and coronary heart disease risk. *Psychosomatic Medicine, 54,* 447–461.

Joiner, T., & Coyne, J. C. (1999). *The interactional nature of depression: Advances in interpersonal approaches.* Washington, DC: American Psychological Association.

Kaplan, J. R., Chen, H., & Manuck, S. B. (2009). The relationship between social status and atherosclerosis in male and female monkeys as revealed by meta-analysis. *American Journal of Primatology, 71,* 732–741.

Kiesler, D. J. (1983). The 1982 interpersonal circle: A taxonomy for complementarity in human transactions. *Psychological Review, 90,* 185–214.

Kiesler, D. J. (1996). *Contemporary interpersonal theory and research: Personality, psychopathology, and psychotherapy.* New York: John Wiley & Sons.

Kiesler, D. J., & Auerbach, S. (2003). Integrating measurement of control and affiliation in studies of physician-patient interaction: The interpersonal circumplex. *Social Science and Medicine*, 57, 1707–1722.

Kubzansky, L. D., Cole, S. R., Kawachi, I., Volonas, P., & Sparrow, D. (2006). Shared and unique contributions of anger, anxiety, and despression to coronary heart disease: A prospective study in the normative aging study. *Annals of Behavioral Medicine*, 31, 21–29.

Lackner, J. M., & Gurtman, M. B. (2005). Patterns of interpersonal problems in irritable bowel syndrome patients: A circumplex analysis. *Journal of Psychosomatic Research*, 58, 523–532.

Lett, H. S., Blumenthal, J. A., Babyak, M., Strauman, T., Robbins, C., & Sherwood, A. (2005). Social support and coronary heart disease: Epidemiologic evidence and implications for treatment. *Psychosomatic Medicine*, 67, 869–878.

Linden, W., Phillips, M. J., & Leclerc, J. (2007). Psychological treatment of cardiac patients: A meta-analysis. *European Heart Journal*, 28, 2972–2984.

Matthews, K. A., Glass, D., Rosenman, R., & Bortner, R. (1977). Competitive drive, Pattern A, and coronary disease: A further analysis of some data from the Western Collaborative Group Study. *Journal of Chronic Disease*, 30, 489–498.

Matthews, K. A., & Gump, B. B. (2002). Chronic work stress and marital dissolution increase risk of posttrial mortality in men from the multiple risk factor intervention trial. *Achieves of Internal Medicine*, 162, 309–315.

McCabe, P. M., Gonzales, J. A., Zaias, J., Szeto, A., Kumar, M., Herron, A. J., & Schneiderman, N. (2002). Social environment influences the progression of atherosclerosis in the watanabe heritable hyperlipidemic rabbit. *Circulation, 105*, 354–359.

Miller, G., Chen, E., & Cole, S. (2009). Health psychology: Developing biologically plausible models linking the social world and physical health. *Annual Review of Psychology*, 60, 501–524.

Moskowitz, D. S., & Zuroff, D. C. (2005). Assessing interpersonal perceptions using the interpersonal grid. *Psychological Assessment*, 17, 218–230.

Nealey-Moore, J. B., Smith, T. W., Uchino, B. N., Hawkins, M. W., & Olson-Cerny, C. (2007). Cardiovascular reactivity during positive and negative marital interactions. *Journal of Behavioral Medicine*, 30, 6, 505–519.

Nicholson, A., Kuper, H., & Hemingway, H. (2006). Depression as an aetiologic and prognostic factor in coronary heart disease: A meta-analysis of 6,362 events among 146,538 participants in 54 observational studies. *European Heart Journal*, 27, 2763–2774.

Orth-Gomer, K., Wamala, S. P., Horsten, M., Schenck-Gustafsson, K., Schneiderman, N., & Mittleman, M. A. (2000). Marital stress worsens prognosis in women with coronary heart disease: The Stockholm female coronary risk study. *JAMA, 284*, 3008–3014.

Pincus A. L., & Ansell, E. B. (2003). Interpersonal theory of personality. In T. Millon & M. J. Lerner (Eds.), *Handbook of psychology: Vol. 5. Personality and social psychology* (pp. 209–229). Hoboken, NJ: John Wiley & Sons.

Roberts, B. W., Kuncel, N. R., Shiner, R. L., Caspi, A., & Goldberg, L. R. (2007). The power of personality: The comparative validity of personality traits, socioeconomic status, and cognitive ability for predicting important life outcomes. *Perspectives on Psychological Science, 2*, 313.

Roy-Byrne, P. P., Davidson, K. W., Kessler, R. C., Asmundson, G. J. G., Kubzansky, L., Goodwin, R. D., . . . Stein, M. B. (2008). Anxiety disorders and comorbid mental illness. *General Hospital Psychiatry, 30*, 208–225.

Ruiz, J. M., Smith, T. W., & Rhodewalt, F. (2001). Distinguishing narcissism and hostility: Similarities and differences in interpersonal circumplex and five-factor correlates. *Journal of Personality Assessment, 76*, 537–555.

Schmidt, J. A., Wagner, C. C., & Kiesler, D. J. (1999). Psychometric and circumplex properties of the octant scale Impact Message Inventory (IMI-C): A structural evaluation. *Journal of Counseling Psychology, 46*, 325–334.

Schwartz, A. R., Gerin, W., Davidson, K., Pickering, T., Brosschot, J., Thayer, J., . . . Linden, W. (2003). Toward a causal model of cardiovascular responses to stress and the development of cardiovascular disease. *Psychosomatic Medicine, 65*, 22–35.

Scheier, M. F., Matthews, K. A., Owens, J. F., Schulz, R., Bridges, M. W., Magovern, G. J., & Carver, C. S. (1999). Optimism and rehospitalization after coronary artery bypass graft surgery. *Archives of Internal Medicine, 159*, 829–835.

Segerstrom, S., & Smith, T. W. (2006). Physiological pathways from personality to health: The cardiovascular and immune systems. In

M. Vollrath (Ed.), *Handbook of personality and health* (pp. 175–194). Chichester, UK: John Wiley & Sons.

Shankar, A., Koh, W., Yuan, J., Lee, H., & Yu, M. (2009). Sleep duration and coronary heart disease mortality among Chinese adults in Singapore: A population-based cohort study. *American Journal of Epidemiology, 168,* 1367–1373.

Siegman, A. W., Kubzansky, L. D., Kawachi, I., Boyle, S., Vokonas, P. S., & Sparrow, D. (2000). A prospective study of dominance and coronary heart disease in the normative aging study. *American Journal of Cardiology, 86,* 145–149.

Smith, T. W. (1992). Hostility and health: Current status of a psychosomatic hypothesis. *Health Psychology, 11,* 139–150.

Smith, T. W., & Gallo, L. C. (1999). Hostility and cardiovascular reactivity during marital interaction. *Psychosomatic Medicine, 61,* 436–445.

Smith, T. W., Gallo, L. C., & Ruiz, J. M. (2003). Toward a social psychophysiology of cardiovascular reactivity: Interpersonal concepts and methods in the study of stress and coronary disease. In J. Suls & K. Wallston (Eds.), *Social psychological foundations of health and illness* (pp. 335–366). Oxford, UK: Blackwell.

Smith, T. W., & Glazer, K. (2006). Hostility, marriage, and the heart: The social psychophysiology of cardiovascular risk in close relationships. In D. R. Crane and E. S. Marshall (Eds.), *Handbook of families and health: Interdisciplinary perspectives* (pp. 19–39). Thousand Oaks, CA: Sage.

Smith, T. W., Glazer, K., Ruiz, J. M., & Gallo, L. C. (2004). Hostility, anger, aggressiveness, and coronary heart disease: An interpersonal perspective on personality, emotion, and health. *Journal of Personality, 72,* 1217–1270.

Smith, T. W., & Ruiz, J. M. (2002). Psychosocial influences on the development and course of coronary heart disease: Current status and implications for research and practice. *Journal of Consulting and Clinical Psychology, 7,* 548–568.

Smith, T. W., Ruiz, J. M., & Uchino, B. N. (2004). Mental activation of supportive ties, hostility, and cardiovascular reactivity to laboratory stress in young men and women. *Health Psychology, 23,* 476–485.

Smith, T. W., & Traupman, E. K. (in press). Anger, hostility, and aggressiveness in coronary heart disease: Clinical application of an interpersonal

perspective. In R. Allan and J. Fisher (Eds.), *Heart and mind II: Evolution of cardiac psychology.* Washington, DC: American Psychological Association.

Smith, T. W., Traupman, E., Uchino, B. N., & Berg, C. A. (2010). Interpersonal circumplex descriptions of psychosocial risk factors for physical illness: Application to hostility, neuroticism, and marital adjustment. *Journal of Personality, 78,* 1011–1036.

Smith, T. W., Uchino, B. N., Berg, C. A., Florsheim, P., Pearce, G., Hawkins, M., ... Yoon, H. C. (2008). Self-reports and spouse ratings of negative affectivity, dominance and affiliation in coronary artery disease: Where should we look and who should we ask when studying personality and health? *Health Psychology, 27,* 676–684.

Smith, T. W., Uchino, B. N., Berg, C. A., Florsheim, P., Pearce, G., Hawkins, M., ... Olson-Cerny, C. (2009). Conflict and collaboration in middle-aged and older married couples: II. Age, sex, and task context moderate cardiovascular reactivity during marital interaction. *Psychology and Aging, 24,* 274–286.

Smith, T. W., Uchino, B. N., Florsheim, P., Berg, C., Hawkins, M., Henry, N., ... Yoon, H. C. (2009). *Affiliation and control during marital disagreement, history of divorce, and asymptomatic coronary artery clarification.* Manuscript submitted for publication.

Suls, J., & Bunde, J. (2005). Anger, anxiety, and depression as risk factors for cardiovascular disease: The problems and implications of overlapping affective dispositions. *Psychological Bulletin, 131,* 260–300.

Suls, J., & Wan, C. (1993). The relationship between trait hostility and cardiovascular reactivity: A quantitative review and analysis. *Psychophysiology, 30,* 615–626.

Tindle, H. A., Chang, Y., Kuller, L., Manson, J., Robinson, J., Rosal, M., ... Matthews, K. A. (2009). Optimism, cynical hostility, and incident coronary heart disease and mortality in the Women's Health Initiative. *Circulation, 120,* 656–662.

Traupman, E., Smith, T. W., Uchino, B. N., Berg, C. A., Trobst, K., & Costa, P. T. (in press). Interpersonal circumplex octant, dominance, and affiliation scales for the NEO-PI-R. *Personality and Individual Differences.*

Trobst, K. K. (2000). An interpersonal conceptualization and quantification of social support transactions. *Personality and Social Psychology Bulletin*, 26, 971–986.

Troxel, W. M. Buysse, D., Hall, M., Matthews, K. A. (2009). Marital happiness and sleep disturbance in a multi-ethnic sample of middle-aged women. *Behavioral Sleep Medicine*, 7, 2–19.

Troxel, W. M., Cyranowski, J., Hall, M., Frank, E., & Buysse, D. (2007). Attachment anxiety, relationship context, and sleep in women with recurrent major depression. *Psychosomatic Medicine*, 69, 692–699.

Uchino, B. N. (2004). *Social support and physical health: Understanding the health consequences of physical health.* New Haven, CT: Yale University Press.

Uchino, B. N. (2006). Social support and health: A review of physiological processes potentially underlying links to disease outcomes. *Journal of Behavioral Medicine*, 29, 377–387.

Uchino, B. N., Smith, T. W., Holt-Lunstead, J., Campo, R. A., & Reblin, M. (2007). Stress and illness. In J. T. Cacioppo, L. G. Tassinary, & G. G. Bertson (Eds.), *Handbook of psychophysiology* (pp. 608–632). New York: Cambridge University Press.

Watson, D., & Clark, L. A. (1984). Negative affectivity: The disposition to experience aversive emotional states. *Psychological Bulletin, 96*, 465–490.

Whipple, M. O., Lewis, T., Sutton-Tyrrell, K., Matthews, K. A., Barinas-Mitchell, E., Powell, L., & Everson-Rose, S. A. (2009). Hopelessness, depressive symptoms, and carotid atherosclerosis in women: The Study of Women's Heath Across the Lifespan (SWAN) heart study. *Stroke, 40*, 3166–3172.

Whiteman, M. C., Deary, I., Lee, A., & Fowkes, F. (1997). Submissiveness and protection from coronary heart disease in the general population: Edinburgh Artery Study. *Lancet*, 350, 541–545.

Wiggins, J. S., & Trapnell, P. D. (1996). A dyadic-interactional perspective on the five-factor model. In J. S. Wiggins (Ed.), *The five-factor model of personality* (pp. 88–162). New York: Guilford Press.

Wiggins, J. S., Trapnell, P. D., & Phillips, N. (1988). Psychometric and geometric characteristics of the revised Interpersonal Adjective Scales (IAS-R). *Multivariate Behavioral Research, 23*, 517–530.

Williams, P. G., Smith, T. W., Gunn, H., & Uchino, B. N. (in press). Personality and stress: Individual differences in exposure, reactivity, recovery, and restoration. In R. Contrada & A. Baum (Eds.), *Handbook of Stress.*

Williams, P. G., Smith, T. W., & Jordan, K. D. (2010). Health anxiety and hypochondriasis: Interpersonal extensions of the cognitive-behavioral perspective. In J. G. Beck (Ed.), *Interpersonal perspectives in the anxiety disorders* (pp. 261–284). Washington, DC: American Psychological Association.

Williams, R. B. (2008). Psychosocial and biobehavioral factors and their interplay in coronary heart disease. *Annual Review of Clinical Psychology, 4*, 349–365.

VI INTERPERSONAL THERAPEUTIC INTERVENTIONS

28 INTERPERSONAL ISSUES IN TREATING CHILDREN AND ADOLESCENTS

Natalie M. Costa

Kristy E. Benoit

Thomas H. Ollendick

INTRODUCTION

Psychopathology in childhood and adolescence can take many and diverse forms, with the most common being in the domains of internalizing disorders such as anxiety and depression and externalizing disorders such as attention deficit hyperactivity disorder and oppositional defiant disorder (Breton et al., 1999; Ollendick & Hersen, 1998). Moreover, these disorders have been found to be highly prevalent (Kessler & Wang, 2008) and to have a complex etiology with genetic, social, behavioral, and familial processes related to temperament, emotion regulation, parenting practices, and impaired peer relationships all being implicated. Unfortunately, current diagnostic classification systems are relatively silent as to the role of interpersonal processes in the development and expression of psychopathology in childhood and adolescence; rather, these systems place the locus of childhood psychopathologies squarely "in" the child (Ollendick, Costa, & Benoit, in press). Although these disorders

frequently occur in interpersonal contexts or situations (e.g., family, peers, schools, neighborhoods), there is little to no mention of interpersonal processes that might serve to occasion the disorders or qualify their expression in our diagnostic systems. However, there are specific treatments, such as Interpersonal Psychotherapy, that are interpersonal in nature, as well as treatments that invoke interpersonal processes, such as Cognitive-Behavioral Therapy and Family Therapy. Given the presence of treatments that directly or indirectly target interpersonal processes, there is a need to better understand and include interpersonal processes in both our conception and classification of child and adolescent psychopathology.

In the present chapter, we hope to lay the foundation for inclusion of interpersonal processes in future diagnostic systems, as well as the treatment of these disorders. We have three primary goals: (1) to review normative interpersonal development, (2) explicate interpersonal processes that may lead to the development and expression of psychopathology in childhood and adolescence, and (3) explore the implications of interpersonal processes in the treatment of these disorders.

NORMATIVE INTERPERSONAL DEVELOPMENT

In order to understand the various childhood psychopathologies from an interpersonal approach, an appreciation of normative interpersonal development is useful. There are three key processes thought to be at the center of normative interpersonal development: temperamental style, emotion regulation skills, and relationships with significant others such as parents and peers. Children's temperamental style and emotion regulation skills play a key role in how children respond to behavioral and emotional stimuli; and those responses, in turn, affect their interpersonal development. Children's relationships with significant others such as their parents and peers play a powerful role in the socialization of emotion and provide a context in which to form new relationships throughout life. Each of these processes will be discussed briefly.

Temperament has been defined as "constitutionally based individual differences in reactivity and self-regulation, influenced over time by heredity, maturation, and experience" (Rothbart & Ahadi, 1994). Reactivity involves positive and negative reactivity and behavioral inhibition to novel or intense stimuli. Children's temperament can evoke certain reactions from others and shape children's preferences for particular people, contexts, and future interpersonal relationships (Thompson, Easterbrooks, & Padilla-Walker, 2003). For example, a highly active and energetic child might be perceived and treated dissimilarly by two different caretakers, creating two very diverse "interpersonal environments" for the child. Also, within the context of temperament, children have to learn to regulate or control emotional arousal, otherwise known as emotion regulation or effortful control (Rothbart & Bates, 1998). Emotion

regulation includes two primary processes, attentional control and inhibitory control. When children are able to adapt their temperament through emotion regulatory skills, they are able to respond appropriately in interpersonal contexts, demonstrate flexibility, and resolve conflicts. Such interpersonal skills then lay the foundation for more successful interpersonal relationships.

The parent-child attachment is considered to be one of the most influential and important relationships in development. The type of attachment children have is characterized by the amount of security and trust they feel towards their caregiver (Bowlby, 1973). Securely attached children are more self-confident, trusting, and competent in their attachments to others (Thompson, 2001). The feelings that securely attached children have about their ability to handle stress or interact with their environment are not thought to be solely "in" the child, but rather embedded in the parent-child context. The interpersonal relationship between parent and child is also important for emotion socialization, as children learn from their parents how to behave competently in social contexts (Thompson, 1994). Emotion socialization occurs via parental practices and behaviors that influence how a child experiences, expresses, and regulates emotion (Eisenberg et al., 2001b), which in turn furthers interpersonal development.

As children progress into middle childhood, peer relationships begin to take on a more important role than the parent-child relationship due to the dramatic change in children's social contexts and actions. From a developmental perspective, one of the most important tasks of middle childhood is to learn acceptable ways of interacting with peers. Although interpersonal abilities and skills accrued from a secure attachment and healthy parental socialization of emotion affect this learning, the majority of learning occurs within the context of peer groups. As such, interactions with peers are thought to play an important role in children's interpersonal development. Certain social skills are necessary in order for children to form successful peer relationships (Rubin, Bukowski, & Parker, 1998). These social skills include, but are not limited to, the ability to: (a) understand the thoughts and feelings of others; (b) begin, maintain, and end interactions in a positive way; (c) appropriately express emotions and behaviors; and (d) inhibit behaviors that might be construed as negative by others. Peer acceptance is thought to be, in part, a function of these social skills. Hence, in the final analysis, normative interpersonal development consists of children possessing the social skills that enable them to form peer relationships and be accepted by their peers.

INTERPERSONAL PROCESSES LEADING TO THE DEVELOPMENT OF CHILD AND ADOLESCENT PSYCHOPATHOLOGY

Thus far, we have focused on normative interpersonal development and its role in normal psychological adjustment. This discourse begs the question of what happens when these developmental processes go awry. Although there are many possible answers to this question, one possibility is that children who do not demonstrate normative interpersonal functioning subsequently evince heightened levels of psychopathology both of the internalizing and externalizing variant (see Muris & Ollendick, 2005). We will provide evidence for this hypothesis by reviewing how the key processes thought to be at the center of normative interpersonal development (i.e., temperament, emotion regulation, parenting practices, and peer relationships) relate to child and adolescent internalizing psychopathology (anxiety and depression) and externalizing psychopathology (disruptive behavior disorders).

Temperament

Internalizing psychopathology. According to Clark and Watson's (1991) tripartite model of anxiety and depression, temperamental styles associated with negative emotional reactivity (NER)/negative affectivity (NA), positive emotionality/positive affectivity (PA), and behavioral inhibition (BI) are all important in understanding the internalizing disorders. NER/NA refers to a heightened temperamental sensitivity to negative stimuli. In contrast, positive emotionality reflects the extent to which children are receptive to reward, sociable, and sensation-seeking, and actively involved with their environment (Rothbart & Bates, 1998). The third temperamental style, BI, is defined as an overt representation of a psychological and physiological state of uncertainty that results from exposure to unfamiliar objects, people, and stressful situations (Kagan, 1994). According to the tripartite model of anxiety and depression, NER/NA is a nonspecific factor that is common to both depression and anxiety, low positive emotionality is linked specifically to depression, and BI is linked specifically to anxiety (Seligman & Ollendick, 1998).

Children with high levels of NER/NA tend to experience a broad range of negative affect such as fear/anxiety, sadness/depression, guilt, and self-dissatisfaction (Watson & Clark, 1984). Moreover, the propensity to experience high levels of negative affect while subsequently experiencing low levels of positive emotionality are linked to the dysphoric and anhedonic symptoms of depression (Compas, Connor-Smith, & Jaser, 2004). High levels of NER/NA combined with low levels of positive emotionality may lead to overly negative interpretations of events or trigger rejection by others, thereby increasing social isolation, which can lead to poorer interpersonal relationships and the development of depression over time.

Children with high levels of BI tend to restrict exploration, avoid novelty, and withdraw, or cling or depend on parents when exposed to unfamiliar stimuli (Kagan, Reznick, & Gibbons, 1989). In Kagan and colleagues' (1987, 1988) seminal studies, inhibited children evidenced higher rates of all anxiety disorders than uninhibited children seven to eight years later. Moreover, the presence of BI during childhood was found to predict adolescent anxiety problems (Dumas, LaFreniere, & Serketich,

1995), as well as depressive disorders (Ollendick & Hirshfeld-Becker, 2002).

Externalizing psychopathology. Whereas NER/NA exhibited as fear or sadness are particularly relevant to internalizing behaviors, NER/NA exhibited as frustration, irritability, and anger are related to externalizing behaviors (Eisenberg, Fabes, Guthrie, & Reiser, 2000; Owens & Shaw, 2003; Robins, John, Caspi, Moffitt, & Stouthamer-Loeber, 1996; Rothbart & Bates, 1998). Propensity for anger and overt expression of frustration may translate to a higher incidence of aversive, provocative, and destructive behaviors. In turn, children with high NER may be more likely to spark coercive interactions if paired with unresponsive parents because they place exceptional burdens on caregivers (Shaw, Bell, & Gilliom, 2000). Coercive interaction patterns in toddlerhood appear linked to increased child noncompliance, negativity, and eventual externalizing behavior problems.

Although positive emotionality has not been specifically examined in children with externalizing forms of psychopathology, behavioral disinhibition (BD) has been examined as a temperamental style potentially related to the development and expression of oppositional and conduct problems in children. In contrast to BI, BD is the tendency to exhibit increased exploration, spontaneity of speech, and approach in unfamiliar situations (see Hirshfeld-Becker et al., 2002). In fact, early studies have shown that BD in toddlerhood is associated with elevated risk for disruptive behavior disorders at age 6 (32%) and age 10 (44%; Hirshfeld-Becker et al., 2007). Studies have not yet followed these youngsters into adolescence, but the early findings suggest an increased trajectory of problems for these at-risk youth.

Emotion Regulation

Internalizing psychopathology. As noted earlier, emotion regulation includes two primary processes: attentional control and inhibitory control. Attentional control may reduce internalizing psychopathology by facilitating children's ability to shift attention away from distressing thoughts, events, and objects, and modulate negative emotional arousal (Eisenberg et al., 2004). Low attention focusing has been linked to higher levels of anxiety and fearfulness in children (Lemery, Essex, & Smider, 2002). Furthermore, children who develop internalizing behavior problems may grant attention to many minor stressors at one time and have difficulty shifting attention away from arousing stimuli. As such, the inability to control attending to distress may fail to decrease emotional arousal. Persistently high levels of fearful and/or sad emotional arousal may then lead to childhood internalizing problems. Conversely, inhibitory control may be a precursor to developing internalizing psychopathology due to inadequate or overly rigid control over emotion (Calkins & Fox, 2002). Individuals who excessively restrain their personal emotional experiences may find themselves ill-equipped to respond spontaneously and begin to avoid social situations (Eisenberg et al., 2000). High degrees of inhibition also may decrease an individual's exposure to novel situations, resulting in few opportunities to practice and receive feedback about emotion regulation skills. High levels of inhibitory control have been associated with fearfulness, avoidant behavior, social withdrawal, and low assertiveness (Kagan, 1998).

Externalizing psychopathology. Support for the role of emotion regulatory skills in externalizing psychopathology is not surprising given that difficulty managing emotions is included in most definitions of externalizing behavior problems (e.g., Cole, Zahn-Waxler, Fox, Usher, & Welsh, 1996). In contrast to the overcontrol often associated with internalizing behavior problems, externalizing behavior problems tend to be linked to undercontrol (low inhibitory control; e.g., Eisenberg et al., 2000). Undercontrolled individuals fail to restrict the expression of emotion and are at increased risk for evoking hostile responses from others. Children low in attentional control also exhibit difficulties due to reduced ability to modulate affective arousal, integrate information, and plan effectively (Eisenberg et al., 2004). For example, low attentional regulation has been demonstrated to be related to anger proneness, externalizing psychopathology, conduct disorders, and aggression (O'Brien & Frick, 1996). Disruptive behavior problems may therefore develop when children cannot adequately refocus attention away from distressing stimuli and sufficiently stop themselves from acting out when experiencing the negative emotions such stimuli prompt. For example, Eisenberg and colleagues (2000, 2001a) have consistently found an association between externalizing problems and lower levels of attention shifting and focusing among school-aged children.

Parenting

Internalizing psychopathology. Over the past decade, parenting behaviors have emerged as an important causal factor in the emergence of anxiety and depression in children (McLeod, Weisz, & Wood, 2007; McLeod, Wood, & Weisz, 2007). The constellation of parenting behaviors that seems to increase risk for anxiety is characterized by high levels of parental control (behavioral and psychological) and rejection/criticism. Dumas et al. (1995) found that psychological control and higher levels of restriction were associated with higher levels of anxiety in children. Siqueland, Kendall, and Steinberg (1996) demonstrated that mothers of children with anxiety disorders were rated by independent observers as more psychologically controlling than mothers of control children. Moreover, Ollendick and Horsch (2007) showed that mothers of highly fearful children were overly controlling, a phenomenon that was especially evident in mothers who were also anxious themselves. Numerous studies have shown that higher rates of rejection and criticism are also associated with and predictive of child anxiety (Dumas et al., 1995) Overall, these parenting

behaviors are thought to hinder the ability to develop solutions to face fear, decrease self-efficacy, and undermine emotion regulation by increasing sensitivity to anxiety, thereby increasing anxiety (Gottman, Katz, & Hooven, 1997).

The group of parenting behaviors associated with increased risk for childhood depression is similarly characterized by unresponsiveness and high levels of psychological control, emotional insensitivity, and rejection (McLeod, Weisz, et al., 2007). Depressed mothers seem to use more psychological control in that they are less sensitive to their children's emotional state and less responsive toward and supportive of their children (Cummings & Davies, 1999). For example, Burge and Hammen (1991) demonstrated that depressed mothers display more negative or critical affect and less responsivity and involvement in parent-child interaction tasks. Additionally, compared to interactions between control mothers and their children, interactions between depressed mothers and their children are less frequent, less consistent, and more lax in discipline (Downey & Coyne, 1990). These parenting behaviors can increase children's risk for depression by leaving children feeling unworthy and undeserving of love and affection. In turn, they may decrease children's sense of self-worth and self-esteem, leading them to adopt an internal locus of control and a reduced sense of self-efficacy, thereby increasing the likelihood of depressive symptoms (Cummings & Davies, 1999).

Externalizing psychopathology. Several parenting behaviors have been hypothesized to contribute to the development of externalizing psychopathology in early childhood. These parenting behaviors are characterized by maternal unresponsiveness (Carlson, Jacobvitz, & Sroufe, 1995), inconsistent behavioral control (Belsky, Woodworth, & Crinic, 1996), and lack of positive involvement (Pettit, Bates, & Dodge, 1997). These types of parenting behaviors may evolve to become a coercive pattern of interactions between children and their parents (Patterson, 1982). Furthermore, these coercive patterns contribute to the development and maintenance of externalizing psychopathology in early to middle childhood (Patterson, Reid, & Dishion, 1992). Brook, Zheng, Whiteman, and Brook (2001) demonstrated that parenting behaviors that were classified as low in positive affectivity—and also high in negative affectivity, psychological control (i.e., control through the use of guilt), and coercive control atttempts—were significantly related to the toddler's level of aggression. Furthermore, Pettit and Dodge (1993) showed that coercive control and overresponsiveness were related to both teacher and mother report of higher child externalizing behaviors during kindergarten and first grade. They also demonstrated that negative coercive family interactions and parenting behaviors had the strongest association with child externalizing behaviors. The observation that different parenting behaviors can lead to child externalizing problems fits well with the view of developmental psychopathology that multiple pathways are possible to any one disorder.

Peer Relationships

Internalizing psychopathology. Downey and Feldman (1996) have proposed a Rejection Sensitivity (RS) model to explain why children who experience rejection in important relationships go on to develop interpersonal difficulties and subsequent psychopathology. Their model proposes that repeated experiences of rejection can result in children always expecting rejection in interpersonal situations, an idea termed "rejection sensitivity." The constant expectation of rejection in social situations increases the likelihood that the rejected child will react in a heightened emotional state of either anxiety or anger. As a result, over time, the child becomes hypervigilant to rejection cues, prompting the child to interpret neutral behaviors as rejecting. Then,

faced with self-induced perceptions of rejection, the child adopts behaviors such as withdrawing, as a defense against anxiety or anger (Downey, Mougios, Ayduk, London, & Shoda, 2004).

In terms of internalizing psychopathology, the RS model helps to explain how peer rejection is linked to the development of anxiety or depression through the feelings of loneliness that occur when one is ostracized by others. RS can result in children developing maladaptive behaviors in social situations, such as social awkwardness and withdrawal, which hinder their chances of developing positive interpersonal relationships (London, Downey, Bonica, & Paltin, 2007). The combination of heightened RS and a lack of positive relationships contributes to the development of loneliness and subsequent anxiety or depression over time. Several empirical studies have demonstrated links between peer rejection and internalizing psychopathology (Kiesner, 2002; Ladd & Troop-Gordon, 2003).

Externalizing psychopathology. As previously stated, the RS model also helps to explain how peer rejection is linked to the development of externalizing psychopathology, such as anger, aggression, oppositional defiant disorder, or antisocial behavior. Whereas some children may respond to rejection with anxiety or social withdrawal, other children respond to rejection with extreme forms of anger and aggression. This type of aggressive behavior often alienates them from their peers, increasing peer rejection. Caspi, Elder, and Bem (1987) hypothesized that children who frequently engage in confrontive aggression among peers develop a style of responding to interpersonal contingencies that, over time, causes them to develop broader and more serious forms of maladjustment, such as externalizing problems. Empirically, longitudinal studies have shown that aggression and peer rejection in grade school uniquely contribute to the development of externalizing psychopathology in adolescence (P. A. Cowan & Cowan, 2004).

THE ROLE OF INTERPERSONAL PROCESSES IN THE TREATMENT OF CHILDREN AND ADOLESCENT PSYCHOPATHOLOGY

Thus far, we have focused on delineating the processes of normative interpersonal development and demonstrating how these factors may be related to the onset and maintenance of both internalizing and externalizing forms of childhood psychopathology. We now turn our attention to the role that interpersonal processes play in the treatment of children and adolescents with these disorders. We should note from the onset, however, that although all of the psychotherapies include interpersonal elements in the therapeutic process (i.e., relationship and alliance factors), most interventions have largely conceptualized disorders as intrapersonal and not interpersonal in nature (Woody & Ollendick, 2006). Furthermore, and of critical importance, the majority of interventions do not target the interpersonal processes that we have earlier specified to be important in the development of childhood psychopathology.

Cognitive-Behavioral Therapy (CBT)

In-Albon and Schneider (2006) identified 24 randomized clinical trials examining the treatment of anxious children with a variant of CBT. The vast majority of these trials examined the effects of CBT delivered individually to children; parents and peers were only minimally involved in most instances. Overall, about 67% of the treated children were diagnosis-free at posttreatment, compared with less than 10% of those in control conditions. Group CBT has also been found to be highly effective in treating anxious children (Flannery-Schroeder & Kendall, 2000; Manassis et al., 2002); however, no differences have been found between individual and group CBT. These findings are somewhat surprising given the potential utility of peers as socialization agents for children and the opportunity

for the treated children to acquire and use appropriate social and emotion regulation skills within the group context.

A number of other studies have shown that individual or group CBT supplemented with family and/or parent anxiety management strategies may also be beneficial. For example, Wood, Piacentini, Southam-Gerow, Chu, and Sigman (2006) showed that family-focused CBT produced superior outcomes to individual CBT with anxious children. Rather than simply training parents to help their anxious child deal with anxiety in a more adaptive manner (as most family-enhanced CBT treatments do), individual CBT was supplemented with an intervention focused on parenting practices found to be directly related to the development and maintenance of childhood anxiety disorders; namely, parental intrusiveness and failure to grant autonomy. For the enhanced group, 79% were diagnosis-free at posttreatment compared to 53% in the individual CBT group.

In addition to parental involvement, a few treatments have examined the role of peer participation in the treatment of children with anxiety disorders. From an interpersonal perspective, we might expect that treatments involving peers would be particularly effective. For example, Beidel, Turner, and Morris (2000) evaluated the efficacy of Social Effectiveness Therapy for Children (SET-C) in the treatment of social phobia in children. This intervention consists of group social skills intervention, peer generalization activities, and individualized in vivo exposure exercises. When compared to an active intervention designed to address test anxiety, SET-C children demonstrated enhanced social skills, reduced social anxiety, and increased overall social functioning; moreover, 67% no longer met diagnostic criteria for social phobia compared to 5% of children in the comparison condition.

Similar results with CBT have been found in the treatment of depression and the externalizing disorders. In the realm of depression, the TADS (Treatment of Adolescent Depression) team (2007) recently compared CBT to fluoxetine and a combination of the two. Although they found that the latter two treatments had better outcomes at week 12 of treatment, there was no difference among the three treatments after 36 weeks of treatment. All, including CBT, were equally effective. Finally, in the area of disruptive behavior disorders, Anger Control Training (Lochman, Barry, & Pardini, 2003) was found to be superior to a no-treatment control condition in reducing disruptive behavior (Robinson, Smith, & Miller, 2002).

Interpersonal Psychotherapy

In contrast to CBT, which targets cognitions and behaviors in the child, Interpersonal Psychotherapy for Adolescents (IPT-A; Mufson, Moreau, Weissman, & Klerman, 1993) focuses on the interpersonal context in which depression is expressed (Fombonne, 1998). In line with our description of normative interpersonal development, IPT was influenced by the importance Bowlby (1973) and others afforded the attachment relationship in early life. The first phase of IPT-A entails identifying the specific interpersonal areas that relate to the adolescent's depressive symptomatology (Fombonne). The therapist and client then agree to work on one of five interpersonal problem areas: role disputes, role transitions, single parent families, interpersonal deficits, and grief. Given that these areas typically involve parents and/or peers, this approach reflects the importance we have given to these relationships in the onset and maintenance of depression in youth. The goals of IPT-A are to reduce depressive symptoms and improve interpersonal functioning (Verdeli, Mufson, Lee, & Keith, 2006). It accomplishes these aims by helping adolescents to understand the reciprocal relationship between their depressive symptoms and interpersonal events, and develop productive means of communicating feelings and solving interpersonal problems.

Mufson, Weissman, Moreau, and Garfinkel (1999) demonstrated that a group treated with IPT-A had greater reductions in depression and superior increases in global and social functioning, as compared to a group that was clinically monitored. Rossello and Bernal (1999) compared IPT-A to both CBT and a wait-list control condition. Results showed that the two active treatment groups improved more than the control group on depressive symptoms. The IPT-A group was also superior to the control group on increases in social functioning and self-esteem. Lastly, Mufson et al. (2004) compared two groups of depressed adolescents, one treated with IPT-A and one treated in school-based clinics with treatment as typically delivered in the community. The IPT-A group demonstrated greater reductions in depressive symptoms and greater improvement in both global and social functioning at posttreatment, as well as fewer symptoms at 16-week follow-up.

While IPT-A research has not specifically assessed change in attachment as a treatment outcome variable, Ravitz, Maunder, and McBride (2008) used IPT's theoretical ties to attachment theory to investigate this possibility in an adult sample. They found that only adults who either partially or fully responded to IPT showed significant reductions in attachment anxiety and attachment avoidance. The authors reasoned that the tasks of IPT helped to increase the experience of security in relationships, and thus may have helped modify the client's internal working model. Given the theoretical importance we have afforded attachment in the development of child psychopathology, similar outcome variables should be assessed in child and adolescent studies as well.

Parent Management Training and Problem-Solving Skills Training

In the area of disruptive behavior disorders, Parent Management Training (PMT) is recognized as one of the most empirically validated treatments (Brestan & Eyberg, 1998). PMT draws on social learning theory and teaches parents techniques that will change the behavior of their child (Kazdin, 2005). The main mechanism through which change occurs is operant conditioning, and key principles include positive reinforcement, consistent discipline, and increased parental involvement. Skills are practiced via role-play, feedback, and modeling. In keeping with our theoretical focus on parental relationships, this treatment targets change in parenting behavior as a means of changing child behavior. PMT has been delivered in a wide array of research programs and under a variety of names (Kazdin, 1997). In a recent review, Eyberg, Nelson, and Boggs (2008) found that children treated with PMT evidenced improvement in their disruptive behavior to within nonclinical levels both at home and at school; gains were maintained at least one to three years following treatment, and, in some instances, improvements in sibling behavior and maternal psychopathology were noted.

An additional treatment that has been combined with PMT is Problem-Solving Skills Training (PSST). In this arena the therapist works more exclusively with the child, teaching problem-solving skills such as identifying problems, generating solutions, weighing the pros and cons of each option, deciding on a solution, and evaluating the outcome (Eyberg et al., 2008). Therapists use techniques such as practice, modeling, role-playing, feedback, and social reinforcement. The idea is to gradually build from more benign problems to complex interpersonal situations. As such, PSST focuses on both peer and parental relationships, and may also help to hone emotion regulation skills. For instance, as children become more adept at generating solutions before lashing out in anger, their inhibitory control necessarily increases. PSST has been found to be superior to relationship therapy (Kazdin, Bass, Siegel, & Thomas, 1989) and when PSST is combined with PMT, improvement

is better than in a PMT-only group (Kazdin, Siegel, & Bass, 1992).

In terms of processes of change, Kazdin and Wassell (2000) showed that in a treatment that included PMT, PSST, or both, improvement in child symptoms was associated with decreases in parents' depression and stress, as well as improved family relationships and functioning. However, studies examining more fine-tuned processes are rare. A notable exception is a recent investigation into parent-child interaction patterns both preceding and following treatment in a combined PMT/CBT format (Granic, O'Hara, Pepler, & Lewis, 2007). These authors demonstrated that improvement in child externalizing behavior was significantly related to increased emotional flexibility in the parent-child dyad when engaging in problem solving. Even though these dyads expressed the same amount of negative emotion as at pretreatment, they appeared to have learned the skills required to repair conflicts and shift from negative to positive interaction patterns. These intriguing results provide preliminary evidence that PMT may improve emotion regulation skills in parents and children alike.

Family Therapy

One treatment modality that has received significantly less research is that of family therapy. This term has been used to describe a broad range of therapy modalities (David-Ferdon & Kaslow, 2008); however, we will focus on studies in which both parent and child are present and family dynamic interactive patterns are the explicit treatment target. In the area of child and adolescent depression, the dearth of research on family therapy is surprising given the evidence linking family factors to the onset, maintenance, and relapse of the disorder. Attachment-Based Family Therapy (ABFT; Diamond & Siqueland, 1995), which draws on attachment theory, emotion-focused therapy, and contextual therapy, is an important exception. ABFT assumes that children are inhibited from developing internal and interpersonal coping skills when they experience poor attachment bonds, high conflict, harsh criticism, and low affective attunement. This negative family environment prevents the development of skills required to protect against various stressors. More importantly, ABFT asserts that by resolving attachment failures, teaching parents to become better caregivers, and helping adolescents and parents rebuild trust and communication, depression will be reduced and relapse prevented. These goals are achieved through relational reframing, alliance building, reattachment, and promotion of competency. Diamond, Reis, Diamond, Siqueland, and Isaacs (2002) demonstrated that adolescents treated with ABFT had a higher rate of remittance, and greater reductions in depressive symptoms and family conflict, as compared to a wait-list control group. The ABFT group also showed a marginally significant increase in perceived positive attachment to mothers.

Another variant of family therapy is Systems Integrative Family Therapy (SIFT), which focuses on family dysfunction. The aim is to help families understand the connections between the child's depression, problematic family scripts, and insecure family attachment patterns (Carr, 2008). SIFT promotes more secure attachments and re-edited family scripts that better manage stress and transitions. Trowell et al. (2007) recently compared this treatment to a Focused Individual Psychodynamic Psychotherapy (FIPP), which centered on interpersonal relationships, life stresses and dysfunctional attachments. There were no significant differences between the two groups, with approximately 75% being diagnosis-free at posttreatment in both. Given these promising results and the ties between this treatment and the theoretical importance of parenting relationships, it will be important that future studies compare SIFT to more well-established treatments.

CONCLUSION

The study of interpersonal relationships and childhood psychopathology is clearly in its own stage of infancy. Unfortunately, the majority of work in terms of interpersonal psychology and the main theoretical perspectives in this arena have focused largely on adults. Little attention has been given to how these perspectives apply to children and adolescents. As a result, much work remains to be done in this area and we cannot simply expect that these adult models can be productively applied to children and adolescents. Youth are not miniature adults and a truly developmentally based perspective will be required. Nonetheless, important interpersonal factors such as temperament, emotion regulation, parental behaviors, and peer relationships have been identified and associated with the development and expression of both internalizing and externalizing psychopathology in childhood and adolescence. Despite these advances, these interpersonal processes have been largely ignored in the development of treatment interventions with few notable exceptions. Accordingly, researchers are beginning to make the argument that these factors should be integrated into treatments for children and adolescents (Hannesdottir & Ollendick, 2007).

While many interventions for children and adolescents are not theoretically driven by interpersonal processes, most treatments are interpersonal in their execution (Ollendick & Shirk, in press). For example, the therapeutic alliance, which refers to the quality and nature of the interaction between the patient and therapist, has been shown to be reliably related to treatment outcome in such diverse areas as CBT for adolescent depression (Shirk, Gudmundsen, Kaplinski, & McMakin, 2008), CBT for anxious youth (Creed & Kendall, 2005), PMT for oppositional and aggressive youth (Kazdin & Whitley, 2006), and family therapy (Karver, Handelsman, Fields, & Bickman, 2006). In addition, interpersonal considerations often help clinicians to understand and adequately treat child and adolescent psychopathology, particularly when it comes to determining the function of a significant behavior. For example, treatment can be applied more sensitively if the clinician is able to determine the interpersonal function of a child's oppositional and defiant behavior, be it the desire for nurturance from unresponsive caretakers, the wish for autonomy from overcontrolling parents, the dismissal of rejection from peers, or some other factor.

In short, much work remains to be done in synthesizing the role of interpersonal processes in the theory, diagnosis, and treatment of childhood psychopathology. Future research, for example, should more adequately examine how teaching parents and others to interact differently with temperamentally difficult children, fostering more refined emotion regulation skills in youth, instructing on optimal parenting strategies, and addressing peer rejection might improve outcomes in the treatment of children and adolescents with diverse forms of psychopathology. Our extant strategies effectively deal with about 60 to 80% of the youth and families we treat; however, a significant minority does not respond to these efficacious interventions. We can and must do better in the next generation of treatment studies. It is our contention that greater attention to interpersonal processes will afford us the opportunity to do so.

References

Beidel, D. C., Turner, S. M., & Morris, T. L. (2000). Behavioral treatment of childhood social phobia. *Journal of Consulting and Clinical Psychology, 68,* 1072–1080.

Belsky, J., Woodworth, S., & Crnic, K. (1996). Trouble in the second year: Three questions about family interaction. *Child Development, 67,* 556–578.

Bowlby, J. (1973). *Attachment and loss: Volume 2. Separation anxiety and anger.* New York: Basic Books.

Brestan, E., & Eyberg, S. (1998). Effective psychosocial treatments of conduct-disordered children and adolescents: 29 years, 82 studies, and 5,272 kids. *Journal of Clinical Child Psychology, 27,* 180–189.

Breton, J.-J., Bergeron, L., Valla, J.-P., Berthiaume, C., Gaudet, N., Lambert, J., . . . Lepine, S., (1999). Quebec child mental health survey: Prevalence of DSM-III-R mental health disorders. *Journal of Child Psychology and Psychiatry, 40,* 375–384.

Brook, J. S., Zheng, L., Whiteman, M., & Brook, D. W. (2001). Aggression in toddlers: Associations with parenting and marital relations. *The Journal of Genetic Psychology, 162,* 228–241.

Burge, D., & Hammen, C. (1991). Maternal communication: Predictors of outcome at follow-up in a sample of children at high and low risk for depression. *Journal of Abnormal Psychology, 100,* 174–180.

Calkins, S. D., & Fox, N. A. (2002). Self-regulatory processes in early personality development: A multilevel approach to the study of childhood social withdrawal and aggression. *Development and Psychopathology, 14,* 477–498.

Carlson, E., Jacobvitz, D., & Sroufe, L. A. (1995). A developmental investigation of inattentiveness and hyperactivity. *Child Development, 66,* 37–54.

Carr, A. (2008). Depression in young people: Description, assessment and evidence-based treatment. *Developmental Neurorehabilitation, 11,* 3–15.

Caspi, A., Elder, G. H., & Bem, D. J. (1987). Moving against the world: Life-course patterns of explosive children. *Developmental Psychology, 23,* 308–313.

Clark, L. A., & Watson, D. (1991). Tripartite model of anxiety and depression: Psychometric evidence and taxonomic implications. *Journal of Abnormal Psychology, 100,* 316–336.

Cole, P. M., Zahn-Waxler, C., Fox, N. A., Usher, B. A., & Welsh, J. D. (1996). Individual differences in emotion regulation and behavior problems in preschool children. *Journal of Abnormal Psychology, 105,* 518–529.

Compas, B., Connor-Smith, J., & Jaser, S. S. (2004). Temperament, stress reactivity, and coping: Implications for depression in childhood and adolescence. *Journal of Clinical Child and Adolescent Psychology, 33,* 21–31.

Cowan, P. A., & Cowan, C. P. (2004). From family relationships to peer rejection to antisocial behavior in middle childhood. In J. B. Kupersmidt & K. A. Dodge (Eds.), *Children's peer relations: From development to intervention* (pp. 159–177). Washington, DC: American Psychological Association.

Creed, T. A., & Kendall, P. C. (2005). Therapist alliance-building behavior within a cognitive-behavioral treatment for anxiety in youth. *Journal of Consulting and Clinical Psychology, 73,* 498–505.

Cummings, E. M., & Davies, P. T. (1999). Depressed parents and family functioning: Interpersonal effects and children's functioning and development. In T. Joiner & J. C. Coyne (Eds.), *The interactional nature of depression: Advances in interpersonal approaches* (pp. 299–327). Washington, DC: APA Books.

David-Ferdon, C., & Kaslow, N. (2008). Evidence based psychosocial treatments for child and adolescent depression. *Journal of Clinical Child and Adolescent Psychology, 37,* 62–104.

Diamond, G. S., Reiss, B., Diamond, G. M., Siqueland, L., & Isaacs, L. (2002). Attachment-based family therapy for depressed adolescents: A treatment development study. *Journal of the American Academy of Child and Adolescent Psychiatry, 41,* 1190–1196.

Diamond, G., & Siqueland, L. (1995). Family therapy for treatment of depressed adolescents. *Psychotherapy: Theory, Research, Practice, and Training, 32,* 77–90.

Downey, G., & Coyne, J. (1990). Children of depressed parents: An integrated review. *Psychological Bulletin, 108,* 50–76.

Downey, G., & Feldman, S. (1996). Implications of rejection sensitivity for intimate relationships. *Journal of Personality and Social Psychology, 70,* 1327–1343.

Downey, G., Mougios, V., Ayduk, O., London, B., & Shoda, Y. (2004). Rejection sensitivity and the defensive motivational system: Insights from the startle response to rejection cues. *Psychological Science, 15,* 668–673.

Dumas, J. E., LaFreniere, P. J., & Serketich, W. J. (1995). "Balance of power": A transactional analysis of control in mother-child dyads involving socially competent, aggressive, and anxious children. *Journal of Abnormal Psychology, 104,* 104–113.

Eisenberg, N., Cumberland, A., Spinrad, T. L., Fabes, R. A., Shepard, S. A., Reiser, M., ... Guthrie, I. K. (2001a). The relations of regulation and emotionality to children's externalizing and internalizing problem behavior. *Child Development, 72,* 1112–1134.

Eisenberg, N., Fabes, R. A., Guthrie, I. K., & Reiser, M. (2000). Dispositional emotionality and regulation: Their role in predicting quality of social functioning. *Journal of Personality and Social Psychology, 78,* 136–157.

Eisenberg, N., Losoya, S., Fabes, R., Guthrie, I., Reiser, M., Murphy, B., ... Padgett, S. J., (2001b). Parental socialization of children's dysregulated expression of emotion and externalizing problems. *Journal of Family Psychology, 15,* 183–205.

Eisenberg, N., Spinrad, T. L., Fabes, R. A., Reiser, M., Cumberland, A., Shepard, S. A., ... Murphy, B. (2004). The relations of effortful control and impulsivity to children's resiliency and adjustment. *Child Development, 75,* 25–46.

Eyberg, S., Nelson, M., & Boggs, S. (2008). Evidence-based psychosocial treatments for children and adolescents with disruptive behavior. *Journal of Clinical Child and Adolescent Psychology, 37,* 215–237.

Flannery-Schroeder, E. C., & Kendall, P. C. (2000). Group and individual cognitive-behavioral treatments for youth with anxiety disorders: A randomized clinical trial. *Cognitive Therapy and Research, 24,* 251–278.

Fombonne, E. (1998). Interpersonal psychotherapy for adolescent depression. *Child Psychology and Psychiatry Review, 3,* 169–175.

Gottman, J., Katz, L., & Hooven, C. (1997). *Meta-emotion: How families communicate emotionally.* Mahwah, NJ: Erlbaum.

Granic, I., O'Hara, A., Pepler, D., & Lewis, M. (2007). A dynamic systems analysis of parent-child changes associated with successful "real-world" interventions for aggressive children. *Journal of Abnormal Child Psychology, 35,* 845–857.

Hannesdottir, D. K., & Ollendick, T. H. (2007). The role of emotion regulation in the treatment of child anxiety disorders. *Clinical Child and Family Psychology Review, 10,* 275–293.

Hirshfeld-Becker, D. R., Biederman, J., Faraone, S. V., Violette, H., Wrightsman, J., & Rosenbaum, J. F. (2002). Temperamental correlates of disruptive behavior disorders in young children: Preliminary findings. *Biological Psychiatry, 50,* 563–574.

Hirshfeld-Becker, D. R., Biederman, J., Henin, A., Faraone, S. V., Micco, J. A., van Grondelle, A.,

... Rosenbaum, J. F. (2007). Clinical outcomes of laboratory-observed preschool behavioral disinhibition at five-year follow-up. *Biological Psychiatry, 62,* 565–572.

In-Albon, T., & Schneider, S. (2006). Psychotherapy of childhood anxiety disorders: A meta-analysis. *Psychotherapy and Psychosomatics, 14,* 1–10.

Kagan, J. (1994). Inhibited and uninhibited temperaments. In W. B. Carey & S. C. McDevitt (Eds.), *Prevention and early intervention: Individual differences and risk factors for the mental health of children* (pp. 35–41). New York: Brunner/Mazel.

Kagan, J. (1998). Biology and the child. In W. Damon & N. Eisenberg (Eds.), Handbook of child psychology: Vol. 3. Social, emotional, and personality development (pp. 177–235). New York: John Wiley & Sons.

Kagan, J., Reznick, J. S., & Gibbons, J. (1989). Inhibited and uninhibited types of children. *Child Development, 60,* 838–845.

Kagan, J., Reznick, J. S., & Snidman, N. (1987). The physiology and psychology of behavioral inhibition. *Child Development, 58,* 1459–1473.

Kagan, J., Reznick, J. S., & Snidman, N. (1988). Biological bases of childhood shyness. *Science, 240,* 167–171.

Karver, M. S., Handelsman, J. B., Fields, S., & Bickman, L. (2006). Meta-analysis of therapeutic relationship variables in youth and family therapy: The evidence for different relationship variables in the child and adolescent treatment outcome literature. *Clinical Psychology Review, 26,* 50–65.

Kazdin, A. (1997). Parent management training: Evidence, outcomes, and issues. *Journal of the American Academy of Child & Adolescent Psychiatry, 36,* 1349–1356.

Kazdin, A. (2005). *Parent management training: Treatment for oppositional, aggressive, and antisocial behavior in children and adolescents.* New York: Oxford University Press.

Kazdin, A., Bass, D., Siegel, T., & Thomas, C. (1989). Cognitive-behavioral therapy and relationship therapy in the treatment of children referred for antisocial behavior. *Journal of Consulting and Clinical Psychology, 57,* 522–535.

Kazdin, A., Siegel, T., & Bass, D. (1992). Cognitive problem-solving skills training and parent management training in the treatment of antisocial behavior in children. *Journal of Consulting and Clinical Psychology, 60,* 733–747.

Kazdin, A., & Wassell, G. (2000). Predictors of barriers to treatment and therapeutic change in outpatient therapy for antisocial children and their families. *Mental Health Services Research, 2,* 27–40.

Kazdin, A. E., & Whitley, M. K. (2006). Pretreatment social relations, therapeutic alliance, and improvements in parenting practices in parent management training. *Journal of Consulting and Clinical Psychology, 74,* 346–355.

Kessler, R. C., & Wang, P. S. (2008). The descriptive epidemiology of commonly occurring mental disorders in the United States. *Annual Review of Public Health, 29,* 115–129.

Kiesner, J. (2002). Depressive symptoms in early adolescence: Their relations with classroom problem behavior and peer status. *Journal of Research on Adolescence, 12,* 463–478.

Ladd, G. W., & Troop-Gordon, W. (2003). The role of chronic peer difficulties in the development of children's psychological adjustment problems. *Child Development, 74,* 1344–1367.

Lemery, K. S., Essex, M., & Smider, N. (2002). Revealing the relationship between temperament and behavior problem symptoms by eliminating measurement confounding: Expert ratings and factor analyses. *Child Development, 73,* 867–882.

Lochman, J. E., Barry, T. D., & Pardini, D. A. (2003). Anger control training for aggressive youth. In A. E. Kazdin & J. R. Weisz (Eds.), *Evidence-based psychotherapies for children and adolescents* (pp. 263–281). New York: Guilford Press.

London, B., Downey, G., Bonica, C., & Paltin, I. (2007). Social causes and consequences of rejection sensitivity. *Journal of Research on Adolescence, 17,* 481–506.

Manassis, K., Mendlowitz, S. L., Scapillato, D., Avery, D., Fiksenbaum, L., Freire, M., ... Owens, M. (2002). Group and individual cognitive-behavioral therapy for childhood anxiety disorders. A randomized trial. *Journal of the American Academy of Child & Adolescent Psychiatry, 41,* 1423–1430.

McLeod, B. D., Wood, J., & Weisz, J. (2007). Examining the association between parenting and childhood anxiety: A meta-analysis. *Clinical Psychology Review, 27,* 155–172, 986–1003.

Mufson, L., Dorta, K., Wickramaratne, P., Nomura, Y., Olfson, M., & Weissman M. M. (2004). A randomized effectiveness trial of interpersonal psychotherapy for depressed adolescents. *Archives of General Psychiatry, 61,* 577–584.

Mufson, L., Moreau, D., Weissman, M. M., & Klerman, G. L. (1993). *Interpersonal psychotherapy for depressed adolescents.* New York: Guilford Press.

Mufson, L., Weissman, M., Moreau, D., & Garfinkel, R. (1999). Efficacy of interpersonal psychotherapy for depressed adolescents. *Archives of General Psychiatry, 56,* 573–579.

Muris, P., & Ollendick, T.H. (2005). The role of temperament in the etiology of child psychopathology. *Clinical Child and Family Psychology Review, 8,* 271–289.

O'Brien, B. S., & Frick, P. J. (1996). Reward dominance: Associations with anxiety, conduct problems, and psychopathy in children. *Journal of Abnormal Child Psychology, 24,* 223–240.

Ollendick, T. H., Costa, N. M., & Benoit, K. E. (in press). Interpersonal processes and the anxiety disorders of childhood. In G. Beck (Ed.), *Interpersonal processes in the anxiety disorders: Implications for understanding psychopathology and treatment.* Washington, DC: APA Books.

Ollendick, T. H., & Hersen, M. (Eds.) (1998). *Handbook of child psychopathology.* 3rd ed.. New York: Plenum Press.

Ollendick, T., & Hirshfeld-Becker, D. (2002). The developmental psychopathology of social anxiety disorder. *Biological Psychiatry, 51,* 44–58.

Ollendick, T. H., & Horsch, L. M. (2007). Fears in clinically referred children: Relations with child anxiety sensitivity, maternal overcontrol, and maternal phobic anxiety. *Behavior Therapy, 38,* 402–411.

Ollendick, T. H., & Shirk, S. R. (in press). Clinical interventions with children and adolescents: Current status and future directions. In D. H. Barlow (Ed.), *Oxford handbook of clinical psychology.* New York: Oxford University Press.

Owens, E. B., & Shaw, D. S. (2003). Predicting growth curves of externalizing behavior across the preschool years. *Journal of Abnormal Child Psychology, 31,* 575–590.

Patterson, G. R. (1982). *A social learning approach: Vol. 3. Coercive family process.* Eugene, OR: Castalia.

Patterson, G. R., Reid, J. B., & Dishion, T. J. (1992). *Antisocial boys.* Eugene, OR: Castalia.

Pettit, G. S., Bates, J. E., & Dodge, K. A. (1997). Supportive parenting, ecological context, and children's adjustment: A seven-year longitudinal study. *Child Development, 68,* 908–923.

Pettit, G. S., & Dodge, K. A. (1993). Family interaction patterns and children's conduct problems at home and school: A longitudinal perspective. *School Psychology Review, 22,* 403–420.

Ravitz, P., Maunder, R., & McBride, C. (2008). Attachment, contemporary interpersonal theory and IPT: An integration of theoretical, clinical, and empirical perspectives. *Journal of Contemporary Psychotherapy, 38,* 11–21.

Robins, R. W., John, O. P., Caspi, A., Moffitt, T. E., & Stouthamer-Loeber, M. (1996). Resilient, overcontrolled, and undercontrolled boys: Three replicable personality types. *Journal of Personality and Social Psychology, 70,* 157–171.

Robinson, T., Smith, S. W., & Miller, M. (2002). Effect of a cognitive behavioral intervention on responses to anger by middle school students with chronic behavior problems. *Behavioral Disorders, 27,* 256–271.

Rossello, J., & Bernal, G. (1999). The efficacy of cognitive behavioral and interpersonal treatments of depression in Puerto Rican adolescents. *Journal of Consulting and Clinical Psychology, 67,* 734–745.

Rothbart, M. K., & Ahadi, S. A. (1994). Temperament and the development of personality. *Journal of Abnormal Psychology, 130,* 55–66.

Rothbart, M. K., & Bates, J. E. (1998). Temperament. In W. Damon (Series Ed.) and N. Eisenberg (Vol. Ed.), *Handbook of child psychology: Vol. 3. Social, emotional, and personality development* (5th ed., pp. 105–176). New York: John Wiley & Sons.

Rubin, K. H., Bukowski, W., & Parker, J. G. (1998). Peer interactions, relationships, and groups. In W. Damon (Series Ed.) and N. Eisenberg (Vol. Ed.), *Handbook of child psychology (5th ed.): Vol. 3. Social, emotional, and personality development* (pp. 619–700). New York: John Wiley & Sons.

Seligman, L. D., & Ollendick, T. H. (1998). Comorbidity of anxiety and depression in children and adolescents: An integrative review. *Clinical Child and Family Psychology Review, 1,* 125–144.

Shaw, D., Bell, R., Gilliom, M. (2000). A true early starter model of antisocial behavior revisited. *Clinical Child and Family Psychology Review, 3,* 155–172.

Shirk, S. R., Gusmundsen, G., Kaplinski, H. C., & McMakin, D. L. (2008). Alliance and outcome in cognitive-behavioral therapy for adolescent depression. *Journal of Clinical Child and Adolescent Psychology, 37*, 631–639.

Siqueland, L., Kendall, P. C., & Steinberg, L. (1996). Anxiety in children: Perceived family environments and observed family interaction. *Journal of Clinical Child Psychology, 25*, 225–237.

The TADS Team. (2007). The treatment for adolescents with depression study (TADS): Long-term effectiveness and safety outcomes. *Archives of General Psychiatry, 64*, 1132–1144.

Thompson, R. A. (1994). Emotion regulation: A theme in search of definition. In N. A. Fox (Ed.), *The development of emotion regulation: Biological and behavioral considerations.* Monographs of the Society for Research in Child Development, 59 (2-3, Serial No. 240), 25–52.

Thompson, R. A. (2001). Childhood anxiety disorders from the perspective of emotion regulation and attachment. In M. Vasey & M. Dadds (Eds.), *The developmental psychopathology of anxiety* (pp. 160–182). New York: Oxford University Press.

Thompson, R. A., Easterbrooks, M. A., & Padilla-Walker, L. (2003). Social and emotional development in infancy. In R. Lerner, M. Easterbrooks, & J. Mistry (Eds.), *Handbook of psychology: Developmental psychology* (pp. 91–112). Hoboken, NJ: John Wiley & Sons.

Trowell, J., Joffe, I., Campbell, J., Clemente, C., Almqvist, F., Soininen, M., ... Tsiantis, J. (2007). Childhood depression: A place for psychotherapy: An outcome study comparing individual psychodynamic psychotherapy and family therapy. *European Child & Adolescent Psychiatry, 16*, 157–167.

Verdeli, H., Mufson, L., Lee, L., & Keith, J. (2006). Review of evidence-based psychotherapies for pediatric mood and anxiety disorders. *Current Psychiatry Reviews, 2*, 395–421.

Watson, D., & Clark. L. A. (1984). Negative affectivity: The disposition to experience aversive emotional states. *Psychological Bulletin, 96*, 465–490.

Wood, J. J., Piacentini, J. C., Southam-Gerow, M., Chu, B. C., & Sigman, M. (2006). Family cognitive behavioral therapy for child anxiety disorders. *Journal of the American Academy of Child and Adolescent Psychiatry, 45*, 314–321.

Woody, S. R., & Ollendick, T. H. (2006). Technique factors in treating anxiety disorders. In L. Castonguay & L. E. Beutler (Eds.), *Principles of therapeutic change that work* (pp. 167–186). New York: Oxford University Press.

29 THE THERAPEUTIC ALLIANCE RESEARCH AND THEORY

Louis G. Castonguay

Michael J. Constantino

James F. Boswell

David R. Kraus

One could argue that at its essence psychotherapy is, or at least always involves, an interpersonal process. Not surprisingly then, relationship concepts such as the therapeutic alliance have received considerable attention in the psychotherapy literature. Theorists from varied psychotherapeutic approaches have long recognized the client-therapist alliance as a crucial component of change. To our knowledge, all scholars who have attempted to identify variables that cut across theoretical orientations have highlighted the alliance as a common factor in psychotherapy (e.g., Frank, 1961; Garfield, 1980; Goldfried, 1980; Strupp, 1973). Reflecting its salience in the study and practice of psychotherapy, most current treatment manuals emphasize the importance of establishing and maintaining a positive alliance, including modalities that have not traditionally highlighted the patient-therapist relationship as a central change mechanism (see Castonguay, Constantino, McAleavey, & Goldfried, in press).

There also appears to be an increasing consensus in the field with respect to the characteristics that define the alliance. As we have written elsewhere, "It is generally agreed that the alliance represents interactive, collaborative elements of the relationship (i.e., therapist and client abilities to engage in the tasks of therapy and to agree on the targets of therapy) in the context of an affective bond or positive attachment" (Constantino, Castonguay, & Schut, 2002, p. 86). Empirically, the alliance has been the most frequently studied therapy process, a trend facilitated by the development of numerous psychometrically sound instruments to measure this construct from client, therapist, and observer perspectives (see Constantino et al., 2002; Horvath & Greenberg, 1994). Although several of the alliance scales have been psychoanalytically anchored, at least one of them, the Working Alliance Inventory (WAI; Horvath & Greenberg, 1989), captures a trans-theoretical perspective. Thus, the alliance can and has been measured in many forms of therapy.

The goals of this chapter are to review briefly what we see as the main empirical findings on the alliance to date and to highlight what we think are the most important future research directions for the alliance, to help us better understand this construct both theoretically and clinically.

ALLIANCE AND OUTCOME

It is now well established that the alliance correlates positively with therapeutic change across a variety of clinical problems, treatments, and theoretical perspectives (Castonguay & Beutler, 2006a; Castonguay, Constantino, & Grosse Holtforth, 2006). Based on multiple meta-analyses, the weighted r effect size for the alliance-outcome association ranges from .22 to .26 (see Horvath & Bedi, 2002; Martin, Garske, & Davis, 2000). Although the size of this relationship is not large, it appears to be robust. Furthermore, the effect might be considered substantial for a variable being measured within the complex entity of psychotherapy (Horvath & Bedi, 2002).

Evidence also suggests that the alliance is particularly predictive of outcome when measured early in treatment and that poor early alliance predicts client dropout (see Constantino et al., 2002). Additionally, although most therapists might feel that they are generally able to judge accurately the quality of the relationship that they have with their clients, research suggests that client and therapist views of the alliance diverge (especially during the early part of therapy), and that the client's perspective tends to be more predictive of outcome (again, this is most pronounced early) (see Horvath & Bedi, 2002). There is some evidence that similarity between client and therapist alliance ratings at the middle and late phases of treatment is positively linked with outcome (see Horvath & Bedi, 2002). Client perspectives of the alliance tend to be more predictive of outcome than therapist perspectives. Nonetheless, there is preliminary evidence indicating that the alliance-outcome association is primarily driven at the therapist level. Using multilevel modeling techniques, Baldwin, Wampold, and Imel (2007) found that differences between therapists in their average client-rated alliance accounted for more variance in the alliance-outcome correlation than differences between clients with the same therapist.

Although the alliance has been linked with outcome, the causal direction of this relationship has not been clearly established (c.f., Barber, 2009; DeRubeis & Feeley, 1990; Feeley, DeRubeis, & Gelfand, 1999). However, the fact that the alliance measured early in treatment is the strongest predictor of posttherapy change increases the likelihood that its quality precedes, rather than follows, substantial improvement. More convincingly, some studies have found that the alliance predicts change subsequent to when it is measured and when controlling for previous change (e.g., Barber, Connolly, Crits-Cristoph, Gladis, & Siqueland, 2000; Castonguay et al., 2008; Klein et al., 2003), further suggesting that the alliance-outcome association is not just an artifact of clients getting better over time (see also Baldwin et al., 2007). In several other studies, however, the alliance has failed to correlate with subsequent change when accounting statistically for prior symptom change (e.g., Barber et al., 1999; Gaston, Marmar, Gallagher, & Thompson, 1991).

A recently emerging direction is to examine the alliance as a mediator of other process-outcome associations. For example, analyzing data from the Treatment of Depression Collaborative Research Program (TDCRP; Elkin, 1994), Meyer and colleagues (2002) found that the alliance mediated the association between clients' pretreatment expectations for change and treatment outcome. Hardy et al. (2001), in a study of cognitive therapy for depression, found that the relationship between clients' underinvolved style and outcome was mediated through the therapeutic alliance. Because alliance quality in these studies was measured at a time between the process variable and outcome variable, the findings again suggest that the alliance precedes improvement as a potential mediator, or mechanism, of change (see Kraemer, Wilson, Fairburn, & Agras, 2002).

In recent developments, experimental trials have implicated a positive impact of training on and implementation of alliance-fostering interventions (e.g., Crits-Christoph et al., 2006; Grawe, Caspar, & Ambühl, 1990) and alliance-repair strategies (e.g., Castonguay et al., 2004; Constantino et al., 2008; Muran, Safran, Samstag, & Winston, 2005), thus lending additional support for the causal influence of the alliance. These experimental trials, while promising, are generally prelim-inary and require replication in both controlled research and real-world settings to determine more convincingly that such techniques have direct, unique, and causal effects on client improvement.

As reviewed above, researchers have begun to address the issue of the direction and nature of the alliance's impact on treatment process and outcome. It is probable, however, that if and when a resolution is achieved, the consensus will be more complex than an "either/or" type of answer (e.g., "the relationship is, above all, the only factor that counts in therapy" or "alliance is only an artifact of client improvement"). The process of change, in our view, involves the synergistic relationships among different variables.

ALLIANCE PATTERNS

Some evidence suggests that different patterns of alliance development may be linked with positive outcome (Kivlighan & Shaughnessy, 2000; Patton, Kivlighan, & Multon, 1997; Stiles et al., 2004; Tracey

& Ray, 1984). However, these findings have demonstrated some inconsistency (c.f., Bachelor & Salamé, 2000; Krupnick, Sotsky, Simmens, & Moyer, 1996) and, thus, more studies are needed to form more definitive conclusions regarding such dynamic patterns. These studies would provide useful information to clinicians who could use different types of alliance patterns as feedback on the progress of therapy. For example, if a high-low-high alliance pattern reliably predicts good outcome, then a therapist need not be alarmed by a decrease in alliance scores during treatment. Instead, it may reflect that things have to get worse before they get better, including in the client-therapist relationship. Findings from such studies may in turn generate investigations to determine if and how different alliance patterns may be a cause, an effect, and/or a reflection of improvement.

Additional research should also be conducted on the effect of tracking and responding to the alliance during therapy. In an innovative study, Whipple et al. (2003) examined the impact on treat-ment outcomes of providing therapists with feedback on various client-rated dimensions (including alliance quality) and recommending clinical strategies (Clinical Support Tools; CSTs) to address potential problem areas. Compared to a no-feedback control group, clients in the feedback plus CSTs group attended more sessions and demonstrated more symptom reduction. These promising findings should generate further studies on the effects of helping therapists to monitor and react therapeutically to alliance feedback.

ALLIANCE DEVELOPMENT

Related to the issue of alliance patterns is the question of how the alliance develops. There is preliminary evidence that therapists who undergo a structured clinical training (including strategies for building rapport, developing collaboration, making empathic connections, and exploring clients' relational problems, including as they manifest in the client-therapist exchange) establish better alliances than therapists with unstructured training (Hilsenroth, Ackerman, Clemence, Strassle, & Handler, 2002). However, more research is needed to determine the impact of specific alliance-fostering guidelines defined both within and across therapy approaches.

In our efforts to better understand how the alliance develops, it might be wise to pay particular attention to its very first step. Some researchers have argued that the early alliance may distinguish itself from later alliance in terms of the impact, manifestations, and sources of alliance ruptures that tend to occur (MacEwan, Halgin, Constantino, & Piselli, 2009; Maramba, Castonguay, Constantino, & DeGeorge, 2009). Furthermore, it is important to understand how client and therapist characteristics might influence the development of a collaborative engagement and positive attachment early in treatment.

PREDICTORS OF ALLIANCE

Research indicates that alliance quality correlates positively with some client characteristics and behaviors (e.g., psychological mindedness, expectation for change, quality of object relations) and negatively with others (e.g., avoidance, interpersonal difficulties, depressogenic cognitions) (see Constantino, Castonguay, Zack, & DeGeorge, in press; Constantino et al., 2002). Furthermore, some of these associations hold even when accounting for symptom change prior to when the alliance is measured, suggesting that the variance explained in the alliance is not solely attributable to symptomatic improvement (e.g., Connolly Gibbons et al., 2003; Constantino, Arnow, Blasey, & Agras, 2005).

Research also suggests that certain therapist characteristics and behaviors are positively associated with quality alliances (e.g., warmth, flexibility, trustworthiness;

see Ackerman & Hilsenroth, 2003). In a study on the early alliance, Constantino et al. (2005) found that alliance quality was positively associated with clients' perceptions of their therapists treating them as they tend to treat themselves (perhaps meeting the clients' need to have their self-concepts verified by others). Certain therapist characteristics and behaviors may also contribute to alliance difficulties (e.g., rigidity, criticalness, inappropriate self-disclosure; see Ackerman & Hilsenroth, 2001). In a theoretically driven study examining interpersonal history and in-session behavior, Henry, Strupp, Butler, Schacht, and Binder (1993) showed that therapists who are hostile toward themselves appear to be particularly at risk for countertherapeutic interactions with their clients. Similarly, Rosenberger and Hayes (2002) examined in a single-case study how the alliance can be affected if the material discussed in the session touches the therapist's own unresolved issues.

GENERAL GUIDELINES FOR FUTURE RESEARCH

Despite the many alliance-focused studies mentioned above, much more research is required to more fully understand its determinants, correlates, and consequences. As one future direction, more conceptual and empirical efforts are needed to clarify the relationship between the alliance and other relational constructs. For example, how distinct is the alliance from therapist empathy, and how much of the outcome variance explained by each of these two constructs is common to both or unique to each (e.g., DeGeorge et al., 2008)? More studies are also needed to clarify the relationship between the alliance and techniques prescribed by different orientations. For example, based on their review of the literature, Crits-Christoph and Connolly Gibbons (2002) concluded that too few studies have been conducted on the relationship between interpretation and alliance to derive reliable conclusions.

Whatever future research reveals, the technique-alliance relationship is likely to be complex. This has been underscored in several qualitative studies suggesting that when faced with alliance ruptures or therapeutic impasses, therapists' increased or rigid adherence to prescribed techniques or the therapeutic rationale may not only fail to repair such ruptures, but also exacerbates them (Castonguay, Goldfried, Wiser, Raue, & Hayes, 1996; Piper et al., 1999). These qualitative analyses are consistent with Schut et al.'s (2005) findings that a higher concentration of interpretations not only related negatively with outcome, but also corresponded to disaffiliative interpersonal processes before and during interpretations.

We also believe that the field should pay attention to specific therapist and client populations. Perhaps one route to better understanding alliance development, maintenance, and negotiation is to study expert therapists to determine, for example, how they first establish a good alliance, the flow of the alliance during treatment with more or less responsive clients, how they attempt (successfully and unsuccessfully) to repair breaches of alliance, how they find balance between the skillful use of techniques and the provision of therapeutic acceptance and support, and how they address all of these complex issues with different types of clients.

More research also needs to be conducted with minority clients. For example, it seems important to explicate culture-specific markers of alliance rupture (Constantino & Wilson, 2007). Furthermore, although there is a small literature that suggests that ethnic minority clients are more likely to terminate therapy prematurely than Caucasian clients (especially when being treated by Caucasian therapists), the reasons for this phenomenon are not well known. It is possible that the link between ethnicity and dropout is mediated by alliance quality.

More alliance research is also needed with personality-disordered clients (Bender, 2005). In their review of the literature, Smith, Barrett, Benjamin, and Barber (2006) found that studies with personality-disordered clients have suggested that the alliance is linked with outcome, and that alliance repair techniques appear to be promising. Many questions, however, remain open for exploration. Interpersonal dysfunction, for example, is a core component of most personality disorders. Although quality of object relations has been shown to predict the alliance (Piper et al., 1991), results of studies attempting to link clients' pretreatment interpersonal relationships with alliance quality have been mixed (Clarkin & Levy, 2004). Some authors have hypothesized that the relationship between attachment and outcome is mediated by alliance quality (Clarkin & Levy, 2004). Related to this hypothesis, client attachment has been linked with treatment response in borderline personality disorder (Fonagy et al., 1996), and has elsewhere been found to predict alliance rupture frequency (Eames & Roth, 2000). Thus, future research should focus on testing hypothesized mediators more directly in order to increase our understanding of potential change mechanisms in the treatment of personality disorders. For example, how do interpersonal factors specifically influence alliance development? Other pertinent research questions might include: Do different types of alliance ruptures and alliance patterns tend to emerge for different types of personality disorders? Are different strategies of intervention required for different personality disorders with regard to the establishment and repair of the alliance?

It also seems important to determine the type of clients for whom the addition of alliance repair techniques might not be necessary, or not sufficient to improve the effectiveness of therapy. Given that many clients benefit from treatment protocols that do not explicitly prescribe alliance repair interventions, the addition of such interventions may not show significant incremental change for these clients. Furthermore, alliance ruptures may not be the reason (or at least not the only reason) that some individuals fail to respond to empirically supported treatments. With such clients, alliance ruptures, if and when they emerge, may be a reflection of other issues, or may simply be less important than other treatment difficulties. For example, the recognition of empathic failure may not add much to a therapist's effectiveness when treating a person with substance abuse who is not willing to change his/her drinking behavior.

In contrast, the addition of alliance repair techniques might be particularly beneficial for some individuals. For example, cognitive behavior therapists treating depressed clients with high levels of reactance (i.e., reluctance to being controlled by others) should be aware that directive treatments do not fare well with these clients (Beutler, Blatt, Alimohamed, Levy, & Angtuaco, 2005). However, it is possible that reactant clients might still benefit from cognitive behavioral therapy if it is used by a therapist who is mindful of, and ready to deal with, clients' potential negative reactions to perceptions of being controlled (see Castonguay, 2000; Goldfried & Castonguay, 1993). Alliance repair techniques may also be particularly beneficial for clients with moderate problems of attachment or interpersonal relationships. These strategies may pave the way for corrective relational experiences and the disconfirmation of cyclical maladaptive patterns.

CONCLUDING THOUGHTS

Although much more research is needed, enough studies have been conducted on the therapeutic alliance to derive one clear conclusion: it should no longer be viewed as a "nonspecific" variable, i.e., a variable for which the nature and impact is not yet understood (see Castonguay 1993; Castonguay & Grosse Holtforth, 2005). Contrary to the way relationship factors have been viewed for many years, the alliance has now been clearly operationalized. It is fair to say that it has been measured, in a reliable way, more frequently than most other process variables (including

psychotherapy techniques). We also know that the alliance correlates with outcome, and that there is some suggestion that the alliance may have a specific, causal impact on client improvement.

As we mentioned earlier, however, the cause and effect relationship between alliance and outcome has not been firmly established. Scholars from different orientations have argued that there are two ways through which the alliance can contribute to client improvement (see Constantino et al., 2002). First, the alliance can have an indirect effect by facilitating the implementation of techniques. If clients feel respected by their therapists and/or agree with the proposed treatment goals and tasks, then they are likely to be engaged in the therapeutic process aimed at or required by the prescribed interventions. Second, the alliance can have a direct curative value. For example, psychodynamic and cognitive-behavioral scholars have argued that the therapeutic relationship provides an optimal context for corrective experiences, where the client is treated differently from the way he or she is treated by other significant persons, and can learn new ways of relating with self and others (e.g., Alexander and French, 1946; Castonguay et al., in press). This is also consistent with Rogers's (1951) assertion that if therapists genuinely accept their clients for who they are, clients will treat their experience with the same level of acceptance and, thus, integrate aspects of self that were previously denied (which in turn will result in decreased psychological suffering).

However, we believe that much more theoretical and empirical effort is needed to clarify further the relationships between alliance and improvement. As Horvath (2005) has argued, there needs to be heightened theoretical discourse and debate around the construct of the client-therapist relationship. There is also a dire need for more theory-driven research of alliance-outcome linkages. Hilliard, Henry, and Strupp (2000) provided one good example of a study that placed the hypotheses, measures, and findings within a specific (psychodynamically oriented) theoretical framework that involved early interpersonal histories, the quality of the therapeutic alliance during therapy, and treatment outcome. The authors found that the early interpersonal histories of both the clients and therapists had various types of direct or indirect influences on the process and outcome of treatment. More work of this nature is needed, along with investigations that recognize the complex interaction of relational, technical, and participant variables in the process of change (Castonguay & Beutler, 2006).

References

Ackerman, S. J., & Hilsenroth, M. J. (2001). A review of therapist characteristics and techniques negatively impacting the therapeutic alliance. *Psychotherapy: Theory, Research, Practice, Training, 38*, 171–185.

Ackerman, S. J., & Hilsenroth, M. J. (2003). A review of therapist characteristics and techniques positively impacting the therapeutic alliance. *Clinical Psychology Review, 23*, 1–33.

Alexander, F., & Frech, T. M. (1946). *Psychoanalytic therapy: Principles and applications.* New York: Ronald Press.

Baldwin, S. A. Wampold, B. E., & Imel, Z. E. (2007). Untangling the alliance-outcome correlation: Exploring the relative importance of therapist and patient variability in the alliance. *Journal of Consulting and Clinical Psychology, 75*, 842–852.

Barber, J. P. (2009). Toward a working through of some core conflicts in psychotherapy research. *Psychotherapy Research, 19*, 1–12.

Bachelor, A., & Salamé, R. (2000). Participants' perceptions of dimensions of the therapeutic alliance over the course of therapy. *Journal of Psychotherapy Practice and Research, 9*, 39–53.

Barber, J. P., Connolly Gibbons, M. B., Crits-Cristoph, P., Gladis, L., & Siqueland, L. (2000). Alliance predicts patients' outcome beyond in-treatment change in symptoms. *Journal of Consulting and Clinical Psychology, 68*, 1027–1032.

Bender, D. S. (2005). Therapeutic alliance. In J. M. Oldam, A. E. Skodol, & D. S. Bender (Eds.), *The American Psychiatric Publishing textbook of personality disorders* (pp. 405–420). Washington, DC: American Psychiatric Publishing.

Beutler, L. E., Blatt, S. J., Alimohamed, S., Levy, K. N., & Angtuaco, L. A. (2005). Participants' factors in treating dysphoric disorders. In L. G. Castonguay & L. E. Beutler (Eds.), *Principles of therapeutic change that work* (pp. 13–63). New York: Oxford University Press.

Castonguay, L. G. (1993). "Common factors" and "nonspecific variables": Clarification of the two concepts and recommendations for research. *Journal of Psychotherapy Integration, 3*, 267–286.

Castonguay, L. G. (2000). A common factors approach to psychotherapy training. *Journal of Psychotherapy Integration, 10*, 263–282.

Castonguay, L. G., & Beutler, L. E. (Eds.) (2006a). *Principles of therapeutic change that work.* New York: Oxford University Press.

Castonguay, L. G., & Beutler, L. E. (2006b). Common and unique principles of therapeutic change: What do we know and what do we need to know? In L. G. Castonguay & L. E. Beutler (Eds.), *Principles of therapeutic change that work* (pp. 353–369). New York: Oxford University Press.

Castonguay, L. G., Constantino, M. J., Boswell, J. F., Przeworski, A., Newman, M. G., & Borkovec, T. D. (2008, June). *Alliance, therapist adherence, therapist competence, and client receptivity: New analyses on change processes in CBT for generalized anxiety disorder.* Paper presented at the 39th annual meeting of the Society for Psychotherapy Research, Barcelona, Spain.

Castonguay, L. G., Constantino, M. J., & Gross Holtforth, M. (2006). The working alliance: Where are we and where should we go? *Psychotherapy: Theory, Research, Practice, Training 43*, 271–279.

Castonguay, L. G., Constantino, M. J., McAleavey, A. A., & Goldfried, M. R. (in press). The alliance in cognitive-behavioral therapy. In J. C. Muran & J. P. Barber, (Eds.), *The therapeutic alliance: An evidence-based approach to practice and training.* New York: Guilford Press.

Castonguay, L. G., Goldfried, M. R., Wiser, S., Raue, P. J., & Hayes, A. M. (1996). Predicting the effect of cognitive therapy for depression: A study of unique and common factors. *Journal of Consulting and Clinical Psychology, 64*, 497–504.

Castonguay, L. G., & Grosse Holtforth, M. (2005). Change in psychotherapy: A plea for no more "non-specific" and false dichotomy. *Clinical Psychology: Science and Practice, 12*, 198–201.

Castonguay, L. G., Grosse Holtforth, M., Coombs, M. M., Beberman, R. A., Kakouros, A. A., Boswell, J. F., . . . Jones, E. E. (2005). Relationship factors in treating dysphoric disorders. In L. G. Castonguay & L. E. Beutler (Eds.), *Principles of therapeutic change that work* (pp. 65–81). New York: Oxford University Press.

Castonguay, L. G., Schut, A. J., Aikins, D., Constantino, M. J., Laurenceau, J. P., Bologh, L., & Burns, D. D. (2004). Integrative cognitive therapy: A preliminary investigation. *Journal of Psychotherapy Integration, 14*, 4–20.

Clarkin, J. F., & Levy, K. N. (2004). The influence of client variables on psychotherapy. In M. J. Lambert (Ed.), *Bergin and Garfield's handbook of psychotherapy and behavior change* (5th ed., pp. 194–226). New York: John Wiley & Sons.

Connolly Gibbons, M. B., Crits-Christoph, P., de la Cruz, C., Barber, J. P., Siqueland, L., & Gladis, M. (2003). Pretreatment expectations, interpersonal functioning, and symptoms in the prediction of the therapeutic alliance across supportive-expressive psychotherapy and cognitive therapy. *Psychotherapy Research, 13*, 59–76.

Constantino, M. J., Arnow, B. A., Blasey, C., & Agras, W. S. (2005). The association between patient characteristics and the therapeutic alliance in cognitive-behavioral and interpersonal therapy for bulimia nervosa. *Journal of Consulting and Clinical Psychology, 73*, 203–211.

Constantino, M. J., Castonguay, L. G., Angtuaco, L. A., Pincus, A. L., Newman, M. G., & Borkovec, T. D. (2005, June). *The impact of interpersonal-intrapsychic complementarity on the development and course of the therapeutic alliance.* Paper presented at the 36th annual meeting of the Society for Psychotherapy Research, Montreal, Canada.

Constantino, M. J., Castonguay, L. G., & Schut, A. J. (2002). The working alliance: A flagship for the "scientist-practitioner" model in psychotherapy. In G. S. Tryon (Ed.), *Counseling based on process research: Applying what we know* (pp. 81–131). Boston: Allyn & Bacon.

Constantino, M. J., Castonguay, L. G., Zack, S. E., & DeGeorge, J. (in press). Engagement in psychotherapy: Factors contributing to the facilitation, demise, and restoration of the working alliance. In D. Castro-Blanco & M. S. Karver (Ed.) *Elusive alliance: Treatment engagement strategies with high-risk adolescents.*

Washington, DC: American Psychological Association Press.

Constantino, M. J., Marnell, M., Haile, A. J., Kanther-Sista, S. N., Wolman, K., Zappert, L., & Arnow, B. A. (2008). Integrative cognitive therapy for depression: A randomized pilot comparison. *Psychotherapy: Theory, Research, Practice, Training, 45*, 122–134.

Constantino, M. J., & Wilson, K. R. (2007). Negotiating difference and the therapeutic alliance. In J. C. Muran (Ed.), *Dialogues on difference: Studies in diversity in the therapeutic relationship* (pp. 236–242). Washington, DC: American Psychological Association.

Crits-Christoph, P., Connolly Gibbons, M. B., Crits-Christoph, K., Narducci, J., Schamberger, M., & Gallop, R. (2006). Can therapists be trained to improve their alliances? A preliminary study of alliance-fostering psychotherapy. *Psychotherapy Research, 16*, 268–281.

Crits-Christoph, P., Connolly Gibbons, M. B., Narducci, J., Schamberger, M., & Gallop, R. (2005). Interpersonal problems and the outcome of interpersonally oriented psychodynamic treatment of GAD. *Psychotherapy: Theory, Research, Practice, Training, 42*, 211–224.

Dalenberg, C. J. (2004). Maintaining the safe and effective therapeutic relationship in the context of distrust and anger: Countertransference and complex trauma. *Psychotherapy: Theory, Research, Practice, Training, 41*, 438–447.

DeGeorge, J., Constantino, M. J., Castonguay, L. G., Manning, M. A., Newman, M. G., & Borkovec, T. D. (2008, June). *Empathy and the therapeutic alliance: Their relationship to each other and to outcome in CBT for generalized anxiety disorder.* Paper presented at the 39th annual meeting of the Society for Psychotherapy Research, Barcelona, Spain.

DeRubeis, R. J., & Feeley, M. (1990). Determinants of change in cognitive therapy for depression. *Cognitive Therapy and Research, 14*, 469–482.

Eames, V., & Roth, A. (2000). Patient attachment orientation and early working alliance—A study of patient and therapist reports of alliance quality and ruptures. *Psychotherapy Research, 10*, 421–434.

Elkin, I. (1994). The NIMH Treatment of Depression Collaborative Research Program: Where we began and where we are. In A. E. Bergin & A. L. Garfield (Eds.), *Handbook of psychotherapy and behavior change* (4th ed., pp. 114–149). New York: John Wiley & Sons.

Feeley, M., DeRubeis, R. J., & Gelfand, L. A. (1999). The temporal relation of adherence and alliance to symptom change in cognitive therapy for depression. *Journal of Consulting and Clinical Psychology, 67*, 578–582.

Fonagy, P., Leigh, T., Steele, M., Steele, H., Kennedy, R., Mattoon, G., . . . Gerber, A. (1996). The relation of attachment status, psychiatric classification, and response to psychotherapy. *Journal of Consulting and Clinical Psychology, 64*, 22–31.

Frank, J. D. (1961). *Persuasion and healing.* Baltimore: Johns Hopkins University Press.

Garfield, S. L. (1980). *Psychotherapy: An eclectic approach.* New York: John Wiley & Sons.

Gaston, L., Marmar, C. R., Gallagher, D., & Thompson, L. W. (1991). Alliance prediction of outcome beyond in-treatment symptomatic change as psychotherapy processes. *Psychotherapy Research, 1*, 104–113.

Goldfried, M. R. (1980). Toward the delineation of therapeutic change principles. *American Psychologist, 35*(11), 991–999.

Goldfried, M. R., & Castonguay, L. G. (1993). Behavior therapy: Redefining clinical strengths and limitations. *Behavior Therapy, 24*, 505–526.

Grawe, K. (1997). Research-informed psychotherapy. *Psychotherapy Research, 7*, 1–19.

Grawe, K., Caspar, F. & Ambuhl, H. (1990). Differentielle Psychotherapieforschung: Vier Therapieformen im Vergleich: Prozessvergleich. [Differential psychotherapy research: Four types of therapy in comparison: Process comparison] *Zeitschrift fur Klinische Psychologie, 19*, 316–377.

Grosse Holtforth, M., & Castonguay, L. G. (in press). Relationship and techniques in CBT: A motivational approach. *Psychotherapy: Theory, Research, Practice, Training.*

Hardy, G. E., Cahill, J. Shapiro, D. A., Barkham, M., Rees, A., & Macaskill, N. (2001). Client interpersonal and cognitive styles as predictors of response to time-limited cognitive therapy for depression. *Journal of Consulting and Clinical Psychology, 69*, 841–845.

Henry, W. P., Strupp, H. H., Butler, S. F., Schacht, T. E., & Binder, J. L. (1993). The effects of training in time-limited dynamic psychotherapy: Changes in therapist behavior. *Journal of Consulting and Clinical Psychology, 61*, 434–440.

Hill, C. E., Kellems, I. S., Kolchakian, M. R., Wonnell, T. L., Davis, T. L., & Nakayama, E. Y. (2003). The therapist experience of being the target of hostile versus suspected-unasserted client anger: Factors associated with resolution. *Psychotherapy Research, 13*, 475–491.

Hilliard, R. B., Henry, W. P., & Strupp, H. H. (2000). An interpersonal model of psychotherapy: Linking patient and therapist developmental history, therapeutic process, and types of outcome. *Journal of Consulting and Clinical Psychology, 68*, 125–133.

Hilsenroth, M. J., Ackerman, S. J., Clemence, A. J., Strassle, C. G., & Handler, L. (2002). Effects of structured clinician training on patient and therapist perspectives of alliance early in psychotherapy. *Psychotherapy: Theory, Research, Practice, Training, 39*, 309–323.

Horvath, A. O. (2005). The therapeutic relationship: Research and theory. An introduction to the Special Issue. *Psychotherapy Research, 15*, 3–7.

Horvath, A. O., & Bedi, R. P. (2002). The alliance. In J. C. Norcross (Ed.), *Psychotherapy relationships that work: Therapists contributions and responsiveness to patients* (pp. 37–69). New York: Oxford University Press.

Horvath, A. O., & Greenberg, L. S. (1989). Development and validation of the Working Alliance Inventory. *Journal of Counseling Psychology, 36*, 223–233.

Horvath, A. O., & Greenberg, L. S. (1994). *The working alliance: Theory, research, and practice.* New York: John Wiley & Sons.

Kivlighan, D. M., & Shaughnessy, P. (2000). Pattern of working alliance development: A typology of client's working ratings. *Journal of Counseling Psychology, 4*, 362–371

Klein, D. K., Schwartz, J. E., Santiago, N. J., Vivian D., Vocisano, C., Castonguay, L. G., . . . Keller, M. B. (2003). The therapeutic alliance in chronic depression: Prediction of treatment response after controlling for prior change and patient characteristics. *Journal of Consulting and Clinical Psychology, 71*, 997–1006.

Kraemer, H. C., Wilson, G. T., Fairburn, C. G., & Agras, W. S. (2002). Mediators and moderators of treatment effects in randomized clinical trials. *Archives of General Psychiatry, 59*, 877–883.

Krupnick, J. L., Sotsky, S. M., Simmens, S., & Moyer, J. (1996). The role of the therapeutic alliance in psychotherapy and pharmacotherapy outcome: Findings in the National Institute of

Mental Health Treatment of Depression Collaborative Research Program. *Journal of Consulting and Clinical Psychology, 64,* 532–539.

MacEwan, G. H., Halgin, R. P., Constantino, M. J., & Piselli, A. (2009). *Efforts of psychotherapists in the first session to establish a therapeutic alliance.* Manuscript submitted for publication.

Maramba, G. G., Castonguay, L. G., Constantino, M. J., & DeGeorge, J. (2009). *Beliefs and early alliance ruptures.* Manuscript submitted for publication.

Martin, D. J., Garske, J. P., & Davis, M. K. (2000). Relation of the therapeutic alliance with outcome and other variables: A meta-analytic review. *Journal of Consulting and Clinical Psychology, 68,* 438–450.

Meyer, B., Pilkonis, P. A., Krupnick, J. L., Egan, M. K., Simmens, S. J., & Sotsky, S. M. (2002). Treatment expectancies, patient alliance, and outcome: Further analyses from the National Institute of Mental Health Treatment of Depression Collaborative Research Program. *Journal of Consulting and Clinical Psychology, 70,* 1051–1055.

Muran, J., Safran, J., Samstag, L., & Winston, A. (2005). Evaluating an alliance-focused treatment for personality disorders. *Psychotherapy Theory, Research, Practice, Training, 42,* 532–545.

Newman, C. F. (1997). Maintaining professionalism in the face of emotional abuse from clients. *Cognitive and Behavioral Practice, 4,* 1–29.

Norcross, J. C. (Ed.) (2002). *Psychotherapy relationships that work: Therapist contributions and responsiveness to patients.* New York: Oxford University Press.

Patton, M. J., Kivlighan, D. M., Jr., & Multon, K. D. (1997). The Missouri psychoanalytic counseling research project: Relation of changes in counseling process to client outcome. *Journal of Counseling Psychology, 44,* 189–208.

Piper, W. E., Azim, H. F. A., Joyce, A. S., McCallum, M., Nixon, G. W. H., & Siegal, P. S. (1991). Quality of object relations versus interpersonal functioning as predictors of therapeutic alliance and psychotherapy outcome. *Journal of Nervous and Mental Disease, 179,* 432–438.

Piper, W. E., Ogrodniczuk, J. S., Joyce, A. S., McCallum, M., Rosie, J. S., O'Kelly, J. G., & Steinberg, P. I. (1999). Prediction of dropping out in time-limited, interpretive individual psychotherapy. *Psychotherapy: Theory, Research, Practice, Training 36,* 114–122.

Rogers, C. R. (1951). *Client-centered therapy.* Boston, MA: Houghton Mifflin.

Rosenberger, E. W., & Hayes, J. A. (2002). Origins, consequences, and management of countertransference: A case study. *Journal of Counseling Psychology, 49,* 221–232.

Smith, T. L., Barrett, M. S., Benjamin, L. S., & Barber, J. P. (2006). Relationship factors in treating personality disorders. In L. G. Castonguay & L. E. Beutler (Eds.), *Principles of therapeutic change that work* (pp. 219–238). New York: Oxford University Press.

Stiles, W. B., Glick, M. J., Osatuke, K., Hardy, G. E., Shapiro, D. A., Agnew-Davies, R., ... Barkham, M. (2004). Patterns of alliance development and the rupture-repair hypothesis: Are productive relationships U-shaped or V-shaped? *Journal of Counseling Psychology, 51,* 81–92.

Strupp, H. H. (1973). On the basic ingredients of psychotherapy. *Journal of Consulting and Clinical Psychology, 41,* 1–8.

Tracey, T. J., & Ray, P. B. (1984). The stages of successful time-limited counseling: An interactional examination. *Journal of Counseling Psychology, 31,* 13–27.

Whipple, J. L., Lambert, M. J., Vermeersch, D. A., Smart, D. W., Nielson, S. L., & Hawkins, E. J. (2003). Improving the effects of psychotherapy: The use of early identification of treatment failure and problem-solving strategies in routine clinical practice. *Journal of Counseling Psychology, 50,* 59–68.

30 INTERPERSONAL INTERVENTIONS FOR MAINTAINING AN ALLIANCE

Catherine Eubanks-Carter

J. Christopher Muran

Jeremy D. Safran

Jeffrey A. Hayes

THERAPEUTIC INTERPERSONAL INTERVENTIONS: RESOLVING ALLIANCE RUPTURES

A substantial body of research has provided evidence that the therapeutic alliance is one of the most robust predictors of outcome (Horvath & Bedi, 2002; Martin, Garske, & Davis, 2000). Over the past two decades, a "second generation" (Safran, Muran, Samstag, & Stevens, 2002) of alliance research has sought to clarify how the alliance develops, why strains or ruptures occur, and how the alliance can be repaired. In this chapter, we review theory and research on alliance ruptures and their resolution, summarize points of consensus, and suggest future directions for this growing area of study.

ALLIANCE RUPTURES

Theory and research on alliance ruptures have been strongly influenced by Bordin's (1979) conceptualization of the alliance as being composed of interrelated factors: the agreement between patient and therapist on the *tasks* and *goals* of treatment and the affective *bond* between patient and therapist. This definition highlights the interdependence of relational and technical factors: It suggests that the meaning of technical factors can only be understood in the relational context in which they are applied. It also highlights the importance of ongoing *negotiation* between patient and therapist on the tasks and goals of therapy. This negotiation is always taking place. When treatment is proceeding smoothly, negotiation may occur without conscious awareness. For example, a therapist may decide not to use a particular intervention because he or she has a sense the patient will not find it helpful, or the patient may decide to try a homework activity even though he or she has some doubts about its usefulness. However, there are moments when the negotiation process breaks down. This phenomenon has been described in various ways: as challenges (e.g., Harper, 1989a, 1989b), misunderstanding events (e.g., Rhodes, Hill, Thompson, & Elliott, 1994); impasses (e.g., Hill, Nutt-Williams, Heaton, Thompson, & Rhodes, 1996), alliance threats (e.g., Bennett, Parry, & Ryle, 2006), and markers of enactments (e.g., Safran, 2002). In this chapter, we refer to these breakdowns in negotiation as *ruptures* (see Safran, Crocker, McMain, & Murray, 1990; Safran & Muran, 1996, 2000; Safran, Muran, & Samstag, 1994). We define a rupture as a deterioration in the therapeutic alliance, manifested by a lack of collaboration between patient and therapist on tasks or goals, or by a strain in the emotional bond. Although the word "rupture" connotes a major breakdown in the relationship, the term also applies to minor tensions of which one or both of the participants may be only vaguely aware.

Note that our definition of ruptures related to tasks and goals focuses on lack of collaboration rather than lack of agreement. This reflects our experience that not all disagreements between patients and therapists are ruptures. A patient can express disagreement with the therapist in a collaborative way in the course of negotiation. For example, a patient can disagree with a therapist's interpretation of the patient's behavior and then collaborate with the therapist to reach a shared understanding of the patient's actions. An emphasis on collaboration over agreement is also helpful in instances when a patient has concerns about a task or goal, but expresses agreement with the therapist in an effort to appease the therapist or to avoid

conflict. These surface-level agreements are actually examples of withdrawal ruptures, described below.

Our conceptualization of alliance ruptures is informed by a relational or interpersonal understanding of the psychotherapy process as a negotiation between the patient's desires or needs and those of the therapist (Mitchell, 1993; Mitchell & Aron, 1999). This perspective holds that learning to negotiate the needs of the self versus the needs of others is both a critical developmental task and an ongoing challenge of human existence. Many of the problems people bring into therapy are influenced by difficulties they have negotiating between their needs and the needs of others in interpersonal relationships. Ruptures in the alliance mark when there is a tension between the patient's and therapist's respective desires (see Safran & Muran, 2000). Ruptures can provide a window into the patient's (and the therapist's) dysfunctional interpersonal or relational schemas and behaviors. In a study of ruptures in psychodynamic therapy, Sommerfeld, Orbach, Zim, & Mikulincer (2008) found a significant association between the occurrence of ruptures and the appearance of dysfunctional interpersonal schemas involving the therapist, identified using the core conflictual relationship theme method (CCRT: Luborsky & Crits-Christoph, 1998). This suggests that when ruptures occur, dysfunctional interpersonal schemas are likely to be active; thus, ruptures provide critical opportunities to identify, explore, and change patients' self-defeating patterns of thought and behavior.

Safran et al. (1990) initially identified seven different types of rupture markers. However, influenced by an unpublished coding manual developed by Heather Harper (Harper, 1989a, 1989b), Safran and Muran (1996) began to categorize rupture markers into two overarching subtypes: *withdrawal* and *confrontation* ruptures. These two subtypes can be differentiated by drawing on Horney's (1950) neurotic trends. In withdrawal ruptures, the patient either moves *away* from the therapist (e.g., by avoiding the therapist's questions), or the patient moves *toward* the therapist, but in a way that denies an aspect of the patient's experience (e.g., by being overly deferential and appeasing). In confrontation ruptures, the patient moves *against* the therapist, either by expressing anger or dissatisfaction in a noncollaborative manner (e.g., hostile complaints about the therapist or the treatment) or by trying to pressure or control the therapist (e.g., making demands of the therapist). Withdrawal ruptures mark the pursuit of relatedness at the expense of the need for self-definition; confrontation ruptures mark the expression of self-definition at the expense of relatedness (Safran & Muran, 2000).

There is some evidence that the types of ruptures that tend to emerge may depend on the characteristics of the clinical population or of the treatment. Withdrawal ruptures may be more common than confrontation ruptures in samples of anxious and avoidant patients, as was found in a preliminary investigation of 20 patients with Cluster C personality disorders and Personality Disorder NOS receiving cognitive behavioral therapy, or CBT (Eubanks-Carter, Muran, Safran, & Mitchell, 2008). Less directive treatments may tend to lead to ruptures where the patient wants more direction or structure, whereas more directive treatments may tend to lead to ruptures where the patient resists direction and structure, as Ghadban (2004) found in an analysis of patients' descriptions of rupture events. Within treatments, individual therapists who are more or less directive may also find that they tend to encounter ruptures that correspond to their personal style.

Clinical Significance of Ruptures

Alliance ruptures are clinically significant events because they can lead to premature termination or treatment failure. Research on the therapeutic alliance has shown that weakened alliances are correlated with unilateral termination by the patient (Horvath & Bedi, 2002; Martin, Garske, & Davis, 2000; Samstag, Batchelder, Muran, Safran & Winston, 1998; Tryon & Kane, 1990, 1993, 1995). In a study of 128 patients with Cluster C personality disorders and Personality Disorder NOS, Muran et al. (2009) found that higher rupture intensity, as reported jointly by patients and therapists, was associated with poor outcome on measures of interpersonal functioning. Failure to resolve these ruptures was predictive of dropout.

Ruptures seem to occur very frequently. Muran et al. (2009) found that in the first six sessions of treatment, ruptures were reported by 37% of patients and 56% of therapists. Similarly, Eames and Roth (2000) demonstrated that patients reported ruptures in 19% of the sessions, whereas therapists reported ruptures in 43% of the sessions. Patients may underreport ruptures due to a lack of awareness of them or discomfort with acknowledging them. Similar findings have been reported with studies using observer measures of ruptures. Using transcripts of therapy sessions, Sommerfeld et al. (2008) found that patients reported ruptures in 42% of sessions, whereas observers identified ruptures in 77% of sessions. Eubanks-Carter, Muran, Safran, and Mitchell (2008) had observers code ruptures from video recordings of sessions, and found that patients self-reported ruptures in 35% of sessions, while observers identified at least one rupture marker in every session.

Challenges for Therapists

Therapists need to manage ruptures successfully in order to resolve them and re-engage the patient in the tasks of therapy. However, there is evidence that rupture resolution is a challenging task (Eubanks-Carter & Muran, 2009; Safran, Muran, Samstag, & Stevens, 2001). First, when patients are reluctant to voice their concerns and complaints, therapists may have difficulty recognizing a problem in the alliance. In a qualitative study of patient interview, Rennie (1994) found that patients were afraid of criticizing their therapists, and tended to be deferential in an effort to protect the alliance. In two studies of covert processes in therapy with integrative therapists, Hill and colleagues (Hill, Thompson, Cogar, & Denman, 1993; Regan & Hill, 1992) found that patients were likely to conceal negative thoughts and feelings from their therapists, and therapists were unable to guess the majority of what patients left unsaid. In two additional studies, Hill and colleagues demonstrated the negative consequences when therapists failed to recognize patients' concerns. Rhodes et al. (1994) examined instances in which patients reported feeling misunderstood by their therapists. When patients did not voice their dissatisfaction, therapists failed to recognize that their patients were unhappy with treatment, and the patients often ended the treatment prematurely. In a qualitative analysis of therapists' recollections of rupture events that ended in termination (Hill et al., 1996), Hill and colleagues found that patients did not reveal their dissatisfaction until they had terminated therapy, which often took therapists by surprise.

Ruptures also present challenges to therapists when therapists *are* aware of a problem in the alliance. In the Vanderbilt I study (Henry, Schacht, & Strupp, 1986), therapists responded to patients' negative feelings by expressing their own negative feelings in a defensive fashion. Vanderbilt II sought to rectify this problem by training therapists in a manualized form of time-limited dynamic therapy that was designed to reduce expression of therapist hostility toward difficult patients by focusing on the management of interpersonal patterns in the therapeutic relationship (Henry, Schacht, Strupp, Butler, & Binder, 1993; Henry, Strupp, Butler, Schacht, & Binder, 1993; Strupp, 1993). However, the training led to an *increase* in hostile messages and complex communications (interpretations that can be seen as either helpful or critical—or both), possibly leading to poor outcome (Henry, Schacht & Strupp, 1986, 1990). There was also a trend toward less

warmth/friendliness and greater expression of negative attitudes, behaviors that have been found to negatively impact the alliance (Ackerman & Hilsenroth, 2001).

The unexpected findings of Vanderbilt II may be a result of therapists responding to alliance ruptures by adhering more rigidly to the treatment protocol, rather than responding sensitively to patients' concerns. Castonguay, Goldfried, Wiser, Raue, and Hayes (1996) found similar results in their study of cognitive therapists' focus in the treatment of depression. When cognitive therapists focused on distorted cognitions (an intervention that they expected to enhance treatment), the effect on outcome was negative. A qualitative analysis revealed that in poor outcome cases, therapists often attempted to address ruptures by increasing their adherence to the cognitive model (e.g., challenging distorted cognitions), rather than responding flexibly. Piper and colleagues observed a similar response to ruptures in their studies of psychodynamic therapy. Piper, Azim, Joyce, and McCallum (1991) found that for patients with a history of high-quality object relations, a greater use of transference interpretations was associated with a weaker alliance and poorer outcome. The authors hypothesized that therapists were offering more transference interpretations in an unsuccessful attempt to repair a weakened alliance. Piper and colleagues supported this hypothesis in a study of the final therapy session in a sample of 22 patients who had dropped out of psychodynamic treatment (Piper, Ogrodniczuk, Joyce, McCallum, Rosie, O'Kelly, & Steinberg, 1999). The last sessions prior to dropout typically began with patients expressing dissatisfaction or disappointment with treatment, to which therapists responded with transference interpretations. As the patients continued to withdraw or express resistance, therapists continued to focus on transference issues. Sessions often ended with patients agreeing to continue therapy—but then dropping out of treatment. Thus, therapists' efforts to resolve ruptures by increasing their use of treatment interventions only served to exacerbate the strain on the alliance and push the patient further away.

RUPTURE RESOLUTION

Unresolved ruptures can be obstacles to successful treatment and can contribute to patient dropout; however, they can also provide powerful opportunities for therapeutic change. By addressing a rupture, a therapist can increase the patient's awareness of his or her self-defeating relationship patterns. The resolution process can also serve as a corrective emotional experience (Alexander & French, 1946) by providing the patient with the experience of working through areas of disagreement and moments of misattunement in order to preserve and even strengthen a valued relationship (Safran, 1993; Safran & Segal, 1990/1996). Indeed, there is growing evidence that resolving ruptures not only helps to avoid dropout, but can lead to improved outcome. Lansford (1986)'s study of six patients in short-term dynamic therapy found that successful efforts to address and repair alliance ruptures in short-term therapy were predictive of good outcome. Similarly, Muran et al.'s (2009) study of 128 patients in three different treatments for personality disorders found that both patient and therapist reports of rupture resolution were related to higher treatment retention. Further evidence of the relation between rupture resolution and good treatment outcome is provided by studies of patient-rated alliance patterns across time. Some studies have found evidence that "U-shaped" alliance patterns in which the alliance is high at the beginning of treatment, declines in mid-treatment, and then rises again at the end of treatment, are related to good outcome (Golden & Robbins, 1990; Kivlighan & Shaughnessy, 2000; Patton, Kivlighan, & Multon, 1997). More recent studies have found that steep, "V-shaped" alliance patterns of brief,

localized rupture-repair events were more predictive of change than global high-low-high patterns, and were associated with greater treatment gains (Stiles et al., 2004; Strauss et al., 2006).

A Taxonomy of Rupture Resolution Strategies

Although empirical research on rupture resolution is still in an early stage (see Eubanks-Carter, Muran, & Safran, 2010, for a review), theorists from a range of therapeutic orientations have long recognized the value of addressing ruptures and have proposed strategies for resolving them successfully. Elsewhere, we have synthesized these contributions in the form of a taxonomy of different types of rupture resolution interventions (Safran & Muran, 2000). The taxonomy is organized according to whether the strategies concern ruptures related to therapy tasks and goals or the therapeutic bond. In addition, the taxonomy is organized according to whether strategies address the rupture in a direct manner or whether they take an indirect approach. Finally, the taxonomy also distinguishes between strategies that address ruptures at a surface or manifest level and those that seek to address ruptures at a level of greater depth that requires some degree of inference.

In everyday practice, many of the most common rupture resolution interventions are directed at the surface level. For ruptures related to tasks and goals, a direct, surface-level approach would be to clarify the tasks and goals and provide a rationale for them. For example, if a patient expressed reservations about doing thought records (worksheets used to track automatic thoughts and the emotions associated with them), a therapist might demonstrate how to complete a thought record and explain how the task will help the patient to identify and challenge dysfunctional cognitions. An indirect, surface-level approach would be to simply change the task without explicitly discussing the change, such as changing the homework assignment from a thought record to another task that the patient was more willing to perform. Alternatively, the therapist might reframe the task by presenting it in a manner that is more agreeable to the patient, such as describing the thought record as a way to better understand oneself.

For ruptures related to the bond, an example of a direct, surface-level approach would be to clarify a misunderstanding. For example, a therapist notices that a patient is withdrawn and initiates an exploration of what the patient is thinking and feeling in the moment. When the patient acknowledges feeling criticized by something the therapist said, the therapist sensitively and nondefensively clarifies what he or she was trying to communicate, but does not try to link the misunderstanding to an underlying theme. An indirect, surface-level approach would be to validate the patient's strong reaction to the therapist's words by noting that the patient's feelings are understandable and serve a valuable protective function.

Surface-level strategies can repair many alliance ruptures and at times are the most appropriate interventions. However, a number of theorists focus on rupture resolution strategies that aim to effect change at the level of underlying meaning (Safran & Muran, 2000). For ruptures pertaining to tasks and goals as well as ruptures related to the bond, direct approaches at this level involve exploring core relational themes, or interpersonal schemas, that shape the patient's perceptions of the world and lead to the self-defeating behaviors that form the basis of the patient's interpersonal difficulties. The goal is to expand the patient's awareness of his or her internal processes and how he or she interacts with others, a process referred to as decentering (Safran & Segal, 1990/1996). Through expanded awareness, the patient can begin to change interpersonal patterns that had become habitual and automatic. For example, discussion of a patient's refusal to complete homework assignments may lead to exploration of the theme of the patient's sensitivity to feeling controlled and dominated by others. A narcissistic

patient's criticism of the therapist as unempathic may lead to exploration of the patient's belief that he or she is special and cannot be understood by ordinary people.

Indirect approaches that operate at the level of underlying meaning seek to provide the patient with corrective relational experiences that disconfirm the patient's maladaptive interpersonal schemas (Safran & Muran, 2000). For instance, a patient who was neglected by her parents asks the therapist for advice. An example of an indirect response to this patient would be to simply provide advice, instead of directly exploring the meaning of this request. By providing support in a compassionate way, the therapist gives the patient a new relational experience that challenges the patient's expectations that others would be reluctant to help her. This disconfirmation of her beliefs provides the patient with the opportunity to develop more adaptive beliefs that will lead to interpersonal behaviors that elicit more positive responses from others.

For all rupture resolution strategies, the therapist's ability to attune to the patient's negative emotions and to tolerate and process the therapist's own response to the impasse in a nondefensive manner also provides an important new relational experience (Safran & Muran, 2000). This type of containment, to use Bion's term (1962, 1967, 1970), can help patients learn that neither they nor their relationships will necessarily be destroyed by painful, aggressive feelings. The role of emotional attunement in the therapeutic relationship may be similar to the process of attunement in early parent-child relationships. As Tronick (1989) and Beebe and Lachman (2002) have shown in their research on mother-infant dyads, there is an ongoing oscillation between periods in which mother and infant are affectively attuned, and periods in which they are miscoordinated. Healthy dyads are able to repair these moments of misattunement. Tronick (1989) suggests that this process of miscoordination and repair serves an important purpose: the baby learns to see the mother as potentially available, and to see the self as capable of establishing authentic emotional contact in the face of differences. In the same way, working through alliance ruptures may help the patient to develop healthier interpersonal schemas. The patient can gradually develop a schema that represents the other as potentially available, and the self as capable of negotiating relatedness, even in the context of ruptures (Safran, 1993; Safran & Segal, 1990/1996).

There is a growing body of empirical support for resolution strategies that address ruptures in a direct manner. Rhodes et al. (1994) found evidence that directly addressing ruptures in the bond at the surface level by resolving misunderstandings was associated with retention in treatment. Foreman and Marmar (1985) and Lansford (1986) found that directly addressing ruptures by exploring core relational themes led to improvement in the alliance and better outcome. Crits-Christoph et al. (2006) also found evidence supporting direct exploration of core relational themes in a pilot study of a training program to improve therapists' abilities to maintain strong alliances with patients with major depression. Five therapists were trained to respond to ruptures directly by encouraging patients to express their underlying feelings and the interpersonal issues connected to them. Crits-Christoph et al. found that the training resulted in increases in alliance scores that were moderate to large in size but not statistically significant, as well as small improvements in depressive symptoms and larger improvements in quality of life. However, there was variability among the therapists in the study, with one therapist showing decreased alliance scores after the training. This finding is another example of how increasing therapists' awareness of ruptures can be detrimental to outcome.

Empirically Based Models of Rupture Resolution

Most of the research on rupture resolution strategies centers around resolution models that have been developed using the "task analytic paradigm." This paradigm analyzes the processes involved in producing change (Greenberg, 1986; Rice & Greenberg, 1984; Safran, Greenberg, & Rice, 1988). Task analysis begins with a theory-based model; this model is progressively refined and revised based on analysis of psychotherapy process data. The model that has had the greatest impact on psychotherapy theory and research is the stage process model of Safran and Muran, which was developed through a series of small-scale studies (Safran et al., 1990; Safran & Muran, 1996; Safran et al., 1994). This model focuses on resolving ruptures at a depth level by exploring core relational themes using metacommunication, or communication about the patient-therapist interaction. In this model the process of rupture resolution begins with Stage 1, when the therapist recognizes a rupture and tries to remedy it by inviting the patient to explore the event. Stage 2 involves exploration of the nuances of the patient's and therapist's perceptions of the rupture. Exploration can lead the patient to become concerned that the therapist will reject him or her; this concern often leads the patient to try to avoid further exploration of the rupture event. Stage 3 involves the exploration of such avoidance maneuvers and their function. The model regards problematic interpersonal behaviors as the patient's ineffective responses to an underlying wish or need; the progression in rupture resolution is to clarify this wish or need (Stage 4) (Safran & Muran, 1996, 2000).

The nature of the clarification in Stage 4 usually differs based on whether the rupture is a withdrawal or a confrontation. In the resolution of a withdrawal rupture, clarifying the underlying wish or need involves helping the patient move from qualified to clearer expressions of self-assertion. Confrontation ruptures, by contrast, often begin with the patient asserting a complaint; clarifying the underlying wish or need here involves helping the patient gain access to more vulnerable feelings. For example, exploration of a patient's complaints about his therapist's competence may reveal that the patient desperately hopes that the therapist can help him, but is afraid that he cannot be helped. The therapist's goal would be to help the patient to express his vulnerable feelings of hopelessness and desperation in a direct way that enhances the dyad's ability to work together constructively. Sometimes confrontations are mixed with withdrawal, and in such instances the resolution process begins much like the withdrawal resolution process, where the therapist task is to facilitate self-assertion. The essential task for the therapist in resolving either withdrawal or confrontation ruptures is to support clarification of wishes and needs by empathizing and validating, remaining open and nondefensive, and taking responsibility for problems in the relationship where appropriate (Safran & Muran, 2000).

In order to further additional research on the rupture resolution model, Safran, Muran, and colleagues have developed a short-term, alliance-focused psychotherapy treatment that is informed by their rupture resolution research findings: Brief Relational Therapy (BRT; Safran & Muran, 2000; Safran, 2002). Through close attention to ruptures, therapists and patients in BRT work collaboratively to identify and understand the patient's problematic interpersonal patterns and to experiment with new ways of interacting. The emphasis in BRT is on helping the patient develop a generalizable skill of awareness, or mindfulness, often through the use of metacommunication in which the therapist explicitly draws the patient's attention to the interpersonal patterns that are emerging in the patient-therapist interaction. A clinical trial comparing BRT with CBT and a short-term dynamic treatment in a sample of 128 patients with Cluster C personality disorders and Personality Disorder NOS (Muran, Safran, Samstag, & Winston, 2005) found that BRT was as effective as CBT and short-term dynamic psychotherapy on standard statistical analyses of change, and was more successful than the other two treatments with respect to retention.

With another sample of patients with personality disorders, Safran, Muran, Samstag, and Winston (2005) reported additional evidence that BRT successfully keeps challenging patients engaged in therapy. In the first phase of the study, 60 patients were randomly assigned to one of two standard treatments—short-term dynamic therapy or CBT—and their progress was monitored. Eighteen potential treatment failures were identified. In the second phase of the study, these patients were offered the opportunity to change treatments. The 10 patients who agreed to the change were randomly assigned either to BRT or to the other standard treatment (CBT or dynamic therapy). The results showed that BRT had significantly fewer dropouts than the standard treatment condition.

BRT's success at reducing dropout provides indirect support for Safran and Muran's rupture resolution model. Additional support is provided by Castonguay, Constantino, Newman, and colleagues' efforts to integrate Safran and Muran's rupture resolution strategies into cognitive and cognitive behavioral therapy. In an effort to improve cognitive therapists' ability to respond to alliance ruptures, Castonguay developed Integrative Cognitive Therapy for Depression (ICT: Castonguay, 1996), which integrates Safran, Muran, and colleagues' rupture resolution strategies (Safran & Muran, 2000; Safran & Segal, 1990/1996), as well as strategies developed by Burns (1989), into traditional cognitive therapy (CT). When ruptures are identified, the therapist breaks from the cognitive therapy protocol and addresses the rupture by inviting the patient to explore the rupture, empathizing with the patient's emotional reaction, and reducing the patient's anger or dissatisfaction by validating negative feelings or criticisms and taking at least partial responsibility for the rupture. In a pilot study, Castonguay et al. (2004) found that patient symptom improvement was greater in ICT than a wait-list condition, and compared favorably to previous findings for cognitive therapy. In a randomized trial comparing ICT to CT, Constantino et al. (2008) found that ICT patients had greater improvement on depression and global symptoms and more clinically significant change than CT patients. ICT also yielded better patient-rated alliance quality and therapist empathy. There was a trend toward better patient retention in ICT than in CT.

A similar effort to integrate rupture resolution strategies into CBT for Generalized Anxiety Disorder (GAD) was undertaken by Newman, Castonguay, Borkovec, Fisher, and Nordberg (2008). The researchers tested the efficacy of an integrative treatment package consisting of CBT and an interpersonal/emotional processing module that included rupture resolution methods drawn from Safran and Muran's work (Safran & Muran, 2000). The study found that the integrative treatment yielded a higher effect size than the average effect size of CBT for GAD in the treatment literature, with continued gains at one-year follow-up. An NIMH-funded study led by Muran and Safran (Muran, Safran, Gorman, Eubanks-Carter, & Banthin, 2008) is currently underway to see if, similar to Castonguay and colleagues' findings, integrating rupture resolution training into CBT training improves therapy process and outcome.

Building on the work of Safran and Muran, three additional studies have used the task analytic paradigm to examine rupture resolution: Agnew, Harper, Shapiro, and Barkham (1994) examined one case of psychodynamic-interpersonal therapy for depression; Bennett et al. (2006) examined six cases of cognitive analytic therapy for patients with borderline personality disorder; and Aspland, Llewelyn, Hardy, Barkham, and Stiles (2008) examined two cases of CBT for depression. Similar to Safran and Muran, Agnew et al. and Bennett et al. found support for therapist acknowledgement of the rupture, followed by collaborative exploration with the patient. However, in contrast to Safran and Muran's focus on the patient-therapist interaction, Agnew et al. and Bennett et al.

supported linking the rupture to parallel situations outside of therapy. In contrast to the direct resolution approaches described by the other studies, Aspland et al. found support for an indirect approach to rupture resolution. In the two cases they analyzed, therapists resolved task-related ruptures by ceasing to rigidly focus on the task, and instead attending more closely to the patient's experience through summarizing, exploring, and validating.

Summary

Research on alliance ruptures has yielded evidence that ruptures are common clinical phenomena that when unaddressed can lead to poor outcome and premature termination. Therapists often have difficulty recognizing ruptures, and when they do become aware of a problem in the alliance, they can have difficulty responding in a flexible, sensitive manner. Successful resolution of ruptures can occur through direct attention to ruptures, or through strategies that address ruptures indirectly; resolution strategies can focus on the surface level of the relationship problem, or they can address underlying core relational themes (Safran & Muran, 2000). Future research on the relationship between ruptures and patient variables such as diagnosis or attachment style (see Eames & Roth, 2000), as well as therapist variables such as personality characteristics or directiveness, should increase our knowledge of which resolution strategies are most effective in a given situation.

Regardless of which resolution strategy therapists choose, there is a consensus across different studies of rupture resolution processes (e.g., Safran & Muran, 2000; Agnew et al., 1994; Aspland et al., 2008; Bennett et al., 2006) of the importance of therapists accepting responsibility for their contributions to ruptures and being willing and able to negotiate with their patients on the tasks and goals of treatment. This is consistent with an interpersonal view of the alliance as a mutual, dynamic process in which both parties are active participants. These areas of consensus have important implications for therapist training (Muran, Safran, & Eubanks-Carter, 2010). Therapists need to develop awareness of their own experience in the session, so that they can use their reactions to patients to help them identify when a rupture is occurring. Therapists need to be skilled in regulating their own emotions in the context of a rupture so that they do not respond defensively. Therapists also need to possess interpersonal sensitivity so that they can communicate to patients that they hear and understand their concerns.

The literature on alliance ruptures and their resolution is still at an early stage. Most of the empirical studies in this area rely on small samples. The use of different forms of treatment and different clinical populations can make it difficult to make comparisons across studies. In addition, there is a lack of consensus about how to measure ruptures and resolution processes. However, there are promising efforts to develop and refine methods for identifying ruptures and resolutions based on fluctuations in alliance scores (Eubanks-Carter, Gorman, & Muran, 2010; Stiles et al., 2004, Strauss et al., 2006), as well as efforts to develop and refine observer-based methods (Eubanks-Carter et al., 2009; Sommerfeld et al., 2008). These methodological advances will provide the tools researchers need in order to increase our understanding of how ruptures impact the patient-therapist relationship, and what strategies and skills therapists need in order to resolve ruptures successfully.

References

Ackerman, S. J., & Hilsenroth, M. J. (2001). A review of therapist characteristics and technique negatively impacting the therapeutic alliance. *Psychotherapy: Theory, Research, Practice, Training,* 171–185.

Agnew, R. M., Harper, H., Shapiro, D. A., & Barkham, M. (1994). Resolving a challenge to the therapeutic relationship: A single-case study. *British Journal of Medical Psychology, 67,* 155–170.

Alexander, F., & French, T. M. (1946). *Psychoanalytic therapy.* New York: Ronald Press.

Aspland, H., Llewelyn, S., Hardy, G. E., Barkham, M., & Stiles, W. (2008). Alliance ruptures and rupture resolution in cognitive-behavior therapy: A preliminary task analysis. *Psychotherapy Research, 18,* 699–710.

Beebe, B., & Lachman, F. M. (2002). *Infant research and adult treatment.* Hillsdale, NJ: Analytic Press.

Bennett, D., Parry, G., & Ryle, A. (2006). Resolving threats to the therapeutic alliance in cognitive analytic therapy of borderline personality disorder: A task analysis. *Psychology and Psychotherapy: Theory, Research, and Practice, 79,* 395–418.

Bion, W. R. (1962). *Learning from experience.* New York: Basic Books.

Bion, W. R. (1967). Notes on memory and desire. In E. B. Spillius (Ed.), *Melanie Klein today* (Vol. 2, pp. 17–21). London: Routledge.

Bion, W. R. (1970). *Attention and interpretation.* London: Heinemann.

Bordin, E. (1979). The generalizability of the psychoanalytic concept of the working alliance. *Psychotherapy: Theory, Research, and Practice, 16,* 252–260.

Burns, D. D. (1989). *The feeling good handbook.* New York: William Morrow.

Castonguay, L. G. (1996). *Integrative cognitive therapy for depression treatment manual.* Unpublished manuscript, The Pennsylvania State University.

Castonguay, L. G., Schut, A. J., Aikins, D., Constantino, M. J., Lawrenceau, J. P., Bologh, L., & Burns, D. D. (2004). Repairing alliance ruptures in cognitive therapy: A preliminary investigation of an integrative therapy for depression. *Journal of Psychotherapy Integration, 14,* 4–20.

Castonguay, L. G., Goldfried, M. R., Wiser, S., Raue, P., & Hayes, A. M. (1996). Predicting outcome in cognitive therapy for depression: A comparison of unique and common factors. *Journal of Consulting and Clinical Psychology, 64,* 497–504.

Constantino, M. J., Marnell, M. E., Haile, A. J., Kanther-Sista, S. N., Wolman, K., Zappert, L., & Arnow, B. A. (2008). Integrative cognitive therapy for depression: A randomized pilot comparison. *Psychotherapy: Theory, Research, Practice, Training, 45,* 122–134.

Crits-Christoph, P., Gibbons, M. B., Crits-Christoph, K., Narducci, J., Schamberger, M., &

Gallop, R. (2006). Can therapists be trained to improve their alliances? A preliminary study of alliance-fostering psychotherapy. *Psychotherapy Research , 16*, 268–281.

Eames, V., & Roth, A. (2000). Patient attachment orientation and the early working alliance—A study of patient and therapist reports of alliance quality and ruptures. *Psychotherapy Research, 10*, 421–434.

Eubanks-Carter, C., Gorman, B. S., & Muran, J. C. (2010). *Quantitative methods for detecting change-points in psychotherapy research.* Manuscript submitted for publication.

Eubanks-Carter, C., Muran, J. C., & Safran, J. D. (2009). *Rupture Resolution Rating System (3RS): Manual.* Unpublished manuscript, Beth Israel Medical Center, New York.

Eubanks-Carter, C., Muran, J. C., & Safran, J. D. (2010). Alliance ruptures and resolution. In J. C. Muran & J. P. Barber (Eds.), *The therapeutic alliance: An evidence-based guide to practice* (pp. 74–94). New York: Guilford Press.

Eubanks-Carter, C., Muran, J. C., Safran, J. D., & Mitchell, A. (2008, June). Development of an observer-based rupture resolution rating system. In J. C. Muran (Chair), *Recent developments in rupture resolution research.* Panel conducted at the annual meeting of the Society for Psychotherapy Research, Barcelona, Spain.

Fitzpatrick, M. R., Iwakabe, S., & Stalikas, A. (2005). Perspective divergence in the working alliance. *Psychotherapy Research, 15*, 69–79.

Foreman, S. A., & Marmar, C. R. (1985). Therapist actions that address initially poor therapeutic alliances in psychotherapy. *American Journal of Psychiatry, 142*, 922–926.

Ghadban, R. (2004). *Cluster analysis of patient-reported therapeutic alliance ruptures across three treatment modalities.* An unpublished dissertation, New School University, New York.

Golden, B. R., & Robbins, S. B. (1990). The working alliance within time-limited therapy. *Professional Psychology: Research and Practice, 21*, 476–481.

Greenberg, L. S. (1986). Change process research. *Journal of Consulting and Clinical Psychology, 54*, 4–9.

Greenberg, L. S., Rice, L. N., & Elliott, R. (1993). *Facilitating emotional change: The moment-by-moment process.* New York: Guilford Press.

Greenberg, L. S., & Safran, J. D. (1987). *Emotion in psychotherapy.* New York: Guilford Press.

Harper, H. (1989a). *Coding Guide I: Identification of confrontation challenges in exploratory therapy.* Sheffield, UK: University of Sheffield.

Harper, H. (1989b). *Coding Guide II: Identification of withdrawal challenges in exploratory therapy.* Sheffield, UK: University of Sheffield.

Hatcher, R. L., Barends, A., Hansell, J., & Gutfreund, M. J. (1995). Patients' and therapists' shared and unique views of the therapeutic alliance: An investigation using confirmatory factor analysis in a nested design. *Journal of Consulting and Clinical Psychology, 63*, 636–643.

Henry, W. P., Schacht, T. E., & Strupp, H. H. (1986). Structural analysis of social behavior: Application to a study of interpersonal process in differential psychotherapeutic outcome. *Journal of Consulting and Clinical Psychology, 54*, 27–31.

Henry, W. P., Schacht, T. E., & Strupp, H. H. (1990). Patient and therapist introject, interpersonal process, and differential psychotherapy outcome. *Journal of Consulting and Clinical Psychology, 58*, 768–774.

Henry, W. P., Schacht, T. E., Strupp, H. H., Butler, S. F., & Binder, J. L. (1993). Effects of training in time-limited dynamic psychotherapy: Mediators of therapists' responses to training. *Journal of Consulting and Clinical Psychology, 61*, 441–447.

Henry, W. P., Strupp, H. H., Butler, S. F., Schacht, T. E., & Binder, J. L. (1993). Effects of training in time-limited dynamic psychotherapy: Changes in therapist behavior. *Journal of Consulting and Clinical Psychology, 61*, 434–440.

Hill, C. E., Nutt-Williams, E., Heaton, K. J., Thompson, B. J., & Rhodes, R. H. (1996). Therapist retrospective recall of impasses in long-term psychotherapy: A qualitative analysis. *Journal of Counseling Psychology, 43*, 207–217.

Hill, C. E., Thompson, B. J., Cogar, M. C., & Denman, D. W. (1993). Beneath the surface of long-term therapy: Therapist and client report of their own and each other's covert processes. *Journal of Counseling Psychology, 40*, 278–287.

Horney, K. (1950). *Neurosis and human growth.* New York: W. W. Norton.

Horvath, A. O., & Bedi, R. P. (2002). The alliance. In J. C. Norcross (Ed.), *Psychotherapy relationships that work* (pp. 37–70). New York: Oxford University Press.

Kivlighan, D. M., & Shaughnessy, P. (1995). Analysis of the development of the working alliance using hierarchical linear modeling. *Journal of Counseling Psychology, 42,* 338–349.

Kivlighan, D. M., & Shaughnessy, P. (2000). Patterns of working alliance development: A typology of client's working alliance ratings. *Journal of Counseling Psychology, 47,* 362–371.

Lansford, E. (1986). Weakenings and repairs of the working alliance in short-term psychotherapy. *Professional Psychology: Research and Practice, 17,* 364–366.

Luborsky, L., & Crits-Christoph, P. (1998). *Understanding transference: The core conflictual relationship theme method* (2nd ed.). Washington, D.C.: American Psychological Association.

Mallinckrodt, B., & Nelson, M. L. (1991). Counselor training level and the formation of the psychotherapeutic working alliance. *Journal of Counseling Psychology, 38,* 133–138.

Martin, D. J., Garske, J. P., & Davis, M. K. (2000). Relation of the therapeutic alliance with outcome and other variables: A meta-analytic review. *Journal of Consulting and Clinical Psychology, 68,* 438–450.

Mitchell, S. A. (1993). *Hope and dread in psychoanalysis.* New York: Basic Books.

Mitchell, S. A., & Aron, L. (1999). *Relational psychoanalysis: The emergence of a tradition.* Hillsdale, NJ: Analytic Press.

Muran, J. C., Safran, J. D., & Eubanks-Carter, C. (2010). Developing therapist abilities to negotiate alliance ruptures. In J. C. Muran & J. P. Barber (Eds.), *The therapeutic alliance: An evidence-based guide to practice* (pp. 320–340). New York: Guilford Press.

Muran, J. C., Safran, J. D., Gorman, B. S., Eubanks-Carter, C., & Banthin, D. (2008, June). Identifying ruptures and their resolution from post-session self-report measures. In J. C. Muran (Chair), *Recent developments in rupture resolution research.* Panel conducted at the annual meeting of the Society for Psychotherapy Research, Barcelona, Spain.

Muran, J. C., Safran, J. D., Gorman, B. S., Samstag, L. W., Eubanks-Carter, C., & Winston, A. (2009). The relationship of early alliance ruptures and their resolution to process and outcome in three time-limited psychotherapies for personality disorders. *Psychotherapy: Theory, Research, Practice, Training, 46,* 233–248.

Muran, J. C., Safran, J. D., Samstag, L. W., & Winston, A. (2005). Evaluating an alliance-focused treatment for personality disorders. *Psychotherapy: Theory, Research, Practice, Training, 42,* 532–545.

Newman, M. G., Castonguay, L. G., Borkovec, T. D., Fisher, A. J., & Nordberg, S. S. (2008). An open trial of integrative therapy for generalized anxiety disorder. *Psychotherapy: Theory, Research, Practice, Training, 45,* 135–147.

Patton, M. J., Kivlighan, D. M., & Multon, K. D. (1997). The Missouri Psychoanalytic Counseling Research Project: Relation of changes in counseling process to client outcomes. *Journal of Counseling Psychology, 44,* 189–208.

Piper, W. E., Azim, H., Joyce, A. S., & McCallum, M. (1991). Transference interpretations, therapeutic alliance, and outcome in short term individual psychotherapy. *Archives of General Psychiatry, 48,* 946–953.

Piper, W. E., Ogrodniczuk, J. S., Joyce, A. S., McCallum, M., Rosie, J. S., O'Kelly, J. G., & Steinberg, P. I. (1999). Prediction of dropping out in time-limited, interpretive individual psychotherapy. *Psychotherapy, 36,* 114–122.

Pollack, J., Flegenheimer, W., Kaufman, J., & Sadow, J. (1992). *Brief adaptive psychotherapy for personally disorders: A treatment manual.* San Diego, CA: Social & Behavioral Documents.

Regan, A. M., & Hill, C. E. (1992). Investigation of what clients and counselors do not say in brief therapy. *Journal of Counseling Psychology, 39,* 168–174.

Rennie, D. L. (1994). Clients' deference in psychotherapy. *Journal of Counseling Psychology, 41,* 427–437.

Rhodes, R., Hill, C., Thompson, B., & Elliott, R. (1994). Client retrospective recall of resolved and unresolved misunderstanding events. *Counseling Psychology, 41,* 473–483.

Rice, L. N., & Greenberg, L. S. (1984). *Patterns of change: Intensive analysis of psychotherapy process.* New York: Guilford Press.

Safran, J. D. (1993). Breaches in the therapeutic alliance: An arena for negotiating authentic relatedness. *Psychotherapy: Theory, Research, Practice, Training, 30,* 11–24.

Safran, J. D. (2002). Brief relational psychoanalytic treatment. *Psychoanalytic Dialogues, 12,* 171–195.

Safran, J. D., Crocker, P., McMain, S., & Murray, P. (1990). Therapeutic alliance rupture as a therapy event for empirical investigation.

Psychotherapy: Theory, Research, and Practice, 27, 154–165.

Safran, J. D., Greenberg, L. S., & Rice, L. N. (1988). Integrating psychotherapy research and practice: Modeling the change process. *Psychotherapy, 25,* 1–17.

Safran, J. D., & Muran, J. C. (1996). The resolution of ruptures in the therapeutic alliance. *Journal of Consulting and Clinical Psychology, 64,* 447–458.

Safran, J. D., & Muran, J. C. (2000). *Negotiating the therapeutic alliance: A relational treatment guide.* New York: Guilford Press.

Safran, J. D., Muran, J. C., & Samstag, L. W. (1994). Resolving therapeutic alliance ruptures: A task analytic investigation. In A. O. Horvath & L. S. Greenberg (Eds.), *The working alliance: Theory, research, and practice* (pp. 225–255). New York: John Wiley & Sons.

Safran, J. D., Muran, J. C., Samstag, L. W., & Stevens, C. (2001). Repairing alliance ruptures. *Psychotherapy: Theory, Research, Practice, Training, 38,* 406–412.

Safran, J. D., Muran, J. C., Samstag, L. W., & Stevens, C. (2002). Repairing alliance ruptures. In J. C. Norcross (Ed.), *Psychotherapy relationships that work: Therapist contributions and responsiveness to patients* (pp. 235–254). New York: Oxford University Press.

Safran, J. D., Muran, J. C., Samstag, L. W., & Winston, A. (2005). Evaluating alliance-focused intervention for potential treatment failures: A feasibility study and descriptive analysis. *Psychotherapy: Theory, Research, Practice, Training, 42,* 512–531.

Safran, J. D., & Segal, Z. V. (1990/1996). *Interpersonal process in cognitive therapy.* New York: Basic Books. (2nd ed., Northvale, NJ: Aronson).

Samstag, L. W., Batchelder, S. T., Muran, J. C., Safran, J. D., & Winston, A. (1998). Early identification of treatment failures in short-term psychotherapy: An assessment of therapeutic alliance and interpersonal behavior. *Journal of Psychotherapy Practice & Research, 7,* 126–143.

Sommerfeld, E., Orbach, I., Zim, S., & Mikulincer, M. (2008). An in-session exploration of ruptures in working alliance and their associations with clients' core conflictual relationship themes, alliance-related discourse, and clients' postsession evaluation. *Psychotherapy Research, 18,* 377–388.

Stiles, W. B., Glick, M. J., Osatuke, K., Hardy, G. E., Shapiro, D. A., Agnew-Davies, R., ... Barkham, M. (2004). Patterns of alliance development and the rupture-repair hypothesis: Are productive relationships U-shaped or V-shaped? *Journal of Counseling Psychology, 51,* 81–92.

Strauss, J. L., Hayes, A. M., Johnson, S. L., Newman, C. F., Brown, G. K., Barber, J. P., ... Beck, A. T., (2006). Early alliance, alliance ruptures, and symptom change in a nonrandomized trial of cognitive therapy for avoidant and obsessive-compulsive personality disorders. *Journal of Consulting and Clinical Psychology, 74,* 337–345.

Strupp, H. H. (1993). The Vanderbilt Psychotherapy Studies: Synopsis. *Journal of Consulting and Clinical Psychology, 61,* 33–36.

Tronick, E. (1989). Emotions and emotional communications in infants. *American Psychologist, 44,* 112–119.

Tryon, G. S., & Kane, A. S. (1990). The helping alliance and premature termination. *Counselling Psychology Quarterly, 3,* 233–238.

Tryon, G. S., & Kane, A. S. (1993). Relationship of working alliance to mutual and unilateral termination. *Journal of Counseling Psychology, 40,* 33–36.

Tryon, G. S., & Kane, A. S. (1995). Client involvement, working alliance, and type of therapy termination. *Psychotherapy Research, 5,* 189–198.

31 INTERPERSONAL PSYCHOTHERAPY (IPT)

Meredith Gunlicks-Stoessel

Myrna M. Weissman

Interpersonal psychotherapy (IPT) is a time-limited psychotherapeutic intervention that was developed in the 1970s by the late Gerald L. Klerman, Myrna M. Weissman, and their colleagues as a treatment for depression (Weissman, Markowitz, & Klerman, 2000). The original treatment manual was published in 1984 (Klerman, Weissman, Rounsaville, & Chevron, 1984) and was updated with the results of more recent efficacy studies in 2000 (Weissman et al., 2000). A quick guide for clinicians that contains detailed treatment procedures and scripts was published in 2007 (Weissman, Markowitz, & Klerman, 2007). Throughout these updates, the basic procedures of IPT have remained unchanged. IPT is based on the principle that regardless of the underlying cause of the psychiatric disorder, such as depression, the onset of symptoms occurs within an interpersonal context. The goal of IPT is to decrease depressive symptoms by understanding and managing the interpersonal context in which they developed.

IPT's efficacy has been demonstrated in numerous clinical trials, leading to modifications of the treatment for subtypes of mood disorders and different age groups, as well as for nonmood disorders (Weissman et al., 2000). It is listed as a recommended treatment for depression by the American Psychological Association and the American Psychiatric Association (American Psychiatric Association, 2006; Chambless et al., 1998; Chambless et al., 1996), as well as the Royal College of Psychiatrists and the National Institute of Clinical Excellence (NICE) in the United Kingdom. IPT has been adapted and tested in alternative formats, including group therapy (Wilfley et al., 2000), couples therapy (Foley et al., 1989), and therapy delivered via the telephone (Miller & Weissman, 2002). It also has demonstrated effectiveness in controlled clinical trials in a number of settings ranging from primary care to school-based mental health clinics, to villages in developing countries (Bolton et al., 2003; Mufson, Dorta, Wickramaratne, et al., 2004; Schulberg et al., 1996). It has been translated into a number of languages and is being adapted for use in other countries. The International Society for Interpersonal Psychotherapy provides information on the application of IPT and promotes collaboration in IPT treatment, research, and training.

THE THEORETICAL AND EMPIRICAL BASIS FOR INTERPERSONAL PSYCHOTHERAPY

The theoretical basis for IPT comes from the work of Adolf Meyer, Harry Stack Sullivan, and other interpersonal theorists who proposed that interpersonal disruptions are a reflection of personality and are associated with psychiatric symptoms. Meyer (1957) viewed psychopathology as an expression of an individual's attempts to adapt to his or her environment. He further posited that the manner in which the individual attempts to negotiate his or her environment is determined by prior experiences within his or her family and social/cultural context. Sullivan (1953) also emphasized the need for a person's actions to be understood from both their historical and present interpersonal context. He believed that a significant component of psychiatric illness develops out of, and is perpetuated by, problems in interpersonal interactions. Consistent with these theories, IPT focuses on helping patients to increase their understanding of the interpersonal event that triggered their depression, and how changing their communication and relationship patterns can lead to changes in their symptoms.

IPT also has primary roots in attachment theory. Bowlby (1978) argued that people have a need to develop strong bonds to significant others. When these bonds are disrupted, the individual experiences emotional distress. IPT recognizes and addresses the role of attachment in the onset of depression by targeting interpersonal disputes, transitions, and grief in relationships that may affect the patient's attachment experiences and contribute to the development of psychopathology.

There is strong empirical support for an interpersonal perspective on depression (Hammen, 1999; Rudolph et al., 2000). Interpersonal stressors, as compared to noninterpersonal stressors, have been found to be more strongly linked to the onset of depression (Rudolph et al., 2000). Recent research has begun to address the question of why some individuals are more vulnerable to developing depression in the face of life stress than others (Caspi et al., 2003). Caspi and colleagues (2003) have identified a functional polymorphism in the promoter region of the serotonin transporter gene that, if present, places individuals at heightened risk for developing depression if they experience a negative life event. IPT addresses the interpersonal stressors that are associated with the depression and provides patients with skills that will be helpful in both current and future interpersonal contexts.

For a more thorough discussion of the theoretical and empirical rationale for IPT, please see the original 1984 treatment manual (Klerman et al., 1984)

COURSE OF TREATMENT

IPT has been developed and tested for a number of psychiatric disorders. In this chapter, we focus on the strategies and techniques for treating depression, since depression is the diagnosis for which IPT was developed, and it has the largest evidence base. Additional information about IPT for other disorders, as well as more detailed treatment procedures, illustrative scripts, and case material can be obtained from the IPT manual and the clinician's quick guide (Weissman et al., 2000; 2007).

IPT is a time-limited treatment that was originally designed to be delivered once a week for 12 to 20 weeks, although the treatment schedule can be more flexible. In the efficacy studies, treatment length has ranged from eight weekly sessions to three years of monthly sessions. What is important is that the therapist and patient agree on the length of treatment from the beginning in order to focus the treatment goals and assess progress towards the goals within a set time frame. The time limit places pressure on both the patient and the therapist to act. The IPT therapist's stance in the therapy is active, collaborative, supportive, and hopeful. The IPT therapist asks questions, makes suggestions (but does not tell the patient what to do), and helps the patient consider options for managing the interpersonal problem. Any effort that the patient makes toward generating or trying out options is greeted with enthusiasm from the therapist. At all times, the therapist should be focused on working on the identified interpersonal problem area.

IPT is divided into three treatment phases: the initial phase, the middle phase, and the termination phase. The initial phase is spent identifying the interpersonal problem area or life event that is linked to the onset or maintenance of the patient's depression. The middle phase addresses the problem area by helping the patient make changes in his or her communication and behavior in relationships. The termination phase is focused on reviewing changes in the patient's depressive symptoms and relationships, discussing anticipated future difficulties, and discussing warning signs of depression relapse.

IPT is based on a medical model of depression, meaning that depression is viewed as a treatable illness and the patient's impaired functioning is blamed on the depression rather than on the patient. It targets depressive symptoms and current interpersonal difficulties, but does not aim to treat personality. In IPT, patients are taught to look at the relationship between the onset of depression symptoms and current interpersonal functioning. The focus of the treatment is on the "here and now" rather than on exploring early origins of maladaptive interpersonal styles. While discussions of the past are not discouraged, the past is discussed only in the context of how it is related to current problems. IPT is not a transference-based treatment. The therapist-patient relationship can be used to give the patient feedback on current interpersonal behavior, and to discuss how the patient's interpersonal patterns with the therapist play out in other relationships, but the therapist-patient relationship is not traced to origins in the patient's early experiences.

INITIAL PHASE

The goals of the initial phase of treatment are to determine the patient's diagnosis,

provide psychoeducation about depression and assign the patient the "sick role," conduct the interpersonal inventory to develop an understanding of the patient's social functioning and interpersonal relationships in association with symptom onset, identify the interpersonal problem area(s), and make the treatment contract.

Determine the Patient's Diagnosis

The first session of IPT resembles the initial intake interview conducted in most psychiatric settings. The therapist should conduct a careful diagnostic interview to assess for DSM-IV-TR (American Psychiatric Association, 2000) or ICD-10 (World Health Organization, 1992) psychiatric illnesses, as well as history of prior episodes of mood disorders, medical history, prior psychiatric treatment, and a brief family history. For patients who are depressed, standardized rating scales, such as the Hamilton Rating Scale for Depression (Hamilton, 1967) or the Beck Depression Inventory-II (Beck, Steer, & Brown, 1996) are useful for evaluating the severity of depression symptoms, helping the patient to understand that depression is a real illness that can be measured and quantified, and tracking the patient's progress over the course of treatment.

Provide Psychoeducation About Depression

Once the depression diagnosis has been made, the therapist should educate the patient about depression, including describing its associated symptoms and behaviors. For example, patients may not realize that a decline in work performance may be a function of reduced concentration, anhedonia, fatigue, and other symptoms of depression, rather than an indication that the patient is lazy or inept.

In IPT, depression is viewed a treatable medical illness. IPT therapists describe the biological underpinnings of depression and explain the interaction between a biological vulnerability to depression and stressful interpersonal events. This helps take the blame off the patient for causing the depression. While patients with other medical illnesses generally recognize that they are ill and attribute functional impairments, such as a decline in work performance, to the illness, depressed patients tend to blame themselves for their difficulties. This is addressed in IPT by assigning the patient the "sick role." This involves explaining that, the same as someone with a medical illness, individuals who have symptoms of depression may not be able to do as many things or do things as well as they did before the depression developed. For example, they may have more difficulty at work, they may have more trouble managing household tasks, and they may withdraw socially. While depressed individuals may have more difficulty doing these things, it is important for them to try to do as much as possible. The goal of the sick role is for patients to try to do as many of their usual activities as possible, with the acknowledgement and acceptance that they might not do these things as well as before the depression developed. This helps patients to feel less critical of performance or outcome and to feel success at merely extending effort. Throughout the treatment, the therapist aims to "blame the depression" when patients struggle and credit patients when they succeed. This helps patients understand that it is not their fault that they are depressed, but that they are capable of doing things to help themselves recover from their depression.

Conduct the Interpersonal Inventory

The interpersonal inventory is used to identify the interpersonal issues that are most closely related to the onset or persistence of the patient's depression and are most affected by the patient's depression. The therapist begins by inquiring about the important people in the patient's life, either alive or deceased, making sure to discuss the relationships that the patient feels are most related to his or her mood in either positive or negative ways. For each relationship, the therapist inquires about the frequency and content of their interactions, terms and expectations for the relationship, positive and negative aspects of the relationship, how the relationship has changed since the patient became depressed, and changes the patient would like to make in the relationship.

Identify the Interpersonal Problem Area(s)

Based on the interpersonal inventory, the therapist helps the patient understand the relationship between the onset of depressive symptoms and interpersonal events. The therapist identifies one of four interpersonal problems areas that will be the focus of treatment. The four interpersonal problem areas are grief due to death, interpersonal role disputes, interpersonal role transitions, and interpersonal deficits.

Grief due to death. Grief is selected as the problem area when the patient experiences the death of a loved one and the loss is associated with prolonged grief, significant depressive symptoms, and impairment in functioning. Grief over losses that are not due to death, such as the end of a romantic relationship, are conceptualized within the problem area of interpersonal role transitions, which is described later in the chapter. The goal of IPT for patients with this problem area is to facilitate the mourning process and to develop or improve other relationships that can fill in some of the support, nurturance, companionship, or guidance that has been lost.

Interpersonal role disputes. An interpersonal role dispute occurs when an individual and at least one significant other have nonreciprocal expectations about the terms and/or guidelines for behavior within the relationship. Some examples of common role disputes that patients experience include arguments with a spouse regarding the division of household labor or amount of time spent with friends, disagreements between an employer and employee regarding the appropriate level of supervision, or disagreements with a sibling regarding care for an elderly ailing parent. Interpersonal role dispute is selected as the problem area if the patient's depressive episode coincides with a relationship conflict. The goal of treatment is to help the patient develop skills to resolve the dispute, if possible. If resolution is not possible, the goal is to help the patient develop strategies for coping with the relationship.

Interpersonal role transitions. A role transition involves adjustment to a life change that requires an alteration of behavior from an old role to a new role. Role transitions can be biologically determined (pregnancy, childbirth) or a result of social and cultural practices (marriage, retirement). In addition to these more normative transitions, patients may also experience unexpected events that require them to relinquish an old social role and take on a new one, such as a sudden illness of a loved one, changes in family structure due to divorce, or the ending of a romantic relationship or significant friendship. Both positive and negative life changes can lead to depression because they involve a loss of familiarity and comfort with the current stage or role. The goal of IPT for patients experiencing a role transition is to help the patient mourn the old role and develop the skills they need to manage their new role more successfully.

Interpersonal deficits. Interpersonal deficits refer to patients who are experiencing feelings of loneliness, a paucity of relationships, or have underdeveloped social and communication skills that impair their ability to have positive relationships. The goal of treatment for these patients is to help them develop the interpersonal skills needed to have more satisfying relationships and reduce social isolation. Due to the time-limited nature of IPT, it is best suited for patients whose interpersonal deficits are not pervasive or are a consequence of their depression or a specific stressor. Patients with severe or pervasive social skills deficits may need more intensive treatment.

Make the Treatment Contract

Once the problem area(s) have been identified, the patient and therapist make a verbal treatment contract. This contract specifies the patient's and therapist's roles in treatment, the interpersonal problem area(s) that will be the focus of treatment, and the practical details of the treatment.

MIDDLE PHASE

During the middle phase of treatment, the therapist and patient begin to work directly on the identified interpersonal problem area(s). This is accomplished by further clarification of the problem area, identifying effective strategies for managing the problem, and practicing and implementing the strategies. Some of the therapeutic techniques are specific to the identified problem area(s), and others are used across problem areas. When the therapist starts to help patients work on their communication and relationship functioning, it is helpful to begin with an area that is manageable and has a high likelihood of success. This generates hope in the patients that the strategies they learn can help facilitate change in their relationships and improve their mood.

We provide brief descriptions of the techniques below. More thorough descriptions of the techniques, as well as illustrative scripts and case material, can be found in the *Clinicians' Quick Guide to Interpersonal Psychotherapy* (Weissman et al., 2007).

General Techniques

Encouragement of affect and linkage with interpersonal events. Encouragement of affect refers to techniques used to help the patient become aware of, acknowledge, and accept emotions about events and relationships, and understand their impact on relationships. When patients discuss emotionally laden material, the therapist should allow time for the expression of feelings and may also encourage the process by making empathic statements such as "That sounds very upsetting" or "I can see how hard that was for you."

Constant attention to the link between mood and interpersonal events is the essential element of IPT. The purported mechanism of action in IPT is that as patients learn to negotiate interpersonal experiences more effectively, their mood improves (Markowitz et al., 2006). Iteratively, an improvement in depressive symptoms also allows patients to manage interpersonal events with greater facility. This theme of the link between interpersonal events and mood recurs throughout treatment. IPT does not focus on experiences in childhood or the distant past, but rather focuses on recent experiences that are linked to the onset or maintenance of the depression. The IPT therapist helps the patient to observe that recent negative interpersonal events are associated with a decline in mood and that positive changes that the patient makes in his or her relationships are linked with an improvement in mood.

Communication analysis. The purpose of communication analysis is to explore the patient's patterns of interacting with others in order to identify ways in which the patient's communication is ineffective, and the skills the patient needs to master to have better communication. Communication analysis involves asking the patient to describe, in detail, an interpersonal event that happened during the week. Together, the therapist and patient analyze the communication to help the patient recognize the impact of his or her words on others, the feelings he or she conveyed verbally and nonverbally, the feelings that arose during the interaction, and changes in the communication that could have altered the outcome of the interaction and the patient's associated feelings. This is accomplished by asking questions such as: How did the discussion start? When and where did it take place? What exactly did the patient say? What did the other person say back? Then what happened? How did that make the patient feel? How does the patient think it made the other person feel? Is that the outcome the patient wanted?

Once the therapist has a clear understanding of the interaction, the therapist and patient discuss how altering the communication at various points might

have led to a different outcome and different emotional experience. This includes discussion of things the patient could have said or done differently.

Decision analysis. Decision analysis is used to help the patient consider options for addressing a particular interpersonal dilemma. This is similar to problem-solving techniques that are used in other treatments, but is focused more specifically on addressing interpersonal difficulties. Decision analysis involves selecting an interpersonal situation that is causing the patient problems, determining the goal, generating potential solutions, and evaluating and selecting a strategy to try. The therapist stresses the importance of the patient trying out these options to assess the impact on the patient's mood. Initially, the therapist may need to be relatively active in helping patients generate options, as depressed patients often have difficulty envisioning solutions to their problems. Over the course of therapy, the goal is for the patient to take an increasingly more active role in generating and selecting options for themselves.

Role-playing. Role-playing is a way for patients to practice the communication and interpersonal problem solving skills that they have learned in order to feel more comfortable using them in real life. The therapist and patient may choose to talk through the scenario before doing the role-play so the patient feels more prepared. It can be helpful to give the patient the opportunity to play both roles to better understand the other person's perspective and to help the therapist understand the patient's experience of the other person. It is also helpful to try the role-play more than once, with different outcomes to the interactions, both positive and negative, so that the patient can become more skilled in handling different kinds of situations that might develop.

Problem-Area Specific Techniques

Grief due to death. The treatment goal for patients with the identified problem area of grief is to facilitate resolution of the grieving process. This involves reviewing in detail the patient's relationship with the deceased, including both positive and negative aspects of the relationship, conflicts in the relationship, and special qualities of the relationship. As part of the exploration of the patient's relationship with the deceased, the therapist should also gently encourage expression of affect about the relationship and its loss. Treatment also involves helping the patient to connect symptoms of depression and current behaviors to feelings surrounding the death. As the treatment progresses, the therapist helps the patient develop skills for communicating about the loss and associated feelings, and applying those skills to other significant relationships in the patient's life. The therapist also helps the patient develop new relationships or further develop existing relationships to fill in some of the support that was lost with the death of the loved one.

Interpersonal role disputes. For patients experiencing an interpersonal role dispute, the dispute may be in one of three stages: renegotiation, impasse, or dissolution. A patient and significant other are in the renegotiation stage if they are still communicating with one another and are attempting to resolve the conflict. In the impasse stage, the patient and significant other are no longer attempting to discuss the conflict, and social distancing (or "the silent treatment") commonly occurs. In the dissolution stage, the patient and significant other have already decided that the dispute cannot be resolved and they have chosen to end the relationship. For patients whose disputes are in the renegotiation or impasse stages, the goal of treatment is to help the patient define and resolve the dispute. This involves working with the patient to identify and explore the dispute, identify existing patterns of communication, and use communication analysis and decision analysis to teach new communication skills and generate solutions to the dispute. If complete resolution of the problem does not appear to be possible, the therapist works with the patient to develop strategies for coping with the relationship that cannot be changed. This may include developing other relationships

that can provide a means of support. It can be helpful to point out to the patient that while a relationship may not be able to be changed completely, simply decreasing the frequency or intensity of conflict can lead to improved mood. If the dispute is in the dissolution stage, treatment focuses on mourning the loss of the relationship. This involves exploring the dispute and lost relationship, developing an understanding of what occurred, and helping the patient to feel comfortable and competent to establish new relationships.

Interpersonal role transitions. Treatment for patients experiencing an interpersonal role transition involves identifying and defining the role transition, helping the patient relinquish the old role and accept the new one, and helping the patient develop a sense of mastery and competence in the new role. The therapist and patient discuss the meaning of the transition to the patient, feelings and expectations about the old and new roles, and gains and losses associated with the transition. The therapist also helps the patient to learn new communication and interpersonal problem solving skills needed to manage the new role and develop relationships that can provide ongoing support around the transition.

Interpersonal deficits. Treatment of this problem area begins with a thorough review of current relationships, to identify and label repetitive interpersonal problems, and connect feelings and depression symptoms to problems in relationships. If the patient does not have many current significant relationships, the therapist can review past relationships to look for patterns of difficulty as well as strengths upon which to build. The therapist can also use his or her own relationship with the patient to explore the patient's interpersonal deficits. The therapist then teaches the patient new skills for building and maintaining relationships and uses role-plays to help the patient practice the new skills. The therapist then helps the patient to identify existing relationships that he or she would like to build upon and/or new people with whom the patient would like to form relationships. It is important with these patients to focus on strengths as much as on deficits. The therapist should highlight skills the patient has used in other relationships, or in the therapy session, to help the patient build a sense of confidence and competence and to reinforce positive communication patterns.

TERMINATION PHASE

The termination phase of IPT is similar to termination phases of other treatments and has several goals. First, it is important to review the course of the patient's depressive symptoms and how these symptoms have changed, also noting the warning symptoms of depression that are particular to that patient, so he or she will be aware if the depression recurs. A second objective of the termination phase is to review the changes that have occurred in the patient's communication style and relationship functioning, link these changes to the improvement in the patient's mood, and highlight the skills and strategies the patient developed that were particularly useful. It is also helpful to discuss potential future situations that the patient anticipates having difficulty with and reviewing strategies that the patient can use to negotiate those situations. As part of termination, it is also important to discuss the feelings the patient has about ending the treatment and the relationship with the therapist. Finally, it is important to discuss the possibility of recurrence of depression and strategies for managing such a recurrence.

EFFICACY AND EFFECTIVENESS OF IPT

Major Depressive Disorder (MDD) in Adults

IPT was originally developed as a maintenance treatment to be implemented following acute phase treatment with medication (Klerman et al., 1974; Paykel et al., 1975). The first clinical trial that included IPT as a treatment option was an eight-month trial of 150 women who had responded to an acute four- to six-week treatment of amitriptyline. Women were randomized to receive eight months of treatment with weekly IPT, amitriptyline, pill placebo, IPT plus amitriptyline, IPT plus pill placebo, and no treatment. Medication was the most effective for preventing depression relapse. IPT was most effective for improving social functioning, the effects of which were not observed until six to eight months following initiation of IPT (Weissman et al., 1974). Patients who received IPT plus amitriptyline had the best outcomes.

The efficacy of IPT as an acute treatment for MDD was demonstrated in a randomized trial of IPT, amitriptyline, a combination of IPT and amitriptyline, and nonscheduled control treatment (DiMascio et al., 1979; Weissman et al., 1979). There were no significant differences between IPT and amitriptyline in level of depressive symptoms posttreatment. Combined IPT-amitriptyline was more effective than either monotherapy, and all active treatments were more effective than the nonscheduled control. At a one-year naturalistic follow-up, many patients treated with IPT had maintained their improvement, and they demonstrated significantly better social functioning than patients treated with amitriptyline alone (Weissman, Klerman, Prusoff, Sholomskas, & Padin, 1981).

IPT was also tested as an acute treatment in the multisite National Institute of Mental Health Treatment of Depression Collaborative Research Program (NIMH TDCRP; Elkin et al., 1989). Patients were randomized to receive IPT, cognitive behavioral therapy (CBT), imipramine, or pill placebo. Patients with milder depression (Hamilton Rating Scale for Depression < 20; (Hamilton, 1960) improved equally regardless of the treatment they received. Among the more severely depressed patients (Hamilton $\geq$ 20), IPT and imipramine had comparable effects and were more effective than CBT and placebo.

IPT has also been tested as a longer-term maintenance treatment for patients with recurrent depression (Frank, 1991; Frank et al., 1990). Patients who had remitted with a combination of IPT and high-dose imipramine were randomized to receive three years of monthly IPT, imipramine, pill placebo, imipramine plus monthly IPT, or monthly IPT plus pill placebo. Imipramine was the most effective treatment for preventing relapse, and IPT was more effective than placebo.

IPT also has demonstrated efficacy among different populations of depressed adults including patients who are HIV-positive (Markowitz et al., 1998), women with peripartum and postpartum depression (O'Hara et al., 2000; Spinelli & Endicott, 2003), and depressed patients who present to primary care settings (Schulenberg et al., 1996).

GERIATRIC DEPRESSION

There have been several studies demonstrating the efficacy of IPT as an acute and maintenance treatment for depressed geriatric patients. The Prevention of Suicide in Primary Care Elderly: Collaborative Trial (PROSPECT) tested IPT alone or in combination with an SSRI, as compared to usual care delivered in primary care practices (Alexopoulos et al., 2005). They found that patients who received IPT showed greater reductions in depressive symptoms and suicidal ideation than patients who received usual care. In another study, geriatric patients who had remitted with an acute treatment of IPT plus nortriptyline were randomized to maintenance treatment with nortriptyline, placebo, IPT plus placebo, or IPT plus nortriptyline (Reynolds et al., 1999). Combined treatment had the lowest recurrence rates, and each monotherapy was statistically superior to placebo.

ADOLESCENT DEPRESSION

IPT has been adapted as a developmentally appropriate treatment for depressed adolescents (Mufson, Dorta, Moreau, & Weissman, 2004). The adolescent adaptation (IPT-A) has the same treatment goal of reducing depressive symptoms by improving interpersonal relationships and social functioning. The relationship problems targeted in IPT-A are identical to IPT, but are age-appropriate. IPT-A has been adapted to address interpersonal issues that are more relevant to adolescence, including

parental separation or divorce, negotiation of peer relationships and peer pressure, and the development of romantic relationships. Some of the techniques used to work towards improving adolescents' relationship functioning and decreasing depressive symptoms have been modified so that they are more developmentally appropriate. The treatment also includes work on more basic social skills and perspective-taking skills.

The efficacy and effectiveness of IPT-A have been examined in three randomized controlled clinical trials (Mufson, Dorta, Wickramaratne, et al., 2004; Mufson, Weissman, Moreau, & Garfinkel, 1999; Rossello & Bernal, 1999). Depressed adolescents treated with IPT-A demonstrated fewer depressive symptoms, better social functioning, and better global functioning at the completion of treatment than adolescents in control conditions.

IPT-A has been adapted for use as a preventative intervention for adolescents who have elevated symptoms of depression but do not meet criteria for a current depressive episode (Young, Mufson, & Davies, 2006). The intervention, entitled Interpersonal Psychotherapy—Adolescent Skills Training (IPT-AST), is delivered in a group format and focuses on psychoeducation and skill-building that can be applied to multiple relationships, rather than a particular problem area. A recent study found that adolescents who received IPT-AST had significantly fewer depressive symptoms and depressive diagnoses and had better overall functioning post-treatment than adolescents who received school counseling (Young et al., 2006).

OTHER PSYCHIATRIC DISORDERS

Frank and colleagues have adapted IPT as an adjunctive psychotherapy for patients with bipolar disorder. Interpersonal and Social Rhythm Therapy (IPSRT) includes an additional focus on the disruptions in daily routines commonly observed in bipolar patients. The treatment focuses on the links between mood symptoms and quality of relationships, the importance of maintaining regularity in daily routines, and the identification and management of potential precipitants of rhythm disruption. IPSRT has demonstrated efficacy as a maintenance treatment when combined with medication (Frank et al., 2005).

IPT has been found to be an effective treatment for bulimia, although it appears to be less effective than CBT (Agras et al., 2000; Fairburn et al., 1993; Wilfley et al., 2002). It does not appear to be effective for substance dependence (Carroll et al., 2004; Carroll, Rounsaville, & Gawin, 1991; Rounsaville et al., 1983). Adaptations for anxiety disorders, including social phobia, panic disorder, and posttraumatic stress disorder, have been developed and are in the pilot stage of evaluation (Bleiberg & Markowitz, 2005; Lipsitz et al., 2006; Lipsitz et al., 1999).

INTERNATIONAL DISSEMINATION OF IPT

As evidence of the efficacy of IPT for depression and other psychiatric disorders has continued to grow, dissemination efforts have also dramatically increased. IPT has been incorporated into training programs in Canada, Europe, Australia, and New Zealand. IPT has been translated into Italian, French, German, Spanish, Dutch, Japanese, and Chinese.

Clinical trials of IPT in developing countries have been completed. Two large clinical trials have been completed in Uganda (Bolton et al., 2007; Bolton et al., 2003). In one study, 177 depressed adults living in villages in rural Uganda were randomized to receive IPT delivered in group format by trained locals or treatment as usual (TAU), which consisted of no treatment except hospitalization for suicidality or psychosis (Bolton et al., 2003). Adults treated with IPT demonstrated significantly greater reductions in depression symptoms, and improvements in social functioning, than adults in the TAU condition, and these results were maintained at six-month follow-up. These findings have been replicated with adolescent survivors of war and displacement in camps for internally displaced persons in northern Uganda (Bolton et al., 2007).

INTERNATIONAL SOCIETY FOR INTERPERSONAL PSYCHOTHERAPY

In 2000, the International Society for Interpersonal Psychotherapy (ISIPT) was formed with the goal of promoting the dissemination of IPT; establishing training and accreditation pathways; and promoting international cooperation in IPT treatment, research, and training. More information about IPT and the Society can be obtained from the ISIPT web site: www.interpersonalpsychotherapy.org.

References

Agras, W. S., Walsh, B. T., Fairburn, C. G., Wilson, G. T., & Kraemer, H. C. (2000). A multicenter comparison of cognitive-behavioral therapy and interpersonal psychotherapy for bulimia nervosa. *Archives of General Psychiatry, 57,* 459–466.

Alexopoulos, G. S., Katz, I. R., Bruce, M. L., Heo, M., Ten Have, T., Raue, P., . . . The PROSPECT Group (2005). PROSPECT Group: Remission in depressed geriatric primary care patients: A report from the PROSPECT study. *American Journal of Psychiatry, 162,* 718–724.

American Psychiatric Association (2000). *Diagnostic and statistical manual of mental disorders, Text revision (4 ed.).* Washington, DC: Author.

American Psychiatric Association (2006). Practice guidelines for the treatment of psychiatric disorders: Compendium 2006. Arlington, VA: Author.

Beck, A. T., Steer, R. A., & Brown, G. K. (1996). *Manual for Beck Depression Inventory (2nd ed.).* San Antonio, TX: The Psychological Corporation.

Bleiberg, K. L., & Markowitz, J. C. (2005). A pilot study of interpersonal psychotherapy for post–traumatic stress disorder. *American Journal of Psychiatry, 162,* 181–183.

Bolton, P., Bass, J., Betancourt, T., Speelman, L., Onyango, G., Clougherty, K., . . . Verdeli, H. (2007). Interventions for depression symptoms among adolescent survivors of war and displacement in northern Uganda. *Journal of the American Medical Association, 298,* 519–527.

Bolton, P., Bass, J., Neugebauer, R., Verdeli, H., Clougherty, K. F., Wickramaratne, P., . . . Weissman, M. (2003). Group interpersonal psychotherapy for depression in rural Uganda: A randomized controlled trial. *Journal of the American Medical Association, 289,* 3117–3124.

Bowlby, J. (1978). Attachment theory and its therapeutic implications. *Adolescent Psychiatry, 6,* 5–33.

Carroll, K. M., Fenton, L. R., Ball, S. A., Nich, C., Frankforter, T. L., Shi, J., & Rounsaville, B. J. (2004). Efficacy of disulfiram and cognitive behavior therapy in cocaine-dependent outpatients: A randomized placebo-controlled trial. *Archives of General Psychiatry, 61,* 264–272.

Carroll, K. M., Rounsaville, B. J., & Gawin, F. H. (1991). A comparative trial of psychotherapies for ambulatory cocaine abusers: Replase prevention and interpersonal psychotherapy. *American Journal of Drug and Alcohol Abuse, 17,* 229–247.

Caspi, A., Sudgen, K., Moffitt, T. E., Taylor, A., Craig, I. W., Harrington, H., . . . Poulton, R. (2003). Influence of life stress on depression: Moderation by a polymorphism in the 5-HTT gene. *Science, 301,* 386–389.

Chambless, D. L., Baker, M. J., Baucom, D. H., Beutler, L. E., Calhoun, K. S., Crits-Christoph, P., et al. (1998). Update on empirically validated therapies, II. *Clinical Psychologist, 51,* 3–16.

Chambless, D. L., Sanderson, W. C., Shoham, V., Bennett Johnson, S., Pope, K. S., Crits-Christoph, P., . . . Woody, S. R. (1996). An update on empirically validated therapies. *Clinical Psychologist, 49,* 5–18.

DiMascio, A., Weissman, M. M., Prusoff, B. A., Neu, C., Zwilling, M., & Klerman, G. L. (1979). Differential symptom reduction by drugs and psychotherapy in acute depression. *Archives of General Psychiatry, 36,* 1450–1456.

Elkin, I., Shea, M. T., Watkins, J. T., Imber, S. D., Sotsky, S. M., Collins, J. F., . . . Parloff, M. B. (1989). National Institute of Mental Health Treatment of Depression Collaborative Research Program: General effectiveness of treatments. *Archives of General Psychiatry, 46,* 971–982.

Fairburn, C. G., Jones, R., Peveler, R. C., Hope, R. A., & O'Connor, M. (1993). Psychotherapy and bulimia nervosa: Longer-term effects of interpersonal psychotherapy, behavior therapy, and cognitive behavior therapy. *Archives of General Psychiatry, 50,* 419–428.

Foley, S. H., Rounsaville, B. J., Weissman, M. M., Sholomskas, D., & Chevron, E. (1989). Individual versus conjoint interpersonal psychotherapy for depressed patients with marital disputes. *International Journal of Family Psychiatry, 10,* 29–42.

Frank, E. (1991). Interpersonal psychotherapy as a maintenance treatment for patients with recurrent depression. *Psychotherapy, 28,* 259–266.

Frank, E., Kupfer, D. J., Buysse, D. J., Thase, M. E., Mallinger, A. G., Swartz, H. A., Fagiolini, A. M., . . . Monk, T. (2005). Two-year outcomes for interpersonal and social rhythm therapy in individuals with bipolar I disorder. *Archives of General Psychiatry, 62,* 996–1004.

Frank, E., Kupfer, D. J., Perel, J. M., Cornes, C., Jarrett, D. B., & Mallinger, A. G. (1990). Three year outcomes for maintenance therapies in recurrent depression. *Archives of General Psychiatry, 47,* 1093–1099.

Hamilton, M. (1960). A rating scale for depression. *Journal of Neurology, Neurosurgery, and Psychiatry, 23,* 56–62.

Hamilton, M. (1967). Development of a rating scale for primary depressive illness. *British Journal of Social and Clinical Psychology, 6,* 278–296.

Hammen, C. (1999). The emergence of an interpersonal approach to depression In T. Joiner & J. C. Coyne (Eds.), *The interactional nature of depression: Advances in interpersonal approaches* (pp. 21–35). Washington, DC: American Psychological Association.

Klerman, G. L., DiMascio, A., Weissman, M., Prusoff, B., & Paykel, E. S. (1974). Treatment of depression by drugs and psychotherapy. *American Journal of Psychiatry, 131,* 186–191.

Klerman, G. L., Weissman, M. M., Rounsaville, B. J., & Chevron, E. S. (1984). *Interpersonal psychotherapy of depression.* New York: Basic Books.

Lipsitz, J. D., Gur, M., Miller, N. L., Forand, N., Vermes, D., & Fyer, A. J. (2006). An open pilot study of interpersonal psychotherapy for panic disorder (IPT-PD). *Journal of Nervous and Mental Disease, 194,* 440–445.

Lipsitz, J. D., Markowitz, J. C., Cherry, S., & Fyer, A. J. (1999). Open trial of interpersonal psychotherapy for the treatment of social phobia. *American Journal of Psychiatry, 156,* 1814–1816.

Markowitz, J. C., Bleiberg, K. L., Christos, P., & Levitan, E. (2006). Solving interpersonal problems correlates with symptom improvement in interpersonal psychotherapy: Preliminary findings. *Journal of Nervous and Mental Disease, 194,* 15–20.

Markowitz, J. C., Kocsis, J. H., Fishman, B., Spielman, L. A., Jacobsberg, L. B., Frances, A. J., . . . Perry, S. W. (1998). Treatment of depressive symptoms in human immunodeficiency virus-positive patients. *Archives of General Psychiatry, 55,* 452–457.

Meyer, A. (1957). *Psychobiology: A science of man.* Springfield, IL:Thomas.

Miller, L., & Weissman, M. (2002). Interpersonal psychotherapy delivered over the telephone to recurrent depressives: A pilot study. *Depression and Anxiety, 16,* 114–117.

Mufson, L., Dorta, K. P., Moreau, D., & Weissman, M. M. (2004). *Interpersonal psychotherapy for depressed adolescents (2 ed.).* New York: Guilford Press.

Mufson, L., Dorta, K. P., Wickramaratne, P., Nomura, Y., Olfson, M., & Weissman, M. M. (2004). A randomized effectiveness trial of interpersonal psychotherapy for depressed adolescents. *Archives of General Psychiatry, 61,* 577–584.

Mufson, L., Weissman, M. M., Moreau, D., & Garfinkel, R. (1999). Efficacy of interpersonal psychotherapy for depressed adolescents. *Archives of General Psychiatry, 56,* 573–579.

O'Hara, M. W., Stuart, S., Gorman, L. L., & Wenzel, A. (2000). Efficacy of interpersonal psychotherapy for postpartum depression. *Archives of General Psychiatry, 57,* 1039–1045.

Paykel, E. S., DiMascio, A., Haskell, D., & Prusoff, B. A. (1975). Effects of maintenance amitriptyline and psychotherapy on symptoms of depression. *Psychological Medicine, 5,* 67–77.

Reynolds, C. F., Frank, E., Perel, J. M., Imber, S. D., Cornes, C., Miller, M. D., … Kupfer, D. J. (1999). Nortriptyline and interpersonal psychotherapy as maintenance therapies for recurrent major depression: A randomized controlled trial in patients older than 59 years. *Journal of the American Medical Association, 281,* 39–45.

Rossello, J., & Bernal, G. (1999). The efficacy of cognitive-behavioral and interpersonal treatments for depression in Puerto Rican adolescents. *Journal of Consulting and Clinical Psychology, 67,* 734–745.

Rounsaville, B. J., Glazer, W., Wilber, C. H., Weissman, M. M., & Kleber, H. (1983). Short-term interpersonal psychotherapy in methadone-maintained opiate addicts. *Archives of General Psychiatry, 40,* 629–636.

Rudolph, K. D., Hammen, C., Burge, D., Lindberg, N., Herzberg, D., & Daley, S. E. (2000). Toward an interpersonal life-stress model of depression: The developmental context of stress generation. *Development and Psychopathology, 12,* 215–234.

Schulberg, H. C., Block, M. R., Madonia, M. J., Scott, C. P., Rodriguez, E., Imber, S. D., …

Coulehan, J. L. (1996). Treating major depression in primary care practice. *Archives of General Psychiatry,* 913–919.

Spinelli, M. G., & Endicott, J. (2003). Controlled clinical trial of interpersonal psychotherapy versus parenting education program for depressed pregnant women. *American Journal of Psychiatry, 160,* 555–562.

Sullivan, H. S. (1953). *The interpersonal theory of psychiatry.* New York: W. W. Norton.

Weissman, M. M., Klerman, G. L., Paykel, E. S., Prusoff, B., & Hanson, B. (1974). Treatment effects on the social adjustment of depressed patients. *Archives of General Psychiatry, 30,* 771–778.

Weissman, M. M., Klerman, G. L., Prusoff, B. A., Sholomskas, D., & Padin, N. (1981). Depressed outpatients: Results one year after treatment with drugs and/or interpersonal psychotherapy. *Archives of General Psychiatry, 38,* 51–55.

Weissman, M. M., Markowitz, J. C., & Klerman, G. L. (2000). *Comprehensive guide to interpersonal psychotherapy.* New York: Basic Books.

Weissman, M. M., Markowitz, J. C., & Klerman, G. L. (2007). *Clinician's quick guide to interpersonal psychotherapy.* New York: Oxford University Press.

Weissman, M. M., Prussoff, B. A., DiMascio, A., Neu, C., Coklaney, M., & Klerman, G. L. (1979). The efficacy of drugs and psychotherapy in the treatment of acute depressive episodes. *American Journal of Psychiatry, 136,* 555–558.

Wilfley, D. E., Mackenzie, K. R., Welch, R., Ayres, V. A., & Weissman, M. M. (2000). *Interpersonal psychotherapy for group.* New York:Basic Books.

Wilfley, D. E., Welch, R. R., Stein, R. I., Borman Spurrell, E., Cohen, L. R., Saelens, B. E., … Matt, G. E. (2002). A randomized comparison of group cognitive-behavioral therapy and group interpersonal psychotherapy for the treatment of overweight individuals with binge-eating disorder. *Archives of General Psychiatry, 59,* 713–721.

World Health Organization (1992). The ICD-10 classification of mental and behavioral disorders: Clinical descriptions and diagnostic guidelines. Geneva: World Health Organization.

Young, J. F., Mufson, L., & Davies, M. (2006). Efficacy of Interpersonal Psychotherapy—Adolescent Skills Training: An indicated preventive intervention for depression. *Journal of Child Psychology and Psychiatry, 47,* 1254–1262.

32 TIME-LIMITED DYNAMIC PSYCHOTHERAPY

Hanna Levenson

Over 25 years ago, Hans Strupp and Jeffrey Binder (1984) developed Time-Limited Dynamic Psychotherapy (TLDP) as a way to help therapists treat clients who evidenced difficulties forming positive therapeutic alliances due to their life-long dysfunctional interpersonal difficulties. These clients, who were often hostile, negativistic, overly dependent, and/or help-rejecting, got under the skin of their therapists.[1] When confronted with such clients, Strupp and colleagues (e.g., Henry et al. 1993a; Henry et al. 1993b) found that therapists had trouble modulating their negative emotional responses in session and therefore had a high likelihood of responding in an unhelpful complementary fashion—for example, client's hostility begetting therapist's hostility. Therapists working with these difficult clients often responded in belittling and invalidating ways—ways that clearly were not therapeutic.

Acknowledgments: Some sections of this book chapter are reproduced from *Brief Dynamic Psychotherapy*, by H. Levenson. Copyright © 2010 by the American Psychological Association. Reproduced with permission. No further reproduction or distribution of APA content is permitted without written permission from the American Psychological Association.

TLDP, which has its origins in psychodynamic theory (specifically, object relations), was designed to examine and shift clients' recurrent, dysfunctional, interpersonal patterns that might be activated in trying to form a relationship with the therapist. It was thought that if the client could be helped to see the self-defeating nature of these patterns, and to understand their significance in terms of "chronic maladaptations," changes in the patient's manner of relating, cognitions, and feelings would occur. A critical aspect of TLDP as outlined by Strupp and Binder (1984) was that "the patient-therapist relationship is conceived of as a *dyadic system* in which the behavior of *both* participants is continually scrutinized by the participants themselves. The overarching goal of TLDP is to mediate a constructive human experience which results in improvements in the quality of the patient's interpersonal relations" (emphases added, p. xiv). Thus, TLDP privileged "contemporary transactions" in the therapy room as a vehicle for creating shifts in interpersonal functioning and for understanding their meaning. In sum, Strupp and Binder (1984) considered psychotherapy to be "basically a set of interpersonal transactions" (p. 29).

Previous types of brief dynamic therapies (12 to 25 sessions) usually limited treatment to highly functioning adults (e.g., above-average intelligence, psychologically minded, introspective) (Levenson, Butler, Powers, & Beitman, 2002). But TLDP was designed to be applicable to a broader range of clients, particularly those who had difficulties achieving good working alliances with their therapists. Furthermore, TLDP melded psychodynamic approaches with more systems orientations. Rather than seeing individuals as fixated at an early stage of development and therefore needing to "work through" these childhood conflicts in therapy, TLDP views the client's problems in living as perpetuated in a dynamic system of interactions that becomes maintained in the present. In other words, the client's dysfunctional interpersonal style is seen as inviting the very response from others that is most unrewarding and (though familiar) maladaptive.

A particularly important feature of TLDP is its firm empirical base built over years of research. (See later section on empirical evidence.) In fact, Strupp and Binder's (1984) seminal text introducing TLDP, *Psychotherapy in a New Key*, began as a treatment manual for a NIMH grant to assess the degree to which such here-and-now interpersonal therapeutic strategies could be taught.

In 1995, I wrote *Time-Limited Dynamic Psychotherapy: A Guide for Clinical Practice*. As the title indicates, that book was designed to translate TLDP principles and strategies into pragmatically useful ways of thinking and intervening for the practitioner. In that book, I gave even more weight to the role of experiential learning. This focus on experiential learning (as opposed to insight) highlights the affective-action component of change. Within the therapy room, the client's worst fears (or expectations) of how he or she will be treated by the therapist have the opportunity to be disconfirmed within the client-therapist transactions. The client's new experiences of self coming forward in

a healthier and more adaptive way, and of therapist (as other) responding in a growth-promoting way, result in powerful learning similar to that achieved through exposure treatment.

In my most recent book on TLDP, I highlight attachment theory and experiential-affective approaches to increase the efficacy and power of the interpersonal approach of TLDP (2010). *Attachment theory* helps explain why people behave as they do—what motivates them. An *experiential-affective emphasis* focuses the therapeutic process of change—what needs to shift for change to occur. The interpersonal frame forms the conceptual basis of the therapy—what is the medium in which the therapy occurs. Each of these components will be briefly examined so that the reader will understand this more current, integrated version of TLDP.

INTEGRATIVE VIEW OF TLDP

Attachment Theory

The literature on attachment theory and its application to understanding human development is enormous and spans nearly 40 years (Obegi & Berant, 2008). Bowlby's (1969, 1973, 1980) monumental work on attachment, separation, and loss outlined the process by which humans are hardwired to maintain physical closeness to the caregivers on whom their very survival depends. "Bowlby viewed the human infant's reliance on, and emotional bond with, its mother to be the result of a *fundamental instinctual behavioral system* that, unlike Freud's sexual libido concept, was relational without being sexual" (Mikulincer & Shaver, 2007, p. 7, emphasis added). Not only did Bowlby break with the psychoanalytic tradition of his day, which "infuriated" the psychoanalytic community (Lewis, Amini, & Lannon, 2001, p. 70), but he also was rejected by the behaviorist camp because he saw that the infant's bond to mother went far beyond a simple reinforcement paradigm.[2]

Bowlby and his collaborator Mary Ainsworth (1969) went on to describe and assess the *attachment patterns* of infants—with some infants able to be soothed by mother after a momentary absence (securely attached), while others were unable to be comforted and remained hyperaroused (anxiously/ambivalently attached) or exhibited little visible distress (avoidantly attached). From the idea of proximity seeking, Bowlby later developed theories of how attachment needs and behaviors extend throughout the life cycle—"from cradle to grave" (Bowlby, 1988)—with adults turning to adults especially in times of stress—not for survival needs, but for a sense of felt security (Stroufe & Waters, 1977). For more on an attachment theory approach to psychotherapy, see Chapters 2 and 13 in this volume.

Bowlby's formulations about *internal working models* helped explain how these attachment patterns persist over time. He postulated that unconscious representational models of the self and attachment figures were developed based on the child's experience with caregivers. This internalized set of expectations comes to color how one sees the world and how one treats oneself. Securely attached children who have been responded to in a contingent, caring manner grow up expecting that they will be safe in the world and that all aspects of self can be noticed and appreciated. Insecurely attached children learn that when they are threatened or stressed, they cannot count on others for comfort or safety. They learn (often before the development of language and higher-order conceptual abilities) that there are parts of them that cannot be accepted by significant others. Because these internal working models affect one's perceptions, and are derived and perpetuated out of awareness, it is hard to correct them. Negative expectations often blind one to what otherwise would be disconfirmatory incoming information, and behavior emanating from such templates often invites others to respond in ways that validate one's dysfunctional working model.

Although there is no specific "attachment therapy" per se, Bowlby (1988) did outline therapeutic tasks that would be helpful in getting people to reappraise and restructure their internal working models. Of particular relevance for TLDP is that Bowlby considered an examination of the transference and countertransference, in the here and now of the sessions, to be of paramount importance. In his seminal book, *A Secure Base*, he (1988) recognized Strupp's work as being consistent with his ideas.

Interpersonal/Relational Theory

Harry Stack Sullivan usually gets the credit for highlighting the relevance of the interpersonal dimension for psychotherapy. Like Bowlby, Sullivan challenged the Freudian position that the discharge of biological drives was fundamental for personality development. Rather, he maintained that humans have an innate drive for interpersonal relatedness. In fact, he defined psychiatry as "the field of the study of interpersonal relations" (1954, p. ix). Even personality was defined as *"the relatively enduring pattern of recurrent interpersonal situations which characterize the human life"* (1953, p. 111).

Sullivan was one of the first to see the importance of the social field for understanding the therapeutic endeavor, taking into account what was being contributed by both patient *and* therapist. "The psychiatrist cannot stand off to one side and apply his sense organs, however, they may be refined by the use of apparatus, to noticing what someone else does, without becoming personally implicated in the operation" (1954, p. 3). Sullivan coined the term *participant-observer* to underscore how the therapist in each session occupies two roles simultaneously—that of an expert, trained observer, as well as that of an emotionally involved participant.

Research using ways to code interpersonal transactions (e.g., Structural Analysis of Social Behavior; Benjamin, 1974, 1993; see Chapter 20 in this volume) led to a fuller understanding of what transpires in therapeutic interchanges, and how a little negative in-session process goes a long way to undermining the successful outcome of therapy.[3] For example, therapists who treat themselves in a hostile fashion treat their clients in a more disaffiliative manner; clients who are treated in a hostile manner by their therapists treat themselves in a more critical manner (Henry, Schacht, & Strupp, 1990). These results suggest that the way we treat ourselves is how we treat others, and how we treat others is the way they come to treat themselves, creating an inextricable feedback loop of self and other dysfunction.

Horowitz and Vitkus (1986) examined how these interactive patterns maintain mental illness. For example, a depressed person seeks help from another person in a deflated, submissive manner. This other person is pulled to respond to the depressed person's passivity from the complementary dominant position—perhaps giving advice or telling the person to "buck up." However, this dominant stance only encourages the depressed person to be even more submissive, thereby heightening the depressed affect, and completing what has become known as a "vicious circle" (Wachtel, 1982).

This interpersonal lens is part of a larger paradigm shift from a *one-person to a two-person perspective* that has been occurring within psychoanalytic thinking and practice for the past 30 years (Levenson, 1995). This relational view acknowledges the observer-participant stance; that transference is not a pathological process of patient projections onto a neutral therapist, but rather plausible perceptions of the therapist's behavior and intent; and that countertransference is not a personal and professional failure on the part of the therapist, but rather a manifestation of his or her role responsiveness (Sandler, 1976), or even interpersonal empathy (Strupp & Binder, 1984).

Modern psychoanalytically oriented therapists, interpersonal neuroscientists, and developmental theorists (e.g., Cosolino, 2006; Fonagy & Target, 2006; Gallese, 2001;

Schore, 2006; Siegel, 1999), using functional MRI studies, single neuron recordings, moment-to-moment assessments of mother-infant interchanges, and primate research, have begun to conclude that "*relationships are a fundamental and necessary building block in the evolution of the human brain*" (Cosolino, 2006, p. 13, emphasis added). The caregiver (e.g., mother) provides the distressed infant with an emotional response that is a nuanced reflection of the infant's distress intermingled with the mother's more organized self state, which then becomes represented to the infant as his or her own mental state.[4] In fact, Fonagy (2003) states that "this 'inter-subjectivity' is the bedrock of the intimate connection between attachment and self-regulation" (p. 115), which brings us to the third theoretical thread of TLDP—how change takes place through experiential-affective learning.

Experiential-Affective Learning

Emphasizing the importance of experiential learning is not a new idea. Early on it was (and continues to be) identified as one of the common factors occurring in effective psychotherapies (Levenson, 2003). The "more numerous and more intense the experiential, as opposed to the purely cognitive components of learning, the more likely they are to be followed by changes in the patient's attitudes or behavior" (Franks, 1982, p. 25). Feelings, according to Damasio (1999), are representations of how our bodily states have shifted. Before language allowed us to have the experience of conscious, explicit memories, we could "remember" past events as a "felt sense" (Gendlin, 1996) through bodily sensations or feelings.

Helping clients become aware of, experience, and process their feelings and emotions has been underscored by all experiential approaches (Greenberg, Rice, & Elliott, 1993). The days of thinking it was healthy to "let it all hang out" are over. Today's signs of mental health include not only the ability to be emotionally aware and intelligent (Goleman, 1995), but also the importance of being able to regulate one's emotional life (Schore, 2003). Siegel (1999), writing on what he calls the neurobiology of interpersonal experience, opines that when caregivers help "metabolize" their child's feelings, they actually help the child develop healthy brain structures and processing capacities, which then foster the child's interpersonal and intrapsychic functioning throughout the lifespan.

Summary

This revised version of TLDP strengthens the interpersonal focus by being more explicit about its underpinnings in attachment theory and the centrality of dyadically created, experiential, emotionally based learning.

TLDP PRINCIPLES AND GOALS

TLDP Principles

There are nine basic principles that are central to the integrated version of TLDP. These will be briefly reviewed. For a fuller description, the reader is referred to Levenson (2010).

Principle 1: People are innately motivated to search for and maintain human relatedness. In TLDP, the search for and maintenance of connections with others is a major motivating force. Empirical research has demonstrated, and theoretical perspectives articulate, that we are hardwired to gravitate toward others.

Principle 2: Maladaptive relationship patterns underlie many presenting symptoms. Early experiences with caregivers help build or discourage mental structures and processes that will help the child develop a capacity for self-reflection (mentalization), emotional regulation, and coherent autobiographic narratives (Fonagy, Jurist, & Target, 2002; Siegel, 1999). These early experiences foster ways of understanding and interacting with one's interpersonal world that become schematized, encoded networks of affective, cognitive, and experiential data that help the child interpret the present, understand the past, and anticipate the future.

For example, a former client of mine (let us call him "Mr. Johnson") had parents who treated him in an authoritarian and harsh manner. Consequently, as a young boy, Mr. Johnson became a placating and anxiety-ridden child. The more he was wary and meek, the less his parents (particularly his father) punished or humiliated him, and the more attention he received (particularly from his mother). His early experiences led him to expect that others were not trustworthy and would be there for him only to the extent that he was submissive. Mr. Johnson adopted a deferential style because it was a way he could maintain a modicum of attachment to his parents while lessening the danger of physical and emotional abuse. He entered therapy as an adult because he suffered from depression, loneliness, and resumption of his binge drinking.

Principle 3: Relationship patterns persist because they are maintained in current relationships and are consistent with the person's sense of self and other (circular causality). The premise in TLDP is that while a dysfunctional pattern of interaction may have (in most cases) begun in the past, it is maintained in the present in relationship to others and oneself. According to the principle of circular causality, one person's message to another "imposes a condition of emotional engagement" (Kiesler, 1996, p. 209) that then results in a corresponding (complementary) response imbued with emotion that gives the other a sense of intention, precipitating another affective response, and so on.

If we return to my example of Mr. Johnson, in life he manifested his submissive style with his wife, children, and coworkers. His wife interpreted his behavior as "passive-aggressive" and was tired of his "do-nothing" attitude, which she perceived as a rejection of her at best and as a hostile act at worst. She tried to get him to be "more of a man" by demanding more from him. Mr. Johnson, on the other hand, felt cowed by his wife's "nagging," and felt even more disgusted with himself, resulting in increased caution and passivity, which further infuriated his wife, and so on. In the end, Mr. Johnson's childhood view of how the interpersonal world works (e.g., demanding, unsafe) and his own sense of self (e.g., a failure, inadequate) was validated over and over again *in the present*.

Hence, a dysfunctional dance results where all parties maintain a reciprocal system not of their conscious choosing— participating unwittingly in self-defeating behaviors and unrewarding transactions, fostering more attachment fears and longings. The focus on the present for understanding why such dysfunctional patterns are maintained is of critical importance for treating such difficulties in a brief time frame. If the maladaptive style is maintained in the person's current life, then *the therapist can work in the present* to effect affective, cognitive, and behavioral changes, rather than focusing on "working through" childhood conflicts that have become "fixated" at an early developmental level.

Principle 4: Clients are viewed as stuck, not "neurotic." From a TLDP perspective, clients are seen as doing the best they can with what they have. They have developed certain patterns of relating for self-protection. These security operations ("defenses") were once adaptive (e.g., as a child, Mr. Johnson's meek attitude kept him from getting beaten), but now they have become part of a vicious cycle where the individual ends up recreating the very situation that he or she most fears.

Principle 5: In TLDP, the focus is on shifting maladaptive relationship patterns, one's sense of self, and attendant emotions. The TLDP therapist needs to become aware of relationship themes in the person's life that may be maintaining patterns of dysfunction leading to symptoms. This can be accomplished not only through conscious reflection (e.g., asking clients about their experiences of problematic transactions with others), but also through observing the client's interpersonal behavior in session, paying attention to the feeling tone of the interactions and listening (with the "third ear"; Reik, 1948) to the use of metaphor, images, and other unconsciously conveyed information.[5] Attending to moment-by-moment shifts in the client's affective state is invaluable for discerning his or her implicit, maladaptive patterns. Furthermore, the therapist's own emotional experiences during the therapeutic hour are invaluable sources of information of what it feels like to be in a relationship with the client and may also reflect the client's self states (i.e., projective identification).

For clients who have particularly *rigid and pervasive dysfunctional strategies* and/or extreme difficulties in affect regulation, often the very issue that is problematic in the outside world is played out within the crucible of the therapeutic relationship. Reenactments occur in session, where the therapist has the opportunity not only to observe the maladaptive interactive sequence in real time, but also to experience first-hand (and often quite powerfully) what it is like to relate to that person and to *react* in ways that are complementary to the client's presentation. I have termed the extent to which the therapist becomes "hooked" (Kiesler, 1996) into the client's pattern as *interactive countertransference* (Levenson, 1995). Thus, the client's transference is not seen as a distortion of the therapist's behaviors (as with Freud's conceptualization), but rather as a reasonable reading of some of the therapist's intentions, feelings, and actions.

Returning to the case of Mr. Johnson, there were times when his vague responses in session (e.g., "I don't know") with long sighs and plaintive looks, evoked my frustration, which was then manifested in the therapeutic hour by the tone of my voice (e.g., a bit sarcastic) and word choice (e.g., a bit patronizing). For example, in the second session Mr. Johnson was describing how his grown daughter had left him all alone to go off boating with "her other friends. They go out on the bay—[pejoratively] 'baying it.' And I just feel left out!" When I replied, "Well, you are!," he lamented, "Yeah, I'm really left out...." As his voice trailed off with a resigned, lamenting quality, I responded matter-of-factly, "The least she could do after you went to all the trouble of raising her and giving her things was stick around for the rest of your life." My intent was to empathically validate his sense of loss (and underlying anger), but the phrasing and tenor of my statement revealed how I had become emotionally hooked into responding in a complementary fashion.

My unintentionally treating Mr. Johnson as if he were a recalcitrant child at times was a perfect fit for his woe-is-me, needy presentation. In TLDP it is first assumed that the therapist's mode of responding is an authentic and genuine reaction to the pushes and pulls from interacting with the client (and vice versa) and not a manifestation of classic countertransference.[6] Of course, it is critical that the therapist eventually unhooks him or herself from this dysfunctional dynamic, but as a first step it is necessary to examine how one might be cocreating the harmful transactional pattern in the session. Then the therapist can engage the client to change the nature of the interaction behaviorally, emotionally, and/or reflectively. (For more on therapeutic strategies, see section below.)

It should be noted that not all clients push and pull their therapists so strongly that they recreate a series of dysfunctional transactions (reenactments) with them (Binder, 2004). Those clients whose working models are more nuanced, flexible, and permeable (Kelly, 1955) need fewer security operations; they are more self-reflective. Consequently they are able to form therapeutic alliances more readily, developing a secure base with their therapists from which to examine their interpersonal patterns.

Principle 6: TLDP is concerned with interactive processes rather than with specific content. The TLDP therapist focuses on repetitive, interpersonal cycles or patterns of emotionally based behavior rather than on specific content (e.g., "wanting to have more friends"). Even when the client talks about something that sounds very intrapsychic (e.g., "low self-esteem"), the TLDP therapist will understand the problem in terms of attachment-based, affectively charged, interpersonal patterns.

Principle 7: TLDP focuses on one chief problematic relationship pattern. While there may be other issues, the TLDP therapist is attempting to make changes in the client's most pervasively dysfunctional style of relating with its attendant emotions. To convey the idea of a chief relationship pattern, Strupp has used the metaphor of a leitmotif—the music that gets played whenever an opera singer takes center stage. In TLDP we are trying to change the client's "theme song" with the idea that subsidiary melodies will shift accordingly.

Principle 8: The therapist is both an observer and a participant. When the TLDP therapist is more in the expert observer mode, he or she can take on the role of choreographer, coach, teacher, guide, or even cheerleader. From this position, the therapist can help clients access, process, label, and reflect on their emotional-interpersonal lives and construct ways for them to take risks to "do it differently." When the therapist is more in the participant mode, the experience is of non-self-conscious, emotional engagement with the client—a sense of "implicit relational knowing" (Stern et al., 1998). Both of these modes are essential for achieving the goals of TLDP.

There is an excellent *New Yorker* cartoon that nicely illustrates this dual therapeutic stance. An Elizabethan drama is taking place on stage with one character saying to the other, "But wait. Ellen doth approach!" And sure enough, Ellen is walking from the audience up onto the stage. The title under the cartoon is "Audience participation." Ellen was once the observer, and now she is going to become a part of the action.

Principle 9: Change will continue after the therapy is over. Simply, the goals of TLDP are to get someone on a new path—thinking, feeling, and behaving differently about self and others. (For more on goals, see the next section.) The intention is to interrupt the clients' repetitive, ingrained styles of being in the world and jog them out of their circular ruts onto a bridge to somewhere more secure and enlivening. To achieve this purpose, the therapist gives them opportunities in the session and in their lives to experience interactions in a more rewarding way and to have a more revitalized sense of self. When the sessions end, hopefully the clients' new attitudes and behaviors (toward self and others) will continue to be manifested in their lives, and reinforced through others' responses and their own resonating selves. This expectation is in accord with systems theory (Bertalanffy, 1969). Just as one invites others to participate in a vicious cycle, one can encourage others to be part of *victorious cycles*, where positive change continues after the session is over.

GOALS

There are two main goals for TLDP: (1) to provide positive new experiences (of self and other) and (2) to provide new understandings (of self and other). Thus, change occurs *experientially and cognitively* and *within and between*. While I will present these goals each in its own section, they are really part of the same phenomenon—two sides of the same coin—one melding into the other like an Escher print. The reason I separate them out is to serve as a heuristic device—to help the therapist formulate and intervene with a clearer conceptualization.

New Interpersonal Experiences

This goal emphasizes the affective-action-oriented component of change—feeling differently and acting differently. The TLDP therapist encourages any feelings, thoughts, or actions that will result in a more functionally adaptive, authentic manner of being in the world and interacting, rather than the client's more typically inflexible, constricted repertoire. To foster a new relational experience, clients are encouraged to take risks in behaving outside their customary pattern with their therapists and others. Again to return to Mr. Johnson—if he could be helped to assert his needs over time to another person (e.g., his therapist, his

wife), he would be taking a risk (based on his present working model) that he would be attacked. If the therapy went well, he could have a *series of new experiences* in which he feels himself as more empowered and sees that he is not punished. If Mr. Johnson's dysfunctional pattern were learned and maintained interpersonally, he can *un*learn it interpersonally.

There are parallels between this type of experiential learning and other therapeutic processes (e.g., exposure therapy, control-mastery therapy). In fact, Alexander and French's (1946) concept of a *corrective emotional experience* is very much at the root of this TLDP goal. As those psychoanalysts stated over fifty years ago, "This [change] cannot be done as an intellectual exercise; it has to be lived through, i.e., felt, by the patient and thus become an integral part of his emotional life" (p. 63). Or as so simply and eloquently put by Frieda Fromm-Reichmann, "What the patient needs is an experience, not an explanation."

In addition to creating new *interpersonal* experiences through risk-taking, the therapist can also transform emotions directly by "changing emotion with emotion" (Greenberg, 2002). For example, a positive emotional state can be promoted directly. By introducing a new (incompatible) feeling, an old feeling can be altered. For example, in working with Mr. Johnson, I began validating and heightening glimmers of his nascent anger at the way his daughter was treating him. ("She is out with her other friends, forgetting me, and it hurts.") By the end of a 20-session therapy, Mr. Johnson felt entitled to be "righteously angry." This emphasis is in line with recent emphasis on fostering positive emotions in therapy rather than focusing on eliminating negative ones (Fredrickson & Branigan, 2005). Another way to transform emotions directly is through a safe enough, attuned relationship with one's therapist. This empathic connection is not only thought to make clients "feel better" in a general sense, but also may help promote neural activation and emotional regulation (Siegel, 2006).[7]

New Interpersonal Understandings

The second goal of TLDP is to help the client reflect on and make meaning of their emotional-relational experiences. This goal also includes intrapersonal and interpersonal perspectives. From the *intrapersonal understanding perspective*, the therapist closely tracks moment-to-moment feeling states that are being evoked and expressed in sessions and fosters an appreciation of the relevancy and meaning of these experiences. For example, I helped Mr. Johnson put his vague sense of unease at being left alone by his children into a feeling language ("I am really angry") and helped him identify the attachment significance of the fear of expressing such anger ("I am really scared that if I am angry with them, they will really abandon me!"). By putting such a felt sense into words, Mr. Johnson was able to think about himself in a new way which led to his having more coherent narratives (Siegel, 1999) about his life that incorporated parts of himself that had previously been disowned.

From the *interpersonal understanding* perspective, the therapist invites clients to stand back from interactions with others, and helps them identify and comprehend their patterns and the reasons for developing and maintaining them. To accomplish this, the therapist often uses rather common intervention techniques such as reflection, clarification and interpretation—although the last is used with particular care because of its likelihood of being interpreted as blaming or shaming (Henry, Strupp, Schacht, & Gaston, 1994). In addition, talking with clients about what patterns are occurring in the room with their therapists (i.e., *metacommunicating*) provides clients with opportunities to see how their lifelong patterns are emerging in the here-and-now of the sessions. Therapist and client can then discuss and examine what has been cocreated between them.[8]

Again, going back to Mr. Johnson, I became aware in the sessions of my frustration and of fantasizing telling him to "get a life!" One of the ways to deal with my negative (and predictable) countertransference (I was becoming his wife!) was to invite him to discuss what was transpiring between us (unlike his wife). On one particular occasion, I became aware that my tone was condescending. I immediately switched gears from the topic at hand and asked Mr. Johnson how he felt about the way I had just talked to him. In a later session, I self-disclosed that I felt that I treated him like a child at times, and he revealed that he sometimes used his "whiny" voice to elicit attention.

Rapprochement

Interweaving back and forth between some form of reflective and experiential learning addresses both top-down processing (focusing on the client's conceptual framework) and bottom-up processing (accessing emotional experience directly). When I am addressing psychodynamically trained therapists, I stress the goal of a new relational experience because it helps remind them that "the supply of interpretations far exceeds the demand" (Strupp, personal communication) or, to paraphrase the old maxim, "an experience is worth a thousand words." Similarly, when I am working with therapists who are cognitively trained, I emphasize the centrality of emotion in effecting change.[9]

FORMULATION AND INTERVENTION STRATEGIES

Formulation: The Cyclical Maladaptive Pattern

In all short-term therapies, defining a focus has been found to be the most common feature (Levenson, et al., 2002). For TLDP the focus is achieved through the Cyclical Maladaptive Pattern or CMP (Schacht, Binder, & Strupp, 1984). The CMP was developed as a way to describe clients' dysfunctional interpersonal cycles or patterns and is comprised of four categories that are used to organize information about the client. In addition, I have added a fifth category—the therapist's interactive countertransference (Levenson, 1995).

Category 1: Acts of the self. This category includes the client's thoughts, feelings, motives, perceptions, and behaviors of an interpersonal nature. For example, "I believe people are basically evil" (thought). "I am afraid to go for a job interview" (feeling). "I start crying when my boss criticizes me" (behavior). Sometimes these acts are conscious and sometimes they are out of awareness, but all usually pertain to emotions that are aroused, disowned, disavowed, and/or distorted due to underlying, unmet attachment needs.

Category 2: Expectations of others' reactions. This category contains all the statements having to do with how the client imagines others will react to him or her. "If I go for a job interview, I will be humiliated." "My boss will fire me if I make one small mistake." Often the client's attachment fears and longings are revealed in terms of what they expect will occur if they are more fully themselves.

Category 3: Acts of others toward the self. This category consists of how the client perceives he or she was and is being treated by others. "When I applied for the job, I never heard back from the interviewer." "When I made a mistake at work, my boss glowered at me all day."

Category 4: Acts of self toward the self (introject). This category contains the client's thoughts, feelings, and behaviors concerning oneself—when the self is the object of the action. "When I didn't get the job, I berated myself for being so stupid as to think I was worth hiring." "Every time I make a mistake at work, I get a migraine." For this category (as well as all the others), the therapist needs to be aware of how the person's demeanor (in addition to, or even in spite of, content) conveys critical information for discerning underlying emotional distress. According to TLDP, the way someone treats oneself is largely, if not solely, a function of how they were treated by others. There is a marvelous *New Yorker* cartoon that

simply and immediately conveys this principle: A dog looks into a mirror after having ripped up pieces of paper that lay strewn around (with a telltale piece in his mouth), and says to his reflection, "Bad dog!"

Category 5: Therapist's interactive countertransference. For this category, the therapist needs to focus on his or her reactions to the client (at a behavioral and affective level). What are you aware of feeling as you sit in the room with the client? What are you pushed or pulled to do? What is going on at a visceral level? What are you thinking? What images come to mind? Ivy (2006), in writing on the characteristics of a good formulation, commented that my inclusion of the therapist's emotional responsiveness to the client as a source of information distinguishes it from earlier ways of formulating psychodynamically that assume a more detached and neutral therapist.

Formulation Steps[10]

Once one has sufficient data for each of the CMP categories, the therapist begins to link the components together to tell a story. This story forms a narrative of how people manifest inflexible behaviors, self-defeating expectations, and dysfunctional interactions with others that lead to, and have been perpetuated by, negative self-appraisals. The focus is on redundant themes emerging in the material, connected through their emotional significance. The CMP delineates the client's internalized working model to better understand historical and contemporary factors. This method of formulation is critical in the practice of TLDP. The CMP should provide a blueprint for the entire therapy—describing the nature of the problem, outlining the goals, suggesting where the client and therapist may become emotionally dysregulated, guiding particular interventions, enabling the therapist to anticipate reenactments, and providing a way to assess whether the therapy is on the right track.

So what would the CMP look like for Mr. Johnson? A simplified version for the purposes of this chapter might be something like: Mr. Johnson is a depressed, lonely, and deferential man (Acts of the Self), and expects others to take charge at best and to be punitive at worst (Expectations of Others). By his account, he had an authoritarian, harsh father and a forceful wife who took advantage of, and further fostered, his submissiveness (Acts of Others). With his vulnerable self-concept confirmed, Mr. Johnson periodically drank himself into oblivion, which led him to feel even more inadequate (Acts of the Self toward the Self). All of this heightened his passivity and depression (returning full circle to Acts of Self). In the room with Mr. Johnson, I felt pulled to force him into action.[11] While at times I felt quite sorry and protective of him, more often I felt frustrated by his "yes, but" attitude (Interactive Countertransference).

From the CMP formulation, the therapist should be able to ascertain the goals for treatment. What *new experiences and new understandings* of both an intrapersonal and interpersonal sort does the client need that would most likely subvert or interrupt his or her maladaptive, vicious cycle—diverting him or her out of a dysfunctional rut and onto a more productive path? With Mr. Johnson, for example, my goals were to help him feel more empowered, to act more assertively, and to understand what had contributed to and maintained his passive style.

Throughout the entire process of formulating and intervening, the therapist must take into account *cultural aspects* that are assumed to permeate all formulations and interventions (Ridley & Kelly, 2007). The client's and therapist's gender, race, ethnicity, sexual orientation, socioeconomic status, age, disability status, and so on must be considered separately and in combination. How do these worldviews influence the client's and therapist's working models, and how do these worldviews then interact as part of the therapeutic process?

Going back to my work with Mr. Johnson, how did our difference in ages (he was old enough to be my father), gender, employment status (he was retired and on welfare and I was an employed psychologist), and societal timeframe (he grew up in the Depression era and I was part of the 60s generation), impact the therapist-client power differentials implicit in any psychotherapy? Could there be some transference-countertransference reenactments that might need to be seen using a cultural (rather than purely idiosyncratic) lens?

Intervention Strategies

The TLDP perspective is that all interventions are relational acts (Norcross, 2002). Interventions are not considered "disembodied techniques" (Butler & Strupp, 1986), but rather strategies that are inextricably embedded in the interpersonal relationship. Theoretically, from an assimilative viewpoint (Messer, 1992), any type of intervention that would facilitate the goals of new experiencing and understanding could be used. I feel free to use whatever is in my therapeutic armamentarium to foster the attachment-based, experiential, interpersonal goals. In addition to traditional psychodynamic interventions (e.g., clarification, confrontation), I have used empty-chair work, body focusing, behavioral rehearsal, psychoeducation, suggestion, and homework, to name a few. However, the therapist must always assess the degree to which a particular technique might hamper or even controvert the goals for treatment. For example, giving Mr. Johnson assertiveness exercises to help him combat his timidity might seem like a good idea. But the therapist would need to judge the degree to which doing this homework (i.e., being a *compliant good patient*) might undermine his experience of being more in control and the master of his own destiny (one of the goals for the therapy). In fact, my giving him such an assignment might even be an acting-out of my interactive countertransference.

There are eight broad categories of TLDP intervention strategies. Those that are directed toward (1) maintaining the therapeutic alliance, (2) accessing and processing emotion, (3) exploring empathically, (4) focusing on the therapeutic relationship, (5) examining cyclical patterns, (6) inquiring in a focused manner, (7) promoting change directly, and (8) discussing the time-limited aspects of the work. The reader is referred to Levenson (2010) for a fuller discussion of each of these.

With regard to some general intervention procedures, in TLDP as in all briefer forms of therapy, the therapist must be able to intervene even when there is insufficient information. Interventions do not need to be "correct" in any absolutist sense; they can be thought of as invitations to think about something differently or try out something differently. Staying close to what is observable, and slowing down the interactions so that the client can catch up to his or her own emotional actions and reactions, are helpful in this regard.

In addition, when commenting on patterns that emerge in session or out, the therapist must wait for sufficient repetitions so that the redundancy is clear not only to him or herself, but also to the client. "Premature" transference interpretations are jarring to clients; they also are experienced as blaming and/or belittling (Henry et al., 1993b; Piper, Azim, Joyce, & McCallum, 1991), and thus should be used with caution.

EMPIRICAL RESEARCH

Does Brief Dynamic Therapy Work?

Perhaps it should be stated at the outset that almost all psychotherapy research in the United States is based on brief therapies that last fewer than 20 sessions (Lambert, Bergin, & Garfield, 2004). *Thus when we talk about research studies on brief therapy, to a large extent we are referring to what we know about therapy in general.* Findings from a number of studies from the 1950s to present have repeatedly shown that the more therapy, the better (Hansen, Lambert, & Forman, 2002; Knekt et al., 2008; Seligman, 1995), However, when one looks at the *rate of change over time,* what is apparent is

that significant and meaningful change can occur within a relatively short period. It has been estimated that 50% of clients show clinical improvement by sessions 8 to 16, 60 to 70% within 13 sessions, and 75% by session 26, which is within the time frame of most brief dynamic therapies (Hansen, Lambert, & Forman, 2002; Howard, Kopta, Krause, & Orlinksy, 1986; Kadera, Lambert, & Andrews, 1996). Encouragingly, therapists who have received specific training in brief dynamic theory and intervention are more helpful to clients (Anderson & Lambert, 1995; Hilsenroth et al., 2006).[12]

Meta-analytic studies (statistically combining findings from a number of studies on the same topic) indicate that brief dynamic psychotherapy is superior to waiting-list control groups, has equivalent outcomes to other psychotherapies and medication, and has stable effects (Anderson & Lambert, 1995; deMatt et al., 2008; Knekt et al., 2008; Leichsenring, Rabung, & Leibing, 2004). When one considers the unit of change per monetary expenditure, brief dynamic therapy comes out ahead of longer-term approaches (Piper et al., 1984). Finally, additional meta-analytic studies on brief therapy have shown that the more the therapist encourages expression of affect, the better the outcome (Diener, Hilsenroth, & Weinberger, 2007).

Research on TLDP

TLDP has a long tradition of empirical research. Stemming from a series of studies begun in the early 1950s, Strupp (1955a, 1955b, 1955c, 1960) found that the therapists' personal feelings about clients were manifested in their interventions. In the 1980s he demonstrated that clients who were mistrusting, hostile, and/or negative had poor outcomes because they were unable to form working alliances with their therapists. As previously stated, these findings led to the development of TLDP and launched a series of studies on therapeutic outcome, process, and training.

Looking at studies on *outcome*, it has been found that clients become significantly more securely attached following treatment (Travis, Binder, Bliwise, & Horne-Moyer, 2001). Levenson and Overstreet (1993) found that 60% of male outpatients who were diagnosed with personality disorders had positive interpersonal and/or symptomatic outcomes following an average of 14 sessions of TLDP, and 70% felt their problems had lessened (Levenson & Bein, 1993). A long-term follow-up study showed that these gains were maintained and slightly bolstered. Another outcome study (Junkert-Tress, Schnierda, Hartkamp, Schmitz, & Tress, 2001) revealed positive outcomes at termination and at long-term follow-ups.

With regard to studies on the therapeutic *process* of TLDP, results indicate that the more therapists treat their clients in a disrespectful fashion, the poorer the outcome, and the more clients reflect this negativity in self-blame (Henry, Schacht, & Strupp, 1990; Hilliard, Henry, & Strupp, 2000. Remember the dog in the mirror? In addition, therapists who themselves have poor introjects treat their clients in a disaffiliative manner and also have negative outcomes (Quintana & Meara, 1990). In two studies (Hartmann & Levenson, 1995; Johnson, Popp, Schacht, Mellon, & Strupp, 1989), reliable TLDP relationship themes could be identified, and Hartman and Levenson (1995) found that those therapists who consistently stayed focused on topics relevant to their clients' CMPs, had better outcomes.

Strupp and colleagues' research on the effects of TLDP *training* on therapist variables and process remains one of the few studies in this important area. In their oft-quoted studies of 16 experienced psychiatrists and psychologists learning TLDP, they found that following training, therapists' interventions were more in keeping with TLDP methods (Henry et al., 1993b). A similar positive training effect was also found for prepracticum counselor trainees (Multon, Kivlighan, & Gold, 1996). However, further research (Bein et al., 2000) suggested that many of the clinicians in the former study may not have reached an acceptable level of TLDP mastery.

An inspection of differences due to trainer effects (Henry et al., 1993b) suggested that training in TLDP (and perhaps other approaches as well) should be directive, specific, and challenging. (For more recommendations on training in brief dynamic psychotherapy, see Levenson and Strupp, 1999.) Similarly, Hilsenroth (2007) advocated for more "focused, intensive, and task-specific instructional methods" (p. 41). Another study found TLDP skills were particularly enhanced with live supervision (Kivligan, Angelone, & Swofford, 1991). Levenson and Bolter (1988) found that following a seminar and group supervision in TLDP, psychiatry residents and predoctoral psychology trainees' brief therapy attitudes and values became more positive. The same finding held with professional clinicians who were attending day-long brief therapy workshops (Neff et al., 1997).

LaRue and Levenson (2001) sought to study long-term training effects. Their study is remarkable in that they contacted practicing psychiatrists and psychologists who had received TLDP training almost a decade earlier when they were trainees at a large medical center. Findings indicated that most of these clinicians ($N = 90$) were still using TLDP formulation methods and intervention strategies in their daily work. Interestingly, they were also integrating TLDP ways of working into their longer-term therapies.

While there is a paucity of research on TLDP with people from different cultures, Wong and colleagues (2003) found that among Asian American students, only those who were more identified with Asian (versus white, European-American) values rated a cognitive therapy treatment rationale as more credible than that for TLDP. With regard to age factors, Nordhus and Geir (1999) reported using TLDP with an elderly population, and Flasher (2000) makes a case for using TLDP with children. Levenson and Davidovitz (2000), in a national survey of 3,400 therapists, found males preferred shorter-term models and spent more time doing brief therapy than their female counterparts; however, the questions were framed generically and not specific to TLDP.

Brief Therapy Is Not for Everyone

Despite the rich clinical and empirical evidence, let me be clear that TLDP is not a panacea. It is not designed to be used with everyone by everyone. There are some problems and issues that do not lend themselves to a brief dynamic treatment (e.g., severe depression, impaired reality testing, ongoing management issues such as chronic suicidal behavior). And there are some therapists who are not well suited by temperament and/or training to do the interactive, directive, self-disclosing, emotionally focused work required by TLDP.

SUMMARY

Time-limited dynamic psychotherapy (TLDP) was designed to help therapists treat difficult clients. TLDP views the client's problems in living as being maintained in a maladaptive dynamic system of interactions that becomes maintained in present relationships. The goals are to disrupt these transactional patterns and alter the client's internal working models of self and other. This chapter presents a revised, integrative view of TLDP that strengthens its interpersonal focus by being more explicit about its attachment theory base and the centrality of dyadically created, experiential, emotionally based learning. This relational model highlights the therapist's participant-observer stance; it also conceptualizes *transference* as plausible perceptions of the therapist's behavior and *countertransference* as a form of role responsiveness that can help a therapist understand a client's dilemma. A method of formulating, and strategies for intervening, are described with clinical examples and supporting empirical evidence.

In closing, I would like to urge that we move away from a research emphasis based solely on so-called empirically supported therapies that are designed to specify particular treatments for specific diagnoses. Research on brief therapy as practiced (rather than solely on controlled trials with carefully selected clients) should be applauded (and funded). Empirical investigation of intervention strategies and theories of change that therapists can use to inform their clinical work are needed (Westen, Novotny, & Thompson-Brenner, 2004). In fact, anything that encourages clinicians and researchers to carry on meaningful conversations should be promoted (Talley, Strupp, & Butler, 1994). In addition, I suggest that we investigate how best to teach brief dynamic principles to therapists and trainees. The need for brief interventions will only grow. We need to learn how best to inform a new generation of practitioners to practice competently in a time-effective manner.

References

Ainsworth, M. D. S. (1969). Object relations, dependency and attachment: A theoretical review of the infant-mother relationship. *Child Development, 40,* 969–1025.

Alexander, F., & French, T. (1946). *Psychoanalytic therapy: Principles and applications.* New York: Ronald Press.

Anderson, E. M., & Lambert, M. J. (1995). Short-term dynamically oriented psychotherapy: A review and meta-analysis. *Clinical Psychology Review, 15,* 503–514.

Barlow, D. H. (2000). Unraveling the mysteries of anxiety and its disorders from the perspective of emotion theory. *American Psychologist, 55,* 1247–1263.

Bein, E., Anderson, T., Strupp, H. H., Henry, W. P., Schacht, T. E., Binder, J. L., & Butler, S. F. (2000). The effects of training in time-limited dynamic psychotherapy: Changes in therapeutic outcome. *Psychotherapy Research, 10,* 119–132.

Bein, E., Levenson, H., & Overstreet, D. (1994, June). Outcome and follow-up data from the VAST project. In H. Levenson (Chair), *Outcome and follow-up data in brief dynamic therapy.* Symposium conducted at the annual international meeting of the Society for Psychotherapy Research, York, England.

Benjamin, L. S. (1974). Structural analysis of social behavior. *Psychological Review, 81*, 392–425.

Benjamin, L. S. (1993). *Interpersonal diagnosis and treatment of personality disorders.* New York: Guilford Press.

Bertalanffy, L. V. (1969). *General systems theory* (rev. ed.). New York: Braziller.

Binder, J. L. (2004). *Key competencies in brief dynamic psychotherapy.* New York: Guilford Press.

Binder, J. L., & Strupp, H. H. (1997). "Negative process": A recurrently discovered and underestimated facet of therapeutic process and outcome in the individual psychotherapy of adults. *Clinical Psychology: Science and Practice, 4*, 121–139.

Bolter, K., Levenson, H., & Alvarez, W. (1990). Differences in values between short-term and long-term therapists. *Professional Psychology: Research and Practice, 21*, 285–290.

Bowlby, (1969). *Attachment and loss: Vol. 1. Attachment.* New York: Basic Books.

Bowlby, J. (1973). *Attachment and loss: Vol. 2. Separation anxiety and anger.* New York: Basic Books.

Bowlby, J. (1980). *Attachment and loss: Vol. 3. Loss, sadness, and depression.* New York: Basic Books.

Bowlby, J. (1988). *A secure base: Clinical applications of attachment theory.* London: Routledge.

Burum, B. A., & Goldfried, M. R. (2007) The centrality of emotion to psychological change. *Clinical Psychology: Science and Practice, 14*, 407–413.

Butler, S. F., & Strupp, H. H. (1986) "Specific" and "nonspecific" factors in psychotherapy: A problematic paradigm for psychotherapy research. *Psychotherapy: Theory, Research and Practice, 23*, 30–40.

Cosolino, L. (2006). *The neuroscience of human relationships: Attachments and the developing brain.* New York: W. W. Norton.

Damasio, A. (1999). *The feeling of what happens.* New York: Harcourt, Brace.

DeMaat, S., Dekker, J., Schoevers, R., van Aalst, G., Gijsbers-van Wijk, C., Hendriksen, M., . . . de Jonghe, F. (2008). Short psychodynamic supportive psychotherapy, antidepressants and their combination in the treatment of major depression: A mega-analysis based on three randomized clinical trials. *Depression and Anxiety, 25*, 565–574.

Diener, M. C., Hilsenroth, M. J., & Weinberger, J. (2007). Therapist affect, focus, and patient outcomes in psychodynamic psychotherapy: A meta-analysis. *American Journal of Psychiatry, 164*, 936–941.

Flasher, L. V. (2000). Cyclical maladaptive patterns: Interpersonal case formulation for psychotherapy with children. *Journal of Contemporary Psychology, 30*, 239–254.

Fonagy, P., Gergely, G., Jurist, E. L., & Target, M. (2002). *Affect regulation, mentalization, and the development of the self.* New York: Other Press.

Fonagy, P., & Target, M. (2006). The mentalization focused approach to self-psychology. *Journal of Personality Disorders, 20*, 544–576.

Frank, J. D. (1982). Therapeutic components shared by all psychotherapies. In J. H. Harvey & M. M. Parks (Eds.), *Psychotherapy research and behavior change: The Master Lecture Series* (pp. 9–37). Washington, DC: American Psychological Association.

Fredrickson, B. L., & Branigan, C. A. (2005). Positive emotions broaden the scope of attention and thought-action repertoires. *Cognition and Emotion, 19*, 313–332.

Gallese, V. (2002). The "shared manifold" hypothesis. *Journal of Consciousness Studies, 8*, 33–50.

Gendlin, E. T. (1996). *Focusing-oriented psychotherapy: A manual of the experiential method.* New York: Guilford Press.

Goleman, D. (1995). *Emotional intelligence.* New York: Bantam Books.

Greenberg, L. S. (2002). *Emotion-focused therapy: Coaching clients to work through their feelings.* Washington, DC: American Psychological Association.

Greenberg, L. S., Rice, L. N., & Elliott, R. (1993). *Facilitating emotional change: The moment-by-moment process.* New York: Guilford Press.

Hansen, N. B., Lambert, M. J., & Forman, E. M. (2002). The psychotherapy dose-response effect and its implications for treatment delivery services. *Clinical Psychology: Science and Practice, 9*, 329–343.

Harlow, H. F. (1959). Love in infant monkeys. *Scientific American, 200*, 68–86.

Hartmann, K., & Levenson, H. (1995, June). *Case formulation and countertransference in time-limited dynamic psychotherapy.* Presentation at the annual meeting of the Society for Psychotherapy Research, Vancouver, British Columbia.

Henry, W. P., Schacht, T. E., Strupp, H. H., Butler, S. F., & Binder, J. L. (1993a). Effects of training in time-limited dynamic psychotherapy:

Mediators of therapists' responses to training. *Journal of Consulting and Clinical Psychology, 61,* 441–447.

Henry, W. P., Strupp, H. H., Schacht, T. E. & Gaston, L. (1994). Psychodynamic approaches. In A. E. Bergin & S. L. Garfield (Eds.), *Handbook of psychotherapy and behavior change* (4th ed., pp. 143–189). New York: John Wiley & Sons.

Henry, W. P., Strupp, H. H., Butler, S. F., Schacht, T. E., & Binder, J. L. (1993b). Effects of training in time-limited dynamic psychotherapy: Changes in therapist behavior. *Journal of Consulting and Clinical Psychology, 61,* 434–440.

Henry, W. P., Schacht, T. E., & Strupp, H. H. (1990). Patient and therapist introject, interpersonal process, and differential psychotherapy outcome. *Journal of Consulting and Clinical Psychology, 58,* 768–774.

Hilliard, R. B., Henry, W. P., & Strupp, H. H. (2000). An interpersonal model of psychotherapy: Linking patient and therapist developmental history, therapeutic process, and types of outcome. *Journal of Consulting and Clinical Psychology, 68,* 125–133.

Hilsenroth, M. J., Defife, J. A., Blagys, M. D., & Ackerman, S. J. ((2006). Effects of training in short-term psychodynamic psychotherapy: Changes in graduate clinician technique. *Psychotherapy Research, 16,* 293–305.

Horowitz, L., & Vitkus, J. (1986). The interpersonal basis of psychiatric symptoms. *Clinical Psychology Review, 6,* 443–469.

Howard, K. I., Kopta, S. M., Krause, M. S., & Orlinsky, D. E. (1986). The dose-effect relationship in psychotherapy. *American Psychologist, 41,* 159–164.

Ivy, G. (2006). A method of teaching psychodynamic case formulation. *Psychotherapy: Theory, Research, Practice, Training, 43,* 322–336.

Johnson, M. E., Popp, C., Schacht, T. E., Mellon, J., & Strupp, H. H. (1989). Converging evidence for identification of recurrent relationship themes: Comparison of two methods. *Psychiatry, 52,* 275–288.

Junkert-Tress, B. Schnierda, U., Hartkamp, N., Schmitz, N., & Tress, W. (2001). Effects of short-term dynamic psychotherapy for neurotic, somatoform, and personality disorders. *Psychotherapy Research, 11,* 187–200.

Kadera, S. W., Lambert, M. J., & Andrews A. A. (1996). How much therapy is really enough?

The Journal of Psychotherapy Practice and Research, 5, 132–151.

Kelly, G. (1955) *Psychology of personal constructs.* New York: W. W. Norton.

Kiesler, D. J. (1996). *Contemporary interpersonal theory and research.* New York: John Wiley & Sons.

Kivligan, D. M., Jr., Angelone, E. O., & Swofford K. (1991). Live supervision in individual counseling. *Professional Psychology: Research and Practice, 22,* 489–495.

Knekt, P., Lindfors, O., Härkänen, T., Välikoski, M., Virtala, E., Laaksonen, M. A., ... the Helsinki Psychotherapy Group. (2008). Randomized trial on the effectiveness of long- and short-term psychodynamic psychotherapy and solution-focused therapy on psychiatric symptoms during a three-year follow-up. *Psychological Medicine, 38,* 689–703.

Lambert, M., Bergin, A., & Garfield, S. (Eds.) (2004). *Handbook of psychotherapy and behavior change* (5th ed.). Hoboken, NJ: John Wiley & Sons.

LaRue, T., & Levenson, H. (2001, August). *Long-term outcome of training in time-limited dynamic psychotherapy.* Paper presented at the American Psychological Association Convention, San Francisco, CA.

Leichsenring, F., Rabung, S., & Leibing, E. (2004). The efficacy of short-term psychodynamic psychotherapy in specific psychiatric disorders: A meta-analysis, *Archives of General Psychiatry, 61,* 1208–1216.

Levenson, H. (1995). *Time-limited dynamic psychotherapy: A guide to clinical practice.* New York: Basic Books.

Levenson, H. (2003). Time-limited dynamic psychotherapy: An integrationist perspective. *Journal of Psychotherapy Integration, 13,* 300–333.

Levenson, H. (2010). *Brief dynamic psychotherapy.* Washington, DC: American Psychological Association Press.

Levenson, H., & Bein, E. (1993, June). *VA short-term psychotherapy research project: Outcome.* Paper presented at the annual meeting of the Society for Psychotherapy Research, Pittsburgh, PA.

Levenson, H., & Bolter, K. (1988, August). *Short-term psychotherapy values and attitudes: Changes with training.* Paper presented at the American Psychological Association Convention, Atlanta, GA.

Levenson, H., Butler, S., Powers, T., & Beitman, B. (2002). *Concise guide to brief dynamic and interpersonal psychotherapy.* Washington, DC: American Psychiatric Press.

Levenson, H., & Davidovitz, D. (2000). Brief therapy prevalence and training: A national survey of psychologists. *Psychotherapy, 37,* 335–340.

Levenson, H., & Overstreet, D. (1993, June). *Long-term outcome with brief psychotherapy.* Paper presented at the annual meeting of Society for Psychotherapy Research, Pittsburgh, PA.

Levenson, H., & Strupp, H. H. (2007). Cyclical maladaptive patterns: Case formulation in time-limited dynamic psychotherapy. In T. D. Eells (Ed.), *Handbook of psychotherapy case formulation* (2nd ed., pp. 164–197). New York: Guilford Press.

Levenson, H., & Strupp, H. H. (1999). Recommendations for the future of training in brief dynamic psychotherapy. *Journal of Clinical Psychology, 55,* 385–391.

Lewis, T., Amini, F., & Lannon, R. (2001). *A general theory of love.* New York: Vintage Books.

Messer, S. B. (1992). A critical examination of belief structures in integrative and eclectic psychotherapy. In J. C. Norcross & M. R. Goldfried (Eds.), *Handbook of psychotherapy integration* (pp. 130–165). New York: Basic Books.

Meltzoff, A. N., & Moore, M. K. (1977). Imitation of facial and manual gestures by human neonates. *Science, 198,* 75–78.

Mikulincer, M., & Shaver, P. R. (2007). *Attachment in adulthood: Structure, dynamics, and change.* New York: Guilford Press.

Multon, K. D., Kivlighan, D. M., & Gold, P. B. (1996). Changes in counselor adherence over the course of training. *Journal of Counseling Psychology, 43,* 356–363.

Neff, W. L., Lambert, M. J., Lunnen, K. M., Budman, S. H., & Levensen, H. (1997). Therapists' attitudes toward short-term therapy: Changes with training. *Employee Assistance Quarterly 11,* 67–77.

Norcross, J. C. (Ed.) (2002). *Psychotherapy relationships that work.* New York: Oxford University Press.

Nordhus, I. H., & Geir, H. N. (1999). Brief dynamic psychotherapy with older adults. *In Session: Psychotherapy in Practice, 55,* 935–947.

Obegi, J. H., & Berant, E. (2008). Introduction. In J. H. Obegi & E. Berant (Eds.), *Attachment theory and research in clinical work with adults* (pp. 1–14). New York: Guilford Press.

Panksepp, J. (1998). *Affective neuroscience: The foundations of human and animal emotions.* New York: Oxford University Press.

Piper, W. E., Azim, H. F. A., Joyce, A. S., & McCallum, M. (1991). Transference interpretations, therapeutic alliance, and outcome in short-term individual psychotherapy. *Archives of General Psychiatry, 48,* 946–953.

Piper, W. E., Debbane, E. G., Bienvenu, J. P., & Garant, J. (1984). A comparative study of four forms of psychotherapy. *Journal of Consulting and Clinical Psychology, 52,* 268–279.

Quintana, S. M., & Meara, N. M. (1990). Internalization of the therapeutic relationship in short term psychotherapy. *Journal of Counseling Psychology, 37,* 123–130.

Reik, T. (1948). *Listening with the third ear.* New York: Grove Press.

Ridley, C. R., & Kelly, S. M. (2007) Multicultural considerations in case formulation. In T. D. Eells (Ed.), *Handbook of psychotherapy case formulation.* New York: Guilford Press.

Sandler, J. (1976). Counter-transference and role-responsiveness. *International Review of Psychoanalysis, 3,* 43–47.

Schacht, T. E., Binder, J. L., & Strupp, H. H. (1984). The dynamic focus. In H. H. Strupp & J. L. Binder, *Psychotherapy in a new key: A guide to time-limited dynamic psychotherapy* (pp. 85–109) New York: Basic Books.

Schore, A. N. (1994). *Affect regulation and the organization of self.* Hillsdale, NJ: Erlbaum.

Siegel, D. J. (1999). *The developing mind: Toward a neurobiology of interpersonal experience.* New York: Guilford Press.

Siegel, D. J. (2007). *The mindful brain.* New York: W. W. Norton.

Stern, D. N., & Process of Change Study Group (1998). The process of therapeutic change involving implicit knowledge: Some implications of developmental observations for adult psychotherapy. *Infant Mental Health Journal, 19,* 300–308.

Stroufe, L. A., & Waters, E. (1977). Attachment as an organizational construct. *Child Development, 48,* 1184–1199.

Strupp, H. H. (1955a). An objective comparison of Rogerian and psychoanalytic techniques. *Journal of Consulting Psychology, 19,* 1–7.

Strupp, H. H. (1955b). The effect of the psychotherapist's personal analysis upon his techniques. *Journal of Consulting Psychology, 19,* 197–204.

Strupp, H. H. (1955c). Psychotherapeutic technique, professional affiliation, and experience level. *Journal of Consulting Psychology, 19,* 97–102.

Strupp, H. H. (1960). *Psychotherapists in action: Explorations of the therapist's contribution to the treatment process.* New York: Grune & Stratton.

Strupp, H. H. (1980). Success and failure in time-limited psychotherapy: A systematic comparison of two cases (Comparison 1). *Archives of General Psychiatry, 37,* 595–603.

Strupp, H. H., & Binder, J. L. (1984). *Psychotherapy in a new key.* New York: Basic Books.

Sullivan, H. S. (1953). *The interpersonal theory of psychiatry.* New York: W. W. Norton.

Sullivan, H. S. (1954). *The psychiatric interview.* New York: W. W. Norton.

Talley, P. F., Strupp, H. H., & Butler, S. F. (Eds.) (1994). *Psychotherapy, research, and practice.* New York: Basic Books.

Travis, L. A., Binder, J. L., Bliwise, N. G., & Horne-Moyer, H. L. (2001). Changes in clients' attachment styles over the course of time-limited dynamic psychotherapy. *Psychotherapy, 38,* 149–159.

Tronick, E. Z. (1989). Emotions and emotional communication in infants. *American Psychologist, 44,* 112–119.

Ursano, R. J., & Hales, R. E. (1986). A review of brief individual psychotherapies. *American Journal of Psychiatry, 143,* 1507–1517.

Wachtel, P. L. (1982). Vicious circles: The self and the rhetoric of emerging and unfolding. *Contemporary Psychoanalysis, 18,* 259–272.

Westen, D., Novotny, C. M., & Thompson-Brenner, H. (2004). The empirical status of empirically supported psychotherapies. *Psychological Bulletin 130,* 631–663.

Wong, E. C., Kim, B. S. K., Zane, N. W. S., Kim, I. J., & Huang, J. S. (2003). Examining culturally based variables associated with ethnicity. *Cultural Diversity and Ethic Minority Psychology, 9,* 88–96.

NOTES

1. Although I wrote the phrase ("got under the skin of") as a common figure of speech, it may not be only a metaphor. Neuroscientific theory and empirical research suggest that we emotionally experience others not by observing their actions and making sense of them cognitively, but rather by having a bodily sense.

2. At the time, Bowlby felt very supported by Harry Harlow's now classic studies (1959) with rhesus monkeys, in which monkeys preferred to spend their time with an "artificial cloth mother" even though they were fed by a "wire mesh mother."

3. The title to Binder and Strupp's 1997 paper says it all: "'Negative Process': A Recurrently Discovered and Underestimated Facet of Therapeutic Process and Outcome in the Individual Psychotherapy of Adults."

4. This "reflection" may have a neurological basis in that humans as well as monkeys have mirror neurons that get activated when observing someone performing an action and trigger our motor system to become "active *as if* we were executing that very same action" (Gallese, 2001, p. 37). Some have posited that this resonance provides the underpinnings of empathy.

5. Freud well understood that the therapist needed something more than the clients' conscious recollection to understand the meaning of their symptoms. He used the construct of "transference" to refer to the likelihood that client would react toward the therapist as significant figures from childhood. This was a brilliant and useful idea—to see how the client could be "telling" the therapist about central conflicts and dilemmas through reenactments in the sessions. However, the one-way, projective implication of the concept would characterize psychoanalytic thinking for decades to come.

6. TLDP does acknowledge that therapists also have "classic countertransferences" (Levenson, 1995)—that is, the therapists' own idiosyncratic conflicts having to do with their unique psychologies that are inappropriately played out with the client. These are the therapists' personal issues that need to be discussed in

their own therapies/consultations. This is in contrast to interactive countertransferences that are viewed as cocreated responses to the pushes and pulls from clients.

7. The new experience should not be thought of as occurring with one-trial learning. Rather it is comprised of a set of experiences *throughout the therapy* in which the client has a different appreciation of him or herself, of the therapist, and of the interaction between them.

8. However, not all clients will act out a dysfunctional dance in the room with their therapists. Such clients have more nuanced flexible and permeable patterns and can be more self-reflective. They can more easily achieve a platform of trust and safety (a secure base) with their therapists from which to examine interpersonal patterns in the "real world."

9. It is worth noting that practitioners and theorists in cognitive-behavioral fields are now acknowledging the *central role of emotions* (Barlow, 2000; Burum & Goldfried, 2007).

10. For more detailed information on steps in TLDP formulation, the reader is referred to Levenson (2010) and Levenson and Strupp (2007).

11. As one student, who saw a video of Mr. Johnson's and my interaction, put it, "You wanted to give him an emotional hot-foot."

12. These findings pertain only to brief dynamic therapies of approximately 12 to 25 sessions. They do not hold for "ultra-brief" approaches (five or fewer sessions, common in managed-care settings), where clinical improvement is markedly lower (Hansen, Lambert, & Forman, 2002).

33 GROUP THERAPIES

William E. Piper

John S. Ogrodniczuk

This chapter addresses the important role that interpersonal processes play in the successful functioning of group therapy and in the achievement of favorable outcome in group therapy. Group therapy is a form of psychosocial treatment that is customarily conducted by one or two therapists in conjunction with three or more patients (also commonly referred to as clients). Under the guidance of the therapist, who follows a particular theoretical and technical approach, the members of the group communicate and interact with each other in ways specified by the theoretical orientation that are believed to be therapeutic. Interpersonal processes may serve to specify the nature of the patient's presenting complaints and problems (e.g., chronic relationship difficulties), the etiology of the problem (e.g., parental abuse), the nature of the treatment (e.g., interpersonal group therapy), and the evidence of success (e.g., mutual improvement in one's partner relationship). Over time, each member of the group establishes a unique relationship with each of the other members of the group. These relationships are usually quite revealing in regard to how the patient perceives and interacts with others and the nature of the patient's problems. By definition, group therapy is inherently interpersonal.

Most historians attribute the origins of the group therapies to the work of Joseph Pratt (1922), a Boston physician, who used inspirational and psycho-educational techniques with groups of tuberculosis patients. As Scheidlinger (1993) pointed out in a chapter on the history of group therapy, the refinement of the group therapies as a treatment technique was largely an American phenomenon. Many were derivatives of psychoanalytic theory and technique, while others developed more independently. An example of the latter was the work of military psychiatrists in England, who were forced to use group therapy with large numbers of military personnel. Development of various group techniques in mid-century reflected the rivalry between Jacob Moreno, who founded psychodrama, and Samuel Slavson, who founded activity therapy.

UNSTRUCTURED TIME AS A DIFFERENTIATOR OF GROUP THERAPIES

The degree to which group therapy models permit unstructured time during therapy sessions reflects the extent to which the models make use of interpersonal processes within the group as therapeutic mechanisms. More unstructured time allows for greater opportunity for interpersonal processes to develop in the group. For some approaches to group therapy (e.g., most interpersonal forms and most psychodynamic forms), the therapist provides unstructured periods of time when patients are told that it is up to them to decide what they wish to talk about in the group. Some therapists expect each session to begin this way. During these periods of unstructured time, the therapist carefully focuses on the nature of the patient's interactions and relationships with members of the group (including himself) in the context of the patient's relationships outside the group. In response to the unstructured open discussion, which may be punctuated by silences, the therapist attempts to provide meaningful interventions (e.g., clarifications, confrontations, and interpretations) about what has transpired. Adherents of this approach believe that, in the immediacy of the here-and-now, interpersonal events and the attempt to understand them has a powerful impact on the patient. In regard to therapy process, the interactions may represent work or nonwork processes. In regard to outcome, the interactions may represent signs of improvement or deterioration. In contrast, therapists in other forms of group therapy, for example, cognitive-behavioral, do not provide unstructured periods of time that give rise to meaningful interactions among the group members. Instead, the therapist tends to work with one patient at a time, while the other patients mainly observe. Sometimes this approach is referred to as individual therapy in a group. Although this approach can be quite useful for certain disorders, it unnecessarily limits the therapist's ability to use interpersonal phenomena within the group for therapeutic purposes.

EFFECTIVENESS OF GROUP THERAPY

There is considerable evidence for the efficacy of the group therapies. In 1980,

Smith, Glass, and Miller published an extensive meta-analytic review of 475 controlled outcome studies of psychotherapy. Approximately one-half were studies of group therapy. The evidence clearly indicated that group therapy was effective compared to control conditions and had similar outcomes to individual therapy. More recently in a review of 107 studies and 14 meta-analytic reviews across six disorders and four patient populations of the group therapy outcome literature, Burlingame, McKenzie, and Strauss (2004) came to similar conclusions. However, despite the large volume of outcome data collected and the general strength of the methodology of the studies, most studies were subject to the possibility of confounding. For example, in comparisons between the individual and group therapies, the data for the two types of therapy have usually come from separate studies. Thus, differences between the two studies other than the two types of therapy could have been responsible for the reported findings. To control for this possibility, McRoberts, Burlingame, and Hoag (1998) reviewed only 23 studies where the two forms of therapy were in the same study. The overall finding of similar positive outcomes for the two forms of therapy did not change.

Given the fact that multiple patients can be treated in a group and outcomes between individual and group are comparable, group therapy appears to be a time-efficient therapy. That is clearly the case for the therapist. For example, rather than schedule eight patients for 50 minutes each, where the total therapist time would be six hours and 40 minutes, the therapist can schedule all eight patients for a 90-minute group therapy session. Thus, the total therapist time would be 90 minutes. This represents a considerable saving of time for the therapist. However, it is important to note that, in the case of the patient, a greater commitment of time is associated with group therapy, that is, 90 minutes rather than 50 minutes.

Beginning approximately in the late 1960s and early 1970s, a transformation began to emerge in the psychotherapy field about what could be accomplished with short-term forms of psychotherapies. Although there were dissenters, an era of optimism began to prevail that cut across different orientations of therapy, for example, behavioral, dynamic, and experiential. As time went on, the vast majority of therapies were completed in twenty sessions or fewer. Many of the therapies were time-limited, which meant that both patient and therapist agreed on the length of therapy prior to its onset. Advocates of brief therapies believed that a time limit creats a beneficial pressure on both parties to get busy and work hard before time runs out. The situation appeared to be even more challenging for the participants in the case of short-term group therapy, where patients competed not only with the clock, but with the other patients. Despite the appearance of a greater handicap for group therapy patients, most meta-analytic reviews of the outcome literature have reported few differences in outcomes between short-term individual and group therapies (see Burlingame et al., 2004). The presence of unique therapeutic factors in group therapy (discussed later in this chapter) may compensate for the time demands of short-term group therapy.

PATIENTS' CONCERNS ABOUT GROUP THERAPY

Despite the fact that the evidence that supports the applicability, efficacy, and efficiency of short-term group therapy is substantial, in particular when compared to individual therapy, it has been the authors' and others' experience that there is a rather strong tendency on the part of patients and therapists to prefer individual therapy if given the choice. This preference has been reported in a number of studies (Alvidrez & Azocar, 1999; Budman, Demby, Redondo, Hannan, Feldstein, Ring, et al., 1988; Robinson, 2002; Sharp, Power, & Swanson

2004). There are a number of possible reasons for the preference. We have formulated our impressions based upon our discussions with patients about their preferences and experiences in group therapy.

Compared to individual therapy, patients seem to anticipate and experience less control in a group. This is because many people, not just two, influence the flow of events. There is also a diminished sense of individuality. The patient must accept that he or she is part of a group as well as being an individual. There is also more difficulty in understanding the events that transpire in a group therapy session. In groups, the discussion often jumps from person to person and topic to topic. Careful reflection about the associations can be revealing, but in the fast pace that characterizes many therapy sessions, immediate understanding can be difficult. Because of the greater number of people in a group, there is less privacy. The patient in group therapy is continuously exposed to others. Confidentiality is impossible to guarantee in a group. There is also a diminished sense of safety for many patients in a group. This is related to the control issue, but more explicitly to the fact that criticism may come from many different directions from a number of different people. Being overwhelmed with criticism in a group is a common anticipatory fear of patients. In summary, issues related to a lost or diminished sense of control, individuality, understanding, privacy, and safety can lead to greater anticipatory and experienced anxiety for patients in group therapy when compared to individual therapy. Although reasonable, our informal clinical impressions are in need of research verification.

THERAPISTS' CONCERNS ABOUT GROUP THERAPY

The therapist's preference is just as important, perhaps even more so. The first question raised by a therapist is usually "What can be accomplished for my patient in a group that lasts a relatively short time?'' Even when the therapist is reassured concerning issues of effectiveness, applicability, and efficiency, factors that concern the patient may also concern the therapist. There is little doubt that the therapist has less control of events with a group of patients than with a single patient. Similarly, a diminished sense of individuality and less understanding of events are common experiences for the therapist in a group. The therapist is more exposed in a group and may also feel more open to criticism and attack. For all of these reasons, the therapist may similarly anticipate and experience greater anxiety in the case of group therapy relative to individual therapy.

In addition, groups are more challenging to organize. An entire set of patients must be assembled to begin at the same time. That requires a substantial supply of referrals, which may be difficult to achieve in a small clinic or in private practice. Most short-term therapy groups are homogeneous in terms of patient composition, which may make it even more difficult to obtain a sufficient number of appropriate referrals in a timely fashion. Because of the group nature of the situation, decisions of individual patients have an impact on the rest of the patients. For example, if one or two patients suddenly change their minds about starting or about continuing, once started, the onset of the group or the very life of the whole group can be affected. For all of these reasons, the task of running therapy groups no doubt seems formidable, and at times, beyond the therapist's control. Unfortunately, training in conducting group therapy is usually far less intensive than training in individual therapy in training programs for mental health professionals such as psychiatrists, psychologists, and social workers.

THERAPEUTIC FACTORS AND DIFFERENT FORMS OF GROUP THERAPY

Given these concerns and practical difficulties involved with creating a therapy group, one might expect findings that favored individual therapy over group therapy. However, it is important to recognize that there are a number of unique interpersonal processes in group therapy that may serve to compensate for the above concerns. These processes have been designated as therapeutic factors. Among the most well-known therapeutic factors for group therapy are the 11 described by Yalom and Leszcz (2005). Seven of these factors seem to be unique to group therapy, because they rely on the presence of other patients.

Perhaps one of the most important therapeutic factors in group process is *Interpersonal Learning*. It involves a set of assumptions and a sequence of activities that follows from the therapist providing nonstructured periods of time, as described at the beginning of this chapter. Yalom and Leszcz assume that ''A freely interactive group, with few structural restrictions, will, in time, develop into a social microcosm of the participant members'' (p. 31). This means that each patient will begin to interact with the other members of the group in the ways in which they have interacted with people outside the group. Thus, patients need not describe their maladaptive interpersonal behaviors in their group because they will soon demonstrate them to everyone in the group. The other members of the group can then provide feedback to the patient describing their maladaptive interpersonal behaviors. Ideally, the patient will modify his or her interpersonal behavior outside the group as well as inside the group. Thus, the patient will have learned to avoid continuation of his or her maladaptive behavior and undesirable outcomes. In addition, the other members of the group can offer praise and encouragement for the new behaviors, which strengthens the probability of their future use.

The other six therapeutic factors are the following: *Universality* is the recognition that others have similar problems. *Altruism* refers to patients helping each other. *Recapitulation of the Family Group* refers to the extent to which patients perceive other patients in the group in terms of roles occupied by members of their families. *Socializing Techniques* refer to patient attempts to help other patients learn social skills. *Imitative Behavior* refers to the processes of modeling and following. *Group Cohesiveness* refers to the bonds that unite patients in a group.

Although the beneficial results of such factors are quite plausible, definitive research involving experimental manipulation of the factors, and observation of their effects on outcome, have been lacking. Unfortunately, studies of the therapeutic factors have mostly been limited to obtaining ratings of the perceived usefulness of the factors from the perspectives of the patient and therapist. However, ratings of high usefulness (or importance) by no means indicate that the factor was highly useful or important. These studies are far from the kind of research that would help group therapists understand if or how the therapeutic factors affect therapy outcome.

Because of the emphasis attributed to interpersonal interactions and subsequent interpersonal learning, Yalom and Leszcz's approach is often referred to as interpersonal group therapy. A second major approach to group therapy that emphasizes interpersonal interactions and interpersonal processes is that of Rutan and Stone's Psychodynamic Group Psychotherapy (2001). Similarities between the two approaches are as follows: Both believe in the importance of interpersonal relationships and group therapy's power to improve interpersonal relationships. Both facilitate unstructured interaction in the group. The therapist does not impose a pre-set agenda of topics. Themes emerge from the group interaction. Both believe in the importance and impact of here-and-now interaction in the process of helping patients change. Both view the group as a social microcosm. Both value long-term group therapy. It allows a full range of life events and anniversaries to occur during the patients' tenure in the group. Both believe that most interpretation (process commentary) should be provided by the therapist. Both believe in the

importance of examining transference in the group. Both believe in the importance of focusing on affective and cognitive processes.

Differences between the two approaches are also apparent. Yalom and Leszcz emphasize the importance of the present (here-and-now) events in the group relative to the past. The origins of the patient's problems are not emphasized. Rutan & Stone emphasize linking past figures, current figures (external to therapy), and therapy figures (therapist, other patients). This is the so-called "triangle of insight" (Malan, 1979, p. 80). Yalom and Leszcz view transference as important, but only as one example of interpersonal distortion. Lateral transferences to and from other patients are of considerable importance. Rutan and Stone regard transference to the therapist as the central axis of distortion to be understood. Yalom and Leszcz regard interpretation as one of many useful techniques. Rutan and Stone regard interpretation as the most important technique. Yalom and Leszcz advocate occasional therapist self-disclosure of personal reactions and feelings and more frequent disclosure concerning here-and-now events. Rutan and Stone advocate avoidance of therapist self-disclosure. Yalom and Leszcz advocate limited use of mass group commentary (group-as-a-whole interventions). It is used primarily to deal with resistance (obstacles, anti-group norms). Rutan and Stone emphasize the therapeutic power of group interventions.

A third major approach to group therapy that emphasizes interpersonal interactions and interpersonal processes is Object Relations Group Therapy. This approach focuses on the internal world of the patient. According to the theory, the patient holds internal images (or representations) of himself or herself, others, and their relationships. The representations can be whole or part images. As described by Brabender (2002), one's object relations are formed early in life and are modified on the basis of our interactions with others. Subsequently, they influence our perceptions and interactions with others in our external world. Melanie Klein (1948) was perhaps the earliest and most influential spokesperson for object relations theory. According to Klein, maturity depends on the successful transition from the paranoid-schizoid position to the depressive position. This involves giving up primitive defenses such as projection and splitting and achieving object constancy (e.g., understanding how people have both positive and negative qualities). In the depressive position, the patient is able to experience guilt and the need for reparation. Wilfred Bion (1959) was the earliest object relations theorist who applied object relations theory to groups. His basic assumptions (dependency, fight/flight, and pairing) are well known to group therapists across theoretical orientations. They are very useful in recognizing when one's group is caught up in a defensive mode of interaction. In such a situation, group interventions have been found to be useful in helping move the group to a work mode of interaction.

Another approach to "interpersonal" group therapy is Wilfley, MacKenzie, Welch, Ayres, and Weissman's Interpersonal Psychotherapy for groups, abbreviated as IPT-G (2000). It is an adaptation of Klerman, Weissman, Rounsaville, and Chevron's individual therapy, known as Interpersonal Psychotherapy (IPT), to the group situation (1984). The fact that both Yalom and Leszcz's approach, and Wilfley et al.'s approach, are referred to as interpersonal group therapy is rather confusing. The two approaches are actually quite different, technically. The IPT-G of Wilfley et al. is a short-term, time-limited group therapy (it avoids long-term treatment). It focuses on depression and four problem areas that can lead to depression (grief, role disputes, role transitions, and interpersonal deficits); it avoids open topic agenda. It focuses on current, external relationships (avoiding focus on past relationships, here-and-now relationships, transference, and intrapsychic events). The therapist is active and directive (avoids passive-receptive therapist role). It attempts to achieve symptom relief and

interpersonal change (avoids attempts to achieve personality change).

BASIC RELATIONSHIP VARIABLES IN GROUP THERAPY

Stemming from the variety of interpersonal interactions in groups among patients and therapists are several basic types of interpersonal relationships or attachments. Some appear to represent group level concepts such as group climate or group cohesion, while others appear to be individual level concepts such as the therapeutic alliance. The alliance usually focuses on the working relationship between the patient and the therapist. It is measured with a questionnaire concerning a patient's working relationship with the therapist. In contrast, cohesion is usually defined as the attractiveness of the group to its members, or a bond between members of the group. There are different ways to measure cohesion. One way is to have the patient rate his or her bond to each of the other patients in the group, which are then averaged. This is the individual's collective rating of the others in the group. Another way is to average the other member's rating of their bond to the patient. This is the collective rating of the patient by the other members of the group. In addition, one can obtain the average of each patient's bond to the group as a whole. It has been our experience that examining the relationship of these three different concepts and measures with other relevant concepts such as therapy outcome has been productive. MacKenzie (1981) describes group climate as an environmental press that is capable of facilitating or impeding goal attainment. He viewed it as fairly independent of the therapist's influence.

It is possible for a group to have strong cohesion, but weak alliance. In this case, the patients in the group have bonded in opposition to the therapist. While this state of events could be useful in the development of cohesion, if it persisted for a long period of time, treatment outcome would probably be poor.

The therapist in a therapy group can make either individual or group interventions. An example of the latter might be "The group is having difficulty examining the impact of the absent members today." A therapist with an individual patient can make individual interventions, but is unable to make group interventions given that there is no group.

Unfortunately, difficulties concerning how to label, define, and measure these interpersonal constructs and understand their relationship with each other have hampered progress concerning what they represent and to what other variables they are related. Indirect evidence of considerable overlap among such constructs as alliance, group cohesion, and group climate has additionally been provided by studies that compared the abilities of the constructs to predict therapy outcome. For example, in a predictor study carried out by Joyce, Piper, and Ogrodniczuk (2007), a patient-rated measure of the alliance was significantly related to three of five measures of cohesion. The correlation coefficients ranged from .27 to .49. In a second study that reported correlations between alliance and cohesion (van Andel, Erdman, Karsdorp, Appels, & Trijburg, 2003), the correlations were even higher, ranging from .65 to .73, and in a third study (Marziali, Munroe-Blum, & McCleary, 1997) the correlation was .65. Considering this set of correlation coefficients, the amount of common variance shared by the two constructs ranged from 7 to 53%, the latter being quite substantial. Despite the apparent overlap in concepts such as the alliance and group cohesion in the Joyce et al. study, the investigators found a significant direct relationship between the alliance and outcome, but not for group cohesion and outcome.

Although there are significant definitional and measurement difficulties with the construct of cohesion, it has received considerably more attention than alliance in the group therapy literature, perhaps because of its greater heuristic value to clinicians and researchers. In many ways, the construct of alliance has been eclipsed by the construct of cohesion, which has been heralded as one of the most important therapeutic factors in group therapy (Yalom & Leszcz, 2005). As Burlingame, Fuhriman, and Johnson (2002) have argued, cohesion in group therapy is *the* therapeutic relationship.

Yet, there remains difficulty in concluding whether the patient-to-therapist aspect of cohesion differs appreciably from the patient-therapist alliance. To date, there is a lack of consensus of how to define the alliance and cohesion in order to clearly differentiate these two interpersonal constructs. Given the variety of constructs that appear to overlap with the alliance, some investigators have attempted to discover more basic underlying factors through various types of correlational and factor analyses.

Our review of the literature revealed only one study that had the expressed purpose of directly discovering basic underlying factors (components) from a larger set that included the alliance in group therapy (Johnson, Burlingame, Olsen, Davies, and Gleave, 2005). In the Johnson et al. study, four constructs (group climate, cohesion, alliance, and empathy) across three types of relationships (patient-to-patient, patient-to-group, and patient-to-therapist) were included in the analyses. Three multilevel structural equations were tested using self-reports from a large sample of group participants. Unfortunately, and despite the fact that many of the correlations between pairs of the variables were substantial, none of the three equations provided a good fit with the data, not even the model hypothesized to have one factor. Given this problem, the investigators conducted an exploratory factor analysis. The analysis revealed that the group members distinguished their relationships in groups primarily by the quality of the relationships rather than who was involved. These included positive bonding, positive working, and negative relationships. Although the components were meaningful, they cannot be regarded as valid until verified by confirmatory analysis or replicated with an independent sample.

Clinicians who regularly practice short-term group therapies have emphasized the importance of the therapist "hitting the ground running," that is, quickly getting off to a good start. In regard to the alliance, this means establishing a strong alliance with the therapist and strong bonds of cohesion with the other patients early in therapy. With this thought in mind, some investigators have focused on the level of alliance early in group therapy and its relationship with therapy outcome at the end of therapy. For example, Piper, Ogrodniczuk, Lamarche, Hilscher, and Joyce (2005) found a significant direct relationship between patient-rated alliance measured after one-third of therapy (session 4 of 12) and therapy outcome. Other studies that have found a direct relationship between early alliance and favorable outcome are those of Taft, Murphy, Musser, and Remington (2004) and Lorentzen, Sexton, and Hoglend (2004).

Many of the studies that have focused solely on the alliance have revealed a significant relationship with favorable outcome. Also, studies that have pitted alliance against cohesion in regard to strength of relationship to outcome have favored the alliance. There do not appear to be any studies that have favored cohesion.

FACTORS THAT INFLUENCE RELATIONSHIP VARIABLES IN GROUP THERAPY

While most research on interpersonal relationship variables in group therapy has examined their impact on treatment outcome, a few studies have investigated factors that influence the relationship variables. These studies have focused on the therapeutic alliance in group therapy. It is not unreasonable to assume that there may be a causal sequence whereby predictors

in some way bring about an increase in alliance, which in turn brings about favorable outcome. Thus, Johnson, Penn, Bauer, Meyer, and Evans (2008) investigated predictors of the alliance in two forms of treatment (Group CBT and Group Supportive Therapy) for schizophrenic patients who had treatment-resistant auditory hallucinations. The investigators found that baseline autistic preoccupation and poor social functioning were negatively associated with mid-treatment group alliance. Mid-treatment group alliance was positively associated with group insight. Furthermore, a strong alliance was associated with increased attendance and compliance with treatment. The authors pointed out some implications regarding group composition. For example, patients appeared to form stronger alliances when in a group where the other patients were high in insight rather than low in insight.

Taking a similar approach, Taft et al. (2004) attempted to identify predictors of working alliance in cognitive behavioral therapy groups for men who had been violent with their partners. Working alliance was measured by the Working Alliance Inventory (Horvath & Greenberg, 1989). Motivational readiness to change (Prochaska & DiClemente, 1982) was the strongest predictor of the working alliance. Psychopathic personality traits were a strong negative predictor of the alliance. Other significant correlates of alliance were: low level of borderline personality traits, low level of interpersonal problems, self-referral, marriage, age, and income.

Although predictor studies are a useful initial step, they usually do not provide information about how predictor variables bring about favorable change. In search of explanatory mechanisms that could make the findings involving alliance and other variables easier to understand, investigators have explored mediator relationships. They have usually used the statistical procedure developed by Baron and Kenny (1986). For example, in the previously mentioned study by Taft et al. (2004), the investigators selected alliance as the dependent variable and then investigated such variables as personality characteristics, interpersonal characteristics, readiness to change, and certain demographic variables as potential mediators of the relationship between psychopathic characteristics and alliance. In addition to being the best predictor of the alliance, motivational readiness to change mediated the relationship between psychopathic characteristics and the working alliance.

Taking a different perspective, Abouguendia, Joyce, Piper, and Ogrodniczuk (2004) selected patient-rated alliance as a potential mediator between expectancy of outcome and actual therapy outcome. Patients who met criteria for complicated grief were assigned to one of 16 therapy groups. Using Baron and Kenny's procedure, their study served as a cross validation for a study previously conducted by Joyce, Ogrodniczuk, Piper and McCallum (2003). There were important differences in the main characteristics of the two studies. In the Joyce study, the patients were psychiatric outpatients who experienced a wide range of difficulties (e.g., anxiety, depression, low self-esteem, and interpersonal problems) rather than complicated grief, and the treatment was short-term individual therapy, rather than short-term group therapy. Despite these major differences, the findings of the studies were similar. For both studies, the alliance emerged as a significant mediator of the relationship between expectancy of outcome and actual, reported therapy outcome.

INTERPERSONAL PROCESSES AND THERAPIST TECHNIQUE IN GROUP THERAPY

Therapists may find it useful to focus on specific interpersonal events in the group by indicating how they capture the attention and participation of all patients. This is accomplished by making a group intervention; that is, an intervention that addresses the group as a whole. The usefulness of making a group intervention was actively debated in the literature during the 1960s and 1970s. In a useful article, Horwitz (1977) clarified a number of possible advantages and disadvantages associated with group interventions. They are paraphrased below. If used judiciously, advantages include:

- In a group, there are always differences in how much time is devoted to individual patients. Concern about such differences can be alleviated by the use of accurate group interventions that indicate shared conflicts.
- There is decreased therapist misunderstanding if the therapist indicates how an individual patient's dynamics in the group are actually shared among most, if not all, patients.
- Group interventions heighten the sense of universality, which is regarded as a useful therapeutic factor in group therapy.
- The therapist's use of group interventions can facilitate a reduction in the patients' anxiety about expressing unacceptable wishes.
- The therapist's use of group interventions can facilitate a level of regression that is useful to explore.

However, if group interventions are used too frequently:

- They become restrictive and work against the presence of other types of interventions.
- The needs of individual patients are ignored.
- Idealization of the therapist is facilitated.
- The therapist transference overshadows peer transference.

Since the debates of the 1960s and 1970s, regarding the use of group interventions, the field has witnessed an increasing acceptance of group interventions, at least theoretically. In contrast, there has been some reluctance and resistance in using them technically, particularly in the case of short-term group therapy. This has reflected concern by therapists that patients would feel neglected and not attended to sufficiently. It has likely also reflected the concern of the therapists given the brevity of therapy and the group situation. However, our research group has had the opposite impression after conducting nearly 90 short-term therapy groups since 1986 for patients who met criteria for complicated grief. Rather than feeling neglected, many patients have experienced group interventions as being directed to them despite the fact that specific reference to them may not have been made.

We believe that the manner in which group interventions are delivered makes a considerable difference in how they are received and whether they lead to work or resistance. Evidence of this has come from a study in the United Kingdom and our own experience in Canada. Malan, Balfour, Hood, and Shooter (1976) conducted a follow-up study with psychiatric outpatients who had been treated in therapy groups that emphasized group interventions at the Tavistock Clinic in London. Many patients expressed frustration and disappointment with the therapists and their technique. The therapists were perceived to be cold, distant, passive, and noncaring. Patients found the therapists' interventions difficult to understand and were considerably irritated when the therapists refused to explain what they meant. Consequently, the patients harbored resentment toward the clinic.

According to Malan et al., the therapists had rigidly used techniques that had been borrowed from long-term, individual psychoanalytic therapy (e.g., therapist abstinence) or from study groups (e.g., repeated group-as-a-whole interpretations of transference) that were designed to teach participants about group dynamics. Such groups had been led by Bion (1959), who carefully restricted himself to group-as-a-whole interventions. Unfortunately, his interventions tended to come across as oracular pronouncements. The Tavistock model represents an extreme form of using group-as-a-whole interventions. Although they appear to be useful to participants who wish to learn about group dynamics, they do not appear to be useful to psychiatric outpatients who were seeking help for their problems in a therapy group.

The negative impact of the model on patients may, in part, have been due to the style in which group-as-a-whole interventions were delivered rather than the content of the interventions. Typically, the Tavistock group therapist or study group leader avoids eye contact with group members, remains relatively expressionless, speaks in a definitive manner, and, if requested, refuses to repeat interventions or elaborate upon them. This is in sharp contrast to a therapist who makes eye contact with patients when making group-as-a-whole interventions, allows facial expressiveness, offers the group intervention in a tentative manner, repeats the interventions when asked, and is willing to elaborate on the intervention to improve understanding. These stylistic differences may seem trivial or minor in nature. However, it has been our experience that they can make a great deal of difference in how well the interventions are received and understood, and how well they elicit work oriented responses. They can serve to engage the patients in therapeutic processes rather than distance patients from them.

A perennial question that group therapists must address is "What are criteria of patient suitability for one's therapy group?" Currently, and especially in the case of short-term group therapies, therapists select patients on the basis of their common predominant problems. For example, our research and clinical team selects patients for their groups if they meet criteria for complicated grief. In addition to shared problems, there are several general criteria that help facilitate work and favorable outcome. They are summarized by Woods and Melnick (1979). They include (a) minimum interpersonal skill, (b) commitment to changing interpersonal behavior, (c) susceptibility to group influence, and (d) willingness to help others. We have come to believe that the best measure of how patients will behave in a current group is one that focuses on the patient's behavior in a previous group. Therefore, we take a careful history of the patient's previous experience in therapy groups.

Over time in a therapy group, patient roles typically form. The roles sometimes serve as factors that strengthen resistance to work in the group. Yalom and Leszcz (2005) identify a number of such roles, for example, the monopolizer, the help-rejecting complainer, and the silent patient. In our own work with short-term therapy groups for patients with complicated grief, we have identified a number of additional such roles. From our perspective, we believe that the roles, for example the professor, the emotional conductor, and the cruise director, serve a defensive function for all of the members of the group. Often the roles express the patient's wishes about the behavior of the therapist (Bahrey, McCallum, Piper, 2001).

SUMMARY

This chapter has considered the many different ways that interpersonal processes are relevant and important to group therapy. They can be used to conceptualize patient problems, etiological factors, approaches to treatment, and signs of improvement. They are highly relevant to distinguishing forms of group treatment that provide individual therapy in a group context versus those that capitalize on group phenomena that arise from the interactions among group members. Evidence of the applicability, efficacy, and efficiency of group therapy was cited briefly. Both patient and therapist concerns about group therapy were discussed, as well as therapeutic factors unique to group therapy, which may serve to mitigate participants' concerns. Two frequently discussed relationship constructs (alliance and cohesion) that rely

on interpersonal concepts were briefly reviewed. Four major approaches to group therapy that very much use interactional concepts were covered. Group interventions have been highlighted as an example of a therapist technique that makes direct use of interpersonal processes in the group.

Although short-term group therapy appears to be an underutilized therapy (Piper, 2008), as its unique positive qualities become better known, we can expect that its prevalence will continue to increase. As emphasized repeatedly in this chapter, to date the biggest impediment to understanding the nature and relevance of interpersonal concepts in group therapy is a lack of systematic research. Few researchers have focused on the dynamics of this complex interpersonal enterprise in terms of understanding four factors: its indications (For whom is group therapy best suited?); its organization (How should a group be composed to maximize its benefits?); its operations (What goes on in group therapy that makes it work?); and its delivery (How can a group leader be most effective?). Group therapy is diverse, operating on various levels and engaging multiple players, goals, roles, and relationships. Complex, programmatic lines of research are required to appropriately address such questions. Few such programs exist. Nevertheless, despite the limitations in our knowledge about the complex dynamics of group therapy, it is clear that it is a unique interpersonal environment that has powerful therapeutic properties.

References

Abouguendia, M., Joyce, A. S., Piper W. E, & Ogrodniczuk, J. S. (2004). Alliance as a mediator of expectancy effects in short-term group psychotherapy. *Group Dynamics: Theory, Research, and Practice, 8,* 3–12.

Alvidrez, J., & Azocar, F. (1999). Distressed women's clinic patients: Preferences for mental health treatments and perceived obstacles. *General Hospital Psychiatry, 21,* 340–347.

Bahrey, F., McCallum, M., & Piper, W. E. (1991). Emergent themes and roles in short-term loss groups. *International Journal of Group Psychotherapy*, *41*, 329–345.

Baron, R. M., & Kenny, D. A. (1986). The moderator-mediator variable distinction in social psychological research: Conceptual, strategic, and statistical considerations. *Journal of Personality and Social Psychology*, *51*, 1173–1182.

Bion, W. R. (1959). *Experiences in groups and other papers*. New York: Basic Books, Inc.

Brabender, V. (2002). *Introduction to group therapy*. Hoboken, NJ: John Wiley & Sons.

Budman, S. H., Demby, A., Redondo, J. P., Hannan, M., Feldstein, M., Ring, J., et al. (1988). Comparative outcome in time-limited individual and group psychotherapy. *International Journal of Group Psychotherapy*, *38*, 63–86.

Burlingame, G. M., Fuhriman, A., & Johnson, J. (2002). Cohesion in group psychotherapy. In J. Norcross (Ed.), *A guide to psychotherapy relationships that work* (pp. 71–88). Oxford, UK: Oxford University Press.

Burlingame, G. M., MacKenzie, D., & Strauss, B. (2004). Small group treatment: Evidence for effectiveness and mechanisms of change. In A. E. Bergin & S. L. Garfield (Eds.), *Handbook of psychotherapy and behavioral change* (5th ed., pp. 647–696). Hoboken, NJ: John Wiley & Sons.

Horowitz, L. (1977). A group-centered approach to group psychotherapy. *International Journal of Group Psychotherapy*, *27*, 423–439.

Horvath, A. O., & Greenberg, L. S. (1989). Development and validation of the working alliance inventory. *Journal of Counseling Psychology*, *36*, 223–233.

Johnson, J. E., Burlingame, G. M., Olsen, J. A., Davies, D. R., & Gleave, R. L. (2005). Group climate, cohesion, alliance, and empathy in group psychotherapy: Multilevel structural equation models. *Journal of Counseling Psychology*, *52*, 310–321.

Johnson, D. P., Penn, D. L., Bauer, D. J., Meyer, P., & Evans, E. (2008). Predictors of the therapeutic alliance in group therapy for individuals with treatment-resistant auditory hallucinations. *British Journal of Clinical Psychology*, *47*, 171–183.

Joyce, A. S., Ogrodniczuk, J. S., Piper, W. E., & McCallum, M. (2003). The alliance as mediator of expectancy effects in short-term individual therapy. *Journal of Consulting and Clinical Psychology*, *71*, 672–679.

Joyce, A. S., Piper, W. E., & Ogrodniczuk, J. S. (2007). Therapeutic alliance and cohesion variables as predictors of outcome in short-term group psychotherapy. *International Journal of Group Psychotherapy*, *57*, 269–296.

Klein, M. (1948). *Contributions to psycho-analysis, 1921–1945*. London: Hogarth.

Klerman, G. L., Weissman, M. M., Rounsaville, B. J., & Chevron, E. S. (1984). *Interpersonal psychotherapy of depression*. New York: Basic Books.

Lorentzen, S., Sexton, H. C., & Hoglend, P. (2004). Therapeutic alliance, cohesion and outcome in a long-term analytic group. A preliminary study. *Nordic Journal of Psychiatry*, *58*, 33–40.

MacKenzie, K. R. (1981). Measurement of group climate. *International Journal of Group Psychotherapy*, *31*, 287–295

Malan, D. H. (1979). *Individual psychotherapy and the science of psychodynamics*. Cambridge, London: Butterworths & Co.

Malan, D. H., Balfour, F. H. G., Hood, V. G., & Shooter, A. (1976). Group psychotherapy: A long-term follow-up study. *Archives of General Psychiatry*, *33*, 1303–1315.

Marziali, E., Munroe-Blum, H., & McCleary, L. (1997). The contribution of group cohesion and group alliance to the outcome of group psychotherapy. *International Journal of Group Psychotherapy*, *47*, 475–497.

McRoberts, C., Burlingame, G. M., & Hoag, M. J. (1998). Comparative efficacy of individual and group psychotherapy: A meta-analytic perspective. *Group Dynamics*, *2*, 101–117.

Piper, W. E. (2008). Underutilization of short-term group therapy: Enigmatic or understandable? *Psychotherapy Research*, *18*, 127–138.

Piper, W. E., Ogrodniczuk, J. S., Lamarche, C., Hilscher, T., & Joyce, A. S. (2005). Level of alliance, and outcome in short-term group therapy. *International Journal of Group Psychotherapy*, *55*, 527–550.

Pratt, J. H. (1922). The principles of class treatment and their application to various chronic diseases. *Hospital Social Service Quarterly*, *6*, 401–411.

Prochaska, J. O., & DiClemente, C. C. (1982). Transtheoretical therapy: Toward a more integrative model of change. *Psychotherapy: Theory, Research & Practice*, *19*, 276–288.

Robinson, S. (2002). What gets measured, gets delivered? *Psychoanalytic Psychotherapy*, *16*, 37–57.

Rutan, J. S., & Stone, W. N. (2001). *Psychodynamic group psychotherapy* (3rd ed.). New York: Guilford Press.

Scheidlinger, S. (1993). History of group psychotherapy. In H. I. Kaplan & B. J. Sadock (Eds.), *Comprehensive group psychotherapy* (3rd ed.). New York: Williams & Wilkins.

Sharp, D. M., Power, K. G., & Swanson, V. (2004). A comparison of the efficacy and acceptability of group versus individual cognitive behaviour therapy in the treatment of panic disorder and agoraphobia in primary care. *Clinical Psychology and Psychotherapy, 11,* 73–82.

Smith, M. L., Glass, G. V., & Miller, T. I. (1980). *The benefits of psychotherapy.* Baltimore, MD: The Johns Hopkins University Press.

Taft, C. T., Murphy, C. M., Musser, P. H., & Remington, N. A. (2004). Personality, interpersonal, and motivational predictors of the working alliance in group cognitive-behavioral therapy for partner violent men. *Journal of Consulting and Clinical Psychology, 72,* 349–354.

van Andel, P., Erdman, R. A. M., Karsdorp, P. A., Appels, A., & Trijsburg, R. W. (2003). Group cohesion and working alliance: Prediction of treatment outcome in cardiac patients receiving cognitive behavioral group psychotherapy. *Psychotherapy and Psychosomatics, 72,* 141–149.

Wilfley, D. E., MacKenzie, K. R., Welch, R. R., Ayres, V. E., & Weissman, M. M. (2000). *Interpersonal psychotherapy for group.* New York: Basic Books.

Yalom, I. E., & Leszcz, M. (2005). *The theory and practice of group psychotherapy* (5th ed.). New York: Basic Books.

34 SUMMARY AND CONCLUDING REMARKS

Leonard M. Horowitz

Stephen Strack

Nearly three score years ago, our academic fathers brought forth to this discipline a new theory, an *interpersonal* theory, conceived in academic freedom and dedicated to the proposition that interpersonal concepts and principles will ultimately yield important insights into human behavior. Since then, the interpersonal approach has provided a new perspective for personality, social, and clinical psychology. When our academic forefathers began their project, academic psychology in North America was dominated by a Gettysburg-like struggle between two rival camps—that of behaviorism (with its relentless focus on observable stimuli and responses) and that of psychoanalytic theory (with its equally relentless focus on internal states, conflicting motives, and strategies for reducing anxiety). As we scan the achievements described in the chapters of this book, we can only applaud the strides we have made in combining the best of the two prior rivals.

Why is the interpersonal approach so appealing, and how has it furthered the goals of psychology? We begin this final chapter by noting its two principal virtues. First, the interpersonal approach today is compatible with every modern psychological approach, integrating them into a whole greater than the sum of the parts. Its propositions concern all principal types of psychological constructs—behavioral, cognitive, motivational, and affective—in a way that synthesizes the concepts, paradigms, and empirical findings of narrower approaches. Second, it provides its own distinctive set of theoretical concepts and propositions—plus implications that can be tested empirically.

This final chapter is therefore organized into two parts. First we show that the interpersonal approach is integrative. Then we present eight propositions that summarize the distinctive contributions of the interpersonal approach represented in this handbook.

THE INTERPERSONAL APPROACH
AS AN INTEGRATIVE THEORY

The interpersonal approach today is probably the one systematic approach that best integrates modern thinking about human nature and interpersonal interactions. Like the biological approach, it assumes that innate (temperamental) differences among infants also shape the infant's environment (Costa & McCrae, Chapter 6). Therefore, infants who are distress-prone may come to differ considerably in their expectancies about, perceptions of, and feelings toward other people. W. A. Collins, Maccoby, Steinberg, Hetherington, & Bornstein (2000) summarized studies documenting this effect—showing that constitutional factors shape a child's environment and affect subsequent relationships. Van den Boom (1994), for example, has shown that, from birth on, parents treat "difficult" (distress-prone, hard-to-soothe, colicky) infants differently from the way they treat "easy" infants. Her data show that parents of difficult infants, not wishing to "rock the boat," are less apt to interact socially with the child when the child is quiet. As a result, by the time those infants are 1 year old, they frequently show an avoidant attachment style in the Strange Situation. However, parents can be trained in ways to handle difficult infants so that the infants are socially more gratifying. Parent-training when the infant is 6 months old leads to considerably greater caretaker-child social interaction, greatly reducing the likelihood of an avoidant attachment style. This result shows how a biological (temperamental) characteristic observed early in life can shape the infant's environment in ways that affect the child's first major relationship.

Like the modern cognitive-behavioral approach, the interpersonal approach emphasizes interpersonal cognitions. For example, hyperaggressive schoolboys seem to have a *readiness* to perceive the neutral acts of peers as reflecting hostile intentions. More than other children, they seem to *expect* peers to harbor hostile intentions.

This expectancy leads aggressive children to interpret a peer's accidental act to be intentionally hostile. That interpretation, in turn, arouses the child's anger (Dodge & Cole, 1987; Hudley & Graham, 1993), leading the child to retaliate. Does a purely cognitive explanation, by itself, adequately explain the aggressive child's hyperaggression? We think not. If it did, why would the child's perception lead to *anger*, which is generally considered to be a reaction to a frustrated motive (Lazarus, 1991)? The full explanation would seem to require some reference to a frustrated motive as a reason to seek revenge—perhaps a self-protective motive to display strength to counter a peer's intentional display of contempt or disrespect. In other words, the interpersonal approach treats interpersonal cognitions as profoundly important, but it adds *motivation* and *affect* to the interpretation as well.

Like the humanistic approach, the interpersonal approach emphasizes concepts such as *self*, *self-image*, *self-ideal, and image of others*. These concepts, however, are not viewed as *static* cognitions, such as a set of expectancies or schemas; rather, the self is viewed as a dynamic theory about oneself that needs periodic updating. For example, alternate hypotheses about the self (one desirable, one undesirable) might compete with one another. By acting in a way that confirms a desirable hypothesis or disconfirms a competing undesirable hypothesis, a person can save face or protect oneself from a threatening alternative (Horowitz, 2004). Higgins (1987) has emphasized two desirable cognitions—the "ideal-self" and the "ought-self"; both serve as motivating guides to a person's actions. When the person's actions expose a discrepancy between less desirable features of one's "actual self" and corresponding features of either desirable guide, the person experiences negative affect. However, people do discover ways to refute undesirable or unwanted information so as to prevent such discrepancies. Several chapters in this handbook describe the ways in which people construct a self-image (Blatt & Luyten,

Chapter 3) and/or protect themselves from unwanted inferences (Shaver & Mikulincer, Chapter 2; Murray & Holmes, Chapter 12). People also provide two broad types of support to partners to help them maintain a positive self-image (Collins, Ford, & Feeney, Chapter 13; Levenson, Chapter 32; Gunlicks-Stoessel & Weissman, Chapter 31). This struggle itself, however, seems to compromise our physical health, thereby setting a price that we pay as a result of the struggle (Smith & Cundiff, Chapter 27).

Finally, like the psychodynamic approach, the interpersonal approach assumes that individuals differ in the nature and strength of specific interpersonal motives. The topic of interpersonal motives—particularly *conflicting* motives and *frustrated* motives—helps explain the source of specific interpersonal problems (Grosse Holtforth, Thomas, & Caspar, Chapter 7). As Costa, Benoit, and Ollendick (Chapter 28) have observed, knowing that a child with an oppositional/defiant disorder is angry, rebellious, or mistrusting provides very limited insight into the child's defiant behavior. From the child's anger, we can infer only that some important motive is being frustrated. But which motive is it—a desire to be treated with more love, acceptance, and understanding? A desire to be granted more autonomy? A desire to be more effectively guided and managed? Until the frustrated motive is identified, one has little hope of restoring peace and composure to a greatly distressed child.

Thus, the interpersonal approach harmonizes well with all other theoretical approaches and may therefore be considered the one genuinely *integrative* approach: With its own distinctive framework of concepts, it incorporates wisdom from relevant "part-theories" (Clarkin, Levy, & Ellison, Chapter 23). Especially in clinical psychology, where theories today tend to overemphasize and overstate one simple explanatory mechanism by ignoring mechanisms proposed by other theories, the interpersonal approach seeks to restore a balance of theoretical mechanisms.

DISTINCTIVE PROPOSITIONS OF THE INTERPERSONAL APPROACH

In this section, we examine eight propositions that are unique to the interpersonal approach. We illustrate each with content from the *Handbook*.

Proposition 1: Two Primary Dimensions Organize the Content of Many Interpersonal Domains.

Various chapters of this handbook have referred to a basic framework that organizes the content of diverse interpersonal domains. This framework consists of the two dimensions, *communion* and *agency*, which emerge when we systematize interpersonal behaviors as well as interpersonal problems, traits, values, social allergens, personality measures, and personality disorders. One might ask why the two interpersonal themes are so ubiquitous. In our view, the reason is clear: Communion and agency are relevant to a broad array of purposes needed for sustaining life—achieving safety and survival, gaining knowledge, reproducing the species, parenting the young, and so on. No matter which life-promoting function we consider, all of us need to know when it serves our purposes to connect trustingly with others versus remaining apart; we also need to know when it is better to exercise control (influence) over others versus follow the lead of (yield to) others. As Simpson, Griskevicius, and Kim (Chapter 5) describe, we are biologically endowed with motives to behave in ways that sustain life. That motivational basis of life manifests itself as communion and agency. Furthermore, the advantages of diversity are guaranteed by the diversity of temperaments present at birth (Costa & McCrae, Chapter 6), reflecting diversity among people in the strength of communal and agentic motives.

Generally speaking, interpersonal theorists find communion and agency—the fundamental motivational abstractions—to be particularly useful in constructing a theory.

Why is that? As noted above, communion (ranging from *keeping separate* to *connecting*) and agency (ranging from *yielding* to *influencing*) seem to have direct evolutionary significance for survival. For that reason, elements in the two-dimensional space of interpersonal traits (such as *extraverted*) are conveniently interpreted in terms of the two organizing classes of motive: Extraverted people, in theory, are motivated by a combination of communal and agentic motives— to *influence* others to *connect* with them. But if we organize our theoretical framework around (say) the dimensions *extraversion* (ranging from *introverted* to *extraverted*) and *agreeableness* (ranging from *disagreeable* to *agreeable*), elements of the space (such as the trait *controlling*) have to be viewed as a combination of (a) extraverted tendencies and (b) disagreeable tendencies—less compelling in explaining motivational or evolutionary purposes.

Nonetheless, it is very clear that *extraversion* and *agreeableness* (the interpersonal factors) do emerge as the first two factors when *all* traits (including intrapersonal traits) are subjected to a factor analysis. How might we reconcile the two frameworks conceptually? It is possible that *communion* and *agency* provide the more useful framework when human motivation is the basic explanatory focus, but that *extraversion* and *agreeableness* provide the more useful framework when the biology of temperament is the basic explanatory focus.

Communion and agency also appear as major themes in broader issues of human nature. Shaver and Mikulincer (Chapter 2) and Collins, Ford, and Feeney (Chapter 13) describe a related distinction in attachment theory: An infant's initial bonding with the caretaker (communion) is followed by the emergence of autonomy (agency), observed in the infant's exploratory behavior. Blatt and Luyten (Chapter 3) use the two abstractions to describe the two fundamental lines of psychological development throughout life, namely, relatedness (communion) and self-definition (agency). Their theory helps us organize and explain

individual differences in dysfunctional as well as adaptive behavior.

The standard measure of adult attachment, Experiences in Close Relationships (ECR), contains two orthogonal scales derived from a factor analysis: *Avoidance* and *Anxiety*. The Avoidance scale, named for the negative pole of a *communal* dimension, assesses whether a person prefers closeness or distance in relationships; that preference seems to depend upon the person's *image of others* as trustworthy or not (Bartholomew and Horowitz, 1991). In contrast, the Anxiety scale, named for the negative pole of an *agentic* dimension, assesses whether a person feels competent, confident, and efficacious in the ability to sustain a close relationship; that self-perception depends upon the person's *image of self* as relatively competent (able) or inadequate (unable). In a similar vein, Fournier, Moskowitz, and Zuroff (Chapter 4) have related *communion* and *agency* to the concepts of *security* (safety in relationships) and *self-esteem* (a sense of efficacy or competence). Finally, the discussion of social support by Collins, Ford, and Feeney (Chapter 13) also uses the distinction to differentiate between two forms of social support—(1) *safe haven* support (*communal* support that relieves distress) versus (2) secure base support, which encourages autonomous (*agentic*) behavior. Both forms have consequences for physical health. Smith and Cundiff (Chapter 27) show the price people pay in cardiovascular functioning when they lack either type of support—leaving the person isolated (in one case), or chronically frustrated by a spouse's interfering dominance (in the other case).

Proposition 2: Behavior Is Ambiguous If We Do Not Know Which Motive Is Driving It.

Some interpersonal behaviors are easily located within a two-dimensional space because observers readily agree about the person's intentions. However, it is not uncommon for two observers to rely on different cues and disagree with each other about their interpretation of a behavior. Leising and Borkenau (Chapter 10) and Gifford (Chapter 11) describe the diversity of cues—some valid and some not valid, some utilized and some not utilized—leading different observers to different interpretations. Gifford also notes how misleading nonverbal cues can be, especially if the target person chooses to mislead observers. Even in close relationships, as Murray and Holmes (Chapter 12) explain, trust ultimately requires a "leap of faith." Still, the more we have observed a person's behavior in different situations and contexts, the more certain we feel about inferring a motivational "common denominator" that helps us interpret a person's behavior. No wonder neighbors are often incredulous upon learning that "that nice young man" has committed a savage act.

Ambiguity is particularly evident when we try to interpret psychopathology from limited observations. In this respect, personality disorders differ conceptually from clinical (Axis I) disorders. Personality disorders do frequently allow an observer to detect a motive behind observed behavior. In contrast, Axis I disorders usually do not reveal a motive behind the syndrome. Let us begin with personality disorders. As Clarkin, Levy, and Ellison (Chapter 23) note, every personality disorder is defined by a list of *pervasive* characteristics. The term *pervasive* implies multiple observations across diverse occasions, situations, and contexts. Hill, Pilkonis, and Bear (Chapter 17) indicate that a pervasive behavior is sometimes all the more pervasive in that it occurs in situations and contexts that violate social conventions (for example, seeking intimate support in the workplace). The sheer number of observable characteristics that must be met to meet the criteria of a personality disorder enables us to find a motivational common denominator—a theme that parsimoniously explains the individual's overarching purpose. That common denominator enables us to locate the observed behavior uniquely in the two-dimensional interpersonal space. And

that location, in turn, allows interpersonally trained observers to agree about the frustrated motive behind the person's problem.

In contrast, clinical (Axis I) disorders are defined in terms of syndromes that typically reflect a relatively specific *problem of self-regulation*, such as a problem regulating one's depression, obsessive thoughts, compulsive acts, restricted eating, and so on. A person's frustrated motives or unsolvable conflict may certainly be related to the syndrome; but the definition of the disorder focuses on the specific uncontrollable syndrome (e.g., obsessive thought, depressed mood), not on pervasive behavior across different situations and contexts. If some frustrated motive or motivational conflict is relevant to the syndrome, it may be unique to that particular person; the type of frustrated motive may differ from person to person with the same syndrome.

Pincus and Wright (Chapter 22) discuss this issue in detail under the heading of *pathoplasticity*: For different people, the *same* syndrome may arise from *different* sources of stress; and *different* syndromes may arise from the *same* source of stress. As Pincus and Wright show, a syndrome does not have a one-to-one relationship to a particular cause. Consider the syndrome we call *anorexia nervosa*. Competing theories exist concerning its cause: For example, Minuchin, Rosman, and Baker (1978) emphasize an intense communal motive (to restore harmony within the family), whereas Bruch (1982) emphasizes an intense agentic motive (to attain a greater sense of autonomy and control). Either (or both) purposes may be correct in explaining anorexia nervosa in different cases. In this sense, the observed syndromal behavior—self-starvation—is an observed behavior—but it cannot be located graphically "once and for all" within the two-dimensional interpersonal space because the interpersonal motive behind self-starvation itself differs across cases.

Costa, Benoit, and Ollendick (Chapter 28) use the Oppositional Defiant Disorder as an example of the same principle. A child's behavior suggests that the child is angry—and chronic, pervasive anger implies a severely frustrated motive. However, chronic and pervasive anger (an affect) does not identify *the frustrated motive* that would disambiguate the child's (oppositional/defiant) behavior. Without more details about the child's life circumstances, we cannot tell *a priori* the reason for such pervasive anger: In some cases, an oppositional child may want more nurturance from unresponsive caretakers (a communal motive). In other cases, an oppositional child may want more autonomy (an agentic motive) from overcontrolling caretakers. A therapist must therefore understand the case-specific issues if the therapist is to help the child resolve the oppositional/defiant syndrome; that understanding is at least as important as any therapeutic procedure directed at the self-regulation of anger.

Proposition 3: To "Understand" a Behavior Well, We Need to Know More Than Its Two Coordinates.

Two contributors to the *Handbook* have observed important limitations of a two-dimensional interpersonal analysis. Benjamin (Chapter 20) convincingly shows the value of a third dimension for understanding interpersonal problems and goals of people in treatment. Her added dimension is dichotomous—a *focus on the partner* versus a *focus on the self*. With this addition, the SASB model broadens the range of interpersonal behaviors to include not only complementary pairs such as "A manages/controls B" and "B yields/submits/complies." It also includes "A endorses freedom for B" and "B freely comes and goes." Either pair might describe a client's treatment goal—for example, "B wants more autonomy" or "B wants more guidance/direction/control."

Jones and Paulhus (Chapter 15) call attention to another limitation of a two-dimensional analysis. They identify a "dark triad" of personalities—individuals whose personalities are usually called (a) psychopathic, (b) narcissistic, or (c)

Machiavellian. All three personalities are located in Quadrant II (negative communion, positive agency), so they would seem alike as personalities that exploit other people (unempathic manipulation). But individuals in the three groups differ in their reasons for exploiting others. Jones and Paulhus identify more specific motives for exploiting others—(a) to attain present versus future gains and/or (b) to sharpen the person's own self-image (identity). The psychopathic individual exploits others in order to attain immediate (present-tense) gratification; the Machiavellian individual is working toward the future in order to amass gains towards significant future power. The narcissistic individual exploits others in order to promote a self-image (in the present) that provides superior standing in the eyes of others—and by implication, in the person's own eyes.

Proposition 4: The Two Primary Dimensions Provide a Sophisticated Analytic Method for Psychometrics.

The content of an interpersonal domain— for example, interpersonal *behaviors, traits, values, motives, problems*—may be used to construct a test. As described by Gurtman (Chapter 18) and Locke (Chapter 19), each element of the domain (e.g., traits) may be located in the two-dimensional space using the two sets of factor loadings as coordinates. The graph may then be subdivided into equal regions (octants) to define eight interpersonal variables. In this way, Wiggins (1979) constructed the Interpersonal Adjectives Test (IAT), selecting items from each octant to assess a theoretical variable corresponding to that octant.

Wiggins's IAS subscale, Warm-Agreeable, for example, is high in communion—it contains traits such as *kind* and *sympathetic*; the *Self-assured-Dominant* subscale is high in agency—it contains traits such as *dominant* and *assertive*. The subscale *Gregarious-Extraverted* is high in both communion and agency—it contains traits such as *jovial* and *extraverted*. The eight sub-scales each assess one of eight theoretical variables. In this system of eight variables, how should we conceptualize the two fundamental dimensions by which each variable is defined? If we regard the dimensions as *motivational*, an important implication follows: The variable *Warm-Agreeable* arises from strong communal motivation; the variable *Self-assured-Dominant* arises from strong agentic motivation; and the variable *Gregarious-Extraverted* arises from a mixture of both.

The two underlying dimensions, communion and agency, are perpendicular (orthogonal) on the graph: That is, traits exist for every combination of (high, medium, or low) communion and (high, medium, or low) agency. When we say that two dimensions are orthogonal, we mean that they are uncorrelated: People's scores on *Warm-Agreeable* (communal) are theoretically uncorrelated with their scores on *Self-assured-Dominant* (agentic).

Although *Warm-Agreeable* and *Self-assured-Dominant* are uncorrelated, each should correlate substantially with the variable *Gregarious-Extraverted* (+C/+A) because that variable results from both types of motivation. That is, *Gregarious-Extraverted* is partly communal and partly agentic, so it shares *half* of its variance with *Warm-Agreeable* (entirely communal). If two variables have half of their variance in common, r^2 should be .5—and r should be $\sqrt{.5} = .71$. Theoretically, then, those two variables should show a correlation coefficient of .71. *Gregarious-Extraverted* shares the other half of its variance (the agentic half) with *Self-assured-Dominant*, so, theoretically, those two variables should also show a correlation coefficient of .71. In this way, we can determine the value of r that is expected theoretically between each pair of variables in the set of eight. For some pairs, r should be positive; for some, it should be negative; for some it should be 0.

Therefore, the eight variables, as a theoretical set, are said to constitute a *nomological net* or *network* Because they are composed of two underlying factors, they are lawfully related to one another. (For more details, see Locke, Chapter 19, and Gurtman, Chapter 18.) Therefore, when a researcher constructs a new test of a single interpersonal variable and needs to validate it, it is possible to locate the new test within the nomological net operationalized by a suitable set of eight subscales (variables) that span the space. For example, suppose a researcher generated a measure of "generosity"—let's call it Test G. Test G might be administered to a large group of participants, together with a corresponding test such as Wiggins's IAT. Scores on Test G could then be correlated with scores on each of the eight subscales. If Test G does, in fact, assess an interpersonal construct, it should correlate most positively with one of the subscales: Let us say that it correlates most positively with the *Warm-Agreeable* subscale. This correlation suggests that Test G is communal. Test G should also correlate positively with two other subscales that are high in communion—namely, *Gregarious-Extraverted* and *Accommodating-Trusting*. However, Test G should have a zero correlation with orthogonal subscales (the ones composed, respectively, of positive agency and negative agency). Finally, Test G should correlate negatively with the three remaining subscales, which are all negative in communion.

If all of the measures—Test G and the eight subscales of the IAS—were theoretically ideal measures, there would be no error of measurement: Every measure would show the effect of communion, agency, or both (nothing else). However, psychological measurement is never that precise. In the *ideal* case, we could specify exact correlations between Test G and each of the eight subscales. In that case, we could show that the correlation coefficients would form a perfect "cosine curve" (see Figure 34.1): The correlation coefficients between Test G and the individual sub-scales would range from +1 through 0 to −1. For more details, see Gurtman (1993). In practice, however, measurement error adds noise to our measures, and noise

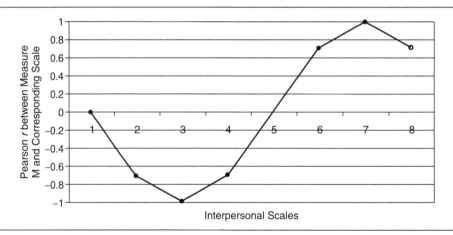

FIGURE 34.1   Ideal Cosine Curve (No Error of Measurement): Ranges from $r = -1$ through $r = 0$ to $r = +1$

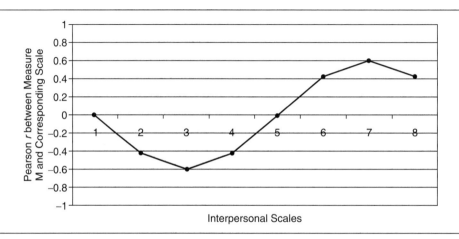

FIGURE 34.2   Cosine Curve with Reduced Amplitude: Ranges from $r = -.6$ through $r = 0$ to $r = +.6$

reduces the amplitude of the cosine curve: The curve might therefore range from $+.6$ through 0 to $-.6$ (see Figure 34.2). Despite the noise, however, the shape of the cosine curve would still be evident—no subscale would be out of order—but the curve's amplitude would be reduced. In this way, Measure G would be located within a theoretical *nomological network* of interpersonal variables—positively related to relevant variables, negatively to "opposite" variables, and unrelated to irrelevant variables. By placing Test G in this nomological net of variables, we are able to establish both convergent and discriminant validity for Test G.

Proposition 5: Complementarity Frequently Characterizes a Behavioral Exchange.

Several chapters in this handbook have referred to the principle of complementarity, a distinctive principle that is unique to the interpersonal theory: When one partner displays a behavior that is graphically located at $[x, y]$, the other partner tends to react with a behavior located at $[x, -y]$. Sadler, Ethier, and Woody (Chapter 8) summarize the substantial empirical evidence for the principle. Their own study— and that of Fournier, Moskowitz, & Zuroff (Chapter 4)—are sophisticated demonstrations of the principle.

How is complementarity to be explained? One interpretation draws upon a motivational explanation. Because behavior is *motivated*, the motive that drives a behavior located at [x, y] is satisfied if the partner provides (a) a similar degree of communion (a person who wishes to connect with a partner wants that partner to willingly connect), and (b) a reciprocal degree of agency (a person who wishes to influence a partner wants that partner to yield to influence). In other words, to satisfy the communal and agentic motives behind a behavior at [x, y], the partner must respond with a behavior at [x, −y]. To read the person correctly, a partner must be very attentive to valid cues—and then utilize those cues to interpret the behavior correctly (Gifford, Chapter 11; Leising & Borkenau, Chapter 10). Rollings, Cuperman, and Ickes have also demonstrated (Chapter 9) how greatly people differ in their ability to "read" a partner correctly and draw accurate inferences.

Reading a partner correctly. Reading a person's intention correctly is not always easy, and an interpersonal invitation may easily be misread. After all, without valid cues that are sufficiently salient, behavior can be ambiguous, therefore subject to alternate interpretations. When Person A invites a particular reaction from Person B, B might be unclear as to what A intends: "Is A offering me nurturance or trying to manipulate me?" An internal dialogue like the one postulated for trust (Murray & Holmes, Chapter 12) can become complex indeed, and subtle factors may complicate the picture further. Thus, a partner may be puzzled by an invitation for an intimate exchange that occurs in a business setting: Hill, Pilkonis, and Bear (Chapter 17) have described the often-overlooked importance of social domain as a complicating factor. When an employee at the workplace invites intimate support for a personal problem from a coworker, the inappropriateness of the invitation (at least from the coworker's perspective) may produce unhappy consequences for the employee.

Complementarity and partner violence. Bartholomew and Cobb (Chapter 14) describe factors that lead to violence in close relationships. This phenomenon may sometimes involve a misreading of cues and noncomplementarity. Suppose two partners (one with an anxious attachment style, the other with an avoidant attachment style) were in a romantic relationship. The anxious partner might readily (mis)interpret cues from the other's avoidance as signs of romantic disinterest and feel rejected; and the avoidant partner might readily (mis)interpret cues from the other's anxious complaints as excessive demands for closeness. One can easily imagine an escalation of cues from each that are misinterpreted, leading each to judge the partner's intentions incorrectly. The partner's intentions/motives are thus misread and frustrated, inducing anger, and (in the presence of other risk factors) leading to explosive violence.

Complementarity and social allergens. When a strong motive drives a behavior—but the partner withholds a desired complementary reaction—the person's motive is apt to be frustrated, and negative affect results. Social allergens (O'Connor, Chapter 16) include behaviors produced by Person A that come to irritate (arouse anger in) Person B. According to O'Connor, one possible explanation is that the partner's irritation or anger may arise from a frustrated motive: Perhaps the offending person keeps "inviting" partners to provide a particular type of reaction that some partners, for their own reasons, do not wish to provide. Wants, requests, or demands—such as "admire me," "connect with me," "take care of me," or "don't bother me"—may be at odds with the partner's own wishes. The partner then experiences a motivational dilemma—"Shall I forego my own wishes for my partner's sake or not?—and the conflict induces internal distress.

The process observed in social allergens may be related to psychopathology in two ways. (1) In some cases distressed individuals—for example, depressed, phobic, dependent, narcissistic, or with-drawn people—find themselves in the role of the "offending" person as they (paradoxically) seek support from potential support-providers who eventually reject them. Segrin (Chapter 25) has described this process for depressed individuals. (2) In other cases, overly accommodating individuals—for example, excessively compliant or nurturant people—may find themselves in the role of offended or irritated person, as they extend themselves and sacrifice personal wishes in order to satisfy other people's "wants" (or so they perceive them). Then they feel exploited, conflicted, and distressed.

Proposition 6: Dyadic Interactions Help Explain the Origin, Maintenance, and Effect of an Axis I Syndrome.

Interpersonal factors contribute in at least three important ways to the development and consequences of a syndrome. Those factors have also been discussed in this handbook.

1. *Vulnerability arises from an interaction between temperament and particular (interpersonal) environments.* People differ innately in their sensitivity to environmental threat. Because of differences in people's innate readiness to perceive and react to danger, the environment of a sensitive child would, in general, provide many more opportunities for stress than that of a less reactive child. And if that environment repeatedly confirmed actual danger through interpersonal interactions—for example, criticism, scolding, indifference, neglect—then interactions would become emotionally charged, further justifying the child's vigilance against danger. Such children in particular would become vulnerable to future emotional distress and psychopathology.

Costa, Benoit, and Ollendick, in reviewing the literature on disorders of childhood (Chapter 28), have highlighted the importance of temperament—innate individual differences such as those manifested in the child's reactivity and poor self-regulation. They note that temperamental differences are modifiable, both by maturation and by experiences involving other people (particularly parents and peers). Similarly, Alden and Regambal (Chapter 26) summarize a large body of literature showing that dynamics within the family of origin are associated with the later emergence of an anxiety disorder. The clearest example appears in the *social anxiety disorder*, where three parent-child patterns are common precursors of psychopathology—(1) parental intrusiveness and control; (2) parental hostility, abuse, and neglect; and (3) limited socializing among family members. Alden and Regambal also note that a child's early wariness and behavioral inhibition seem to *invite* (or provoke) controlling parental behavior—overprotection, intrusiveness, and derisiveness. And those behaviors, in turn, seem to solidify and sustain a child's innate social reticence.

2. *Frequently an interpersonal event precipitates a syndrome.* For vulnerable people, interpersonal events frequently become the first trigger for an Axis I syndrome. One of the clearest instances is associated with *post–traumatic stress disorder.* As Nugent, Amstadter, and Koenen (Chapter 24) note, an *interpersonal* trauma (e.g., rape) is much more likely to precipitate a post–traumatic stress disorder than an equally horrific—but noninterpersonal—natural disaster. Likewise, a panic disorder leading to agoraphobia may first arise after the person receives news of an impending interpersonal danger—for example, evidence that a spouse contemplates ending the marriage, or news that a parent is now terminally ill (see Horowitz, 2004). Similarly, after a painful interpersonal rejection, a young woman's dieting may escalate to life-threatening proportions in anorexia nervosa.

3. *Others react negatively to a syndrome.* A syndrome also seems to have its own interpersonal effects on other people, further sustaining or even exacerbating

the psychopathology. Segrin (Chapter 25) has summarized the voluminous literature showing the negative effect that a person's depression may have upon others. Depressed people exhibit such characteristics as reductions in eye contact, positive facial expression, gestures, and head nodding, as well as slowed speech with fewer words and longer pauses, excessive reassurance-seeking, and the display of negative affect. Partners initially empathize, but, over time, they come to feel more depressed themselves and then tend to reject the depressed person. That rejection can exacerbate the depressed person's problem by removing former sources of potential support and by confirming the person's negative self-view.

Because psychopathology so often seems to emerge from specific types of interpersonal interactions, it is crucial that our discipline construct ways to assess a person's principal interactional patterns and vulnerability. Schauenburg and Grande (Chapter 21) have described a semistructured interview, the Operationalized Psychodynamic Diagnosis, through which people describe their important relationship patterns—for example, what the relationship is like and how the person regards others and behaves toward them. The interview also assesses the effect of their behavior upon the interviewer as well as the "quality" of the person's self-image and image of others. Benjamin's methods (Chapter 20) also provide an important advance in assessing clinically relevant interpersonal interactions.

Proposition 7: In Contrast, Most Personality Disorders Each Reflect a Specific Vulnerability.

Clarkin, Levy, and Ellison (Chapter 23) describe the growing consensus that personality disorders reflect a person's difficulties with (a) a specific concern about the self and/or (b) chronic interpersonal interactions that are problematic. These two types of difficulties seem to go hand-in-hand. Because of the person's interpersonal history, the person has apparently become highly sensitive to some particular interpersonal threat—for example, abandonment, isolation, rejection, humiliation, criticism, disrespect, exploitation. Each particular vulnerability affects the person's self-image, producing a distressing (affect-laden) set of cognitions. To protect oneself, the person adopts strategies that seem to backfire over time. Grosse Holtforth, Thomas, and Caspar (Chapter 7) have described in detail how a vulnerability can manifest itself as a threat of specific unsatisfied motives. The specificity of these motives helps clarify and focus the work of treatment,

As suggested earlier, each type of vulnerability probably arises from an interaction between a biologically based sensitivity (e.g., a sensitivity to threat or anxiety) and a particular class of childhood experiences (e.g., humiliating criticism). People probably adopt strategies to protect themselves from hurtful interactions by drawing upon their own innate biological capacities (strengths). For example, a person who, for biological reasons, finds it easy to sustain focused concentration would be well equipped to adopt the focused attentional strategies of someone with an obsessive-compulsive personality disorder. With those strategies the person could avoid errors, loss of control, or other lapses that might lead to criticism, reproach, or shame.

Each major type of vulnerability is quite specific. The vulnerability of someone with a borderline personality disorder (BPD) specifically concerns a threat of abandonment. Although some highly vulnerable people are fortunate to find a partner whom they can trust, others do not. In those cases, the self-protective motive manifests itself as a vigilance for cues of potential abandonment by significant others; the person seems particularly "ready" to detect those cues. This readiness seems to produce greater monitoring, rapid judgments from limited cues, and precautionary steps to prevent (or undo) impending abandonment.

When we assign the diagnosis of BPD to someone, how important for the diagnosis is the particular vulnerability associated with BPD, namely, *frantic efforts to avoid real or imagined abandonment*? Would we make the diagnosis if we had no evidence that the person was concerned about abandonment? Suppose a person met all nine criteria of the borderline personality disorder—with one exception: The person denied any concern or worry about—or desire to avoid—real or imagined abandonment. True, the person might exhibit all forms of interpersonal commotion associated with BPD (meeting eight of the nine criteria), and the diagnostic manual requires no more than five criteria. But in this case the interpersonal linchpin—the vulnerability that integrates the criteria—is not present. How would we then explain the person's multiple instabilities—unstable relationships, paranoid ideation, mood shifts, identity shifts, impulsive acts? Would we simply follow the diagnostic rule—any five or more of the nine criteria—and apply the diagnostic label anyway? Or would we question the validity of the informant's self-awareness and self-report? We might find ourselves hypothesizing that the person does experience a concern about abandonment, but, for reasons expected to emerge during treatment, the person cannot presently recognize, acknowledge, or express the concern in words. But now suppose that, after 20 years of treatment, we have to admit that the person is, in fact, simply not concerned about abandonment. Because the essential interpersonal linchpin is clearly absent, we might ask whether BPD has been an accurate diagnosis. Some interpersonal theorists might well argue that BPD was simply incorrect as a diagnosis for this case: The fundamental explanatory construct for BPD—a severe vulnerability around fears of abandonment—is missing, so in this particular case, some other mechanism (perhaps an entirely biological mechanism) is needed to explain the very atypical "nine minus one" pattern.

To say that an interpersonal vulnerability organizes the criteria for a corresponding personality disorder means that a person might have two personality disorders (two coexisting vulnerabilities). That is, the person might have acquired two vulnerabilities independently, each leading to a set of strategies for protecting the self from that potential set of hurts; and the person would then qualify for two personality disorders. The histrionic personality disorder, for example, frequently co-occurs with the borderline personality disorder (Davila, 2001; Watson & Sinha, 1998). Whereas a borderline diagnosis suggests that the person seeks to avoid abandonment, a histrionic diagnosis suggests that the person seeks attentional engagement from others as a way of connecting with others. Similarly, the histrionic and narcissistic personality disorders reflect different vulnerabilities (one primarily communal, the other primarily agentic). In that case, an overlapping strategy (attention-seeking) can serve both purposes. Attention-seeking can serve (a) a communal strategy for *connecting* with others ("Did you notice my new hat?") as well as (b) a self-enhancing strategy for attaining admiration and respect ("Have you ever seen a more beautiful hat than mine?"). In brief, as Clarkin, Levy, and Ellison have noted (Chapter 23), concomitant personality disorder diagnoses frequently occur. In such cases, both problems need to be understood and addressed in treatment.

Proposition 8: Successful Psychotherapies Must All Address Interpersonal Issues.

No matter what form of psychotherapy researchers examine, the quality of the client-therapist relationship is usually one of the best predictors of a treatment's success for outcome (Castonguay, Constantino, Boswell, & Kraus, Chapter 29). Eubanks-Carter, Muran, Safran, and Hayes (Chapter 30) have described the kinds of events in a dyadic treatment that threaten the therapeutic alliance (and, therefore, the therapeutic outcome). Whenever a client shows signs of dissatisfaction with the treatment or with the therapist's behavior—even if the client has not articulated those signs clearly—wise therapists make it a point to find an opportune moment to investigate the reason for the client's dissatisfaction. In our view, a negative reaction always indicates that some goal or motive of the client's is being frustrated and needs to be articulated and discussed. Ignoring such dissatisfactions promotes a breach in the therapeutic relationship. It is especially noteworthy that inexperienced therapists often respond to a client's complaint about the treatment with an intervention prescribed by the treatment manual—e.g., the therapist ascribes the complaint to the client's dysfunctional belief (in a cognitive therapy) or to negative transference (in a psychodynamic therapy). Such unwelcome responses tend to exacerbate the problem.

Sophisticated forms of interpersonal treatments have been described in this handbook. In general, these treatments explicitly examine the nature of dysfunctional interaction patterns. Levenson (Chapter 32) has described time-limited dynamic psychotherapy (TLDP) as a way to expose a *maladaptive interpersonal cycle* that is responsible for the client's psychological problems. It broadly formulates the client's problem and investigates manifestations of the problem in significant relationships (including the one with the therapist). Interventions are then designed to modify the maladaptive pattern in the client's current life. Gunlicks-Stoessel and Weissman (Chapter 31) describe the basic principles of Interpersonal Therapy (IPT) and corresponding interventions of IPT. Current interpersonal problems are identified, clarified, and addressed with specific problem-focused techniques. Interestingly, when depression is the presenting complaint, the IPT strategically ascribes the syndrome to the client's illness, in order to relieve the client of a sense of responsibility that normally leads to feelings of blame, shame, or guilt. IPT also attempts to educate the client about depression, and, from the beginning of treatment, an IPT therapist encourages (and gives credit to) the client for taking steps to overcome depression.

Finally, Piper and Ogrodniczuk (Chapter 33) describe the role of interpersonal issues in group therapy. Forms of group therapy in which clients interact with each other offer an ideal setting for clients to examine interpersonal processes that affect their own lives and to experiment with novel ways of interacting. It is interesting that a group member's working relationship with the therapist (the therapeutic alliance) is a better predictor of treatment outcome than the group members' alliances with each other (the group cohesion). Thus, in group therapy, as in individual therapy, a dyadic (therapist-client) relationship seems to have a special role in producing change.

To summarize, the scope of these eight propositions is far ranging. They address basic interpersonal mechanisms and processes in diverse contexts. Clearly, the interpersonal approach has touched a substantial variety of topics that are important to personality, social, abnormal, and clinical psychology. Hopefully, this handbook will help others better appreciate the goals and meaning of an interpersonal approach.

References

Bartholomew, K., & Horowitz, L. M. (1991). Attachment styles among young adults: A test of a model. *Journal of Personality and Social Psychology, 61*, 226–244.

Bruch, H. (1982). Anorexia nervosa: Therapy and theory. *American Journal of Psychiatry, 132*, 1531–1538.

Collins, W. A., Maccoby, E. E., Steinberg, L., Hetherington, E. M., & Bornstein, M. H. (2000). Contemporary research on parenting: The case for nature and nurture. *American Psychologist, 55*, 218–232.

Dodge, K. A., & Cole, J. D. (1987). Social-information-processing factors in reactive and proactive aggression in children's peer groups. *Journal of Personality and Social Psychology, 53*, 1146–1158.

Gurtman, M. B. (1993). Constructing personality tests to meet a structural criterion: Application of the interpersonal circumplex. *Journal of Personality, 61,* 237–263.

Higgins, E. T. (1987). Self-discrepancy: A theory relating self and affect. *Psychological Review, 94,* 319–340.

Horowitz, L. M. (2004). *Interpersonal foundations of psychopathology.* Washington, DC: American Psychological Association.

Hudley, C., & Graham, S. (1993). An attributional intervention to reduce peer-directed aggression in African American boys. *Child Development, 64,* 124–138.

Lazarus, R. S. (1991). *Emotion and adaptation.* New York: Oxford University Press.

Minuchin, S., Rosman, B. L., & Baker, L. (1978). *Psychosomatic families.* Cambridge, MA: Harvard University Press.

Van den Boom, D. (1994). The influence of temperament and mothering on attachment and exploration: An experimental manipulation of sensitive responsiveness among lower-class mothers with irritable infants. *Child Development, 65,* 1457–1477.

Wiggins, J. S. (1979). A psychological taxonomy of trait-descriptive terms: The interpersonal domain. *Journal of Personality and Social Psychology, 37,* 395–412.

AUTHOR INDEX

SUBJECT INDEX

Abandonment, 589
  depression, 43
  Intimate Partner Violence (IPV) and, 235, 237, 238, 244
Abnormality
  interpersonal description of, 360
  in interpersonal diagnosis, 364
Accommodating-Trusting, 585
Accuracy, 157. *See also* Achievement, 175
  empathic (*see* empathic accuracy, 143)
  problems, lens model used for, 180
  study of, 365
Accuracy criterion, 160
Achievement
  defined, 176
  dependents of, 178
  enhancing or compromising, 176
  in lens model, 175
  matched links and, 177
  strength of, 179
  study of, 176
Acquaintanceship effects in empathic accuracy, 146
Act-by-act behavioral complementarity, 128, 134
Action verbs, 58
Active love, in SASB model, 328, 333
Activity, 93
Adaptations, 76
Adaptive inferential feedback, 436
Adaptive landscape notion, 79, 80
Adaptive personality development, 38
Adolescents. *See* Child and adolescent psychopathology; Children, 493
Adoption studies, 100
Adult attachment
  standard measure of, 582
  style
    individual differences in, 211
    influence of child-rearing variables on, 96
    poisonous pedagogy (PP), 99

Adult Attachment Interview, 393
Adult behaviors, 99
Adult Personality Functioning Assessment (APFA), 290, 294
Affection
  in circular models, 347
Affiliation
  control vs., 60
  conveyed in interpersonal communication, 362
  coronary heart disease and, 475, 476, 478
  cross-spectral analysis of, 137
  need for, nonverbal communication and, 172
  in SASB model, 333
  situational, bias in, 129
Affiliative behaviors, 97
  enduring traits as independent predictors of, 98
Affirm, in SASB model, 328, 338
Agency
  coronary heart disease risks and, 475
  in interpersonal diagnosis, 359
  in interpersonal goals, 108, 109
  interpersonal pathoplasticity and, 369
  interpersonal theory and, 38, 47
  intraindividual variability and, 371
  IPC inventories of, 314, 320
  metaconcept of, 60
  in models of personality, 79
  motives of, 109
  in person-situation integration, 373
  self-definition, 8
  summary and conclusions, 581
  vs. unmitigated/mitigated agency, 111
  values, 116
Agentic dimension of IPC, 58
Aggregated situational mutual influence, 128